Strategic Marketing Management

SECOND EDITION

Strategic Marketing Management

Carol H. Anderson

Rollins College, Crummer Graduate School of Business

Julian W. Vincze

University of New Brunswick, Saint John, and Rollins College, Crummer Graduate School of Business

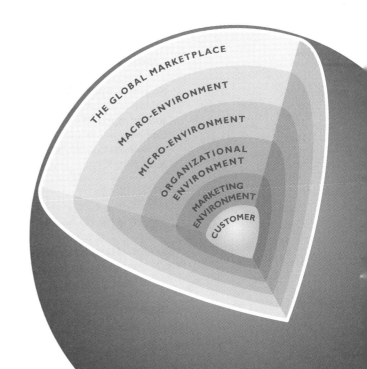

HOUGHTON MIFFLIN COMPANY

Boston   New York

Editor-in-Chief: George T. Hoffman
Associate Sponsoring Editor: Susan M. Kahn
Associate Editor: Jessica Carlisle
Senior Project Editor: Tracy Patruno
Senior Manufacturing Coordinator: Priscilla Bailey
Marketing Manager: Steven W. Mikels

Cover painting: © Craig Antrim

Printed in the U.S.A.

Library of Congress Catalog Card Number: 2002116444

ISBN: 0-618-33807-1

1 2 3 4 5 6 7 8 9   QUV   07 06 05 04 03

BRIEF CONTENTS

CONTENTS

● PART FOUR   **Managing Marketing Efforts**   **483**

● **PART FIVE   CASES**   **551**

Marketers live in exciting times. There are always new strategic challenges to face and new frontiers to conquer. Many of these challenges are brought to the forefront in this text and in the accompanying cases. In today's global society, marketing activities touch and influence people's lives, as individuals and businesses attempt to sell, buy, or exchange goods and services. Globalization offers a greater worldview, and will continue to affect the marketing process over the long term as organizations of all sizes and types identify new opportunities for overseas expansion. Converging technologies, the Internet, and other technological advances continue to make the marketing function one of the most dynamic and exciting aspects of an organization—one that each of us experiences daily. In addition, the way we do business has been greatly affected by changing organizational structures, and a mandate from the public for more ethical and socially responsible corporate behavior.

In *Strategic Marketing Management,* marketing is viewed as a dynamic process designed to achieve distinctive strategic competence and global advantage. This is accomplished through value-added marketing activities and operations that are designed to create and sustain long-term relationships. Our goal is to help present and future marketing managers achieve success by taking the best from traditional marketing theory and combining it with contemporary, innovative approaches to meeting challenges in a fast-paced, often uncertain environment.

An excellent collection of carefully selected full-length cases is included in the second part of the book. The combined text and case book enhance pedagogy by providing opportunities for insightful analysis of real-life marketing situations and the application of contemporary marketing theory and practice to a variety of organizations. Students have fewer books to buy and tote around, and instructors find it easier to integrate cases and theory when both are available in one volume.

In addition, a shorter mini-case at the end of each chapter, called *Marketing Management in Action,* offers students and instructors an analytical approach to applying marketing concepts presented in the chapter. These shorter cases can be used for in-class instruction, small-group exercises, or out-of-class assignments. They are designed to make classroom instruction more interesting and meaningful, and provide a basis for lively discussion. Case analysis generally can be more focused on specific marketing concepts related to the case situations. Each mini-case is carefully articulated with the concepts in the accompanying chapter. Study questions at the end of each mini-case form a helpful basis for discussion; teaching suggestions related to these questions are provided in the Instructors Resource Manual.

Appendix A, "Development, Implementation, and Evaluation of a Marketing Plan," contains a complete outline and instructions for creating a viable marketing plan. Sections of the marketing plan can be coordinated with chapter assignments throughout a semester.

● KEY FEATURES

The key features of this text can be organized around its thematic emphasis on strategic marketing decisions, change and innovation, coverage of cutting-edge topics, integrated approach, and chapter pedagogy.

Emphasis on strategic marketing decisions.   Text discussion and applications focus on strategic decisions made at the business unit (SBU) level of an organization. Tactical decisions that are required to implement a strategic marketing plan are discussed relative to elements of the marketing mix. Chapter 3, "Strategic Market Planning," presents approaches to achieving sustainable competitive advantage through strategic marketing decisions. Accountability for the longer-term strategic plan is emphasized in Chapter 15, "Control and Measurement of Marketing Performance."

Emphasis on Change and Innovation.   In addition to providing current and comprehensive coverage of marketing management concepts, the text focuses on change and the need for innovation. We emphasize the need for marketing managers to recognize, embrace, and manage change in today's global business environment, which is buffeted by many forces: globalization of markets; increased computerization and database capabilities; emerging and converging technologies; an information age economy; changing organizational structures; and increased attention to security, ethics, and social responsibility issues.

Dramatic changes in the marketing environment and the changing role of marketing in society pose serious challenges for marketing managers. Successful marketing strategies and tactics require innovative solutions and proactive decisions to deal with the forces of risk, uncertainty, and change. The marketing planning process must include the building of longer-term strategic alliances and closer relationships with all constituencies. Customer satisfaction is increasingly focused on an organization's ability to deliver quality and value. Cross-functional integration of marketing functions, and integration of marketing with other business functions are a necessity for planning and execution.

Two unique chapters highlight the key theme and emphasis of this text: Chapter 2, "Forces of Change and Their Impact on the Marketing Process," and Chapter 15, "Control and Measurement of Marketing Performance." In addition, Chapter 3, "Strategic Market Planning," provides insights into the "big picture"—the strategic decisions that drive tactical marketing activities.

Coverage of Cutting-Edge Topics.   Two other special chapters have been included because of their critical importance to successful marketing management: Chapter 9, "Services Marketing Strategy;" and Chapter 13, "Direct Marketing."

We also focus on many key and current topics in marketing management practice, including change management, total quality management, continuous process improvement, reengineering, cross-functional work teams, information technology advances, decision support systems, electronic communications revolution (electronic commerce and electronic marketing), virtual offices and virtual organization design, relationship marketing (customers, employees, suppliers, and all other stakeholders), ethical and social issues, changing role of marketing in society, the marketing research process, and creative problem solving. Both qualitative and quantitative aspects of marketing decisions are presented throughout the book.

Integrated Approach. A conceptual environmental model represents the integration of marketing management elements and functions within an organization and its micro- and macro-environments. This global model will help students to grasp the complexities and interconnectedness of today's business world and to recognize the role of marketing management within a global economy. Within this environmental context, an "ecocycle" model portrays the business phases generally followed by marketing organizations.

Chapter Pedagogy. The text includes a wide variety of elements to enhance understanding, facilitate analysis, and illustrate relevance.

- *Opening vignettes* for each chapter focus on contemporary marketing experiences or activities of actual companies and illustrate the relevance of chapter content.

- *Margin definitions* provide a convenient glossary of key terms for quick reference.

- *Boxed inserts* provide additional up-to-date examples to illustrate the relevance of chapter concepts. Highlighted inserts are entitled:

  "Innovate or Evaporate"—focusing on innovative approaches taken by marketers

  "Marketing and Entrepreneurship"—focusing on successful marketing strategies for small businesses

  "Managing Change"—focusing on marketing decisions made by organizations in a time of change and uncertainty

  "Marketing in the Global Village"—focusing on decisions made from a global marketing management perspective

  "It's Legal But Is It Ethical?"—focusing on marketing management decisions made within the parameters of ethical and socially responsible behavior

  "Marketing In the Information Age"—focusing on the use of databases, communications technology, and electronic commerce in marketing

- A chapter *summary* presents an overview of the major concepts discussed in the chapter, providing an excellent "advance organizer" before reading the chapter and a review after reading the chapter.

- End-of-chapter study *questions* are thought provoking, facilitate deeper understanding of chapter content, and provide a good basis for enlightened class discussion.

- End-of-chapter experiential *exercises* offer "hands-on" learning opportunities to apply concepts discussed in the chapter to real-life situations.

- Clear and abundant *figures and tables* emphasize key points and provide further explanation of text discussion to facilitate comprehension and learning.

- Timely and relevant closing cases called Marketing Management in Action at the end of each chapter offer "mini-cases" that are action-oriented and decision-focused experiential learning tools that provide an interesting basis for analysis and discussion. Study questions at the end of each short case offer additional insights, with suggested answers provided in the Instructors Resource Manual.

ORGANIZATION OF THE BOOK

The first section of the book is devoted to a discussion of marketing theory and applications. The second section of the book contains 22 classroom-tested marketing cases that provide comprehensive examples of marketing strategies and tactics.

Part One is an introduction to strategic marketing management. The changing role of marketing in contemporary organizations is discussed in Chapter 1. Chapter 2 emphasizes the forces of change that operate in the marketing environment and their impact on marketing management decisions.

Part Two presents the challenges that face marketers in their attempts to achieve and sustain competitive advantage. Discussion includes strategic market planning (Chapter 3), marketing intelligence and creative problem solving (Chapter 4), and developing an understanding of customer characteristics and buying behaviors (Chapters 5, 6, and 7).

Part Three focuses on marketing mix strategies and their implementation. Chapters 8 and 9 provide a basis for managing goods and services through product management and service strategies respectively. The importance of efficient and effective distribution channels and supply chain management is emphasized in Chapter 10. Integrated marketing communications strategies and tools are discussed in depth in Chapters 11 and 12, followed by the increasingly important direct marketing approach (Chapter 13) that includes strategic elements of both distribution and integrated marketing communications. The factors that must be considered in the development of pricing strategies are presented in Chapter 14.

In Part Four, discussion returns to the broader view taken in Part One and addresses the issues of controlling and measuring the results of marketing activities (Chapter 15), and establishing organizational structures that will facilitate successful marketing ventures (Chapter 16).

Part Five contains 22 comprehensive cases for analysis of a variety of marketing situations. The case collection is current, with all situations taking place in the late 1990s and 2000s. Cases cover a wide range of industries and organizational sizes, as well as for-profit, nonprofit, product, service, consumer and business-to-business marketing environments. Some cases contain important ethical and social responsibility issues, and most are decision-centered rather than descriptive. All have been classroom tested and have proven to be interesting and challenging to students. Many of these cases provide an opportunity to integrate multiple marketing topics for a better sense of how the marketing mix elements work together. Many cases also provide sufficient data for quantitative analysis related to marketing, accounting, or finance.

A COMPREHENSIVE INSTRUCTIONAL RESOURCE PACKAGE

Strategic Marketing Management is supported by an excellent package of teaching and learning aids, including the following:

Instructor's Resource Manual and Test Bank. Many useful features are provided in the *Instructor's Resource Manual* to enhance the quality of instruction: chapter summary, chapter learning objectives, annotated chapter outlines, answers to end-of-chapter questions that provide a basis for stimulating classroom discussion, and suggestions for completion of the applied end-of-chapter experiential exercises.

In addition to these basic features, additional experiential exercises are included for use in applying chapter concepts in class, along with a listing of available transparencies for each chapter and a selected bibliography of suggested articles and books for additional insights. There is also a list of appropriate cases from the textbook, which correspond to the topics covered. In addition, we have also provided a list of Harvard Business School cases that can be coordinated with each Chapter.

Another section of the *Instructor's Resource Manual* is devoted to effective use of the cases included in the book, including:

- General case teaching and analysis guidelines
- A comprehensive matrix that indicates where each case can be used with textbook topics
- An extensive teaching note for each case

Teaching notes often include summaries, background company information, answers to discussion questions, and additional references and resources.

The next part of the manual is devoted to an extensive test bank to assist the instructor in assessing student performance. There are approximately 1600 items created in the form of true/false, multiple choice, matching, and short-answer essay questions. Answers are provided for all questions as well as text page references. In addition, all multiple-choice questions have been labeled as testing knowledge, comprehension, or application of the concepts presented in the text.

HM Testing on CD ROM. This computerized version of the Test Bank allows instructors to select, edit, and add questions, or generate randomly selected questions to produce a test master for easy duplication. Online Testing and Gradebook functions allow instructors to administer tests via their local area network or the World Wide Web, set up classes, record grades from tests or assignments, analyze grades, and produce class and individual statistics. This program can be used on both PC and Macintosh computers.

PowerPoint Slides. A package of approximately 350 PowerPoint slides is available for use by adopters of this textbook and is available on the Instructor Web Site. Slides include chapter figures as well as additional exhibits that highlight chapter concepts. Instructors who have access to PowerPoint can edit slides to customize them for their classrooms. Slides can also be printed for lecture notes and distribution.

Color Transparencies. In addition to the PowerPoint slides, a package of color transparencies accompanies the book. These are replicas of many of the PowerPoint slides, which include art and tables from the textbook as well as additional exhibits.

Videos. A selection of videos is available to adopters. Videos are selected to correspond with the concepts and topics highlighted in each chapter. A video guide is included to facilitate selection of the video for a particular instructional unit.

STUDENT AND INSTRUCTOR WEB SITES

Specially designed Web pages enhance the book content and provide additional information, guidance, and activities.

The student site includes learning objectives, chapter outlines, ACE Self Tests, and convenient web links to the organizations highlighted in the text. There are additional exercises designed to further test students' understanding of concepts as well as recommended Internet sites for research on many marketing management topics.

The instructor site provides lecture notes, comprehensive case teaching notes, and PowerPoint slides. There are also additional cases, caselets, scenarios, and/or critical incidents that can be used for testing purposes or to provide additional examples of course concepts.

 YOUR COMMENTS ARE VALUABLE TO US

We consider ourselves fortunate to be members of a discipline where so many exciting things are happening and where so many individuals have been willing to share their knowledge and expertise with us. We have attempted to write a book that will convey both the theory and the "nuts and bolts" applications of strategic marketing management to students of marketing. Your feedback would be most welcome, and we look forward to your valued comments, suggestions, and criticisms, because our challenge is to continue to create better teaching materials for students and faculty.

ACKNOWLEDGMENTS

It is said there is nothing new under the sun, and perhaps this book is another testimony to that statement. Leading researchers and thinkers in marketing and other disciplines have inspired much of the content of this text. They have made available a plethora of marketing thought through publications, seminars, conferences, and personal conversations. We have attempted to distill many of these notable contributions to marketing and other disciplines and to combine them with current business practices and an understanding of pedagogy, to deliver a book that is interesting, easy to read, and at the same time stimulates deeper levels of introspection and understanding. Contributions to this book have come from a variety of sources, including our students, colleagues, publisher, reviewers, and families. We apologize in advance for any names that may be inadvertently omitted.

Students.   We continue to be inspired by students who hold us accountable for excellence in education. Learning in our classrooms is a two-way street where we learn a great deal from our students while we teach them about marketing. Many students at the Crummer Graduate School, that we have had the privilege of teaching are practicing managers, who bring a wealth of experience and insights to classroom discussions. *Strategic Marketing Management* is greatly influenced by many years of teaching experience in public and private business schools, where we have learned from past successes and failures in an attempt to find the best teaching methods and materials to maximize student learning. We believe that this relationship with our students provides the type of feedback that has made it possible for this book to fill a gap in marketing education.

Crummer Graduate School of Business at Rollins College and Other Colleagues. We owe a debt of gratitude to many professional and personal influences that have helped us form our views of the marketing discipline over the years. In particular, we appreciate the encouragement of our Deans and colleagues at the Crummer Graduate School who strongly support a professional and technical environment that encourages and supports textbook writing.

Houghton Mifflin Editors. We believe we have worked with the best folks in the industry over these past months, starting with V.P., and Editor-in-Chief George Hoffman. We owe a special debt of gratitude to Jessica Carlisle, our Associate Editor, who helped everyone stay focused and on course. To her goes much of the credit for the professionalism of the final product. Tracy Patruno, Senior Project Editor, coordinated production of the book, and the team at Nesbitt Graphics contributed to the professional appearance and readability of the book as well as developed the art program.

Case Contributors. We appreciate the willingness of leading case authors in marketing to share their excellent cases with the authors of this textbook. Students and instructors will benefit greatly from the professional contributions of the following case writers:

Adrian Sargeant Henley
Management College

Frank Shipper
Salisbury State University

Charles Manz
University of Massachusetts, Amherst

Alexander Wood
University of Central Florida

John J. Lawrence
University of Idaho

Linda J. Morris
University of Idaho

Joseph J. Geiger
University of Idaho

Robin Habeger
Iowa State University

Kay M. Palan
Iowa State University

John H. Friar
Northeastern University

Raymond M. Kinnunen
Northeastern University

Vishal Aggarwal
Keane, Inc.

John K. Ross, III
Southwest Texas State University

Michael J. Keefe
Southwest Texas State University

Bill J. Middlebrook
Southwest Texas State University

Steven J. Maranville
University of Saint Thomas

Madeleine E. Pullman
Southern Methodist University

Timothy T. Dannels
Iowa State University

Marilyn L. Taylor
University of Missouri at Kansas City

George M. Puia
Indiana State University

Krishnan Ramaya
University of Southern Indiana

Madelyn Gengelbach
University of Missouri at Kansas City

George C. Rubenson
Salisbury University

Robert J. Mockler
St. John's University

Dorothy G. Dologite
City University of New York-Baruch College

Paul Poppler
St. John's University

Rebecca J. Morris
University of Nebraska at Omaha

Anne T. Lawrence
San Jose State University

Craig A. Hollingshead
Marshall University

W. Blaker Bolling
Marshall University

Richard L. Jones
Marshall University

Ashli White
Marshall University

Katherine Campbell
University of Maryland

Duane Helleloid
University of Maryland

Natalya V. Delcoure
Northeast Louisiana University

Lawrence R. Jauch
Northeast Louisiana University

John L. Scott
Northeast Louisiana University

Jeffrey A. Krug
University of Illinois at Urbana-Champaign

William A. Andrews
Stetson University

Ram Subramanian
Grand Valley State University

Lars Larson
Grand Valley State University

David M. Currie
Rollins College

Reviewers. We appreciate the time and effort spent by reviewers on our manuscripts throughout the developmental process. Their willingness to share a wealth of marketing knowledge and insights enhanced the quality of the book. Our thanks to the following reviewers:

Mark Alpert
University of Texas at Austin

Craig Andrews
Marquette University

Martin Bressler
Houston Baptist University

James Camerius
Northern Michigan University

Jack Forrest
Cumberland University

Frank Franzak
Virginia Commonwealth University

James Gaius Ibe
Morris College

Wolfgang Grassl
Hillsdale College

Randall Hansen
Stetson University

Patricia Hambrich
Boston University

Joel Herche
University of the Pacific

Katryna Johnson
Concordia University

Craig Kelley
California State University,
Sacramento

Constantine Katsikeas
University of Wales, Cardiff

Peter LaPlaca
University of Connecticut

Thomas Marpe
Saint Mary's University of Minnesota

Anil Mathur
Hofstra University

Michael Shapiro
Dowling College

Robert Stephens
Macon State College

James H. Underwood, III
University of Southern Louisiana

Rao Unnava
Ohio State University

Brian Van der Westhuizen
California State University

Family.   Our families deserve a huge "thank you" for their support. Their love and encouragement throughout each edition of this text has been invaluable. In particular, we want to express our appreciation to our spouses, Alexander ("Lex") Wood and Linda Vincze, for their patience and understanding.

To all those named above, and to all those unnamed contributors to this book, we express our deep appreciation for the many ways in which you helped to bring this project to reality.

Carol Anderson Wood

Julian W. Vincze

● CAROL H. ANDERSON

Dr. Carol H. Anderson is a graduate of Texas A&M University (Ph.D. and MBA in Business Administration), University of Houston (M.Ed. in Curriculum and Instruction, and Vocational Education certification), and Cornell University (B.S.). She is Professor of Marketing Emerita at Rollins College and Southern Illinois University at Carbondale. Previous university faculty teaching positions include the Crummer Graduate School of Business at Rollins College, and Southern Illinois University at Carbondale. She also has taught at the University of Houston, and Texas A&M University. Dr. Anderson has been honored with numerous outstanding teaching awards from students and colleagues, including SIU's university-wide Outstanding Undergraduate Teacher in 1989; Outstanding Teacher in the SIU College of Business and Administration for several years; and the Crummer Graduate School's Welsh Award for outstanding faculty 1993 and 2000. Teaching experience includes MBA, Ph.D., and undergraduate courses across the marketing curriculum, as well as global and domestic student practica (consulting projects).

Dr. Anderson's teaching philosophy is student-oriented with a focus on practical applications of marketing theory, including hundreds of comprehensive strategic marketing plans and research projects for area companies and nonprofit organizations. She has held merchandising positions with Neiman-Marcus, Saks Fifth Avenue, and Mercantile Stores, Inc. Dr. Anderson's research and publications have focused primarily on strategic marketing management issues, marketing education, ethics, entrepreneurship, and marketing for nonprofits. She has published articles in professional journals such as the *Journal of Retailing, American Journal of Small Business (Entrepreneurship: Theory & Practice),* and the *Journal of Marketing Education,* and a retail managment textbook, as well as numerous presentations at professional meetings.

Dr. Anderson's professional association memberships include the American Marketing Association, World Association for Case Research and Application, Society for Case Research, Midwest Marketing Association (Past President), and Midwest Business Administration Association (Past President).

● JULIAN W. VINCZE

Julian W. Vincze is Director of Graduate Programs in Management, University of New Brunswick, Saint John. Former positions include V. P. Academic Programs, Euratio Academy, Zurich, Sophia Antipolis (France) and New York, specializing in leadership concepts and cross-cultural mergers/acquisitions/reorganizations. Also Emeritus Professor of Marketing at the Crummer Graduate School of Business at Rollins College (Orlando, Florida) he has co-authored nine textbooks in strategic management and marketing management. Dr. Vincze's other publication credits include chapters contributed to textbooks, eighteen published business cases, several articles and software reviews.

Dr. Vincze's undergraduate degree is from the University of Montana, his Master of Business Administration degree is from the University of Western Ontario in London, Canada, and his Ph.D. from the University of Bradford (Management Center) at Bradford, United Kingdom. He has industrial experience in the United States, Canada, and the European Community and has held long term academic positions in the United States and Canada, and "visiting" appointments in the United Kingdom, the Netherlands, Australia, and in Croatia.

Dr. Vincze's extensive practical and graduate teaching experiences enabled him to provide leadership in internationalizing the curriculum at the Crummer School and in 1992 he received the Charles A. Welsh Award for outstanding faculty performance. He also received research awards in 1986, 1992, 1993, 1996 & 1997. In 1993 Professor Vincze was awarded a Texas A&M/University of Hawaii CIBER (Center for International Business Studies) fellowship for FDIB (Faculty Development in International Business) Asia Program. In 2002 he was awarded a Fulbright Senior Scholar Award for Croatia.

Dr. Vincze has been active in several professional associations holding various leadership positions such as National Program Chairman and member of the Board of Governors for the Academy of Marketing Science (AMS), and Vice President of the Case Clearing Center for the North American Case Research Association (NACRA). Dr. Vincze remains active in several associations including the World Association for Case Research and Applications (WACRA).

Case	The Changing Role of Marketing	Forces of Change	Strategic Market Planning	Marketing Intelligence	Consumer Buying Behavior	Business Buying Behavior	Market Segmentation	Product Strategy	Services Marketing	Distribution Strategy	IMC Strategy	IMC Tools	Direct Marketing	Pricing Strategy	Control Marketing Performance	Marketing-Oriented Organization	Social Issues/Ethics	International	Innovation	Entrepreneurial
1. Botton Village	✓					✓	✓	✓		✓	✓		✓			✓	✓	✓	✓	✓
2. W. L. Gore & Associates, 1998	✓	✓				✓									✓	✓			✓	
3. Service in the Skies		✓		✓		✓	✓	✓					✓		✓		✓	✓		✓
4. Cowgirl Chocolates		✓		✓		✓			✓		✓			✓					✓	✓
5. Calgene Inc.: Marketing High-Tech Tomatoes	✓	✓	✓		✓	✓	✓		✓	✓				✓		✓	✓		✓	
6. 3DV-LS: Assessing Market Opportunity	✓	✓	✓		✓	✓	✓					✓	✓						✓	✓
7. Rayovac Corporation: "Recreating a Proud America Brand"	✓	✓			✓				✓	✓	✓	✓						✓		
8. DeCopier Technologies, Inc.		✓			✓	✓								✓					✓	✓
9. Circus Circus Enterprises, Inc. (1998)	✓	✓	✓	✓		✓	✓	✓							✓	✓	✓			
10. Priceline.Com: Act III	✓	✓			✓	✓	✓	✓	✓				✓	✓				✓	✓	✓
11. Black Diamond, Ltd.: Hanging on the Cutting Edge	✓	✓	✓	✓	✓	✓	✓			✓						✓			✓	

	The Changing Role of Marketing	Forces of Change	Strategic Market Planning	Marketing Intelligence	Consumer Buying Behavior	Business Buying Behavior	Market Segmentation	Product Strategy	Services Marketing	Distribution Strategy	IMC Strategy	IMC Tools	Direct Marketing	Pricing Strategy	Control Marketing Performance	Marketing-Oriented Organization	Social Issues/Ethics	International	Innovation	Entrepreneurial
21 America Online		✓			✓		✓	✓	✓				✓	✓			✓	✓	✓	✓
22 Kentucky Fried Chicken and the Global Fast-Food Industry	✓	✓					✓	✓	✓									✓		

An Introduction to Strategic Marketing Management

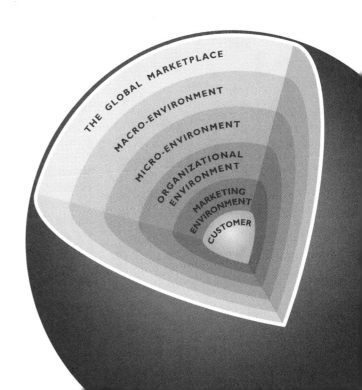

The Changing Role of Marketing

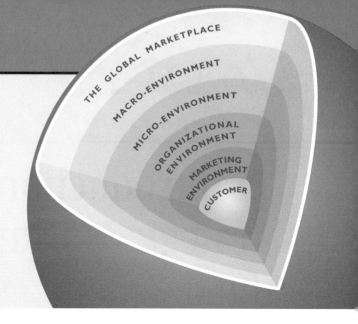

Overview

There are marketers that make things happen. There are marketers that watch things happen. And then there are marketers that ask, "What happened?"

Wake Up and Smell the Coffee—It's Starbucks

An important contributor to the world economy, the coffee industry involves many levels of domestic and international strategic marketing management. Coffee is a ubiquitous beverage served in even the remotest parts of the world. More than 400 billion cups of coffee are consumed each year—greater than any other beverage except water. Per capita consumption in the United States is nearly 11 pounds of coffee each year, second only to the Scandinavian countries (Finland, Sweden, and Norway), where per capita consumption exceeds 22 pounds of coffee annually. Brazil, Vietnam, and Columbia lead the rest of the world in growing and exporting coffee beans. The United States leads the world in coffee bean imports, with nearly 23 million 60-kilo bags of coffee beans annually, followed by Germany and France with nearly 14.5 million and 6.7 million 60-kilo bags, respectively.

Starbucks, the industry leader in gourmet coffees, opened its first store in Seattle's Pike Place Market in 1971. At that time, U.S. coffee consumption had declined from its peak in the 1960s, when 75 percent of the population were coffee drinkers. Coffee consumption continued to fall until the 1980s and has remained relatively stable since then. In 2002, 52 percent of American adults (107 million people) drank an average of 3.3 cups of coffee each day. Another 28 percent (57 million people) drank coffee occasionally. (Europeans consume two to three times more coffee than Americans.) Since Starbucks started selling gourmet coffee by the pound, overall demand for specialty coffees (including gourmet, flavored, and organically grown blends) has risen steadily. There were 21 million gourmet coffee drinkers in 1999, an increase from 4.5 million in 1993. Although a coffee cult had existed for years in the Pacific Northwest, it was the growth of coffeehouses such as Starbucks that increased consumer awareness and interest, leading to an increased national demand for premium coffee.

In a world where coffee has become a commodity, Starbucks has pursued a successful strategy of preemptive moves (first-to-market) and differentiation to become the United State's number one specialty coffee retailer, and has made a major impact on the international marketplace. Starbucks has been positioned as "a part of its customers' lives . . . the 'third place' in their daily existence—a familiar and welcoming refuge from work or home where they could relax in a safe public setting and enjoy a sense of community." The company's differentiation strategy is based on using the highest quality ingredients in all of its products, practicing environmental and social responsibility with each of its stakeholders and in each of the communities that it serves, treating coffee making as a brand of cooking, marketing a value-laden brand, and building strong relationships with employees and customers. Starbucks considers its product to be the "coffeehouse experience," whether the experience is in the coffeehouse or replicated somewhere else. A company executive says, "We'll rarely talk just about the product. Starbucks is a place that allows the customer experience to happen. Things in the store are just props to the experience." This underscores the importance of customer relationships to the success of Starbuck's business.

Howard Schultz, current chief global strategist and chairman of the board, joined Starbucks as director of retail operations and marketing in 1982. Starbucks began providing coffee to fine restaurants and espresso bars that year. In 1983, Mr. Schultz traveled to Italy, where the popularity of espresso bars in Milan transformed his vision for the company. He believed that a similar coffee bar culture could be developed in Seattle. The concept was tested successfully in a new location in downtown Seattle in 1984. However, the owners of Starbucks did not share Schultz's vision, so he left the company and founded his own coffee bar, Il Giornale. By 1987, Il Giornale had grown to three locations, and Schultz took advantage of an opportunity to purchase Starbucks' Seattle stores, roasting plant, and brand name from his former employers, changing his company name to Starbucks. As the major shareholder and CEO of Starbucks, Schultz's early strategy and key hires facilitated the company's early growth. His first-to-market strategy was pursued throughout the Pacific Northwest and then in Chicago and California, proving that the concept could succeed beyond Seattle.

Although Schultz needed a constant infusion of cash for the company's ambitious growth plans, he did not want to borrow from banks. Nor did he see franchising as an option—after carefully selecting and roasting beans, he did not want the ultimate product ruined by inattention to detail at the store level. Therefore, Starbucks decided to take the company public on June 26, 1992, and returned to the markets to raise additional capital after the IPO. Growth throughout the United States relied primarily on a cluster strategy, moving into major urban markets and opening up stores in close proximity to one another. A hub-and-spoke pattern evolved, with each urban market becoming the starting point for expansion into suburbs and smaller metro areas. Starbucks used little traditional advertising (an average of $1 million per year for the past 20 years—a fraction of the amount spent by other leading brands). Emphasis was placed on two factors: the ability of the actual stores to increase awareness of the brand, and the ability of customers to get Starbucks wherever they were. By 1996, Starbucks owned over 1,000 U.S. stores, and opened its first international store in Tokyo, Japan. In 2001, Starbucks opened its 300th Japanese location and celebrated 5 years of business in Japan. The success of a coffee shop in a country where the national drink is green tea demonstrated the potential for the concept in other cultures.

At the end of fiscal year 2001, Starbucks' profits increased 32 percent to $181.2 million on sales of $2.6 billion, compared to $94.6 million on sales of $2.2 billion in year 2000. Eighty-four percent of net revenues came from company-operated retail stores. The balance came from the company's specialty operations (business alliances, international retail store licensing, grocery channel licensing, warehouse club accounts, direct-to-consumer joint ventures, and other initiatives). By early 2002, Starbucks was opening new stores daily, with plans to open approximately 1,200 stores in fiscal 2002. The company served an average of 18 million customers a week throughout the world, with stores in 20 countries on four continents.

As of August 2002, Starbucks operated 5,506 stores in locations such as freestanding stores, office buildings, shopping centers, airport terminals, and supermarkets. Some locations serve lunch; some provide "hot spots" for computer connections. They also provide the Starbucks Card, a prepaid electronic card for online or in-store purchases, which can also be used as a gift card. Business-to-business services include office beverage and delivery service, business gifts, and food service. In the grocery stores, consumers can buy Starbucks coffee in gourmet flavors (alliance with Kraft Foods), ice cream (alliance with Dreyer's Grand Ice Cream, Inc.), bottled Frappuccino (alliance with PepsiCo), and Double Shot (premium espresso in 6.5-ounce can).

Starbucks has expanded rapidly and with great success during both good and bad economic times since Howard Schultz's purchase of the company in 1987. *Business Week* named Starbucks the fastest-growing global brand in 2001, and Interbrand, a New York-based brand-valuation firm, ranked the company's brand 88th in the world with an assessed brand value of $1.8 billion. Company executives and industry analysts ask: "How does Starbucks continue to grow the business?" The company wishes to "grow big and yet stay small," and depends on Starbucks' unique culture and relationships with its customers, employees, suppliers, and alliance partners as the driving force for continued growth.

Researchers at Booz Allen Hamilton and Northwestern University's Kellogg School of Management recently surveyed 113 executives who were a representative sample of Fortune 1000 companies. The researchers found that top-performing companies "focus extraordinary, enterprise-wide energy on moving beyond a transactional mind-set as they develop trust-based, mutually beneficial, and long-term associations, specifically with four key constituencies: customers, suppliers, alliance partners, and their own employees." Starbucks fits this new model of the relationship-centric organization, constantly accruing "relational capital," defined by the researchers as the "value of a firm's network of relationships with its customers, suppliers, alliance partners, and employees."

A key factor in Starbucks' success has been its recognition of the importance of these relationships, particularly with its employees. In particular, the role of the baristas (coffee brewers or partners) is critical in creating a comfortable, stable, and entertaining environment for customers. Employees are effective communicators of the brand; and money that other companies might spend on advertising is invested in employee training and benefits. The company environment encourages empowerment, communication, and collaboration. All employees, regardless of position, are considered "partners" and receive stock options. Decision-making is decentralized and regionalized, with relational capital built through two-way communication of the company's culture, values, and best practices across all levels and units of the organization. However, the company has experienced "growth pains" as some managers and employees who feel overworked and underpaid sued Starbucks in 2001 for allegedly refusing to pay legally mandated overtime. Starbucks settled the suit for $18 million, but many employees still feel frustrated in what they consider "fast food" jobs.

A key component of Starbucks' strategy is creating relationships with customers at the store level—particularly relationships established between customers and the barista. Baristas receive extensive training, and are taught to anticipate customers' needs. They provide feedback on a regular basis that may lead to new products, or improved approaches to providing customer satisfaction. The "Starbucks Card" also provides the basis for a loyalty program in the future.

Starbucks relational model emphasizes the development of long-term relationships with its vendors and partners, rather than making decisions on the basis of lowest cost. The company looks for quality first, then service, and finally cost. Although they negotiate very hard, they will not compromise quality or service to obtain a lower price. Supplier selection involves employees from various functional areas, to understand how the entire supply chain can affect Starbucks operations. They choose vendors and partners that can grow with them. Included with suppliers are the coffee growers. As a solid supporter of the Fair Trade movement, Starbucks pays a premium price for its coffee and is committed to social and environmental issues in countries where their coffee is grown.

In order to develop the Starbucks brand outside its own retail stores, the company leverages its increasingly strong brand through alliances to sell Starbucks coffee and to create new products under the Starbucks name. To counter the risk of losing direct control over its brand, partners are carefully chosen based on their reputation, commitment to quality, and willingness to train their employees the Starbucks way. Close, collaborative relationships are established and nurtured within this aspect of the relational model. Licensing agreements provide Starbucks with more control of its brand than it would have with franchising arrangements.

The challenge facing Starbucks is how to maintain the differentiation of a brand through customer experiences, and the internal and external relationships that make those experiences a reality. They are facing the test of whether relationships that are built on trust—one cup of coffee, one customer, and one store at a time—can be sustained through growth to a projected 10,000 to 20,000 retail locations, and an increase in employees from 25,000 to 50,000.

Howard Schultz says, "There is no doubt in my mind that Starbucks can realize its financial goals. A more fragile issue is whether our values and guiding principles will remain intact as we continue to expand." Another issue in the U.S. market is the shifting customer base from the Baby Boom generation to Generation Xers—some of whom are social activists with a negative attitude toward the power and image of the Starbucks brand, and designer coffee at high prices.

Sources: Ranjay Gulati, Sarah Huffman, and Gary Neilson, "The Barista Principle: Starbucks and the Rise of Relational Capital," *Strategy + Business* (Issue 28, Third Quarter 2002), pp. 58–69; Jake Batsell, "Starbucks Turned a Shot Into a Grande," *The Seattle Times* (November 4, 2001), http://www.seattletimes.com; "World of Coffee," www.msnbc.com (August 25, 2002); "Coffee Crisis," www.msnbc.com (August 25, 2002); www.starbucks.com (August 25, 2002); www.hoovers.com (August 25, 2002); Stanley Homes and Geri Smith, "Planet Starbucks: To Keep Up the Growth, It Must Go Global Quickly," *BusinessWeek* (September 9, 2002), pp. 100–110.

Excitement . . . challenge . . . opportunities for creativity . . . meaningful contributions to society. Marketing management offers all of these—and more—to for-profit and nonprofit organizations in the twenty-first century. Marketing activities occur at the *cutting edge,* that is, between an organization and its customers, suppliers, and other constituencies. Thus, the high visibility of marketing management decisions lays them open to constant external and internal scrutiny. Opportunities abound for alert and innovative managers to develop and maintain successful enterprises. However, these opportunities are not without risk, as firms find themselves operating at an accelerated pace in an increasingly complex and uncertain global marketplace.

The marketing function constantly undergoes significant changes due to a variety of simultaneous and rapidly occurring environmental pressures. Some of the most noteworthy catalysts for change in recent times include

- increased globalization of markets on both the supply and demand sides,
- implications of new and converging technologies, advances in telecommunications, and the Internet,
- computer applications and the creation and uses of extensive databases,

- redesigned organizational structures,[1] and
- increased emphasis on national and global security, business ethics, and social responsibility.

Global competition has intensified because of mergers, acquisitions, joint ventures, and other alliances formed by major marketing firms in industries such as automobiles, appliances, and food products. Worldwide telecommunications are at the forefront of the global business revolution, with partnerships being formed among telephone and cable companies and a wide spectrum of publishing and entertainment enterprises. The Internet brings markets and suppliers much closer together. The growth of computing power has a major impact on low-tech as well as high-tech businesses. Computer power levels the playing field between large and small businesses by generating mutual advantages in creating new product designs, higher efficiency in production, shorter order lead times, innovative marketing programs, closer long-term buyer-seller relationships, and other widely used applications. Organizations are leaner, with fewer layers. A smaller number of workers can accomplish more work in less time with more flexibility as they communicate across departments, companies, and nations by computer, fax, Internet, and other information technology. These revolutions—and others yet to come—will continue to provide both opportunities and threats for marketing managers in the twenty-first century.

MARKETING AND MARKETING MANAGEMENT DEFINED

The definition of *marketing* is shifting rapidly from the traditional, transaction-based view of microeconomics and production efficiency to marketing as a mutually beneficial exchange process built on long-term relationships between buyers and sellers. While both customers and products have a major influence on marketing decisions, companies are devoting more attention than ever before to customers' wants and needs. Likewise, marketing efforts are more focused on attracting, retaining, and developing profitable relationships with employees, suppliers, customers, and others.

How is *marketing* defined? The term can be defined as narrowly or as broadly as you like. The simplest definition of marketing is: Find a need and fill it! Many people equate marketing with personal selling and advertising, but marketing encompasses much more than this. The American Marketing Association's (AMA's) definition has evolved over the years to reflect the realities of the marketplace. Early definitions focused on selling goods that had already been produced, with little recognition of customers' wants and needs or the use of marketing in nonprofit organizations. In 1960, the AMA defined *marketing* as

> the performance of business activities that direct the flow of goods and services from product to consumer to user.[2]

In 1985, the AMA definition was broadened to view marketing as a system and marketing activity as a process that can be performed by nonprofit organizations as well as by businesses selling goods and services for profit:

> Marketing is the process of planning and executing the conception, pricing, promotion, and distribution of ideas, goods, and services to create exchanges that satisfy individual and organizational objectives.[3]

Based on the daily decisions and activities of contemporary marketing managers, we believe that the definitions of marketing and marketing management have extended further to encompass more aspects of the organization and its environment. Borrowing heavily from Frederick E. Webster, we believe that

> **Marketing** is the management function responsible for assuring that every aspect of the organization focuses on customer relationships by delivering superior value, recognizing that the organization's ongoing relationships with customers are its most important asset.[4]

Marketing
Management function responsible for developing and maintaining customer relationships through superior value.

Schultz expands this definition by focusing on what marketing is supposed to do: "create value for customers and prospects; for companies, channels and distributors; for shareholders; and for economies, societies, and yes, even governments and trading partners." Thinking about marketing as value creation "promotes a different mindset among those who practice it, manage it, approve it as an organizational activity and enjoy the benefits."[5]

Marketing management
Continuous process at all organizational levels and across business functions from formulation to implementation of marketing strategy.

Marketing management is a continuous and pervasive process that occurs at all levels of an organization and across all business functions. At the total organizational level, marketing management involves creating and maintaining the organization's culture—a set of values and beliefs about the necessity of satisfying customers' needs. These values and beliefs dictate that long-term cooperative relationships should be built and maintained through an analysis of market structure, customer behavior, and positioning within the value-adding process. At the strategic business unit (SBU) or divisional level, marketing management involves strategy— defining how the organization is to compete within the market and focusing on market segmentation and targeting, positioning of goods/services, and deciding when and how to partner. At the operating level, marketing management develops tactics—specifics about the marketing mix (product offerings, place/distribution policies, pricing, promotion/communication)—and manages customer and reseller relationships. Each level of marketing management and activities must be developed in continuity with the preceding level as the organization moves from formulation to implementation of marketing strategy. This includes the integration of marketing with other business functions at both the strategic and tactical levels.

Marketing in a Multilayered Environment

The environment in which marketing occurs likewise can be viewed from a number of levels, starting with an individual customer and expanding to a broader view of the entire global marketplace, as shown in Figure 1.1.

The Customer at the Core. At the heart of the marketing environment is the customer or primary purchasing unit, the reason for an organization's existence. A customer may be an individual consumer or a single company, nonprofit organization, or government agency that is the buyer or receiver of goods and services produced for its benefit. When aggregated into markets, the number and types of these customers, their locations, buying habits, and wants and needs are of particular

FIGURE 1.1

A Model of the Marketing Environment

interest to marketers who are interested not only in their present characteristics but also in the direction that these will take in the future.

The following discussion of environmental influences is organized according to internal and external factors. In reality, however, it is not possible to neatly separate one from the other in an interactive twenty-first century marketplace. The marketing mix is only part of a complex network system that consists of the marketer, customer, and employee, all of whom must be coordinated, related, and work together if the marketing process is to work. The concept of "employee" is broadly defined to include not only the company's sales force and other employees, but also retailers, distributors, agents, and other facilitators who create value for one another.[6]

The Internal Marketing Environment.   Various aspects of the marketing function create a unique environment within an organization. The marketing function is closest to customers and consists of all the influences and actions taken by the marketer to satisfy customer needs. The firm's mission and marketing strategy provide a basis for designing the **marketing mix**—the combination of products (goods and services), prices, promotion (communications), and place (distribution) decisions that make up a particular marketing program design.

The Internal Organizational Environment.   Marketing and other functional activities are performed within an integrated organizational environment. Business functions other than marketing include accounting, finance, human resources, operations, information systems, and other areas required for operating an efficient and effective marketing organization. These functions may be extended to encompass

Marketing mix
The "4 P's" of product, price, place (distribution), and promotion (communications).

other areas such as research and development (R&D), manufacturing, purchasing, and other functions with the potential to have a positive or negative impact on marketing strategy outcomes.

The External Micro-Environment.   The external micro-environment consists of relationships among customer markets, competitors, suppliers, marketing intermediaries and distribution channels, and any other public or private entity that may have a direct influence on a firm's ability to market its products.

Customer markets are diverse in their characteristics and in their demand for goods and services, making it necessary for marketing managers to monitor them constantly. For example, as consumers of all types exhibited a growing preference for wireless handheld telephones with Internet applications over the more traditional cellular telephones, the markets for wireless phones experienced significant growth.

Marketers may be faced with both direct and indirect *competition.* For example, Starbucks faces direct domestic and global competition from other coffee purveyors such as AFC Enterprises, Diedrich Coffee, and New World. Indirect competition may come from retail shops such as Panera, whose focus is more on food and bakery items. Of course, any beverage that can be substituted for coffee (e.g., tea), can be considered a competitor as well.

A vast array of *suppliers* provides the goods and services that are needed for the manufacture, production, and sale of finished goods, as well as the general operation of a business. For example, Starbucks must purchase not only the coffee beans that are the core of their business but also dairy products, tea, equipment for processing the "green" coffee beans, store fixtures, tables and chairs, dishes and silverware, paper products and cleaning supplies, and many other items.

Marketing intermediaries include wholesalers and retailers (middlemen) that form channels of distribution to move products from producers to final customers (see Chapter 10). Other intermediaries transport goods and services to and from the business via trucks, planes, trains, or ships—or perhaps via telephone lines, Internet, cable, or satellite. Intermediaries also may provide financing, credit, risk insurance, a wide range of business services, and other critical resources that can have a direct effect on the success of the business. Sales of Starbucks' coffee and other products are facilitated by local retail shops and trucking lines that transport the coffee from the farms to exporters, and eventually to Starbucks cafés. Lending institutions may provide the necessary financing for inventories held by manufacturers, wholesalers, and retailers. Insurance companies cover potential losses that the business and its partners may incur. Facilitating services also may include media advertising, market research, outside sales representatives, and many others.

There are many *public and private entities* within a firm's micro-environment that can have an impact on marketing efforts. Examples include political activist groups such as political action committees (PACs), the Sierra Club, antiabortionists or pro-choice groups, the tobacco lobby, the American Association of Retired Persons (AARP), the Better Business Bureau, and a variety of others. Many organizations have experienced market success or failure as a result of the efforts of such groups. Successful global companies such as Nike and Starbucks, for example, are often the targets of activist groups because of their size and visibility. Starbucks formed a department of corporate social responsibility in 2001 in an effort to be open and direct regarding social issues. They have teamed up with fair trade and environmental groups to make a positive contribution in the markets where they operate.

The External Macro-Environment.   Forces in the macro-environment can have a major impact on marketing outcomes and management decisions, but they are largely beyond the control of the firm. These forces include the demographics of the marketplace, economic factors, physical or natural conditions, technological advances, legal and political constraints, and social or cultural issues.

Marketers must constantly monitor and respond to the *demographics of the marketplace.* Shifting populations throughout the world create new opportunities and problems as the number of potential customers increases or decreases in a particular area. Demographics are analyzed in terms of changes and trends in age distribution; population size, growth rates, and mobility; household structure (including gender roles, working members, etc.); immigration and emigration patterns; ethnic markets; level of education; the nature of various market segments; and other factors of interest to the marketer.

Some *economic factors* that can affect marketing strategy and buyer responses to marketing efforts include income levels and social class distribution, demand for various goods and services, interest rates, savings and debt levels, inflation, taxes, employment, and international currency exchange rates. For example, the financial crisis in Asia during the late 1990s demonstrated that a severe financial crisis in one part of the world can have a significant impact on business conditions throughout the rest of the world. More recent economic downturns in Latin America and other areas have also affected world trade.

The *physical environment and natural conditions* will continue to have a major impact on marketing decisions into the twenty-first century. Natural events such as hurricanes, tornadoes, earthquakes, floods, wildfires, and *el Niño,* that occur in all areas of the world affect the availability of resources to create and buy goods and services. (The impact of *el Niño* was felt throughout many nations in the late 1990s with its devastating weather patterns and disruption of normal daily lifestyles for a multinational marketplace.) Environmentalists demonstrate concerns over the condition of our planet in terms of renewable and nonrenewable resources (e.g., alternative energy sources, availability of raw materials, and air and water pollution), resulting in more government regulation throughout the world, and increased use of wind, water, and solar power. Each of these factors can have an effect on marketers and their customers.

Technological advances and the rate of change associated with technological innovations represent one of the most dynamic environmental influences on marketing management decisions and the daily lives of a worldwide marketplace. Issues faced by marketers in the technological environment include R&D expenditures, rapidly changing lifestyles and business operations, changing market boundaries, new forms of communication and data transmission, automation, and so forth. Each technological breakthrough has the potential to affect the marketing mix directly or indirectly, including areas such as product design (e.g., computer-assisted design) and production (e.g., robotics), communications media (e.g., the Internet), distribution (e.g., catalogs, direct marketing, mobile commerce, and the Internet again), and pricing (e.g., higher technology generally results in increased efficiency, decreased costs, and lower customer prices). New and emerging technologies also can enhance service performance by shortening the response time needed to handle customer complaints, tracking merchandise shipments to provide customers with immediate order status information, and generally enabling the firm to be more customer-oriented.

The *legal and political environment* both protects and frustrates marketers and their customers. Protection is provided for customers in terms of product safety, fair pricing practices, truth in advertising, the right to redress when treated unfairly, and other actions that might be harmful to the buyer. Protection also is provided for one business against another regarding unfair restraint of trade, contractual relationships, and so forth. Frustrations occur in the amount of "red tape" or details required to produce and sell goods and services in the United States and throughout the world. Fiscal policies, tariffs, foreign trade agreements and market entry requirements, import/export restrictions, government type (e.g., democratic versus totalitarian), growth of public interest groups (e.g., PACs), domestic and international security concerns, and many other legal and political environmental factors affect marketing decisions.

Social/cultural issues comprise another macro-environmental force that is of particular interest to marketers. The norms, beliefs, behaviors, values, and attitudes of individuals and organizations are beyond the direct control of marketers. Although these may shift over time for a given segment of the population, changes occur rather slowly and must be monitored and understood by marketers. The cultural revolution in China and other developing countries has major implications for marketers from all over the world who plan to do business there. Within the social/cultural environment, marketers are interested in present and emerging gender roles, social and household roles, ethnic and nationalistic allegiances, environmental concerns, consumer attitudes toward business (and vice versa), attitudes toward materialism and self, and many other factors related to culture, subculture, and social behavior. Knowledge of these environmental factors can be used to determine what products to market and how to market them to a desired target market.

Each of the internal and external environmental forces just described is discussed in more detail with relevant topics later in the book. Chapter 2 discusses the role played by various environmental factors in bringing about or responding to the challenges of a changing world. As you read about change, keep in mind the "ripple effect" that a major change in one aspect of the dynamic global marketing environment shown in Figure 1.1 can have on other environmental factors at every level.

Marketing as Value Exchange

Marketing is the process of *value exchange*—the exchange of tangible goods, services, ideas, time, and other intangibles that represent value—between two or more parties. The key to a successful exchange is that each party has something of value desired by the other. For an exchange or transaction to occur, relationships must be established at some level between buyer and seller. This, in turn, requires that the parties communicate and deliver value. Of course, each party must be free to accept or reject the offer and must believe that dealing with the other is both acceptable and desirable. Marketers are increasingly aware of the fundamental need to stress mutual benefits to facilitate an exchange. When all parties involved experience a sense of fulfillment, a transaction can be considered successful.

Many types of "buyers" and "sellers" may be involved in marketing transactions. Examples include manufacturer and retailer, retailer and consumer, dentist and patient, hair stylist and client, teacher and student, voters and elected officials, congregation and clergy, worker and employer, community residents and police, and donors and the needy.

The level of satisfaction experienced by each partner in an exchange directly correlates with the ability of each to identify and satisfy the needs of the other. If both sides do not define *need* similarly, dissatisfaction may result. It is the role and responsibility of each buyer and seller to ensure satisfaction and to deal with dissatisfaction appropriately when it occurs. This may result in a series of multiple exchanges over time and ideally lead to a positive long-term relationship between buyer and seller.

The quality of exchange relationships underlies the profitability of many small businesses. Whereas customers often feel "unimportant" or as if they are just a "number" to a large business, many small businesses are more inclined to cater to individual customer needs. People in small businesses may call customers by name and provide extra personal services that increase the value of the transaction to the buyer. This, in turn, generates repeat business and referrals through word-of-mouth. Of course, many large businesses are able to develop more personal customer relationships with computer-assisted sales support (e.g., American Airlines' AAdvantage frequent flyer numbers allow American Airlines personnel to call customers by name and have more personal information about a vast array of customers).

While the focus of this text is primarily on organizations that engage in marketing for profit, the nonprofit sector has become more attuned to the need for marketing strategies to achieve a variety of objectives such as fund-raising, volunteer involvement, and acceptance by target audiences. Successful marketing efforts by nonprofits such as the American Red Cross, food banks, and homeless shelters also must stress mutual benefits that will result in an exchange or transaction in which all concerned find an acceptable level of satisfaction. Nonprofit institutions are concerned with competing with other organizations for needed funds, particularly in times of economic downturns. Professional fund-raisers understand that successful fund-raising requires the customization of proposals, a dynamic marketing orientation, and emphasis on mutual benefits to stimulate an exchange.[7]

● EVOLUTION OF THE MARKETING CONCEPT

"Build it and they will come" represents the mentality of the earlier views of marketing, with an emphasis on production and selling. Historically, marketing's role has been to sell all the goods and services a firm could produce, often using aggressive tactics or a "hard sell" to do so, with little regard for the customer's perspective. Within this context, the marketing function was narrowly defined and generally performed from either a mass-marketing perspective ("one size fits all") or a sales and advertising perspective in order to create a market. This approach tended to limit the scope of marketing activities and to isolate marketing management from other management aspects of the business.

Marketing concept
Organizations must be customer-focused, market-driven, global in scope, and flexible in delivering superior value.

More recently, the **marketing concept** generally has come to reflect the belief that organizational goals are best achieved by determining the needs and wants of target markets and delivering these benefits and satisfactions more effectively than competitors. Historically, companies have used five different approaches in marketing their products or services. A sixth approach follows a redefined marketing concept. The choice of marketing approach represents the philosophy that drives the organization's marketing activities, as follows:

1. *Production concept.* Firms following the production concept in conducting their activities will strive for high production efficiency, wide distribution, and low-cost operations, based on the premise that customers will opt for products that are widely available and low in cost.

2. *Product concept.* Firms using the product concept focus on producing good products and continuously improving them, in the belief that customers will buy the "best" products, that is, products that offer the most quality or performance.

3. *Selling concept.* Based on the belief that customers will not buy enough of the firm's products if left to their own devices, the selling concept focuses on selling and promoting the company's product aggressively rather than making what will sell.

4. *Marketing concept.* When a company follows the marketing concept, it must deliver what the market needs and wants and do so more efficiently, effectively, and with more value added than its competitors. Both internal and external marketing efforts are necessary. This philosophy is based on

   - a market focus (the firm cannot be everything to everyone);
   - customer orientation (this means taking customers' points of view to attract, retain, and satisfy them—including a global perspective);
   - coordinated marketing (this involves coordinating among marketing functions and between marketing and other company units); and
   - profitability (how else can organizations achieve their goals?).

5. *Societal marketing concept.* Organizations following the societal philosophy recognize the need to focus on the long-term consequences of their marketing activities. An expansion of the marketing concept, it includes consideration of the well-being of customers and society as a whole. The organization's responsibility is to determine the needs, wants, and interests of target markets and to deliver the desired satisfactions more effectively and efficiently than competitors. This should result in preservation or enhancement of the well-being of consumers and society.[8]

6. *The "new" marketing concept.* The evolving and expanded role of marketing is driven by a redefined marketing concept. Organizations that adopt the "new" marketing concept for long-term profitability and survival must be customer-focused, market-driven, global in scope, and flexible in their ability to deliver superior value to customers. At the same time, customers' preferences and expectations may change continuously as customers are exposed to new product offerings and communications. Further, this concept holds that

   - value is defined in the marketplace—not in the factory;
   - customer knowledge and customer and employee loyalty go hand-in-hand in building long-term relationships;
   - innovation and continuous improvement apply more to processes than to products (although products are often a by-product); and
   - the age of mass production has yielded to the era of mass customization.

In short, customer value—as defined by customers and other stakeholders—must be the central element of all business strategy. "In the end, the survivors

FIGURE 1.2

The Marketing Mix Within an Interactive Marketing System

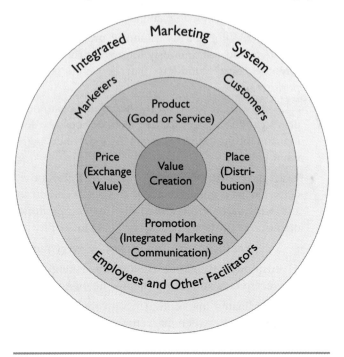

will be organizations that have the ability to reinvent themselves as market conditions change and make a full commitment to the new marketing concept."[9]
As Schultz states, focus on the traditional marketing mix must shift to a coordinated view of the marketer, the customer, and the employee if the marketing
process is to work.[10]

● THE MARKETING MIX

The marketing mix includes the basic tools used by marketing managers to sell
goods and services to target customers (Figure 1.2). Elements of the marketing mix
include the organization's *product* (good or service), *price* (value), *place* (distribution channel, location), and *promotion* (integrated marketing communications)—
sometimes referred to as the "4 P's." Marketing managers must design and
coordinate these elements within their marketing programs to achieve synergy in
the marketplace.

Product (Good or Service)

The good or service offered by an organization represents more than manufacturing or production specifications. It is a bundle of benefits that is being delivered to
meet the needs of the organization's customers. In the past, superior product design
or performance was thought to be sufficient to attract large numbers of customers

at the expense of competitors. Today, however, customers and suppliers are becoming involved in product development and management. They are being brought into the design process by many manufacturers to maximize market acceptance and purchase. Product positioning strategies have become more finely tuned to customer needs and perceived benefits, frequently from a value-added perspective.

Services may be the major offering (i.e., a service product) of marketing organizations such as airlines and banks, the telephone company, or your favorite dry cleaner. On the other hand, services may be viewed as ancillary to the sale of tangible products such as automobiles, televisions, and appliances. In either case, there is an increased effort to deliver higher-quality services and to make them tangible with clues that the consumer can recognize as a way to differentiate one firm's product or service from that of another. Services also can be considered a major marketing tool within the marketing mix. Additional services offered with the sale of goods or other services have become an important asset in building customer loyalty and gaining long-term competitive advantage.

Product proliferation in both goods and services has made it more difficult for marketers to maintain brand identity and for consumers to decide among options that are available to them. The computer industry is an excellent example of this trend with the increasingly shorter time to market of new hardware and software and related peripheral products.

Price (Value)

Price is basically the amount a customer is willing to give up to obtain a desired good or service. Traditional pricing approaches tended to be cost-based and adjusted according to demand and price elasticity, indicators of what the customer was willing to pay. Today, the focus is on pricing strategies such as everyday low prices, price-quality-value, and value-added. These are but a few of the "buzz words" that characterize the current and evolving approach to pricing. Consumers and organizational customers want real value for their money. However, value is determined by the relationship between quality and price; the better the quality for the price charged, the higher is the perceived value of the purchase. Value may also include nonmonetary factors such as time and effort expended by the customer.

Place (Distribution)

The place or distribution element of the marketing mix refers to the channels and/or locations that sellers use to reach their buyers. For example, direct sales from manufacturer to final customer represent the shortest channel. Longer channels may involve manufacturer, one or more wholesalers or agents, retailers, and final consumers.

As buyers and sellers strive to decrease the time to market for their products, distribution channels have become shorter. One result is a trend toward more discount operations, such as Sam's Warehouse Clubs and Best Buy. Specialty superstores handle large volumes of merchandise and thousands of customers. Barnes & Noble superstores, for example, represent one of the fastest-growing trends in storefront book retailing, with stores that range from 20,000 to 40,000 square feet and 100,000 titles that are sold at a 10 to 20 percent discount. They also feature food and entertainment.[11] Amazon.com, a fast-growing online bookseller, also represents an important trend in distribution via the Internet.

The growth of direct marketing represents another major change in distribution strategies, where the middleman is eliminated wherever possible—generally resulting in a cost reduction. Information technology, efficient management of customer databases, and a "poverty of time" on the part of many customers have fueled this trend, which is expected to escalate. Database marketing allows firms to respond to market needs for goods and services and to build closer relationships with their customers.

Promotion (Integrated Marketing Communications)

The promotional or communications mix consists of all the tools that an organization uses to communicate with its customers: advertising, personal selling, sales promotion, direct marketing, and publicity/public relations. All organizations involved in moving a product through the channels of distribution are involved in communications strategies as they sell to buyers at the next level. However, today, many of the traditional communications methods are being challenged.

With the advent of sophisticated multimedia opportunities, marketers have expanded their ability to communicate with their target customers. In addition to the traditional print and electronic media (i.e., newspapers, magazines, direct mail, radio, television), today's marketing messages can be transmitted by interactive television, home shopping networks, direct-mail video catalogues, computer services, m-commerce, and other electronic avenues. The globalization of markets challenges marketing managers to design and execute effective communications programs for foreign audiences at home and abroad.

⬤ MARKETING MANAGEMENT IN THE TWENTY-FIRST CENTURY

Managers of a broad range of contemporary organizations have come to recognize the importance of marketing. Involvement of marketing managers throughout the entire strategic planning process (described in Chapter 3) and effective implementation of tactical marketing decisions are critical for short-run survival and long-run sustainable competitive advantage. Marketing also contributes to an organization's survival during severe economic downturns and a subsequent decrease in financial resources, increased numbers and types of competitors, a more highly diversified customer base, disasters, and other dynamic environmental factors.

The Importance of Marketing Relationships

Relationship marketing
Activities focused on building long-term relationships with customers.

Contemporary marketing management can be viewed as a value-adding process directed toward **relationship marketing.** If marketing management is to achieve distinctive strategic competence and global advantage, it requires designing marketing operations that will create and sustain long-term relationships. The model in Figure 1.3 represents a critical set of relationships whose combined efforts carry out this dynamic process.

FIGURE 1.3

The Marketing Global Superhighway

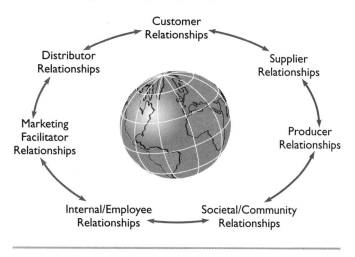

This process involves all the activities that marketers perform to ensure that mutually beneficial relationships endure in the constantly evolving global business environment. As you can see, relationships are the key: relationships with customers, suppliers, producers, employees, distributors, and marketing facilitators. Marketers need to be innovative, flexible, creative, and both proactive and reactive in their marketing decisions if these relationships are to be mutually beneficial and add value. R&D is one area where such relationships have proved effective. Close collaboration among internal business units and external sources of expertise has proved effective in decreasing time to market and increasing customer satisfaction. For example, companies such as General Electric use product development teams that bring together researchers, manufacturers, and marketers to develop new products. Lockheed Martin Aeronautics Co., a unit of Lockheed Martin Corp., is a global enterprise that focuses primarily on the research, design, development, manufacturing, and integration of advanced technology systems, products, and services. The company formed an alliance with Korea Aerospace Industries (KAI) and the Republic of Korea Air force to design, develop, and build the new supersonic T-50 advanced jet trainer airplane.[12]

The importance of relationships in the marketing process becomes even more compelling in view of the highly volatile and uncertain global business and legal/political environments. The nature and strength of these relationships, as well as the overall management of the marketing process, are affected significantly by such changes as the technology explosion characterized by the enhanced information-transfer capabilities of the Internet and wireless technologies.

The activities performed by marketing managers, although also constantly evolving, generally may be categorized as researching, planning, formulating strategy, developing marketing programs and budgets, and implementing, controlling, and evaluating the programs and results. While each of the relationships shown in the model is important, the unity (or integration) of the total marketing process is equally important to businesses. General Motors, Macy's, Sears, and other power marketers suffered financial reverses in recent years, not only because of forces beyond their control (e.g., the economy) but also because of their lack of focus on core businesses and key customers. Although these firms subsequently have turned their businesses around, opportunities were missed as a result of a lack of understanding of the market and an inability to deliver what the market needed. When a firm loses touch with its customers or fails to remember its core business, the buyer-seller relationship is in jeopardy.

It is within this "marketing global superhighway" that specific marketing activities are performed and managed. These activities are both external and internal, domestic and international. They vary from those noted earlier to a broader definition of marketing that includes networking, building and maintaining strategic alliances, continuous process improvement, R&D, and involvement in product design, as illustrated in preceding examples. In addition, throughout the marketing management process, marketers must be continuously sensitive to social responsibility issues and the expectation of highly ethical behavior. The latter has become a more important issue within the context of corporate scandals and negative performance.

Changes in Organizational Structure

The problems of recession, restructuring, downsizing/rightsizing, and privatizing have led to a new marketing environment where organizations are flatter and time horizons are shorter. Many companies have removed one or more layers of middle management, so managers tend to be younger and to have a new sense of time horizon. Such managers tend to belong to several teams and are expected to perform as **cross-functional team** players who are involved in a variety of business areas such as cost reduction and logistics. At the same time, they must maintain a clear sense of goals, product positioning, and business positioning. Marketing imagination must be applied to areas that go far beyond the traditional demand stimulation and order-getting.[13]

> **Cross-functional teams** Project management teams made up of members from many functional areas (marketing, accounting, engineering, production, etc.) who work together to achieve a common goal.

Historically, most marketing transactions have been market-based and carried on within the constraints of traditional bureaucratic hierarchical organizations. Today, a new breed of marketing organization has emerged in the form of strategic partnerships and networks. The transformation that is taking place includes a shift from a microeconomic model that emphasizes transactions and profit maximization to the management of strategic partnerships. In order to deliver superior value to customers, firms are positioning themselves between vendors and customers in the **value-adding process.** Relationships with customers are becoming the key strategic resource of the business.[14]

> **Value-adding process** All actions and organizations involved in transferring goods and services, as well as satisfaction, from suppliers to end-customers.

Changes in the Marketing Function.   Changes in organizational structures, market demand, and technology not only have redefined the marketing function but also have altered the way in which marketing decisions are made and executed. For example, marketing decisions may be made within the framework of a matrix or cross-functional organization where marketing is integrated with other functional areas, or marketing tasks may be assigned to outside experts due to the cost-effectiveness and popularity of project teams and outsourcing.

Decisions within each aspect of marketing management are associated with some element of risk. As a result, the role of marketing research has been reoriented in many firms to meet the challenges of decreased financial resources, a more

INNOVATE OR EVAPORATE*

Marketing Giant P&G Bends Its Own Rules with the Fast-Growing SpinBrush

 Inspiration for new innovations often comes from unlikely places—such as walks through the aisles of Wal-Mart. John Osher, an entrepreneur who had spent most of his career inventing things and selling them to large companies, invented the nation's best-selling toothbrush (manual or electric) in 1998, and closed a deal to sell it to Procter & Gamble in January 2001. Osher and three other Cleveland-area entrepreneurs had previously invented the Spin Pop, a lollipop attached to a battery-powered handle. The candy spins when a button is pressed. The Spin Pop was sold to Hasbro for millions, and the four men were looking for another application for their innovative technology.

The idea for their next innovation came from one of their group walks through the aisles of a local Wal-Mart. They observed that electric toothbrushes—such as Sonicare, Interplak, and others—were priced at $50.00 or more, and therefore held only a fraction of the large toothbrush market. They decided to create an electric toothbrush that would sell for $5.00 (batteries included), using the Spin Pop technology. This was only $1.00 more than the most expensive manual brush, making it attractive for customers to trade up. The next 18 months were spent in designing and sourcing a high-quality brush that could retail for $5.00. Their planned exit strategy was to sell the invention to Procter & Gamble once they could prove that the product would sell. They could not afford to advertise the brush with a $5.00 price, and were determined not to raise the price to give them the margin needed for promotion. They adapted the marketing technique they had used for the Spin Pop, with packaging that invited the consumer to "Try Me" by pressing on the package in the store. They also

hired a former Clorox salesman with years of experience selling to Wal-Mart and other large chains. They first tested SpinBrush in October 1999 in a midwestern discount chain, Meijer Inc., where it outsold the top-selling manual toothbrush by nearly 3 to 1. By early 2000, the group had convinced Walgreen and Wal-Mart to carry the brush. Ten million SpinBrush units were sold in 2000, compared to 3 million electric toothbrush units in the U.S. market. With this sales history, the group was ready to approach P&G.

Osher and his colleagues noticed that Colgate toothpaste was edging out Crest from its long-standing market leader position, which it had held since the early 1960s. Colgate launched Total, and marketed it with a new theme of whitening while Crest continued to pitch its cavity-fighting message. In 1998, Colgate's market share increased by 5.6 percent, giving the company 29.6 percent of the market. P&G's share of the market shrank to 25.6 percent during the same period, making the company a likely buyer for the SpinBrush if a deal could be worked out. Colgate had also recently launched the ActiBrush electric toothbrush at $19.95, and it was rapidly gaining market share.

Osher arranged an appointment with P&G in July 2000. Darin Yates, a brand manager on the Crest team with approval to negotiate a purchase, was impressed with focus group responses. Out of a panel of 24 members of a focus group who evaluated the SpinBrush, 23 raved about the brush, and begged to take it home. With such favorable consumer reaction, Yates moved quickly to buy SpinBrush and close the deal within six months. Since the October 2000

*The box title is attributed to James M. Higgins, *Innovate or Evaporate* (Winter Park, FL: New Management Publishing Company, 1995).

(continued)

focus group, the $5.00 SpinBrush has become the best-selling toothbrush in the United States—manual or electric. P&G posted over $200 million in global sales, helping Crest to become the company's twelfth billion-dollar brand. Crest was also able to reclaim the title of Number One oral-care brand in the United States.

The four entrepreneurs' $1.5 million investment was parlayed into a $475 million payout. Alan G. Lafley, who became chief executive of P&G in June 2000, refocused the company on brands that drive the greatest earnings, including Pampers, Tide, and Crest, staying closer to P&G's core strengths in hair and oral care, in a drive to balance sales and profit growth. (In addition to SpinBrush, Lafley purchased Clairol for $4.9 billion.)

The strategic approach taken by Lafley with SpinBrush breaks many of P&G's traditional practices:

- *Product development strategy:* SpinBrush was not invented within P&G. It was purchased from a group of independent entrepreneurs who developed and tested the product outside the company.

- *Product marketing strategy:* Three of the inventors were hired by P&G for the first year to help with everything from packaging to logistics. They became part of a 27-person team headed by Yates. They had authority to bend any P&G rules that interfered with the business. They also could go higher within the company to resolve any conflicts. As Osher said, "My job was to not allow P&G to screw it up." The SpinBrush founders wanted to keep the business entrepreneurial, but questioned the product's ability to reach its potential when it became fully integrated into P&G's big-company culture.

- *Pricing strategy:* Product introduction started with an aggressive low-end pricing strategy that made it more difficult for new entrants to gain market share, rather than starting at the high end and lowering prices as competitors entered the market. (The inventors insisted on maintaining the $5.00 price, including batteries.)

- *Promotional strategy:* To maintain the low $5.00 price, P&G opted not to use an expensive launch campaign for the first seven months, but to use packaging as their "silent salesperson." The unique package allows customers to turn on the brush in the store, and see for themselves what the brush can do. This is counter to the usual P&G product rollout with heavy TV advertising from the beginning and a price that is high enough to cover the advertising expense.

- *Competitive strategy:* Early in 2002, Colgate launched Motion—a SpinBrush look-alike at the same $5.00 price. Competition also led Colgate to drop the price of ActiBrush from $19.00 to $12.00. P&G added new models to the SpinBrush line, including some with replaceable heads, car-shaped models for children, and others.

As of August 2002, P&G was selling SpinBrush in about 35 countries—the fastest global rollout of a product ever. P&G made a dramatic departure from its usual new product development and marketing strategy in its acquisition of SpinBrush. The 165-year old company harnessed its strategic advantage in the marketing and distribution of products to the innovation and risk-taking of a small startup that was not constrained by a large company culture.

Source: Robert Berner, "Why P&G's Smile Is So Bright," *BusinessWeek* (August 12, 2002), pp. 58–60.

diverse customer base, intense competition, shorter product life cycles, and other concerns. Market researchers have become recognized partners in making marketing decisions in many industries, taking on the role of expert predictive consultants who share risk and accountability as they try to understand their customers and determine strategic direction.

Changes in the Relationship Between Marketing and Other Business Functions.   The distinct traditional functional boundaries of the past are becoming blurred as organizations develop more flexible structures to deal with the rapid changes in their operating environments. As Webster notes,

> . . . the intellectual core of marketing management needs to be expanded . . . to address more fully the set of organizational and strategic issues inherent in relationships and alliances. . . . We are now considering phenomena that have traditionally been the subject of study by psychologists, organizational behaviorists, political economists, and sociologists. The focus shifts from products and firms as units of analysis to people, organizations, and the social processes that bind actors together in ongoing relationships.[15]

This statement recognizes the changes that are taking place—or should be taking place—at each level of an organization: corporate, strategic business unit (SBU), and operating levels. Although the three key dimensions of marketing—culture (basic set of customer-oriented values and beliefs), strategy, and tactics—can be found at all organizational levels, they are emphasized at the corporate, SBU, and operating levels, respectively.

In this new role, marketing managers are integral members of cross-functional networks of specialists formed as a partnership rather than a hierarchy. Marketing managers cannot work in a vacuum; marketing decisions have an impact on, and are impacted by, decisions made by financial, accounting, operations, human resources, and other functional managers. Thus, a synergy can be realized from an internal confederation of managers who work together to achieve a common goal—for both external and internal (employee) customers and partners.

The relationship between marketing and other business functions includes an expanded role for the organization's customers. Whereas customer surveys and other research were used primarily to determine marketing strategies in the past, customers are now providing important input into decisions in other functional areas. For example, a growing number of manufacturers are bringing their customers into the design process for new products and services at an early stage. This trend is consistent with a customer orientation and the desire to reduce risk associated with the development and introduction of new products.

Marketing and Entrepreneurship

While many start-up and small firms have benefited from planned marketing programs, others have ignored the need for marketing until it was too late. However, more small business owners and entrepreneurs are recognizing the need to coordinate marketing with manufacturing, distribution, operations, financial, and other decisions. As Hisrich points out, the relationship between marketing and entrepreneurship is important because the entrepreneur must use marketing appropriately to launch and develop new ventures successfully, many entrepreneurs have a limited understanding of marketing, and entrepreneurs are often poor planners and managers.[16]

On the other hand, successful entrepreneurs have learned to use marketing to their advantage. America's fastest-growing companies include entrepreneurial firms such as teen retailer Hot Topic and Chinese fast food chain P.F. Chang's. Both firms have prospered by "dominating modest-sized niches and serving them with

MARKETING AND ENTREPRENEURSHIP

Hot Topic—One of America's Fastest Growing Retailers in Lean Economic Times

 A clearly defined niche strategy has propelled Hot Topic, an edgy alternative to mainstream stores for teens, into one of America's fastest growing companies since it opened its first store in California in 1989. As you move about one of the company's stores, you may see SpongeBob SquarePants school folders, dragon hemp necklaces, cupcake-pink hair dye, an Invader Zim journal, and Incubus or Misfits T-shirts among other trendy items. About 75 percent of Hot Topic's merchandise is not available anywhere else in their areas.

Hot Topic's teenage customers are fiercely loyal, and most say it is the only place they shop. According to Michael Wood, vice president of Teenage Research Unlimited, the store caters to what he calls "edge teens." This group is often in the vanguard of fashion, and they are passionate about their favorite bands—whose T-shirts occupy a large amount of wall space in the stores. It is not just the outcast teens who shop in Hot. Topic stores; you may find a 30-something-year-old buying a trendy T-shirt to go with his khakis. As Wood says, "Teens love stores that belong to them, and this is one of those stores."

Hot Topic has continued to attract a steady stream of new customers. This has earned it a place on Fortune's fastest growing company list for three consecutive years. Its 400-plus stores generated $415 million in sales in 2002, a 146 percent increase over 2001—without losing track of its niche. Almost fanatical attention is paid to customer feedback. CEO Betsy McLaugh-

lin studies 1,000 of the shopper "report cards" received by Hot Topic each week. Trendiness is supported by short order lead times that enable stock replenishment in 14 to 60 days. The stores also stay in step with current teen trends. For example, as the Goth trend lost popularity, Hot Topic stores replaced their gloomy, gated entrances with a more inviting, club-inspired tunnel motif.

A second niche that CEO McLaughlin has set her sights on is the plus-size women's apparel market (sizes 14–26). This is an underserved, potentially lucrative market segment that represents about 25 percent of women aged 15–34 who are size 14 or larger—9.5 million customers in the United States alone. Hot Topic added a plus-size page to its website in 1999. Within hours, orders were coming in at a rapid rate. After this response, McLaughlin decided to spin the plus-size concept out as another retail chain called Torrid. Beyond the demographics, plus-size women have become more self-confident, and want trendy, form-fitting clothing that they will travel some distance to find. Both niches are carefully monitored for customer preferences and trends in their respective markets, leading to long-term growth for this entrepreneurial firm.

Source: Matthew Boyle, excerpt from "Rapid Growth in Rough Times: Fortune's 100 Fastest Growers Prove There Is Still Life in the Fast Lane," *Fortune: 100 Fastest Growing Companies* (September 2, 2002). Copyright © 2002 Time Inc. All rights reserved.

voracious drive." Others have used their size to dominate weaker firms in a weaker economy. In the case of Hot Topic, the company is not only ranked number 10 among the fastest-growing companies, but also has a strong balance sheet and a long-tenured management team. Since the first store opened in California in 1989, a deep loyalty has grown among suburban teens who prefer Hot Topic's edgy alternative to mainstream stores. Store atmosphere is clearly targeted toward teens, from merchandising to visual displays, and music that relates to many of the T-shirts and other items carried in the stores.[17]

Marketing in Nonprofit Organizations

Numerous nonprofit organizations, such as the American Red Cross, churches, art museums, foundations, hospitals, and schools, have used marketing tools to reach their respective audiences for some time—but on a more ad hoc, informal basis. As managers of these nonprofit organizations encounter new, more complex problems in their respective marketplaces, there is an increasing trend to formalize the marketing function with assigned responsibility and specified position within the organizational structure. These managers are recognizing the need to analyze their markets, resources, and mission as a basis for marketing strategy decisions. For example, market analysis is focused on identification of markets and their needs, customer behavior and satisfaction, and attitude/awareness. Resource analysis includes recognition of internal strengths and weaknesses relative to external opportunities and threats. Mission analysis focuses on defining the organization's business mission, customers/needs served, competitors, and market positioning.[18]

Volunteers make up one of the most important market segments for nonprofit organizations, but they are becoming more difficult to recruit because many would-be volunteers are faced with time and money constraints.[19] The emerging type of volunteer is eager to help but is also "careerist and project-oriented." This creates the need for a different type of marketing approach, where meeting the needs of volunteers and tapping the resources of corporate America have become major keys in marketing programs. Organizations such as Boy Scouts of America, Ronald McDonald House, and Big Brothers/Big Sisters of America have had to scramble to attract and keep their volunteers. New York City's Boy Scouts council has started paying college students above the minimum hourly wage to lead troops, in response to the tripling of its ratio of scouts to adult volunteers in five years. Many nonprofit organizations are using marketing tactics to recruit minorities, retirees, and teens as volunteers while extending their agencies' operating hours to evenings and weekends, designing low-commitment, flexible service opportunities, and developing new relationships with corporations. As one nonprofit director said, "People want to do something that's going to make them feel good quickly," which sounds very much like a direct application of the marketing concept.

The International Scope of Marketing

As domestic firms face heightened competition from developed and developing countries, their need for effective marketing becomes evident. Developing markets for American products and emerging foreign competition from Japan, China, South America, Asia, and other parts of the world have brought about changes in marketing. For example, product and packaging designs have been adjusted, international distribution channels have been expanded or realigned, promotional methods have been adapted to local audiences, and organizational structures have been redrawn.

Of the world's 500 largest companies, 297 saw their profits fall in 2001. Total earnings were less than half the previous year's earnings. The world economy, terrorism, and dishonest executives affected many international companies. The 24 telecom companies in Fortune's Global 500 list experienced losses that were collectively $78 billion worse than the previous year. However, some of the "old-economy" global stalwarts such as DuPont (No. 172) and Unilever (No. 68) saw their profits surge by 88 percent and 61 percent, respectively. Then there's Wal-Mart (No. 1), the first service company to top Fortune's Global 500 list. The company, whose headquarters are in a modest town in one of America's poorest states, had revenues of $220 billion—exceeding that of any other company in history. Wal-Mart has also maintained a top position in Fortune's Most Admired American Companies listing for many years, placing number 3 in 2002. (Nokia was ranked as the most admired company outside the United States.) Eight criteria are considered for each of the most admired listings: innovation, financial soundness, employee talent, use of corporate assets, long-term investment value, social responsibility, quality of management, and quality of products/services. Wal-Mart has demonstrated its ability to compete successfully under effective leadership in the global marketplace. They have developed winning strategies for growth, and for growing or maintaining market share. They have done this by understanding customer and employee wants and needs, and by targeting customer groups that can be satisfied in a manner superior to competitors' efforts.[20]

● FOCUSING ON CUSTOMER SATISFACTION

Customers experience feelings of either satisfaction or dissatisfaction with each purchase of a good or service. While these feelings may extend from a mere shrug of the shoulders to legal action, it is important to understand the marketing implications of either state. Satisfied customers are repeat customers. They are a good source of new business through word-of-mouth communication. On the other hand, dissatisfied customers tend to buy elsewhere and to share their "bad" experiences with even more potential customers, thus having a negative impact on a company's marketing efforts. **Customer satisfaction** is not easy to define or measure, but in simplest terms, most customers are satisfied when their purchase experiences meet or exceed their expectations.

Customer satisfaction
Difference between expectations and perceived benefits received.

Customer-Oriented Strategies

Customer-oriented strategies are developed with customer satisfaction and company profitability as the primary motivators. Therefore, it is necessary to know precisely who the customers are, why they buy, and what it takes to satisfy them. At both the organizational and consumer levels, many changes have taken place in buying motives and purchase behavior—as well as the customer's role in marketing management decisions.

Customer-oriented strategies
Customer-satisfaction focal point for all long-term plans.

Changes in Markets and Their Buying Behavior.   Shifting demographics, changing family roles, economic concerns, advances in technology—all these factors and many more have contributed to changes in the role of marketing to final consumers. For example, as more women have entered the work force, more men and teenagers have taken on the responsibility of shopping for the family. Customers of all types are increasingly turning to the Internet for their shopping needs. Such trends are growing and have strategic implications for marketing communications, distribution, and other aspects of the marketing mix.

Economic influences have contributed to the growing popularity of shopping at superstores like Barnes & Noble for books, Best Buy for computers, Circuit City for appliances, Home Depot for building supplies, or Toys 'R' Us for games and toys. The significant growth in Hispanic, Asian, and other ethnic markets has prompted manufacturers and retailers to adapt products and marketing communications strategies to meet the needs of these important segments. Further, as marketers distribute their goods and services across international borders, they must implement new marketing strategies that are consistent with local realities.

Organizational buying practices have been affected significantly by world economic and political conditions. Bottom-line profitability, total quality management, and service before, during, and after the sale have become the basis for buying decisions within the context of the optimal price-value-quality relationship and avoidance of risk. In addition, the purchasing process has been streamlined in many instances through telemarketing, computerized ordering systems and inventory control, satellite links, and other advances in technology.

Marketers must constantly monitor changes in markets and their buying behavior in order to understand and act on these changes. Many marketing research tools are available for this purpose, as discussed in Chapter 4. The key is to first understand the customer, then to understand how any changes in the marketing mix might affect customer satisfaction and buying behavior. For example, Starbucks tested its wireless access service in selected stores in the United States and abroad before conducting a rollout of the concept.

Involving the Customer Earlier in the Marketing Process. Customer wants and needs are being considered more seriously than ever before in the design and delivery of both goods and services, as noted earlier. Innovative marketers are accomplishing this in a number of ways, but one of the most important approaches concerns the use of point-of-sale scanning technology to capture, store, retrieve, and use customer-based information.

Involvement of the customer in the design and delivery process is not limited to tangible goods. Services marketers also have found it advisable to include customers in their marketing decisions. For example, financial institutions are implementing marketing technology to understand each customer's needs and wants. In this industry, as in many others, the focus has shifted to the customer rather than the institution and its traditional offerings. Increased competition, deregulation, a proliferation of product and service offerings, and better informed consumers require a more external view for strategy development.

At the industrial level, changing markets and market conditions require shorter response times by manufacturers. Therefore, industrial designers and customers have become more involved in the design and manufacturing process to meet more complex and sophisticated market demands.

Value-Added Marketing Strategies. *Value-added marketing*—the right combination of quality, service, and value—is the key to market success. Customers generally perceive value as high quality at a reasonable price, but not necessarily the lowest price. Quality includes both product features and the quality of service that is delivered before, during, and after the sale. Manufacturers are increasingly concerned with preventing quality glitches before a product reaches the customer. Quality defects found by customers after the sale could drive demanding customers away forever in their quest for quality, service, and value.

In the past, the factors that established "value" were determined at the top of an organization. Today, the ability to deliver added value requires local market input in terms of knowledge, decision making, and procedures. If a company is to deliver value to its customers successfully, it must make a total commitment to making the necessary changes. This may involve the adoption of new attitudes and philosophies, implementation of new approaches to the marketing process, and redesign of the organizational structure. In particular, certain marketing decisions should be decentralized to place them closer to the customer but coordinated through the organization's centralized information system.

Advances in technology have added value to goods and services for overall quality improvement. For example, several banks have placed more emphasis on the human customer relationship management (CRM) component of their operations. They are using new high-tech CRM initiatives—integrating technology with the human touch to improve customer service on the front lines. This move has fostered an entrepreneurial culture among bank managers, and involves applications such as searching its customer database every day to identify large increases in account balances. Bank of America launched customer-focused CRM initiatives to improve service following a number of megamergers.

Quality and value often are defined in terms of service quality. Poor service quality results in customer dissatisfaction and the likelihood that the customer will change suppliers and brands. As noted previously, service evaluation depends on those factors which the customer values as important and may differ by customer segment.

Internal Marketing Strategies.   Organizations are beginning to recognize that one of their most valuable customer segments is their own employees. Comprehensive **internal marketing** programs that motivate employees to focus on the external customer should be directed toward employees at all levels—because service is everybody's business. Leading marketers, such as Southwest Airlines, Wal-Mart, and Starbucks, emphasize marketing to their internal customers—their employees. The payoff comes in the form of more satisfied employees and customers, added value for the brand, and more profitability for the company.

> **Internal marketing**
> Motivating, training, and empowering employees as the organization's internal customers.

Internal marketing can lead to high employee retention, which generally means that a company has a work force that understands its customers' needs and can be highly productive. In other words, to retain valued customers, it is necessary to retain valued employees. Internal marketing includes, but is not limited to, higher pay. Employees are motivated when management listens to and acts on their suggestions for serving internal and external customers more effectively. As described in the vignette at the beginning of the chapter, Starbucks relies heavily on its baristas and other store employees, as well as its suppliers and vendors, to "sell the brand" for Starbucks. This is accomplished with an open communication system, empowerment of employees, ongoing training programs, and excellent incentives for delivering a value-added quality experience to Starbucks customers.

Although we no longer seem to be in an era of guaranteed job security and deeply held company-employee loyalty, many companies have recognized the need to market themselves as desirable places to work. Each year, *Fortune* magazine identifies a list of "The 100 Best Companies to Work For." The 2002 list was compiled from random surveys that had been completed and tallied a few weeks before the September 11, 2001 attacks on the World Trade Center and the Pentagon. Following these attacks, and given previous concerns about an economic slowdown in the United States, *Fortune* set about finding out what makes a company fit for its list of the 100 Best Companies to Work For during a time of budget cuts and layoffs. The top four firms in the 2002 list were Edward Jones, Container Store, SAS Institute, and TDI Industries. Some special features cited by employees of these companies included small-town values, early bonuses to help defray lost commissions, special benefits, respect (felt they made a difference), fitness center, child care, employees called and treated as partners. In general, top companies like Edward Jones avoided layoffs, found creative ways to keep employees satisfied, and created an environment where employees were willing to go the extra mile. Other best companies such as Cisco (No. 15) could not avoid layoffs, but offered generous severance and compassionate alternatives. Agilent Technologies had to cut pay and lay off 8,000 people, but still had workers who loved the company. Some worked without pay and did all they could to increase productivity to help the company. Employees responded this way because of Agilent's efforts to gain its employees' trust as it was on its way up. On the way down, Agilent made a series of smart moves that involved good management, good planning, and empathy. In interviews with dozens of current, former and soon-to-be ex-Agilent employees, almost none had anything negative to say about the company.[21]

● BUILDING MARKETS FOR THE LONG TERM

Marketing managers must build long-term relationships with customers, suppliers, employees, and other important constituents. The traditional transactional approach to marketing is insufficient in most cases today. Instead, it is necessary to build and maintain strategic alliances and functional networks in order to achieve marketing and financial objectives.

Relationship Marketing versus Transaction Marketing

Relationships with customers have become a primary concern of marketers, as described below. The more traditional model of marketing considered a marketer actively involved in managing a marketing mix to match the needs of passive customers in a fragmented market. The focus was on products and transactions. Today's marketers (particularly those in industrial markets) are converting these unrelated market fragments into niches, with more focus on relationships and interactions, because they now have a better understanding of the long-term interactive relationships that are formed between buyers and sellers.

Companies are moving away from the mass-marketing strategies of the past to the practice of *relationship marketing*. Relationship marketing involves treating each customer as a unique segment to maximize customer share. New technologies make it possible to begin outside the company by knowing more about the wants and needs of key customers and then working backward to develop strategies for the marketing organization and brand.

Relationship (or database) marketing, as it is perceived by packaged-goods marketers and retailers, has resulted in a number of changes in the marketing process. Databases contain coded and specified information that makes it possible to tailor marketing decisions to specific customer traits and buying behavior, thus enhancing the opportunity for a long-term relationship between buyer and seller. Customer databases are used frequently as an important tool for direct-marketing programs. Direct marketing can be done without an extensive customer database, but merely contacting customers directly is insufficient to build relationships.

Networking

A number of marketing organizations operate as "network" organizations. Marketing is the function responsible for keeping all partners in the network focused on the customer and informed about competitor product offerings and changing customer needs and expectations.

This view is consistent with a new view of marketing management where the focus is on customer value, and "the process of defining, developing, and delivering customer value." Marketing management should be viewed as a simultaneous combination of strategy, culture, and tactics—organizational processes and capabilities for linking customers with the organization. (Recall that customers can be broadly defined to include stakeholders such as suppliers and other parties that are external to the marketing firm.)[22]

Building and Maintaining Strategic Alliances

Strategic alliance
Formal or informal relationship that in essence creates a new venture within the context of an organization's long-term strategic plan.

The range of marketing relationships extends from a single transaction to vertical integration, as shown in Figure 1.4. A true **strategic alliance** takes the form of an entirely new venture, such as the partnership between a supplier and its customer. Such an alliance should be formed and achieve goals within the context of a

FIGURE 1.4

The Range of Marketing Relationships

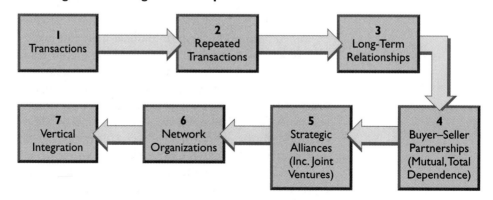

Source: Frederick E. Webster, Jr., "The Changing Role of Marketing in the Corporation," *Journal of Marketing,* Vol. 56 (October 1992), p. 5. Reprinted by permission of the American Marketing Association.

company's long-term strategic plan. Because such strategic alliances are focused on improving a firm's competitive position, they can be viewed as an important marketing phenomenon. Marketing is involved in the formation and management of strategic alliances because of their involvement with customers, resellers, or competitors for the development of new technology, new products, and new markets.[23]

● ORGANIZATION OF STRATEGIC MARKETING MANAGEMENT

Strategic Marketing Management is divided into four major sections as described below.

Part One: An Introduction to Strategic Marketing Management

Chapter 1 sets the stage for the importance of the role of marketing in a time of change. Fundamental marketing management concepts are discussed, including customer satisfaction and relationship marketing. Chapter 2 addresses the increasingly rapid rate of change as it affects strategic and tactical marketing decisions within the context of an ever-changing global environment.

Part Two: Achieving Competitive Advantage

The strategic market planning process is described relative to marketing decisions in Chapter 3, along with strategies for sustainable competitive advantage. Chapter 4 focuses on marketing intelligence and creative problem solving in marketing management decisions. Steps in the marketing research process and research issues are included. Chapters 5 and 6 address consumer buying behavior, and business markets and buying behavior, respectively. The chapters describe the respective purchase decision processes, buying influences, and differences between consumers and organizational buyers. Chapter 7 covers the basics of market segmentation, target marketing strategies, and positioning strategies.

Part Three: Implementing Marketing Mix Strategies

In this section, we address the elements of the marketing mix. Product strategy is discussed in Chapter 8, including product classifications, strategic issues, product life cycle, and branding. Chapter 9 covers the differences between marketing intangible services and tangible goods, the service design process, service quality, and other key topics. Chapter 10 provides an understanding of distribution strategies that must be determined by marketing managers, including channel types, structures, selection, and design. Chapters 11 and 12 describe integrated marketing communications (IMC) strategies and tools, respectively. The communications mix, push versus pull strategies, financial aspects, and management of the IMC mix (personal selling, advertising, sales promotion, publicity/public relations) are discussed. Chapter 13 focuses on direct marketing, and provides information about direct marketing tools and objectives, the direct marketing process, and the integration of direct marketing with other IMC tools and the distribution strategy. Chapter 14 describes the role of pricing in strategic marketing, and at different stages in the product life cycle. Various pricing strategies and issues are included.

Part Four: Managing Marketing Efforts

The need for control and measurement of marketing performance is addressed in Chapter 15. Topics include the control process and strategic planning, levels of analysis, and measures of marketing performance. Chapter 16 discusses the characteristics of a marketing-oriented organization, including organizational structure, integrated management systems, and the virtual organization.

Summary

New opportunities and challenges arise from the rapidly changing environment in which today's marketers operate. Marketing management decisions are affected by both internal and external forces—from a single buyer to a world marketplace. Increased globalization and computerization, new technology, the Internet and wireless technologies, redesigned organizational structures, and social responsibility issues have both positively and negatively affected the marketing management process.

The definition and role of marketing in the organization have shifted from a traditional transaction-based view to one that perceives marketing as a mutually beneficial exchange process built on long-term relationships between buyers and sellers.

Marketing management occurs at three distinct levels: organizational (culture), strategic business unit (strategy), and operating level (tactics). Marketing is the process of exchanging tangible goods, services, ideas, time, and other intangibles that represent value between two or more parties.

The future role of marketing is driven by a newly defined, expanded marketing concept that is customer-focused, market-driven, global in scope, and flexible in its ability to deliver superior value to continuously changing markets.

The marketing mix consists of an organization's products, price, place, and promotion. Each of these strategic elements also has had to respond to environmental changes, and operates within an integrated system.

Changes in organizational structures, market demand, and technology not only have redefined the marketing function but also have altered the way in which marketing decisions are made and executed. The relationship between marketing and other business functions is characterized by increased interdependence as cross-functional teams work together. Entrepreneurships and nonprofit organizations that use marketing tools are achieving greater success in reaching their objectives.

Customer satisfaction is critical in building long-term relationships. Thus marketers must continuously monitor changes in markets and buying behavior and involve the customer earlier in the marketing process.

Value-added marketing strategies center on the right combination of quality, service, and value from the customer's perspective. Customer satisfaction also relies on effective internal marketing to employees who must be trained and empowered to meet customer needs. Internal marketing is a major factor in employee satisfaction and productivity, which translates into higher levels of customer satisfaction and profitability.

Relationship marketing, strategic alliances, and networking are important ways to build long-term relationships with customers, suppliers, and other partners. These relationships are key factors in the new role of marketing in organizations.

Questions

1. List the major forces that make up (a) the internal marketing environment and (b) the external marketing environment. Name internal and external crises that have brought about change in a marketing organization. Evaluate the response of marketing managers to these situations. How would you have responded?

2. Describe the major environmental changes that have an impact on marketing decisions. Identify and analyze a current marketing situation that illustrates a response to each of these environmental pressures.

3. Discuss the evolution of marketing approaches used by organizations to sell their goods and services. Give examples of each concept, explaining why elements of each may continue to exist in today's markets.

4. Create your own definition of *marketing*. How is this similar/dissimilar to the definition given in the text, and why?

5. What does *marketing as value exchange* mean? Describe the "value" you received in a recent purchase of (a) clothing, (b) a restaurant meal, (c) educational services, (d) household products, and (e) a gift for a family member or friend.

6. Discuss the changes that have taken place in organizational structures and the impact of these changes on performance of the marketing function for (a) a new automobile, (b) a new movie release, (c) an existing brand of detergent, and (d) computer software targeted at a manufacturing firm.

7. Define *customer satisfaction*. Based on recent purchases, discuss specific factors that led to your satisfaction and/or dissatisfaction with this experience. What role, if any, does the customer play in ensuring satisfaction?

8. Explain the relationship between internal marketing, customer satisfaction, and profitability.

9. Discuss and give examples of (a) relationship marketing, (b) networking, and (c) strategic alliances.

Exercises

1. Outline a possible marketing mix (product, place, price, promotion/communications) for (a) a new car, (b) a new movie, (c) an existing brand of detergent, and (d) computer software targeted at a manufacturing firm.

2. Contact a nonprofit organization in your community and determine whether and how marketing tools are currently used to achieve its objectives. Include marketing's place in the organizational structure, assignment of responsibility for marketing tasks, and an evaluation of current marketing activities. What are your recommendations for changing or expanding this nonprofit organization's marketing program? Justify your answer.

3. Interview a small business owner or manager regarding the effect of the environmental forces described in the text (globalization, computerization and databases, the Internet, and organizational restructuring) on his or her business from a marketing perspective.

Endnotes

1. Thomas A. Stewart, "Welcome to the Revolution," *Fortune* (December 13, 1993), pp. 66–68, 70, 72, 76, 80.

2. Ralph S. Alexander (chairman), *Marketing Definitions: A Glossary of Terms* (Chicago: American Marketing Association, 1960), p. 15. Reprinted by permission of the American Marketing Association.

3. "AMA Board Approves New Definition," *Marketing News* (March 1, 1985), p. 1. Reprinted by permission of the American Marketing Association.

4. Frederick E. Webster, Jr., "The Changing Role of Marketing in the Corporation," *Journal of Marketing* 56 (October 1992), pp. 1–17.

5. Don E. Schultz, "It's Now Time to Change Marketing's Name," *Marketing News* (October 22, 2001), p. 8.

6. Don E. Schultz, "Marketers: Bid Farewell to Strategy Based on Old 4Ps," *Marketing News* (February 12, 2001), p. 7.

7. G. Worth George, "What Part of No Don't You Understand?" *Fund Raising Management* 23(6) (August 1992), pp. 38–41.

8. Philip Kotler, *Marketing Management: Analysis, Planning, Implementation, and Control,* 8th ed. (Englewood Cliffs, NJ: Prentice-Hall, 1994), p. 29.

9. Frederick E. Webster, Jr., "Defining the New Marketing Concept," *Marketing Management* 2(4) (1994), pp. 23–31.

10. Don E. Schultz, "Marketers: Bid Farewell to Strategy Based on Old 4Ps," *Marketing News* (February 12, 2001), p. 7.

11. Sunita Wadekar Bhargava, "Espresso, Sandwiches, and a Sea of Books," *Business Week* (July 26, 1993), p. 81.

12. *PR Newswire,* "Korea Aerospace Industries and Lockheed Martin Highlight Progress on T-50 Development and Industrial Cooperation," New York (July 24, 2002).

13. Kenneth G. Hardy, "Tough New Marketing Realities," *Business Quarterly* 57(3) (Spring 1993), pp. 77–82.

14. Webster (1992), *op. cit.*

15. Webster (1992), *op. cit.,* p. 10.

16. Robert D. Hisrich, "The Need for Marketing in Entrepreneurship," *Journal of Consumer Marketing* 9(3) (Summer 1992), pp. 43–47.

17. "Rapid Growth in Rough Times: Fortune's 100 Fastest Growers Prove There is Still Life In the Fast Lane," *Fortune: 100 Fastest Growing Companies* (September 2, 2002), www.fortune.com.

18. Philip Kotler, "Strategies for Introducing Marketing into Nonprofit Organizations," *Journal of Marketing* 43 (January 1979), pp. 37–44.

19. Keith H. Hammonds and Sandra Jones, "Good Help Is Hard to Find," *Business Week* (April 4, 1994), pp. 100–101.

20. Matthew Boyle, "America's Most Admired Companies," *Fortune* (March 4, 2002), pp. 64–86; Paola Hjelt, "The Fortune 500," *Fortune* (July 22, 2002), pp. 144+.

21. Robert Levering and Milton Moskowitz, "The 100 Best Companies to Work For: The Best in the Worst of Times," *Fortune* (February 4, 2002), pp. 60+; Daniel Roth, "How to Cut Pay, Lay Off 8000 People, and Still Have Workers Who Love You," *Fortune* (February 4, 2002), pp. 62–68.

22. Frederick E. Webster, "Marketing Management in Changing Times," *Marketing Management* (January/February 2002), pp. 18–23.

23. Webster (1992), *op. cit.*

MARKETING MANAGEMENT IN ACTION: CLOSING CASE

Starbucks: Are Cyber Cafes in Sync with the Coffee Purveyor's Core Business?

On August 22, 2002, Starbucks launched a nation-wide campaign to roll out wireless access service with T1 speeds in 1,200 of its stores in the United States and Europe, with plans to add 800 more stores by the end of the year. In Denver alone, 55 Starbucks coffee shops activated wireless, local area networks ("hot spots") for customers, with modern laptops or handheld computers. Starbucks and T-Mobile also initiated a six-months pilot test in London and Berlin, as a forerunner to global expansion. The project was possible through an existing three-way relationship between Starbucks, T-Mobile International (wireless subsidiary of Deutsche Telecom), and Hewlett-Packard (through existing alliance with Compaq), and was preceded by a 12-month beta test in five cities. This agreement made Starbucks the largest "Wi-Fi" (802.11b) network supplier in the United States.

Starbucks customers can access the network with a wireless-ready notebook computer or Pocket PC. In order to connect, the customer must have a T-Mobile HotSpot account and Wi-Fi capability for their wireless device. They can obtain a free trial of Starbucks' T-Mobile HotSpot service for 24 hours. After that, the company charges ISP prices. T-Mobile also offers a number of Internet access service plans on their Web site, at their stores, and at Starbucks.

According to each of the companies involved in this venture, technology is not the driving factor; it is the push by customers to have wireless Internet access. H-P president Michael Capellas said, "I have always been excited about the ability to tie in all of these devices. But, let's keep this in perspective. What we are doing is building the next generation of Internet access. This is about customers and how can we make it easy for them. The more we can make the technology fade into the background the better." H-P, the preferred technology provider for Starbucks, contributes free, downloadable software (Wireless Connection Manager) to make it easy for mobile users to configure their PDA or notebook computer.

At the time of the Starbucks Wi-Fi launch, T-Mobile had hotspots in airports and some Starbucks locations in San Francisco and New York. They sold a variety of plans and subscriptions to their service. Rapidly increasing use of this technology has created some problems, such as overcrowding among competing 802.11 networks. Starbucks' location in Pioneer Courthouse Square in Portland, Oregon, is at odds with the Personal Telco Project, a grassroots effort to provide free 802.11-based Internet access in a "cloud" around downtown Portland. The park is the site of Portland's first real schoolhouse and is sometimes referred to as Portland's living room, used every day by commuters, tourists, shoppers, and students—and recently competing wireless networks. There are about 70 donated access points for the free 802.11-based Internet project in the area. One of these is in an office over Pioneer Courthouse Square. Potential problems arise when new users come to the park for free access, and end up connecting to the Starbucks/T-Mobile connection. Performance is also affected adversely since both providers are using 802.11 technology, and running in the same 2.4-GHz band. Other Starbucks locations close to neighborhood area networks may face similar problems.

Starbucks chairman and chief global strategist Howard Schultz said, "We have evolved the brand that is the third place people go between home and work. People see us as extension of the front porch or the office. As a result of that, this is a rare opportunity to address our collective vision. Our customers have been waiting for just such an offering: high-speed wireless Internet access in a familiar and widely available location that keeps them connected while on the road, or between the home and office." When asked where the revenue

from this venture will come from, an industry researcher said, "It will be the 'after the morning rush' people providing the revenue . . . It could help Starbucks expand and pull in revenue from the people who will tinker on a laptop . . . and want a cappuccino." However, he suggested that there is only a finite number of customers available who have laptops, who will take them to Starbucks, who have an 802.11 adapter, and who are willing to pay the price for wireless access—particularly when free network access is available. T-Mobile's U.S. operations chairman John Stanton explained that there is frequently no quality commitment with free networks, and customers will prefer his company's network due to its high speeds and ease of use.

An industry analyst suggested that Starbucks should not become too wrapped up in the technology in this venture, and should avoid use of the words "cyber café." The analyst emphasized that Starbucks should "Keep the core business of Starbucks—coffee—and maintain those margins . . . Wireless access should not disturb the Starbucks experience." This is consistent with the words of Howard Schultz at the time of the original Compaq deal in 2001, who said that Starbucks would not become a cyber café at all—but would be the antithesis of that. He described the new Wi-Fi service as "a natural extension of the Starbucks coffeehouse experience."

Signs that make customers aware of the hot spots at relevant Starbucks have promoted the new service. As customers have become aware of the hot spots and have learned how easy they are to use, their response has been very favorable. A Starbucks customer can take his or her laptop and a wireless modem into the store, boot up the computer, and the operating system will identify the 802.11b (Wi-Fi) signal for that site. Then the customer can register with T-Mobile, and surf the Internet, download music files, or send e-mail—while getting his or her daily dose of caffeine.

Starbucks relational model relies greatly on relationships with its customers, employees, suppliers, and alliances. The company seeks feedback from each group about new products and services that will expand the brand. They have found that the customer must be able to see a connection between the core essence of the Starbucks brand

and the proposed new product or service offering. The new offering must also be consistent with the company's mission (see Exhibit 1). Likewise, the wireless Internet service (which Starbucks calls the "world's largest Wi-Fi network") needs to attract the next generation of customers. Based on a research study conducted by Starbucks, 20-something-year-olds who were hypnotized revealed that they already feel uncomfortable in today's Starbucks stores. They do not relate well to the ambiance, music, and price of gourmet coffee. The question is whether the customer service experience can be enhanced by technology without jeopardizing the barista-customer relationship, and whether the values and guiding principles that have driven Starbucks success can be maintained as the company expands into new ventures.

Exhibit 1 Starbucks Mission Statement

Establish Starbucks as the premier purveyor of the finest coffee in the world while maintaining our uncompromising principles while we grow.

The following six guiding principles will help us measure the appropriateness of our decisions:

Provide a great work environment and treat each other with respect and dignity.

Embrace diversity as an essential component in the way we do business.

Apply the highest standards of excellence to the purchasing, roasting, and fresh delivery of our coffee.

Develop enthusiastically satisfied customers all of the time.

Contribute positively to our communities and our environment.

Recognize that profitability is essential to our future success.

Starbucks Environmental Mission Statement

Starbucks is committed to a role of environmental leadership in all facets of our business. We fulfill this mission by a commitment to:

Understanding of environmental issues and sharing information with our partners.

Developing innovative and flexible solutions to bring about change.

Striving to buy, sell, and use environmentally friendly products.

Recognizing that fiscal responsibility is essential to our environmental future.

Instilling environmental responsibility as a corporate value.

Measuring and monitoring our progress for each project.

Encouraging all partners to share in the mission.

Source: www.starbucks.com

Case Study Questions

1. Evaluate Starbucks' current growth strategy, and the ability of this same strategy to sustain brand extension in the future. Are there other strategic approaches that should be considered? (These should be consistent with the company's mission statement, relational model, and core values.)

2. Analyze Starbucks' ability to maintain its focus on its core business—coffee—while expanding into new products, new markets, and new technologies.

3. Discuss the potential challenges that may be faced by Starbucks as wireless access service is added to the menu in its stores. Include the role of store operations, baristas and other employees, suppliers and alliance partners, technological considerations, and other important factors that may combine to create the valued Starbucks "customer experience."

4. Identify the advantages and disadvantages of the three-way strategic alliance between Starbucks, Hewlett-Packard, and T-Mobile in terms of Starbucks' long-term growth and enhancement of its value-added brand.

5. Evaluate the effect of relevant internal and external environmental forces on the success of Starbucks' wireless service venture in its stores. Recommend ways that marketing managers can respond to these forces to ensure success.

6. Consider the concepts of "marketing as value exchange" and "customer satisfaction" as you

make recommendations to Chairman Howard Schultz regarding implementation of the wireless service access in Starbucks coffee shops.

Source: "Starbucks, T-Mobile and HP Launch Their Campaign to Offer T1-Speed Wireless Access In the Mega-Coffee Chain's Stores. But Will Anyone Buy Into This?" Hoovers Online, http://hoovnews.com (August 22, 2002); "Tomorrow the Coffee Shop Chain Will Announce A Deal to Expand Internet Access with Partners T-Mobile and Hewlett-Packard, Perhaps Making Cyber Cafes in the United States a Commodity Instead of an Oddity," Hoovers Online, http://hoovnews.com (August 21, 2002); Steve Caulk, "Hot Coffee, Hot Spot Internet; Denver Starbucks Offering Web Service to Their Customers," *Rocky Mountain News* (August 22, 2002), p. 5B; "Revolutionary Starbucks," *The Times,* London (August 22, 2002), p. 26; Ranjay Gulati, Sarah Huffman, and Gary Neilson, "The Barista Principle: Starbucks and the Rise of Relational Capital," *Strategy + Business* (Issue 28, Third Quarter 2002), pp. 58–69; http://www.starbucks.com; Stanley Homes and Geri Smith, "Planet Starbucks," *BusinessWeek* (September 9, 2002), pp. 100–110.

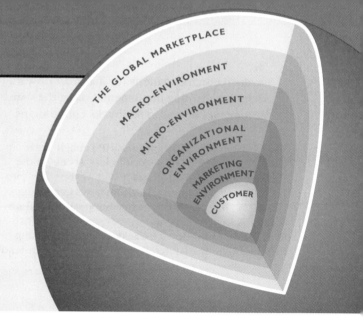

THE GLOBAL MARKETPLACE
MACRO-ENVIRONMENT
MICRO-ENVIRONMENT
ORGANIZATIONAL ENVIRONMENT
MARKETING ENVIRONMENT
CUSTOMER

Forces of Change and Their Impact

Overview

The Marketing Ecocycle

Business Revolutions and Catalysts for Change

Impact of Change on Strategic and Tactical Marketing Decisions

Did the dinosaurs hold management training seminars when their world started changing? "No longer are we guaranteed good weather, plentiful food and big mud holes to wallow in," said the facilitator, a tyrannosaurus. "We have to take responsibility for our own survival. If we don't adapt, we're history." To which a weary brontosaurus, from his perspective in the middle of the food chain, replied, "We've always done things this way. Why change? Besides, you guys are always coming up with these hot survival fads and they never stick. Remember values-based evolution?"[1]

Transformation of a Society: The Hydrogen Economy

Decades ago, Jules Verne suggested that society would be utterly transformed by energy based on hydrogen. Today that possibility seems more realistic than ever. Ford Motor Company Chairman William Clay Ford said that the fuel cell will "finally end the 100-year reign of the internal combustion engine." The first fuel cell was built in 1839, but did not receive much attention as a practical generator until NASA first used it in the U.S. space program in the 1960s.

Fuel cells create electricity through a chemical reaction between hydrogen and oxygen. When pure hydrogen is used as a fuel, water vapor is the only emission—a cleaner, more environmentally friendly alternative to some other energy sources that are currently in use. The use of fuel cells powered by hydrogen is gaining strong support, although this may be a disruptive technology that challenges the "old ways" of generating power and providing electricity. Some reasons for this heightened interest include:

- Energy based on hydrogen provides unprecedented efficiency.
- Hydrogen-powered fuel cells are expected to solve nearly every energy problem.

- Commercial organizations are accelerating the hydrogen economy. The first wave of products is already on the market, and will increase over the next several years. This includes cars and buses powered by fuel cells, and compact electric generators for commercial buildings and houses.
- The technology for generating hydrogen is available now—with "reformers" and "electrolyzers" that are powered by renewable energy sources, such as wind turbines and solar panels.
- Major oil companies are betting heavily on the future use of hydrogen. Many of the largest manufacturers, such as United Technologies, General Electric, DuPont, and every major automobile company, also are planning to use fuel cells powered by hydrogen in future products.

Despite the many positive arguments for the widespread use of hydrogen-powered fuel cells, many issues must be resolved. The major barriers are cost, infrastructure, time, and government support. Time can be shortened by making hydrogen from natural gas (methane). (Methane is currently used in plastics, hydrogenated vegetable oil, and other products.) Although its use can be supported strategically, methane is environmentally unfriendly because it generates carbon dioxide. Experts believe the first task is to equip gasoline service stations to fuel the hydrogen-powered cars that are coming onto the market, because the existing infrastructure is limited and widely dispersed. Therefore, the lack of a hydrogen infrastructure to supply fuel to these vehicles must take high priority. The cost barrier could be addressed by higher levels of spending by industries or the government to accelerate low-cost mass production of fuel cells. In addition to technical hurdles that must be overcome, the public's perception of hydrogen-powered fuel cells is not always favorable or accurate.

The September 11, 2001 terrorist attacks on the United States provided an incentive for a more rapid shift away from methane to renewable sources like solar and wind. Royal Dutch/Shell, an oil giant that is investing heavily in hydrogen for the future, believes that nearly half the world's entire energy supply may come from renewable sources by the middle of this century. As one looks around the world, it is apparent that oil is being displaced by other sources of power. In Scandinavia, three major companies plan to build a pilot plant where wind power will be used to make hydrogen. The implications of switching to this technology are significant. Denmark obtains 15 percent of its power from the wind, making it the world wind-power leader. The advantages include the ability to store hydrogen in large quantities, making it suitable for use in fuel cell–equipped buildings and vehicles. For example, the technology is used in Daimler-Chrysler's hydrogen-powered buses in Europe.

Wind power can be generated in many areas of the United States. For example, North and South Dakota have strong winds, and "if studded with twirling wind turbines, could become the Saudi Arabia of hydrogen." Other potential hydrogen sources include the 55 major dams along the Columbia River and its tributaries in the Pacific Northwest, and the volcanoes in Hawaii for their geothermal energy.

Solar power has gained in popularity as an energy source. Customers can buy a solar photovoltaic system at some Home Depot stores in California, and solar roofing is available from companies such as United Solar Systems. Throughout the world, photovoltaic sales increased by 38 percent in 2001. Although the cost of solar energy is decreasing, it is still too expensive to be considered a major replacement for grid-supplied electricity.

In contrast to solar power, wind power costs have dropped 90 percent since 1980. (Monster turbines are credited with this drop.) Wind power usage throughout the world has increased 25 percent each year for the past decade—faster than solar, which has grown 20 percent, or any other energy source. It is estimated that Europe's wind capacity alone could reach 60 billion watts by 2010. This is enough power to serve 75 million people. The United States is catching up quickly, but still lags behind the Europeans. Most of the growth in use of wind power in the United States is in the thrifty heartland, where an Iowa school district was first to adopt the technology for its schools. An increasing number of midwestern towns, school districts, and farmers were then inspired to use wind power. According to a wind power consultant, the systems generally break even within a decade, then "continue to whirl out cash year after year." Two Minnesota farmers were among the first to try this technology. They let an energy company plant seventeen wind turbines on six acres of their family farm. These turbines together can generate up to ten megawatts—enough to power 4,000 homes. The brothers now have installed two 750-kilowatt turbines of their own, and will sell the output to the local utility. They expect each turbine to generate $25,000 each year after reaching breakeven in about 12 years.

With the exception of hydropower, renewable energy provides only 2 percent of the electricity used in the United States today—but there is great potential for its use in the future. A federal study found that the harnessable wind power in the midwestern and western states alone is capable of supplying "as much electricity over a 15-year period as all of Saudi Arabia's vast oil reserves if they were burned in power plants." Large energy companies such as ABB, Royal Dutch/Shell, and BP (which now stands for "beyond petroleum"), are making major investments in wind power. BP has strengthened its position in solar power to become the third largest photovoltaics maker, behind Sharp and Kyocera of Japan.

Experts describe a very different energy industry in the next two decades, with a diverse group of large players. William Ford's prediction that fuel cells will become the twenty-first century's answer to the internal combustion engine is on its way to becoming a reality. Sunbeam's Coleman Powermate unit is marketing small, portable power modules that contain fuel cells. Other companies are preparing to market larger fuel systems to homeowners and small businesses. Some have been installed in pilot programs, and full-scale rollouts are expected in the next several years. The market for fuel cells is estimated to reach $2.4 billion in sales by 2005, up from $218 million in 2000. Energy crises, such as the electricity shortage experienced by Californians in 2001, have created more interest in fuel-cell technology as an alternative to present energy sources. Although many people are unaware of it, energy companies are already serving an existing market for fuel cells. A United Technologies unit, International Fuel Cells, has been using fuel-cell systems to provide "uninterruptible" power to buildings in South Windsor, Connecticut. It is now

using its 200-kilowatt PC25 systems to provide electricity to everything from a bank in Omaha to a police station in New York City's Central Park. (The system enabled the city to avoid a $1.2 million power-line upgrade.)

Automotive manufacturers are investing heavily in fuel-cell technology, and experts expect that fuel-cell cars will lead the hydrogen economy by the end of this decade. Ford and Daimler-Chrysler committed $750 million to a joint venture with Ballard Power Systems to develop fuel-cell cars by 2004. In summer 2002, Ford Power Products (powertrain sales office of Ford Motor Co.) unveiled the first hydrogen-fueled internal combustion engine, the Ecostar hydrogen generator developed in collaboration with Ballard. General Motors (GM) and Toyota formed an alliance for the same purpose. GM announced it would have generators similar to the Ford-Ballard technology available in 2005. Other auto manufacturers that have joined the race include Honda, Renault-Nissan, Hyundai, and Volkswagen. Detroit, Michigan has become a research center for breakthrough technology that may change the automotive industry forever. Analysts estimate that an investment of $500 million to $1 billion is being made in these projects each year.

There is a downside to a speedy adoption of hydrogen fuel-cell technology. A widely accepted way to carry large amounts of hydrogen around in vehicles is still needed, although hydrogen can be compressed, making it possible for cars to have special tanks with pressurized hydrogen. Several companies are working diligently on this problem. A partnership between General Motors and Quantum Fuel System Technologies Worldwide, Inc. received certification from a top German safety institute in summer 2002 for the first high-pressure hydrogen storage tank, ultimately capable of allowing fuel-cell vehicles to achieve a 300-mile driving range. Quantum has benefited from its experience in aerospace applications where weight is critical. Research efforts are focused on producing an efficient, lightweight onboard storage system with sufficient capacity for longer distance driving.

Because it will take some time to put the necessary infrastructure in place, it will be at least a few years until the corner gas station will be equipped to sell hydrogen. For those who want to gas up their fuel cells at home, Stuart Energy

Systems of Toronto is developing an efficient electrolyzer that only requires a garden hose for water and an electrical outlet to generate enough hydrogen overnight to fuel your car for the next day. If you do not want to carry an onboard hydrogen tank in your vehicle, cars can carry compact reformers that can synthesize gas from either gasoline or methanol (wood alcohol). Gasoline reformers, which still need further development, are costly, bulky, energy consuming, and complex. Methanol is less polluting to reform into hydrogen than gasoline, but it is very toxic.

In spite of the potential problems with hydrogen technology, industry leaders such as Bill Ford believe that fuel cells will ultimately replace the piston engine. The main reason is that fuel cells offer a 100 percent increase in fuel efficiency. Moreover, fuel-cell technology is developing rapidly in comparison to the piston engine, which relies on a mature technology that is becoming increasingly difficult to improve. Daimler-Chrysler is making a major effort to launch fuel-cell cars between 2003 and 2005. The first cars will not appear in dealer showrooms, but will be sold as "fleet" vehicles, such as taxis, that can be gassed up at their home bases. The fuel-cell car market is not expected to reach more than 5 percent of the 850,000 vehicles sold in the United States each year until after 2008. That is, unless the federal government takes measures to put the hydrogen economy on the fast track. This can be done through the creation of tax incentives and seed funding for faster development of wind, solar, and other renewable energy technologies, research and development grants, mandates for electric utilities, and by switching federal vehicle fleets to fuel-cell technology—which in turn would help the industry achieve the economies of scale needed to drive down costs. Industry leaders are encouraged by President Bush's hydrogen fuel-cell initiatives described during his 2003 State of the Union address.

According to energy expert Amory Lovins, "Using hydrogen to combine such renewable energy sources with highly efficient fuel-cell cars could deliver a double whammy to oil's hegemony... That's because the cars' fuel cells could be used both for transportation and, when parked, to generate electricity to feed into the grid." He refers to these vehicles as dual-use "Hypercars."

Alternative sources of energy, such as fuel-cell technology, have the potential to change our economy, our environment, and our daily lives in significant ways. The concepts of a marketing ecocycle, creative destruction, and crisis and renewal are discussed in this chapter. They are vividly illustrated by the accelerating acceptance of fuel cells powered by hydrogen. Consider the companies, industries, organizations, and individuals whose lives would be different if the United States and other countries convert to renewable energy sources.

Source: David Stipp, "The Coming Hydrogen Economy," *Fortune* (November 12, 2001), pp. 90–100; Mary Sell, "Ford, Energy Company Show Off Hydrogen-Powered Generator," *The Grand Rapids Press* (August 8, 2002), p. A30; "A Quantum Leap for GM's Hydrogen System Project," *Business World* (August 14, 2002); Steve Lohr, "Fuel-cell Work is Helping Build Research Prowess for Detroit," *The New York Times* (July 15, 2002), p. 3+; Anonymous, "Whatchamacallit?; The Jargon Patrol," *Irish Times*, Dublin, July 24, 2002, p.54.

Change is inevitable, as the saying goes, and nowhere does it seem to be more evident than in the marketing environment. The impact of change is felt throughout the world as marketing managers make far-reaching strategic and tactical decisions to avoid the fate of the dinosaurs. Successful marketers concentrate on building solid internal and external relationships as a foundation for dealing with the opportunities and risks inherent in coping with change. To compete in a rapidly changing global environment, the marketing process relies on managing information effectively and capitalizes on the use of cross-functional teams, integrative and interactive marketing, and strategic partnerships such as the AOL Time Warner alliance.

● THE MARKETING ECOCYCLE

Complex natural systems experience a continuous process of change from birth to maturation and throughout their continued development, ultimately facing a crisis of some sort. Crisis may lead to extinction (like the dinosaurs), or it can be viewed as "creative destruction" that leads to the renewal or rebirth of the system. Survival depends on the ability of the system to renew (or reinvent) itself and once again emerge as a living, vibrant system. This process of change and renewal is referred to as an *ecocycle,* which can be pictured in the form of an infinity loop (as shown in Figure 2.1, where it is applied to a marketing organization).

David Hurst adapted the theory of natural systems to explain the process of crisis and renewal experienced by most organizations as they evolve.[2] The general management literature tends to focus on the rationality of managers and the stability of organizations. However, when unexpected random events do occur, it is helpful to view organizational change as an ongoing process—one that should be expected and welcomed for the creative opportunities it provides. This means "that a manager's influence is often occasional, indirect, and delayed rather than constant, direct, and immediate. It recognizes that managers may often be constrained in their ability to act and confused as to what to do."[3] This approach enables marketing managers to view the process of crisis and renewal as a way to maintain continuity during periods of change. Natural ecocycles show us that patterns tend to form "rhythms of life" as they repeat themselves. The key for marketers is to be able to recognize that these patterns will recur.

The Natural Ecocycle

> **Natural ecocycle**
> Continuous loop of birth, conservation, creative destruction, and renewal followed by natural organisms.

A **natural ecocycle** has four basic phases: birth, conservation, creative destruction, and renewal. These phases are continuous, with some part of the system in every phase at any one time. Hurst uses the forest ecosystem to illustrate the phases in the natural ecocycle.[4] Although the continuous loop has no absolute beginning or end, this chapter will provide a simple description of the complex process by starting with the birth phase of the conventional forest life cycle. (Later an extended ecocycle model will be applied to managing change in marketing organizations.)

Phase 1: Birth.   Ecologists call this the *stage of exploitation,* where a number of processes occur simultaneously, leading to rapid colonization of the forest. Resources are plentiful and readily available, and little investment is required to harvest them (e.g., fallen trees). Eventually, this space also becomes crowded with natural growth.

Phase 2: Conservation.   As the forest space becomes more crowded, competition intensifies, and there is a need for more efficiency. A greater investment is needed for survival, and resources are used to defend territories. The entire system is becoming more tightly connected, and resources are more constrained. Hierarchical structures emerge that dominate the system and control the niches beneath them (e.g., a very large tree). The ecosystem is more homogeneous and specialized, making it more vulnerable to catastrophe (e.g., forests containing only limited species of trees that are susceptible to disease and insects). This reduced flexibility, variety, and resilience of the forest can result in catastrophe if there is a disaster (e.g., a forest fire).

Phase 3: Creative Destruction.   Continuing with the example of the forest fire, the system is only partially destroyed in order to be renewed. The existing highly developed, tightly connected hierarchical structure is shattered. Those that will survive are those mobile enough to escape (e.g., forest animals), those prepared for the situation, and those that are lucky. The forest ecosystem is out of equilibrium, and even small events occurring in the system can create large changes in outcomes.[5]

Phase 4: Renewal.   This phase represents the reconception of the system. The dynamics are difficult to observe because the large, conservative hierarchical systems that dominated the ecosystem in phase 2 have now been reduced to small-scale, widely scattered structures. Resources become loosely connected to one another, forming a large-scale network. Once again, conditions favor fast growth because resources are more accessible and little investment is required to harvest them. The ecospace now can be recolonized by a large variety of small-scale organisms in this far-from-equilibrium system within the natural constraints of the overall environment.

The Marketing Organization Ecocycle

Marketing organization ecocycle
An adaptation of the natural ecocycle with the addition of the human ability to take conscious, rational action.

The difference between a natural system, such as a forest, and a marketing organization is the ability of humans to take conscious, rational action. Thus Hurst adds rational action to the emergent and constrained action components of the natural ecocycle.[6] The **marketing organization ecocycle** illustrated in Figure 2.1 and discussed below extends the model and applies it to managing change in the

FIGURE 2.1

Marketing Organization Ecocycle

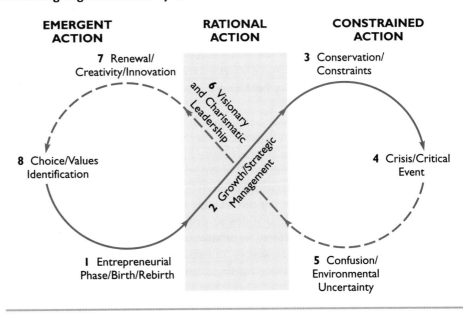

marketing environment. The rational action component is expanded to incorporate the problem-solving process under proactive and reactive conditions.

Like complex natural ecosystems, the marketing management process can be viewed as a continuous system of change and renewal following the natural rhythms of an organization's existence. Note that Figure 2.1 is comprised of two half-loops. The solid-line portion of the loop is similar to a traditional S-shaped life-cycle curve. This is generally a period of growth and planning where outcomes are somewhat predictable. Outcomes are less predictable in the dotted-line portion of the loop, which represents crisis and renewal in response to change in the organization's environment.[7] Both loops represent a learning curve under different conditions and with different motivations.

Phases of the marketing organization ecocycle are discussed briefly below and are illustrated with familiar marketing examples. However, the processes of integration and disintegration that characterize the system make it difficult to follow the progress of any one organization through the entire ecocycle. The phases are numbered for discussion, but in reality, the marketing management process is a continuous loop without a clearly defined beginning or end.

Phase 1: Entrepreneurial Phase.   In the formative start-up (or a later regenerative stage), the organizational culture promotes spontaneous behavior and learning. The entrepreneurial organization prospers and grows in a seemingly unplanned way, eventually becoming larger and more structured. Planning tends to be short term and involves tactical decisions (often in the absence of a long-term strategy to provide direction).

For example, in Nike's start-up phase, entrepreneurs Phil Knight and Bill Bowerman had the vision and energy to market a high-performance running shoe that soon replaced the ordinary sneaker and created major changes in the athletic shoe industry. Their vision was to gain a competitive advantage over popular German imports by applying high-technology, mass manufacturing, and sophisticated marketing techniques to shoes made at low cost in factories in the Far East. In this early stage, there were no clear guidelines for running the business and no clear boundaries between Nike and its environment. Those who were involved in designing, manufacturing, selling, and wearing the shoes were evolving together through loosely connected relationships and an informal communications network. The entrepreneurs and their employees had a shared vision and enthusiasm for working together to solve problems and to get the job done.[8]

Phase 2: Strategic Growth.   As the organization increases in size and complexity, managers lose the control of the operation that they once enjoyed. More emphasis is placed on formal strategic planning and proactive problem solving. Companies formalize those things which work well into a strategy that can be repeated in different situations. Nike's growth during the 1970s was based on extending the strategy that gained it a leading position in high-performance track and field shoes to products for other sports. A flexible organization and a little investment in production facilities enabled Nike to move from basketball to tennis, football, soccer, and other activities. There were few precedents for Nike to follow in developing the aggressive marketing strategy that was working so well for it. Nike was among the first to capitalize on the endorsements of professional athletes and coaches and to sponsor the Olympic Games and other events. Learning by trial and error led to repeatable strategies in a largely untapped sports shoe market. However, with this success came increased competition and a more sophisticated consumer. Specialization increased, and new materials and production methods required more efficiency.

Phase 3: Conservation/Constraints. Behavior of the marketing organization becomes constrained in the face of increased competition (and possible lack of competitive edge), scarcity of resources, and environmental threats (e.g., recession, new legislation, entry of formidable competitors). Some would argue that constraints keep the business from straying from its mission. Conversely, constraints may inhibit innovative processes and the ability to adapt to change. Nike went public in 1980, and revenues were growing. However, performance was constrained by several factors: global dominance of Puma and Adidas, and missed opportunities in the growing women's market and the jogging craze of the early 1980s. Nike stayed with its core strategy of focusing on high-tech shoes for the serious athlete, and became the preeminent international brand of athletic footwear and apparel. By the mid-1990s, Nike ran into financial constraints as consumers moved away from athletic shoes to other types of footwear, and the Asian market collapsed. Inventory gluts in the United States and Japan forced 1,600 jobs to be cut, and stock prices to slide.[9]

Phase 4: Crisis/Critical Event. The organization now finds itself vulnerable. Any crisis can threaten its survival. On the positive side, a crisis can shatter the constraints that hampered the organization in phase 3. Unwieldy hierarchies are flattened, formal policy manuals are discarded, unions and employees may join forces with management to save the firm, and new channels of information are opened. The typical result is a renewed focus on the core business and a downsizing of the operation. (Note that critical events may occur during all phases of the ecocycle in a learning organization. Further, marketing managers may create their own preemptive crises by restructuring the business, bringing in a new style of management, or other means for the purpose of using innovative processes to renew the organization.)

As Nike increased its global presence, it became the object of damaging news reports that told of the conditions under which products manufactured by Nike and other companies were made in developing nations. Human rights groups accused Nike of using low-wage employees, some of them said to be underage, in deplorable working conditions. Nike responded by cooperating with the activists and exceeding their demands by improving wages and health and safety standards, and allowing human rights groups to monitor Nike's foreign plants. Nike faced a serious problem as it dealt with this public relations nightmare, along with the Asian economic crisis and declining sales of traditional athletic shoes.[10]

Phase 5: Confusion/Environmental Uncertainty. In this phase, the organization moves from what appears to be the end of its life cycle into the early stages of the renewal curve of the ecocycle. (This process is similar to the evolution of social and political systems that have arisen from oppression or other crises.) Confusion and uncertainty prevail as managers attempt to adapt to change so as to salvage the operation. In response to the crisis, additional constraints may be generated internally or externally through changes in the corporate culture, mergers and acquisitions, shortage of resources, and other factors. The challenge is to use creative problem solving to find a more innovative way to do business.

To improve the company's financial position in 1999, Nike recognized a need for continued growth in European sales, and a strong increase in sales in Asia where recession was a threat. One analyst said that the company could meet its growth targets if outside factors went Nike's way. Changing consumer tastes in the United States would have to shift "back toward sports-related casual clothes, and away from the more popular styles sold at stores such as The Gap and Abercrombie & Fitch." Nike's Michael Jordan brand helped propel the company to market leadership in the 1990s, but by the end of the decade, it had lost its popularity among fad-conscious trendsetting teens. Nike officials were faced with the challenge of developing a future plan for their brand—one that would maintain their core values and adhere to their mission to market high-quality athletic shoes and clothing.[11]

Phase 6: Visionary and Charismatic Leadership.   Many organizations have been able to turn devastating crises into memorable successes through the efforts of charismatic leaders. Management experts maintain that organizations survive during this period because of leadership and shared values.

Phil Knight, CEO of Nike, Inc., is well known as a charismatic leader—one who has been able to maintain his company's innovative culture throughout changing business cycles. From the fast-growing 1970s, to taking the company public in 1980, gaining global dominance for the Nike brand, and successfully combining its athletic performance wear and casual clothing and shoes, Knight has led the way with a creative and dedicated team.

Phases 7 and 8: Renewal/Creativity/Innovation and Choice/Values Identification.   The close relationships and interdependence of these learning-curve phases and the entrepreneurial/rebirth phase described earlier make it difficult to separate them for discussion. The renewal phase is characterized by a creative problem-solving process in which alternatives are explored and evaluated. Choices are made among the alternatives, generally consistent with the values of the organization. The examples of the charismatic leadership of General Electric's Jack Welch, Microsoft's Bill Gates, and Nike's Phil Knight, illustrate the need to create an environment that encourages creativity and innovation. Each of these organizations has recognized the need to maintain maximum flexibility and personal initiative in order to develop the new ideas needed for success. For example, during its renewal phase, Nike has shown an ability to "break down the fences" in its now much larger, more formal organization. Novelty continues to be introduced to the enterprise through methods such as the "Launch Group" that successfully took the Air Jordan shoe to market, intentionally disrupting the formal system to retain an entrepreneurial spirit. Phil Knight said that one of the biggest challenges is that success breeds failure. "The more successful you are, the less innovative you are." As a result, opportunities for growth are more limited. Knight seems to enjoy the challenge of change. As he said, "One of the frustrating and enjoyable things is that every six months there is a new life. There is no formula. Basically you have to keep creating, otherwise you will fail. There is no easy answer."[12]

Most start-up organizations have clearly defined values that drive their organizational and marketing decisions. Unfortunately, some lose their sense of core values during the growth cycle, making it difficult to maintain their identity during times of crisis. In the renewal phase, the organization has a new opportunity to define (or redefine) the values that drive the business. This may mean new products, new markets, and more creative use of the marketing mix.

Creative Destruction and Innovation

Constant change in the environment ultimately affects the life of a marketing organization, just as it does in any natural or human ecocycle. We have seen that it is sometimes beneficial to create a crisis to ensure the ongoing viability of a company. Many innovative marketing opportunities have emerged from internal and external environmental threats. Wars have led to new technology and communications devices. Weather-related disasters have created ideas for new housing materials, and automobile and airplane accidents have created ideas for safer cars and planes. Bankruptcies have enabled companies to reorganize and reinvent themselves. AT&T's divestiture of the "Baby Bell" subsidiaries in the 1980s created smaller, more flexible organizations that can adapt to a changing environment more easily and can capitalize on the changes with new marketing innovations.

Remember that changes are inevitable and that crises will occur. Whether these events will result in creative destruction—or just total destruction—is up to the ability of marketing managers to exploit positive events and to create marketing opportunities out of negative crises.

● BUSINESS REVOLUTIONS AND CATALYSTS FOR CHANGE

A number of simultaneous revolutions are at the forefront of a vast spectrum of change: *globalization of markets, growth of information technology and computer networks, converging technologies, redesigned organizational structures,* and *the information age economy* that is a product of these revolutionary forces.[13] (These "winds of change" are illustrated in Figure 2.2.) Another important catalyst for change evolved from the September 2001 terrorist attacks on the United States, and unethical corporate practices that came to the forefront in 2001 and 2002. The result was increased emphasis on national and global security, business ethics, and social responsibility. As shown in Table 2.1, if marketers are to survive and prosper in the twenty-first century, they must continue to reorient themselves to anticipate change, capitalize on marketing opportunities, and minimize the negative consequences of unwelcome surprises that occur within the context of the environmental forces described earlier.

Globalization

Globalization
A world view of a global marketplace implying world standards and common customer needs across nations.

Today's marketers operate in a global economy. Whether a company restricts itself to domestic markets, several international markets, or markets to the entire world, the effect of **globalization** cannot be avoided. It may appear in the origin of finished goods or component parts, product design, distribution strategies, new foreign competition, products to satisfy multicultural ethnic markets, or other forms. Thus the globalization of markets requires an understanding of both customers and products and the need for a good fit between the two. McDonald's, Coca-Cola, and Honda have successfully entered many diverse markets with a basic corporate mission and

FIGURE 2.2

Business Revolutions and Change

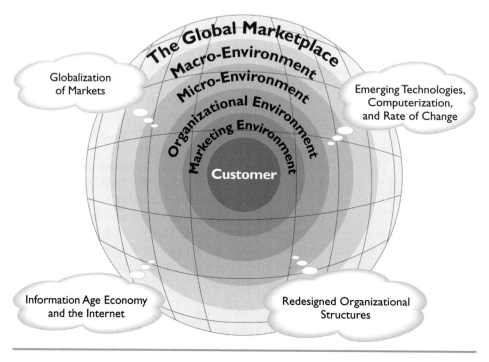

TABLE 2.1

Convergence of Business Revolutions and Environmental Factors

	Business Revolutions				
Environmental Factors	*Globalization of Markets*	*Growth of Information Technology and Computer Networks*	*Redesigned Organizational Structures*	*Information Age Economy*	*Security, Ethics, and Social Responsibility*
Customer (Buying Unit)	Increasingly diverse national and ethnic mix of customers	Internet shopping; purchase of high-tech products	Customer may be included in marketing management decisions	Increased opportunities for direct marketing	Need to build customer confidence; new/improved security goods and services; employees as customers

TABLE 2.1 *(continued)*

Convergence of Business Revolutions and Environmental Factors

	Business Revolutions				
Environmental Factors	**Globalization of Markets**	**Growth of Information Technology and Computer Networks**	**Redesigned Organizational Structures**	**Information Age Economy**	**Security, Ethics, and Social Responsibility**
Marketing Function ("4 P's")	McDonald's restaurant location decisions; Coca-Cola's ad campaigns	Shorter product life cycles and new product development time; marketing research	Networks and cross-functional teams	DSS; two-way communication; better information for management decisions	Integrated Marketing Communication (IMC) message and positioning; responsible pricing strategies, product design, distribution channels, etc.
Organizational Environment (All Business Functions)	Integration of business functions to produce global products (such as "world car")	DSS; internal communication (LANs)	Flatter organizational structures; more use of project teams (e.g., Chrysler)	Quick access to business data for planning (e.g., sales, accounting, financial)	Accounting under fire for Enron, et al. impacts marketing and product/company perceptions; financial "propriety"; operations (security, travel, etc.); human resources—honest employees, company values
Micro-environment (Direct influence on marketing functions; Marketer can exert some control)	NAFTA trade agreement; new marketing intermediaries and distribution channels	Cellular phones and wireless communication	Increased outsourcing to suppliers and marketing intermediaries	More current and accurate competitive information	Security, privacy issues, databases; new markets for producing, buying, and selling goods and services

(continued)

TABLE 2.1 *(continued)*

Convergence of Business Revolutions and Environmental Factors

	Business Revolutions				
Environmental Factors	**Globalization of Markets**	**Growth of Information Technology and Computer Networks**	**Redesigned Organizational Structures**	**Information Age Economy**	**Security, Ethics, and Social Responsibility**
Macro-environment (Marketer cannot directly control these forces)	AT&T's Network Systems Group's joint venture in China and other countries	Alliances among technical companies	Flatter organizations due to increased computerization; increased importance of organizational culture	Information superhighway market information regarding market and demographic trends; timely capture of economic data, etc.	Global security and global issues; impact on world trade and business relationships

set of core values that translate across national boundaries, cultures, and stages of economic development. (See Figure 2.3.) On a much smaller scale, a locally owned Mexican restaurant or jewelry importer also exhibits the effects of globalization.

The North American Free Trade Agreement (NAFTA) created an economic partnership to expand trade across the U.S., Mexican, and Canadian borders. Canada, one of the most important customers of the United States, is buying even more from American producers—from heavy machinery to baby carriages, as well as large increases in telecommunications equipment, music tapes, and CDs, for example. Mexican companies have bought more made-in-the-U.S.A. products from manufacturers such as Caterpillar, which experienced a significant increase in exports to Mexico. The emergence of the European Common Market and other trade agreements, such as the General Agreement on Tariffs and Trade (GATT), make international trade easier and more desirable as new markets open to companies throughout the world.

Today, consumers and organizational buyers judge suppliers by world standards. When a company can enter almost any market, success is judged by who is the best in the world. The key is to determine the world standard and benchmark against world champions in every facet of the business (e.g., product design, manufacturing, distribution, and customer satisfaction). It is also important to watch for trends or events that may change these standards and then set goals that stretch performance. At one time, German automobiles were considered top quality in the world; then the Japanese entered overseas markets with models that offered superior customer value—high quality for the price. Detroit's Big Three auto makers believe that today they are positioned to deliver a world standard of quality at the best price in the world. The winners are determined in the constantly changing global

FIGURE 2.3

McDonald's Establishments Throughout the World

McDonald's Corporation Worldwide Sales and Revenues for Years 2000 and 2001 (Dollars in millions)

Countries	2000		2001	
	Sales	Operating Income	Sales	Operating Income
United States	$19,572.8	$1,773.1	$20,051.5	1596.0
Europe	9,292.8	1,180.1	9,411.7	1063.2
Asia/Pacific	7,051.4	441.9	6,621.9	370.5
Latin America	1,790.0	102.3	1,733.2	10.9
Other*	2,474.2	94.1	2,812.1	11.7
Total Systemwide Sales	$40,181.2		$40,630.4	
Corporate Operating Income**		(261.8)		(355.3)

* Includes systemwide sales for Partner Brands
** Includes operating losses for Partner Brands

McDonald's Corporation Restaurants Throughout the World (as of December 31, 2001)*

U.S. (13,099)	Europe	(5,794)	Asia/Pacific	(6,771)	Latin America	(1,581)	Other	(2,848)
	United Kingdom	(1,184)	Japan	(3,822)	Brazil	(568)	Canada	(1,223)
	Germany	(1,152)	Australia	(715)	Mexico	(235)	Other McDonald's	(550)
	France	(913)	China	(430)	Argentina	(211)	Partner Brands**	(1,075)
	Italy	(320)	Taiwan	(351)	Other	(567)		
	Spain	(309)	South Korea	(324)				
	Sweden	(240)	Philippines	(237)				
	Netherlands	(212)	Hong Kong	(198)				
	Poland	(189)	Other	(694)				
	Austria	(154)						
	Other	(1,121)						

*Number of establishments in parentheses; 30,093 restaurants system wide in 121 countries as of December 31, 2001.
**Partner Brands as of December 31, 2001 include Aroma Café (44), Boston Market (657), Chipotle (177), and Donatos Pizza (197).
Source: www.mcdonalds.com/corporate; www.hoovers.com.

marketplace, where more strategic alliances and mergers of auto makers are expected to follow the megamergers of the 1990s.

Opportunities to trade in goods and services in the global economy are not restricted to large corporations. Opportunities abound for smaller entrepreneurial firms as well, as shown by the worldwide market success of David Montague's folding mountain bikes, described in the Marketing in the Global Village box on the next page.

Trends in the U.S. Market

A discussion of global markets would not be complete without acknowledging some significant trends in domestic U.S. markets. This subject will be discussed further with buying behavior issues in Chapters 5 and 6, and segmentation in Chapter 7. However, within the context of global market changes, the U.S. market is a leading consumer of the world's goods and services—and changes in the U.S. market affect production and distribution decisions made by businesses throughout the world.

The U.S. marketplace emerged as an increasingly complex, multidimensional, multicultural customer base in the 1990s, and the trend is expected to continue throughout the twenty-first century. The traditional "typical American" no longer exists, and a new middle-class profile is evolving. Several population trends are discussed based on comprehensive U.S. Census 2000 data.

The American population has undergone significant changes over the past decade, according to statistics from the 2000 U.S. Census. Although final tabulations and analyses of Census survey data may take several years for completion, early estimates and projections identify several trends that are noteworthy within the context of marketing to consumers and businesses in a global economy. In comparison to the 1990 U.S. Census, today's Americans are:[14]

- more diverse.
- more apt to be multiracial.
- less apt to live in a traditional household.
- having fewer children.
- better educated.
- getting older.

The United States has an increasingly mobile population. During the 1990s, 13 million people emigrated from other countries to the United States. (Another 73 million people moved across state lines.) The immigrants from abroad tend to be younger than the population in general. They prefer to relocate to areas where they have friends and family, and where they can speak their native language. They retain many of their ethnic food preferences and lifestyle characteristics as an important part of their culture. They are attracted to regions with a significant proportion of people from their original country. In 2000, at least 10 percent of the population in 15 states was foreign-born, compared to only five states in 1990. For example, one of every four California residents is foreign born. Each state tends to attract a different mix of people: Mexicans generally dominate groups in California, Texas, and Illinois; Chinese and Indians are more prominent in New York; and Cubans are a prominent group in Florida. Percentages of foreign-born individuals in each of the United States are illustrated in Figure 2.4. (Washington, D.C., and Hawaii are not represented on the map.)

Hispanics and Asians make up the fastest growing minority segments. Perhaps the most significant finding of the 2000 Census is the rise in numbers of Hispanics to become the largest minority population in the United States, with numbers very

MARKETING IN THE GLOBAL VILLAGE

Global Bicycle Peddler: David Montague

The information age and advances in technology have leveled the playing field for entrepreneurial firms like Montague Corp., a manufacturer of unique folding mountain bikes. Co-owner David Montague claims that he was weaned on a fax machine, an important tool for sometimes daily transmitting of design changes back and forth between three continents. The bicycle company designs its bikes in Cambridge, Massachusetts, manufactures them in the Far East, and sells most of them in Europe. The information technology that underlies the new global economy makes it possible for niche businesses like Montague Corp. to compete globally.

In 1984 when the first Montague prototype was built, the design was praised by *Bicycling* magazine as being the best for a full-size, high-performance bicycle that folds. In 1992, Montague Corp. entered a joint venture with BMW, manufacturer of German cars. BMW sold 10,000 bicycles in Germany alone in one year. BMW was the official mountain bike sponsor for the 1996 Olympic Games in Atlanta. As part of its promotional effort, BMW provided 1,500 specially designed Official Olympic Games mountain bikes to the Atlanta Committee of the Olympic Games. Montague also produces bikes for Toyota, and other car and bicycle manufacturers have since formed partnerships to link high-performance cars and bicycles as a relationship marketing tool. As David Montague said, "We've come a long way since the early days. But the industry we've changed isn't the bicycle industry, but the car industry."

When Montague started its alliance with BMW in 1992, not a single car company sold bicycles. By 1994 every carmaker in Europe was selling a bicycle with their name on it. Over the

years Montague has occupied an almost unique niche with their simple, sturdy, high-performance bicycles that fold. The company considers the folding aspect secondary to performance, and designs bikes with consumer lifestyles in mind (i.e., easy to store, particularly in apartments, and easy to transport on buses and trains throughout the world).

In 1994, Montague took an entrepreneurial idea for a folding, electric-assisted bicycle to the U.S. Defense Advanced Research Products Agency (DARPA), a Pentagon-based agency that funds development of a broad range of concepts. As a result, the company obtained a contract to develop a bicycle (called Tactical Electric No Signature Mountain Bike, or TENS MTB), the first electric bicycle to be built for military use. It is used for many purposes by the U.S. Marine Corps., U.S. Paratroops, Military Police, and U.S. Army Special Forces.

The popularity of folding bicycles throughout the world is growing rapidly. Although it is difficult to obtain exact numbers, experts estimated that global sales of folding bikes in 2000 were between 600,000 and 1.5 million. Sales to Japanese customers represented about one third of the total, followed by Europe. The European market is particularly ideal for light and compact folding bikes because of its sophisticated public transportation system. Critical events such as the earthquake that hit Los Angeles, California in the late 1990s, and energy crises have fueled demand throughout the world for this type of bicycle.

Sources: John Michael Welch, "Folding Bikes: Moving Beyond 'Niche,'" *Bike Europe, Elsevier Business Information* 4(2) (March 2000); bicycle@montagueco .com; Alan Farnham, "Global—or Just Globaloney?" *Fortune* (June 27, 1994), pp. 97–100; Christen Kinsler, "(Two-)Wheeling and Dealing," *Ward's Auto World* (September 1996), p. 112.

FIGURE 2.4

U.S. Foreign-born Population by State

In 2000, the foreign-born represented at least 10 percent of the population in 15 states (including Washington, D.C., and Hawaii, not represented on the map), compared with just five states in 1990.

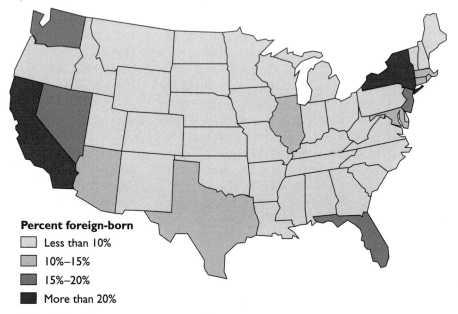

Percent foreign-born
- Less than 10%
- 10%–15%
- 15%–20%
- More than 20%

Source: William H. Frey, "Migration Swings," *American Demographics* (February 2002), pp. 18–21. Copyright © 2002 Media Central, a *Primedia* Company. All rights reserved.

close to those of the African-American population. The Hispanic market in the Northeastern, Midwestern, Southern, and Western U.S. regions is illustrated in Table 2.2. In the Midwest alone, the number of Hispanics increased by 1.4 million

TABLE 2.2 Hispanic Heritage

The Hispanic market has ceased to be a matter of regional concern. In the Midwest, for example, the Hispanic population rose by 1.4 million people.

	Total Hispanic Population, 2000	*Total Hispanic Population, 1990*	*Percent Change*
United States	35,305,818	22,354,059	57.9%
Northeast	5,254,087	3,754,389	39.9%
Midwest	3,124,532	1,726,509	81.0%
South	11,586,696	6,767,021	71.2%
West	15,340,503	10,106,140	51.8%

Data Source: U.S. Census Bureau.
Source: Alison Stein Wellner, "The Census Report," *American Demographics* (January 2002), pp. S3–S6. Copyright © 2002 Media Central, a *Primedia* Company. All rights reserved.

people. For a number of years, the U.S. Bureau of the Census has been plagued with the problem of classifying individuals who claim more than one race as their heritage. For the first time, new categories were added to the survey form to allow people to identify with more than one race (some included seven). Many chose either United States or America when asked about their ancestry or ethnic origin on the Census 2000 forms. The most common multiracial classification selected on the 2000 census was "white and some other race," with about 32 percent of self-declared multiracial people (primarily Hispanic) in this category. The states with the largest multiracial populations are shown in Table 2.3. A more diverse and more mobile population requires different goods and services, and different marketing approaches to meet their needs. For example, geographic shifts, along with demographic trends, influence marketing decisions for leisure-time activities, food and other product assortments, retail expansion, and other customer-focused strategies.

The traditional American family and household structure experienced changes during the past decade. There were 105.5 million households in 2000, 15 percent more than in 1990. However, the number of traditional family households grew more slowly (11 percent) than non-family households (23 percent), as illustrated in Table 2.4. Each segment is a lucrative market, and marketers must be aware of the changing composition of these households. For example, more than 60 million households do not include children. Many individuals delay marriage until their mid-20s and more are deciding not to have any children. Other nontraditional households include a variety of cohabitation arrangements.

Based on the 2000 Census, the new "key demographic" will most likely move to an older age group as Baby Boomers join the ranks of the middle-aged. The fastest

TABLE 2.3 Blended Look

States with the largest multiracial populations.

State	Multiracial Population	% of U.S. Multiracial Population
New York	590,182	9%
Texas	514,633	8%
Florida	376,315	6%
Hawaii	259,343	4%
Illinois	235,016	3%
New Jersey	213,755	3%
Washington	213,519	3%
Michigan	192,416	3%
Ohio	157,885	2%
Oklahoma	155,985	2%

Data Source: U.S. Census Bureau.

Source: Alison Stein Wellner, "The Census Report," *American Demographics* (January 2002), pp. S3–S6. Copyright © 2002 Media Central, a *Primedia* Company. All rights reserved.

TABLE 2.4 U.S. Household Changes

Family households still outnumber non-family households but grew at a slower rate in the past decade.

	1990	*2000*	*% Growth*
Family households	64.5 million	71.8 million	11%
Non-family households	27.4 million	33.7 million	23%
Total households	91.9 million	105.5 million	15%

Data Source: U.S. Census Bureau, *Forecast* analysis
Source: Alison Stein Wellner, "The American Family in the 21st Century," *American Demographics* (August 2001), p. 20. Copyright © 2001 Media Central, a *Primedia* Company. All rights reserved.

growing age group, the 50 to 54 age cohort, grew by 55 percent to nearly 18 million people. The second fastest group, aged 45 to 49, grew by 45 percent or 6.2 million people. As illustrated in Table 2.5, the 40 to 59 year old age group grew by more than 20 million people between 1990 and 2000.

These population shifts have many implications for marketing. For example, there is a growing need for more goods and services targeted to an older population and more factual, youth-oriented advertising messages for a younger population that is turned off by outrageous claims and "hype." Baby-boomers and the youth market are computer- and technology-literate, increasing the demand for a wide range of products for the home and office. As more people are employed in the service and

TABLE 2.5 Middle-Age Spread

The number of people between the ages of 40 and 59 in the United States increased by more than 20 million over the past decade.

Age	Population 2000	Population 1990	% Change 1990–2000
9 and younger	39,725,303	36,453,622	9%
10–19	40,747,962	34,868,264	16.9%
20–29	38,345,337	40,333,357	−4.9%
30–39	43,217,052	41,826,004	3.3%
40–49	42,534,267	31,488,359	35.1%
50–59	31,054,785	21,882,269	41.9%
60–69	20,338,992	20,727,902	−1.9%
70–79	16,273,254	14,116,192	15.3%
80 and older	9,184,954	7,073,904	30.9%

Data Source: U.S. Census Bureau
Source: Alison Stein Wellner, "The Census Report," *American Demographics* (January 2002), pp. S3–S6. Copyright © 2002 Media Central, a *Primedia* Company. All rights reserved.

entertainment industries, businesses will need to adapt their business hours to accommodate those who work in other than 9-to-5 jobs. Clearly, there is a growing market for ethnic foods, literature, entertainment, and other goods and services. Many of these are narrowly targeted and create opportunities for entrepreneurial niche marketers.

Marketers also are faced with changes in the distribution of income and how these changes affect spending patterns among various market segments. Middle-aged wage earners make up the top-earning households. Although many household incomes have dropped in real terms as a result of corporate downsizing, recessions, and the terrorist attacks of September 11, 2001, households headed by 45- to 54-year-olds have median incomes considerably higher than the national average.

Trends in personal income and buying power indicate the importance of value pricing strategies at all income levels, offering best quality at a fair price. Consumers are keeping durable products such as cars and appliances for a longer time, creating a greater need for maintenance services and parts businesses. Homes are claiming more of the consumer dollar for home repairs, remodeling, furnishings, and land-scaping, spurring growth in the do-it-yourself (D-I-Y) market and fueling the expansion of D-I-Y power retailers such as Home Depot and Lowe's.

From the "land of plenty" mentality of the 1980s when conspicuous spending was the norm, consumers of the 1990s showed a tendency to be more practical and value conscious. Consumers continue to follow this trend in the twenty-first century. Consumer researchers describe present American workers, parents, and single adults as "stressed out" due in large part to the uncertainties of job insecurity, heightened awareness of terrorism, and longer working hours. The result is a search for healthy ways to relax. Opportunities abound for both for-profit and nonprofit organizations that can respond to the contemporary American mindset. Marketers of personal care services (e.g., spa vacations, physical fitness, yoga) and outdoor activities have capitalized on this trend. Many leisure activities are targeted to families and couples by for-profit companies like Club Med and hotel chains and nonprofit organizations like Little League, churches, scouting, and the YMCA. Stressed consumers find relief in a simple cup of gourmet tea or by visiting one of the increasingly popular coffeehouses that provide a contemporary answer to the happy hour of the 1980s. The rapid expansion of Starbucks and other coffeehouses into malls, bookstores, and other locations illustrates a successful response to changing consumer lifestyles.

Along with less conspicuous consumption, today's value-oriented buyers seek honest bargains but not necessarily "cheap" prices. They want value at a fair price and a quality product that will last. Mass merchandisers and off-price retailers responded quickly to this mood by positioning themselves successfully on the dimensions of price, value, and quality. This strategy appeals to both aging baby-boomers and to a marketing-averse younger generation.

As men and women take on more of each other's life roles and responsibilities, the changing dynamics between the sexes shape consumer attitudes, making it necessary for marketers to use different approaches to sell their products. For example, traditional advertising that is gender-specific is shifting to reflect changing male-female roles.

In summary, most of the changes in the U.S. marketplace have occurred because of population shifts in the distribution of age, ethnic groups, income levels, and consumer lifestyles. These trends have an impact on consumer, industrial, governmental, and nonprofit organizations as they attempt to design the most effective marketing mixes. Using the impact of an aging population as an example, retailers and manufacturers must adjust product assortments to the needs of the elderly. This affects not only retail distribution strategies (e.g., location, delivery, and hours) but also the need for safer, more convenient packaging, lighter-weight materials, and labels that are easy to read. Health care and insurance providers are experiencing a significant upswing in demand for their services by middle-aged baby-boomers and their parents.

New and Emerging Technologies

Rapidly emerging technologies redefine our economy as companies develop new goods and services and find new ways to conduct business. Creative use of technology is essential to successful marketing as we enter the twenty-first century. The impact of computers and advances in telecommunications extend from the workplace to the home and leisure activities and permeate our educational system. Customer databases, computer networks, and other technological advances overcome the constraints of geography and time and provide a competitive edge to their users. Microprocessors, innovative software, and laser optics have taken marketers of tangible goods and intangible services into the information age. Work can be performed literally anywhere with a computer and communications software as management structures flatten, networks and team efforts become the norm, and strategic alliances extend the capabilities of the traditional marketing organization.

Technology and the External Environment.   Outside the firm, many environmental forces have an impact on, and are affected by, technology. Whole industries have been created, re-created, or obliterated by advances in computer power and telecommunications. Cellular telephones and wireless communications, interactive video games, location-based entertainment, more powerful and smaller computers, and computer software are but a few examples of fast-growing, technology-based industries. Product life cycles are shortening as new technology makes the old obsolete, making the new product development process a critical marketing function for those who compete in this fast-paced, high-tech market.

The entertainment industry is redefining and re-creating itself as strategic alliances are formed among cable and telephone companies, television station owners, computer firms, movie producers, publishers, and a host of other support organizations as they develop home-based and location-based entertainment venues to appeal to various population segments. Advances in technology also make it convenient for customers to shop or conduct business from their homes or offices, thus changing the distribution system for many goods and services. Online shopping has become increasingly efficient, convenient, and user-friendly. Emerging technology includes standardized software for Web shopping, standard protocol for credit card purchases on the Web (secure electronic transaction, or SET), new merchant-ware for both consumers and business customers, digital IDs, and other technology to make shopping on the Web safer and easier. The growth in on-line shopping has created lucrative opportunities for many companies.

Emerging information and communications technologies have brought together partners from many diverse organizations. Although many of the technology alliances are occurring among larger companies, a number of entrepreneurs have found exciting opportunities as well. Regardless of company size, most marketers will experience increasing consumer acceptance of three marketer-friendly technologies: broadband Internet; wireless; and interactive television (iTV) services. These technologies will play an increasingly important role in Web retailing, the use of interactive commercials, and realization of the capability of Personal Digital Assistants (PDAs). These new technologies are weaving marketing into consumers' daily lives, and the pace of acceptance is expected to escalate as the technologies move from interesting novelties to integrated tools. Broadband technology allows a marketer to speed up delivery of large amounts of data, which in turn makes online marketing easier and faster, and opens up many creative opportunities. Forrester Research predicted that more than 18 million U.S. homes (29% of all online U.S. households) would have broadband Internet connections by the end of 2002—an increase of 72 percent over 11 million homes in 2001. Wireless Internet connections for laptop computers and PDAs also present many opportunities for wireless advertising, wireless e-commerce, and wireless CRM (customer relationship management) applications. iTV also has gained a larger audience. More consumers subscribed to iTV in 2002 than previously, with 18.4 million U.S. households forecasted by Jupiter to have iTV service (about 17% of all U.S. households, up 135 percent over 2001. iTV enables consumers to request information or make a purchase without calling an 800 number or finding mail-order addresses. It also can be used for many other applications, such as video-on-demand (VOD) service, whereby marketers can send promotional videos directly to consumers.[15]

Transportation methods have benefited from innovative technologies as well. For example, computers are used extensively in designing automobiles and are responsible for many of the features we take for granted in our cars. Aircraft navigation and communications are made easier and safer with high-tech know-how. Innovative applications of existing technology result in new marketing opportunities and a redefined competitive environment. For example, the Eurotunnel that was built as a joint venture between Great Britain and France enables passengers to go from London to Paris by train through a tunnel under the English Channel in about the same time as going by plane, including taxi and airport waits. The 3-hour trip makes it easy for a Parisian to shop at Harrods and a Londoner to visit the Louvre for the day. This not only presents new market opportunities but also creates a new competitive environment within the transportation industry as airlines and railways seek new ways to market their services in a changing world.

Technology and the Internal Environment.   The introduction of new technology may serve as creative destruction, that is, the crisis phase of the marketing organization ecocycle. Leading firms such as Bank of America and American Airlines gained competitive advantage by introducing information technology to their operations. As early as 1950, Bank of America management recognized the need to use technology for a more efficient business operation when a rapid increase in check usage was straining the bank's ability to keep up with demand. The check-clearing process was done manually, going through at least two banks, perhaps requiring the efforts of seven or more employees over more than two days. The implementation and continuous upgrading of an information technology system continue to improve the bank's performance and have facilitated a marketing orientation.

In a similar scenario, American Airlines was having problems about the same time with its manual system of matching passenger lists with seat inventory and obtaining timely flight information, as demand for airline services escalated. American's technological solution was in the development of the computerized SABRE system that handles telephone calls, makes passenger reservations on American and other airlines, and handles other services. The technology adopted by these industry leaders significantly changed the basis of competition within the banking and airline industries, as their information technology applications continued to evolve and competitors emulated their successes with their own applications. Today, the ability to obtain and use timely, accurate information is essential for maintaining a marketing orientation.

Technology and Today's Marketing Orientation: Building Relationships. As markets change, new products proliferate, competition accelerates, and the pressure on profit margins intensifies, marketing managers must keep up with all aspects of their internal and external environments. The increased capacity of computers and the ability to manage huge databases have made marketing research easier and have facilitated providing timely environmental information for decision support systems. The focus should be on building relationships with customers, suppliers, and other stakeholders by using information effectively in all aspects of the business, such as creating innovative products to satisfy customer needs, managing inventory, evaluating suppliers, and monitoring market trends and competitors' actions.

All elements of the marketing mix (product, promotion or communications, place or distribution, and price) have been affected by emerging technologies, as shown by the examples in Table 2.6. Some of the most obvious changes have occurred in promotional and distribution methods, largely due to the capabilities of interactive electronic media.

The Information Age Economy

Tremendous changes will continue to take place in the ways that workers, customers, suppliers, and others communicate with one another. Internet, World Wide

TABLE 2.6

Technology and the Marketing Mix

Marketing Mix Element	Technology/Application
Product (Goods and Services)	Computer-assisted product design, automobile design Inventory management, retail, manufacturing
Promotion (Communications)	Personal selling, video conferencing Advertising, Internet, instant messaging Sales promotion, electronic "virtual" displays Reseller support, automatic on-line ordering
Place (Distribution)	To customers via the Internet Warehouses, automated package moving equipment Transportation, package tracking
Pricing (Value)	Demand forecasting, computerized models Cost accounting under different scenarios, computerized models

Information superhighway
Convergence of telephones, computers, television, cable, and other electronic technologies to provide instantaneous interactive communication.

Web, WAN and LAN networks, e-mail, e-commerce, cyberspace, telecommuting, wireless, and mobile computing are all a part of the **information superhighway.** The convergence of telephones, televisions, and computers introduced a new information age economy that affects the way people work, interact with one another, make purchases, and pursue leisure activities. Many of the former constraints of time and distance have all but disappeared.

How does the information superhighway affect marketing activities? It has brought about changes in markets and in the marketing mix in a "chicken and egg" relationship, since changes in one tend to bring about changes in the other. For example, consumers are purchasing more personal computers and other high-tech equipment for their homes, and more organizations are realizing the advantage of conducting business from networked facilities or virtual offices. As on-line business activities, purchasing, and entertainment venues increase, the need to reduce fraud has spawned growth in the security industry. Recognition technology has gained acceptance in response to this need, using technologies such as biometrics to identify people through various bodily characteristics. Automated services enable a company to lower operating costs.

The information superhighway not only makes change possible but also makes change necessary in all elements of the marketing mix. Advanced information technology will continue to affect decisions about product design (or redesign), development, and overall product management; communication tools and media; place or location and distribution channels; and pricing strategies. This emerging technology has proliferated a vast array of new products and services on the market. Each new product, in turn, opens up other marketing opportunities and challenges in business-to-business as well as consumer markets.

Many new media forms are available for marketers to use to reach their customers with advertising messages. New information technology such as that related to Web sites, the Internet, and mobile or wireless communication can be used by a company to support its salesforce's interaction with customers and the company. Likewise, marketing efforts play a major role in promoting the benefits of the new high-tech products, increasing demand and widening distribution.

The information superhighway is a major distribution channel for many products because customers make purchases via on-line computer and home-shopping networks. It also has made possible more effective worldwide electronic tracking of shipments. Major package-delivery companies use computerized tracking to locate a package anywhere in their worldwide system at any time and provide customers with software to make shipping preparation more efficient. Electronic kiosks have become popular in malls, where customers can bank or make purchases on-line, review real estate, or download new software and charge it to their accounts on the spot. In addition to customer convenience, this type of distribution system lowers costs by selling direct, thus keeping consumer prices down.

Changing Management Structure

Extensive computerization and advances in information technology have changed the way that work is organized in marketing and other business functions. In the past, most companies of any size were managed through a complex hierarchy with narrowly defined lines of reporting and decision making. Marketing departments tended to work as a staff function with little or no meaningful interaction with other functional divisions. Today's organizations are considerably flatter and less hierarchical as technological capabilities allow marketers to make quick, well-informed responses to their markets. As a result, the traditional role of middle managers has been eliminated or redefined as organizations become downsized or rightsized.

Concurrent with the flattening of the middle-management level of the organizational hierarchy, firms are placing greater reliance on computers to gather and analyze information. There is a greater focus on sticking to core competencies internally and outsourcing noncore work. Product management is a popular approach to executing organizational tasks and may be performed by internal project teams or outside experts. While there is a trend toward using outside consultants in marketing and other areas, the career path to the top of many organizations includes managing an important project.

Project-based (versus position-based) work is not new, having been used for decades in such industries as construction, the movie industry, and many professional services. For example, an experienced outside project leader can be hired to help reorganize a firm's distribution strategy. New cars can be designed and produced by deploying cross-functional "platform teams" rather than using the traditional method of passing work through the corporate hierarchy. Project-based work also increases the sales of supporting products. Project management can allow mass customization of a basic product, such as computer software, to solve the problems of a particular customer.

Many leading companies believe that the ability to reconfigure their organizational designs when and how needed is critical to success in the information age. Those who have revolutionized their organizational processes successfully include General Electric, Allied Signal, Ameritech, and Tenneco.[16] As General Electric's CEO, John F. Welch, said,

> You've got to be on the cutting edge of change. You can't simply maintain the status quo, because somebody's always coming from another country with another product, or consumer tastes change, or the cost structure does, or there's a technology breakthrough. If you're not fast and adaptable, you're vulnerable. This is true for every segment of every business in every country in the world.

And this is particularly true in the consumer appliance industry, where GE has been a long-time market leader.

Firms that choose to operate in highly flexible structures where information can be obtained readily from an office computer rather than going up, over, and down the organization should meet the following requirements that are consistent in organizations where change is managed successfully:

- First, everyone from the top executive to the entry-level hourly worker should share the same vision and company values so that they can all work toward achieving the same objectives.

- Second, managers and employees must view change as an ongoing process of adaptation to market needs and company capabilities—rather than a one-time occurrence.

- Third, a customer orientation must drive the business—determining what products should be produced, when, where, and how they should be sold so as to deliver the greatest value and satisfaction to customers.

• Fourth, flexibility infers the need for "all-purpose" managers who can function as team members in multiple areas. In some cases, work may be performed in a matrix organization where marketing and other functions are integrated throughout the company. The focus tends to be on skill and ability rather than on position in the company.

How have radical changes in organizational structures affected the marketing function? Marketers have been able to decrease time to market for new products, improve production efficiency, and monitor changes in their markets or company as a result of smaller, more flexible organizations and because of easier access to timely information.

As marketing firms develop more customer-oriented processes, it becomes necessary to break down the walls that traditionally separate marketing from production, engineering, research and development, finance, and other functional groups in order to implement marketing strategies successfully. As discussed earlier, cross-functional project or work teams have gained popularity as part of an overall customer-oriented process, where the reward system emphasizes teamwork over individual contributions to the success of a project. Marketing professionals play an important role on the project team, often bringing in the customers themselves to participate in the process.

Project teams
Cross-functional work groups organized and empowered to carry out a particular project.

Project teams for product development may be formed with people from areas such as engineering, design, manufacturing, marketing, finance, and a broad range of specialists. An executive may serve as "godfather" to the group, but the actual work is directed by leaders below that rank, and the group decides how it wants to be organized to get the work done. Management works out a contract with the team and then sets it loose. The team has the power to create the product without interruption and work out disputes among themselves, as well as the responsibility for meeting the budget. This type of teamwork makes the marketing process more effective because marketing personnel are able to provide input about customers' needs, with the result being a product that has a high probability of success in the marketplace.

Security, Ethics, and Social Responsibility. Concerns about security, ethics, and social responsibility are not new to marketers. However, the terrorist attacks of September 2001 and the corporate scandals of 2001 and 2002 brought each of these to the forefront in both short-term marketing tactics and long-term strategic market planning.

In the weeks following the terrorist attacks of 9/11, many referred to the mood of the population as "the new normal." The first reaction by consumers and advertisers was to focus on patriotism and American values, to downplay obvious commercialism, to search for spiritual meaning, and to help others. Staying in touch with family and friends became more important than ever, and trust became a critical component of personal and business relationships. Products that made people feel more secure (e.g., guns, security devices) flooded the market ready for eager buyers, and people bought new home furnishings as they chose to spend more time at home with family and friends. Soon after the attacks, consumers found comfort in patronizing brands and businesses that they trusted and considered reliable.

A year after the terrorist attacks, Americans had not forgotten the tragedy and the lost lives, but they had returned to near-normal routines. The long-term impact is unknown, but within a relatively short time, American consumers were once again buying luxury products, airline passengers were flying again, comfort foods were giving in to healthier fare—although many of the same fears and attitudes were still present. Advertisers recognized these shifts in attitudes and new sensitivities, and most developed communications that were appropriate—many with patriotic or family value themes. Six months after 9/11, *Advertising Age* commissioned researchers to determine the impact of the attacks. They feared that people would be reluctant to travel, spend money, eat out, shop in malls, or leave home. However, the research showed just the opposite, proving the "resilience of Americans and consumerism." Sixty-two percent said that they were going about living their lives, even though thoughts of terrorist threats marred their daily routines. Patriotic products, music, TV programs, and events buoyed the spirit of the American population. Marketers need to constantly monitor possible shifts in attitudes and values, and their effect on shopping behavior in situations such as this. In spite of these devastating events—or perhaps because of them—the U.S. population accelerated a trend (that began before September 11, 2001) toward Americana themes in home furnishings, clothing, and food. Target's "AmericaLand" product line had been in the works for two years, featuring a flag-inspired designer collection of clothing, accessories, home goods, and sporting gear. Other retailers were also quick to market red, white, and blue products, topped by the American flag.[17]

A need for trust and security was evident following news about corporate scandals at companies such as Enron, Arthur Andersen, WorldCom, Qwest, and others. Customers and employees were hurt by the dishonesty and misdeeds of irresponsible company executives, and were uncertain about their own futures. According to *Advertising Age*, consumer spending was affected more by the economy than by 9/11. The resulting layoffs and devalued stocks and retirement funds have had a long-term effect for many people, clearly demonstrating the impact of unethical, irresponsible behavior. However, crises can lead to opportunities for marketing professionals. They can enhance their strategic role within the company by working to improve or protect the firm's reputation, or they can work with customers or clients to build confidence. Experts say that marketers can take specific steps to deal with a scandal's backlash against business and executives, such as the following:[18]

- Create or revisit the company's crisis management plan.
- Establish a closer working relationship with senior management, and other executives in investor relations.
- Enhance internal marketing efforts.

IMPACT OF CHANGE ON STRATEGIC AND TACTICAL MARKETING DECISIONS

The preceding discussion indicates that changes in the marketing environment bring about changes in long-range organizational strategies and day-to-day tactics as marketers position themselves to remain competitive. In some cases marketers are the primary catalysts for change, although they may be responding to perceived opportunities in the environment. New product development and distribution technology illustrate the creation of goods and services that revolutionize what and how customers buy. When new products such as cellular telephones, CD-ROMs, fiberoptics, and microwave ovens were first introduced, they contributed to major lifestyle changes and spawned many new product lines that continue to evolve. In other cases, marketers respond to change with strategies such as mass merchandising and value pricing for cost-conscious consumers, convenience products for hectic lifestyles, automobiles to meet the specific needs of families and single individuals, or travel and hospitality services for busy executives.

While both strategies and tactics affect relationships inside and outside the firm, **strategies** are associated primarily with building external relationships because of their long-term implications. **Tactics** tend to be associated more with building internal relationships in order to encourage creativity and motivate employees to execute the tactical decisions successfully. (Strategies and tactics are discussed further in the next chapter.)

Strategies
Long-term plans associated primarily with building external relationships consistent with organizational mission.

Tactics
Shorter-term plans associated with building internal relationships and motivating employees to carry out strategic intent.

Building Internal Relationships

The process of changing organizational structures to meet the needs of a changing marketplace requires the implementation of effective internal marketing programs to promote the company's vision and goals to its internal customers. Part of the internal marketing effort is focused on cross-functional teams that have a major impact on marketing personnel as they become involved in all customer-related aspects of the organization. Such marketing personnel may work on several projects at one time, sharing their expertise in identifying the match between the company's products and its markets. Working on a project from beginning to end gives marketing professionals better insights into corporate strengths and weaknesses and a better understanding of the goals to be achieved by the marketing mix. The internal marketing effort should be focused on gaining loyalty to the project and company, as well as to the employee.

Marketing research, consumer studies, and the salesforce provide invaluable feedback for managing new and existing products. Honda makes changes in its automobile designs in response to information obtained from focus groups and customer surveys to satisfy its markets. USAA, an insurance and financial services company that markets primarily to military officers and their families, surveys one-half million customers a year to determine their present satisfaction and their future insurance and financial needs as a basis for product and service development. Many companies keep track of customer complaints and telephone requests in order to know their customers better and take action when needed. Restaurants, hotels, and other service firms ask customers to complete questionnaires at the point of sale to indicate their level of satisfaction with the service experience.

Although the primary objective of marketing research may be to build relationships with external customers and sell products, another important objective should be to use the results in internal marketing programs in order to improve service quality and responsiveness to customer needs as part of the overall marketing mix. Internal marketing research also should be used to assess employee satisfaction, to identify human resource needs (e.g., training, flexible scheduling, child or elder care, etc.), and to obtain employees' suggestions for improvement in all facets of the business.

Building External Relationships

Establishing long-term external relationships is particularly important in times of significant environmental changes. Many formal and informal corporate relationships have emerged as a result of the converging business revolutions described earlier. A marketing company cannot be global without foreign partners, whether it is in manufacturing, distribution, or other areas. The fast-paced advances in information technology and computerization have created alliances among firms in the computer, telecommunications, cable, entertainment, and other industries as they position themselves at the on-ramp of the information superhighway.

External relationships with customers bring them into marketing decisions at an early stage to help ensure the success of products and marketing programs. Customers give valuable input into product design, promotional plans, and other decisions. Likewise, today's relationships with suppliers bring them into the planning phase for new or improved products, production methods, customer service, and other areas. A number of facilitators, such as transportation companies, financial institutions, and other outside service providers, also help marketers monitor and deal with change.

Strategic alliances form the basis for many external relationships throughout the world, extending from formal, contractual arrangements to a simple handshake. A number of strategic mergers and acquisitions have occurred in recent years in what might be considered the most volatile industries: defense, telecommunications, transportation, health care, financial services, food, and entertainment. Changes in the marketing environment have spurred companies to seek partners with expertise, product lines, or market access that they themselves may be lacking or to create a formidable dominance in a lucrative market. Some of the mergers and acquisitions that occurred in the 1990s include Martin Marietta and Lockheed (now Lockheed Martin) in response to the transformation of America's defense industry and the need to operate more efficiently. Other mergers created a formidable combination of cable, media, and content in the entertainment industry; hospital chains became larger to be in a stronger position to deal effectively with the new managed health care environment; and others. These new combinations have reshaped major industries with far-reaching consequences for the companies involved and their customers, suppliers, employees, shareholders, and other business partners.

The number of informal relationships has increased significantly, as companies of all sizes and types seek partnerships that can improve their ability to serve customers profitably. **Supply chain links** and entities involved in the logistics of moving materials, parts, and products to customers through distribution channels have changed from being operations-intensive to being a critical strategic element. Thus many business relationships are formed to facilitate supply chain management. A large percentage of the gross domestic product (GDP) is spent by American companies to wrap, bundle, load, unload, sort, reload, and transport goods. A company that is competitive on product, low cost, quality, service, and other benefits desired by customers can lose that competitive advantage if it does not manage its logistics effectively. The grocery industry alone believes it can eliminate unnecessary steps and redundant stockpiles to reduce its annual operating costs by 10 percent, or $30 billion, in the way it handles its logistics. For example, a typical box of cereal may take 104 days to get from factory to supermarket as it passes through a linked series of wholesalers, distributors, brokers, diverters, and consolidators

Supply chain links
Suppliers, intermediaries, logistics, and facilitators involved in moving goods and services from producer to buyer.

and their warehouses. Automotive suppliers are expected to produce ideas to cut costs for U.S. auto makers. Most companies have cut production costs drastically but still can reduce unnecessary supply chain costs by reducing duplication and inefficiency.

The enormity of the logistics situation and the need for close external relationships between suppliers and shippers can be illustrated by picturing a 23-ton rig laden with odometers and speedometers headed for a General Motors Saturn assembly plant in Tennessee. This is just one link in a supply chain that covers more than 99,000 miles every day—or 36 million miles a year. If this delivery is delayed, entire production lines, Saturn retail showrooms, and other supply chain partners will suffer. Saturn's world-class logistics system links suppliers, factories, and dealers to turn its parts inventory 300 times a year—almost once a day.

Identifying Opportunities in a Time of Change

It has been said that there are three kinds of marketers (as noted in Chapter 1): those who make things happen, those who watch things happen, and those who ask what happened. Obviously, being able to make things happen requires the ability to identify opportunities and act on them promptly. The key is to have a system in place to monitor environmental trends and events on a continuous basis, thus making it easier to recognize opportunities at an early stage. Of course, feasible opportunities should be consistent with a well-articulated vision and mission for the business. Companies use many approaches to identify opportunities, including the following:

- Formal scanning through internal marketing information systems (MIS) and external data services
- Secondary and/or primary research studies
- Internal company databases (customer and supplier information)
- Industry and/or trade association market data
- Consumer publications, particularly advocate or political types

  Two other indicators of new opportunities (or threats) are as follows:

- Adversity—A negative event or poor performance that has a negative impact on sales and profits may force attention toward finding new opportunities.
- Changes in competitive set from either inside or outside the industry

Once opportunities have been identified for action, marketers must design and implement effective marketing programs. Some key factors to consider in capitalizing on opportunities for growth are listed below.

- The new opportunity must be compatible with the organization's core competencies and its values and mission, especially in a volatile, rapidly changing environment.
- Top management commitment, sufficient capitalization, and human resource potential are essential.
- The organization must seek expertise in the new business, whether it is outsourced or developed in-house.

- The corporate culture must support the creativity, innovation, and stamina needed for the new venture.

- The company must know its product and the benefits that it provides for customers.

- Perhaps most important of all, marketers must listen to customers and understand their wants and needs.

Managing Change

Leading marketers such as Southwest Airlines, Home Depot, Microsoft Corp., Hewlett-Packard Co., and Levi Strauss & Co. prospered in recent years by making ongoing adjustments and managing change effectively. A rapidly changing world market provided Microsoft with tremendous multinational opportunities for its software business in developing economies such as China, Latin America, Eastern Europe, and Africa, as well as developed economies such as Europe and Japan. Microsoft's sales offices and wholly owned subsidiaries can be found throughout the world. A highly successful strategy is achieved by fostering independent local software developers and distributors in countries with vast growth potential such as India and China.[19,20]

Many large firms such as Sears, General Motors, and IBM experienced setbacks before becoming successful in their attempts to make much needed changes. The hot-growth companies tend to act small while thinking big. Home Depot carved out a unique market niche for itself, and revenues and profits climbed as other retailers' sales suffered.

Hewlett-Packard operates in an industry with an extremely short product life cycle where constant change is a necessity. H-P constantly innovates with new products in new markets. In March 1994, the company introduced the world's best-selling computer printer, a black and white inkjet model. The following October H-P introduced a newer model that offered an optional color printing kit at just $49 more than the older monochrome model. As H-P's chief executive says, "We've developed a philosophy of killing off our own products with new technology. Better that we do it than somebody else." H-P revamped its product development to shorten the time to bring a new product to market from 6 years to less than 9 months. To accomplish this takes a sincere commitment to change.[20,21]

The success stories of companies that have prospered in dynamic, changing environments suggest that they possess a number of common characteristics.[21,22] Lessons to be learned about managing change in a marketing organization include the following:

- Focus on your customers and understand your markets; this should drive internal organizational changes.

- Listen to customers to learn how they define customer value and satisfaction and how they perceive your company versus its competitors.

- Welcome change and be prepared to review and update goals and procedures continuously.

- Inform everyone in the company why change is necessary, communicate the vision for the future, and provide all necessary information to remove the fear and uncertainty that accompany change.

INNOVATE OR EVAPORATE*

The Chocolate Meltdown

 Masterfoods USA, formerly known as Mars, is a family-owned global marketer that spends millions of dollars to keep the names of its popular candy brands before customers. M&Ms (the world's number 1 chocolate candy), Snickers, Milky Way, and other Mars candies are part of American culture, eaten "straight" as candy or added to other food concoctions. While Mars is an industry leader in confectionery, pet food, and other food-related businesses, in the mid-1990s it faced problems in developing successful new products and disdained sharing ideas or forming alliances to improve its competitive position.

Mars continued to emphasize quality control and manufacturing efficiency, but growth was inhibited by a process technology that resulted in a serious lack of new hit products. Mars focused on global expansion, continually seeking converts to its brands in one country after another but not worrying about losing brand loyalty in existing markets. Hershey and other competitors took market share from Mars through aggressive marketing and acquisitions. Hershey increased both market share and profits in a flat market and also bought Cadbury's U.S. confectionery operation and two other brands to gain even more market dominance—while Mars stood pat. Although it attempted to adjust to change, Mars did not develop and manage its supply chain relationships successfully. In particular, the company did not react well to innovations in the retail and wholesale distribution chain, where consolidation had shifted buying power to large supermarket chains and mega-wholesalers that demand lower costs from suppliers. Mars enraged some segments of the trade by making abrupt policy

*The box title is attributed to James M. Higgins, *Innovate or Evaporate* (Winter Park, FL: New Management Publishing Company, 1995).

changes that reduced retailers' profits by not supplying enough product to fill the orders they took, focusing on production rather than sales, eliminating some promotional deals, and taking an imperialist approach to management that stifled innovation and growth.

By 1998, Mars had revitalized its position as the number 2 candy maker in the $21 billion U.S. candy industry, second only to Hershey. Mars was rated by the *Forbes Private 500* as the sixth-largest U.S. company. Mars regained momentum by launching creative new advertising campaigns and introducing successful extensions of its leading candy brands. New promotions included the 1997 Super Bowl campaign and promoting M&Ms as the "official candy of the millennium" (MM is the Roman numeral for 2000). Another new product extension, M&Ms Crispy Chocolate Candies, was developed for introduction during the 1999 Super Bowl—supported by a $70 million advertising and promotional campaign. The tag line for the launch: "The Feeding Frenzy Has Begun."

The "feeding frenzy" continued as Mars changed its corporate name to Masterfoods USA to better represent its role as a major international food company—rather than just a chocolate company. In 2001, Mars placed first among 15 Virginia firms on the *Forbes Private 500* list. With sales of $15.5 billion, net income of $1.35 billion, and operating income of $2.3 billion, the company was ranked fourth among the 500 largest private companies. New products and product extensions have been introduced by Mars with more on the way, but the most popular candy in the world—M&Ms—has enjoyed the greatest visibility. Each day over 400 million M&Ms chocolate candies are produced, totaling more than 146 billion each year.

As a way to help America after the September 11, 2001 attacks, M&M Chocolate Candies teamed up with the American Red Cross to support the ARC Disaster Relief Fund. One hundred

(continued)

percent of the company's profits of a specially created Red, White, and Blue M&Ms product (over $3 million) were donated to the campaign. In 2002, the largest promotional program in the company's 61-year history illustrated the global power of the M&Ms brand with a Global Color Vote to determine the world's choice for a new color M&M from purple, pink, or aqua, to add to the current mix of red, yellow, orange, green, blue, and brown candies in each package. Millions of people from 78 countries around the world (some who had never voted in a political election in their own countries)—more than the number of people who live in Ireland and Norway—participated by phone, mail, and the World Wide Web in the Global Color Vote. The winning choice was purple, and a gala event was held in New York City to celebrate purple's win.

Masterfoods USA (Mars) continues to revitalize and grow its brands, and maintain its brand equity (27 percent of the U.S. chocolate market) relative to Hershey (43 percent) and Nestle (12 percent). Mars—and its M&Ms power brand—has proven its continued ability to innovate and grow in a highly competitive market.

Sources: Bill Saporito, "The Eclipse of Mars," *Fortune* (November 28, 1994), pp. 82–92; www.hoovers .com/premium/profiles; Laura Liebeck, "Novelty Hasn't Worn Off for Candy Manufacturers," *Discount Store News* (July 13, 1998), pp. 8, 110; Anya Sacharow, "Mars' Stars," *Brandweek* (May 25, 1998), pp. I-28–I-30; "World Votes Purple Into the "M&M's Bag," *PR Newswire* (June 19, 2002), p. 1; Becky Ebenkamp, "Purple People Voter," *Brandweek* (June 3, 2002), p. 17; http://www.mms.com (M&M website); Anonymous, "M&Ms Turn Red, White, and Blue," *Candy Industry* (December 2001), p. 122; Tom Shean, "15 VA. Firms Place On Forbes List of 500 Largest Private Companies," *Virginia-Pilot* (November 29, 2001), p. D1; Mike Beirne, "New Mars Mission," *Brandweek* (October 15, 2001), p. 3.

- Decentralize authority for quicker decision making, and place high value on teamwork versus individualism.

- Recruit, hire, train, and reward skilled people at all levels who are versatile and responsive.

- Empower your people to make decisions related to their areas of responsibility, and make clear what results are expected.

- If you lack the expertise to take advantage of opportunities that fit your corporate goals, obtain it by outsourcing, acquisition, or strategic alliances.

- Remove all walls between functional areas in the company, and develop cross-functional or project teams.

- Involve suppliers and other important stakeholders in providing input for dealing with change, and create alliances and include them in project teams.

- Don't lose sight of the company's core values in the process of making changes; successful companies realize that some things should never change.

Summary

As shown in this chapter, the marketing environment is changing faster than ever. Organizations that continuously monitor change are in a better position to capitalize on new opportunities and minimize risk. Those which remain passive and do not adapt to change face possible extinction. Many environmental forces can have an impact on marketing decisions. The process of change and renewal in marketing organizations can be compared with the phases of an ecocycle of complex natural systems where survival depends on the ability of the system to emerge from crisis as a living, vibrant system.

The challenges faced by marketers today are fueled primarily by concurrent business revolutions: the globalization of markets; the growth of information technology and computer networks; converging technologies; the information age economy; redesigned organizational structures; and security, ethics, and social responsibility. The globalization of markets requires an understanding of customers, products, and the fit between the two, whether the marketer is dealing across continents or across town.

American consumers buy a significant amount of the world's goods and services. Thus it is important to look at changes in the U.S. market, where the "average American" no longer exists due primarily to population shifts in the distribution of age, ethnic groups, income levels, and consumer lifestyles.

New technology is a catalyst for change in the types of goods and services that are produced and the ways they are marketed. Technological advances in computerization and telecommunications have affected organizations in the way that work is performed, buying and selling activities take place, and relationships are built. Rapid advances in technology have brought about many strategic alliances in entertainment, telecommunications, computers and software, and other industries. Technological progress has opened the information superhighway, where telephones, television, and computers converge to communicate instantaneously around the world, creating a new distribution channel for goods and services.

Changing management structures are evolving to enable organizations to deal effectively with environmental change. Today's organizations are flatter, less hierarchical, and more likely to use integrated cross-functional teams to manage projects. Computers and their ability to handle large databases efficiently have lessened the need for traditional middle managers by using more project managers and task-oriented work groups. The focus is on flexibility so that changes can be made quickly in response to the marketplace.

Changes in the environment affect both marketing strategies and tactics. Internal marketing programs are necessary to motivate internal customers (employees) to execute external programs successfully and build long-term relationships with customers. Shortened product life cycles, particularly for high-tech or fashion products, require a constant long-term strategic vision and the ability to adapt short-run tactics as needed.

There are many approaches to identifying opportunities in a constantly changing environment, including formal and informal scanning techniques, databases, and a variety of primary and secondary research methods. Identification of opportunities is only the first step. It is also necessary to manage the change that accompanies taking advantage of new opportunities. Hot-growth companies tend to act small while thinking big. They have a vision for the future but do not neglect customers, suppliers, and other important stakeholders in the present.

Questions

1. Explain the concept of a marketing organization ecocycle. Using a familiar company or nonprofit organization, describe the phases that make up the continuous process represented by the ecocycle.

2. Discuss the business revolutions that have led to major changes in marketing, as described in

this chapter. Are there others that should be included? Explain and justify your answer.

3. Describe a recent international event that has influenced the marketing process for a familiar company or product category and has created a need to adapt the marketing mix to this new situation in order to be competitive in a global marketplace.

4. Discuss the major trends that marketers need to monitor in a wide range of technological developments and information processing. Explain how each can influence a specific marketing decision (e.g., product specifications, distribution methods, promotional media, pricing strategy, and others).

5. Illustrate how the building of internal and external relationships between marketers and their internal and external constituents can contribute to successful marketing management in a time of change.

Exercises

1. Interview a marketing professional from a local company about possible crises or environmental changes that have made it necessary for him or her to change some aspect of his or her marketing organization and/or marketing mix.

2. Sketch the marketing organization ecocycle, and using the experience of actual companies, describe (a) the best-case scenario and (b) the worst-case scenario for how these companies managed change in their internal or external environments.

3. Describe the ways that marketing managers can identify opportunities in a time of change as they are discussed in the chapter. Create your own innovative method for identifying potential crises and opportunities, and explain how you would implement this method to manage change in your own organization.

Endnotes

1. Hal Lancaster, "Managing Your Career: The Right Training Helps Even Dinosaurs Adapt to Change," *Wall Street Journal* (March 28, 1995), p. B1.

2. David K. Hurst, *Crisis and Renewal: Meeting the Challenge of Organizational Change* (Boston: Harvard Business School Press, 1995). Much of this section of the chapter is based on Hurst's organizational ecocycle model and examples.

3. *Ibid.*, p. 2.

4. *Ibid.*, pp. 97–103 and Fig. 5-1, p. 97.

5. Further explanation of the far-reaching impact of natural events can be found in the chaos theory (e.g., the flapping of a butterfly's wings in South America can cause strong wind currents in Europe) or the Japanese concept of *tsunami*. The latter term refers to a huge sea wave in the ocean caused by a submarine disturbance such as an earthquake or a volcanic eruption.

6. See Hurst, *op. cit.*, Organizational Ecocycle, Fig. 5-2; organizational ecocycle model illustrated (p. 103) and model components described (pp. 103–115). The eight phases in Hurst's model are (1) strategic management, (2) conservation, (3) crisis, (4) confusion, (5) charismatic leadership, (6) creative network, (7) choice, and (8) entrepreneurial action.

7. See Hurst, *op. cit.*, Model of Organizational Change, Fig. 3-3 (p. 72), discussion (pp. 71–73), and Fig. 5-2 (p. 103) and discussion of types of rational action (pp. 105–113). Hurst maintains that these two half-loops represent two different types of rationality: instrumental means-end rationality in the life-cycle phase (1. strategic management) and values-based rationality in the renewal phase (2. charismatic leadership).

8. Source of many Nike examples used with discussion of ecocycle model: Hurst, *op. cit.*, pp. 35–49, 105–106, 114–115, 165–166, and others.

9. Adrian Murdoch, "Just Doing It," *Accountancy* (March 1999), pp. 30–31; Jo Wrighton and Fred R. Bleakley, "Philip Knight of Nike—Just Do It!" *Institutional Investor* (January 2000), pp. 22–24.

10. Murdoch, op. cit., pp. 30–31; Wrighton and Bleakley, *op. cit.*, pp. 22–24.

11. Gina Binole, "Nike, Jordan Go Stylishly Forth," *The Business Journal* (May 28, 1999), p. 1; Andy Dworkin, "Nike Presents New Strategies to Hit Profit Goals," *The Oregonian* (September 25, 1999), p. E01.

12. Murdoch, *op. cit.*, pp. 30–31; Wrighton and Bleakley, *op. cit.*, pp. 22–24.

13. Thomas A. Stewart, "Planning a Career in a World without Managers," *Fortune* (March 20, 1995), pp. 72–80.

14. William Frey, H., "Migration Swings," *American Demographics* (February 2002), pp. 18–21; Alison Stein Wellner, "The Census Report," *American Demographics* (January 2002), pp. S3–S6; Gardyn, Rebecca, "Unmarried Bliss," *American Demographics* (December 2000), pp. 56–61.

15. Steve Jarvis, "A Whirlwind of Technologies May Sweep Up Marketers," *Marketing News* (June 7, 2002), pp. 8, 12.

16. Stratford Sherman, "A Master Class in Radical Change," *Fortune* (December 13, 1995), pp. 82–90.

17. Elizabeth Large, "Patriotic Glitter Fading as Americana Items Endure," *Journal-Gazette* (July 11, 2002), p. 1D; anonymous, "Living On After 9/11," *Advertising Age* (March 11, 2002), p. 18.

18. Deborah L. Vence, "How to Be A Hero," *Marketing News* (September 2, 2002), pp. 1, 13–14.

19. Brent Schlender, "Microsoft: First America, Now the World," *Fortune* (August 18, 1997), pp. 214–217.

20. Wendy Zellner, Robert D. Hof, Richard Brandt, Stephen Baker, and David Greising, "Go-Go Goliaths," *Business Week* (February 13, 1995), pp. 64–70.

21. Noel M. Tichy, "Revolutionize Your Company," *Fortune* (December 13, 1993), pp. 114–118.

22. Zellner et al., *op. cit.*

MARKETING MANAGEMENT IN ACTION: CLOSING CASE

Radio Sawa: A New Station for a New Generation

"Oh kiss me, beneath the milky twilight, lead me on the moonlit floor, lift your open hand, strike up the band and make the fireflies dance…"

Then, as the American pop sounds of "Kiss Me" by the band Sixpence None the Richer fade, Arabic pop music kicks in. Among the featured artists is the Egyptian singer Amr Diab, who croons: "Habibi, Habibi, Habibi ya nour el-ain, Ya sakin khayali …" ("My darling, my darling, my darling, the light of my eyes, you live in my dreams…")

This is the sound of Radio Sawa, whose name means "Radio Together" in Arabic, which is targeted toward Arab youth. Radio Sawa is a venture of the Middle East Radio Network (MERN), a pilot project of the Voice of America. MERN operates as an independent, bipartisan body that is responsible for all U.S. government-sponsored international broadcasting. The moving force behind Radio Sawa has been Norman J. Pattiz, chief executive of the largest U.S. radio company, Westwood One, Inc. and chairman of the Mideast subcommittee of the U.S. government's Broadcasting Board of Governors (BBG). Pattiz joined the BBG (oversees all nonmilitary international broadcasting, including Voice of America) long before September 11, 2001. From the beginning, he promoted the idea of using a commercial radio format, such as that developed for Radio Sawa, as the future of the Voice of America. When VOA was canceled, most of its Arabic-language news staff that had previously worked on VOA's shortwave radio programming joined Radio Sawa.

Pattiz was sent on a fact-finding trip by the BBG to assess the effectiveness of VOA in the Middle East. In November 2001, he testified before the House Committee on International Relations that VOA had little or no impact on its audience in the region. VOA used one standard format of Arabic programming, broadcast over shortwave to all 22 countries in the region. The VOA signal came from the Island of Rhodes and was barely audible to the 1 to 2 percent of the population that listened to VOA Arabic.

Pattiz sold the U.S. Congress on the idea of using the simple theme of the young and lovelorn to "sell" the United States to Arab youth. About 60 percent of the population in the Middle East is under the age of 30—a potential audience of 300 million young people. After the September 11 attacks, MERN moved up its launch date to March 2002 from summer 2002. Listeners can receive the programs via AM, FM, and satellite dishes. With an initial budget of over $30 million, Radio Sawa started broadcasting to the Arab world in March 2002. Within three months, it was the number one radio station in eight Arab countries—reaching 10 times the audience that Voice of America reached in 50 years.

Radio Sawa's format is a major change from the traditional VOA shortwave and AM radio broadcasts beamed to the Arabic-speaking world. The heavy component of news, analysis, and cultural programming that was characteristic of VOA's format has been eliminated in favor of the "bubble-gum pop music of stars like Britney Spears and the Lebanese singer Rashid al-Majid." Programming consists of 85 percent pop music, 15 percent government-generated news, and no commercials, 24 hours a day. The news portion of the programming is fast-paced, substantive, and uncensored—intended to counter the coverage of events by Arab media giant al-Jazeera and others.

Market research has been used extensively to fine-tune Radio Sawa's programming and content. The latest research techniques have been used to determine which tunes to play and how often. Three quarters of the listeners in Radio Sawa's target age group of 17- to 28-year-olds told researchers that they wanted to hear both Arab and Western music. The results indicated that a large, younger Middle Eastern audience "has one foot placed in the past but also one foot firmly in the future." "This allows the station to broadcast both Western and Arabic music, and provide a pro-American message, without being soft on the problems in the Middle East at the same time." Pattiz said, "We are for the first time successfully using a Western format to attract a Middle Eastern audience in order to deliver the largest possible public diplomacy mission ever" … "We don't dispute that young people are listening for the music, but we're also getting our message out there."

Although some people have negative attitudes toward Radio Sawa's approach (too much music, not enough news, etc.), marketing research is credited to a large extent for the station's success. Those respondents who stated that Sawa was their first choice for news increased from 1 percent on July 1, 2002 to 18 percent by August 12, 2002. During the same time the audience for BBC news fell from 15 to 5 percent. The station has received volumes of feedback from listeners—much of it through thousands of e-mails. Most of the feedback has been positive, but some has not been so complimentary (such as the father who was concerned that Sawa was corrupting the youth).

Pattiz' goal was to attract an audience—which Radio Sawa has been doing extremely well. He also wanted to create good feelings about Americans among the station's audience; however, a Gallup poll showed that Arabs' feelings about Americans were at a very low level. The long-range strategic plan is to build an audience, and then present an increasing number of programs, more dialogues, more discussions of policy, more interviews with people who are relevant and important to the station's target market. Those responsible for the success of Radio Sawa recognize that it will take months—if not years—to know whether American news can be successfully marketed to an audience that enjoys listening to pop music on their radios.

A large part of Radio Sawa's success depends on obtaining permission to use transmitters in key areas and custom tailoring programs to specific regions. With the permission of local governments, Radio Sawa sends FM broadcasts from four places in the Arab world: Amman, Jordan (radio signals reach Palestinians in the West Bank); Kuwait City; and Dubai and Abu Dhabi in the United Arab Emirates. AM signals are sent from the Greek Island of Rhodes, and can reach as far as Egypt. In June 2002, the United States was given permission by the Horn of African nation Djibouti to construct a long-range AM radio transmitter that allows Radio Sawa to broadcast into Egypt, Saudi Arabia, Sudan, and Yemen, and to operate two FM radio stations in Djibouti itself. Also, in August 2002, by agreement with the Government of Cyprus, the station began broadcasting over a new medium wave (AM) transmitter that will provide broad reach in the region. Some of America's Middle East allies, such as Egypt, have not permitted the transmission of Radio Sawa's signal. However, it is becoming increasingly difficult for governments to prevent the flow of information from sources such as Radio Sawa. Clearly, today's information technology overcomes the old problems of jamming shortwave broadcasts from the outside world.

Many young people in the area, particularly those who are more educated and more cosmopolitan, like to listen to both languages. However, some object to the news content and consider it America-centric. Seven teenage girls sipping sodas at the Planet Hollywood in Amman recently were heard to swoon over Radio Sawa—but not for the news. "I like that they put good English songs on and good Arabic songs," a 14-year-old said. "But there is too much news. It's boring. Maybe older people would like it." But the girls' table fell silent when they were told that Uncle Sam sponsors Sawa—although the station announces this clearly. "I hate Bush," declared a 13-year-old. "We should be telling the Americans what is happening here," said another teenager. "They don't understand us… they think they know us. I have nothing against Americans, I just don't like the way they think."

The audience finds the music format with its alternating Western and Arabic pop appealing, in contrast to local stations that play only Arabic music. As one listener said, "I like it a lot. First of all, there's no one talking, it's just continuous music. The Arabic music is songs you'd hear at clubs. The English is whatever's popular at the moment. … There are no ads, and maybe one news bulletin." However, while people are listening to the music, it is not clear whether they hear the news—and if they do hear the news, whether they like it. They key question is whether Radio Sawa's audience is tuning in just for the music, and tuning out the station's newscasts, which offer factual information about events of the day in and out of the Arab world, and clarification of U.S. policies. The influential Egyptian newspaper *Al Ahram* said that "a major failing of the U.S. government broadcasts is that while they attempt to let Arabs know about Americans, they are not doing anything about explaining Arabs to Americans." It concludes: "Chances are the Arab youth will… take the U.S. sound and discard the U. S. agenda."

Radio Sawa executives intend to layer in more news and public affairs programming over time after they have built their audience, and have already started to lengthen the newscasts. U.S. critics who have not yet found bias in Sawa's brief newscasts still question whether the station will be able to hold its audience if political pressure to give taxpayers their money's worth leads to broadcasting more speeches and statements by the American government (as promised to Congress).

If, as some critics assume, Radio Sawa will not have a significant effect on converting Arabs to support U.S. policies, then some other type of programming and format may be needed. However, those involved in the project believe that if the station can capture a substantial audience, perhaps it will be useful in opening up a dialogue with a young Arab audience. In addition to radio, other forms of communication, such as television, exchanges from one person to another, and enabling the professional training of a free press in the Arab world, will expose audiences to a diversity of opinion.

An increasingly popular alternative form of communication, particularly among Radio Sawa's young target audience, is the Internet. On June 14, 2002, Radio Sawa announced that it was launching streaming audio on the station's Internet site (http://www.radiosawa.com). Norman Pattiz stated, "We always envisioned Radio Sawa as being a station where we have a lot of interaction with our listeners… Our Internet site will help us do that. It will help us stay in touch and communicate with our audiences." Streaming audio will extend Radio Sawa's reach to listeners around the world, not just those in the Middle East.

According to a July 2002 report from the United Nations Development Programme (UNDP), the world's lowest level of information "connectivity" (percentage of those with access to a personal computer and who use the Internet) is found in the Arab countries. However, where there are not severe restrictions on Internet usage, the medium is growing significantly—particularly among younger, urban, upper-income Middle Easterners who are PC-literate. A New York-based Committee to Protect Journalists stated that there were an estimated four million Internet users in the Arab world; and this figure was expected to double by the end of 2002. Although not as widespread as television, and financially not feasible for many, the Internet provides access to a broad range of news and information that was previously unavailable. Likewise, there is competition between Middle East sites in both Arabic and English (as well as an increase in French for North Africa). Online competition for the audience that is targeted by Radio Sawa includes major media such as al-Jazeera (aljazeera.net) and CNNarabic.com, as well as private Web sites—each with its own point of view to express to the world.

Ongoing field research is conducted regularly to determine the most effective way to present news and editorials. Pattiz explained, "We cannot talk at these people. We can't pontificate. We can't create a connection with a listener by telling them a bunch of stuff in a totalitarian manner." As one writer said, "Reaching a skeptical Arab audience with the straight story about America is a daunting challenge."

Sources: http:/www.ibb.gov/radiosawa; Felicity Barringer, "U.S. Messages to Arab Youth, Wrapped In Song," *The New York Times* (June 17, 2002), p. A8+; Melissa Sekora, "The Sounds of Sawa," *National Review Online* (http:/www.nationalreview.com) (July 19, 2002); John Hughes, "Rays of Hope In Reaching the Young Arab Mind," *Christian Science Monitor* (July 17, 2002); Sonni Efron, "Middle Eastern Youth Tune in to U.S.-Sponsored Radio Show," *The Detroit News* (September 1, 2002); U.S. Department of State, International Information Programs (usinfo.state.gov); Diana West, "With a Transistor Radio," *The Washington Times* (June 28, 2002); "Changing Trends In Middle East Media Since 11 September—Analysis," *BBC Monitoring Middle East—Political,* London (July 12, 2002); "US-Funded Mideast Radio Network to Broadcast from Djibouti," *ABC Online* (http://www.abc.net.au/news) (June 2, 2002).

Case Study Questions

1. Analyze the effect of each of the business revolutions on Radio Sawa's long-range strategic plan and shorter-range tactics. Include globalization, technology, information age, organizational considerations, and the concepts of ethics and social responsibility in your analysis.

2. Determine the impact of political and economic change on the creation of Radio Sawa. How have these changes affected programming and format decisions by the station? What changes have occurred, and are expected to occur, in the target audience?

3. Discuss the idea of identifying opportunities in a time of change, and managing that change within the context of this case.

4. Describe the marketing organization ecocycle as it applies to Voice of America and Radio Sawa. Can Radio Sawa be considered a form of "creative destruction?" What are the future implications, if any, for the Voice of America?

5. Assume that you are in charge of creating and disseminating messages about America and its people to other countries that may not view America favorably. Describe and defend the methods that you would use to achieve audience satisfaction, and to build long-term relationships with Radio Sawa's audience.

Achieving Competitive Advantage

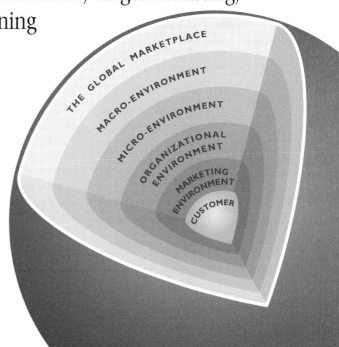

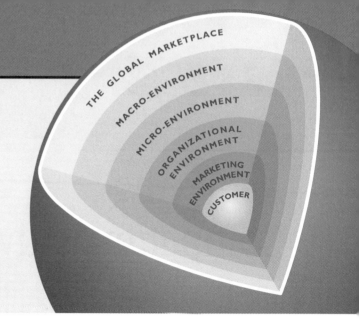

CHAPTER 3

Strategic Market Planning

Victorious warriors win first and then go to war, while defeated warriors go to war first and then seek to win.[1]

Overview

Marketing Management Decisions and Strategic Planning

Strategic Market Planning: A Multilevel Process

The Strategic Planning Process

Planning for the Long Term

Strategic Planning and the Challenge of Change

Strategic Planning and a Customer Orientation

A Bumpy Ride for the Airlines: Competitive Strategy Post-9/11/01

According to the Air Transport Association, U.S. airlines lost $7.7 billion in 2001, and projected a $5 billion loss for 2002. The terrorist attacks against the United States using hijacked planes on September 11, 2001 exacerbated profitability problems already faced by most major domestic airlines. The entire airline industry was grounded for four days following the attacks. This event resulted not only in significant losses in revenue, but also significant added costs for security and other operating expenses. When flights resumed, passengers and flight crews were hesitant to fly again. Many of those who did fly were concerned about safety. The September 11 events hastened restructuring efforts already underway by many companies to stabilize operations. As revenues continued to drop, the suffering airlines announced layoffs of over 140,000 employees, reduced the number of available flights, and cut back on services in an attempt to lower costs and regain profitability. Airline managers, industry groups, and the U.S. government all sought remedies for the deplorable situation. Much of the strategic thinking of the past no longer seemed relevant, and new strategies had to be formulated for an uncertain world.

Catastrophic events in the operating environment quickly changed the strategies and key success factors of airline competitors.* Two major factors contributed to the shifting competitive positions of various airlines: changes in business travel habits; and

*This strategic challenge can be viewed within the framework of the "crisis and renewal" phase of the marketing organization ecocycle, discussed in Chapter 2, and the "strategic inflection point," discussed later in this chapter.

better-informed travelers. Prior to 9/11, many companies cut travel costs by seeking lower airfares, and insisting on more restricted fares, largely due to dissatisfaction with a complex airfare pricing structure for business travelers. As one writer stated, "Business travel is being 'Wal-Marted' by low-cost carriers," who accounted for nearly 20 percent of U.S. domestic air capacity in 2002. For example, Southwest Airlines surpassed Northwest Airlines, Continental Airlines, and US Airways Group in terms of revenue passenger miles flown domestically. In addition to an increased demand for lower-price airfares, travelers, travel agents, and corporate travel managers have become more knowledgeable about prices. In particular, they have used the Internet to find and take advantage of deeply discounted fares.

While all airlines have attempted to control costs and increase profits, the smaller discount carriers have been more successful in executing a low-cost, low-price strategy. The large full-service airlines were faced with enormous fixed costs that were not easy to reduce: expensive hub-and-spoke route systems; and expensive labor contracts that depended on high-margin business fares. The high-cost business models were not attracting the new breed of low-fare business travelers to their previous levels. The larger airlines' pricing structure did not appeal to the economical consumer, in spite of the additional comfort and amenities that accompanied unrestricted fares (at about four times the cost of a restricted fare). Major carriers were caught in a pricing quandary. If they lowered business fares, they needed to raise leisure fares, and this would put them in competition with discounters. In addition, the new security measures were not only costly for the airlines, but also made travel less convenient— no matter what price was paid for the trip.

In the post-9/11 environment, the leading low-fare airlines (Southwest, ATA, JetBlue, AirTran, and Frontier) took business away from the five largest U.S. airlines (American, United, Delta, Northwest, and Continental), in terms of passenger traffic. The strategic competitive advantage that low-fare carriers have had over full-service carriers includes younger fleets requiring less maintenance, and younger labor forces unencumbered by undesirable labor contracts. Low-fare carriers tend to use only one airplane model,

which minimizes maintenance, operating, and training costs, in contrast to the six or seven types of aircraft flown by the big carriers. Low-cost carriers also have maintained fast-paced schedules with minimal time between flights. They also have benefited from consumers' easier access to fare information on the Internet.

For the past 30 years, Southwest Airlines has been a model airline among the discount carriers, maintaining profitability in turbulent times. However, another profitable discount airline, Jet-Blue Airways, has proven to be an industry leader since its inaugural flight from New York City's JFK International Airport to Ft. Lauderdale, Florida in February 2000. According to the company's April 2002 prospectus, "*JetBlue is a low-fare, low-cost passenger airline that provides high-quality customer service primarily on point-to-point routes. We focus on servicing underserved markets and large metropolitan areas that have high average fares, and we have a geographically diversified flight schedule that includes both short-haul and long-haul routes.*"

JetBlue started its operation with $130 million, the most initial capital for any startup U.S. airline. As of mid-2002, JetBlue offered one-class service to about 20 eastern and western U.S. cities and Puerto Rico, operating about 108 flights daily. The airline's main hub is at JFK Airport in New York, with a second hub at Long Beach Airport outside Los Angeles. While other airlines cut back operations, JetBlue has aggressively added routes, terminal slots, and airplanes. They saw an opportunity for success based on their ability to stimulate demand through low fares, and to address increasing customer dissatisfaction with airline travel. They have accomplished this by offering a "high-quality flying experience, emphasizing safety, security, reliability, customer service, and low fares." The company has identified its major competitive strengths as low operating costs, new all-Airbus A320 fleet of about 25 planes (and contracts for as many as 132 additional Airbus A320s), a strong brand, strong service-oriented company culture, competitive position in New York (nation's largest travel market), proven management team (CEO David Neeleman and other officers experienced in airline operations), and extensive use of advanced technology. They have pursued a hybrid marketing strategy of low cost and differentiation. Elements of JetBlue's strategy include stimulation of demand with low fares and superior product offering; emphasis on low operating costs (largely accomplished with technology), focus on point-to-point service to large metropolitan areas with high average fares, or highly traveled markets that are underserved (with the intent to further penetrate key markets with additional flights per day); and differentiation of product and service by providing a unique high-quality flying experience that includes new aircraft, simple and low fares, leather seats, free LiveTV at every seat, pre-assigned seating, reliable performance, and high-quality customer service.

The airline industry faces many strategic challenges in the years to come. Will major airlines redesign their strategies to be more competitive with the low-fare airlines? Will the future belong to the smaller, low-fare, low-cost carriers like Southwest or JetBlue? JetBlue CEO David Neeleman said his airline's greatest challenge is to stay small as the company moves forward. "Small," according to Neeleman, means that JetBlue must maintain a "homey, corporate culture that centers on customer-as-VIP and is sustained by core values of 'safety, caring, integrity, fun and passion.'"

Sources: Trottman, Melanie, and Scott McCartney, "The Age of 'Wal-Mart' Airlines Crunches the Biggest Carriers," *The Wall Street Journal,* June 18, 2002, pp. A1, A6; *Air Transit World* (ATW), http://www.atwonline.com, June 21, 2002; Ward, Rodney, "September 11 and the Restructuring of the Airline Industry," *Dollars and Sense* (May/June 2002), pp. 16–20+; Fiorino, Frances, "JetBlue Pursues Growth While Staying 'Small,'" *Aviation Week and Space Technology* (June 10, 2002), p. 41; *JetBlue Prospectus,* JetBlue Investor Relations, http://investor.jetblue.com, April 11, 2002, and other company information; "JetBlue Airways Corporation," *Hoovers Online,* www.hoovers.com, June 21, 2002.

Strategic market planning is about having a vision for the future and a winning plan in place before battling competitors in the marketplace. The strategic planning process is critical to achieving long-term success in meeting the challenges of a rapidly changing and uncertain environment.

● MARKETING MANAGEMENT DECISIONS AND STRATEGIC PLANNING

The strategic planning process and the marketing process are closely related, since marketing management decisions must be consistent with a firm's overall business strategy. Although strategic market planning can occur throughout the marketing organization ecocycle, it is most noticeable in the growth phase,[2] where conscious, rational decisions are made to guide the direction of the company. (See Figure 2.1 on page 41.)

Strategic decisions are related to an understanding of customers' needs, competitors' activities, and the financial implications of each decision. In turn, tactical marketing plans are based on a clear vision of the firm's overall business strategy and an understanding of its marketing strategies. Both strategic and tactical planning must be responsive to changes in the marketplace. For example, IBM's Global Small and Medium Business group decided in 2002 to pursue a more aggressive growth strategy in the small-to-midsize business (SMB) market. There are 400,000 SMB enterprises worldwide with 100 to 1,000 employees, and millions more with fewer than 100 employees. Although fragmented and often difficult to deal with, this customer group has been underserved and represents a $300 billion marketing opportunity for IBM, Microsoft, Linux, and other competitors. IBM's offer includes tailored technological solutions from IBM Global Services and support through IBM.com in areas such as e-business assistance, customer relationship management (CRM), supply chain, wireless technology, and security applications. Tactics used to implement this market growth strategy included a $100 million marketing campaign with the goal of educating customers that "Together with our business partners, we will provide solutions that will provide a competitive advantage for customers in the marketplace." Further, a dedicated team within each of the company's major product groups was given responsibility for creating and delivering solutions for this market. Salesforce activities, distribution channel operations, and other day-to-day decisions provide tactical support for IBM's market growth strategy.[3]

There are many definitions of *strategy,* depending on one's point of view. As can be seen in the preceding example, further confusion arises because there often is a fine line between the point where "strategy" ends and "tactics" begin. Since business-level strategy is the focus of this book, the following definitions of *strategy* and *tactics* provide a basis for discussion.

Strategy

Strategy
Explicit statement that provides direction for coordinated business decisions, a longer-term vision for the future.

The term *strategy* is used interchangeably with *competitive strategy* or *business strategy*. **Strategy** embodies a firm's objectives and reasons for being in business. It includes corporate policies, resource allocations, customer markets, and the competitive environment in which it chooses to operate. A firm's strategy is its vision of its future. It is an explicit statement that provides direction for coordinated business decisions in marketing and other functional areas.

Strategy can be defined by four basic dimensions that apply to all businesses and by two additional dimensions that apply to multiple businesses. The typical business strategy includes a specification of the following[4]:

1. *The product market in which the business will compete.* For example, JetBlue Airlines has chosen to compete in the domestic, short-haul and long-haul passenger transportation market serving underserved markets and high-average-fare metropolitan markets.

2. *The level of investment in a strategic unit.* For firms such as JetBlue, a strategic unit may be determined on the basis of geography; for example, how many flights and how many planes should be committed to the New York City-Long Beach, California route?

3. *Functional area strategies required for competing in the chosen product market.* JetBlue must design an effective marketing mix, consisting of strategies for promotion, pricing, distribution, and airline services.

4. *Underlying strategic assets and skills that give the firm a sustainable competitive advantage.* As discussed in the opening scenario of this chapter, JetBlue has a low-cost, efficient operation and motivated employees and has received many accolades for its exceptional service and high-quality performance.

Two other dimensions must be determined for firms having multiple business units:

1. *How the firm's resources will be allocated across business units.* For example, AMR Corporation must allocate financial resources and personnel across American Airlines, American Eagle (its regional carrier), and other business units in which it has an interest (e.g., Worldspan computer reservation service and any code-sharing alliances with non-U.S. carriers).

2. *How to create synergies across the businesses (i.e., creation of value by complementary business units).* American Eagle short-haul shuttle service passengers find it convenient to connect with American Airlines flights to more distant destinations. American Airlines benefits from shared facilities, maintenance, ticketing, and so forth.

Tactics

Tactics
Plan for the shorter-term, day-to-day operating decisions, what to do.

Whereas *strategy* refers to the longer-term, broader statement of direction for an organization, **tactics** refers to the shorter-term, day-to-day operating decisions. In other words, *strategy* refers to a broadly stated plan of action, that is, "what to do," that enables a firm to compete successfully in its environment. *Tactics* refers to "how the strategy will be carried out." Military strategy analogies often are used to explain the difference between these two concepts.

A frequently quoted Chinese strategist, Sun Tzu, laid the foundation for Eastern military strategy with his *Art of War,* written in 500 B.C. Sun Tzu's premise is that winning requires good strategy and that those who are well skilled in battle can overcome their enemy's army without fighting. "The ultimate strategy is to subdue the enemy's army without engaging it. To take cities without laying siege to them. To overthrow his forces without bloodying swords." This represents the strategic perspective—*doing the right thing* (marketing *strategy*).

On the other hand, the German general Carl von Clausewitz provides a foundation for Western military strategy in his book, *On War,* written in the eighteenth century. His premise is that winning is based on fighting the big battle, that is, *doing things right* (action-oriented marketing *tactics*).[5]

This chapter provides an overview of the strategic planning process, the challenge of changing strategic planning, and the integration of a customer orientation into the strategic planning process. Marketing management decisions are made within the context of a firm's strategic plan and are designed to carry out its strategic intent and achieve its strategic objectives.

● STRATEGIC MARKET PLANNING: A MULTILEVEL PROCESS

Regardless of the size or scope of an organization, strategic planning generally occurs at several levels: corporate, division or strategic business unit, and functional or operating level. (See Table 3.1.) Managers at these levels are responsible for making a group of interdependent decisions that vary somewhat at each level. At the corporate level, managers have primary responsibility for satisfying customers and

TABLE 3.1

Marketing, Strategic Planning, and Organizational Levels

Level in Organization	Marketing Input	Marketing Task Description
Corporate	Customer viewpoint and competitive analysis for corporate-level strategy	Corporate marketing decisions for entire company consistent with mission (longer-term planning; growth policies)
Business Unit	Each division focuses on its own set of customers and competitors for its own business unit(s)	Strategic marketing for each business unit or profit center; drives tactical plan at operating level
Operating/Functional	Design of marketing mix and implementation of tactical marketing plans (4Ps)	Marketing management—shorter-term implementation of strategy within given product/market

Source: Adapted from *Marketing Planning and Strategy,* 4th edition, by Subhash Jain, ©1993. Reprinted with permission of South-Western College Publishing, a division of International Thomson Publishing. Fax 800 730-2215.

for the financial performance of the entire company over the long term. They also are responsible for the relationships among divisions of the company and the organization's culture and values in the greater society. Corporate-level tactics become the strategy that drives decisions at the next lower level, the division or strategic business unit (SBU).

Divisional managers are most concerned with strategies for their separate business unit(s) or profit centers that are operated within the larger corporation. Each division has its own mission and objectives within the parameters of the corporate strategic plan, but its focus may be on a different set of customers and competitors than the other divisions of the company. Each division typically has responsibility for the implementation and control of its strategic plan. Divisional tactics formulate the strategy for the next lower level, the functional or operational level.

Functional-level managers take a shorter-term view of strategy than managers do at higher levels in the business, although the day-to-day decisions must be made within the requirements of the corporate and divisional strategies. Functional managers are responsible for determining the tactical marketing plan for achieving the functional-level strategy (which is the same as the divisional-level tactical plan). The tactical plan includes identification of the market segment(s) to be pursued and the appropriate marketing mix (i.e., product, pricing, promotion, and distribution) to reach the desired market(s). In some organizations, the strategic process continues on to lower-level department or group managers who have accountability for carrying out the functional-level strategy.

The primary focus of this book is on the business unit level, where marketing strategy is developed and executed. At this level, there are three major forces that must be taken into consideration: the company, its customers, and its competitors—the *strategic 3Cs.*[6] Marketing strategies address the questions of how the firm can most effectively differentiate its offerings from those of competitors and match the firm's resources and strengths to the needs of the marketplace. The ability to accomplish this allows a company to deliver the greatest value and satisfaction to its customers within a defined marketing environment.

● THE STRATEGIC PLANNING PROCESS

The strategic planning process involves a number of fundamental steps, although managers may differ somewhat as to the exact nature or order of each step. In fact, strategic planning generally follows an iterative process, rather than following a specified sequence, as new information is made available that may affect decisions made in a preceding step.

At the very beginning of the strategic planning process, it is important to develop a strategic vision for the company. The vision statement provides long-term strategic direction, encompassing core values (guiding principles) and the company's core purpose or reason for being in business. Once the strategic vision is determined, the strategic planning process continues with a clear understanding of the firm's mission and philosophy, to ensure consistency between the vision/mission and both long- and short-range plans. Both an external environmental analysis (i.e., customers, competitors, and market) and an internal self-analysis must be performed to make informed strategic decisions. Based on the firm's corporate mission and performance objectives and the results of the environmental analyses, the next step is to determine strategic objectives and define the broad strategy to achieve those objectives. This step is followed by a plan for implementation and tactics (marketing mix strategy), execution of the plan, and evaluation and control measures. (See Figure 3.1.) At this point, it is important to note that small businesses and nonprofit organizations benefit from strategic market planning, as well as larger businesses.

Mission-Driven Strategic Planning

| **Mission statement** Defines the reasons for the business's existence in the present and in the future. |

The **mission statement** clearly defines (and in some cases redefines) the reason for a business's existence in the present and in the future, as illustrated in Figure 3.2. Thus the mission statement provides guidelines for strategic planning. Strategic marketing decisions will be based on answers to these questions:

1. What business are we in? (What is the customer orientation? Who and where are our customers? Which ones will we serve and how will we serve them?)

2. What business will we be in? (What is our response to the environment? What are the customer needs to be served? How will these needs be satisfied?)

3. What business should we be in? (What are the product/market opportunities for new or existing customers? What is the product/market "fit" with present customers?)

The business mission, then, is a general statement about the strategy of a business. It addresses the scope of the business (product markets in which it does and does not want to compete), direction for future growth, general idea of the functional area strategies, and the strengths (key assets and skills) that provide a basis for differentiation and form the basis of the business.

FIGURE 3.1

Strategic Planning Process

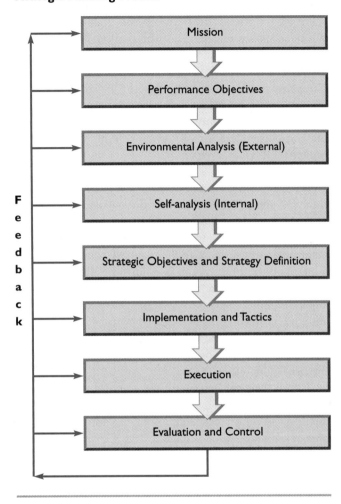

FIGURE 3.2

Mission Statement

Southwest Airlines is dedicated to the highest quality of Customer Service delivered with a sense of warmth, friendliness, individual pride, and Company Spirit.

We are committed to provide our Employees a stable work environment with equal opportunity for learning and personal growth. Creativity and innovation are encouraged for improving the effectiveness of Southwest Airlines. Above all, Employees will be provided the same concern, respect, and caring attitude within the Organization that they are expected to share externally with every Southwest Customer.

Source: Reprinted with permission of Southwest Airlines.

Strategic Readiness.   Classic marketing concepts such as "strategic windows"[7] and "marketing myopia"[8] demonstrate that the advantage of developing a strategic plan is twofold. A "strategic window" represents a short period of time when there is an optimal "fit" between the organization's capabilities and a new opportunity to satisfy the needs of the market. *Marketing myopia* refers to missed opportunities caused by focusing on the product at the expense of paying attention to the customer and the needs of a changing marketplace. The plan provides a blueprint for long- and short-term decisions that allow marketing managers to maximize opportunities and minimize threats. Since it is not possible to foresee all possible opportunities and threats, a formal strategic plan provides a basis for making better decisions in unexpected circumstances, that is, for being in a state of **strategic readiness.**

Strategic readiness
Ability to take advantage of unexpected market opportunities by having a long-term strategic plan and vision in place.

Strategic vision
Longer-term, futuristic perspective; requires patience and determination.

Strategic opportunism
Focus on present, and seizing market opportunities in a dynamic, uncertain environment.

Strategic Vision versus Strategic Opportunism.[9]   The strategic process is influenced greatly by an organization's structure, systems, and culture, and by the personnel who are responsible for planning and implementation. **Strategic vision** takes a longer-term, futuristic perspective and requires considerable patience and determination to adhere to the planned strategy. In contrast, **strategic opportunism** focuses on the present and positions the firm in a dynamic, uncertain environment where the future is relatively unpredictable. Each has its advantages and disadvantages: Strategic vision provides managers and employees with a sense of purpose and direction, whereas strategic opportunism emphasizes flexibility and responsiveness as new opportunities arise. Skillful managers can benefit from a combination of these approaches by being ready to seize opportunities that are consistent with the firm's long-range vision.

Henry Ford can be counted among the earliest U.S. strategic visionaries with the advent of his "horseless carriage" in the early 1900s, and the company's mass production assembly lines. Since then, the auto industry has experienced many examples of both strategic vision and strategic opportunism as the leaders vie for market share. Ford and General Motors have jockeyed for the market leader position for decades, but the last time Ford outsold GM was in 1930, and at times GM has enjoyed as much as a 2 to 1 advantage over Ford, particularly during the 1950s and 1960s. Ford's long-time strategic vision throughout the past century and continuing into the twenty-first century has been customer-oriented, with an understanding of shifting customer tastes, market needs, and the market's demand for quality.

In the 1990s, strategic opportunism was combined with strategic vision as Ford responded to consumer needs by producing smaller, more fuel-efficient vehicles, and focusing on quality improvement ("Quality is job one.") During this same period, Ford further diversified its product line to include new truck models and utility vehicles. The company's growth strategy was focused on building market share and brand loyalty through quality products and service. Ford was expected to overtake GM for the number one position in the auto industry, because of its proactive response to four major challenges to the auto industry over the past quarter century: fuel economy, quality, shift in buyer tastes, and more intense competition.

Ford's strategic vision and ability to take advantage of market opportunities were severely impacted by safety issues related to Ford Explorers and Firestone Wilderness tires in 2000 and 2001. When Firestone tires suddenly lost their treads, the SUVs rolled over, with serious consequences to drivers and passengers. Company sales and profitability suffered due to customers' concerns about the vehicles' quality

MARKETING **IN THE** GLOBAL VILLAGE

Mexican "Ants" Build Homes—One Bag of Cement at a Time

Mexico is a nation of 100 million people, with a growing shortfall of about six million housing units. While many people want to build their own homes, 70 percent of workers earn between $1,500 and $15,000 a year in this developing economy, and must pay steep prices for many necessities due to market domination by oligopolies. Would be do-it-yourselfers (called "ants" by the Mexicans) find it difficult to save enough money to build a new home. Instead, low-income homebuilders buy cement one 110-pound bag at a time, building as much of their home as they can afford over an extended period of time. This vast market provides a profitable strategic opportunity for suppliers of home building materials sold in small quantities.

Cemex SA, the world's third largest cement supplier ($6.9 billion in sales in 2001) and the top seller of cement in the United States, pursues this strategy to dominate markets from California to Cairo. The company holds a 60 percent share of the Mexican cement market, where it makes huge profits by aggressively marketing its product to low-income consumers, mostly through 5,000 neighborhood distributors.

According to industry analysts, Cemex's cement prices in Mexico are the highest of any major market in the world. Price comparisons are difficult, because in the United States cement is usually sold in bulk by the ton. A ton in the United States costs about $82, compared with $160 in Mexico, and production costs are lower in Mexico than in the United States. Cemex argues that such comparisons are meaningless, because cement is sold as a commodity in the United States and as a "branded product" in Mexico (even though Cemex's per-bag prices are generally higher in Mexico than in other developing countries).

Residents and activists from the construction industry have tried to fight against exaggerated prices for cement, and have lobbied for cheaper cement prices—but to no avail. Chairman Lorenzo Zambrano denies any price gouging, and defends the fairness of Cemex's pricing strategy on the basis of the expense of delivering millions of bags to remote areas over rough terrain and poor roads. A government investigation found no wrongdoing or monopolistic behavior by the company, and President Vicente Fox referred to Cemex as "one successful company." In a 2000 survey, Price-waterhouseCoopers rated Cemex the region's most admired company. Financial performance has been outstanding, with profit* in the Mexican market at 46 percent of total revenue in 2001 (nearly twice the U.S. figure reported). Although Mexico represented 38 percent of Cemex's global revenue, it contributed 52 percent of the total $2.3 billion in profit earned in 2001. Mr. Zambrano attributed this performance to efficiency and low-cost operations. He maintained that the perception of high prices is due to the "overvalued" peso. Financial success has enabled Cemex to afford a large number of acquisitions throughout the world to increase its global dominance.

Cemex's marketing (operating) strategy supports the company's business level growth strategy of selling cement in small quantities to individuals. This target market comprises about 85 percent of all cement sold in Mexico. Tactics that are used to carry out this strategic intent on a day-to-day basis include all elements of the marketing mix. In addition to single-bag packaging of cement, and a high-margin pricing strategy, promotional tools (IMC) are focused on the low-income market. For example, when workers return with cash from working in the United States at Christmas, Cemex representatives often meet them at airports with booklets that

*Profit calculated before taxes, interest, depreciation, and amortization.

(continued)

contain construction tips. The company promotes its brand much like sellers of soap or soda. In addition to its airport greeters, Cemex holds block parties, and puts its brand name on professional soccer jerseys and on T-shirts handed out to religious pilgrims. Neighborhood distributors (many in remote areas) earn points toward vacations, trucks, and other incentives for increasing sales.

A recent "ant-marketing" campaign was focused on signing up individual distributors for a free membership in its Construrama network. Cemex gave each dealer a new computer, and half the cost of new Construrama signage and store painting. Distributors also benefitted from Cemex's purchasing clout when buying other products at low wholesale prices.

Source: Peter Fritsch, "A Cement Titan in Mexico Thrives by Selling to Poor," *The Wall Street Journal* (April 22, 2002), pp. A1, A12.

and safety, and to the cost of replacing millions of Firestone tires on the popular Explorer SUV and Ranger pickup models. The relationship between long-time business partners, Ford and Firestone, also suffered.

Performance Objectives

Once the mission statement has been determined, the next step is to establish the goals and objectives that the strategic plan is expected to accomplish. Performance objectives generally are stated in measurable terms, such as return on investment or other profitability or productivity measures that are to be accomplished within a specified period of time. Strategic objectives can be determined for separate divisions, departments, or other organizational units. Objectives established for one level or business unit should support and be compatible with those of other levels or units of the business.

Environmental Analysis (External)

One of the purposes of strategic market planning is to be able to anticipate and respond to environmental changes that may affect the firm. Managers need a clear understanding of the firm's external and internal environments to plan and carry out strategies successfully. Several analytical tools and frameworks are available to use in strategic market analysis and planning as indicated in the following pages. An important source of information throughout the strategic market planning process is found in the marketing information system and the management decision support system, as discussed in Chapter 4. It is particularly useful for conducting an ongoing environmental analysis.

Macro-environment
External forces over which a company has little or no control.

The external environment consists of a **macro-environment** (i.e., economic, legal/political, sociocultural, demographic, physical, and technological—factors over which the company has little or no control) and a **micro-environment** (i.e., competitors, markets, suppliers, and intermediaries—sometimes referred to as the *operating or task environment*). In this chapter, our focus is on the major external environmental factors that influence the strategic planning process: the firm's customers,

Micro-environment
Operating or task environment (competitors, markets, suppliers, and intermediaries).

its competitors, the market, and an organized procedure for environmental scanning and forecasting.

Customers. Successful marketing strategies in both consumer and business-to-business marketing focus on ways to satisfy customer needs and how to do this better than competitors. In order to achieve its strategic intent, a firm first must know *who* makes up its customer base, where they are located, and how to reach them. Questions that should be answered about present and prospective customers, and some ways to obtain answers to these questions, include the following:

- Which customers are the best prospects today, and which will be the most profitable over the long term? What shifts are likely to occur in the present customer mix? Information sources may include consumer surveys, company records, geo-demographic studies, or commercial databases.

- Do the identified customers fall into segments that can be differentiated from one another on similar traits? Information sources may include geographic, demographic, product use, buying patterns, brand loyalty, or competitive positioning studies.

- What are the key buying motives for each customer segment? What do they perceive as "value"? Are perceptions of value changing? Information sources may include focus groups, consumer panels, attitude surveys, or in-depth interviews.

- What are the major causes of customer satisfaction and dissatisfaction from the present company and its competitors? Information sources may include customer satisfaction studies, service quality studies, and repurchase records.

- What customer needs are not being satisfied at present? Given the level of demand and intensity of competition, is it feasible to pursue products or markets to fulfill these unmet needs? Can analyze with Porter's 5-Forces model; conduct demand analysis and sales forecasting.

Major do-it-yourself home improvement retailers Home Depot, Inc. and Lowe's experienced rapid growth over the past decade. They profited from understanding their customers' characteristics and buying motives, and they know how to satisfy the wants and needs of different market segments. Initially, home improvement retailers catered mainly to construction companies, home repair businesses, commercial contractors, and other business customers. Over time, as home owners performed more of their own remodeling, upgrading, and repair tasks, they became a profitable segment for discount home improvement products.

Home Depot, Inc. caters to several customer groups: retail do-it-yourselfers; customers who buy products, such as flooring, and have a contractor recommended by Home Depot do the installation or construction work; and professional contracting customers. These segments are easily differentiated from one another, and the company's marketing mix is altered sufficiently to cater to the specific needs of each customer group. In each case, the overriding buying motive is value, generally defined as excellent quality at a reasonable price. Value perceptions have come to include more emphasis on convenience and service—particularly for homeowners who want to improve their homes, but do not have time to carry out the necessary tasks. Home Depot's commercial customers have a dedicated team of sales associates to meet their needs for service and promptness. Orders also may be delivered to the job site.

Both Home Depot, Inc. and Lowe's recognized an unmet need among female customers. Although men have traditionally performed most of the actual home improvement tasks, it is more often women who have initiated the task and made major purchase decisions. Recognizing this trend led both companies to a greater focus on female customers. They instituted training classes targeted toward women to teach them how to perform home improvement tasks. Lowe's redesigned store layouts to be more appealing to female customers, adding wider aisles, improved product arrangement, and a generally more attractive shopping environment. Home Depot, Inc. opened specialty retail outlets that concentrate on a limited product line, including new upscale Expo Design Center Stores, an exclusive retailer of interior design services, and installation and remodeling products. In each case, these retailers recognized important customer groups, identified their value perceptions and unmet needs, and developed strategies to capitalize on the opportunities to satisfy these customers.

Manufacturers of trucks, vans, and sport utility vehicles (SUVs) experienced large sales increases during the 1990s as consumers traded in their traditional passenger cars for more rugged vehicles. Some industry observers considered this phenomenon a cultural shift. That is, families with small children needed small minivans; families with older children preferred a more powerful, more stylish SUV. When grown children left home, they may have driven off in their own pickup or smaller SUV, and the parents switched to a luxury car. In response to a shift in consumer preferences, auto manufacturers developed more luxurious SUVs during the 1990s and beyond that combine sporty styling with luxury, such as the Ford Expedition, Lincoln Navigator, Mercedes M-class, and others. Shifting consumer preferences such as this have strategic implications for product/market expansion, competitive positioning, performance objectives, and other strategic planning decisions.

Competitors.   Marketers seek to achieve a sustainable competitive advantage in the markets in which they operate. Therefore, it is necessary to know the identity of key competitors, to understand their strategies, and to anticipate their tactics. While attention typically is focused on direct competitors, it is also wise to monitor indirect competitors who have enlarged their own customer base or have found new ways to satisfy unmet customer needs. Competitors may be selling the same or similar (substitute) products. They may be selling these products through the same distribution channels or reaching customers in an entirely different and innovative way. It is important to recognize all primary sources of competition that can affect a firm's position in the marketplace and to determine the competitive assets and skills that each possesses.

Some questions that should be answered about competitors, and examples of tools that can be used in this analysis, are provided in the following section.

- Who are the present competitors? How do they rank in order of threat to our market position? What strategies are they pursuing? What are their key success factors? Can use five-factor model; analysis of competitive strengths and weaknesses/competitive rivalry.

- Who are the potential competitors? What are their strategies and objectives? What barriers to entry exist to protect our position? Use five-factor model to determine potential entrants and entry barriers.

- What new products or technologies are gaining a competitive edge? Use five-factor model to analyze substitute products and customer power.

If the firm is considering entry into a new industry or product line, similar questions must be answered within the new competitive set.

Five-factor model of profitability
Framework for assessing strength of present and potential competition.

The **five-factor model of profitability** is a popular framework for assessing the strength of competition.[10] (See Figure 3.3.) At the core of the model is the competition among existing firms within a given industry. The intensity of competition depends on the number and relative size of competitors, degree of similarity of their products and strategies, high versus low fixed-cost structure, level of commitment to the business, and entry and exit barriers. The five-forces model also directs marketing managers' attention to the threat of potential entrants, the threat of substitute products, and the bargaining power of both customers and suppliers.

The U.S. athletic shoe industry provides an excellent example of a highly competitive marketing environment. Industry leaders, such as Nike, Reebok, Adidas, and Fila, have dominated the market for many years. However, because of the low-cost

FIGURE 3.3

Five-Factor Model of Profitability

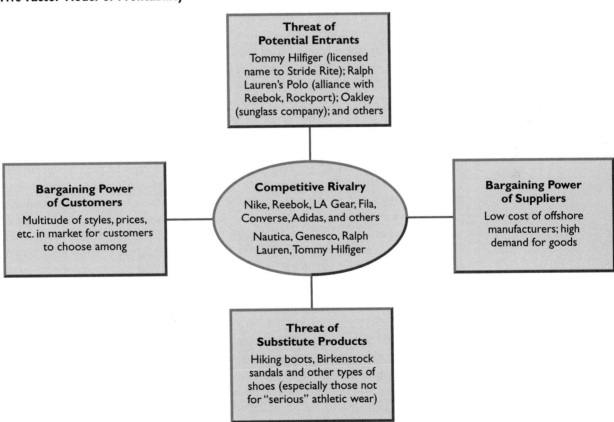

Source: Model adapted from Michael Porter, "Industry Structure and Competitive Strategy: Keys to Profitability," *Financial Analysis Journal* (July–August 1980), p. 33.

production and high-profit potential of athletic shoes, many other firms have entered the market, with others planning to follow. Newer entrants include clothing companies such as Nautica and Tommy Hilfiger and sunglass manufacturers such as Oakley, as illustrated in Figure 3.3.

The Market.   The strategic planning process must take into consideration the primary characteristics of the market segment(s) in which the company chooses to compete. In particular, it is necessary to know the present and potential size of the market, the rate and direction of growth, and relevant trends that may influence strategy development and execution. Market analysis is combined with analysis of customers and competitors in order to determine key success factors, cost bases and perceptions of value, distribution systems, and relative channel position. Questions involving each of these factors must be answered and considered in the strategic planning process, as illustrated in the following example.

Small banks seemed to have an uncertain future in recent years as many retail banks consolidated into a few large national players, and expanded into insurance, investment banking, and other services. As banks became larger, they placed more emphasis on cutting costs. This involved closing tens of thousands of branches, requiring higher account minimums, and charging ATM fees. Once-loyal customers became dissatisfied with the quality of service, and personal relationships deteriorated.

Small community banks have found a lucrative niche in serving the needs of this disenchanted market segment. Small banks often provide a personal touch by serving Starbucks coffee, offering free baby-sitting and investment advice, and other amenities. Some offer free checking, no minimum balance, extended hours, and give away free promotional items. They cater to the markets that have been of less interest to the large banks, including small businesses, minorities, and rural areas. Small banks' profits and loan growth outpaced those of giants like Bank of America and Wells Fargo from 1997 to 2002. Small-bank profits grew at 11.8 percent annually during this time versus 8.5 percent for their larger counterparts. Deposits at smaller banks have grown 5 percent annually since the mid-1990s, while large banks' growth has been flat. Small banks have shown resilience to an uncertain economy, partially because their customers tend to be local businesses that have less exposure to broad economic cycles. Many also have executives with megabank experience. Of course, not all small banks have been successful, but the market for their services has remained relatively constant—attracting the attention of the larger banks that previously abandoned[11] retail banking customers—small-to-mid-sized businesses and individuals.

Environmental Scanning and Forecasting.   In addition to being informed about the micro- or operating-environment factors discussed earlier, marketing managers also must be informed about the macro-environment—forces such as economic conditions, legal and political influences, sociocultural trends, and technological developments. These forces are beyond the direct control of the firm but can shape the development of strategy and its results.

Environmental scanning and forecasting can take a number of forms. The basic requirements include the management of a relevant database and the continuous gathering and interpretation of meaningful data. Computerized decision models are used to facilitate this process.

Environmental scanning and forecasting
Continuous gathering and interpretation of meaningful information about the environment.

Bankers, for example, should monitor the impact of the economy on consumer spending patterns, savings levels, and so forth. The legal and political environment must be monitored to determine the effect of present and pending legislation regarding financial services and taxation. Further, sociocultural trends may lead to different uses of individual and family funds. Technological developments, such as more powerful computers and software, security enhancements, and advances in online banking, also must be analyzed as part of the strategic marketing planning process.

Organizational Analysis (Internal)

In order to determine the best strategic fit between a firm and its environment, it is necessary to conduct a self-assessment of the firm's resource strengths and competitive weaknesses. Each firm has a set of resources that determine its strategic position versus competitors in its industry: financial, physical, human, technological, and organizational resources. The firm's self-assessment can be accomplished by analyzing internal databases (i.e., sales records, customer and competitive data, research and development reports, financial performance for each product category, and so forth) to determine its key success factors and areas that need improvement.

Financial Resources.   A firm's current financial position may determine the level of commitment that can be made for a particular strategic option—or it may place constraints on funds for desirable strategic options. Financial analysis includes a review not only of the present financial assets but also of the sources and uses of those assets, as reported in the firm's financial statements. Sources include sales, interest, dividends, investments, and borrowed funds. Uses may include inventories, promotion and other marketing expenses, interest, taxes, dividends, and other types of financial outlay.

Many companies cut back on expenses, particularly for marketing programs, when faced with declining sales or profits. Spending for advertising and sales force activities may be cut by companies faced with decreased earnings or slow growth. However, this often is done at the expense of attracting much needed business, making it difficult to carry out the firm's strategic intent over the long run.

Physical Resources.   Analysis of physical resources includes an understanding of those required for successful implementation of marketing strategy. This involves an assessment of resources presently available versus those needed in the short and long term, including property, plant (buildings, etc.), and equipment, as well as inventory. For example, the airlines discussed in the opening scenario count among their physical resources their fleet of airplanes, terminal locations and equipment, maintenance facilities, and related equipment. Physical resources related to an airline's corporate headquarters also may be included.

Human Resources.   The talents and abilities of its managers and all other personnel are an indicator of a firm's ability to carry out its strategic intent successfully. A broad definition of a firm's human resources may be extended to include outside specialists, key suppliers or customers, or others who are involved in some way in strategic planning and implementation.

The effect of an organization's human resources goes beyond profitability to a more inclusive measure of corporate reputation. Each spring *Fortune* magazine publishes a list of the most admired corporations in America, based on responses from 10,000 executives, directors, and security analysts across 58 industries. Companies are ranked on eight key attributes: innovation, financial soundness, use of corporate assets, long-term investment value, social responsibility, quality of products/services, quality of management, and employee talent. The last two attributes are directly related to the effect that an organization's managers and employees can have not only on financial performance, but also on the firm's overall reputation. In 2002, General Electric, Walgreen, and Citigroup were selected as the three most admired among U.S. companies from all industries for quality of management. Intel, General Electric, and Walgreen were selected as the three most admired for employee talent. Each of these companies has maintained its reputation among the most admired for many years. One would expect that "quality of management" includes honesty and integrity. However, this attribute was apparently missing for some previously "most admired" companies who fell to the bottom of the list in 2002. Employees, stockholders, suppliers, and customers of companies such as Enron, Arthur Andersen, Global Crossing, WorldCom, and Tyco, suffered great losses because of questionable business practices on the part of their managers. *Fortune's* 2003 list of "America's Most Admired Companies" was led by Wal-Mart, followed by Southwest Airlines. General Electric dropped to the number five position.[12]

Technological Resources.   Technological resources may be related to both products and processes. Technology may be the product in a high-tech company that markets products such as computer hardware and software, telecommunications, or laser applications. On the other hand, technology may be a strategic strength or weakness on the production line in a manufacturing firm or used to manage large databases in an accounting firm or marketing research service, for example. In these companies, technology can include patents and processes, as well as general know-how.

Many firms achieve a competitive advantage through strategic use of technology. For example, JetBlue Airways uses advanced technology in many ways. Pilots use laptop computers in the cockpit during the flight to access electronic flight manuals and to calculate the weight and balance of the aircraft. Security cameras are placed in the cabin of each JetBlue aircraft with a live feed to the cockpit crew while in flight, and to the central operations center at JFK Airport when on the ground. Technology also adds value to the customer experience with free LiveTV at every seat, a ticketless reservation system, and operations efficiencies.[13]

Organizational Resources.   The strategic planning process includes an analysis of a company's structure, systems, and procedures. Structure includes the various business units or divisions that make up the company and the degree of centralization for decision making. The organizational structure should be conducive to development of a strategic marketing plan, and it also should support implementation of that plan.

Strategic Objectives and Strategy Definition

Once management has a clear understanding of its external and internal environments, the next step is to establish realistic objectives to be achieved by the strategic plan. These are generally stated in terms of marketing objectives and financial objectives. Financial objectives generally are stated in terms of profitability, performance, or productivity (e.g., 18 percent return on investment). Marketing objectives generally are stated in such terms as sales, market share, customer satisfaction, or communications objectives (e.g., 25 percent market share, 30 percent increase in brand awareness). After the strategic objectives are established, the overall strategy that will be used to accomplish these objectives must be defined. This is a broad statement for the longer term and is used to drive the details of the specific short- and long-range plans.

Implementation and Tactics

The implementation phase of the strategic planning process is concerned with the allocation of resources needed to carry out the tactical, day-to-day strategic intent. Tactics are the short-range plans that are designed to carry out the goals of the broader strategic plan. Elements of the marketing mix—product, price, communication, and distribution—form the basis for tactical plans targeted at selected market segments.

Resource Allocation. Implementation involves top management commitment to make available the tools that are necessary to carry out the strategic plan. This refers to the level of financial, human, physical, and other resources that will be used for the planned marketing activities during the execution phase. *Financial resources* relate to budget details, decisions about internal versus external sources of funds to support the budget, and a timeline for obtaining and using these funds. *Human resources* involve all levels of personnel that hold some responsibility for execution of the strategy—from top management accountability to entry-level employee specifications. *Physical resources* refer to the property (e.g., land, buildings, etc.), equipment, or other tangible capital goods that are instrumental in executing the strategy.

Target market(s)
Homogeneous group(s) of customers that a company chooses to serve.

Target Market and Marketing Mix. A critical aspect of the strategic planning process is identification of the **target market(s)** that the company will serve. There must be a strategic fit between the customers who are selected and the design of the marketing mix to reach each segment. The tactical plan is based on decisions regarding the design of the marketing mix. The product, communication, pricing, and distribution strategies must provide a consistent, synergistic approach to carrying out the strategic intent during the execution stage. For example, JetBlue Airlines' focus on point-to-point service, low prices, selected routes and destinations, and promotional messages are consistent and effective in achieving the company's objectives.

Execution

For many, the execution phase is the make-or-break stage for the strategic plan. Execution involves the physical performance of the tasks and activities identified in the implementation stage. Successful execution of the plan should achieve the strategic objectives specified previously. It is important to note that the best of strategies can fail if implemented poorly. Likewise, a poor strategy may lead to success if executed well.

Samsung Electronics' strategic objective is to become number one in its industry throughout the world, and Korea's first great global company. This includes taking on Japanese brands that have dominated the market for many years. To accomplish this objective, CEO Yun Jong Yong had to shake up a complacent corporate culture, and overcome a cheap brand image of earlier products that flooded the U.S. market (12-inch black-and-white Sanyo television sets in the 1970s; discounted microwaves and other products in the 1980s and early 1990s).

Some actions taken by Samsung management to execute their strategic plan include:

- Forming alliances with companies such as Dell Computer (to supply components for Dell PCs), Sprint (the I300 Smart Phone), Hewlett-Packard, Compaq, and IBM.

- Pulling Samsung products out of large discount chains like Wal-mart and Kmart, and moving upmarket to Best Buy, Circuit City, and other specialty stores.

- Becoming a truly innovative company, creating cutting-edge technology across a spectrum of product lines; and achieving fifth place ranking in patents in the world in 2002.

- Building strong global market positions as first in memory chips and thin-film displays, and fourth in handset production.

- Spending $400 million on a stylish marketing campaign in 2002, including a high profile role at the Salt Lake City Winter Olympics.

- Developing a company that looks and operates more like a Western-style multinational, including the addition of non-Korean managers to its board, and a management team that includes non-Korean business experience, particularly U.S. experience, and proficiency in English.[14]

Evaluation and Control

In this phase of the strategic planning process, actual results are compared with the planned marketing and financial objectives established in an earlier stage. Results of the plan can be monitored during and after execution. If measured during execution, midcourse corrections may be made. It is not enough to know *whether* the objectives were achieved; it is perhaps more important to know *why* the objectives were or were not achieved. Control mechanisms should be in place before the plan is executed, and all involved parties should be accountable for their part in making the plan work. Continuing the preceding example, Samsung may gain insights from evaluating its new product-development process, marketing strategies, and other factors involved in shortening the time to market for its new products.

PLANNING FOR THE LONG TERM

Over the long term, strategic marketing planners must focus on two major considerations: developing basic strategies to maintain a sustainable competitive advantage and making a distinction between strategic and tactical decisions. Most marketing management decisions have long-term consequences and so must be consistent with a firm's overall strategic intent.

Sustainable Competitive Advantage: Basic Strategies

Sustainable competitive advantage
Long-term success based on unique assets and skills that determine strategic thrust.

The most common routes to **sustainable competitive advantage** involve one or more of the following basic strategies: differentiation, low cost, focus, preemptive move, and synergy. Each of these is described in the following sections and illustrated in Table 3.2.

Differentiation
Strategy based on distinguishing a company's offering from that of competitors based on value-added benefits.

Differentiation. With **differentiation,** one company's product (goods and/or services) is distinguished from that of its competitors by giving customers more value and greater perceived benefits than they could obtain elsewhere. Differentiation can be on the basis of both objective (e.g., measurable performance, added design features) and subjective (e.g., prestige, style) dimensions. When these differentiating factors clearly give a significant advantage over competitors, they can be

TABLE 3.2

Basic Strategies for Sustainable Competitive Advantage

Basic Strategy	*Description*	*Example*
Differentiation	Strategy for distinguishing one company's product from its competitors' on the basis of greater perceived benefits and/or more value	New Balance Athletic Shoes differentiates its brand from competitors, and has the most loyal footwear customers, with a unique product that is available in varying widths, from AA to extra-wide 6E.
Low Cost	Marketer achieves cost advantage by controlling costs of production, product components, marketing programs, etc.	JetBlue Airways and Southwest Airlines control operating costs with no-frills flights, online ticketless reservation services, and efficient hub-and-spoke terminals, permitting lower ticket prices and/or higher profit margins.
Focus	Concentration of the business on specific market segment(s) and/or product group(s)	While many automotive manufactureres have diversified their product lines, Bayerische Motoren Werke AG (BMW) has continued to focus on a premium line of luxury vehicles, particularly the BMW 7-series.
Preemptive Move	First-mover advantage from being first to enter market with a new product, innovation, etc.; creates barriers to entry for competitors	Microsoft gained a long-lasting first-mover advantage through alliances with computer manufacturers who installed Microsoft software on new PCs.
Synergy	Combining the assets and skills of two or more business units by sharing business functions, customers, marketing personnel, etc.	Ford Motor Company achieves synergy by using the same platform for its Thunderbird, Lincoln LS, and Jaguar S-Type; and Volkswagen uses the same 4-wheel drive system (AWD) for Passat and Audi models.

used effectively in the firm's product positioning statements. A differentiation strategy based on dimensions that are important to customers offers an effective way to create value.

Low-cost strategy
Strategy based on ability to add value to the product and/or processes that results in lower prices and/or higher operating margins.

Low Cost.   A **low-cost strategy** should not be confused with the idea of being inexpensive. Today, the ability to gain a cost advantage by controlling costs of production, delivery, product components, and other expenses has become crucial for competitive superiority. Customers demand more value for their money, causing marketers to examine creative ways to deliver value to their customers. While value does not necessarily mean that the customer will pay less for a good or service, it does generally imply value added at some point in the process of manufacturing and/or delivering the good or service to the customer.

Focus strategy
Strategy that concentrates on specific market segment(s) and/or product group(s).

Focus.   A **focus strategy** involves concentration of the business on specific market segment(s) and/or product group(s). Focus can be combined with other strategic marketing techniques, such as differentiation or low cost, to achieve sustainable competitive advantage.

Preemptive move strategy
First-mover advantage, first to enter the market.

Preemptive Move.   A **preemptive move strategy** involves gaining strategic advantage by being the first to enter the market with a new product, a new use for an existing product, a new distribution method, or other innovation. This strategy can create barriers to entry for companies that attempt to follow the first mover into the market.

Synergy
Two or more business units combining assets and skills to achieve strategic advantage.

Synergy.   Firms that are comprised of two or more business units often can obtain **synergy** by combining the assets and skills of these units to achieve strategic advantages. This may involve sharing certain business functions, such as centralized accounting, production, and so forth. They also may be able to offer multiple products or services to the same customer, that is, one-stop shopping, by using the same salesforce to cross-sell each company's offerings.

Strategic versus Tactical Marketing Decisions

At this point in the chapter, it seems appropriate to re-emphasize the differences between strategic and tactical marketing decisions. It is also important to recognize the interdependent relationship between these two concepts. The launch of the Gillette Company's Mach3 razor is a classic example of the relationship between strategy and tactics. Gillette's long-term marketing strategy is focused on achieving or enhancing worldwide leadership in existing or new core consumer product categories in which the company chooses to compete, including razors and blades. In the case of the Mach3 razor, implementation was carefully planned and executed to ensure a successful launch. The razor had become a commodity that was difficult to differentiate, so Gillette created a new category with the Mach3—the shaving system—which they controlled. Product and market research spanned 7 years, with development costs of $750 million. Product testing, customer preferences and ratings, and other research were clearly focused on the market and what customers wanted. Research revealed that men around the world—across countries and ethnic groups—desired the same thing from a shave: "the closest shave in fewer strokes—with less irritation." Once this value proposition was developed, it became a global product positioning statement that drove the tactical plan. Examples of tactics used to achieve the strategic objectives included $300 million in initial marketing campaigns; sufficient manufacturing capability to avoid shortages at the outset; packaging, point-of-sale, and other promotional and support material that was the same throughout the world, but simply translated into 30 languages; a single marketing and advertising campaign for every market with minor local adjustments and translations; and a profitable price point based on pre-testing price sensitivity with consumers. The strategic objective for the Mach3 to be the top-selling razor and blade in North America and Europe was achieved in just 6 months, by appealing to a new group of consumers and upgrading Sensor Excel (previous model razor) customers.[15]

● STRATEGIC PLANNING AND THE CHALLENGE OF CHANGE

Forces of change and their impact on the marketing management process were discussed in the preceding chapter. In this chapter we look at the impact of change on strategy development. In the past, strategic plans could be developed with some level of confidence for perhaps 5 to 10 years. Today, however, the rate of change in most industries is such that the strategic planning horizon is more likely to be 3 to 5 years maximum, with periodic reassessment during this time to determine the need for strategic realignment. Events such as the terrorist attacks against the World Trade Center and the Pentagon caused many firms to reconsider their strategies and the strategic planning process. In dealing with change, an organization needs to consider several factors:

- What changes are occurring in the ways that firms are approaching strategy development?
- What roles do flexibility and adaptability play in long-range planning?
- Who are the firm's stakeholders, and what levels of involvement do they have or should they have in determining strategic direction for the long term?
- With ethics and social responsibility issues permeating the business environment, how should these concepts be integrated into practice through the strategic planning process?
- What is the role of marketing information systems in strategic market planning, and what criteria should be considered in determining the types of data to include?

Changes in Approaches to Strategy Development

The complexity and uncertainty that face most business organizations today in their rapidly changing operating environments have had a major impact on the strategic planning process. As a result, managers experience the frustration of not being able to predict the future with a desirable degree of accuracy and not having sufficient time to engage in necessary long-range planning activities.

Dr. Andrew Grove, Chairman of Intel Corp., suggests a methodology for distinguishing a **strategic inflection point** (turning point) from the "normal hurly-burly of corporate life."[16] The threats of change can be converted into opportunities by

Strategic inflection point
The point at which the threats of a changing environment can be converted into opportunities by following certain actions.

FIGURE 3.4

Strategic Inflection Point: A Six Forces Adaptation of the Five Forces Model

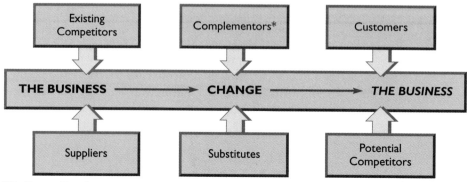

*Significance: Complementors counteract substitution.

(a) Imbalance of Environmental Forces (Substitutes)

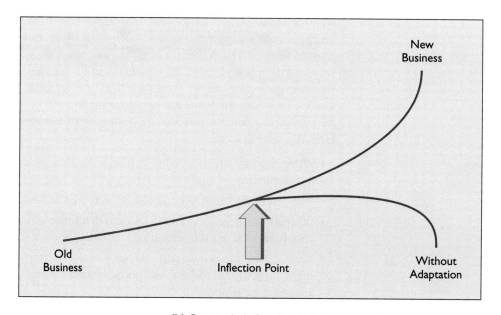

(b) Strategic Inflection Point

Source: Adapted from Andrew S. Grove, "Navigating Strategic Inflection Points," *Business Strategy Review* (Autumn 1997), pp. 11–18. Copyright London Business School. Reprinted by permission of Blackwell Publishers.

following a generic series of actions. The *five forces model* that is used to analyze the competitive environment was presented in Figure 3.3. These forces include suppliers, buyers, potential entrants, and substitutes, with the fifth comprised of the force of rivalry and competition within the industry. A more recent update of this model has added a sixth force—*complementors*. (See Figure 3.4.) This force is described as both subtle and significant. It is the dependence developed in a business on other companies whose products work in conjunction with its own, creating a synergistic effect.

An example is found in the relationship that was created between Microsoft (software) and Intel (microprocessors) in the personal computer industry. Neither company would have been as effective without the other. Where these forces are more or less in equilibrium with one another, the industry environment remains relatively favorable. However, when one of these forces becomes significantly larger or more powerful than another force, the environment is less favorable. For example, a substitute may be introduced to the market with a force that is many times greater than existing forces, distorting the usual way of doing business. (See Figure 3.4a.) The result is generally a change in the framework in which the business operates, eventually leading to a different type of framework where the business operates under a different set of influences. Essentially, the business is reinvented and becomes a completely different structure. Grove refers to the period of time during the transition as the *strategic inflection point.* (See Figure 3.4b.) "During a Strategic Inflection Point, the way a business operates, the very structure and concept of the business, undergoes a change. But the irony is that at this point itself nothing much happens. That is the nature of an Inflection Point: it is a kind of a gentle curve. Yet at a point where nothing else happens, you must determine whether the future trajectory of that curve is going to head up or down."[17]

When a firm is at a strategic inflection point, the effect is so subtle that the change may be missed. Some changes, such as market saturation or erosion of market share, may occur over a relatively long period of time, making it difficult to determine where to implement a strategic shift. However, environmental scanning and market research can reveal the need for new strategic approaches. Intuit, a software company that markets the software, QuickBooks, targeted a core market comprised of over six million small businesses with fewer than 20 employees. Because Intuit had saturated this market, CEO Steve Bennett recognized that growth had to occur in a new market—all businesses that employ up to 250 employees, which amounts to an $18 billion software market made up of 24 million firms. The software products for this vast market are priced between $500 and $7,000 depending on application and degree of customization tailored to selected industries. In part, the need for change was brought about by the growth of previous small business customers who now had more employees and had an unmet need for more developed software.[18]

Although he does not guarantee a precise formula, Grove identifies some warning signs that indicate a strategic inflection point in a time of change:

- *Try the "silver bullet test."* If you anticipate a change in your key competitor, imagine that you have a silver bullet that you can use to shoot one competitor. If you have only one choice, which one will it be? You must decide. When this answer changes to another competitor, this is a good indication that you are passing through a strategic inflection point. One of the signs that you are facing a different business scenario is when the people who threaten you change.

- *Do you have that feeling that the people around you have "lost it"?* If so, apply the "silver bullet test" to complementors—those on whom you are most dependent to make your product work best. Listen for people to use phrases that represent a whole new vogue; if these words sounds like gibberish to you, there may be cross-currents going on in your organization that need to be analyzed.

When you or someone else doesn't "get it," maybe the "it" is no longer what you used to talk about—a warning sign that something is changing.

- *Listen to the bearers of bad news (i.e., what people think is going wrong) in your organization.* Those who are closest to a problem (e.g., technology, sales or customer situation) generally see the first signs of a strategic inflection point. Sales organizations are particularly good at this.

- *Use debate as an important measuring tool for sorting through the "is it" or "is it not" questions.* This process helps to remove the inconsistencies and identify important events and changes.

Identification of strategic inflection points is one of a number of methods used to identify "turning points that can make or break even the strongest of businesses." The important lesson is that marketing managers need to take actions to "convert the threats of change into opportunities." Each of the forces in the traditional five forces model must be monitored, along with the sixth force—complementors—in order to develop a winning strategy.

Complexity and Uncertainty

The complexity and uncertainty that characterize most industries today—particularly in high-technology areas such as telecommunications and computer hardware and software and others such as managed health care—have caused many firms to reassess their long-term strategies. In these industries, the legal/political ramifications are evolving and uncertain, and competitive actions and reactions are not always predictable.

Complexity refers to the intricacies and interrelationships of a company and the industry in which it operates, making it difficult to analyze, understand, or solve complicated problems. Strategic marketing management requires the ability to separate elaborately intertwined environmental forces to simplify their analysis to the extent possible.

Uncertainty refers to vagueness and doubt about a company's industry and general operating environment—not being sure what is happening now or what is going to happen in the future. Several scenarios generally are possible, ranging from worst case to most optimistic. The question is, Which is most likely to occur, and how soon?

Industries with a high level of complexity and uncertainty include those related to telecommunications, computers, and software. Government regulations, strategic alliances among competitors, rapid advances in technology, and other factors present both threats and opportunities. The September 11, 2001 terrorist attacks on America introduced a new level of complexity and uncertainty to the nation's businesses. An uncertain future was faced by companies that were displaced from the World Trade Center in New York City on that date, along with many others throughout the country. Makeshift offices were set up in remote locations, and complex security systems were put into place to protect workers and customers from potential disasters. Kenneth Chenault, CEO of American Express Co., was one of many business leaders who demonstrated a willingness to tackle important issues in the middle of a crisis. Chenault and his team made hundreds of ad hoc decisions, guided by two overriding concerns: employee safety and customer service.

AmEx helped 560,000 stranded cardholders get home, often taking them across the country on chartered buses and airplanes. The company waived millions of dollars of delinquent fees for late payment, and increased credit limits for clients who were without cash. Prior to September 11, the company's charge card and travel agency (number one in the world in both categories) were already suffering from a slowing economy, and the threat of terrorism further exacerbated the company's financial problems. American Express Travel Related Services, Financial Advisors, Express Bank, and online financial service operations are complex operations, along with the company's services in travel, charge cards, travelers' checks, and magazines. The challenge is to manage complex operations in an uncertain business environment, while maintaining the company's core values and strategic intent.[19]

Poverty of Time

Traditionally, small business managers have less time available for strategic planning than do managers in large businesses. In larger firms, the strategic planning process tends to be more formal, often with individuals or departments charged with this responsibility. Further, stockholders, lenders, and other interested parties demand evidence of accountability that may be found in a firm's strategic marketing plan. The rate of change and resulting volatility in business environments increase the need to anticipate the future in order to maximize opportunities and minimize threats. Many firms have turned to outside analysts who are knowledgeable about their industry and experts in strategic planning to facilitate this process. Many of the major consulting firms and former "Big Six" accounting firms have expanded their services to fill this need. Regardless of the size of the business, time must be made available for reflection and planning for the future.

The Importance of Flexibility and Adaptation

The strategic planning process establishes clear guidelines for future marketing decisions, but at times this formal process may result in establishing directives and constraints that make it difficult for a firm to adapt to changing circumstances. Therefore, a realistic strategic plan should allow for needed flexibility and provide parameters for adapting to new situations. This requires easily understood guidelines that cover a relatively broad range of decisions—particularly focused on the firm's mission and objectives to maintain consistency and take advantage of the company's core competencies.

The rapid growth of Internet commerce has tested the flexibility of many organizations and their ability to adapt to an entirely new way of doing business. One major challenge is that the Internet is a global marketplace, introducing new competition and new markets to firms throughout the world. Small local marketers no longer must worry only about local competition. They suddenly are thrust into the world of international commerce, requiring a new approach to strategic market planning. Foreign companies have discovered the lucrative American market, and U.S. companies that adapt to doing business on the Internet can benefit from new markets, less regulation, and expanded business relationships.

INNOVATE OR EVAPORATE*

The Inspired Chef: Somthing's Cooking at Whirlpool Corp.

 The world's largest manufacturer of home appliances, Whirlpool Corp. entered the twenty-first century faced with strategic challenges: a slowdown in growth; falling profits; and another cyclical downturn. Although the company was generating annual sales of over $10 billion, management recognized the need to become more innovative in developing new businesses. Otherwise, there would be no creative ideas for the next generation of products. How does a 90-year-old corporate structure get beyond its basic lines of refrigerators, washing machines, and ovens to develop innovative business ideas for today's markets? A 75-member Innovation Team (an international cross-section of 75 people from all levels of the organization) was formed to look throughout the company for ideas that could generate material business growth. Everyone was responsible for innovation. No boundaries were set, and no proposals were rejected out of hand. Each new idea had to undergo rigorous evaluation sessions, with considerable emphasis placed on expected customer reactions to the new business idea.

Inspired Chef was one of the innovative ideas that survived the rigorous new product evaluation process at Whirlpool. This idea was the brainchild of a KitchenAid Division executive, Josh Gitlin, who recognized the trend toward "extreme nesting" (people spending more time at home engaged in decorating, cooking, and entertaining). This trend offered a promising opportunity to "sell the culinary passion that goes along with owning all of these complex kitchen tools." Here's how the concept works: Inspired Chef contracts with chefs and culinary school grads to give cooking class-dinner parties in customer's homes. The chef furnishes all foods and equipment, along with a catalog filled with KitchenAid products. Part of the tuition goes to Whirlpool, who also had created a new distribution channel for its appliances. The lowest price is $29 for the Spanish dinner party, where guests can learn to cook paella—and if they are so inclined, they can buy a paella pan.

Gitlin's new business idea entered the experimental stage in August 2000, when funding and personnel were made available. Gitlin became founder and president of the new unit. Within a year, Inspired Chef's staff had grown to seven people and nearly 60 instructors who were teaching classes in six states, and the company implemented a national rollout. The company's Web page offers information about culinary classes, KitchenAid and other products, instructors, and recipes. Whirlpool's new way of thinking about innovation has become pervasive throughout the company, and this may be its greatest opportunity for long-term success.

*The box title is attributed to James M. Higgins.

Source: Fara Warner, "Recipe for Growth," *Fast Company* (October 2001), pp. 40–41; www. inspiredchef.com.

Stakeholder Involvement

Stakeholders
All external and internal parties involved in the life of an organization.

Many firms bring their important stakeholders into the strategic planning process. These valued **stakeholders** may include customers, suppliers, employees at various levels in the organization, consultants, and others. Their contributions may be in the nature of market feedback; projections about product supply and demand; and information about competitors, technological breakthroughs, legal and political activities, and other environmental issues. A firm's overall marketing effort should include the development of strategic relationships with key stakeholders that can provide useful insights throughout the strategic planning process. Information gained from each of these sources can be included in the marketing decision support system (MDSS), discussed in Chapter 4.

Integrating Ethics and Social Responsibility

If a direction for ethics and social responsibility is not integrated into the strategic market planning process from the very beginning, the organizational culture may not provide the needed direction for ethical and socially responsible marketing programs.[20] As an organization focuses on profits, productivity, and efficiency—outcomes that are necessary for success—it may lose sight of its basic core values that define acceptable limits for strategic and tactical decisions. (See Figure 3.5.) The fall of Enron, Arthur Andersen, WorldCom, and other corporations in 2001 and 2002 indicated a lack of ethical values that were clearly understood and enforced—and subsequently caused financial disasters.

Ethical behavior is fundamental to building trust and long-term relationships between a company and its employees. A code of ethics sets standards and provides

FIGURE 3.5

Integration of Ethical and Socially Responsible Plans into Strategic Decision Making

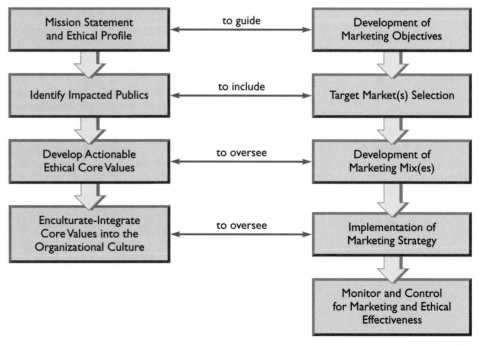

Source: Adapted from Donald Robin, and R. Eric Reidenbach (1987), "Social Responsibility, Ethics, and Marketing Strategy: Closing the Gap Between Concept and Application," *Journal of Marketing* 51(1) (January 1987), pp. 44–58. Reprinted by permission.

FIGURE 3.6

American Marketing Association Code of Ethics

Members of the American Marketing Association (AMA) are committed to ethical professional conduct. They have joined together in subscribing to this Code of Ethics embracing the following topics.

Responsibilities of the Marketer

Marketers must accept responsibility for the consequences of their activities and make every effort to ensure that their decisions, recommendations, and actions function to identify, serve, and satisfy all relevant publics: consumers, organizations, and society. Marketers' professional conduct must be guided by:

1. The basic rule of professional ethics: not knowingly to do harm;
2. The adherence to all applicable laws and regulations;
3. The accurate representation of their education, training, and experience; and
4. The active support, practice, and promotion of this Code of Ethics.

Honesty and Fairness

Marketers shall uphold and advance the integrity, honor, and dignity of the marketing profession by:

1. Being honest in serving consumers, clients, employees, suppliers, distributors, and the public;
2. Not knowingly participating in conflict of interest without prior notice to all parties involved; and

3. Establishing equitable fee schedules including the payment or receipt of usual, customary, and/or legal compensation for marketing exchanges.

Rights and Duties of Parties

Participants in the marketing exchange process should be able to expect that:

1. Products and services offered are safe and fit for their intended uses;
2. Communications about offered products and services are not deceptive;
3. All parties intend to discharge their obligations, financial and otherwise, in good faith; and
4. Appropriate internal methods exist for equitable adjustment and/or redress of grievances concerning purchases.

It is understood that the above would include, but is not limited to, the following responsibilities of the marketer:

In the area of product development management:

- Disclosure of all substantial risks associated with product or service usage
- Identification of any product component substitution that might materially change the product or impact on the buyer's purchase decision
- Identification of extra-cost added features

(continues on next page)

guidelines for acceptable behavior. The American Marketing Association's Code of Ethics is shown in Figure 3.6.

STRATEGIC PLANNING AND A CUSTOMER ORIENTATION

It has become increasingly evident that a successful strategic plan must start with the customer. Marketing opportunities are based on an identification of market wants and needs, an understanding of how customers make buying decisions, how they use the goods and services they buy, and their level of commitment to current brands. The strategic planning process should incorporate the following:

FIGURE 3.6 *(continued)*

American Marketing Association Code of Ethics

In the area of promotions:
- Avoidance of false and misleading advertising
- Rejection of high pressure manipulations, or misleading sales tactics
- Avoidance of sales promotions that use deception or manipulation

In the area of distribution:
- Not manipulating the availability of a product for purpose of exploitation
- Not using coercion in the marketing channel
- Not exerting undue influence over the resellers' choice to handle a product

In the area of pricing:
- Not engaging in price fixing
- Not practicing predatory pricing
- Disclosing the full price associated with any purchase

In the area of marketing research:
- Prohibiting selling or fund raising under the guise of conducting research
- Maintaining research integrity by avoiding misrepresentation and omission of pertinent research data
- Treating outside clients and suppliers fairly

Organizational Relationships

Marketers should be aware of how their behavior may influence or impact on the behavior of others in organizational relationships. They should not encourage or apply coercion to obtain unethical behavior in their relationships with others, such as employers, suppliers, or customers.

1. Apply confidentiality and anonymity in professional relationships with regard to privileged information.
2. Meet their obligations and responsibilities in contracts and mutual agreements in a timely manner.
3. Avoid taking the work of others, in whole, or in part, and represent this work as their own or directly benefit from it without compensation or consent of the orginator or owner.
4. Avoid manipulation to take advantage of situations to maximize personal welfare in a way that unfairly deprives or damages the organization or others.

Any AMA members found to be in violation of any provision of this Code of Ethics may have their Association membership suspended or revoked.

Source: Reprinted by permission of the American Marketing Association.

- Outstanding approaches to delivering customer satisfaction
- A plan for value creation from the customers' perspective
- Plans for continuous quality improvement in products and processes
- The ability and willingness to re-engineer and/or redesign as indicated by the marketing environment or internal conditions.

Customer Satisfaction

The ultimate success of a strategic marketing plan lies in the amount of customer satisfaction and profitability that it can generate. A strategy that results in high levels of customer satisfaction gives a firm one of the greatest long-term assets it can have: loyal customers who return time and again for repeat purchases. However, the ability to deliver customer satisfaction must start with a customer focus, and this business philosophy must start with top management. This requires giving attention to the quality not only of the goods and services offered by the business but also of the

FIGURE 3.7

The Value Chain

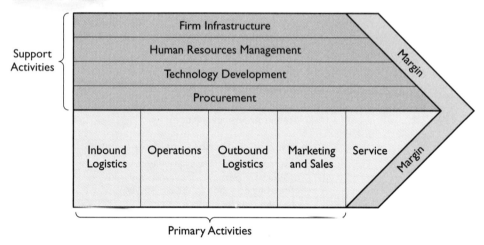

Source: Reprinted with the permission of the Free Press, a Division of Simon & Schuster, Inc. from *Competitive Advantage: Creating and Sustaining Superior Performance* by Michael E. Porter. Copyright ©1985, 1988 by Michael E. Porter.

processes involved before, during, and after a sale, as indicated in Chapter 1 and throughout this book.

Value Creation

Value is "in the eye of the beholder." It is important to consider the perspective of the final consumer or business customer when deciding how to add value to a company's goods and services. The value added to a sale differentiates one company's offering from that of a competitor. It provides the basis for a positioning strategy that can be used in product design (or redesign) and marketing communications. While many firms pursue a low-cost strategy and many purchase decisions are made on the basis of price, the most successful approaches include a competitive advantage obtained through a value-added strategy. Customer value may be created in a variety of ways, such as exceptional customer service, product assortments, unusual product design features, unique packaging, creative distribution methods, and higher-quality component parts and materials.

> **Value chain**
> Set of primary and secondary activities concerned with creating and delivering value for customers.

Porter's **value chain**[21] includes both primary and secondary activities that create value for customers. (See Figure 3.7.) The value chain reveals ways to obtain competitive advantage through differences in primary and secondary value-creating activities. Primary value activities include inbound and outbound logistics, operations, marketing and sales, and service. Secondary value activities include procurement, technology development, human resource management, and the firm infrastructure. Each of these activities may be a strength or weakness when compared with competitors.

One way to add value is through more convenient, lower-cost distribution methods. In the United States and throughout the world, shopping centers and malls have responded to customers' demands for one-stop shopping and discount centers. In Japan, the number of supermalls is expanding. The Japanese make up only 2 percent of the world's population but purchase two thirds of the world's branded products. Known for their demand for quality, Japanese consumers now are also demanding lower prices. Japan's economic difficulties of the 1990s and post-2000 created customer resistance to the higher prices they once paid without question during the affluent 1980s. Japanese consumers have turned to discount outlets and shopping in stores overseas or ordering from foreign catalogs to obtain value. It is estimated that Japanese shoppers spend over $40 billion overseas each year. One response to this trend is the development of supermalls in Japan. These supermalls offer a variety of retail shops, dining, and leisure activities, with emphasis on lower prices and more value for the money. Economies of scale are obtained through increased efficiency in inbound and outbound logistics (e.g., highway access, containerized shipping), spreading fixed costs over a larger operation, and other value-added activities.[22]

Summary

The strategic planning process and marketing management are closely related, since marketing management decisions must be consistent with a firm's overall business strategy. A formal strategic plan provides a basis for making better decisions in all circumstances because strategic decisions are based on an understanding of customers' needs, competitors' activities, and the financial implications of each decision. The firm's overall business strategy and an understanding of its marketing strategies drive tactical marketing plans. Both strategic and tactical decisions must be responsive to changes in the marketplace.

Strategic plans are developed at several levels of an organization: corporate, division or strategic business unit, and functional or operating level. The focus of this book is on the business unit level. Stages in the strategic planning process include determination of the firm's mission and corporate performance objectives, analysis of external and internal environments, marketing objectives and strategy, implementation and tactics, execution of the plan, and evaluation and control measures.

The major external environmental factors to be analyzed in the strategic planning process are the firm's customers, competitors, and market where it will compete. Marketing managers must continuously scan the external environment to identify

opportunities and threats and to be able to identify market trends and forecast demand. The major internal factors that should be included in a firm's self-analysis are competitive strengths and weaknesses related to its financial, physical, human, technological, and organizational resources.

Marketing planners must design strategies that will give them a sustainable competitive advantage over the long term. The most common routes taken to achieve strategic advantage involve one or more of the following basic strategies: differentiation, low cost, focus, preemptive move, and synergy.

The forces of change discussed in the preceding chapter and the rate at which these changes occur have a significant impact on the strategic market planning process. The approach to strategy development has changed due to the rate of change, environmental complexity and uncertainty, inability to accurately predict the future, and time constraints faced by managers for planning activities. Because of this, many marketing managers have had to settle for shorter planning horizons and allow for flexibility needed to adapt to new circumstances.

Many firms gain insights and support from customers, suppliers, employees, and other important stakeholders throughout the strategic planning process. Firms also are finding it expedient to integrate ethics and social responsibility into their strategic market planning and include core values to help define acceptable limits for strategic and tactical decisions. Because a successful strategic plan must start with the customer, the strategic planning process should include outstanding approaches to delivering customer satisfaction, a customer-oriented plan for value creation, and the ability and willingness to change with market conditions.

Questions

1. Explain the relationship between the strategic market planning process, the marketing management process, and the success of an organization. Use an existing nonprofit or for-profit organization to illustrate your answer.

2. Discuss the purpose of a formal strategic plan for a high-tech telecommunications company that is faced with the challenge of managing change in a volatile, uncertain marketing environment. Would your answer be different for a manufacturer of a low-tech, staple product such as paper goods for an office? Why?

3. Describe each of the stages in the strategic planning process. Explain how aspects of this process might be different for a cellular telephone company versus the American Red Cross.

4. Give an example of each internal and external environmental force that can affect the success of a marketing program, and state why it is important to analyze each of these. Which of these forces can be controlled (at least to some extent) by the organization, and what are some ways that this can be accomplished?

5. Identify a recent macro- or micro-environmental change that has had an impact on marketing decisions. Explain how this has affected product design or availability and pricing, promotion, or distribution strategies. (Be sure to differentiate between strategy and tactics and between organizational levels in your answer.)

6. Describe the major strategic approaches that marketers can use to achieve sustainable competitive advantage over the long term. Give a specific example of how each has been used by a marketer of goods or services and why you think it has been successful (or unsuccessful).

7. Record the details of a recent purchase experience, and analyze your perceptions of whether the organization's marketing strategy is based on a customer orientation. Why and how should the customer be considered in developing a strategic marketing plan?

8. Explain the role that core values and ethics should play in developing a strategic marketing plan. How can these concepts be integrated into the strategic plan and effectively implemented on a day-to-day basis?

Exercises

1. Obtain annual reports or other company literature from a variety of companies (e.g., auto manufacturers, packaged food products, tobacco, telecommunications, banks, etc.). Identify their mission and/or vision statement, objectives, and long-term strategies, and evaluate their effectiveness.

2. Determine the mission statement, objectives, and long-term strategies for a nonprofit organization such as the American Cancer Society, a church, or the Girl or Boy Scouts of America. Discuss the differences, if any, in the purposes of strategic planning for the types of organizations discussed in this exercise and Exercise 1.

3. Select an industry that is experiencing a rapidly changing environment (e.g., telecommunications, converging technologies, software, security goods and services, etc.). For this industry, analyze the following:

   a. Major competitors in the industry and their relative position in terms of market share and profitability.

   b. Industry growth rates (size and direction) and emerging trends that will affect future strategic decisions (either positively or negatively).

   c. Key success factors to ensure profitability over the long term.

   d. Comparative strengths and weaknesses of each of the industry competitors described in part a and your opinion of whether their relative positions are subject to change.

4. Visit the Web sites of the companies discussed above. Analyze the content of these Web sites to determine how they support the company's strategy and how use of this medium offers them a competitive advantage with their customers.

5. Develop a strategic marketing plan for an entrepreneurial venture in which you are interested (or for an organization to which you belong). What advice would you give to someone else about pitfalls and challenges that were encountered in this planning process?

Endnotes

1. Quote taken from *Bartlett's Book of Business Quotations,* compiled by Barbara Ann Kipher (Boston: Little, Brown and Company, 1994), p. 265.

2. The *growth phase* as used here refers to the early stages of the firm when it is emerging from its start-up phase or to any point in the organizational cycle where strategic marketing decisions are made. This may apply to strategic growth plans, new product development policies, and so on.

3. Ed Scannell, "IBM Goes After Small Business Big Time," *InfoWorld* (April 18, 2002), http://ww1.infoworld.com.

4. David A. Aaker, *Strategic Market Management,* 6th ed. (New York: Wiley, 2001), pp. 4–6.

5. Gerald A. Michaelson, "Winning the Marketing War," in Jeffrey Heilbrunn (ed.), *Marketing Encyclopedia: Issues and Trends Shaping the Future* (Chicago: American Marketing Association, 1995), pp. 170–172.

6. Subhash C. Jain, *Marketing Planning and Strategy,* 4th ed. (Cincinnati: South-Western Publishing, 1993), pp. 23–25.

7. Derek F. Abell, "Strategic Windows," *Journal of Marketing* (July 1978), pp. 21–26. (A strategic window represents a short period of time when there is an optimal "fit" between the organization's capabilities and a new opportunity to satisfy the needs of the market.)

8. Theodore Levitt, "Marketing Myopia," *Harvard Business Review* (July–August 1960), pp. 45–56. *Marketing myopia* refers to missed opportunities caused by focusing on the product at the expense of paying attention to the customer and the needs of a changing marketplace.

9. Aaker, *op. cit.,* pp. 142–148.

10. Michael E. Porter, "Industry Structure and Competitive Strategy: Keys to Profitability," *Financial Analysis Journal* (July–August 1980), p. 33.

11. Mara Der Hovanesian, Heather Timmons, and Chris Palmeri, "For Small Banks, It's a Wonderful Life," *BusinessWeek* (May 6, 2002), pp. 83–84.

12. "America's Most Admired Companies," *Fortune,* March 4, 2002, pp. 64–90; "America's Most Admired Companies," *Fortune,* March 3, 2003, pp. 64–94.

13. JetBlue Airways Prospectus Summary, *Prospectus, Investor Relations,* http://investor.jetblue.com, April 11, 2002.

14. William J. Holstein, "Samsung's Golden Touch," *Fortune* (April 1, 2002), pp. 89–94.

15. Glenn Rifkin, "Mach 3: Anatomy of Gillette's Latest Global Launch," *Strategy + Business* (Second Quarter 1999, Issue 15), pp. 34–41.

16. Andrew S. Grove, "Navigating Strategic Inflection Points," *Business Strategy Review* (Autumn 1997), pp. 11–18.

17. *Ibid.*

18. Erika Brown, "Small Is Big," *Forbes* (May 2002), pp. 88+.

19. John A. Byrne and Heather Timmons, "Tough Times For A New CEO," *BusinessWeek* (October 21, 2001), pp. 64–70.

20. Donald Robin and R. Eric Reidenbach, "Social Responsibility, Ethics, and Marketing Strategy: Closing the Gap Between Concept and Application," *Journal of Marketing* 51(1) (January 1987), pp. 44–58.

21. Michael E. Porter, *Competitive Advantage: Creating and Sustaining Superior Performance* (New York: Free Press, 1985), Chap. 2.

22. Virginia Kouyoumdjian, "Supermalls Build on New Shopping Strategy," *Wall Street Journal* (September 29, 1997), p. B12.

MARKETING MANAGEMENT IN ACTION: CLOSING CASE

eBay Inc.: The Challenge of Balancing Growth and Social Capital

Within a few years, the Internet auction site, eBay, became the preeminent industry leader in the trading and selling of goods online. The company went public in September 1998. While other dot.com firms struggled and crashed, eBay continued to gain new buyers and sellers, strengthen its brand name, and expand internationally. In 2001 alone, eBay traded $9 billion worth of goods, approximately 20 percent of all consumer e-commerce that year. Automobiles alone were estimated to represent over $1 billion of that amount. Profits nearly doubled from the previous year to $90 million, with revenues of $750 million (about 8 percent of all goods traded on the site). The market addressed by eBay in 2002 was estimated at $1.7 trillion. By 2005, eBay expects to achieve $3 billion in revenue and $1 billion in profits, but will need to triple the number of its registered buyers and sellers to 150 million to meet this goal. In addition, eBay has attempted to keep its stock at a high price/earnings ratio of about 80 (based on 2002 estimates), but the methods the company is using to drive growth have begun to cause problems between eBay and its core customers.

CEO Meg Whitman states that eBay's quest is "to build the world's largest online trading platform where practically anyone can trade practically anything." In addition to its strong position in automobiles and collectibles, eBay has become the largest online seller of computers, photo equipment and supplies, and sporting goods. By spring 2002, eBay was selling a motorcycle every 18 minutes, a laptop computer every 30 seconds, and a book every four seconds. You can buy everything from glass eyeballs, to timeshares, to restaurant equipment, or any of over 18,000 other categories of goods and services from this electronic bazaar.

eBay is close to being a virtual corporation, since it has no inventory, no warehouses, and no sales force. However, it is "social capital" (trust, goodwill, credibility) that is largely responsible for eBay's success. This intangible asset allows eBay to benefit from the creativity of the millions of entrepreneurs on its site, who must meet the demands of even more numerous buyers who are drawn to the site. As of mid-2002, there were 42 million registered users, and the number continues to grow. eBay takes advantage of the low communication and transaction costs of the Internet to bring buyers and sellers together. Customers perform many of the functions that a traditional retailer would handle for its customers, such as introducing countless new products and marketing techniques, paying shipping costs, and handling customer service. eBay makes money by taking a commission on every trade (typically 1 to 5 percent), listing fees, and other charges. The company benefits further from network effects: the more buyers who go to eBay, the more sellers are attracted, who then attract more buyers, and so on, with the site becoming a much larger source of supply and prices becoming more competitive. Rajiv Dutta, eBay's CFO, explains that there is an enormous amount of subtlety and complexity underneath this system, and that the company is not so much a conventional company as a self-regulating, complex system. When comparing eBay to a traditional retailer such as Wal-Mart, Dutta says that eBay has no real cost of goods, and customer acquisition is driven primarily by word-of-mouth. He further points out that Wal-Mart has nearly $16 billion in long-term debt and eBay has virtually none. Since eBay is free of many of the costs that most other corporations must bear, it is able to generate an increasing amount of cash. Operating margins went from slightly negative in 1999 to 19 percent in 2001, compared to Wal-Mart's operating margin of about 5 percent. Dutta forecasts operating margins to hit 30 to 35 percent by 2005 (the basis for the $1 billion operating profit target noted above).

However, eBay's future success depends on more than financial performance. It must maintain and extend the social capital that has been created through the network effects and the interactions among the millions of people who trade on its site, and continue to convert it into profits. An important source of social capital is eBay's feedback system, where buyers and sellers can rate each other. Although the posting of negative feedback is very rare (less than 1 percent), sellers are afraid of getting negative comments and take measures to avoid them by being brutally honest about any defects in their wares. One seller who does 600 auctions a week in collectibles such as Barbie dolls and *Star Wars* figures says every time a seller gets a negative feedback, that seller's sales go down.

Social capital, just as other forms of capital, earns a return. Some of the returns to eBay include thousands of small pricing and product selection innovations made by members in tune with the economy; ability to meet unmet customer needs and develop products that might otherwise be overlooked; users create markets where none existed before, then absorb expenses such as inventory, marketing, and shipping, and help with customer support. In an ongoing effort to keep its community of users happy, the company spends considerable time listening to customers and regularly observing trends on its site through focus groups, comments on discussion boards, and other means.

eBay's organizational structure is designed as a collection of start-ups. Each major category and each country has its own manager, and these managers are "the stewards of social capital on their turf." They are experts in their particular markets who are responsible for growth in their respective niches—and making sure nothing impedes trade there. They provide feedback upward in the organization to indicate when a new category is needed. Whitman says that the company decides to expand the trading platform based on where users want to go. One of these newer directions is toward adding fixed-price components to its site (in direct competition with Amazon.com). In 2000, eBay acquired Half.com, a fixed-price online store for discounted commodity goods, and integrated it into the eBay site. As of spring 2002, about 19 percent of all sales on eBay were fixed-price rather than auction.

In eBay's quest for growth, the company has been attracted to large corporations like Disney, IBM, and Home Depot, among others. These companies use eBay to sell discontinued goods, excess inventory, and returned items. Even Dell uses eBay

as a channel to sell refurbished off-lease PCs, and governments use eBay to liquidate foreclosed assets. As of spring 2002, the large sellers accounted for less than 3 percent of total eBay sales—but eBay wants to expand their offerings, particularly to the fixed-price, in-season items that represent most of the economy. As eBay marketing VP Bill Cobb tells reluctant corporate sellers, "We have the technology, the marketplace, and the buyers. Why are you going to do it on your own? Nobody visits your site." Large companies that have their own Web sites find that eBay is a good alternative channel for auctioning goods that they would prefer not to sell on their company site. For example, Disney uses eBay to auction collectors' items such as ride vehicles from its theme parks and movie props, and IBM sells laptops that are reaching the end of their product cycle for about $1,000 each. In fact, IBM has found that eBay auctions are bringing new clients to IBM rather than taking sales from IBM.com.

The question is whether the forces that are driving eBay's growth will pull it in so many directions that its valuable social capital will be undermined. Growth in listings (a major contributor to revenue) has slowed dramatically, after phenomenal increases in 1999 and 2000. To achieve its financial goals by 2005, eBay will need to expand aggressively into new categories, geographies, formats, and customer types. However, rapid growth poses a threat to its social capital. The expansionary strategies already in use have begun to alienate existing users. eBay has tried to avoid taking sides between buyers and sellers when a problem arises, but the sellers are objecting to this neutrality position—particularly the "Powersellers" who sell more than $2,000 a month on eBay. If these sellers expect preferential treatment from eBay, large companies such as IBM may expect even more. However, eBay insists that it will treat everyone the same, and maintain a level playing field. "Our vision of eBay consists of a marketplace where your next door neighbor can compete side by side with large corporations," Whitman says. You can find IBM laptop listings from the $86 billion corporation alongside auction listings from small sellers, and it is impossible to tell who is the seller of each listing.

The level playing field approach may create another problem, if customers stop benefiting from the relationships they develop through eBay. For example, in the original collectibles and antiques categories, such an efficient market was created that average selling prices declined 30 percent in one year. Another problem was created when eBay implemented a controversial standardized checkout feature that automatically exchanges information between the buyer and the seller after an auction. This was a change from its original practice whereby buyers and sellers e-mailed one another after an auction to make arrangements for delivery and payment. eBay made the feature optional when sellers objected because they thought the company was trying to come between them and their customers. Smaller sellers also fear the effect of large corporate sellers on their online businesses. Much of eBay's social capital comes from the fact that it is a place where people can transact with people, not with large, impersonal corporations.

The future of eBay hinges on its ability to grow and appeal to a diverse group of constituents without depleting its social capital, which remains a key factor in its success. The challenge is to expand into new categories without leaving the core business behind, or antagonizing important customer groups. Social capital is not a resource that appears on a company's balance sheet, and often the company does not know it is missing until it is already gone.

Case Study Questions

1. Describe and evaluate the basic strategic thrust(s) that are used by eBay to achieve a sustainable competitive advantage.

2. Determine the major environmental forces that can affect eBay's ability to successfully implement its marketing strategy. How should eBay respond to these forces?

3. Describe eBay's present and potential customers, and analyze the ability of eBay to serve these customers in terms of segments, motivations, and unmet needs.

4. Analyze eBay's strategic moves toward large business sellers and fixed-price sales. What criteria should be used to make these decisions?

5. Assuming that eBay sellers are also customers, identify the criteria that might be used by small entrepreneurial sellers versus large corporate sellers when they select eBay as a distribution channel for their goods.

6. Conduct a competitive analysis for eBay and others in this industry. Include present and potential, and direct and indirect competitors. Evaluate the strengths and weaknesses of each competitor, including eBay, based on what you consider to be the key success factors in this industry.

7. Create a value chain for this business and industry, based on Porter's value chain. Note that the nature of this business, and the vast network of business partners, may necessitate a different value chain model. What changes, if any, would you make?

8. Identify the problem/challenge/opportunity that is faced by eBay today. You have a meeting with CEO Meg Whitman tomorrow morning to present your recommendations for a marketing strategy that will facilitate growth (new product lines and/or new geographic markets); but will not negatively impact the "social capital" that the company has developed successfully.

Sources: Erick Schonfeld, "eBay's Secret Ingredient," *Business 2.0* (March 2002), pp. 52–58; Mohammed, Rafi A., Robert J. Fisher, Bernard J. Jaworski, and Aileen M. Cahill, *Internet Marketing: Building Advantage in a Networked Economy* (McGraw-Hill, Boston, MA 2002), pp. 58–67; and www.hoovers.com.

CHAPTER 4

Marketing Intelligence and Creative Problem Solving

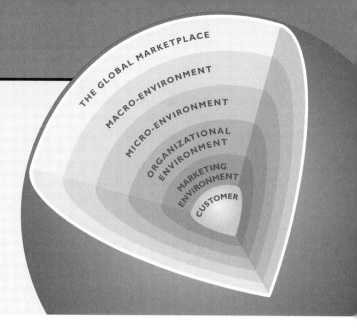

Overview

Marketing Management Decisions and Creative Problem Solving

The Marketing Research Process

Key Information for Marketing Decisions

Sources of Information

Issues in Marketing Information Acquisition and Use

The passion for original Coke was something that just caught us by surprise. The simple fact is that all of the time and money and skill poured into marketing research on the new Coca-Cola could not measure or reveal the depth and emotional attachment to the original Coca-Cola felt by so many people.[1]

Data Mining: Improving the Odds with Harrah's Customer Tracking System

Harrah's Entertainment, Inc. needed to increase revenues, and recognized the importance of improving customer loyalty and repeat visits to its casinos. The solution was a highly targeted direct marketing campaign called Total Rewards that evolved through cooperation between Harrah's IT and marketing departments, starting in the late 1990s. Total Rewards (originally Total Gold) is supported by an extensive customer database. Customers use magnetized plastic cards (i.e., frequent gambler cards) when they visit the casinos, and the resulting data enable Harrah's to target narrowly defined market segments with an appropriate marketing mix. Until several years ago, the company was an also-ran chain of casinos. With its data warehousing and data mining ability, Harrah's turned its extensive knowledge about its customers into increased customer loyalty and repeat business. As of 2002, Harrah's had become the second-largest casino operator in the United States (after MGM Entertainment), and had the industry's highest 3-year return on investment.

The Total Rewards card makes it possible to track both high and low spenders, and both are of interest to Harrah's for predicting their long-term potential as customers. Twenty-five million holders of these personalized Total Rewards cards use them willingly to earn free trips, meals, hotel rooms, and other gifts while they test the odds of slot playing. In response to the suggestion that the program is deceptive, marketing director Rich Mirman said, "If they don't want their play tracked, they don't have to use the card." He added that Harrah's would never sell its customer lists to anyone. When asked whether Harrah's was getting people to actually increase their overall gambling, Loveman said, "It's all about customers bringing their existing gaming business to us... It's rarely about more gambling. It's a lady who lives in Philadelphia, comes to Atlantic City ten times a year, visits Harrah's three times, but now she's got a reason to come to Harrah's six times."

As a slot player moves from one machine to another with his Total Rewards card, he inserts the card into each machine that he plays. A tangle of computers in a Harrah's office in Memphis, Tenn., records an astonishingly detailed account of each second he spends at the casino. The database gathers information on which machines customers play, how many machines they play, how many separate wagers they place, and the total amount of money they deposit in the machines. This is in addition to personal demographic information included on the card, and already warehoused in Harrah's customer database. Harrah's uses the data to refine its database of 90 different demographic segments. Each segment is targeted with customized direct mail incentives that are designed to motivate a particular customer to visit any of Harrah's 25 properties in the United States. (See Exhibits 1 and 2.)

Harrah's reason for gathering such extensive information for its new data mining and tracking system is a very practical one. The majority of its 2001 revenue of $3.7 billion (11 percent increase from 2000 results) and more than 80 percent of its operating profit came from slots and other electronic gaming machines. More than half of the revenue generated at the three Harrah's casinos in Las Vegas came from already known players outside Nevada.

Former Harvard business professor Gary Loveman devised Harrah's database system. Loveman, now the company's chief operating officer, maintains that the company's recent financial success is based on "getting to know [customers] so well through data profiling that he can give them the perfect reasons—a steak here, a free hotel room there—not to spend money at other casinos, where the odds, after all, aren't any better.... All we used to know was how much money we made on each machine, but we couldn't connect

what kind of customer used them. Now, I can get on the system and say. 'Where are all the 60-or-older females from North Carolina playing?' Boom I'll know. This is the replacement of intuition and hunch with science."

Previously, Harrah's growth in revenues came from building new casinos, but as more competition entered the market, just expanding the number of casinos was not enough. In addition, each Harrah's casino operated and marketed itself independently of the rest of the chain. Each property considered that it owned its customers, and did not take advantage of the strength of the entire chain. In addition, customers were not receiving consistent service and treatment from one property to another. By 1997, CEO Phil Satre realized that finding a way to keep the chain's 25 million slot players loyal to Harrah's was the key to both capturing the largest share of customers' wallets, and providing a sustainable competitive advantage. The company then began devising a way to electronically link all of Harrah's players' clubs so that, for example, a riverboat gambler in Mississippi could redeem his Total Reward points for free meals, rooms, or shows at a Harrah's in Las Vegas or any other city. In 1998, Gary Loveman was given the task of combining card data from each casino into a central marketing "brain" for the company.

Today, Harrah's works on the premise that customers will become "brand loyal" if given the right inducements. Over 40,000 gaming machines in 12 states are linked in its network, and revenue from customers who gambled at more than one Harrah's casino increased by $100 million in the first 2 years of the program. Harrah's "wallet share" of every dollar spent by customers in casinos increased from 36 percent to 42 percent. Each percentage point increase in its share of customers' overall gambling expenditures coincides with an additional $125 million in shareholder value.

Harrah's software identifies the most likely big spenders by starting with just four bits of information: gender, age, where they live, and what they play. Appropriate marketing strategies are then designed for the big spenders—usually implemented through direct mail—to "maximize every relationship." Harrah's decided very early to treat each customer as a long-term acquaintance. They analyzed gigabytes of customer data that were collected by player tracking systems at the various Harrah's properties during the previous 5 years. They found that 80 percent of company revenues, and almost 100 percent of profits, came from the 30 percent of their customers who spent between $100 and $500 per visit to a Harrah's casino. These customers were typically locals who made frequent visits to Harrah's properties in their region.

According to Harrah's database, profiles of the ideal Harrah's customer indicate that age and distance from the casino are the leading predictors of how often a customer will visit, the kind of game he will play, and the number of coins he plays per game. Loveman describes the perfect player as "a 62-year-old woman who lives within 30 minutes of Kansas City, Mo., and plays dollar video poker." She also has a substantial amount of disposable cash, spare time, and easy access to a Harrah's riverboat casino. Once high-value customers are identified, Harrah's places them into one of its corresponding 90 demographic segments. Customers who do not live near Harrah's properties generally receive direct mail discounts or comps on hotel rooms or transportation. Local or regional "drive-in" customers generally receive food, entertainment, or cash incentives. Most offers have tight expiration dates. The company tracks response rates and return on investment for each offer, then adjusts its future campaigns accordingly. Credits toward comps are based on the amount of "coin-in," or approximately one reward credit for each $10.00 gambled.

Source: Joe Ashbrook Nickell, "Welcome to Harrah's," *Business 2.0* 3(4) (April 2002), pp. 48–54; www.harrahs.com; Christopher T. Huen, "Harrah's Bets on IT to Understand Its Customers," *Information Week* (December 11, 2000), pp. RB10–RB12.

EXHIBIT 1

Main Technology Components of Harrah's Nationwide Customer-Tracking Network

Magnetic Card Readers that are installed on all of company's 40,000 plus gaming machines capture a customer ID from each card. A small LCD screen flashes a personalized greeting and the customer's current reward points.

Electronic Gaming Machines: Each gaming machine is computerized and networked, and captures transaction data which is relayed to Harrah's mainframe computers.

Onsite Transaction Systems: Each casino property has IBM-based transaction systems that store all casino, hotel and dining transaction data.

National Data Warehouse: All of Harrah's mainframe systems and customer data are linked by a Unix-based data center in downtown Memphis. This database sends customer history and reward-point tallies to the onsite mainframe systems, and these then relay the data to card readers.

Predictive Analysis Software: Nearly instantaneous customer profiles, created by software that was developed by SAS and Harrah's, are used to design and track marketing initiatives and their results.

Source: Joe Ashbrook Nickell, "Welcome to Harrah's," *Business 2.0* 3(4) (April 2002), p. 54.

EXHIBIT 2

Harrah's Customer Tracking System

WHO GETS THE FREE STEAK?

Here's how Harrah's customer-tracking system predicts which of its slot players
are likely to win the most revenue.

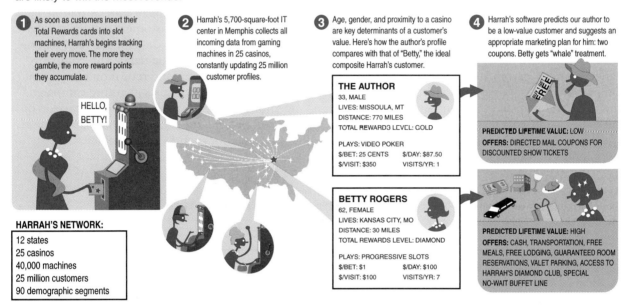

1 As soon as customers insert their Total Rewards cards into slot machines, Harrah's begins tracking their every move. The more they gamble, the more reward points they accumulate.

HELLO, BETTY!

HARRAH'S NETWORK:

12 states
25 casinos
40,000 machines
25 million customers
90 demographic segments

2 Harrah's 5,700-square-foot IT center in Memphis collects all incoming data from gaming machines in 25 casinos, constantly updating 25 million customer profiles.

3 Age, gender, and proximity to a casino are key determinants of a customer's value. Here's how the author's profile compares with that of "Betty," the ideal composite Harrah's customer.

THE AUTHOR
33, MALE
LIVES: MISSOULA, MT
DISTANCE: 770 MILES
TOTAL REWARDS LEVEL: GOLD

PLAYS: VIDEO POKER
$/BET: 25 CENTS $/DAY: $87.50
$/VISIT: $350   VISITS/YR: 1

BETTY ROGERS
62, FEMALE
LIVES: KANSAS CITY, MO
DISTANCE: 30 MILES
TOTAL REWARDS LEVEL: DIAMOND

PLAYS: PROGRESSIVE SLOTS
$/BET: $1 $/DAY: $100
$/VISIT: $100   VISITS/YR: 7

4 Harrah's software predicts our author to be a low-value customer and suggests an appropriate marketing plan for him: two coupons. Betty gets "whale" treatment.

PREDICTED LIFETIME VALUE: LOW
OFFERS: DIRECTED MAIL COUPONS FOR DISCOUNTED SHOW TICKETS

PREDICTED LIFETIME VALUE: HIGH
OFFERS: CASH, TRANSPORTATION, FREE MEALS, FREE LODGING, GUARANTEED ROOM RESERVATIONS, VALET PARKING, ACCESS TO HARRAH'S DIAMOND CLUB, SPECIAL NO-WAIT BUFFET LINE

Source: Joe Ashbrook Nickell, "Welcome to Harrah's," *Business 2.0* 3(4) (April 2002), p. 54. Copyright © 2002 Time Inc. All rights reserved.

Successful organizations know how to create and satisfy customers better than their competitors. Whether organizations are large or small, for-profit or non-profit, or represent any of a vast number of industries or social causes throughout the world, their long-term profitability and survival depend on a thorough understanding of the environment in which they operate. This includes customers, competitors, suppliers, employees, and all the other external and internal stakeholders and environmental forces described in preceding chapters. Because customers and their needs and wants keep changing, critical marketing intelligence must be gathered continuously through ongoing data collection and research activities to provide insights for marketing management decisions.

This chapter focuses on the important role of timely and accurate market information in marketing management decisions and creative problem solving that will deliver value to satisfied customers. The relationships between the creative problem-solving process, the marketing research process, and marketing intelligence are discussed, as well as the sources, types, and uses of marketing information and issues that should be considered in the acquisition and use of marketing information. (See Figure 4.1.) Market intelligence should focus not only on "what is"—the existing solutions to customers' problems—but also on "what isn't"—those

FIGURE 4.1

Problem Solving, Research, Information, and Decisions

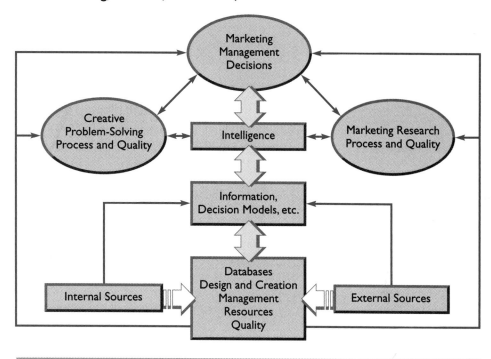

FIGURE 4.2

Finding a Match Between an Organization and Its Market

new ideas, products, processes, and methods which provide innovative break-throughs to satisfy needs that the market may not even recognize until a solution becomes available. As illustrated in Figure 4.2, what the market needs and is willing to pay for must be reconciled with what the firm has the ability and willingness to provide.[2]

● MARKETING MANAGEMENT DECISIONS AND CREATIVE PROBLEM SOLVING

Marketing managers are challenged with the need to make many diverse decisions, many of which require an understanding of new products, new applications, new markets, new competitors, or new methods of doing business. In order to remain competitive and arrive at innovative solutions, it is necessary to take a creative approach to problem solving. When we refer to a "problem," we are considering opportunities as well as threats. By definition, a *problem* is a "...question proposed for solution or consideration ... a question, matter, situation, or person that is perplexing or difficult...."[3] In the following sections we will explore some of the approaches to obtaining inputs for creative problem solving.

Need for Marketing Intelligence in a Changing World

Marketing intelligence system
Process of gathering information about customers, competitors, and other relevant data from the external environment.

drives the strategy!

A **marketing intelligence system** is designed to monitor the external environment for emerging trends or events.[4] In a customer-oriented organization, customers and competitors are the primary focus of this system. Marketing intelligence comes from a variety of sources such as sales representatives, other channel members, suppliers, outside information providers, and public information.

The need for high-quality marketing intelligence is greatest during times of significant change (i.e., the stage of crisis or creative destruction) in order to maintain an upward growth curve—or perhaps to slow down a decline as a business and/or its environment changes. The concept of a strategic inflection point was introduced in Chapter 3 to illustrate the make-or-break point where change affects the organization and creative solutions to problems must be sought aggressively if the company is to survive. As the rate of change accelerates and an organization's environment becomes more complex and uncertain, the need for accurate, timely, useful information increases exponentially. "Business as usual" will cease to exist unless innovative solutions are found to deal with changes that affect the company.

For example, *diversity* is a key word in our vocabulary today. It permeates the life of every contemporary institution and indicates the wide range of information needed to understand the differences that must be addressed by marketing managers. Barabba[5] organizes the stakeholders of an extended organization (or enterprise) into three major groups of individuals or entities that can affect or be affected by the decisions of the enterprise. These include

- the customer (consumers and others in the distribution system that are served by the organization),
- the community (consumers in a societal context, government entities that attempt to represent them, special interest groups, and competition for customer and community resources), and
- the organization or enterprise (everything on the opposite side of the customer and the community, such as suppliers, investors, and others).

Marketing intelligence can be used to understand the relationships between these groups and the differences represented in their values. Key factors that have increased the need for a more frequent and timely use of information include access to high-quality and timely data of all competitors simultaneously, need for a broader array of information for a more diverse marketplace, shorter time for making decisions, shorter time that data are valid due to rapid changes in the market, and the many attractive options that a firm can implement in its marketing programs.[6]

Responsibility for Marketing Decisions

In a customer-oriented marketing organization, everyone makes marketing decisions. These may range from a top-level executive who has the final go/no-go decision for a corporate acquisition to a front-line customer service representative who must solve a problem "on the spot." In fact, personnel in all functional areas of a firm make marketing-related decisions; it is not just the responsibility of the marketing department. The activities of all areas must be integrated to achieve organizational objectives, and this requires the use of marketing intelligence throughout the entire firm.

Organizational Level. The three decision-making levels of a firm were discussed in Chapter 3 relative to the multilevel strategic planning process: corporate, division or strategic business unit (SBU), and functional or operating level. The types of decisions and information needs vary with each level of the hierarchy, as illustrated by the examples in Table 4.1.

Functional Area. Our primary concern in this chapter is with the types of decisions and information needs that are characteristic of the functional or operating level of the firm. In today's environment of integrative management and cross-functional work teams, all individuals involved in a task or project need to

TABLE 4.1

Organizational Level and Information for Marketing Decisions

Level	Examples	
	Decision Areas	*Information Needs*
Corporate Level	Satisfying customers and achieving financial objectives; long-term financial performance; establishing and enforcing corporate ethics and responsibility	Market intelligence for strategic growth plans; performance data for SBUs; market forecasts; industry trend analysis
Division or SBU Level	Strategies for separate SBUs or profit centers (may focus on different set of customers, competitors and products than other divisions of the company)	Market demand; competitive intelligence; site-selection/location analysis; operating level performance data; industry trends
Functional/ Operating Level	Tactical marketing plan to achieve the functional-level strategy; profitable market segments to pursue; appropriate marketing mix; details on product performance	Target market characteristics and response patterns; return on advertising expenditures; customer satisfaction research; front-line employee productivity (sales, etc.); detailed data on product performance

understand the market(s) they serve—both qualitatively and quantitatively. The decisions made by each functional area can have an impact on each of the others. For example, a decision to market a new product may be supported by positive results from a product test by the research and development (R&D) department and a market feasibility study. Primary research may be conducted with potential customers to determine the most appropriate marketing mix (i.e., product features, pricing and distribution strategies, and promotional mix). Other functional areas that will need to analyze information related to their role in this process include human resources (e.g., personnel for production and sales), accounting and finance (e.g., expenses, cost basis, profitability targets and ratios), production (e.g., demand schedule, operations efficiency), and others.

Marketing misses have occurred, and automobile manufacturers have lost billions of dollars in sales because they either misjudged what consumers wanted, or procrastinated about creating new designs. For example, General Motors conceptualized the minivan long before its introduction by Chrysler in the 1980s. In the late 1970s, focus groups made up of buyers of full-size vans rejected the slimmed-down vehicle as too small. The interpretation of market research data by some of the more influential GM managers of the time indicated that the market would not support the minivan, and that it was not financially feasible. Rival Chrysler Corp. put a similar minivan into production soon after that, and wide acceptance of the minivan by consumers is history.[7]

How Marketing Decisions Are Made

There are probably as many ways to make a decision as there are decision makers. As markets become more global and competition becomes more intense, marketing managers have fewer strategic and tactical options available to them than previously. Unfortunately, it is not always possible to make decisions with the confidence provided by "perfect" information. In the ideal world, some assumptions about the ability to support marketing management decisions with high-quality market intelligence might include the following:[8]

- There is adequate time for accurate research conducted at a reasonable price.
- Existing information relevant to the problem is brought to the manager's attention early enough to determine other information needed for the decision.
- The need for a research effort can be communicated early enough for a quality research project.
- The managers responsible for making a decision and the researchers who are responsible for gathering the marketing intelligence each have a good understanding of what is needed and the processes followed by each party.
- Research results are unambiguous and clearly support a particular decision.
- The most desirable decision is also feasible to implement and can be implemented with a clear understanding of the degree of uncertainty and/or risk involved.

What managers appear to be searching for in their quest for high-quality marketing intelligence is a set of assumptions and decision rules that will provide some reasonable degree of assurance for their decisions. For those managers who make a series of similar decisions, these assumptions and decision rules can be applied to multiple situations when proven to work successfully. Decision-making and research needs are determined to a large extent by the degree of complexity and uncertainty involved and the time available for making an informed decision.

Routine versus Complex Decisions.   Routine decisions often are "programmed"; that is, they are guided by policies and predetermined guidelines. They usually are made by fewer decision makers to cover a shorter time period. Routine decisions also typically are made in recurring or similar situations where market conditions and company factors are quite predictable.

Complex decisions tend to involve new situations where there is little or no previous experience in making similar decisions. These situations may involve a high degree of risk, require a high level of investment, or be subject to a rapid rate of change such as that brought about by accelerated technological changes. When one or more of these conditions are present, it is considerably more difficult to make a well-informed decision, and there is a greater need for marketing intelligence.

Time Factor.   Complex decisions obviously require more time for information gathering and analysis and more time for planning whenever possible. One of the greatest challenges to marketers in the twenty-first century will continue to be the drive to get new products to market faster and more successfully than competitors. Shortened product life cycles and time frames for making decisions require high-quality information and an efficient decision support system to expedite the decision process and reduce risk.

Creative Problem Solving (CPS)

Most marketing textbook chapters that address marketing research and decision making tend to do so from a quantitative perspective. While quantitative inputs may be essential for a complete understanding of the situation, managers also must use qualitative inputs that cannot be measured with a high degree of accuracy. Often these inputs are referred to as a manager's judgment or intuition that may require **creative problem solving**—"stepping outside the box" to find creative solutions to business problems and opportunities. The usefulness of marketing intelligence is only as valuable as the decision maker's ability to look at the data in new ways and to consider new possibilities, that is, "color outside the lines," to come up with innovative solutions.

Creative problem solving "Stepping outside the box" to find creative solutions to business problems and opportunities.

A nationwide study found that 89 percent of the advertising, marketing, and marketing research professionals who responded to a survey frequently use intuition to guide some part of their decision making. One explanation is that marketing professionals do not have the time to gather data to support every decision in today's fast-paced, downsized, and urgent business environment.[9] Minivans are common today, but when Chrysler decided to produce a minivan in the 1980s there was no precedent to support this decision. The limited amount of research that was available indicated that the market for this automobile was very small—30,000, with 20,000 of these sold as panel vans. Lee Iacocca believed in the minivan in spite of the uncertainty about whether it would be successful, and made a decision to go forward with the minivan, based to a large extent on intuition.[10]

FIGURE 4.3

Stages in the Creative Problem-Solving (CPS) Process

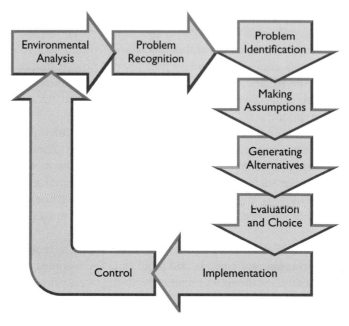

Source: James M. Higgins, *101 Creative Problem Solving Techniques: The Handbook of New Ideas for Business.* Winter Park, FL: New Management Publishing Company, Inc. Figure 2-1, p. 18, 1994. Reprinted by permission.

Higgins[11] states: "Problem solving is an integral part of organizational life. Every time a manager or leader directs people in producing a product or service, problems are being solved, decisions made. Every time any member of an organization thinks of a new way to reduce costs, invents a new product or service, or determines how to help the organization function better in some way, problem solving is taking place. But, whether the problem solving occurring in these situations is truly creative is another question. . . . [T]he development of creative problem-solving skills is a necessity, not a luxury. . . . The most innovative individuals and organizations are the ones most likely to prosper." The emphasis here is on taking a *creative* approach to solving problems using an eight-stage process, as illustrated in Figure 4.3. A brief description and an example of the analytical and creative process of each of the eight stages[12] are provided below.

Stage 1: Analyzing the Environment.   Both the external and internal environments must be monitored constantly to identify problems and opportunities so that managers can respond quickly to change and new business opportunities and can resolve problems successfully. In a customer-oriented organization, everyone should assume responsibility for being informed about what is happening—or what is about to happen—around him or her. For example, automobile manufacturers became aware that Baby Boomers were a potential market for the minivan, but they felt the need to know more about the buying motives of their present and potential customers.

Stage 2: Recognizing a Problem. Before a problem or opportunity can be solved or identified, the decision maker must be made aware of it. The awareness may come from formal or informal environmental scanning or from a vague, intuitive feeling that something is "wrong" or that an exciting opportunity is "around the corner." Sometimes problem recognition occurs with a sudden flash of insight, but more often a period of time is required for subconscious processing of environmental information, followed by conscious analysis of the qualitative and quantitative indicators. Lee Iacocca recognized that the traditional van driver might be ready for a more stylish, yet utilitarian vehicle.

Stage 3: Identifying the Problem. In this stage, the symptoms are separated from the real problem so the problem-solving process can focus on establishing objectives and determining decision criteria to use in evaluating the available options. Problem identification is primarily a rational process, but intuitive thinking also is involved. Questions should be answered about the past and present status and what is anticipated for the future. In this stage of the CPS process, managers should have a clear idea of the real problem by gaining insights about what has happened, who was affected, where it happened and where it had an impact, how and why it occurred, and what could be done to be more successful. General Motors misjudged consumer wants for a minivan type auto in the 1970s, but Chrysler took the risk of producing a replacement for the station wagon.

Stage 4: Making Assumptions. Before generating alternatives, assumptions must be made about future conditions that are related to the problem situation. Assumptions need to be made about internal resources (e.g., financial, human, physical, etc.) required to solve the problem or take advantage of the opportunity or the anticipated support of managers and others. Assumptions also need to be made about the external macro- and micro-environments regarding economic conditions, market demand, competitive reaction, and other factors. In the case of the Chrysler minivan, the company assumed that conditions for growth would remain positive and that brand equity would encourage purchases.

Stage 5: Generating Alternatives. The generation of alternatives involves both rational and intuitive thinking. Those alternatives which are already known can be listed and contemplated through rational thought processes. Managers who limit possible alternatives to those which are already known miss a chance to come up with innovative solutions through creative problem-solving processes. The quantity of new alternatives is more important in this stage, the point at which people tend to be most creative. Rather than worry about the quality of each idea that is being generated, this stage gives people a chance to brainstorm and to come up with unique alternatives.

Stage 6: Choosing Among Alternatives. The process of choosing among available alternatives involves systematic evaluation of each available option to determine whether it meets the criteria established in the problem identification stage. Considerable attention should be given to the outcomes that would be expected with each alternative, its chances of success, and the resources needed for implementation. Although rational thinking plays a major role in evaluating and choosing among acceptable alternatives, intuition and judgment (often based on years of experience) also enter into the choice process—particularly where the decision is very complex and insufficient information is available to make a rational decision.

Stage 7: Implementing the Chosen Solution.   Stages 1 through 6 provide a sound basis for carrying out the chosen solution to the problem. At this point, the problem has been clearly identified, and a well-thought-out plan should be in place for action. The establishment of objectives to be achieved by the plan and a time line for accomplishing them provide much-needed direction. In addition, specific individuals should be made accountable for their areas of responsibility for executing the planned solution and be given the support of key individuals in the organization. Successful implementation requires constant attention to details and awareness of potential obstacles that may hinder the success of the plan. Continuing with the Chrysler minivan example, the company needed to ensure that every detail of the chosen solution was carried out as planned—from product design and production to distributors and sales personnel to customer service and so on.

Stage 8: Control.   When we think about "creative" problem solving, we sometimes ignore the need for control and evaluation of the plan once it is under way. A clear idea was formed during the preceding stages of the CPS process about the nature of the problem and the most likely solution. The control stage offers an opportunity to

---

INNOVATE OR EVAPORATE*

Beyond Focus Groups—Hanging Out with Snowboarders and Teenagers In Video Arcades

Auto manufacturers remember a number of missed marketing opportunities for new vehicle concepts—opportunities that were missed because of poor-quality research, or misinterpretation of data. At the 2000 Detroit Auto Show, critics made negative comments about Ford Motor Co.'s futuristic "24/7" concept car. The car came complete with wireless data links and Internet access to keep drivers connected around the clock. Ford's then chief-executive officer, Jacques Nasser, was more concerned about what teen-agers thought of the concept—and they loved it. Nasser recognized the importance of knowing the opinions of a generation that was hardly old enough to drive. He and his "top lieutenants" took an innovative research approach by immersing themselves into the youth market. Nasser stopped by a video arcade in Miami, and invited a group of teens to attend the auto show as guests of Ford Motor Co. He also spent an evening hanging out with teens in Tokyo, and did so in California, Florida, New York, Toronto, London, Stockholm and France, learning about their preferences for cars.

The teenage consumers who are still too young to drive will be an important market for Detroit automakers. They are expected to be more affluent than their parents' generation, and most do not remember the poor reputation for quality that many Baby Boomers associate with Detroit's cars. The automakers see this as a chance to counter the market impact of imports that have attracted young drivers with their lower prices and unique designs.

General Motors decided to go beyond focus groups and to use more innovative research techniques. To visualize older GM brands from the perspective of a younger person, the company created life-size Nintendo-like superheroes to inspire its in-house auto designers: a black-clad hero wielding a saber for Cadillac (for its new high-tech image); an athletic girl on a snowboard for Saturn. Other nontraditional research methods pursued by the Big Three automakers included "chatting up kids at skateboarding competitions, plowing through consumer electronics and clothing for design inspiration and listening closely to ethnographers."

Auto executives have learned that they cannot rely on their own viewpoint when making marketing decisions. Ford developed a sport utility vehicle, nicknamed the "Youth Oriented Derivative," with two doors plus a small half door (similar to that on the Saturn "three door" coupe). The car bombed in research, and Ford's head of global marketing said that feedback from kids was painful. One teenager said, "That looks like the kind of car that a bunch of 45-year-old guys would think is cool." Research indicated that what the young buyers wanted was a four-door vehicle with rugged functional SUV-like looks—not a two-door car with "bubble" styling—and it could not look like a toy.

Today's youth culture is more complex and market-savvy than previous generations. Young drivers are influenced by music, fashion, sports, entertainment, and technology when making purchases. Based on an understanding of these buying criteria, Ford included a more powerful engine, a compact-disk player, and 15-inch aluminum wheels as standard equipment on its Focus ZX-3 hatchback that sells for just under $13,000.

GM's research was focused on finding out what it takes to be first with Generation Y. They were surprised at young consumers' reactions when they took one car model to a snowboarding event. The car did not seem safe to the teens because its hood had been shortened to make more room inside. GM's market-research chief said that we often "think of youth as a bunch of crazy skateboarders," but they've grown up wearing helmets and elbow pads, and safety is important to them in cars. Based on GM's research, the company developed a fleet of high-concept cars such as the Pontiac Piranha, a sporty coupe that links to the image of extreme sports.

A major marketing research problem for Detroit automakers is that most young consumers still prefer imports, particularly Volkswagen AG and Honda Motor Co. models that they consider "cool." As one consultant said, "We're moving into a fashion and entertainment economy." GM used a creative research approach to better understand cultural nuances. The company sent Dindo Cajulis, a 33-year-old car buff, to the "Hot Import Nights" car show in San Bernardino, California, where he was to show off a stylized bright orange, souped-up Pontiac minivan that GM believed would attract the attention of young hot-rodders that gravitate toward smaller imports like Honda Civics. The minivan drew huge crowds of young drivers, as Mr. Cajulis "hung out" with his "customized GM Sunburst Montana, describing it in detail to curious spectators and picking up feedback to pass along to GM. 'I'm their eyes and ears,' he says of the No. 1 auto maker."

In summary, automakers have found it necessary to incorporate the creative problem-solving process into their overall research efforts to gain a more in-depth understanding of potential customers. Information obtained from qualitative research, in combination with quantitative research results, has provided GM, Ford, and other automakers with valuable insights for better informed marketing decisions.

*The box title is attributed to James M, Higgins.

Source: Gregory L. White, Joseph B. White, and Sholnn Freeman, "What's A Cool Car? The Question Is Driving U.S. Auto Makers Wild—Beyond Focus Groups, Officials Hang Out in Video Arcades and Chat Up Snowboarders," *The Wall Street Journal* (August 9, 2000), p. B1+.

know whether the actions taken actually solved the problem and whether the plan was executed appropriately. Creative problem solving in this stage consists of recognizing those things which work and—building on this knowledge—making them work even better. CPS also involves recognizing deficiencies in the solution and creatively adapting new thinking to improve the success of the plan.

THE MARKETING RESEARCH PROCESS

The CPS process and the marketing research process are closely related, and both processes influence the quality of the management decision process. It is important to have a clear understanding of the purpose of the research and the nature of the decision in the beginning of the process (i.e., the intended use of results). High-quality marketing intelligence and a poor-quality decision process, and vice versa, do not lend themselves to successful creative problem solving. Each stage of the research process must be approached creatively.

Marketing research specialists tend to follow a sequence of steps in designing and executing a research project. The exact order or description of each step may vary by researcher and project, but the research process generally includes the activities described below and illustrated in Figure 4.4.

Step 1: Recognize the Need for Research

The first step in any marketing research effort is to be aware that unresolved problems or opportunities exist and that available information cannot provide satisfactory answers. Sometimes this recognition is brought about by a crisis, or it may be a by-product of other research or just a vague sense that there are issues that need to

FIGURE 4.4

Steps in the Marketing Research Process

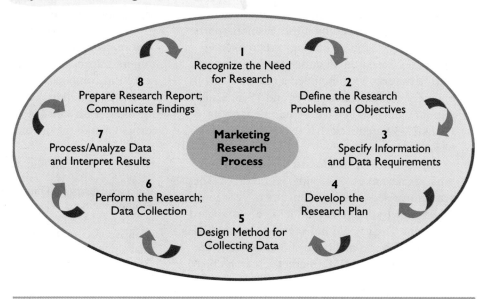

1 Recognize the Need for Research

2 Define the Research Problem and Objectives

3 Specify Information and Data Requirements

4 Develop the Research Plan

5 Design Method for Collecting Data

6 Perform the Research; Data Collection

7 Process/Analyze Data and Interpret Results

8 Prepare Research Report; Communicate Findings

Marketing Research Process

be addressed. For example, Harrah's Entertainment was concerned about sales in its chain of casinos and realized that it really did not understand the buying habits of its key customers—only how much money they made on each slot machine.

Step 2: Define the Research Problem and Objectives (Purpose)

As James Thurber said, "It is better to know some of the questions than all of the answers."[13] What is it that managers really need to know? What are the specific managerial decisions that require the insights provided by the research results? The vaguely stated issue in step 1 above can be restated as: Although we tripled the number of casinos we operated between 1990 and 1997, the market became much more competitive. We needed to increase the loyalty of our 25 million players. (See stages 2 and 3 in the CPS process.)

Step 3: Specify Information and Data Requirements

The type of information needed for an informed decision must be determined before going any further in the research process. This information should be focused directly on the identified research problem and not a "shotgun approach" to gathering any and all available data. The quality of the research and the quality of the management decision will be much higher if the focus is on meaningful data inputs. Continuing with the example of Harrah's research needs, the company needed information about consumers, their buying habits, brand loyalty to Harrah's casinos, and slot machine usage. The necessary information may be obtained from **primary data** (e.g., observation, survey questionnaires, personal interviews). Other information might include an assessment of distribution effectiveness and competitive activity that could be obtained from **secondary data** (e.g., company's records, data warehouse, industry reports). Steps 2 and 3 are where the most errors are apt to occur, because the value of the research is seriously threatened if the basic research problem and the information needed (research questions) are not identified correctly.

Primary data
Information gathered specifically for a current marketing management decision.

Secondary data
Information from published or other sources that was gathered for another purpose.

[handwritten margin notes: surveys, face-to-face talking to someone, databases]

Step 4: Develop the Research Plan

In this stage the preliminary data-collection method is determined, such as whether it will be obtained by primary research or from secondary sources. A schedule for performing the research activities and a budget are developed. (This happens throughout the CPS process.) In Harrah's case, a comprehensive approach to collecting consumer data on a continuous basis was developed.

Step 5: Design the Method for Collecting Data

This step involves designing the data collection method, including data sources, questionnaire or data-collection instruments, sampling design, and sample size. Primary data may be collected by mail, telephone, or personal interviews, whereas secondary data may be obtained from internal or external information sources. The questionnaire or other type of data-collection instrument is developed consistent with the research method to be used. A representative sample of the population is identified. The number of respondents also is determined at this point, with the number large enough to ensure useful data but small enough to meet time and budget constraints. (This is necessary throughout the CPS process.) Harrah's developed a sophisticated electronic data collection method based on its Total Rewards cards. All customers who were willing to use the cards in the casinos were included in the sample.

Step 6: Perform the Research

At this stage in the research process the researcher is responsible for the actual work involved in data collection. The research plan must be followed as planned to maintain consistency of the data, and research quality must be monitored and controlled. The questionnaires or other data-collection instruments must be administered according to plan, and precautions must be taken in their handling to avoid potential errors and bias. The key here is to *listen to* (or *see*) the respondent's viewpoint. (This occurs throughout the CPS process.) Harrah's use of its Total Rewards cards to gather data provides an actual representation of its customers, their slot machine preferences, and their response to direct marketing campaigns.

Step 7: Analyze the Data and Interpret the Results

The researcher is responsible in this stage of the research process for reviewing the data-collection instruments and culling out any that are not usable. The data are coded and prepared for analysis (i.e., the data usually are input into a computer program for statistical analysis). The data are then tabulated, analyzed, and organized in a format for interpretation. The results generally formulate a pattern that provides insights about the issue being investigated. At this stage precautions must be taken to remain objective and avoid misinterpretations of the data. (See steps 1 through 6 in the CPS process.) Harrah's analyzes players' gambling habits from the information logged into its database from Total Rewards cards and other personal data entries to determine which customers to market to, and with which offers.

Step 8: Communicate Findings

In the final stage of the research process the researcher prepares a final report and presents the findings to those who will use the information for decision making. This usually involves both a formal written report and a presentation. The focus of this report should be on the agreed-on information that addresses the research problem and objectives. The interpretation of the results also includes the researcher's recommendations for action. (See steps 7, 8, and beyond in the CPS process.) At Harrah's, this is an ongoing process. As more data are added to its database, they are mined for insights that will lead to more successful target marketing and marketing programs.

● KEY INFORMATION FOR MARKETING DECISIONS

Marketing decisions involve one or more of the internal and external environmental factors described in preceding chapters. (See Figure 4.5.) The driving forces of change discussed earlier (i.e., globalization, computerization, information age and

FIGURE 4.5

Global Marketing Environment and Marketing Intelligence

technology, management hierarchies, and security and corporate responsibility) have created a situation where high-quality marketing intelligence is essential for long- and short-term decisions. Further, merely having the information is insufficient if it is not used *creatively.* Rapid changes in the marketing environment have created the need for shorter planning horizons and less certainty about the "right" decision. These conditions require finely tuned creative and conceptual skills, as well as the ability to process information and make informed judgments. The question is, of all the information that is available to managers, what information do they really need? The basic types of information needed are related primarily to external opportunities and threats and internal strengths and weaknesses, as discussed next.

External Opportunities and Threats

External information needed by marketing managers falls into two general categories: opportunities and threats. The key external factors that must be analyzed include the market, its customers, and the firm's competitors. Some types of external information needed by managers are described in the next section, followed by a discussion of possible sources of information.

Market and Buyer Analysis. An organization must be fully informed about current trends in its market(s) and anticipate changes that may occur. The first research task is to define the market for the firm's goods or services, followed by determining the **market demand** and **market potential**—the present and projected rates and directions of growth for the identified market. The next task is to determine the characteristics and buying habits of consumers (e.g., needs and wants, buying preferences, lifestyles, etc.) and organizational customers (e.g., industry, size, location, etc.) in the segment(s) of interest. Once the firm has a solid understanding of the dimensions and characteristics of its market and the buying behavior of its present and potential customers, it is ready to develop marketing programs to satisfy market demand.

Competitive Analysis. Elements of competitive analysis were described in Chapter 3 within the context of Porter's "five forces" model. Marketing intelligence must include information about both *direct* and *indirect* competitors. **Direct competitors** serve the same target market(s) and satisfy the same basic needs. Competition may be on the basis of preferred brands or distribution channels, selective product characteristics, or various product forms that satisfy a generic need. For example, consider the need for transportation. For the buyer of an automobile, direct competition on the basis of brands might include Mercedes Benz, BMW, and Cadillac purchased through competing distribution channels (e.g., manufacturer dealership, CarMax, or an independent auto-buying club). Competition in the auto industry is particularly intense on the basis of product characteristics (e.g., engine type, alternative fuel hybrids, fuel economy, safety features) and forms (e.g., sport utility vehicle, minivan, truck, four-door passenger). Automobile manufacturers and their advertising agencies rely on information about prior and forecasted sales, demographic and psychographic market characteristics, and other data in their decisions about how to design and market their diverse range of products.

Indirect competitors may be from the same or other industries and appeal to customers with substitute products or ways of doing business. For example, not only do auto manufacturers and dealers face competition from each other; they also face competition from other modes of transportation. In some areas, motorcycles have gained a larger share of the market. Many urban dwellers rely on mass transit buses or trains or choose to carpool with neighbors. Travel by air or rail offers a competing solution to automobiles for long-distance travel. Other indirect competitors to the auto industry are the auto repair shops and mechanics that keep older cars running longer, diminishing the owner's need for a new car. Researchers must be creative in knowing and anticipating the sources of indirect competition.

Internal Strengths and Weaknesses

An analysis of an organization's internal strengths and weaknesses relative to competitors provides an understanding of its ability to compete successfully for customers and build market-share profitably. The internal information most commonly used for marketing decisions includes an analysis of the firm's major resources, such as financial, human, and technological resources, as well as the effectiveness of its marketing activities.

Market demand
Present customer needs to be fulfilled by a product category based on ability and willingness to buy.

Market potential
Maximum sales and profit that can be reasonably expected under given conditions.

Direct competitors
Serve the same target market and satisfy the same customer needs.

Indirect competitors
May be from same or other industries and appeal to customers with substitute products or business methods.

Financial Resources. The firm's internal databases include a record of its assets and liabilities. Assets are most often in the form of physical properties and equipment, investments, inventories, cash, accounts receivable, and so forth. Liabilities consist of debt in the form of loans, taxes, and other financial obligations. Financial ratios can be calculated from the accounting statements and financial records and compared with industry ratios for determination of the firm's financial position relative to competitors.

An analysis of financial resources also should include an analysis of the level of risk faced by the firm and/or its industry. In a rapidly changing business environment, volatility and uncertainty make it difficult to assess risk, but all available information should be used to make decisions that will have an impact on the firm's bottom line. This includes an assessment of the firm's ethics in financial dealings and reporting.

Human Resources. Information is needed about the firm's personnel requirements for carrying out its mission and the ability of present managers and employees to satisfy customers and deliver a profit to the company. Personnel records and management reviews can provide much of the information for this type of analysis. The corporate scandals of 2001 and 2002 demonstrated the effect of the unethical behavior of executives and others on corporate performance. The basic question to be answered is, Can our people provide a competitive advantage with our customers? If so, how are they doing it? And what can they do better?

Technological Resources. As you will recall from Chapter 2, the major environmental forces driving change in all types of businesses include increased computerization, emerging technologies, the information superhighway, the information age economy, and security and social responsibility. The marketer who falls behind in these areas has little chance of survival and profitability over the long term. In a customer-oriented organization, information technology can be used advantageously to monitor the market, gather customer data, and create a marketing information system. Marketing intelligence in this area should focus on what technological applications are available, what they can do to enhance performance of the firm, and whether they will provide a competitive advantage.

Marketing Effectiveness. An important task of marketing research is to track the effectiveness of current (and planned) marketing programs. One analytical method that is used for this purpose is to conduct a **marketing audit**,[14] which is a thorough, systematic, objective evaluation of an organization's marketing environment, objectives, and strategies. The purpose is to identify potential problems and opportunities so that the company's marketing performance can be improved.

A marketing audit may examine any or all aspects of an organization's marketing situation. This includes factors within the marketing environment (macro- and micro-environments), marketing strategy, marketing organization, marketing systems, marketing productivity, and marketing function. (See this chapter's Appendix for a comprehensive list of questions that may be asked in each area.) One of the most compelling questions for any marketing manager is whether or not marketing programs are working. The marketing audit is an excellent way to determine answers to this question, since it can be used to assess the effectiveness of all elements of the marketing mix (i.e., products, price, distribution, and promotional tools). An audit

Marketing audit
Thorough systematic evaluation of an organization's environment, objectives, and strategy.

should be conducted periodically and used to track important outcomes such as brand equity, customer satisfaction, and other items of ongoing interest.

 ## SOURCES OF INFORMATION

Marketing intelligence is obtained from a wide spectrum of sources through both formal and informal methods. In its basic form, it consists of data and facts (or items assumed to be factual) about the realities of the marketplace. Data are analyzed and converted into information that is useful for management decisions. However, many factors can intervene in the process of moving from a mass of data to a wise managerial decision. One of the most compelling factors is the potential difference between the orientations of the information user and the information provider, referred to by Barabba and Zaltman as the "law of the lens."[15] These differences may consist of interpretations of the marketing situation or research expectations, conflicts of interest regarding the purpose or outcomes of the research, internal versus external perspectives on the problem, or other differences that may be relevant to the gathering or use of the data. The transition from data to decisions and the difference between the domains of making decisions and producing information are illustrated in Figure 4.6. Data that in some way represent the realities of the marketplace

FIGURE 4.6

The Information Pyramid and the "Law of the Lens"

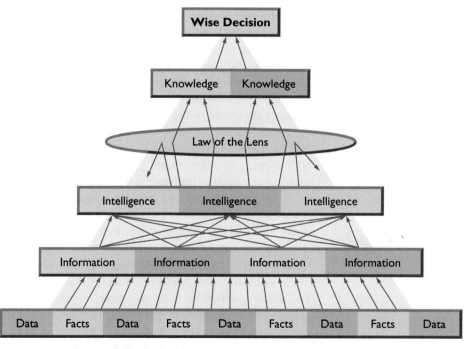

Source: Reprinted by permission of Harvard Business School Press. From *Hearing the Voice of the Market* by Vincent P. Barabba and Gerald Zaltman. Boston, MA: 1991, p. 44. Copyright ©1991 by the President and Fellows of Harvard College. All rights reserved.

can be gathered in any form and entered into an organization's information system, but the data may not be meaningful, accurate, or believable. When the data are interpreted in a meaningful way, they can be classified as information. When the information is believed to be true, it becomes intelligence that is easily understood, timely, reliable, and valid for use in management decisions.

Databases

Successful marketing organizations generally create and maintain databases that can manage the wide range of information that comprises their marketing intelligence systems. The two primary types of databases used by marketing managers are the marketing information system (MIS) and the marketing decision support system (MDSS). Data inputs may range from complex mathematical forecasting models to rumors and intuitive interpretations. They may be focused on one product in a narrowly defined geographic market segment, or they may cover multiple products throughout a global marketplace. The difficulty is in knowing what is a true reflection of reality. As Will Rogers once said, "It's not what we don't know that gives us trouble. It's what we know that ain't so."[16]

MIS—marketing information system
Formal complex of people, equipment, and procedures designed to provide timely, accurate, and useful information to marketing decision makers.

Marketing Information System (MIS). The **MIS** is a formal complex of people, equipment, and procedures designed to gather, organize, structure, analyze, evaluate, and distribute timely, accurate, and meaningful information to marketing decision makers. The data inputs may originate from inside or outside the company and involve a planned, continuous, orderly collection, analysis, and organization of relevant data for both short- and long-term decisions. We usually associate the use of a computer with an MIS, but reference libraries and even well-organized file cabinets can constitute important information for management decisions.

MDSS—marketing decision support system
A coordinated system of data and tools by which internal and external information is turned into a basis for marketing action.

Marketing Decision Support System (MDSS). The **MDSS** is a coordinated collection of data, systems, models, analytic tools, and computing power by which an organization gathers information from the internal and external environment and turns it into a basis for marketing action.[17] An MDSS is differentiated from an MIS and other technologically based systems by its humanistic focus on extending the problem-solving capabilities of marketing managers. An MDSS is essential in highly competitive markets where decisions must be made more quickly, more frequently, and with less tolerance for error. An MDSS is computer-based (for speed and data manipulation), interactive (online systems), flexible (for data access and integration from multiple sources), and discovery-oriented (looking for trends, identifying potential problems, and searching for answers to new questions based on the information provided), and is relatively easy to use. The three essential components of a MDSS are databases, a user interface, and a library of analytical and modeling tools.

Decision models are available from commercial sources or are developed in-house to address issues such as the allocation of organizational resources (e.g., retail site selection, new production equipment, or other investments). Models also are used to determine the efficiency and effectiveness of promotional activities, including advertising (e.g., media placement and expenditures, measures of audience size and characteristics), salesforce allocation, and productivity, warehousing operations, and many other applications.

TABLE 4.2

Types and Uses of Databases

Types of Databases	Uses/Applications
Internal Data and Information	
Sales records	Employee scheduling, sales events
Credit records	Direct marketing, consumer research
Inventory records	Sales histories, vendor and SKU analysis
POS scanner data	Inventory control, reordering, merchandising
Reservation system	Employee scheduling, purchasing
External Data and Information	
North American Industrial Classification System (NAICS—formerly SIC—codes)	Coding system facilitates search for industry information; standards for comparison
Directories	Trade and professional association listings, company information, etc.
Various business information sources	Listings of company and industry data sources
Indexes to business literature and publications	Guide to periodical literature, business journals, and other media
Government databases	U.S. Census Bureau population statistics, Commerce Department trade data, FTC regulations, etc.
Commercial databases (e.g., Arbitron, Nexis/Lexis, etc.)	Specialized by company and market information, audience statistics, etc.

Point-of-sale (POS) system
Scanner system used to collect data at retail checkouts.

Types and Uses of Databases.   Many types of databases serve the decision-making needs of managers. In a marketing-oriented company, databases are focused directly or indirectly on satisfying the customer. Some of the more widely used databases and their applications are presented in Table 4.2. For many organizations, data gathered internally for one purpose might provide an additional source of revenue when sold to outside users, such as the scanner data gathered through a **point-of-sale (POS) system** in retail stores and computerized airline reservation systems, such as Sabre and Galileo.

The users of databases are as diverse as the databases themselves, with each user having unique needs that must be met with marketing intelligence. A user may be a manufacturer, retailer, advertising agency, marketing research firm, or other marketing-oriented organization. Within a marketing organization, databases may be used to forecast market demand for a given product within a specified time frame, determine design features and production schedules to meet demand, develop pricing models for new and existing products, assess the effectiveness of promotional campaigns, and determine the efficiency and effectiveness of distribution channels.

Our emphasis here is on information systems used by marketing managers and executives, but another important type of information system is gaining acceptance by customer-oriented firms. Customer-contact personnel tend to occupy the lowest tier in a hierarchical organization, yet their impact on customer satisfaction often is greater than that of any other group. Companies that invest in cutting-edge **front-line information systems (FIS)** achieve significant gains in service quality and reliability and subsequently high levels of customer satisfaction. FedEx, Frito-Lay, and Hertz are examples of companies that equip their front-line personnel with technologies that improve their performance, and they also tend to have high levels of employee satisfaction. The data gathered at the FIS level can provide inputs for the upper management levels.[18]

Database Design and Creation

Perhaps the most important aspect of a **database** is its initial design and creation. At this point, the managers who will use the information must be able to communicate effectively with those responsible for providing the information so that the resulting database will be informative and useful. The design and creation of the database should be user-oriented and focused on helping the organization achieve its mission while satisfying its target market(s). The design should include both internal records and external marketing intelligence, and meet the requirements of the information user and provider for making both strategic and tactical decisions.

Internal Records. A large quantity of internal data is generated in the course of doing business. Examples of data include routine departmental and functional area records such as marketing, accounting, finance, production, personnel, and so forth. Data may also include order processing records, sales figures, inventory status, customer accounts (receivables), supplier invoices (payables), and other data that will be useful for management decisions. Internal records can be used to compile sales and cost data, to calculate productivity measures and scheduling of activities and employees, and to determine budgets and future courses of action in many areas.

External Marketing Intelligence. Marketing intelligence can be obtained from either primary or secondary sources. Primary data provide answers to a specific marketing management problem. For example, a utility company may send a questionnaire to its customers to determine their level of satisfaction with the utility's services, or a market study may be conducted to determine the positioning of a company's product relative to its competitors. Strategic tracking studies are another form of primary data that are used to monitor consumer awareness, perceptions, and behavior through rapid changes in marketing technology, media, and distribution channels. They also can be used to track the effects of marketing programs as they are introduced, the evolution of brand awareness and brand image over time and how it is affected by competitors, advertising recognition and recall, characteristics of the optimal target market, and other useful information.[19] Data generally are collected by telephone or mail, with the quality of the research determined by its design and execution. As with other research methods, tracking studies can be good or bad depending on the sampling plan, questionnaire design, interviewing procedures, and data processing, but their real value is their ability to provide longitudinal data.

Front-line information system (FIS)
Data provided to customer-contact personnel to improve customer service.

Database
Organized collection of a wide range of information used for decision making.

Often it is possible to obtain the needed marketing information from secondary data that have been compiled previously for some purpose other than the present management decision without conducting primary research. Secondary information is readily available from a variety of online and easily accessible databases such as library and online data sources, commercial or syndicated sources, government agencies, and others.

Information Requirements. As shown in Figure 4.6, the "law of the lens" serves as a filter between the perspectives of the information user and the information provider. It is difficult under the best of conditions to design useful databases, develop an effective research methodology, and interpret the results in a way that will be a true representation of marketplace reality. Precautions should be taken to ensure that a database's underlying data and information are as accurate and unbiased as possible so that they can be integrated into the decision process with some degree of confidence.

The marketing manager must specify the types of decisions to be made and the specific types of information needed to make those decisions. This must be communicated clearly to the information provider (e.g., researcher, information systems personnel, etc.) to be used as a basis for system design and data-collection methods. Likewise, the two parties should have a common understanding about the type of information needed, how it will be used, how it will be obtained, and the format that will provide the most useful information. The process of determining information requirements is complicated by personal biases that may introduce subjectivity into the research process. Further, the manager of a database must consider whether the user is internal to the organization or one or more external parties with a variety of needs. A database may consist of proprietary internal and external data that are intended only for use in-house, or it may contain commercial data or information that is intended for sale to outside parties. In the first case, the user and the support system can be narrowly defined, but in the commercial sector the users and their applications may be more diverse and require more fine-tuning and technical support tailored specifically to different organizations and industries. The key is to recognize the actual customer of the research and to provide satisfaction through the research process and results.

Database Management

It is important to recognize that databases and the technology that makes possible the efficient management of large databases are merely tools to be used by managers. ". . . [M]odern database management abetted by technology should be more than 'list maintenance.' Systems should constantly analyze and highlight strategic opportunities the firm can exploit. Surviving in the fast-action markets of the future will demand it."[20]

Some potential pitfalls in database management include information overload and "analysis paralysis," unhelpful data, inward focus, and lack of commitment. Databases can become extremely large and unwieldy, containing data and information that are not relevant to the decisions they are meant to support. A periodic review of the database relative to management requirements can expose unhelpful data that should be eliminated and missing data that should be added in the appropriate format. The key to successful database management is to remember that data and information are tools to be used by managers. They are not solutions in themselves and should be designed and controlled from a marketing perspective supported by efficient and effective information technology.

Market Measurement and Forecasting Demand

Marketing managers must be able to estimate the results of their strategic or tactical decisions, often under different competing scenarios. Databases such as the MDSS can provide essential information for estimating market demand, market potential, and actual market size, as well as the company's present and desired market-share position for a given product or product category. Databases also are useful tools in forecasting future sales and profit figures for a given product or business unit within a specified time period and with a given level of marketing effort.

Forecast
What a firm expects to achieve under given conditions.

Market potential is the maximum that can be reasonably expected (usually stated in dollar or unit sales) under given conditions. A **forecast** is what the firm expects to achieve under given conditions and may provide target performance standards for the company, its business units, and individual personnel.[21] Potentials and forecasts can be calculated at several levels: industry and/or market, company, and product. Market potential estimates are used for decisions such as market entry or exit, location of a business facility, and as inputs for sales forecasts. Forecasts are used primarily to answer "What if" questions, set budgets, and establish a basis for monitoring deviations from forecasted sales. Data used to estimate market potential may come from government sources, trade associations, private companies, financial analysts, surveys, and other sources.[22]

● ISSUES IN MARKETING INFORMATION ACQUISITION AND USE

The issues involved in acquiring and using marketing information are too numerous to discuss in this chapter, but some of the primary challenges include the decision as to whether to conduct marketing research with internal personnel or to use outside information providers. In addition, decisions must be made regarding the scope or extent of the research and the nature of organizational resources that will be involved. Other major issues include the quality of research methodology and results and the legal and ethical implications of all marketing intelligence activities.

In-house or Outsource Research Task

Marketing managers must assess the advantages and disadvantages of obtaining information from internal or external information providers. Criteria for making this decision include cost, time, objectivity, and expertise.

Extent/Scope of Research

The amount of information that is needed for a particular decision will vary, but the decision process is expedited when measures are taken to ensure that available information is relevant to the problem under consideration. Creative problem solving and the steps in the research process can be applied to this decision, starting with a clear problem definition and an understanding of the most useful data sources. Where existing information provides sufficient input for a quality decision, further data collection may not be necessary. Available secondary information also can help identify specific primary research needs within a more limited scope.

Organizational Resources

Within the context of organizational resources, a number of issues can create constraints on the acquisition and use of marketing information. It is important to assess the expertise of in-house personnel; the quality of existing MDSS, MIS, or other databases that are used as management tools; the financial resources available for gathering and managing information; the amount of time that is available for gathering information to make a timely decision; and the ability and objectivity of management to use and act on the information.

In-house Expertise.   The research task should be clearly defined to guide the responsibilities of personnel who are assigned to obtaining marketing information. Likewise, criteria must be established for personnel hiring and performance for those people and departments involved in information gathering and research activities. Efforts should not be confined to marketing but should be integrated across all relevant functional areas, such as accounting, finance, operations, human resources, information systems, or others that may be involved in providing or using data for marketing decisions.

MDSS/MIS Availability (and Appropriateness/Quality).   The marketing decision support system and the marketing information system become an issue when the quality of the data and information is in question. All personnel who are involved in this process must have a mutual understanding of the importance of integrating qualitative and quantitative information into a useful format for analysis and decision making. Technology and the information system that it supports are useful tools but not an end in themselves in ensuring that their outputs will be appropriate or of high quality.

Financial Resources.   Gathering information and maintaining a useful database require considerable financial resources. Costs can include the purchase of more sophisticated computer hardware or a specialized database from an outside source, the hiring of a consultant to gather and analyze needed information, or the support of an internal department or individual who is responsible for designing and maintaining the database. The quality of management information is related in large part to the organizational commitment to allocating funds to decision support systems and their maintenance.

Time Available to Make Decision.   Deadlines for making decisions become an issue when the marketing manager has insufficient information to make an intelligent decision. Managers are making more decisions than ever and have a shorter time in which to make them. This requires a readily available information system that is timely, accurate, and useful. Depending on the time available, more research can be conducted and more information added to provide additional insights into the problem. Often, the optimal decision cannot be made with the time and resources available. When the time that is available for decisive action is limited, insufficient financial resources and other constraints become a larger issue.

Managerial Objectivity and Ability to Use/Act on Information. Assuming that all the preceding issues have been resolved, there is still the issue of whether managers who are responsible for interpreting information and making strategic or tactical decisions can remain objective throughout the process. Each decision maker has his or her personal set of experiences, biases, and motives that may enter into the decision (consciously or subconsciously). Some major marketing mistakes have been made because of the inability to remain objective about the fate of a particular product or company unit.

Research Quality/Quality of Information

Quality issues related to marketing intelligence can be broken down into three major types: quality of the research process, quality of the data and information obtained, and quality of the management decision process. Marketers are concerned with the quality of the goods and services they sell and the quality of production and other organizational processes. The same level of concern must be applied to the quality of marketing research and information used by managers to make marketing-related decisions, as well as to the quality of the overall decision-making process. A close relationship exists between the management decision and the allocation of resources to support that decision. For example, if the decision is to increase market share for a line of computers, the decision is not complete unless it also includes a plan for implementation and identifies the resources necessary to carry out the plan. Quality of the research also should reflect a balanced view of the information from the perspectives of the customer and the company and the information user and provider.

International Marketing Research

While the fundamental principles of obtaining and using marketing intelligence for management decisions apply to both domestic and international research, the process is more complex in international markets. Some issues that are more problematic in international research include the difficulty of making cross-cultural comparisons, social and language differences, and the availability and accuracy of secondary data. Costs tend to be higher because of the need for specialized research designs to accommodate country differences, training, acquiring population data, and so forth. Despite the challenges of international marketing research, however, it does offer considerable insight into potential opportunities and problems in overseas markets.

Legal and Ethical Issues

Legal and ethical issues abound in the acquisition and use of marketing intelligence. Government regulations and legal guidelines provide both protection and constraints for a company and its customers. As communication and database technologies become more sophisticated and widely used, security and privacy issues become a greater concern. Ethical and bias issues are present throughout the entire marketing research and decision-making process.

Regulatory Issues.   Government regulations, industry standards, and legal guidelines present many challenges for marketing intelligence users and providers. The major federal government regulations emanate from the Federal Trade Commission (FTC) and the Federal Communications Commission (FCC). The FTC Act, Section 5, declares unfair or deceptive acts to be unlawful. Such deception includes the use of research as a sales ploy or as a "foot in the door" technique. Other regulation may come from federal, state, and local governments or private property (e.g., shopping malls) where research may be conducted. Industry standards also exist to provide objective criteria for professional behavior and guidelines for companies that may not have their own code for conducting research.

Privacy Issues.   Privacy is a concern that is embodied in both regulatory and ethical issues. The problem is present in the gathering and manipulating of marketing intelligence related to both consumers and business-to-business marketing. One of the most frequent abuses of privacy by marketing researchers is the promise of anonymity while gathering data and then identifying the respondent in a way that is harmful or inappropriate. For example, an unsuspecting respondent may be placed on a sales list with personal data, and perhaps that list also would be sold to another party.

Ethical Issues.   The term *ethics* often is used interchangeably with *moral values* and bears a strong relationship to the way one person treats the rights of another. Research ethics include honesty throughout the research process, not manipulating methodology or data to achieve desired results, and basically respecting the rights of respondents and all involved in the process to avoid deception and fraudulent practices. Marketing information can be used and abused in consumer and business-to-business markets, but marketing managers and researchers also are faced with an ever-increasing need to know more about their competitors. The question becomes how to obtain useful customer and competitive information and how to do so legally and ethically.

Bias Issues.   All sources of potential bias related to the researcher and the research process should be avoided to ensure high-quality marketing intelligence and decisions. Those who handle data and information have many opportunities to introduce bias into every stage of the CPS process and the marketing research process. Unbiased research relies on carefully listening to respondents and objectively processing the data and making inferences from it. Research bias also can be controlled by presenting all relevant information to the information user (i.e., reporting exactly what the respondents said) and being truthful with the handling and analysis of the data (no data left out of the analysis or misinterpreted). It is virtually impossible to completely eliminate all sources of bias in a research project or database, but a wholehearted attempt should be made to remove every source of bias that is possible. This is essential for providing data that are reliable and valid for management decisions.

IT'S LEGAL BUT IS IT ETHICAL?

Beware of Leechware

During the dot.com era, banner ads were one of the most frequently used forms of advertising by Internet marketers, but they were not as successful as many expected. As a result, some on-line marketers have embraced more aggressive tools for advertising—called "*leechware*" or "*spyware.*" Leechware is a piggyback software that is installed on an unsuspecting user's computer. This software generally comes intertwined with the hottest download, file-swapping site, or most popular software of the moment. It may be bundled with other software, or disguised as a "Web enhancer" that can monitor a user's online activities and display those ads that are of most interest to the user.

The most common type of leechware, Gator.com, tracks the URL a user visits and displays pop-up banner ads related to the content of the site. Beermat Software's "politically incorrect but hugely popular drug-dealing game" called Dope Wars had millions of downloads. The game's new 2.1 version came bundled with Gator.com and Cydoor Technologies—programs that infiltrate the user's hard drive to provide "services" he or she may not want. These programs monitor users' Internet activity and display targeted pop-up ads on their screens, even when they are not playing the game. It is very difficult—if not impossible—to uninstall this software once it is on the user's hard drive, even if the software (e.g., game) to which it was attached is deleted. Ian Wall, founder of Beermat Software, responded to complaints about the spyware that was attached to Dope Wars 2.1 software within a week after its release. He severed his relationships with Cydoor and other leechware companies, keeping only Gator as an optional download. He wrote an e-mail in which he cited "lingering technological issues" and "a small but vociferous group of people who make a big fuss about 'spyware' being the biggest threat to Life on Earth As We know It."

Another popular file-swapping site, Kazaa, has an abundance of bundled leechware. (The company faced a court order to stop providing free copyright-protected music in early 2002.) Ari Schwartz, associate director of the Center for Democracy and Technology, said "A lot of companies see this as a model for the future." Advocates of leechware technology consider it beneficial to both the customer and the advertisers—combining the effectiveness of one-to-one marketing with the efficiency of mass marketing. They also point out that such software keeps the site free to its users. Consumers only receive advertising and coupons they may be interested in; marketers increase efficiency by advertising only to those who are likely prospects. According to Scott Eagle, Gator's chief marketing officer, "On-line publishers are failing because they're publishing irrelevant advertising.... We add value by popping up information and advertising at the appropriate time, to a user who's far more likely to be interested." Unfortunately, many unsuspecting Internet users are totally unaware that the leechware software is being installed on their computers, because it is bundled stealthily with many popular Internet downloads or innocuous-looking pop-up ads. Once installed, leechware is extremely difficult to remove. Leechware companies have been careful to protect themselves with vague licensing agreements that users typically ignored. Others hide it in privacy agreement statements, which also are largely ignored.

Many consumers and consumer advocates are troubled that disclosures about the invasiveness of this software are often vague, or obscured in licensing agreements. James Love, director of the Consumer Project on Technology, said, "These are very abusive practices ... The fact that this has gone so far with so many different players is indicative of how weak the government is in dealing with software companies." He has asked the U.S. Federal Trade Commission (FTC) to "create full standard disclosures for laypeople."

(continued)

The new generation of leechware has fostered the growth of stealth advertising. For example, eZula's Top Text software makes it possible for the company to sell words on Web pages that become links to eZula's advertisers. However, no compensation is given to the publishers of these Web pages. Many find this practice very offensive, which leads Web sites such as Scamware.net and eZulafacts.com to give the appearance that they are warning consumers. Even Microsoft's Windows XP was supposed to come bundled with a similar technology called "Smart Tags," but the company was pressured not to include this spyware in the final product.

Gator went further by creating a pop-up banner ad to track users' online activities and present them with related ads that were actually existing banner ads. The Interactive Advertising Bureau (IAB), which is allied with DoubleClick (the largest Internet sales network), called this practice a "dirty trick" and threatened to involve the FTC in the situation. The IAB charged that Gator was "falsely implying relationships that do not exist." They charged Gator with violating contract, trademark, and copyright interests. Gator responded by filing a federal lawsuit asking for protection of its right to use the existing banner ads. Gator and the IAB settled their differences, and Gator tabled its lawsuit with plans to use a "new pop-up banner ad that works on behalf of Web publishers." However, Gator's CEO Jeff McFadden restated his faith in "behavioral targeting." Scott Eagle, Gator's marketing director,

said, "The big issue is, who owns the desktop?... We believe the consumer does, and the consumer has a right to invite Gator to provide content." Gator users do have at least two chances to stop a download before the spyware invades their hard drive, which is more forthright than many of their competitors, who conceal their leechware on users' hard drives, and then report back users' movements.

Privacy and ethical issues abound with the use of leechware, and privacy advocates are disturbed by the trend. Special-interest groups have lobbied the FTC to provide protection for the public. Their concerns are that if leechware can monitor Web-surfing habits, then it also can violate users' privacy by tracking sensitive personal information. Most customers are uncomfortable with sharing this information with unknown parties, and certainly do not want the information that is being gathered to be used for unethical purposes.

It should not be a surprise to marketers, and the public in general, that leechware technologies and related advertising techniques have raised serious concerns about personal privacy and ethical issues. If used ethically, however, the information that is provided by leechware can be a valuable tool for direct mass marketers and users of the Internet.

Source: David Howard, "Radar—Along for the Ride," *SmartBusinessMag.com* (February 2002), pp. 22–24.

Summary

Timely, accurate, high-quality marketing intelligence has become a necessity in a rapidly changing world and increasingly complex marketing environment. Marketing decisions are made throughout all levels of an organization, from long-range strategic plans at the top management level to a front-line customer-contact employee's on-the-spot decision.

The quality of information available for management decisions is enhanced by integrating creative problem-solving techniques with the marketing research process. Whereas quantitative inputs may be essential for a complete understanding of a problem or situation, managers also must use qualitative inputs that cannot be measured with a high degree of accuracy. This involves creative problem solving—"stepping outside the box" to find creative solutions to business problems and opportunities.

The marketing research process is closely related to the creative problem-solving process. It involves eight steps: (1) recognizing the need for research, (2) defining the research problem/objective, (3) specifying the information required, (4) developing the research plan, (5) designing the method for collecting information, (6) performing the research, (7) analyzing the data, and (8) communicating the findings.

Marketing decisions require both external and internal information. External information focuses on environmental opportunities and threats, with an emphasis on analyzing the market and buyers and competitors. Internal information focuses on the company's strengths and weaknesses versus those of competitors. Areas of inquiry generally include financial, human, and technological resources and the effectiveness of marketing programs.

Marketing intelligence is gathered from a variety of sources through formal and informal methods. In its most basic form, it consists of data and facts about the marketplace. When the data are analyzed and interpreted in a meaningful way, they become information. Information that is believed to be true becomes intelligence that is easily understood, reliable, and valid for use in management decisions. Data and information are aggregated into databases such as a marketing information system (MIS) or marketing decision support system (MDSS) that are capable of supporting decision models for a variety of purposes.

Issues involved in the acquisition and use of marketing information include whether to conduct the research in-house or through an outside provider, the extent and scope of the research, availability and quality of organizational resources, quality of information and the research process, challenges of international research, and legal, ethical, and bias concerns.

Questions

1. Explain the importance of timely and relevant information inputs for marketing management

decisions. Give an example to support your answer.

2. Describe the basic problem-solving process, and give a detailed example of how this might be used in making a decision about how to introduce a new product to the market. (Select a specific product and target market.) At what stage(s) do you believe it is most important to be creative?

3. Describe the complete marketing research process, and give a detailed example of how this might be used by a regional fast-food restaurant that is considering expanding its locations to other regions of the United States. How would this process differ if the restaurant were planning to open new locations in Europe?

4. Discuss the uses and sources of information about the external environment that might be included in a marketing intelligence system for a personal digital assistant (PDA) manufacturer. Select one specific type of information and show how the PDA manufacturer would use this in making a decision about new product features.

5. Describe internal environmental information that might be used by the PDA manufacturer in conjunction with the external information described in Question 4, and show why this would be useful.

6. Give an example of a database that is used by marketing managers, and list several specific applications of the data that it contains. Explain how the data are converted to information, the information to intelligence, the intelligence to knowledge, and the knowledge to wise management decisions.

7. Debate the advantages, constraints, and issues involved in the acquisition and use of information gained through marketing intelligence.

Exercises

1. Choose one article in current business media that illustrates the use of marketing information

in a decision related to a product, distribution channel, promotional campaign, or pricing strategy. Critique the research or data-gathering approach taken by management in terms of its appropriateness for this marketing decision. What additional information, if any, should the company have obtained? Defend your answer.

2. Industrial buyers face considerable uncertainty in their selection of goods and services, and the problem is greater in international trade due to differences in culture, language, and distance. National product standards have been imposed to create artificial barriers that restrict trade among countries. The International Standards Organization (ISO) was created by 89 member nations to develop product and service standards (ISO 9000) that would be acceptable to all members. The result was that any product or service that meets the ISO 9000 standards could be distributed in all the member nations without being subjected to other national requirements. Locate a complete description of the ISO 9000 standards, and determine the relationship between these standards and the specific type(s) of marketing intelligence that might be related to fulfilling the requirements for a multinational manufacturer of tennis shoes.

3. Develop a five-item survey to determine consumer preferences for soft drinks (following the marketing research process described in this chapter). Administer the survey to ten of your friends, and tabulate and analyze your results. What inferences can be made from this ministudy? What measures can be taken to ensure a better-quality research project?

Endnotes

1. Donald R. Keogh, President of Coca-Cola Company, "Coca-Cola Company, Form 10-K" (Washington, D.C.: Securities and Exchange Commission, September 16, 1996).

2. Vincent P. Barabba, *Meeting of the Minds: Creating the Market-Based Enterprise* (Boston: Harvard Business School Press, 1995), pp. 61-67.

3. *Webster's New World College Dictionary,* 3d ed. (New York: Macmillan, 1996), p. 1072.

4. Alexander Hiam and Charles D. Schewe, *The Portable MBA in Marketing* (New York: Wiley, 1992), p. 126.

5. Vincent P. Barabba, *op. cit.,* pp. 138-141.

6. Vincent P. Barabba and Gerald Zaltman, *Hearing the Voice of the Market: Competitive Advantage Through Creative Use of Market Information* (Boston: Harvard Business School Press, 1991), pp. 23-24.

7. Gregory L. White, Joseph B. White, and Sholnn Freeman, "What's A Cool Car? The Question Is Driving U.S. Auto Makers Wild—Beyond Focus Groups, Officials Hang Out in Arcades and Chat Up Snowboarders," *The Wall Street Journal* (August 9, 2000), p. B1+.

8. Barabba and Zaltman, *op. cit.*, pp. 33-34.

9. Thomas R. Keen, "What's Your Intuitive Decision-Maker Quotient?" *Marketing News* 30(22) (1996), p. 6.

10. Stephen Sharf, "Real Celebrities," *Ward's Auto World* (September 2000), p. 21.

11. James M. Higgins, *101 Creative Problem Solving Techniques: The Handbook of New Ideas for Business* (Winter Park, FL: New Management Publishing Company, 1994), Chap. 2, pp. 17-33 (quote, p. 17).

12. For further discussion, see *ibid.,* pp. 20-28.

13. James Thurber, quoted in *Bartlett's Book of Business Quotations,* compiled by Barbara Ann Kipfer (Boston: Little, Brown, 1994), p. 92.

14. Philip Kotler, William Gregor, and William Rodgers, "The Marketing Audit Comes of Age," *Sloan Management Review* (Winter 1977), pp. 25-43. [In Philip Kotler, *Marketing Management: Analysis, Planning, Implementation, and Control,* 11th ed. (Englewood Cliffs, NJ: Prentice-Hall, 2003), pp. 698-699.]

15. Barabba and Zaltman, *op. cit.,* pp. 41-45.

16. Quoted in Barabba and Zaltman, *op. cit.,* p. 137.

17. For further discussion of MDSS, see William R. Dillon, Thomas J. Madden, and Neil H. Firtle, *Marketing Research in a Marketing Environment,* 3d ed. (Homewood, IL: Irwin, 1994), Chap. 22, pp. 645-664, which is the source of much of the information in this section; also see John D. C. Little, "Decision Support Systems for Marketing Managers," *Journal of Marketing* 43(3) (Summer 1979), p. 9-26.

18. Jagdish N. Sheth and Rajendra S. Sisodia, "Improving Marketing Productivity," in Jeffrey Heilbrunn (ed.), *Marketing Encyclopedia: Issues and Trends Shaping the Future* (Chicago: American Marketing

Association, and Lincolnwood, IL: NTC Business Books, 1995), p. 234.

19. Jerry W. Thomas, "Strategic Marketing Tracking Shows How Efforts Pay Off," *Marketing News* 29(34) (August 28, 1995), pp. 34ff.

20. Bob Donath, "Business Marketing 2000: The Marketing Millenium Flowers," in Heilbrunn, *op. cit.,* p. 157.

21. For further discussion, see Donald R. Lehmann and Russell S. Winer, *Analysis for Marketing Planning,* 3d ed. (Burr Ridge, IL: Irwin, 1994), Chap. 6, pp. 112; and Kotler, *op. cit.,* Chap. 10, pp. 244–262.

22. For further discussion, see Donald R. Lehmann and Russell S. Winer, *Analysis for Marketing Decisions,* 3d ed. (Homewood, IL: Irwin, 1994), Chap. 6, pp. 116ff.

APPENDIX: COMPONENTS OF A MARKETING AUDIT

Part I. The Marketing Environment Audit

Macro-environment

A. Demographic

What major demographic developments and trends pose opportunities or threats to this company? What actions has the company taken in response to these developments and trends?

B. Economic

What major developments in income, prices, savings, and credit will affect the company? What actions has the company been taking in response to these developments and trends?

C. Environmental

What is the outlook for the cost and availability of natural resources and energy needed by the company? What concerns have been expressed about the company's role in pollution and conservation, and what steps has the company taken?

D. Technological

What major changes are occurring in product and process technology? What is the company's position in these technologies? What major generic substitutes might replace this product?

E. Political

What changes in laws and regulations might affect marketing strategy and tactics? What is happening in the areas of pollution control, equal employment opportunity, product safety, advertising, price control, and so forth, that affects marketing strategy?

F. Cultural

What is the public's attitude toward business and toward the company's products? What changes in customer lifestyles and values might affect the company?

Task Environment

A. Markets

What is happening to market size, growth, geographical distribution, and profits? What are the major market segments?

B. Customers

What are the customers' needs and buying processes? How do customers and prospects rate the company and its competitors on reputation, product quality, service, sales force, and price? How do different customer segments make their buying decisions?

C. Competitors

Who are the major competitors? What are their objectives, strategies, strengths, weaknesses, sizes and market shares? What trends will affect future competition and substitutes for the company's products?

D. Distribution and Dealers

What are the main trade channels for bringing products to customers? What are the efficiency levels and growth potentials of the different trade channels?

E. Suppliers

What is the outlook for the availability of key resources used in production? What trends are occurring among suppliers?

F. Facilitators and Marketing Firms

What is the cost and availability outlook for transportation services, warehousing facilities, and financial resources? How effective are the company's advertising agencies and marketing research firms?

G. Publics

Which publics represent particular opportunities or problems for the company? What steps has the company taken to deal effectively with each public?

Part II. Marketing Strategy Audit

A. Business Mission

Is the business mission clearly stated in market-oriented terms? Is it feasible?

B. Marketing Objective and Goals

Are the company and marketing objectives and goals stated clearly enough to guide marketing planning and performance measurement? Are the marketing objectives appropriate, given the company's competitive position, resources and opportunities?

C. Strategy

Has the management articulated a clear marketing strategy for achieving its marketing objectives? Is the strategy convincing? Is the strategy appropriate to the stage of the product life cycle, competitors' strategies and the state of the economy? Is the company using the best basis for market segmentation? Does it have clear criteria for rating the segments and choosing the best ones? Has it developed accurate profiles of each target segment? Has the company developed an effective positioning and marketing mix for each target segment? Are marketing resources allocated optimally to the major elements of the marketing mix? Are enough resources or too many resources budgeted to accomplish the marketing objectives?

Part III. Marketing Organization Audit

A. Formal Structure

Does the marketing vice president have adequate authority and responsibility for company activities that affect customers' satisfaction? Are the marketing activities optimally structured along functional, product, segment, end-user, and geographical lines?

B. Functional Efficiency

Are there good communication and working relations between marketing and sales? Is the product-management system working effectively? Are product managers able to plan profits or only sales volume? Are there any groups in marketing that need more training, motivation, supervision, or evaluation?

C. Interface Efficiency

Are there any problems between marketing and manufacturing, R&D, purchasing, finance, accounting, and/or legal that need attention?

Part IV. Marketing Systems Audit

A. Marketing Information System

Is the marketing intelligence system producing accurate, sufficient, and timely information about marketplace developments with respect to customers, prospects, distributors and dealers, competitors, suppliers, and various publics? Are company decision makers asking for enough marketing research, and are they using the results? Is the company employing the best methods for market measurement and sales forecasting?

B. Marketing Planning Systems

Is the marketing planning system well conceived and effectively used? Do marketers have decision support systems available? Does the planning system result in acceptable sales targets and quotas?

C. Marketing Control System

Are the control procedures adequate to ensure that the annual plan objectives are being achieved? Does management periodically analyze the profitability of products, markets, territories, and channels of distribution? Are marketing costs and productivity periodically examined?

D. New-Product Development System

Is the company well organized to gather, generate, and screen new-product ideas? Does the company do adequate concept research and business analysis before investing in new ideas? Does the company carry out adequate product and market testing before launching new products?

Part V. Marketing Productivity Audit

A. Profitability Analysis

What is the profitability of the company's different products, markets, territories, and channels of distribution? Should the company enter, expand, contract, or withdraw from any business segments?

B. Cost-Effectiveness Analysis

Do any marketing activities seem to have excessive costs? Can cost-reducing steps be taken?

Part VI. Marketing Function Audits

A. Products

What are the company's product-line objectives? Are they sound? Is the current product line meeting the objectives? Should the product line be stretched or contracted upward, downward, or both ways? Which products should be phased out? Which products should be added? What are the buyers' knowledge and attitudes toward the company's and competitors' product quality, features, styling, brand names, and so on? What areas of product and brand strategy need improvement?

B. Price

What are the company's pricing objectives, policies, strategies, and procedures? To what extent are prices set on cost, demand, and competitive criteria? Do the customers see the company's prices as being in line with the value of its offer? What does management know about the price elasticity of demand, experience-curve effects, and competitors' prices and pricing policies? To what extent are price policies compatible with the needs of distributors and dealers, suppliers, and government regulation?

C. *Distribution*

What are the company's distribution objectives and strategies? Is there adequate market coverage and service? How effective are distributors, dealers, manufacturers' representatives, brokers, agents, and others? Should the company consider changing its distribution channels?

D. *Advertising, Sales Promotion, Publicity, and Direct Marketing*

What are the organization's advertising objectives? Are they sound? Is the right amount being spent on advertising? Are the ad themes and copy effective? What do customers and the public think about the advertising? Are the advertising media well chosen? Is the internal advertising staff adequate? Is the sales-promotion budget adequate? Is there effective and sufficient use of sales-promotion tools such as samples, coupons, displays, and sales contests? Is the public relations staff competent and creative? Is the company making enough use of direct, online, and database marketing?

E. *Sales Force*

What are the sales force's objectives? Is the sales force large enough to accomplish the company's objectives? Is the sales force organized along the proper principles of specialization (territory, market, product)? Are there enough (or too many) sales managers to guide the field sales representatives? Do the sales-compensation level and structure provide adequate incentive and reward? Does the sales force show high morale, ability, and effort? Are the procedures adequate for setting quotas and evaluating performance? How does the company's sales force compare to competitors' sales forces?

Source: Philip Kotler, *Marketing Management,* 11th ed. (Englewood Cliffs, NJ: Prentice-Hall, 2003), pp. 698–699.

MARKETING MANAGEMENT IN ACTION: CLOSING CASE

McDonald's Wants to Know What Ails Sales

In April 2002 McDonald's reported disappointing profits for the sixth consecutive quarter. As management of the largest burger chain in the world continually failed to meet its own final projections, top analysts became wary and downgraded the company's stock. Institutional investors such as Fidelity Investments began selling their shares, and clients were no longer interested in investing in McDonald's. This lackluster performance raised many questions in an economic environment where many competing franchise restaurant chains were attracting investors. In spite of its heavy weighting of McDonald's data, the S&P Restaurant index was up 18 percent in the previous year. Wendy's soared 57 percent, and Tricon Global (KFC, Pizza Hut, Taco Bell) hit a 52-week high with stock up 65 percent for the year. McDonald's stock increased less than 4 percent from April 2001 to April 2002, to sell at $28—42 percent off from its 1999 high. This is quite a change from what one institutional investor called "the quintessential growth stock"—one that could be depended upon to deliver 12 to 15 percent growth in earnings from one year to the next.

McDonald's and investors wanted to know what happened to the company that has been "one of the bluest of blue chips" of the Dow Jones industrial average since 1985. Jack Greenberg, chief executive of McDonald's, instituted an expensive new food-preparation system to improve the worst of the fast-food chain's problems. Sales had stagnated and customers complained of "slow service, rude employees, and cardboard-tasting food." McDonald's management was confident that the problems could be solved, and that sales would rebound, but investors and analysts were not convinced.

One problem was related to McDonald's rapid growth strategy in a market that was rapidly becoming saturated. Between 300 and 350 new restaurants were planned by the end of 2002, compared to 1,130 in 1995. Overseas expansion outpaced domestic expansion, but in spite of growth, international stores were not showing consistent profitability. They were plagued with issues such as

mad cow and hoof-and-mouth disease, weak foreign currencies, and high commodity costs.

A second problem was related to the competitive environment. Many believed that competitors such as Burger King and Wendy offered hotter and tastier food products. These chains have had a long history of scoring higher than McDonald's in customer satisfaction surveys. McDonald's placed last among fast food restaurants on the University of Michigan's American Customer Satisfaction index every year since the survey began in 1992. Complaints included the comment that pictures in advertisements did not accurately represent the real food.

McDonald's reached a strategic inflection point in 1996, when they lost market share to Burger King and Wendy's, and experienced their fourth consecutive quarter of declining same-store sales. The company made changes in management and in operations in an attempt to improve performance, including "Made for You," a new system to improve the quality of food preparation. The equipment enabled stores to customize preparation of sandwiches and offer freshly toasted buns. This massive upgrade of equipment was necessary to bring operations standards up to the level of competition. These improvements were expected to increase profits 10 to 15 percent a year, according to Jack Greenberg, then head of McDonald's USA. The stock market reacted positively. Then, "Made for You crippled the service times," according to a long-time McDonald's operator. He said that the new system typically doubled the average service time to two to three minutes per order, and sometimes as much as 15 minutes. As a McDonald's franchisee said, "When . . . 100 people walk in, you've got to have some food ready . . . Made for You doesn't allow that." Three years after the new system was introduced, McDonald's quarterly same-store sales (a key industry measure) increased an average of 1.5 percent compared to the industry average of 2.3 percent. McDonald's also suffered up to 3 percent loss in "customer counts" (average number of diners who enter each restaurant) in each of the three previous years. During the same period, Wendy's sales rose

FIGURE 1

We Love to See You Smile?

McDonald's Weaknesses	McDonald's Strengths
Greeted customer with smile—64%	Gave correct order—96%
Repeated order for accuracy—52%	Received order in less than three minutes—72%
Mentioned food promotion or supersize—36%	Said, "Thank You"—72%

Source: Feedback Plus—visit of 25 McDonald's in New York, Chicago, Dallas, and Los Angeles Regions, November 7–15, 2001. Reported in: Shirley Leung, "McDonald's Asks Mystery Shoppers What Ails Sales," *The Wall Street Journal* (December 17, 2001), pp. B1, B3. Reproduced with permission of Dow Jones & Co. Inc. in the format textbook via. Copyright Clearance Center.

4.4 percent. McDonald's largest shareholder sold 60 percent of its holdings (75 million shares) in 2001 and 2002. Other major shareholders also cashed out most of their stock, and negative reviews from the financial community affected the company's brand reputation, causing the value of the McDonald's name to fall by $2.5 billion in 2001.

Mike Roberts, head of McDonald's USA, was optimistic about the company's ability to overcome some of its disappointing financial results by increasing the number of transactions in 2002. However, this required the cooperation of the company's 2,600 franchisees, who were infuriated by the "Made for You" system. It cost them more than they expected, and it slowed their service time. Many franchisees were also concerned about what one called "panic-driven discounting" or "value meals" that were priced too low.

Roberts recognized that slow service was the main complaint from U.S. customers, and company executives took aggressive steps to give faster and more personalized service. An analyst noted, "Strategies are in place to improve operations, such as restaurant assessments, a toll-free customer satisfaction phone line, manager incentive programs and the continued rollout of new products." McDonald's spent over $20 million in the first quarter of 2002 to give U.S. franchisees money to help defray the costs of new equipment, such as a split-function ordering system designed to reduce service time.

McDonald's sent 22,000 "mystery shoppers" to 13,000 domestic restaurants in 2002 (including 10,400 run by owner-operators) to evaluate service, cleanliness, and food quality using a single set of standards and measurements. *The Wall Street Journal* conducted its own study by hiring Feedback Plus, Inc. from Dallas, one of the largest mystery shopping companies in the United States, to visit and provide results on 25 McDonald's restaurants in four markets: Dallas, Chicago, New York, and Los Angeles. The average for all fast food and sit-down restaurants evaluated by Feedback Plus was 80 percent. McDonald's scores (about 81.9 percent) were higher than Wendy's International Inc. (80.7 percent), Diageo PLC's Burger King (80.1 percent), and Tricon Global Restaurants Inc.'s Taco Bell (77.1 percent). See Figure 1 for an example of the data obtained by Feedback Plus.

McDonald's use of mystery shoppers was part of a major effort to upgrade operations, which also included:

- An ongoing initiative to drive domestic sales and profits with improved execution at the restaurant level.

- A rigorous training program for the company's new operations consultants.

- Evaluations of each restaurant in 2002 based on:

  Four reviews, including two unannounced visits.

  Three to five mystery shopping reports each quarter (more than 200,000 by year-end).

Source: David Stires, "Fallen Arches," *Fortune* (April 29, 2002), pp. 74–76; Amy Zuber, "McD to Post 6th Quarterly Decline, Concedes Service Woes," *Nation's Restaurant News* (April 1, 2002), pp. 1, 55; Shirley Leung, "McDonald's Asks Mystery Shoppers What Ails Sales," *The Wall Street Journal* (December 17, 2001), pp. B1, B3.

Case Study Questions

1. Describe the management problem(s) that face McDonald's in the situation portrayed in the case. Explain how you would use the creative problem-solving process as a management tool to determine the type of market intelligence needed for an informed decision. (Include all steps, and specific types of information.)

2. Identify the marketing research problem(s) facing McDonald's at the time of the case. Using each of the steps in the marketing research process as a framework, recommend the best research approach for obtaining the required marketing intelligence.

3. Determine the type of internal and external information that would be helpful for McDonald's in their effort to overcome the identified problem(s).

4. Identify sources where each of the types of information discussed in Question 3 might be found. Discuss briefly how to evaluate the quality of these sources.

5. Discuss the role of databases in the problem-solving process, and show specifically how internal and/or external databases might be useful in the case situation.

6. Evaluate the use of "mystery shoppers" as a research tool, and critique the types of questions included in the mystery shopper evaluations. Do the questions address the problem(s) that you identified? What would you do differently, if anything?

7. Based on your analysis of the case, recommend a marketing research plan for McDonald's.

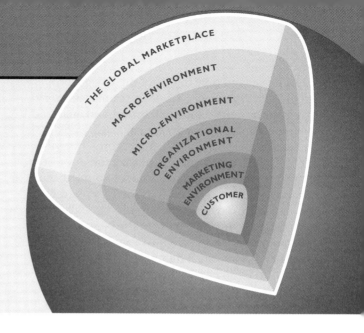

THE GLOBAL MARKETPLACE
MACRO-ENVIRONMENT
MICRO-ENVIRONMENT
ORGANIZATIONAL ENVIRONMENT
MARKETING ENVIRONMENT
CUSTOMER

CHAPTER 5

Understanding Consumer Buying Behavior

Overview

The Consumer Buying Process

Social and Cultural Influences on Buying Behavior

Individual Influences on Buying Behavior

Consumers and Products

Consumers and Situations

Relationship Marketing

Southwest Airlines insists on capitalizing the word customers *wherever it is used—in ads, brochures, even the annual report. The practice may seem picayune, but what better way to flag employees and the public that the Customer matters?[1]*

American Consumer Values After 9/11

Marketers faced many new challenges in the wake of the terrorist attacks of 9/11. There were noticeable changes within days of the tragedy in the ways that consumers expressed their personal values and changed their typical shopping behavior. Retailers were challenged to maintain inventories for some high-demand products. Media programming and advertising content also underwent considerable scrutiny and change.

Consumer Values and Shopping Behavior

Consumers' shopping behavior changed significantly immediately after the tragedy. People rushed to buy guns, television sets, gasoline containers, bottled water, gas masks, and security devices. They were concerned about security at home, at work, and in shopping malls.

Waves of patriotism spurred sales of the American flag—and retailers found it difficult to keep up with demand. Products that symbolized Americana, and almost anything that was red, white, and blue, sold out quickly. Americans of all ethnic groups were proud to wear shirts displaying the American flag or other patriotic symbols. Drivers across the country flew flags from their vehicles, and bumper stickers proclaimed their love for their country.

A look at Wal-Mart's sales data for the week after the attacks gives some insights into the psyche of the American consumer during that time. Wal-Mart, the world's largest retailer, has a computer system at its Bentonville, Ark. headquarters, with data storage capacity second only to that of the U.S. government. Sales from every Wal-Mart scanner in every store are instantly tabulated, sorted, and analyzed by the computer system. In an average week 100 million customers visit Wal-Mart stores, but sales were down 10 percent on Tuesday, the day of the attack. At stores around New York and northern Virginia, sales were as much as 30 to 40 percent lower for the day, compared to the same day a year earlier. Many Wal-Marts in the New York and Washington areas were "ghost towns" during the day, except for a small number of customers who wanted to be in familiar surroundings and to watch the television sets. One manager reported that "One guy came in and stayed six hours, he was so nervous." Customers began flooding back to the stores in the evening to buy staples and emergency supplies. For example, sales of gas cans jumped 895 percent; gun sales increased 70 percent; ammunition sales went up 140 percent; sales of TV sets jumped 70 percent; and antenna sales increased 400 percent. Wal-Mart sold 116,000 American flags on Tuesday, the day of the attacks, and 200,500 flags on Wednesday. Every U.S. Wal-Mart store was out of flags, and had five vendors promising new shipments as soon as possible.

By Thursday after the attacks, shopping patterns and sales were closer to normal, and stores braced for a better-than-normal weekend. Customers returned, and boosted sales 25 percent over the previous year's figures. Managers noticed that electronics sales were up significantly, and that more couples were shopping together than usual. Sales for the month of September 2001 were estimated at 4 to 6 percent ahead of September 2000. Lee Scott, Wal-Mart's chief executive, said "The data tells us that American citizens are determined to lead their lives as normally as possible, and we're seeing that in our stores . . ." On 9/11 a Wal-Mart store manager in Union, New Jersey, was preparing to open a new store the next day, but shifted his efforts in response to an urgent request by the Red Cross for bottled water, T-shirts, socks, and underwear for rescuers. He filled trucks with supplies, and sent them to an emergency command center. The manager opened his new store as planned, but increased his order of American flags from 50 to 4,500, and invited a color guard from a local veterans group to the opening.

Impact on Media Content

Television and radio programming was focused almost exclusively on the terrorist attacks and related news for a week or more after 9/11. Programs that could be considered offensive were either off the air, or edited to be more acceptable. Family values, patriotism, and spirituality became prominent themes as people tried to make sense of what had happened, and figure out how it would affect their lives.

Most of the scheduled advertising was cut from days of continuous television news programming. This was done as a matter of respect for victims and expediency for continuous news coverage. Some advertising was considered inappropriate or offensive, given the tragedy. Content was edited carefully to avoid offensive or insensitive material. For example, Daimler-Chrysler's Chrysler Group was ready to launch an ad for the new Jeep Liberty sport-utility vehicle. The ad showed the Jeep driving up the side of the Statue of Liberty, and the twin towers of the World Trade Center were in the background. The company scrambled to pull the ad out of some magazines, and made changes to the original. They kept the idea of showing a Liberty (Jeep) scaling a statue of the same name, but reversed the angle so the background was water. Many companies were ready to launch new products, and were caught in the midst of expensive advertising campaigns that had to be aborted—at least temporarily. All advertisers had to be careful about when to re-launch their advertising, and what images to use in America's new circumstances—particularly those firms whose products and promotional messages were geared toward fun and indulgence. Many companies used their advertising media for noncommercial patriotic themes and expressions of appreciation to the workers at Ground Zero. Campbell Soup Company had budgeted more money for marketing in September 2001 than in the past, but decided to hold off on all advertising after the attacks. As a Campbell spokesman said, "I don't think we have anything that's inappropriate but we want to be sensitive." Instead, the company donated beverages, hot soup, and bread to workers in the rescue and recovery effort.

Print and electronic media purchases and rentals also reflected changes in consumer shopping patterns. Demand was high for books on prophecy, faith, and spirituality. Books on Amazon.com's best seller list for the week included "Germs" and "Twin Towers: The Life of New York City's World Trade Center." Borders Group, Inc. had large numbers of requests for anything by or about Nostradamus.

Americans returned to movie theaters in normal numbers soon after the attacks; others bought or rented videos—often to escape from relentless around-the-clock news coverage. Blockbuster experienced a surge in store traffic that started on Tuesday afternoon and continued through the weekend, as people chose to watch movies in their own homes or with friends.

Many teens and preteens turned to favorite Web sites or magazines as their way of coping with the tragedy. Pleasant Company, a Mattel Inc. subsidiary that makes the American Girl dolls and books, created a special section on its Web page called "How to Cope," in response to a flood of e-mails from preteen girls searching for answers about fear, terrorism, and racial discrimination. AOL Time Warner Inc.'s *Teen People* magazine received thousands of e-mails from teenagers in the weeks after the attacks.

The "New Normal" for American Consumers

According to research commissioned by *Advertising Age* in March 2002, six months after the terrorist attacks, 80 percent of adults still felt the effect of 9/11 in their daily lives; 23 percent focused on the memory once a day; and 62 percent admitted that their daily routines were marred by thoughts of terrorism—but that has not stopped them from living a normal life. American consumers have demonstrated their resilience as they continue to travel, eat out, shop in malls, and leave home. The economy has had a greater influence on consumer spending than 9/11, but a combination of the two factors has caused consumers to focus more on value and practicality than in recent years. Increased sales of comfort foods and products for entertaining at home reflect a desire to spend more time with families and friends, as "Americans have moved past grief and toward a new normalcy."

Sources: Ann Zimmerman and Emily Nelson, "In Hour of Peril, Americans Bought Guns, TV Sets," *The Wall Street Journal* (September 18, 2001), pp. B1, B6; Matthew Rose, "Demand for Books on Prophecy, Faith, Surges After Attack," *The Wall Street Journal* (September 17, 2001), p. B8; Betsy McKay, Vanessa O'Connell, and Joseph B. White, "New Campaigns Are Put on Hold, Ads Are Pulled in Disaster's Wake," *The Wall Street Journal* (September 17, 2001), p. B8; Amy Merrick, "Youths Turn to Web, Magazines," *The Wall Street Journal* (October 18, 2002), pp. B1, B4; Anonymous, "Living on After 9/11," *Advertising Age* 73(10)(March 11, 2002), p. 18+; Hillary Chura, "The New Normal," *Advertising Age*, 73(10)(March 11, 2002), pp. 1, 4.

Successful marketers recognize the importance of putting the customer first—always. Leading marketing and management gurus have maintained for many years that the primary objective of a business is to create customer satisfaction—with profit as a reward rather than an objective. In other words, when the customer is satisfied, everyone benefits—the company and its stockholders, suppliers, employees, and others. A satisfied customer finds value in a firm's goods and services and is willing to pay a reasonable price for them.[2] Thus marketing strategy must be based on a thorough understanding of customers' needs, wants, and buying behavior, as well as how they define *value* in a rapidly changing marketplace.

Discussion in preceding chapters has paved the way for developing an understanding of **consumer behavior,** defined as "the study of the buying units and the exchange processes involved in acquiring, consuming, and disposing of goods, services, experiences, and ideas."[3] Note that this definition includes acquisition, consumption, and disposition in the exchange process for both tangible and intangible items. Likewise, this definition applies to both for-profit and nonprofit consumers.

Consumer behavior
Study of buying units and exchange processes involved in acquiring, consuming, and disposing of goods, services, experiences, and ideas.

Consumer researchers are interested not only in how, why, where, and when customers buy but also in how they use the goods and services after purchase (perhaps for new uses or in different ways than originally intended) and how they dispose of goods once they no longer have a use for them (e.g., recycle, resale, etc.).

Previous chapters have stressed the importance of monitoring changes in the marketing environment to assess the potential for new market opportunities or threats to the organization. Timely and accurate environmental information is a critical element in market forecasting and developing strategic and tactical plans. Throughout this book, marketing is discussed from the perspective of customer-oriented value exchange, where long-term relationships benefit all parties involved in the exchange process as each party receives something of value from the other. The relationship between the study of consumer behavior and the strategic planning process is illustrated in Figure 5.1.

If value is the key to satisfying exchange relationships, then who defines *value*? In the past, the seller defined value—generally in terms of product features, low price, distribution method, and other company-oriented criteria. Today, however,

FIGURE 5.1

Consumers and Strategic Planning

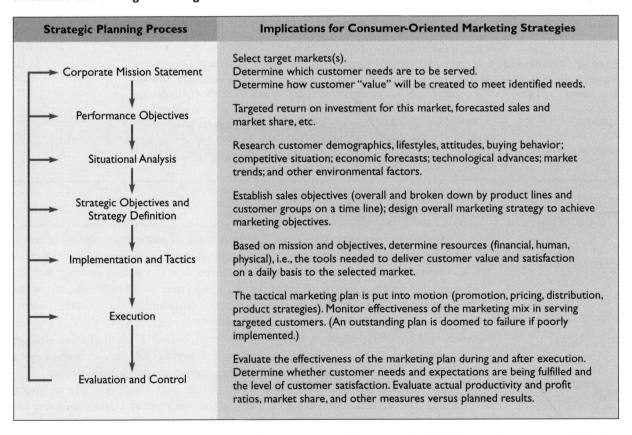

Source: Adapted from Anderson, Carol H. (1993), *Retailing: Concepts, Strategy and Information,* St. Paul, MN: West Publishing Company, Exhibit 6-1, pp. 225, 227.

Customer value
All the benefits derived from a total product and all the costs of acquiring those benefits.

value is defined in the marketplace by the customer. **Customer value** can be defined as "all the benefits derived from a total product and all the costs of acquiring those benefits."[4] This definition is in keeping with the new marketing concept that creates customer value throughout the entire marketing process by combining a customer orientation with total quality management principles. The result is a higher level of satisfaction among customers, employees, suppliers, and others, as well as higher profits for the company and its shareholders.

In this chapter we will discuss the consumer buying process, buying influences and motivations, and relationship marketing as it applies to final consumers. Successful marketing programs rely on a clear understanding of consumer needs and preferences relative to all aspects of the marketing mix—starting with the product offer and extending to an understanding of consumer responses to various pricing, distribution, and promotional strategies.

THE CONSUMER BUYING PROCESS

Consumer buying process
Five stages in consumer purchase decisions: need recognition, information search, evaluation of alternatives, purchase decision, and postpurchase evaluation.

The **consumer buying process** generally consists of five stages of related activities: (1) recognition of a need, (2) search for information, (3) evaluation of alternatives, (4) choice/purchase, and (5) postpurchase evaluation. (See Figure 5.2.) Consumers may expend a great deal of effort when making a purchase decision, or they simply may treat the purchase as a routine problem-solving situation where

FIGURE 5.2

Consumer Buying Process and Level of Involvement

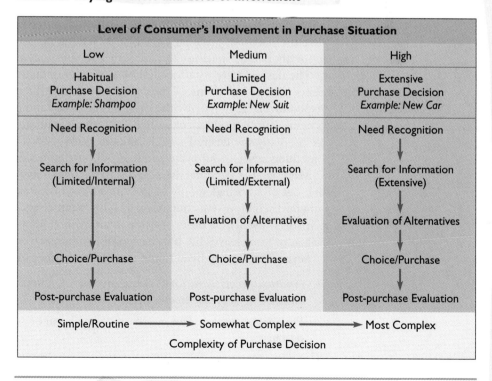

minimal effort is required. The level of complexity of consumer decision making is directly related to the consumer's level of involvement[5] with the purchase situation (rather than involvement with the product or product class). Consumer decision making is categorized as habitual, limited, or extended. The more involved the customer is in the purchase situation, the more complex is the decision process. Likewise, lower involvement results in routine or limited effort in arriving at a decision, as shown in Figure 5.2.

While we tend to think of this process in terms of specific products or brands, it also applies to the consumer's choice of specifically where and how to shop (e.g., retail store, home shopping network, etc.). In fact, many purchases start with the selection of a shopping center or store rather than with a particular product or product category. In Figure 5.3, a hypothetical automobile purchase is used to illustrate the various stages of the consumer buying process as they are described in the following sections.

Recognition of a Need

The purchase decision process starts with the recognition of a deficiency or felt need. This may be a specific need for a specific product (e.g., a required textbook for school) or an ill-defined sense of wanting or needing something (e.g., need for recreation to relieve stress from work or intense study or desire to munch on snack food). Social, physical, or psychological stimuli in the consumer's environment can create a sense of imbalance that is likely to awaken a consumer need—thus starting the consumer buying process, as illustrated by the automobile purchase example in Figure 5.3.

When a consumer perceives that a significant difference exists between the actual and desired situation relative to a potential purchase, he or she is motivated to solve the purchase problem. However, this difference must be sufficiently large and important enough to cause the consumer to take action. (See Figure 5.4.)

The desired state is influenced by a number of factors, with the consumer's reference groups being one of the most important influences. Consumer choices are shaped to a large degree by the opinions of family and friends, as well as the desire to emulate role models, celebrities, and others whom the consumer aspires to be like. Similarly, the desired state is influenced by a consumer's desire to experience something new—to innovate and to do or have something different.

Major factors affecting the actual state include a recognized deficiency (i.e., running out of a normal supply of goods), a state of physical or emotional disequilibrium or discomfort (e.g., hunger, headache, weather changes, unexpected invitation to a social event), or dissatisfaction with a previous purchase (i.e., postpurchase evaluation) that leaves the purchase problem unresolved.

Seven factors have been found to influence either the desired or actual state:[6]

1. *Financial considerations.* These involve the effect of a present or anticipated increase or decrease in income.

2. *Previous decisions.* The purchase of one good or service often triggers related purchases.

3. *Family characteristics.* Different goods and services are appropriate for changing family life cycle stages.

FIGURE 5.3

Consumer Buying Process for an Automobile

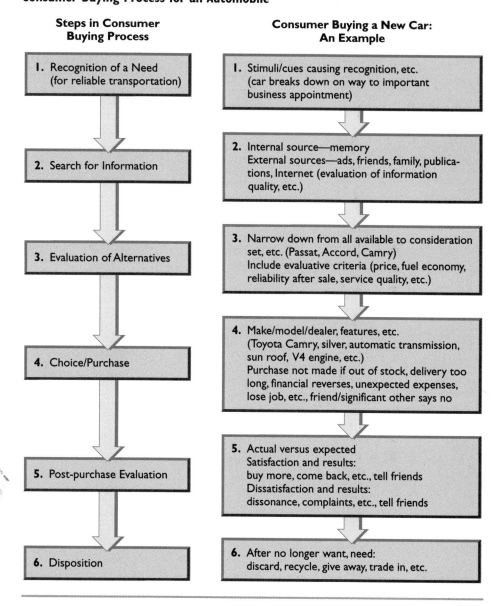

	Steps in Consumer Buying Process	Consumer Buying a New Car: An Example

1. Recognition of a Need (for reliable transportation)
2. Search for Information
3. Evaluation of Alternatives
4. Choice/Purchase
5. Post-purchase Evaluation
6. Disposition

1. Stimuli/cues causing recognition, etc. (car breaks down on way to important business appointment)
2. Internal source—memory
   External sources—ads, friends, family, publications, Internet (evaluation of information quality, etc.)
3. Narrow down from all available to consideration set, etc. (Passat, Accord, Camry)
   Include evaluative criteria (price, fuel economy, reliability after sale, service quality, etc.)
4. Make/model/dealer, features, etc. (Toyota Camry, silver, automatic transmission, sun roof, V4 engine, etc.)
   Purchase not made if out of stock, delivery too long, financial reverses, unexpected expenses, lose job, etc., friend/significant other says no
5. Actual versus expected
   Satisfaction and results:
   buy more, come back, etc., tell friends
   Dissatisfaction and results:
   dissonance, complaints, etc., tell friends
6. After no longer want, need:
   discard, recycle, give away, trade in, etc.

4. *Culture and social class.* These serve as a point of reference for what and where to buy.

5. *Individual development.* Different needs are based on physical and psychological development.

6. *Current situation.* This includes time constraints, weather, distance, and type of purchase.

7. *Marketing efforts.* These involve awareness and the desire for a new product as a result of promotional efforts.

FIGURE 5.4

Recognition of a Consumer Purchase Problem

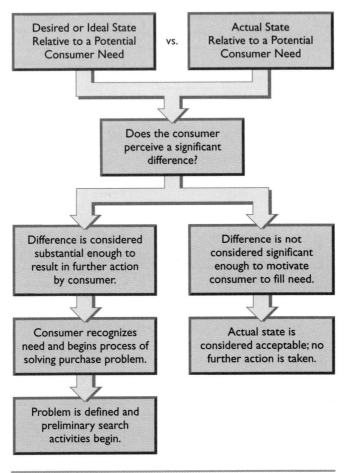

Search for Information

The consumer process may not go beyond the recognition of a need in circumstances such as the following: (1) the need is not imminent, and search can be postponed, (2) the need is not important enough to warrant action, or (3) insufficient time, money, or dealer access makes it impossible to act when the need is identified. But, once a consumer need has been recognized, the consumer may or may not engage in search activities, the next step in the consumer process. (See Figure 5.5.)

There are several types of consumer search activities: internal, external, prepurchase, and ongoing search. Prepurchase search may be either internal or external. It may or may not be focused on a specific consumer need, although search efforts are directed toward making a better purchase decision to solve a purchase problem.

Internal search consists of searching one's memory for relevant experiences and information that can be applied to the present purchase problem. This is the predominant type of search activity engaged in for most consumer purchases. Thus

Internal search
Searching one's memory for relevant experiences and information to solve a purchase problem.

FIGURE 5.5

Consumer Information Search

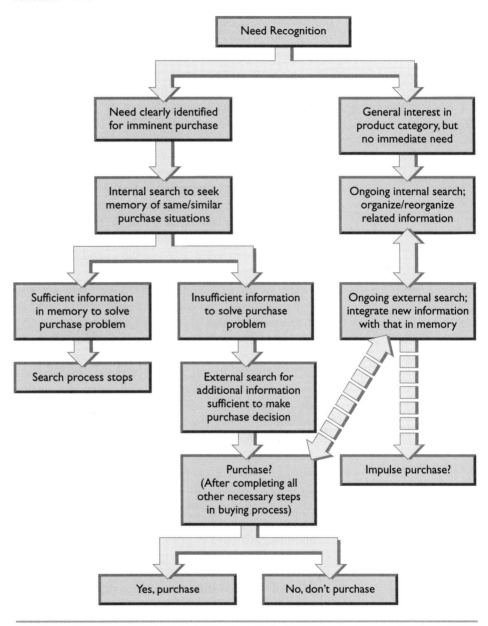

it is important for marketers to keep potential customers constantly informed about their products and brands and to encourage repeat purchases that require little or no search effort.

External search is a more complex process that involves a proactive approach to obtaining information from personal, social, government, marketing, and other sources. The information obtained through external search may result in additional search as the consumer gains new information and learns about other alternatives to solve the purchase problem.

External search
More proactive, complex process of obtaining information from personal, social, government, marketing, and other sources.

Many consumers engage in ongoing search to learn more about a certain product class, gathering information to use in future purchases. For many people, ongoing search is a pleasurable activity that enables them to build a base of information for future use. It also gives them status among their friends and family as an opinion leader who is knowledgeable about a particular product class—such as cars, health foods, or travel destinations. Ongoing search is particularly evident among the growing number of collectors—those who are constantly looking for, selecting, and purchasing previously discarded items. Collectibles run the gamut from baseball trading cards to vintage automobiles, teddy bears to milk pitchers in the shape of cows, and almost anything imaginable.

The challenge to marketers is to motivate the consumer to make a purchase based on the recognized need. Thus marketers must make it easy for consumers to obtain the necessary information to make an informed decision. Much of this information is provided in advance of the recognized need—and in fact may trigger the felt need through advertising, sales presentations, advance publicity, trial, and other methods. Providing information early in the consumer buying process is an important element of internal search, to keep a company's products and brands at the top of the consumer's mind and thus have an impact on the final purchase decision. Most consumer search efforts consist of searching one's memory for similar buying experiences and stored information that is relevant to the present situation. When information stored in memory is insufficient or unreliable, the consumer will consult external sources.

Information sources for external search include personal or group sources, marketing sources, public or independent sources, and personal experience. One of the most effective methods of promoting an organization's products and services is through word of mouth among family, friends, acquaintances, and other reference group members with whom the customer comes in contact. Although personal sources tend to have the highest level of credibility with consumers, they are the most difficult for marketers to manage effectively.

Marketing sources include advertising, salespeople, catalogs, online computer services, packages, displays, and so forth. Information from marketing sources is generally targeted toward prospective customers through the most appropriate media, stores, and other means of communication. McDonald's advertising can be found on television and radio stations, in newspapers and magazines, direct mailings, heavy couponing, point-of-sale materials, and sales promotion activities. The fast-food chain supports many local events and benefits from positive word-of-mouth promotion among its customers. McDonald's also communicates with PC users through the company's Web site, www.mcdonalds.com, which includes links to an international restaurant locator, information about the Ronald McDonald House Charities (RMHC) at www.rmhc.com, and corporate information. There is a special site for children called "Ronald and Friends" (www.ronald.com), introduced as "The Internet's Land for Fun" where children can play games, print out pages to color, and engage in other forms of play. A Parent's Page is included to urge parents to monitor and supervise their children's online activities. McDonald's communicates with its viewers not only with words, but also logos and character icons that are interwoven into the content of each Web page.[7]

Public sources of information are made available to consumers through publications such as *Consumer Reports* and information disseminated by government agencies, newspaper articles, and publicity. Consumers tend to view this information as the most objective and reliable, since it is made available by an independent source and is not paid for by the marketer.

The amount of effort that the consumer is willing to expend in information search is determined by factors such as the amount of experience in making similar purchases; the search cost in terms of time and money; the amount of financial, social, physical, emotional, or other risks involved in making the "wrong" decision; and the degree of difference among the various purchase options.

Evaluation of Alternatives

Once the consumer has gathered the necessary information from internal and/or external sources to determine the alternatives available to satisfy a recognized consumer need, the next step is to weigh the identified alternatives according to a set of important criteria. (See Figure 5.6.) Both objective and subjective criteria may be used in evaluating purchase alternatives.

Objective criteria may include specific product features, such as price, design characteristics, warranty, performance measures, or other factors that can be compared easily across products, brands, and companies. In selecting a new home, a young family with children may focus on the price of the home, required down payment, mortgage terms, property taxes, distance to schools, quality of schools, and so forth.

Subjective criteria are more elusive, since they tend to focus on symbolic aspects of the product, style, and perceived benefits that the consumer expects to obtain from the purchase, such as status or pleasure. For the family purchasing a home, subjective criteria might include an element of nostalgia (past memories of a similar childhood home), feelings of safety or status, aesthetic responses to architectural features and landscaping, odors detected in the house, and a reaction to neighbors they happen to meet.

Quality and value, perhaps the most important purchase criteria considered by consumers, may be viewed as either objective or subjective components of a value-added strategy. These are discussed later in this chapter within the context of building relationships with customers.

Although consumers may consider a wide range of criteria in the process of evaluating purchase alternatives, the importance of each of these criteria may be weighted quite differently. In most buying situations, only a few salient criteria are used by the consumer in making the final purchase decision. Evaluative criteria apply not only to the goods and services being considered for purchase but also to entire product classes, brands, companies, countries of origin, and retail outlets.

Choice/Purchase

After the consumer has gathered information during the search process and ranked the various alternatives based on important purchase criteria, he or she is prepared to make a purchase decision. All potential brands and products can be placed into two major categories: an awareness set (products and brands known to the consumer) and an unawareness set (products and brands unknown to the consumer). The awareness set can be broken down further into three subcategories: *consideration set* (also called the *evoked set,* products and brands that the consumer actually would consider buying), *inert set* (products and brands that the consumer

FIGURE 5.6

Evaluation of Alternatives

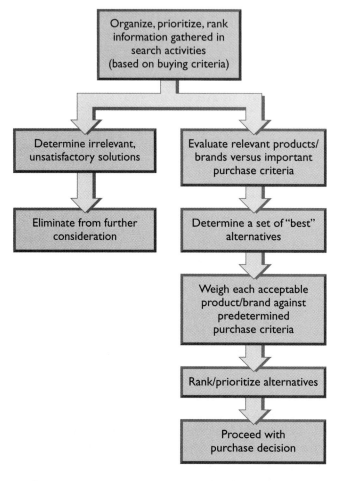

Note: This process also applies to selection of retailer and purchase method.

is indifferent toward, holding neither a strongly positive nor strongly negative attitude toward them), and *inept set* (products and brands that are known but are totally unacceptable to the consumer).

The extra baggy grunge look and hip-hop fashion became the consideration set for apparel worn by Generation X consumers in the 1990s. Conservative clothing could be classified as the inept set—totally unacceptable to this market. As youth fashions evolved into the late 1990s, grunge and hip-hop fashions gave way to styles inspired by 1950s, 1960s, and 1970s films and memorabilia—a sort of "retro" look (e.g., Converse high-top sneakers) or "thrift shop" or army surplus image. These fashions, too, have passed from the consideration set into the inert or inept categories for Generation Y (10–24 year-olds). Because fashion cycles are relatively short, new designs must be created constantly to satisfy customers and maintain brand loyalty.

Within this discussion, it is assumed that a choice is made and a purchase is completed at this point in the consumer buying process. However, a consumer may make a choice but not actually purchase for several reasons: the retailer is out of stock on the item, the customer may find a better (previously unknown) alternative at point of purchase, the customer has insufficient funds or credit is not available, someone else (e.g., friend, salesperson) makes negative comments about the customer's choice, and other factors.

Postpurchase Evaluation

The consumer buying process does not stop with the purchase act. In creating customer value, marketers find that follow-up after the sale is an essential element in delivering customer satisfaction and building long-term relationships. The level of customer satisfaction is determined by the difference between expectations and performance. When the marketer delivers more than the customer expects, the result is a higher level of satisfaction. Likewise, when the actual performance of a product or sales experience does not meet customer expectations, dissatisfaction results, as shown in Figure 5.7.

Successful marketers measure customer satisfaction in several ways. For example, hotels make customer response surveys readily available in guest rooms, and restaurants provide them on tables or with the check. Investment companies, banks, and a vast array of consumer product companies invite customers to provide feedback on their products and purchase experiences. The availability of 800 numbers, interactive Web sites, knowledgeable and well-trained customer service representatives, salespeople, and managers provides customers with ways to communicate both positively and negatively with the company. Satisfied customers are repeat customers. It is much less expensive to convert dissatisfied customers into satisfied customers than it is to attract new customers. Thus marketers need to know how they are evaluated after the sale.

● SOCIAL AND CULTURAL INFLUENCES ON BUYING BEHAVIOR

Consumers function not only as individuals but also as members of a complex society that has a significant impact on purchase decisions. Therefore, the buying process is influenced by factors in the consumer's external environment as well as factors internal to the individual. Although many of these influences are beyond the direct control of the marketer, they must be considered carefully in designing effective marketing programs.

Consumer socialization
Process whereby people acquire the knowledge, skills, and attitudes necessary to perform as consumers.

Human behavior, including consumer behavior, is learned through a socialization process starting at a very young age and continuing throughout one's life. **Consumer socialization** is the process that enables people to acquire the knowledge, skills, and attitudes necessary to perform as consumers. Cultural values and norms are transmitted to the individual through direct or indirect interaction with other members of society, referred to as *socialization agents*. Direct socialization may occur through contact with friends, family, peers, or other "up-close" relationships. Indirect socialization may occur through the media, business efforts, the government, or other sources that do not have direct contact with the person being socialized. Marketers who know and understand their customers can be major agents in the

FIGURE 5.7

Postpurchase Evaluation

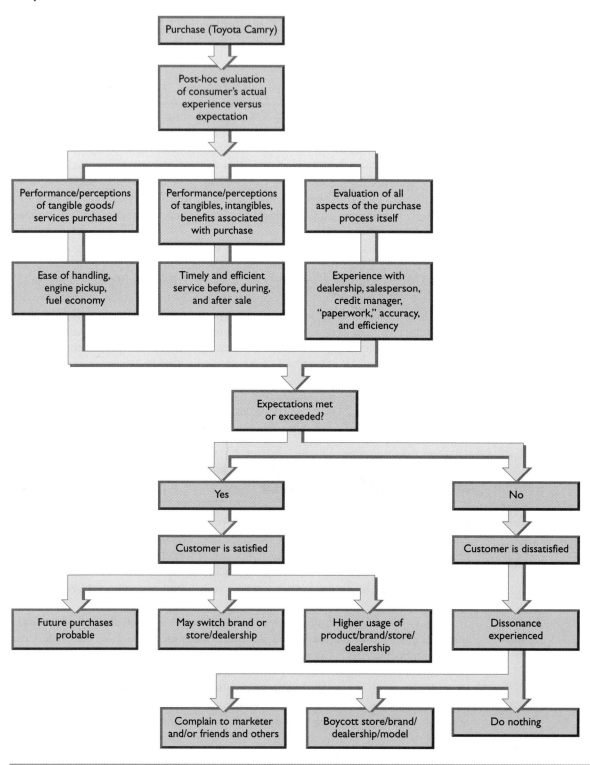

consumer socialization process as they develop long-term relationships consistent with cultural norms.

Cultural and Social Status

An individual's culture, subculture, and social class are considered the most important societal influences on buying behavior. A person's needs, wants, behaviors, and values are shaped by the society in which he or she lives.

> **Culture**
> The complex of learned values and behaviors shared by a society.

Culture.   A **culture** is defined as "the complex of learned values and behaviors that are shared by a society and are designed to increase the probability of the society's survival."[8] Culture supplies the individual with enduring core values and boundaries for behavior. Since culture is learned behavior, its influence is subject to change with new knowledge and experience; however, this process is very slow and complex.

MARKETING IN THE INFORMATION AGE

Online Banking: Technology and CRM

Consumers throughout the world have been quick to embrace the Internet and e-commerce as an integral part of their lives. However, large numbers of potential e-commerce customers are reluctant to make purchases on the Internet. Although the number of people who are getting online has grown slightly (34 percent in 2002 versus 31 percent in 2001), the number of users who actually made a purchase in 2002 remained stagnant at 15 percent, the same percentage as in 2001.

Data contained in the third annual Taylor Nelson Sofres (TNS) Interactive "Global e-Commerce Report" of 42,000 people across 37 countries indicated that growth in online users in June 2002 was hampered primarily by fears about online payment security. E-tailers failed to assure a large number of consumers that it is safe to shop online in the Information Age. Thirty percent of Internet users who had not shopped online were reluctant to give their credit card details; and 28 percent felt safer shopping in stores. For the third consecutive

year, the United States had the largest proportion of Internet users who were online shoppers (32 percent—1 percent lower than 2001). They also were the biggest spenders at an average $162 during the four weeks studied, compared to the worldwide figure of $99. Online shopping gained the most usage for 2002 in South Korea, Norway, and France. The greatest declines were in Ukraine, Australia, Czech Republic, and Finland.

One form of e-commerce that has increased in popularity is online banking, although growth has been slower than many analysts expected. The two-way flow of information between a bank and its customers enables the customer to have instant account information and access to a variety of transactions, and allows them to interact with the bank online. The bank has access to a wealth of financial and personal information about its customers that it can use to build closer relationships through customer relationship management (CRM) programs. As banks have merged and expanded, focus on a close relationship with local customers has shifted to the problems of

(continued)

developing close relationships with a customer base that is sprawled over multiple regions, with different responses to marketing programs.

The advantages of using high-tech methods to distribute goods and services are often diminished if there is not an opportunity for customer feedback. Online surveys are one way to gather immediate information about customers' satisfaction with the online banking process, services offered, the bank's reputation, and so forth. Advances in technology and low cost make this approach effective in gathering information for CRM programs. Customer satisfaction is key to customer relationship marketing, and customer service is continually identified as a weak spot for financial institutions. Many banks have been focused on internal issues over the past decade, driven largely by mergers, cost cutting, and reengineering, and customer service received little attention. At the same time, the industry has raised fees to increase noninterest income.

Poor customer service has led many of the best customers to transfer their accounts to other financial services providers, particularly nonbank brokerage and mutual fund companies. A 2001 survey found that nearly half of customers agreed "it wouldn't take a lot" for them to move their money to another institution—if the other institution really treated them well. To stop this loss of disenchanted customers, banks have recognized the need to improve their customer feedback mechanisms, and to do so at the time and place of transactions. Bankers have adopted a wide range of information-gathering techniques including complaint data analysis; call center exit surveys; employee feedback groups; customer focus groups, and online surveys. These approaches are supplemented with more traditional market research tools. CRM relies on these data when developing customer loyalty programs that are based on a clear understanding of customers' thoughts and feelings.

The newer data-gathering techniques used by banks are intended to obtain more in-depth information about consumer reactions and emotions closer to the time and place of a transaction (i.e., immediacy). The key to getting feedback with a minimum of distraction is to intertwine queries into the usual customer–bank interaction. Responses are fresher, and banks can leverage the contacts they already have with their customers without bothering them. This must be done carefully because online surveys have the potential to annoy customers if they are too much like "spam" mail.

As more customers use Internet banking, the online survey becomes a valuable tool for immediate customer feedback. First Union's Web site, for example, offers the opportunity to make service-related comments, on the homepage or mortgage applications. A select group of customers, such as those who use the bill-pay service, may receive additional targeted surveys. According to Gayle Wellborn, senior vice president in First Union's e-channel division, "We've incorporated a lot more of the customer's voice in the design and creation of products and services up front." There is a caution when using online surveys, however. Between 15 and 25 percent of American households have at least tried online banking, but a lower percentage uses it on a regular basis. Customer information added to the company's database may be skewed and not accurately reflect the opinions of their larger customer base.

Effective marketing in the Information Age is based on strategies that build trust and long-term relationships. The information that goes into CRM databases must be representative of targeted customers. The company must listen carefully to what customers have to say, and take the appropriate actions to improve customer satisfaction.

Source: Johanna Knapschaefer, "Reading the Customer," *Banking Strategies* 78(1) (January/February 2002), http://www.bai.org/bankingstrategies/2002-jan-feb/; "Cyber-nervous" *Marketing News* (August 19, 2002), p. 3.

Cultural values are disseminated primarily through three basic institutions: the family, educational institutions, and religious organizations. With the decline of the traditional American family and the values associated with it and the movement of many young people away from religious organizations, schools have become an important force in the transmission of cultural values.

Consumer behavior is affected by three broad categories of values that vary across cultures:[9] self-oriented, environment-oriented, and other-oriented values. These categories can be broken down as follows:

- *Self-oriented values.* Self-oriented values are objectives and approaches to life that are desirable to individual members of society. They can be classified as active/passive, material/nonmaterial, hard work/leisure, postponed/immediate gratification, sensual gratification/abstinence, and humorous/serious.

- *Environment-oriented values.* Environment-oriented values prescribe a society's relationship with its economic, technical, and physical environments. They can be expressed as maximum/minimum cleanliness, performance/status, tradition/change, risk-taking/security, problem-solving/fatalistic, and admire/overcome nature.

- *Other-oriented values.* Other-oriented values are a society's view of appropriate relationships between individuals and groups within that society, such as individual/collective, limited/extended family, adult/child, competition/cooperation, youth/age, and masculine/feminine.

Subculture
Identifiable subgroup within a culture that shares values and patterns of behavior that are distinguishable from the overall culture.

Subculture. Diverse populations can be categorized into subcultures. A **subculture** is an identifiable group "within a culture that shares distinguishing values and patterns of behavior that differ from the overall culture."[10] The more heterogeneous a population, the more subcultures that can be identified within it. Each subculture determines its own set of values and acceptable behaviors, which are followed to varying degrees by its members. Subcultures may be identified on the basis of race, nationality, religion, age, geographic location, and other dimensions. Because buying motives and behaviors tend to be relatively consistent among the more narrowly defined subcultures, they are attractive target markets for marketing efforts. See Table 5.1 for a comprehensive subculture comparison of age-cohort groups.

Social class
An individual's status in society generally based primarily on occupation, education, and income.

Social Stratification. Social status or **social class** represents another important societal influence on buying behavior. While social class structure is less evident in the United States than in many other countries, marketers and social scientists find it useful to determine a person's social status based on occupation, education, income, and other relevant dimensions. Although several acceptable systems are used to measure social class, they generally result in three broad class designations (upper, middle, and lower class) that can be subdivided further as shown in Table 5.2.

Consumption behavior is influenced significantly by the amount of prestige or esteem associated with a particular social class. Those within a certain social class tend to be similar in their purchase behaviors for goods and services—particularly visible items such as clothing, houses, cars, and recreational activities (e.g., restaurants, sports, travel, and other leisure activities). Although two consumers in different social classes may have the same amount of money to spend, they can be expected to spend it differently. For example, two teenage girls—one upper class and one lower middle class—may be shopping for gifts for family members.

TABLE 5.1

Subculture Comparisons Across Age-Cohort Groups

Characteristic	Cohort Group		
	Depression Cohort (GI Generation)	*World War II Cohort (Depression Generation)*	*Postwar Cohort (Silent Generation)*
Years born	1912–1921	1922–1927	1928–1945
Age in 2002	81–90	75–80	57–74
Attitude toward money	Positive toward saving; negative toward debt; carry financial scars	Keep spending down and savings up; self-denial	Balance between saving and spending
Attitude toward sex	Intolerant	Ambivalent	Repressive
Music preferences	Big Band Era	Swing	Frank Sinatra (youngest segment was the "cool generation," first to dig folk, rock)
Other	First to be strongly influenced by contemporary media (radio, movies)	Shared experience of common enemy and common goal; intensely romantic	"War babies"; long period of economic growth and social stability; global unrest and nuclear threat

The lower-class teenager may have more money to spend because her family expects her to work after school to earn money for many of her own consumer needs (as well as do well in school), whereas the upper-class teenager may have only money from allowances or occasional jobs because more of her time is focused on academic achievement, personal development, and social activities.

Many children's clothes and toys are targeted at different social segments. For example, the ever popular Winnie-the-Pooh merchandise can be found at a variety of retailers. The older, original characters' merchandise is found at exclusive, higher-priced stores such as FAO Schwartz and Tiffany. The "newer" Winnie-the-Pooh and friends' merchandise can be bought at lower-priced stores such as Kmart, Wal-Mart, and Target.

Group Influences

Consumers belong to a variety of groups—each with its own way of influencing purchasing behavior. Since it is difficult, if not impossible, for a consumer to act in complete isolation from others, it is important for marketers to understand the role of group influence in the consumption process. Individuals look to group members to define what is acceptable and unacceptable according to the group's norms, values, and beliefs. The groups that have the greatest impact on the formation of attitudes and behavior are *reference groups* and *family*. However, the influence of either of these groups is strengthened or weakened by the individual's *role* (real or perceived) and relative *position* within each group.

TABLE 5.1 *(continued)*

Subculture Comparisons Across Age-Cohort Groups

Characteristic	Cohort Group			
	Baby-Boomers I Cohort (Woodstock Generation)	Baby-Boomers II Cohort (Zoomers)	Generation X Cohort* (Baby-Busters)	Generation Y Cohort ("Youthquake")
Years born	1946–1954	1955–1965	1966–1976	Population burst from ±1980 to present
Age in 2002	48–56	37–47	26–36	11–25 years Under 10 years
Attitude toward money	"Spend, borrow, spend"	"Spend, borrow, spend"; debt acceptable to maintain lifestyle	"Spend? Save? What?"	Both groups indulged by parents
Attitude toward sex	Permissive	Permissive	Confused	Indications are they will be similar to baby-boomer parents
Music preferences	Rock and roll	Rock and roll	Grunge, rap, retro	Varied
Other	Vietnam divides leading-edge and trailing-edge baby-boomers; Kennedy and King assassinations had major impact; economic good times and optimism for early baby-boomers	Youthful idealism disappeared with Watergate; later baby-boomers exhibited narcissistic preoccupation with self; age of downward mobility	Slacker set, cynicism and pessimism; latchkey kids of day care and divorce; political conservatism; "What's in it for me?"	Technologically adept; education a priority; environmentally conscious; achievement oriented; tolerant of diversity; socially "in-the-know"; greater gap between the "haves" and "have-nots"

*Birth years vary for Generation Xers; some experts designate the years from 1961–1981.

Sources: Adapted from Faye Rice, "Making Generational Marketing Come of Age," *Fortune* (June 26, 1995), pp. 110–114; Melinda Beck, "Next Population Bulge Shows Its Might," *Wall Street Journal* (February 3, 1997), pp. B1, B5; Jonathan Kaufman, "At Age 5, Reading, Writing, and Rushing," *Wall Street Journal* (February 4, 1997), pp. B1, B2; Ellen Graham, "When Terrible Twos Become Terrible Teens," *Wall Street Journal* (February 5, 1997), pp. B1, B8; and other sources.

Reference groups
Groups that become a point of reference for an individual's behavior, beliefs, and attitudes.

Reference Groups.   People generally have a number of **reference groups** (or individual reference persons) that they use as a point of reference for their own behavior, beliefs, and attitudes. Consumers adopt and imitate the values of these groups but may look to different reference groups at different times based on proximity, purchase situation, and product class.

TABLE 5.2

Social Class Hierarchy

Upper Americans (about 14 percent of population)

Upper-uppers (0.3 percent)
Inherited wealth (i.e., old money), old aristocratic family names, charitable giving, multiple homes, prestigious schools, fine jewelry, luxury vacations, investments, imitated by other classes

Lower-uppers (1.2 percent)
High income or wealth earned through business or professions (i.e., new money; newer social elite), most moved up from middle class, active in social and civic affairs, achievement oriented, purchases represent status

Upper-middles (about 12.5 percent)
Well educated, intellectual elite, and professionals; lifestyle involves private clubs ("joiners"), causes, arts; quality homes (in "right" neighborhood); quality clothes, furniture, appliances

Middle Americans

Middle class (32 percent)
Both average-pay white- and blue-collar workers; live on "better side of town" and try to "do the proper things" (respectability); focus on family; most have completed high school and may have some college; aim children toward college

Working class (38 percent)
Average-pay blue-collar workers and/or those who lead a "working-class lifestyle"—regardless of income, education, or employment; tend to stay close to home and parents and relatives, and to live in older parts of town; comprise mass market for consumer goods

Lower Americans

Upper-lower (9 percent)
"Working poor"; living standard just above poverty level; not on welfare; unskilled and poorly paid but striving to move up to higher class; behavior may be judged "crude" or "trashy"

Lower-lower (7 percent)
On welfare (public aid or charity), visibly poverty stricken; out of work or working "dirtiest jobs"; includes indigents, criminals; some are prone to every form of instant gratification if money is available; others struggle to achieve what they believe will be their heavenly reward for resisting earthly temptations

---

Sources: Adapted from Richard P. Coleman, "The Continuing Significance of Social Class in Marketing," *Journal of Consumer Research* 10 (December 1983), pp. 265–280; and Del I. Hawkins, Roger J. Best, and Kenneth A. Coney, *Consumer Behavior: Building Marketing Strategy,* 8th ed. (Boston, MA: Irwin McGraw-Hill, 2001) p. 122.

Primary reference groups
Influential individuals that the customer interacts face-to-face with most frequently.

The proximity of reference groups can be described as either primary or secondary. **Primary reference groups** may be formal or informal and include individuals the customer interacts with most frequently on a face-to-face basis, such as family, friends, and co-workers. (Family influences on purchase decisions are discussed later in this section.) Reference group influence is most noticeable in the purchase of highly visible goods and services that are intended to show conformance to the norms of a particular group.

Secondary reference groups
Groups that influence consumer decisions despite the fact that there is little or no interpersonal contact with the consumer.

Secondary reference groups may or may not involve formal membership and generally are those with whom the consumer has little or no interpersonal contact. Membership groups include those of which an individual is automatically a member (such as gender, age, marital status, social status) or may be those which a person joins and "belongs to." Groups that an individual belongs to may be primarily personal (e.g., social club, church, work group, college class) or nonpersonal (e.g., American Automobile Association, frequent fliers program, political party).

Reference Groups Can Be Positive or Negative. A *positive reference group* represents desirable values and beliefs and is one to which a person aspires to belong, that is, an *aspiration* group. For example, people tend to dress like others they admire in their work group, particularly those with higher status. Cosmetic manufacturers are benefiting from a worldwide trend among young women to emulate American women in using makeup. Avon is selling lipsticks and other beauty aids in "back road" areas of eastern Europe, veiled Muslim women in Kurachi and ex-Communists in Prague are buying American beauty brands with reformulated products and colors that appeal to local preferences, and Max Factor sells Vidal Sassoon hair products in the Far East (adding a pine aroma to some shampoos). These and other examples of American-type cosmetics sold overseas illustrate the concept of *mass customization,* adapting one basic product with minor modifications to satisfy the needs of a target market—in this case markets that see attractive American women as a reference group.

In contrast, a *negative reference group* is one that a person dissociates with as having totally unacceptable norms, beliefs, and behaviors, that is, a *dissociative* group—or a negative point of reference. For example, motorcycle manufacturers have been faced with the problem of dissociating their brands from Hells Angels or other bikers with a negative image. Negative reference groups occur in every strata of society. Teenagers avoid cars or clothing that they associate with older people. Even small children influence purchases based on reference group perceptions, as experienced by OshKosh B'Gosh, Inc., a manufacturer of work clothes. In the 1980s, well-dressed babies wore tiny bib overalls and work clothes from OshKosh. However, the company's image became closely associated with children's clothes, making it difficult for OshKosh to sell clothes to anyone else. A line of older children's clothes failed because they refused to wear baby clothes. The negative image also caused line extensions in adult apparel to fail.

Family of orientation
Family an individual is born into; shapes long-term attitudes and behavior.

Family Influence. Consumer decisions are influenced by two types of family: family of orientation and family of procreation. The **family of orientation** is the one that an individual is born to or adopted into and that shapes attitudes and behavior that tend to endure from childhood throughout one's lifetime. Parents give their children their first lessons in consumer behavior—the best kinds of food to eat, brands to buy, movies to see, television to watch, stores to shop in, and generally what is acceptable and unacceptable consumer behavior. A large percentage of a family's shopping is done by teenage children of working parents. This early influence carries on when the child is grown and no longer has to shop to please his or her parents.

Family of procreation
Family that an individual starts with his or her own spouse and children.

The **family of procreation** is formed when the individual starts his or her own family and has a spouse and children. Consumer needs, wants, and buying roles change as new families are formed. Changes in today's lifestyles have a major impact on traditional consumer roles of the past. It is important for marketers to know and understand the various consumer roles played by family members and how these affect purchase behavior.

Family purchase decisions are influenced by size of the family and stage in the family life cycle, as illustrated in Table 5.3. Census data and marketing research indicate that it is more appropriate today to extend the family life cycle concept to the broader concept of a household life cycle. Households are the basic unit of consumption in the United States, making it essential to understand their composition. As noted in Chapter 2, the number of single-person households has increased significantly, along with an increase in nontraditional households (single parent with children, same-sex couples, cohabiting singles, and so forth). This trend must be monitored by marketers to determine consumer preferences for brands and goods and services, packaging specifications, distribution methods, and other marketing mix decisions.

Life Roles and Status in Groups. Each person plays many roles throughout his or her lifetime. Some of these endure over a long period of time (e.g., son, daughter, mother, father), whereas others exist for a relatively brief time (e.g., president of a professional association, work supervisor). Each of the roles that a person performs—often simultaneously—has a set of expectations (and consumer needs) associated with it that have a major influence on buying behavior.

Individuals with the highest status in a group tend to set and enforce the group norms for most aspects of personal behavior. Those with lower status are most likely to adopt the values and behaviors of the group leader. Parents set the expectations for children in a family—what they will eat or wear and what is acceptable behavior at home and away from home. The status of religious leaders, politicians, sports heroes, musicians, actors/actresses, and other prominent individuals provides a reference point for their followers, thus influencing the purchase (or avoidance) of many goods and services. Consumers are most likely to make purchases that communicate their status (real or perceived) to others, that is, status symbols. As marketers build relationships with their customers, it is important to know and understand their life roles and the status associated with these roles to create customer value consistent with these roles.

● INDIVIDUAL INFLUENCES ON BUYING BEHAVIOR

Most of the influences just described are external in nature, although some have internal influence implications through interaction with one another. When we consider consumers as individuals, the primary influences on buying behavior are related more to personal characteristics and psychological factors. These are internal to the individual and thus more resilient to persuasive marketing tactics that are intended to change consumer attitudes and behaviors.

Personal Influences

Personal characteristics include age and stage in life cycle (discussed with family influence), occupation, economic circumstances, lifestyle, personality, and self-concept.

Life cycle stage
Family or household status, along with age, related to consumer lifestyles and preferences.

Age and Life Cycle Stage. A person's age and **life cycle stage** dictate to a large extent distinct needs and preferences for food, clothing, leisure activities, medical care, and other consumer goods and services. Young, active singles and families are

TABLE 5.3

Family/Household Life Cycle and Buying Behavior

Stage in Household Life Cycle	Buying Behavior
Younger (under 35)	
Single I/unmarried	May live at home, alone, or share residence; active social life; spends money on recreation, clothing, basic furniture.
Young married (or cohabitating) couple (< 35)	Highest purchase rate of durables (cars, appliances, electronics, etc.) and vacations; financially more secure than they can expect in future.
Full nest I (female < 35, children < 6)	Low liquid financial assets; home-buyers, child-related products, health care, etc.
Single parent I (children < 6)	Low liquid assets; child-oriented purchases; convenience goods and affordable services.
Middle-aged (35–64)	
Single II/unmarried	Many types: may be divorced, widowed, or never married; differing lifestyles which may or may not involve expenses for previous family, dating, and individual indulgences (expensive cars, luxury vacations, etc.).
Delayed full nest I (female > 35, children < 6)	Better liquid asset position; heavy purchases of children's clothing, educational products, preventative health care, and family vacations.
Full nest II and III (couple with children > 6 at home)	Generally better off financially; active lifestyle; purchase "large size" packages, larger quantities of food, cleaning materials; buy sporting goods, larger vehicles, lessons, etc.
Single parent II (children > 6 at home)	May have less disposable income; active lifestyle for children and parent; may be juggling work, family, and social life; spending patterns will depend on financial status, but primarily children/family-oriented.
Middle-aged couple (< 65, no children at home, empty nest I)	Generally better off financially; may both be working; buy more expensive cars, home furnishings, vacations, and leisure activities; may be in new marriage and establishing new household.
Older (over 64)	
Single III/unmarried (no children at home)	Includes never married bachelor, divorced, widowed; consumer characteristics determined by status of health and wealth; expenditures for medical care, wellness programs, entertainment (and dating), or just for mere subsistence.

(continued)

TABLE 5.3 *(continued)*

Family Household Lifecycle and Buying Behavior

Stage in Household Lifecycle	Buying Behavior
Older (65 and over)	
Older couple (no children at home, empty nest II)	Similar to middle-aged couple in many respects; may be retired (with fixed income); more expenses for health care, leisure activities, vacations; may be helping to support children, grandchildren.
Other	Note that households are the primary consumption unit in society and that there is a great deal of diversity in the makeup of traditional and nontraditional households. Marketers must consider these factors, along with lifestyle, income, and other indicators when planning marketing programs.

Sources: Adapted from John C. Mowen and Michael Minor, *Consumer Behavior,* 5th ed. (Englewood Cliffs, NJ: Prentice-Hall, 1998), pp. 525–527; Mary C. Gillis and Ben M. Enis, "Recycling the Family Lifecycle: A Proposal for Redefinition," in A. Mitchell (ed.), *Advances in Consumer Research,* Vol. 9. (Ann Arbor, MI: Association for Consumer Research, 1982), pp. 271–276; Del I. Hawkins, Roger J. Best, and Kenneth A. Coney, *Consumer Behavior: Implications for Marketing Strategy,* 8th ed. (Chicago: Richard D. Irwin, 2001), p. 191; and other sources.

good customers for fast-food restaurants and takeout and catered food—most likely healthy and gourmet. Singles are a good market for sports cars, and young families buy a large percentage of the minivans and sport utility vehicles sold in the United States. Middle-aged consumers may opt for sit-down restaurants or gourmet food prepared at home from "scratch." Many prefer comfortable four-door luxury cars with safety features. Age also is related to a predisposition toward spending and saving. The oldest U.S. consumers grew up in the Depression era and tend to save their money and postpone gratification obtained through purchases. In contrast, baby-boomers have demonstrated a preoccupation with themselves and have incurred a high level of debt. Generation X, among the youngest members of the population, are cynical consumers. Many have money to spend (because a large number are still living with parents), but research indicates that they have a deep distrust of business and a strong dislike of marketing "hype." Their younger brothers and sisters, Generation Y, are computer savvy and more sophisticated than many of their predecessors (see Table 5.1).

Likewise, each stage in the life cycle has its own set of related consumer wants and needs. As a person changes status from a young, unmarried single to marital or cohabitation status, personal and household needs change, and new product categories are sought in the marketplace. When babies and children are added to the family or household, more new consumer decisions must be made, and so on throughout the life cycle as the children grow up and leave home and the adults are left with an "empty nest." Eventually, the life cycle ends with a single household member once again—only at this time the person is most likely elderly and seeks an entirely different array of consumer goods and services, depending on his or her health, economic situation, and personal interests.

Occupation and Economic Status. Consumers typically purchase clothes, automobiles, homes, and other products that are consistent with their work roles. For example, a sales manager for a major computer manufacturer would be likely to buy good-quality business suits and accessories (as well as name-brand sports clothes for informal sales meetings), an upscale automobile model, a home in a "good" neighborhood, personal computer(s) and accessories, software, membership in local organizations, and quality family vacations. The production-line worker who makes the computers is most likely a good customer for work clothes, leisure wear, outdoor sporting equipment, pickup trucks, sport utility vehicles, and do-it-yourself home improvement products.

The sales manager and the production worker in the preceding example may earn about the same income but will spend it differently. Occupation and income are closely related and are major determinants of a person's socioeconomic status and ability to spend money. They are primary indicators of household income, personal debt, savings, and general ability and willingness to spend money for a wide range of consumer goods and services.

Lifestyle
The manner or style in which people live, how they use their time and money, and how they think.

Lifestyle. In the past, marketers relied heavily on their knowledge of a market's demographic characteristics in designing marketing strategies. Today, demographics are considered only part of the picture; **lifestyles** have become an important variable in understanding consumer behavior. Lifestyles are simply the way people live—how they use their time and money and how they think. Lifestyles are related to a person's attitudes, interests, and opinions (AIOs), which transcend social class, income, demographics, and other familiar ways of categorizing consumers.

Individuals from diverse backgrounds can be aggregated into one market segment for various products. Examples abound in the markets for pickup trucks (driven by blue-collar workers, corporate CEOs, farmers, young women, and a broad cross section of consumers). Other product categories that appeal to consumer lifestyles include athletic shoes for active sports or casual nonathletic wear, health clubs, wireless phones, and most beverages.

Personality. An individual's personality has a major influence on consumer choices but is difficult to measure or to use directly in marketing programs. However, it is known that a personality type tends to be consistent and goal directed to create similar responses to similar situations. Personality traits are formed at an early age and do not change easily.

There are a number of reliable methods of measuring personality traits and behaviors related to these traits. Traits can be described in bipolar adjectives, with an individual's personality described on a continuum between extremes, such as conservative/liberal, reserved/outgoing, tough-minded/tender-minded, or independent/dependent. Although it is not efficient to measure the personality type of each consumer in a market, his or her responses and behaviors can be predicted with a high degree of accuracy.

Marketers can apply an understanding of attitudes and behaviors that are associated with certain personality traits to designing products, promotional campaigns, packaging, and other aspects of the marketing mix. This is particularly evident in marketing personal care products and beverages. Brands and marketing communications for a popular beverage can be designed to appeal to an outgoing personality, for example, by stressing group activities and acceptance. In contrast, marketing communications for the same product targeted toward a more reserved personality would stress enjoyment of the beverage in a quiet, comfortable setting.

Self-concept
Self-image, attitude toward oneself.

Self-concept.   An individual's **self-concept,** or self-image, plays a major role in consumer decisions. People make purchases based on attitudes toward themselves—who they think they are or would like to be or how they think others see them. Many purchases are made to move a consumer's actual self closer to the ideal self. Self-help goods and services (health, fitness, personal grooming, books, seminars, etc.) have experienced increased sales as consumers attempt to improve their self-concepts.

Brand images are built on self-concept to a large extent. For example, low-income consumers buy national brands of canned goods rather than generics to indicate a higher-status self-concept. High-visibility products are influenced most by self-concept. In our upwardly mobile society, people tend to consume at the next higher level. For example, a person who considers himself or herself to be an innovative consumer is a good prospect for high-fashion clothing and home accessories, unusual artwork and jewelry, exotic vacations, gourmet food, and alternative fuel cars. The innovator will pay more and expend more effort in the consumer buying process to be the first to own a new product. (Recall the "mad rush" to be the first owners of each new edition of Windows software.)

People who view themselves as economical consumers will search for good deals that offer high quality at low prices. A resurgence in used-car sales and increased traffic at thrift shops are strong indicators of a frugal self-concept (as well as an economic necessity in many cases today).

Self-concept can influence decisions about what not to buy. Brand loyalty and self-concept are closely related, so any brand that is inconsistent with a person's self-image will not be acceptable. Likewise, if role models and celebrities used in advertising and personal selling are inconsistent with an individual's self-concept, the message will be "tuned out" or viewed negatively. Consumer preferences and reactions should be determined in advance of marketing campaigns.

Psychological Influences

Psychological influences include motivation, perception, learning and memory, and beliefs and attitudes. Each of these is discussed briefly in this section.

Motivation.   Recognition of a consumer need will not automatically lead to purchase. The consumer must be motivated to take action to remove the sense of imbalance caused by the actual and desired state of affairs. Motives are internal drive states that direct an individual's behavior toward satisfying his or her felt needs. As a result, marketers need to understand the motives that underlie consumer decisions.

Hierarchy of needs theory
An explanation of motivation whereby the individual moves from lower to higher levels of need, having the greatest motivation to satisfy the lowest-level needs first.

While there are many theories of motivation, many marketers find it useful to apply Abraham Maslow's **hierarchy of needs theory** to marketing decisions.[11] This theory explains motivation in terms of a hierarchy, moving from lower to higher levels of needs, as shown in Figure 5.8. Individuals generally will not be motivated to satisfy a higher-level need until they have satisfied the lower-level, or more basic, need below it.

It is possible to regress in this hierarchy. That is, if someone has reached the point of self-actualization but suddenly is affected by a natural disaster (i.e., hurricane, fire,

FIGURE 5.8

Maslow's Hierarchy of Needs: Their Role in Consumer Buying Behavior

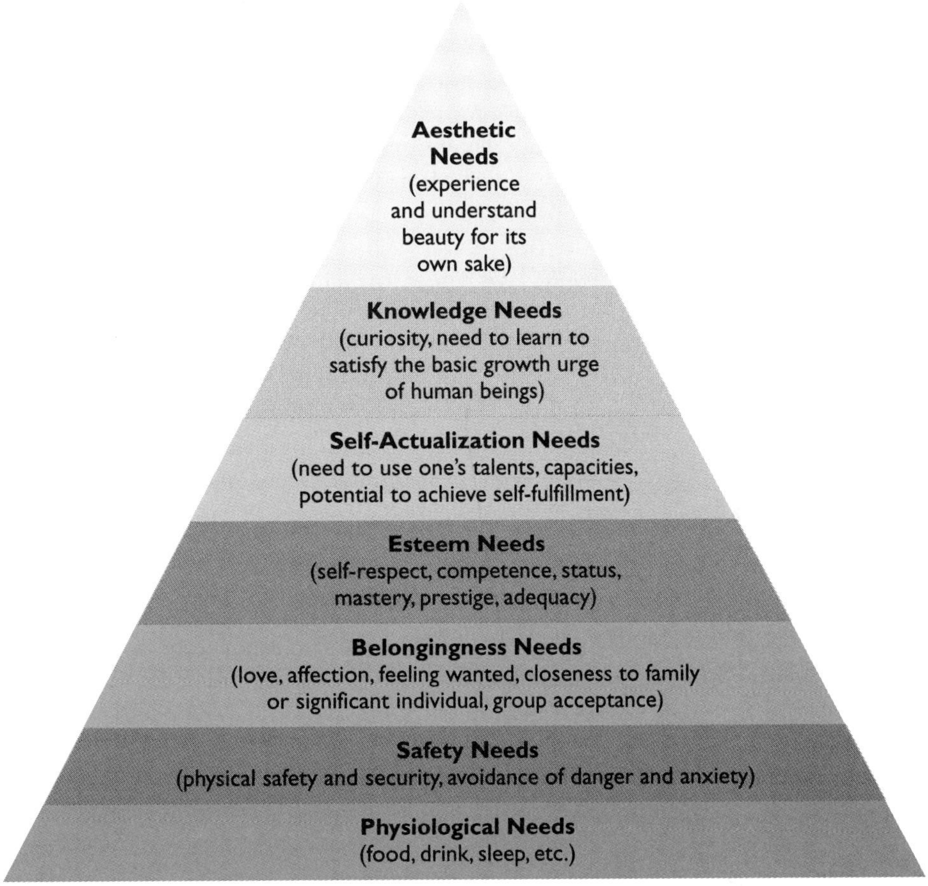

Aesthetic Needs
(experience and understand beauty for its own sake)

Knowledge Needs
(curiosity, need to learn to satisfy the basic growth urge of human beings)

Self-Actualization Needs
(need to use one's talents, capacities, potential to achieve self-fulfillment)

Esteem Needs
(self-respect, competence, status, mastery, prestige, adequacy)

Belongingness Needs
(love, affection, feeling wanted, closeness to family or significant individual, group acceptance)

Safety Needs
(physical safety and security, avoidance of danger and anxiety)

Physiological Needs
(food, drink, sleep, etc.)

Note: Aesthetic Needs and Knowledge Needs are difficult for most individuals to achieve and are not included in many representations of Maslow's hierarchy of needs.

earthquake) or a man-made disaster (i.e., terrorist attack, business failure), he or she will experience basic lower-level needs and concentrate on satisfying the need for shelter, safety, and so forth. Economic setbacks also can cause a consumer to revert to fulfilling lower-level needs. For example, the conspicuous consumption of the 1980s turned to desire for value and practicality in purchases due to corporate downsizing and layoffs, rising prices, and other uncertainties in the 1990s and into the new millenium. (However, luxury and uniqueness are still powerful motivators.)

Perception.   Perception and motivation work hand in hand to direct consumer actions. As stated earlier, problem recognition starts with an internal (hunger, cold, loneliness, happiness) or external environmental stimulus processed through one or more of the five senses: vision (magazine advertisement), hearing (radio commercial, friend's suggestion), smell (bread baking), taste (food sample), and touch (fine fabric). The stimulus may or may not motivate the consumer to make a purchase decision, depending on how the stimulus is converted into information and perceived by the individual.

Perception
The way people are exposed to information, pay attention to it, and make sense of it.

Perception is the way that people are exposed to information, pay attention to it, and make sense of it to understand and function in the world around them. Because effective communication is critical in executing successful marketing strategies, marketers are challenged to understand how consumers receive, interpret, and remember information about their products and brands. It is tempting to aggregate individual perceptions into one overall brand image, for example. However, in reality, each individual may hold a different perception of the same object due to three perceptual processes: selective attention, selective interpretation, and selective retention.

Selective attention
The way people screen out and pay attention to only those stimuli that are relevant to them.

Selective attention allows people to screen out and pay attention to a small portion of the hundreds of thousands of stimuli that bombard them each day. The question is: Which stimuli or messages will a person notice? In general, people are most likely to notice stimuli that are related to a current consumer need (advertisement for new tires to replace a set of tires that is defective on their car), those that are significantly different in intensity from the usual (lower price than anticipated, brighter color in ad, contrasting sound of voice or music in commercial), and those that they have a predisposition to notice and are particularly interested in at the time (tire ads will stand out among ad clutter on a page full of ads).

Selective interpretation
How individuals interpret or distort information any way that they please.

Selective interpretation allows individuals to interpret or distort information any way that they please. They may accept or discount information based on their own beliefs and attitudes. If the company advertising the tires, for example, is believed to be unethical in its service policies, the low price and other aspects of the ad will be interpreted in a way that supports the prior belief. Marketing messages must be designed to make the point intended as simply as possible and should be tested in advance for possible misconceptions.

Selective retention
The ability that allows individuals to choose what to remember from the masses of information they receive.

Selective retention refers to an individual's ability to choose what to remember and what to forget from the masses of information encountered each day. People tend to remember best those bits of information that support their preconceptions and discount information that is contrary to what they already believe. Therefore, one of the most challenging marketing tasks is to reinforce positive perceptions and overcome negative perceptions through all forms of personal and nonpersonal communication.

Learning and Memory.   Consumer behavior, like all human behavior, is largely learned. However, individuals can learn only what they perceive and thus experience. Perception, therefore, plays an important part in the learning process. Individuals learn values, attitudes, behaviors, preferences, meanings, and feelings from their culture and social class, reference groups (family, friends), institutions (school, church, government), commercial sources, and their own personal experiences. Learning results in changes in long-term memory and related changes in the individual's behavior. When an individual is motivated to act on a recognized need, the buying process becomes a learning experience. Motivation is greater in high-involvement purchase situations, making learning more focused and memory more lasting.

There are many theories of learning that are useful in understanding buyer behavior. One of these is *learning through association,* a method whereby individuals are able to make connections between stimuli or generalize from one situation to another similar situation. An example is the extension of a positive brand image to new products and services sold under the same brand. Disney uses this strategy successfully by extending customer loyalty across a broad range of entertainment venues (theme parks, movies, videos), licensed products (apparel, toys, memorabilia), resorts, cruises, and time-share vacations, hotels, cable television, and other goods and services. Likewise, consumers learn to discriminate among stimuli (brands, similar products, etc.) to choose among alternatives and either associate with or dissociate from various objects. Comparative advertising is one method used to help consumers make distinctions between favorable and unfavorable aspects of competing products, although the advertiser's product is presented most favorably.

When learning takes place, the information is accumulated in either short- or long-term memory. Short-term memory may be referred to as a working memory, a dynamic thought process that interprets previously stored information and experiences to solve current problems. Long-term memory consists of numerous types of information that is stored indefinitely in a person's mind. Marketers want customers to hold positive perceptions of their products and brands in long-term memory to build brand loyalty and long-term relationships between buyer and seller. Along with understanding what and how consumers remember, marketers also are concerned with what and how consumers forget. For products that are purchased frequently and consumed rapidly, marketers must keep their brand at the top of the consumer's mind. Reminder advertising helps consumers learn through repetition and is a deterrent to brand switching.

Attitudes and Beliefs. An individual's education and experiences combine to form attitudes, which may be either positive or negative. **Attitudes** are made up of three components: cognitive (beliefs), affective (feelings), and behavioral (actions). Consistency among all three components is essential if an attitude is to endure and cause the person to behave in a relatively consistent manner. For example, heavy smokers tend to believe that smoking is not harmful, feel relaxed when smoking, and therefore buy and smoke cigarettes. In order for an attitude change to take place, the smoker will need to be convinced that smoking will shorten his or her life and/or use some means to produce negative feelings about smoking (develop bad cough) and/or stop buying and smoking cigarettes. When one component is out of sync, the rest will adjust to form a new attitude. If the smoker learns that he or she must quit to prevent serious illness, then new beliefs and feelings will be formed to support the new, nonsmoking behavior. Attitudes also include an ethical or moral component that affects buying decisions.

Beliefs are closely related to perception, learning, and memory, discussed earlier. Individuals form beliefs based on their perceptions of information stored in memory, but these beliefs may not be consistent with reality. For example, the smoker just described may base his or her beliefs on isolated bits of information that support the belief that smoking is not harmful. Marketers are particularly interested in the beliefs that consumers hold about their products, brands, and companies (i.e., image)—because these beliefs have a major impact on the consumer's willingness to buy.

Attitudes
Made up of three components (beliefs, feelings, and actions) that must be consistent if they are to endure over a long time.

Beliefs
Deeply held knowledge and opinions that may or may not be consistent with reality.

CONSUMERS AND PRODUCTS

Products that are the object of a purchase decision have a significant influence on the buying process. The classification of a good or service affects the amount of time and effort expended by a consumer in reaching a purchase decision. (Recall the discussion of the extent of the purchase decision process earlier in the chapter.) The steps in the buying process that are most affected are the amount and depth of information search, evaluation and ranking of available alternatives, and postpurchase evaluation. If the product is complex, expensive, unfamiliar, has a high element of risk (e.g., financial, social, physical, psychological) associated with it, and/or has many viable alternatives available to the consumer, the purchase decision will be more extensive.

Conversely, a simple, uncomplicated, low- or no-risk product can be purchased with relatively little effort in a more habitual or routine manner. The purchase of Band-Aids would be a routine purchase compared with an extensive decision process for choosing a surgeon. Selecting a dinner wine for special dinner guests (who are wine connoisseurs) is a much higher involvement and more extensive buying process than purchasing a regular brand of diet soda for everyday personal consumption.

Purchases are influenced by the relationship between consumers' life roles and the products they need to fulfill their responsibilities in each role. For example, a 32-year-old married man may be a sales manager who covers a three-state area for his company. He also has two children, aged 6 and 4. In his professional role, important product groups (or role-related product clusters) may include business suits and accessories, briefcase, notebook computer, online data services, good-quality wristwatch, and a late model "upscale" automobile. As the father of two children, his role-related product clusters may include child-oriented entertainment, fast-food restaurants with playground facilities, children's furniture, medical insurance, and so forth.

CONSUMERS AND SITUATIONS

The purchase situation is another important influence on the consumer buying process. There are several ways of categorizing situations related to the overall consumption process. Three broad categories include the communications situation, the purchase situation, and the usage situation.[12] (The disposition situation may also be included.) While the present discussion focuses on the purchase situation, let us consider each of the others briefly. The communications situation determines whether and how consumers hear or listen to marketing communications. People respond differently to marketing communications based on their moods, physical states, whether they are alone or with someone, and how much "clutter" surrounds the message. To be most effective, communication should be received by a reader or listener who is a highly motivated potential buyer—and with no other competing messages or "noise" to distract the consumer. However, this is rarely possible.

The usage situation also affects buying behavior, because people may buy different brands and quality of products for different occasions. For example, a jumbo package of inexpensive paper napkins for everyday family use is a routine purchase compared with high-quality paper dinner napkins purchased for a special occasion. (However, if the special occasion was to honor local environmental agency directors, cloth napkins probably would be more politically correct.)

The most frequently used classifications of situational influences on consumer buying behavior are physical surroundings, social surroundings, time or temporal perspectives, task definitions, and antecedent states,[13] as shown in Table 5.4. *Physical surroundings* include location, interior and exterior appearance, lighting, color, sound, climate, equipment, and all objects present in the environment. These factors combine to give customers an impression of spacious versus crowded conditions, pleasing atmospherics, and so forth, which, in turn, affect the customer's willingness to buy.

Social surroundings include all persons present in the situation. People tend to buy better-quality and more prestigious brands when buying for special people or important occasions. Within the shopping environment, other shoppers, salespeople, and others affect purchases. Obnoxious behavior on the part of salespeople and other shoppers may cause the consumer to leave without purchasing. Shopping environments that include pleasant, helpful salespeople are conducive to buying. Friends who accompany the shopper also can exert a positive or negative influence on purchases. Social surroundings are evident in the "pub" scene. To capitalize on the impact of atmosphere and image on social behavior, the Irish Pub Co. began to create and sell a completely finished pub to customers throughout the world. By late 1996, the company had exported more than 1,000 new Irish pubs to 35 countries, with strong support from Guinness PLC. Guinness assists with finding investors, site selection, and other forms of assistance—but does not have a financial interest in Irish Pub Co. The real payoff to Guinness is increased beer exports through expanded distribution channels, although some U.S. bars consider this unethical competition.[14]

TABLE 5.4

Situational Influences on Consumer Behavior

Consumer Situation	Characteristics	Influence on Buying Behavior
Physical surroundings	Present one-bedroom apartment is "cramped" when couple has new baby	Purchase new home with room for baby and child-related purchases
Social surroundings	Rude, noisy customers and salespeople in crowded retail clothing store	Leave without purchasing or purchase less than planned; may not return
Temporal perspectives	No time to shop for significant other's birthday gift	Call florist; shop on-line for special gift
Task definition	Need to take care of lawn (at that new home)	Purchase lawn mower, edger, fertilizer, weed killer, etc.
Antecedent states	Stressed out, overworked, fatigued, in a "bad mood"	Indulge self with special purchase to "feel better," or order takeout food and video and become a "couch potato" for the evening

Temporal perspectives refer to the amount of time available for shopping and how soon the purchase must be made. An emergency medication or a flat tire on the highway requires immediate attention—little search activity, few or no alternatives to evaluate, and a choice to be made as quickly as possible. On the other hand, shopping for replacement furniture or appliances that are presently usable is not as critical. The typical purchase process will involve extended search and careful evaluation of alternatives.

Task definitions refer to the reason for buying the good or service—generally viewed in terms of using different evaluative criteria and shopping behavior when buying for oneself versus buying for another person.

Antecedent states are temporary moods or conditions that affect the consumer and influence purchases. For example, unseasonably hot weather may cause a consumer to postpone the purchase of winter clothing. A consumer who is feeling happy and energetic may be more inclined to make impulse purchases, and so forth.

● RELATIONSHIP MARKETING

Relationship marketing
Building long-term buyer-seller relationships by understanding and fulfilling customer needs better than competitors do.

Today's successful marketers focus on **relationship marketing,** that is, developing continuous buyer-seller relationships consistent with the intent of the new marketing concept and market-driven management.[15] Discussion in this section includes the role of quality and satisfaction in developing repeat business rather than attracting one-time transactions. Further, the practice of relationship marketing is considered relative to the final consumer, the subject of this chapter. Buyer-seller relationships in the organizational markets will be discussed in the next chapter.

Buyer-Seller Relationships

Marketing was described in Chapter 1 within the context of value exchange. Recall that marketing exchanges can occur between a wide variety of buyers and sellers. Sellers may be for-profit or nonprofit organizations, commercial businesses, government agencies, and others. They may sell tangible goods, intangible services, or both to final consumers.

Consumers typically purchase goods and services for their own personal or household use. Buyers (customers, clients) in consumer markets are numerous—posing special problems for the seller who must determine how to create a lasting basis for a relationship with each and every one. They tend to purchase in smaller quantities and more frequently than organizational buyers, necessitating a greater number of contacts and a more personal relationship between the parties.

Sellers must have a thorough understanding of their markets to create value and deliver satisfaction to consumers. This is particularly difficult in highly competitive, mature markets where differentiation is based on giving greater value and doing it better than competitors. Marketers who are helpful to their customers on an ongoing basis have loyal customers who come back repeatedly for related products. Helpfulness takes many forms: making adequate information available before and during the sale, answering customers' questions intelligently and honestly, dealing

IT'S LEGAL **BUT IS IT ETHICAL?**

Just Another Used Car Story?

Consumers purchase thousands of used cars and trucks each year, generally seeking value at a low, or reasonable, price. However, many used vehicles are wrecks that were salvaged in an effort by insurance companies to recover some of their losses. As a result, insurers have encouraged a little-known industry that sells poorly repaired vehicles to unsuspecting consumers, without disclosing the history of the wreck. *Consumer Reports* researchers analyzed an important subset of the 393,000 passenger vehicles involved in fatal accidents from 1993 through 1999. The study focused on a subset of 58,000 late-model cars and trucks that police determined had disabling damage at the accident scene, and for which the researchers could obtain information about the vehicle's history.

Consumer Reports' study concluded that a severe crash does not deter a wreck from being resold and back on the road. Over 40 percent of all passenger vehicles that were involved in fatal crashes were rebuilt, and given new titles for use on public roads. Not all vehicles that police identify as having disabling damage end up being a total loss, according to definitions used by states and hundreds of insurance companies. The analysts focused on 41,800 vehicles that an insurer considered "totaled," indicated by the terms "salvage," "junk," "dismantled," or "non-legal highway" as their first title following the fatal crash date. About 20 percent (8,300) of these vehicles were later retitled for use on public roads. Titles subsequently were "washed" of the salvage history for about one third (2,500) of these cars. Six percent of the cars studied by *Consumer Reports* had their title "washed," and there was no indication on the latest title that the vehicle had been totaled and then rebuilt.

The age and low mileage of newer vehicles makes them more attractive to used-car buyers, so they are more likely to be rebuilt. About one fourth of totaled vehicles within one model year were retitled for the highway, compared to 15 percent that were 5 model-years old. Richard Morse, former chairman of the National Highway Traffic Safety Administration's (NHTSA's) Motor Vehicle Titling Registration and Salvage Advisory Committee remarked, "That's a lot of cars." He stated that hard numbers on rebuilt vehicles were scarce, and that the agency's reform efforts with Congress were impeded by a lack of information. The president of Consumers for Auto Reliability and Safety said, "These numbers are a big red flag for used-car buyers. They validate the concern that tremendously damaged cars do go back on the highway."

The *Consumer Reports* study analyzed detailed information contained in a computerized database maintained by NHTSA's Federal Fatality Analysis Reporting System (FARS) about every fatal U.S. motor vehicle accident. Although most FARS data are public and available on the Internet or CD-ROM, the entire vehicle identification numbers (VINs) are not released because they are considered personally identifying information. No information about the vehicle's title history is included in the FARS data.

Providers of vehicle title-history information, such as Carfax (which maintains a 1.6 billion record database), have records that include VINs and vehicle histories—but do not include the detailed accident information that is in the FARS database. Carfax does have accident data from some states, however. The *Consumer Reports* study was able to join data for the first time from the FARS and Carfax databases, through a special agreement among the three parties to preserve the confidentiality of the FARS VINs (which were

(continued)

never seen by Consumers Union). The results apply only to those fatal crashes studied by the analysts, which they consider to be conservative since they excluded any titles with incomplete information.

The Highway Loss Data Institute (HLDI) and its affiliate, the Insurance Institute for Highway Safety (IIHS), are private nonprofit groups with a combined $14.6 million annual budget provided mainly by 75 insurance companies. Their mission is "finding out what works and what doesn't work to prevent motor-vehicle crashes in the first place." Their goal is "to reduce human and property losses from automobile accidents." The institutes analyze the human, vehicular, and environmental factors associated with accidents by performing crash tests and researching the damage claims by make and model. (IIHS data are used in *Consumer Reports'* auto safety assessments.) The institutes have millions of records on loss claims related to about two thirds of all insured late-model cars and trucks in the United States. This enables them to gather useful information about the models that are most often involved in accidents. They also could answer questions about how many totaled vehicles have been rebuilt and put back on the road, and related patterns or trends that merit further atten-

tion. Brian O'Neill, president of the institutes, said, "There is no evidence that the safety of rebuilt vehicles is a major problem. . . . Is it possible that repairs are related to vehicle performance during a crash? That's impossible to know . . ." HLDI has VINs and other basic details for all cars and trucks that were totaled in collisions. These data could be merged with Carfax's extensive database of title histories to provide a comprehensive picture of rebuilt wrecks. However, they would not release individual records. O'Neill said, "Knowing that there are that many rebuilt vehicles doesn't tell you very much." He pointed out that some wrecks are bought by car thieves, who remove the VIN plate and place it on a stolen car of the same make, model, and year, but he had no information on how frequently this happened. Other insurance industry service providers and sellers of vehicle history reports have databases that could be combined with government and other available data to give a more accurate picture of what happens to rebuilt wrecks. The question that remains unanswered for many consumers is "Are they in jeopardy or being cheated when they buy a used car?"

Source: "Wrecks in Disguise," *Consumer Reports* (January 2002), pp. 28–36.

with problems and complaints promptly and fairly, following up after the sale to say "thank you," and offering continued service.

Although successful companies thrive on close relationships with their customers, relationship marketing can be costly in terms of time, money, and effort required to build close ties with customers. Therefore, it is important to determine the desirable levels of relating to customers. Five levels of relating to customers include basic, reactive, accountable, proactive, and partnership.[16] The *basic level* involves a one-time transaction—the sale is made, and no attempt is made to follow up, particularly if customers are numerous and profit margins are low. At the *reactive level,* customers are encouraged to contact the salesperson or company if they have any complaints or questions. *Accountability* defines the level of the relationship when the salesperson follows up after the sale for feedback on whether customer expectations were met and what improvements are needed. This is characteristic of high-margin sales and few customers. The fourth level is *proactive,* where the salesperson continues to contact the customer every so often with product information updates and news of new products. The closest buyer-seller relationship is a *partnership.* The company works with the customer on an ongoing basis to find ways to satisfy the customer's needs better.

Quality, Satisfaction, and Long-Term Relationships

Membership can provide the basis for long-term buyer-seller relationships. Programs for frequent fliers and frequent guests abound in the travel and hospitality industries. Club marketing programs are targeted toward video game buyers (Nintendo), buyers of decorative accessories for the home (Lladro, Precious Moments figurines), high spenders in department stores, major depositors in banks, and so on. Membership lists allow the marketer to maintain close two-way communication with customers, generally providing opportunities for feedback through an 800 telephone number, surveys, and personal phone calls. In an increasing number of cases, relationship marketing is occurring on the Internet and other interactive electronic telecommunications systems. As long as the marketer delivers quality, value, and satisfaction, customers will remain members. If their participation and recommendations are ignored, they will seek a marketer who will listen and act on their needs.

Relationship Marketing and the New Marketing Concept

The marketing concept is operationalized through implementing organization-wide total quality management and creating exceptional value for customers. A key element of the new marketing concept is delivering quality to the marketplace—but who defines quality? Many organizations define quality in terms of products, processes, or people—such as precise engineering specifications, productivity in the manufacturing process, or organizational excellence within the context of human resources. While all these aspects of quality are important, they are insufficient if the customer is not considered first.

The new marketing concept suggests that the "true definition of quality is meeting and exceeding customer expectations."[17] The problem, of course, is that customers continue to change and increase their expectations. Thus quality and value are defined in the marketplace—a dynamic process that requires constant monitoring. Consumers continue to have higher expectations because of their own needs and wants and the promises and present performance of companies and their competitors. This is where total quality management (TQM) and continuous innovation from the customer's perspective are essential to maintain a competitive edge. Within this context, quality applies to all aspects of the marketing mix: product design and production process, efficient and effective distribution channels, marketing communications and promotional strategies, value pricing, and level of service provided before, during, and after the sale. The net result should be the ability to deliver quality that equals or exceeds customer expectations.

Delivering Customer Value Through Market-Driven Management

Marketers can implement the new marketing concept and compete successfully for long-term relationships with customers in a global marketplace by following fifteen key ideas:[18]

1. *Create customer focus throughout the business.* Everyone in the organization puts the customer first—starting with top management.

2. *Listen to the customer.* Encourage and listen to individual consumer feedback to gain valuable information about the customer and the company.

3. *Define and nurture your distinctive competencies.* Maximize your competencies by fitting your company's capabilities to the needs of your target market.

4. *Define marketing as market intelligence.* Up-to-date, complete, and accurate customer and competitor information provides understanding for customer-oriented decisions.

5. *Target customers precisely.* Know which customers should be yours and which are better suited to competitors (and why).

6. *Manage for profitability, not sales volume.* Profit is an indicator of a company's ability to create and deliver value to the customer and to do so efficiently.

7. *Make customer value the guiding star.* Customer value should be incorporated in the company's mission statement; value should be defined based on market intelligence.

8. *Let the customer define quality.* Quality, defined as meeting customer expectations, must be translated into specific product performance characteristics.

9. *Measure and manage customer expectations.* Know what the customer expects, be sure the expectations are realistic, and avoid overpromising.

10. *Build customer relationships and loyalty.* Customers are a company's most important business asset. Long-term buyer-seller relationships require time and effort. (However, some customers prefer price-based transactions to long-term relationships.)

11. *Define the business as a service business.* Value goes beyond the product purchased to include a bundle of services that determine customer satisfaction/dissatisfaction.

12. *Commit to continuous improvement and innovation.* Customers' constantly changing definitions of value and a company's commitment to delivering superior customer value make it necessary to continuously create new products and add customer value.

13. *Manage culture along with strategy and structure.* Top management must instill the entire organization with a customer orientation that focuses the firm outward on consumers and competitors.

14. *Grow with partners and alliances.* Customer-focused organizations deliver greater customer value by forming strategic partnerships to extend their core competencies.

15. *Destroy marketing bureaucracy.* Marketing and the customer should be the responsibility of everyone throughout the firm, not only that of a marketing department.

Summary

Every organization relies on its greatest asset—customers—for success. The market-driven organization delivers value to its customers, understanding that value is defined in the marketplace and not in the factory. Marketers who thoroughly understand their customers are able to design products and marketing programs that deliver value, quality, and satisfaction.

The study of consumer behavior includes the acquisition, consumption, and disposition of goods and services by final consumers, or buying units, that purchase for their own use. At the heart of this process is a customer-oriented value exchange. The consumer buying process consists of a series of related activities: recognition of a need, search for information, evaluation of alternatives, choice/purchase, and postpurchase evaluation. The extent of this decision-making process may be habitual (or routine), limited, or extended, based on the complexity of the decision, level of consumer involvement, perceived risk, and so forth. This process applies to brands, stores, and shopping formats, as well as to individual products.

Buying behavior is affected by a number of cultural, social, and group factors. A person's culture, subculture, and social class are considered the most important societal influences on consumer behavior. A person's needs, wants, behaviors, and values are shaped by the society in which he or she lives. Individuals look to their reference groups to define what is acceptable or unacceptable according to the group's norms, beliefs, and values. Reference groups may or may not involve membership or face-to-face contact, and their influences may be positive or negative.

Individual influences on buyer behavior include both personal characteristics and psychological influences. Personal factors are represented by a person's age and life cycle stage, occupation and economic status, lifestyle, personality, and self-concept. Psychological influences include motivation, perception, learning and memory, and attitudes and beliefs.

Purchase decisions also are affected by product characteristics and the nature of the purchase situation. Product influences include the type of good or service being purchased, extent of the buying process, level of perceived risk, and the relationship between the product and consumers' needs. The purchase situation affects consumer decisions on the basis of social influences and physical surroundings, time perspective, task objectives, and antecedent states.

An emphasis on relationship marketing is consistent with the new marketing concept and market-driven management and is an underlying theme in the study of consumer behavior presented in this chapter. The focus is on continuously delivering value to consumers who will return for repeat business rather than concentrating on one-time transactions. Relationship marketing relies on a thorough understanding of consumers and a two-way communication process. Quality, value, and satisfaction are the cornerstones of relationship marketing. Long-term buyer-seller relationships are built not only on having superior products and processes and high quality at fair prices but also on perceptions of ethics and level of trust between the two parties.

Questions

1. Describe the stages in the consumer buying process for a major purchase, such as an expensive automobile or a new home.

2. Compare the buying process just described with the buying process for (a) a new suit and (b) a six-pack of soda. Explain the differences.

3. For a recent purchase that you have made, identify the key information sources and influences that affected your decision to buy (or not to buy) the good or service.

4. Give examples of how marketing efforts made (or could have made) a difference in the purchase process and final outcome described in Question 3.

5. Explain the concept of customer value and describe its relationship to the new marketing concept.

6. Give a specific example of each of the seven factors that influence the actual or desired state to trigger recognition of a customer purchase problem. Describe marketing actions that can be directed toward helping consumers recognize and resolve each of these deficiencies or felt needs.

7. As a marketing manager for a brand of packaged foods, you are responsible for developing consumer-oriented marketing programs. Within this context, evaluate the following influences on consumer purchases.

   a. Culture and subculture

   b. Social class

   c. Reference groups

   d. Personal characteristics

   e. Psychological factors

   f. Product characteristics

   g. Purchase situation

8. Find examples of relationship marketing in the business media and evaluate their effectiveness in terms of developing long-term buyer-seller relationships and delivering customer value.

Exercises

1. Identify and analyze five advertisements for consumer products in current media in terms of the following:

   a. Stage in the consumer buying process that is targeted

   b. Social and cultural influences that are represented

   c. Group influences that are represented explicitly or implicitly

2. Interview three individuals who represent distinctly different ages and life cycle stages regarding factors that influence their choice of (a) snack foods, (b) vacation destinations, and (c) automobiles. Analyze the differences (and similarities) in terms of the implications for marketing strategy.

3. Identify two examples of relationship marketing, and evaluate each one as to whether you believe it will or will not succeed in developing long-term buyer-seller relations, the potential ethical issues, and the ability to deliver bona fide customer value.

Endnotes

1. Alan Deutschman (ed.), *Fortune Cookies: Management Wit and Wisdom from Fortune Magazine* (New York: Vintage Books, 1993), p. 15.

2. For additional discussion, see Frederick E. Webster, Jr., *Market-Driven Management: Using the New Marketing Concept to Create a Customer-Oriented Company* (New York: John Wiley & Sons, 1994), Chap. 1.

3. John C. Mowen and Michael Minor, *Consumer Behavior*, 5th ed. (Englewood Cliffs, NJ: Prentice-Hall, 1998), p. 5.

4. Del I. Hawkins, Roger J. Best, and Kenneth A. Coney, *Consumer Behavior: Implications for Marketing Strategy*, 8th ed. (Chicago: Richard D. Irwin, 2001), p. 7.

5. *Purchase involvement* is defined as "the level of concern for, or interest in, the purchase process triggered by the need to consider a particular purchase." It is considered a temporary state experienced by the buyer, based on the interaction of characteristics of the individual, product, and situation. See Hawkins et al., *ibid.* (p. 425), for further discussion.

6. Carol H. Anderson, *Retailing: Concepts, Strategy and Information* (St. Paul, MN: West Publishing Company, 1993), pp. 235–237; based on Gordon C. Bruner II and Richard J. Pomazal, "Problem Recognition: The Crucial First Stage of the Consumer Decision Process," *Journal of Consumer Marketing* 5(1) (Winter 1988), pp. 53–63.

7. www.mcdonalds.com, www.rmhc.com, www.ronald.com (September 20, 2002).

8. Peter D. Bennett (ed.), *Dictionary of Marketing Terms* (Chicago: American Marketing Association, 1988), p. 50.

9. Del I. Hawkins, Roger J. Best, and Kenneth A. Coney, *Consumer Behavior: Implications for Marketing Strategy*, 8th ed. (Chicago: Richard D. Irwin, 2001), pp. 44–50, 80–85.

10. Bennett, *op.cit.*, p. 196.

11. Abraham H. Maslow, *Motivation and Personality* (New York: Harper & Row, 1954).

12. Hawkins et al. (2001), *op. cit.,* pp. 478–481.

13. *Ibid;* Russel Belk, "Situational Variables and Consumer Behavior," *Journal of Consumer Research* 2 (December 1975), pp. 157–163; John C. Mowen, *op. cit.,* pp. 452–473.

14. Charles Goldsmith, "Prefab Irish Pub Sells Pints World-Wide," *Wall Street Journal* (October 25, 1996), pp. B1, B8; Scott Cherry, "Pub Par; Kilkenny's Bring a Touch—and a Taste—of the Old Sod to Tulsa," *Tulsa World,* p. 19; "Philly Pubs Take Stout Stand Against Guinness' Support for Startup Bars," *Dayton Daily News* (March 19, 2000), p. 6F.

15. See Frederick E. Webster, Jr., *op. cit.,* Chaps. 3, 5, and 9, for further discussion of concepts discussed in this section.

16. Philip Kotler, *Marketing Management,* 11th ed. (Englewood Cliffs, NJ: Prentice-Hall, 2003), pp. 76–78.

17. Webster, *op. cit.,* p. 67.

18. *Ibid.,* Chap. 9.

MARKETING MANAGEMENT IN ACTION: CLOSING CASE

Shopping with The Fickle, Fashion-Conscious Teens of Generation Y

With money to spend, U.S. teen and pre-teen consumers flock to the rapidly growing number of trendy teen-oriented apparel shops in local malls. According to a study conducted by Teenage Research Unlimited, America's 32 million teens spent an average of $104 a week in 2001—a total of $172 billion: more than the annual gross domestic product of industrialized nations like Israel, Chile, or Portugal. Gen Y shoppers under the age of 20 spend five times more in inflation-adjusted dollars than their parents did at the same age. Because teens spend so much money they are attractive to marketers, prompting marketing researchers to study this group's spending patterns, lifestyles, attitudes and opinions, and shopping preferences for a wide variety of products. Apparel retailers who cater to teenagers have found that they have very different ideas about fashion even within their own age group, and that their taste can change very quickly.

Of most interest to market researchers are the 71 million young people born between 1977 and 1994, who are now coming of age. These young people, known as Generation Y,* are the children of Baby Boomer parents. They have been heralded as the next big generation—an extremely powerful group whose numbers can transform every stage it goes through—just as the 78 million Baby Boomers, born between 1946 and 1964, did before them.

The Three Waves of Generation Y

Gen Y is a very large generation that can be divided into three different life stages to better understand their attitudes, lifestyles, and consumer behavior. These stages (or waves) and selected consumer characteristics are based on several research studies. The age categories are useful for gaining a better understanding of different consumer groups within Gen Y. However, each retailer defines an age range for its own target market that may not exactly coincide with the age range for each wave described below.

The First Wave: Gen Y Adults, ages 19 to 25 (born between 1977 and 1983) represent 36 percent of the generation. They have a very positive attitude toward money, and their ability to earn it and to afford the lifestyle they grew up in. When asked to name one thing that would improve their lives forever, most answered, "having more money." They enjoy spending money, and many have three or more credit cards. A large number of Gen Ys in this group are full-time undergraduate college students with a total purchasing power of $105 billion, and average monthly discretionary spending of $179. Their average annual personal earnings were

$5,140 in 2001, with about 60 percent of the students earning this money through part-time jobs.

The Second Wave: Gen Y Teens, ages 13 to 18 (born between 1983 and 1989) represent 34 percent of the generation. These teens spent $155 billion in 2000, an increase of $2 billion from 1999. Teenage Research Unlimited (TRU) estimates the average teenager's weekly spending at $84, with $57 coming from his or her own money. Most of their spending is on clothing; Harris Interactive found that 75 percent of girls' expenditures and 52 percent of boys' are for apparel. Teens have very few fixed expenses, and many have jobs at restaurants or retail stores, so most of their income is disposable—mostly spent for clothing. In spite of teens' love of shopping and spending, 18 percent own stocks or bonds. In a nationwide study of over 2,000 12 to 19 year olds, 30 percent wanted to get their own credit card, and 42 percent of the 18 and 19 year olds already had cards in their own name. Many used a variety of debit cards and pre-loaded cards such as the American Express Cobalt Card.

The Third Wave: Gen Y Kids, ages 8 to 12 (born between 1990 and 1994) represent 30 percent of the generation. This group, often referred to as "'tweens," may have even more spending power than their older brothers and sisters. According to a study conducted by the Wonder Group, today's 'tweens spend an average of $4.72 each week of their own money. Most of this is from an allowance, but a large amount also comes from cash gifts—particularly from grandparents. The 'tweens not only spend a total of $10 billion out of their own pockets from allowances or gifts—but they also influence additional spending of about $260 billion annually. They are considered the most influential group, because they still have to convince their parents to get the things they want. Today's parents have become "cooperative partners" in this effort—where "the 'tween and the mom act as one consumer."

The Teen Age Consumer

Teenagers' fickle fashion sense is a primary motivator for buying more clothes. They also are "hard" on their clothes, given their active lifestyles. Many are involved in active or extreme sports. Boardwear and footwear retailers Quiksilver and Vans Inc. consider their demographic to be very brand-conscious, and not as concerned about swings in the economy. Boardwear refers to surfboard, skateboard and snowboard wear—casual clothing worn by U.S. teens who consider themselves to be surfers, skaters, and snowboarders either to participate in the sport or to party.

Teens are very hard to reach with their wide range of opinions and preferences. For example, some Gen Y consumers dress to look like the rappers and hip-hop artists on music videos. Some want to mimic the look of their favorite singer or actor; others want to create their own individualized look. Some like to be the target of advertising directed at them; others are insulted by the direct approach. Some love brand names; others hate brand names.

The group has not been easy for retailers to figure out. They are the most ethnically and racially diverse generation in the United States, and have very different definitions of what's cool at any given time. They are suspicious of advertising and resist being influenced by it, particularly ads they consider phony or slick. They want honest, intelligent ads that teach them something. They enjoy humor in ads, but not at the expense of others. They like their senses stimulated with loud music and lots of merchandise, according to a spokeswoman with the International Council of Shopping Centers. As one expert observed, they are "addicted to clothes, music, and being cool."

Gen Y teens are an important target market for Gucci, Prada, Fendi, Louis Vuitton, Armani, and Versace. Professor James Twitchell of the University of Florida said, "Gen Y is inundated with an increasing flow of stories about these objects from advertisers. It's not just that they have more disposable income. They have more disposable time to consume not just the objects, but the meanings of the objects."

When asked about their reactions to the 9/11 terrorist attacks, Gen Y consumers said they felt "angry and worried," and that they were spending more time watching TV and spending time with friends—but they hadn't cut back on their trips to the mall or the money they spent on clothes and other objects for themselves. This generation is truly dedicated to shopping.

The Retailers' ("Teentailers") Challenge

Specialty retailers who focus on teen apparel are expanding rapidly, and are the most popular tenants in many malls, making up an increasingly larger percentage of the overall store mix. Teen retailers find synergy in numbers of competitors in the same mall from the cross-traffic among younger customers. Teen-oriented stores have experienced robust sales and have been making ambitious expansion plans. Some are well-known, long-time retailers who are tapping into this lucrative market. Others are newcomers that see a huge growth opportunity in the teen market. Some of the more popular chains include Reno-based Hot Cats that targets 12 to 24 year olds; Carlsbad, California-based No Fear that targets 15 to 25 year old males; New Albany, Ohio-based Abercrombie & Fitch Co. (and its lower-priced spin-off store Hollister Co. that targets 14 to 18 year olds). Other teen-focused chains include Wet Seal Inc., Vans Inc., Quiksilver Inc.; skateboard-themed Industrial Rideshop; Agaci Too for young women; Pacific Sunwear; Robert Wayne Footwear; Hot Topic subsidiary Torrid that targets larger sizes; and many others.

The big challenge for "teentailers" is to predict fashion trends for their Gen Y customers. National and local retailers, such as the Buffalo Exchange new and used clothing chain, want to know what makes their teenage customers "tick." To find out what clothes and other products appeal to this group, the Tucson-based retailer "gathered a group of young fashion hounds to document the hippest clothing trends in Tucson." Using cameras, notebooks and sketchpads, the teen trend-spotters tracked what teenagers considered hot and reported back to the store's executives. Rebecca Block, vice president of Buffalo Exchange Ltd., said, "For us, that generation is such a huge population …. We want to give them what they want."

Retailers and manufacturers try to build brand loyalty—but today's teens are the opposite of their label-conscious predecessors. They often cut off the labels when they buy brand names. There doesn't seem to be any real agreement among the Gen Y teens as to the hottest fashion. Abercrombie & Fitch illustrate this diversity of opinion when it comes to its upscale, casual clothing. One teenager said, "All the hot guys wear Abercrombie … It's an image. Everyone shops for the look." But another teen said,

"It's too prepped out … It's like, 'Look at me, I can spend.' It's like making the whole world look the same."

Teen retailers must constantly reinvent themselves, in part because most teens are computer-literate and are inundated with information—causing their tastes to change quickly. Many retailers and mall operators use regular teen focus groups to try to keep up with these rapid changes. Some focus group results included a request for concerts and a skateboard park at a mall. Others resulted in adding to their stores "overstuffed couches, photograph sticker and CD machines, Internet kiosks, rock-climbing walls and TV monitors that feature the latest music icons belting out subtle marketing themes." Sears Roebuck and Co. sponsored a 37-city tour by Grammy-winner Christina Aguilera in 2000. In their 850 stores, they had a Christina-themed "experience" area and sold CDs cut for Sears by Aguilera.

The dilemma faced by teen retailers is that Generation Y fashion preferences are fickle, fast moving, and difficult to predict. Mistakes can be costly. For example, Pacific Sunwear of California Inc. found that a purchase of the wrong style of shorts dragged down same-store sales nearly 10 percent in spite of sales increases in other categories. On a much larger scale, many traditional retailers suffered in the early 1990s recession when young consumers flocked to thrift shops and army surplus stores to buy so-called grunge wear. That fashion revolt was a blow to surf-themed outfitters like Quiksilver. A consumer backlash against neon in surfwear in 1992 resulted in the worst year Quiksilver had experienced as a public company, and the change to a more diversified product mix.

A spokesman for the National Retail Federation said, "If [retailers] can get to [Gen Y teens] young in terms of brand loyalty, they're going to keep them for the rest of their lives." Building that brand loyalty requires constant vigilance and the willingness to make changes quickly.

*Generation Y is also known as Gen Y, Echo Boomers, Millennials, Generation Next, Bubble Generation, and Clickeratti.

Source: Anonymous, "Show Me the Money: Divvying Up the Gen Y Spending Pool," *American Demographics* 23 (9) (September 2001), p. 49; Pamela Paul,

"Getting Inside Generation Y," *American Demographics* 23(9) (September 2001), pp. 42–49; Jennine Relly, "Generation Y: Corporations, Local Retailers Focus on Vast Pool of Teen, Pre-teen Buyers," *Arizona Daily Star* (April 15, 2001), p. D1; Maureen Tkacik, "Youth Apparel Chains Are Booming—Survey Shows Teens Tend to Spend Most of Their Income on Clothing," *Wall Street Journal Europe* (July 6, 2001), p. 23+; Chris Jones, "Southern Nevada Mall Shops Cater to Generation Y," *Knight Ridder Tribune Business News* (September 6, 2002), p. 1.

Case Study Questions

1. Describe each of the steps (as you perceive them) in a teenager's (13 to 19 years old) decision process for a typical clothing purchase. At each stage in this process, suggest at least one way that retailers and manufacturers can influence the teen's decision.

2. Choose the most relevant influences on teenagers' purchase decisions from the list below. Discuss how each influence affects a teenager's decision to purchase clothing or accessories, and how teen retailers can apply an understanding of these influences to develop successful marketing strategies:

   a. Social and cultural influences
      1. Culture and subculture
      2. Values
      3. Reference groups
      4. Social class

   b. Psychological influences
      1. Motivation
      2. Perception
      3. Learning and memory
      4. Attitudes and beliefs

   c. Individual influences
      1. Age and life cycle
      2. Economic status (and occupation if applicable)
      3. Lifestyle
      4. Personality
      5. Self-concept

   d. Marketing influences

3. Explain how situations can influence a teenager's decision to purchase a new outfit. Consider physical and social surroundings, time, antecedent states, and task or activity. How can marketers apply an understanding of this influence?

4. Critique the statement, "If [retailers] can get to [Gen Y teens] young in terms of brand loyalty, they're going to keep them for the rest of their lives."

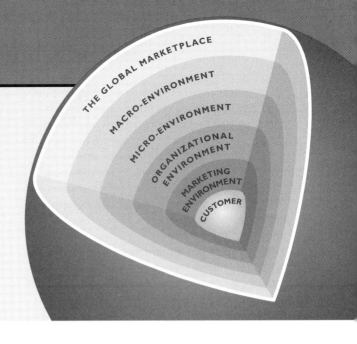

CHAPTER 6

Business Markets and Buying Behavior

Purchasing is by far the largest single function at AT&T. Nothing we do is more important.[1]

The U.S. Automotive Industry: World-Class Buyers and Sellers

What would life be like without cars and trucks and other vehicles? Imagine a world without cars, pickup trucks, minivans, or sport utility vehicles to transport a lone driver, a family of five, or a complete soccer team. Imagine a world without trucks to deliver mail, catalog orders, or a major piece of machinery that will keep the production line moving efficiently in the factory. The prospect of a nation at a standstill on its streets and highways dramatizes the importance of the automotive industry as a leading indicator of the health of the U.S. economy.

The consumer market for automobiles represents only the tip of the iceberg in the number and complexity of transactions related to the automotive industry. To satisfy the direct needs of the marketplace for transportation and its indirect needs for a variety of other goods and services, car and truck manufacturers throughout the world are involved in extensive buying and selling activities at all levels of distribution.

Organizational purchasing is driven by *derived demand*. That is, final consumers or other businesses "demand" vehicles for personal and commercial purposes from a manufacturer or dealer. In turn, the manufacturer must purchase the necessary goods and services to meet this demand. If customers cannot or will not buy a manufacturer's products, there is no need to make the purchases necessary to produce them.

Automobile manufacturers must purchase raw materials and component parts needed to produce a product for resale. This may include steel, plastics, rubber, leather, paint, tires, glass, and other items to complete a particular automotive design. Many suppliers of basic and custom goods depend on the business they derive from automobile makers. For example, a small company whose core business is sun visors may sell custom accessories for sport utility vehicles, light trucks, and vans. Major tire manufacturers such as Goodyear or Michelin derive their sales from new car sales and from the aftermarket. Each of these suppliers is influenced by events and trends in the macro- and micro-environments.

Manufacturers must understand the needs and wants of their customers in order to forecast demand levels and anticipate style preferences. For example, during the mid-1990s, trucks and sport utility vehicles gained popularity among "nontraditional" truck customers. Minivans, which had been in demand for several years, began to take on the image of old station wagons. Demand for sport utility vehicles—including larger models and high-priced luxury models—escalated in the first decade of the twenty-first century. At the same time, manufacturers experienced a decrease in demand for sports cars. (To overcome this trend, some manufacturers capitalized on nostalgia by reincarnating popular models from the past, such as the Corvette and the Volkswagen Beetle.)

Changes in the marketing environment have directly influenced the types of organizational purchasing decisions that need to be made. Globalization of the automotive industry has dramatically influenced organizational purchasing because of its effect on competition in this market. Final consumers can select a wide variety of makes and models from manufacturers throughout the world. Manufacturers can buy parts from the most profitable sources and assemble vehicles in overseas markets to meet the needs of their overseas customers. The effects of technology and computerization also influence organizational buying behavior. For example, consumers can now choose high-tech options such as an in-car satellite navigator, an infrared night-vision screen, collision-avoidance radar, radar-enhanced cruise control, and programmable traffic signs. Inventory-control issues involve having sufficient inventory on hand when it is needed and not having valuable financial resources (and space) tied up in inventory longer than necessary. Government rules and regulations for safety features, fuel emission standards, and other concerns also must be considered.

All these factors need to be addressed by organizational buyers in the automotive industry today. The ongoing challenge for marketing managers is to ensure that these organizational buyers will be strategically positioned to respond to changes as quickly as they happen.

Consumers and their buying behavior were discussed in the preceding chapter. Our attention now turns to buying behavior in business or organizational markets. Like the consumer market, the business market is made up of both buyers and sellers. However, rather than buying for personal consumption or household use, the organizational buyers who comprise the business market acquire goods and services to be used directly or indirectly in their own operations, which they in turn sell, rent, or provide to other organizations. Within this context, the buyer purchases on behalf of a business, government agency, institution (such as a school or church), or other organization (such as the Red Cross or other nonprofit organization).

This chapter focuses on external buyers, but it should be noted that many organizations have suppliers who provide goods and services to internal customers who also have the option of purchasing from competing suppliers outside the organization. Although some unique dynamics are involved in this type of purchase decision, traditional organizational buying concepts can be applied for a better understanding of the process.

● SCOPE OF BUSINESS MARKETS

The business market can be described in terms of customer types, market size and trends, and the major industries that comprise the overall market. For example, retail buyers purchased goods and services from an array of producers and wholesalers in 1997 that resulted in $2,578 billion in retail sales to final consumers. Food services and drinking places accounted for $258 billion in an innovative growth market.[2] A few of the industries that serve this market include agriculture (e.g., meat, produce, dairy), beverages, baking, paper goods, plastics, kitchen equipment, computers, and other providers of goods and services.

Major industries comprising the business market include agricultural services, mining, construction, manufacturing, transportation, wholesale trade, retail trade, finance and insurance, and services. The magnitude of business purchases for each of these industries is reflected in their annual sales shown in Table 6.1.

Types of Customers

The organizations described in this section represent both buyers and sellers of a wide array of goods and services. However, we are most concerned here with purchase or acquisition. Business customers can be classified into four major groups (although these may overlap at times): business and commercial organizations, reseller organizations, government organizations, and institutional organizations.[3]

Business and Commercial Organizations. Lockheed-Martin Corp. may buy metals from a mining company, or an insurance company may buy computers from IBM for use by secretaries in its corporate office, or Birds-Eye may buy fruits and

TABLE 6.1

Major U.S. Industries*—Number of Establishments and Business Receipts, 1997†

Industry	Establishments (1,000)	Business Receipts (billion dollars)
Agriculture, forestry, fishing	117	51
Mining	27	173
Construction	669	835
Manufacturing	394	3,991
Transportation, public utilities	302	1,264
Wholesale trade	531	4,223
Retail trade	1,592	2,578
Finance, insurance, real estate	678	2,468
Services	2,554	2,657

*Corporations, partnerships, and nonfarm proprietorships.
†Excludes investment income except for partnerships and corporations in finance, insurance, and real estate.
Source: Statistical Abstract of the United States, 2000, Table 869.

vegetables from a farmer to process in its frozen food business. In each case, the buyer is making a purchase in order to directly or indirectly produce another good or service—such as airplanes, insurance contracts, or food products. Most of these organizational customers can be classified as either **original equipment manufacturers (OEMs)** or user customers. Most organizational customers may be classified as both OEMs and users. For example, Birds-Eye not only buys produce from its suppliers but also needs equipment, products, and services to clean and maintain its manufacturing facilities.

> **Original equipment manufacturers (OEMs)** Buy component parts from a commercial supplier; these parts become part of a finished product sold to another organization or consumer.

An OEM buys component parts from a commercial supplier. These component parts then become part of the finished product that is sold to another organization or consumer. For example, as a buyer, Dell Computer Corp. may buy microchips from a business-to-business supplier to use in the manufacture of its computers. The microchip would then become an integral part of Dell's final product. OEMs also may be purchasers of services that become part of an "extended" product, such as Kitchen Aid purchasing General Electric's service capability to fulfill Kitchen Aid's appliance warranty obligations.

User customers purchase equipment, supplies, and services that are used directly or indirectly in the production of other goods and/or services that are sold to other organizations and/or to the consumer market. For example, a builder may purchase a power saw for carpenters to use in the construction of a building, or the builder may buy liability insurance to cover workers in case of an accident. Neither the saw nor the insurance policy becomes an actual part of the finished product, but both are necessary purchases for completion of the building that is being sold to another customer.

Reseller Organizations.   Retailers and wholesalers are **intermediaries** in the distribution system, buying goods from manufacturers and producers to resell at a profit to their customers. They also purchase a variety of goods and services that are needed for their daily business operations. While resellers are closely related to the consumer market, they also represent a large share of the business customers that make up the total business marketing system. (Retailers and wholesalers will be discussed further in Chapter 10 within the context of distribution strategy.)

> **Intermediaries** Organizations such as retailers and wholesalers that buy from manufacturers and producers to resell at a profit to their customers.

Retailers constitute an important group of customers in the business-to-business markets. As shown in Table 6.1, retailers purchased goods for resale to final consumers in 1997 that resulted in business receipts of $2,578 billion across 1,592 million retail establishments. In addition, these same retailers purchased a vast array of goods and services for their stores and retail systems, such as information systems, visual merchandising, fixtures, flooring, lighting, office supplies, and utilities. Retail buyers are customers of both manufacturers and wholesalers.

> **Middlemen** Wholesalers that buy from manufacturers or producers and resell at a profit to retailers.

Wholesalers serve as **middlemen** in the distribution channels, buying from manufacturers or producers and reselling at a profit to retailers. Wholesalers may carry many lines of merchandise and create assortments that are targeted to particular retail customers. Since wholesalers generally are involved in physical distribution activities, they are good customers for materials-handling equipment, trucks, warehousing supplies, and so forth. As noted in Table 6.1, 531 million wholesale establishments accounted for $4,223 billion in business receipts in 1997 in the United States.

MARKETING **AND** ENTREPRENEURSHIP

Europe's Rust Belt Finds New Source of Business Via the Internet

 The 160 workers on the factory floor of Z.R.E. Grodeck* spend most of their time forging, banging, and welding pieces of metal into finished products such as "boilers, racks, pumps, and other parts for the heavy industry that the Internet revolution was expected to make us forget." Many smokestack industries in formerly Communist countries are struggling to survive, and must compete with cheaper labor in Asia and India, but Z.R.E. Grodeck logged on to the Internet and found a new source of business.

The Internet is slowly making its way to businesses in Eastern and Central Europe, and Z.R.E. Grodeck, acquired two years ago by New Jersey-based Universal Process Equipment Inc., was one of the earliest Internet business-to-business pioneers in Poland. The company used a personal computer to dial up a business-to-business Web site in the United States, and bid on contracts for American manufacturers that wanted less expensive sources for labor-intensive products. In 2001, Z.R.E. Grodeck built hundreds of metal frames for moving sheets of glass around a factory. The frames were produced in a Polish factory, and used by a British glassmaker, Pilkington, in American plants.

Poland's current dot.com prosperity is based on a realistic assessment of the rapid rise and fall of Silicon Valley and the Nasdaq index. They also avoided the business-to-consumer online businesses that crashed in the United States. Polish efforts and investments have been focused on adapting traditional business to the Internet, and bringing "clicks" to "bricks." Most of their early Internet activity was done to supplement a traditional company's primary activity.

* The initials Z.R.E. are initials for the Polish translation of the Electric Equipment Manufacturing Company.

One of the barriers to a rapid increase in the use of the Internet in Poland is connectivity. In a population of 39 million people, only 5 to 8 percent have regular Internet access, and much of that is through old, unreliable phone lines. The country's healthy economy, and growth in the Internet and other technological advances, is moving Poland closer to the living standards of Western Europeans. Poland's overall economy grew 4.1 percent in 2000, making it one of the strongest economies in the region. Industry analysts estimate the country's Internet sector to be valued in the hundreds of millions of dollars. At present, only a small percentage of business activity comes from Internet-related and information technology companies. However, more portals are being opened, old media are moving online, new products are being developed, and investors are eager to support entrepreneurial ventures.

Although they have suffered some ups and downs in the stock market, 15 Polish high-tech companies have been listed on the Warsaw Stock Exchange over the past five years. (The exchange generally follows Nasdaq technology trends, although the Polish economy is not very dependent on the Internet.) Some of the frenzied investment that preceded the downfall of many Silicon Valley dot.coms has been avoided in Poland, because there simply is not a great deal of money to spend. There are no large numbers of individual investors, there is little money in savings accounts, and bank interest rates are close to 20 percent. The scarcity of investment dollars from the general population has made it necessary for Poland's start-up Internet ventures to obtain financing, but this also keeps growth somewhat controlled. Venture capital for Polish high-technology businesses has come from sources such as the United States, Britain, and large Polish businesses. Marcin Hejka, strategic investments manager for Eastern Europe at Intel

(continued)

Capital, a division of Intel Corporation, said, "The quality of business plans and new opportunities in the region is growing." He added, "If a company has a good idea, the right team and the right product, it shouldn't have trouble attracting venture capital investors" in Poland. The large number of smart, relatively low-paid engineers in Poland and nearby regions offers an advantage to high-technology entrepreneurs.

A small number of entrepreneurial venture capitalists in Poland have seized the opportunity to invest in high-technology companies. Rafal Styczen made his first fortune at the age of 24 when he floated his first company, ComArch in Krakow, on the Warsaw exchange. In addition to ComArch, which designs and assembles computer systems for businesses, Styczen started the Internet Investment Fund in Krakow to invest in Poland's new economy. The fund started nine companies, which he believes have been successful because the lack of stock market exposure has allowed them to "develop sensibly . . . and to make their money selling products and services, not shares." Some of Styczen's entrepreneurial ventures include:

- *Billbird* (www.mojerachunki.p1)—automates Poland's outdated bill-paying system where

payers often have to spend hours in line at post offices to pay their bills with cash.

- *SynergiXmedia*—creates and sells interactive Web sites.
- *E-Center in Krakow*—provides a home, hardware, and technical support for Web site operators.
- *Interactive Medicine*—online service for dentists to handle bookkeeping and manage drug and equipment orders.

With entrepreneurial businesses such as Z.R.E. Grodeck, and eager large and small venture capitalists, Poland's Internet market is positioned for growth. As Matt Rothman, chief executive of Softbank Emerging Markets said, "What is developing in Central Europe is in many cases going to leapfrog developments elsewhere, and the market is just starting. . . . So a lot of things that were tried and rejected in the U.S. will be avoided here, and you'll come up with more appropriate and localized solutions that I think will have a lot of success."

Source: Peter S. Green, "A High-Tech Lifeline in Europe's Rust Belt," *The New York Times* (April 29, 2001), p. 3.5+.

Government Organizations.   There are thousands of government organizations at the federal, state, and local levels. Governmental customers vary widely in size, scope, and purchasing processes. However, they collectively form one of the largest markets in the world for goods and services, accounting for purchases in the trillions of dollars.[4] The magnitude of government purchases represents everything from stealth bombers for the U.S. Department of Defense to paper clips for the mayor's office in Cut-and-Shoot, Texas. State and local government consumption expenditures accounted for $1,150.8 billion in 2000, as shown in Table 6.2.

Government consumption expenditures at the federal level reached $590.2 billion in 2000. Federal government purchasing units may be classified as either defense or nondefense. Government purchases for the civilian sector include goods and services for departments, administrations, agencies, boards, commissions, executive offices, and other independent establishments that serve the nonmilitary needs of the American population. Examples of nonmilitary governmental purchases include office supplies and furnishings, computers and telecommunications systems, vehicles, and research-oriented goods and services. Federal military customers include the U.S. Army, Navy, and Air Force, and the Defense Supply Agency that centralizes much of the buying for the armed services. These purchases include a wide range of

TABLE 6.2

Federal, State, and Local Government Consumption Expenditures (billions of dollars)*

	1995	2000
Federal Government	521.5	590.2
National defense**	350.6	375.4
Consumption expenditures	297.5	321.9
Durable goods	21.0	22.5
Nondurable goods	6.3	10.4
Services	270.2	289.0
Nondefense	170.9	214.8
Consumption expenditures	141.8	171.8
Durable goods	0.9	1.3
Nondurable goods	6.5	6.9
Services	134.3	163.6
State and Local Government	850.5	1,150.8
Consumption expenditures	694.7	929.0
Durable goods	12.7	16.9
Nondurable goods	72.9	110.9
Services	609.0	801.2

*Does not include gross investment in structures, equipment, and software.

**Data prior to increased expenditures to combat terrorism at home and abroad following September 11, 2001.

Source: U.S. Bureau of Economic Analysis, http://www.bea.doc.gov/bea/dn/nipaweb/index.htm, U.S. Census Bureau, Statistical Abstract of the United States: 2001, Table No. 417, p. 260.

products related to the military mission (e.g., armaments) and to military personnel (e.g., commissary assortments, housing, personal services).

America's fifty state governments are important customers for education, roads, institutions (e.g., hospitals, prisons), water, airports, and various maintenance and redevelopment projects. Local government customers may be classified further as counties, municipalities, townships, and special districts. Although metropolitan counties are greatly outnumbered by rural counties, their purchases represent most of the county-level governmental expenditures. Most of the purchases made by counties, municipalities, and townships tend to be related to building and maintaining streets and highways, providing police and fire protection, creating and maintaining parks and recreational facilities, solid-waste removal, and water supply and treatment. Counties also make purchases related to the preservation of natural resources. In addition, special districts are formed to provide certain functions, such as water supply systems or fire protection. The district governmental unit must purchase the goods and services needed to perform these specialized functions successfully.

Foreign governments are also a large market for U.S. manufacturing output and services. Industries such as defense, aircraft, and telecommunication have prospered by selling to overseas customers. This trend is expected to continue. Buyers that represent overseas businesses, institutions, and governments may have a different set of buying criteria than domestic buyers. They may require product modifications to meet their government standards and local customer demands. The ordering process, payment method, and other aspects of the sales transaction also may need to be tailored to the buyers' needs.

Institutional Organizations. All organizational customers that are not considered commercial businesses (OEMs, users) or government purchasers constitute the institutional market. While the classifications are not always clear-cut between private, government, and institutional organizations, institutional customers can be public or private, for-profit or nonprofit, large or small, domestic or international. Schools, churches, professional associations, little league teams, disaster-relief agencies, hospitals and health care facilities, and a diverse group of other institutions make up a large part of the organizational market. Thus it is necessary to consider their buying needs and behaviors.

Changes in Market Size and Trends

Total business receipts for private U.S. firms in business and organizational markets in major industries reached $18,242.6 billion in 1997. Combined business receipts for 2,123 U.S. retail establishments and wholesale businesses were $6,801 billion in 1997.[5] Each of these markets has undergone significant changes that have affected buyers and sellers alike.

● DIFFERENCES BETWEEN ORGANIZATIONAL AND CONSUMER BUYING BEHAVIOR

Businesses, governments, and institutions each have their own patterns of buying behavior. However, the broadly defined organizational buying process differs from the consumer buying process in a number of ways. In comparison with consumer purchases, the marketing challenges inherent in organizational purchases can be considered from both external and internal perspectives.[6] In general, an organization's external buyer-seller relationships are based on **derived demand,** a more complex buying and selling process, and a more concentrated customer base. In contrast, consumers and households buy for their own use, engage in a less complex process than organizations, and represent a diverse group of customers.

Internally, organizational buyers tend to place more emphasis than final consumers on technology and superior performance, customization to meet specific requirements, and the order-fulfillment process, which may include manufacturing to order rather than filling an order from an existing inventory of finished goods. These differences are due in large part to the nature of derived demand.

In contrast to final consumers, organizational buyers tend to buy more technical products, with less standardization, in larger quantities, and with more emphasis on services offered with the product. Organizational buyers have more opportunities to negotiate prices and to purchase direct from the manufacturer or through shorter distribution channels. Promotion to organizations tends to be concentrated on using the company's salesforce, trade media, and trade shows. In addition, organizational purchases generally are more complex, more direct, more structured and formal, involve more people in the process, and are based on longer-term relationships.

In terms of characteristics, organizational buyers differ from consumers in that they generally

- are more specialized in the types of goods and services they purchase,

- function as a member of a team or buying center,

Derived demand
Goods demanded by consumers or organizational buyers creating a need for purchases by manufacturers or dealers to provide goods and services to satisfy this demand.

INNOVATE OR EVAPORATE*

Innovation Is Necessary—but Insufficient

 After two decades of intense industry building, the biotech industry has taken off. According to an Arthur D. Little study, growth in the pharmaceutical industry is estimated at 7 to 8 percent over the next five years. In comparison, the biotech industry growth is likely to be 15 percent a year. Thirty biopharmaceuticals are on the market, with about 700 more in various stages of development. The compelling challenge to producers is to maneuver promising drugs through the hurdles of the U.S. Food and Drug Administration (FDA) approval process and manufacturing problems.

Immunex Corp. obtained FDA approval for its breakthrough drug for rheumatoid arthritis, Enbrel, in 1998, one of the first major biotech successes. In 2000, sales of Enbrel reached $650 million, $150 million above company estimates, and company stock price reached $80. In spite of the marketing success of Immunex's innovative new product, it was the manufacturing process that became its downfall. The company lost about $200 million in sales in 2001 because its production capacity was insufficient to meet demand. The stock price dropped as low as $11. A biotech giant, Amgen Inc., bought Immunex for $25 a share in December 2001. A new Enbrel plant was under construction in Rhode Island, but would not be operational for added production to meet demand until 2003.

Nearly every month, some promising new biologic drug runs into manufacturing or approval problems. These protein-based drugs are difficult to manufacture, wherein lies the problem—the more successful the product in the marketplace, the worse the production bottleneck. As Peter B. Davis, chief financial officer of Berkeley, Calif. biotech firm Xoma Ltd. said, "While there have been big advances in discovery technologies,

*The box title is attributed to James M. Higgins.

there has not been a corresponding increase in development capacity.... Now, the worry is less whether [the industry] can find a molecule than what to do with the molecule it finds."

According to a recent report from US Bancorp Piper Jaffray, currently every operational biotech plant is working at or near capacity. The 99 biotech drugs that are in late stages of clinical development are expected to yield up to 40 new drugs that will go on the market by 2005, which presents a serious manufacturing problem. Two major obstacles must be overcome when building a new biologics plant: complex technical problems, and cost ($300 to $500 million). There is a big difference between discovering a new drug and making one; and manufacturing generally is not a biotech's forté.

Traditional drug companies that have been manufacturing pharmaceuticals for years are not immune from production problems either. The FDA fined Schering-Plough Corp. $500 million for inadequate quality control at four plants, and delayed approval for Clarinex, an important new allergy drug. The agency also cited industry leader Pfizer Inc. for quality control problems at an Indiana plant, and doctors ran out of routine shots for children because of manufacturing problems for a range of vaccines made by Merck, Wyeth, and Aventis.

Traditional drugs are considered easy to make, compared to the complexity of biotech drugs that are built from fragile molecules meant to act like the body's natural disease-fighting proteins. The protein-based drugs cannot be swallowed as pills, and so must be injected directly into the bloodstream—which presents another challenge. If you can make one pill, a chemical entity, you can make millions just like it. In contrast, biologics are made from living cells or bacteria, which are more difficult to control in the manufacturing process. For two to three weeks, cells with the appropriate proteins are grown in

(continued)

fermentation tanks. The protein is extracted and purified for two to four more weeks. Then the protein is put into vials, and rigorous quality tests are performed for up to two months. When the company moves from the research and early market entry stages to mass production, the whole process may need to be altered significantly, because even minor changes can affect how the drug acts in the body. Although the FDA approved the drug in an earlier stage, the agency may require more clinical trials to be sure that changes in manufacturing for larger quantities have not changed how the drug performs.

Some biotech firms avoid dealing with manufacturing problems by outsourcing production to contract manufacturers. However, the contract firms can demand stringent contract terms and may not want to deal with small biotech companies. Moreover, the FDA also has delayed approval of breakthrough drugs because of quality concerns with the contract manufacturer. Hopefully,

the manufacturing problems will ease as production capacity increases. Piper Jaffray estimates that 938,000 liters of biotech production (200% increase in capacity) will be added in the next four to five years. Most of the increased production is attributed to a few large compnies—who may also experience further delays in getting their drugs to market. Small biotechs with a successful new product may have to come up with an innovative solution for their own manufacturing challenges.

The challenges facing the young biopharmaceutical industry do not end with the discovery of an innovative drug and the approval of the FDA. The marketing of an innovative product will be undermined by a lack of process innovation in manufacturing and marketing.

Source: Catherine Arnst and Arlene Weintraub, "Biotech: The Challenges Facing This Young Industry Don't End with Drug Discovery and Approval," *The BusinessWeek 50* (Spring 2002), pp. 195–196.

- purchase goods and services for use in providing goods and services for their own customers,
- are more professional and better trained,
- buy in larger quantities,
- purchase from fewer sellers,
- use shorter distribution channels,
- buy from manufacturers and distributors who are centrally located,
- negotiate prices and other terms of sale,
- form long-term relationships with key suppliers,
- require at least some level of customization in their purchases,
- emphasize specifications and performance,
- are more concerned with technology and rate of change, and
- require more services with their purchases.

● THE BUSINESS-TO-BUSINESS BUYING PROCESS

While various types of organizations and buying situations tend to follow a similar series of steps in the purchasing process, there are differences in the approaches used by business, industrial, governmental, and institutional buyers. Organizational structure and buyer characteristics also affect the organizational buying process and decision making. Each of these factors affects marketing strategy decisions for both the buyer and the seller.

Steps in the Buying Process

Assuming that buying responsibility and authority are established within an organization, its buyers or purchasing agents tend to follow a similar sequence of decisions and actions. Within different types of organizations and buying situations, the purchase process varies in degree of formality, complexity, number of people involved, and amount of effort required to make a good decision. Since there are certain basic activities that must be undertaken to complete a purchase, organizational buyers generally follow some or all of the steps shown in Figure 6.1 when making purchase decisions.

FIGURE 6.1

The Organizational Buying Process

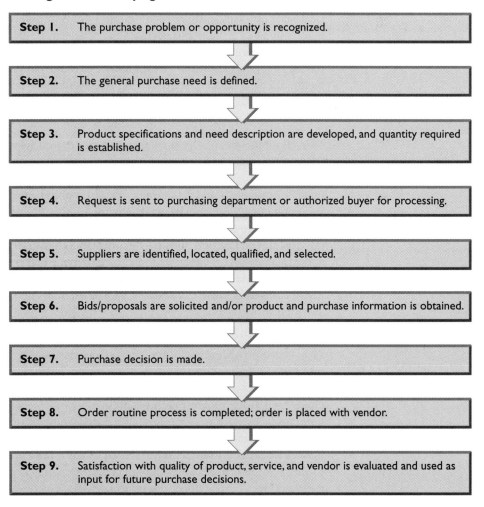

Step 1. The purchase problem or opportunity is recognized.

Step 2. The general purchase need is defined.

Step 3. Product specifications and need description are developed, and quantity required is established.

Step 4. Request is sent to purchasing department or authorized buyer for processing.

Step 5. Suppliers are identified, located, qualified, and selected.

Step 6. Bids/proposals are solicited and/or product and purchase information is obtained.

Step 7. Purchase decision is made.

Step 8. Order routine process is completed; order is placed with vendor.

Step 9. Satisfaction with quality of product, service, and vendor is evaluated and used as input for future purchase decisions.

Organizational Differences

Although most organizational buying decisions can be described in terms similar to those illustrated in Figure 6.1, there are several differences in the approach to purchasing used by buyers in business and commercial organizations, reseller markets (retailers and wholesalers), government agencies, and institutions. A few of these differences are described in this section.

Business and Commercial Organizations. Business and commercial organizations include OEMs, users, and a variety of industrial and producer customers, as discussed earlier. OEM, producer, and industrial purchasing agents make buying decisions that range from complex to routine. Purchases may include heavy and light equipment, computer systems, materials to use in production, consumable supplies for daily operations, and outside services. The more intricate nature of the buying decisions leads to more emphasis on customization, company-determined specifications, short lead times (so that production is not held up), many vendors (whose performance is carefully monitored), and a considerable amount of bidding and negotiation.

Users' purchases are focused on equipment, supplies, and services that are used to create other goods and services for resale. The nature of this buying process tends to be more routine and involve maintenance of a safety stock, automatic ordering, and other means of streamlining the purchasing process. Reordering may be facilitated by a direct satellite or computer link between buyer and seller for automatic order placement.

Reseller Markets. The buying process followed by retailers and wholesalers in the reseller markets requires considerable negotiation and quantity buying. These buyers must be fully aware of events and trends throughout their distribution channels. Both retailers and wholesalers must be able to forecast demand accurately at the consumer level and be well informed about the goods and services that are available at the manufacturer or producer level that can satisfy the needs of the retail customers. Further, both parties must be able to determine the most effective and efficient buyer-seller relationships that will deliver the most value to the customer while yielding acceptable profit margins to the retailers and wholesalers. In many cases, this need has resulted in a retailer assuming the role of a wholesaler, and vice versa.

Government Agencies. Purchases of goods and services for all levels of government agencies (and federal purchasing in particular) typically involve more layers of approval—first that the item is "needed" and then for the actual terms of the purchase itself. Government purchases frequently involve solicitation of numerous bids, with price being a major selection criterion; adherence to federal, state, or local legislation regarding the purchasing process; voluminous amounts of forms and paperwork, that is, bureaucratic "red tape"; and more attention to a vendor's ability to meet predetermined product specifications than to product superiority or marketing efforts. Finally, governmental purchases always are open to public scrutiny, creating a need for adherence to all legal and ethical rules of conduct.

Institutions.   The buying process followed by institutions is as diverse as the nature and number of institutions in the market. A small nonprofit agency, for example, may have an extremely informal, last-minute approach to purchasing. Conversely, a larger nonprofit organization such as the American Red Cross may have a more formal, standardized procedure. Some churches follow strict financial guidelines in purchasing goods and services that support their mission; others do not.

Most educational institutions have become more accountable and professional in carrying out the purchasing function. Decreased enrollments and increased operating costs in schools have focused attention on balancing institutional budgets in order to reach their strategic goals. While tuition has increased at many schools, this alone cannot cover historic expense levels. Thus school purchasing agents are pressed to find the most value for their money, with cost and adherence to institutional policies providing the major buying criteria.

These problems have become magnified in today's health care systems. Hospitals, nursing homes, and other health care providers need to provide adequate care for patients while keeping costs down in a relatively uncertain, rapidly changing environment. The need to benefit from economies of scale and keep costs down has led to mergers, acquisitions, and other horizontal and vertical alliances that have changed the purchasing process. Today's health care organizations have placed more restrictions on purchasing agents in their selection of goods and services, choice of vendors (often from preferred lists), specifications for order completion, shipping, and other details.

Some differences exist between the buying process followed by for-profit and nonprofit organizations. For-profit institutions have bottom-line responsibility, and purchases must be made at a price that not only covers the cost of the good or service but also results in profitability for the firm. On the other hand, nonprofit organizations are more interested in breaking even—not spending more than they receive.

Nonprofit buying can be categorized in several ways, using a rather liberal interpretation of *buying*. First, there is the purchase of typical goods and services to fulfill the nonprofit's strategic mission for its target market. Obviously, these purchases must be made under the most advantageous terms possible (low price, long payment period, etc.). Second, there is the solicitation of "free" goods and services from the community, the recruitment of volunteers, and the solicitation of donors. Third, nonprofits buy the goodwill of the community by "selling" the organization's services to its intended client base. Although little or no money is exchanged in the last two situations, there is a cost attached to "buying" the desired outcomes from each of these markets. Many recipients of the services provided by nonprofit organizations need to be convinced to participate. Those who populate the homeless shelters, for example, may not recognize—or accept—the need for job training and health care.

● ORGANIZATIONAL STRUCTURE AND BUYER CHARACTERISTICS

Many business-to-business buying situations require close relationships between the buyer and seller. Marketers who desire to sell their goods and services to organizational customers must recognize not only the need to deliver value and quality, but also the need to pay attention to the human aspect of the transaction.

TABLE 6.3

The Changing Role of Organizational Buyers

Changes in purchasing by businesses and other organizations include:

More emphasis on profitability. The bottom line must be enhanced by each transaction.

Increased use of the computer. Forecasting and maintaining inventories to determine purchase needs; tracking market trends and supplier performance; computer may replace salesperson in many instances.

Improved technology. Shipping and receiving efficiencies; better warehouse facilities for purchases; rate of change and continuous need to upgrade in many product categories; Internet plays a major role.

Consolidation, mergers, acquisitions. Business partners may change, long-term relationships may no longer be valid, and new strategic partnerships may need to be forged.

Distribution factors, relative channel power. Both buyers and sellers may cover larger territories; channel power shifting in many cases from sellers to buyers (e.g., large grocery and consumer goods manufacturers and supermarkets); shorter time to market.

Dynamic/changing global marketplace. Larger international base of customers, suppliers, and competitors; opportunities to cut purchase price through overseas purchasing; potential lack of reliability in dealing with overseas vendors; more regulations to contend with; global influence on product choices in consumer markets.

Organizational structure. Decentralization in many firms pushes purchasing decisions down to lower organizational levels; group decision making for major purchases (may include outside consultants, such as software providers and others with particular technical expertise); trend toward team emphasis and cross-functional project teams (that may become involved in purchase decisions).

In general, the world has become more complex for business-to-business buying and selling. The good news is that this complexity is made more manageable with the capabilities of the computer, databases, and other technological advances.

They also need to understand the implications of organizational structure for the organizational buyer as well as his or her role in the buying center. Table 6.3 outlines some of the changes taking place for organizational buyers.

Organizational Structure

Just as consumers make most of their buying decisions within the structure of a household, the business-to-business buying process occurs within an organizational structure that may allow much or little latitude for the buyer. The structure determines who is involved in a purchase decision, who actually makes the decision of what to buy, and who is responsible for actually making the purchase. Further, the structure determines the specific procedures and the formality of the buying process.

One approach to understanding the composition of the purchasing organization is to view it as a *buying center,* discussed next. Keep in mind, however, that the size of an organization may determine the scope of a buyer's responsibilities and the degree of formality that is exhibited.

Key Players in the Buying Center

Buying center
All those who participate in the purchasing decision-making process and who share common goals and risks arising from the decisions.

The decision-making unit of an organization is generally referred to as the **buying center,** defined as "all those individuals and groups who participate in the purchasing decision-making process, who share some common goals and the risks arising from the decisions." The buying center is made up of individuals who are involved in six buying roles.[7] These roles include users or initiators, influencers, deciders, approvers, buyers, and gatekeepers, as described below using the purchase of a new security system for a corporate headquarters.

Users or Initiators. Generally, the person who will benefit most from the acquisition of a good or service will start the purchase process. However, the purchase also may be initiated by another individual who recognizes the same need and realizes the benefits of the acquisition. For example, a top executive discovers that sensitive company information has somehow leaked out to competitors, and is somewhat aware that installation of a security system could fulfill this need.

Influencers. As the name implies, influencers affect the buying decision. Typically, as the purchase becomes more complex and expensive and affects more people, more individuals are involved with the potential to impact the final decision. They may set specifications for the good or service and may suggest viable alternatives for the purchasing agent to consider. This is particularly true for highly technical purchases that may be influenced by anyone from a production-line worker to a top manager. In the case of a security system purchase, influencers can include anyone with computer and surveillance systems or law enforcement expertise, users who have specific requirements for the system, and the financial officer who must consider this acquisition (and its administration and maintenance) within budgetary constraints.

Deciders. Deciders are individuals who can approve or disapprove of the proposed purchase—including requirements for product specifications and terms of sale, selection of preferred suppliers, and making the final determination of whether or not to buy. Note that despite their significant role in the purchasing process, deciders generally do not sign the purchase order. For the security system, a decider may be a software designer in the research and development department who needs to maintain better control over electronic communications with clients. Because of the software designer's ability to satisfy customers and build long-term relationships that result in high profitability for the company, his or her opinions will weigh heavily in the purchase decision.

Approvers. Approvers are individuals who make a "go" or "no go" decision about proceeding with the purchase process and who decide whether activities are conducted appropriately. If the security system purchase is being influenced by the need of the research and development department (see "Deciders" above), an approver might be the vice-president for marketing or another top-ranking executive.

Buyers. Buyers (or purchasers) may be one or more individuals, a buying center, or a purchasing department. Buyers have the responsibility and authority to select suppliers, negotiate terms of sale, and otherwise complete the details of the purchase according to specifications. For the security system purchase, a purchasing agent may choose between Symantec and Cisco to supply the specified hardware and software, and may negotiate the final terms with their sales representatives after obtaining their offers or bids.

Gatekeepers. Certain individuals in an organization are in a position to control information flows to those involved in purchase decisions. They have the ability to screen information about suppliers, products, or other aspects of a purchase and can determine whether or not to keep the "gate" open or shut for information. Further, they can decide what, if any, information to share with others involved in the buying decision. For example, a receptionist or secretary may decide for some reason to block a Symantec sales representative's attempts to communicate with the buying center or may fail to deliver requested product information to the purchasing agent. Thus the buyer may interpret the absence of information as Symantec's lack of interest in the sale—when the gatekeeper actually has controlled the critical information.

● TYPES OF BUSINESS PURCHASE DECISIONS

Like final consumers, the amount of effort expended in the purchasing process can extend from a routine purchase that requires only a few simple decisions to an extremely complex buying situation that involves more decisions and more effort. In business-to-business markets, buying situations can be classified into three major groups or buy classes: straight rebuy, modified rebuy, and new task.[8]

Straight Rebuy

Straight rebuy
Routine ordering process, simplest organizational purchase.

The **straight rebuy** is the simplest type of purchase made by organizational customers. It generally involves a routine ordering process, often with the most commonly used goods and services ordered automatically by computer or satellite link. In many instances, regular suppliers on a preferred list may be authorized to replenish inventory on frequently consumed items that meet predetermined specifications and to place the order based on prior approval. This type of purchasing situation implies that the buyer has had considerable experience with the product and supplier, as well as the prescribed buying routine. It requires close relationships with trusted suppliers who can deliver quality products on time (just-in-time delivery) to keep inventories at a minimal level while preventing stockouts and work slowdowns.

Modified Rebuy

Modified rebuy
Routine buying procedures altered in some way, requiring consideration of other alternatives.

The **modified rebuy** occurs when the routine buying procedures are altered in some way, requiring the purchasing agent to consider several alternatives. A number of changes can occur: The vendor may be out of stock or discontinue the original routinely purchased item, features or specifications included in the original item need to be changed in some way, or the purchasing process itself may be changed. The result is that additional alternatives must be considered before a final purchase decision is made, often involving limited search efforts and the input of several internal and external parties.

New Task Purchases

New task purchase
Unfamiliar or infrequent purchase situation, most extensive and complex.

As the name suggests, a **new task purchase** involves buying a good or service that is relatively unfamiliar—one that has never been purchased before or one that is purchased very rarely. The purchase process tends to be extensive, generally starting with an internally recognized need and ending with an evaluation of either the good or service purchased and the supplier from whom it was purchased. A new task purchase is characterized by the expenditure of more time and search effort and the involvement of more individuals at all stages of the decision. Of course, the most expensive, complex, and/or risk-prone decisions require the most time, effort, and involvement. These buying decisions follow the most formal procedures, such as those illustrated previously in Figure 6.1.

Extended Taxonomy of Purchase Decisions

Bunn (1993) extended the three Webster and Wind (1972) classifications of business-to-business purchase decisions to six categories: casual, routine low priority, simple modified rebuy, judgmental new task, complex modified rebuy, and strategic new task.[9] The categories are distinguished from one another by a set of situational characteristics and buying activities. Situational characteristics include purchase importance, task uncertainty, extensiveness of choice set, and buyer power. Key buying activities include search for information, use of analysis techniques, proactive focus, and procedural control.

The extended taxonomy of buying decisions provides a useful basis for market segmentation strategies and a mechanism for developing adaptive selling approaches based on more narrowly defined buying situations and buying decision approaches. These approaches are described in Figure 6.2. The results of a study by Wilson, McMurrian, and Woodside suggest that framing of buying problems by organizational buyers is layered and more complex than related taxonomies developed by Bunn and others. It is important, therefore, to understand that organizational buyers' preferences for vendors and value-added customer services are also affected by how they view the buying problem.[10]

● MAJOR INFLUENCES ON PURCHASE DECISIONS

Business-to-business buying decisions are not only more complex than consumer decisions, but they also are subject to numerous internal and external influences. Many of the personal, interpersonal, organizational, and environmental factors that affect organizational purchases are beyond the direct control of the purchasing agent but must be factored into the final buying decision.

External Environmental Influences

Today's business-to-business marketers frequently operate in constantly changing, highly volatile, and uncertain environments, where risk involved in the purchasing function takes on more significance than ever. Market demand, competitive strategies, technological advances, economic conditions, and the regulatory environment each have a major impact on buying decisions made by professional purchasing agents.

FIGURE 6.2

Taxonomy of Business-to-Business Buying Decisions

	Descriptions of Buying Decision Approaches					
Variables	**1** **Casual**	**2** **Routine** **Low Priority**	**3** **Simple** **Modified** **Rebuy**	**4** **Judgmental** **New Task**	**5** **Complex** **Modified** **Rebuy**	**6** **Strategic** **New Task**
Situational Characteristics						
Purchase Importance	Of minor importance	Somewhat important	Quite important	Quite important	Quite important	Extremely important
Task Uncertainty	Little uncertainty	Moderately uncertain	Little uncertainty	Great amount of uncertainty	Little uncertainty	Moderately uncertain
Extensiveness of Choice Set	Much choice	Much choice	Narrow set of choices	Narrow set of choices	Much choice	Narrow set of choices
Buyer Power	Little or no power	Moderate power	Moderate power	Moderate power	Strong power position	Strong power position
Buying Activities						
Search for Information	No search made	Little effort at searching	Moderate amount of search	Moderate amount of search	High level of search	High level of search
Use of Analysis Techniques	No analysis performed	Moderate level of analysis	Moderate level of analysis	Moderate level of analysis	Great deal of analysis	Great deal of analysis
Proactive Focus	No attention to proactive issues	Superficial consideration of proactive focus	High level of proactive focus	Moderate proactive focus	High level of proactive focus	Proactive issues dominate purchase
Procedural Control	Simply transmit the order	Follow standard procedures	Follow standard procedures	Little reliance on established procedures	Follow standard procedures	Little reliance on established procedures

Source: Bunn, Michele (1993), "Taxonomy of Buying Decision Approaches," *Journal of Marketing,* Vol. 57 (January), p. 47. Reprinted by permission of the American Marketing Association.

The U.S. Postal Service planned to increase postage rates well before the terrorist attacks of 9/11, but this horrific event had a devastating effect on not only the USPS, but all postal and delivery services. Millions of letters and parcels were either delayed or never delivered (many ended up in the rubble of the World Trade Center). The problem was exacerbated by the discovery of anthrax powder in mail delivered to government offices and other locations. The shutdown of the U.S. air-traffic system, and tighter security at U.S. Customs checkpoints at borders, ports, and airports, paralyzed millions of packages, high-priority mail, and other cargo. Increased security restrictions also slowed deliveries and pick-ups by United Parcel Service, FedEx, and other airfreight carriers.

These events are a vivid reminder of the havoc that unexpected events can play with otherwise healthy business operations. The slowdown in mail and package delivery, and the permanent destruction of some pieces, caused a ripple effect throughout the world. All types of for-profit businesses, nonprofit organizations, and customers were affected. The return to "normal" operations was remarkably quick, but the damage had been done to revenues and profits for the USPS and the other carriers, as well as their business customers. Many businesses switched their package deliveries from the USPS to other shippers such as UPS and FedEx. Many marketing strategies and tactics that were based on the delivery-business-as-usual were changed to reflect the new realities. Catalog companies and other direct marketers were hit hard with increased postal rates, and security concerns. Credit card issuers and processors first had their business disrupted in the aftermath of September 11, and then by the anthrax scare, causing them to promote online bill presentment and payment, and electronic banking. Numerous individuals and businesses have found the Internet to be a desirable alternative to the traditional "paper-based" communication—changing the dynamics of a variety of businesses and industries.[11]

Market Demand. Since business-to-business purchases are based on derived demand, the business and consumer markets essentially dictate what is produced and purchased by organizational customers. Buying goods and services to use for production or resale requires the ability to forecast accurately what the market wants and needs. Market demand and product influences (discussed later in this chapter) interact to influence the purchase process and buying decisions.

Competition. Organizational markets tend to have fewer, but larger and more powerful, competitors than consumer markets. Thus the dynamics between buyers and sellers may be subject to their relative power position. Competition can be viewed from the perspectives of both the buyers and sellers. On the seller side, numerous competitors who offer similar goods or services offer the organizational buyer more opportunities to negotiate favorable terms of sale, capitalizing on supply and demand. With fewer sellers, of course, there is less room for negotiations and deals.

On the buying side, purchasing decisions are influenced by the nature of the firm's competitors, their location, and their present (and planned) actions. Organizational buyers must be knowledgeable about trends and events in their industries in order to develop sustainable competitive strategies. Within this context, purchases take on strategic importance in achieving organizational objectives. The entire purchasing process also is affected by the relative sizes of the parties involved. For example, mass merchandisers and discount chains have more buying "clout" compared with small retailers and suppliers. A large retailer can make demands on manufacturers and other suppliers in terms of specifications, order terms, delivery, and exclusivity. Most suppliers cannot afford to lose their largest customers and will cater to their demands, often making purchases more difficult and expensive for smaller customers.

Technology and the Rate of Change. Organizations must continuously be on the cutting edge of technological change in determining which goods and services they will buy and sell. Purchasing agents must stay informed about the latest technological advances in everything from computer systems to order forms. Changing technologies result in the need to update present production equipment, computer systems, and other inputs needed by the organization to remain competitive—as well as components for higher-tech products demanded by the marketplace. Computers, software, and related technologies are perhaps the most visible examples of the short life span of many technological advances. For example, the switchover to the Pentium chip in the mid-1990s adversely affected sales of Intel's older microprocessors. Later, the MMX chip, Windows NT, and Windows XP had a similar impact on sales of the Pentium technology. In addition to the increased capability of software and hardware, the "trickling down" of computer technology to more unsophisticated home users has had an impact on hardware design, with computers and other equipment being produced with more "stylish" designs.

Economic and Financial Conditions.   Business-to-business markets have undergone drastic economic shifts and volatile financial conditions during the past two decades. This has affected buying decisions in several ways. First, in a serious economic downturn, purchasing budgets may be frozen and budgets reallocated so that funds for purchasing new goods and services are not available. Second, having the financial strength to make purchases does not remove the element of risk associated with making a "bad" buying decision—particularly with large-ticket capital investments. Third, purchases made in response to derived demand from the organization's customers and their customers may decline, diminishing the need for new purchases.

Regulatory and Political Influences.   In comparison with final consumers, organizational buyers must observe more rules and regulations while engaged in purchasing activities. Regulations include fair trade practices, competitive actions, price discrimination, affirmative action requirements, security regulations, and other legislation. Political and ethical influences, such as the corporate scandals of 2002, also affect business-to-business buying decisions. Although a practice may be legal, it may be contrary to the current political climate or ethically unacceptable to a firm's stakeholders. Purchasing in a global marketplace requires knowledge of each country's laws and politics and the ethical norms of that culture.

Internal Organizational Influences

Just as household factors influence consumers' buying decisions, organizational characteristics influence buying decisions made by business-to-business buyers. Purchasing decisions must be made within the context of a firm's mission and objectives, company policies and procedures, and formal and informal systems. The size and structure of an organization also affect purchases in terms of whether buying is centralized or decentralized or oriented toward a dominant organizational function. For example, a production orientation would suggest that those involved in this function would dominate purchase decisions.

As noted previously, organizational buying involves joint decision making. The buyer must reach consensus with a variety of individuals from other functional areas and levels of the organization. Implicit in this team approach to buying is recognizing who really makes the buying decisions—whether it is the person who is authorized to sign the order or someone else who makes the decision behind the scenes.

Organizational buying policies and preferences include guidelines that must be followed by purchasing agents. In an age of just-in-time (JIT) delivery, increased attention to quality and value, and the building of long-term strategic relationships between buyers and sellers, this may include a requirement to purchase only from a list of preferred providers, with departure from this list requiring upper-level approval. Buyers evaluate their vendors on dimensions such as reliability, trust, price, performance, and convenience of transactions and buy from those that score the highest on important factors.

Profit goals affect the price that can be paid for goods and services, with an established profit-margin goal entering into the cost equation. (See Chapter 14 for further discussion of pricing concepts.) A tradeoff must be made between price and performance at times, with the deciding factor often being the ability to maintain quality standards and to satisfy key customers.

Personal Influences

Personal traits and interpersonal dynamics among the members of the buying center influence all individuals involved in organizational buying processes. Although organizational considerations dominate buying decisions, the effect of personal traits on the decision process and interactions among joint decision makers cannot be ignored.

Demographic, psychographic, and sociologic characteristics affect organizational buying decisions in many of the same ways that they affect consumer decisions. The buyer's experience, position in the company, age, education, personality type, cultural background, perceived competence, ethical behavior, and attitudes toward risk affect his or her approach to purchasing. Personal motivation and perceptions of his or her role in the organization and other life roles also influence an organizational buyer's decisions.

In interactions with joint decision makers, organizational buyers are influenced by many interpersonal factors. Relative position or status within the organization, degree of responsibility and authority, ability to empathize with others, and ability to persuade internal and external parties in the decision-making process all play a key part in purchases.

Product Influences

As discussed earlier in the context of types of organizational purchases, the nature of the good or service being purchased affects the buying process. Commodities such as paper products or telephone services are purchased on a routine basis, requiring the input of fewer individuals and little extra effort once the initial product specifications and providers have been determined. While routine product purchases typically involve smaller items and lower unit values, they usually are purchased in large quantities, making it necessary to negotiate favorable prices, delivery, and other terms of sales.

The purchase of products that are more complex, expensive, or riskier involves more extensive decision making. More individuals participate in the decision, both from inside and outside the company. Buyers must expend more time and effort in gathering relevant information and evaluating potential suppliers. They also must negotiate for more favorable terms such as guarantees, service after the sale, or price breaks.

● RELATIONSHIP MARKETING

Relationship marketing was discussed in Chapter 5 as it applies to consumer markets. Here we will consider buyer-seller relationships within the context of business-to-business markets. Although many of the buying and selling units represented in business markets may be viewed as large, faceless conglomerates, relationships are not built between buildings and production lines and systems. They are built between the people who inhabit those buildings and operate within those systems from a market-driven perspective. Relationship marketing transcends organizational size or age, industry, nationality, or other characteristics; the need to build long-term relationships between buyers and sellers is universal.

Buyer-Seller Relationships

The highest levels of customer satisfaction are obtained from a series of relationships between buyers and their suppliers throughout entire channels of distribution. The very nature of business-to-business transactions is adversarial, yet suppliers and their customers must view one another as partners if they are to be profitable over the long run. While the new marketing concept puts the customer first,[12] it is helpful to view both buyers and sellers as customers who function as partners in building a lasting and mutually advantageous exchange relationship.

According to Webster,[13] relationship marketing is essentially a question of attitude, where the customer is a business partner rather than an enemy. This view of relationship marketing puts the customer first—before the company, before the product, and perhaps at the expense of a sale. Positive long-term relationships with customers require a high level of trust, cooperation, interdependence, and focus on customer satisfaction. In professional services marketing, for example, relationships are based on a mutual set of expectations and a belief in the other's integrity, competence, and confidentiality, where appropriate. However, it should be noted that it is not feasible to build relationships with all customers or all suppliers—some are not viable candidates for long-term relationships.

Quality, Satisfaction, and Long-Term Relationships

Organizational buyers develop loyalty to suppliers who provide them with quality, value, and service that meet or exceed their expectations. This loyalty results in a long-term, ongoing relationship that is valuable to both parties. Loyal buyers are more willing to pay premium prices or to ask for special inducements to buy from a supplier they view as a partner. The revenue stream from this partnership extends to future purchases of the same good or service or to additional revenues and profit from other products sold by the company. Additionally, a satisfied customer will tell other potential customers, generating highly believable word of mouth that will encourage others to buy.

Relationship Marketing and the New Marketing Concept

Fifteen guidelines for implementing the new marketing concept were described in Chapter 5.[14] Each guideline applies to building buyer-seller relationships in organizational markets as well as in consumer markets. From the perspective of an organizational buyer, the seller's focus should be on creating customer value, targeting the most viable customers, sharing goals and competencies, obtaining input from buyers about their expectations and definitions of quality and value, and making a commitment to continuous improvement and innovation that benefits customers.

Some illustrations of business-to-business relationship marketing include joint ventures between buyers and their key suppliers to develop innovative products or processes, JIT delivery systems, more efficient distribution channels, and possible cost savings. Marketing tactics (e.g., personal selling, advertising, customer loyalty programs) are geared toward the extra effort required to develop long-term buyer-seller relationships rather than closing a single sale. The U.S. Postal Service (USPS) implemented a customer-oriented strategy in the 1990s in an attempt to overcome past "bureaucratic" images of its service. Both the number and quality of services were increased to supplement the traditional core business of letter and parcel delivery service, creating a more customer-focused organization. Many of these services were in direct competition with those offered by full-service packing and shipping companies like Mail Boxes, Etc. and delivery services like FedEx and Airborne Express. The added services also provided another source of revenue, as the volume of first-class mail slows due to competition from faster communications devices such as fax machines and e-mail. The USPS also announced that it was in the business of processing bills for corporations, in direct competition with banks and other private companies that vie for bill-processing contracts.[15] The service was launched with American Express Company as the first customer. The USPS took over the customer bill payments for American Express at its Staten Island, New York, processing center, in anticipation of expanding this service to other customers. While competitors maintain that the USPS has an unfair advantage, the agency maintains that such services are an extension of the services it provides to its customers.

Summary

In contrast to consumers who purchase for their own use, organizational buyers purchase goods and services to be used directly or indirectly in their own operations. In turn, they sell, rent, or provide goods and services to other organizations. Organizational buyers purchase on behalf of a business or commercial enterprise, government agency, institution, nonprofit, or other type of organization.

Major industries comprising the business market include agriculture, forestry and fisheries, mining, construction, manufacturing, transportation and public utilities, wholesale and retail trade, finance, insurance, real estate, and services. Most organizational customers can be classified as both original equipment manufacturers (OEMs) or user customers. An OEM buys component parts from a commercial supplier to use in the OEM's finished products that are sold to another customer. User customers purchase equipment, supplies, and services that are used directly or indirectly in the production of other goods and services that are sold to other organizations and/or to the consumer market. Reseller organizations include retailers and wholesalers who are intermediaries in the distribution system. Governmental customers vary in size, scope, and purchasing processes but comprise one of the largest markets throughout the world. Institutions are made up of purchasers that are neither commercial nor governmental. They can be public or private, for-profit or nonprofit, large or small, domestic or international.

Organizational buying patterns differ from those of consumers in several ways. An organization's purchases are based on derived demand and involve a more formal and complex process, with more individuals involved in buying decisions. More attention is given to specifications, performance, the order-fulfillment process, and building long-term relationships. Customers tend to be concentrated by industry and geography, and purchases tend to be less standardized, more technical, and in larger quantities.

The organizational buying process is a sequence of decisions and actions that are followed in varying degrees depending on the nature of the purchase and the type of organization. Buying decisions are made within the boundaries of an organizational structure that determines who has responsibility for purchasing and what procedures will be followed. A buying center approach, comprised of individuals who perform the roles of users or initiators, deciders, approvers, buyers, and gatekeepers, may be used for purchasing.

Organizational purchases can range from routine decisions that require little effort to extremely complex decisions that involve a great deal of effort. Buying situations can be classified as straight rebuy (routine, automatic), modified rebuy (changes to familiar purchase), or new task (relatively unfamiliar purchase). These basic decision types can be extended to a taxonomy of six types, based on situational characteristics (purchase importance, task uncertainty, extensiveness of choice set, and buyer power) and buying activities (search for information, use of analysis techniques, proactive focus, and procedural control).

Factors in both the external and internal environments affect organizational purchase decisions. External factors include market demand, competition, technology and the rate of change, the economy, and the regulatory environment. Internal factors include the firm's mission and objectives, policies and procedures, formal and informal systems, size, and organizational structure. Other influences on buying decisions include personal characteristics and the nature of the good or service being purchased.

Buyer-seller relationships are an important aspect of organizational purchasing. Despite the adversarial nature of many business-to-business purchase situations, formal or informal partnerships are formed on the basis of customer satisfaction and high-quality goods and services. This type of relationship marketing is consistent with the marketing concept.

Questions

1. Discuss each of the stages in the buying process for organizational purchases. Illustrate with an actual or hypothetical company purchase of new office equipment.

2. For the purchase just described, identify (a) the key information sources that would most likely be consulted and (b) the primary influences that can affect this purchase decision.

3. Create a scenario to explain how a supplier may have to deal with a buyer's expectations (and vice versa) in an industrial, organizational, or governmental buying situation.

4. What impact, if any, does the type of purchase or product class have on purchase behavior in the scenario described in Question 3?

5. Compare and contrast the complete purchasing decision-making process for an individual versus a company for specific products such as (a) security system, (b) truck, (c) light bulbs, and (d) long-distance telephone service. (You may wish to present your answer in a comparative table or flowchart.)

6. Discuss the implications of situational characteristics and buying activities for marketing strategies or tactics within each of the buying decision approaches presented in Figure 6.2.

7. As the sales manager for a computer software company, explain how you would approach the key players in a target customer's buying center to convince them to buy your product.

8. Describe and give an example of the relationship between quality, satisfaction, and long-term relationships between buyers and sellers.

Exercises

1. Find business-to-business advertisements in trade publications or general business media. Critique the effectiveness of these on the basis of your perception of the following:

a. Type of organization targeted

b. Influences used to encourage customer response

c. Type of purchase decision

2. Interview a retail buyer or industrial purchasing agent regarding the changes that are occurring in the buying process in his or her company and industry. Also determine how he or she is meeting the challenge posed by these changes.

3. Obtain a copy of an RFP (Request for Proposal) from a government agency or other organization that is seeking bids for specific goods and/or services. Determine how this process is different from the usual nonbidding purchase process and the decision maker(s).

Endnotes

1. S. Tully, "Purchasing's New Muscle," *Fortune* (February 20, 1995), p. 75. (A statement made by AT&T's executive vice-president for telephone products to indicate the importance of purchasing in the organizational hierarchy.)

2. Economic Census Summary (NAICS Basis) 1997, Table 721, U.S. Census Bureau, *Statistical Abstract of the United States: 2001*, p. 481.

3. Robert W. Haas, *Business Marketing Management: An Organizational Approach*, 5th ed. (Boston: PWS-Kent Publishing, 1992), Chap. 1.

4. U.S. Bureau of Economic Analysis, http://www.bea.doc.gov/bea/dn/nipaweb/index.htm, U.S. Census Bureau, *Statistical Abstract of the United States: 2001*, Table 417, p. 260.

5. Economic Census Summary, *op. cit.*, p. 480.

6. See V. Kasturi Kangan, Benson P. Shapiro, and Rowland T. Moriarty, Jr., *Business Marketing Strategy: Cases, Concepts and Applications* (Chicago: Richard D. Irwin, 1995), Chap. 1; and John C. Mowen and Michael Minor, *Consumer Behavior*, 5th ed. (Englewood Cliffs, NJ: Prentice-Hall, 1998), pp. 537–539.

7. Frederick E. Webster, Jr., and Yoram Wind, *Organizational Buying Behavior* (Englewood Cliffs, NJ: Prentice-Hall, 1972), pp. 78–80.

8. For further discussion, see Patrick J. Robinson, Charles W. Faris, and Yoram Wind, *Industrial Buying and Creative Marketing* (Boston: Allyn & Bacon, 1967).

9. Michele D. Bunn, "Taxonomy of Buying Decision Approaches," *Journal of Marketing* 57 (January 1993), pp. 38–56.

10. Elizabeth J. Wilson, Robert C. McMurrian, and Arch G. Woodside, "How Buyers Frame Problems: Revisited," *Psychology & Marketing* 18(6) (June 2001), pp. 617–655.

11. Rick Brooks, "A Day of Terror: Air-Cargo Systems Face Logjam Following Halt of Airline Traffic," *Wall Street Journal* (September 12, 2001), p. A3; Jane Adler, "Suddenly, Security," *Credit Card Management* 14(11) (January 2002), pp. 30–37; Paul Miller, "Parcel Carriers Meet the Challenge," *Catalog Age,* 18(12) (November 2001), p. 19; David Biederman, "USPS Asks for $5 Billion," *Traffic World,* 265(47) (November 19, 2001), p. 12.

12. For further discussion of relationship marketing and the new marketing concept, see Frederick E. Webster, Jr., *Market-Driven Management: Using the New Marketing Concept to Create a Customer-Oriented Company* (New York: John Wiley & Sons, 1994).

13. *Ibid.,* p. 142.

14. *Ibid.,* Chap. 9.

15. Staff Reporter, "Postal Service Seeks Business of Processing Bills for Corporations," *Wall Street Journal* (June 11, 1997), p. B15.

MARKETING MANAGEMENT IN ACTION: CLOSING CASE

Pushing Microsoft "Office" Out of the Office

When you are already considered a monopoly, where do you go for new business? Jeffrey S. Raikes, a key executive and software guru at Microsoft, is dedicated to growing the company's business. In the 1990s, he created Microsoft Corp.'s Office software by combining the company's word-processing and spreadsheet programs. Since its inception, Office has generated over $60 billion in sales, quietly becoming Microsoft's "other, quieter monopoly," along with the Windows operating system. Following his success with Office, Raikes became responsible for the company's vast sales operation, eventually becoming one of the top executives at Microsoft.

Now Raikes has returned to Office to reinvent his own creation—tackling a crucial assignment that is the key to future growth. The growth rate for sales of Office software had slowed to 1 percent in the year ended June 30, 2002. With his new strategy, Raikes expects to double the annual sales growth of Office to $20 billion by 2010. To accomplish this goal, he and his staff will launch new products, ranging from a new tablet computer to programs designed to enable workers to analyze large amounts of data in a short time.

In addition to new products, he was figuring out how to reinvigorate his old business in Office, when he was influenced by comments made by Jack Welch during a speech. According to Welch, dominant companies in slow-growing businesses should redefine their market. The resulting share of the larger market will be smaller, but opportunities will grow. Raikes decided to look far beyond the 40 million customers in America who "work overtime on PowerPoint and Excel." His new Office software would be targeted toward anyone who used information, whether or not they created it. He envisioned new customers in the ranks of workers who are not typical Office users, such as pilots, nurses, factory workers, and truck drivers—a market estimated to be 117 million people in the United States. Raikes faces many challenges in this new endeavor. As new markets are pursued, new competitors must be confronted, such as Hyperion Solutions Corp. in business-intelligence software and SAP in business applications. In new areas where a market has never been established, it is difficult to sell technology to people who must be convinced they need it.

Raikes is taking an innovative approach to discovering new product ideas. Four hundred sales advisors were hired to work closely with corporate customers and show them how to maximize the capability of current Microsoft software. Another team is spotting the "white spaces" or gaps between present product categories for which new programs can be invented. The Center for Information Work was established as a prototype of the office of the future, and a place to test the company's latest innovations. Raikes plans to spend $3 billion on Office over the next five years, with plans to create specialized versions of the software for new segments of users. Microsoft has embarked on several strategic initiatives that are expected to boost Microsoft sales by up to $20 billion in the next

eight years—with half of the amount coming from doubling sales of the Office suite:

1. Expand into new markets with "run-the-business" Office applications for small and mid-size business users; applications include programs in areas such as payroll, accounting, and inventory management; goal is to double Office sales to $20 billion by 2010.

2. Create new applications for new markets, such as business-intelligence software for analyzing data; plans to invent brand new product categories for workers who must interpret all the data their companies gather.

3. Create programs for small companies; build on capabilities of two acquisitions—Great Plains Software and Navision, who are leaders in small business software; goal is to increase sales from $300 million to $10 billion by 2010.

4. Launch Tablet PC in November 2002; requires a special tablet version of Office to take advantage of the handwriting features; Tablet has a keyboard, and users can store and recall handwritten notes.

Raikes' strategic vision has captured the attention of Wall Street. As Goldman, Sachs & Co. analyst Richard Sherlund said, "I'm glad somebody's got fire in the belly." His targets may be audacious, but his dream of a whole new generation of software is an inspiration to the 7,500 people who work for him. Office sales are expected to grow 10 percent during the 2002 fiscal year. However, much of this may be due to Microsoft's new licensing terms, which have prompted customers to buy the most recent version of the software. After that, Office will need compelling new features to sell company-wide upgrades. Microsoft will face new competitors as it pursues each of its strategic initiatives. This includes competition from well-established specialists in each of its new markets as it transitions from selling commodity software to also selling complex applications. Raikes helped build Microsoft from its beginning in 1981, when the company had only 100 employees and annual sales were $12 million. He ran the Word and Excel divisions in the early days, and these two software programs changed the way work was done. His new focus is on reducing "what he calls a worker's 'time to insight.'" He believes the result "could give you, in effect, a 28-hour day." Raikes is enthusiastic about his work, and has the experience and desire to accomplish his goals—as daunting as the task may seem. (He is independently wealthy, with $350 million in Microsoft stock, but is highly excited about what he is doing for the company.)

Raikes looks in many places for inspiration, including his own everyday experiences. Frustrations of dealing with paper-based documents, such as those used for his children's school applications, have led to one of the first new products his engineers are working on. The product is a "paperless workflow application designed to allow organizations to dispense with paper forms and heaps of retyping." Other ideas come from customers, such as JetBlue Airways. Pilots are required to update their flight manuals each time policies change, according to Federal regulations. This can occur several times a week and is very time-consuming. Most pilots keep the information in a notebook, and rip out the pages replaced by the updates. Every JetBlue pilot is issued a computer, and manuals are automatically updated every morning on a Web site that uses Word and Office Web software. The airline saves 10,000 man-hours each year with this innovation. Office software does not need new capabilities to make it more useful for customers such as JetBlue; they just have to show customers that they can do much more with the software they have (and then they will be encouraged to buy the latest versions). Based on the JetBlue success, 400 "grassroots sales advisors" were hired to meet directly with workers (bypassing corporate technology departments).

A major problem facing Raikes is how to market new-to-the-market applications, such as the ability to collaborate on a document simultaneously. He says, "A lot of what we can do with software is stuff that customers don't think to ask for. . . . This makes it harder to describe what software does—and harder to sell it." To overcome some of this problem, the Microsoft Center for Information Work opened in September 2002, featuring technologies such as the "RingCam." RingCam is a teleconferencing technology created by Microsoft Research that will soon be ready for the market. It is described as looking "a bit like a small table lamp, [with] five cameras circling the top and eight tiny microphones around the base to give a 360-degree view of a room." Microsoft's software matches the audio and visual feeds so that the person who is speaking appears automatically on the computer screens of people who are accessing the meeting from another location.

Raikes' innovative ideas also apply to established markets. For example, Microsoft's business-intelligence software is expected on the market within two years. The application is designed to "help people extract data from various computer systems, run it through sophisticated analytic programs, and produce reports to guide their decisions." Competition in this $3.8 billion market includes Hyperion and Business Objects. Raikes believes Microsoft's competitive advantage will be in creating programs that are easier for workers to use within the familiar Office applications. He said, "We can create business intelligence for the masses."

Since the downturn in the technology sector, corporate customers have not been as eager to buy the latest technology, but Raikes says he can afford to wait. "A lot of times, people will overestimate how quickly things might change in the short term. . . But they will also underestimate how quickly things will change in the long term." When they are ready to buy, Microsoft will be ready to sell a whole new generation of software. The key question for Microsoft, and for the rest of the industry, is whether Raikes can hit the jackpot again with a new generation of Office.

Source: Jay Greene, "Beyond the Office: How Microsoft Aims to Broaden the Reach of Its Business Suite," *BusinessWeek* (September 16, 2002), pp. 54–56.

Case Study Questions

1. Identify the different types of organizational buyers that might be interested in learning more about the capabilities of their present Microsoft Office software (assuming they are either unaware that this application is included in their present program, or have not tried to use it for their business needs). Explain how this knowledge might translate into future sales for at least one of the types of organizational buyers that you identified.

2. Analyze the process that would most likely be followed by an organizational buyer versus a final consumer when purchasing the Tablet PC. What are the implications for marketing mix design and implementation?

3. Describe the role of key players in a buying center relative to a purchase of Microsoft Office software. How does each person's role change, if at all, when purchasing a complex new-to-the-market Microsoft software product versus "commodity software" such as an existing version of Office.

4. Select one of the new products planned by Microsoft as described in the case. Explain how the type of buying decision affects Microsoft's marketing strategy for selling this new product to a new target market both in terms of the three major classifications of purchase deci-

sions, and the extended taxonomy presented in Figure 6.2.

5. Select one type of organizational buyer from your answer to Question 1. Which internal and external influences do you believe would have the greatest (negative and/or positive) effect on the purchase decision discussed in Question 4? Why?

6. Based on information in the case, does Microsoft practice relationship marketing? Give examples to illustrate your answer, and discuss other ways that the company can build long-term buyer-seller relationships.

7. What do you believe are Microsoft's greatest challenges in bringing these new products to market, and how can Mr. Raikes overcome these obstacles?

CHAPTER 7

Market Segmentation, Target Marketing, and Positioning

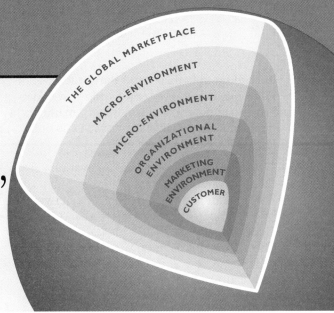

A new population force is emerging in our society, increasingly demanding rapid response, easy access, and a sense of control. Already shaping our online environments, its members are drawing on their experiences in cyberspace to form their expectations for everyday life. It is the e-generation ... defined not by common demographics but by a common set of experiences.[1]

Marketing to Low-Income Markets: Third World Buyers at the "Bottom of the Pyramid"

The end of the Cold War brought about a significant economic and social transformation with many new growth opportunities for multinational corporations. However, "the prospect of millions of 'middle-class' consumers in developing countries, clamoring for products from multinational corporations (MNCs) was wildly oversold." The Asian and Latin American financial crises also affected the attractiveness of emerging markets. The September 11th attacks further compounded the risk-reward debate for entering global markets.

The magnitude of the opportunity in emerging markets is actually much larger than originally thought, but the opportunity lies in the billions of *aspiring poor* who are becoming a part of the market economy for the first time. Companies with the resources and the persistence to compete at the bottom of the world economic pyramid can expect to reap rewards in growth, profits, and immeasurable contributions to mankind. MNCs have a unique opportunity to develop and test environmentally sustainable technologies and products in developing countries that do not have the basic infrastructure to meet the needs of the population. This often leads to innovations that eventually can be marketed to the whole world. Tier 4 market opportunities also enable the world's wealthiest companies to make an important socially responsible contribution by selling to the poor and helping them out of their desperate circumstances.

According to Prahalad and Hart, reaching the two thirds of the world's population that constitute the huge potential of the B2–4B* market will require significant changes in how MNCs operate. These changes include:

- The development of radical innovations in technology and business models.
- A reevaluation of the relationships between price and performance for goods and services.
- The attainment of a new level of capital efficiency, and new approaches to measuring financial success.
- A move from a "bigger is better" mentality to an "ideal of highly distributed small-scale operations married to world-scale capabilities."
- The ability to produce and distribute products and services in "culturally sensitive, environmentally sustainable, and economically profitable ways."

Four tiers of consumers can be identified according to annual per capita income (based on purchasing parity in U.S. $). Tier 1 at the top of the pyramid represents 75 to 100 million people with annual per capita income of more than $20,000, Those with annual per capita income between $1,500 and $20,000 are considered Tiers 2 and 3, a population of 1,500 to 1,750 million. Tier 4 represents the market potential of the world's poorest consumers—4 billion people with an annual per capita income of less than $1,500.

Marketers need to reevaluate long-held assumptions about Tier 4, such as:

1. The poor are not our target customers; we can't profitably compete due to our cost structure.
2. The poor cannot afford, or have no use for, goods and services sold in developed markets.
3. Only those consumers in developed markets appreciate and will pay for new technology; the poor can use the old technology.
4. The bottom of the pyramid is not important to the long-term viability of our business; leave them to governments and nonprofits.
5. Managers are not motivated or excited about business challenges with a humanitarian dimension.

6. It is difficult to find talented managers who want to work at the bottom of the pyramid.

To many, the pursuit of business at the bottom of the pyramid defies conventional managerial logic, but there is tremendous potential for profitable growth opportunities. Two of the Tier 4 MNC pioneers are Hindustan Lever Ltd. (HLL) and Nirma Ltd. in India.

Hindustan Lever Ltd. (HLL) is a subsidiary of Great Britain's Unilever PLC, and widely considered the best-managed company in India. HLL served India's small elite who could afford MNC products for over 50 years; then observed the success of Nirma Ltd. who offered detergent products to poor consumers, mostly in rural areas. In 1995, HLL recognized the opportunity to serve this market, and made significant changes to its business model. The company adapted its detergent formula to the needs of poor people who washed clothes in rivers and other public water systems. Packaging was changed to smaller single-use containers (because of limited money for purchase, and possible lack of refrigeration), but prices were in line with the larger packaging sold to other markets. They decentralized production to benefit from a large labor pool in rural India, and also adjusted distribution and pricing strategies for Tier 4 consumers. Nirma Ltd. is a local Indian firm that began rural distribution of detergent products in the 1990s in India, creating a new business system, new product formulation, low-cost manufacturing, and establishing a wide distribution network. Their success in this market inspired HLL to enter. Now, Nirma and HLL each hold a 38 percent market share for their detergent products.

Other MNCs that have experienced success with innovative products and processes in Tier 4 markets include I.M. Singer & Company, Grameen Bank Ltd. in Bangladesh, Standard Bank of South Africa Ltd., Citigroup Inc., and Monsanto Company. Each of these companies devised an innovative approach to credit availability and lending to the world's poorest families to enable them to buy the goods and services they need. Another MNC with a strong presence in Tier 4 markets is Hewlett-Packard Company. HP has articulated a vision called "World e-Inclusion" that focuses on providing technology, products, and services appropriate for the needs of the world's poor.

Working with global and local partners, HP plans to sell, lease, or donate $1 billion in satellite-powered computer products and services to underserved markets in Eastern Europe, Africa, Asia, Latin America, and the Middle East. A spokesperson for Hewlett-Packard said, "HP's involvement in poor . . . areas has opened doors to businesses from more traditional segments as well" because governments and organizations are aware that HP is willing to work differently and understand the local culture. Many others have joined the ranks of these successful MNCs in serving Tier 4 markets. Most have made innovative contributions of essential services to the local infrastructure and quality of life, such as water, electrical systems, and refrigeration. Many of these innovations have been adapted for use in other countries, and have created new businesses for MNCs.

Although Tier 4 markets offer opportunities for small local organizations as well as the larger MNCs, Prahalad and Hart offer some compelling reasons why MNCs should pursue potential consumers at the bottom of the pyramid:

1. *Resources:* few local entrepreneurs have the managerial or technological resources to create the necessary infrastructure.
2. *Leverage:* MNCs can transfer knowledge from one market to another.
3. *Bridging:* MNCs are in the best position to unite the range of actors needed to develop the Tier 4 market (e.g., commercial infrastructure, access to knowledge, managerial expertise and imagination, financial resources).
4. *Transfer:* Many of the innovations created for the bottom of the economic pyramid can be adapted for use in the resource- and energy-intensive markets of the developed world, a potential advantage for environmentalism.
5. *Build a local base of support:* Empowering the poor often threatens the existing power

structure; MNCs must build a local base of support.
6. *Conduct R&D focused on the poor:* Identify unique requirements of the poor according to region and by country, and learn useful principles and potential applications from local practices.
7. *Form new alliances:* Provides opportunity to gain insight into developing countries' culture and local knowledge, and to improve the MNC's own credibility; helps to manage and learn from economic, intellectual, racial, and linguistic diversity.
8. *Increase employment intensity:* Contrary to typical thinking in terms of capital intensity and labor productivity, Tier 4 logic requires that the production and distribution approach must provide jobs for many—increase employment intensity, raise income levels among the poor, and groom them to become new customers.
9. *Reinvent cost structures:* Cost levels must be reduced dramatically relative to Tier 1 (highest income market) to create goods and services that the poor can afford; business process must focus on functionality, rather than on the product itself, including lower investment costs, and more use of information technology.

The emergence of the Tier 4 market is not only an opportunity for MNCs, but it is also an opportunity for "business, government, and civil society to join together in a common cause." There is a chance to dissolve the conflict between advocates of free trade and global capitalism on the one hand, and environmental and social sustainability on the other. There is also an opportunity to overcome the notion that the corporate sector should serve only the wealthy, and that governments and nonprofit organizations should take care of the poor and the environment.

---

*B2–4B refers to the emergent trend of businesses selling to the bottom of the economic pyramid (the 4 billion people worldwide who live in abject poverty and subsist on less than $1,500 a year), or selling to pre-markets that have not developed sufficiently to be considered a consumer market.

Source: Dana James, "B2–4B" Spells Profits: Billions of Third World Buyers Are Rich Opportunity," *Marketing News* (November 5, 2001), pp. 1, 11–12, 14; C.K. Prahalad and Stuart L. Hart, "The Fortune at the Bottom of the Pyramid," *Strategy + Business* 26 (First Quarter 2002), pp. 55–67.

The rate of change in the twenty-first century is expected to outpace the magnitude and speed of change experienced by marketers in the late twentieth century. New product proliferation, shifting population demographics, and a promising but increasingly complex world marketplace challenge marketers to make informed decisions about the customers they will serve. Selection of a target market is a conscious choice, made on the basis of organizational goals and values and the attractiveness of each customer group. A mistake in this area could be extremely costly. As Frederick E. Webster has observed:

> The most important strategic choice any company makes is choosing the customers it wishes to do business with. It is a choice that defines the business.... Changing the definition of the served market changes the definition of the business. Customers shape the business, which is why customer choice is the critical strategic decision. If management has not defined a strategic vision of what it wants to be, and who is the desired customer, it has no control over the forces shaping its business. A business that tries to be all things to all customers is not a business at all, because it has failed to define its product/market scope.[2]

⬤ THE BASICS OF MARKET SEGMENTATION

An organization can approach its market in one of two primary ways. It may choose to sell to everyone in the market, aggregating all types of customers into one mass market. Or it can choose to segment a large market into smaller groups.

Mass Marketing

Mass marketing
Attempt to sell to everyone in the market assuming that demand is homogeneous; one marketing mix is used for all customers.

Mass marketing is appropriate when demand is homogeneous, or every potential customer has the same basic need that can be satisfied in the same basic way. In many ways, this resembles a "shotgun approach," where one marketing mix is used for all customers in hopes that everyone will buy. A mass-marketing strategy can be applied successfully where customers' wants and needs are similar across the market, goods and services can be standardized, and customers can be expected to respond in similar fashion to marketing programs. For example, the manufacturers of staple food items, such as sugar or salt, can be said to practice mass marketing by having their products packaged in only one size and color.

In today's marketplace, companies are more apt to use a market-segmentation strategy because not everyone in the market qualifies or is interested in buying the good or service offered, nor can the company satisfy the wants and needs of every customer. As a result, most organizations choose to target those segments of the market which they can serve most successfully.

Market Segmentation

Market segmentation
Process of dividing a large market into smaller groups or clusters of customers with similar characteristics.

Market segmentation is the process of dividing a large market into smaller groups or clusters of customers. The similarities within each segment make it possible for marketers to reach all members of a particular segment effectively with one basic marketing mix. That is, customers are expected to respond similarly to the same product features, promotional campaigns, distribution methods, and pricing strategies. Groups of customers may be located in the same geographic area or share similar buying habits, media preferences, or product usage, for example.

Why Subdivide Markets?

The business revolutions described earlier in this book contribute to an increased interest in subdividing the market into identifiable segments. Globalization has opened up world markets to more competitors, with a more diverse customer base in both consumer and organizational markets. Customers have more choices of goods and services to buy than ever before, and more companies are eager to fulfill their needs. Increased computerization, technological advances, and an information age economy make it possible to gather and manipulate enormous databases. These databases provide up-to-the-minute information about customer traits, their buying habits, and other data that can be linked to additional databases containing more personal information. Using these data, a marketer can reach a narrowly defined segment of customers with a marketing program tailored to their wants and needs.

    A number of benefits are derived from following a market-segmentation strategy. The most obvious benefit is the ability to use a specially designed marketing mix to target a smaller market with greater precision. Hence the term **target marketing.** Target marketing is more costly than mass marketing, but it is more precise and allows the marketer to deploy resources where they can be most effective—the traditional efficiency versus effectiveness argument. Segmentation permits closer relationships between buyer and seller and the ability to identify new marketing opportunities—perhaps a chance to satisfy a need that is not presently being fulfilled.

Target marketing
Using a specially designed marketing mix to target a smaller market with greater precision; permits closer buyer-seller relationships.

Customer Value and Target Marketing

Organizations must have a clear understanding of *value* as the customers in its target market define it. Customer satisfaction is related closely to perceptions of the value or benefits received from products, brands, stores, suppliers, and other sources. To ensure satisfaction, marketing managers must be able to identify and rank the factors that contribute to exceptional value as perceived by customers. A company not only must be able to deliver the value that its customers expect, but also must be able to do so better than the competition if its target marketing strategy is to be successful.

● TARGET MARKETING STRATEGIES

Target marketing strategies are developed in accord with customer demand patterns relative to customers' wants and needs for particular goods or services. During the segmentation process, estimated market-demand figures are used to forecast expected sales and profitability for each segment. The nature of customer demand determines the type of marketing strategy to be pursued and whether to target the entire market (mass marketing, as discussed earlier) or one or more distinctly different segments of the market (multiple- or single-segment target marketing).

A Multisegment Marketing Strategy

Multiple segmentation
Focus on two or more distinguishable market segments; each segment is treated as a unique market, with its own unique marketing mix.

Marketers may choose to focus their target marketing strategy on two or more distinguishable market segments. This strategy is referred to as **multiple segmentation,** or a clustered or selective specialization strategy. Each segment is treated as a unique market, with its own unique marketing mix.

There may or may not be synergies among the different targeted segments, but each is selected for its own attractive opportunities relative to company objectives. For example, photography companies focus on multiple segments such as travelers, professional or hobby photographers, and active elderly people. Ford Motor Co. targets multiple customer groups based on lifestyles and demographics through product design, pricing approaches, positioning, and promotional strategies. The Ford Taurus appeals to distinct market segments such as companies purchasing for business use, young families, singles, and older adults. Likewise, Ford targets different models such as the Mustang convertible, Explorer sport utility vehicle, Focus, and others to one or more customer groups based on the benefits desired by each segment.

A multisegment strategy is effective when there are two or more distinct segments. Extra costs are incurred because each segment requires a different target marketing approach. However, this strategy also increases the opportunity for marketers to maximize the return from each segment while spreading risk if any segment fails to perform as planned.

A Single-Segment Marketing Strategy

A concentrated target marketing strategy may be used for a single market segment with a distinct set of needs. Two approaches to a single-segment strategy are niche marketing and one-to-one marketing, as discussed next.

Niche marketing
Marketing effort highly focused on a single segment that seeks special benefits; seller must have distinct advantage over competitors and provide superior goods and services.

Niche Marketing. **Niche marketing** is a strategy that is highly focused on a single segment that seeks special benefits. Customers in a niche market will go to considerable effort and pay higher prices to obtain the good or service they demand. There are numerous examples of niche marketing strategies. A niche market with special needs includes youthful wheelchair users, many of whom are victims of urban violence and do not want the prototypical chrome wheelchair of the past. To satisfy the needs of this market, several wheelchair manufacturers have developed sporty, collapsible, lighter-weight models that are highly maneuverable and come in bright colors—more like a sports car.

Ford Motor Company's Jaguar division targets upscale drivers who want a sporty, high-performance car. Loan companies and pawnshops (often unscrupulously) target low-income customers who have high debt levels. Health food stores such as Whole Foods Market (based in Austin, Texas) target upper-income, health-conscious consumers who want high-quality, unique food products. Think about the possible niche markets you might be a member of for business or personal purchases. What makes each niche unique?

Marketers who pursue a niche marketing strategy must have a distinct advantage over competitors and must be able to satisfy customers with superior products and services. Niche marketing can be a successful strategy for small firms that need to focus their marketing efforts because of limited resources and abilities. This strategy allows smaller firms to compete successfully with larger firms. Nevertheless, smaller firms may find it difficult to compete with larger competitors on a more extensive scale.

One-to-One Marketing. Over the past several decades, market-selection strategies have evolved from mass marketing to market segmentation to niche marketing. Fueled by comprehensive databases and communications technology, marketers have progressively become more informed about their individual customers and can narrow down markets more precisely. The result is the implementation of one-to-one marketing strategies, where mass customization and **micro-marketing** dominate. This strategy is an extension of multisegment or niche marketing where the needs of a single customer are given special consideration. Related concepts include relationship marketing, database marketing, and customer-satisfaction initiatives. The extreme case is one customer (or buying unit) and one customized product such as a house, wedding gown, or telecommunications system. More often, one-to-one marketing is practiced within existing segments to satisfy the needs of individual buyers.

> **Micro-marketing**
> Precise segmentation strategy that capitalizes on databases and information technology to implement one-to-one marketing or mass customization.

Examples of one-to-one marketing can be found in every industry where unique customer demands exist. Lands' End Direct Merchants offers customers the option of designing their own custom-fit jeans and chinos at their Web site, www.landsend.com, where you can provide your own measurements, order a color swatch, and set up your account to reorder the same style, or order another pair with different features or measurements. Levi Strauss & Company, considered by many to be a mass marketer of jeans, uses laser technology to custom fit jeans for its customers. In an interview with the *Financial Times,* Don Peppers said that three technology capabilities are needed for an organization to establish a relationship with its customers: database for instant access to individual customer records; Internet for efficient interactivity; and mass customization (which Peppers calls computerized standardization). The key is to know your customers' wants and needs and customize products, services, and messages to each customer.[3]

● THE MARKET-SEGMENTATION PROCESS

The market-segmentation process starts with a commitment to provide satisfaction to one or more groups of customers. Decisions about the products to be offered and the customers to be served also must be consistent with the organization's operating policies, performance goals, and ability to provide the desired benefits. Effective market segmentation requires an understanding of the product (good or service) that is being marketed—in particular, the product's intended use for a given market and its distinctive characteristics or specifications.

Marketing managers also must consider environmental factors throughout all steps in the market-segmentation process. The selection of the most attractive and profitable segments to serve starts with a clear understanding of the organization's internal and external environments. This knowledge is needed to assess competitive strengths and weaknesses and external opportunities and threats in the customer segments that the organization pursues. It is assumed that the marketer has

FIGURE 7.1

The Market-Segmentation Process

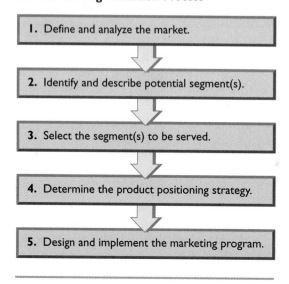

1. Define and analyze the market.

2. Identify and describe potential segment(s).

3. Select the segment(s) to be served.

4. Determine the product positioning strategy.

5. Design and implement the marketing program.

full knowledge of the current situation or will obtain the necessary information prior to, and during, the process of selecting one or more market segments to target.

The process of dividing markets into meaningful segments involves five major activities. (See Figure 7.1.) However, the sequence of these steps and their description may vary from one marketing situation to another. The important point is that all the tasks enumerated here must take place sometime during the segmentation process. Often this process is iterative; that is, new information is discovered that requires going back to a previous step in order to re-examine the process or the results.

1. Define and Analyze the Market

Before a market can be analyzed, its parameters must be determined within the organization's mission and business definition, as well as its strategic intent. Markets may be defined according to characteristics that can include or exclude customers from a group (e.g., types of customers, types of products, geography, channel position). Once the overall market boundaries have been delineated, the market size and growth rate, competitive environment, and other issues must be ascertained relative to the organization's objectives. The challenge in this step is to define the market narrowly enough to create a focused marketing strategy for the selected segment(s) and at the same time to define the market broadly enough to include attractive new opportunities.

2. Identify and Describe Potential Segments

The next step is to decide what dimensions or variables would be most useful for selecting members of potential market segments. Potential market segments are identified on the basis of the selected dimensions, and relevant data are collected and analyzed for each segment. To the extent possible, these variables are selected in advance, either *a priori* or based on preliminary marketing research results.

Next, final consumers or organizational customers are aggregated into homogeneous groups, and a profile of the characteristics of each group (segment) is developed. The attractiveness of each segment is evaluated, and segments are ranked according to their desirability. This process may require several research approaches, such as gathering secondary marketing intelligence, conducting a survey or focus groups, or analyzing databases.

3. Select the Segment(s) to Be Served

In this stage of the segmentation process, the final target market selection is made. Each segment is evaluated against predetermined criteria that reflect the organization's ability to serve the market profitably while providing customer satisfaction. Each segment is then ranked according to its performance on each criterion, and specific target market(s) are selected. Finally, the segmentation strategy is determined.

4. Determine the Product Positioning Strategy

Products and markets are closely intertwined, making it imperative to determine the best "fit" between the two. At this point, possible positioning concepts or alternative approaches for each target market are determined according to the features most desired by customers. From the possible alternatives, the most desirable positioning strategy is selected. This strategy must take into consideration factors such as competitors' positioning strategies, the market situation, and overall organizational goals.

5. Design and Implement the Marketing Program

In this stage, the tactical marketing plan is developed, and objectives are determined for the marketing program. The marketing-mix strategy is designed and developed to communicate the positioning concept to the target market. All elements of the marketing program design must be consistent with the selected positioning strategy. The final step in the segmentation process is to implement the marketing program for each target market and to control and evaluate its effectiveness in achieving the planned goals.

Criteria for Effective Segmentation

The development and implementation of a market segmentation strategy can incur greater costs (e.g., market research, separate promotional campaigns and distribution channels, etc.) than a mass-marketing strategy. Therefore, each segment must meet the following basic criteria.

1. The Organization Must Be Able to Identify and Measure Each Segment. Some segmentation variables are relatively easy to identify. For example, it is relatively easy to count the number of consumers who are teenagers or under age 30, assuming the necessary population data are available for that market. Obviously, it must be possible to identify relevant dimensions before they can be measured objectively.

It is more difficult to identify and measure variables such as personality traits, brand loyalty, or cultural values. For example, it is more difficult to count the number of people who are extroverts versus introverts. The latter would require psychological research conducted with a representative sample of the identified segment. While this lifestyle characteristic can be used in promotion and product development, it is not possible to identify every extrovert and introvert for one-to-one marketing opportunities. Personal characteristics are most often inferred from other measures that may be more subjective and intuitive. However, both objective (quantitative) and subjective (qualitative) information must be considered in a description of a potential market segment.

2. The Market Must Be Substantial Enough. The segment must be sufficiently large, with substantial potential to generate desired revenue and profit levels. Multiple criteria are used to measure the size and profitability of an identified segment, including the present size and sales potential of the segment, its growth potential in revenues and number of customers, and the degree of fit with the present organizational product line and resources. In addition to the attractiveness of a given segment, the organization also must consider its ability to create customer value and long-term satisfying relationships with customers in the segment.

In many developing economies, personal consumption is outpacing rapid growth in the gross domestic product (GDP)—figures that can be calculated and estimated from available data. It is possible to measure the increase in the number of middle-class workers with purchasing power parity of $10,000 to $40,000 in the world's largest emerging markets such as China, Indonesia, India, South Korea, Turkey, South Africa, Poland, Argentina, Brazil, and Mexico—according to the U.S. Department of Commerce. However, there is disparity in the definition of middle class. McKinsey & Co. estimated that in China middle-class household incomes are more than $1,000 per year. A former privatization minister in Poland estimated middle-class income there at $3,000 a year, and a market research firm in Indonesia defined middle class there as a family with more than $140 in shopping bills in a month. Data indicate that the developing countries are the fastest growing market for U.S. exports. Demographic data such as these can be obtained or estimated with some degree of accuracy, although people often underreport their income in surveys.[4]

3. The Organization Must Be Able to Reach Customers. Some markets are very attractive and indicate significant potential for future growth but are not easily accessible to the company and its products. Accessibility includes the ability to reach the market segment through distribution channels, advertising media, personal selling, and other aspects of the marketing mix. Barriers between a company and potential customers in a given market segment also may include unfavorable laws and regulations, trade barriers, economic factors, or other factors.

The tobacco industry and producers of alcoholic beverages have a large potential market of underage smokers and drinkers that many would like to reach in order to establish brand preference at an early age. However, U.S. legal constraints provide a barrier to this market. The populations of China and Russia are enormous, and their buying power is increasing rapidly. However, marketers may not be able to reach their sales and profit objectives as quickly as they would like because of an inadequate infrastructure to support the business (e.g., transportation, telecommunication, media for advertising) or other reasons.

4. Customers in the Selected Segment Must Be Responsive. The targeted customers must have the money and willingness to buy the good or service offered. In other words, if the company is to achieve success with its marketing programs, its plan must be realistic and actionable. Positive, negative, or indifferent market response may be due to several factors, such as the relative strengths and weaknesses of the company and its products versus those of competitors.

For many years, personal computers were priced too high for many consumers. In 1997, manufacturers marketed a large number of PCs for less than $1000. The market response was positive, and many first-time computer owners were born, thus opening up the market for related merchandise such as games, word-processing software, and Internet connections, and an enduring market for low-priced PCs. The PC market is very competitive, and any company entering the market must have a unique selling point against its competitors, including perceived superior value for the price paid.

5. Characteristics of the Segment Are Relatively Stable Over a Long Period. A segmentation decision is a long-term strategy, so it should be consistent with the organization's mission and longer-term strategic objectives. The degree of anticipated volatility and uncertainty in the market is directly related to the ability to forecast demand patterns and plan future actions. Many firms delay or abandon decisions to enter markets where conditions will have a negative impact on profits. Conditions such as closed manufacturing plants and high unemployment without any indication that the economy will improve or political upheaval and military action in war-torn countries like Afghanistan and Iraq make it difficult to predict future purchase behavior and revenues. Segments with intensive competition for their business also may exhibit a lack of stability for the long term and therefore be less attractive.

● SELECTION OF MARKET SEGMENTS

Following identification of the overall market to be pursued, the next step is to group customers within that market into more narrowly defined segments. Variables used to determine membership in a segment should be chosen for their usefulness in forecasting sales and predicting customer response to the company's offer.

A unique target marketing strategy is designed to appeal to each market segment based on the set of common characteristics shared by individuals in that segment. Although a single characteristic such as geographic location may be the predominant basis for selecting a given market segment, it is more likely that a combination of variables will be considered. For example, the number of people in a household (or business) and level of income may be considered in addition to geographic location.

Bases for Segmenting Consumer Markets

Target marketing decisions are based on attributes of the customers in a selected market. The problem is that there are many possible ways to divide a market, often making it difficult to know which are the most appropriate. Creative problem-solving techniques can be applied to gain competitive advantage through innovative segmentation, targeting, and positioning approaches.

The elderly population is an attractive target market for a variety of goods and services. The traditional image of a decrepit senior citizen has been challenged by the healthy, active lifestyles of many of today's seniors. As Baby Boomers grow older over the next few decades, their large numbers and their different attitude toward age will make them an attractive segment for many marketers. They also show signs of continuing self-indulgent consumption. Today's elderly (over-60s) are wealthier and healthier than ever, and have more time to spend their money. The poverty rate among Americans over 65 has fallen from 35 percent in 1960 to 10.2 percent in 2002. Over-50s own three quarters of all financial assets and account for half of all discretionary spending in developed countries, and they control most of the wealth in the United States.[5]

Marketers use demographic, socioeconomic, and geographic data extensively to describe their markets. This type of descriptive information is quantifiable and relatively easy to obtain and verify, but it provides only a general description of a customer group. For example, consider the diverse characteristics of all members of your age and income group in your city or community. Are they all prospective customers for the same goods and services that you own or plan to buy? Imagine all the possible segments that can be identified for a basic good or service such as a quart of milk or automotive repair.

To gain more insights into differences among customers within a broadly defined segment, marketers expand the quantitative market definition with relevant qualitative information such as behavioral, situational, psychographic (lifestyle), and psychological descriptors, as well as the benefits or satisfactions that are sought by customers. Attractive senior segments for fitness equipment can be determined by a combination of quantitative and qualitative data. Quantitative data might include U.S. Census population counts for individuals age 60 to 75 by gender, income, and geographic location. Qualitative data might include lifestyle analysis and focus groups to identify attitudes toward health, daily activities, and brand preference.

Demographic and Socioeconomic Descriptors.   The most frequently used demographic variables include age, gender, marital status, household (or family) size, stage in the household life cycle, religion, race or ethnic group, and nationality. Variables that describe consumers' socioeconomic status include income, occupation, education, social class, and asset ownership. Both demographic and socioeconomic characteristics are preliminary indicators of how purchases are made and how they are used. Clearly, many of these categories are interrelated and must be considered simultaneously to provide a better understanding of buyer behavior. Multiple demographic and/or socioeconomic descriptors—such as age, income, household life cycle stage, and social class—may be used to describe a market segment. Although useful, these dimensions do not reveal important differences among consumers in terms of their attitudes or preferences that often transcend demographic categories.

Demographic data based on U.S. Census Bureau Census 2000 race and age classifications for the total population are illustrated in Figure 7.2. The charts indicate the racial diversity of the United States, and potential market segments based on race. One of the most important findings of Census 2000 was the increase in the Hispanic population to 35 million people from 22 million in 1990, an increase of 57.9 percent in 10 years, making this segment the largest minority group in the United States—narrowly bypassing the Black/African American segment with a population of 34.7 million. The Black population increased between 15.6 percent and 21.5 percent for those marking only Black and those marking Black and another race, respectively. Although the Asian American population represented only 3.6 percent of the U.S. population in 2000, this was a significant increase from 1990. The segment defining themselves as "Asian only" increased by 48.3 percent to 10.2 million. When Asian background was combined with another race, the number increased to 11.9 million, a 72.2 percent increase over 10 years. For the first time in the history of the U.S. Census, a person could indicate multiple races on the survey, resulting in 63 possible combinations in the race category. When combined with the Hispanic ethnicity question (e.g., Hispanic and Black, Hispanic and White), the total number of race and ethnicity categories rose to 126. Demographers have long anticipated that the Hispanic and Asian populations would have significant increases due to higher immigration rates, and this is expected to continue. Nearly 7 million people (2.4 percent of the U.S. population) selected two or more race categories, posing a challenge to marketers who emphasize race in segmentation decisions. (See Figure 7.2.) The size of the Baby Boomer generation (1946–1964) and Generation Y (1977 to present) population also provides many opportunities for marketers, as depicted in Figure 7.2.[6]

Geographic Descriptors. Many market segments are selected because of their geographic location for several reasons. Customers for a company's goods and services tend to be concentrated in a particular geographic area. Products may be developed for use in a particular physical environment (e.g., snowboards are more popular in Denver than in Miami, and earthquake insurance is in greater demand in California than in Vermont). Decisions about the locations of retail stores and the distribution centers that serve them are made relative to concentrations of desirable retail customers. Other reasons for geographic segmentation include media availability (e.g., effective television or newspaper coverage to reach the targeted customers) and efficient uses of company resources (e.g., salesforce coverage, customer service).

Geographic variables may range from the location of a small group of key customers to the entire world. In market-segmentation decisions, it is more meaningful to aggregate populations from smaller to larger geographic areas. Some levels of geographic segmentation include country (United States), region of the country (southwestern United States), state (Texas), county (Harris), metropolitan area (Houston), zip code, and neighborhood. The size and density of the population also are used to identify customer segments. For example, Wal-Mart's winning strategy for many years was to locate stores in small towns with populations under 20,000. Finally, climate and seasonal changes are related to many consumer needs and wants in different areas, such as the demand for four-wheel-drive vehicles in snow and rugged terrain and convertibles in sunny climates. Approaching

FIGURE 7.2

U.S. Population by Race and Age

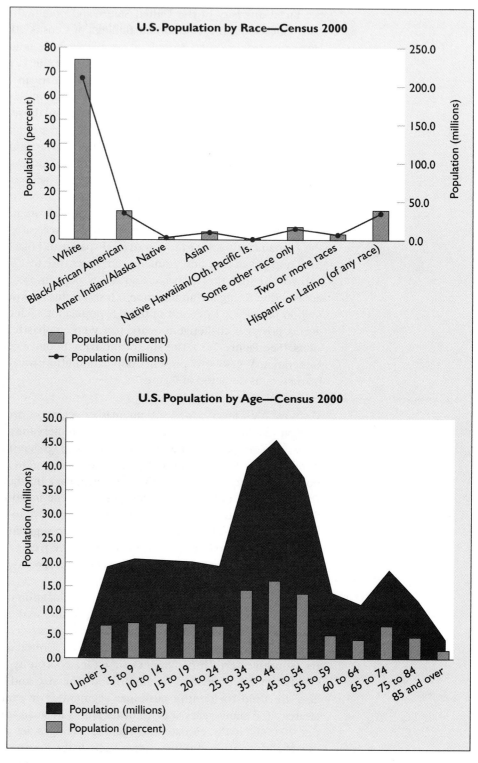

Source: U.S. Census Bureau, American FactFinder, DP-1. Profile of General Demographic Characteristics: 2000, www.census.gov.

MARKETING IN THE GLOBAL VILLAGE

Have Cult, Will Travel: Krispy Kreme Doughnuts Cross the Border

Have you heard the story about "the woman who was driving by a Krispy Kreme outlet and swerved across traffic, rolling her car, when she saw the 'Hot Doughnuts Now' sign light up"? Such stories are part of the spreading urban legend repeated by the Krispy Kreme "cult" that has grown up around the brand in the United States. One of the cult icons is the bright red "Hot Doughnuts Now" sign that lights up outside the stores to let people know a new batch of doughnuts is ready. Krispy Kreme has achieved the status of a "cult brand," one of those rare brands that "seizes the imagination of a small group who spread the word, make converts, and help turn a fringe product into a mainstream name."

Krispy Kreme Inc. is a Winston-Salem, North Carolina-based company that has been making and selling its signature doughnuts since it was founded in 1937. In 2002, Krispy Kreme had a chain of about 240 shops in 34 states and Canada, and was planning further expansion. The company also sells its products to grocery and convenience stores, and sells ingredients and equipment to franchisees. The company has experienced an enviable growth record, with sales of $394.4 million in 2002 (1-year sales growth of 31.2 percent), and net income of $26.4 million (1-year net income growth of 79.9 percent).

Krispy Kreme follows a geographic segmentation strategy at the level of country, state, city, and neighborhood. Most of the company's stores are in heavy-traffic locations. Retailers such as grocery stores, convenience stores, gas stations, truck stops, and others also sell Krispy Kreme doughnuts. Customer segments include characteristics such as degree of brand loyalty and rate of usage (preferably).

● CANADIAN MARKET ENTRY

In December 2000, Toronto-based KremeKo won the development rights for new Krispy Kreme stores in central and eastern Canada. KremeKo also holds the development rights for Ontario, Quebec, and the four Atlantic provinces. (ICON Doughnut Development Co. of Chicago owns the rights for Vancouver; Seattle; Portland, Oregon. Anchorage, Alaska; and Honolulu, Hawaii.) This was the company's first venture outside the United States, and it was a huge success. Krispy Kreme conducted research on the market and their potential customers and competitors. The implementation of the marketing plan for this international market segment was carefully planned and executed.

Implementation and Marketing Mix

New Customers and Cultural Sensitivity. Although the brand had a long-standing reputation in the United States for its great-tasting doughnuts, the personal in-store experience, and a fun brand character, there was no guarantee that the brand would be relevant to the Canadian market. KremeKo was challenged with making a 64-year-old brand, with its nostalgic American roots, appeal to Canadians. It was important to convey the uniqueness of the Krispy Kreme brand to new Canadian customers, a "heavy user" segment that is reported to consume more doughnuts per capita than the people of any other country. (Some say that doughnut brand loyalty is part of their national identity.)

New Competitors. A Canadian doughnut chain owned by Wendy's International Inc., Tim Hortons, is KremeKo's major competitor. As Krispy Kreme moves north into Canada, Tim Hortons is moving south into the United States, opening stores in Buffalo, New York and Detroit,

(continued)

Michigan. The Canadian chain opened 30 stores in Buffalo alone over the past 5 years, with plans for at least 9 more. Market research firm NPD Group Canada Corp. says that Canada has more doughnut shops per capita than any other country on earth—one for every 9,000 of its 30 million residents, compared to one U.S. shop for every 26,000 Americans. The doughnut shop is an important aspect of social life in this market, and both firms see room for expansion. Other competitors include Coffee Time, Dunkin' Donuts, Baker's Dozen, and Robins Donuts. Krispy Kreme only sells doughnuts, and has no plans to add sandwiches, soup, bagels, or other food items, so does not feel threatened by the existing 3,200 doughnut shops. As CEO Morris said, "I believe that what we're doing is so unique and so different that the category itself will expand… I saw it in coffee, and I believe it's the same thing here." (Morris was formerly with Starbucks.) He believes the category has room for about 50 Krispy Kreme stores in Canada.

Promotion.   Public relations dominated the Integrated Marketing Communications (IMC) strategy used by Krispy Kreme to enter the Canadian market. Mat Wilcox, a public relations (PR) agent for Canada, said, "You actually have to go to a store to experience a 'Krispy Kreme moment.' I went to Los Angeles (to visit a store). I asked everyone around me, 'What's the big deal?' And every single one of the people had a story to tell. It is a very personal experience; it's a personal brand. The passion for it is very difficult to reflect through advertising or any other marketing component." Roly Morris, president and CEO of KremeKo said after his first visit to a Krispy Kreme store in California, that he had never seen such excitement and anticipation of customers in view of the in-store "doughnut-making theater." (A glassed-in wall allows customers to view the doughnut making process while hundreds of fresh doughnuts roll by on a large conveyor belt.) The PR plan promoted the folklore and generated word-of-mouth excitement before a new store opening by using billboards and free offers of coupons and T-shirts to anyone promising to be an "ambassador" for the brand. They also distributed thousands of doughnuts in strategic locations and to media outlets before the first store opened. (An estimated 5,000 doughnuts were given away last year.)

Media hype and free doughnuts played a major part in KremeKo's promotional strategy, but the focus of the PR strategy was the community. The company makes a grass-roots connection by hiring employees who represent different cultures, and by developing fund-raising projects in their communities. The night before the first Canadian store opened, about 200 fans lined up outside. On opening day people lined up for as long as an hour, and were treated to free coffee and entertainment by a local children's group. The media gave enthusiastic coverage to the event.

Distribution.   KremeKo is able to select its own suppliers in Canada, and does not have to source from a central supplier, as its U.S. stores must do. Flexibility with supplier selection indicates the willingness to adapt to the needs of a new foreign market. A wholesale operation is planned for the Canadian stores in 2003 to sell fresh doughnuts to retail outlets.

● KRISPY KREME GOES GLOBAL

Based on marketing research and their experience with the first store in Canada, Krispy Kreme will focus on five countries in 2003: Japan, South Korea, Australia, Spain, and the United Kingdom, with other countries under consideration for the future. They believe that these countries represent attractive expansion opportunities. The first franchise agreement outside the United States was awarded to Borderless Australia, an Australian firm that was given development rights for Australia and New Zealand. Krispy Kreme's priority expansion plans are focused on markets with over 100,000 households. Dense population characteristics enable economies of scale in their local operations infrastructure and brand-building activities.

The pace of the international rollout has been intentionally slow, to make sure the company understands the culinary tastes of foreign markets, and to identify complementary beverages or products that will appeal to those markets. For example, they need to find a way to alleviate health concerns about doughnuts in countries such as Japan, where consumers are aware that American and European cuisines may not be a good influence on their diets and health.

Source: www.hoovers.com; www.krispykreme.com; Angela Kryhul, "The Krispy Cult," *Public Relations Report,* www.marketingmag.org (January 28, 2002); Joel Baglole, "Hole New Border Battle Cooking: Krispy Kreme Vying With Canadian Chain," *The Record* (August 24, 2001), p. B01; Andy Georgiades, "Krispy Kreme Sees Sweet Spot In Toronto Area," *The Wall Street Journal* (June 12, 2002), p. B1+; "Krispy Kreme Awards Development Rights to Australia and New Zealand," *Canada NewsWire* (June 5, 2002), p. 1; Richard Craver, "Krispy Kreme Plans to Go Global," *Knight Ridder Tribune Business News* (May 10, 2002), p. 1.

geographic segmentation in this manner permits the marketer to identify variables that may have an impact on buying decisions differently within the larger geographic area.

Behavioral and Situational Descriptors. The ways consumers buy and use goods and services provide useful dimensions for breaking up a larger market into smaller segments. Purchase behavior variables include the consumer's status as a present, past, or future user or nonuser of the product class, brand, or supplier.

An emerging segment of the population, which is referred to as the "e-Generation," draws on experiences in cyberspace to form their expectations for everyday life. The e-Generation, representing a market segment that is prevalent across all age groups and Web site content, is defined by a set of common experiences, not by demographics. Their most powerful behavioral characteristic is time sensitivity, in terms of convenience and efficiency. The e-Generation's online interactions in cyberspace ripple throughout other consumer contact channels, including telephone calls to follow up on something they saw on a Web site or searching the Web for information featured on television.[7]

Degree of loyalty to the brand, the product category, and the company also are useful variables for deciding which markets to target. Frequent fliers and frequent shoppers are rewarded with free goods and premiums to motivate them to buy more because large numbers of loyal, heavy users ensure long-term profitability.

Buyers may be segmented on the basis of situational factors such as the nature of the purchase occasion (e.g., a special event) or the consumer's readiness to make this purchase decision. Airlines combine geographic and demographic variables for target marketing decisions. Present and prospective airline passengers are segmented according to air travel routes, places of departure, and destinations. They also are segmented on the basis of demographics such as first class, business class, and coach and on passenger loyalty and frequent flier status. Each combination of variables (e.g., New York to Los Angeles business travelers who are members of the airline's frequent flier program versus a one-time pleasure traveler flying coach) may require a different marketing approach.

Psychological and Psychographic Descriptors.   These dimensions are useful for planning marketing activities but are difficult to measure directly. Among the more commonly used psychological variables are personality types, consumer motivations and needs, and attitudes. Marketers can determine typical profiles of their prospective customers within a market segment and use this information to determine product positioning, promotional messages, media, and distribution strategies, for example.

Consumer lifestyles (psychographics) have gained increased attention in recent years as an important predictor of buying behavior. Lifestyles tend to transcend age, gender, income, and other segmentation dimensions. The 1990s saw a major shift toward healthier living across all generations and income levels. The general population became more interested in a variety of sports, and professional sports gained in popularity among a diverse group of players. Fitness clubs and health-food stores grew significantly during this time, along with the producers of all health-related goods and services. Increasingly active lifestyles have opened up new marketing opportunities for diverse demographic groups and created a need for a better understanding of their needs and buying motives.

Benefits Sought.   Benefit segmentation is related to the previous two groups of segmentation variables but is considered separately because of its importance to customers. Any one customer might be seeking an endless list of benefits, but most are seeking quality, value, and service combined with other wanted benefits. Two major benefits that are demanded by consumers today are goods and services that provide convenience and self-improvement. In today's fast-paced society, consumers depend on many convenience goods and services. This trend has generated many new businesses and has changed the way many existing businesses operate to meet this demand. Banks have opened more branch offices, expanded the number of ATMs in remote locations, added online banking services, and provided service from mobile units and in churches. Many service businesses have extended their hours to accommodate workers who work other than from 9 to 5. Sales of prepared and partially prepared gourmet foods have grown in response to the needs of busy people who like to serve quality food.

Self-improvement benefits transcend all demographic, geographic, behavioral, psychological, and other categories and have proliferated to include many new products. Markets desiring educational improvement extend from preschool children to senior citizens. For-profit and nonprofit organizations alike are pursuing this market with a vast array of classes, programs, books, videos, and enlightening experiences. The same is true for physical fitness, spiritual growth, and a myriad of other benefits that various market segments are eager to buy.

Bases for Segmenting Business-to-Business Markets

Many of the general segmentation variables that are used in consumer markets also can be used to divide organizational markets. However, the specific variables within each dimension are selected for their predictability and marketing applications for business and organizational customers.

Demographic Descriptors.   The most widely used demographic variable for segmenting businesses is the industry classification. The **North American Industry Classification System (NAICS)** is a standardized method of classifying businesses to provide uniformity in business reporting and to facilitate the aggregation of data for an entire industry. (NAICS is a replacement for the previously used Standard Industrial Code (SIC), and is more comprehensive. Comparative tables can be used to relate previous SIC classifications to their new NAICS counterpart.) A company selling office equipment may sell similar supplies to a school, automobile manufacturer, hospital, and cheese processing firm but treat each segment as a different target market. Information about each group of customers can be tracked conveniently by using its industry classification. The NAICS is represented by numerical classifications ranging from two to seven digits, with the two-digit number being the broadest industry definition and the seven-digit number the narrowest definition. For example, the NAICS primary metal manufacturing industry is group 33; computer and electronic product manufacturing is group 341; computer and peripheral equipment manufacturing is listed under both 3411 and 34111; electronic computer manufacturing is classified as 334111; and notebook computer manufacturing is also classified as 334111.[8] For many businesses, data are available for only a two- or three-digit classification.

Market segments often are selected on the basis of the size of an organization. Size may be measured according to sales volume, number of employees, and number of locations. Age of an organization generally is related to its size, measured in terms of years in business. This helps to distinguish between start-up ventures and established businesses, for example.

The way a product will be used by the customer is another way to distinguish among market segments. In the business-to-business market, the primary end-uses are related to the type of customer: original equipment manufacturers (OEMs), aftermarket user (parts and repairs), wholesale trade (resale to another member of the distribution channel), and retail trade (resale to final consumers). Marketers who target other businesses not only must satisfy the needs of their immediate customers but also must be aware of derived demand from the final purchaser. For example, manufacturers of plumbing supplies need to monitor trends in the construction and remodeling of business and residential properties to determine patterns of future demand for kitchen and bathroom fixtures.

Geographic Descriptors.   Location is an important variable for segmenting organizational markets. Many industries are concentrated in one geographic area, such as automobiles in Detroit, furniture in North Carolina, computer software in Silicon Valley, California, and fine-quality watches in Switzerland. A synergy can be obtained through geographic segmentation where many similar customers are located in close proximity. It is more efficient and cost-effective to serve this type of market, particularly when a high level of service is required or when shipping high-volume or heavy goods that have a low unit value. Industry concentrations also provide opportunities for related businesses that locate in the same area to sell goods and services to the primary industry.

North American Industry Classification System (NAICS) Standardized method of classifying businesses to provide uniformity in business reporting and to facilitate aggregation of data for an entire industry; a useful basis for determining market segments to target.

MANAGING CHANGE

Dynamic Segmentation Strategies for Dynamic Customers

Segmentation strategies are used to classify customers and markets to achieve marketing and communication efficiencies. Consumers, businesses, nonprofit organizations, cities, states, nations, and other entities are placed in segments where customers in each segment share similar characteristics and responses to marketing programs. In spite of its wide use, segmentation strategies do not always work as planned. As Don E. Schultz said, "Yet, for all its recognition and acceptance as a key tool, segmentation approaches often fail. And, unfortunately, many marketers don't know they are failing until it's too late—that is, after the advertising campaign or the promotional program has been implemented."

Often some variable in the marketing mix—pricing strategy, advertising, or other promotional tool—is blamed for a marketing failure. Marketers may never learn that their segmentation approaches are not working. As Schultz said, "[Marketing managers] go for months and even years using fallacious segmentation approaches that make no difference in the marketplace."

Many traditional segmentation approaches are failing for several reasons. First, segmentation plans tend to be developed from the perspective of the marketer rather than that of the customer. Demographics such as age, sex, and income may be helpful in selecting advertising media and distribution channels, but do not offer deep insights about how customers within a given segment make buying decisions. The demographic segmentation schemes are not based on actual behaviors, particularly buying behaviors, and therefore are not as useful as they might be. Behavioral databases have been improving for use in segmentation decisions, but experts say they need further development to be truly useful for successful implementation.

Segmentation is static. Initial assignment to a group during the segmentation process generally remains the same until the person, company, or geographic area moves (changes) into another category (e.g., person's age groups, company size, median income of a geographical area). There is a tendency to put a segmentation plan in place, and then not make any major changes in the marketing program that was initially designed for that group. The only thing that changes is the customer (e.g., young girls act like teens earlier and have to wait 5 years to be "segmented" into the next category; a company acquires a competitor and adds new products to its line, but is not receiving marketing information relative to this new line; median incomes drop significantly in a city, but the goods and services targeted toward this demographic segment are beyond the ability of residents to purchase). Each of these changes suggests the need for special attention to marketing mixes that are relevant to each customer segment as it evolves.

Schultz is convinced that the next big challenge marketers face is to develop dynamic segmentation approaches that can be tailored to the changes that occur in customers' lives. As he said, "…the classifications are static while customers and prospects are jumping all over the place." Business is lost when a company does not know and understand its customers—particularly those who have been loyal in the past, but whose needs have changed—causing them to shop elsewhere.

Dynamic segmentation can be a useful tool, but many marketers argue that it is not feasible in today's market. This may be true in some cases, but some marketers have found it to be practical. Tesco, the U.K. supermarket operator with about 7 million customers, uses a frequent shopper card to gather data and read market basket purchases on every shopping occasion. Tesco uses its database to reclassify customers every week and creates a new customer classification or segmentation scheme for those who no longer "fit" in their previous segment. In this way, Tesco can recognize and understand changes in buyer behavior in a real-time, ongoing basis, and stay "in step" with their customers' lives. The retailer has the ability to capture the dynamic nature of the customer in a constantly updated database, and incorporate this information into effective marketing programs. Tesco moved to number one in food store sales in the United Kingdom by matching the dynamics of its customers to a dynamic segmentation strategy, and adapting creative marketing strategies to these changes. A visit to Tesco's Web site, www.tesco.com/clubcard, illustrates the importance of the Tesco frequent shopper card. There are many incentives to use the Clubcard, including the opportunity to earn extra points and save money, and to earn air miles and other deals. The concept is extended to exclusive free clubs: Kids Club; Baby Club; Toddler Club; Tesco Clubcard World of Wine; and the Healthy Living Club—all further applications of an effective segmentation strategy.

Source: Don E. Schultz, "Behavior Changes; Do Your Segments?" *Marketing News* (July 22, 2002), pp. 5–6; www.tesco.com; www.tesco.com/clubcard.

Overseas market segments can be analyzed according to geographic characteristics, usually considered with other variables such as economic conditions or population size. For example, manufacturers of bulldozers, dump trucks, and other construction equipment experienced strong sales gains during Europe's economic recovery in the mid-1990s. Sales growth in heavy construction equipment spurred investment in manufacturing plants, new product development, and other new business opportunities in Europe.[9]

Behavioral and Situational Descriptors. Organizational customers for many products can be classified on the basis of technology, such as high-tech/low-tech, innovative, or conservative. The types of products desired and the ways they are marketed differ among these segments. For example, a telecommunications company that markets integrative systems will likely have more potential customers among high-tech, innovative firms that desire state-of-the-art connectivity with employees and customers.

It is useful to identify the heavy, medium, and light users, as well as the nonusers, of a product. The marketing effort then can be focused on selling additional goods and services to the heavy users (while rewarding them for their purchases), increasing sales to medium and light users, and converting nonusers to users. Related to users' demand level is usage rate and frequency and order size. Customers who use a product rapidly, purchase frequently, and buy in large quantities offer economies of scale and profitability.

Other behavioral and situational dimensions for business markets are related to the customer's organization. It is important to know how the buying process is carried out, starting with the structure of the buying organization and identification of the appropriate buying unit, such as a buying committee or a purchasing agent. The organization's purchasing may be centralized or decentralized. Furthermore, the organization's purchasing policies may affect segmentation decisions, such as whether its purchasing is done through sealed bids, selections are made from a list of preferred providers, or there is an existing close relationship between the customer and supplier. In terms of targeting a particular buying unit, it may be useful to segment on the basis of who has the most influence on purchase decisions. These individuals may be production or marketing personnel, technical experts in the area, or others. They may or may not be the final decision maker, but they may be targeted because of their influence on the purchasing process.

The situation in which purchases are made, the type of purchase, and the customer's state of readiness to buy also can be used to select market segments. Buying situations include the nature of the purchase (e.g., a routine stock refill or a complex purchase), whether it is a new application or technology, and whether the product is customized for the buyer. In addition, segments may be selected on the basis of customers' readiness to buy the product, such as those who are fully informed and desire to buy the product immediately versus those who are unaware or poorly informed about its benefits. Homeowners in Florida who are concerned about an impending hurricane season are ready and anxious to buy disaster supplies such as plywood to cover windows, flashlights, and bottled water. Suppliers can target manufacturers, and manufacturers can target retailers that cater to these concerned homeowners with appropriate product assortments, timely deliveries, and sales efforts targeted toward specific customer buying situations.

Psychological and Psychographic Descriptors. These variables may apply to the individual or group that makes the final buying decision or may reflect the characteristics or culture of the organization as a whole. Attitudes toward the product, brand, or seller can provide insights for segmentation, including attitudes toward risk, innovation, economic motives, and so forth. Knowledge of customer groups that exhibit similar attitudes makes it possible to design a marketing program tailored to each group. The degree of loyalty that customers exhibit toward a company also provides a useful segmentation dimension. For instance, segments may be identified according to whether they are loyal, repeat buyers or have negative or indifferent attitudes toward the company and its products.

Although more difficult to isolate as a segmentation variable, personal traits of the individual(s) responsible for making a purchase are considered for organizational customers just as they are for consumers. Personal characteristics include factors such as decision-making style, experience related to the purchase, and knowledge of the product category and its application. For example, a purchasing agent who is innovative and willing to take risks on new products will go through a different decision process than a buyer who is conservative and risk averse.

Benefits Sought. Some of the benefits most frequently sought by organizational customers include value (defined as low or fair price and high quality), service, and delivery. Customers can be segmented on the basis of economic motives and price sensitivity. An expensive, high-fashion apparel manufacturer would consider retailers such as Neiman Marcus to be a more desirable market segment than discounters such as Kmart. An important selling point for many suppliers is the ability to provide goods and services that can cut costs and enhance the bottom line. As products become more complex and businesses outsource more functions, the availability of service before, during, and after the sale becomes a key factor in making a purchase decision. This is particularly true in high-tech markets where customers may be grouped according to the need for a service representative or on-site consultant as part of the sales deal.

Logistics represent a major expense for many firms, making transportation costs and convenience another important benefit for customers. Segments can be identified according to delivery distances from distribution centers, order quantity or dollar value to qualify for delivery services, and so forth. Many companies open new factories or distribution centers to serve new markets. Others may expand their target market by using rapid-response commercial delivery services. FedEx, for example, warehouses repair parts for certain customers in its centrally located facility in Memphis, Tennessee.

Combining Variables to Identify Segments

From the many possible variables that can be used to segment a larger market into smaller groups, there is no one variable that is comprehensive enough to do this effectively. The segmentation process must start with the most important dimension(s) that will provide a starting point for further analysis of the market. The next step is to continue to refine the market definition with a series of predictive variables, until this is no longer useful. For example, a firm such as Microsoft that develops computer software for workplace applications may start by gathering data for a specific type of workforce such as airline pilots. The focus would become narrower based on variables that predict purchase, such as company size, level of technology and acceptance of software innovations, specific types of software applications needed, and Microsoft's ability to provide the desired benefits using the Microsoft Office platform.

While individual segments are selected on the basis of unique dimensions that distinguish one group from another, the company must be able to manage multiple segments simultaneously. Microsoft may also target nurses, delivery truck drivers, and others. The basic software product may be customized to meet the needs of each target market, but the marketing efforts would need to be tailored to each group. Smaller segments can be combined into a larger segment where there are sufficient similarities, and synergies can be obtained for marketing activities such as similar promotional media, distribution channels, salesforce coverage, or manufacturing processes.

International Implications of Market Segmentation

The increased globalization of markets brings new approaches to international market segmentation. Rather than consider an individual country as a single segment with similar needs and wants, marketers find it more meaningful to identify similarities among consumers across multiple international markets. One segment that has attracted the attention of marketers is the teenagers of the world, who have a similar desire for products that symbolize an American Western lifestyle. From country-western bars in Berlin to rock music in Tokyo, teenagers are responding to global marketing appeals.

The spending power of American teens and 'tweens is well known to marketers, but their 8- to 14-year-old counterparts in Europe are also becoming a major economic force. They wear American fashions, listen to American music, and eat at American fast-food restaurants. The Euroteen generation may be more American than the generations that preceded them, but they have strong national loyalties, and do not like to be seen as an American with an accent. They are more tech-savvy than American teens and 'tweens, but use that media channel differently. They are responsive to promotions, and have money to spend (mainly from jobs and allowances). A spokesman for Burger King in Europe said, "The teen market is a growing and active one, and we actively promote to them."

Marketers find it necessary to tailor their marketing mix when marketing to European teens. National attitudes affect perceptions of marketing messages differently in different countries. Teens in these countries use the Internet, but they consider it "too American," and say they would rather buy a local product over the Internet than an American one. Wireless marketing is more advanced in Western Europe, which provides opportunities for marketers. While tailoring the marketing mix by country is a challenge, marketers such as McDonald's have found that a prize with a Happy Meal may be a word puzzle on the menu tray, or a small stuffed animal—much less than Americans have come to expect. The challenge is to communicate brand attributes in a way that is in tune with the culture and language of European teens—a market-by-market approach. As the head of online and interactive business development for Fox Kids Europe said, "Keep it local. Make it relevant to the kids and 'tweens in their respective countries." (Fox broadcasts to 54 countries in 17 languages and operates 14 localized Web sites.)[10]

Technology and Marketing Intelligence as Segmentation Tools

Segmentation decisions require an in-depth knowledge of the market, gained from marketing research and the company's marketing intelligence (MIS) and decision support (MDSS) systems. Marketers in the twenty-first century have access to more personal information about customers than ever before. Databases provide highly specialized details about all participants in the market, as discussed in Chapter 4. Information technology capabilities make it possible to process huge amounts of data and analyze them with complex statistical procedures quickly and efficiently. Target market selection depends on the ability to convert these data into information and information into knowledge that will enable wise decisions based on demand forecasts for each market segment.

Management Tools

A number of management tools provide inputs for segmentation decisions, including psychographic and geodemographic methods.

VALS. VALS™ (Values and Lifestyles), from SRI Consulting, is a frequently used consumer lifestyle and psychographic classification system. VALS taps relatively enduring psychological characteristics and several key demographics to classify consumers into eight groups with distinctive mindsets. Two concepts are key to understanding the VALS scheme: self-orientation (principle-, status-, and action-oriented) and resources. The self-orientation describes the patterns of attitudes and activities that help people reinforce, sustain, or modify their social identities. Resources (age, education, income, health, self-confidence) reflect the individual's ability to express his or her self-orientation. The eight VALS consumer groups are depicted in Figure 7.3. Through a partnership with Simmons, NY, about 20,000 U.S. adults are surveyed to identify their product, service and media preferences and VALS-type. GeoVALS™ provides estimates of the percentages of the VALS groups by zip code and block group. JapanVALS™ is a system developed specifically for Japan.[11]

FIGURE 7.3

VALS Consumer Lifestyle Segments

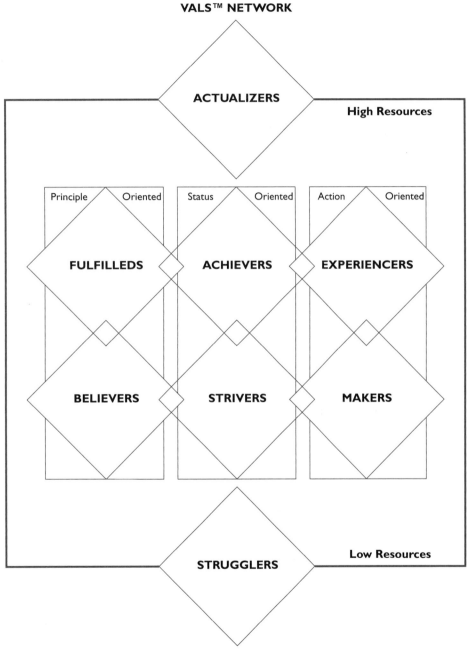

PRIZM and GLOBAL SCAN.   Two popular systems of geolifestyle or geodemographic analysis are the PRIZM (Potential Rating Index by Zip Market) system from Claritas Inc. and GLOBAL SCAN system from Backer Spielvogel Bates Worldwide (BSBW). The rationale for using geodemographic analysis to segment markets is that people who share similar cultural backgrounds, socioeconomic status, and perspectives tend to gravitate to the same neighborhoods. Over time, these individuals tend to emulate their neighbors, adopting similar social values, preferences, expectations, and consumer buying behaviors.

The PRIZM system can profile every neighborhood in the United States in terms of 62 lifestyle clusters organized into 12 broad social groups, each having similar within-group lifestyles but with heterogeneity between groups. PRIZM does not measure values and attitudes.[12]

Although VALS and PRIZM are oriented toward the United States, BSBW's GLOBAL SCAN extends lifestyle analysis beyond the United States. Each year GLOBAL SCAN surveys 15,000 consumers in 14 countries to measure over 250 value and attitude components, in addition to buying preferences, media usage, and demographics. GLOBAL SCAN is based on three critical factors: nationality, demographics, and values and their relative importance. Core values are intrinsic to a person's identity and inherent beliefs, go much deeper than behavior or attitude, and are more enduring over the long term. From the survey data, BSBW can identify five global lifestyle segments (strivers, achievers, pressured, adapters, and traditionals) that are present in all 14 countries, although the proportion in each category may vary by individual country. Marketers can use lifestyle analysis to develop cross-cultural marketing strategies tailored to those lifestyle segments that cut across cultures. For example, the median age of GLOBAL SCAN's "strivers" is 31 years. They are young people living hectic lives; they work hard to achieve success, but they have difficulty meeting their goals. They are further characterized as materialistic, seeking pleasure and instant gratification, and seeking convenience in all aspects of their lives because they are short of time, money, and energy.[13]

● ETHICAL ISSUES IN MARKET SEGMENTATION

The decision to focus marketing efforts on one or more groups of customers can raise several ethical and social responsibility issues. The nature of target marketing is that some customers are "in" and some are "out" of the group. This can present an ethical dilemma, as witnessed by the social pressures and long legal battles faced by the tobacco industry during the 1990s over the targeting of cigarette ads to children and minorities. The beer and alcohol industries have faced similar public censure for targeting underage drinkers, minorities, and "winos" with their promotional programs, and more recently, parents of obese children have brought lawsuits against McDonald's for unfairly influencing their children to eat fatty foods.

The R.J. Reynolds Tobacco Co. (RJR) planned to introduce Uptown cigarettes to the market in 1989, targeted toward black smokers. Although RJR's research supported this product introduction, RJR canceled its plans because of a public outcry against Uptown and its planned advertising campaigns. Likewise, Heileman Brewing Co. targeted PowerMaster, an extrastrong malt liquor, toward its heavy users—blacks in low-income neighborhoods. An industry commentator said, "The category was developed for a consumer who wanted a fast buzz, so the advertising plays that up."

When Heileman announced plans to introduce PowerMaster, it caused an uproar among antialcohol groups and black leaders. They expressed deep concerns about the targeting of this malt liquor toward communities that suffered disproportionately from alcohol and other drug problems. PowerMaster was withdrawn from the market. Although the underlying rationale for the Uptown and PowerMaster strategies was carefully thought out and executed by the firms, their target marketing practices were severely criticized by the public. Research conducted by Smith and Cooper-Martin[14] to determine ethical concerns related to target marketing found that consumers' criticisms are greatest when the targeted customers are particularly vulnerable and/or the product is particularly harmful.

POSITIONING STRATEGIES

Positioning
Customer perceptions of a product image or benefits that distinguish it from the competition; it's what you do to the mind of the prospect, not what you do to the product.

Just what is **positioning?** The concept of positioning was introduced and made popular by Ries and Trout, whose classic definition states, "Positioning starts with a product. A piece of merchandise, a service, a company, an institution, or even a person. Perhaps yourself. But positioning is not what you do to a product. Positioning is what you do to the mind of the prospect. That is, you position the product in the mind of the prospect. So it's incorrect to call the concept 'product positioning.' You're not really doing something to the product itself."[15]

Positioning versus Differentiation

Product differentiation
Refers to enhancing the product itself with special features, additional services, or other characteristics.

Product positioning often is confused with segmentation and product differentiation. The concepts are related but not identical. Positioning refers to customer perceptions of a product image or benefits that distinguish it from the competition. A widely accepted view of **product differentiation** is that it refers to the product itself, where the product offer includes features that are different from the usual offerings of competitors. Differentiation may be on the basis of physical differences such as special product enhancements or additional services included with the product or other characteristics that give the company a competitive edge. Another view of differentiation is related to marketing communications, where advertising messages, packaging, and other marketing tactics are used to make the company's product appear superior to that of the competition. Others relate product differentiation to segmentation strategies, that is, offering different products to different market segments.

The Positioning Process

The positioning process consists of a set of key elements that provide a foundation for designing the marketing mix consistent with the chosen market-segmentation strategy.

- Identify the target market(s) to be pursued.
- Determine the specific customer needs, wants, and benefits desired by each target market.
- Analyze the attributes and perceived images of each present and potential competitor in each target market.

FIGURE 7.4

Perceptual Mapping and Positioning Decisions

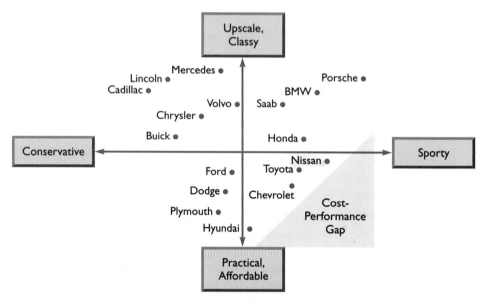

Source: Alexander Hiam and Charles D. Schewe, *The Portable MBA in Marketing* (New York: John Wiley & Sons, 1992), p. 227. Copyright ©1992 by John Wiley & Sons. Reprinted by permission of John Wiley & Sons, Inc.

- Compare your position with that of competitors on each important dimension desired by customers. (This may be done using a technique called *perceptual mapping,* as shown in Figure 7.4.)

- Identify a unique position that offers a combination of benefits that are desirable to the target market and that are not offered by competitors.

- Design a marketing program that will persuade customers that there are good reasons to buy from the communicating firm rather than from its competitors.

- Continue to assess and reassess present and potential target markets and competitors, as well as the marketing efforts to reach them.

- Continue to monitor the market for segments with unmet needs where there is an opportunity for your firm to introduce a better offering that will displace, or replace, present competitors.

Customer Value and Positioning

Webster[16] extends the definition of positioning to include **value proposition,** or the way that the organization plans to deliver superior value to customers. The positioning statement—or value proposition—is the result of the strategic decision-making, analytical, conceptual, and creative processes that put into words the image that marketers want customers to have of their product, brand, or company. The positioning statement becomes the selling proposition to prospective customers,

Value proposition
Part of the positioning strategy, how the organization plans to deliver superior value to its customers; the image that marketers want customers to have of their product, brand, or company.

offering a reason to buy the company's product rather than that of competitors. The value-proposition concept focuses on creating customer value and goes beyond the classic definition that positioning is based solely on communication. The value statement also can be used internally to communicate to the entire organization the reason they are in business, thus focusing everyone's efforts on a common purpose of satisfying the targeted customers. Long-term, sustainable competitive advantage can be realized from the positioning statement if the organization's resources, knowledge, and skills support it. The value proposition or positioning statement addresses three questions:[17]

1. *Who is the target customer?* (Defined in the market-segmentation process.)
2. *Why should the customer buy?* (Benefits to customer, why company's product is superior to competitors.)
3. *What are we selling?* (Definition of the product from the viewpoint of the customer.)

Volkswagen used nostalgia symbols to position its new Beetle with the tag line "Less flower. More power" and a bud vase "perfect for a daisy plucked straight from the 1960s" built into the dashboard. The position is a combination of romance and reason—modern convenience in an old-style package. The original Beetle was the first car driven by many baby-boomers and an icon of the 1960s. Baby-boomers are again the primary target market, and the appeal of the Beetle is both emotional and economical. From the perspective of today's target market, the car is positioned as an inexpensive-to-own, fun-to-drive symbol of baby-boomer youth in the "Age of Aquarius"—an era of rebellion against conventions.

Creative problem-solving techniques can be applied to answering six questions posed by Trout and Ries[18] for those wanting to apply positioning thinking to a brand or company:

1. *What position, if any, do we already own in the prospect's mind?* (This should be determined from the marketplace. Spend the money for research, if needed.)
2. *What position do we want to own?* (Use creative problem solving and the best information available to determine the best position from a long-term point of view.)
3. *What companies must be outgunned if we are to establish this position?* (Try to select a position that no other company "owns" rather than going head-to-head against a market leader.)
4. *Do we have enough money to occupy and hold the position?* (Do not try to achieve the impossible without sufficient money to establish a position—and to hold it.)
5. *Do we have the guts to stick with one consistent positioning concept?* (Having few but strong marketing programs provides consistency for the positioning statement and makes more efficient use of the marketing budget.)
6. *Does our creative approach match our positioning strategy?* (The positioning strategy should drive the creative strategy, such as advertising, not the other way around.)

Key Variables for Positioning

Several approaches can be used to position a company's product in the minds of consumers. Each approach must take into consideration the nature of the customer, the product, and the unique selling proposition that will set the company's product apart from its competitors.[19] Some of the most common positioning strategies are based on attributes of the product or brand, price and quality, use or application, product user, product class, or competitor. Since positioning is customer-focused, another approach that is used successfully involves positioning by benefits, problem solutions, or basic needs.

Positioning on Product Attributes.   A frequently used positioning strategy is to associate a company's product or brand with an attribute or product feature. The simplest approach is to select one dimension that is most important to customers, such as toothpaste that fights cavities. However, some companies choose more than one dimension to attract more customers. In addition to being positioned as a cavity fighter, Crest's positioning strategy for its toothpaste includes the benefits of tartar control, cleaning power, and taste. Marketers are cautioned, however, that positioning on too many attributes can lead to a confused image of the product and can detract from a unique selling proposition.

Positioning on Price and Quality.   Price indicates quality for many consumers and relates to perceptions of value received. High quality at a fair (not necessarily the lowest) price indicates excellent value. Higher prices also can signal a higher level of service and performance when the customer finds it difficult to judge quality. Gasoline prices are consistent with octane levels or expected quality of performance. Theater seating is priced according to the desirability of seat locations. The Ferrari automobile is positioned as a luxury sports car. Higher prices of organically grown foods indicate higher-quality, more healthful produce.

Positioning on Use or Application.   Products can be positioned according to the way they are used by customers. Many products are positioned according to a special use, such as laundry detergents that contain bleach for extra cleaning power, Arm & Hammer baking soda as an odor-killer in refrigerators, or legal services that focus on international law. Successful positioning strategies focus on a unique selling proposition, but this may be extended to multiple uses. For instance, baking soda is used not only for cooking but also for relief from insect bites and as an ingredient in many industrial and consumer products to enhance their performance.

Positioning by Product User.   This strategy involves associating the product with a class of customers who use the product, perhaps by using a celebrity endorser who symbolizes the attributes of the product. Nike sells athletic shoes to multiple market segments using a desire to enhance athletic performance (or status for owning the shoes that are icons of this accomplishment) as a selling proposition.

Positioning on Product Class.   Product class associations are used to position a product with both direct and indirect competitors, such as healthy drinking "waters" like Evian, Perrier, and Clearly Canadian or sports utility vehicles like the Ford Explorer, Chevy Blazer, Jeep Cherokee, and Nissan Pathfinder.

Positioning Against Competitors. Competitive positioning is considered in all positioning strategies, but explicit reference to a particular competitor can take advantage of an entrenched position. Avis, Inc., a car rental company, "tries harder" than first-place Hertz Corp. Amazon.com, the pioneer Internet bookseller, is positioned as a high-tech competitor against other book retailers like Barnes & Noble Inc. or Waldenbooks.

Positioning by Benefits, Problem Solutions, or Basic Needs. The growth of ethnic diversity in the United States has brought with it the challenge of serving customers whose lifestyles, languages, and buying preferences may be very different from an organization's existing customer base. Banks, among other businesses, have extended their target markets to include the special needs of ethnic and minority populations. MetroBank, founded by Taiwanese Americans in 1987, is one of the fastest growing banks in Houston, Texas. MetroBank is positioned as a banker for a multicultural client base, in recognition of the mutual problems—and mutual opportunities—shared by newcomers to America. The bank has been able to capitalize on the swiftly changing demographics of the nation's fourth largest city by carving out a special niche with pent-up demand for banking services.[20]

Summary

One of the most important strategic choices any organization can make is choosing the customers it wants to serve. This decision defines the scope of the business and provides direction for marketing programs. An organization can use a mass-marketing approach to serve everyone in the market. This strategy is advisable where customers' needs and wants are similar across the market, goods and services can be standardized, and customers can be expected to respond in similar fashion to marketing programs. Alternatively, an organization can choose to serve one or more distinctively different segments of the market—a single- or multisegment approach. Each segment has its own distinctive needs and wants and requires a specialized marketing approach. Niche marketing and one-to-one marketing are two approaches to single-segment markets.

Steps in the market-segmentation process include market definition and analysis, segment identification and description, segment selection, product positioning strategy, and marketing program design and implementation. Criteria for effective segmentation include segments that are identifiable, measurable, and reachable. The segment also must be large enough to be profitable, customers must be responsive to the company's offer, and segment characteristics should be relatively stable over time. Commonly used quantitative bases for segmenting consumer markets include demographic, socioeconomic, and geographic data. These data usually are combined with relevant qualitative information such as behavioral, situational, psychographic, and psychological descriptors, as well as the benefits or satisfactions sought by customers. Organizational markets are segmented on many of the same dimensions, but specific variables are selected for their predictability and marketing applications within a business-to-business context.

Segmentation can be viewed from a global perspective. Rather than consider each country as an individual segment, marketers look for similarities among customers across multiple international markets. Technological advances facilitate the segmentation process through databases and marketing intelligence capabilities. Likewise, customers' level of technology is itself an important segmentation variable. Ethical issues in target marketing focus primarily on the exploitation of vulnerable customers and the sale of harmful products.

Positioning strategies are used to differentiate a firm's offering from that of the competition. Positioning is not what you do to the product; it is your place in the mind of the customers. The process starts with the customer value proposition that addresses three key questions: Who is the target customer? Why should the customer buy? What are we selling? Variables that are used frequently for positioning include product attributes, price and quality, use or application, product user, product class, positioning against competitors, and positioning by benefits, problem solutions, or basic needs.

Questions

1. Describe the role of market segmentation in an overall marketing strategy. Illustrate with a specific example.

2. Discuss the different approaches to target marketing and the conditions where each approach is appropriate.

3. Explain the process that you would follow when determining a market-segmentation strategy for a new line of exercise equipment. Would the process be different for the services of a nonprofit disaster relief organization? Justify your answer.

4. What specific criteria were used to select the most attractive market segments discussed in Question 3? Explain the rationale for using these criteria.

5. Assume you are the marketing manager for a line of home entertainment equipment. Discuss the impact of the segmentation variables described in the text on your selection of the most attractive consumer and organizational markets to target, including:

   a. Changing demographics and buying behavior (e.g., gender influences, age groups, income, education).

   b. Changing geographic influences (e.g., population movement, population density, climate, international).

   c. Changing behavioral and situational influences (e.g., ways of shopping, value equation, time, awareness, brand loyalty).

   d. Changing psychographic and psychological factors (e.g., lifestyles, motivation, attitudes).

   e. Changing preferences for benefits (e.g., convenience, economy, self-improvement, relaxation, challenge).

Exercises

1. Find examples in the media that illustrate the relationship among market segmentation, target marketing, and positioning. This may be in the form of an article, television program, advertisement, packaging, or other format. Critique the way this relationship is represented in the source selected. What would you do differently? Why?

2. (a) Analyze population data in a representative source such as U.S. Census Bureau reports, the *Statistical Abstract of the United States,* or other government documents to determine major population shifts that are occurring in the United States. Interpret your findings relative to market projections for a specific good or service that might be useful in developing a target marketing strategy. (b) Analyze industry data to determine trends occurring in one or more organizational markets, using government or trade association data sources. Interpret your findings relative to market projections for a specific good or service that might be useful in developing a target marketing strategy.

3. Using personal or media sources, develop and conduct a survey to determine the role of the following in segmentation strategy decisions:

   a. Global economy

   b. Technology

   c. Changes in the marketplace related specifically to a company or its products

   d. Ethics and social responsibility

   e. Innovation

   f. Other contemporary issues

Endnotes

1. David Edelman, Carlos Bhola, and Andrew Feller, "Keeping Up With the 'e-Generation,'" *Marketing News* 31(18) (September 1, 1997), p. 2.

2. Frederick E. Webster, Jr., *Market-Driven Management: Using the New Marketing Concept to Create a Customer-Oriented Company* (New York: John Wiley & Sons, 1994), pp. 95–96.

3. Don Peppers and Martha Rogers, *The One to One Future: Building Relationships One Customer at a Time* (New York: Currency Doubleday, 1993); Rod Newing, "Learning to Treat Different Customers Differently: Don Peppers of the Peppers and Rogers Group," *Financial Times* (London) (July 5, 2000), p. 23; Lands' End Direct Merchants, Catalog (Fall 2002).

4. Rahul Jacob, "The Big Rise: Middle Classes Explode Around the Globe, Bringing New Markets and New Prosperity," *Fortune* (May 30, 1994), pp. 74–90.

5. "Business: Over 60 and Overlooked; Marketing to the Old," *The Economist* (London) 364 (8285) (August 10, 2002), p. 55.

6. U.S. Census Bureau, American FactFinder, DP-1. Profile of General Demographic Characteristics: 2000, www.census.gov; *Statistical Abstract of the United States,* www.census.gov; Nicholas Kulish, "Population of Asian-Americans Surges, 1 of 4 Persons Is Minority, Census Shows," *The Wall Street Journal* (March 3, 2001); and other sources.

7. Edelman, Bhola, and Feller, *op. cit.*

8. U.S. Census Bureau, U.S. Department of Commerce, Economic Analysis—Census 2000, NAICS, www.census.gov.

9. Greg Steinmetz, "Europe Is Becoming Solid Ground for Earth Movers," *Wall Street Journal* (May 3, 1995), p. B3.

10. Lisa Bertagnoli, "Continental Spendthrifts: Influential Euroteen Demo Has U.S. Marketers' Attention," *Marketing News* (October 22, 2001), pp. 1. 15.

11. For further discussion, see T. P. Novak and B. MacEvoy, "On Comparing Alternative Segmentation Schemes," *Journal of Consumer Research* (June 1990), pp. 105–109; M. F. Riche, "Psychographics for the 1990s," *American Demographics* (July 1989), pp. 25ff; Values and Lifestyles Program, *Descriptive Materials for the VALS2 Segmentation System* (Menlo Park, CA: SRI International, 1989); and Del I. Hawkins, Roger J. Best, and Kenneth A. Coney, *Consumer Behavior: Building Marketing Strategy,* 7th ed. (New York: McGraw-Hill, 1998), pp. 438–445.

12. Hawkins, Best, and Coney, *ibid.,* pp. 445–446; and Tom Miller, "Global Segments from 'Strivers' to 'Creatives,'" *Marketing News* 32(15) (July 20, 1998), p. 11.

13. Hawkins, Best, and Coney, *op. cit.,* pp. 447–449.

14. Craig N. Smith and Elizabeth Cooper-Martin, "Ethics and Target Marketing: The Role of Product Harm and Consumer Vulnerability," *Journal of Marketing* 61(3) (July 1997), pp. 1–20.

15. Jack Trout and Al Ries, *Positioning: The Battle for Your Mind* (New York: Warner Books, 1986), p. 2.

16. Webster, *op. cit.,* pp. 106–108.

17. *Ibid.,* pp.107–108.

18. Jack Trout and Al Ries, "The Future of Positioning," *AMA Marketing Encyclopedia: Issues and Trends Shaping the Future,* edited by Jeffrey Heilbrunn (Chicago: American Marketing Association, 1995), pp. 51–52.

19. See David A. Aaker and J. Gary Shansby, "Positioning Your Product," *Business Horizons* 24(3) (May-June 1981), pp. 56–62; and Alexander Hiam and Charles D. Schewe, *The Portable MBA in Marketing* (New York: John Wiley & Sons, 1992), pp. 223–226.

20. Rick Wartzman, "How Tiny MetroBank Wins Big by Catering to an Ethnic Market," *Wall Street Journal* (January 15, 1996), pp. A1, A7, www.metrobank.com.

MARKETING MANAGEMENT IN ACTION: CLOSING CASE

Hispanic Youth and Culturally-Focused Media

"We couldn't pick up where we were in our general market advertising," said Don Calhoon, Wendy's executive vice president of marketing. "[Brand awareness was] so low that the opportunity becomes extremely large." Fast-food retailer Wendy's International did not specifically target a major campaign toward Hispanics and Latinos until 2002. Faced with hardly any brand awareness among Spanish-dominant consumers who regularly patronize McDonald's and Burger King fast-food restaurants, Wendy's committed a national advertising budget to reach Hispanics. The budget of about $10 million (3.5 percent of its total media budget) was allocated to Spanish-language TV, radio, and in-store displays, placing Wendy's fourth in spending by fast-food restaurants. (McDonald's spent $27 million on this market in 2001; Burger King spent $20 million in 2001; and Tricon Global Restaurants [parent of KFC, Taco Bell, and Pizza Hut] also spent heavily.) "We have been, I guess you could say, a little bit slow to the gate, but our goal is to build a strong relationship with this consumer," said Michelle Fedurek, vice president for media services at Wendy's International. For the first time, Wendy's is devoting part of its national ad budget to campaigns in Spanish. Previously, Wendy's ran ads targeted toward consumers in 27 local markets. Based on market research, the new national campaign is designed to introduce the Wendy's brand to the Hispanic consumer, recognizing that although Hispanics do not really know who Wendy's is, once they do know about the restaurant chain, they will try it, and like it.

The 2000 U.S. Census was a wake-up call for marketers to recognize the country's fast-growing Hispanic and Latino population, with a projected high growth rate for this ethnic group. Census results revealed that there are about 35 million Hispanics, or 12.5 percent of the American population. The dearth of solid information about this influential market has led firms such as Arbitron and Nielsen Media Research to find better ways to collect data on Hispanics. In particular, market researchers have recognized a need for better data on Hispanics' media consumption habits. A great deal of progress has been made in multicultural marketing and research. However, marketers still want more in-depth information on the dominance of the Spanish language, biculturalism, psychosocial motivators, and other in-depth research studies similar to those for the mainstream American market and for African Americans. Some feel that language preference data is seriously lacking.

The need for better information on the Hispanic market becomes evident when comparing Hispanic and mainstream advertising expenditures. Spending on Hispanic ads was forecast to rise 4 percent in 2002, compared to little or no change in general media advertising. It is important to note that the increase applies to a fairly small amount in advertising dollars when compared to mainstream market ad buys. The total Hispanic ad budget for 2001 was $2.2 billion, compared with mainstream ad expenditures of $233.7 billion. Hispanic advertising budgets are forecast to increase significantly because of the Census 2000 data, and the likelihood of continued increase in number of Hispanics due to immigration and high birth rates. An increase in numbers of TV viewers for Hispanic media results in better rating points for Spanish-language broadcasting, which means advertisers will have to pay more for ads. The percentage change in number of Hispanic TV households (63.2 percent) compared to total U.S. TV households (13.3 percent) is shown in Figure 1. Advertisers are also influenced by median household incomes, which the 2000 Census reported to be $33,447 for Hispanics, compared with $44,226 for white households, and $30,439 for Black households.

Advertising's most attractive market is found in abundance in this huge population. In comparison to the general market, they are about 10 years younger, have larger households (by one more person per household), are more traditional (including larger percentage of conventional nu-

FIGURE 1

TV NATION
Between 1993 and 2002, the number of Hispanic TV households increased a dramatic 63.2 percent, while the total number of U.S. TV households increased by only 13.3 percent.

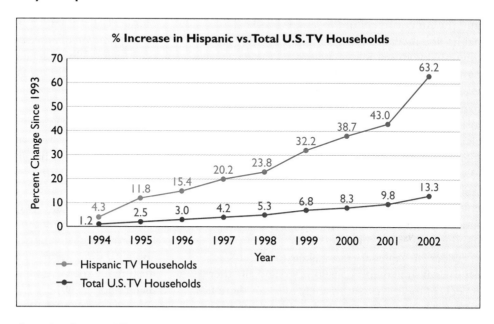

Source: Joan Raymond, "¿Tienen Numeros?" *American Demographics* 24(3) (March 2002), pp. 22–25. Copyright © 1992 by John Wiley & Sons. This material is used by permission of John Wiley & Sons, Inc.

clear families), and their buying power reached $424 billion in 2002—a 25 percent increase from $342 billion in 2000.

By 2005, Hispanic youths are expected to outnumber Blacks to become the largest ethnic youth population (17 percent of those under 18 and 45 percent of all minority minors in the United States). By 2010, one child in five will be Hispanic, according to forecasters. This is a 22 percent increase in 9 years, compared to a decline of 5 percent for white youth during the same period. Many consumer trends start in top urban markets, and these trends are heavily influenced by Hispanic and Latino youth who make up the majority. For example, 58 percent of the under-20 youth in Los Angeles are Hispanic, with their share expected to increase to 80 percent by 2003.

A one-size-fits-all market segmentation approach cannot be taken with the young Hispanic population. Those under the age of 18 are one of

the largest and most complex demographics in America, and are not mirror images of their parents and grandparents who felt more compelled to become more "American." The 18 and under segment, representing 35 percent of all Hispanics, prefers to be both bilingual and bicultural. They want the best of both worlds—Hispanic and American. They are not content with just the Spanish-language media channels that entertain and inform their parents, and merely translating general market strategies into Español miss their mark unless they also reflect cultural preferences. Young people of all ages are difficult to reach, but Hispanic youth are even more difficult to target because they are both bilingual and bicultural. They have a growing number of media channels at their disposal, and because more than three quarters of them are bilingual, they have more media options than their non-Hispanic counterparts. Marketers talk about marketing to the individuality of today's youth, but often do not realize that for young Latinos, their bilingualism is a large part of their individuality.

As Olivia Llamas, project director for the Yankelovich Hispanic MONITOR said, "One of the biggest misperceptions about U.S. Hispanic teens is that they will eventually be completely assimilated into the American culture, in language, social habits, and media consumption, and become indistinguishable from their general market counterparts." She added that marketers that think that eventually they will only need to advertise to Hispanic youth in English would find that they are not losing their language or culture. They are proud to claim their culture, with 54 percent of Hispanic teens identifying themselves as "Hispanic Only," or "More Hispanic than American." Another 36 percent consider themselves equally grounded in both cultures, 6 percent consider themselves "more American than Hispanic," and only 4 percent identify themselves as "American Only."

Older Hispanics are more likely to prefer Spanish to English in media consumption and all other aspects of their lives. Surprisingly to some, there has been a significant increase in Spanish-language preference among Hispanic youth in recent years, but marketers should not make any assumptions. According to the MONITOR, 29 percent of 16- to 24-year-olds prefer Spanish, a 23 percent increase over 1997. Although 45 percent of this group prefers English, 65 percent tune in to Spanish-language TV for 1.7 hours a day. Fifty-nine percent listen to Spanish-language radio. Hispanic households tend to watch more TV, on average, than other groups. Spanish versus English advertising effectiveness studies by the Roslow Research Group in 2000 indicated the following among the general Hispanic population, and Hispanic teens:

- Commercials in Spanish were 61 percent more effective at increasing ad awareness levels than commercials in English (40 percent more effective for teens).

- Commercial messages in Spanish are communicated 57 percent more effectively than commercials in English (16 percent for teens).

- Ads received in Spanish are four times more persuasive than commercials in English (twice as persuasive for teens).

In general, Hispanics are more apt to make purchase decisions based on advertising, and are highly brand loyal. "For an advertiser to be effective with today's Hispanic youth market, he needs to be everywhere they are, and with a message that is relevant to them, both in Spanish and in English," said Monica Gadsby, senior vice president and director of Hispanic media for Starcom. Those marketers who include Spanish-language TV in teen-targeted schedules will optimize delivery of Hispanic teens, and increase total teen market reach by up to 4 to 5 percentage points.

Major TV networks have added new program content to attract Hispanic advertisers and viewers. For example, CBS aired Spanish and bilingual ads during their primetime broadcast of the Latin Grammy Awards, and Nickelodeon was the first major English-language cable network to accept bilingual advertising during regular programming. However, English-language media tend to cost about 10 times more than Spanish-language media, making it expensive for traditional Hispanic advertising budgets. Where English-language broadcast networks may have 300 or more advertisers, their Spanish-language counterparts tend to attract about 100. (The disparity in ad costs causes many Spanish-language stations to feel inadequately compensated for their ability to deliver a large and increasingly affluent audience.) Hispanic TV media has become a more prominent choice for both Hispanic and mainstream advertisers who want to reach Hispanic youth. The two largest TV competitors for viewers and advertising dollars in this market are Univision and Telemundo (acquired by NBC in April 2002).

It is important to keep in mind when making media choices that reaching the segment—and getting through to them—are two different things. Speaking their language is insufficient, if the message is not "in-culture," a term coined by Hispanic marketing strategist Isabel Valdes. Core values that distinguish Hispanic youth from their general market counterparts include "Familismo," or a strong family orientation that influences how they use and respond to media. For example, Hispanic teens are more apt to watch TV with their parents than non-Hispanic teens, and 50 percent of Hispanic teen girls and 27 percent of Hispanic teen

FIGURE 2

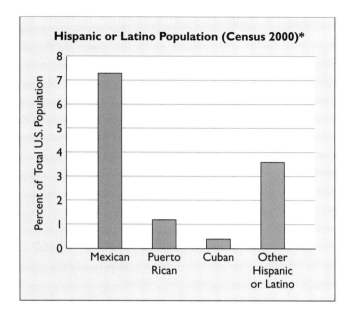

Hispanic or Latino Population (Census 2000)*

*Total Hispanic or Latino population represents 35.3 million people or 12.5 percent of the total U.S. population.
Source: U.S. Census Bureau, DP-1. Profile of General Demographics Characteristics: 2000, Census 2000 Summary File 1, www.census.gov.

boys admire their mothers more than any other person in their lives. Marketers also need to recognize nuances that differentiate youth from different countries. Messages should capture cultural, religious, and idiomatic differences when targeting specific geographic market segments. The MONITOR found that 54 percent of Hispanics felt there were some important differences between themselves and other Hispanic groups. (See Figure 2 for the 2000 Census breakdown of the Hispanic population.) The 2002 World Cup soccer matches attracted a huge number of Hispanic viewers. However, marketers who use a soccer theme in all their Hispanic advertising are not recognizing that while soccer works for some, most East Coast Hispanics are from the Dominican Republic and Cuba, where baseball is king. As the Hispanic youth market grows, it will be need to be segmented further into subcultures that are more in tune with the lifestyles, interests, and attitudes of each group. Ethnic youth identify with multiple categories, but although they may consider their Hispanic heritage as their major identity, marketers should not assume that it is their only identity.

Wendy's first Hispanic ad spots in 2002 used humor to show that the Wendy's name is virtually unknown to Spanish-dominant consumers. In one spot, a suspicious wife jealously attacked her businessman husband for writing another woman's name into his planner every day at lunchtime— only to find out that Wendy's is a fast-food restaurant. The Spanish language tagline "En Wendy's comer es mas rico" can be translated roughly as "At Wendy's eating is more enjoyable/tastes better."

Wendy's still faces the challenge of catching up with its fast-food competitors. In a Yankelovich Monitor poll of 1,206 Spanish-speaking consumers, 61 percent had visited a McDonald's in the past 30 days, 45 percent had eaten at Burger King, and 23 percent mentioned KFC, Taco Bell, Pizza Hut, or Domino's Pizza. McDonald's has marketed to Hispanics for decades, but has recently implemented strategies to differentiate itself from the increasing competition. Burger King placed more emphasis on a new Hispanic campaign as part of its relaunch, and smaller fast-food chains such as Subway Restaurants and others have also increased their ads targeted at Hispanics.

"Telling the story about Wendy's and introducing the concept is only part of a bigger picture," Mr. Calhoon said. "Future media buys will align with specific properties, including the World Cup and Latin award shows," he said.

Source: Joan Raymond, "?Tienen Numeros?" *American Demographics* 24(3) (March 2002), pp. 22–25; Rebecca Gardyn, "Habla English?" *American Demographics* 23(4) (April 2001), pp. 54–57; Anonymous, "Hispanic-American TV Booms," *Broadcasting & Cable* 132(21) (May 20, 2002), p. 29; Anonymous, "Hispanic Media and Advertising Growth (and Effectiveness)," *Growth Strategies* 941 (May 2002), p. 4; Kate MacArthur, "Beefing Up Hispanic," *Advertising Age* 73(9) (March 4, 2002), p. 28; Stuart Elliott, "Hispanic Networks Hone An Edge in a Race for TV Ad Dollars," *The New York Times* (May 30, 2002), p. C.7.

Case Study Questions

1. Discuss the pros and cons of subdividing the American youth market into subsegments when designing marketing communication strategies.

2. Defend the use of a multisegment strategy versus a mass marketing approach by marketers such as Wendy's and McDonald's.

3. What characteristics of the youth market should be used to assign people to one segment or another? Explain your answer. Would the basis for segmentation be different for Hispanics versus non-Hispanics?

4. Describe the steps in the market segmentation process that Wendy's might use to develop a target marketing strategy for young Hispanics. Identify a specific segment.

5. Analyze the ability of the segment defined in (3) above to meet the criteria for effective segmentation discussed in the chapter.

6. How can technology, such as the Internet, be used to effectively reach Hispanic youth?

7. Design a marketing communications program for Wendy's, including the following:

   a. product differentiation,

   b. product positioning and customer value,

   c. description of a potential television commercial targeted toward Hispanic youth, and

   d. specific media that is appropriate for the TV commercial described above.

8. Marketers can take another view of segmentation relative to media choices. They may choose Spanish-language only, English-language only, or combined Spanish and English advertising media. They may choose local markets only, or national campaigns. What specific criteria should Wendy's use when deciding among media such as Univision, Telemundo, major mainstream networks, or smaller highly targeted stations?

Implementing Marketing-Mix Strategies

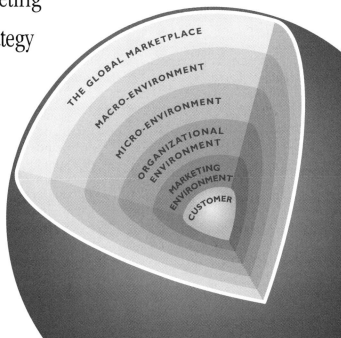

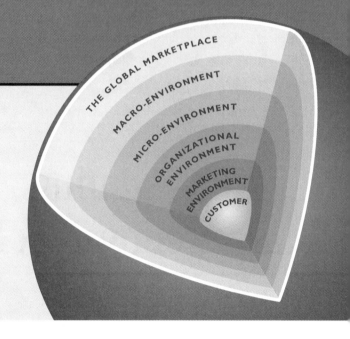

Product Strategy

There is nothing more difficult to take in hand, more perilous to conduct, or more uncertain in its success, than to take the lead in the introduction of a new order of things.[1]

Making Cheese "Fun" Is Serious Business—Call It "Triggering the Drool"

Two years ago, with the mandate from his bosses at Kraft Foods Inc.'s flagship cheese division to "Make this work," research chef Todd Menaker set out to create a new pizza-flavored American-cheese snack called *Rip-Ums*. "So many things make your brain scream 'pizza,'" Mr. Menaker said. "Do you start with an oregano note? Or caramelized onion crust?"

For product-developers at Kraft, cramming the entire "flavor profile" of a slice of pizza into a piece of cheese is a complicated process. But it is a vital part of Kraft's strategy to stay ahead of the embattled packaged-food industry. Various companies have faltered trying to make packaged foods like soups or cereal stay relevant to the on-the-go U.S. customers who snack more and cook less. Big U.S. food companies have been posting annual volume gains recently of about 1%, but Kraft's volume has been twice that. A big part of this success has been reinventing venerable brands with new twists like Jello-O X-Treme fruit gel cups and Mini Oreos. But to continue this performance requires Kraft to squeeze growth out of cheese, its biggest business with about $6 billion in 2001 sales. Americans already consume 30.5 pounds per person, which is up from 13.9 in 1975 but it is far from the 51 pounds per year in France.

Kraft's 537 cheese products—such as Velveeta Hot Mexican cheese loaf, Athenos blue cheese, and Cracker Barrel sharp cheddar—are but a few that contribute to their $34 billion domestic volume. Kraft's cheese market share is about 40%. And, for years, sales have been growing at 5% annually until they flattened in 2001. Kraft believes there is still room for growth in domestic as well as international cheese markets, but believes the key to driving sales is figuring out new uses, messages, and imagery for cheese as tastes and trends shift. "We call it 'triggering the drool,'" says Michael Pellegrino, Kraft's vice president for cheese marketing. An important part of the process of driving sales is making cheese fun. Kraft's new *Rip-Ums* cheese sticks combines two products designed to appeal to kids: American cheese and string cheese. "I play with these all the time," says Mr. Menaker. Each *Rip-Ums* stick is pre-cut so it can be ripped into 12 strips. After peeling them apart, Mr. Menaker formed them into circles before popping them into his mouth.

Developing and marketing new products is risky and expensive. Kraft spends about $360 million a year on research and development (R&D) and competitors are quick to imitate any new hits. But Kraft is confronting some challenging trends: Americans are eating more snacks and "comfort foods," but they are also increasingly interested in healthy or "good for you" foods. At the same time, the evolving American palate is increasingly craving specialty cheeses. Even Wal-Mart is selling brie and Asiago to the masses. "We're coming full circle now in terms of what was popular decades ago," says Steve Pimentel, a food-merchandising manager for discount retailer Costco Wholesale Corp. "We ate Wonder bread, processed hams, coffee in a can and used technology to chap things up to make them taste better. Now, people see all the artisan breads and specialty coffees and are like, 'Wow, I can roast my own beans.'" These days, Costco notes that its best-selling parmesan cheese is aged for 2 years—not the Kraft sprinkle-from-the-jar variety.

A few years ago, Kraft noted a surge in demand for string cheeses, a $400 million sales category. But in spite of this popularity, Kraft realized there wasn't much difference between brands. They reasoned that any new Kraft string-cheese products would have to be novel enough to excite kids and technically unique to discourage knock-offs. "Food has to be entertaining," says Janis Smith-Gomez, a senior Kraft business director for cheese. "Other companies usually do that through prizes and toys.

Here we try to do it with the actual product." A possible solution emerged from Kraft's Worldwide Cheese council, an internal think tank that meets as many as three times per year to swap ideas about new products, licensing opportunities, and technology. Kraft's U.K. division already sold a string-cheese-like processed cheese product, but it lacked the flavor of American cheese, which Kraft's research showed was a favorite snack for American children. And U.S. households that include children spend 45% more on cheese than childless households. So Kraft's challenge was to develop the correct flavors and "mouth feel." Melanie Turenne, food manager and section manager, says nailing the American-cheese flavor was easy. But developing the second version of *Rip-Ums,* the pizza variety, went through five different permutations before getting approval from a test-panel of children.

Kraft recently started the market roll-out of *Rip-Ums* as a part of the fastest growing category, the so-called impulse-driven snacks, the kind that shoppers often grab at the last moment as they near the cash register. *Rip-Ums* are designed to be consumed on its own, rather than on a "cheese carrier" such as a cracker. This will allow *Rip-Ums* to compete with other types of portable, no-assembly-required snacks such as cookies and potato chips. In fact, Kraft has recently made several market introductions of innovative products. In 2000 Kraft unveiled Philadelphia cream-cheese snack bars with first-year sales of $60 million, and is now adding a cream-cheese brownie bar. Because consumers demanded more convenience, Kraft's bagged cheeses now come in 12 varieties, designed for both lunch boxes and party trays. Even 50-year-old Cheez Whiz has been repositioned more as a dip than as a sauce. Kraft is also working hard to give cheese a healthier, sexy image. The opening Internet page at www.kraftcheese.com shows an amorous young couple placing yellow cheese cubes in each others' mouths. "Love it... Gotta have it?" asks the text.

By marketing its cheese so aggressively, Kraft says it is helping families here and abroad combat what it calls the "calcium crisis." Despite the fact that a 21-gram *Rip-Ums* snack contains 7 grams of fat, Kraft says its cheese products are a good way to deliver calcium to women and children who are often deficient in the nutrient. "We want to establish simple eating rituals to help build stronger bones," says Mary Kat Haben, president of Kraft's cheese, meals, and enhancers group.

Source: Shelly Branch, "At Kraft, Making Cheese 'Fun' Is Serious Business," *The Wall Street Journal* (May 31, 2002), pp. A1, A6.

As illustrated by the Kraft example, the product often is the principal means by which a company provides consumer satisfaction that in turn drives sales. Sometimes, the package in which a product is contained may also satisfy a need for convenience or safety, such as a plastic container for shampoo. The brand identity of a product also can add meaning—perhaps assurance or social status. The seller of a product may include a service, such as delivery or financing. All these things enhance consumers' satisfaction and are, by definition, part of the company's product strategy. At the corporate level, product strategy is the engine that drives the rest of the marketing strategy; without it, there is nothing to distribute, nothing to promote, nothing to price, and nothing to satisfy customers. At the divisional level, product strategy is equally important as the basis for divisional overall marketing strategy and marketing activities. From a tactical viewpoint, product offerings determine the remainder of the marketing-mix aspects of distribution, pricing, and communication plans and actions.

⬤ WHAT IS A PRODUCT?

Product
A physical commodity or an idea, cause, or other intangible that provides customer satisfaction.

The term **product** refers not only to a physical commodity but also to anything offered by an organization to provide customer satisfaction. A product can be a single commodity, a group of commodities, a product-service combination, or even a combination of several tangible goods and intangible services. Or a product can be an idea, a cause, or any other intangible factor that satisfies customers of nonprofit or for-profit organizations.

Theodore Levitt was one of the first to suggest a useful term to describe this concept of a product:[2] the *augmented product*, which is the aggregate of physical, psychological, and sociologic satisfactions that a buyer obtains. When an industrial marketer sells a major item of machinery, the product may be augmented in several ways. A small electric motor manufacturer may (1) provide financing, (2) ensure a constant supply of maintenance and replacement parts, (3) guarantee the performance of the motors for a specified period of time, (4) make technicians available to advise customers on the installation and use of the motors, and (5) train the customer personnel who actually will operate the motors. The customer does not simply buy an electric motor; the customer purchases a core product augmented by financial, warranty, service, and training benefits.

⬤ CLASSIFICATION OF GOODS

A tradition of classifying goods and services exists in marketing. The two most commonly used classification schemes are those adopted by the American Marketing Association's Committee on Definitions. The first classification scheme applies to consumer goods and is based on purchasing patterns (i.e., convenience goods, shopping goods, and specialty goods).[3] The second classification scheme applies to both consumer and organizational goods and is based on the rate of consumption and tangibility (i.e., nondurable goods, durable goods, and services). The next sections will describe the particular attributes of consumer and organizational goods.

Consumer Goods: Convenience, Shopping, and Specialty Goods

Consumer goods can be classified into three subtypes: convenience goods, shopping goods, and specialty goods. (See Table 8.1.) **Convenience goods** are goods that the shopper desires to buy with a minimum outlay of time and effort. Items stocked in convenience stores typically include confections, bread, milk, beer and soda, cigarettes, and magazines. **Shopping goods** are goods that consumers wish to compare with other available offerings before making a selection. Household furnishings, clothing, and recreation equipment are in this group. **Specialty goods** are goods that buyers are willing to go to considerable lengths to seek out and purchase. Such goods may be custom made, or they simply may be very successfully differentiated products such as a high-performance tennis racquet or high-fashion designer apparel.

Organizational Goods

Organizational goods are goods, such as chemicals, component parts, office supplies, and so on, that are purchased by businesses in order to produce other goods or for operating a business. Organizational goods, including those purchased by governments and nonprofit organizations, represent marketing opportunities that are as important as those for consumer goods. The methods of organizational marketing are somewhat specialized, but in general, the concepts presented in this book are valid for the organizational marketer as well as for the consumer goods marketer.

Agricultural, Other Extractive Products, Raw Materials.   Farms, forests, mines, and quarries provide raw materials. Most agricultural products and all extractive products undergo some processing before consumption. Demands for extractive products are derived from the demands for the goods into which they are transformed.

Manufactured Organizational Products.   Manufactured products are those which have undergone some processing. There are several specific types of manufactured organizational goods. *Semimanufactured goods* are raw materials that have gone through some stages of manufacturing but require further processing before they can be used. *Parts or components* are manufactured items that are ready to be incorporated into other products. *Process machinery or installations* are major pieces of equipment used in the manufacture of other goods. *Accessory equipment* involves lesser items of a productive nature. *Operating supplies* are materials used in the course of business that are destroyed or consumed in the process.

Unique Characteristics of Organizational Goods.   Organizational goods are different from consumer goods, although the basic nature of their marketing is similar. First, many organizational goods are highly technical products. Even a commodity-type

---

Convenience goods
Consumer items purchased with a minimum outlay of time and effort.

Shopping goods
Consumer items purchased after comparison with other available offerings.

Specialty goods
Consumer items purchased for specific attributes after considerable effort.

Organizational goods
Goods purchased by businesses in order to produce other goods or for operations.

TABLE 8.1

Classes of Consumer Goods—Some Characteristics and Marketing Considerations

	Type of Product		
	Convenience	*Shopping*	*Specialty*
Time and effort devoted by consumer to shopping	Very little	Considerable	Cannot generalize; consumer may go to nearby store and buy with minimum effort or may have to go to distant store and spend much time and effort
Time spent planning the purchase	Very little	Considerable	Considerable
How soon want is satisfied after it arises	Immediately	Relatively long time	Relatively long time
Are price and quality compared?	No	Yes	No
Price	Usually low per unit	High	High
Frequency of purchase	Usually frequent	Infrequent	Infrequent
Importance	Unimportant	Often very important	Cannot generalize
Marketing Considerations			
Length of distribution channel	Long	Short	Short to very short
Importance of retailer	Any single store is relatively unimportant	Important	Very important
Number of outlets	As many as possible	Few	Few, often only one in a market
Stock turnover	High	Lower	Few; often only one in a market
Gross margin	Low	High	High
Responsibility for advertising	Producer's	Retailer's	Joint responsibility
Importance of point-of-purchase display	Very important	Less important	Less important
Brand or store name importance	Brand name	Store name	Both
Importance of packaging	Very important (silent salesperson)	Less important	Less important

Source: Adapted from William J. Stanton, Michael J. Etzel, and Bruce J. Walker, *Fundamentals of Marketing,* 9th ed. Copyright ©1991, New York, McGraw-Hill, Inc., pp. 171, 174. Used with permission of the authors.

product such as copper tubing is the result of highly sophisticated metallurgical and process research. Many organizational products are extremely expensive or are purchased in such large quantities that very large sums of money are involved. Organizational products, other than rapidly changing high-technology products, tend to have longer life expectancies than consumer products. Introductions often are slower paced, growth is achieved over a long period of time, and mature organizational products flourish for years before going into decline. Relatively few organizational products are perishable, although some, such as chemicals, do lose their purity or potency over time. Some organizational products are toxic, flammable, or dangerous in some other way; hence they require extremely careful handling in transit, storage, and use. Organizational products, far more than consumer goods, create serious environmental problems in waste disposal. For example, the storage of spent nuclear fuel cell rods is problematic because they are highly toxic to humans for hundreds of years.

The Demand for Organizational Goods.   The demand for organizational products is derived—that is, it stems from the existence of a demand for something else. The demand for a machine tool exists because there is a demand for the item that the tool can make. There is a demand for oil rig replacement parts because there is a demand for crude petroleum. Derived demand tends to be highly cyclic, because relatively modest changes in final demand can drastically affect the derived demand.

For example, an industrial company that sells plastic injection-molding machines has a large customer that regularly buys about $150,000 worth of equipment for expansion and replacement of old machines. If this customer experiences a 15 percent decline in demand, the organization may decide not to increase capacity or to replace older machines. Instead of buying $150,000 worth of new molding equipment, it may buy only $50,000 worth. This 15 percent decline for the plastics manufacturer turns out to be a 66.7 percent decrease for the machinery company. Of course, if the customer's business were to increase by 15 percent, the equipment manufacturer's sales would be proportionately higher. Derived-demand relationships may result in drastic swings in the sales of organizational products—swings that make both forecasting and marketing planning very difficult.

The Marketing Mix for Organizational Goods.   The marketing-mix concept is applicable to organizational marketing. However, the character of the organizational marketing mix may be quite different from the consumer product marketing mix. Because organizational products are often complex and technical in order to meet rigid specifications established by industrial buyers, there is much more customizing of organizational products than of consumer products. This results in very broad product lines that reflect thousands of relatively minor differences in customers' requirements.

While new product development is important in organizational marketing, it often tends to be more technically driven than market directed. True, organizational product managers and sales personnel work closely with key customers in the development of new products to meet customers' needs, but a substantial number of ideas for new products are generated within the seller's research and development (R&D) and engineering departments.

Capital goods
Items categorized as
business assets and
capitalized for accounting
purposes.

Organizational products often require extensive after-sale service. This is especially true of **capital goods,** such as stamping machinery, printing presses, or mainframe computers. Organizational products are often augmented products that include technical consultation, maintenance and repair service, and purchase financing.

The distribution channels for organizational goods are very specialized. This means that industrial companies may lose direct control of their products once they are sold. Many companies that sell through distributors do not know what happens to their products once they have been shipped from the factory. In part to overcome this problem, some industrial firms have acquired their own distributors. Others have used franchising or other contractual arrangements to establish some vertical control over their channels of distribution.

Organizational marketers generally make extensive use of personal selling and comparatively little use of integrated marketing communication. This may be the single most obvious difference between the consumer product marketing mix and the organizational marketing mix. Industrial firms do advertise, but the use of mass communication is limited, and the amounts of money spent on it are considerably less than in consumer goods marketing.

The pricing of organizational products is extremely complex, largely because of the many variations in customer status and product lines that are involved. In the extreme, a price is established for each transaction. Price is always subject to negotiation, even if the seller wants to establish some uniformity in the pricing approach. Reliance on a limited number of large customers (whether users or resellers) gives the buyer a great deal of bargaining power.

These differences in product, distribution, communications, and pricing strategies for the organizational marketer are important because they lead to different overall marketing strategies than those used in consumer goods marketing. But the planning process by which the organizational marketing strategy is developed and the concepts on which the organizational marketing program are based are not fundamentally different.

PRODUCT STRATEGY ISSUES

Developing a product strategy is not easy. Several elements are involved, and many appear to be hopelessly entangled. With a systematic approach to strategy design, these entanglements can be straightened out. First, the various issues involved in developing product strategy must be isolated and broken down into their components. By concentrating separately on each of these important issues, it is discovered that each is related to some other issue. The elements of product strategy are not terribly complicated, once these relationships are recognized. Developing product strategy becomes a process of making decisions about the individual issues that are discussed next.

Determining the Product Line

The basic question of paramount importance in developing product strategy is: What products should we sell? But the fundamental marketing opportunity is not to sell things but rather to provide satisfactions. Thus the question probably should be rephrased to: What satisfactions or benefits should we provide? In most organizations, satisfactions are delivered via products, services, or product-service combinations.

The first step in deciding what to sell is identification of a product's potential ultimate consumers through analysis of the marketing situation. The marketing strategist should then select the target market segment. Having identified the consumer, the product planner's second step is to determine the use (satisfaction) specifications that the product will have to meet. Unfortunately, this important step often is omitted. Product planners may be tempted to jump immediately to the design of product characteristics, which could be a critical mistake. Product designers need to know exactly what the product is supposed to do, how the product will be used, how often, and with what efficiency it is supposed to operate. From a marketing strategy viewpoint, it is not as important to know what a product is capable of doing as it is to understand what consumers expect it to do and to create a "fit" between the two.

However, it is not sufficient simply to satisfy ultimate consumers. A product must provide satisfactions for wholesalers and retailers as well. These are not consumption satisfactions but reseller satisfactions. For a product to fit into a retail assortment, it must match the reseller's expectations in terms of inventory requirements, stock turnover, margin, packaging, and so forth. If it fails to meet these needs, the product will not be stocked.

The final step in answering the question of what products a company should sell involves matching both the customers and the resellers with appropriate product quality characteristics. Generally, product quality design involves developing three important characteristics: performance, cost, and appearance. These characteristics may affect both the product and its package. The form of a product (its specifications) should match its function, and its function is to satisfy consumers and resellers. It must do so profitably. This is the product's principal function from the manufacturer's viewpoint. In addition, other objectives may dictate product functions. For example, it may have to be made in existing facilities, or it may have to be designed to fit into a line of products. Or the products may have to meet legal or other constraints.

Determining the Width and Depth of a Product Line

Product mix
The composite of products a company offers.

Product line
Those items in the mix that are closely related.

Product width
Refers to how many different products are offered.

Product depth
Refers to how many items of each type are sold.

Line extension
Process of building either the depth or the width of a product offering.

Determining the appropriate product line means making decisions concerning the number of different items in each product line and the number of different lines to be handled. See, for example, Table 8.2. The composite of products a company offers is called its **product mix.** Those items in the mix that are closely related are referred to as a **product line.** For example, Procter & Gamble has an extensive mix of products ranging from beauty care to food and beverage and health care. Its line of products is extensive and well illustrates the concepts of width and depth. **Product width** refers to how many different products are offered, and **product depth** defines how many items of each type are sold. Procter & Gamble's product line has a fairly broad width, with five major categories and 26 subcategories. Product depth varies within each category. For example, as indicated in the Fabric and Home Care Products category in Table 8.2, the Laundry category includes 27 product brands, the Hard surface cleaners category includes nine, and the Bleach category has only one.

The process of building either the depth or width of a product offering is **line extension.** Why should a company offer so many products? Is such diversity necessary?

TABLE 8.2

Procter & Gamble's Global Business Units/Brands

Fabric and Home Care	
Bleach and prewash additives	Ace
Care for special fabrics	Dryel, Febreze
Dish care	Cascade, Dawn, Dreft, Fairy Dish, Hederol, Ivory Dish, Jar, Mintax, Yes
Fabric conditioners	Azurit, Bounce, Downy, Lenor Fabric Conditioner
Hard surface cleaners	Ace, Comet, Flash, Maestro Limpio, Maestro Lindo, Mr. Clean, Mr. Proper, Viakal
Household cleaner	Swiffer
Laundry	Ace Detergent, Alfa, Alo, Alomatik, Ariel, Bold, Bonus, Bonux, Cheer, Dash, Daz, Dreft, Era, Fairy, Gain, Gaofuli, Ivory Snow, Jet, Monogen, Mr. Clean, Myth, Panda, Perla, Tide, Tix, Vizir, Yes
P&G Chemicals	Fatty Acids, Fatty Alcohols, Glycerine, Methyl Esters, Tertiary Amines

Beauty Care	
Cosmetics	Cover Girl, Ellen Betrix, Max Factor, SK-II
Deodorants/anti-perspirants	Old Spice, Secret, Sure
Fragrances	Giorgio Beverly Hills, Herve Leger, Hugo Boss, Laura Biagiotti-Roma, Mossimo, Old Spice, Red
Hair care	Blendax, Head & Shoulders, Infasil, Innerscience, Pantene Pro-V, Pert Plus, Physique, Principal, Rejoice, Rejoy, Vidal Sassoon, Wash & Go
Skin/beauty care	Camay, Ellen Betrix, Fairy, Infasil, Ivory, Muse, Noxzema, Olay, Safeguard, Seiv Alfaz, SK-II, Zest

Health Care	
Water filtration	PUR
Health/oral care	AZ, Blend-a-Med, Blendax, Crest, Fixodent, Gleem, Hipoglos, Ipana, Kukident, Medinait, Metamucil, NyQuil/DayQuil, Pepto-Bismol, Scope, Vicks VapoRub
Pet health and nutrition	Eukanuba, Iams
Prescription drugs	Actonel, Asacol Delayed-Release Tablets, Cacit, Dantrium, Dantrium IV, Didrokit, Didronel, Digozine, Dytide H, Macrobid, Macrodantin, Neoduplamox, Previscan, Ultradol

TABLE 8.2 *(continued)*

Procter & Gamble's Global Business Units/Brands

Food and Beverage	
Beverages	Brothers, Folgers, Millstone, Punica, Sunny Delight
Fat substitute	Olean
Peanut butter	Jif
Shortening and oil	Crisco
Snacks	Pringles

Baby, Feminine, and Family Care	
Baby bibs, diapers, and baby wipes	Bibsters, Cutie, Dodot, Dodotis, Luvs, Pampers, Prima, Kids Fresh, Luvs Ultra Thicks, Pampers Baby Fresh
Feminine protection pads, pantiliners, and tampons	Alldays, Always, Ausonia, Evax, Lines, Orkid, Otros Dias, Salvaslip, Tampax, Whisper
Incontinence	Attento, Linidor, Salvacamas
Paper towels, toilet tissue, and facial tissue	Bounty, Charmin, Puffs, Codi, Loreto, Royale, Tempo

A consumer generally buys only one product at a time unless the products are complementary in nature. However, because different customers have different requirements, it may be necessary to offer a number of products to satisfy several different market segments.[4] This is obviously necessary when opening or entering a new market; however, it is not as easy as it might seem. Both Post Cereals and Quaker Oats Co. have introduced new lines of breakfast cereals to bolster sales of their established products.

However, the addition of new products cannot go on endlessly or the company may find that it is in competition with itself (referred to as *cannibalization*).[5] This can be done purposely, as when a new product is introduced as a substitute for an older one. Or it may be done to dominate a category by marketing two brands or products rather than just one. Ultimately, the manufacturer must decide on an optimal width and depth of line that is most profitable in the long run. Theoretically, a company should continue to add products as long as incremental revenues generated by the new product are greater than the incremental costs of adding it. Occasionally, a product may be added even though its contribution to profit is negligible. Offering a full line to serve retailers or providing special products for the handicapped are examples.

A critical factor in establishing an effective product mix is consistency. The term *line* means the products must be meaningfully related. The Procter & Gamble product mix is a good example. Products may be related by using common manufacturing processes. Some of Procter & Gamble's products are manufactured by essentially the same methods. The products in a line may move through the same distribution channel. This is true of all the company's Food and Beverage products. Finally, the items in a line are consistent if they have similar end-use or consumption patterns.

Attempting to market a diverse line of products can be confusing and wasteful if not handled carefully. Successful firms have decentralized marketing responsibility and do not attempt to market disparate items such as batteries and razors as part of a single line. Such decentralization is practiced by Gillette Co. with success as it organizes into three core business units—grooming, portable power, and oral care.[6]

When to Introduce or Delete Products

As highlighted earlier, many firms struggle with deciding when new products should be developed and introduced in today's highly competitive marketplace. There is little choice because rapid technological obsolescence forces every seller to consider the necessity of introducing new products to survive and grow. Even without technological obsolescence, declining competitive distinctiveness demands a planned program of new products to maintain market share. A benchmarking study of 161 business units uncovered the key drivers of new product performance. Two key performance dimensions—profitability and impact—defined the "performance map." Four key drivers of performance were identified, namely, a high-quality new product process, the new product strategy for the business unit, resource availability, and R&D spending levels.[7]

The issue of dropping unprofitable products was mentioned previously. However, candidates for deletion should be identified well in advance of when they are to be dropped. The deletion of "sick" products and the timing and method of their withdrawal from the company's line are all-important aspects of the problem. Abandonment, however, is not the only strategy available for the mature product.[8] It may be the last resort. Alternative approaches include product improvement, repackaging, private branding, and so on.

The timing of changes in the product line is always difficult. New products may not be available when the company would like to introduce them. Developing new products usually takes longer than anticipated, and sometimes a competitor actually beats the company to the punch. The timing of product deletions is also difficult because sales departments are reluctant to abandon products that are producing any sales. A product should be dropped when it ceases to contribute to overhead. In practice, this situation is hard to detect. If no replacement is available, it may be best to continue to sell unprofitable items rather than having a gap in the product line. New products should be developed while older ones are in their declining stages, and introduction of the replacement product should be timed to coincide with or lead removal of the old.

Packaging

Jobbers
Specialized resellers who act as marketing agents for manufacturers.

Packaging is always important in developing product strategy.[9] Most consumer goods are packaged in one way or another, and many industrial products also are packaged—especially shelf items that are sold through warehouse distributors and **jobbers.** Creating an effective package is complicated. There are many factors to consider; only the most important can be touched on here.

Environmentalists have attacked packaging, especially of beverage containers. One-way (nonrecyclable) containers—cans and nonreturnable bottles—have been outlawed in some areas. Product-development engineers have designed remarkable package improvements in response to environmentalists' concerns. Reusable and recyclable containers, self-disposing closures, and biodegradable package materials

IT'S LEGAL BUT IS IT ETHICAL?

Ready-to-Wear Watchdogs

The first generation of garments that couple nanotechnology—the science of making electronics on the tiniest of atomic scales—with high-tech fabrics to create "smart clothing" is beginning to roll out. Motorola Inc. is developing clothing that can "talk" to washing machines, giving instructions on how the garment should be washed. DuPont Co. and Burlington Industries Inc. see potential for a huge new market in clothing that looks like the same old thing but functions more like an appliance. Features such as expanding the waistline of your slacks with a push of a button, or adjusting the color of a sweater to match other garments you are wearing, or tracking a wandering child through a global-positioning system woven into his jacket, or baby sleepwear that sounds an alarm if breathing stops all may be coming soon.

At Nano-Tex Inc., a company using nanotechnology to engineer fabric that resists wrinkles and stays drier, with laboratories outside San Francisco, researchers play basketball every day in the same socks, engineered with molecular-scaled sponges that absorb the rancid hydrocarbons responsible for body odor. The sponges are designed to release the smelly stuff only when they meet a detergent in water. David Stone, chief scientific officer, says that with this new fabric "you could wear the same gym suit three or four times" without offending other players. DuPont researchers are attempting to engineer new fibers that can function as conductive "wires" as well as react to electricity, heat, or pressure. The researchers have tinkered with the traditional circular shape of fibers to make them oval, square, or triangular to enable microscopic "wings" of different materials to be added to the core fiber. This engineered fiber can then be made to contract or expand, loosening or tightening clothing, or making it warmer or cooler as the wearer desires. These engineered fibers are already appearing in some new high-performance fabrics and will eventually enhance fashion as well as function. DuPont expects such research to renew its fibers business. Their now-tiny "textronics" or smart fabrics division is considered the ideal opportunity to leverage DuPont's expertise in chemistry, textiles, and electronics.

Massachusetts Institute of Technology (MIT) scientists researching the electronics aspects are trying to find ways to meld devices like phones and computers into garments and have attracted funding from several corporate sponsors. In 2000, Philips NV, in cooperation with Levi Strauss & Co., briefly test-marketed a jacket with built-in cellphone and MP3 player, but the system proved too cumbersome, observers reported. And in 2001, MIT researcher Steven Schwartz tested in Russia a "smart" space suit outfitted with wearable computers. Built in collaboration with Boeing, the suit was designed to monitor the astronaut's condition while providing information and feedback during space walks. Sensatex Inc., a New York technology start-up, hopes to market an athletic T-shirt that will monitor heart rate, track body temperature and respiration, and count how many calories the wearer is burning. It could warn of a potential heart attack or heat prostration. The prototype smart T-shirt, which is expected to sell for $200, looks and feels like a soft, ribbed-cotton knit. But the cotton and spandex cloth is interwoven with conductive fibers that receive and transmit data from embedded sensors to a special receiver the size of a credit card. The "transceiver," worn at the waist, stores the information and can transmit it for playback to a cellphone, personal computer, or wrist-mounted monitor. Sensatex says it will focus on the fitness market, and chief executive Jeffrey Wolf says he is working with sports organizations to test professional players.

Such detailed monitoring ability brings to mind certain ethical concerns for some people.

(continued)

The benefits of "smart" clothing can be readily evaluated and offer some extremely valuable safety factors for infants, toddlers, the elderly and frail, and competitive athletes. But the "big brother is watching" syndrome that defenders of the right to personal privacy often assert may also be a legitimate concern.

Source: Susan Warren, "Ready-to-Wear Watchdogs," *The Wall Street Journal* (August 10, 2001), pp. B1, B3.

have been developed, often at considerable expense. A recent concern over packaging is safety, particularly for hazardous or toxic products.

Package design is closely related to product image and promotion. These relationships must be considered whenever self-service and mass merchandising are involved. For example, impulse buying appears to be the result of delivering a sensory cue at the point of sale. Unique packaging may be the only technique available for attracting consumers to certain products. Various brands of detergents, dehydrated milk, salt, sugar, and other staples, which are almost identical in content, may be differentiated effectively by packaging. Major promotional programs for firms such as Coca-Cola and Pepsico also may be based on packaging.[10] In another example, many supermarket chains have realized that "store" brands with innovative packaging can be a vital component in effecting and maintaining store image.[11]

Manufacturers should never ignore the packaging requirements of resellers. From a retailer's point of view, good consumer packaging has display impact. It moves merchandise off the shelves. In addition, resellers' mechanical requirements must be met. Packages must be appropriately sized. They should shelve or stack conveniently and should be easy to price mark. Packages also should be strong enough to withstand routine handling by store personnel and shoppers.

Cost is the final important consideration in packaging. Very elaborate packaging is costly. For products such as aerosol insecticides and shaving cream, the cost of the container may be greater than that of the contents. The cost of packaging always must be considered in relation to its contribution to marketing strategy.

Product Safety

When the use or misuse of a product harms a consumer, the courts have held that manufacturers (and recently, wholesalers and retailers) are liable for the injury or damage inflicted.[12] Claims for heavy damages and extremely liberal awards have caused drastic increases in premiums for product liability insurance and have made manufacturers more reluctant to introduce new, "untried" products.

When product safety problems were experienced by pharmaceutical and personal care product companies, then Procter & Gamble Co. decided to take its tampon product Rely off the market. G. D. Searle also withdrew a pair of products, attempting to curtail mounting litigation costs. Another drug maker, A. H. Robbins, filed for bankruptcy, as did Manville Corp. in a similar case involving asbestos.[13]

A discussion of product strategy would be incomplete without a reference to the tampering with drug and food products that occurred in the early to mid-1980s. In 1982, the first cyanide-tainted capsules of Johnson & Johnson's Tylenol were discovered. For the next few years, similar situations arose with Johnson & Johnson's products as well as those of other companies. Eventually, most companies abandoned the capsule package and determined ways in which tampering could be stopped or at least detected.[14]

Product Liability

Product liability is a major concern to marketing managers. Lawsuits and the high cost of insuring against them have forced managers to find ways of dealing with the liability issue. Various strategies have been employed. Some companies have withdrawn products; others have attempted to raise prices to finance the added cost. Where possible, changes in product and packaging have been made.[15] But not all claims for injury end up in the courts. Data dealing with the increase in product liability are hard to obtain, but it is a serious problem. The escalation in insurance premiums testifies to this. Fred Morgan indicated that in 1982, 96 percent of all claims were settled without a court verdict. Nevertheless, court decisions establish the boundaries within which out-of-court settlements are reached. After inspecting the case law dealing with product liability litigation, Morgan had several conclusions to offer. (See Table 8.3.)

Warranty—Post-Sale Services

Because a firm is in business to provide satisfaction, its marketing effort is not complete until satisfaction has been delivered. When satisfaction is not completely delivered at the time of purchase, post-sale servicing becomes necessary. When a product is intended to provide longer-term satisfaction, it is probable that an effective warranty and service policy also will be included in the marketing mix. Sears, Roebuck and Co. has found it effective to remind its customers, "We Service What We Sell"; General Motors Corp. emphasizes its Mr. Goodwrench program; and all car manufacturers promote warranties of their products.

Building post-sale services into the product strategy is a powerful marketing technique. However, some managers think of customer service and customer complaint handling as the same thing. This is not so. Active consumer satisfaction policies add to the effectiveness of marketing programs. Companies such as American Express, General Electric, Whirlpool, General Motors, IBM, and Procter & Gamble incorporate after-sale service programs as important elements in their marketing strategies, and many firms such as 3Com have revised their programs to become more solutions oriented rather than just service oriented.[16]

Marketing consumer durables and most industrial products involves post-sale servicing. For example, the marketing of equipment installations often requires that the seller supply technical service for setup, maintenance, and repair. This type of activity is important in keeping the customer "satisfied" and encourages repeat purchases. Its effect on longer-run marketing success makes post-sale servicing a vital part of the continuing marketing program.

Product life cycle (PLC) Graphically portrays the sales history of a product into four stages: introduction, growth, maturity, and decline.

 # THE PRODUCT LIFE CYCLE

The **product life cycle (PLC)** is one of the most frequently encountered concepts in marketing management. Levitt popularized the concept; others have criticized or elaborated on it.[17] The PLC portrays graphically the sales history of a product from

TABLE 8.3

Pertinent Observations Concerning Product Liability

Fred Morgan offers the following conclusions reached after inspecting the case law that has accumulated on product liability litigation:

1. Companies can be held liable for damages under negligence and warranty pleadings resulting from marketing communications—statements by salespersons, advertised messages, and packaging and labeling.
2. Marketing communications can result in liability because of innocent misrepresentation of facts.
3. Because strict liability is based on a product defect, advertising and personal selling activities are generally irrelevant in a strict liability pleading.
4. Courts have interpreted defective labels, warnings, and packaging as defective products, thereby establishing strict liability actions.
5. Distributors—retailers and wholesalers—are generally not liable for the misrepresentations of manufacturers. Distributors' communications to customers can, however, misrepresent the product.
6. Distributors are less likely to be found liable for product-related damages than manufacturers because the former are often able to assign the defense to the latter.
7. Distributors who brand products as their own are treated as manufacturers, thereby exposing themselves to manufacturers' liability under all theories of liability.
8. One channel member's warranty generally does not bind another channel member unless the latter, either explicitly or through its actions, has adopted the warranty.
9. The negligent acts of one channel member can result in other channel members being held liable if they should have anticipated the negligent act.

Addendum

A decision (*Sindell* v. *Abbott Laboratories et al.*) established a new doctrine of causation in product liability. Under this doctrine, the manufacturers of a product, if found guilty of charges of negligence filed against them, would be assessed damages in proportion to their market share, even though the plaintiff could not identify which of those manufacturers produced the particular product that caused the injury.*

---

*See Mary Jane Sheffet, "Market Share Liability: A New Doctrine of Causation in Product Liability," *Journal of Marketing* (Winter 1983), p. 35.
Source: Fred W. Morgan, "Marketing and Product Liability: A Review and Update," *Journal of Marketing* (Summer 1982), p. 69. Reprinted by permission of the American Marketing Association.

the time it is introduced to the market until the point when it is withdrawn. (See Figure 8.1.) There are four major stages to the PLC: introduction, growth, maturity, and decline.

- *Introduction*—a new product is presented to the marketplace. Initial distribution is obtained, and promotion is initiated.

- *Growth*—consumers and the trade accept the product. Initial distribution is expanded, promotion is increased, repeat orders from initial buyers are obtained, and word-of-mouth advertising leads to more and more sales.

- *Maturity*—competition becomes intense. Toward the end of this period, competitors' products cut deeply into the company's market growth.

FIGURE 8.1

Product Life Cycle

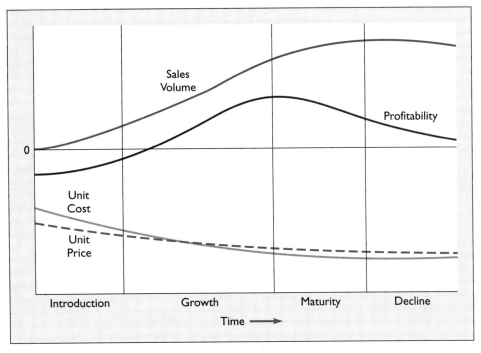

- *Decline*—the product becomes obsolete, and its loss of competitive advantages results in sales decreases. Decline is accelerated by disintegration in product distinctiveness, evidenced by obsolescence. A final stage, called *dropout,* occurs when the product is deleted or abandoned.

Figure 8.1 shows the behavior of cost and profit over the PLC. During introduction, high development and market-entry costs result in losses. Profits swell during the growth stage, but in decline, squeezed profit margins due to severe price competition result in losses.

Are Product Life Cycles Real?

Both a theoretical life cycle model and a real-world PLC exist. Reality seldom conforms to theory.[18] Marketing executives believe in the PLC concept—but streetwise marketers point out that unusual circumstances may interfere with expected life cycle behavior. William Jensen, a marketing manager at *Time* magazine, expressed it well: "The life cycle of a product is dependent on the actions and decisions of people, both of buyers and sellers, not on a set of formulae independent of the fickle fingers of consumers."[19] Torelli and Burnett examined over 1,000 industrial businesses to determine the extent PLCs exist. They concluded that market growth rate is only one of the aspects determining the shape of the real-world sales curve. The shape and duration of the life cycle also depend on such factors as market innovation, market concentration, competitive entry, and spending on R&D and marketing.[20]

Implications of the Product Life Cycle for Marketing Managers

The PLC's usefulness is its application as a guide to marketing strategy. Changes in the marketplace require marketing managers to adapt to these developments. Marketing managers recognize the usefulness of the PLC concept as a tool for planning and decision making. For example, retailers and manufacturers have identified the need for tracking capabilities of products throughout the supply chain. Full product life cycle management is cradle-to-grave management of a product as it progresses through the logistics pipeline.[21] Harrell and Taylor report that the concept has validity for predicting the sales volume of a product class. They also note that the PLC's greater significance is to highlight factors that influence the shape and amplitude of volume projections, in order to assess opportunities and risks realistically.[22]

Attempts to generalize about the appropriate strategy for each stage of the PLC have been made. Most are matrices showing the various stages of the PLC and the strategies typically associated with each. An example of this approach is shown in Figure 8.2.[23] The product is the firm's chief competitive weapon, so contending with the PLC is best accomplished by making changes in the product itself.

Product strategy is most critical in the first and last stages of the PLC. A new product is necessary for the PLC to begin. The competitive distinctiveness or technological superiority of a new product determines its success in the introductory stage. New products are the ultimate solution to maturity and decline problems when decisions must be made on abandoning a declining product. However, the strategies of marketing mature products are not restricted to the elimination of such products. (Please refer to preceding discussion.)

Although a product strategy matrix as shown in Figure 8.2 is useful, it is not a "roadmap" for market mixing.[24] For example, one cannot simply determine the life cycle stage, follow the column down to the product strategy row, and find the correct thing to do. The matrix merely displays what is generally done. Every marketing situation is unique, and the marketing manager must be alert to the many factors that influence strategy at any given time. And the stage in the PLC is only one factor.

Why Do Life Cycles Occur?

Two theories have attempted to explain the product life cycle. The first is the consumer adoption process; the second is adoption theory.

The Consumer Adoption Process.   An explanation of the PLC is found in the **consumer adoption process,** the process whereby consumers become aware of and eventually adopt a new product. As more and different people move through the adoption process, sales increase until the market is saturated. This process usually takes time. People become aware of new products only after they have been on the market for some time, and they accept such innovations gradually. Everett Rogers has identified the steps in this innovation adoption process as follows:

Consumer adoption process
The process by which consumers become aware of and adopt new products.

1. *Awareness.* The individual becomes aware of the innovation but lacks information about it.

2. *Interest.* The individual is stimulated to search for information about the innovation.

FIGURE 8.2

Product Life Cycle Strategies

Sales	Introduction	Growth	Competitive Turbulence	Maturity	Decline

Characteristics

	Introduction	Growth	Competitive Turbulence	Maturity	Decline
Sales	Low	Rapidly rising	Slowing	Peak sales Cyclicality sets in	Declining
Prices	High	Lower than introduction	Low	Low	Falling
Profits (per unit)	Negative	High and rising	Declining	Average	Declining
Customers	Innovators	Early adopters	Early majority	Middle majority	Laggards
Competition	Few	Growing number of imitators	Shakeout begins	Declining numbers	Further decline

Strategies

	Introduction	Growth	Competitive Turbulence	Maturity	Decline
Overall	Create awareness and trial R&D and engineering are critical	Market share penetration	Protect and strengthen niche	Protect share—manage for earnings Emphasize competitive costs	Reduce expenditures and harvest
Product	Basic	Offer extensions, features, service	Tighten line, improve quality	Diversity of brands and models	Phase out weak items
Price	Cost plus	Market broadening	Match or beat competitors	Defensive	Maintain profit margins
Distribution	Selective	Build intensive coverage	Strong dealer support	Intensive and extensive	Selective
Communications	Create awareness	Stimulate wider trial	Maintain consumer franchise	Stress brand differences and benefits	Phase out maintenance only
Manufacturing	Subcontract Short runs Overcapacity	Centralize Shift to mass production Undercapacity	Long runs Some overcapacity Stability of manufacturing process	Many short runs Decentralize	Revert to subcontracting

Source: From *Analysis for Strategic Market Decisions,* 1st edition, by G. Day. Copyright © 1986. Reprinted with permission of South-Western College Publishing, a division of International Thomson Publishing. Fax 800-730-2215.

3. *Evaluation.* The individual considers whether to try the innovation.

4. *Trial.* The individual tries the innovation on a small scale to test its usefulness.

5. *Adoption.* The individual decides to make use of the innovation on a regular basis.[25]

Adoption theory
Refers to the spread of a new idea from introduction to final general acceptance.

Adoption Theory. **Adoption theory** provides further insight into the PLC by its extension into the *diffusion process.* This refers to the spread of a new idea from its introduction to its final general acceptance. Such a spread would follow a normal pattern of communications, except some people are more prone than others to accept new products and ideas.[26] Rogers classifies the adopters of innovations using five categories:[27]

1. *Innovators* are the first people to accept a new product. There are relatively few of them. Only about 2.5 percent of all adopters fall into this category.

2. *Early adopters* constitute about 13.5 percent of innovation acceptors.

3. The *early majority adopters* are those who precede the other half of innovation acceptors. About 34 percent of adopters fall into this class.

4. *Late majority adopters* also account for about 34 percent of all innovation acceptors.

5. The last 16 percent of the adopting public, classified as *laggards,* constitute a more extreme segment. These people are often price conscious and wait until an innovation has passed well into its mature stage before adopting it.

The distribution of adopter types provides further insights into the PLC when it is retabulated on a cumulative basis. Retabulation suggests that by the time innovators have purchased the new product, only 2.5 percent of its eventual total market has been realized. Adding the early adopters, the saturation rises to 16.0 percent. Not until the laggards have stepped into the market is 100 percent achieved. These data are shown in Figure 8.3. The bars are "smoothed" by averaging the adoption percentages over the range, which gives a curve that remarkably resembles the PLC curve.

The implications of adoption theory for product strategy are clear. The secret of getting a new product underway is to get innovators to try it—and then to quickly capture early adopters. Because these people tend to be highly influential opinion leaders, the importance of getting them to buy the product is apparent. Promoting to opinion leaders and, through them, to the larger market is described as a two-step communication process. The next stage involves making the product readily available to the early and late majority. Laggards generally will come along by themselves. The diffusion process also helps explain the difficulties companies encounter in the decline period of the PLC. What happens is that many original customers begin experimenting with competitors' products.

TEST MARKETING

In the past, test marketing was used principally as a screening device. Products that were unsuccessful in a test market simply did not get the opportunity for national marketing. Marketing managers extrapolated the results of the test to the national

FIGURE 8.3

Cumulative Distribution of Innovation Adopters

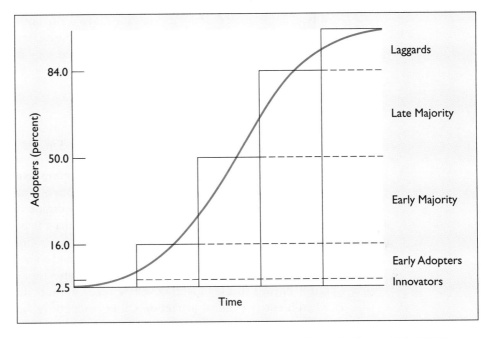

Source: Adapted with the permission of The Free Press, a Division of Simon & Schuster Adult Publishing Group from *Diffusion of Innovations,* Fourth Edition by Everett M. Rogers. Copyright © 1995 by Everett M. Rogers. Copyright © 1962, 1971, 1983 by The Free Press.

Test marketing
Investigates marketability of products and variables such as differing prices or communication themes or media mixes.

market and made a final "go/no go" decision. Today, however, **test marketing** is expected to investigate variables in the marketing plan other than just the product, such as differing prices or differing communications themes or media mixes.

Product modification might be recommended as a result of test marketing, but this is no longer the principal reason for test marketing. One company emphasized that test marketing is not a screening device by stating, "It should be undertaken with the prior knowledge that all the important odds for success are high."[28]

Advantages of Test Marketing

What specific questions can be answered by test marketing?[29] First, the overall workability of the marketing plan can be evaluated. A test market is like a shakedown cruise for a new ship. Grocery manufacturers actually use test marketing as the first step in a planned program of market entry. True, minor adjustments in subsequent markets of the **rollout** (market-by-market introduction) may occur, but the rollout is planned from the day the product is first introduced into the first test market.

Rollout
A market-by-market introduction of a new product.

A second question that test marketing can answer involves evaluating alternative allocations of the budget. The level of spending can be varied in each of several test markets and differences in consumer response measured. Similarly, apportionment of the budget among various elements of the mix may be tested. In one market, the principal effort may be directed toward in-store promotions and merchandising deals.

In another market area, the main thrust of the introduction may be consumer sampling and mass-media advertising. Different advertising media may be tested in the different markets. Radio and newspapers may be used in one area; television in the other. These experiments are always carried on under tightly controlled conditions. Store-audit data and warehouse-withdrawal information, brand-awareness studies, coupon redemptions, and other measures are used to judge the relative effectiveness of various approaches to market entry.

Disadvantages of Test Marketing

There are several reasons for deciding not to pursue test marketing.[30] First, test marketing is expensive. Therefore, many companies now use test marketing as the first phase of national distribution. Second, test marketing takes time to complete—the average duration appears to be about 6 months. This is more than enough time for dangerous developments to occur. For example, the distinctiveness of the innovation can decay drastically. It will no longer be a new product when it goes into the national market. Third, test marketing is criticized because it prematurely informs competitors of a company's plans. Test marketing is very visible, and a good marketing intelligence system will immediately report its existence to a competitor's management. The least that can happen is that competitors will be ready to meet the threat of the new product when it enters national marketing. Other competitive tactics, however, may be more disastrous. Some competitors "jam" a test market by purposely altering their marketing programs in tested areas. Competitor reactions are not limited to just jamming test market results, however. A small competitor actually may be able to beat a national marketer to full-scale distribution while the larger seller is still involved with testing.

Successful companies have been speeding up the new product introduction process—a process once believed to take up to 2 years to complete. Some companies are eliminating test marketing altogether. Others are compressing or dispensing with steps that provide information that is useful but not critical to the new product's marketing plan. Windows of opportunity for new products open and close swiftly. David Miller, a client services director at ad agency Ogilvy & Mather, points out that when multinationals such as Procter & Gamble, Unilever, and Kraft Jacob Suchard develop a new product, they plan to sell it in at least 30 to 40 markets, so they are basically using countries as their test markets.[31]

● LAUNCHING NEW PRODUCTS

As illustrated by the Mini example in the Marketing in the Global Village scenario, one of the first major decisions in launching a new product is timing. We mentioned that the strategic window of opportunity for new products is open for a limited time. However, many new product opportunities remain viable long enough for a company to decide between an early or a late entry. Although it is possible to identify the advantages of both early and late entry, it is very difficult to predict accurately what will be the outcome of either strategy, because the market forces are so dynamic.[32] A recent examination of early entry by Szymanski and colleagues concluded that, on average, market order entry exerted a significant and positive direct impact on market share. However, they also stated that pioneer advantage was augmented by service quality, vertical integration, R&D expenditures, shared

MARKETING IN THE GLOBAL VILLAGE

High Style in a Tiny Package

Top European automakers are betting that little cars can coexist with SUVs on U.S. roads. They're expecting fashion-conscious American customers to spend $20,000-plus for tiny compact cars packed with high-tech features and high-style interiors. These cars in Europe have already become a major market segment because buyers find them easy to park in congested cities and they appreciate the stingy use of gasoline. "This is a good trend," says Wolfgang Reitzle, head of Ford Motor Co.'s luxury division, who plans to use their Volvo brand to expand into the premium compact market. Volkswagen AG's Audi Brand and Daimler-Chrysler AG's Mercedes also have plans to bring little European models over to the U.S. market.

The first little luxury model in the U.S. market is the "Mini" by BMW Group AG, which reinvented the 1960s British classic. Although a four-seater, the "Mini" is less than 12 feet long and only 4 feet 7 inches tall. With the doors open, it is wider than it is long. But although the original was bare-bones transportation—even a heater was optional—the new "Mini" is loaded with options such as heated mirrors, a computer navigation system, an air-conditioned glove box, rain-sensing windshield wipers, and an eight-speaker sound system. Gregory L. White, staff reporter for the *Wall Street Journal*, writes that the "Mini" screams fashion statement and when viewed from the front seems to smile cutely, while the roof (which is available in different colors from the body), looks like a cap. Inside, the look to White is retro, with brushed-metal trim and a speedometer the size of a salad plate in the middle of the dashboard, while other gauges rise from the steering column in round pods.

"There are people who may well be able to afford a larger car, but for whatever reason they just don't want one," says "Mini" spokesman Michael McBale. "They want all the good things that come with a small car—the responsiveness, the handling—but they don't want the flimsiness." The "Mini" won't bear the BMW emblem, but will have the German engineering that has made BMWs the performance benchmark for many auto enthusiasts. Introduced in the United Kingdom and Europe in 2001 with great success, the "Mini" arrived in the United States in April 2002 with a starting price under $18,000. Tom Lueck, Internet sales manager at Bob Smith BMW near Los Angeles, noted that the prelaunch enthusiasm was as strong as it had been for the hugely popular Z3 roadster that arrived in 1996.

BMW officials insisted that the "Mini," with six air bags and an optional computerized antiskid system, will be able to hold its own with the hulking SUVs and pickups on American roads. But at 2,316 pounds, the "Mini" is a shrimp compared to the Ford Excursion and other large SUVs that weigh three times as much. There is also the risk that introducing smaller, lower-priced models of elite brands will dilute their exclusive status among buyers of their much more expensive and profitable core models. Wendelin Wiedeking, president and CEO of Porsche AG, which isn't planning smaller, cheaper cars, says, "As a luxury brand, if you lower your price range, it gets more risky." But Audi with its A3 model, BMW with a model planned to be smaller than the 3-series, Mercedes with its A-class compacts, and Daimler-Chrysler with its two-seat Smart car all are indicating an interest in testing the U.S. market. Andreas Renschler, head of the Smart unit, says customers returning from Europe frequently ask Daimler-Chrysler whether they can get the Smart car in the United States. "If the customer wants to buy it, we should go" to the United States, he says.

Source: Gregory L. White, "High Style in a Tiny Package," *Wall Street Journal* (October 17, 2001), pp. B1, B4.

facilities, shared customers, market growth rate, and immediate customer purchase frequency.[33] This and other research suggests that entry timing is not always the critical factor.[34] A long-run leadership position is usually attained by the firm that develops the strongest competitive advantage.

Once the decision to enter has been made, there are several choices open to the marketer. Two of these are of primary importance. First, a decision must be made either to market to a selected segment or to approach the market as a whole. The second is between a rollout (market-by-market) introduction or an attempt to obtain immediate national or global distribution. This decision must be made on the basis of potential in the segments being considered and on the relative profitability of developing separate strategies for each segment. Test marketing might be used to resolve this issue. Careful analysis of all available data should indicate the approach to take. If true segments exist, and if the cost of preparing individualized programs can be justified, a segmented approach is desirable, since the appeal of the product and its promotion can be keyed more closely to specific consumer needs than they can in an undifferentiated marketing program.

The choice between a rollout program and one of national marketing rests on a number of other factors. If new distribution is necessary, national marketing cannot be achieved quickly, but market potential may dictate a national effort. If the total amount of business to be had is spread very thinly, it may not be worth trying to cultivate any particular market intensely. Another factor that may influence the decision to go national is the threat of potential competition. A market-by-market introduction may take as long as 18 months to complete—plenty of time for competitors to enter the picture. Finally, if a marketing program is to rely heavily on national advertising media, the waste involved in going through a series of local markets may be substantial.

● BRAND STRATEGIES

The primary focus of product strategy for some firms is to build brand equity (the set of assets or liabilities associated with a brand),[35] whereas others use branding strategies to strengthen product image. Bagozzi and colleagues suggest that firms that employ a brand strategy must decide on several factors, such as whether to use individual brands for each product or a family of brands. For example, Kellogg Co. promotes Kellogg's Rice Krispies or Kellogg's Frosted Flakes (a family brand strategy), whereas General Foods Corporation, with its Jell-O, Maxwell House Coffee, or Log Cabin syrup brands, promotes individual brand names.

Companies that use *multiple brand names* for related products decide to allow their products to succeed or fail on their own merit. Some advantages of using multiple brand names are (1) a firm can separate in customers' minds each product it markets, (2) product(s) can be targeted at specific market segments, and (3) the impact of one failed product is minimized. Also, managers must decide on what brand names to use in order to achieve forceful symbolic impacts on customers. Additionally, managers must decide where to market, that is, what market segments to pursue at what locations. And finally, managers must decide on the appropriate marketing-mix elements—price, distribution, and communications.[36]

Other factors that increase brand image are (1) product quality—products that perform beyond customer expectations (e.g., Lime Away and Kleenex); (2) consistent advertising—communications that effectively highlight a brand's competitive advantages, both often and well (e.g., Tide and Lexus); (3) distribution effectiveness—customers are exposed to the brand when shopping (e.g., Dentyne chewing gum); and (4) brand personality—the brand represents a specific image (e.g., Levi's).[37] For example, the brand strength of Coca-Cola is widely attributed to its universal awareness, availability, and trademark—all of which resulted from strategic decisions made previously by Coca-Cola's corporate managers.

The brand name is the most important aspect of brand-building, serving as a unique identifier. A **brand** can be a name, term, design, symbol, or other feature that identifies one firm's product or service as different from all other goods and services. The legal term for *brand* is **trademark**.[38] An effective brand name can evoke feelings of security, trust, and confidence, as well as other desirable characteristics.[39] Many firms use branding strategies to carry out market-development strategies such as line extensions that use a brand name to facilitate entry into new market segments (e.g., Ice Beer or Concentrated Tide). A similar strategy is *brand extension,* where a current brand is used to enter a completely different product class (e.g., Arm and Hammer Baking Soda Chewing Gum, a tooth cleaner sold only in the toothpaste aisle).

Brand Equity Explained

Many firms realized that brand names were valuable assets and that successful brand extensions could lead to additional loyalty and profits. However, ineffective brand extensions can damage brand association, since brand perceptions are transferred from one product to the other.[40] **Brand equity** is the set of assets (or liabilities) associated with a brand that add (or subtract) value.[41] The value of brand equity depends on the marketplace's relationship with the brand. Figure 8.4 lists the elements of brand equity that are determined by the consumers' assessment of the product, the company that manufactures and markets the product, and other factors that affect the product between manufacturing and consuming.

Aaker, a recognized authority on brand equity, notes that the assets and liabilities of brand equity differ from context to context. He suggests that they be grouped into the following four categories for active management: perceived quality, brand awareness, brand associations, and brand loyalty. *Perceived quality* affects return on investment directly because the cost of retaining customers is reduced, and perceived quality affects return on investment indirectly because it allows a higher price to be charged and enhances market share while not increasing costs.[42] Perceived quality also may drive stock return, a measure that reflects long-term performance.[43]

Brand awareness differentiates brands along a recall/familiarity dimension—people like the familiar. Second, brand awareness via name recognition may signal commitment and substance—both attributes valued by consumers. Third, the prominence of a brand will determine if it is recalled at key times in the purchasing process. An extreme example of this is brand dominance, where the brand is the only one recalled when the purchasing process is initiated. Brand awareness can be extremely durable and very difficult to dislodge. The name *Datsun* was as strong as *Nissan* 4 years after the name change occurred.[44]

Brand association is anything that is directly or indirectly linked in the consumers' memory to the brand. Product attributes and customer benefits are the associations with obvious value because they provide customers with reasons to buy and a basis for brand loyalty. However, strong brands go beyond product attributes

Brand
A name, term, design, symbol, or other feature that identifies and differentiates one firm's product or service from all others.

Trademark
The legal term for *brand*.

Brand equity
The set of assets (or liabilities) associated with a brand that add (or subtract) value.

FIGURE 8.4

Elements of Brand Equity

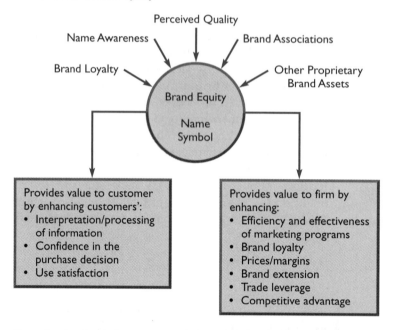

Source: Reprinted with the permission of The Free Press, a Division of Simon & Schuster Adult Publishing Group from *Managing Brand Equity: Capitalizing on the Value of a Brand Name* by David A. Aaker. Copyright © 1991 by David A. Aaker.

to differentiate on associations such as organizational associations, brand personality, symbols, emotional benefits, and self-expressed benefits. Determining the brand's identity or vision—the associations that the brand aspires to represent (as opposed to the image or existing associations)—is key to creating and managing this brand asset. Also, creating a brand identity or vision may provide a good framework for making business strategy decisions.[45]

Brand loyalty is customers' resistance to switching brands, and it significantly reduces the marketing costs of doing business. Loyalty can be based on habit, performance, or switching costs. It provides enormous competitive advantage as a market-entry barrier and provides trade leverage such as preferred shelf space. In the extreme, it may determine customers' store choices. A large base of satisfied customers provides a brand with an image of being successful, accepted, and enduring. And finally, brand loyalty provides a firm with the time needed to respond to competitive actions.

It is important to note that both consumer and industrial products possess brand equity. However, several differences exist between the two sectors.[46] Industrial products are often branded using the firm's name. Thus loyalty (or disloyalty) to the brand may extend across all the firm's product lines. Also, because firm rather than brand loyalty exists, positioning new products differently than existing products may be difficult or almost impossible. Finally, loyalty to industrial products includes the firm, its products, and the resellers who distribute the product. Therefore, attempts to change brand image must take into consideration distributor image.

Private Labels or Store Brands

Private labels are used by many retail firms to produce and market their products. For example, Sears, Roebuck and Co. has its own store-brand products, Kenmore for major appliances, designed to compete with national brands. Store-brand strategy is important for industries where the middleman has gained distribution control. The success of discount and specialty stores, such as Target Stores, Wal-Mart Stores, Inc., Old Navy, and others, has accelerated the use of private or store brands. If manufacturers refuse to supply resellers with private branded merchandise, these resellers simply may go into manufacturing themselves. House brands are packaged distinctively in upscale containers.

The quality of house-brand products equals or exceeds offerings by national brands, and the number of consumers who say this has increased steadily in the last decade.[47] Why? Because private-label brands are being marketed as value brands, as products equivalent to national brands but lower in price. For example, J.C. Penney Company, Inc. developed its private-brand jeans Arizona into annual sales surpassing $500 million. Private-brand sales of grocery products exceeded $30 billion and are continuing to grow.[48] As noted by Professor Gene German, retail executives from supermarkets, drug stores, and mass merchandise firms were asked to forecast the growth in sales of private-label products during 2001. Retail executives from mass merchandisers were the most optimistic with a forecast of 15.9 percent growth, followed by drug store executives who forecast 8.1 percent growth, and supermarket executives who projected a 6.7 percent growth of private label products in their stores.

What does this mean for marketing strategists? Certainly it is a signal to national manufacturers that competition from store brands will continue to increase. Retailers will focus more on their own brands and less on manufacturer brands, especially on nationally advertised brands that have weak marketing or small market shares. These weaker brands will be in jeopardy of being eliminated from retail stores. Retailers will use this space for the increasing number of store brands offered to consumers.[49]

Even though consolidation within the supermarket industry has occurred and "supercenters" have come about to heighten product marketing, these trends may strengthen private brands rather than weaken them.[50] However, national manufacturers' brands are fighting back with aggressive defense of their brands' market shares. The ultimate winner is likely to be the consumer. Shopping at mass merchandisers such as Target Stores or Wal-Mart Stores, Inc. enables consumers to choose from a wide array of both national and store brands, giving them the best of both value and variety.

Summary

We began this chapter with a definition of product and noted that products are classified in several ways. The major distinctions are between consumer and organizational goods and between products and services. Several unique characteristics of organizational products are their technical complexity, high cost, and longer life expectancy. The demand for organizational products is also derived, meaning it stems from the existence of a demand for something else. The marketing mix for organizational goods may be quite different from the consumer product marketing mix because of the unique characteristics of these products.

A number of important marketing management issues surface when developing product strategy. Critically important is development of the product line, which begins with identification of consumer needs. Other product-strategy issues include decisions on the width and depth of the line and the timing of changes. Product strategy also involves related issues of packaging, product safety (and the related issue of product liability), and post-sale services.

The position of a product in its life cycle is a prime determinant of product strategy. Some generalizations about appropriate strategies related to specific product life cycle stages can be shown through a product strategy matrix. Although the matrix can be a useful tool, it is not to be used as a roadmap for market mixing. Each marketing situation is unique and involves its own special strategies.

Two theories have attempted to explain the product life cycle: the consumer adoption process (involving the stages of awareness, interest, evaluation, trial, and adoption) and adoption theory (which classifies adopters of innovations as innovators, early adopters, early majority, late majority, and laggards).

Although test marketing was used in the past to screen out products that were likely to be unsuccessful, test marketing is used today to evaluate the workability of the marketing plan. Some objections to test marketing are that it is expensive, time-consuming, and may tip off competitors about the new product.

Launching new products can be a challenge with respect to timing of the product introduction, choice of target market segment, and whether to employ product rollout or introduce the product nationally or globally.

The final topic discussed in the chapter was brand strategy, with brand equity being a key aspect of developing sustainable competitive advantage. Private labels or store brands are also used by many retail firms to market their products.

Questions

1. Select a product that you would like to own, such as a personal computer or a sailboard. Draw up a list of your personal use specifications for this product. Write down explicitly what you expect the product to do. Match these use specifications with the characteristics of two or three alternative products that you find for sale. What conclusions do you draw from this comparison?

2. An automobile can be considered an augmented product. Why?

3. Name three products that you believe are in (a) the introductory stage, (b) the growth stage, (c) the maturity stage, and (d) the decline stage of the PLC. Explain the logic of your classifications.

4. Describe the adoption process and relate it to the product strategy that (a) an early entrant and (b) a late entrant in the microwave oven business might employ.

5. Why do some products diffuse more rapidly than others? For example, new clothing styles are adopted quickly by a large portion of the population, whereas products such as Teflon-coated kitchenware take many years to become widely accepted. Explain your thinking.

6. Describe thoroughly the various elements involved in brand equity. How important is brand equity in relation to product strategy?

Exercises

1. Many companies describe their product offerings in their annual reports. Obtain an annual report (or visit a Web site) of a consumer products company and review the company's product mix. In your analysis, apply the concepts of width and depth presented in this chapter.

2. Choose a well-known firm from an industry such as personal computers, bottled water, or beer. Next, analyze the current stage of the

industry's life cycle and the current stage in the life cycle of the company chosen. Then analyze how the firm's product-strategy component of its marketing strategy has changed over the last 10 years. If possible, also perform this exercise for the top two or three major competitors in the industry.

3. Choose a high-tech firm with local operations. Contact their CEO or CFO or COO and ask him or her to describe what changes have occurred in the products marketed by the company during the last 5 years (or while he or she has been in charge). After listening closely to the answer, ask about the driving force behind these changes—technological advances or customer needs.

Endnotes

1. Niccolo Machiavelli, *The Prince*, 1532, as quoted in *Bartlett's Book of Business Quotations*, compiled by Barbara Ann Kipher (Boston: Little, Brown and Company, 1994), p. 22.

2. Theodore Levitt, *Marketing for Business Growth* (New York, McGraw-Hill, 1975), p. 9.

3. This is the classification accepted by the Definitions Committee of the American Marketing Association. Its origin has been traced to M. T. Copeland, "Relation of Consumers' Buying Habits to Marketing Methods," *Harvard Business Review* (April 1923), p. 282. Modifications have been proposed over the years. For example, see Leo Aspinwall, *Four Theories of Marketing* (Boulder, CO: privately published, 1961). See also *Journal of Marketing*, July 1986, and elsewhere for more recent classification systems; and see also Philip Kotler, *Marketing Management*, 11th ed. (Englewood Cliffs, NJ: Prentice-Hall, 2003), pp. 410–412.

4. Zeynep Gurhan-Canli and Durairaj Mahaswaran, "The Effects of Extensions on Brand Name Dilution and Enhancement," *Journal of Marketing Research* (November 1998), pp. 464–473.

5. Robert A. Kerin, Michael G. Harvey, and Majes T. Rothe, "Cannibalism and New Product Development," *Business Horizons* (October 1975), p. 25.

6. See www.gillette.com/products.

7. Robert Cooper and Elko J. Kleinschmidt, "Winning Businesses in Product Development: The Critical Success Factors," *Research Technology Management* (July–August 1996), pp. 18–22.

8. Michael C. Neff and William L. Shanklin, "Creative Destruction as a Market Strategy," *Research Technology* (May–June 1997), pp. 33–40.

9. For a discussion of six critical elements in packaging, see Tom Cook, "Packaging Plan Affects How Well a Product Will Sell," *Marketing News* (May 23, 1986), p. 27.

10. Havis Dawson, "Right Package Deal," *Beverage World* (June 15, 1998), pp. 30–34.

11. Dean Harrison, "Private Label Evolution," *Frozen Food Age* (March 1998), pp. 4–6.

12. For a review of legal issues in marketing, see Dorothy Cohen, *Legal Issues in Marketing Decision Making* (Cincinnati: South-Western College Publishing, 1995).

13. Karl A. Boedecker, Fred W. Morgan, and Allen B. Saviers, "Continuing Duty to Warn: Public Policy and Managerial Views," *Journal of Public Policy & Marketing* (Spring 1998), pp. 127–131.

14. For selected reports on the Tylenol tamperings and other similar incidents, see Dennis Kneale, "Rivals Go after Tylenol's Market, but Gains May Be Only Temporary," *Wall Street Journal* (December 31, 1982), p. 31; Nancy Giges, "J&J Begins Its Drive to Keep Tylenol Alive," *Advertising Age* (October 11, 1982), p. 1; Judith Garner, "When a Brand Name Gets Hit by Bad News," *U.S. News and World Report* (November 8, 1982), p. 71; "2-Time Loser," *Advertising Age* (February 17, 1986), p. 1; and "O-T-C Capsule Terrorism Escalates," *Advertising Age* (March 24, 1986), p. 1. Or, for a recent article on pharmaceutical product developments (and packaging), see Tracy Harmon Blumenfeld and E. Michael D. Scott, "Rethinking the Product Development and Marketing Paradigm," *Pharmaceutical Executive* (May 1998), pp. 59–70.

15. Michael Brody, "When Products Turn into Liabilities," *Fortune* (March 3, 1986), p. 20.

16. Jeff O'Hair, "New 3Com Program: Revamped Resell Certification Plan to Focus on 'Total Solution' and Support," *Information Week* (January 26, 1998), pp. 125–126.

17. Theodore Levitt, "Exploit the Product Life Cycle," *Harvard Business Review* (November–December 1965), p. 81; Mark Duda and Jane S. Shaw, "Life Cycle Assessment," *Society* (November–December 1997), p. 51.

18. Some writers have been disturbed at the lack of sufficient empirical evidence to support the notion that products go through the classic life cycle

stages; the concerned reader is directed to: Laura M. Birou, Stanley E. Fawcett, and Gregory M. Magnan, "The Product Life Cycle: A Tool for Functional Strategic Alignment," *International Journal of Purchasing and Materials Management* (Spring 1998), pp. 37–51.

19. William N. Jensen, "'Life and Death' for Any Product," *Advertising Age* (October 27, 1986), p. 72.

20. Hans B. Torelli and Stephen C. Burnett, "The Nature of Product Life Cycles for Industrial Goods Businesses," *Journal of Marketing* (Fall 1981), p. 98.

21. D. W. Wyland, "Keep Your Product in Play: Introducing Full Life-Cycle Management," *Chain Store Age* (September 1998), p. 186.

22. Stephen G. Harrell and Elmer D. Taylor, "Modeling the Product Life Cycle for Consumer Durables," *Journal of Marketing* (Fall 1981), p. 68.

23. Besides the source indicated for Figure 8.2, one can find similar treatment in Kotler, *op. cit.*

24. For a particularly strong criticism of the use of the product life cycle strategy matrix, see Nariman K. Dhalla and Sonia Yuspech, "Forget the Product Life Cycle Concept," *Harvard Business Review* (January–February 1976), p. 105.

25. The most complete discussion of the adoption and diffusion processes is found in Everett M. Rogers, *Diffusion of Innovations* (New York: Free Press, 1962). Another study of adoption is found in James H. Donnelly, Jr., and M. T. Etzel, "Degrees of Product Newness and Early Trial," *Journal of Marketing Research* (August 1972), p. 295.

26. A growing chain of personal influence and communication might well explain the growth in the first stages of the product life cycle. If each person who hears about an innovation tells only two others about it each week, within 10 weeks more than 1000 people will have learned about it. Of course, like the broken chain letter, the process collapses when noncommunicators slip into the network.

27. Everett Rogers, *Diffusion of Innovations* (New York: Free Press, 1962), pp. 156ff.

28. *Test Marketing* (Toledo, Ohio: National Family Opinion Research, undated).

29. Anonymous, "Test Marketing," *Advertising Age* (February 13, 1986), p. 11; also Anonymous, "Test Marketing a New Product: When It's a Good Idea and How to Do It," *Profit-Building Strategies for Business Owners* (Scarsdale, NY: 1993), 23(3), p. 14.

30. Anonymous, "Why New Products Are By-Passing the Market Test," *Management Today* (October 1995), pp. 12–13.

31. *Ibid.*

32. Shi Zhang and Arthur B. Markman, "Overcoming the Early Entrant Advantage: The Role of Alignable and Nonalignable Differences," *Journal of Marketing Research* (November 1998), pp. 413–436.

33. David M. Szmanski, Lisa C. Troy, and Sundar G. Bharadwaj, "Order of Entry and Business Performance: An Empirical Synthesis and Re-Examination," *Journal of Marketing* (October 1995), pp. 17–27.

34. For other studies that suggest that the pioneering firm has a decided long-run market share advantage, see Roger A. Kerin, P. Rajan Varadarajan, and Robert A. Peterson, "First-Mover Advantage: A Synthesis, Conceptual Framework, and Research Propositions," *Journal of Marketing* (October 1992), pp. 33–52; and Peter N. Golder and Gerard J. Tellis, "Pioneering Advantage: Marketing Logic or Marketing Legend," *Journal of Marketing Research* (May 1993), pp. 158–170.

35. Mats Urde, "Brand Orientation: A Strategy for Survival," *Journal of Consumer Marketing* Vol. 11(3) (1994), pp. 18–32.

36. Richard P. Bagozzi, Jose Antonio Rosa, Kirti Sawheny Celly, and Francisco Coronel, *Marketing Management* (Englewood Cliffs, NJ: Prentice-Hall, 1998), p. 318.

37. James Lowry, "Survey Finds Most Powerful Brands," *Advertising Age* (July 11, 1988), p. 31.

38. Peter D. Bennett (ed.), *Dictionary of Marketing Terms,* 2d ed. (Chicago: American Marketing Association, 1995), p. 27.

39. Terrance Shimp, *Promotion Management and Marketing Communications,* 2d ed. (Hinsdale, IL: Dryden Press, 1990), p. 67.

40. David A. Aaker and Kevin Lane Keller, "Consumer Evaluation of Brand Extensions," *Journal of Marketing* (January 1990), pp. 27–41.

41. A detailed discussion of brand equity is given by David A. Aaker, *Managing Brand Equity* (New York: Free Press, 1991).

42. Robert Jacobson and David A. Aaker, "The Strategic Role of Product Quality," *Journal of Marketing* (October 1987), pp. 31–44.

43. David A. Aaker and Robert Jacobson, "The Financial Information Context of Perceived Quality," *Journal of Marketing Research* (May 1994), pp. 191–201.

44. Aaker, *op. cit.*, p. 57.

45. For a complete discussion of brand equity, the reader should examine David A. Aaker, *Strategic Market Management*, 5th ed. (New York: John Wiley & Sons, 1998), pp. 175–180.

46. A complete discussion of brand equity is available in Geoffrey L. Gordon, Roger J. Calantone, and C. A. di Benedetto, "Brand Equity in the Business-to-Business Sector: An Exploratory Study," *Journal of Product & Brand Management* Vol. 2(3) (1993), pp. 4–16.

47. Joe Berry, "National Brands on the Rebound but the War Is Far from Over," *Brandweek* (February 27, 1995), pp. 17–18.

48. A discussion of private label brands can be found in Hillary Miller, "Store Brands Are Looking Good," *Bev-erage Industry* (April 1995), pp. 60–61; or in Marcia Mogelonsky, "When Stores Become Brands," *American Demographics* (February 1995), pp. 32–36.

49. Gene German, "Are Consumers Buying More Private Label (or Store Brand) Products?," *Ag Dm Newsletter,* June 2002; see www.exnet.iastate.edu/agdm/articles/other/Gerjune02.html; also **Smart Marketing** (June 2001), monthly newsletter, Cornell University.

50. Jeffery D. Zbar, "Industry Trends Hold Private Label Promise," *Advertising Age* (April 3, 1995), p. 31.

MARKETING MANAGEMENT IN ACTION: CLOSING CASE

If Simmons Is a Power Brand, Does That Help Sales Volume?

"Most people have a very myopic notion of what branding is," says Dr. David A. Shore, associate dean at Harvard Business School. Scoffing at the common perception that branding is all about awareness, Shore says awareness is almost irrelevant. What matters, he says, is "strategic awareness." Shore notes that, "When I ask people if they ever heard of Simmons mattresses, they say yes. When I ask them about other brands, they say Sealy and Serta or Stearns & Foster. But when it comes to buying a mattress, people are more influenced by the salesperson than by the power of the brand." According to Dr. Shore, this is because people can't see any distinction between those brands, and thus there is high brand awareness but low strategic awareness. People don't seem to know what brand their mattress is and have no idea of what brand they would buy to replace their current mattress.

Dr. Shore suggests that most manufacturers have a brand, but the question is how much brand equity has the manufacturer built in the marketplace. Most companies test for brand awareness, but that doesn't necessarily relate to sales volumes; as Shore points out, in Denmark McDonald's has a higher brand awareness than Burger King, but young adults show a strong preference for Burger King. Shore says that in some industries one brand may score the highest awareness and another brand may enjoy an even higher preference, but a third brand can achieve the highest sales. Thus, Shore reasons, a company should measure its brand equity against competitive brands every 6 months, asking the key questions: Do your customers ask for your brand by name? Do customers see a difference between your brand and a competitive brand? Is the customer willing to purchase your brand?

Shore suggests sales managers should think not about awareness but about quality, because "It's all about perceived quality." Manufacturers invest millions of dollars in developing products to the highest levels of quality, but many customers are unable to assess quality. They substitute consistency, dependability, and trust as indicative of quality. A second substitute is longevity and a third is singular distinction, says Shore, emphasizing singular. By trying to be all things to all people, you end up being nothing to anyone. When companies emphasize too many benefits, then none of them stands out. Shore's example of stressing the singular distinction is Volvo. He says they have built a very safe car and everything they do reinforces that image. They have an integrated identity campaign and they coordinate communications to reinforce the same theme in the marketplace. "If you do this," says Shore, "the marketplace will begin to believe that theme." He cites brands that command a premium price because of their perceived quality, such as Zantac. The magazine *Selling Power* checked the price of 60 Zantac 150 mg, listed at www.drugstore.com for $101.37, while the generic equivalent, Ranitidine 150 mg, sells for only $10.98, which seems to support Shore.

But what is the essence of a brand? "Brands represent what people (customers) think about the product and the feelings they experience when they think about the product," says Shore. Suggesting that the sale is made in the customer's mind and heart, Shore notes, "I would argue that typically it's not the product or service. It's something that surrounds it. For example, Nike doesn't sell sneakers, it sells heroism." Therefore, we need to decide what we want customers to think about. At the fundamental level, a brand to Shore "is more than name recognition and a promise to the customer. A good brand makes people willing to pay more, travel further, and wait longer. [But] taking charge of a brand image is often more challenging than herding cats."

Shore cautions that many companies delegate branding to their advertising agencies. Although ads may be a tactical component of branding, Shore explains, "I see branding as a larger umbrella under which communications, marketing, advertising, and sales fall." Suggesting that branding begins with a positioning statement, Shore notes it should say "here is what we want to own in the minds of the marketplace."

But to Shore, "The sales force is the most visible manifestation of the brand. Salespeople need to say with a singular voice, 'This is who we are and, by extension, this is who we are not.' The critical element that power brands have is trust, and a sales force needs to become the trusted advisor to the customer." To emphasize his point about trust, Shore says, "This is an extraordinary responsibility.

The sales force has the moral equivalent of a guidance counselor who clearly understands what the brand is and knows not to extend it too far and not to over promise."

Shore offers a formula for integrating brand power with sales power by using the acronym ASK. "The first letter, 'A,' is for affective feelings, for example, when people shop on Fifth Avenue in New York, or on Rodeo Drive in Beverly Hills, what counts is the emotional experience involved in the purchase, not the price of the product." The second letter, "S," is for skills: "the ability to deliver on the promise, the ability to skillfully assess and serve the needs of the customer." The third letter, "K," is for knowledge. Shore explains, "The more knowledgeable someone is about you, the more brand savvy, the more customers will look at you. The problem is that at first glance all brands look very similar. That's why you need strategic awareness—so you can get a share of the market."

Source: Gerhard Gschwandtner, "How Power Brands Sell More," *Selling Power* (April 2001), pp. 68–73.

Case Study Questions

1. What is the definition of a "Power Brand"?

2. Do you agree that "brand awareness" is not sufficient measurement for market success? Why? Or, why not?

3. How does Dr. Shore describe the relationship between a "Power Sales Force" and a "Power Brand"? Do you agree with this description?

4. Is Simmons a power brand?

5. Name some brands you believe are worthy of the "Power Brand" label.

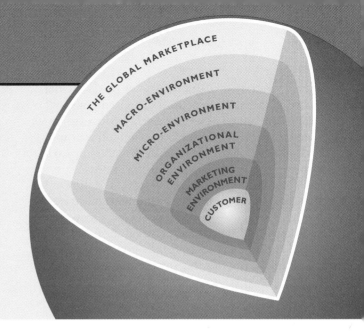

CHAPTER 9

Services Marketing Strategy

Delivering great service, one customer at a time, day after day, month after month, is difficult. Nothing . . . suggests that the excellent service journey is easy. It is not. But it is immensely rewarding, not just financially, but spiritually. Excellence nourishes the soul.[1]

Banks Rediscover Retail Customers and Focus on Service

During the stock market boom of the 1990s, banks shifted their focus away from services for retail banking customers to concentrate on more lucrative commercial lending, investment banking, and stock brokerage services. During this period, many banks closed branches, increased fees on retail accounts, and placed less emphasis on retail banking services. This strategy was profitable as long as the economy and the stock market performed at record-high levels. However, as Wall Street began to show signs of a bear market in 2001 and 2002, and low interest rates reduced income from lending, bankers recognized the need to improve customer satisfaction and improve profitability. In this environment, banking services have been refocused on retail consumers.

Bank of America Changes Service Strategy

Bank of America, for example, launched a $70 million consumer-focused advertising campaign to "drive deposit growth and deepen customer relationships." The underlying marketing objective was to attract more retail customers. Within a 12-month period, the bank eliminated all fees for Internet banking, began opening branches on Saturday mornings, provided a money wire service for Mexican immigrants, and introduced a new service to protect credit-card holders from fraud and theft. Initiatives such as these resulted in 490,000 new checking accounts (compared with 193,000 for all of 2001), 28 million household customers, and 4,226 branches in 21 states. In 2003, Bank of America expects to break its own record by attracting 1 million accounts, mostly by building new branches and improving customer service. In an effort to improve service quality, the Gallup Corporation polled the bank's customers on their satisfaction with customer service. Branch bank employees were rewarded for improved performance. Analysts credit Kenneth Lewis, Bank of America's chief executive as of April 2001, with this turnaround. As one analyst said, "When it comes to customer service, Bank of America has really turned the corner . . . Three or four years ago, this was not known as a customer-friendly bank."

In the service industry it is often difficult to maintain a differentiation strategy because competitors can quickly copy new ideas. The banking industry is no exception. In the Carolinas, for example, after Bank of America announced Saturday banking hours in July 2002, nearly every other bank in the state (e.g., Wachovia, First Citizens, BB&T) followed suit. The same situation occurred when Bank of America did away with its monthly fee for online bill payment.

Growth Strategies in the Retail Banking Industry

Banks can pursue a number of strategies to attract more customers and to improve customer service.

Build more branch banks and/or increase the hours of operation. As banks attract new customers and retain their existing customers, they are increasingly successful at selling them more credit cards, mortgages, and other products. One proven way to gain more banking customers is to increase the number of branch banks and other opportunities for banking services. For example, Bank of America announced plans in October 2002 to open 550 additional branches nationwide over 3 years. An increasing number of bank branches (e.g., JP Morgan Chase, Commerce Bank, U.S. Bank) have extended their hours of operation to Sunday. More branches are located in supermarkets, malls, and retail stores in order to reach customers in the evening and on weekends when banks are typically closed, and growth is particularly strong in supermarket branches.

Add new and/or improved services. New services designed by the Bank of America to at-

tract new customers and retain present customers include the introduction of services such as Total Security Protection, which provides free protection against credit-card theft, loss, and fraud (October 2002), and Saturday banking hours in the Carolinas, with other banks to follow (July 2002).

Several banks have added greeters or concierges in an effort to be more user-friendly. For instance, J.P. Morgan Chase in New York has uniformed greeters who meet customers and escort them to their desired area. In Atlanta, Bank of America introduced "mobile tellers" who select customers out of long queues and process their transaction then and there.

Seattle, Washington-based Washington Mutual Inc. (WaMu) designed new branches and retrofitted old ones to resemble a Gap retail store. Each "store" branch has a concierge, and customers receive timely help from tellers and managers who stroll about in khakis and casual shirts to help customers. WaMu takes its "store" concept further than most of its competitors. Bank customers can purchase an array of products, such as calculators, piggy banks, books about financial topics, dolls, Slinkys, and even a WaMu-branded action figure with mix-and-match outfits. Some WaMu branches have a play area with television, electronic games, and toys to entertain children while parents conduct their banking business.

Change the fee structure. Bank of America provided free Internet banking for its customers by removing its $5.95 monthly fee for online bill payment. An announcement in May 2002 that the bank would provide free online bill payment for new customers, resulted in an increase from 1 million to a record 1.5 million active, online bill payers in the first 6 months of the promotion. During the same 6-month period, the overall number of Online Banking subscribers increased from 3.1 million to 4.35 million. The company also extended payment schedules for customers who were behind on their loans. According to a spokesman, "We want to be the bank that helps our customers even during tough times . . . So that when they are back on their feet, we have loyal customers."

Some banks help customers avoid high service fees by informing them about available alternatives. Bank One's Louisiana operation reduced the number of account closings with a campaign targeted toward its 10,000 customers in the state who already maintained the higher minimum balance for a low-fee checking account. Customers were called and offered a free upgrade with lower fees, resulting in fewer account closings.

Concentrate on lucrative and/or underserved market segments. In April 2002, Bank of America introduced its SafeSend service targeted toward its Hispanic customers, to allow them to wire money to Mexico by telephone or the Internet. The bank also began accepting the Mexican consular ID card from those immigrants without traditional identification.

Annette Kellermann, Accessible Banking Program Manager for Bank of America, stated, "Bank of America is committed to making banking accessible to all of its customers." In keeping with this commitment, the bank installed over 300 bilingual Talking ATMs in Florida in 2002, with plans to increase its total number of Talking ATMs to over 7,000 coast-to-coast by the end of 2005. Talking ATMs are easy to use for routine transactions. They use private, spoken instructions through a headset, and deliver every function available at non-talking ATMs. Bank of America and Wachovia Corp. also implemented programs to provide customers who are blind or visually impaired with alternative formats of written bank customer communications. Documents may be requested in Braille, large print, or audio formats at no charge.

Other potentially lucrative markets include people at both ends of the economic scale. For example, St. Paul, Minnesota-based Bremer Bank has offices in Minneapolis where it offers wealth advisory services to retain its 18,000 affluent customers and to increase the bank's trust, investment, and insurance businesses. The privately held company pursues this strategy to remain competitive in the face of bank consolidation and mergers. At the other end of the economic spectrum are those customers who never manage to pay off their debts and who frequently bounce checks. According to the executive director of the National Association of Consumer Advocates in Washington, D.C., these customers are among the most profitable bank customers. They tend to be attracted by checking accounts with low minimum balances, but may pay a penalty as high as $30 for a bounced check.

In summary, the banking industry pursues a variety of strategies to achieve growth and customer satisfaction in this highly competitive environment. However, the services offered must be relevant to the needs of consumers. Service quality must go beyond cheerful greetings and a proliferation of branches; and a strategy based on meaningful differentiation is essential to achieve a sustainable competitive advantage.

Source: Chris Serres, "Bank of America Tries to Beef Up Customer Service," *Knight Ridder Tribune Business News,* Washington (October 26, 2002), p. 1; Dee DePass, "Bremer to Open Minneapolis Office to Focus on Its Wealthier Customers," *Star Tribune,* Minneapolis, MN (October 30, 2002), p. 3D; "First Six Months of Free Online Bill Payment at Bank of America Achieves Rapid Growth to 1.5 Million Bill Payers," *PR Newswire,* New York (October 30, 2002), p. 1; Michelle Higgins, "Banks Rediscover Service," *Wall Street Journal* (May 29, 2002), pp. D1, D2; Calmetta Coleman, "Banks Cozy Up to Customers," *Wall Street Journal* (April 26, 2001), pp. B1, B4; "Bank of America Installs More than 300 Bilingual Advanced Technology ATMs in Florida," *PR Newswire,* New York (October 29, 2002), p. 1; Vickie Beck, "Wachovia Makes Plans to Aid Blind," *Tampa Tribune,* Tampa, FL (October 30, 2002), p. 5.

First impressions are crucial for all types of marketing efforts, but services marketers are most vulnerable to customer perceptions that lead to satisfaction or dissatisfaction. A negative first impression may lead to a one-time transaction or none at all, whereas a positive impression generally leads to repeat business.

Although tangible goods and intangible services are both referred to as *products,* in this chapter we emphasize the marketing of services that comprise an organization's core business. However, considerable attention also is given to those additional services which have become increasingly important to the sale of all types of products in both business-to-business and consumer markets at all levels of distribution.

● SERVICES: A MAJOR FORCE IN THE U.S. ECONOMY

The service sector of the U.S. economy contributed an estimated 22.6 percent of the Gross Domestic Product in 2001.[2] (Expenditures for selected service industries are shown in Table 9.1.) Services experienced significant increases in number of establishments, revenues, number of paid employees, and annual payroll over the past decade. (See comparative figures for 1992 and 1997 in Table 9.2.) The number of civilians employed in service occupations increased 31.9 percent from 13,857,000 in 1983 to 18,278,000 employed in 2000. The greatest growth in service employment during this period was among Hispanic workers.[3] The U.S. Department of Labor estimates that employment in major service occupations will reach 31,163,000 jobs by 2010, an increase of 19.5 percent over 2000.[4]

An increasing number of services have evolved in response to a focus on productivity and profits by organizations and the poverty of time experienced by active, overly busy consumers. For example, many of the activities that consumers once performed for themselves are now included with the sale of goods and services or sold separately as a convenience to the customer. This includes services such as personal shopping, delicatessen meals, take-out food, pickup and return of cars for repair, lawn services, house cleaning, and grocery deliveries. Both marketers and customers are trying to find ways to make buying easier (while holding prices down at the same time!).

TABLE 9.1

Gross Domestic Product: Expenditures for Selected Service Industries, 1990–1999 (billions of real 1996 dollars)

Service Industry	1990	1995	1998	1999	Percent Change 1998–1999
Business services	241.3	313.9	417.4	463.5	11.04%
Health services	423.2	444.3	462.0	463.5	0.32%
Other services	191.3	199.9	233.9	241.9	3.42%
Legal services	108.8	105.1	107.0	111.9	4.58%
Auto repair, services, and garages	61.9	65.9	74.8	78.3	4.68%
Amusement and recreation services	45.0	55.6	67.4	70.7	4.90%
Hotels and other lodging places	55.2	62.7	65.5	67.3	2.75%
Educational services	50.3	58.5	61.2	61.2	0.00%
Personal services	46.4	48.1	52.2	53.1	1.72%
Social services & membership organizations	38.0	49.3	52.0	53.0	1.92%
Motion pictures	21.2	23.6	27.8	27.2	−2.16%
Total—all services listed	1,361.9	1,510.4	1,704.4	1,772.6	4.00%

Source: U.S. Census Bureau, *Statistical Abstract of the United States: 2001*, Table No. 641, p. 418.

TABLE 9.2

U.S. Service Industry: Comparative Statistics 1992 and 1997*

	1992	1997	Increase	Percent Change
Number of Establishments	1,825,435.0	2,077,666.0	252,231.0	13.82%
Sales/receipts/revenues/shipments (bil $)	1,202.6	1,843.8	641.2	53.32%
Annual payroll (bil $)	452.7	688.9	236.2	52.18%
Paid employees (1,000)	19,290.4	25,278.4	5,988.0	31.04%

*Taxable firms only; data based on 1987 SIC code.
Source: "Business Enterprise, Table No. 722. Comparative Statistics for the United States (1987 SIC Basis): 1992 and 1997," U.S. Census Bureau, *Statistical Abstract of the United States: 2001*, p. 483.

MANAGING CHANGE

High-Quality Service at Everyday Low Prices

Today, not only the higher-priced marketers are expected to provide outstanding service; the cost-cutting manufacturers and distributors also must please customers with excellent service (and low prices). Staples, a fast-growing office supply superstore, has competed successfully with Office Depot and Office Max by pleasing customers with services that set Staples apart from the competition.

A small business owner walked into a Staples store to buy map pins, expecting the typical discount store lack of service. The store did not have the unusual variety of map pins that he needed— but he was surprised at the store's extra efforts to satisfy his needs. The sales associate immediately contacted the manufacturer of a similar pin and faxed information on the pins to the customer's office—all for an order of no more than $20. Several months later when the customer returned to the store, the sales associate impressed him by remembering his name. The business owner is now a regular Staples shopper and spends a couple of thousand dollars a year at the store.

How does Staples do this? The company focuses on developing a service culture that sets it apart from other office supply retailers. Its sales associ-

ates use a massive database (including data from a membership card) to know their customers well, and this is but a part of an enterprise-wide integrated information technology (IT) system designed to give Staples customers a consistent and seamless experience. As Paul Gaffney, CIO at Staples, said, "When you do the right thing for your best customers, good things happen." Customer service drives an overarching IT strategy to help achieve the company's mission. Staples' online kiosk, Access Point, is an example of the enterprise focus on the customer. Access Point kiosks, installed in all of Staples' 1,040 stores, were created by connecting the company's e-commerce website (Staples.com), with its point-of-sale (POS) system, order management system, distribution system, and supply chain. People throughout the company, from areas such as retail, catalog, online, finance, distribution, merchandising, and training, and others, collaborated to design the system.

According to Gaffney, "We're letting customers do business the way they want to do business, not the way we want them to." The Access Point system allows customers to buy an item such as office furniture at the kiosk, pay with a credit card, and take a bar-code

(continued)

printed receipt to the cashier to pay in real-time. Kiosks also provide customers with a library of information about products and services, access to an inventory of 45,000 online products, and the ability to build PCs to order (allowing over 35 percent of the stores to sell computers without carrying them in the store). While the multimillion-dollar Access Point system was developed to improve customer service, Staples also benefited by introducing many customers to Staples.com. According to company estimates, a customer who shops in both stores and one other channel (Staples.com or catalog) has a "lifetime value" of two and a half times that of a store-only shopper.

System integration also includes consolidation of the Staples and Quill fulfillment center facilities. (Quill is a mail-order office products company that was acquired by Staples in 1998.) Gaffney's strategy involves standardization, and reducing the number of direct linkages between systems and the number of different technologies required to keep the staff proficient in order to increase productivity.

Other service-oriented initiatives by Staples include the addition of a fleet of mobile technicians who perform computer installations, instruction, and repairs. The company also provides banking opportunities within selected stores, such as its alliance with FleetBoston Financial Corp. Small business banking services are available in "Fleet Small Business Zones" in Staples stores in the northeastern United States, and Internet banking services are available in some Canadian stores through a kiosk program with Canadian Imperial Bank of Commerce.

With technology as an integrated support system, the company creates customer-friendly stores, encourages managers to spend time with customers, gives incentives to employees for outstanding service, and treats its people as it would like them to treat Staples' customers.

Source: Rahul Jacob, "How One Red Hot Retailer Wins Customer Loyalty," *Fortune* (July 10, 1995), pp. 72–79; Todd Datz, "Strategic Alignment; Your Business Processes Can't Enable Superior Customer Service or An Efficient Supply Chain Without Integrated Systems," *CIO,* Framingham 15 (21) (August 15, 2002), pp. 1–64+; Mairi MacLean, "Retail Sales: It's All in the Details: Staples Perfecting Science of Tracking Customers' Habits," *Edmonton Journal,* Edmonton, Alta. (March 8, 2002), p. F1; Chris Reidy, "Staples Enters Into Alliance with FleetBoston Financial for Banking Services," *Knight Ridder Tribune Business News,* Washington (July 11, 2002), p. 1.

Growth in the service industry has taken many forms, affecting all categories of goods and services and all stages of the purchasing process. Service marketers have added or increased customer services such as shopping convenience through location or distribution strategies (e.g., Internet, ATMs, branch banks, branch warehouses, just-in-time delivery), longer business hours, one-stop shopping, better trained sales and service personnel, more liberal warranties or adjustment policies, improved customer service response systems (personal, telephone, on-line), and availability of information before, during, and after a sale.

Current trends are expected to continue and to escalate in the direction of more services at higher quality, performed to build long-term relationships with satisfied—perhaps even pampered—customers. Value beyond price and quality will continue to be defined and redefined in the minds of buyers and will drive the types of services that are offered. Major service trends that are expected to escalate include increases in Internet shopping and banking; automation and integration of service processes; and computer-related services. Converging technologies in entertainment, information, and communication will fuel growth in many industries. A growth trend also will continue for the outsourcing of home and office services, and for private and public security services, among others.

● CHARACTERISTICS OF SERVICES VERSUS GOODS

The unique characteristics of services, in contrast to physical products, present special challenges to marketing managers. Services are intangible, variable (or inconsistent), inseparable, and perishable.[5] Each trait affects the design and delivery of successful customer service programs, as shown in Figure 9.1.

Services Are Intangible

Intangibility
Services cannot be seen, felt, tasted, heard, or smelled by customers before purchase, making them more difficult to evaluate than tangible goods.

Since services have **intangibility,** meaning they cannot be seen, felt, tasted, heard, or smelled before purchase, customers find them more difficult to evaluate than goods. For example, a customer cannot see, feel, or otherwise sense the extraction of a wisdom tooth by an oral surgeon before the procedure is completed, nor the value of dental insurance or regular dental checkups until they can be experienced. Similar experiences from the past, word-of-mouth from others, and an individual's imagination are major sources of prepurchase evaluation. The oral surgeon's facilities, employees, communications, equipment used to perform the service, symbols and logos, and even price can be used to give the service tangibility. For example, neatly dressed, professional personnel, a clean and comfortable waiting room and surgery

FIGURE 9.1

Unique Service Characteristics: Marketing-Mix Implications

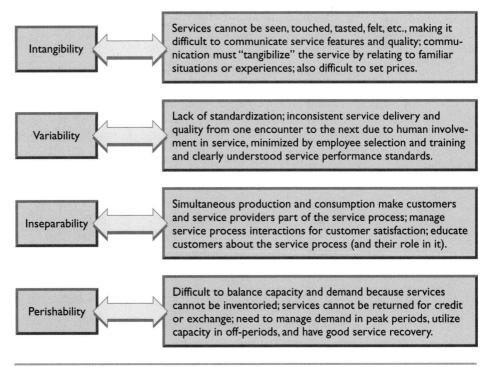

area, accurately written instructions, and even the "age" of the magazines in the waiting room can provide physical evidence of service quality for this dental service.

Services Are Variable

Services are performed—or supported in some way—by human beings, making it nearly impossible for them to be delivered consistently from one customer and/or employee to the next. **Variability,** or inconsistencies, can be overcome by using quality control measures, increasing customer satisfaction by having effective service systems in place, monitoring customer satisfaction regularly, and managing the behavior of customers and employees in each service encounter.

One area where service quality varies is in handling customer complaints. At different times in the same business environment different employees may handle the same type of complaint differently with different customers. In one situation, the complaint-handling process may flow quickly and efficiently, increasing the customer's satisfaction and likelihood of making additional purchases. In another situation, the same customer may be treated rudely or even accused of trying to take advantage of the company's service policies—effectively showing that customer that he or she is not important.

Variability
Services are affected in some way by human beings, and therefore it is nearly impossible to achieve consistent service delivery from one customer and/or employee to the next.

Service and Delivery Are Inseparable

Customers are involved at some level in the service delivery process, giving the services the quality of **inseparability.** Because services are consumed as they are performed, it is difficult to separate the service provider from the service itself, making people a part of the product. For example, a telephone company's truck or a company's physical facilities are seen as part of the service received by a customer; that is, they are inseparable. The service personnel become the business in the customer's eyes; therefore, poor service creates the image of an undesirable store or other business, as described in the following scenario, illustrating a service that accompanies the purchase of tangible goods.

Mary Smith is returning a wedding gift to the housewares department of a well-known department store, expecting to make another selection. The salesperson that she approaches does not want to deal with a return, so she rudely sends Mary to customer service in another part of the store—meanwhile approaching another customer who looks like a better prospect for a sale. When Mary arrives at customer service, two employees seem inconvenienced by Mary's request as they discuss their lunch plans. Neither they nor the salesperson asks Mary if she would like to make another selection. The irony is that the store's liberal return policy is tainted by the "don't care" attitude of employees who actually perform the service, and the retailer misses an opportunity to make an additional sale and build a long-term relationship with the new bride for future purchases.

Inseparability
Services are consumed as they are performed, and customers are involved at some level in the service process, making the customer, the service provider, and the service itself inseparable.

Services Are Perishable

Services cannot be inventoried, except for the equipment and supplies necessary for their performance. They are time-dependent; if they are not used one day, they cannot be inventoried for the next. Service marketing managers must balance consumer

Perishability
Services cannot be inventoried, except for the equipment and supplies needed for their performance; they are time-dependent.

demand for services with the availability of service employees and facilities. When demand is steady, **perishability** is not a problem because employee schedules can be adjusted to meet forecasted needs. However, service marketers do experience fluctuation in demand, making it difficult to schedule the necessary resources. For this reason, many service providers find it more profitable to maximize use of part-time employees and contract out some services, such as accounting or promotion.

● LEVELS OF SERVICE

There are two basic levels of service: primary services and ancillary services. Managers must decide on whether and how the responsibility for service performance will be shared by the company and its customers. Often, pricing strategies are tied to the degree of full service or self-service performed across both primary and ancillary customer service offerings.

Primary Services

Core services
Major activity of a business or organization.

Primary services
Considered essential to completion of a transaction and necessary to make and keep a sale.

Core services refer to the major activity of a business (or nonprofit organization). **Primary services** are considered to be essential services that are the basis of a transaction and necessary to make and keep a sale.

Let us take two examples of relatively complex products. For customers purchasing intangible investment services, the use of a brokerage account to buy and sell stocks is a primary service. For those purchasing a complex tangible good, such as a computer for the first time, important primary services may include knowledgeable sales assistance, the availability of credit and extended warranties, and the ability to return defective merchandise. Similarly, The Pep Boys—Manny, Moe, & Jack, an automotive store, sells auto parts to mechanics and do-it-yourselfers. They sell tangible brand-name and private-label automotive parts, and also offer on-site service facilities as a primary service.

Ancillary Services

Ancillary services
Offered as an expected or optional supplement that adds perceived value to the primary purchase but may not be required as a necessary or usual part of the sale.

Ancillary services are offered as expected or optional supplements to the primary purchase. The customer generally expects them, although they are not required as a necessary or usual part of a sale. However, ancillary services do add perceived value for the customer and contribute to the marketer's image and competitive position.

Many services previously considered "extra" are now demanded by consumers as "essential" to a sale, increasing the number of extras required to differentiate one firm's offering from that of competitors. Examples of expected consumer services include carryout at most supermarkets, convenient free parking, credit, and alteration or assembly services provided by a retailer. Business-to-business customers expect prompt delivery, favorable credit terms, and responsive customer service, perhaps through a 24-hour 800 number "hotline."

Optional services are another form of ancillary service that customers may or may not pay for. For example, many retail consumers welcome a personal shopping service that is performed on a formal or informal basis. Personal notification of the arrival of special merchandise, gift registries, or a travel agency may be attractive to an important customer segment. Customer experiences in department stores, specialty shops, and shopping malls have raised awareness and perceptions of service across all types of retailers. Baby-sitting services have become popular among shoppers. Resorts, hotels, and shopping malls have expanded their services to include something for the entire family, in response to the active, time-poor lifestyles of their customers who want to maximize opportunities for family fun.

The cosmetics industry has long provided a high level of personal sales assistance (beauty consultants, cosmetologists) in department stores. However, a large percentage of cosmetic products are sold through drugstore chains and mass merchandisers, generally known for their self-service formats and lack of personal service. To differentiate in this highly competitive beauty market where the same products are sold in thousands of outlets, drugstore chains and mass merchants have recognized the need for a higher level of customer assistance. Some drugstores believe that a cosmetician may be just as influential in attracting and retaining customers as a pharmacist. Increased attention to retail services in this market has led to more training and better compensation and rewards for service personnel. It also has resulted in the use of point-of-sale data for employee scheduling at peak service times, better point-of-sale displays for customer assistance, and more emphasis on the services of beauty consultants and cosmeticians in drugstores and mass discount chains.[6]

Organizational customers are expecting and demanding an increasing number of optional services with primary product purchases. These may include on-site training or assistance with inventory management, marketing, and technical expertise. A number of business marketers have developed consulting services to satisfy many of these customer needs. In many cases, these ancillary services evolve into a new core business. For example, large accounting firms have added investment advising to their traditional accounting and financial services, with the permission of the Securities and Exchange Commission (SEC). For some accounting firms, investment advising has become a separate business-often a subsidiary such as Arthur Andersen's Accenture that enables the firm to provide "one-stop" service to its accounting clients. Recent questionable corporate accounting practices highlight the shared responsibility for ethical behavior between advisors and clients.

● SERVICE AS VALUE

What differentiates a desirable purchasing experience from an undesirable experience? Today's consumers and organizational buyers not only want the opportunity to buy quality products at the right price, but they also expect to buy from qualified personnel with maximum benefits and minimum effort. They demand *value*—an intangible concept that is frequently defined in terms of exceptional customer service that accompanies exceptional product quality and value-based prices.

At the consumer level, many competing marketers offer similar brands and merchandise selections to the same group of customers, giving them many shopping alternatives. Successful retailers, such as Nordstrom, Inc., differentiate themselves by competing on the basis of superior customer service to build long-term customer relationships. This is often the only dimension that distinguishes one marketer's offerings from those of a competitor.

The Importance of Strategic Planning

The strategic planning process followed by marketers of services and goods is similar. It starts with the business philosophy or mission, which provides the basis for the company's objectives and other elements of the strategic plan. For example, a luxury cruise line might follow this strategic planning process:

Strategic Planning Process	Strategic Marketing Example
1. Corporate mission statement	Cruise line; luxury travel to exotic locations
2. Performance objectives	$50 million in sales; 10% return-on-investment
3. Situational analysis	Increase in older, affluent population; globalization of business; availability of cruise ships, hospitality crew, port access; presently operating under capacity
4. Strategic objectives and strategy definition	Increase number of first-time passengers and build loyalty for repeat business; offer cruise plus land travel packages
5. Implementation and tactics	Budget and prepare promotion to travel agents; direct mail to professional group membership lists
6. Execution	Launch advertising campaign in select media; mail promotional literature to carefully screened mailing list; sell cruises to ship capacity
7. Evaluation and control	Assess increase in number of passengers, customer satisfaction and intent to repeat purchase, achievement of sales and return on investment targets

In developing its marketing strategy, a service organization must have a clear understanding of how it is (or should be) positioned relative to the competition and what competitive moves are taking place. The company also must decide whether it wants to be a service leader or follow the leader.

Service image
Competitive positioning conveyed by everything that represents the company and its service products; dimensions used in positioning should be valued by customers.

Competitive Positioning. Since marketers do not operate in a vacuum, they must monitor their competitors constantly. Essentially, services should be positioned competitively in every aspect of the service product itself and in all methods the company uses to communicate the service's features and benefits to its target market. In other words, the **service image** (position) can be managed effectively by careful attention to the actual service design and performance and to everything that represents the service to customers (written and verbal communications, physical evidence, etc.). The customer should believe that the service he or she is receiving is superior on relevant dimensions to that provided by the competition.

Service Leadership versus Follow-the-Leader.   Marketers of services also must decide whether to position their company and service products as leaders in the industry or to wait for competitors to set the standards and follow their lead. Market-entry strategies are beyond the scope of this chapter, but the companies that are first to market are not always those which emerge as service leaders. For example, CompuServe was first to market with Internet on-line services but eventually was eclipsed by America Online and other service providers who set the parameters for quality service. There are many other well-known and not so well-known examples that demonstrate this type of service leadership. Among them are Southwest Airlines, a service leader among both discount- and regular-fare airlines, Nordstrom department stores, and smaller computer companies that have out-serviced industry giant IBM.

Benefits of Exceptional Customer Service

Marketers of both goods and services have learned that one of the most effective ways to differentiate themselves from competitors is through exceptional customer service offered with each purchase. The "extras" provided by customer service add to the cost of doing business, but customer-oriented businesses have found that the benefits of offering a range of services desired by customers generally far outweigh the costs for the following reasons:

1. Services attract and keep customers.
2. Service is instrumental in recovering lost or about-to-be-lost sales.
3. There is a strong relationship between levels of service quality and levels of customer satisfaction.
4. Customer service activities generally lead to a profitable return on investment over the long term.
5. Services play a major role in the marketing mix.

Attracting and Keeping Customers.   Services such as availability of credit, convenient locations and hours, knowledgeable salespeople, no-hassle return privileges, responsive service personnel, and free delivery add value to purchases. The service relationship between buyers and sellers is ongoing, as illustrated in the following retail examples for an automotive repair business and an apparel retailer.

Before the sale, media advertisements, signage, and sales assistance provide both types of customers with the necessary purchase information. During the sales process, the apparel customer may be given assistance in selecting and trying on appropriate garments and having them fitted for alterations. The auto repair customer may be shown a diagram that explains the problem area in the car and the tradeoffs for different methods of repairing the problem and may be given a "loaner" car to drive during the repair process. Both customers may use a credit card for payment.

After the sale, the altered garment or the repaired auto may be delivered to the customer's home, and the salesperson may call to thank the customer for the business, offer future assistance, or tell the customer about an upcoming special sales event. In addition to these expected or essential services, other optional services may provide a sustainable competitive advantage in any type of business. For the apparel customer, extras might include baby-sitting, unusual merchandise assortments, or locating items in a competing retail store. For the auto repair customer, extras might include vacuuming the interior of the car and checking the oil and tire pressure.

Recovering Lost or About-to-Be-Lost Sales.   Customers who are frustrated, upset, disappointed, or otherwise negatively affected by a buying experience usually want to know that someone cares about their problem, will listen to their dilemma, and will try their very best to do something about it. Customers have more economic power than ever before, patronizing the businesses that are best at problem resolution.

The Staples sales associate described earlier recovered the sale of map pins to the small business customer by going the "extra mile" in service—and not only saved the $20 sale but also developed a long-term relationship with a customer who now spends 100 times that amount every year.

A Sears, Roebuck and Co. sales associate recovered the sale of a broken garage door opener by taking prompt action to correct the problem. Another Sears representative called 2 days later to see if the problem had been resolved and offered extended warranties on the garage door opener and other Sears items. The retailer admitted the mistake, fixed it quickly, and exceeded the customer's expectations, leaving a positive impression.[7]

Linking Customer Satisfaction to Service Quality.   Customer expectations about the types of services that should be offered and their criteria for performance of these services have a major impact on the level of satisfaction or dissatisfaction felt with the total purchase experience. This can be represented as

Customer satisfaction = (service expectations − perceived service performance)

Customer satisfaction
Difference between customers' service expectations and perceptions of service actually received.

If performance exceeds expectations, then satisfaction should be high. Conversely, if service expectations are not met (or are unrealistic), dissatisfaction will result. Loyal, satisfied customers give a marketer a long-term competitive advantage. Of course, expectations vary according to retail type; for example, less service is expected from an off-price retailer and more from a boutique.

Realizing a Profitable Return on Investment.   Most businesses achieve successful results when they invest in customer service activities. Just as services are designed to satisfy the needs of different customers, the costs of these services vary according to business type, service product assortment, and customer base. However, the cost to provide a service may not be proportionate to the perceived value placed on it by a customer.

Performing a Major Role in Marketing.   Because of their contribution to sales and profitability, services are an important component of the overall marketing mix. Having the right products in the right place at the right price and right time is critical for marketing success, along with the effective use of promotional tools. However, these factors are insufficient without the added value offered by integrating wanted customer services into the overall marketing-mix strategy.

MARKETING IN THE INFORMATION AGE

USAA Leverages Processes for Strategic Advantage

The re-engineering of many businesses from a purely functional organization to a structure that focuses on creating an efficient horizontal workflow often changes the way work processes are performed. In a service organization, processes are the dominant factor in customer and employee satisfaction, because it is the processes that provide evidence of service quality.

United Services Automobile Association (USAA) is a major provider of insurance and financial services to 4.3 million active and retired military personnel and their families. Robert Herres, former chairman and CEO, said, "At USAA, we have always had processes linking together our basic activities. There's an underwriting process, a rate-setting process, a loss-management process, a catastrophe-management process, as well as the usual collection of functional processes." Although these processes seem to work well, Herres said, "We found that if you really want to exploit new technology—and for us, that includes both communications and information systems—you have to analyze how the work in your organization actually gets done and decide which steps can be tailored to a machine and which are best left to people." He explained that this is accomplished by developing detailed process maps and getting the entire organization to think in terms of processes.

USAA started out as a direct writer of insurance in 1922, operating by mail and telephone from one centralized location in San Antonio, Texas. When the company began to apply new technology, it discovered that many traditions had built up over the years in its administrative organization, creating a number of unnecessary steps. Paper was lost or hard to find—or not even missed. The existing processes had to be re-evaluated before they could be integrated with modern information systems.

Herres said, "Technology also forced us to think about how and where our processes intersect. Alignment across businesses is critical for us because our goal is to exploit the efficiencies of centralized information management while we decentralize service delivery." In order to leverage technology across the company, someone has to ensure that one area of the company (such as insurance) is not creating systems and processes that do not interface well with the corporate system. For example, most of USAA's customers move once every 3 years, and when the company was confronted with a seemingly simple—but inefficient—system of changing addresses, necessary systems and processes were established so that a customer could call any of USAA's lines of business and have an address change posted immediately in all business sectors across all parts of the organization.

USAA recognizes the need for interconnectivity between systems as it expands each of its businesses. A customer information file (CIF) built in the 1980s has proven valuable as the company adds new systems and processes. The CIF is accessed by customer service applications in every business unit at USAA, simplifying the data-entry process when customers call for service.

USAA gained a well-respected customer service edge with its personalization strategy, winning prestigious awards from organizations such as J.D. Power and Associates and Ward's 50 for outstanding performance and customer relations. However, the company continually recognizes the need to address internal system problems to maintain high service quality standards. In 1998 USAA launched a data management program to streamline internal data, expanding the CIF, storing less information in disparate silo databases and storing more information centrally in an integrated data clearinghouse.

With growth in its different business sectors, and the introduction of the USAA.com Web site in 1999, USAA wants its members to see a unified company when they do business. In its first year, the data management program that lets customers do business over the USAA.com Web site conducted more than 6.3 million transactions. Earl King, senior VP of business integration at USAA, stated that success of the system goes beyond financial returns. "The real opportunity isn't in the savings . . . The real opportunity is to more easily integrate business processes, to allow us to become a company that meets our mission of showing customers we're one organization linked together to solve their needs."

"As technology improves and the pace of change accelerates, all processes (management, business, and work processes) become faster moving and more interactive. Decision-making cycles tighten, feedback loops are shorter, and there's less room for error. The risks go up because you can get left behind a lot more quickly."

Source: David A. Garvin, "Leveraging Processes for Strategic Advantage," *Harvard Business Review* (September–October 1995), pp. 77–90; Andy Patrizio, "Home-grown CRM," *Insurance & Technology,* New York, 26 (3) (February 2001), pp. 49–50; "USAA Insurance Named to Ward's 50—Again," www.usaa.com (November 5, 2002); "USAA Receives J.D. Power and Associates Award," www.usaa.com (November 5, 2002); USAA Company Capsule, www.hoovers.com (November 5, 2002).

 ## SERVICE MARKETING ISSUES

The unique characteristics of intangible services often make it more difficult to target customer groups and to anticipate how they will respond to service offerings. Some approaches to marketing primary and ancillary services to defined market segments are described below. In addition, several other factors need to be considered relative to the purchase of services. Perceived risk, service attributes, brand and service provider loyalty, and the diffusion of innovations (adoption process) are discussed briefly.

Market Segmentation

Successful services marketing starts with an understanding of customers' wants and needs. This includes identifying the customer group(s) to be served, their particular service needs, and how they make their buying decisions.

The general bases for market segmentation discussed earlier in this book can be applied to final consumers and business customers for both goods and services. The characteristics of these segments provide direction for the service marketing mix. Some useful bases for identifying customer segments for a variety of services include:

Demographic	*Consumer:* Income, age, family life cycle (e.g., child care and child-sized bathrooms for younger customers, wheel chairs and rest areas for senior citizens)
	Business: Company size, location, number of employees (e.g., assistance with inventory management or promotion for smaller customers)
Geographic	*Consumer:* Proximity to the store, type of neighborhood (e.g., delivery services and catalog or telephone shopping services for distant customers)

	Business: Concentration relative to an industry, sales territory characteristics, etc.
Psychographics/ lifestyle	*Consumer:* A combination of similar demographic and psychological characteristics (e.g., activities, interests, opinions); tendency to follow similar consumer behavior patterns (e.g., personal shopping and delivery for time-poor dual-career couples with children, to satisfy their need for convenience)
Benefits sought	*Consumer:* Expect certain benefits from the purchase of primary services and from the services that accompany the purchase of physical goods. Benefits may include convenience, avoidance of risk (e.g., warranties, money-back guarantees), or exceptional value for the price.
	Consumers: May seek other benefits such as status or enhancement of personal image.
	Businesses: May seek benefits such as improved productivity, efficiency, and increased profits.
Price sensitivity	*Consumers:* Demand for retail services, such as sales assistance, delivery, or warranties, is related to their sensitivity to charges for these services (e.g., "economic shoppers" prefer self-service and cash-and-carry transactions to keep the purchase price as low as possible).
	Businesses: Seek value through added services, such as assistance with promotional events or inventory management.

Perceived Risk

Perceived risk
Higher levels of risk or uncertainty experienced by customers when buying services versus tangible goods due to factors such as lack of information, experience, and standardization.

Buyers tend to feel a higher level of **perceived risk** when buying services than when buying tangible goods for several reasons: lack of purchase information, customer involvement, inability to return or exchange, and lack of standardization.[8]

Lack of Purchase Information. Service customers are hampered in their purchase decisions by a relative lack of evaluative criteria for judging the quality of a service and the benefits that it offers. They also typically suffer from a lack of purchase information. This inability to evaluate many service attributes before purchase, or even after purchase, can lead to a higher level of perceived risk by the buyer. Financial services are one area where customers may feel a sense of inadequacy in making a purchase decision. For example, many South Africans were introduced to banking services for the first time in 1996 in locations where people previously were considered too poor or illiterate to be valuable customers for a bank. The ability to open a bank account and to use an ATM were new experiences for this vast, underdeveloped market, where people needed an easy, safe way to stash and access cash. Bank employees helped customers with usage information as long as needed, with the goal of educating them to help themselves.[9]

Customer Involvement. The personal nature of many services, requiring a high degree of **customer involvement** in the production process, can cause anxiety about potential risk (e.g., a complex medical procedure). The simultaneous production and consumption of many services lead to differences in purchase behavior, such as more attention given by customers to characteristics of service providers and other customers. These factors are inseparable components of the total service experience. For example, beauty salons cater to a wide range of customers with different hair and skin characteristics and different styling preferences. Customers often develop a personal relationship with a stylist and enjoy the social aspects of a visit to the salon.[10]

> **Customer involvement**
> In the simultaneous production and consumption process for services, increases the level of customer anxiety and perceived risk.

No Returns or Exchanges. Since many services are consumed as they are produced (e.g., dental services, computer repair), a dissatisfied customer cannot return or exchange defective work in the same way he or she can return a shirt or copy machine. Guarantees and service warranties may be offered but may be difficult to implement satisfactorily. For example, customers of a beauty salon cannot return a bad permanent to get a new hairdo. Restitution can be made, but not without possible embarrassment and inconvenience. To overcome this type of perceived risk, many service marketers are pursuing a differentiation strategy that provides more warranties and guarantees for the quality of their work.

Lack of Standardization (Variability). Because services tend to be more variable and less standardized than products, customers attach considerably more risk to their purchase. Service outputs usually are not as consistent as manufactured products. On the other hand, variability can be an advantage where a service can be customized to the needs of the individual buyer. While the hair stylists described earlier can customize their services for a wide variety of customers, they are expected to provide the same quality of service every time a customer visits their salon, regardless of the specific service provided.

Evaluation of Service Attributes

Purchase behavior is influenced by the degree to which services lend themselves to evaluation. Three attributes of services influence the evaluation process: search properties, experience properties, and credence properties.

Search Properties. Attributes of a service that a customer can discern prior to purchase, such as price or location, are referred to as **search properties.** For example, a medical patient facing the prospect of surgery may be limited to prehospitalization service attributes such as appearance of the physical facilities, hospital personnel, and "paperwork."

> **Search properties**
> Attributes of a service that the customer can discern prior to purchase.

Experience Properties. **Experience properties** are those attributes that can be discerned only during or after the service has been performed. For our surgery patient, this may be an evaluation of the physical comfort or discomfort that was experienced, the concern demonstrated by the surgeon and the hospital staff, and response to care-related questions.

> **Experience properties**
> Attributes that can be discerned only during or after the service has been performed.

Credence Properties. Some service attributes cannot be determined with any accuracy, even after the service has been performed. For example, the surgery patient is generally not a medical expert who can determine the medical success of the procedure. Rather, **credence properties** must be inferred from a subjective evaluation of the entire process.

Credence properties
Service attributes inferred from a subjective evaluation of the entire process.

Brand and Service Provider Loyalty

Differences in the ways customers purchase goods and services are due to psychological involvement, personal interaction, and fewer impulse purchases. Loyal customers feel more confidence and less risk in repeat purchases from the same service provider.

Psychological Involvement. The fact that most services require participation of the customer to some degree increases the personal level of psychological involvement in the service process. When combined with a relatively high level of perceived risk and inadequate information before the purchase, loyalty to a service provider is likely to occur. When purchasing services, such as those of a physician or long-distance telephone company, a customer may lack prepurchase information about possible substitute services and may be influenced not to change or consider other providers due to perceived costs of time and money.

Personal Interaction. The inseparability, at some level, of the service provider and customer should lead to a relationship of mutual trust. As each party gains a better knowledge of the other's ability and needs through personal interaction, a higher level of loyalty evolves. Companies that maintain meaningful databases on their customers can have an advantage in building brand loyalty through personal relationships with their customers

Fewer Impulse Purchases. Customers are more likely to make impulse purchases for physical goods than for intangible services because of the perceived risk factor. This is particularly true for first-time service purchases, which generally come about after a need has been recognized and a search for information about alternatives has occurred. Once a customer has had a good service experience, it becomes time-consuming to revisit the alternatives, and brand loyalty minimizes perceived risk associated with the service.

Adoption Process for Innovations

Service innovations tend to be diffused into the market at a slower rate than goods innovations. It can be difficult to implement change due to customers' resistance to trying an unproven service or method of delivering the service. The **rate of diffusion** depends on the innovation's relative advantage, ability to communicate, complexity, compatibility, and ability to test or sample. Figure 9.2 provides a graphic example of the rate of acceptance and adoption of Internet shopping services.

Rate of diffusion
Pace at which innovations are accepted by the target market.

Adoption process
Length of time for a segment of the market to accept and purchase new services.

The **adoption process** is shortened when customers perceive that an innovation offers greater benefits than existing alternatives. However, service innovations tend to be adopted more slowly than physical product innovations because it is more difficult to evaluate their relative advantages in advance. In part, this is due to the difficulty in communicating intangible benefits that cannot be displayed, seen,

FIGURE 9.2

Adoption Process for Service Innovations*

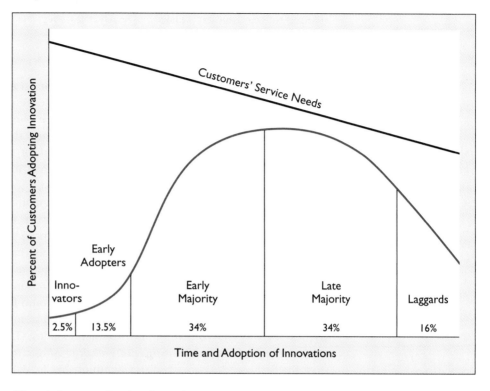

Example: Internet online shopping service.
Adapted with the permission of The Free Press, a Division of Simon & Schuster Adult Publishing Group, from *Diffusion of Innovations,* Fourth Edition by Everett M. Rogers. Copyright © 1995 by Everett M. Rogers. Copyright © 1962, 1971, 1983 by The Free Press.

touched, or tested in advance. (The communication task is easier when the service can be explained relative to a tangible good.)

The complexity of a service also slows down the adoption process. Innovative approaches to financial services (such as online banking and investing), for example, contain features that are complex and difficult to explain to a prospective customer. The length of time that it takes for customers to adopt a service innovation also depends on its compatibility with the customers' past experience and existing values relative to this purchase. Finally, the customers' ability to try out the service, risk-free, before purchase affects the time to adoption. It is difficult for a consumer to "sample" a new haircut or tooth extraction in advance or for a company to try out an entire local-area network (LAN) system on its own premises before commitment to the innovation. Therefore, marketers must "tangibilize" these benefits to the extent possible.

● THE SERVICE DESIGN PROCESS

The service design process starts with a determination of the right type(s) of services to offer, which in turn depends on customer segments to be served, nature of the service, pricing strategy, level of complexity or uncertainty of purchase (including perceived risk), and the firm's resources. Services marketing managers also must decide how many services to offer and at what level. Finally, managers must determine the details involved in actually delivering the service, that is, what is needed to carry out each task.

Determining Customer Targets

As discussed previously, the needs and wants of the target market should drive service marketing decisions. Different segments have different service needs, ability or willingness to pay, and profitability potential for the firm.

The travel and entertainment industries recognize the need to cater to shifts in their target markets. Intrawest, owner of a network of North American ski resorts from West Virginia to California and Canada, believes it has the formula for luring the most desirable skiers. These skiers typically like to take vacations at "destination" resorts such as Blackcomb and Whistler Mountains located 90 miles north of Vancouver, B.C., Canada, and spend four times more than day-trippers on items other than lodging and lift tickets. Whistler-Blackcomb provides multilingual ski instructors to serve destination skiers from places other than North America. Intrawest focuses on enhancing uniqueness while assuring guests of uniform excellence. The company's strategy is to create destinations—total mountain villages that extend beyond the usual ski resort concept. Whistler-Blackcomb features not only traditional skiing and resort amenities, but has also captured X-treme sport enthusiasts with activities such as snowboarding and mountain biking. They received top rankings with *TransWorld Snowboarding and Freeskier Magazine,* and were selected to co-host the first ever X Games Global Championship in May 2003.[11]

Wal-Mart Stores, Inc., and Bloomingdale's Inc. generally target two different customer segments, although a large number of customers (known as *cross-shoppers*) may shop in both stores. Thus there is a difference in retail services demanded by customers from a mass merchandiser like Wal-Mart and a department store like Bloomingdale's. At Wal-Mart, the self-service format emphasizes availability of merchandise assortments, easy unassisted shopping (information in shopping carts, convenient layout, wide aisles, easy-to-read signs), informed help from nonsales employees, a large number of checkout registers, and empowered employees to carry out the store's "customer is always right" philosophy. In contrast, Bloomingdale's has responded to the service needs of its clientele by replacing many part-timers with full-time salespeople, offering Godiva chocolates, and sending thank-you notes to preferred shoppers. Bloomingdale's also holds private shopping nights where the store gives "gifts of service" such as free alterations and free delivery.

Determining the Nature of the Service

The type of service has an impact on service design. Primary (core) services related to medicine, investments, software design, and other relatively complex areas require considerable support services and qualified customer contact personnel. On the other hand, automated services, such as ATMs, require more design effort behind the scenes than at the point of customer contact. Restaurant services run the gamut from extensive personal service in a fine-dining sit-down establishment to the less personal, automated service at a fast-food drive-through restaurant.

The design of ancillary services follows the same logic as that for core services. If the support service is relatively complex and is instrumental in providing differentiation from competitors, it will require a more elaborate service design (people, equipment, processes). Large, heavy items such as furniture and appliances may require the design of delivery and repair services. Apparel retailers may need to incorporate alteration services, and a bicycle shop or toy store may need to assemble purchases. Each aspect of a primary or ancillary service must be designed to deliver customer satisfaction.

Determining Pricing Strategy

The ideal position for a service marketer is to achieve differentiation based on exceptional, high-quality service while maximizing profits and minimizing costs. The pricing strategy that will deliver these results is based on all elements of the service design (e.g., complexity, customization, resource requirements, etc.), along with the marketer's ability to contain costs without sacrificing quality. However, pricing strategy also depends on what the market is willing to pay, as well as competitors' pricing strategies.

Pricing decisions must be made for ancillary services that are performed to enhance the value of a core service or good. For example, upscale retailers are expected to offer a wide range of services at no additional charge to justify their higher pricing structure. Examples include free alterations, intensive effort to locate wanted merchandise if not available locally, personal shopping, and lenient merchandise return privileges. Upscale consumers also may expect the unexpected— optional services such as special store hours, refreshments while shopping, and a comfortable place to relax, with a phone or fax machine available. Pricing decisions for ancillary or supporting services present the dilemma of whether to charge a fee or not. Marketers at all levels of the channel react to customer demands for service, believing that these services will build sales and develop long-term relationships. However, additional sales may come at too high a price if the firm does not consider the cost of providing these services and the impact on profits. Table 9.3 illustrates the relationship between customer classifications, the cost to serve each segment, and the net realized price.

Pricing strategies can be determined according to customer segments, based on amount and frequency of purchases, types of services (or goods) purchased, new

TABLE 9.3

The Customer-Cost-Price Relationship

Customer Type	Average Cost of Customer Service to Marketer	Price of Service to Customer
New customer	High	Low to moderate
Frequent buyer/heavy user	Low	Varies
High-tech		
Informed/sophisticated	Low	Low
Naive/beginner	High	High to moderate

versus potential buyers, and so forth. Assuming that the services offered are considered necessary to make the sale, then other questions must be answered about the effect of service fees on buying, such as: Will a "heavy user" of a good or service stop buying if he or she has to pay for a particular service? And what is the company-wide impact on all purchases made by that customer? Should the fee be adjusted? Are there other services that are more important?

The cost of providing a service is directly related to the level of service provided. Some of these costs are wages for personnel (sales, service performance, credit, etc.), physical facilities (initial cost, maintenance, use of non-sales-producing space), necessary technology and equipment (computers, databases, production equipment, etc.), and cost of price adjustments or allowances. When customer dissatisfaction is caused by poor service or service that is not valued by the customer, both direct and indirect costs are affected.

Direct costs are associated with actual service performance, making customer adjustments in terms of repeating the service or refunding payment, honoring warranties and guarantees, and costs (mostly marketing) of attracting new customers on the basis of service. *Indirect costs* include customer turnover rate (dissatisfied customers buy less or stop buying) and word-of-mouth referrals (satisfied customers are the best form of advertising, negative word of mouth travels fast from dissatisfied customers).

A potential cost is related to the firm's lack of customer orientation. Managers must heed their customers' complaints and suggestions for customer service improvements and/or innovations. Otherwise, this oversight may result in lost business. Another indirect cost that often is overlooked and difficult to measure is loss of productivity as a result of the time and energy required by service managers and employees to "put out fires" for customers when no quality service plan is in place.

Addressing Complexity or Uncertainty

Complex services (home building, investments) and physical goods (automobiles, electronics, computers) frequently require extensive sales assistance, demonstrations, and service guarantees. Complexity is related to a feeling of uncertainty or risk when purchasing expensive or complex products. Thus the marketer needs to assure the customer that the company stands behind the purchase (e.g., after-sale assistance, help phone number, no-risk returns).

Health care needs often are related to high levels of complexity and uncertainty. Most patients find the details of medical problems difficult to understand, and treatments are not guaranteed to cure. As a result, medical practitioners need to provide patients with information that they can understand in order to remove as much anxiety as possible. They also should demonstrate a personal interest in follow-up procedures to reduce the uncertainty felt by the patient.

Assessing the Marketer's Resources

The ideal is not always achievable. Customers may want more services at a higher level than it is reasonable for the services marketer to provide. Services require human, financial, and physical resources (personnel, facilities, equipment) that may be needed elsewhere. A small service business, for example, may have to outsource ancillary customer services such as accounting, delivery, and credit (although there are advantages and disadvantages to contracting out services). Larger service businesses may allocate more resources to physical facilities and expansion in order to offer more services to more customers. The opening scenario for this chapter described the efforts of Bank of America and others to serve new market segments with more branches and more customer-focused services, with the expectation of increases in customers and profitability.

Determining the Number of Services

It is not necessary to offer all possible services to customers. Customer services should be prioritized by their perceived value to customers, with these rankings weighed against the cost of providing each service. Concentration should be on offering those services that make a difference in the consumers' present and future purchase decisions. Note that customers may be willing to pay some or all of the cost of highly desirable services if the value is evident. For example, novice computer users usually need help setting up a new PC and loading software, and perhaps basic instruction. Business customers may require the assistance of a consultant who has identified marketing problems in implementation of the recommended solution. Since the level of service required differs by the experience and/or sophistication of the customer, services can be bundled as a package with several different pricing structures.

Determining the Level of Service

The level of customer service offered by a service provider can extend from full service with maximum assistance before, during, and after the sale to a completely self-service operation where the customer shops relatively unassisted until the sale is finalized. Examples include an upscale restaurant versus a self-service cafeteria line or an automated car wash versus a full-detailing service to clean a car.

The service-level decision must be consistent with the types of services offered and their importance in making a sale and keeping a customer. We previously classified services as essential (primary or core) or expected and optional (ancillary). Recognize that while some services may be essential for one group of customers, they may be optional for another customer segment.

SETTING STANDARDS FOR SERVICE QUALITY

Most customers believe that they have relatively clear definitions of service quality and judge service experiences accordingly. However, when it comes to specifying and describing service design features, the marketer is faced with a much more formidable task. Each detail of the service, both seen (or experienced) and unseen by the customer, must focus on how to deliver quality.

Seven best practices that can be used to achieve better service include: (1) developing a situational service strategy (knowing where you are relative to your competition), (2) integrating customer service throughout every aspect of the business, (3) defining all points of service, and communicating what is expected of employees, (4) holding everyone accountable for quality of customer service, (5) defining, communicating, and executing an all-out recovery strategy, (6) giving customer contact personnel the ability to solve customers' problems immediately, and (7) focusing on continuous improvement in customer service.[12]

One effective approach to designing and delivering quality service is to benchmark against superior service marketers. It is also essential to establish and communicate quality standards, identify actual and potential gaps in service quality, and have an effective service retention and recovery program in operation.

Benchmarking

Benchmark
Compare a company's service performance against the performance of competitors or other business leaders that are recognized for excellent practices.

Companies should **benchmark** their own service performance against the performance of competitors or other leaders in the business world. At the forefront of outstanding customer service are companies such as Nordstrom, Inc., Walt Disney World, Marriott International Inc., and many others. Each industry has a service leader that sets the standard for everyone else. Think about the service marketers that you deal with for personal or business services. Who does customer service right, and who fails miserably? What are the reasons for success or failure in delivering high-quality services?

Nordstrom, Inc., started out as a relatively obscure department store in the Pacific Northwest but has risen to national prominence, outstripping its would-be competitors on a well-deserved and highly publicized reputation for exceptional customer service. How has the company done this? Everyone—even the Nordstrom family—has to start on the selling floor. A decentralized organization pushes decisions as close to the customer as possible. Salespeople are encouraged to provide feedback to management, empowered to take returns, and always expected to do the unexpected for their customers.

Specific standards for service quality should be based on input from customers, employees, and managers who are responsible for carrying out the intent of the service design. Service quality standards must be stated clearly to ensure proper implementation by customer service personnel and to allow accurate measurement of their effectiveness in satisfying customers' service needs and achieving management's performance objectives.

Leading service marketers have identified the key dimensions of service quality. Based on extensive market research with thousands of respondents in different service industries, Zeithaml, Parasuraman, and Berry[13] have narrowed the key factors that influence customers' evaluations of service quality down to five basic dimensions, as shown in Table 9.4. In many studies, reliability has been identified as the number one factor used in assessing service quality. Thus, do what you say you are going to do—and do it better than anyone else—every time!

Planning Service Tasks and Activities

For each individual type of service, management must identify the specific tasks and activities needed to carry it out. An example of customer service activities involved in handling complaints and the resources needed to support them is shown in Table 9.5.

Blueprinting
Similar to flowcharting, provides a visual representation of all steps involved in delivering a service to a customer; can be used to identify failure points in service quality.

Blueprinting. Ideally, of course, problem areas should be recognized before they occur. **Blueprinting** or flowcharting techniques can be used to provide a visual representation of all the steps involved in delivering a particular service to a customer. This makes it possible to discover missing steps or redundancies in the process and to determine necessary remedies and resources.

TABLE 9.4

Dimensions of Service Quality

1. Tangibles	Appearance of the company's physical interior and exterior environment, equipment, personnel, and communications materials. (The customer contact and service areas for selling and performing the service, handling complaints, etc., should be convenient and attractive, with cheerful, positive, well-informed personnel.)
2. Reliability	The marketer's ability to perform the promised service dependably and accurately time after time after time. Do it right the first time and every time thereafter.
3. Responsiveness	The marketer's willingness to help customers and provide the needed service promptly. Resolve the problem quickly and answer the customers' questions intelligently and accurately. Honor promised schedules and follow up as needed.
4. Assurance	Service employees' knowledge and courtesy, their ability to convey a sense of trust and confidence to customers. They should know what they are talking about (or find out from someone who does) and treat the customer with respect.
5. Empathy	The ability of service personnel to convey to each customer that he or she is important and that the service provider and company care about the customer and his or her problem. (This is sometimes difficult when the customer is being unreasonable or obnoxious, but it does pay off in the long run.)

Source: Adapted from Valarie A. Zeithaml, A. Parasuraman, and Leonard L. Berry, *Delivering Quality Service: Balancing Customer Perceptions and Expectations* (New York: Free Press, 1990), pp. 15–33; and Valarie A. Zeithaml and Mary Jo Bitner, *Services Marketing: Integrating Customer Focus Across the Firm,* 2nd ed. (Boston: Irwin McGraw-Hill, 2000), pp. 82–85.

TABLE 9.5

Customer Service Tasks, Activities, and Resources: An Example for Complaint Handling*

Service Tasks, Activities	Resources to Carry Out Service Task
Initial customer contact, communication	Sales or service personnel, physical setting if in person, or telephone or mail response capability
Discuss problem; listen!	Service personnel training, empathy
Identify problem	Knowledge of service process, procedures, and options
Determine alternative solutions	Computer, database, policy manual; trained, empowered employees; availability of relevant information for decision
Choose "best" solution	Training and experience in matching customer needs and service solution
Act quickly to implement solution	Clear implementation guidelines; necessary systems, personnel, and resources available to carry out solution
Follow up contact with customer	System for record keeping, documentation of transaction

*Ideally, customer complaints should be recognized and corrected before the sale is completed. After the sale, remedies are more limited and more expensive.

The process of delivering a particular service to a customer usually involves many discrete activities and individuals. The customer assumes that all elements in this process are working together to solve his or her problem. Frustration mounts when the system breaks down because employees do not communicate with each other about the customer's problem and they do not comprehend the complete service process. To overcome this problem, the marketer can take the customer's perspective to learn where the customer gets "lost" in the system.[14] This can be done by flowcharting each step in the customer's experience to gain a better understanding of the process and by blueprinting (a more sophisticated extension of flowcharting) every activity needed to create and deliver the service. This process also requires identification of the critical linkages between activities. A blueprint of the customer service process for an express mail delivery service and a hotel is illustrated in Figure 9.3. Critical incidents can occur at each point in the process, resulting in customer satisfaction—or in service failure.

Identifying Gaps in Service Quality.   Service-quality problems tend to be related to expectations, perceptions, and communications problems. These problems can be classified into five service-quality gaps that have important implications for marketing managers at all levels of an organization:

Gap 1. Difference between consumer expectations and management perceptions of customer expectations.

Gap 2. Difference between management perceptions of customer expectations and service-quality specifications.

Gap 3. Difference between service-quality specifications and the service actually delivered.

Gap 4. Difference between service delivery and what is communicated about the service to customers.

Gap 5. Difference between consumer expectations about the service and perceptions of the service actually delivered (a summary of gaps 1 through 4).[15]

● SERVICE DELIVERY AND IMPLEMENTATION

The process of delivering high-quality customer service must start with an organizational culture that nurtures a customer-oriented perspective. Marketers not only must identify those services most desired by their customers but also must determine the best ways to deliver high-quality service to achieve customer satisfaction and recognize the important role of customer contact personnel.

Organization Structure and Culture

The organization must encourage and facilitate a service philosophy—from the top managers to the lowest employee. Experience in successful service organizations suggests that if front-line employees are to perform high-quality service, then the entire organizational structure must be designed with a customer-orientation focus. Some successful service organizations also boast an informal structure that makes customer service everyone's responsibility; every employee has ownership when it comes to serving the customers. Further, management must ensure that the necessary support exists for successful implementation of customer service activities.

FIGURE 9.3

Blueprinting the Customer Service Process

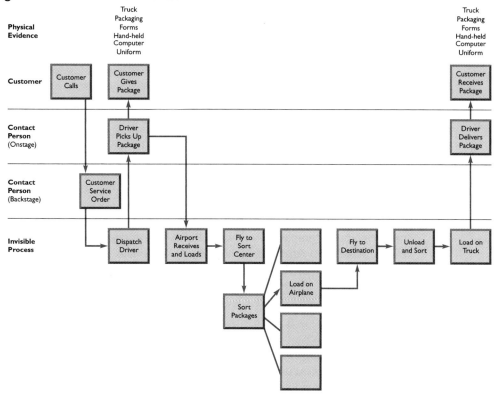

(a) Blueprint for Express Mail Delivery Service

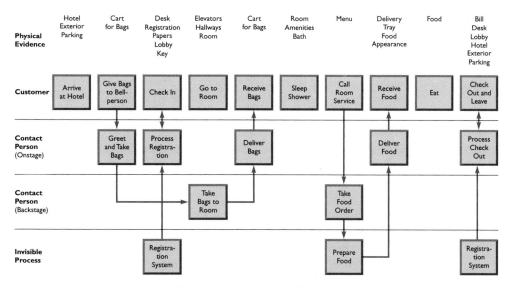

(b) Blueprint for Overnight Hotel Stay

Source: Bitner, Mary Jo, "Managing the Evidence of Service," in *The Service Quality Handbook,* eds. Erberhard & Christopher, New York: AMA, p. 282. The Service Quality Handbook by Richard Scheuing. Reproduced with permission of American Management Association in the format textbook via Copyright Clearance Center.

Top-Management Commitment.   Senior executives have to believe in the benefits of allocating resources to providing exceptional services to customers. Otherwise, the lack of commitment to customers and their service needs will filter down through the entire company. The service commitment can be carried out at different levels, from lowest-level self-service, do-it-yourself, cash-and-carry, bag-it-yourself, no-returns operations to high-level sales assistance, credit availability, exclusive image packaging of purchased goods and services, lenient complaint resolution, and considerable pampering of customers.

Treating Employees as Internal Customers.   To infuse personnel throughout the company with enthusiasm for giving each and every customer top-notch service, many companies treat employees as internal customers. Internal marketing programs are designed to "sell" employees on their company and its products, as practiced by Disney World and Southwest Airlines. When employees have positive attitudes about their company and believe in what it represents, this attitude is conveyed to customers and the community. It has been said that if you can sell the employees on the company, they will sell the customers. In customer service activities this is particularly important because of the human element involved and the fact that many customer services exist to take care of negative customer problems.

Viewing Service as a Performance.   Service firms like Disney World and premium resort hotels refer to their customers as "guests" and to employees as "cast members." To these service-oriented companies, every service activity is a performance and is designed from a dramaturgical (or theatrical) point of view. Elements of a drama can be related to service design and delivery: the setting (servicescape, social and physical characteristics), scene (with script), performance (service delivery), cast of actors and actresses (service providers), and audience (customers). Viewing service as a performance should result in better management of a company's image and higher levels of customer satisfaction.

Ensuring Service Recovery.   An important aspect of the service design and delivery process is the retention of customers. Although retention achieved by providing high-quality service throughout the entire service process is the most desirable way to accomplish this, unanticipated problems can occur. Effective service-recovery procedures must be in place to overcome such problems, regardless of the type of business. A memorable headline, "Puh-leeze, won't somebody help me?"[16] expresses the frustration felt by exasperated service customers every day. A firm's ability to solve customers' problems, give needed assistance, fix disappointments, and give service beyond what is required or expected is instrumental in developing long-term relationships.

Certainly, some mistakes will occur in business transactions; for example, a repair may not be completed satisfactorily, the wrong product may be shipped or arrive late or defective, a salesperson may not call a customer back as promised, the wrong price may be charged, or a billing error may occur. No matter how diligently marketers try to avoid product or service errors, it is virtually impossible to achieve "zero defects." Whether a customer problem seems inconsequential or a complaint seems like whining over a petty issue, it must be resolved. Thus companies must have a plan for service recovery—to win back customers one at a time. Everyone in the organization must be trained and motivated to provide customer satisfaction

TABLE 9.6

Suggested Actions for Successful Service Recovery

Service recovery can be successful when the following actions are taken:

- *Measure the costs of effective service recovery.* The costs of losing a customer include the loss of repeat purchases and negative image and word-of-mouth communications with other customers.

- *Break the silence.* Good service recovery starts with listening to the customer to identify the problem. Since most customers do not complain, marketers must be proactive in identifying the problems that customers may not communicate but that would make them purchase elsewhere.

- *Anticipate needs for recovery.* Managers must continuously review their organization to find potential failure points in marketing, operations, or other areas that affect the performance of high-quality customer service.

- *Act fast.* Customer service problems tend to escalate rapidly, so it is important to identify them quickly (preferably before the customer does) and prove a commitment to the customer by taking care of them immediately.

- *Train employees.* Train customer contact personnel and give them the skills they need to deal effectively with upset customers. Employees should understand the entire service delivery process—not just an isolated function that may seem to have a questionable purpose.

- *Empower the front line.* Customer contact personnel should be empowered and given the authority, responsibility, and incentives to recognize, be concerned about, and take care of customers' problems. (Limits to the monetary value of service recovery actions may be set.)

- *Close the loop.* The customer should be kept informed about corrective actions taken to resolve his or her problem or given an explanation of why the situation can't be "fixed." This can be done by telephone, letter, or asking for feedback or suggestions that have a chance of being implemented.

Source: Reprinted by permission of *Harvard Business Review.* From "The Profitable Art of Service Recovery" by Hart, Christopher, W. L., James L. Heskett and W. Earl Sasser, Jr., July/August 1990. Copyright © 1990 by the President and Fellows of Harvard College; all rights reserved.

and be given the ability to make decisions on the spot. Employee attitudes should never communicate an "I don't care" or "It's not my job" attitude. Suggested actions for successful service recovery are described in Table 9.6, and the high cost of losing just one customer is presented in Figure 9.4.

Personnel Issues

Quality of customer service can be traced to a number of personnel issues: hiring the "right" people, training them properly in customer service techniques, empowering them to respond to customers' needs, and compensating them on customer satisfaction as well as on sales or profits.

Adequate Staffing. Adequate staffing for performance of service activities requires the ability to manage demand and supply. Service marketers experience a frequent imbalance between service cost and productivity. It often seems that customer service needs and problems occur at times when the fewest personnel are available, they are the busiest with other customers, or they are fatigued. Poor service also may result from "slow" times when there are few demands on employees to perform, resulting in potential boredom and low productivity.

FIGURE 9.4

The Importance of Customer Retention

Cost of Losing One Customer

The ripple effect of one unresolved customer problem can be felt throughout an entire marketing organization. There are losses in sales, profits, and employee and customer goodwill when customers are convinced that managers and employees do not care. Psychological and emotional costs are not easy to quantify, but the impact for a hypothetical retailer of losing one customer and the dollars from a particular sale can be calculated as follows:

- One dissatisfied customer will tell 11 others.
- These 11 people will each tell 5 others (67 people told).

Assume that only 1 in 4 decides not to buy from this retailer and would spend an average $50/week:

- Result = 67 people told x 1/4 who won't buy
        = 17 x $50 per week x 52 weeks = $44,200 per year in lost sales

Customer service research suggests that it costs about six times as much in marketing and other costs to attract a new customer as it does to keep an existing customer. For example, one study determined relative costs:

- It costs $19 for a retailer to keep one customer happy
- It costs $118 to attract a new customer into the store
- Total impact: $118 x 17 customers = $2,006 to attract 17 customers.

Source: Adapted from Paul R. Timm, *50 Powerful Ideas You Can Use to Keep Your Customers* (Hawthorne, NJ: Career Press, 1992), pp. 9–12.

The Importance of Training. Customers become frustrated and unhappy when employees are not prepared to perform expected customer services satisfactorily. Service businesses should be committed to providing the necessary training and courtesy skills for all employees who come in contact with customers in person, by telephone, by mail, or by any other means. This includes everyone from the CEO to the janitor—a customer orientation should prevail throughout the company. In addition to product knowledge, service personnel need to be kept informed about company policies and procedures, acceptable ways to deal with customers, and the status of actions taken on any customer preferences and problems with which they are involved.

Employee training can be directed toward overcoming the most common customer service mistakes. Customers want to feel that someone is listening to them and understands and cares about their needs, that they are liked and respected, that their business is appreciated, and that their problems will be solved—but mostly that someone cares and will respond to their concerns.

Marriott International Inc., Walt Disney World, and other marketers known for their commitment to customer service emphasize the importance of finding, training, and keeping the best service workers. Front-line workers, the people who actually face your customers every day, can make or break your business—despite the plans and intentions of top management.[17]

Empowerment. Once customer service knowledge and skills have been developed, service personnel should be empowered to serve and given adequate support to provide satisfying solutions for their customers. Within the context of quality-service design and delivery, Berry[18] says, "Empowerment is a state of mind." An empowered employee experiences feelings of (1) control over how to do the job, (2) awareness of how the work fits into the "big picture," (3) accountability for his or her own work output, (4) shared responsibility for performance of the work group or organization, and (5) equity in the way rewards are distributed based on individual and collective performance.

Some of the benefits of empowerment are that employees feel like part owners of the business; they feel knowledgeable, responsible, and accountable; and they feel good about their jobs and their flexibility in dealing with service problems. A word of caution, however: Empowerment is not for everyone. Training empowered employees costs money, and there is the risk of making the "wrong" customer service decisions. The secret to successful empowerment seems to lie in a commitment to quality service and a deep sense of trust between management and lower-level service personnel.

Compensation, Awards, and Recognition. Many service businesses reward customer contact personnel mainly on the basis of sales figures. However, if a customer orientation is to prevail, then reward systems must go beyond commissions or wages based on sales to include measures of customer service and satisfaction. A combination of compensation based on sales or straight salary and additional awards and recognition for high levels of performance in customer service activities can motivate employees to "put the customer first."

A diverse group of service firms (e.g., fast-food restaurants, banks, hotels, and others) have revamped their pay practices, compensating service employees on the basis of how well they have served customers. They believe in a service ethic that focuses on customer retention: When the customer is happy, the employee is happy, and vice versa, reducing loss of customers and employees.

Summary

The phenomenal growth of the service sector of the U.S. economy is expected to continue in both consumer and organizational markets. However, marketers must consider the unique characteristics of services versus tangible products when making marketing management decisions. The four most prominent differences are intangibility (cannot touch, feel, see, or otherwise experience the service before purchase), variability (inconsistency in service delivery from one time to the next), inseparability (of the service provider, the service process, and the customer), and perishability (cannot inventory for future sale).

Services may be considered primary (necessary for completion of a sale) or ancillary (related to the good or service being sold but not essential for the sale; usually a source of competitive differentiation). Value perceptions of services start with strategic planning and competitive positioning. Exceptional customer service attracts and retains customers, helps in service recovery, and increases customer satisfaction and return on investment.

Services marketing issues include choice of market segments, reduction of customers' perceptions of risk, customers' evaluation of service attributes, brand and service provider loyalty, and the adoption process for service innovations.

The service-design process includes determination of customer targets, the nature of the service, and the pricing strategy. It also addresses the complexity or uncertainty that may be associated with the service and evaluates the resources available to the marketer to deliver a high-quality service. In addition, the number of services and the level of service also must be determined.

Service quality is a major issue and requires well-defined standards and implementation. Service firms may use benchmarking to identify excellent business practices that may apply to their operations. Blueprinting (or flowcharting) of the entire service process can help to identify potential gaps in service quality and failure points that may require service recovery procedures. Service delivery and implementation are affected by the structure and culture of the organization and by personnel issues. Successful service organizations have the commitment of top management, treat employees as internal customers, and view service as a performance. Personnel issues include adequate staffing, training, empowerment of front-line employees, and compensation, awards, and recognition.

Questions

1. Describe the four main characteristics that differentiate the marketing of services from the marketing of tangible goods. Give an example of how each characteristic might affect management decisions regarding the marketing of an automobile versus the marketing of automobile insurance or repair services.

2. Review the opening vignette for this chapter. Critique the strategies used by Bank of America and other banking institutions to increase their customer base, and improve satisfaction among retail customers. Include in your analysis an assessment of the types of primary and ancillary services offered, market segmentation approaches, loyalty programs, complexity or uncertainty in the service process, the use of technology to achieve strategic goals, and issues concerning service quality and delivery.

3. Flowchart a recent service experience, including the initial decision to use this service, all interactions that you had with the service provider, and the outcome (i.e., the service actually received). Identify and evaluate the positive and negative aspects of this encounter, as well as the primary and ancillary services that were involved.

4. Discuss the ways that marketers can benefit by providing exceptional customer service. From the customer's viewpoint, create a "hierarchy of horrors"—five of the worst things that an organization can do to its customers—and how these problems can be eliminated or minimized.

5. Explain the factors that contribute to a customer's perceptions of risk when purchasing services. What are some ways that a marketer can overcome these perceptions in purchase situations such as the following: (a) minor surgery performed by an unfamiliar physician, (b) a long-awaited cruise vacation, (c) a major automobile repair, (d) drycleaning services for an expensive suit, and (e) an overseas airline travel?

6. Analyze your purchase process for (a) financial services, (b) a haircut, (c) home repair, and (d) long-distance telephone service in relation to brand and service provider loyalty. Consider the level of psychological involvement, personal interaction, and the tendency to make impulse purchases.

7. Outline the service-design process that might be followed by managers of an upscale restaurant who must plan, create, and deliver excellent service to their customers—every time. Give an example of each step, and demonstrate the close linkage that exists between the service product and its delivery system.

8. Continuing with your answer to Question 7, consider a restaurant service encounter that you may have experienced. Develop a blueprint that depicts the "frontstage" and "backstage" elements of this service. Identify the potential failure points or gaps in service quality that may be present in this service design and/or its implementation.

9. Discuss the role of the following in the successful delivery of high-quality services to an organization's customers: (a) organizational structure and culture, (b) personnel issues, and (c) planning for service recovery.

Exercises

1. Obtain examples of ways that service firms reward their customers for frequent purchases (e.g., frequent-flier miles, banking award programs, buyer clubs, etc.). Evaluate the nature of each program's appeal and its ability to attract and retain loyal customers. Describe specific actions that have damaged your relationship with a service provider that you previously felt a loyalty toward and whether/how these actions could be avoided or corrected.

2. Review advertisements for service firms, and identify recent technological developments that are being used in the design and delivery of services. For each new or emerging technology, evaluate whether it offers useful enhancements to provide quality service, or is simply a short-term gimmick to attract customers or introduces a new source of frustration or risk.

3. Compile a list of costs for five services that you might use one or more times over the course of a year, including all types of costs that you might incur in buying and using these services. Explain how your price perceptions affect the concept of "value" received compared with interpretations of "value" expressed by the service firm in its marketing communications. If there is a significant discrepancy in the definitions of value by the firm and its customers, how can this gap be overcome?

Endnotes

1. Leonard L. Berry, *On Great Service: A Framework for Action* (New York: Free Press, 1995), p. 3.

2. Robert E. Yuskavage, "Gross Product by Industry," *A Progress Report on Accelerated Estimates*, (June 2002), p. 26; www.bea.doc.gov/bea.

3. U.S. Census Bureau, *Statistical Abstract of the United States: 2001*, Labor Force, Employment, and Earnings, No. 593. Employed Civilians by Occupation, Sex, Race, and Hispanic Origin: 1993 and 2000, p. 382; www.bls.gov.

4. U.S. Department of Labor, Bureau of Labor Statistics, "Table 2. Employment by Major Occupational Group, 2000 and Projected 2010," and "Table 1. Employment by Major Industry Division, 1990, 2000, and Projected 2010," htttp://www.bls.gov/news.release.

5. For further discussion of the differences between physical products and intangible services, see Philip Kotler, *Marketing Management,* 11th ed. (Englewood Cliffs, NJ: Prentice-Hall, 2003), pp. 444–449; Christopher H. Lovelock, *Services Marketing,* 4th ed. (Englewood Cliffs, NJ: Prentice-Hall, 2001), pp. 8–15.

6. Faye Brookman, "Chains: Service Is Key," *Women's Wear Daily* (April 1996), pp. 6, 26.

7. Susan Reda, "Seven Keys to Better Service," *Stores* (January 1996), pp. 32–34.

8. Valarie A. Zeithaml, "How Consumer Evaluation Processes Differ Between Goods and Services," in James H. Donnelly and William R. George (eds), *Marketing of Services* (Chicago: American Marketing Association, 1981), pp. 186–190.

9. Ken Wells, "Its New ATMs in Place, A Bank Reaches Out to South Africa's Poor," *Wall Street Journal* (June 13, 1996), pp. A1, A10.

10. Calmetta Y. Coleman, "Style over Substance: Power of a Good Perm Brings Us Together," *Wall Street Journal* (September 27, 1995), pp. A1, A6.

11. William C. Symonds, "The Club Med of the Ski Slopes?" *Business Week* (March 18, 1996), pp. 64, 66; www.whistler-blackcomb.com (November 5, 2002); www.intrawestvacations.com (November 5, 2002).

12. Reda, *op. cit.;* also see *The Ultimate CRM Handbook: Strategies and Concepts for Building Enduring Customer Loyalty and Profitability*, John Freeland, ed. (Boston: McGraw-Hill, 2003).

13. Valarie A. Zeithaml, A. Parasuraman, and Leonard L. Berry, *Delivering Quality Service: Balancing Customer Perceptions and Expectations* (New York: Free Press, 1990), pp. 15–33; Valarie A. Zeithaml and Mary Jo Bitner, *Services Marketing*, 2nd ed. (Boston: Irwin McGraw-Hill, 2000), pp. 82–85.

14. For further discussion of flowcharting and blueprinting, see Lovelock, *op. cit.*, pp. 129–134, 223–232.

15. Valarie Zeithaml, Leonard L. Berry, and A. Parasuraman, "Communication and Control Processes in the Delivery

of Service Quality," *Journal of Marketing* 52 (April 1988), pp. 35–48; and Zeithaml and Bitner, *op. cit.*

16. Stephen Koepp, "Puh-leeze, Won't Somebody Help Me?" *Time* (February 2, 1987), pp. 28–34.

17. Ronald Henkoff, "Finding, Training, and Keeping the Best Service Workers," *Fortune* (October 3, 1994), pp. 110–122.

18. Berry, *op. cit.*, pp. 208ff.

MARKETING MANAGEMENT IN ACTION: CLOSING CASE

Meals on Wheels: Entrepreneurship and Funding for a Nonprofit

What is "hunger?" Meals on Wheels Association of America defines hunger as

> ... more than just a growling sensation in the stomach; it's an emotional and physical stress that, when prolonged, may cause serious health problems and a substantial loss in the quality of life. Congregate and home-delivered meal programs geared toward ensuring the nutritional well being of the nation's elderly, helping millions of seniors stay happy, healthy, and independent, longer.

Nonprofit organizations such as Meals on Wheels Association of America (MOWAA) depend on funding from private donors and government agencies to support their daily free food service programs for homebound individuals. Lack of funding is a constant problem, but is particularly critical during economic downturns when donations decline significantly. In 2000, Meals on Wheels received an estimated $500 million from federal and state governments and private donors. About one million Americans benefited from the program, but another 100,000 remained on waiting lists. Demand for meals is rapidly outpacing the supply of funding. Thus, many of the more than 4,000 nonprofit agencies in the United States that participate in Meals on Wheels programs have turned to entrepreneurial ventures for the additional funds needed to serve tens of thousands of needy and infirm elderly people.

Many other nonprofits have run for-profit enterprises for years, but Meals on Wheels is a comparative newcomer to catching the entrepreneurial spirit. A group of small MOWAA charities are pursuing entrepreneurial sources of funding, such as selling gourmet foods at retail. However, not everyone is pleased with this ap-

proach. Customers and donors do not always approve of their charity becoming an entrepreneurship; they believe it should not behave like a business. Other service organizations may feel threatened if Meals on Wheels suddenly expands beyond its existing service area, or begins to promote a product for profit. From the perspective of Meals on Wheels personnel, they must decide who among their applicants are the poorest and most infirm. These individuals will get the meals, but those who are less needy (but still hungry), will have to wait. Finally, making the leap from nonprofit to for-profit ventures "takes a level of staffing and sophistication that hasn't been there," according to Connie Benton Wolfe, executive director of the National Meals on Wheels Foundation in Iowa City, Iowa. According to Harvard Business School professor, James Austin, who studies the blurring between nonprofit and for-profit enterprises, "Most new businesses fail ... Finding a nice new source of revenue is far from guaranteed."

As Bob Pratt, chief executive of Volunteers of America in Los Angeles, California, said "We can see the handwriting on the wall. . . . The 35 million elderly today are going to turn into 70 million elderly by 2030, and there's very little provision in public policy or philanthropy for this population. We're going to have to find ways to be more self-sufficient." During an economic slowdown, Mr. Pratt's group, which has delivered meals to the needy since the 1950s, must contend with a drop in both corporate and individual contributions. As a result, charities are scrambling to develop their own income streams. Some have entered the catering business; others are selling gourmet foods through grocery stores. MOWAA's national foundation offers seminars on how to develop so-called private pay programs. If people who can afford to pay for home-delivered meals can pay all or part of the cost, agencies hope they will have enough money to deliver more meals to those who cannot pay.

Marketing initiatives include promotional activities such as the billboards and bumper stickers used by Senior Resource Connection, a local nonprofit in Dayton, Ohio. The message, "Now's the time to tell your parents to eat their vegetables," is targeted toward encouraging adult children to buy the agency's paid-meal service for elderly relatives. Targeting the right market segments with marketing messages is a challenge for nonprofit as well as for-profit enterprises. The Metropolitan Inter-Faith Association in Memphis, Tennessee delivers meals to about 1,500 people each day—but still has a waiting list of over 100 individuals. The agency launched a marketing program to expand their fee-for-service program so that they might serve more of the people on their waiting list. Dianne Polly, the group's program executive of meals and elder outreach said, "... we've decided that adult children are probably the group to target—but we're not finding them. ... Nobody lives in the same town anymore. I mean, my mom lives in Nebraska. Who would know to contact me? And you could sell me on this really easily."

Other ways to increase the amount of funding available for free-meal programs include taking a more businesslike approach to monitoring finances. For example, Senior Resource Center in Montgomery County, Ohio bought a new computer program in the mid-1990s that they used to track funding sources and costs of meals. Chuck Sousa, director of nutrition and service development for the agency, said, "Before that, we didn't really know what a meal cost." About the same time, some customers expressed a willingness to pay for the meal service—some out of pride and others to avoid being put on a waiting list. Within a year, Senior Resource Center was delivering 100 paid meals a month. When the agency aimed a billboard campaign at commuters the following year with messages such as 'Aging parents? We can help,' the number of paid meals increased tenfold to 1,002 meals a month the following year. Mr. Sousa made changes in response to an increase in paying customers, including better

quality serving trays to replace the foil plates that let the food all run together, creating more appetizing menus, and providing customer service training for his staff (e.g., answering the phone politely). In regard to customer service, Mr. Sousa said, "Not-for-profits tend to be like the motor-vehicles office, thinking we're the only one in town, so it doesn't matter how we treat you." As a result of these changes, Senior Resource served 42,240 paid meals at $4.65 each during the year, yielding a profit of approximately $78,500. With this money, the agency subsidized meals for about 60 additional people for a year, shortening the agency's waiting list by half.

Volunteers of America of Los Angeles found several sources that were willing to help with its entrepreneurial ventures. In the late 1990s donors gave the agency $800,000 to launch a gourmet line of fresh soups with the name "La Voa." Young culinary arts students provided the labor; local industrial design students designed striking teal-blue cartons; and major food companies such as Nestle U.S.A. and others provided free professional advice. As of 2001, the venture was not yet profitable, but Volunteers of America continues its quest for profitability. Since soup sells better in the cooler months, the agency developed new entrees to accompany the soups, and asked celebrity chefs such as Julia Child to endorse them. To make better use of its capacity, Volunteers of America of Los Angeles uses its large kitchen, free labor, and expensive vacuum-packing equipment to make and package a line of gourmet pet food under the "Brando's Supper Club" brand. (The agency also provides a companion pet program for seniors with delivery of free or discounted pet food, along with other pet-related services, to help low-income senior citizens keep their pets.)

The number of elderly Americans will continue to grow rapidly over the next several decades, spurred by aging Baby Boomers. Many of these individuals will be among the poor and infirm who will rely on nonprofit agencies (private and government) for their daily meals. (See Exhibit 1: Projected Noninstitutional Population 65+ Years With ADL Limitations.)

As Ms. Benton Wolfe of the National Meals on Wheels Foundation said, "People assume that Meals on Wheels is an entitlement, and it will always be there when they need it. ... They are surprised when they find out there are limitations." Meals on Wheels and its many nonprofit partners such as Volunteers of America of Los Angeles are struggling to overcome these limitations so that they may fulfill their mission to feed the needy.

Source: Kelly Greene, "Meals on Wheels Tries For-Profit Tactics to Grow," *Wall Street Journal* (April 25, 2001), pp. B1, B6; Volunteers of America Greater Los Angeles, www.voala.org; Meals on Wheels Association of America, www.projectmeal.org; Seniors First, Orlando, Florida, www.seniorsfirst.org; U.S. Department of Health and Human Services, Administration on Aging, www.aoa.dhhs.gov/aoa; U.S. Bureau of the Census, www.census.gov.

Case Study Questions

1. Discuss the pros and cons of entrepreneurship ventures by nonprofit agencies such as Meals on Wheels and Volunteers of America. Consider the perspectives of the organization's personnel, customers/clients, donors, and volunteers.

2. Contact a Meals on Wheels program in your community and determine the various services that it offers to elderly people, and how it interacts with other social services agencies to provide necessary services.

3. Describe a typical service design for a Meals on Wheels program based on either an interview with a volunteer or agency executive, or on your own idea of how this should operate to achieve the agency's mission. If possible, create a blueprint of this process and identify potential failure points and gaps in service quality.

4. Define and evaluate the primary and ancillary services provided by Volunteers of America of Los Angeles. Evaluate the "fit" of these services with the agency's mission statement. Also analyze the present and future potential of VOA's gourmet food products. What are your recommendations for improving profitability?

5. Outline the history of today's elderly nutrition programs and MOWAA in the United States since its inception. Now write a short scenario of how you believe MOWAA should carry out its service activities in the future. (See www.projectmeal.org.)

6. Describe the elderly nutrition program sponsored by the U.S. Administration on Aging. (See www.aoa.gov.) What is the role of the private and public sectors in providing nutrition programs for America's aging population?

7. (Optional.) Log on to www.aoa.dhhs.gov/aoa/stats and determine the underlying assumptions for population projections by age for the elderly from 1995 to 2050.

EXHIBIT 3

Projected Noninstitutional Population 65 Years and Over with ADL[1] Limitations

| Year | Number (000) | | Percent of Population[2] | |
	Total With ADL Limitations	Severely Disabled	Total With ADL Limitations	Severely Disabled
1990	6029	1123	18.8	3.5
1995	6712	1265	19.3	3.6
2000	7262	1384	20	3.8
2020	10118	1927	19.2	3.7
2040	14416	2806	21.4	4.2

[1]Individuals with limitations in performing the usual Activities of Daily Living (ADL).
[2]Base also includes institutional population.
Source: U.S. Department of Health and Human Services, Administration on Aging, "Projected Health Conditions Among the Elderly," Table 19—Projections of the Noninstitutional Population 65 Years and Over with ADL Limitations: 1990 to 2040, www.aoa.dhhs.gov/aoa/stats.

CHAPTER 10

Distribution Strategy

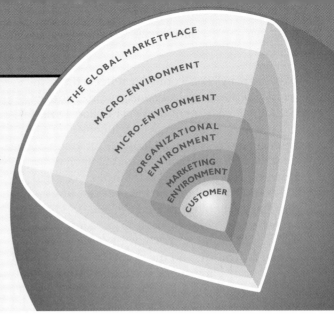

THE GLOBAL MARKETPLACE
MACRO-ENVIRONMENT
MICRO-ENVIRONMENT
ORGANIZATIONAL ENVIRONMENT
MARKETING ENVIRONMENT
CUSTOMER

Overview

Can you sell a product on Tuesday and have it back on the shelf by Wednesday? If your answer is no, then you should be determining now how to make this type of replenishment part of your supply system; otherwise, you are not following the trends of the current leaders.[1]

Managing Distribution: UPS Delivers More Than Packages

UPS used to be the guys who just shipped your stuff. Now they want to be the guys who handle your e-commerce, your warehousing, your logistics, your customer service, and your repair work. And *then* ship your stuff.

Erick Schonfeld, www.ecompany.com (June 2001, p. 91)

The unobtrusive brown vehicles of United Parcel Service, Inc. (UPS) are a familiar sight as they deliver nearly 14 million packages each day throughout the United States and 200 other countries and territories. To deliver these packages, UPS uses a fleet of approximately 80,000 delivery trucks, 240 planes,* 3,200 vans, 12,000 tractor rigs and 73,000 trailers, 429 motorcycles/motor scooters, 5 delivery boats, and 150 other vehicles.† In 2002, the 95-year-old company had 371,000 employees, $30.7 billion in sales, and $2.4 billion in net income. UPS is the world's number one package delivery company, leading in ground-delivery business and gaining on rival FedEx in air delivery. It also competes for package delivery customers with Deutsche Post and its subsidiary DHL, along with smaller competitors throughout the world.

UPS vice chairman Mike Eskew says, "You think you are talking to a trucking company," [but in fact] "you are talking to a technol-

---

* Does not include 384 aircraft leased by UPS.
† "Other vehicles" include bicycles and golf carts; does not include mules, horses, or sleds that are sometimes used to reach remote destinations.

ogy company." This comment reflects the company's corporate strategy and culture. For over a decade, UPS has spent nearly $1 billion a year on information technology, which it considers a key strategic asset. The initial impetus for emphasizing infotech was to streamline internal operations. However, this fortunate decision also prepared the company well for the Internet age. Investments in technology helped UPS nearly double its operating margins from 8 to 15 percent, and boosted sales and profits over the long run. (Economic downturns and the events of September 11 had a negative impact on the entire industry.)

UPS offered package tracking on the Internet in 1995, and found that customers were eager to check the status of their packages themselves. Four million people a day tracked their packages on UPS' Web site in 2001, a significant increase from the 600,000 people who inquired by phone 5 years before. This success led to the establishment of an e-commerce sales force (e-commerce account managers or eCAMs) whose task is to convince business customers to integrate UPS's package-shipment data into their Web sites. In 2001, over 60,000 corporate customers had downloaded the tools provided by UPS.

Additional growth is expected to come from international expansion and from recent acquisitions, such as Mail Boxes Etc. and freight forwarding companies. However, the major thrust for growth beyond the core package delivery business lies in managing complete logistical and supply chain operations for corporations. UPS Logistics, UPS Consulting, eVentures (launched to develop operations supporting e-commerce), and UPS Capital Corporation provide support for managing the "endless loop of goods, information, and capital that all those packages represent." In recent years, UPS has increasingly placed itself at the center of each logistical step in its corporate clients' operations—starting with the shipping of raw materials from suppliers to manufacturers or producers, to ultimately processing the payment for a product's final sale. UPS can help its clients reduce expenses, increase margins, manage their supply chain, store their goods, repair their products, and answer their phones—"a United Parcel Service that places as much emphasis on the service as it does on the parcels." Merrill Lynch estimated that 25 percent of UPS's earn-

ings would come from non-package businesses between 2000 and 2002.

UPS Logistics

UPS Logistics was formed in 1995 as a subsidiary to sell logistics management expertise to other companies. The impetus came from the rise of the Internet and a growing need for technological supply-chain assistance. UPS Logistics CEO, Dan DiMaggio, says the root of supply chain inefficiency is a lack of information—and as supply chains become increasingly complex, it is more attractive to outsource management of the logistics function. UPS Logistics is headquartered in Atlanta, but has facilities around the world. The services provided for its customers range from computer-based systems that may be used for routing and truck loading, or dedicated fleets (some require special equipment) that deliver all types of goods. For example, they deliver supplies to Papa John's Pizza, with the schedule based in part on how fast pizza dough rises during transit.

UPS Logistics takes care of the full order completion process for companies such as Nike's e-business, Nike.com. UPS receives and stocks the inventory of shoes and clothing in UPS's warehouse in Louisville, then ships the goods to customers as instructed by Nike. Finally, they act as Nike's service representatives if a customer calls because the shoes do not fit, or must be returned for credit or exchange.

UPS Logistics also takes delivery of domestic and imported goods, and ships them on to the next link in the supply chain in North America and overseas. The group also maintains parts warehouses for clients, with the largest located at its 550-acre distribution hub in Louisville. Delivery and repair services (particularly for items such as computers and printers) are provided for corporate clients from these locations.

UPS Logistics made an agreement with Ford Motor Co. to manage the transportation and distribution of 4.5 million vehicles a year. One problem tackled by UPS Logistics was the need to reduce the number of days between the time a vehicle rolls out of an assembly plant and is taken off the car-carrier truck at a dealer. Ford's cars and trucks have a high unit value, and no delivery system is quite as complicated, making it imperative to know where the vehicles are at all times.

Twenty-one different manufacturing sites in the United States and Canada produce Ford, Mercury, and Lincoln automobiles and trucks that are hauled by truck or rail to "intermodal consolidation" railroad yards, sorted according to destination, and moved by train or truck to 55 destination railroad ramps around North America, where haul-away rigs are ready to take the vehicles on to 6,000 American dealers. As Eskew says, "While that may sound like a large network to a lot of people, that sounds like a small one to us." For a company that handles 13 million packages a day, 4.5 million cars and trucks do not seem overwhelming to UPS.

Before working with UPS Logistics, Ford knew what was happening at each end of the delivery network, but did not have accurate information about where the vehicles were between the assembly plant and dealership, or when they would be delivered to their destination. Ford was unable to integrate the railroad and trucking company computer systems with its own systems, or to get accurate delivery information to its dealers.

Within 6 months, UPS and Ford employees, together with the factories, railroaders, and truckers at the consolidation and destination ramps, gathered the necessary data and developed a system that can locate a vehicle anytime by its vehicle identification number (VIN). The system, which can cut delivery times by an estimated 40 percent, and typically by 6 days, has been extended to dealers so they can track incoming deliveries. Individual customers also have the capability to track a vehicle ordered from Ford, much the same way they track a UPS shipment.

In 2000, the UPS Logistics Group contributed approximately $1 billion to company revenues, by having timely and accurate information available to shorten delivery times. For example, a dealer who needs a new red Mustang can go online to locate one. In 2001, UPS Logistics' program reduced that Mustang's transit time from 16 days to 12, freed up idle inventory valued at $1 billion, and saved $125 million in annual inventory carrying costs.

Sources: Erick Schonfeld, "The Total Package," *www.ecompany.com Magazine* (June 2001), pp. 90–97; www.ups.com; Philip Siekman, "New Victories In the Supply-Chain Revolution," *Fortune,* www.fortune.com (October 30, 2000); "United Parcel Service, Inc.," *Hoovers Online,* www.hoovers.com (November 11, 2002).

Goods and services can be produced, priced, and promoted effectively—but until they are moved through a distribution system from their source to the final customer, no sales will occur. Poierier and Reiter have stressed the importance of efficient distribution channels to the point of saying that there will soon be a time when every customer purchase will be tracked immediately by all the key players in the distribution network. This means that when a customer buys a box of cereal, pertinent data will be provided simultaneously to every member in the distribution channel—to the farming system that harvests the crops, to the breakfast cereal manufacturer, as well as to the grocery store where the cereal was bought.[2]

DISTRIBUTION CHANNELS: AN OVERVIEW

Channel of distribution
A channel of distribution is an interdependent network of retailers, wholesalers, distributors, and agents who are responsible for moving a good or service from its point of origin to the final customer.

A **channel of distribution** is an interdependent network of retailers, wholesalers, distributors, and agents who are responsible for moving a good or service from its point of origin to the final customer. The distribution channel may consist of one buyer and one seller (direct channel); or it may be made up of multiple buyers and sellers at different levels (e.g., wholesale, retail). Marketing channels also include communication channels and service channels that are designed to facilitate transactions. The importance of the distribution function in marketing is apparent when one considers the magnitude of goods and services that are transported and sold at millions of locations throughout the world. The economic impact of distribution is shown in Tables 10.1 and 10.2 for wholesaling and retailing activities in the United States. Other marketing, manufacturing, and physical distribution functions also contribute to the total economic effect of the distributive process.

Many experts believe that the distribution decision is the most important marketing decision a company can make. The design of an organization's distribution system is a key factor in creating customer value and in differentiating one company's offering from that of another. For example, CarMax, a power retailer in the automotive industry, offers its customers a wide assortment of brands and models from its car lots and over the Internet.

The field of distribution is made up of two distinct branches: channels of distribution and physical distribution.[3] *Channels of distribution* consist of a network of intermediaries that manages a flow of goods and services from the producer to the final customer. The success of this network depends on relationships among manufacturers, wholesalers, retailers, sales representatives, and others. As products move from one intermediary to the next, exchange takes place—exchange of physical goods, intangible services, and value-added dimensions. Marketing activities are performed at each stage.

Physical distribution
Movement of goods and services (logistics) with a focus on transporting and warehousing them through the supply chain.

Physical distribution activities include the actual movement of goods and services (i.e., logistics), with a focus on transporting and warehousing them. Together the channels and physical-distribution functions comprise a comprehensive supply chain that starts with the supplier's suppliers, that is, the materials, parts, and other supplies needed to grow, produce, or manufacture a finished product, as shown in Figure 10.1.[4]

The movement of goods and services can be costly and inefficient, threatening customer satisfaction and profitability. Companies that provide convenience or lower prices through creative distribution solutions have a distinct competitive advantage. Both low-cost and differentiation strategies are achieved through efficient and innovative designs of inbound and outbound logistics, starting with suppliers of the first incoming materials to the supply chain. Automotive manufacturers, such as Ford Motor Co., develop strategic partnerships with suppliers to maintain the lowest possible price structure throughout the whole process. Likewise, wholesale and retail outlets should be selected for both efficiency and effectiveness. Efficient operations use assets advantageously to achieve competitive advantage (regardless of pricing strategy to customers). Effective outlets deliver the most customer value and satisfaction.

Relationship to Organizational and Marketing Strategies

Distribution strategies are concerned with having the right product in the right place at the right time. Marketing strategies are concerned with product-market decisions—which customers to serve and which customer needs to fulfill. The design of a distribution channel is a long-term strategic decision that is difficult to change,

TABLE 10.1

Impact of Wholesaling on the U.S. Economy (1997)

NAICS[1]		Sales ($1,000)	Establishments[2]	Paid Employees
42	**Wholesale trade, total**	**4,059,657,778**	**453,470**	**5,796,557**
421	**Wholesale trade, durable goods, total**	**2,179,717,376**	**290,629**	**3,398,261**
4211	Motor vehicles and motor vehicle parts and supplies	533,352,124	29,328	375,731
4214	Professional and commercial equipment and supplies	367,383,550	45,351	716,113
4216	Electrical goods	357,691,888	38,234	475,766
4218	Machinery, equipment, and supplies	328,968,331	76,643	772,550
4215	Metals and minerals, except petroleum	150,493,610	12,583	174,029
4217	Hardware, and plumbing and heating equipment and supplies	92,189,762	21,194	219,233
4213	Lumber and other construction materials	89,175,875	14,267	155,535
4212	Furniture and home furnishings	75,006,478	15,246	157,465
4219	Miscellaneous durable goods	185,455,758	37,783	351,839
422	**Wholesale trade, nondurable goods, total**	**1,879,940,402**	**162,841**	**2,398,296**
4224	Groceries and related products	588,970,062	41,760	854,919
4227	Petroleum and petroleum products	267,623,942	11,297	137,829
4222	Drugs, drug proprietaries, and druggists' sundries	203,147,771	8,053	190,127
4225	Farm-product raw materials	166,786,245	10,343	97,521
4226	Chemicals and allied products	128,923,496	15,920	165,768
4223	Apparel, piece goods, and notions	124,104,420	20,707	207,574
4221	Paper and paper products	117,062,485	15,848	214,350
4228	Beer, wine, and distilled alcoholic beverages	69,703,203	4,850	151,677
4229	Miscellaneous nondurable goods	213,618,778	34,063	378,531

[1]North American Industrial Classification System 1997 basis.
[2]Table includes only establishments with payroll; nonemployers are not included.
Source: 1997 Economic Census: Wholesale Trade United States, U.S. Census Bureau, Washington, D.C., 1997.

TABLE 10.2

Impact of Retailing on the U.S. Economy (1997)

NAICS[1]		Sales ($1,000)	Establishments[2]	Paid Employees
44–45	**Retail trade, total**	**2,460,886,012**	**1,118,447**	**13,991,103**
441	Motor vehicle and parts dealers	645,367,776	122,633	1,718,963
445	Food and beverage stores	401,764,499	148,528	2,893,074
452	General merchandise stores	330,444,460	36,171	2,507,540
444	Building material and garden equipment	227,566,101	93,117	1,117,912
447	Gasoline stations	198,165,786	126,889	922,062
448	Clothing and clothing accessories stores	136,397,645	156,601	1,280,153
446	Health and personal care stores	117,700,863	82,941	903,694
442	Furniture and home furnishings stores	71,690,813	64,725	482,845
443	Electronics and appliance stores	68,561,331	43,373	345,042
451	Sporting goods, hobby, book and music stores	62,010,926	69,149	560,839
453	Miscellaneous store retailers	78,109,161	129,838	752,986
454	Nonstore retailers	123,106,651	44,482	505,993

[1]North American Industrial Classification System 1997 basis.
[2]Table includes only establishments with payroll; nonemployer firms are not included.
Source: 1997 Economic Census: Retail Trade United States, U.S. Census Bureau, Washington, D.C., 1997.

FIGURE 10.1

Supply Chain

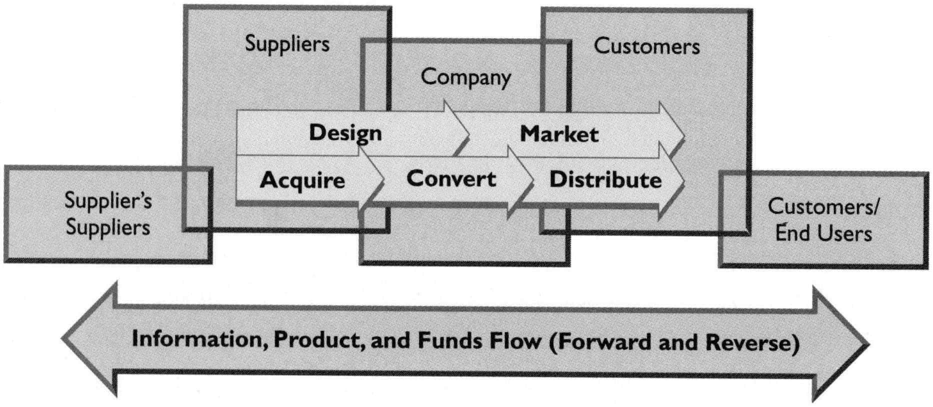

Source: Reprinted with permission of the publisher. From *Supply Chain Optimization.* Copyright © 1996 by Charles C. Poirier and Stephen E. Reiter, Berrett-Koehler Publishers, Inc., San Francisco, CA. All rights reserved. 1-800-929-2929.

requiring careful attention to the selection of channel intermediaries and their ability to add customer value and contribute to the marketer's strategic goals. For instance, IBM chooses distributors that reach its customers most effectively and other intermediaries that add value to the distributive process (e.g., FedEx).

The distribution decision interacts synergistically with product, promotion, and pricing decisions to achieve strategic organizational objectives. The customer is at the center of this integrated process, consistent with the marketing concept. Computerization and automation help achieve the marketer's strategic intent through better inventory management and more efficient distribution systems and facilities.

Need for Channel Intermediaries

If consumers and organizational customers bought each product directly from its original source, the number of contacts required would be cumbersome and inefficient. Stern and El-Ansary identified four reasons for the emergence and arrangement of distribution-oriented **intermediaries.**[5]

Intermediaries
Retailers, wholesalers, and others responsible for the functions involved in moving goods and services from the producer or manufacturer to the final customer.

1. *Intermediaries arise in the exchange process because they make the process more efficient.* As shown in Figure 10.2, without retailers, each final consumer would have to deal directly with each manufacturer, making the process more complex. This basic form of distribution exists in primitive cultures where households exchange excess production with one another.

2. *Intermediaries arise to overcome the discrepancy between the assortment of goods and services generated by the producer and the assortment demanded by the consumer.* Figure 10.2 shows that the addition of wholesalers minimizes the number of contacts between each manufacturer and retailer. Generally, manufacturers produce large quantities of a few goods, and consumers want a small quantity of a wide variety of goods, creating a need for the following activities:

   - *Sorting out.* For example, grading lumber into broad categories for sale: construction lumber, pattern lumber, and specialty products; then sorting by type, size, closeness, strength, and characteristics that affect the appearance and use of the lumber.

   - *Accumulation.* Gathering similar stocks of goods from multiple sources to create one larger homogeneous supply; for example, a pharmaceutical wholesaler accumulates health-related products from numerous manufacturers to provide a complete line of diverse goods to a drug store.

   - *Allocation.* Breaking a large homogeneous supply into smaller lots; for example, a tire wholesaler divides carload lots of automobile tires into smaller quantities for small auto repair shops.

   - *Assorting.* Building up an assortment of products for resale to the next level of customers; for example, a grocery wholesaler buys many types of products from many producers (e.g., cereal, cleaning supplies, produce, beverages) to provide a complete assortment to a grocery store.

3. *Marketing agencies work together in channel arrangements to routinize transactions.* Each purchase includes ordering, valuing the product, and pay-

FIGURE 10.2

The Role of Channel Intermediaries

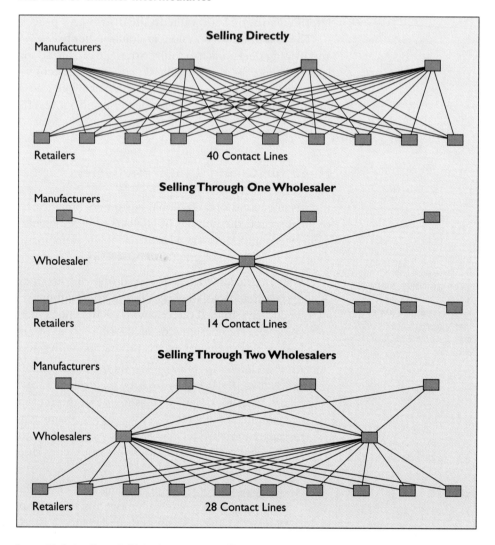

Source: *Marketing Channels,* 3/e by Stern/El-Ansary, © 1996. Reprinted by permission of Prentice-Hall, Inc., Upper Saddle River, NJ.

ment. Some standardized procedures, such as methods of payment, shipping, and communication, are used to overcome the need to bargain in each new situation.

4. *Channels facilitate the search process at all levels.* Manufacturers, wholesalers, and retailers often lack information about customers' wants and needs, and customers often have difficulty finding products to satisfy these needs. Relationships among channel intermediaries make the search process easier. Retailers and wholesalers are organized into industry groups by type of product

FIGURE 10.3

Functions Performed by Distribution Systems

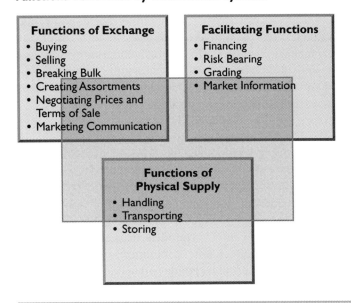

or business format (e.g., department store, auto parts, electronics). Suppliers tend to be geographically concentrated to decrease delivery time and facilitate comparison shopping. Centralized merchandise marts (e.g., Chicago, Atlanta) bring together retail buyers, manufacturers, and wholesalers. Furniture manufacturers are concentrated in North Carolina, software developers in Silicon Valley, and retail malls offer consumers one-stop shopping.

Functions Performed by Distribution Systems

Critical distributive functions that move suppliers and customers closer together include *exchange, physical supply,* and *facilitating activities.* (See Figure 10.3.) The question is not whether these functions will be performed, but rather who will perform them better than the supplier.

Functions of Exchange.   The exchange function represents the gamut of activities that enter into a transaction: *buying and selling, breaking bulk and creating assortments, negotiating prices and terms of sale,* and *marketing communication.* All channel intermediaries use their expertise to match product assortments to the needs of the next level in the channel. They provide information about products and customers—a two-way communication process.

Functions of Physical Supply.   Physical supply involves *handling, transporting,* and *storing* materials. Raw materials and parts suppliers move products to manufacturers, who deliver them to wholesalers, retailers, consumers, or organizational customers. Each level of distribution takes responsibility for receiving and sending goods to the next level, storing inventories where it is most efficient.

Facilitating Activities. All channel participants need the assistance of other organizations to complete their tasks. Experts inside or outside a firm may perform facilitating activities. The major facilitating functions include *financing* (credit, loans), *risk bearing* (hold inventory, title transfer), *grading* (standardizing assortments), *market information* (formal and informal research), and *management services* (consulting, technology, etc.).

● CHANNEL STRUCTURES AND MARKETING SYSTEMS

The distribution system is composed of channel intermediaries (wholesalers, retailers, and other merchants or agents) that provide a link between producers[6] and the final customer. The ideal marketing system uses channels that maximize efficiency and effectiveness, minimize costs, and deliver the greatest customer satisfaction. In addition to goods and services, channel members exchange payment, information, titles, and ownership. Channels are structured differently for consumer and organizational goods because of the nature of transactions and customer needs.

Consumer Marketing Channels

There are four basic producer-to-consumer channel alternatives, as shown in Figure 10.4. The longest, most indirect channel (D) includes the producer, one or more wholesalers or agents, retailers, and consumers. This channel is most appropriate when the producer's objective is to achieve maximum market penetration with intensive distribution. Marketers of frequently purchased products (e.g., snack foods, office supplies) use indirect channels to reach the greatest number of customers where they are located.

The shortest channel (A), from producer to customer, offers the most direct and quickest distribution route because no intermediaries are involved. It is the easiest to manage and control (e.g., Lands' End catalogs, Tupperware's direct salesforce). Technological advances and customers' time concerns have increased the popularity of the Internet, interactive cable, and other time-saving, no-hassle direct selling methods.

Organizational Marketing Channels

Recall that organizational customers include both for-profit and nonprofit entities that produce other goods and services for distribution to final customers. The traditional marketing channels used by industrial firms, manufacturers, growers, and other organizational buyers and suppliers, shown in Figure 10.5, can be adapted to the needs of nonprofit organizations (e.g., the American Cancer Society) and government agencies (Social Security Administration).

FIGURE 10.4

Alternative Distribution Channels for Consumer Goods

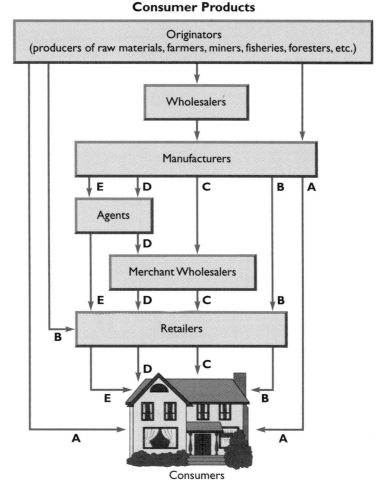

Consumer Products

Source: Hiam & Schewe, *Portable MBA in Marketing,* NY: John Wiley & Sons, 1992, p. 329. Copyright © 1992 by John Wiley & Sons. This material is used by permission of John Wiley & Sons, Inc.

The most direct channel (F) is from producers to organizational customers (e.g., auto parts manufacturer to automobile manufacturer). Many industrial products require personal selling by a knowledgeable salesforce, particularly when a high level of customization is needed (e.g., high-tech applications, unique production equipment).

The most extensive channel (H) might involve a logging company that cuts logs and ships them to a sawmill to be made into lumber and graded for furniture quality. The lumber is passed along to an industrial distributor or agent for sale to a furniture manufacturer, who in turn distributes the finished products through wholesalers, agents, or retailers to final customers. Obviously, it would be inefficient

FIGURE 10.5

Alternative Distribution Channels for Organizational Goods

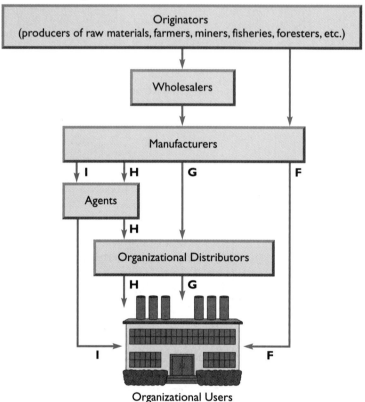

Source: Adapted from Hiam & Schewe, *Portable MBA in Marketing,* NY: John Wiley & Sons, 1992, p. 331. Copyright © 1992 by John Wiley & Sons, Inc. This material is used by permission of John Wiley & Sons, Inc.

for the furniture manufacturer to grow the forest and complete all the premanufacturing distribution activities.

Multiple Channels

Many consumer and organizational product marketers use multiple distribution channels. For example, suppliers of motor parts may distribute directly to washing machine manufacturers, indirectly to appliance repair companies through wholesalers, and to final consumers through do-it-yourself hardware stores and catalogs. Direct channels are more effective and efficient for selling to large customers, and indirect channels are more suitable for intensive distribution to large numbers of smaller customers.

Hershey Foods Corp.'s traditional distribution strategy focused on grocery store sales and seasonal bagged items. Hershey maintained leadership in the U.S. candy market for many years, with 30 percent market share in 2002. When Rick Lenny became Hershey's CEO in 2001, he recognized that advertising and new product development needed to be revitalized for the brand to reach its potential. The confectionary market was faced with increasing competition, declining growth rate, and other competition from candy-like snack items marketed by food company rivals.

Hershey was overly dependent on its large bags of Hershey's Kisses, Reese's Mini-Cups, and other items packaged for the holidays, while competitors focused on more profitable single impulse-type items. Lenny, formerly with Kraft and Nabisco, saw an opportunity to improve performance by focusing on a few top brands, following the Kraft style of power brand management. Changes were made in personnel, structure, and strategies to support new product and distribution decisions. Hershey's new distribution strategy emphasized convenience stores such as 7-Eleven Inc. and "single-serve" candy items. During the spring 2002 Easter holiday season, 7-Eleven managers estimated that Hershey's new distribution strategy resulted in as much as 200 percent increase in candy sales in their stores.

Pursuit of multiple channels may require multiple marketing approaches. For example, Hershey continues to sell its large packages of chocolate candies in grocery stores, drug stores, mass merchandisers, and elsewhere, but has adapted its product and packaging to be more competitive in the convenience store channel. Single candy bars (or small packages) are higher priced, highly profitable, fast-selling impulse items in these high-traffic, high-margin stores. Advertising had to support the convenience store channel and "single-serve" candy items, by boosting its TV advertising profile, and returning to movie tie-ins such as those with "E.T." and "Spider-Man." Hershey expanded its multiple channel strategy further late in 2002 with a 2,500-square-foot retail store in New York's Times Square. The 150-foot-tall structure retails Hershey's confections—everything from Kisses to Jolly Rancher candies, directly to consumers.[7]

International Channels

International channel decisions are related to market-entry strategies and legal and political constraints. A U.S. manufacturer can approach direct distribution in two ways: sell U.S.-made goods directly to an overseas customer or produce goods in the foreign country and sell directly to targeted customers. (See Figure 10.6.) This strategy requires an alliance with a foreign business or government that enables the firm to produce and sell its goods and services in that market. The major American automobile manufacturers establish manufacturing and/or assembly plants overseas to bring their products closer to consumers. Non-U.S. automobile makers manufacture automobiles in the United States to create a shorter distribution channel to American consumers. Manufacturing in a foreign country also may require the establishment of regional supply networks to complete the supply chain.

Longer channels require a broader view of the total distribution process. International distribution typically starts with the manufacturer and its exporting organization (internal or external) within its own country and ends with the final

FIGURE 10.6

International Channels of Distribution

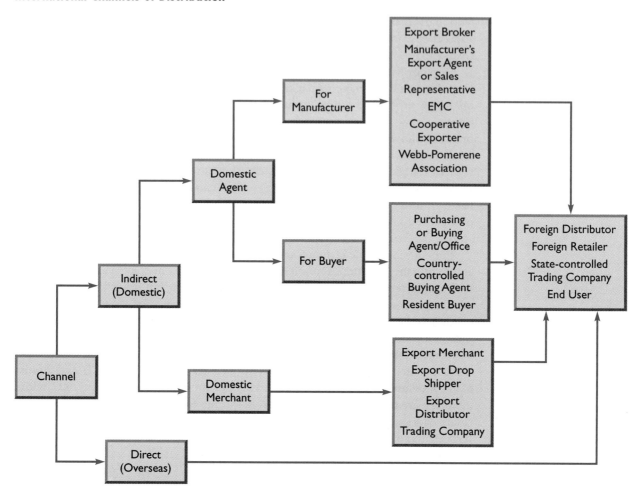

Source: International Marketing, 3/e, by Onkvist et al. © 1997. Reprinted by permission of Prentice-Hall, Inc., Upper Saddle River, NJ.

foreign customer. In between are the various middlemen (e.g., wholesalers, agents, retailers) and other intermediaries such as physical distribution companies, freight forwarders, marketing experts, and financial and risk insurance providers. The longer the channel, the less control any one member can exercise over others.

Overseas distribution may include an unorthodox channel. For instance, hundreds of neighborhood "gasboys" use their pickup trucks to deliver canisters of gas, widely used as cooking fuel, to large numbers of customers in areas such as the suburbs of São Paulo, Brazil. The gas-balloon deliveryman, as he is called, is a trusted community member who has excellent rapport with his customers. For this reason, he is central to the marketing efforts of multinational companies in Brazil. They find him to be "an extremely valuable tool" when they want to introduce new products to this population. This distribution channel has been used by

Nestlé to distribute packets of Nestlé flavoring, Johnson floor wax, and Procter & Gamble and Unilever laundry detergents to thousands of households.

In Brazil, stoves are operated with gas rather than electricity, making the "gas balloon" a kitchen fixture. One company, Ultragaz SA, distributes gas to about 18 million households each month—about 15 percent of all Brazilian homes. The company has national market coverage and an extensive database. This makes their sales people an attractive means for testing food, household goods, and toiletries on a mass scale or to target more narrowly defined consumers by income group or geographical area. Brazil's gas deliverymen usually serve the same district for several years and gain the trust of entire communities. They are trusted and welcome in their customers' homes. Hanno Ponder, president of Sara Lee Corp.'s personal-care division in Brazil said, "These guys go into people's homes. . . . They get our product right into the hands of consumers."

Ultragaz started product samplings for multinationals in 1995, charging just five cents to deliver each unit of a product with its existing staff, and the deliverymen are not paid extra. The service is viewed as a way to improve relationships with customers by giving them presents. The gas-balloon delivery system does not work in Brazil's largest cities where more households, particularly in high-rise apartment buildings, use piped gas. It is not useful to reach highest income consumers—but multinational marketers find it very effective in the areas served by Ultragaz. While the channel provided by neighborhood gasboys is used primarily as a sampling strategy within a larger promotional strategy, it provides important support for the company's overall distribution strategy.[8]

International distribution affects nearly every company, regardless of its involvement in importing or exporting. As suppliers extend their distribution overseas, they are faced with more complex and costly channel decisions, longer lead times, and problematic cultural differences among channel members.[9] These issues are counterbalanced by growth opportunities in a global marketplace. For example, upscale jeweler Tiffany & Co. entered the Japanese market in 1972 as a wholesaler. Tiffany remained a small player until the "bubble economy" of the 1980s increased the popularity of foreign luxury brands. However, Tiffany's retailer, Mitsukoshi Ltd., continued to promote more moderately priced items, leading Tiffany to open its own boutiques in 1993 and more department store outlets. Japanese consumers continued to buy expensive jewelry during the 1998 economic crisis, supporting Tiffany's decision to continue to open new shops to fill the demand for luxury goods in Japan's $25 billion a year jewelry market. Tiffany renewed its Japan distribution arrangement with Mitsukoshi Ltd. in 2001. Twenty-seven of the 47 Tiffany & Co. selling locations in Japan are operated as boutiques in Mitsukoshi stores. In fiscal years 1998, 1999, and 2000, more than one fourth of Tiffany's company-wide sales came from its Japanese stores and boutiques.[10]

● CHANNEL MEMBERS

Wholesalers and retailers, the keys to most distribution strategies, provide the focus of this section. Manufacturers (and their suppliers), physical distribution providers, and other facilitators also are an integral part of the distribution system. The role played by each channel member and major types, strategies, and trends within each group are discussed next.

Wholesalers

Wholesalers
Buy inventories from one business and sell to another to provide a link between two or more producers or intermediaries.

Wholesalers buy inventories from one business and sell to another to provide a link between two or more producers or intermediaries. They may or may not take physical possession of goods. Wholesalers are adapting to a changing environment to remain viable as major channel players, although many marketing firms have eliminated the middleman by performing the distribution function themselves. Few consumers are aware of the many services performed by wholesalers to simplify their purchases and of the impact of this diverse sector on the U.S. economy. Wholesaling involves about 453,470 firms, employs nearly 6 million people, and sells over $4 trillion in manufactured products and raw materials. (See Table 10.1.)[11]

The three major types of wholesalers are manufacturers' sales branches and offices, agent middlemen (agents and brokers), and merchant wholesalers. The most direct and least complex wholesaler arrangement is through manufacturer-owned sales branches and offices. It is also the most costly and least efficient method.

Manufacturers' Sales Branches and Offices. This type of wholesaling organization is owned and operated by the manufacturer but managed separately from the manufacturer's production facility. Manufacturers' sales representatives sell directly to customers through the company's sales branches. This arrangement allows manufacturers to control the quality of personal selling, promotional activities, and other marketing functions through their own salesforce and to maintain closer control over inventory and production.

Agent Middlemen. Independent sales representatives act as agents and brokers for manufacturers. Agent middlemen generally represent a number of noncompeting lines. They differ from merchant wholesalers in that they sell the manufacturer's goods but do not take title (official ownership). Agents and brokers facilitate exchange by bringing buyers and sellers together and offering limited service to customers, for which they usually receive a commission based on sales. Agent middlemen are important business partners for small manufacturers, usually specializing in a particular type of product or customer and customizing their services to buyers' and suppliers' needs. They also can offer a number of complementary goods to the same geographically concentrated customers.

Merchant Wholesalers. These independently owned businesses represent the greatest proportion of all wholesalers. They are primarily concerned with purchasing goods from one or more suppliers and selling them to other businesses. They take title to the goods they sell and may take possession. Most are "full service" wholesalers that offer a wide range of sales support and facilitating services to suppliers and customers. The primary service provided by wholesaler-distributors is to ensure that the right goods are in the right place, at the right time, and at the right price. Services may include repackaging, help in marketing, financing, technical assistance, and other value-added services.

The major strength of merchant wholesalers is their ability to match the needs of business customers and consumers with the output of diverse manufacturers. Producers find it more cost-effective to use merchant wholesalers to get their products to customers than to maintain their own sales branches and sales representatives. The services provided by merchant wholesalers allow manufacturers to concentrate on production, while channel intermediaries assume responsibility for inventory management and its associated risks.

Role of Wholesalers.   A number of wholesalers perform many distribution functions that otherwise would be performed by channel members that precede or follow them. Wholesalers add value to the distribution process and final cost structure in a number of ways. One of their primary roles is to manage inventory at different phases of the supply chain, including warehousing, transporting, taking ownership and title to goods, quick-response ordering, and other activities. Wholesalers also deal in information services and providing market research, accounting, and inventory data forward and backward in the channels.

Wholesaling Strategies.   Strategies pursued by wholesalers can be explained in part by three major theories of market coverage, consistent with the distribution strategies of other channel intermediaries. Intensive, exclusive, or selective market-coverage patterns refer to the placement and number of distributors that will sell a particular good or service. These theories of market coverage also can be applied to the nonprofit sector (e.g., food banks, bloodmobiles, government services). The desired level of coverage can be accomplished by selling through a series of intermediaries (wholesalers, agents, brokers, retailers). At the retail level, coverage includes store and nonstore formats, direct sales, electronic commerce, and other methods of reaching consumers.

Intensive distribution
When marketer uses every available outlet to reach its customers.

Intensive distribution provides the most comprehensive market coverage. The marketer uses every available outlet to reach its customers. For example, drug wholesalers carry broad assortments of pharmaceuticals and other products that they distribute to drugstores and health care facilities. Convenience stores use an intensive distribution strategy to sell frequently purchased, rapidly consumed, low-involvement products, like soda and snacks, through outlets located near consumers.

Exclusive distribution
When only one or a few distributors are allowed to carry one or more product lines from a supplier.

An **exclusive distribution** strategy is selected when only one or a few distributors are permitted to carry one or more product lines from a supplier. Generally, the goods are perceived to be more upscale, expensive, high-involvement purchases. Their quality image is enhanced or maintained by the distributor's image. Wholesalers and retailers may decide to serve an exclusive clientele (although there are legal limits). This strategy is appropriate for specialty goods where the customer is highly involved in the purchase situation or the product category.

Selective distribution
Limits distribution to a few types of intermediaries or retail outlets.

Selective distribution combines the features of intensive and exclusive distribution strategies and is used to limit distribution to a few types of intermediaries or retail outlets. For example, manufacturers and wholesalers may restrict coverage to selected retail stores based on their merchandising strategies or locations. A manufacturer may select only those wholesalers which can represent the company's products favorably to other channel members and final customers.

MANAGING CHANGE

Vendor-Managed Inventory and Integrated Supply

 Wholesalers must satisfy the needs of both customers and suppliers in a constantly changing environment. The concept of supply-chain management gives a new twist to the way wholesalers and other channel members conduct their business, with some implementing a *vendor-managed inventory* (VMI) system. VMI "is the streamlining and integration of the purchasing, receiving, stocking and payables function between wholesalers and key manufacturers."

Many wholesalers have responded to customers' need for cost reductions by assuming more responsibility for inventory management and integrated supply. More wholesalers are extending the concept to a vendor-based VMI because they believe that the greatest potential for cost reduction obtained from vendors lies in process—not product—costs. For decades, businesses have understood and applied product-cost management and cost behavior to the variable costs of production in terms of direct costs of labor, materials, and overhead. Today's managers are paying more attention to nonproduct or process costs through techniques such as activity-based costing and process re-engineering.

A vendor-based VMI removes redundant costs for duplicate efforts in purchasing, selling, invoicing, receiving, and warehousing the products or other functions performed by both the wholesaling firm and its vendors. "The managerial challenge is to streamline the supply chain (reduce duplicate functions) while maintaining flexibility and accuracy for the affected processes." For example, original equipment manufacturers (OEMs) and electronic-manufacturing service (EMS) companies have found it profitable to reduce their inventory risk by outsourcing activities that are not a part of their core competencies. Under a VMI

agreement, the supplier holds a dedicated inventory at a customer's manufacturing site or nearby warehouses.

VMI partners must be chosen carefully, considering the vendor's history of reliability, company policies, and business practices—as well as the wholesaler's readiness and ability to engage in this system. The financial payoff is in cost savings related to the processes of purchasing, stocking, and paying for inventory. However, the cost savings can contribute to the wholesaler's profitability only if the labor costs associated with redundant functions also are reduced. The profitability of a VMI venture also is affected by the accuracy and reliability of information provided by all parties involved in the agreement. VMI is most successful when customers constantly work with suppliers, and when constant attention is given to aspects of the system that need fine-tuning.

According to Dee Biggs, director of customer logistics with Welch's, the Concord, Massachusetts-based food and beverage manufacturer (e.g., grape juice), "keeping customers happy often boils down to efficient processes for managing back-office concerns such as inventory." Biggs sees VMI as a critical component of customer management. "The relationships we form with clients are very important to us—our foremost concern is to maintain the strength of these partnerships. As a result, we need the best possible means of executing and improving our VMI initiative."

Sources: Scott Benfield, "Developing a Backdoor Vendor-Managed Inventory," *Supply House Times* 41(3) (May 1998), pp. 78–82; Gina Roos, "Supply Chain's Vendor-Managed Inventory," *Electronic Engineering Times* (October 14, 2002), p. 100; Roberto Michel, "Supply-Side Smoothness," *MSI* (August 2002), pp. 44–48.

Trends and Issues in Wholesaling. The major business revolutions described earlier in this book (globalization, increased computerization, advances in technology, and changing management hierarchies) are related to many of the changes and challenges confronting wholesalers. For instance, many buyers and sellers are using shorter distribution channels, cutting out many traditional intermediaries. The need for shorter delivery times and lower costs provides the motivation for shorter channels, facilitated by computerization and automation.

Globalization of business, unstable economic conditions, and financial crises throughout many parts of the world create challenges for wholesalers that are engaged in international distribution. Add to this the increasingly intense competition among distributors and potential ethical problems related to the scramble for business. Industry consolidation among both producers and retailers has created larger firms that are capable of managing their own supply chains and distribution functions. Other problems include the high cost of sales calls, the general decline in employee productivity, and management of relationships between producers and wholesalers.

Communication between the wholesaler-distributor, suppliers, and customers is another key issue for merchant wholesalers. For example, they forecast sales demand and provide market information backward in the channel as input for product development and production schedules and provide information about products and services forward in the channel to potential buyers. The valuable services performed by merchant wholesalers make a major contribution to the total U.S. economic output (gross domestic product, or GDP).

Retailers

Retailers serve final consumers by being both buyers and sellers of goods and services. As a seller, a retailer must understand the desires and expectations of its target market. As a buyer, a retailer must identify and negotiate with those suppliers that can satisfy the retailer's customers and return a profit to the company. Retailing involves all the activities needed to sell goods and services to final consumers—the end of the supply chain.[12] We are involved with many forms of retailing in our daily lives—from the traditional supermarkets or department stores to Internet commerce and roadside fruit stands.

Distributive functions performed by retailers include the creation of product assortments to satisfy the needs and wants of an identified target market. Retailers break large shipments into smaller sizes and quantities that are suitable for use by individuals or households. They provide consumers with useful information to facilitate their purchase decisions, and they develop strategies that make it relatively convenient for consumers to shop. Of increasing importance to consumers, market-focused retailers offer quality products at competitive (or fair) prices. Purchases made by final consumers drive demand backward through the supply chain to originators of goods and services; that is, nothing moves until something is sold.

Retailers can be classified according to form of ownership and control or strategic positioning, as shown in Table 10.3. An understanding of the characteristics of each classification is important for designing suitable retailing strategies.

TABLE 10.3

Retail Classifications

Ownership and Control	Strategic Positioning
Independent ownership, one-store operation	Margin-turnover classification
	Tangible goods versus services
Chain organization	Type of merchandise carried: general merchandise
Leased department	
Vertical marketing system (VMS)	Type of merchandise carried: food-based retailers
Franchise	
Others	

Classifying Retailers by Ownership and Control.   Forms of retail ownership and control range from a small, independent, "mom and pop" operation, such as the corner grocery store in a small town, to a large retail conglomerate made up of multiple retail chains with many stores in each chain, like Target Corporation (Target Stores, Mervyn's, Marshall Field's, Rivertown Trading).

Independent Ownership, One-Store Operation.   This type of retailer is legally described as a sole proprietorship, partnership, or corporation. Many are family-owned small businesses that play a critical role in distributing goods at the retail level, making up a majority of all retail establishments.

Chain.   Chain organizations share common ownership of two or more stores with generally similar merchandise assortments, store appearance, and operating formats. Chain sizes range from an independently owned chain of two stores to very large chains like Wal-Mart Stores, Inc. (largest retailer in the United States and world) and METRO AG (fifth largest retailer worldwide and leader in Europe). METRO AG's primary market is Germany, with a global strategy of operating stores throughout Europe, Asia, North Africa, and North America to take advantage of the purchasing power in newly industrialized countries.[13]

Leased Department.   Departments in a larger store may be leased to an "outside" company (lessee) with expertise in a particular line of goods (e.g., cosmetics, shoes, or repair services). The lessee owns the merchandise inventory that is available for sale to customers, assumes responsibility for personnel, pays the retailer a percentage of sales generated by the department, and operates the business according to store policies and operating guidelines (e.g., hours of operation, credit policies).

Vertical Marketing System (VMS).   In conventional marketing channels, supply-chain intermediaries operate as independent firms. No channel member has excessive control over others. Any number of producers, wholesalers, and retailers can be coordinated and controlled by the same organization in a VMS. VMS arrangements may be formal or informal, including single ownership of two or more phases of production and/or distribution, contractual franchise arrangements, or other methods giving one channel member control over others. (VMS channels are discussed later in this chapter.)

Franchise.   A retail franchise is a contractual arrangement between a sponsoring organization (franchisor) and an independent owner (franchisee). Fast-food chains such as McDonald's and Kentucky Fried Chicken (KFC) are prominent franchise systems. Other types of franchises range from child care centers, cleaning services, lawn care services, and auto parts stores to beauty shops and funeral homes. Worldwide franchising statistics vary, but franchising is growing rapidly throughout the world, including Europe. Results of a survey conducted by the European Franchise Federation indicated there were nearly 3,700 franchisors and 145,000 franchised units in 1997 in Europe. Franchising accounted for nearly 41 percent of all retail sales ($800 billion annually) in 1996, with an estimated 550,000 franchised businesses and 8 million employees.[14]

The four major types of franchise systems are manufacturer-sponsored retailer franchise (automobile dealerships), manufacturer-sponsored wholesaler franchise (Pepsi-Cola bottlers and distributors), wholesaler-sponsored retailer franchise (True Value hardware), and service-firm-sponsored retailer franchise (McDonald's restaurants).

Other Forms of Ownership and Control.   Other retail classifications based on ownership include those owned by consumers, government, farmers, and public utilities.

Consumer-Owned Cooperatives.   These cooperatives are formed by final consumers who join forces and pay a fee to operate their own retail outlet. They can obtain lower prices by purchasing in larger quantities, but the process of buying and breaking larger purchases into smaller amounts for each member requires considerable effort. Grocery co-ops are the most prevalent, but some financial co-ops (e.g., credit unions) and public utility co-ops also are in operation to save money for their members.

Government-Owned Retail Establishments.   These are operated primarily to serve the needs of a particular segment of the population. Examples include the base exchanges and commissaries found on or near military installations for the benefit of the U.S. armed forces.

Farmer-Owned Retail Establishments.   The familiar farmers' market can be found in local marketplaces operated by independent farmers and merchants who combine their fruits and vegetables, and sometimes baked goods and handicrafts, to sell directly to consumers. The "store" may be an open area, partially covered, or the back of a pickup truck. The atmosphere is reminiscent of the cracker-barrel general stores of colonial times. Consumers get fresher produce directly from the farm, usually at lower prices, and farmers get instant cash and generally higher margins than those obtained from supermarkets.

Public Utility–Owned Retail Establishments.   These retail organizations sell appliances and other products related to the type of utility they operate. An electrical utility may sell appliances, and telephone companies sell phones and accessories through their own retail outlets.

Classifying Retailers by Strategic Positioning.   Retail organizations also can be classified according to profit margin–inventory turnover ratios, product strategies, and types of merchandise carried (general or food-based).

Margin-Turnover Classification.   Retailers can be classified according to a strategic combination of two dimensions: gross profit margin and inventory turnover ratio. *Gross margin* is equivalent to the average markup percentage (based on retail price) or the difference between the price paid by customers and the cost of the goods paid to suppliers. *Inventory turnover* refers to the number of times during a year that the average amount of inventory on hand is sold.

Tangible Goods versus Service Strategy.   Strategic positioning by retailers may be based on the level of service provided to customers and/or the emphasis on tangible goods versus services in their product assortments. One group of retailers sells services to its customers through separate businesses. For example, Gymboree operates 575 children's clothing stores in the United States, Canada, United Kingdom, and the Republic of Ireland. The retailer also extends its brand by franchising more than 500 Gymboree Play & Music Programs in 20 countries throughout the world. As an extension of the Gymboree brand, the additional service offered to young children and their parents by franchisees consists of interactive children's play and music programs, combined with learning.[15] Another strategy is to limit service offerings to those that facilitate the sale of tangible goods (e.g., delivery, bagging groceries). The customer may or may not pay for facilitating services.

Retailers of General Merchandise.   General merchandisers include all nonfood retailers such as department and specialty stores. Other general merchandisers that usually offer a price advantage include full-line discount stores, off-price retailers, and flea markets and resale shops.

Department Stores.   These retail organizations carry an extensive assortment of noncompeting lines organized into departments. They may be part of national or regional chains, a local independent retailer, or a strategic business unit within a large conglomerate. Criteria established by the U.S. Bureau of the Census for a business to be considered a department store include a minimum of 25 employees and a broad-based merchandise assortment of specified merchandise categories. Department stores typically have higher markups to cover the costs of higher levels of customer service, more elaborate store environments, and other operating expenses.

Specialty Stores.   Specialty stores offer a limited number of lines of goods or services but generally offer customers a wide selection within these specialized lines. Most specialty stores are small or medium-sized establishments or boutiques carrying few lines. Specialty retailers are found in just about every line of goods and services imaginable—and the trend continues to grow. Examples include retailers that concentrate assortments on apparel and accessories, electronics, specialty foods, greeting cards, automotive repair, and so forth.

Full-Line Discount Stores. These types of discount stores carry a wide assortment of merchandise, differing from department stores by charging lower prices. Other strategic differences related to lower prices include lower profit margins, higher inventory turnover, limited or self-service, no-frills store decor, and less expensive locations. Examples include Wal-Mart Stores, Inc., Kmart Corp., and Target Stores.

Off-Price Retailers. These may be manufacturer-owned factory outlets (e.g., Liz Claiborne, Inc., Hartmarx, and Burlington Coat Factory), off-price chains (e.g., T.J. Maxx and Marshalls Inc.), or independent stores that promote national brands at exceptionally low prices. An expanded form of the off-price retailer concept is an off-price mall containing multiple outlets, such as the Belz Outlet Mall or the Sawgrass Mill Mall, both with locations in Florida.

Flea Markets and Resale Shops. These are organized and expanded forms of garage sales and yard sales that appear in every community. These retailers have gained popularity in recent years among both buyers and sellers. Flea markets, which usually are located in out-of-the way, low-cost locations, rent space to individual vendors for a given period of time. Typical merchandise includes antiques, used household items, tools, and other goods. Resale shops operate more like a traditional retailer, being selective in the items they take to sell and arranging their merchandise in attractive displays. Many resale shops take items on consignment, keeping a percentage of the sales price and giving the remainder to the original owner. People from all economic levels are creating a growth market for retailers like Grow Biz International (operating under franchised names such as Once Upon A Child, Play It Again Sports, Plato's Closet, and Music Go Round), and Goodwill Industries (a nonprofit charitable organization).

Food-Based Retailers. Food retailers can be classified according to the width and depth of their merchandise assortments, pricing strategy, and level of service provided to customers. The major types of food-based retailers include the conventional supermarket, combination store, superstore, box (limited-assortment) store, warehouse store, convenience store, and hypermarket, as discussed below.

Conventional Supermarkets. These stores combine low prices and convenient locations, resulting in higher sales volume and inventory turnover. They offer a full line of groceries, meat, and produce and a limited assortment of general merchandise but find it difficult to compete with other food retailers (e.g., Kroger, Albertson's, Safeway) that offer lower prices, larger selections, or more convenience.

Combination Stores. These stores are primarily food-based retailers but are combined with a general merchandise store or a drugstore. The two types of stores are operated as one from the perspective of the customer. Examples include Albertson's and its subsidiary, Jewel.

Superstores. These stores are larger (up to 30,000 square feet or more) and more diverse than conventional supermarkets and generate high sales volumes.

Superstores carry many nonfood items (e.g., greeting cards, floral arrangements, housewares), along with specialty food products (e.g., baked goods, deli items, seafood). Kroger Co. and Wal-Mart Stores, Inc., have developed superstore formats that combine supermarket and nonfood merchandise. (The term *superstore* also refers to large power retailers, discussed later in this chapter with retailing trends.)

Box (Limited-Assortment) Stores.   These stores carry a limited line of goods (usually nonperishable), particularly low-priced private labels and generic brands. Customers select merchandise directly from cut cases or shipping cartons and generally bag their own groceries at stores such as Aldi.

Warehouse Stores.   Warehouse stores carry a wider assortment of goods than box stores but focus on a limited number of brands of dry goods with very few perishable items. Warehouse stores such as Costco and Sam's Club are able to buy special deals from their suppliers in order to attract customers with low prices. Merchandise assortments may vary from one day to the next in these no-frills, efficient, low-cost operations that combine the superstore and warehouse store concepts.

Convenience Stores.   Stores such as 7-Eleven follow a location strategy that makes frequently purchased consumer goods available in neighborhoods and other high-traffic areas near their customers. Higher prices are paid for convenient locations and longer operating hours.

Hypermarkets.   These are very large stores, typically ranging from 100,000 to 300,000 square feet in size. They are a combination supermarket and full-line discount general merchandise store with a central checkout, an extension of the French *hypermarché*. Carrefour SA and Royal Ahold N.V. are leading international retailers in this category. Others, such as Wal-Mart Stores, Inc., have developed this type of store, but with mixed results.

Retailing Strategies.   Two broad theoretical concepts drive retailing strategies: theories of institutional (structural) change and store location. *Theories of structural change* include the retail life cycle concept, wheel of retailing, retail accordion, dialectic process, adaptive behavior, and scrambled merchandising. Retailers who understand these theories can develop proactive and adaptive strategies that enable them to remain profitable in a rapidly changing environment.

Retail life cycle
Changes in the structure of retail institutions over time; four stages are innovation, accelerated development, maturity, and decline.

The **retail life cycle** is similar to the product life cycle (see Chapter 8) but refers specifically to changes in the structure of retail institutions over time. Like products, retail institutions progress through four identifiable stages of indeterminate length from inception to demise: innovation, accelerated development, maturity, and decline, as illustrated in Figure 10.7a.[16]

Wheel of retailing theory
Upward spiral of retail innovators that enter the market as low-priced operators but become more upscale over time, making way for new low-priced operators.

The **wheel of retailing theory** describes the evolution of retail institutions as a wheel-like or cyclic progression. It explains the upward spiral of retail innovators who enter the market as low-priced, low-margin, no-frills, low-status operators. Over time, competitive pressures cause the retailer to add more upscale products, more services, and more attractive store surroundings. This results in loss of the original price-conscious consumers, making way for new low-price innovators to enter the market. (See Figure 10.7b.)

FIGURE 10.7

Theories of Structural Change in Retailing

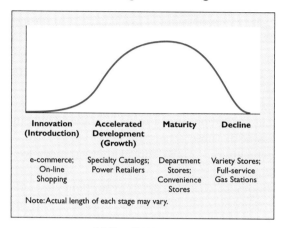

(a) Retail Life Cycle

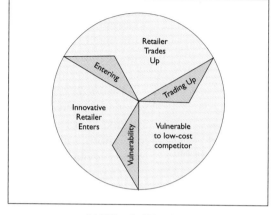

(b) Wheel of Retailing

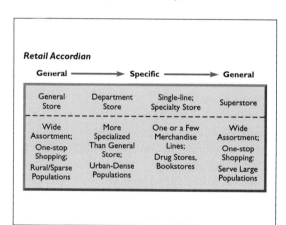

(c) Retail Accordion

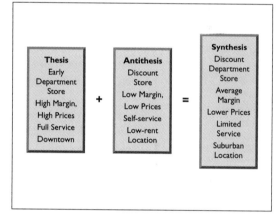

(d) Dialectic Process

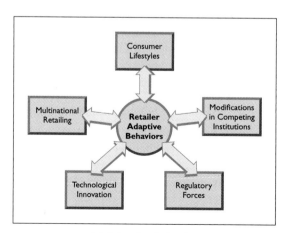

(e) Adaptive Behavior

Retail accordion
General-specific-general pattern of the expansion and contraction of merchandise lines.

The **retail accordion** concept refers to a general-specific-general pattern of expansion and contraction of merchandise lines, although each type of store exists today. The general store that offered broad assortments of unrelated merchandise to early American colonists lost popularity as department stores emerged to fill more specialized needs. Eventually, a broad spectrum of specialty stores evolved to fill these same needs, focusing on a single product line or a few related lines of merchandise. The accordion idea continues as superstores and mass merchants offer one-stop shopping to a diverse customer base. (See Figure 10.7c.)

Distinctly different forms of retail institutions emerge as old and new, or substantially different, types of retail institutions adapt to one another. This can be explained as a **dialectic process** with three stages: thesis (original form of retail operation), antithesis (completely different form), and synthesis (innovative combination of old and new), as shown in Figure 10.7d.

Dialectic process
Emergence of retail institution in three stages: thesis (original form), antithesis (different form), and synthesis (innovative combination of old and new).

The **adaptive behavior theory** of changing retail institutions has its roots in Darwin's theory of natural selection (survival of the fittest). Retailers who anticipate changes in their environments and develop winning competitive strategies will survive and prosper. In an overcrowded retail marketplace, often the only place to gain new business is to take it away from competitors. (See Figure 10.7e.)

Adaptive behavior theory
Similar to Darwin's theory of natural selection (survival of the fittest).

Scrambled merchandising refers to the practice of adding unrelated goods and services to a retailer's traditional product assortment to increase sales and profits through quick selling of higher-margin items that often are purchased on impulse. Examples include the addition of sunglasses and snack foods at a gasoline service station and milk and eggs at a drugstore.

Scrambled merchandising
Adding unrelated goods and services to a traditional retail assortment to increase sales and profits.

Store Location Strategies.   Store location strategies are related closely to manufacturer and wholesaler distribution strategies and to the evolution of retail structures. The complex theories of retail location and site selection are beyond the scope of this chapter. However, location can be viewed from the perspectives of competition and development. Strategic positioning involves not only perceptual comparisons with competitors but also physical placement of retail facilities relative to those of other retailers that compete for the same consumer dollars. For example, fast-food restaurants find it advantageous to locate relatively close to one another. Most discount stores and mass merchandisers operate in free-standing locations with large parking areas, preferably near a large shopping mall in a high-traffic location. Stores that sell shopping goods such as jewelry, furniture, and cars tend to locate near one another to facilitate customers' need to compare merchandise and deals. Malls and strip shopping centers are homes to many specialty retailers and large department stores.

Trends and Issues in Retailing.   The retailing industry is experiencing change in three major areas: store formats and operations, channel relations, and customer characteristics. The trend in *store formats and operations* is toward more nonstore retailing, greater specialization, and more superstores. Many retailers and their customers bypass physical storefronts altogether with direct-response techniques, such as direct marketing (e.g., telemarketing, catalogs, vending machines, and computerized and electronic commerce). Perhaps the most compelling trend is the rapid acceleration of electronic commerce, made possible by advances in technology, communications, the Internet, and customer databases.

Specialty stores that serve nearly every product category and consumer lifestyle are proliferating. Many are small boutiques that carry everything from sunglasses to souvenirs of your favorite sports team. Others are megaretailers that focus on one product category. Category killers like Borders book stores and Home Depot carry large assortments of a particular product line and sell at low prices, making it difficult for department stores and smaller specialty stores to compete with them in that category. Following the "bigger is better" trend, acquisitions and mergers in all retail categories have accelerated retail consolidation for greater domestic and global coverage. At the other end of the spectrum, entrepreneurs continue to develop innovative concepts that change the usual way of doing business, such as selling airline and event tickets over the Internet, fast-food delivery services, and one-product kiosks in malls.

Retailers are under pressure from all sides to cut operating costs by adopting operating methods that are more efficient or lose their competitive advantage. Point-of-sale scanning, computerized order processing, improvements in logistics, and other state-of-the-art applications have become more sophisticated. More demands are placed on suppliers to provide services such as prewrapping delicatessen products or preticketing apparel. At the same time, consumers demand greater value and lower prices, making it necessary to increase profit margins by lowering costs, partially through performing more of the distribution functions in-house.

Trends in *channel relations* focus on heightened competition, building stronger relationships with suppliers and customers, and developing synergies in the supply chain. Many channel relationships have been formalized through acquisitions and mergers that increase consolidation within the industry. Many of these changes are evolving in response to the demands of a changing marketplace.

Shifts are occurring in *customer characteristics.* Customers are better informed and more value conscious. They come from increasingly diverse ethnic and socio-economic backgrounds and have different shopping preferences. They expect more service, more convenience or hassle-free shopping, and lower prices. Increasingly, retail customers expect to be entertained while shopping and are attracted to the ambiance of the store environment, although they shop in both discount stores and upscale stores for home and personal products.

Other Channel Intermediaries and Facilitators

In addition to wholesalers and retailers, the supply chain includes producers and manufacturers that must determine the most suitable channel strategy for their goods and services and do so in cooperation with other channel members. Physical distribution firms move products from one intermediary to the next until they reach final consumers or organizational customers. They are involved in forecasting market demand, obtaining and processing orders, managing and storing inventory, packing and shipping, and delivering orders to diverse buyers.

⬤ CHANNEL SELECTION AND DESIGN

The design of a distribution channel is an important strategic decision because customers must be able to purchase goods and services when and where they find it most satisfying and convenient. Marketing intelligence data can be used to determine customers' buying habits and channel preferences as input for channel design decisions. Channel structure also depends on the firm's resources and objectives. For instance, the opportunity to distribute computer software directly over the Internet may provide a shorter lead time and a better return on assets than distributing through wholesalers or storefronts.

Bucklin[17] explains channel structures in terms of four service level outputs: spatial convenience, lot size, waiting or delivery time, and product variety. *Spatial convenience* refers to the degree of market decentralization or a distribution strategy that is designed to reduce customers' travel time and search costs through convenient locations of intermediaries. As customers place greater value on travel time and search costs, the channel becomes more decentralized and requires more channel intermediaries.

Lot size refers to the number of units that a customer will purchase at any one time. Products that are consumed quickly and replenished frequently require higher levels of service outputs to maintain inventories. When customers can rely on their suppliers to maintain an inventory of wanted items, they can purchase in smaller quantities and hold smaller inventories. The smaller the lot size that is available in a channel, the higher is the service output of that channel, and the higher is the price that can be charged to customers for convenience.

Waiting time or *delivery time* is the time a customer must wait between ordering and receiving goods. Longer waiting times generally mean that the customer will experience greater inconvenience and will need to plan purchases in advance. However, when the customer is willing to wait longer to receive purchases, prices usually are lower.

Product variety
Width and depth of retail assortments.

Product variety refers to the width and depth of assortments. When customers demand a broad assortment of goods, channel members must carry a higher level of inventory. This results in higher channel output and higher distribution costs.

As customers require a higher level of service outputs, the channel expands to include more intermediaries to provide the necessary marketing functions and flows. When channel outputs are higher, customers will pay higher prices for additional service and convenience. Conversely, channel outputs and prices are lower when customers provide more of the marketing functions themselves.

Channel Objectives

Inventories will reside in a channel where it is most cost-effective for all channel members to deliver the level of service outputs demanded by customers. Multiple distribution channels may be needed where diverse markets are targeted, each with its own unique demands and objectives. For example, a pharmaceutical manufacturer may distribute painkillers to final users through a variety of wholesalers or agents to drugstore pharmacies, hospitals, doctors' offices, nursing homes, and direct-marketing channels.

Distribution objectives must be consistent with overall marketing and company objectives (e.g., targeted sales levels and profit margins) and product characteristics. Frequently cited objectives include intensity of market coverage; degree of control over inventory and its management; minimization of time or distance; ability to move bulky, customized, or high-cost products; opportunity to provide high levels of customer service; and supplier cooperation. In addition to achieving the company's distribution objectives, channel design must consider company policies and organizational structure (for managing the distribution function). It also must conform to legal and regulatory requirements, such as refraining from unfair restraint of trade and creating conditions for unfair competition.

Channel Length and Number of Intermediaries

The number of intermediaries required to achieve the desired intensity of distribution determines channel length. Three channel alternatives related to coverage include intensive, selective, and exclusive distribution. Channels designed for *intensive* distribution include the maximum number of intermediaries and outlets to accomplish the widest coverage possible (e.g., convenience goods). To achieve a *selective* distribution strategy (e.g., shopping goods), a company will choose a limited number of distributors in a more narrowly defined market. An *exclusive* distribution strategy (e.g., specialty goods) is focused on an even narrower market, defined according to geography or type of outlet. When designing the structure of a distribution channel, suppliers must choose among a number of intermediaries that have direct or indirect access to the desired target market. Selected factors that influence the length of distribution channels are listed in Table 10.4.

Selection Criteria for Channel Members

Criteria must be established for selecting each channel intermediary, based on the company's distribution objectives and the number of intermediaries needed to achieve these objectives. Five key factors dominate the criteria for including a channel member in the company's distribution structure: market coverage, costs and other economic criteria, control, flexibility/adaptability, and overall ability to add value.

Market Coverage.   Channel intermediaries should be selected for their ability to achieve the company's distribution objective of reaching the greatest number of potential customers with the fewest transactions. For example, Pepsico Inc. uses bottling companies, distributors, and a vast array of retailers and vending machines to reach soft drink customers. The selection of intermediaries depends on the size of a trade area, number and location of potential customers, and purchasing process pursued for each product line.

Costs and Other Economic Criteria.   The cost of achieving desired market coverage must be consistent with distribution strategy objectives and should not be greater than the benefits to the company and its customers. Shorter channels may not be the least expensive when all channel functions are considered. If, for example, the objective is to open a new market for auto parts in a developing country, then the channel design might include a combination of export and import companies, local manufacturers and wholesalers, retailers, and other intermediaries. These companies will share marketing functions and use their individual expertise to gain acceptance from this developing consumer market.

Control.   There is a potential loss of control over a product's sales and distribution when channel intermediaries are used. Wholesalers or distributors that carry lines

TABLE 10.4

Factors Influencing Distribution Channel Length

	Factors	*Channel Length*
Market	1. Number of potential exchanges 2. Expected size of exchange 3. Geographic concentration of market	1. Many = long; few = short 2. Small = long; large = short 3. Concentrated = short; dispersed = long
Marketing mix	1. Unit price 2. Perishability 3. Width of product line 4. Technical, specialized, or customized products 5. Product type 6. Promotion/communication	1. High = short; low = long 2. Perishable = short; nonperishable = long 3. Wide = short; narrow = long 4. Specialized = short; not specialized = long 5. Commodity = long; specialty = short 6. Communication aimed toward consumers = long; aimed toward intermediaries = short
Organization	1. Number of other products or lines 2. Financial resources 3. Level of control desired 4. Management skill	1. Many = short; one/few = long 2. Strong = short; weak = long 3. High level of control = short; low level of control = long 4. Skilled = short; not skilled = long
Intermediary	1. Economy in services required 2. Availability of intermediaries	1. Efficient intermediaries = long; inefficient intermediaries = short 2. Available = long; unavailable = short
Regulatory environment	1. Regulatory restrictions	1. Heavy restrictions = long; light restrictions = short

Source: From Hiam & Schewe, *Portable MBA in Marketing*, NY: John Wiley & Sons, 1995, pp. 336–338, Exhibit 12.4. Copyright © 1995 by John Wiley & Sons, Inc. Reprinted by permission of John Wiley & Sons, Inc.

from a number of manufacturers may neglect one line for others that are more profitable. Of particular concern is the quality of service that will be provided before, during, and after a sale by the intermediary. This is particularly true for high-tech and complex products that may require a specialized salesforce and in-depth product knowledge. More control can be achieved with fewer intermediaries, by performing many distribution functions in-house, and by adherence to established standards.

Flexibility/Adaptability.   Considerable financial and human resources are used to create and maintain long-term channel relationships, which may or may not involve formal contracts. Organizations must be able to respond to changes in the market or company, particularly in industries characterized by rapid change and environmental uncertainty. For example, automotive superstores like AutoNation

INNOVATE OR EVAPORATE*

Alternative Music Distribution Channels

Mainstream musicians distribute their sounds through retail outlets such as Tower, Target, or Sam Goody, but where do you buy recordings of the newer, harder-to-find alternative sounds? The distribution of music is "a fragmented and faddish business where being seen as alternative—having street cred"—can be paramount while the definition of "alternative" is constantly shifting. Smaller bands and record labels that perform all genres of music (rock, rap, country, jazz) complain about the difficulty of getting their music "out there." They find that alternative distributors are a favorite option.

Fans of cult bands, local music makers, and new sounds are most likely to buy their recordings in small, independent retail shops. These shops buy from alternative record distributors with grassroots names such as Caroline Distribution and Alternative Distribution Alliance (ADA). These channels gain legitimacy through the ownership and support of Warner EMI Music, a joint venture between Time Warner and EMI Group. Alternative distributors keep their identities and their marketing strategies separate from their parent companies, creating a dual distribution system tailored to the needs of customers and suppliers. This allows the larger record labels to work with smaller bands that otherwise would not be worth their while.

Jim Powers, owner of Minty Fresh Inc., a Chicago-based independent record label, says that his company chose ADA as a distributor because "their sales people are into new music and can articulate their passions to the retailer." Rather than sell on the basis of sales figures and product endorsements that might convince a discounter like Target to stock a CD, the key selling point for alternative distributors and independent retailers is the sound of the music itself.

What strategies are available for distributing music? Distributors take the CDs or DVDs from warehouses and get them into record stores. Most of the powerful major music labels have their own distribution systems, shipping billions of copies of CDs and DVDs by Madonna, Boyz II Men, and Aerosmith to major retailers. In contrast, alternative distributors deal primarily with independent retailers that will give store space to an innovative new band with a cult following. This channel has lower sales potential but a more profitable customer base of loyal followers and little competition from the larger distributors—making it a lucrative proposition. ADA's 30 sales representatives covered 5800 independent retailers in 1998, introducing them to niche bands that their customers would not find anywhere else—a way to "champion certain bands instead of focusing on the more generic big hits." The ADA salesforce, stationed all over the country, can save money and increase sales by introducing more than one band at a time to independent retailers.

The success of alternative music distribution channels depends on personal relationships between distributors and customers, and learning what their clientele likes and dislikes. Alternative distributors are "taking the smaller labels and getting them to market, which might not otherwise happen," says a music industry attorney in New York.

*The box title is attributed to James M. Higgins, *Innovate or Evaporate* (Winter Park, FL: New Management Publishing Company, 1995).

Sources: Margaret Littman, "No Alternative: Reality Counters Perception in Music Distribution Biz," *Marketing News* 32(16) (August 3, 1998), pp. 1, 13; www.caroline.com; www.ada-music.com; "Warner Music Group and EMI to Form World's Premier Music Group," *Business Wire* (January 24, 2000).

(www.autonation.com) created problems for traditional car dealerships by amassing large inventories of multiple brands of automobiles and selling cars over the Internet. Some resourceful manufacturers and dealers instituted one-price policies and went on-line to compete with these large retailers. Likewise, computer software developers adapted to market needs by letting customers download software products directly from the Internet.

Overall Ability to Add Value.   Several questions should be answered about an intermediary's ability to add value to the product being marketed or to the distribution process:

1. Can the intermediary perform the necessary distribution tasks that will fulfill our company objectives and customer needs? (Example: Installation and maintenance contracts.)

2. What is the intermediary's ability to add value to perceptions of our product's image in the marketplace? (Example: Distributing jewelry through Tiffany's versus Kmart.)

3. Can the intermediary provide high-quality service outputs within the context of location, quantity, waiting time, and assortment? (Example: A system developed by stamps.com allows customers to use the Internet to buy postage. Viable U.S. Postal Service stamps can be printed onto envelopes.)[18] The U.S. Postal Service also sells stamps and other shipping support services via the Internet.

Evaluation of Channel Efficiency and Effectiveness

Marketers must constantly assess the efficiency and effectiveness of individual channel intermediaries as well as the entire channel. In general, channel members must achieve the goals set out for them in their arrangements with the supplier and must satisfy the criteria established for their selection. Several broad measures are discussed below: market coverage, economic performance, marketing effectiveness, and overall ability to add value.

Market Coverage.   Effective distribution is obtained when the supplier has achieved the desired level of coverage in the designated target market(s). This may include having enough retail intermediaries to reach a substantial number of consumers and enough wholesalers, agents, brokers, or other middlemen to reach desired organizational customers. Other coverage measures include a proactive and well-informed salesforce, product inventories that are available when and where needed by final customers, and sufficient attention given by the intermediary to marketing the supplier's product (i.e., evidence that the intermediary considers it important).

Economic Performance.   Costs of distribution at each channel level and with each intermediary can be determined as a percentage of sales, unit costs, operating profits, contribution margins, marketing program costs, and return on dollars spent for reseller support. Economic measures can be applied to each level of reseller to assess their contribution to strategic channel goals.

Marketing Effectiveness.   Marketing program elements are assessed for their effectiveness in accomplishing sales objectives, with particular emphasis on the communications mix. For instance, personal selling can be evaluated on ability to meet sales objectives. Advertising and other communication efforts can be evaluated on sales and other measures of audience response. Pricing strategies can be reviewed relative to demand elasticity and market characteristics.

Channel members should be evaluated on inventory turnover rate, delivery record, customer service, and other relevant criteria. Studies conducted by KPMG Consulting, Deloitte & Touche, and Consumer Goods Manufacturer agreed that effective supply-chain management relies on efficient inventory management and that optimal inventory levels (minimum levels necessary to support customer service objectives) can improve cash flows and ability to respond to market demands. The KPMG study emphasizes the importance of integration: "Integrating and involving supply chain partners are essential to achieving a competitive advantage in the marketplace."[19]

Overall Ability to Add Value.   Some ways that channel members can add value to the distribution process include the ability to adapt to changing market conditions, to provide market data, and to deliver high-quality customer service. For example, the intermediary must be able to adapt to the entry of a powerful new competitor, or to the problems of a faltering economy, by maintaining customer relationships and providing competitive service. Value also is added through timely and accurate market feedback (e.g., sales trends, customer preferences, competitive actions). Level of commitment to customers can be determined from indicators of high-quality customer service, determined from customer satisfaction surveys, complaints, and level of commitment to training the salesforce and service personnel.

● CHANNEL MANAGEMENT

Channel management includes a broad range of issues and responsibilities, following the general marketing management process described in Chapter 3. Four issues are discussed in the following sections: channel power and relationships, vertical marketing systems, legal and ethical concerns, and emerging channel structures.

Power and Relationships

Distribution channels rely on a series of relationships among intermediaries. Most channel members are independent organizations with their own objectives and ways of conducting business, but each wants to control its own distribution activities and set standards for its business partners. Ideally, all members in the same channel will operate in an environment of cooperation and mutual trust, but it is more likely that they will have conflicting goals and market orientations. The overriding concern is with control, that is, which member will dominate the distribution channel and set the standards for others in the supply chain.

Channel power
Control and dependence in relationships in the channels of distribution.

Channel power refers to control and dependence in channel relationships— "...the ability of one channel member to get another channel member to do what the latter would not otherwise have done."[20] The member with the most relative power can use any means to influence or control the policies and marketing strategy of another. Bases of power include rewards, coercion, expertness, reference identification, and legitimacy. *Rewards* are economic advantages that accrue if the channel leader's wishes are followed (e.g., assignment of exclusive territories for limiting the number of competing product lines carried). *Coercive power* involves any negative sanction or punishment possible to get other channel members to conform (e.g., late shipments, price increases). *Expert power* is based on a channel follower's perception that the channel leader has special knowledge that will be beneficial. Small retailers may depend on large wholesalers for market information and management assistance. *Referent power* is gained from a superior image or association, based on pride in a present or anticipated relationship (e.g., a car dealer may prefer to open a prestigious Jaguar dealership versus a Kia dealership). *Legitimate power* is based on the belief that the channel leader possesses the right to exert influence on other channel members and to expect compliance (e.g., ownership or contractual agreements, relative size, market position). Note that channel power is relative, and all members have some degree of power, due to their interdependence. The power bases usually work in combination to achieve the channel's strategic objectives.

Vertical and horizontal **channel conflicts** are inevitable in a changing, competitive environment, but conflict must be managed so that previously adversarial suppliers can achieve positive outcomes. Researchers found that a supplier's market-oriented behaviors have a significant effect on all other major channel relationship factors, specifically the market orientation of distributors, the level of trust and commitment, cooperative norms, and satisfaction with financial performance.[21]

Vertical Marketing Systems

A **vertical marketing system (VMS)** is an organized form of channel control involving any number of intermediaries (as described earlier within the context of retailing). A channel may be completely or partially integrated. A fully integrated channel has all stages of production and distribution under one ownership or control. It is more common to have partial integration (forward or backward), such as producer-wholesaler, producer-retailer, or wholesaler-retailer. Advantages of a VMS include more cost-effective and profitable distribution alternatives, less interfirm conflict, economies of scale, better bargaining power in negotiations, guaranteed supply, and more opportunity to innovate. The three major forms of VMS are corporate, administered, and contractual.

Corporate backward integration occurs when retailers own producers or wholesalers that precede them in the channel (e.g., Kroger owns processing facilities). In **corporate forward integration,** manufacturers own their own retail or wholesale outlets or distribution centers (e.g., Radio Shack Corporation). An **administered VMS** closely resembles a conventional marketing channel, where each member remains independently owned and autonomous but collaborates with the others in marketing activities (e.g., Procter & Gamble Co. and retailers). A **contractual VMS** consists of independently owned firms at different levels of production and distribution that integrate their programs through a formal contract. The three major types of contractual VMS channels are wholesaler-sponsored voluntary chains (e.g., Western Auto), retailer-sponsored cooperative groups (e.g., Ace Hardware), and franchises (e.g., Jiffy Lube, Dunkin' Donuts).

Legal and Ethical Issues

All distribution channel members are subject to the requirements of antitrust and fair dealing legislation in the United States (e.g., Sherman Antitrust Act, Federal

---

Channel conflicts
Vertical and horizontal differences of opinion among channel members.

Vertical marketing system (VMS)
Organized form of channel control involving any number of intermediaries; integration may be partial or complete.

Corporate backward integration
Retailers own producers or wholesalers that precede them in the channels of distribution.

Corporate forward integration
Manufacturers own their own retail or wholesale outlets or distribution centers.

Administered VMS
Resembles a conventional marketing channel; each member remains independently owned and autonomous but collaborates with others in marketing activities.

Contractual VMS
Independently owned firms at different levels of production and distribution that integrate programs through a formal contract.

Trade Commission Act). They also are subject to international and foreign laws when involved in overseas transactions. Basically, the control that one channel member exerts over another may be considered illegal if it creates a monopoly, restrains trade, or reduces competition (e.g., a large retailer's excessive demands on a small supplier that can be viewed as restraint of trade).

Many ethical issues arise in distribution activities. These are concerned primarily with the buying and selling process and fair treatment of customers and business partners. Unethical marketing activities often focus on how the marketing mix is used to influence customers, suppliers, and others. Areas of particular concern include deceptive advertising, packaging, and labeling; high-pressure sales techniques; product quality and safety; unfair pricing methods; and overcharging. Channel members also are expected to be socially responsible by maintaining a safe environment and contributing to the economic and social well-being of the community.

Trends in Distribution Channels

Technology growth in international markets, and changes in government regulation (including security) will continue to drive the major changes in channel relationships. In addition, channel design will focus on creating shorter lead times and order-processing cycles and will place more emphasis on service and customer satisfaction. More attention also will be given to increased domestic and global competition and to developing and maintaining strategic alliances.

Technology. Marketers will continue to emphasize the need to reduce the number of links and to trim costs in the supply chain. Sophisticated computer applications and data interchange technologies will play an increasingly important role in efficient inventory management and cost-reduction strategies. The combination of converging technologies and integrated distribution channels has led to significant changes in the traditional producer-controlled channels. The management of distribution channels has become increasingly Internet-based, including functions such as analyzing customer demand, purchasing supplies, factory and warehouse scheduling of raw materials and finished goods, order tracking from original suppliers to final customer, and market research and product design.

Often, an external consultant provides the needed expertise in distribution and supply chain management. For example, UPS Logistics Group (UPS subsidiary that provides consulting services throughout the world) helped Ford Motor Co. shorten the number of days between the time when a car rolls out of an assembly plant and the time it comes off the car-carrier truck at a dealership. UPS Logistics also provides the full-order completion process for companies such as Nike.com's Internet business, and operates a repair business for several high-tech companies within their warehouse complex.

More automation will be used in materials handling, warehousing, and physical distribution processes. Bar-coding and radio frequency technologies are becoming more sophisticated, monitoring the movement of everything from freshly picked apples to containerized freight on a ship. Technology has been, and will continue to be, the predecessor of creative destruction (crisis and renewal) described in Chapter 2, and will present major challenges for continuous improvement in a competitive marketplace.[22]

International Markets.   Although overseas markets offer new distribution opportunities, the challenges of international channels are more complex. Primary concerns are the need to minimize delivery lead time and variability and to develop better ways to decrease distribution costs. Multinational companies will increase their marketing efforts in developing nations, including the need to provide an infrastructure and create a consumer economy.

Companies must gain a better understanding of cultural variations among foreign customers and suppliers and of cross-cultural channel management. Channel members do not need to be directly involved in overseas markets to be affected by international distribution trends. Virtually every channel member has some association with foreign suppliers or customers, global communication technology (e.g., Internet), and foreign competition.

Changing Regulatory Environment.   Deregulation and changing regulations in many industries in the United States and abroad will continue to bring about changes in channel management. In the United States alone, the communications, transportation, and financial industries have undergone significant regulatory changes, generally creating a more competitive and volatile business environment. Transnational trade agreements such as NAFTA and others will continue to open new markets and present new distribution challenges. Distributors must have the flexibility to adapt to these changes.

Other Trends.   Manufacturers, wholesalers, and retailers are placing greater emphasis on knowing their customers—their operations and buying patterns. Each channel member must add value to the supply chain beyond parts and finished goods, to maintain satisfied customers. Retailers and distributors have more influence in their distribution channels. Once-dominant manufacturers work more closely with middlemen, to know their end customers better and to create channel-wide efficiencies. The percentage of family-owned and small (0 to 3 branches) distributorships rose significantly in 2002. The number of middle-sized distributorships decreased, but growth occurred in large distributorships, many through acquisitions or mergers.

Retail trends include the new lavish megastores that showcase the products of Hermes, Gucci, Louis Vuitton, Nike, Lego, and other companies. At the other extreme, outlet centers and discount houses are growing rapidly, and many lower-priced retailers offer upmarket amenities to attract customers. Retailers' "store brands" have gained popularity, and in many cases have become national brands (e.g., Sears' Craftsman tools, Kenmore appliances). Store brands improve retail profit margins and build customer loyalty. Other retail trends include the growth of regional malls that attract customers from all segments of the population. More retailers are pursuing a multi-channel strategy by direct selling through catalogues or the Internet, or kiosks within a store or mall, as well as traditional storefronts.

Finally, the need for security throughout all distribution channels has become a major issue for marketers in the post-9/11 world. Federal, state, and international authorities have taken measures to ensure the safe shipment of cargo (and the safety of individuals involved in distribution). Although these precautions are necessary, they often create costly slowdowns in production and shipping, making it difficult to control costs and efficiencies.[23]

Summary

A channel of distribution is a set of interdependent organizations that combine their efforts to make goods and services available to end-customers. The activities of distribution channels (intermediaries between producers and customers) and physical distribution (logistical movement of goods and services) make a major economic contribution. Channel intermediaries make the exchange process more efficient, match supply and market demand, routinize transactions, and facilitate customers' search processes. Functions performed by distributors include exchange, physical supply, and facilitating activities.

The primary channel intermediaries are wholesalers, retailers, and other merchants or agents. Consumer and organizational channels may be direct or indirect. Direct channels are the shortest and quickest because no intermediaries are involved. Indirect channels use one or more intermediaries, resulting in longer lead times and less control. Multiple channels can be used to reach diverse customer groups. International channels are more complex and costly than domestic channels.

Wholesalers may provide full service, partial service, or no service. The three major types of wholesalers are merchant wholesalers, manufacturers' sales branches and offices, and agent middlemen. Market-coverage strategies may be intensive, exclusive, or selective and can be applied to both the for-profit and nonprofit sectors. Trends and issues in wholesaling include shorter distribution channels, globalization, technological advances, increased competition, industry consolidation, and other factors.

Retailers offer assortments of goods and services to meet the demands of final consumers and can be classified according to form of ownership and control or strategic positioning. Retailers can be classified further in terms of general merchandisers and food merchandisers, as well as location strategies. Three major areas of change in retailing include store formats and operations, channel relations, and customer characteristics.

Channel structure is determined by four service level outputs: spatial convenience, lot size, waiting time, and product variety. Channel length is determined by desired market coverage and types of intermediaries needed. Selection criteria for channel members include market coverage, costs, control, flexibility, and ability to add value to the process. Channel efficiency and effectiveness are evaluated against the same criteria. Channel management focuses on channel power and relationships, vertical marketing systems, legal and ethical concerns, and emerging channel structures within the competitive environment.

Questions

1. Describe the role and contributions of a distribution system in the U.S. economy and in the world economy. Include an explanation of the difference between distribution channels and physical distribution activities and how each fits into the supply-chain concept.

2. (a) Name all potential intermediaries that might comprise a complex distribution channel, and list the general characteristics of each intermediary. (b) Describe the general functions performed by channel members.

3. Select a specific industry, such as personal computers, snack foods, or children's apparel, and determine at least two different distribution channels that might be pursued by a producer in these industries. Justify each channel alternative selected.

4. For one of the channels selected in Question 3, describe the specific functions that each identified intermediary would perform most effectively. What advantages, if any, can be achieved by a vendor-managed inventory system?

5. Describe the major types of wholesalers and the services typically performed by each type. Explain the relationship between type of wholesaler and market-coverage strategy. Can a producer use more than one type of wholesaler to distribute the same product to different target markets? Explain.

6. Repeat Question 5, substituting retailer for wholesaler.

7. Assuming that you are a marketing manager for a producer of home-improvement supplies, discuss the criteria that you would use in selecting and evaluating channel members. What factors would be important in determining channel length (number of intermediaries) needed?

8. Discuss the five major issues in channel management, and describe a specific example of how each might have an impact on distribution methods 10 years from now.

Exercises

1. Visit a warehouse or distribution center in your community. Determine the role that this facility plays in the total distribution process for a particular type of merchandise. Evaluate the use of technology.

2. Determine the economic contribution of the various categories of wholesalers and retailers by accessing U.S. Bureau of the Census data on the Internet (Census of Retailing; Census of Wholesaling). Plot the trends in each category on a graph, and identify any major changes that may be occurring. What are your predictions for the future of each type of intermediary based on census data?

3. Find an example of an international manufacturer, wholesaler, or retailer in current business media. Identify the channel(s) of distribution used by this channel member to move goods from producers to customers in another country. Discuss possible problems that might be encountered in this process, including cultural differences, legal and political concerns, and so forth.

Endnotes

1. Charles C. Poireier and Stephen E. Reiter, *Supply Chain Optimization: Building the Strongest Total Business Network* (San Francisco: Berrett-Koehler Publishers, 1996), p. 244.

2. *Ibid.*

3. Alexander Hiam and Charles D. Schewe, *The Portable MBA in Marketing* (New York: John Wiley & Sons, Inc., 1992), p. 320.

4. For further discussion of the supply-chain model, see Poirier and Reiter, *op. cit.,* Chap. 1.

5. Louis W. Stern and Adel I. El-Ansary, *Marketing Channels* (Englewood Cliffs, NJ: Prentice-Hall, 1988), p. 5.

6. *Producer* is used in this discussion as a general term to represent all originators of goods and services, including producers of raw materials, farmers and growers, manufacturers, etc.

7. Shelly Branch, "Hershey Turns to Convenience Stores to Sweeten Revenue," *Wall Street Journal* (March 29, 2002), p. B4.

8. Miriam Jordan, "Fuel and Freebies," *Wall Street Journal* (June 10, 2002), p. B1, B6.

9. See Michael R. Czinkota, "Export/Import Marketing: Lessons for Domestic Markets," and John T. Mentzer, "Channel Management 2000," in Jeffrey Heilbrunn (ed.), *AMA Marketing Encyclopedia* (Chicago: American Marketing Association, 1995), pp. 118–119 and 127–132.

10. Yumiko Ono, "Tiffany Glitters, Even in Gloomy Japan," *Wall Street Journal* (July 21, 1998), pp. B1, B18; "Tiffany Renews Japan Distribution Agreement with Mitsukoshi Limited," *Business Wire,* New York (August 2, 2002), p. 1.

11. *1997 Economic Census: Wholesale Trade United States,* U.S. Census Bureau, Washington, D.C., 1997.

12. In many cases the supply chain extends the distribution process to product resale and recycling, such as used items sold in resale shops or automobile trade-ins, that result in multiple sales and purchases of the same item.

13. Metro AG, Hoover's Online, http://www.hoovers.com (November 10, 2002); "Wal-Mart Teams with CITIC to Expand Into China's East," *China Online News,* Hoover's Online, http://www.hoovers.com (October 11, 2002).

14. Robin Lee Allen, "The NRN 50—The Franchisees: Foodservice's Theory of Evolution: Survival of the Fittest," *Nations Restaurant News* (January 1998), pp. 12–15ff; European Franchise Survey, European Franchise Federation (August 1997), Franchising Research web site: http://www.wmin.ac.uk.

15. "Gymboree Franchise Information," www.Gymboree.com (November 10, 2002).

16. For a complete discussion of the retail life cycle concept, see W. Davidson, A. Bates, and S. Bass, "The Retail Life Cycle," Harvard Business Review (November–December 1976), pp. 89–93.

17. Louis W. Stern (1988), op.cit; Louis W. Stern and Adel I. El-Ansary, Marketing Channels, 4th ed. (Englewood Cliffs, NJ: Prentice-Hall, 1992), p. 1.

18. Matthew Nelson, "E-stamp Receives Big Backing for Net-Based Postage Sales, InfoWorld (September 29, 1997), p. 68; www.stamps.com; www.usps.com/buystamps.htm).

19. Anonymous, "SCF Surveys Study Inventory and Integration," Transportation & Distribution 39 (6) (June 1998), p. SCF15.

20. See Stern and El-Ansary (1988), op. cit., pp. 266–281; and Adel I. El-Ansary and Louis W. Stern, "Power Measurement in the Distribution Channel," Journal of Marketing Research 9 (February 1972), pp. 47ff.

21. Judy A. Siguaw, Penny M. Simpson, and Thomas L. Baker, "Effects of Supplier Market Orientation on Distributor Market Orientation and the Channel Relationship: The Distributor Perspective," Journal of Marketing 62 (July 1998), pp. 99–111.

22. Philip Seikman, "New Victories In the Supply-Chain Revolution," Fortune (October 30, 2000), www.fortune.com; Ian Mount and Brian Caulfield, "The Missing Link: What You Need to Know About Supply-Chain Technology," ecompany.com (May 2001), pp. 82–88.

23. "Industrial Distribution Magazine Survey Reveals Industrial Distributors Battered But Not Broken," PR Newswire (September 23, 2002), p. 1+; "56th Annual Survey of Distributor Operations," Industrial Distribution Magazine, (September 22, 2002); Tischelle George, "Information Week 500—Distribution: Middleman's Mantra: Know Thy Customers," InformationWeek (September 2002), p. 91; Barry Tarnef, "Bolstering Cargo Security," World Trade, Vol. 15, Issue 11 (November 2002), pp. 54–55.

MARKETING MANAGEMENT IN ACTION: CLOSING CASE

Mothers Work, Inc.: The Care and Nurturing of a Maternity Fashion Retailer

Rebecca Matthias, Mothers Work, Inc., President and COO, and Dan Matthias, Chairman and CEO, constantly face the question of how to continue the growth of their successful maternity fashion retail business. Growth over the past two decades has been fueled by the addition of new stores, acquisitions of existing stores, store expansions, and increased sales volume. The company planned to open 60 new stores by the end of 2002, and continues to explore new avenues for growth.

Rebecca Matthias, a civil engineer in Philadelphia, was pregnant with her first child in the early 1980s. She needed to dress appropriately for the business world, but could not find suitable maternity clothes for career wear. Thus the most successful maternity fashion apparel retailer in the United States was born in 1982. Matthias first launched Mothers Work, Inc. as a mail order catalog, operating from her closet with $10,000 of her own savings. Business was so successful that she outgrew her closet, and moved her operation to her parents' house, then to a loft in an old building. Her husband Dan Matthias gave up his job as a computer specialist and joined her in the business. Mothers Work, Inc. went public in 1993.

Mothers Work is considered the leading designer, manufacturer, and marketer of maternity fashion apparel in the United States. The company operates from more than 900 locations throughout the country, outpacing its competition with one third to one half of the U.S. maternity clothes market. Mothers Work owns three leading brands: Motherhood Maternity[1]; Mimi Maternity; and A Pea In the Pod. Maternity fashions are also sold through direct mail orders and the company's Internet site, Maternitymall.com. Motherhood Maternity, the middle-market line in fashion and price, offers

[1] The Motherhood Maturity and A Pea In the Pod lines were acquired by Mothers Work, Inc. in 1995, and have been greatly expanded since that time. This was the beginning of segmenting the lines by price points. Raising the price level at Pea and lowering prices sharply at Motherhood positioned the company to pursue the "Sears-type customer" or as Rebecca Matthias said, "to compete with the real big guys out there where there's a big market." This strategy nearly doubled Motherhood's revenues, leading to cost reductions through high-volume purchasing. According to Dan Matthias, "The approach is lower the price, get the volume, then get the margin."

EXHIBIT I

Real Time Retailing®—Getting Product to the Stores Quicker

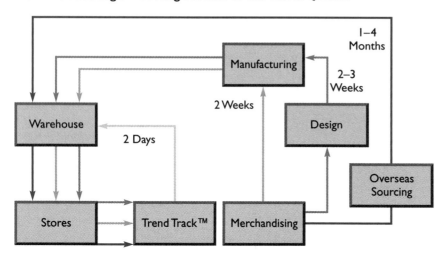

Design	Identify fashion trends and translate into brand designs.
Merchandising, Planning and Distribution	Merchant and buyer teams determine assortment (e.g., styles, price points, colors, where the product should be produced) and manager planning (i.e., ensure the right supply is in the right place at the right time).
Manufacturing	Domestic and international cutting, trimming and assembly
Overseas Sourcing	International manufacturing to minimize cost and maximize delivery
Warehouse	Ship and receive all merchandise to and from international sources, the stores, direct mail and the Internet.
Trend Track™	Proprietary, real-time computer system to track all information by location, size, color and replenishment requirements.

Source: Courtesy of Mothers Work Inc.®, The World's Largest Maternity Authority Retailer. Copyright © 2003. All rights reserved.

---

better quality maternity apparel at lower prices, in competition with maternity departments at Sears, Penney's, and Target. Mimi Maternity is a youthful "with it" line targeted toward image-conscious customers who value more fashionable apparel, and usually shop in stores such as Bloomingdale's. A Pea In the Pod is a high-fashion chain that offers luxury and top-designer maternity fashions "in a pampering environment." A customer can pay anywhere from $450 for a dress at A Pea In the Pod store to $16.90 at Motherhood Maternity. The company also has discount shops in factory-outlet malls, and operates leased spaces for its brands in department stores such as Macy's and Babies "R" Us.

MaternityMall.com is an Internet site that offers customers the best maternity fashions, information, and baby products online. In January 2002, Mothers Work acquired the 170-store iMaternity chain from a major competitor, and renamed the stores Motherhood Maturity. The company continues to publish a catalog, but mainly to drive store traffic. It is placed in ob-gyn doctors' offices, and contains a $10-off coupon for in-store purchases.

The company's philosophy revolves around "giving the customer the fashion she wants, when she wants it." Mothers Work supports its philosophy with proprietary systems that can track and respond to consumer demand quickly: a supply chain with a high degree of vertical integration, world wide sourcing, and proprietary "Real Time Retailer" computer systems. (See Exhibit 1.) Rebecca and Dan Matthias operate their business from the second floor of a block-sized plant in downtown Philadelphia. The company's vertically integrated supply chain starts with the designers working on the same floor of the headquarters building, which also includes a vast central warehouse serving 726 company-run retail outlets. Each store has point-of-sale cash registers that relay sales data back to the headquarters computer for rapid inventory replenishment. The headquarters building also houses an expansive fabric-cutting room. Sewing shops, owned by others but carefully monitored by Mothers Work, are located all over—some close to the Philadelphia headquarters, others out of town or in some 20 countries in Latin America, Asia, and the Middle East.

Rebecca and Dan Matthias recognize that their philosophy of "give the lady what she wants when she wants it" leaves a relatively narrow window for when a pregnant woman wants new maternity clothes. Nearly four million babies are born in the United States each year; and some three million women are pregnant on any given day. Those in the first trimester usually still fit in their regular clothes, and those in the last weeks of their pregnancy are less apt to purchase maternity wear except for a special event. The company has found that first-time mothers are the best customers. As Rebecca Matthias—mother of three—says, "Repeat offenders don't buy that much." She also says that the newly pregnant woman can be a great customer, "like a woman whose house has just burned down. She needs to replace her jeans, her underwear, her social gown, the clothes she wears to the grocery. And she needs to buy for more than one season."

The stores must have the right garment on hand when a maternity customer walks in because this continually changing group of approximately 1.5 million consumers cannot wait until next month or next season for a new dress, pair of jeans, or other needed clothing. The challenge is to have the desired merchandise on the selling floor when the customer walks in the door—without overloading the inventory and taking markdowns on merchandise that does not sell. Mothers Work carries about 12,000 stock-keeping units (SKUs) or individual items on its inventory list. Dan Matthias says, "It's

kind of like a hardware store: low volume, high assortment." Mothers Work must overcome the same hurdles as other women's apparel retailers: multiple seasons; changing fashions; and unexpected winners and losers. The company works on a "pull" or replenishment strategy: stores receive a basic inventory, and when an item sells, headquarters sends out a replacement. A three-level supply chain supports this strategy: domestic production mostly a short distance from the Philadelphia headquarters and warehouse (where about 60 percent of the high-end clothing is made); production in the Caribbean area and Mexico; and distant sewing plants that are mostly in Asia. A large amount of the fabric sewn by local and Caribbean suppliers is purchased and cut by Mothers Work in Philadelphia before being sent to the sewing shops. The strategy of always keeping some domestic production has paid off for the company, such as filling an inventory gap when an item sells faster than expected. For example, a sale of two $11.90 T-shirts for $19.90 was more successful than anticipated. Although the special price cut its margins, a plant outside Philadelphia produced an extra 100,000 T-shirts in a month.

The stores' point-of-sale terminals capture individual customer information (about 170,000 new names per month), create mailing lists according to baby's due date, and send and receive digital photos that help managers set up store displays (and can show headquarters what the stores look like). However, their main purpose is to provide daily sales reports that trigger stock replenishment. (Some stores receive as many as five replenishments in a week.) The replenishment process takes place each weekday evening at the company warehouse, with computerization playing a major role. For example, the computer issues an internal order to top up the picking stations for items like sweaters that can be packed flat, and instructs workers to move the required number of sweaters from the inventory area to one of thousands of bins stacked in rows in the order fulfillment area. By early the next weekday morning, the computer double-checks the number of sweaters in each bin, and adds more if needed. Next, it issues "pick lists" of sweaters that must be shipped to a given store to replenish its inventory. The process goes something like this in the warehouse's main order-picking section for sweaters and other flat-packed items (6,200 SKUs): Rectangular carriers travel on overhead rails to the bins. Pickers, each responsible for a section of an aisle of bins, are waiting at their stations. As a carrier moves along, a computer-operated green light in front of each bin alerts the picker to add a particular size and color of sweater (say large, purple), and to push a button when she has done so. If the light stays on, she must continue picking large purple sweaters for that store until the light goes out. Once all the items in her section for that store's order are picked, the carrier moves on, and is replaced by another bin and its glowing green light. At the end of the line, the carrier is zipped shut by workers and the zipper tabs are locked with a seal to make it easier to spot in-transit theft when the carrier arrives at the store. The carrier (one of 24,000 in the system) is emptied at the store and returned to Philadelphia for another order. A separate, automated "hanger sortation" system is housed in a 22,000-square-foot plus area of the building for picking garments such as suits and dresses, which are put on hangers, and then shipped in flat boxes. Dan Matthias estimates that 99.5 percent of what the stores need is available to ship when they need it. Each week, Mothers Work reviews and analyzes all store inventories to identify where specific items are moving—or not moving. For example, with stores in different climates, cotton skirts that are not selling in early fall in a Boston store might be transferred to an Orlando store where cotton skirts are still selling well.

In 2001, Mothers Work, Inc. netted sales of $388.3 million, a 1-year sales growth of 6 percent. Net income was $3.5 million, which took into consideration the costs incurred in acquisitions and other expansion expenses. The company's financial performance and prospects for the future led to a consensus "buy" recommendation for Mothers Work, Inc. stock by the five analysts who cover it, according to a June 22, 2002 Standard & Poor's report. (Go to hoovers.com for financial data.)

Given Mothers Work's outstanding performance and its large market share, Rebecca and Dan Matthias must decide where to go from here. They deviated from their core business in 1996 with the acquisition of Episode, a chain of regular women's wear. It was liquidated in 1998 at a cost of over $20

million. Their current strategy is to stay closer to the core business that they know well. They have considered international expansion, but are concerned about any venture that is not related to the pregnant American woman. As Rebecca says, "We learned our lesson when we went astray. There's a lot more easy money to be made here before we tempt fate elsewhere." Anticipating a post-9/11 baby boom, along with other companies that sell baby-related goods, Mothers Work geared up with added financing to take advantage of this potential opportunity. Meanwhile, they continue to develop their Internet strategy through Motherswork.com to capture even more of the $1 billion a year maternity-wear market.

Sources: Philip Siekman, "New Victories In the Supply-Chain Revolution," *Fortune* (October 30, 2000); www.motherswork.com; "Mothers Work, Inc.," *Hoovers Online*, www.hoovers.com; Eddie Baebb, "A New Format Fails to Deliver," *Crain's Chicago Business*, 24(47) (November 19, 2001), p. 3; Peter Van Allen, "Mothers Work Isn't Done," *Philadelphia Business Journal* 21(19) (June 28, 2002), p. 3.

Case Study Questions

1. Evaluate the complete distribution system and supply chain used by Mothers Work, including the advantages and disadvantages of vertical integration.

2. What are the benefits, if any, of outsourcing more of Mothers Work's operations?

3. Analyze and discuss the present distribution channels used by Mothers Work. Should the company consider other distribution channels, such as international?

4. You are meeting with Rebecca and Dan Matthias tomorrow morning. At this meeting, you will present your recommended strategy for growth, and a plan for implementing your strategy. Prepare an outline of your recommended plan.

Integrated Marketing Communications Strategy

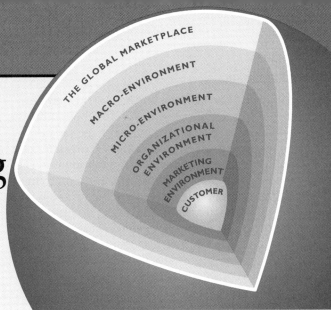

THE GLOBAL MARKETPLACE
MACRO-ENVIRONMENT
MICRO-ENVIRONMENT
ORGANIZATIONAL ENVIRONMENT
MARKETING ENVIRONMENT
CUSTOMER

Never promise more than you can perform.[1]

Was the mLife Advertising/rebranding Campaign a Bold Strategy?

The vague "What is mLife?" TV, print, online, and outdoor campaign that began in mid January 2002, was crafted by Ogilvy & Mather, and ran taglines like "Is mLife fattening?" In the week just before Super Bowl 2002, it became cool to trash the 'teaser' campaign. Everyone thought it was backed by insurance giant MetLife. But when the six 60 second spots (that's $2 million apiece, down 15 percent from the 2001 ad price) were broadcast during the Super Bowl game it turned out that AT&T Wireless was launching one of the most expensive and extensive rebranding campaigns in a long time.

When it switched from the teasing question stage of the campaign to the branding phase, AT&T tried to get consumers to think more about what they could do with their cell phones and how wireless services like text messaging could add value to their lives. The new ads for mLife (short for mobile life) showed slice of life, scenes with happy people talking about how mLife had helped them stay connected and live more freely. In short they were attempting to create an emotional appeal. But some people wondered if consumers ever could really feel emotional about a cell phone!

Many people in the ad industry harshly criticized the teaser campaign for being exorbitant in a down economy and it didn't help the situation that the 'creative' aspects were also attacked. The point of a teaser campaign is to stimulate curiosity—it is not a call to action. But mLife was widely insulted for being overly vague. One marketing expert even used a January 2002 issue of the *Wall Street Journal* as a basis for the cry of "Cut the cord on mLife."

Bold Branding

However John Gaffney writing for Business 2.0 (www.business2.com), gives AT&T big points for bold branding. Gaffney notes that the old concept of using advertising to shape consumer perception of your product, in an environment where marketers are paying more attention to accountants than to creative directors, was a bold move. The mLife campaign wasn't designed with next week's sales goals in mind. Gaffney thinks that took guts and suggests marketers who think branding campaigns are best left to the 90s should reconsider.

According to Jupiter Media Metrix, the mLife campaign has worked on at least one level in that traffic to the mLife website soared 1,900 percent after the Super Bowl spots. The site logged 34,000 unique visitors on Saturday, February 2, and 681,000 on Super Bowl Sunday. Yes, the numbers did drop to 567,000 on Monday, but that is still healthy traffic for a corporate website. Moreover, in excess of 36 percent of all visitors registered to receive more information about AT&T Wireless services and products. According to Mark Seigel, an AT&T Wireless spokesperson, this result "blew away" the company's expectations. Jupiter Media Metrix said the mLife campaign earned AT&T the biggest jump in Web traffic of any advertiser during the Super Bowl.

Gaffney believes the mLife campaign was a big roll of the dice in an ad market that was very tight and was an effort to differentiate itself from Cingular, Sprint, and Verizon. Seigel said the aim was to get consumers to care about more than the latest calling plan prices—a wireless war that's squeezing profits. Was the teaser campaign's millions of dollars of expenditures extravagant? Perhaps. But AT&T thinks advertising can get the job done.

Source: John Gaffney, "Marketing Focus: AT&T's mLife in Hell," *Business 2.0* (February 11, 2002).

Perhaps AT&T has rediscovered a way for integrated marketing communications (IMC) to help differentiate or rebrand. Ogilvy and Mather analyzed the communications needs of the targeted customers and used an integrated marketing communications mix of advertising, direct marketing, and publicity, to effectively send the emotional message of maximum convenience and flexibility. AT&T also needs to structure the remaining marketing mix elements—product strategy, pricing strategy, and distribution strategy—to be compatible with this overall marketing strategy.

● INTEGRATED MARKETING COMMUNICATIONS

Designing the integrated marketing communications activities of an organization pushes the manager to the forefront of marketing knowledge. Innovation and creativity make the difference between humdrum marketing and truly outstanding communication of the intended message to target audiences. The term **integrated marketing communications (IMC)** is used in marketing to cover all types of marketing activities designed to stimulate demand. We refer to these various demand-creating activities as the *communications mix.*

The American Productivity & Quality Center (APQC) developed a more concise definition of integrated marketing communications as follows: "IMC is a strategic business process used to plan, develop, execute and evaluate coordinated, measurable, persuasive brand communication programs over time with consumers,

> **Integrated marketing communications (IMC)** Used in marketing to cover all types of marketing activities designed to stimulate demand; sometimes referred to as the *communications mix.*

customers, prospects and other targeted, relevant external and internal audiences."[2] If we simply substitute the word *marketing* for *brand* in this definition, the concept of IMC broadens to encompass the entire scope of marketing communication activities in both the consumer products market and the business-to-business market.

Communications Theory

Communications theory has important applications in all areas of IMC and marketing strategy. Simply stated, *communication* is the transmission of messages. Therefore, the ultimate success of an IMC program rests on its ability to deliver a core message to a target market.

The Communications Flow.   IMC activities involve a forward communications flow. Manufacturers *communicate to* wholesalers, retailers, and ultimate consumers. Resellers *communicate to* their customers. Backward flows of communications also exist and are critical to understanding customers and markets. Communications also can flow horizontally. Retailers exchange ideas among themselves. Consumers are notoriously inclined to spread marketing information. In fact, we even talk about word-of-mouth advertising as if it were a type of communications medium. A 2002 study by Yankelovich Inc., a market research consultancy, indicated that 57 percent of African Americans get advice about a product through someone they know while 48 percent of Hispanics gave the same response. But relatives pass on knowledge at the rate of 44 percent for African Americans and 62 percent for Hispanics. Emanuel Rosen, who wrote the book, *The Anatomy of the Buzz: How to Create Word-of-Mouth Marketing,* says one of the challenges is finding opinion leaders, whom he also calls "network hubs," and persuading them to test a product. Felipe Kor-zenny, president of Cheskin Research Inc., a multicultural market research firm, seems to agree when he said, "Penetrating a community through opinion leaders makes for a good chance that the product will be adopted."[3] In almost all communication situations there is a feedback loop that provides information about the effectiveness of the flow of communications.

Elements of Communication.   There are four important elements that help us understand the relation of communications to IMC: the source, the message, the medium, and the receiver.

1. The *source* is the initiator of the message, often a manufacturing or service establishment wanting to transmit some information to customers or resellers.

2. The *message* is the commercial idea being communicated. In advertising, it is the copy; in selling terms, it is the "sales pitch." The message is the substance of what flows from sender to receiver.

3. The *medium* delivers the message. In advertising, the medium may be a television show, a newspaper, a magazine, or any number of other forms. In personal selling, the salesperson is the medium.

4. The *receiver* is the person (or persons) to whom the message is directed. In most cases the receiver is a potential customer. However, a receiver also can be a purchase influencer or a reseller, who then is expected to become a sender to retransmit the message to yet another audience.

The role of these four communications elements is illustrated in Figure 11.1. The source is an organization, for example, Ford Motor Co. The medium is national network television. The vehicle is "Monday Night Football." The message is an endorsement by a famous quarterback of the company's Taurus automobile. The receiver is a potential customer at home who views the commercial.

Types of Communications.   Figure 11.1 is an oversimplification of a highly complex mass communications system, which is illustrated in Figure 11.2.

- *Specific communications.* Specific communications involve the direct transmission of a message from a single source to a single, specific receiver. For example, a salesperson at a Ford dealership in Orlando telephones a customer in the suburbs who owns a Ford Escort purchased several years previously. The salesperson thinks that the customer might be ready for a new car, possibly a Taurus. This specific communication in shown in Figure 11.2a.

- *Selective communications.* Selective communications involve directing messages through a single medium to a limited number of receivers. For example, after talking on the telephone, the salesperson might send a colorful brochure showing the new Taurus to everybody who purchased an Escort 3 years earlier. Figure 11.2b illustrates this communications flow.

- *Mass communications.* Mass communications involve the use of one or more media to reach large numbers of receivers. Figure 11.2c shows such a communications program. Now, instead of the salesperson being the source, the dealer fills this communications role. Three radio stations are selected as media for the commercial message to the entire market. Each radio station reaches some, but not all, of the potential customers. However, every potential buyer is exposed to at least two radio stations.

Distortion and Noise.   Not every message reaches its intended receiver, and some arrive hopelessly distorted. *Distortion* is most likely to occur in long communications flows involving several successive media vehicles. Using persons to transmit messages often creates distortion. A manufacturer whose product is purchased and resold first by a wholesaler and then by a retailer has little control over the sales message delivered to the ultimate consumer. This is the reason manufacturers attempt to reach consumers through a controlled IMC campaign.

Noise, or confusion, is an even more serious problem.[4] It can arise because of faulty transmission, faulty reception, or interference. A small newspaper advertisement

FIGURE 11.1

The Communication System

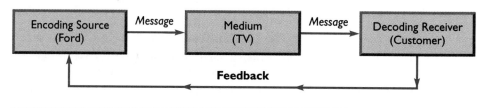

FIGURE 11.2

Three Types of Communication: (a) specific communications, (b) selective communications, (c) mass communication

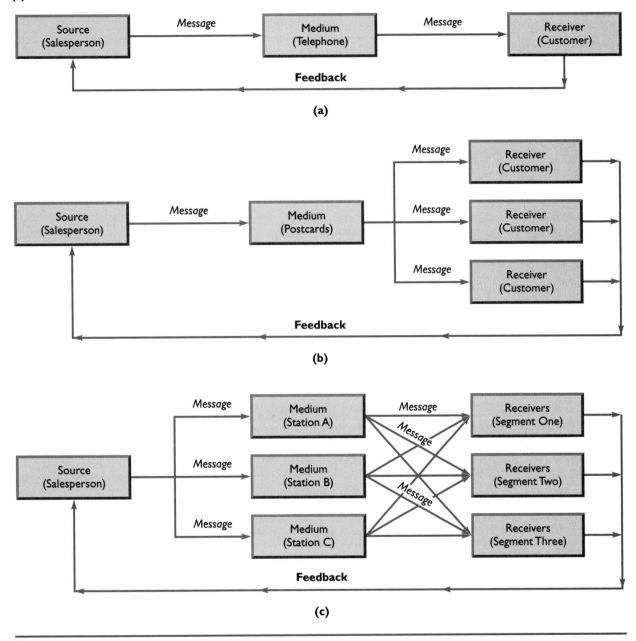

crowded in among many others on a cluttered page certainly will be lost. Bad reception and interference are even more likely in broadcast communications. Consumers are not especially interested in advertising and thus do not pay close attention to it. They frequently turn down the volume or switch the radio or television channel whenever a commercial starts. The popularity of the television remote control stems from the convenience of "zapping" commercials both on the air and when a show is being replayed from a videocassette recorder.[5] However, even if the message comes through, the noise level at the receiving end is very high.

The loudest and most serious noise results from competitive interference. The typical consumer is exposed to many communications flows simultaneously. Often these are directly competitive. Look at a newspaper and note how many directly competing advertising messages it contains. In the same way, how many fast-food or cosmetics commercials do you see in one evening of television watching?

How can a marketer overcome this type of interference? By communicating meaningfully to the right people, at the right time, and with the right message. Effective communication, however, demands conspicuous creativity and requires consistent and persistent efforts. The noise at any one time is too great for marketers to expect immediate results. Over the period of an entire IMC campaign, and certainly in the long run, a well-conceived, continuous, and creative communications program can achieve its objectives.

The Communications Mix

Communications mix Any communications activity designed to stimulate demand—specifically, advertising, salesforce activity, sales promotion, direct marketing, and publicity/public relations.

Various elements of IMC are combined in the **communications mix.** Specifically, this mix includes advertising, salesforce activity, sales promotion, direct marketing, and publicity/public relations. The term *mix* implies that there are different ways of blending these ingredients as part of an overall IMC program. It also suggests a synergism, in which the total IMC effect is greater than the sum of its parts. In short, the communications mix is an overall creative plan as well as a thoughtfully designed combination of selected ingredients.

Advertising. *Advertising* is the public communication of messages to select audiences to inform and influence them. Advertising messages are identified with the advertiser and involve payment to the medium employed, whereas public relations/publicity does not. Advertising is often mass communication. Although some advertising is directed to specific individuals (e.g., in the use of direct mail, trade publications, and professional publications), most advertising messages are placed in public media to be seen by large numbers of people.

Salesforce Activity. Simply stated, *salesforce activity* is any person-to-person or telephone-based activity by a firm's representative that is intended to deliver value to customers. From a management perspective, this involves selecting, training, organizing, deploying, motivating, and supervising a team of field salespersons and establishing account management policies to guide field and internal behaviors. From a salesperson's perspective, this involves all sales process activities associated with personal selling plus related activities required to build relationships and satisfy customers over the long term.

Sales Promotion. Because *sales promotion* frequently involves reducing prices to distributors or retailers to motivate them to push the sponsor's products, it is easy to forget that non-price-related sales promotional activities are the predominant forms of sales promotion. Sales promotional activities are intended to have an immediate impact on consumer buying behavior.

Direct Marketing.   *Direct marketing* involves activities designed to reach targeted customers without an intermediary organization being involved. For example, database marketing has enabled customized direct-mail programs to become viable methods to reach individual customers with persuasive communications.

Publicity/Public Relations.   *Publicity* is communication of information that is not paid for and does not identify the source of the message. It is sometimes not included as part of the communications mix because it lacks controllability. Publicity can be used for many nonmarketing communications purposes, for example, in connection with a company's dealings with the financial community or in connection with a collective-bargaining situation. To isolate the part of the publicity that is properly part of the communications mix, we use the term *public relations* (PR).[6] For instance, when a company introduces a new product, it may try to have articles about the product appear in magazines and newspapers.

IMC Objectives

In addition to contributing to the overall marketing effort, the major objective of IMC activities is to influence targeted customer groups. IMC does influence sales. In dot.com or mail-order businesses, IMC is the principal means of marketing. But mostly IMC contributes to sales revenue directly by performing two powerful functions: It *conditions,* and it *reinforces.* IMC activities prepare the way for the salesperson by informing customer prospects of the value of the company's products or services. And IMC reinforces sales efforts by reminder reinforcement and after-sales presentations. Postpurchase communication combats negative evaluation. For undecided customers, IMC keeps the flow of information open until the next opportunity for a sale occurs.

The effects of IMC on actual and potential customers have been stated in different terms by several researchers.[7] Their perspective is that potential customers must progress through several states of awareness before they are ready to buy—as illustrated in Figure 11.3. The total population of potential customers can be classified according to these stages. The goal of IMC is to move potential customers toward the state of conviction and actual use. The classification of awareness levels shown in Figure 11.3 is called the **hierarchy of effects model.**

Hierarchy of effects model
The classification of awareness levels that potential customers must progress through before they are ready to buy.

What marketers really want to accomplish with IMC is (1) to create a unified image and (2) to support relationship building with customers and stakeholders. First, the firm must decide specific targets for the IMC campaign (initiators, users, decision makers, influencers, buyers, or gatekeepers). Next, the firm must set communications goals, which Marian Burk Wood suggests fall into five categories:[8]

1. *Build brand equity.* Use IMC to reinforce your brand's value and identity and encourage stronger preference, which should strengthen relationships competitively.

2. *Provide information.* Offer details about product uses, availability, buying incentives, or convenience of use. Pall Corp., marketer of fluid filtration and purification products, organized its Web site around industry categories rather than internal divisions. This facilitates client browsing through appropriate industry-related Web pages or using the site's search function to find Pall products

FIGURE 11.3

Hierarchy of Effects Model

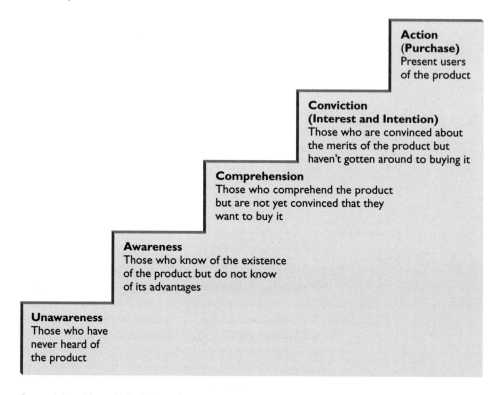

**Action
(Purchase)**
Present users
of the product

**Conviction
(Interest and Intention)**
Those who are convinced about
the merits of the product but
haven't gotten around to buying it

Comprehension
Those who comprehend the product
but are not yet convinced that they
want to buy it

Awareness
Those who know of the existence
of the product but do not know
of its advantages

Unawareness
Those who have
never heard of
the product

Source: Adapted from Colley, R. H., *Defining Advertising Goals for Measured Advertising Results.* Association of
National Advertisers, New York, p. 55. Reprinted by permission.

and technologies appropriate for solving their problems. Also, clients or contacts can e-mail requests for sales consultations.

3. *Manage demand and sales.* Work to stimulate primary demand (for new or innovative products) or selective demand (perhaps for a mature product) or to
temporarily dampen demand when the firm is unable to meet demand (or the
requested shipping dates). American Express Company used IMC tactics to
build selective demand for its corporate card in a highly competitive market affecting customer acquisition, card use, and market share.

4. *Communicate differentiation and enhance positioning.* Convey significant
factors of differentiation and positioning relative to competitors' products. For
example, United Parcel Service (UPS) stresses the range of guaranteed "urgent
delivery" choices such as "same day" and "next day" to differentiate itself from
competitors while positioning itself to meet almost any deadline. This is a powerful image for a delivery firm.

5. *Influence attitudes and behavior.* Promote a favorable inclination toward
your company and products while encouraging some action, such as recommending your services, contacting your representatives, or completing a purchase order. For instance, A.B. Dick supported the introduction of a new

IT'S LEGAL **BUT IS IT ETHICAL?**

Drug Companies Overstep Boundaries

In southern Florida during July 2002, up to 150 people received Prozac in the mail. They had not asked for it, and there are conflicting stories whether there were prescriptions for it. The Florida attorney general's office has issued subpoenas to Walgreen Co., which mailed the drug, as well as to a local hospital, a medical group, four health professionals, and Eli Lilly, maker of Prozac. Eight Lilly employees have been disciplined and Lilly says it believed the doctors knew patients would be mailed the medicine. But physicians' representatives claimed they thought drug vouchers, not the drug, would be sent. Walgreen says they were just following doctor's orders.

Consumer advocates were outraged and said the promotion was another example of drug companies caring more about profits than patients. Privacy proponents feared patients' medical records had been mined for direct advertising campaigns without their permission. Douglas Wood, a partner at Hall, Dickler, Kent, Goodstein & Wood, a law firm specializing in advertising, said, "There is a real hysteria out there about privacy, so that Prozac situation touched a nerve. Pharmaceutical companies are using every angle to advertise. They have just gotten more aggressive—using print, direct mail, coupons. There are many people that just don't like what has happened."

This incident occurred when everyone from doctors, to governors, to senators have been trying to muffle pharmaceutical messages in hopes of protecting patient privacy while lowering skyrocketing prescription drug costs. The Centers for Medicare and Medicaid Services estimated that overall spending on prescription drugs in 2001 rose 16.4 percent to $142 billion. Some industry critics tie ballooning prescription drug costs to surging pharmaceutical promotional spending, which had more than doubled from 1995 to 2001. Research by IMS Health placed current ad spending at $19 billion. But drug companies insist that promotions provide valuable information to doctors and patients, and that drug costs are growing because there are more medicines and people are living longer.

Pharmaceutical companies pay many of the major drugstore chains to contact patients and encourage them to either refill prescriptions, upgrade to a newer version of a medication, or change to a different drug. This practice has spawned a number of "invasion of privacy" suits. New regulations that will set national privacy standards for patient medical records were due to be released by the U.S. President's office in late 2002, and The Health Insurance Portability and Accountability Act will go into effect in April 2003. This may require pharmacies to determine if they need to alter their promotional agreements with drug companies.

Source: Teresa Agovinao for The Associated Press, "Drug companies overstep boundaries," *Marketing News* (August 19, 2002), p. 17.

two-color printing press targeted at small printing firms, corporate printing departments, and large commercial printers by using direct mail, public relations, newsletters, and magazine ads to smooth the way for subsequent sales calls. The company emphasized the key product benefit—making short-run color printing profitable. Although previously known for its duplicating machines, A.B. Dick's IMC campaign established the company as a maker of full-sized printing presses, and this led to 350 orders totaling more than $20 million.

Wood warns marketers against stretching their IMC strategy and budget over four or five objectives and thus diffusing their IMC effectiveness. It is more effective to concentrate on only one or two IMC goals.

● PULL VERSUS PUSH IMC STRATEGIES

Many people think that IMC is directed only toward customers, but important aspects of IMC are directed toward channel intermediaries. Approximately one-third of IMC expenditures is for customer advertising and two-thirds is for sales promotion. The largest portion of these sales promotion expenditures (37 percent of total spending) is for intermediary promotions, whereas the remainder (29 percent of total spending) is for customer advertising. Therefore, approximately 63 percent of total IMC expenditures are aimed at customers and 37 percent at intermediaries.

Pull-through communications
Customer-targeted IMC activities designed to build awareness, attraction, and loyalty and reduce search costs.

Customer-targeted IMC consists of **pull-through communications.** The objective of pull-through communications is to build awareness, attraction, and loyalty and reduce search costs, as shown in Figure 11.4. Successful pull-through communications influence customers to seek out certain products or services, thus pulling the product through the channel. Channel intermediaries or resellers must carry these products in order to attract and satisfy target customers.

Push-through communications
IMC activities directed at channel intermediaries in order to motivate resellers to make products/services available to customers.

In contrast, **push-through communications** are directed at channel intermediaries in order to motivate resellers to make a certain product available to customers. Successful push-through communications result in greater availability, fewer stockouts, effective merchandising (shelf space and visual effects), and better marketing efforts by resellers.

Combining both push- and pull-through communications creates the most effective influence on customer response and market share gains.[9] Figure 11.4 outlines the components of push- and pull-through communications.

Pull-Through Communications

Figure 11.4 illustrates the wide range of alternatives in the IMC mix that can be used for effective communications to create customer pull.[10] A good example of the power of communication is the classic case of L&M cigarettes, which had a 17 percent market share prior to the ban on cigarette television advertising. Following the ban, the company decided not to advertise because its people believed that other advertising media were ineffective. L&M is no longer in the market. Without continued reinforcement of the brand and its positioning, L&M faded from customers' minds and from the marketplace.

Customer-directed sales promotions take a variety of formats such as coupons, rebates, sweepstakes, gifts, and rewards. Catalog retailers such as L.L. Bean, Inc., or Eddie Bauer stimulate customer pull every month with mailings to targeted customers. In addition, salesforce activity, direct marketing, and electronic marketing on the Internet are forms of IMC that take a customized approach to creating customer pull in the marketplace.

Persuasive communications
IMC activities intended to get target customers to take a specific action (to purchase something).

Persuasive communications are intended to get target customers to take a specific action (to purchase something). A firm must be careful in using persuasive

FIGURE 11.4

Push-Pull Communications and Customer Response

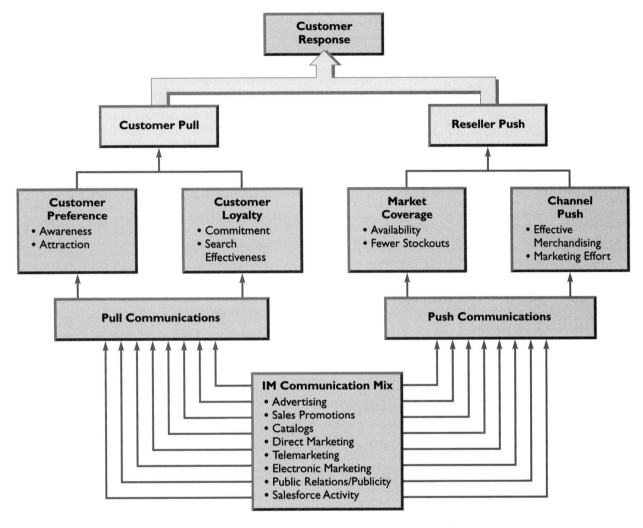

Source: Adapted from Roger J. Best, *Market-Based Management* (Englewood Cliffs, NJ: Prentice-Hall, 1997), p. 253.

communications. If the message is too one-sided in stressing benefits or comparisons with competing products, the message may lose credibility. For example, Paul Wiefels, a marketing consultant, believes that some technology marketers seem too fascinated by their own products. This results in an evangelical zeal that can transform markets, but more often it results in a myopic preoccupation with the trivial and arcane. Consumers are fed product specifications and features instead of useful explanations on how the product might fit into their lives or solve problems at work.[11]

INNOVATE OR EVAPORATE*

E-mail Marketing: Reach Out and Touch Consumers

 Scott Woodside on nearly every page of his Platinum Pen Store Web site invited visitors to join an e-mail list to receive special offers on pens—both the extraordinary and the mundane, because he sold 99-cent pens alongside $9,999 pens. Woodside and many small businesses have found that e-mail marketing is one of the most effective ways to keep customers coming back to their small-business Web sites. It can also be an extremely cost-effective way to keep in closer contact with customers while building brand awareness and loyalty. Shawn Augustson, co-founder of Busy-Cooks.com, puts it this way, "It keeps your visitors involved and informed. Just think about all the sites one visits in a day. You could easily be forgotten about. Your newsletter sort of is a little reminder that you are out there." E-mail marketing in this form is sometimes referred to a "viral" marketing and can cost as little as pennies per message—quite a bargain compared to the $1 or more cost of a traditional direct mail piece. And, response rates on e-mail marketing can be strong—Meta Group reported in 2001 fulfillment rates of 5 percent to 15 percent for e-mail compared to only 1 percent to 3 percent for traditional direct mail.

Deborah Whitman has published a selection of best practices culled from e-mail marketing veterans at smaller companies. She writes that small businesses should create a compelling e-mail communication and send it regularly. Many businesses use newsletters as their e-mail marketing vehicle. A newsletter format can give a friendlier feel while building a relationship with customers. Whitman suggests the following newsletter features can be effective:

- *Include special prices and offers*—the travel newsletter by Gorp.com, an adventure travel company, published a weekly travel newsletter with special discounts and deals on adventure trips.

- *Clever, unique information*—High Country Gardens monthly newsletter offered tips on key gardening tasks.
- *Entice them back to your Web site*—a recent Gorp.com newsletter gave a short paragraph about the best wildflower hikes in the United States and then provided a link to a full article on Gorp's Web site.
- *Share info about new products and services*—some small businesses use their newsletters to share information about new products and services with existing customers.
- *Entertainment*—MyGolf.com included golf jokes as well as about 15 other kinds of jokes in their customized newsletter.
- *Market it well*—many small businesses market their newsletters by saying nothing more than "join our e-mail list," but by using some of the below listed tactics more people should be persuaded:
  - Tell them what valuable information or offers they'll get.
  - Include links to prior newsletters.
  - Give customers many chances to join—put invitations to join your e-mail lists in several places on your Web site.
  - Limit demographic questions—make it easy to join, but follow up with questions in a later e-mail that helps you target messages better.
  - Sign people up offline—have a sign-up sheet or list in your storefront or office where people can easily write in information.
  - Welcome them with the most recent newsletter—each time a new customer joins send a welcome e-mail that includes the most recent newsletter.

*The box title is attributed to James M. Higgins, *Innovate or Evaporate* (Winter Park, FL: New Management Publishing Company, 1995).

Source: Deborah Whitman; "E-mail Marketing: Reach Out and Touch Customers," Net Progress—Online Marketing Website (Spring 2001).

Push-Through Communications

Figure 11.4 illustrates that the same wide variety of pull-through communications activities is available for push-through communications efforts. Push-through communications are directed at channel intermediaries and are designed to motivate resellers to become more aggressive in their customer communications and marketing. As shown in Figure 11.4, the objective of push-through communications is to build more effective reseller efforts so that sponsoring firms are able to obtain better market coverage (number of desired distributors) and better merchandising efforts from resellers. This support of resellers' efforts is sometimes called **trade promotions.**

Trade promotions
IMC push-through communications efforts designed to motivate resellers to obtain better market coverage and better merchandising activities.

IMC and Product Life Cycle Stages

There are limits to what communication can accomplish relative to sales levels at different stages of the product's life cycle (PLC). During the introductory stage of the PLC, a firm builds awareness, comprehension, and interest, but market demands may be small, and only limited sales volumes are achievable.

The growth stage of the PLC offers the best opportunity for sales gains using IMC. A firm must invest in IMC during this phase or miss the best opportunity for sales growth because communication results are more likely to have an impact during this period. As markets mature, there are fewer new customers coming into the market, and the effect of IMC on sales diminishes. In declining markets, the firm needs to cut IMC expenditures because they produce little sales response.

● FINANCIAL ASPECTS OF IMC

IMC activities can involve huge sums. For example, the cost of a 30-second spot on the Superbowl in 1985 was about $500,000. In 2002, the cost was $2 million. In addition, the cost of producing a television commercial is very high. According to one source, a typical commercial in 2001 cost approximately $350,000. Despite these high figures, IMC expenditures in some companies are relatively small when compared with manufacturing and other operational costs. Moreover, this apparent high cost becomes even more modest when the number of consumers reached is considered. For example, if a network television ad is viewed in 20 million homes, the cost of reaching each household is less than 1 cent.

When related to the value of products and services sold, IMC expenditures are not exorbitant. Business-to-business marketing firms, on average, spend less than 1 percent of sales revenue on IMC. Firms marketing consumer goods and services spend in the range of 5 to 10 percent of their sales revenues on IMC—although some companies such as cosmetics firms spend much more.

To measure the effectiveness of IMC, marketers have developed several tools: the customer response index, calculations of communications elasticity, and calculations of communications carryover.

Calculating the Customer Response Index (CRI)

Changes in customer awareness of ads, comprehension of content, and interest or conviction as a result of advertising copy are important factors that affect overall

Customer response index (CRI)
A calculation of the changes in customer awareness of ads, comprehension of content, and interest or conviction that measures overall customer response.

customer response. A tool for measuring overall customer response is the **customer response index (CRI),** which can be calculated using this formula:

$$CRI = \% \text{ aware} \times \% \text{ comprehend} \times \% \text{ interest} \times \% \text{ intentions} \times \% \text{ purchase}$$

Let us assume that the following customer responses occurred after exposure to an ad:

Awareness of the ad was calculated at 63 percent.

Comprehension of the ad was calculated at 54 percent.

Interest in the product was calculated at 77 percent.

Intention to purchase the product was calculated at 68 percent.

Purchase of the product was calculated at 90 percent.

The CRI is calculated this way:

$$CRI = 0.63 \times 0.54 \times 0.77 \times 0.68 \times 0.90$$
$$= 0.16, \text{ or } 16 \text{ percent}$$

Now if the firm and its ad agency believed they could improve "comprehension" from 54 to 67 percent by using a finely tuned communications mix, then the CRI could be improved from 16 to 20 percent:

$$CRI = 0.63 \times 0.67 \times 0.77 \times 0.68 \times 0.90$$
$$= 0.20, \text{ or } 20 \text{ percent}$$

This calculation indicates that improving "comprehension" from 54 to 67 percent should produce an increase in the CRI (and thus a sales increase).

Calculating Communications Elasticity

Communications elasticity
Calculating the change in sales volume per 1 percent change in IMC efforts.

Calculating the change in sales volume per 1 percent change in IMC efforts is a measure of **communications elasticity.** For example, suppose that an increase of 1 percent in communications expenditures produced an estimated 22 percent change in sales volume.[12] Thus a firm with $40 million in sales and a 0.22 communications elasticity could estimate that its sales would increase to $41.67 million with a 20 percent increase in communications, as shown below.

$$\text{Sales} = \text{volume} \times \text{communications elasticity} \times \text{price}$$
$$= 400,000 \times [1 + (0.22 \times 0.20)] \times \$100$$
$$= \$41.67 \text{ million}$$

Calculating Communications Carryover

Communications carryover
A calculation of the effect of IMC expenditures made in one time period on additional sales responses in subsequent time periods.

IMC expenditures made in one time period produce additional sales response in subsequent time periods. This is termed **communications carryover.** Communications carryover coefficients can range from zero to less than one. The average carryover coefficient is approximately 0.5.[13] Therefore, in the period immediately following a communication, a 0.50 sales effect from the preceding period will carry over, and in the second period, a carryover effect of 0.25 occurs, and so on, until after the period 6, when the carryover sales effect is less

FIGURE 11.5

Communications Carryover

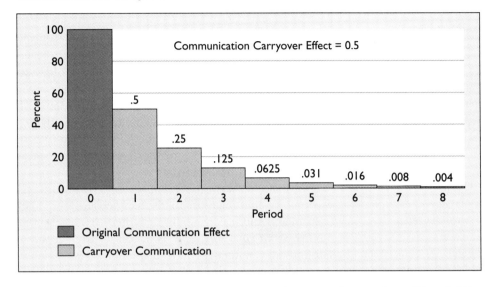

Source: Adapted from Schultz and Block, "Empirical Estimates of Advertising Response Factors," *Journal of Media Planning,* Fall 1986. Reprinted by permission.

than 1 percent. See Figure 11.5 for a graphic representation of this carryover effect.

Budgeting IMC

IMC budgeting decisions constitute one of the most difficult problems in marketing planning. What size budget results in effectiveness? When does the firm reach the level of excess spending? How does a firm ensure that budget constraints relating to operating issues from other functional activities of the firm do not overpower the need for effective IMC? In many firms there are ongoing battles with accounting and/or finance people about how to measure the effective use of IMC dollars and how to record such expenditures on financial statements because of the lag effects of communications carryover. All these issues are important, and the following discussion covers the variety of budgeting approaches available.

Marginal approach
An IMC budgeting method whereby the last dollar spent on IMC activities exactly equals the incremental profit generated by these expenditures.

The Marginal Approach. Theoretically, the IMC budget should be at a level where the last dollar spent exactly equals the incremental profit generated by the expenditure. Application of the **marginal approach** to IMC budgeting assumes that marginal gross profit (selling price minus manufacturing costs) is constant and that sales increases are associated with incremental IMC expenditures.

Measuring the effect of IMC on sales is extremely difficult. One of the major difficulties is that the effectiveness of IMC in a given period is influenced by the carryover effect of IMC done in prior periods (as noted earlier). The classic study attempting to measure cumulative effect was done by K. S. Palda, who used a regression equation that incorporated the lagged effects.[14] Palda determined that in the short run each dollar of IMC (advertising) generated only $0.50 in additional sales but in the long run produced $1.63 in sales. These calculations justify a long-run policy of heavy IMC using the marginal budgeting approach. Unfortunately, most firms do not have sufficient data relative to the lagged effects of their IMC expenditures and therefore use nonmarginal budgeting approaches.

Available Funds Approach.   Using the **available funds approach,** a firm limits its IMC budget to funds it has on hand. This is like saying, "If we have anything left over after we pay all our bills, we'll spend it on IMC." This is committing dollars to all manufacturing, operating, and administrative activities and then spending any remaining funds on IMC. This is sometimes referred to as the *total residual method.* A variation of this approach is the *cash residual method,* where a firm in a weak cash position spends little on IMC.

> **Available funds approach**
> An IMC budgeting method that limits IMC expenditures to funds a firm has on hand.

Does the available funds approach produce the correct budget? It might be wasteful, committing more funds than needed. More likely, however, it generates too few dollars. And it is generally accepted that a minimum level of spending, called the *threshold spending level,* is necessary to have any effect. This method may result in totally ineffective levels of spending.

Competitive Parity Approach.   Some firms are convinced that to maintain market share they need to spend at least as much for IMC as their competitors do. This is called the **competitive parity approach.** To increase market share requires even greater expenditures, so over time the total amount spent on IMC in a given industry will increase. Sometimes the cost of adding market share can be too high. This approach requires that the manager track the amounts that competitors spend on similar brands. Generally, the amounts spent on public media are available for most products sold by leading advertisers.[15]

> **Competitive parity approach**
> An IMC budgeting method whereby a firm spends at least as much for IMC as its competitors do.

Percentage of Sales Approach.   The easiest approach to IMC budgeting is the **percentage of sales approach,** which involves allocating a fixed percentage of sales to IMC. Assuming that money for IMC must be earned before it can be spent, this percentage is based on last year's sales or forecasted current sales. This method has the effect of accelerating IMC when sales are on the increase and reducing it when sales are declining—which may be inappropriate.

> **Percentage of sales approach**
> An IMC budgeting method that allocates a fixed percentage of sales to IMC.

Fixed Sum per Unit Approach.   Similar to the percentage of sales approach, the **fixed sum per unit approach** involves budgeting a specific amount per unit sold. The advantage of using a fixed sum per unit sold is that the appropriation for IMC is not affected by changes in pricing strategy. The fixed sum per unit approach is used frequently in determining industrial product IMC budgets, as well as for consumer durables such as automobiles.

> **Fixed sum per unit approach**
> An IMC budgeting method that designates a specific amount per units sold.

Return on Investment Approach.   The **return on investment (ROI) approach** has been recognized as theoretically advantageous because it considers the IMC budget to be an investment rather than a current expense. Ideally, the budgeted amount should be based on the maximization of profits over a product's total life cycle. The technique demands forecasts of alternative revenues and costs for different levels of IMC expenditures. This makes it comparable with capital-budgeting decisions.

> **Return on investment (ROI) approach**
> An IMC budgeting method that considers IMC expenditures as an investment that should be based on the maximization of profits over a product's total life cycle.

The communications planner chooses among alternative budget levels by comparing the forecasted rate of return for each level. However, the extreme difficulty in forecasting a product's life cycle sales and management's usual reluctance to treat IMC as an investment expenditure make this approach less likely to be used.

Task method approach
An IMC budgeting method that recognizes that IMC expenditures must achieve specified objectives and involves four steps: conduct research, determine objectives, identify IMC tasks, and cost the IMC tasks required.

The Task Method Approach.   The **task method approach** recognizes that IMC expenditures must achieve specified objectives, in the same way that other budgets in the firm do. A comprehensive four-step budget procedure has been developed to emphasize the tasks involved in constructing an IMC strategy:

1. *Conduct research.* The marketing situation is analyzed looking for marketing opportunities and targets.
2. *Determine objectives.* Short- and long-term IMC objectives are set.
3. *Identify IMC tasks.* The message and media required to achieve the IMC objectives are identified.
4. *Cost the IMC tasks.* The costs involved in the strategy are estimated.

Through the use of computerized systems, the task method approach of IMC budgeting has become less costly and more feasible, resulting in a wider base of use.

Summary

Integrated marketing communications (IMC) are all types of marketing activities designed to stimulate demand. These activities are often called the *communications mix.* Communications theory has important applications in all areas of IMC. Most IMC activities involve a forward communications flow to wholesalers, retailers, and consumers; however, backward flows of communications are critical to understanding customers and markets. Understanding the four elements of communication—the source, the message, the medium, and the receiver—can help us to understand how communications relate to IMC. There are three general types of communications—specific communications, selective communications, and mass communications. Some messages do not reach the intended receiver because of distortion or noise.

Various elements of IMC are combined in the communications mix. The term *mix* implies that there are different ways of blending these elements. Specifically, the mix includes advertising, salesforce activity, sales promotion, direct marketing, and publicity or public relations.

The major objective of IMC activities is to influence targeted customer groups. One way to measure the effectiveness of communications is to measure consumer awareness. One classification model that is used to describe customer awareness is the hierarchy of effects model. The two major goals of IMC are (1) to create a unified image and (2) to support relationship building with customers and stakeholders.

IMC strategies can be classified as pull-through strategies or push-through strategies. The objective of pull-through communications is to build awareness, attraction, and loyalty so that customers will seek out certain products or services. Persuasive communications are part of pull-through communications. Push-through communications, sometimes called *trade promotions,* are directed at channel intermediaries in order to motivate resellers to make the product available to consumers. However, there are limits to what communications can accomplish relative to sales levels depending on the stage of the product life cycle (PLC).

IMC activities can involve huge sums, although relative to the value of the products and services sold, IMC expenditures are usually not exorbitant. To measure the effectiveness of IMC, marketers have developed several tools, such as the customer response index (CRI), calculations of communications elasticity (the change in sales volume related to the change in IMC effort), and calculations of communications carryover (how long the message affects sales response after it is withdrawn).

IMC budgeting decisions are difficult because it is not easy to financially record a direct numerical correlation between IMC activities and sales. Some methods that firms use to budget IMC are the marginal approach, available funds approach, competitive parity approach, percentage of sales approach, fixed sum per unit approach, return on investment approach, and task method approach.

Questions

1. Do you agree that the development of integrated marketing strategy pushed marketing managers to the frontiers of marketing knowledge?

2. Suggest ways in which the concepts of specific, selective, and mass communications might be used by a department store in planning an IMC strategy for lawn and patio furniture.

3. As an executive for a large, multidivision organization, recommend an appropriate integrated marketing communications mix for each of the following products: (a) a medicated soap for dry skin, (b) a facial cosmetic that contains sun-blocking additives and comes in various tones, (c) a hair-coloring system that is temporary (washes out with shampoo in three to five applications), is dispensed in a cream form (easy to apply), will not stain clothes, contains no bleach, and is environmentally friendly, and (d) a hair-removal system that is a cream dispensed from a tube, washes off after 5 minutes (while removing the hair), does not harm the skin, and is safe for facial use.

4. You are in charge of designing an IMC strategy for an instant tea designed to be used in preparing iced tea. However, users have reported using the product to prepare hot tea. You have decided to communicate this alternative product use. You have a $5 million budget. How would you decide how much of this amount to spend on this "hot" new product use?

5. Suggest some reasons why it is important to know exactly how a product is distributed before developing an IMC strategy.

6. A marketing consultant was nearly fired on the spot when he suggested that a firm could decrease its overall marketing expenses by increasing its IMC budget. Fortunately, the consultant was able to explain the truth of his position. How would you go about explaining what he meant?

Exercises

1. Identify a firm (either national or local) that within the last 12 months has used a push-through communications strategy effectively. Identify the specific types of IMC activities that the firm used, and explain why you believe this was the correct choice to achieve success.

2. Access the Web site of one of the major agencies or organizations involved in the control of advertising (such as the Federal Trade Commission at http://www.ftc.gov or the National Advertising Division of the Better Business Bureau at http://www.bbb.org). Determine the agency's current position on ethical and legal issues (such as advertising to children). Do a content analysis of media targeted to this audience, and identify advertisements in electronic and/or print media that demonstrate possible infractions of ethics or regulatory policy. Create new ads that will convey the same message in an ethical and responsible manner.

3. Contact a local new or used automobile dealership that you have identified from perusal of the local newspaper as being a heavy advertiser.

Through extensive questioning, identify the specific type of budgeting method the company uses to plan and prepare its IMC activities.

Endnotes

1. Publilium Syrus, "Maxim 528," as quoted in *Bartlett's Book of Business Quotations* (Boston: Little, Brown & Company, 1994), p. 217.

2. Don E. Schultz, "Check Out Your Level of Integration," *Marketing News* (August 18, 1997), p. 10.

3. Deborah L. Vence, "Word of Mouth: How to Generate that Buzz so Effective for Ethnic Markets," *Marketing News* (July 22, 2002), p. 19.

4. For an interesting discussion of clutter in advertising media, see Ralph Andill, "Separating the Message from the White Noise," *Marketing* (April 16, 1998), p. 17.

5. Anonymous, "Zapping," *Marketing* (September 17, 1998), p. 15; Anonymous, "Perimeter Ads Solution to Zapping," *Marketing Week* 20(46) (February 26, 1998), p. 34.

6. Martin L. Bell and Julian W. Vincze, *Managerial Marketing: Strategy and Cases* (New York: Elsevier Science Publishing, 1988), p. 508.

7. Colley's model is found in R. H. Colley, *Defining Advertising Goals for Measured Advertising Results* (New York: Association of National Advertisers, 1961), p. 56.

8. Marian Burk Wood, "Clear IMC Goals Build Strong Relationships," *Marketing News* 31(13) (June 23, 1997), p. 11.

9. For further discussion, see David Reibstein, "Making the Most of Your Marketing Dollars," in *Drive Marketing Excellence* (New York: Institute for International Research, 1994).

10. Gary Lilien, Philip Kotler, and K. Moorthy, *Marketing Models* (Upper Saddle River, NJ: Prentice-Hall, 1992), pp. 329–356.

11. Paul Wiefels, "Change Marketing Tactics as Buyer Attitudes Shift," *Marketing News* 31(12) (June 9, 1997), p. 10.

12. Rajeev Batra, Donald R. Lehmann, Joanne Burke, and Jae Pae, "When Does Advertising Have an Impact? A Study of Tracking Data," *Journal of Advertising Research* 35(10) (September–October 1995), pp. 19–29.

13. Dwight R. Riskey, "How TV Advertising Works: An Industry Response," *Journal of Marketing Research* 34(2) (May 1997), pp. 292–294; and Ron Schults and Martin Block, "Empirical Estimates of Advertising Response Factors," *Journal of Media Planning* (Fall 1986), pp. 17–24.

14. K. S. Palda, *The Measurement of Cumulative Advertising Effect* (Englewood Cliffs, NJ: Prentice-Hall, 1964), p. 80.

15. See *Leading National Advertisers.* This periodical reports the spending by competing brands on measured media: television, radio, magazines, newspapers, and outdoor.

MARKETING MANAGEMENT IN ACTION: CLOSING CASE

"Cisco Internet Generation," an IMC Campaign for Cisco Systems Inc.

Cisco Systems Inc., the San Jose-based network equipment manufacturer, provides hardware designed to provide B2B customers with seamless communication systems. Therefore, its own advertising must be polished and effective and withstand comparison with the best existing B2B ad campaigns by competitors. With its "Cisco Internet Generation" IMC campaign, the company was expecting to create a corporate image of reliability, precision, and innovation through the use of broadcast, print, and Internet advertising.

An earlier TV campaign had centered on the question, "Are you ready?" implying that corporate customers should be sufficiently up-to-date technologically to take advantage of the communications systems Cisco manufactured and marketed. To build on this prior message, all messages on all media of the "Cisco Internet Generation" IMC campaign included the signature tagline, "Empowering the Internet generation." This push by Cisco to build brand awareness using multiple media included print ads, one of which featured three people walking through a rice paddy. Reflected in the water was the image of an airplane. The accompanying text read, "Last year your customers spent $172 billion on business travel." And, shown prominently was a Web address that pointed to Cisco's presentation of video conferencing technology. Many industry observers thought this was an especially adroit message during a time (2000–2001) when business travel budgets were being slashed.

Nancy Hill, president of GMO Hill/Holiday of San Francisco, Cisco's ad agency of record, said the "Internet generation" ads showcased Cisco as an empowering, enabling company that thrived on one-on-one, human interaction. Hill pointed out that in the campaign "... Cisco gets specific about things you can be doing that you have not thought about." In all advertising, technical terms were avoided and the IMC campaign emphasized Cisco's continuing focus on utilization of the Internet as the future of all business. "Right from the beginning, there has always been something in our campaigns that just feels like Cisco," Hill noted. "It is almost always global, and puts a human face on technology."

Combining Approaches

A key to the "Cisco Internet generation" campaign had been the linking of print and broadcast media with an interactive presence, according to Hill. If an ad was targeted at a business strategist, the advertisement would point to a Web site tuned to their level of technical expertise and their mindset. Or, an ad slanted toward an information technology executive, would point to a Web page tuned to the bits-and-bytes mindset. Print ads had appeared in national newspapers, and magazines such as *Information Week, The Industry Standard, Forbes, Fortune, The Economist,* and *The Wall Street Journal.*

Tim Hendrick, VP-account management for JWT Technology, San Jose, said that linking media to Web sites added a call to action to an otherwise broad campaign. Hendrick was doing the same type of broadcast, print, and Web tie-in for his clients and said, "You need to have a response mechanism or call to action, as it's the means to gather information about the b-to-b customer. We've seen a lot of brands come out with advertising that tries to make an impact with the customer. But at the same time, you have to sell product. A link to a Web page is the beginning of that sales cycle."

Tracking Performance

Cisco had worked hard to track the performance of the "internet generation" campaign. An internal tracking study showed that Cisco's unaided brand awareness had risen 80 percent since 1999. Respondents also rated the "internet generation" ads 80 percent higher (more effective) than competitor ads by Lucent Technologies Inc. and Nortel Networks Corp. And the same internal study indicated that Cisco's reputation as an Internet expert was 250 percent higher than Microsoft Corp. and 500 percent higher than IBM Corp. and Lucent Technologies Inc.

Source: John Evan Frook, "Cisco scores with its latest generation of empowering ads," *B to B;* Chicago (August 20, 2001), Copyright Crain Communications, Incorporated.

Case Study Questions

1. Why does the "Internet generation" campaign by Cisco qualify as an IMC campaign?

2. Of the types of media used by Cisco for the "Internet generation" campaign, which do you believe is the most effective in communicating the intended message and images? Which media are the least effective?

3. What are your thoughts about what Tim Hendrick said concerning the "... need to have a response mechanism or call to action ..."?

4. Can a sales cycle begin with a link to a Web page?

5. How effective do you think Cisco's internal tracking study is? Should you accept the stated results without question?

6. Has Cisco's "Internet generation" IMC campaign continued to be successful from 2001 until today?

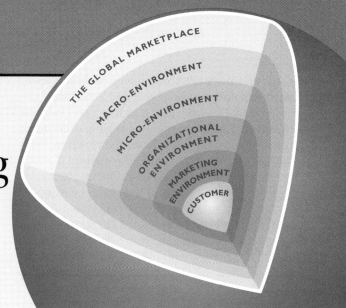

CHAPTER 12

THE GLOBAL MARKETPLACE
MACRO-ENVIRONMENT
MICRO-ENVIRONMENT
ORGANIZATIONAL ENVIRONMENT
MARKETING ENVIRONMENT
CUSTOMER

Integrated Marketing Communications Tools

Overview

Managing Salesforce Activity

Managing the Advertising Program

Publicity, Direct Marketing, and Sales Promotion

The successful sales rep of this decade will be a facilitator, not a pitchman, an expert on the customer's total business who coordinates with colleagues to make buying easy and efficient.[1]

European IMC Constraints

Pharmaceutical companies in the United States use a daily assault of sales people calling on physicians, prescription rebates, TV commercials, and print ads as integral to their integrated marketing communications (IMC) strategies for reaching their customers and consumers. But the European Union's (E.U.) ban on prescription-drug advertising prevents companies from mentioning their products on Internet pages or in brochures. "Even if we get a call from an inquiring consumer, we have to be fairly careful about mentioning any drug," says Rolf Hoemke, communications director at Aventis AG's German unit. "Usually we suggest they consult their doctor." In Europe, Aventis is restricted to using allergy calendars and pollen-count pointers to promote their allergy drug Allegra. This is the same French-German company that spent 101.6 million Euros ($89 million) in 2001 for ads in the United States to make Allegra a household name.

Many argue that the E.U. ban severely limits patient access to information and thereby to full access to drug products. In fact per-capita retail sales of drugs in certain large European countries are far less than in the United States. AstraZeneca PLC's ulcer drug Prilosec, for instance, had 2002 worldwide sales of 6.85 billion Euro; however, although less populated than Europe, the U.S. sales represented two-thirds of that total. Until recently, such arguments have had little impact, but as the Internet and the drug industry open new outlets for health-care information, opportunities are emerging that could allow for more aggressive IMC activities. A March 2002 set of E.U. proposals would allow drug makers to market treatments for AIDS, diabetes, and respiratory ailments on their corporate Web sites, in patient-requested pamphlets, and in other company literature. These diseases were chosen as test cases because treatments don't vary radically from patient to patient. Also, patients with these diseases have been most insistent in requesting information. If approved, the E.U. proposals could be implemented within 2 years; if the trial is judged to be effective, the proposal could be expanded to other drugs. Although these measures fall short of U.S.-style direct-to-consumer IMC marketing, they do indicate the pressure on the E.U. governments to loosen restrictions. The biggest force of pressure is the Internet, which allows consumers to seek information beyond what their doctor tells them.

In many ways, the Internet already has made moot a complete ban on direct-to-consumer marketing strategies, because if consumers don't find information about a certain medicine on a company's E.U. Web site, they can easily get the information by clicking on its U.S. Internet address. But this may cause some confusion, because drug products often have different names in Europe and the United States, and also have different recommended and/or approved dosages. Lars Almblom Jorgensen, executive vice president at Novo Nordisk AS says, "If we close the flow of information in Europe, we just run the risk of letting people get bad or wrong information. Sure, everyone knows we want to sell more insulin. But we also know the expensive part of treatment is when you have to treat a disease that's much worse because it wasn't treated earlier. Information is vital."

Source: Vanessa Fuhrmans and Gautam Naik, staff reporters; "European Drug Makers May Utilize More Aggressive Marketing Tactics," *Wall Street Journal* online, http://online.wsj.com; *European Business News* (March 15, 2002).

As the European Union (E.U.) proposal makes clear, it is becoming obvious that an integrated marketing communications (IMC) approach is critical to developing an effective marketing strategy. Although components of the various IMC tasks may be assigned to different parts of a firm, they must be integrated by a single, overall promotion strategy with a common communications purpose. Chapter 11 identified the entire scope of IMC activities, including salesforce activity, advertising, public relations/publicity, direct marketing, and sales promotion. This chapter examines each of these communications tools in greater depth.

● MANAGING SALESFORCE ACTIVITY

Marketing strategists' decisions related to salesforce activities are people-related and complicated.[2] Our discussion of the sales process focuses on building customer relationships. A model of this sales process is shown in Figure 12.1. According to this model, an organization must determine that its strategic goal is to be customer-focused and ensure that all sales activities are oriented toward this end.

Managing the salesforce involves defining the sales task, investigating the relationship between sales activity and productivity, and determining salesforce structure. It also involves configuring sales territories, determining salesforce size, and addressing human resources issues such as staffing, compensation, direction, and motivation.

FIGURE 12.1

The Sales Process

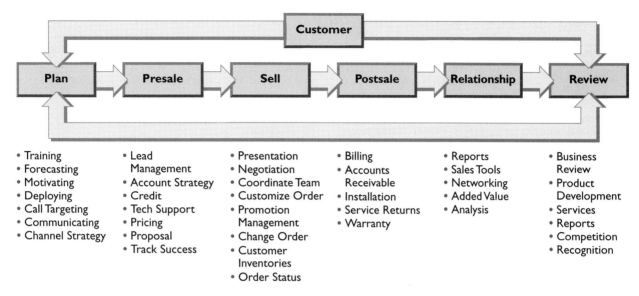

Source: Adapted from Glen S. Petersen, *Higher Impact Sales Force Automation: A Strategic Perspective* (Boca Raton, FL: St. Lucie Press, 1997), pp. 54–65.

Defining the Sales Task

What do salespersons do? Typical salespeople answer by saying, "Too much." One way to determine the sales task for a firm is to consider all the different types of selling and decide which style is best for the firm and its product(s).[3]

> **Relationship selling**
> Developing a relationship with the customer to learn about his or her needs, attitudes, and behaviors.

Relationship Selling.   **Relationship selling** involves building customer relationships and cultivating current and future sales opportunities instead of just soliciting immediate business. In relationship selling, the salesperson works closely with prospective customers and the selling company's research and development (R&D) department. In some situations, such as in the capital goods market, it may take several years to complete a sale. The goal is to create a good working relationship with the customer and build the customer's confidence. Through close cooperation, products or services can be developed to meet the customer's particular need. Doing this requires that the salesperson develop a relationship with the customer to learn about his or her needs, attitudes, and behaviors. As Dan Logan notes, this "... is a continuous process based on understanding your target audience ...," and building this kind of rapport takes dedication and consistency in approach over time.[4]

Laura Liswood believes that "... if customers have [use] one product with you ... there's a 15 percent likelihood they'll stay loyal to you for 5 years. With two products, that rises to 45 percent; with three, it's up to 80 percent." Over time, the entire buyer-seller relationship tends to shift as the product matures. Sellers can capitalize on these changes to strengthen their relationship with their customers.[5] Cross and

INNOVATE OR EVAPORATE*

Sales Force Automation and Global Selling

One of the key differences between selling in the United States and selling in nearly any other country is the length of the sales cycle. Whether the delay is due to cultural tendency to do more research or more socializing, or economic circumstances, or some as yet unknown factor, American salespeople have to pursue more accounts simultaneously to make their sales targets. Mark Zawacki, managing partner at the Palo Alto, California, office of ExpertEyes, a tech consulting firm with offices in London and Ghent, Belgium, says, "Selling in an international context exposes you to more varied and complex sales situations, which accelerates your sales experiences. You need to think a lot smarter and longer-term about how you build your sales pipeline."

Some industry observers believe the answer lies in Sales Force Automation (SFA), but culture and cost may often be key challenges to those introducing SFA in international markets. In many areas of the globe, salespeople prefer the face-to-face approach with clients (whom they treat as their own, not the company's). Language and antiquated technology may be barriers to using the latest software and the cost of upgrading may be prohibitive. The idea behind SFA is using technology to put customer information in the hands of all company employees via database, not just in files for individual salespeople. But some salespeople treat such information as personal proprietary information that is the base for their competitive advantage over other salespeople, both within their own company and with competing firms. They may not understand the benefits to their company of sharing customer information.

One Argentine company successfully overcame these hurdles with a home-grown sales-force automation strategy costing less than $75,000. The 1,000-strong salesforce was automated by purchasing pocket-sized electronic organizers that had been modified so they could capture the significant details of a salesperson's meetings with customers. When the sales reps returned to the office, they downloaded the information into a central database, where it became available throughout the firm. Gustavo Covacevich, CEO of Buenos Aires-based Previnter SA, says, "Immediately, we increased sales activity dramatically. The device generated a daily need for data that could not be faked, and the new tool actually made it easier to manage their client relationships. Activity increased, and productivity increased."

*The box title is attributed to James M. Higgins, *Innovate or Evaporate* (Winter Park, FL: New Management Publishing Company, 1995).

Sources: Lisa Bertagnoli, "Selling Overseas Complex Endeavor," *Marketing News* (July 30, 2001) p. 4; Kathleen V. Schmidt, "Why SFA Is a Tough Sell in Latin America," *Marketing News* (January 3, 2000).

Database-driven marketing
Any marketing process in which useful, behavioral, psychographic, or demographic information about prospects or customers is stored in the company's database and is used to enhance or prolong the relationship or to stimulate sales.

Smith introduce a modification they call **database-driven marketing,** which is an interactive, relationship-building kind of marketing centered around a core of customer information. It is "any marketing process in which useful, behavioral, psychographic or demographic information about prospects or customers is stored in the company's database and is used to enhance or prolong the relationship or to stimulate sales."[6] This type of interaction is a form of **relationship marketing** that can be used to foster customer loyalty.

Relationship marketing
An interactive, relationship-building marketing centered around a core of customer information.

Pretransaction Selling versus Posttransaction Servicing. *Pretransaction selling* is similar in some respects to relationship selling. The objective of pretransaction selling is to evolve a long-standing relationship between the supplier and customer. *Posttransaction servicing* is a different type of selling effort, often assigned to individuals other than those who closed the sale initially. For instance, post-sales servicing of electronic data processing equipment often is assigned to technicians. The objective of post-sales servicing is to keep a customer satisfied.

Cold-Canvas versus Lead Selling. Almost in direct contrast to relationship selling is cold-canvas selling. Salespersons who call on a "shot in the dark" basis, not knowing whether the prospect needs the product, are *cold-canvas selling*. Cold canvassing, or "prospecting" as it is sometimes called, is rare today in consumer markets. Restrictive local ordinances, the mobility of households, the high proportion of working women, and consumers' unwillingness to buy this way have made it difficult and often ineffective. However, in some industrial and wholesale selling, the cold call is still used, since organizational buyers are sometimes receptive to this approach. Some cold calls are also still used by financial services firms based on prequalified lists and by some small businesses who do not seem to acknowledge that this is an inefficient and less effective way to use salespeople.

Lead salespersons only call on prospects known or thought to be interested in buying a company's product or service. Leads can be obtained in many ways. Lists of prospects can be purchased, or respondents to advertising can be contacted. Also, customers suggest names of other prospects. One common prospecting method is the use of an *endless-chain system*. The salesperson attempts to obtain the names of at least two or three new prospects from each person called on. In this way, even if most contacts do not "pan out," there usually is a backlog of prospects to call.

Planned versus Canned Selling. The day of the unplanned, ad-lib sale is past. All sales presentations are planned to some degree. The extreme in planning is the *canned sales pitch.* Salespeople using this approach follow a script, deviating only to adapt the presentation to special circumstances. Relatively unskilled persons can be effective using canned sales, and the approach works in person or on the telephone.

Estee Lauder's sales approach is inscribed in a 150-page basic sales training manual that is utilized in the 100 hours of sales seminars that new sales representatives undergo during their first year of employment. And this is followed-up with annual classes.[7]

Experienced salespeople prefer a more flexible approach. However, a sales plan is still used. It may be elaborate or simple, depending on the sales opportunity and the training and inclination of the salesperson. Some salespeople develop very elaborate customer strategies to identify a sales objective and outline how the sales interview will be conducted.

Missionary versus Transaction Selling. *Missionary salespeople* represent manufacturers, calling on customers, resellers, and purchase influencers to stimulate demand and to assist resellers in developing selling programs for the manufacturer's product. Ordinarily, a missionary salesperson does not accept orders. In contrast, the *transaction salesperson* concentrates on booking business. Contrasting these two types of selling situations is sometimes characterized as "order takers versus order getters." Similar in some respects to competitive selling, transaction selling involves making sales in the face of intense competition. These competitive salespeople often are technically trained and are found mostly in industry. Order salespersons are encountered in the marketing of resale items, especially packaged goods distributed through wholesale-retail trade channels.

Creating the Job Description.   Sales managers agree that many demands are made on salespeople above and beyond selling, such as completing reports, providing estimates, and sometimes even collecting accounts. Many firms also require salespersons to manage their territory and their customers. These numerous demands often lie at the heart of the problems that arise. The IMC view of salesforce activity stresses the importance of contact with customers but also insists that all activities be planned, directed, and controlled in the same way that all aspects of marketing are managed.

The sales task in a business-to-business environment is noted in Figure 12.2. It is a position description for an account executive and entails many responsibilities apart from selling. Firms differ in the specific nonselling demands they make; however, this position description illustrates the scope and character of many typical requirements.

Investigating the Relationship Between Sales Activity and Productivity

Salesforce automation
The creation of electronic information systems that make sales activities more productive and cost-effective.

Current trends to improve productivity have been driven by the industry trends of re-engineering, downsizing, and rightsizing to achieve lean and effective organizations. One result of these trends is **salesforce automation.** Salesforce automation focuses on productivity and cost reduction in order to deliver value to the customer.[8] Once laptop computers became available in the mid-1980s with two-way communications and the ability to update remote user systems, field salesforce automation became a timely activity because information systems (IS) departments had already automated "back room" processes. Previously, IS had avoided sales and marketing functions because it was viewed as a quagmire of open-ended and constantly shifting needs. Glen S. Petersen notes that one of the earliest success stories was Ciba-Geigy, which reported that a 1 percent increase in salesforce productivity generated a 6.7 percent increase in revenue.[9] Moriarity and Swartz, in a *Harvard Business Review* article, concluded that salesforce automation increased sales by 10 to 30 percent and resulted in a return on investment in excess of 100 percent.[10] However, what is the strategic initiative for salesforce automation if it can achieve these results? Petersen suggests two: Market success will be determined by (1) delivering superior value to the customer and (2) capturing maximum profit in the delivery of that value.[11]

The question becomes: Where do we begin? Re-engineering and total quality management initiatives advocate a customer focus, but in practice, these techniques are applied more often to processes that are not connected directly to customers. By contrast, the sales process directly relates to customers, and it is necessary to coordinate all the firm's functional activities with sales to deliver value to customers. It is this perspective that drives the development of effective automation of field salesforce activities.

FIGURE 12.2

Position Description for an Account Executive

Account Executive (AE)

I. Job Summary. The Account Executive (AE) is responsible for managing a module of business accounts in the Business Markets Division (BMD). The AE will be on incentive compensation and accountable for protecting the revenue base, generating new revenues by planning and executing moderately complex sales transactions including voice, data, and network systems as well as packaged solutions.

II. Duties and Responsibilities

 A. Responsible for the management of an assigned module (group of accounts) **45%**
  1. Positioning = interface with assigned business customers/key decision makers
  2. Data gathering = compilation of data determining customers' problems
  3. Data analysis = analyzing all data gathered
  4. Designs = conceptual solutions for business problems
  5. Proposals = prepares and presents final communications solutions to customer
  6. Implementation = monitors support team activities, assigns tasks and follows up
  7. Follow-up = ensures implementation is complete as ordered by customer and customer is satisfied with effect of solution on problem

 B. Account planning **25%**
  1. Develops account plans to identify customer needs and proposes solutions
  2. Based on the plan identifies opportunities and assigns priorities and timelines

 C. Development and general administration **30%**
  1. With sales management develops account management and selling skills
  2. Keeps abreast of trends via trade publications and attending seminars
  3. Prepares correspondence and contracts relative to sales activities

III. Major Problems

 A. Develop and maintain state-of-the-art technical knowledge
 B. Establish and position us in accounts not previously penetrated
 C. Demonstrate to customers that we are credible business solutions resource
 D. Sell product line which is more expensive than competition
 E. Acquire necessary support resources from a limited pool

IV. Key Contacts

 A. Support team—technical sales and implementation support
 B. Customer—sell products and services
 C. Industry association—maintain presence and gather intelligence

V. Knowledge and Skill Requirements

 A. Education—bachelor's degree or equivalent experience
 B. Specialist—basic product, customer, and market knowledge
 C. Technical—AE assessment and testing required
 D. Experience—one year in selling environment

VI. Scope

 A. Incumbent reports to sales manager who supervises a group of AEs
 B. Objective to increase module size by 20–22%

Source: Highly adapted from recruiting information sent to graduate business school Career Centers.

FIGURE 12.3

Networked Sales Automation System

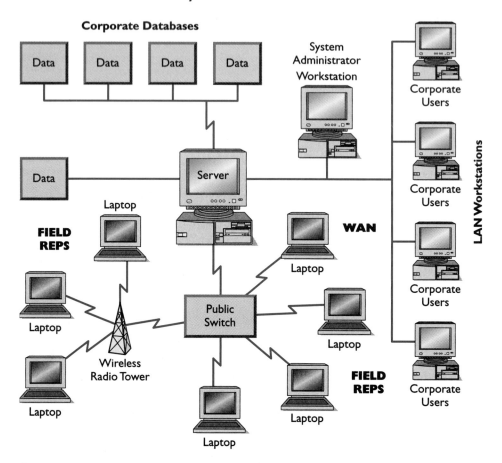

Source: Reprinted by permission from Glen S. Petersen, *High Impact Sales Force Automation: A Strategic Perspective,* St. Lucie Press, Boca Raton, FL, 1997, p. 91. Copyright © CRC Press, Boca Raton, Florida.

Figure 12.3 represents a networked sales automation system where sales reps' laptops are connected with a server via a wide-area network (WAN) or with corporate headquarters via a local-area network (LAN). This automated system can reduce cycle times because the data are timely, accurate, and readily available; leverage efforts can be organized throughout the company via e-mail (electronic messages); and sales reps can be freed from support functions (such as report writing), thus providing more time, energy, and motivation to interact with customers.

Determining Salesforce Structure

> **Direct selling**
> When the firm employs its own salesforce and calls directly on customers.

> **Indirect selling**
> When the firm uses the employees of resellers to solicit sales.

The structure of a firm's salesforce corresponds closely with its channel of distribution. There are two selling alternatives: (1) **direct selling,** in which the firm employs its own salesforce and calls directly on customers, and (2) **indirect selling,** in which the firm uses the employees of resellers to solicit sales.

The existence of a sales department indicates a functionally based organization. This is commonly the case when extensive personal contact with customers is required. Even if indirect selling is used, the outside salesforce must be supervised for effectiveness.

The salesforce can be structured several different ways. When a company's product line is extremely broad, the salesforce can be divided according to product lines. This means that separate salesforces are used, even if they call on the same customers. Another way of organizing the salesforce is geographically. A salesperson is viewed as a manager of a territory, responsible for developing business within it. This works well in companies with short or homogeneous product lines and in markets where extreme market segmentation is not encountered. However, if a territory contains several different types of industries, it is often difficult for one individual to be familiar with the special needs of each. This dilemma leads to the assignment of salespeople on a customer-size basis. Large and small customers tend to demand different services. A fourth basis for the assignment of salespeople can be the level or type of customer. For example, different salespeople might call on manufacturing, wholesale, and retail outlets.

It is common to find various combinations of these methods. Any number of combinations is possible. An extremely large company might combine all four types of sales organization: product, territory, size, and customer.

Configuring Sales Territories

Many marketing strategists use a geographic basis in assigning the salesforce. Widely dispersed customers and high expenses to reach them make geographic assignments economical. Also, it is easier to provide competitive customer service from a local base. This is done best when the salesperson lives in the territory. Increased morale will occur if territory design results in ease of coverage and relatively equal probability of reaching sales goals.

The question is: Which comes first—design of the salesforce or design of the territories? The two are closely related. A salesforce may be designed to serve specific territories, or territories may be adapted to the size and capabilities of the existing salesforce. Because we already looked at the first approach, we will now focus on the second approach.

Fitting the Sales Territory to the Salesforce.   If a company already has a salesforce, it may develop its territories around these people. A manager determines how many territories the salesforce can handle effectively. Then the total market is divided into this number of geographic areas. Alternatively, the optimal size of territory for a single salesperson is determined. The territories are arranged in order of attractiveness to the firm. Next, people are assigned to territories. The first alternative results in thin coverage of most territories. The second alternative may leave markets uncovered if the existing salesforce is small in number. If the first method assigns too large an area, the result is that fewer than optimal calls will be made on some good customers and less frequent calls will be made on all customers. The second method may cover some markets while it develops others intensively. Volume is sacrificed, and competitors may establish a foothold in the uncovered markets.

Salesforce deployment can affect sales productivity. If improved performance is needed but there is no reason to restructure territories, a redeployment of personnel

FIGURE 12.4

Shapes of Sales Territories

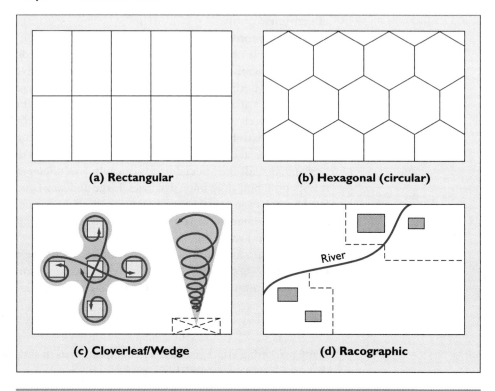

(a) Rectangular   (b) Hexagonal (circular)

(c) Cloverleaf/Wedge   (d) Racographic

may do the trick. There also can be some adjustment in coverage at the same time. Changes in the relative importance of various markets do take place. Salespeople do not like to be moved like pawns on a chessboard. Sometimes, however, contentment with an existing situation can cause low productivity. Redeployment may be the solution.[12]

Configuring the Shape of Territories.   Designing territories involves two problems. One is the shape of the territory; the other is its size. A territory is only part of an entire market, and the parts must fit together. Within this limitation, however, the territorial parts can be of almost any shape—even a jigsaw configuration is possible. Territories are constructed by combining smaller geographic or political units into larger ones. Rectangles are the easiest to construct, but circular areas are the most economical to serve. The smaller the building blocks, the easier it is to obtain the desired configuration. States are often used, but counties are particularly good because they are the smallest areas for which market data are available.

   Figure 12.4 shows how an area might be divided into several geometric territories. In the *rectangular* shape (Figure 12.4a), the market is divided into equal parts by vertical and horizontal lines. The result is artificial and offers no advantages except that the territories are of equal geographic size. The *circular* territory (Figure 12.4b) has this same advantage but also minimizes travel distances if customers are evenly located throughout the territory and the salesperson is located in the center. (Because it is impossible to fill a surface completely by circles, hexagonal territories are shown in the figure.)

Figure 12.4c illustrates two special territorial configurations. The *cloverleaf* design is for a territory with customers clustered in five locations. The salesperson is located at the center and makes trips to the four peripheral markets. The *wedge* design is part of a larger circular territory. The rectangle at the point of the wedge represents a major metropolitan market. Several individuals divide the market, each taking a wedge-shaped territory. This is the most equitable allocation of a market, with the best customers found in the center. No one salesperson gets all the preferred accounts. Each is located at the point of the wedge, concentrating calls in one part of the metropolitan area and making occasional trips to the periphery.

Because customers usually are scattered unevenly, territories with such neat rectangular, circular, cloverleaf, and wedge shapes are rarely possible. Political boundaries and topologic phenomena also make ideal configurations impractical; for example, customers may be concentrated in urban centers that may be historically or accidentally situated. A major river or other travel impediment may cause a deviation from the ideal shape. In practice, designing territories begins with the ideal but ends with compromises to fit each territory to the physical, political, and demographic characteristics of the market. Figure 12.4d illustrates this.

Size of Territories.   The size of a territory depends on several factors. Territories should be about equal—both in revenue potential and in difficulty of servicing. But complete equality is never possible. It is easier to compare performance when territories are approximately equal; in addition, morale is better and bickering over assignments is minimized.

Designing territories that are equal in both potential and workload is problematic because customers are not evenly distributed. There is no solution to the problem. It is solved only by compromise.

Determining Salesforce Size

A firm such as Procter & Gamble Co. has several thousand salespeople. How does the company decide how many salespeople to employ? There are two major approaches to this important question.

Workload Approach.   The number of salespeople a firm needs may be calculated by estimating the extent of the selling task and dividing this task by the amount that a single person can handle.[13] For example, a manufacturer of industrial machinery sells to two types of customers: end-users and dealers. In a selected market there are 500 end-users and 100 dealers. Experience indicates that the average salesperson can make approximately 600 sales calls per year. Management wants to determine the number of salespeople necessary to make 12 calls on each of the end-users and 24 calls on each of the dealers during a single year.

To make this determination, management can use a special formula:

$$N = \frac{\sum_{i=1}^{2} F_i C_i}{K}$$

or

$$N = \frac{F_1 C_1 + F_2 C_2}{K}$$

where N = the number of salespeople
F = the call frequency required for a given customer type
C = the number of customers in a type
K = the average number of calls a salesperson can make during a year

Therefore, inserting these figures into the formula, the equation is worked as follows:

$$N = 1/600[12(500)] + [24(100)]$$
$$= 1/600(6000 + 2400)$$
$$= 14$$

Thus, based on the number of customers to be reached and the average of sales calls made per person per year, the firm decided to assign 14 people to this particular sales task.

Marginal Approach. Marginal analysis enables a firm to determine the optimal size of its sales organization. However, practical applications involve making day-to-day decisions about hiring and releasing personnel. Managers know two basic facts about the size of a salesforce: If an additional person is hired, total sales should increase and so will total selling costs. If a salesperson is dismissed, sales will decline and so will expenses. Thus another salesperson should be hired if the extra person will contribute more in gross profit than in cost. In firing or not replacing salespeople, the opposite reasoning applies: If the cost saved exceeds the gross profit sacrificed, the company is better off with a smaller salesforce.

Staffing and Measuring Performance

Managing the salesforce also involves several key human resource issues. This section discusses issues related to staffing and measuring performance.

Recruiting and Evaluating Applicants. Staffing the salesforce starts with understanding the sales tasks to be performed. Good position descriptions are the first step. The second is identifying abilities and characteristics required for the position. These specifications become the criteria for recruiting and evaluating applicants.

The big question is: What abilities and characteristics make a good salesperson? Some combination of intelligence, personality, and experience is desirable—but determining how to measure these elements and what weights to assign to them is less clear.[14] Various testing and rating devices provide management with a useful tool but cannot substitute for the manager's judgment of the fit between applicant and the job to be filled.

Training.   Once applicants have been hired, they must be trained. Sales training is a complicated subject and beyond the scope of this discussion. In brief, it involves an orientation to the company and its products and also covers the sales requirements needed for the new position. In many companies, sales training lags behind the need for effective new people.

Measuring Performance.   Attempting to distinguish high-performing from low-performing salespeople, Plank and Reid found that what best explained the differences were (in decreasing order of importance) (1) using or processing information, (2) getting information, and (3) giving information.[15] They suggest that today's personal selling position may be conceptualized as the management of personal marketing relationships through effective information management.[16] Instead of focusing on activities, this viewpoint emphasizes a salesperson's mental processes that involve carrying out the position duties effectively. This verifies research by Shapherd and Rentz in 1990 that recognized selling as a complex mental process.[17] However, it is also generally agreed that a customer orientation is the high performer's strongest trait.[18]

Dealing with Turnover.   One of the most serious problems in sales management is the high turnover rate of personnel. Salespeople tend to look for opportunities to earn more money, to get a promotion, or to live in a better part of the country. If not actively seeking a new job, they almost always are willing to listen to an attractive offer. Because turnover affects all companies, sales managers are always trying to find people to fill positions vacated by those who have left or have been discharged. Jones, Kantak, Futrell, and Johnston reviewed the research on salesforce turnover, and concluded that many factors enter into the turnover equation.[19] Their research focused on the interaction of leader behavior and work attitudes as a factor in the relationship of job satisfaction and the propensity to leave. In general, leader behavior and job satisfaction appear to be important influences on the decision to leave a company.

Developing a Compensation Plan

Territorial workload is only one factor affecting the payment of salespeople. To attract and hold good people, a compensation plan must meet the requirements of both the employees and the company. Balancing these two requirements is not easy. Salespeople want an adequate income on a regular basis, and they want to be rewarded for their contribution to the firm. For the firm, sales compensation must retain effective people, stimulate them to be productive, and provide control over the sales effort. Several types of compensation programs are available.

Salary Plan.   A straight salary is good from the salesperson's point of view because it provides a fixed sum at regular intervals. An expense allowance or reimbursement for expenses is also provided. However, there is no direct and immediate reward for exceptional performance. From the company's viewpoint, straight salary is a fixed cost, so as long as sales are satisfactory, costs are controlled. If sales slip, however, a fixed sales cost can become a problem. In addition, straight salary does not motivate extra effort. However, it does allow the employer to require nonselling activities, which people who are paid commission tend to avoid.

Commission Plan.   Under a commission plan, salespeople are paid a fixed or sliding rate based on sales volume or profit contribution. The commission is a reward for doing a job well. It also motivates salespeople to increase productivity. The firm benefits from a performance incentive. And because the commission is calculated on current sales, it pays for itself and is a completely variable cost.

Combination Plan.   A combination plan contains both salary and incentive. The salary is high enough to provide the financial security that employees desire. It is also low enough that its fixed-cost aspect does not affect the firm in periods of declining sales. The incentive is paid in the form of a commission—usually on sales greater than a set quota. Thus the salesperson benefits from extra income for better-than-standard performance, and the firm benefits from a partly variable sales expense and some financial incentive to encourage and control marketing effort.

Directing and Motivating the Salesforce

Directing is providing guidance to the salesforce concerning what tasks to perform. Although the compensation plan and territory design should contribute to the desired goal-directed behavior, some form of written and verbal guidance is necessary. However, one of the key aspects of successfully directing the salesforce is motivation.

> **Motivation**
> The amount of effort a salesperson is willing to expend on each task associated with the job.

Motivation can be viewed as the amount of effort a salesperson is willing to expend on each task associated with the job. The process involved in determining motivation and some of the variables that influence the process are shown in Figure 12.5, which is an adaptation of the work of Churchill, et al.[20] The conceptual framework on which Figure 12.5 is based is known as **expectancy theory,** which indicates that the level of effort expended on each task of a salesperson's job will result in a certain level of achievement. It assumes that this performance will be evaluated and rewarded in some way. The salesperson's motivation is determined by three sets of perceptions: (1) **expectancies**—the perceived linkages between expending greater effort on a task and achieving improved performance; (2) **instrumentalities**—the perceived relationship between higher performance and receiving greater rewards; and (3) **valence for rewards**—the perceived desirability of the rewards that might be received.

> **Expectancy theory**
> The level of effort expended on each task of a salesperson's job that results in a certain level of achievement.

> **Expectancies**
> The perceived linkages between expending greater effort on a task and achieving improved performance.

> **Instrumentalities**
> The perceived relationship between higher performance and receiving greater rewards.

> **Valence for rewards**
> The perceived desirability of the rewards that might be received.

There are two aspects of expectancy perceptions: magnitude and accuracy. The *magnitude* of a salesperson's expectancy perceptions is the degree to which that person believes expending greater effort will influence job performance—the more a person expects greater effort to produce enhanced results, the higher is his or her willingness to devote the efforts necessary. The *accuracy* of expectancy perceptions is how clearly the person understands the relationship between effort expended and results achieved on some performance dimension. If a salesperson's expectancies are inaccurate, he or she spends too much time and energy on activities that have little impact on performance and too little on activities with greater impact. Figure 12.5 indicates that personal and organizational characteristics affect the magnitude and accuracy of expectancy perceptions, as does the individual's perceptions of his or her role in the firm.

FIGURE 12.5

Factors Influencing a Salesperson's Motivation

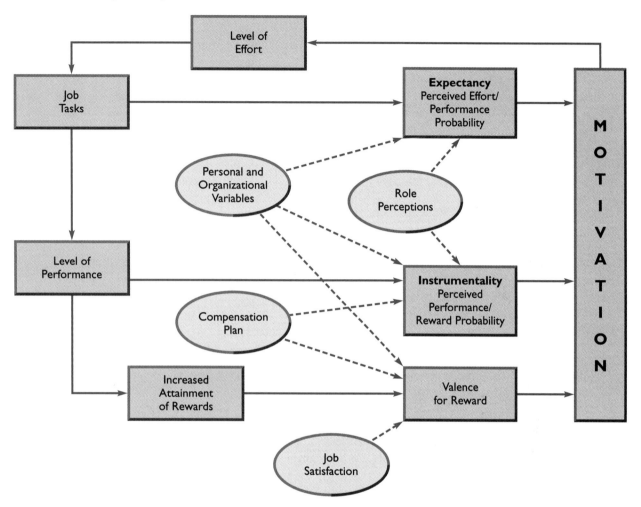

Source: Adapted from Gilbert A. Churchill, Jr., Neil M. Ford, Orville C. Walker, Jr., Mark W. Johnston, and John F. Tanner, Jr., *Sales Force Management,* Sixth Edition, McGraw-Hill, 2001, p. 544. Reprinted with permission of The McGraw-Hill Companies.

Instrumentalities (like expectancies) are a salesperson's perceptions of a probability estimate made about the link between performance and various rewards—an improvement in performance will lead to a specific increased reward such as higher pay or a promotion. If the instrumentality estimate is large, the person believes that there is a high probability that greater performance will increase rewards, and thus he or she will be more willing to expend the effort to achieve better performance. Like expectancies, note that personal and organizational characteristics and the individual's perceptions of his or her role have an impact on instrumentalities. Moreover, the firm's compensation plan influences instrumentality perceptions. The actual link between performance and rewards is determined by

INNOVATE OR EVAPORATE*

Consumer Marketing Changed by Advent of 29.8/7 Media Week

 Consumers have created a 29.8-hour day, according to Renetta McCann, CEO of media planning and buying groups Starcom Worldwide. How can a 24-hour day become 29.8-hours? By multitasking across media.

Do you sit in front of a TV with a magazine or newspaper or today's mail? If you do, that is multitasking. Or, we log onto the Internet with the radio or CD player on at the same time. Teens seem to do all of the above, plus more—a mobile phone to one ear, a CD player at the other, while looking at a favorite magazine. Today media isn't just pervasive; it's all encompassing and fed by our desire to keep in touch and stay current. McCann suggests this has created a "continuous partial attention" situation among consumers. This modern media marketplace presents real challenges because media distribution models assumed discrete media exposures—a single person exposed to a single message through a single medium at a single point in time. McCann's most important message was integration and the increasing need for a fully and totally integrated marketing communication strategy.

*The box title is attributed to James M. Higgins, *Innovate or Evaporate* (Winter Park, FL: New Management Publishing Company, 1995).

Source: Don E. Schultz, "Consumer Marketing Changed by Advent of 29.8/7 Media Week," *Marketing News* (September 24, 2001), p. 11.

---

the firm's policies and procedures; however, salespersons can have inaccurate perceptions that do affect their actions.

Valence for rewards is a salesperson's perception of the desirability of receiving higher rewards. This leads to the question: Do salespersons consider some rewards of more value than others? The traditional view has been that salespeople value monetary rewards as the highest and most motivating.[21] Several studies support this, but increased pay is not the most desired reward by all salespeople in all companies because this may be influenced by the rewards they are currently receiving. In addition, their satisfaction with current rewards is in turn influenced by their personal characteristics, job satisfaction, and the compensation policy of their firm.

The discussion of factors affecting motivation suggests that salespersons' expectancy estimates and reward valences will likely change as their career progresses. As people age and become experienced, their financial obligations change, their skills and confidence tend to improve, and the rewards they receive—as well as their satisfaction with those rewards—change. All these factors can affect expectancies, reward valences, and in turn motivation.[22]

● MANAGING THE ADVERTISING PROGRAM

The second major topic of this chapter is how a firm's marketing strategist utilizing integrated marketing communications (IMC) efforts uses advertising (mass communications). A key question for marketing strategists is how heavily IMC efforts should rely on advertising. Other issues in developing an advertising program involve determining the target customer, the key message, and the medium to be used.

Determining Advertising Opportunities

As mentioned earlier, a critical question for marketing strategists is whether a firm should rely heavily on advertising in its IMC efforts. Five key conditions indicate that a favorable opportunity exists.

1. Favorable Trend in Demand. Effective IMC, especially advertising, is easier when consumer demand is positive. It may be possible to slow the rate of decline of a product or a service when the demand is diminishing, but it is unreasonable to hope that advertising alone can reverse a downward trend.

Advertising can accelerate an increase in demand if the trend is already favorable. For example, most marketers of orange juice for in-home consumption are advertising their reconstituted carton sales rather than frozen concentrated product. This mirrors the trend in actual consumption, since consumers value the convenience of ready-to-drink juice.

MANAGING CHANGE

Ad Agencies' Roles Changing Dramatically in Dot.com Age

Client needs and the risks that accompany them have changed drastically in the last 15 years. Competition, the continuing pressure of industry consolidation, and cost-driven considerations have made it critical that client-agency relationships endure. Media trade publications note there is unrest in ad land as marketers and their "marketing partners" struggle to communicate. For clients and agencies, the predominant view relative to reviews of agency creative assignments is *caveat emptor* or "buyer beware."

What has changed since the freewheeling 1980s? An increasing number of large, brand-driven marketers have found they are in mature markets where sales are declining, and this has driven ad agency industry consolidation to improve the bottom line and to use capital more effectively. In turn, this required agencies to totally focus on business and accountability issues rather than on creativity. The recent rapid expansion of the Internet, and the accompanying explosion in the number of e-commerce firms, has resulted in agencies finding it difficult to adjust to new issues of marketing communication, such as "Brand building is imperative for the Internet." It also adds complexity to any agency review.

Thus, it is not surprising that even legendary long-term advertiser-agency relationships have been hit with a wave of change that has dampened expectations and sometimes resulted in outright ruptures.

Before considering an agency review, perhaps marketers need to ask, "Do I truly need to search for a new agency, or is there something I, as the client, can do differently with my present agency?" A focused and honest self-examination may reveal something to help change the way client and agency do business. Such a self-examination must include clear statements that convey what exactly is expected of the agency. If a review is the decision, then it needs to be defined within parameters that best suit your company's particular needs. Can it realistically be done in-house? Or, are the services of a third-party consulting firm necessary? If a consulting firm is chosen, it should ensure that the review process considers all stakeholders and also multiple marketing communications disciplines before the scale of the review is established.

Source: Arthur Anderson and Lee Anne Morgan, "Agencies' Roles Changing Dramatically in Dot.com Age," *Marketing News* (May 22, 2000), p. 18.

2. Strong Product Differentiation.   If a good or service can be clearly differentiated from competitors' offerings, advertising will be effective. Using comparative advertising, a firm contrasts its products' features with a competitor's brand. Probably the most famous comparative advertising approach ever employed was the "Pepsi Challenge." However, this approach is used across all categories of consumer and industrial products.[23] Taco Bell in December 1997 launched a nationwide television campaign with a variation on comparative ads. Taco Bell's traditional competitors are the major fast-food chains of McDonald's, Burger King, Wendy's, and others who have the "hamburger" as the basic item anchoring their menus. In contrast, Taco Bell's menu is based on traditional Mexican food items such as tacos. By using a Chihuahua that eloquently professes his preference for tacos over hamburgers, Taco Bell differentiated its product and stressed product features all in the same ad.[24]

3. Hidden Attributes.   Advertising opportunities are greater when hidden attributes are more important to the consumer than external features that can be identified readily. To take advantage of hidden qualities, such as flavor in foods, purity in drugs, or cleaning power in detergents, consumers often rely on brand identification and advertising claims when making purchase decisions.

4. Emotional Buying Motives.   The opportunity to motivate or convince consumers through advertising increases when strong emotional buying motives exist. Emotion is a more powerful tool than argument in advertising.[25] Although at odds with the rational problem solving and logical information processing posed in some consumer buying behavior models, ad people are convinced that emotional appeals are more effective. Constable suggests that an emotional relationship between consumer and product leads to increased use, the opportunity for premium pricing, and a more powerful brand.[26]

5. Adequate Funds.   It is the marketing manager's responsibility to determine how elaborate the ad program should be, how much it will cost, and if sufficient funds are available. Unless there are adequate financial resources to support an advertising program of the scope required, an advertising opportunity does not exist.

Whether this and the other four conditions of a good advertising opportunity exist can be determined by a marketing audit and marketing research. In terms of the marketing planning process, a study of the marketing situation should reveal the extent of the required advertising program and whether the firm can afford it.

Identifying the Appropriate Audience(s)

Another key question in developing an IMC program, especially the advertising component, is: With whom should we communicate? All IMC activities are directed at specific target customers. Since most markets are segmented, this means that IMC activities must be directed at the specific market segment(s) the firm is attempting to influence. The need for a feedback loop is evident because the effectiveness of the communication must be evaluated in some fashion.

This does not mean that marketing strategists need only identify a single group of target customers. This is too simplistic for today's highly dynamic, well-informed, and fiercely competitive markets. Many individuals affect the buying process; IMC activities must be planned to reach them all. In addition to customers, purchase influencers must be considered. For example, consumers usually rely heavily on the advice of others in purchasing products such as home interior decorating items or shrubs and flowering trees. Whether these influencers are interior decorators, landscape architects, or relatives and friends, IMC efforts must be designed to reach these individuals. In designing an effective communications mix, it is extremely important to accurately identify those who consume and buy as well as those who influence purchases.

Selecting the IMC Message

What message should be communicated to achieve IMC objectives? The answer to this question is often the key to IMC success. The heart of communication (especially advertising) is transmitting ideas. One purpose of communication is to help customers reach a buying decision. The secret of doing this is to offer solutions to problems. From this follows the importance of understanding consumers' needs. An effective message does not describe the product in great detail; instead, it convinces buyers that the product will satisfy needs. But with the advent of Internet Web sites, some questionable message selection activities have emerged. For example, in the summer of 2000, Kenneth B. Moll, a Chicago lawyer specializing in class actions, was suspended by Illinois regulators for pocketing fees that he was ethically obligated to share. However, while suspended, Moll's six-lawyer firm continued to appeal to clients with a Web site that extolled the firm's "reputation for professional integrity." Therefore, choosing the correct message is both an ethical and a marketing strategy task.[27]

Determining the IMC Media

Deciding which media to use is another important marketing strategy decision.[28] This decision determines whom the messages will reach, and the medium itself influences the effectiveness of communication. For example, the strong effect of television may result more from the power of that medium than from the actual message transmitted. Another reason that such decisions are so important is that media costs often are the largest single item in the IMC budget.

Communication methods vary tremendously from one medium to another. The greatest contrasts are found in comparisons of such obviously different media as newspapers and television. Similar but less dramatic differences also exist among the other major advertising media.

Different messages require different types of media. A message used in radio will be different from one used on a billboard. A media plan should be based on an understanding of the objectives for IMC and how consumers, users, and purchase influencers receive information. Rather than asking, "In what media should we advertise?" the marketing strategists should ask, "Which media (including magazines, newspapers, television, and so forth) reach our ultimate users, purchasers, and purchase influencers?" The IMC strategist works backward from the consumer in selecting media, always matching the characteristics of users, purchasers, and purchase influencers with the audience characteristics of the various available media.

Newspapers. A great variety of newspapers are available: daily newspapers, newspapers published exclusively on Saturday or Sunday, weekly newspapers, religious newspapers, foreign-language newspapers, and newspaper-distributed

TABLE 12.1

Change in Number of Magazine Titles*
By 10 largest categories, 1997 vs. 2001

| Category | Number of Titles | | % Change |
	1997	2001	
Regional interest	759	821	8.1%
Travel	527	706	34.0
Computers, automation	581	699	20.3
Music, music trades	449	521	16.0
Lifestyle	272	467	72.0
Comics	538	449	−16.5
Women's	348	416	19.5
Environment, ecology	328	393	19.8
Management	244	306	25.4
Family	216	289	34.0

*Titles on this list may include Canadian and trade publications in addition to U.S. consumer magazines.
Source: National Directory of Magazines, 2002, Oxbridge Communications, New York.

magazines such as the Sunday supplements. Some are published in the morning, others in the evening. They range in size from the standard 15- by 23-inch newspaper to the smaller tabloid. They can be local, regional, or national in circulation. Some newspapers accept ads in color; others are not equipped to handle color. This list is sufficient to dramatize the variety that we encounter even within a single medium.

Magazines.   As can be seen in Table 12.1, a wide variety of magazines can be used by marketing strategists. The 10 largest categories totalled 5,067 titles in 2001.

Radio.   Over the past decades, network radio has largely been replaced by television network programming, but local radio continues to be a very important communications medium. Industry analysts expect robust results for the handful of big, publicly traded radio groups, driven by large-scale consolidation. Radio continues to attract advertisers who see opportunities to reach audiences more finely targeted.[29] Radio advertising is less expensive than television advertising and offers the ability to reach potential customers in their cars, at the beach, at their workplace, and in other places where television has little effect. In 2001, expenditures were $18.4 billion.

Television.   Television is extremely important as a communications medium in terms of dollars spent. Like radio, television can be divided into *spot* (local) and *network* (national) broadcasting. U.S. households with television (many with multiple sets) have reached saturation, but audiences of the three major networks have declined. Three reasons exist: (1) the growing popularity of programs by independent stations or rival networks; (2) the growth of cable and satellite systems and the rapid proliferation of channels, including the popular movie, sports, and news networks; and (3) the rising incidence of ownership of videocassette recorders (VCRs) and digital recording systems.

For the most part, large firms advertising on television continue to employ prime-time advertising. However, a substantial audience—almost 25 million households—is still tuned in after midnight, and, interestingly, (1) the price of a spot on late-night television can be as low as 10 percent of the prime-time cost, and (2) there appear to be no significant differences in the demographics of the late-night audience—although there is certainly some difference in lifestyle. The net result is that a late-night target audience can be reached at a much lower cost per thousand by using late-night television.

Another factor was the introduction of shorter-length ads, beginning with 15-second commercials. The standard length of commercials traditionally was 60 seconds, but stations allowed advertisers first to place back-to-back "fifteens" and then, by 1985, to air stand-alone 15-second spots.[30] Recently, even shorter lengths of 10 seconds have been reported,[31] as well as use of a 1-second commercial.[32]

Direct Mail.   Any type of mailing, whether a postcard or an elaborate brochure, is classified as direct-mail advertising. Direct mail is an extremely versatile medium that can be used for IMC activities by firms that are large or small and local, regional, or national. (This IMC tool is discussed further with direct marketing in chapter 13.)

Outdoor Advertising.   Despite public pressure to remove outdoor advertising from the U.S. environment,[33] signs and billboards remain an important communication medium.[34] In 2001, advertisers spent about $5.3 billion on out-of-home media. The January 10, 2001 issue of *The Wall Street Journal* (page B12), noted that even as corporate spending on advertising was slowing, a rash of new outdoor advertising space was popping up in downtown urban areas as developers saw easy profit in urban wall displays.[35] Image-conscious firms like Gap, Inc., Calvin Klein, Inc., Apple Computer, Inc., and Disney World paid $100,000 per month (or more) for attention-getting displays in New York's Times Square or along Sunset Strip in Los Angeles. Even Internet trendsetters such as HotBot and Excite! rely on billboards to be visible in the real world.[36]

Three variations of outdoor media are common. The *30-sheet poster* is the standard billboard form, although a smaller 8-sheet poster is now being made in some urban locations. The message is printed on sheets of paper that are pasted on large wooden or metal frames. *Painted posters,* some of which are rotated every 5 or 6 weeks within a market by relocation of the entire display, are the second billboard type of outdoor medium. The third is the *electronic spectacular,* as seen in Times Square or Las Vegas. Stunning novel effects are obtained by the use of motion, sound,[37] smoke, and other dramatic devices.[38]

Transportation Media.   Transportation as a medium uses displayed messages inside and outside public transportation vehicles or on the walls of subway stations, airport terminals, and the like. Interior transportation advertising frequently takes

MARKETING **IN THE** INFORMATION AGE

Kicking Back Against the Power of Consumerism

 Kalle Lasn's business is cultural revolution. Trying to "deInc" the world, he wages a guerrilla war against billion-dollar brands and organizations. Lasn edits *Adbusters,* a 100,000-circulation, trendy, provocative, and strikingly anti-corporate magazine that challenges the advertising industry, and comments on economic and environmental issues. It is devoted to the art of "culture jamming," which is attacking the ad industry and subverting the meaning in a message.

Ad satires in the magazine and their Web site (www.adbusters.org) target corporations and their products—McDonald's, Nike, Absolut vodka, Calvin Klein, Giorgio Armani, Tommy Hilfiger. An example of a spoof ad on a Tommy Hilfiger campaign depicts a herd of sheep and the tag line: "Tommy, follow the flock." A second ad shows a male model with a well-toned torso who peers intently down his fashionable underwear under the headline "Obsession." Their "Absolut" spoof ad tag lines raise questions about alcoholism and impotence.

In his book *Culture Jam: The Uncooling of America,* Lasn writes, "Instead of treating vegetative, corporate-drive TV culture as something to be gently, ironically mocked, it's time to face the whole ugly spectre of our TV-addicted nation, the savage anomie of a society entranced and entrapped and living a lie. It's time to admit that chronic TV watching is North America's number one mental health problem, and that a society in which citizens spend a quarter of their waking lives in front of their sets is in need of a serious shock therapy."

Lasn wants the same access to the airwaves as corporations, to counter what he perceives as the more destructive messages in the media today. He notes that in a "free marketplace of ideas," consumers will have all the facts to make informed decisions about where and how they will spend their money. Some brands have begun to play to the same consumer cynicism and now lampoon one another. Sprite has used anti-advertising techniques for years. Its "image is nothing, thirst is everything" slogan was designed to reassure cynical customers that Sprite does nothing but quench your thirst.

Though it accepts ads, *Adbusters* is choosy: "We do not accept product ads that contradict our central message. For example, we would not take ads for a motor company. But, when it comes to advocacy ads, we accept anything— even if we don't agree with them."

Source: "Sunday Business Post: Kicking Back Against the Power of Consumerism," *Financial Times Information Limited—Europe Intelligence Wire* (September 3, 2002).

the form of placards or *car cards.* Wrigley's chewing gum, for example, has been extensively advertised this way. Exterior or traveling displays appear on the sides of buses, on the backs of taxicabs, and on panels attached to delivery vehicles.

Point of Purchase (POP).   It is extremely difficult to distinguish the use of point-of-purchase (POP) communications from sales promotion. Most firms closely coordinate POP communications with other IMC media use, so the displays involved are considered part of the IMC advertising program. POP materials include advertising attached to the package, window banners, simple or elaborate stages for displaying merchandise, "shelf-talkers," merchandising tags, end-cap displays, floor signs, package stuffers, information booklets, and more recently in-store ultra-thin, battery-powered electronic screens, along with wireless networking.[39] POP communications reduce

TABLE 12.2

U.S. Ad Expenditures by Type of Media,[1] 1997–2001[2]

	1997	1998	1999	2000	2001	% Change, 1997–2001
Newspapers	$41,670	$44,292	$46,648	$49,050	$44,255	6.2%
Magazines	9,821	10,518	11,433	12,370	11,095	12.9
Broadcast TV	36,893	39,173	40,011	44,802	38,881	5.3
Cable TV	7,237	8,547	10,429	15,455	15,536	114.7
Radio	13,491	15,073	17,215	19,295	17,861	32.4
Yellow Pages	11,423	11,990	12,652	13,228	13,592	19.0
Direct mail	36,890	39,620	41,403	44,591	44,725	21.2
Business papers	4,109	4,232	4,274	4,915	4,468	9.0
Billboards	1,455	1,576	1,725	5,176	5,134	252.9
Internet	600	1,050	1,940	6,507	5,752	858.7
Miscellaneous	23,940	25,523	27,571	32,083	29,988	25.3
Total	**$187,079**	**$201,594**	**$215,301**	**$247,472**	**$231,287**	**27.4%**

[1]In millions; expenditures include all commissions as well as art, mechanical and production expenses.
[2]Figures for 2000 and 2001 are final; at press time, projections for 2002 had not been released.
Source: Courtesy of Universal McCann, a unit of McCann-Erickson WorldGroup.

the time gap between exposure to a message and opportunity to purchase and therefore stimulates purchases, especially of impulse items.

Miscellaneous Media.   This classification is a catchall for all the other communications media. These include motion-picture advertising, Yellow Pages listings, skywriting, and so on.[40] The category covers most of the other familiar media, but new methods of communicating are constantly being conceived and used experimentally. One recently perfected example of such experimentation is "virtual billboards," which are becoming a reality at sports events and which bring in new sources of revenue for broadcasters and more exposure for advertisers. Unlike stadium billboards of television "burn-ins," which show scores and statistics to viewers, virtual ads appear to be at the stadium but can only be seen by viewers at home. The ads get bigger or smaller as cameras zoom in or out but are blocked—just like real billboards—when the action moves in front of them. For years, movies have used these special effects. Now, employing the same technology that allows missiles to lock onto targets using laser imaging, these effects are being achieved on live television.[41]

Table 12.2 shows the distribution of advertising expenditures by media in selected years. Methods of reporting data have changed over the years. For example, at one time only media costs were included. Currently, the total outlay, including agency commissions, art, and production, is included in the dollar amounts reported

MANAGING CHANGE

Changing Marketing Horses—Burned Out on the Internet

After looking at your computer monitor for hours on end, do you seem to start to go blind, deaf, and develop an unscratchable itch? Then perhaps you are burned out on the Internet. With hundreds of thousands of people online daily, you would think that marketing to them would be simpler. But due to increased competition, it is often more difficult today than when the Internet was in its infancy.

As a business owner attempting to inexpensively bring attention to your company, what do you do when burnout arrives? How do you keep increasing sales while eliminating online stress? Kenny Love suggests focusing on spending a few "cheap" dollars on offline resources, like the really inexpensive "shopper" newspapers. These are the little, flimsy, tabloid-sized papers not much thicker than toilet paper (in some cases thinner, depending on your brand of toilet paper), and usually distributed all over town. Some names you might recognize are "Pennysaver" or "Thrifty Nickel." Regional and local shopper newspapers are plentiful and have three good traits:

1. Ads are extremely cheap.

2. Published weekly, they get your message out at a speed comparable to e-zines, and have a decent lifespan.

3. Unlike newspapers, where editorials are readers' first interest and ads second, "shoppers" are filled with ads and have no editorials.

Your ads in a shopper newspaper can direct prospective new customers to your Web site or to your autoresponder of sales information. Running your ad several times consecutively will ensure most area readers see your ad. And, because ads are inexpensive, run it again in three or four weeks and you should start to see the result.

Source: Kenny Love, "Changing Marketing Horses," *Internetday.com* (February 14, 2002).

by *Advertising Age*. On this basis, the total advertising expenditures by media for 2001 were estimated at $231.3 billion.

Dealer Promotion Aspects of IMC Media. It is important to remember in selecting IMC media that dealer promotion often is required. Dealer promotion falls into two categories. First, promotional efforts may be aimed directly at resellers as a part of the general program to stimulate sales and build a distribution system. This is called *promotion to the trade*. Promoting to the trade is designed to inform resellers about the manufacturer and the product line and normally includes strong motivational appeals while emphasizing such features as profit margin, merchandise turnover, and selling assistance provided by the manufacturer.

The second category of promotion involving resellers is *advertising through the trade*. When the manufacturer advertises through the trade, the reseller becomes a type of promotion medium. A good example is dealers who *re-advertise* the manufacturer's product under the terms of a cooperative advertising agreement whereby the manufacturer prepares sample advertisements, radio commercials, videotapes, films, etc. for use by resellers. This type of IMC activity extends the manufacturer's communications to ultimate users and develops dealer interest and goodwill.

TABLE 12.3

Advertising Cost per Thousand Selected Magazines

Magazine	Cost	Circulation	CPM
Time	$191,721	4,155,806	$46.13
Newsweek	154,317	3,177,407	48.56
Sports Illustrated	188,839	3,223,810	58.57
Esquire	47,037	674,171	69.77
U.S. News & World Report	112,604	2,224,003	50.63

Source: Compiled from *Ad Age,* June 15, 1998, pp. S1–S28; *Ad Age,* June 29, 1998, p. 22; and *Ad Age,* Special Issue, *The Advertising Century: Money Matters,* "Spending Spree," by Robert J. Cohen, March/April 1999, pp. 126–136.

Evaluating Media Effectiveness: Cost per Thousand, Reach, and Frequency. Can various media be quantitatively evaluated? Yes! One criterion is cost per reader, or as commonly used, the measure is **cost per thousand (CPM).** We compute CPM as follows:

Cost per thousand (CPM)
The cost of reaching 1000 of a medium's consumers.

$$CPM = \frac{\text{page rate} \times 1000}{\text{circulation}}$$

The cost per thousand for a color full-page in *Sports Illustrated Kids* in 2002 was $6.67. We calculate this by multiplying $54,000 (color full-page cost) by 1,000 and dividing that figure by 3,100,000 (circulation). Table 12.2 contains CPM calculations.

Marketing planners may select IMC media with the lowest cost per reader. But CPM calculated costs are seldom the most effective basis for choosing media. Suppose the communication is directed at a special audience—say, for a tennis racquet. The relatively low CPM for *Sports Illustrated Kids,* when compared with other magazines, may encourage the media planner because of the magazine's superior audience environment.

Probably the most damaging criticism of the CPM criterion is that it is an average and not a marginal value. Assume that the media planner using the CPM data in Table 12.3 selects *Time,* and three ads are planned, not just one. Also assume that only one-fourth of the readers actually are exposed to a given ad. This is called the **reach** of the medium. Now we can estimate the CPM for *new* readers for each ad:

Reach
The number of customers (readers/listeners/viewers) actually exposed to a given ad.

	Cost	Reach	CPM
First insertion	$191,721	1,038,951	$184.53
Second insertion	191,721	779,214	246.04
Third insertion	191,721	584,410	328.06

Making the same assumption about *U.S. News & World Report*, we can calculate the CPM for the new readers as follows:

	Cost	Reach	CPM
First insertion	$112,604	556,000	$202.53
Second insertion	112,604	417,000	270.03
Third insertion	112,604	312,750	360.04

Using these calculations, the media planner would place two insertions in *Time* and one in *U.S. News & World Report* in this order: *Time, U.S. News & World Report, Time*—always selecting the magazine with the lowest incremental CPM. The improvement over three insertions in *Time* is significant:

	Total Cost	Total Reach	CPM
Three insertions in *Time*	$575,163	2,402,575	$239.39
Two insertions in *Time* and one in *U.S. News & World Report*	496,046	2,559,625	208.93

The selection of media on the basis of incremental cost is preferable to their selection on the basis of average cost.

Frequency
The number of times an average customer sees an ad in a given time period.

There is another dimension of media selection called **frequency**—the number of times an average reader sees an ad in a given time period. The preceding example assumed the sponsor was interested only in new readers. Sponsors usually want both reach and frequency because many believe that repetition is key to customers learning about brand names or product features or special offers. Using again the assumption that one-fourth of a magazine's circulation sees an ad, running an ad twice in *Time* would produce a reach of 1,818,165. Actually, 1,038,951 people would see the ad each time, but on the second insertion, 259,738 (0.25 × 1,038,951) would see it for the second time. With subsequent insertions, the amount of duplication would increase, and frequency would occur. After six insertions, a few readers (about 1100) will have seen the ad six times, others five times, and so on. The average would be 1.8, which is the frequency of the six-times schedule.

Media Models.   Using computers, marketing and operations research specialists combined information regarding markets and media (as well as subjective judgments) to create a variety of marketing and *media models*. (Readers interested in detailed explanations of 18 marketing models should read Lilien and Rangaswamy, *Marketing Engineering: Computer-Assisted Marketing Analysis and Planning*.)[42] Media models are decision models used to design the media mix. Young and Rubicam, Inc., is credited with the development of the first media model.[43] Within a few years, significant improvements were made in media models. The best known is MEDIAC, developed by Little and Lodish.[44] It searches among alternative advertising schedules to maximize objectives. It does not produce a schedule; it only evaluates alternatives.

Other models have been developed by academics, ad agencies, and media-buying organizations. All use the extensive media information available, including cost data from Standard Rate and Data, Inc., and audience information from Arbitron, Simmons Market Research Bureau, and A. C. Nielsen.[45] Some models attempt to determine the value of a schedule; others attempt to maximize reach and frequency. A model such as ADCAD entails very sophisticated measurements of advertising's effect on consumers' attitudes and is a rule-based expert system that allows managers to translate their qualitative perceptions of marketplace behavior into a basis for deciding on advertising design.[46]

However, despite the technological advances in media models, many organizations' media mixes still are created manually, using available market information and applying an understanding of communications objectives.

PUBLICITY, DIRECT MARKETING, AND SALES PROMOTION

In addition to the use of salesforce activities or advertising, three additional components may be used as integral aspects of IMC and the communications mix. Publicity, direct marketing, and sales promotion all must be considered to ascertain their contribution to achieving marketing strategy objectives established for IMC.

Publicity and Public Relations

Publicity
Any form of nonpaid commercially significant news or editorial comment about ideas, products, or institutions.

The American Marketing Association's official definition of **publicity** is "any form of nonpaid commercially significant news or editorial comment about ideas, products, or institutions."[47] The usual media for publicity are newspapers, magazines, television, and radio. And although not paid for by the firm, it usually supplies most of the information via news releases or other documentation. Because the public generally perceives the media as impartial, information from publicity is viewed more favorably than that from paid advertising, which is viewed as self-serving. Some people may even see publicity as an endorsement of the firm or product or service being discussed. Thus many firms go to considerable time, effort, and expense to ensure that they receive "publicity," that is, mention in the media. However, publicity cannot really be controlled, so what is said and how it is said may result in negative publicity, which can be seriously detrimental to a firm.

Publicity can be a powerful force in a marketing program. Consider, for example, how effective Disney World is in the widespread coverage of its theme park activities in editorial columns and in advertisements of other companies. A spokesperson for the organization once reported that for the opening of the Euro Disney Park it received in publicity the equivalent of over $50 million in media coverage. The reader also will recall that Microsoft Corp. launched Windows 98 with fanfare and intense media coverage, which CEO Bill Gates acknowledged as immensely valuable.

Public relations (PR)
Related to publicity; marketing communications that promote and manage an organization's products and/or image.

Public relations (PR) also can be an effective aspect of communications if creative concepts and tactics are not overemphasized at the expense of being aligned with communications strategy. To achieve this alignment and thus a solutions-orientation for PR, Terry Bader, general manager of Shandwick, a PR agency, suggests that a four-step approach is required. First, PR account representatives need to immerse themselves in the client's industry to understand the competition and the client's marketing goals. Second, after understanding the industry, PR representatives must understand customers' and clients' goals in order to identify issues and opportunities in the situation. Third, PR representatives must develop creative positioning that supports the client's IMC strategy and marketing goals. Fourth, PR representatives must develop tactics compatible with steps 1, 2, and 3.[48]

Direct Marketing

Direct marketing
Interactive system of marketing that uses one or more communications methods to effect a measurable response and/or transaction at any location.

We view **direct marketing** to include all activities that allow a firm to communicate directly with potential customers, who in turn purchase directly from the firm without any intermediaries such as wholesalers or retailers.[49] Catalogs and telephone marketing were the two primary means of direct marketing until 1994, when marketing via the World Wide Web began. Currently, direct marketing is growing in importance and is discussed in depth in Chapter 13.

Sales Promotion

Sales promotion
The use of a variety of short-term communication and incentive methods to stimulate faster and/or greater market response.

Sales promotion is the term used to describe all types of demand stimulation except advertising, publicity, direct marketing, and personal selling. Once the marketing strategy communications objectives are established, then specific communications tasks that sales promotion can accomplish within the overall communications mix are considered. Next, the cost-effectiveness of feasible sales promotion methods is calculated (as explained previously), and a choice is made of those that offer the best results compared with costs.

Sales promotion activities seldom occur alone; they are usually used in conjunction with advertising because the use of both seems to increase their impact. A common ratio of 70:30 is used for consumer goods (70 percent of IMC budget for advertising and 30 percent for sales promotion). Of course, several factors must be considered when using a ratio such as 70:30, including customer behavior and expectations, degree and nature of competition, and stage in the product's life cycle.[50] However, the impact of sales promotion activities is short term, and this factor always must be considered by marketing strategists who rely on sales promotion activities to reach their IMC and marketing strategy objectives.

Available Push Promotions.   The following list contains push techniques (trade promotions) that are available to marketing strategists:

Consumer coupons	Samples of new products
Couponing in retailers' ads	New product introductory events
Premium offers	Prepriced shippers
Money-back offers	Contests
Cents-off promotions	Demonstrations
Tie-in promotions	Fashion shows
Trading stamps	Trade shows
Sweepstakes	Prizes in C.D.s[51]

Additional sales promotion activities and devices include the following:

Motion pictures

Videotapes

Catalogs

Celebrity appearances

Display and dispensing equipment

Visual aids for salespeople

Special deals (2 for 1 or temporary price reductions)

Specialty advertising (calendars, pens, T-shirts, etc.)

Evaluating Push Techniques.   To illustrate how marketing strategists should evaluate customer (consumer and business-to-business) reactions and thus the effectiveness of push techniques, assume that a local dairy offers retailers an extra 25 cents "special deal" above their regular margin of 25 cents per gallon carton. This special deal is intended to stimulate sales of milk. The dairy's sales and distribution costs are 20 cents per gallon carton, and production costs are $1.54. The normal retail selling price to customers is $2.99. In normal (non–trade promotion) months, the dairy generates $1 million in total contribution as calculated below:

$$
\begin{aligned}
\text{Total contribution (current)} &= \text{current volume} \times (\text{retail price} - \text{retail margin} \\
&\quad - \text{sales distribution costs} - \text{unit production cost}) \\
&= 1{,}000{,}000 \times (2.99 - 0.25 - 0.20 - 1.54) \\
&= 1{,}000{,}000 \times 1.00 \\
&= 1{,}000{,}000
\end{aligned}
$$

The dairy should be concerned with how much sales would have to increase for a push (trade promotion) to break even or to produce an increase in contribution. The dairy's net of discounts margin drops from $1.00 to 75 cents per gallon. And, as calculated below, sales would have to increase by 33 percent to 1.333 million gallons for this special deal to break even.

$$
\begin{aligned}
1{,}000{,}000 &= \text{special deal volume} \times (2.99 - 0.25 - 0.20 - 1.54 - 0.25 \text{ added discount}) \\
1{,}000{,}000 &= \text{SD volume} \times 0.75 \\
\text{SD volume} &= 1{,}000{,}000 \div 0.75 \\
\text{SD volume} &= 1{,}333{,}000
\end{aligned}
$$

Unless the dairy is quite certain that sales volumes will increase by 33 percent or more, to meet or exceed the 1.333 million gallon level, it should not use this special deal push communication.

Summary

This chapter discussed using IMC tools for effective marketing. The first major topic was managing salesforce activity, which is focused on building customer relationships, is people-related, and thus is complicated. It involves defining the sales task, investigating the relationship between sales activity and productivity, and determining salesforce structure. Salesforce managers are also required to configure sales territories, determine salesforce size, and address human resources issues such as staffing, compensation, direction, and motivation.

The second major topic was managing the advertising program. Five conditions determine advertising opportunities: a favorable trend in demand, strong product differentiation, hidden attributes, emotional buying motives, and adequate funds. Once advertising opportunities are identified, IMC managers must identify the appropriate audience to target, develop effective ad content (message), and determine an efficient and effective media mix. Our media mix discussions included dealer promotion aspects; evaluating effectiveness via cost per thousand, reach, and frequency; and media models.

The concluding major topics of the chapter were the three additional components that must be considered for their contribution to achieving the objectives of IMC and the communications mix: publicity, direct marketing, and sales promotion. Publicity is any form of commercially significant news about an organization, idea, or product that is presented in the media but not paid for. Public relations involves communicating information about an organization, product, or idea that is supportive of the firm's mission and marketing goals. Direct marketing includes all activities that allow a firm to communicate directly with potential customers. Finally, sales promotion is any type of activity that stimulates product demand that is not specifically advertising, publicity, public relations, direct marketing, or personal selling.

Questions

1. Assume that you are the IMC manager for BMW and that you have the responsibility for recommending next model year's communications mix. Would you use each of the components (tools) of the communications mix? With what objectives in mind? And in what relative weighting?

2. Suppose that you are the senior vice-president of sales and that your analysis of the size of the salesforce and selling effort deployment indicates that your salesforce is the correct size but that the allocation of selling effort needs adjustment in a number of territories. How would you implement such deployment changes?

3. What is the ideal sales compensation plan, and how does it relate to "motivating" the sales force?

4. Discuss the factors that indicate that advertising should be a major component of your IMC plan.

5. List the various media available to be used by IMC, and detail your reasoning in choosing which is the most effective.

6. Which of the "other components" of IMC (publicity, direct marketing, sales promotion) are essential elements (tools) of IMC?

Exercises

1. Conduct an analysis of shifts in media use among electronic and nonelectronic media over the past decade. Based on this study, determine the effect that the Internet and other emerging technologies have had—and will continue to have—on IMC strategies. Prepare a brief forecast of the direction you believe this industry will take during the first decade of the twenty-first century.

2. Design a personal selling plan for a line of laser printers (or other product of your choice). Include the objectives to be achieved by your plan, the specific IMC tools, and the budgeting method that will be used. Demonstrate specifically how these IMC elements will be integrated with each other—and with the rest of the marketing mix.

3. Design a media mix that would be appropriate for promoting a new restaurant or entertainment venue in your community. Obtain audience profiles and rate cards from the media (or published sources such as the Standard Rate and Data Service), and determine the best combination of media that will achieve your objectives. Determine an appropriate budget, and weigh this against the desired media mix and coverage. Where and how will adjustments be made without sacrificing the media impact if desired expenditures are greater than the budgeted amount?

Endnotes

1. *Fortune Cookies: Management Wit and Wisdom from Fortune Magazine* (New York: Time, Inc., 1993), p. 21.

2. Many fine books are available on the subject of sales management, personal selling, and sales promotion. For example, on sales management, see Douglas J. Dalrymple and William I. Cron, *Sales Management: Concepts and Cases,* 4th ed. (New York: John Wiley & Sons, 1992); Thomas R. Wotruba and Edwin K. Simpson, *Sales Management Text and Cases,* 2d ed. (London: PWS-Kent Publishing, 1992); Rolph E. Anderson, Joseph F. Hair, and Alan J. Bush, *Professional Sales Management* (New York: McGraw-Hill, 1988); Richard R. Still, Edward W. Cundiff, and Norman A. P. Govoni, *Sales Management: Decisions, Strategies, and Cases,* 5th ed. (Englewood Cliffs, NJ: Prentice-Hall, 1988); Thomas N. Ingram and Raymond W. LaForge, *Sales Management: Analysis and Decision Making* (New York: Dryden Press, 1989); and Robert R. Hartley, *Sales Management* (Columbus, OH: Merrill Publishing, 1989). On personal selling, see Donald W. Jackson, Jr., William H. Cunningham, and Isabella C. M. Cunningham, *Selling: The Personal Force in Marketing* (New York: John Wiley & Sons, 1988); and Neil M. Ford et al., *Sales Force Performance* (Lexington, MA: Lexington Books, 1984). On salesforce management, see Gilbert A. Churchill, Jr., Neil M. Ford, Orville C. Walker, Jr., Mark W. Johnston, and John F. Tanner, *Sales Force Management,* 6th ed. (Homewood, IL: Irwin, 2001); William J. Stanton, Richard H. Buskirk, and Rosann L. Spiro, *Management of a Sales Force,* 8th ed. (Homewood, IL: Irwin, 1991); and Derek A. Newton, *Sales Force Management: Text and Cases,* 2d ed. (Homewood, IL: Irwin, 1990).

3. Rene Y. Damon, "A Conceptual Scheme and Procedure for Classifying Sales Positions," *Journal of Personal Selling & Sales Management* (Summer 1998), pp. 31–46.

4. Dan Logan; "Integrated Communications Offers Competitive Edge," *Bank Marketing* 26(5) (May 1994), p. 63.

5. Carla B. Furlong, "12 Rules for Customer Retention," *Bank Marketing* 25(1) (January 1993), p. 14.

6. Richard Cross and Janet Smith, "Retailers Move Toward New Customer Relationships," *Direct Marketing Magazine* (December 1994), p. 20.

7. Emily Nelson, "The Art of the Sale," *Wall Street Journal* (November 1, 2001) pp. B1–B6.

8. Glen S. Petersen, *High Impact Sales Force Automation: A Strategic Perspective* (Boca Raton, FL: St. Lucie Press, 1997), p. 1.

9. *Ibid.,* pp. 8–9.

10. Roland T. Moriarity and Gordon S. Swartz, "Automation to Boost Sales and Marketing," *Harvard Business Review* (January–February 1989), pp. 100–108.

11. Petersen, *op. cit.,* p. 33.

12. Melissa Campanelli, "Reshuffling the Deck," *Sales and Marketing Management* 146(6) (June 1994), p. 83.

13. For a thorough discussion of the *workload approach,* which is sometimes called the *buildup method,* the reader may reference any current text in salesforce management, such as Churchill, Ford, Walker, Johnston, and Tanner, *op. cit.,* pp. 233–237.

14. Shonkar Ganesan, Barton A. Weitz, and George John, "Hiring and Promotion Policies in Sales Force Management: Some Antecedents and Consequences," *Journal of Personal Selling & Sales Management* (Spring 1993), p. 15.

15. Richard E. Plank and David A. Reid, "Difference Between Success, Failure in Selling," *Marketing News* (November 4, 1996), pp. 6–14.

16. *Ibid.*

17. David C. Shapherd and Joseph O. Rentz, "A Method for Investigating the Cognitive Processes and Knowledge Structures of Expert Salespeople," *Journal of Personal Selling & Sales Management* (Fall 1990), pp. 55–70.

18. Ronald E. Michaels and Ralph L. Day, "Measuring Customer Orientation of Salespeople: A Replication with Industrial Buyers," *Journal of Marketing Research* (November 1985), p. 443.

19. Eli Jones, Donna Massey Kantak, Charles M. Futrell, and Mark W. Johnston, "Leader Behavior, Work Attitudes and Turnover of Salespeople: An Integrative Study," *Journal of Personal Selling & Sales Management* (Spring 1996), p. 13.

20. Churchill, Ford, Walker, Johnston, and Tanner, *op. cit.,* pp. 540–568.

21. See, for example, Neil M. Ford, Orville C. Walker, Jr., and Gilbert A. Churchill, Jr., "Differences in the Attractiveness of Alternative Rewards Among Industrial Salespeople: Additional Evidence," *Journal of Business Research* (April 1985), pp. 123–138; and Laurence B. Chonko, John F. Tanner, Jr., William A. Weeks, and Melissa R. Schmitt, "Reward Preferences of Salespeople," Research Report No. 91-3, Center for Professional Selling, Baylor University, Waco, Texas, 1991.

22. Refer to material by William L. Cron, Alan J. Dubinsky, and Ronald E. Michaels, "The Influence of Career Stages on Components of Salesperson Motivation,"

Journal of Marketing (January 1988), pp. 78–92; and Churchill, Ford, Walker, Johnston, and Tanner, *op. cit.*, p. 547.

23. Stuart Van Auken and Arthur J. Adams, "Attribute Upgrading Through Across-Class, Within-Category Comparison Advertising," *Journal of Advertising Research* (March–April 1998), pp. 6–16.

24. Gregg Cebrzynski, "Taco Bell Ad: Gordita Whips the Whopper," *Nations Restaurant News* (July 20, 1998), p. 3; and Staff writer, The Associated Press, untitled news item, *Marketing News* (August 31, 1998), p. 7.

25. Linda Westphal, "Use Your 'Emotional Mind' When Writing Copy," *Direct Marketing* (July 1998), p. 66.

26. Cathy Constable, "Use Advertising to Help Make Good Times Better," *Marketing News* (February 2, 1998), p. 4.

27. Richard B. Schmitt, "Lowering the Bar: Lawyers Flood Web, But Many Ads Fail to Tell Whole Truth," *Wall Street Journal* (January 15, 2001), pp. A1–A12.

28. See Jay Klitsch, "Making Your Message Hit Home: Some Basics to Consider When Selecting Media," *Direct Marketing* (June 1998), pp. 32–33; and Robert McKim, "Choosing the Right Media for Your Message," *Target Marketing* (October 1997), pp. 86–91.

29. Brian Steinberg, "Large Radio Concerns Are Expected to Post Robust Second-Quarter Results," *Wall Street Journal* (July 13, 1998), p. B5C.

30. Verne Gay, "TV Stand-Alone 15s Make Inroads at Nets," *Advertising Age* (August 19, 1985), p. 1.

31. Scott Hume, "Doe-Anderson Tries Branding in 10 Seconds," *Adweek* (March 16, 1998), p. 3.

32. Alistair Cristopher, "Blink of an Ad," *Time* (August 3, 1998), p. 51.

33. Ellen Neuborne and Ronnie Weil, "Road Show," *Business Week* (May 8, 2000), pp. 75–90.

34. David Pugh, "The Outdoor Industry Comes in from the Cold," *Marketing Week* (March 14, 1997), pp. 16–22.

35. Sheila Muto, "Signage-itis: More Buildings Sport Billboards," *Wall Street Journal* (January 10, 2001), p. B12.

36. Marc Bunther, "The Great Outdoors," *Fortune* (March 1, 1999), pp. 150–157.

37. Debra Sparks, "Musical Billboards," *Financial World* (February 18, 1997), pp. 48–51.

38. Charles R. Taylor, "A Technology Whose Time Has Come or the Same Old Litter on a Stick? An Analysis of Changeable Message Billboards," *Journal of Public Policy & Marketing* (Spring 1997), pp. 179–186.

39. Steve Jarvis, "POP's Silver Screen," *Marketing News* (November 5, 2001), p. 13.

40. Paul Nolan, "Beach Blanket Billboards," *Potentials in Marketing* (September 1998), p. 10.

41. Staff writer, The Associated Press, "Virtual Billboards Becoming Reality at Sport Events," *Marketing News* (August 31, 1998), p. 11.

42. For an excellent general explanation of marketing and media computer models, see Gary L. Lilien and Arvind Rangaswamy, *Marketing Engineering: Computer-Assisted Marketing Analysis and Planning* (Reading, MA: Addison-Wesley, 1998).

43. See W. T. Moran, "Practical Media Decisions and the Computer," *Journal of Marketing* (July 1963), p. 26.

44. MEDIAC was presented in John D. C. Little and Leonard M. Lodish, "A Media Planning Calculus," *Operations Research* (January–February 1969), p. 1. For a description of how a commercial bank used this media planning model, see Leonard M. Lodish, *The Advertising Promotion Challenge: Vaguely Right or Precisely Wrong* (New York: Oxford University Press, 1986).

45. These are the most widely used media audience research services. Arbitron and A. C. Nielsen provide audience and program ratings for broadcast media. Simmons Market Research Bureau provides print media data as well as information on product use. There are other useful secondary research sources for use in media planning, including Standard Rate and Data Service and Leading National Advertisers.

46. Raymond R. Burke, Arvind Rangaswamy, Joshua Eliasberg, and Jerry Wind, "A Knowledge-Based System for Advertising Design," *Marketing Science* 9(3) (Summer 1990), pp. 212–229.

47. *Marketing Definitions* (Chicago: American Marketing Association, 1960).

48. Terry Bader, "PR Responds to New Demand for Solutions," *Marketing News* 32(14) (July 7, 1997), p. 7.

49. Richard P. Bagozzi, José Antonio Rosa, Kirti Sawhney Celly, and Francisco Coronel, *Marketing Management* (Englewood Cliffs, NJ: Prentice-Hall, 1998), p. 406.

50. Del I. Hawkins, Roger J. Best, and Kenneth A. Coney, *Consumer Behavior: Implications for Marketing Strategy*, 4th ed. (Homewood, IL: BPI/Irwin, 1989), pp. 643–654.

51. Jennifer Ordoñez, "Not Just Cereal Material: Prizes Pop Up in More CDs," *Wall Street Journal* (May 31, 2001), pp. B1–B4.

MARKETING MANAGEMENT IN ACTION: CLOSING CASE

Maserati Returns to U.S. Market

Legendary sport-car maker Maserati made its debut in the U.S. market in March 2002. At one time the sleek, sophisticated, and sexy Maserati models were symbols of effective Italian design capabilities. But in the 1970s, Maserati became insolvent. In September 2001 the first of three new Ferrari-engineered Maserati models was launched in Europe and then in the United States in 2002. To announce their return, Maserati used a massive marketing blitz targeted at the world's rich and famous. Exclusivity is the buzzword of marketing for most luxury brands. Thus, Maserati sponsored sporting and cultural events around the world. It also signed a joint advertising agreement with Italian jewelery firm Bulgari in an attempt to link itself with another luxury-goods brand. Maserati also has planned to advertise in some business newpapers and high-end magazines such as *Condé Nast Traveler, GQ,* and *Architectural Digest.* They have also erected huge billboards (300 square yards or larger) that picture their car against a shiny, silver background in New York's Times Square and Rome's Spanish Steps.

Maserati does most of its advertising in-house with the help of a small design and advertising shop, Seidl-Cluss, based in Stuttgart. Amadeo Felisa, director general of Maserati, says, "The brand has to be revitalized, and to do so we've decided to pursue a different type of marketing that isn't just focused on the product. We are too small to do a sweeping ad campaign. We need to target our audience." This marketing strategy is similar to Porsche, Jaguar, and Ferrari, who shun mass market advertising on the logic that they must target customers who aren't fazed by prices that start at $80,000.00. In 2002, Maserati sold 1,800 cars, but aims for sales of 10,000 by 2006. During the first 2 months of U.S. sales, the count was 800 cars ordered.

Ferrari, its parent, is a good role model: it has extended its brand not only to regular Formula One paraphernalia, but also to products such as Vodafone mobile phones and leather goods, including a shiny "Ferrari Red" pair of shoes. However, some industry experts wonder whether niche marketing is right for Maserati who is trying to re-build its brand from almost nothing in certain markets such as the United States. And, it is competing against other premium car brands, such as Rolls-Royce and Lamborghini, as well as top-end Mercedes and BMW models.

Peter Stephenson-Wright, managing director for automotive accounts at specialized marketing agency Wuderman, notes, "A niche brand still has to get over a certain volume to be financially viable. In order to get critical mass, you've got to get enough material out there so that people get to know it [the brand]."

Source: Alessandra Galloni and Deborah Ball, "After 11 Years, Maserati to Return to U.S.," *Wall Street Journal* (March 25, 2002), p. B11.

Case Study Questions

1. How well known in the U.S. market do you think the Maserati brand is?

2. What is the brand image that you have of Maserati? Are you sure you had a brand image of Maserati before you read the case?

3. Is the luxury auto market saturated with brands?

4. What often happens to sales of luxury-goods brands in times of economic constraints?

5. Do you agree with Peter Stephenson-Wright, who questions whether niche marketing is the appropriate marketing strategy for reintroducing Maserati in the U.S. market?

6. If niche marketing isn't the best marketing strategy for Maserati, what is the best marketing strategy for them?

Direct Marketing

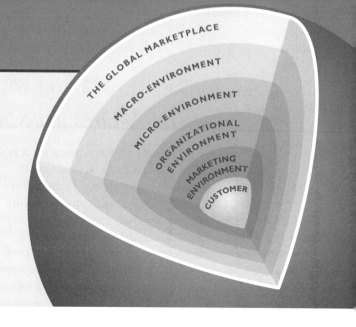

Overview

"It is as simple as turning on your computer, and right there are all the pockets of your financial life on the screen, from your 401(k) and IRA to your brokerage and bank accounts," says Charles Schwab as he describes his vision of how more people will handle their personal finances in a few years. And where does Schwab fit in? "We'll be the consolidator, the integrator. We'll be the utopia."[1]

"Dude, You're Getting a Dell" . . . Computer, and PDA, and Printer, and Digital Camera, and . . .

In 2001, the U.S. computer industry experienced a 4 percent drop in shipments for the first time since 1985. By this time, approximately 60 percent of U.S. households owned at least one computer, and a soft economy made consumers less willing to invest in new PCs and technology upgrades. The business sector delayed technology purchases for corporate use because of post-9/11 and economic concerns. The reluctance of consumers and business customers to buy the latest PC models or add-ons led PC manufacturers to search for new avenues to increased sales and market share.

One strategy for increasing sales was to reduce prices. Dell Computer Corp. launched an aggressive price war that pushed competing PC makers to lower prices on some models to bargain-basement levels. Several models were priced below the $1,000 level that stunned buyers in the mid-1990s. Dell priced its cheapest model, the new SmartStep machine, at $599. Hewlett-Packard and eMachines introduced PC models for $399; Gateway announced a $399 desktop; and notebook PC prices were reduced to $950 for an IBM Thinkpad, and $899 for an H-P Compaq Evo. Dell's long-standing low price strategy has made it the dominant player in the low-end niche for PCs for many years, but competition that previously shunned this market is now actively pursuing the same customers.

Dell Computer Corp.'s strategy for increasing sales and market share goes beyond pricing decisions, however. The company is also placing more emphasis on final consumers, although business customers are still the greatest revenue generators. As part of its consumer marketing strategy, Dell's goal is to dominate that segment of the market just as it does with higher-priced business computers. The company's long-running advertising spots that featured a teenager named Steven, who smooth-talked parents until he could assure their children, "Dude, you're getting a Dell," were clearly a departure from typical business-focused Dell promotions as they focused on consumer media and final consumers.

With more money, experience, and clout than its competitors, Dell has been able to maintain its number one position in PC market share. The company briefly dropped to number two for the first quarter of 2002 when Hewlett-Packard purchased Compaq. At that time, H-P Compaq combined held 17.2 percent compared to 14.4 percent for Dell. However, Dell regained its top position a few months later, largely due to the success of its direct-selling model.

Dell Computer Corp. revolutionized the computer industry by following the principle that customization and direct delivery of computer systems are the best strategy for meeting the needs of business and government customers and final consumers in a rapidly changing global business environment. The business revolves around a direct-selling philosophy that has paid off handsomely for entrepreneurial founder Michael Dell and investors in the company. Dell Computer Corp. was founded in a University of Texas dormitory room in 1984. Since then, sales, profits, and Michael Dell's net worth have increased greatly—counter to the experience of many computer and dot.com rivals. In 2001, Dell ranked 53rd among the Fortune 500 companies, with $31,502.0 million in revenues; $1,246.0 million in sales; and assets of $4,694.0 million. The company was ranked fourth in the overall computer and office equipment sector, following IBM, Hewlett-Packard, and Compaq.

Dell's market leadership is attributed to its direct selling model that eliminates retailers that add time and cost to transactions. Dell believes that working directly with customers provides a better understanding of their needs, and a more efficient way to provide the solutions for those needs. Dell was a leader in commercial migration to the Internet in 1994, and added e-commerce capability in 1996. A year later the company was the first to record $1 billion in online sales. Dell's Internet commerce site, one of the highest volume sites in the world, receives 920 million page requests per quarter, and covers 80 countries, 27 languages/dialects, and 40 currencies. Dell has realized efficiencies from its site, in terms of procurement, customer support, and relationship management.

Dell Computer Corp. achieves sustainable competitive advantage through its ability to design and customize products to meet end-user requirements and to provide them with a wide selection of peripheral software. In addition to its strength in direct selling, Dell maintains market leadership as a result of cost containment, channel domination, continuous innovation, and an ability to meet the needs of its customers with short delivery times. Dell holds little or no inventory, and products are assembled as soon as an order is placed. When the product is completed and checked, it is shipped at once. A just-in-time inventory process that is supported by extensive and efficient supplier relationships and elimination of middlemen through a direct distribution channel enable Dell to be a value-added, low-cost, build-to-order marketer of PCs.

To understand Dell's outstanding results, it is important to consider how the company exploits the direct-selling model for custom-made computers. The company's success is due to being able to operate with no finished goods inventory, using the latest high-margin components, using direct channels to customers, and receiving timely direct payment from large business customers or credit-card companies without waiting for payment from resellers.

As the PC industry matures, and competition becomes more intense, Dell is leveraging its operating philosophy and key assets by adding new products to its consumer and business lines. For business customers, Dell introduced the PowerEdge™ 1600SC, a powerful server for small businesses and corporate workgroups. The company also is focusing on business customers—particularly those that have resisted adding to their technology infrastructure, but need to upgrade in order to remain competitive. New products targeted toward both consumer and business markets include Dell-branded printers and supplies (alliance with Lexmark), handheld PCs, personal digital assistants (PDAs), and others. Other items such as a Dell-branded digital camera are also seen as part of an "overall digital solution," and are in keeping with Dell's core philosophy.

Each of these ventures puts Dell in direct competition with other entrenched companies, but fit its long-term strategy of "entering new markets once the products become commodities and price becomes the major factor in purchasing decisions." Although Dell faces fierce competition, the company's direct sales model and low price strategy continue to be key success factors.

Sources: John Pletz, "Dell Issues Challenge With Its New PDA," *Austin American Statesman* (November 5, 2002), p. D1; John Pletz, "Dell Says It's No. 1 in U.S. Consumer Sales," *Austin American Statesman* (November 13, 2002), p. C1; Bob Keefe, "Dell Aims to Dominate Consumer Market With New Focus," *The Atlanta Journal/The Atlanta Constitution* (December 26, 2001), p. B1; Steve Lohr, "Dell's Results Match Those of a Year Ago," *New York Times* (May 17, 2002), p. C5; "The Fortune 500 Largest U.S. Corporations," *Fortune* (April 15, 2002), pp. F-3, F-48; www.dell.com.

Social and lifestyle changes in consumer markets have escalated the demand for more convenient shopping. Most of today's consumers suffer from a "poverty of time," a result of fast-paced, hectic work lives and lack of time for personal activities. The result is an increase in purchases made from direct-selling, direct-action advertising, and electronic media sources. Likewise, commercial enterprises, government agencies, and nonprofit organizations rely more than ever on direct marketing approaches to buy and sell a vast array of goods and services.

In 2002, U.S. sales revenues that are attributable to direct marketing activities were estimated at more than $2.0 trillion. Direct marketing media expenditures reached $206.1 billion—more than half of all advertising expenditures. More than 16.4 million people were employed in direct marketing in 2002, with nearly 9 million in consumer direct marketing and 7.5 million in business-to-business direct marketing. Direct marketing sales and advertising expenditures are expected to continue to grow at an annual rate of 8.3 percent and 6.5 percent, respectively.[2]

● DIRECT MARKETING DEFINED

Direct marketing
Interactive system of marketing that uses one or more communications methods to effect a measurable response and/or transaction at any location.

The Direct Marketing Association defines **direct marketing** as "... an interactive system of marketing which uses one or more advertising media to effect a measurable response and/or transaction at any location."[3] This definition includes four key elements:

1. Direct marketing is an interactive two-way communication system between a marketer and a prospective customer.

2. The targeted customer is always given an opportunity to respond.

3. The communication can take place wherever and whenever there is access to communications media.

4. All direct marketing activities can be measured.

TABLE 13.1

Consumer and Business-to-Business Direct Marketing Sales: By Marketing Objective and as Percent of Total U.S. Sales

	Sales (Billions of $)*			Compound Annual Growth %	
	1996	*2001*	*2006*	*1996–2001*	*2001–2006*
Consumer					
Direct marketing sales	**$655.10**	**$1,006.80**	**$1,471.10**	**9.00%**	**7.90%**
Direct order	216.9	328.6	471.0	8.7	7.5
Lead generation	313.0	487.1	729.3	9.2	8.4
Traffic generation	124.5	191.1	274.0	8.9	7.5
Total U.S. consumer sales	**$5,550.80**	**$7,484.80**	**$9,540.30**	**6.20%**	**5.00%**
DM consumer sales as percent of total U.S. sales	**11.8%**	**13.5%**	**15.4%**		
Business-to-Business					
Direct marketing sales	**$501.00**	**$858.10**	**$1,307.80**	**11.40%**	**8.80%**
Direct order	146.9	231.9	340.8	9.6	8
Lead generation	318.1	567.3	877.6	12.3	9.1
Traffic generation	36.8	58.9	86.1	9.9	7.9
Total U.S. business-to-business sales	**$11,090.0**	**$14,300.4**	**$18,024.1**	**5.2%**	**4.7%**
DM business-to-business sales as percent of total U.S. sales	**4.5%**	**6.0%**	**7.3%**		

*Sales in current (nominal) dollars, not adjusted for inflation.
Source: Reprinted from *Economic Impact: U.S. Direct and Interactive Marketing Today 2002* with permission from The Direct Marketing Association, Inc.

The Direct Marketing Association applied a media-based definition of direct marketing for the purposes of its 2002 economic impact study:

> Any direct communication to a customer or business recipient that is designed to generate (1) a response in the form of an order (direct order), (2) a request for further information (lead generation), and/or (3) a visit to a store or other place of business for the purchase of a specific product(s) or service(s) (traffic generation).[4]

See Table 13.1 for sales growth related to each objective.

Direct marketing activities include characteristics of both marketing communication and distribution strategies. The resulting process is an integrated marketing program that focuses the resources of an organization on the needs of an individual buyer.

Integrated Marketing Communications Perspective

Direct marketing represents an increasingly important aspect of the integrated marketing communications mix (see Chapters 11 and 12), as well as the overall marketing mix. However, there are some distinct differences between direct marketing and general advertising. Direct marketing involves selling to individuals one

TABLE 13.2

Comparison of Major Economic Growth Categories, Highlighting Growth Surge in Direct Marketing

| | Compound Annual Growth, % | |
Economic Growth Category	1996–2001	2001–2006
Direct marketing ad expenditures	6.8	6.5
Total U.S. ad expenditures	4.4	5.5
Direct marketing sales revenue	10.0	8.3
Total U.S. sales revenue	5.5	4.8
Direct marketing employment	5.7	4.3
Total U.S. employment	2.0	1.3

Source: Reprinted from *Economic Impact: U.S. Direct and Interactive Marketing Today 2002* with permission from The Direct Marketing Association, Inc.

at a time versus selling to broad groups of customers simultaneously, providing all information needed to make a purchase, personalizing communications, providing an immediate response mechanism (i.e., toll-free telephone number, Internet address, or mail response format), and marketing programs that are driven by comprehensive databases.[5] Descriptions of direct marketing strategies include building customer relationships and obtaining direct responses through a variety of marketing communications methods and media.

The typical integrated direct marketing campaign employs multiple direct marketing tools in a sequence of promotional activities. A customer's first exposure to the launching of a new car model may be through newspaper publicity about a local auto show or road test reports in *Motor Trends* magazine. Next, the customer may be exposed to paid advertising in print and broadcast media and is offered an easy response mechanism to obtain additional information (e.g., a toll-free telephone number or Web address). After this response, the customer may receive direct mail brochures, a video, and/or a telephone call to follow up on the inquiry. The next step may be a personal sales encounter, followed by further communication that is designed to elicit a response. Major economic growth categories related to direct marketing are presented in Table 13.2.

Distribution Channel Perspective

Traditional distribution strategies have focused on maximizing efficiency in the selection of channels and intermediaries. Now the focus has shifted to maximizing effectiveness and efficiency through channel designs, such as direct marketing, that excel in meeting the distribution needs of consumers and organizations. This is the shortest channel of distribution from the producer to the consumer or organizational buyer, as described in Chapter 10 (i.e., zero-level channel, nonstore retailing). Direct marketers do not require a retail storefront or traditional sales location. Inventory management remains the responsibility of the seller until the buyer takes possession of the product or experiences the service. In a direct distribution system, the sales process may be initiated by either the seller or the customer, and the good or service is delivered directly to the customer.

As the opening scenario indicated, more and more customers are showing a preference for the direct sales model for computer and network products as they seek more speed and customization for their purchases. The traditional channel for selling expensive, high-tech products has been from manufacturer to distributor to reseller to end-user. Increased direct selling of computers and peripherals by means such as telephone, mail order, and on-line sales ("e-commerce") has eliminated many distributors from the sales process.

Consumer markets are heterogeneous and complex and choose different distribution channels for their shopping activities. However, an increasing number of buyers are finding the Internet to be the most efficient and satisfying place to shop. The Internet has brought attention to its value as a distribution channel because of characteristics that are either unique or shared with other marketing channels. These characteristics include the ability to inexpensively store large amounts of information at different virtual locations; the availability of powerful and inexpensive ways to search, organize, and disseminate information; interactivity; the ability to provide rich perceptual experiences; the relatively low entry costs for sellers; and the ability to provide physical distribution for certain products such as computer software.[6]

FACTORS LEADING TO THE GROWTH OF DIRECT MARKETING

Direct marketing has experienced phenomenal growth as a result of customers' time constraints, an increase in niche marketing, availability of specialized media, computerized databases, advances in technology and electronic media, and global business expansion. The effects of these factors are interrelated, and they tend to work in combination with one another to achieve direct marketing objectives.

Consumers and organizations alike have found it necessary to maximize the use of their time when making purchases. Thus the opportunity to "buy direct" and eliminate unnecessary middlemen, while keeping prices low, has considerable appeal when compared with a lengthy interaction with a sales representative or fulfillment of a multistaged mail or telephone order. **Niche marketing,** by its very nature, is conducive to direct marketing because of the close relationship between buyers and sellers. Focusing on a small niche of the market enables the marketer to become well informed about the needs of customers in that segment and to use direct marketing as an effective quick-response strategy. However, the niche must be large enough to be profitable, have attractive growth potential, and be free of intense competition.

Direct marketing has enjoyed much success because of the availability of specialized media that can carry promotional messages to a narrowly defined population. These media run the gamut from newspapers to the Internet—all highly targeted to a special audience of readers, listeners, or subscribers.

Another key factor in the growth of direct marketing is the proliferation of computerized databases. This information can be found in internal sources such as company records and customer credit-card accounts and in external sources such as

Niche marketing
Focus on a small segment of the market that exhibits homogeneous needs and response to marketing offers.

MARKETING IN THE GLOBAL VILLAGE

Localize—Or Get Lost In Translation!

 According to linguists, only 6 percent of the world's population speaks English as a first language. However, only about 4 percent of all e-commerce sites are written in a language other than English (96 percent were written in English in 1999). Although the World Wide Web has become a major direct marketing medium to reach an international marketplace, it would appear that marketing messages are being lost in translation. Forrester Research found that viewing time on a Web site is doubled when the site is localized for language and culture. For example, Japanese who were addressed in their own language were three times more likely to conduct an online transaction. Experts say that for every $2 million generated in domestic sales, $1 million is lost if the site is not localized for foreigners.

Expensive marketing campaigns are doomed if the target audience does not understand the language, or there are cultural differences that may be misunderstood. Executives at Panasonic, the consumer products division of Matsushita Electric, learned about this first-hand. They had planned to rollout a huge marketing campaign to promote the company's new Japanese-language Web site. Panasonic licensed the famous cartoon character, Woody Woodpecker, to serve as a user guide on the new site. An American staffer discovered a potential problem a week before the marketing blitz was to begin. He alerted his colleagues that the slogan, "Touch Woody—The Internet Pecker," might need some revision for English-speaking markets. This is not a major blow to a large company like Panasonic, but it does reflect a lack of cultural awareness that can cause a loss of customers.

Some analysts predict that within a few years English will no longer be the default language of cyberspace, and that the majority of Web content will be in a language other than English. Those e-commerce companies that localize language and content in communications with overseas customers are more apt to maximize revenues and grow earnings. As Eric Schmitt of Forrester Research says, "When offered in multiple languages, customer-service features like product data sheets and FAQs provide differentiation, build brand loyalty, and cut support costs."

Companies have been adapting their products and processes to foreign markets for a long time, but these traditional localization efforts tended to have set time frames, and needed few updates. Online localization in terms of language and culture is quite different—it will always be a work in process. A Jupiter Communications WebTrack survey of 114 U.S. Web sites found that two thirds had made only a minimal (or no) attempt to make changes for other markets. "Most corporates still fall into two camps: Many are globally aware but Internet-naïve; the rest are Internet-savvy but globally naïve." Professional localization specialists have emerged to help companies adapt to different global markets, including not only language translations, but also cultural concerns such as the use of color (e.g., white represents death in Asia), and legal and regulatory snares (e.g., comparative advertising is banned in Germany).

There are several approaches to localization. Software is available from companies such as GlobalSight, a company that provides "all-in-one" solutions for multilingual e-businesses. BerlitzIT eFlow, a product from Berlitz GlobalNET, performs more specific tasks related to translation and localization projects. There are many other options—some proprietary and some free. Localization can be outsourced or conducted in-house. For example, one company in the metal and steel business prefers to hire its own translators and localization experts and have them work alongside people with industry experience. The company has three translators in Hong Kong and five in China.

Other companies prefer to outsource localization. ScreamingMedia, a New York-based provider of content infrastructure, syndication, and services, hired outsourcer eTranslate. The process was as follows:

- eTranslate consulted with ScreamingMedia on issues of language and culture.

- eTranslate assessed ScreamingMedia's site for localization red flags, including linguistic issues (especially slang), buzzwords, and other idioms that were difficult to translate.

- eTranslate consultants reviewed back-end issues such as how translation might impact the company's database, text embedded in code, etc.

- ScreamingMedia identified Web site files that needed translation, and annotations to help with localization.

- eTranslate isolated translatable text, and created a glossary to guide translators.

- ScreamingMedia received a functioning version of the site for review.

- As of 2001, Screaming Media's site had been translated into German, French, Spanish for South America, Portuguese for Brazil, and British English for the United Kingdom.

No, American English is not the same as British English—as Tanya Field, director of new media for Discovery Networks Europe found out. Field's job entailed working with the growing demand for added support services for its cable programming. As she pointed out, it goes beyond "spelling words with 'ise' instead of 'ize.'" She noted that various familiar topics are viewed differently—such as different perspectives on who really won World War II.

The Internet has fostered a need for speedy multilingual communication. Technological advances, such as browser-enabled translation programs and other software, are making the job easier for direct marketers. Machine translation is insufficient, however. As Jonathan Sage, a PricewaterhouseCooper director of knowledge management for Europe, says, "Any translated communication or document that's headed for clients should always pass through human translators."

Source: Adam Lincoln, "Lost In Translation," *eCFO* (Spring 2001), pp. 39–43.

marketing research and commercial data suppliers. Marketing efforts can be targeted to specific customers based on the detailed personal or company information that is available from databases.

Technology is a major force in the growth of direct marketing. In particular, the tendency of buyers and sellers to complete their transactions directly has evolved as a result of the increased use of computers, advances in worldwide telecommunications capability, and the extensive use of electronic media.

In conjunction with each of the preceding factors, direct marketing continues to experience growth because of the globalization of markets for all types of goods and services. The expansion of U.S. catalogers and mail-order businesses into Europe and other overseas markets, as well as the expansion of foreign mail-order companies into the United States, has accelerated the use of direct marketing channels on a global basis. International direct marketing expenditures and revenues for the top five non-U.S. countries are shown in Table 13.3. Just as in the United States, economic downturns and other disasters affect marketing budgets and sales, as indicated by negative growth figures between 1995 and 2000. Increased use of the Internet, computerized databases, and commercial radio and television is expected to contribute to the increased percentages of growth between 2000 and 2005.[7]

TABLE 13.3

International Direct Marketing Expenditures and Revenues for Top Five Non-U.S. Countries (Ranked by Level of 2001 Forecast) (in millions of U.S. $)

Direct Marketing Expenditures					Annual Growth %	
Country	Market	1995	2000	2005	1995–2000	2000–2005
Japan	Total	$107,851	$67,278	$87,090	−9.01	5.30
	Consumer	$47,660	$31,307	$38,053	−8.06	3.98
	B-2-B	$61,191	$35,971	$49,037	−9.78	6.39
Germany	Total	$29,381	$22,733	$36,886	−5.00	10.16
	Consumer	$13,898	$10,841	$16,859	−4.85	9.23
	B-2-B	$15,483	$11,892	$20,027	−5.14	10.99
United Kingdom	Total	$12,847	$16,530	$24,312	5.17	8.02
	Consumer	$6,320	$8,262	$11,512	5.51	6.86
	B-2-B	$6,527	$8,269	$12,800	4.85	9.13
France	Total	$16,331	$13,969	$21,614	−3.08	9.12
	Consumer	$6,856	$5,359	$7,852	−4.81	7.94
	B-2-B	$9,474	$8,610	$13,762	−1.89	9.83
Italy	Total	$11,942	$11,611	$18,951	−0.56	10.29
	Consumer	$5,742	$5,499	$8,420	−0.86	8.89
	B-2-B	$6,200	$6,112	$10,531	−0.29	11.50

Direct Marketing Revenues					Annual Growth %	
Country	Market	1995	2000	2005	1995–2000	2000–2005
Japan	Total	$900,924	$525,676	$758,426	−10.21	7.61
	Consumer	$462,160	$275,585	$367,820	−9.82	5.94
	B-2-B	$438,764	$250,091	$390,606	−10.63	9.33
Germany	Total	$133,592	$102,348	$188,152	−5.19	12.95
	Consumer	$71,740	$53,969	$92,935	−5.53	11.48
	B-2-B	$61,853	$48,379	$95,217	−4.80	14.50
United Kingdom	Total	$66,477	$97,015	$155,542	7.85	9.00
	Consumer	$37,185	$53,507	$79,597	7.55	8.27
	B-2-B	$29,292	$43,508	$75,945	8.23	11.79
France	Total	$93,793	$98,941	$184,149	1.07	13.23
	Consumer	$43,377	$38,600	$64,866	−2.31	10.94
	B-2-B	$50,416	$60,341	$119,283	3.66	14.60
Italy	Total	$48,852	$50,505	$104,372	0.67	15.62
	Consumer	$26,450	$26,503	$50,978	0.04	13.98
	B-2-B	$22,401	$24,002	$53,393	1.39	17.34

Source: Direct Marketing Association, *op. cit., Economic Impact: Direct Marketing in 30 Countries Worldwide.*

● DIRECT MARKETING TOOLS

Direct marketing tools may be personal (direct selling) or nonpersonal (direct-action advertising, electronic media). While both consumer and organizational purchases can be made directly from a manufacturer or distributor, more business-to-business transactions are made through direct channels, primarily to decrease costs and time and to increase profits. This is due in part to the size, complexity, and specialized nature of many organizational purchases, as well as to the need to understand each customer's situation. See Table 13.4 for a summary of direct marketing sales by medium and market.

TABLE 13.4

Value of Consumer and Business-to-Business Sales Driven by Direct Marketing, by Medium and Market

	Sales (Billions of Dollars)*			Compound Annual Growth %	
	1996	*2001*	*2006*	*1996–2001*	*2001–2006*
Direct Mail	**$34.5**	**$46.5**	**$63.5**	**6.15%**	**6.42%**
Business-to-business	$12.9	$18.4	$26.1	7.38%	7.28%
Consumer	$21.6	$28.1	$37.4	5.39%	5.85%
Magazine	**$7.1**	**$9.8**	**$13.0**	**6.54%**	**5.79%**
Business-to-business	$3.8	$5.3	$7.0	6.87%	5.86%
Consumer	$3.4	$4.5	$6.0	6.17%	5.71%
Newspaper	**$13.9**	**$18.8**	**$24.7**	**6.14%**	**5.65%**
Business-to-business	$5.4	$7.7	$10.5	7.35%	6.58%
Consumer	$8.6	$11.1	$14.2	5.35%	4.99%
Other	**$11.3**	**$15.6**	**$21.8**	**6.74%**	**6.93%**
Business-to-business	$5.0	$7.2	$10.4	7.66%	7.67%
Consumer	$6.3	$8.4	$11.4	5.98%	6.27%
Radio	**$4.9**	**$7.6**	**$10.6**	**9.30%**	**6.95%**
Business-to-business	$2.6	$4.1	$5.7	9.69%	7.20%
Consumer	$2.3	$3.5	$4.9	8.89%	6.65%
Telephone Marketing	**$54.0**	**$76.2**	**$104.8**	**7.13%**	**6.60%**
Business-to-business	$33.7	$48.9	$68.5	7.77%	6.95%
Consumer	$20.3	$27.2	$36.4	6.05%	5.94%
Television	**$15.9**	**$22.3**	**$30.6**	**6.96%**	**6.54%**
Business-to-business	$7.6	$10.9	$15.3	7.53%	6.91%
Consumer	$8.3	$11.4	$15.4	6.43%	6.19%
Total	**$141.6**	**$196.8**	**$269.2**	**6.80%**	**6.46%**
Business-to-business	$70.8	$102.5	$143.6	7.66%	6.99%
Consumer	$70.9	$94.3	$125.5	5.91%	5.88%

*Sales in current (nominal) dollars, not adjusted for inflation.

Source: Reprinted from *Economic Impact: U.S. Direct and Interactive Marketing Today 2002* with permission from The Direct Marketing Association, Inc.

Direct Selling

Methods of **direct selling** include direct mail, catalogs, telemarketing, in-home or in-office sales, and vending machines. Personal direct selling includes telemarketing and personal contact in the customer's home or office. This method is used frequently for many consumer goods and services, such as cosmetics, jewelry, and household goods. Direct mail and catalogs also are used to promote a variety of products, such as apparel and music or books, in the consumer sector. Organizational customers may purchase a wide range of goods such as auto parts and office supplies through direct mail and catalogs.

Direct-action advertising refers to direct-response advertising in both print and broadcast media. Direct marketing activities that use the Internet, television, cable, facsimile, video, and other electronic media continue to gain customers as the general population becomes better informed and has easier access to the technology.

Direct Mail.   This is the most predominant direct-selling method and includes everything from a simple black-and-white postcard to an impressive multicolor professional package. Catalogs, letters, brochures, pamphlets, flyers, and other printed materials, along with computer disks or CDs, videotapes, and other promotional items, are mailed directly to customers.

Benefits of direct mail include the ability to precisely target selected customers through the use of databases and mailing lists, to tailor the marketing message to the specific needs and characteristics of a prospective customer, to create unique, personalized marketing approaches, and to measure customer response rate. Direct mail can be used at all stages in the buying process, from making prospective customers aware of a purchase problem, to providing information during the search process and evaluation of purchase alternatives, to reinforcing a customer's choice after the sale has been made. Direct mail is an effective marketing tool for nonprofit as well as for-profit organizations. Each year Toys for Tots, a U.S. Marine Corps nonprofit charity, runs a direct mail campaign to solicit donations to support its annual toy collection and distribution to needy children. From June through November 2001, 1.5 million pieces were mailed to prospective donors, with August, September, and October being the most intense months. In spite of the terrorist attacks on September 11, Toys for Tots completed its series of mailings that included gifts such as Toys for Tots decals or magnets, holiday-themed stamps, or calendar booklets. The campaign had net revenue of $3.8 million, up from $600,000 the previous year. The gross amount raised exceeded $6 million, and the combined cost of the donor and acquisition campaigns was $2.4 million, which was spent primarily on postage and the acquisition of donor lists. In spite of the national crisis that dominated the media during the campaign, direct mail proved to be an effective marketing tool.[8]

On the other hand, the proliferation of direct mail has become a nuisance for many people as they deal with mounds of "junk mail," giving this tool a negative image and a high probability that it will be thrown away. For example, Reader's Digest Association has faced continued weak responses to direct mail promotions because customers are overwhelmed by the commercial clutter that fills their mailboxes.

Catalogs.   Catalogs have become the most popular form of direct mail for many of the same reasons that all areas of direct marketing have experienced phenomenal growth. Two catalogs that spurred the growth of this industry were those of Montgomery Ward & Co., Inc., and Sears, Roebuck and Co. in 1872 and 1886, respectively.

Many catalogers have rapidly expanded their Internet infrastructures to capture a growing online community. Initially, e-commerce was not profitable for these direct marketers, but competition from other online catalogs and retailers, customer demand, and rising postal rates (plus the post-9/11 anthrax scare) drove most catalogers to integrate the Internet with their traditional catalog business. This proved to be an advantage to augment print catalogs, and help in coping with rising postal rates and a slowing economy. Catalogers with Web sites also benefit in terms of better response time in filling orders and back-orders, addressing customer requests and complaints, and generally more effective customer contact strategies. Almost all of today's catalogers have Web sites, which helps them to remain more profitable during economic downturns and postal rate increases. Nearly all catalogers are multi-channel companies, and more than half are more likely to integrate and manage major catalog functions across channels (e.g., customer service; fulfillment). Annual catalog circulation in 2001 was 4.4 million versus 2.6 million catalogs in 2000. U.S. catalog advertising expenditures reached $14.9 billion in 2002, with an expected increase to $18.3 in 2006. Total catalog advertising expenditures are divided between business-to-business marketers and consumer marketers into one-third and two-thirds respectively. Total sales for the U.S. catalog market are expected to reach $163.1 billion in 2006, an increase from $125.9 billion in 2002. Employment in catalog direct marketing is expected to increase from 500,159 workers in 2002 to 556,041 workers in 2006.[9]

Catalog marketers can cut distribution costs and reach selected customers, and customers can save precious time and shop at their convenience wherever they may be. Catalogs are used by all types of for-profit and nonprofit organizations to reach their consumer and business markets. Many manufacturers, retailers, and distributors use multiple distribution channels that might include catalogs, retail stores, and personal selling. For example, a customer may make a purchase from J.C. Penney Company, Inc., or Williams-Sonoma, by ordering from a catalog, ordering by telephone, ordering online over the Internet, or visiting a store. More catalogs are also being made available to customers on CDs or videos.

Telemarketing. Telephone marketing is an efficient direct marketing tool that includes all direct-response advertising communications, generally using Wide Area Telephone Service (WATS) for outbound (OUT WATS) and inbound (IN WATS) operations or conventional, private line, or other telecommunications services. Telemarketers may outsource or conduct their telephone marketing in-house. Telephone direct marketing generated sales of $719.5 billion in 2002, with approximately 59 percent attributed to the business-to-business sector.[10]

A well-planned telemarketing program uses the latest telecommunications hardware, software, and database technologies, generally as part of an integrated marketing communications program. It focuses on personal interaction and building relationships with customers. Telephone marketing is second only to personal selling as the most intensely personal promotional medium.[11] The advantages of this direct marketing tool include its ability to provide immediate feedback, flexibility, incremental effectiveness when used with other media, methods of building and maintaining customer goodwill, and opportunities to offer higher levels of customer service. In addition, it is a highly productive tool and has a relatively low cost per contact.

Home or Office Personal Selling. Many direct marketing programs are based on personal selling opportunities where a sales representative takes goods and services to a customer's home or office. The most common form of this type of direct marketing is the party plan followed by such firms as Tupperware and Mary Kay Cosmetics and the door-to-door approach used by Avon Products, Inc. As more women have entered the work force in the United States, many of these direct-selling events have moved from the customer's home to the workplace. This is often complemented by the use of a catalog for order placement at a later time when it is convenient for the customer.

Vending Machines. Vending machines have become more sophisticated over the years and offer a wide array of goods and services. They can dispense tangible goods such as hot and cold foods and beverages and cigarettes. They also can dispense service products such as airline insurance policies. They can be operated with coins or a card, and they can make change for a dollar. Some even "talk" to customers via preprogrammed computer chips.

Direct-Action Advertising

Direct-action advertising can be described in terms of direct response in print media and direct response in broadcast media, as detailed below. The objective of direct response is to motivate the customer to purchase the good or service at the time that it is offered. The offer may include incentives to persuade the customer not to delay the buying decision.

Direct Response: Print Media. The most frequently used print media for direct-response campaigns are magazines, newspapers, inserts, and supplements. Magazines and newspapers may include all direct-response space advertising, inserts, and other advertising formats. The direct-response program objectives may be to achieve immediate sales, generate leads, or increase store traffic. Specialty magazines have become an increasingly effective medium for direct-response marketing because of their highly targeted audiences. While their distribution may not be wide, their ability to hit the right audience is cost-efficient and effective. Potential customers can read about a good or service and immediately place an order directly by mail, telephone, facsimile, or Internet. The key to success for marketers using print media to elicit direct response is to select the right magazine or newspaper for their target market and to gain exposure to as many target customers as possible. This is not always easy, because general advertisers also are targeting many of the same customers.

Direct Response: Broadcast Media. In addition to print media, direct-response campaigns also may communicate with customers through broadcast media (television and radio). Television is particularly effective because of its ability to demonstrate products in use and provide a response mechanism such as a toll-free telephone number, a physical location, or a Web site where the customer can place an order. The use of interactive television is expected to increase as the number of computer WebTV systems in households increases. A large number of customers will use set-top boxes to access the Web—and the direct marketing opportunities that the combined television and Internet have to offer. Television direct response advertising contributed $135.4 billion in sales in 2002.

Radio is everywhere—in homes, cars, and offices, at the beach, in the grocery store, and in every other place you can imagine. Customers are tuned in to their radios in large numbers while they work at their home or office, drive their cars, and engage in leisure activities. Although a radio message is usually short and fleeting, it can motivate customer response and support other direct marketing media. Radio commercials provide potential customers with contact information so that they may purchase the item offered from the advertiser or a third party (such as independent distributors). Although radio messages are fleeting, advertisers can select programs that are most listened to by their target market—and therefore achieve higher response rates. Radio direct marketing sales and expenditures are ranked lowest of all media at $56.3 and $7.9 billion respectively.

Electronic Media

Electronic media
Television, cable, Internet, facsimile, video, etc.

Technological advances have accelerated the use of **electronic media** in direct marketing. The most commonly used tools are television, cable, and the Internet. Facsimile, video, and other media also are used in many campaigns. An accelerated rate of technological advances in these media has increased their attractiveness to direct marketers.

Television and Cable.   Both television and cable have been important marketing media for many years. However, advances in the interactive capability of these media have increased their usefulness to direct marketers.

Cable offers direct marketers an array of specialized target markets. Audiences of cable channels such as CNN (news), ESPN (sports), MTV (music videos), and the Weather Channel each share common characteristics that make them attractive targets for certain goods and services. Cable channels also include the Home Shopping Network and other shopping networks that sell directly to customers, often using infomercials extensively in addition to direct advertising. In contrast to the cheap image of home shopping in its early days, today's direct marketers include more upscale products and represent major fashion retailers. Television home shopping is expected to increase with the proliferation of specialized channels and their interactive capability. Whether television and cable are used to elicit direct response or to support other advertising and personal selling efforts, these electronic media are a critical element in an integrated communications mix.

The Internet.   Advances in information technology and the digital revolution have made the Internet the marketplace of choice for many buyers and sellers as they engage in e-commerce. Accessibility and interactivity are the key advantages of the Internet as a direct marketing tool. Reliable statistics on Internet traffic and sales are difficult to find because of the newness and rapid growth of this medium. Some indicators of the magnitude of direct marketing opportunities on the Internet can be found in company examples, sales and marketing costs, and buying activity, as shown in Figure 13.1.

Analysts predict that the phenomenal growth of Internet marketing (e-commerce) will continue well into the twenty-first century, fueling the worldwide

FIGURE 13.1

Business Practices and Trends in Interactive Direct Marketing Media

Selected results from studies reported by the Direct Marketing Association and the U.S. Department of Commerce indicated the following business practices and trends in interactive direct marketing:

Use of Web Site

- According to research conducted by Inktomi and NEC Research Institute, Inc., there were more than one billion unique Web pages in January 2000, compared to 100 million Web pages in 1997.
- In 2001, 34 percent of direct marketers had operated a Web site for five or more years, more than double the number in 2000.
- 71 percent of consumer companies have actively embraced online transactions as an added sales venue, compared with 20 percent of business-to-business marketers (41 percent overall).
- Web sites are used extensively to research general information for personal use, as well as professional and technical information.
- More than half of direct marketers responding to the DMA study reported that e-commerce transactions are making a profit. Others expected to become profitable the following year.

Reasons for Using the Web

- The most compelling reasons that direct marketers leverage interactive marketing media are to maximize benefits in cost savings (43 percent), greater visibility (47 percent), and new business opportunities (61 percent).
- More than 80 percent of direct marketing companies use their Web site primarily for product/service information. However, those direct marketers that target consumers only (64 percent) and those that target both consumers and B-2-B (63 percent) said the primary purpose of their Web site is sales/e-commerce, compared to only 25 percent of B-2-B direct marketers. Seven of 10 reported that lead generation was the primary purpose. Transactions from international customers represent about 10 percent of total transactions for about three-quarters of direct marketing companies.
- Web sites are used more often for customer service fulfillment, including integration into telephone/fax and Internet-based systems, providing product information, processing orders, conducting exchanges and returns for credit, real-time inventory status updates, and e-mail (as well as other channels) communication between customers and service representatives.
- A *Purchasing Magazine* survey found that over one third of business buyers use the Web to conduct at least some of their firm's transactions, and most of the others planned to do so in the near future.

Technology

- Basic technologies of the digital economy (i.e., processing power, data storage, and data transmission) are becoming increasingly more powerful, driven largely by increased use of the Internet for marketing directly to customers.
- Technologies most used by direct marketers are e-mail (96 percent), the Internet (96 percent), and PDF (82 percent).
- 2 out of 3 manage e-mail, Internet, and PDF technologies in-house, as well as their own cookies on consumer sites.
- At least two thirds of direct marketers offer "login" and "e-newsletter" features or functions on their Web sites. Less frequently offered functions involve personalization, pop-up offers, targeted advertising, online chat, and wireless PDA applications.

FIGURE 13.1 *(continued)*

- Most direct marketers (88 percent) use a secure server for their Web sites, with higher usage among consumer direct marketers (92 percent).

Research and Measurement of Results

- The U.S. Government (e.g., Census Bureau, Bureau of Economic Affairs), professional associations (e.g., DSA, DMA), and private research firms are compiling enormous amounts of data on e-commerce in business and consumer markets, but many questions arise about definitions and measurement needed to understand the full impact of the data.

- Only about one third of direct marketers measure the effectiveness of interactive media, but consumer sites (46 percent) measure results more often than B-2-B (30 percent), or those that target both markets (32 percent).

- Top criteria used when measuring the effectiveness of interactive media include sales and leads generated, and "hits" on designated/unique URLs; other criteria include e-mail addresses collected, and costs per site by customer and by visitor.

- Although most have some level of data on customers, only 43 percent of all direct marketers in the DMA study use segmentation techniques on their customer files; most frequently used information includes purchase history, location/zip code, and demographic variables.

- The most frequently tracked types of customer information on direct marketing Web sites are the amount of time a customer spends on the primary Web site (63 percent) and on each area/page (62 percent), and information about the customer's system. Other data collected include the path a customer used to reach the site, user's connection speed, clickthroughs for promotions on company's sites and other sites, links from e-mail, and the promotional source of an order.

- 64 percent cross-sell by both targeting offline buyers online, and online buyers offline, with catalogs (56 percent) and printed promotions (50 percent) the most often used offline method to lure online customers to an offline channel.

- 34 percent track net sales by media sources; the largest share of net sales is attributed to direct mail (27.8 percent), catalogs (27.3 percent), and Web sites (24 percent).

Marketing Tools and Strategy

- Two thirds are aggressively adding e-mail addresses to their databases to use as a marketing tool.

- Banner advertising usage remained consistent with the previous year, with usage still limited.

- Synergy between traditional online and offline direct marketing techniques is more evident, and much of the synergy is related to driving Web site traffic.

- Conventional marketers are adopting a multi-channel strategy that integrates Web sites, physical stores, catalogs, or other channels.

- Most respondents leverage online media to gain new customers, market via e-mail, and retain customers.

- Direct marketers recognize the importance of keeping traditional offline promotional methods in their mix for customer acquisition and retention.

- Competitive pricing information is more readily available to customers than ever, generally making it necessary for Internet marketers to differentiate on factors other than price.

- Direct marketing companies have survived by changing their focus from dot.coms to dot.corps; dot.coms are being integrated into the overall corporate marketing and operations infrastructures.

FIGURE 13.1 *(continued)*

Opportunities

- Exploit technological capabilities to their greatest potential (e.g., quicker move to build broadband infrastructure that permits all individuals to have access to the advanced services that support the Internet).

- Convert more online visitors to online buyers. More Americans are using the Internet, but their online purchases represent only a small percentage of their total purchases.

- Continued increase in online marketplaces (e.g., eBay where consumers sell to other consumers [C2C] and businesses can sell to one another [B2B] or to consumers [B2C]).

- Increase efforts to "localize" Web sites for international customers.

Issues and Potential Problems

- Lack of consumer confidence in Internet commerce with respect to privacy, security, consumer protection, reliability, and intellectual property rights.

- Customer frustration with "junk mail" and "spam," and their apparent inability to stop its flow into their homes and offices.

Source: "The Evolving Online Environment," *U.S. Economy, Digital Economy 2002*, Chapter 2, U.S. Department of Commerce, Economics and Statistics Administration (June 2000), www.esa.doc.gov/508/esa; "DMA's Fifth Annual E-Commerce Survey," *The Direct Marketing Association State of the E-Commerce Industry Report 2002*, Direct Marketing Association, www.the-dma.org.

---

economy. In 2000, 300 million people throughout the world used the Internet, up from 3 million people in 1994. Experts predict that this number will increase to 1 billion by 2005. Over 50 percent of the U.S. population uses the Internet, across all age groups and other demographic and economic dimensions. Electronic commerce among businesses for commercial transactions has improved productivity significantly in creating, buying, distributing, selling, and servicing goods and services. Business-to-business e-commerce is estimated to grow significantly for sales and purchasing. The digital delivery of goods and services via the Internet is expected to continue its growth in the distribution of software programs, newspapers, music CDs, airline tickets, securities, consulting services, entertainment, banking and insurance, education, and health care, for example.[12] In developing direct marketing strategies, marketing managers should consider the following:[13]

- Recognize that consumer markets are heterogeneous and complex and that the Internet is but one of many distribution channels in a vast array of conventional retail channels; also consider consumer and organizational purchasing processes.

- Identify unique characteristics of the Internet as a distribution channel, as well as characteristics that are shared with other marketing channels, as a basis for determining differentiation strategies and maintaining competitive advantage.

- Evaluate the substitutability of the Internet for distribution functions that are performed by traditional channel intermediaries.

- Determine the suitability of the Internet versus other channels for marketing a good or service with certain characteristics.

In addition, those companies who are later adopters of direct marketing via the Internet (e.g., Encyclopedia Britannica) must manage the disruption of traditional business models when Internet-based technology is added to the marketing mix. They must ask how the Web will affect customer needs, sales and marketing, production and operations, and company personnel. As one CEO said when asked how the Internet was changing his company, "It totally changes everything. It changes the way we process and manufacture all the way through to how we market, sell and deliver."[14] Federal Express Corp., Holiday Inns, Inc., and other companies with successful Internet marketing programs tend to agree that "the Internet initiative must bring into the fold information systems, marketing, and customer support among other departments; Web sites must be interactive, allowing the user to take control of the experience; and the strategy must be part of the overall marketing program, not its forgotten stepchild."[15]

Facsimile, Video, and Other Media.   A number of other tools are used in direct marketing programs, generally in combination with other media. Facsimile (fax) transmissions are used to transmit written and graphic communications between two fax machines over telephone lines. American Telephone & Telegraph Co. (AT&T) was among the first to recognize the potential of fax as a direct-response medium, first sending a direct mail piece to business executives whom they urged to respond by fax for further information about AT&T's equipment or services.[16]

Direct marketers often use videocassettes and videodisks in place of print catalogs. Videos have an appeal to marketers of fashion apparel, automobiles, and other goods and services (e.g., insurance, travel destinations) because of their ability to show the good or service in use. They can be used to explain complex details and provide answers to questions frequently asked by buyers.

Kiosks (free-standing sales units) are placed in retail stores and malls and other public locations. Direct purchases may be made either electronically by computer or in person. Customers can use the kiosk to check on the availability of merchandise and to place an order. They can complete financial transactions using banking kiosks and complete a variety of other types of transactions. Direct marketing has an array of media that can be used to elicit a direct response by including a toll-free telephone number, Internet address, or regular telephone number, for example.

● OBJECTIVES OF DIRECT MARKETING

Direct customer response
One-on-one customer contact where the customer responds directly to the seller's offer.

The two major objectives of direct marketing are to build relationships with customers and to obtain a **direct customer response.** However, not every direct marketing campaign is intended to invoke an immediate transaction. Some direct marketing techniques may be used in combination with other elements of the communications mix, such as backup for the salesforce, reinforcement of other media advertising, and other purposes.

Build Customer Relationships

Relationship building is an important element of direct marketing. Because sales representatives, distributors, and others are involved in direct contact with customers, they may be perceived as an extension of the product they are selling. This total product concept must be consistent with the needs of a particular target market, and it must be communicated effectively. To accomplish this, sales and marketing efforts focus on building relationships with the most important and profitable customers.

Relationship marketing
Building long-term customer relationships beyond a single transaction.

Relationship marketing may include the development of a continuous relationship with a number of unique market segments (or individuals), multiple products, multiple channels, and differentiated messages. The marketing program is customized to each segment. Customer loyalty programs, such as frequent-flier awards, often are used to develop long-term relationships, and this enhances the success of direct marketing programs.

Direct Response or Transaction

In addition to building relationships, another objective of direct marketing is to elicit a direct, immediate response from customers—that is, a one-time transaction (that may grow into repeat business if a relationship is established). Avon's door-to-door selling techniques, Tupperware's home parties, Amazon.com's online Internet book sales, direct mail pieces sent to prospective customers, television shopping networks, and telemarketing are examples of methods used to motivate targeted customers to make an immediate purchase or place an order for a specified time of delivery.

The interactive nature of many of the direct-response techniques often allows the seller to tailor the sales message to the needs of the buyer, increasing the probability of closing a sale quickly. The intended purpose of direct-response advertising through any medium is to stimulate a direct order, generate a qualified lead that can result in a sale, or drive store traffic for advertised products.[17]

INTEGRATED DIRECT MARKETING COMMUNICATIONS

Direct marketing tools must be integrated among themselves to create consistency and synergies in their impact on the target audience. Likewise, direct marketing programs should be integrated with other elements of the marketing mix (product, place, price, and promotion) and communications mix (advertising, personal selling, sales promotion, public relations).

Integration Across Direct Marketing Tools

When direct-selling, direct-action, and electronic media are used in combination, the result is greater than when any one medium is used in isolation. Multiple exposures to the same message are more likely to get customers' attention, help them to remember the message, and move them to act on an offer. For example, a retailer may send a direct mail piece to a charge account customer announcing the arrival of a new catalog in the near future, followed by the catalog itself. Next, the customer may receive a telephone call that highlights a particular product in the catalog (that the retailer's database indicates the customer has an interest in). In addition, the customer may see a magazine advertisement that provides a telephone number or Internet address for additional information or placing an order.

Integration with Other Communications Mix and Marketing-Mix Elements

Direct marketing tools have become increasingly important as elements in the overall communications mix (discussed in Chapters 11 and 12). In turn, the communications mix is but one aspect of the overall marketing mix and must be coordinated with product, pricing, and distribution decisions. Retailers, financial institutions, insurance companies, and other industries generally rely on a combination of the direct marketing tools described in this chapter, such as direct mail, personal selling, electronic media, and so forth.

● THE DIRECT MARKETING PROCESS

Direct marketing process
Development and maintenance of customer databases, interactive marketing systems, and procedures for measuring results.

The **direct marketing process** consists of developing and maintaining customer databases, an interactive marketing system, and a procedure for measuring results. Each element of the direct marketing process is related to the primary decision variables that underlie direct marketing programs: the offer (including the product), creative aspects, media (including lists, if appropriate), timing and sequencing, and customer service provisions.[18]

Direct marketing planning should be coordinated with the organization's strategic planning process and should be consistent with other marketing activities in order to achieve a sustainable competitive advantage. An emphasis on low costs of operation, an offering that is uniquely differentiated from that of competitors, a highly focused (or niche) strategy, or some combination of these approaches can lead to long-term competitive advantage.

Customer Databases

Customer database
Computerized record of information such as customers' personal characteristics, buying habits, and past purchase records that is used to develop direct marketing programs.

Those firms with an accurate, up-to-date **customer database** have the potential to dominate a market based on knowledge of their customers' buying habits, motives, lifestyles, and demographics. Within the context of direct marketing, a *database* is a set of records that contains information about customers. Data generally include relevant personal information about individuals or companies and their past buying behavior, for example. Because databases play a critical role in successful direct marketing, they must be developed and managed carefully.

Role in Integrated Direct Marketing. Target marketing strategies depend on a high level of detailed consumer or organizational customer knowledge. As a result, databases have gained importance in determining which direct marketing tools to use and how to combine them most effectively. For example, a database may provide historical customer data that tell which customers are most likely to respond to telemarketing versus direct mail and the types of products they are most likely to buy. It also may provide information about the total sales generated by each medium and its cost-effectiveness.

A database serves a number of purposes. It enables a marketer to identify the most profitable customers and obtain more business from them. It can be used to identify and qualify the best prospects and convert them to customers, identify past

MARKETING AND ENTREPRENEURSHIP

High Impact from Low-Tech Direct Marketing

When buyers enter the annual International Housewares Show in Chicago's 1.3 million-square-foot McCormick Place convention center, they are confronted with more than 60,000 retailers, distributors, and buyers of houseware products from all over the world. More than 2000 exhibitors present an array of eye-catching displays, such as Rubbermaid Incorporated's 10,000-square-foot booth. Then there's Bakertowne Co., Inc., in a 20- by 15-foot booth in the rear of its section, a "small fish in a big pond," said Lou Kahn, the company's vice- president, and there's the 10-by-10-foot booth used to promote Doumar Products' adhesive remover. Both are competing with the industry giants for sales leads and orders.

Being small can be a disadvantage at a large trade show—unless you use smart marketing that allows "firms operating from guppy-size booths to compete with the sharks." The integration of multiple direct marketing tools can make a firm more competitive. For example, Bakertowne Co., Inc., an importer and distributor of houseware and industrial goods, estimates that as much as 15 percent of the contacts made at the show result in new business leads, and many of these leads result in new business deals. Kahn and other

smaller exhibitors find success in using direct marketing techniques before a trade show, such as sending direct mail and scheduling appointments with prospects. Postcard-sized mailers are inexpensive and effective because they can be mailed to prospects before the show and they are easy to read and carry. The cards should tell the prospect about product introductions, giveaways and promotions, and the company's location at the show. Other direct marketing techniques might include attention-getting demonstrations to help generate leads or make a direct sale. Print and broadcast media can be used along with the direct sales approach at the trade show, as well as direct mail pieces, incentives, and so forth. This is particularly cost-effective if you can get coverage (paid ads and/or publicity) for your company and product line on cable stations, in newspapers, or in other media that are likely to be seen or heard by trade show attendees. The trade show itself is a powerful direct marketing medium, but it makes its greatest impact when it is combined with other marketing tools.

Source: Michelle Wirth Fellmann, "Small Booth, Big Show, Big ROI. Really," *Marketing News* 33(3) (February 1, 1999), pp. 1, 16.

customers and reactivate them, and identify the company's most profitable products. A database also provides input for marketing managers who are responsible for developing appropriate promotional, pricing, and distribution policies; identifying new markets and ways to enter them; measuring the results of marketing efforts; increasing productivity; and decreasing costs while increasing sales volume.[19]

Developing and Managing a Database.   A database is more than just a customer list, although the two terms are sometimes confused. A database includes not only demographic characteristics but also customers' buying preferences and behavior, media habits, and other useful information. Direct responses from customers include valuable information that can be added to the database over a long period of time. This information can be used to determine buying trends, additional opportunities, or potential problems that may be experienced with a particular customer or market segment.

In addition to company-generated data that are useful for direct marketing, there are a number of customer lists that can be used. The most common types are potential customers with a demonstrated interest in a product and a willingness to buy, potential customers with similar identifiable characteristics but unknown willingness to buy, and customers who have bought from the company previously. Lists may be created and maintained in-house or rented from outside sources, such as list brokers.

Data warehousing and data mining have become an integral part of direct marketing. Many companies capture information from each customer purchase, telephone customer service call, mail-in response card, interactive e-mail, or other contact situations. Once collected, the data are organized into a **data warehouse,** which is a method of storing massive amounts of data captured from customer interfaces and other sources. **Data mining** involves sophisticated statistical procedures used to extract meaningful patterns from mass amounts of data. Direct marketers can use data/mining techniques to capture, query, and analyze the data to identify potential customers, determine the most suitable offer for each one, enhance customer loyalty, reactivate customer purchases with timely offers, and other purposes.[20] (Refer to Chapter 4 opening vignette about Harrah's data warehousing operation.) Data warehousing and data mining require competent personnel to manage the database, and should be established as an integral part of the company's overall marketing intelligence system (MIS).

> **Data warehouse**
> A method of storing massive amounts of data captured from customer interfaces and other sources.

> **Data mining**
> Sophisticated statistical procedures used to extract meaningful patterns from mass amounts of data.

Interactive Marketing System

> **Interactive marketing systems**
> Technology-based selling systems consisting of computers, software, databases, and telecommunications technology.

Interactive marketing systems have grown from a simple salesperson-customer transaction to technology-based selling systems. Thus computers, software, databases, and telecommunications technologies are combined into one system to enable organizations to sell directly to their customers, particularly those with whom they want to build long-term relationships. Customer relationship management requires a disciplined system that maximizes the value of customer relationships and ensures that individual customer needs are profitably satisfied at the right time, in the right channel, and with the right offer.[21] The components of a hypothetical direct marketing system are illustrated in Figure 13.2. Although direct marketing system designs vary from one situation to another, the basic components generally include an automated, computerized database, efficient telecommunications, an interactive communication system (which includes both inbound and outbound call centers), order-fulfillment facilities and procedures, a well-developed customer service function, and retention and loyalty programs.

The Direct Marketing Association forecast $4.0 billion in expenditures for interactive/online marketing in 2002, with the expectation that this figure would grow 18.9 percent annually to reach $8.4 billion in 2006. Interactive/online sales forecasts for 2002 were at $36.0 billion, with expected annual growth of 20.9 percent to reach $81.1 billion in 2006. Interactive marketing employment is estimated to reach nearly one half million workers in 2006.[22]

Measuring Results

Although direct marketing is an efficient way to serve a chosen target market, it is costly and time-consuming to implement. Therefore, results of a direct marketing program must be monitored to determine whether or not it has been successful—

FIGURE 13.2

Components of a Direct Marketing System

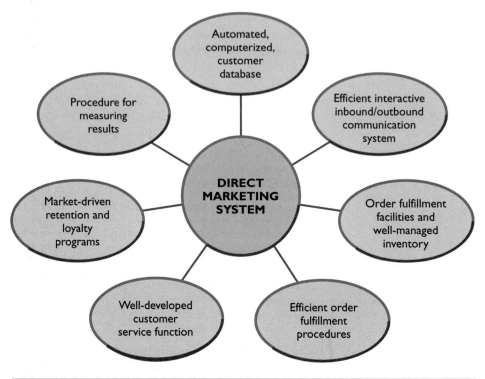

and why. The effectiveness of each tool used in a marketing campaign can be measured individually and collectively to determine the relative contribution that each has made to the final result. For example, test marketing can be used to determine customer reactions to any element of the direct marketing approach, such as media and message reactions, attitudes toward the marketer and the product, and so forth. Measures can be used throughout a direct marketing campaign to analyze customer responses and at the end of a campaign to determine whether sales or other objectives were met.

The results of a direct marketing program can be measured in several different ways. Sales responses can be measured against campaign objectives to determine if they were achieved. A cost-benefit analysis can be performed to determine the efficiency and effectiveness of resources used. Follow-up research can be conducted with customers to determine their level of satisfaction or problems they may have experienced with the purchase or the transaction.

In business-to-business direct marketing, results may be measured with marketing and sales productivity (MSP) systems.[23] Both large and small companies can expect improvements in productivity and effectiveness if they use MSP information networks as management tools to measure automated routine tasks and gather and interpret data. Some examples include salesperson productivity (e.g., sales calls, order entry and status, tracking leads, managing accounts), direct mail and fulfillment, and telemarketing (e.g., merging, cleaning, and maintaining mailing and calling lists, ranking prospects). Measurement of marketing results is discussed further in Chapter 15.

● ISSUES IN DIRECT MARKETING

Direct marketing continues to increase in popularity as a marketing communication and distribution method. However, there are issues and concerns that must be faced by both customers and direct marketing organizations. Key factors that affect decisions by both buyers and sellers are discussed briefly, along with selected legal, ethical, and social issues.

Customer-Related Issues

Although many consumers and businesses are responsive to direct marketing efforts, many others are reluctant to make purchases in this way. The factors that motivate or discourage this type of purchase are discussed next.

Factors Motivating Use.   A number of key factors contribute to consumers' and organizational buyers' decisions to purchase directly from a supplier. Key factors include a desire for quick and convenient order fulfillment, lower prices due to elimination of middlemen, a proliferation of specialized media targeted to their needs and preferences, availability of interactive media for purchasing in homes and offices, and more technologically savvy buyers.

Factors Discouraging Use.   Many of the factors that diminish customers' ability or willingness to purchase directly include lack of comfort with interactive technology, unavailability of direct salespeople in the home or office, preference for hands-on in-store shopping experiences, and privacy or ethical issues (discussed below).

Organization-Related Issues

The major issues involved in the adoption of direct marketing programs by organizations (both for-profit and nonprofit) include use of resources and measures of effectiveness. Others include legal, ethical, and social factors (discussed later).

Resource Utilization.   The need to become more efficient by cutting operating costs is a primary motivator for using a direct marketing strategy. Direct marketing efforts can be targeted precisely toward select groups of customers and individuals with a high expectation of success. The absence of a middleman makes it possible to significantly reduce processing time and transactional costs, although direct marketers are responsible for all marketing functions that are performed by other channel members in traditional distribution channels.

Another key issue revolves around the time and effort that must be put into creating and maintaining a direct marketing system. Further, databases are in constant need of updating and need dedicated effort if their benefits are to be maximized. The main question is whether other selling methods might provide a greater return for the time and money invested.

Effectiveness Measures.   It is often difficult to measure success in direct marketing because the measures themselves are not satisfactory. A comprehensive approach can be taken by breaking down the direct marketing system into its various components and analyzing the effectiveness of each one. For example, sales results, mail or telephone inquiries, or other responses can be used to measure the effectiveness of each direct marketing medium. Message effectiveness might be assessed with communications measures such as recognition or recall tests or attitude measures. Customer service effectiveness can be measured with customer satisfaction surveys and monitoring of transactions.

Legal, Ethical, and Social Issues

Both buyers and sellers have a number of concerns about the legal, ethical, and social aspects of direct marketing. Leading trade associations such as the Direct Selling Association (DSA) and the Direct Marketing Association (DMA) have developed codes of ethics that demonstrate a commitment to both the customer and the seller. Members pledge to adhere to the code's standards and procedures as a condition of admission and continuing membership. The DSA code "ensures that member companies will make no statements or promises that might mislead either consumers or prospective sales people." DSA denies membership to any company involved in pyramid schemes, which are illegal. An independent code administrator who is not connected with any member company is responsible for enforcement, resolving complaints, and deciding on remedies. Member companies must honor the administrator's decisions. The DMA also provides its members with guidelines for business ethics in several ways, including a booklet ("Doing the Right Thing"), and ethical practice guidelines for direct marketing that can be accessed from DMA's Business Assistance site.[24] Two issues are selected for discussion here: invasion of privacy and multilevel marketing (pyramid) schemes.

Invasion of Privacy.   One of the greatest drawbacks to consumers who are inclined to purchase directly is the invasion of their privacy. The ability of direct marketers to create databases that contain all types of personal information is a major concern. The problem is exacerbated by the fact that a company may sell its customer database to another organization, often without its customers being aware of this sharing of personal information. Online direct marketing, in particular, has come under scrutiny for privacy infractions, and suffers from customer mistrust even when privacy policies are clearly stated on a Web site. Respondents to a study conducted by PricewaterhouseCoopers in 2000 indicated that retail Web sites should ask permission before sharing or using any personal information. They also objected to retail Web sites that store their credit card information for future use, and prefer to pay for online purchases via a 1-800 telephone number.[25] The Web affords direct marketers with advanced technology that can store vast amounts of site visitors' information without their knowledge, leading to much debate between marketers, software producers, government officials, and consumers. The cost of providing high levels of privacy can be high for direct marketers, but customers also pay a steep price for lack of security, and are reluctant to participate in many direct marketing opportunities. Another violation of consumers' privacy is the deluge of unwanted advertisements, letters, and other forms of direct marketing. "Junk" mail and "spam" e-mail that fills customers' mailboxes and computers make it difficult for professional direct marketers to be heard in the clutter.

Multilevel Marketing (Pyramid).   With the popularity of direct selling, there has been a growth in multilevel marketing businesses, sometimes referred to as *pyramid schemes.* Many multilevel marketers are responsible and deal within the confines of the law and ethical judgment; others may not. The problem lies with the balance between a focus on sales of a product versus the building of a salesforce that returns profits to each level above it (i.e., a pyramid). In this case, the customers are actually the lower levels of the salesforce that feed orders and profits to those above—making it attractive to continue to recruit large numbers of sales representatives who may be required to purchase and carry an inventory of the product.

● TRENDS IN DIRECT MARKETING

The future of direct marketing appears to be determined by three related factors: databases, technology, and communication. The importance of automated, computerized, comprehensive databases has been stressed throughout this chapter. As markets become more global and populations become more diverse, databases will continue to provide more efficient and effective ways to identify homogeneous market segments that can be targeted with direct marketing programs. The future of database management is intertwined with the future of technology and the improvements that technology continues to provide, such as the linking of multiple databases for more complete customer information and continuous follow-up throughout an entire sales process.

The communications mix is in a state of change because of shifts in media use by buyers and sellers and general advances in telecommunications capabilities throughout the world. In particular, the Internet is expected to make even more inroads as the chosen medium for many shoppers. The proliferation of cable channels, satellite broadcasting systems, and cellular and mobile technology will continue to offer more direct marketing media options. The more that marketers and their customers are linked electronically, the less need there will be for personal contact or in-store transactions. Newspapers and other print media will continue to be challenged by readers and advertisers as to their relevance in today's world. Many have found success by using multiple distribution channels (e.g., print, Internet) to disseminate news and advertising content. The increased power of Internet service providers and those who control Internet "portals," or access points, are influencing increasing numbers of buyers to read, browse, and shop electronically. At the same time, customers expect a satisfactory level of individual attention and service. It is just that the traditional ways of delivering customer satisfaction are giving way to newer, more efficient, and more effective—and better-informed—ways of doing so.

Summary

Direct marketing is an interactive two-way marketing communication system between a marketer and a prospective customer, who is always given a chance to respond. The communication can take place whenever and wherever there is access to communications media. Direct marketing communication is designed to elicit a direct order response, generate sales leads, or generate customer traffic. Direct marketing represents an increasingly important aspect of the integrated marketing communications mix. Direct marketing also can be viewed from a distribution channel perspective, since it represents the zero-level, or shortest, channel between customers and suppliers.

Phenomenal growth in direct marketing is attributable to customers' time constraints, an increase in niche marketing, availability of specialized media and computerized databases, advances in technology and electronic media, and global business expansion.

Direct marketing tools include direct selling (direct mail, catalogs, telemarketing, home or office personal selling, and vending machines), direct-action advertising (direct response in print or broadcast media), and electronic media (television, cable, Internet, facsimile, video, and other media). Media selection is one of the major decisions that must be made by direct marketers, since each medium has its advantages and disadvantages for the product market that is targeted.

The primary objectives of direct marketing are to build relationships with customers and to obtain a direct customer response. Customer relationships are enhanced by customized marketing programs and well-managed databases.

The direct marketing process consists of developing and maintaining customer databases, an interactive marketing system, and a procedure for measuring results. Direct marketing planning should be coordinated with an organization's strategic planning process and should be consistent with other marketing activities.

Accurate, up-to-date customer databases make it possible for direct marketers to dominate a market based on knowledge of their customers' buying habits, motives, lifestyles, and demographics. Databases are used to determine which customers to target and how to reach them (media, message). They are also used to measure the results of a direct marketing campaign. Direct marketing is part of an interactive marketing system of computers, software, databases, and telecommunications technologies.

Although direct marketing is increasing in popularity as a marketing communication and distribution method, there are a number of issues that should be considered. Direct marketing is appealing to consumers and organizational customers who desire speed, convenience, and lower prices—particularly those who are more technologically

savvy. Organizations may find the effort required to create and manage databases to be a negative factor, despite their usefulness. Customers may resist direct marketing efforts because they are uncomfortable with interactive technology, prefer hands-on shopping, or are concerned about privacy issues or multilevel marketing techniques. The future of direct marketing is driven by three related factors: databases, technology, and communication.

Questions

1. Describe the direct marketing strategy pursued by Dell Computer Corp., and analyze the reasons for its success. What future changes, if any, do you believe will be made to this strategy based on current trends? Justify your answer.

2. Based on the Direct Marketing Association's definition of direct marketing, identify and give a current example of each of the four key elements of a direct marketing strategy that were described in the chapter.

3. Explain the relationship between direct marketing and (a) the integrated marketing communications mix and (b) channels of distribution.

4. Identify the factors that have contributed to the phenomenal growth of direct marketing, and discuss your predictions for the future of direct marketing (i.e., media, customers, etc.).

5. Assume that you have been given the responsibility of developing a direct marketing campaign for a new type of insurance policy. Discuss the objectives of your campaign and how you will measure the results.

6. Describe and evaluate the pros and cons of each of the direct marketing tools that can be used for (a) direct selling, (b) direct-action advertising, and (c) electronic media. Give examples to illustrate each tool.

7. Discuss the components of the direct marketing process (databases, interactive marketing system, measurement of results) relative to selling books or other publications to an identified market segment.

8. Evaluate the major issues that confront direct marketers, and discuss how you believe these will impact direct marketing strategies over the next decade.

Exercises

1. Conduct a content analysis of a favorite magazine or newspaper, and evaluate the number of direct marketing communications that appear in that issue. Analyze the following factors: (a) ability to reach and influence the intended target market, (b) appropriateness of the medium and the message, and (c) direct-response mechanism used to attain implied objectives.

2. Identify a direct marketing campaign that appears in multiple types of media. Evaluate each medium used in terms of its ability to create synergy with other media and its impact on the reader/viewer/listener. Provide actual examples, if possible.

3. Contact a direct marketer, and learn the process that was followed for a recent campaign. If possible, obtain examples of campaign materials and critique their effectiveness in achieving direct marketing objectives.

4. Evaluate a Web page for a retailer such as Lands' End or Barnes & Noble in terms of its effectiveness as a direct marketing tool.

Endnotes

1. Erick Schonfeld, "Schwab Puts It All Online," *Fortune* (December 7, 1998), pp. 94–100.

2. Direct Marketing Association, Inc., *2002 Economic Impact: U.S. Direct Marketing Today*, available at http://www.the-dma.org/.

3. Mary Lou Roberts and Paul D. Berger, *Direct Marketing Management* (Englewood Cliffs, N.J.: Prentice-Hall, 1989), p. 2.

4. Direct Marketing Association, *op. cit.*

5. Alexander Hiam and Charles D. Schewe, *The Portable MBA in Marketing* (New York: John Wiley & Sons, 1992), p. 373; Roberts and Berger, *op. cit.*, p. 4.

6. Robert A. Peterson, Sridhar Balasubramanian, and Bart J. Bronnenberg, "Exploring the Implications of the Internet for Consumer Marketing," *Journal of the Academy of Marketing Science* 25(4) (1997), pp. 329–346.

7. Direct Marketing Association, *op. cit.*

8. Glenn J. Kalinoski, "Economic Downturn Doesn't Slow Toys for Tots," www.dmnews.com (March 5, 2002); see Direct Marketing Association, *op. cit.*, the DMA State of Postal and E-Mail Marketing 2002.

9. "Catalog Ad Spending, Sales and Employment," *Economic Impact: U.S. Direct & Interactive Marketing Today, Executive Summary 2002*, Direct Marketing Association (2002).

10. Direct Marketing Association, *op. cit.*

11. For further discussion, see Roberts and Berger, *op. cit.*, Chap. 11.

12. Internet data in this paragraph are taken from Lynn Margherio, Project Director, U.S. Department of Commerce, *The Emerging Digital Economy*, available at http://www.ecommerce.gov. This report includes data from research conducted by Morgan Stanley, Forrester Research, leading financial analysts, and other professional sources.

13. Peterson, Balasubramanian, and Bronnenberg, *op. cit.*

14. Michael Krauss, "The Web and the Company Must Work Together," *Marketing News* 32(19) (September 14, 1998), p. 8.

15. Tom Dellecave, Jr., "The 'Net Effect,'" *Sales & Marketing Technology* (March 1996), pp. 17–21, in John E. Richardson (ed.), *Marketing 97/98, Annual Editions* (Sluice Dock, Guilford, Conn.: Dushkin Publishing Group, 1999), pp. 211–215.

16. Roberts and Berger, *op. cit.*, p. 427.

17. Direct Marketing Association, *op. cit.*, *2002 Economic Impact: U.S. Direct and Interactive Marketing Today.*

18. Roberts and Berger, *op. cit.*, pp. 5–8.

19. *Ibid.*, pp. 147–148.

20. Kotler, Philip, *Marketing Management*, 11th ed. (Upper Saddle River, NJ: Pearson Education, Inc., 2003), pp. 54–56, 125–126.

21. Anonymous, *Customer Relationship Management: Practical Applications*, available at http://www.recsys.com/Relman5.htm.

22. Direct Marketing Association, *op. cit.*, *2002, Economic Impact: U.S. Direct and Interactive Marketing Today.*

23. V. Kasturi Rangan, Benson P. Shapiro, and Rowland T. Moriarity, Jr., *Business Marketing Strategy: Cases, Concepts, and Application.* (Chicago, Ill.: Irwin, 1995), pp. 573–582.

24. "About DSA's Code of Ethics," Direct Selling Association, www.dsa.org; "Ethical Guidelines," The Direct Marketing Association, www.the-dma.org/library/guidelines/ethicalguidelines.shtml.

25. Rafi A. Mohammed, Robert J. Fisher, Bernard J. Jaworski, and Aileen M. Cahill, *Internet Marketing: Building Advantage in a Networked Economy* (New York, NY: McGrawHill Companies, Inc., 2002), p. 260.

MARKETING MANAGEMENT IN ACTION: CLOSING CASE

Nonprofit Direct Marketing: The Good News Jail & Prison Ministry

There are 1.9 million adult prisoners behind bars. Who will bring them the good news of the Gospel?

These are the opening lines on a Web page for the Good News Jail & Prison Ministry, a nonprofit charitable organization. This direct marketing message challenges the viewer to become involved in carrying out the mission of a unique Ministry that exists "to provide spiritually mature, equipped and motivated men and women to serve as Christian Chaplains in Correctional facilities nationally and internationally."

About the Good News Jail & Prison Ministry

Good News Jail & Prison Ministry was incorporated in the Commonwealth of Virginia in 1961 as a nonprofit organization. Its purpose was to organize a visitation program for the benefit of inmates of State institutions; witness to inmates and their families; aid in physical and spiritual rehabilitation of men and women upon their release from an institution; and provide an educational program within the institutions to encourage inmates to continue formal education. The key to achieving these purposes lies in trained, ordained staff chaplains in correctional institutions throughout the United States and overseas. From one chaplain and one institution in 1961, Good News Ministry has grown to over 215 chaplains that serve 179 institutions in 23 states and the countries of India, Nigeria, Latvia, Ghana, Kenya, Siberia, Uganda, Lithuania, and Estonia. For over 40 years, Good News Jail & Prison Min-

istry has provided service for sheriffs, directors of correction, institution staff, and inmates of correctional facilities.

Funding for Good News Ministry comes primarily from gifts and donations, and occasional support from foundations and grants. The Ministry does not accept financial support from federal, state, or local tax revenues—but does provide hundreds of thousands of dollars worth of services each year, at no cost to local taxpayers.

Direct Marketing for Nonprofits: A Broad Perspective

Religious and church-based nonprofit organizations use a variety of marketing tools, including direct marketing media, to reach their constituents. Collectively, nonprofits spend huge sums of money on marketing each year (though many prefer to call it "public relations"). Most nonprofits find that a highly targeted direct marketing campaign is an effective use of their limited budgets. Direct marketing media can be more cost-effective than traditional advertising, and can provide more market coverage at a lower cost—particularly when volunteers do much of the work.

In spite of the need to spend each marketing dollar wisely, many nonprofits do not know whether a campaign actually reached its objectives (assuming that objectives were clearly stated and measurable), or whether their dollars invested in marketing were well spent. In other words, was there a direct link between the time and money spent on the campaign and the desired results of that campaign? Competition among a wide variety of nonprofit organizations is intense, as each one clamors for donors, volunteers, and other resources. Direct marketing media provide a way to break through the clutter—if planned and executed effectively.

Direct Marketing Tools Used by Good News Jail & Prison Ministry

To accomplish its mission, Good News Ministry must seek financial resources, and the personal involvement of many volunteers. A strong direct selling tool used by the organization is its Web site (www.goodnewsjail.org), which is straightforward, to the point, and easy to navigate from one page to another. A number of direct response opportunities are presented online:

- Listen to a radio ministry by clicking on a feature called "Full Pardon" to hear inspiring stories of how God's work has affected the lives of inmates.

- Use a direct e-mail link to communicate with the "Full Pardon" radio ministry.

- Accept a free offer for a booklet, "What Does God Think of Me Now?"

- Locate a chaplain in your area in the United States or abroad.

- Become involved as a Good News Volunteer to help in ways such as teaching a Bible Study, assisting the Chaplain with office work, distributing Bibles, or assisting in worship services.

- Give financial support by completing a personal information form; receive e-mails; make donations anonymously; and log in to sign up for a free account to facilitate future donations.

- Request more information about Good News Jail & Prison Ministry via a 1-800 telephone number, a regular telephone number, e-mail address, or a personal mailing address.

A recent direct marketing campaign implemented by Good News Jail & Prison Ministry was targeted toward donors. The primary objective of this campaign was to raise much-needed money (targeted amount not publicized). Personal selling has been used most effectively for this purpose,

and was Good News Ministry's most effective direct marketing tool in this campaign.

Another objective was to drive people to the Ministry's Web site, where they can take advantage of direct response opportunities. Several direct marketing techniques were used to increase online traffic, such as giving away coasters with Good News Ministry Web site information on them, and distributing a CD made for radio play. Other direct marketing media used by the Ministry to achieve multiple objectives include direct mailings and videos.

The basic message that was communicated across all media used in the donor campaign was "We provide Chaplains to jails and prisons. We turn tax spenders to tax payers." While Good News Jail & Prison Ministry considers the campaign a success, an in-depth analysis of results versus objectives was not available. When asked how well the direct marketing media and plan worked to achieve objectives, one representative of the organization echoed the response of many other nonprofits with the comment, "That I don't know. We are struggling in this area and can use all the help we can get."

Jails and prisons continue to fill to overflowing, and more inmates are being released early and must function as responsible members of the greater society. Thus, the Good News Jail & Prison Ministry is faced with a constant need to raise money from donors, recruit volunteers, increase chaplain participation, build external and internal relationships, and maintain a database of donors, volunteers, and others. Possible target audiences for ongoing and future campaigns include chaplains, present and prospective donors and volunteers, corporations, church groups, and inmates. Campaign objectives may include obtaining a direct response and/or building relationships with targeted groups. These objectives should be established prior to the campaign, preferably in measurable terms that can be used to assess the success of direct marketing media (e.g., number or dollar amount of donations that can be attributed to direct marketing on the Web site, or to personal sales calls; the number of new volunteers or chaplains attributed to a direct mail campaign or personal contacts).

Since direct channels of communication seem to work best for Good News Ministry, direct marketing media can continue to be used successfully. The question is, which direct marketing tools are most appropriate and cost effective, and how can personal selling and nonpersonal direct marketing tools be integrated into an effective campaign? Further, how can Good News Jail & Prison Ministry determine which marketing approach and media did the best job of achieving their objectives for a particular campaign?

Source: Good News Jail & Prison Ministry, www. goodnewsjail.org (November 19, 2002); telephone interviews and e-mail correspondence with Good News Ministry volunteers and organizational representatives (November 19–20, 2002).

Case Study Questions

1. Based on information in the case, evaluate Good News Jail & Prison Ministry's donor campaign in terms of direct marketing objective(s), media, message, and other criteria.

2. What direct selling tools (e.g., direct mail, telemarketing, in-home/in-office) and/or direct action advertising media (e.g., print, broadcast, electronic) would you use for a follow-up campaign—and why? State campaign objective(s).

3. Give specific examples of how direct marketing can be used by the Ministry to achieve each of these objectives within one year: (1) increase number of chaplains from 215 to 230; (2) add 100 new volunteers in the United States; (3) obtain $1 million in new donations.

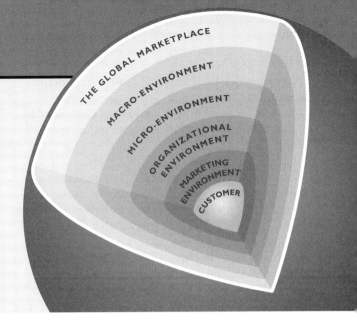

THE GLOBAL MARKETPLACE
MACRO-ENVIRONMENT
MICRO-ENVIRONMENT
ORGANIZATIONAL ENVIRONMENT
MARKETING ENVIRONMENT
CUSTOMER

CHAPTER 14

Pricing Strategy

The value decade is upon us. If you can't sell a top-quality product at the world's lowest price, you're going to be out of the game.[1]

Overview

Palm's Pricing in 2002

If you're shopping for a hand-held computer, it's been easy to find models from Sony, Hewlett-Packard (Compaq), and Palm with all the latest features including color screens, if you're willing to spend $400 to $600. Or, a stripped-down, heavy, low-end model can be found from Handspring and Palm for under $200. But mid-range choices with a decent number of cool features like color have been limited. However, in March 2002, Palm launched model m130 at $279 complete with color screen, and it doesn't feel like a brick in your pocket.

At first glance, the m130 looks like any other bargain-basement, youth-oriented model in Palm's m100 series, with a rounded bottom edge and a rubbery flip lid with a window that flashes the time and date when you press a button. And, its removable faceplate can be replaced with a variety of bright colors. But instead of charcoal gray, the m130 is steel blue and silver, and when you open the lid and turn it on, there is a bright, vivid, backlit color screen. The m130 also has an expansion slot that accepts the same small SD or multimedia cards as Palm's expensive models to allow you to increase memory, add travel information, electronic books, games, or a dictionary and thesaurus. There is also a "Bluetooth" card for wireless connections to certain PCs and other devices.

The main competitor to the m130 is the Handspring Visor Prism at $299. It has been on the market awhile and is thinner and narrower. But it is also heavier—6.9 ounces compared to the m130's 5.4. However, the features available with the m130 are what set it apart at this midprice range. According to tests done by Walter S. Mossberg, writer of the "Personal Technology" column for the *Wall Street Journal*, it is synchronized properly with Palm's desktop software as well as Microsoft Outlook and Lotus Organizer. It is able to beam programs and data to and from other Palms. It comes with a host of add-on software, including a program that lets you read Microsoft Office files. And, it has a photo viewer. Mossberg had only minor complaints, but he did note that Palm already offered some close alternatives to the m130. If you can live with a monochrome screen and AAA batteries instead of color screen and lithium battery, but want all the other features, there is the m125 model at $199. Or if you find the one-inch thickness of the m130 too bulky and again are willing to do without a color screen, there is the m500 at $299.

So what is Palm's pricing strategy in this situation and how does it relate to their overall marketing strategy? Some observers would say it is a "value" pricing strategy because Palm is offering superior product features while undercutting competitors' prices. Others might say no, it is just a product extension or product positioning strategy. Maybe it is both. There seemed to be an unfilled position in the mid-range of prices. There also seemed to be an unfilled position for a relatively full-featured hand-held with the very obvious and desired color screen. Palm put the two together and introduced a product at a price to match the unfilled position. Mossberg says, "...the m130 may be the perfect hand-held for the midrange customer."

Source: Walter S. Mossberg, "Palm's New Hand-Held Is a Light, Color Model Without High Price Tag," *Wall Street Journal* (March 21, 2002), B6.

P alm wisely identified that value pricing would allow it to remain competitive in their industry. The company recognized that customers perceive benefits as having three components: service benefits, brand benefits, and product benefits—and offered its customers increased product benefits. Pricing is certainly one of the most complex and difficult of the strategy-making tasks and bedevils many companies.[2] In this chapter we discuss the formidable task of formulating pricing strategy for the firm. Prior to this point in the book, it would have been difficult to discuss the multiple issues involved in pricing strategy because marketing strategists are required to simultaneously consider the other elements of the marketing mix, which have been discussed in previous chapters. Many of the aspects involved in establishing a pricing strategy depend on managerial decisions made at each of the stages of the marketing strategy process.

● THE ROLE OF PRICE IN STRATEGIC MARKETING

Price
The monetary amount a buyer pays for a good or service and/or the revenue expectation from a sale.

To understand the role of pricing in strategic marketing, we must begin by defining price. Simply stated, **price** is the monetary amount a buyer pays for a good or service. But the real meaning of price is not so simple. Both the buyer and seller have differing views of the meaning of price. An additional complicating factor is *market complexity*. Market complexity is the result of such factors as the proliferation of product/service offerings, the geographic scattering of customers, the segmentation factors operating in most markets, the wide variety of differing conditions affecting market transactions, and the internal pricing conflicts at work in any organization. Market complexity makes setting the right price extremely difficult, yet it is often a

FIGURE 14.1

Components of Pricing Strategy

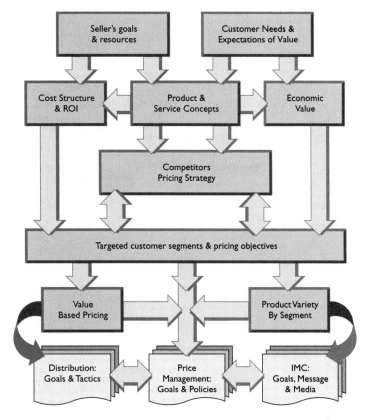

Source: Copyright © 2002. Reprinted by permission of Pearson Education, Inc., Upper Saddle River, NJ. *Strategy and Tactics of Pricing,* 3/e by Thomas T. Nagle and Reed K. Holden.

key factor in the success of a firm's marketing strategy.[3] Moreover, a firm's pricing strategy must be coordinated with indirect and nonprice competitive strategies. (See Figure 14.1.) What happens to a firm that promises value at the right price and then does not deliver? "Unless a brand has substance to support its promises, its equity begins to deteriorate," says Marc C. Particelli of Booz, Allen & Hamilton, Inc. An example is cable-TV giant Comcast Corp., which has a near monopoly and since mid-2000 has raised its prices by 15 percent in the face of economic conditions of uncertainty for many of its customers. The result is many customers are moving to satellite systems from cable.[4,5]

Buyer's versus Seller's Point of View

Purchasing power
The money available to spend for the purchase of desired goods of services.

To the ultimate consumer or organizational customer, the price paid for a product represents giving up something of value (money). This is usually viewed as **purchasing power,** because money spent on one purchase cannot be used for some other purchase. For every consumer, this exchange represents a choice process, choosing among alternatives of what to purchase. Perhaps you may recall your own childhood experience when, for the first time, you stood before the candy display at the local convenience store trying to decide what you would buy with a dollar clutched in your hand. Remember how hard the decision was? Perhaps you can even recall the myriad of conflicting emotions. Regardless of what you finally chose, you may have been reluctant to turn away from the display because buying one item meant that others could not be purchased. As consumers, most of us face these same hard decisions for a lifetime. Even a reseller who buys goods to supply to others views price in this same manner. Paying a price is a choice process of what to buy—and it means giving up something of value.

From the seller's point of view, price can be something quite different. Sellers know that price determines the revenue stream that has a direct impact on profits achieved. Thus, to the selling organization, price is the **revenue expectation** from a sale. Closely related to this revenue expectation viewpoint is the parallel view that price is the **accumulation of costs** incurred in developing, manufacturing, and marketing a product plus some profit margin factor. Financial executives and production personnel most often have this point of view, especially when the firm uses a cost-plus pricing strategy (which will be discussed below). However, marketing personnel must think of price as but one element in the marketing mix and therefore must focus on the total marketing program and how the pricing strategy fits the overall marketing strategy of the organization.

Price is important and cannot be viewed in isolation, especially in highly competitive markets, because it has a direct impact on the other elements of the marketing mix. If a firm's pricing strategy is a significant element of its competitive positioning, and especially if price is a competitive advantage, then price must be viewed as having meaning only in relation to the total marketing program. Therefore, the most appropriate view of price is that it is an integral part of the firm's marketing strategy, which in turn drives the revenue stream and thus makes profits achievable.

Revenue expectation
The price that determines the revenue stream derived from a sale.

Accumulation of costs
Closely related to revenue expectation, but the parallel view that price is the accumulation of costs involved in developing, manufacturing, and marketing the product plus some profit margin factor.

An Example of Pricing Complexity

In many global markets, mobile telephones (referred to as "cell phones" or "handy's" in various parts of the globe) are a fast-selling item often desired for their "prestige" value as much as for their communication benefits. When a global manufacturer such as Nokia establishes a pricing strategy for an individual marketplace, it is a complex task because of the many marketplace factors that vary from one locale to another. Knowledge regarding the conditions where strategies of global pricing of standardization or adaptation are still limited.[6] For example, in the U.S. market, Nokia and all competitors virtually give away the actual cell phone and count on the revenue stream that results from use of the product as their source of income. The telecommunications company that receives the multimonth contract for service must pay a commission or fee to both the manufacturer of the cell phone and to the sales agent who signs up the customer. These long-term service contracts, plus the task of initially programming the cell phone to enable customer use, represent an indirect pricing strategy that must be developed by prior agreement among manufacturer, reseller, and service provider.

Meanwhile, in Australia, Nokia had to develop a totally different pricing strategy because in this market all cell phones ("handy's") are sold at a price that is independent of the price paid to initially program the product and independent of any long-term service provider contract. Thus Nokia's cell phone may sell for A$99 to the customer, while the reseller also charges the customer A$49 for initially programming the phone. In addition, the customer must sign a minimum of a 24-month service provider contract that contains minimum monthly fees, as well as an additional fee based on frequency of use. Thus, while the reseller may advertise in Australia that the Nokia cell phone is priced at only A$99, the real cost to the customer may easily amount to a minimum of A$550 over the 24-month period of the service contract required of every purchaser. To the customer, therefore, the total price is A$550, whereas to the reseller the total revenue (price) from the sale may be only A$99, and to the service provider the revenue stream (price) over 24 months will be a minimum of A$451. What is the revenue stream (price) for Nokia? This depends on the margin available from the sales to the reseller plus whether there are any fees or commissions that accrue from the service contract.

Actual Price

Obviously, many variables affect the actual price a buyer pays. It is virtually impossible for a marketing strategist to anticipate and plan for all these different variables. What the marketing strategist can do is develop a general approach to pricing strategy or a policy that is consistent with the organizational mission and objectives. Such a pricing approach is flexible and allows for minor changes that will be required to adjust the final buyer's price to the prevailing market conditions. In many firms, this price is called the **base price. Actual price** paid by the consumer then becomes the result of extras added to or discounts deducted from the base price.

We can now state that a firm's pricing strategy consists of three elements:

1. The established base price

2. The relationship between prices of the various items in a product/service line, because such pricing requires that differentials exist between items in a multiple line

3. The specific discount structure used to adjust individual prices to actual market conditions

Pricing Conflicts

Although we have become accustomed to encountering conflicts in developing product strategy, in designing channel strategy, and in creating promotional strategy, we must bluntly note that pricing strategy disagreements are more heated than in any other area of marketing strategy. Perhaps this is so because more executives from a variety of functional areas within a firm are involved in establishing pricing as opposed to other areas of marketing strategy. Perhaps it is also so because, as noted earlier, many selling firms use the pricing viewpoint of accumulation of costs. Regardless of the reasons, pricing conflicts arise at the following three levels: within the firm, within the channel system, and between the firm and the business environment (i.e., between the firm and competitors, between the

Base price
The general price established to be consistent with the firm's organizational mission and objectives.

Actual price
The result of extras added to or discounts deducted from the base price paid by the consumer.

firm and government, and between the firm and customers where ethical considerations may be involved).

Conflicts Within the Firm.   There are three types of pricing conflicts that occur within the firm. First, in many firms there is no agreement about the basic function of pricing strategy. Is it to generate sales volume, or is it to produce profits? These two points of view are often incompatible. A second conflict involves individuals within the firm who are concerned with rate of return, payback, or cash flow and who often pressure for high prices because of a concern for high costs and diminishing returns on marketing activities.[7] A third conflict involves individuals who are concerned with market share and increasing volume and who tend to pressure for low prices because of the desired long production runs and economies of scale. The second and third types of conflicts can overlap and obviously need to be resolved.

Conflicts Within the Channels.   Channel members are both buyers and resellers, and it is these two conflicting roles that may cause disagreement with manufacturers' pricing policies. While acting as buyers, channel members almost always desire to have lower prices. While acting as resellers, however, they often desire to maximize revenue flows, which leads to a desire for high prices. A further conflict relates to resale price maintenance. Although some resellers comply voluntarily with manufacturers' suggested retail prices, other resellers may not because of market conditions.

Conflicts with Competitors.   Probably the most obvious, visible, and serious conflicts are conflicts with competitors. In **oligopolistic markets,** this occurs because one firm's prices affect its competitors' sales volumes. In more competitive markets with less product differentiation, pricing strategy may be the key to competitive behavior. However, even in monopolistic markets, competitive pressures may still exist because of potential substitute goods/services or potential competitors.

Oligopolistic markets Markets where one firm's prices affect its competitors' sales volumes.

Conflicts with Governmental Agencies and Public Policy.   A firm's pricing also may result in a conflict with governmental agencies. All pricing strategies must be developed to comply with existing laws and enforcement policies, but what if the result is contrary to the firm's objectives? Pricing that is not legal must be changed, but what about those gray areas that depend on decisions by regulatory agencies or the courts to ascertain legality? In general, a firm will never enjoy a long-term benefit from questionable pricing strategies, and thus such strategies should always be avoided. However, even legal pricing strategies may be viewed as contrary to public policy. Often very visible national or multinational firms who attempt to raise prices find that public opinion will pressure national governments or their agencies to attempt to intervene. One such example is pricing of pharmaceutical products that are viewed as providing a socially desirable benefit. High prices are always subject to public debate and public pressure to ensure that governmental agencies insist on the lowest possible price. In fact, in some countries, the government controls all pricing for pharmaceuticals.

Pricing Strategy as a Competitive Edge

In the twenty-first century, marketing strategists are labeling the 1990s as a decade when pricing became a key competitive weapon. The power of effective pricing strategies to produce results in the marketplace is not equaled by any other component of the marketing mix. Thus pricing must be used with caution because ineffective or improper pricing could effectively destroy an otherwise well-conceived marketing strategy.[8] There are three essential elements to consider when establishing pricing strategy as a competitive component. The first and most important element is the firm's pricing policy, which defines the kind of pricing strategy to be followed. Regardless of whether the firm is marketing high-, medium-, or low-priced products, it must decide if its specific prices will be above, comparable with, or below competitors' prices. Generally, it is not possible for a firm to have extreme pricing positions. For example, a company would not offer some products or services priced below competitors' while also offering other products priced above competitors'.

The second essential element is the relationship of pricing to other marketing-mix factors. As previously noted, pricing cannot be considered alone; it is a component of the marketing strategy. Using direct pricing competition may force compliance by competitors, but indirect and non-price-competitive techniques may be more desirable because the competition may not be able to match such activities. The most desirable competitive approach is to include both price and nonprice elements, particularly exceptional customer service or unique offering.

The third essential element in pricing strategy is the relationship of pricing and the product life cycle. Pricing strategies applicable to each stage in the cycle are significantly different. For example, in the introductory stage, there are two commonly used alternatives to consider: pricing above or below competitive products. The overall span and success of the life cycle are directly dependent on the product's competitive distinctiveness; thus pricing at any stage in the cycle must reflect dynamic customer characteristics and market competitive conditions.

 ## PRODUCT LIFE CYCLE PRICING

Pricing strategy decisions are closely related to the position of the good/service in its life cycle. This section discusses in some detail the pricing strategy that is usually appropriate for each of the stages in the life cycle.

Introductory Stage

The pricing strategy that is appropriate for a new product depends on its degree of distinctiveness (compared with substitutes) and the length of time this distinctiveness is expected to last. If the product has distinctive aspects that are expected to last for more than a few years, then the firm may be able to price at a premium in order to quickly recover development costs and perhaps to maximize shorter-term profits. However, in today's extremely competitive marketplace, it is highly unusual for such a distinctive advantage to last for more than a few months. If the product does not have any distinctive aspects, one should question if the new product

Skimming price
A price comparable with or above that of a competitive product.

Penetration price
A price much lower than that of a competitive product.

should be introduced. However, if it is introduced, it must be priced at or below competing products. This is so because without distinctiveness the product has limited opportunities for success unless it is priced below the competition.

The traditional wisdom is that new products with perishable distinctiveness should be introduced with either a **skimming price** (price above or comparable with the competitive product)[9] or a **penetration price** (price much lower than the competitive product). The choice between skimming and penetration pricing is

---

INNOVATE OR EVAPORATE*

Discount Drugs for Elderly on Low Incomes

Eli Lilly & Co. announced their "LillyAnswers" discount drug plan at a news conference in March 2002 attended by U.S. Health and Human Services Secretary Tommy Thompson. "LillyAnswers" was the lowest-cost industry plan and appeared to undercut substantially discount plans announced in 2001 by Novartis AG and GlaxoSmithKline PLC. It was also viewed as another pharmaceutical industry effort to stave off government-negotiated drug-price controls. "LillyAnswers" required only a $12 monthly payment for major therapies like Humulin and Humalog for diabetes, osteoporosis drug Evista, and psychosis drug Zyprexa, used for dementia in the elderly.

For the pharmaceutical industry, the question is whether the combined efforts of these three firms will suffice to diminish talk in Congress about establishing mechanisms to control the price of drugs for older Americans. "LillyAnswers" applies both to people who are disabled and who are in the Medicare insurance program, and to people over 65 with an annual income below $18,000 per individual or $24,000 per household. Lilly claims the plan will apply to more than 5 million Americans and could save them an average of $600 annually. But few observers think the plan provides a comprehensive solution for older Americans who cannot afford to buy their prescription medications.

John Rother, policy director of the American Association of Retired Persons (AARP) said, "This is a pretty tight definition. It's a relatively small piece of the group who have no drug benefit." He estimated that perhaps 2 million out of about 12 million older people who lack prescription-drug insurance coverage might qualify. But even so, Mr. Rother said the Lilly plan "is raising the bar about how generous these plans are." Lilly's chairman, Sidney Taurel, said, "We decided it was time for us to step in and assist the neediest of people on Medicare. We definitely support a drug benefit for all seniors. We are just being realistic that there is no guarantee something will be enacted this year." Mr. Taurel also noted that the pharmaceutical industry's opposition to a government program isn't to a prescription-drug benefit for older Americans, but rather to one that would involve government purchasing power and price controls.

Lilly's plan came just days after the Bush administration released a modified drug-discount-card proposal for Medicare recipients. In it, pharmacy-benefits management companies would negotiate with drug companies in an effort to drive down drug costs for the elderly. Secretary Thompson said, "The president's proposed drug-discount card is a first step . . . a very important one in the process of providing real reductions in prescription drug costs."

---

*The box title is attributed to James M. Higgins, *Innovate or Evaporate* (Winter Park, FL: New Management Publishing Company, 1995).
Source: Thomas M. Burton, "Lilly to Discount Drugs for Elderly on Low Incomes," *Wall Street Journal* (March 5, 2002), pp. B1, B4.

based on the expected **elasticity of demand.**[10] Demand is said to be *elastic* when relatively small changes in price result in large changes in units sold. On the other hand, demand is said to be *inelastic* when relatively large changes in price result in small changes in units sold. Thus, if demand is inelastic, a skimming price is appropriate, and if demand is elastic, a penetration price is chosen.

> **Elasticity of demand**
> When relatively small changes in price result in large changes in units sold.

Inelastic ---

Growth Stage

Pricing in the growth stage of the life cycle must consider the relationship with competitors. Because competitors have entered the market, the pricing decision must be based on both maintaining market share and the relationship between pricing and the rest of the marketing strategy. Frequently in the growth and early maturity stages, a limited number of firms dominate industry sales. This situation is called an *oligopoly.*

A classic example occurred in the contact lens industry, where Bausch & Lomb, Inc., enjoyed 100 percent of the market for about 3 years after its 1970 innovative introduction. Correctly appraising the situation, Bausch & Lomb used price skimming as its introductory pricing strategy. However, by 1978, when the industry became highly competitive, Bausch & Lomb's market share had dropped to less than 50 percent. In response to this situation, the company announced a significant price reduction (about 25 percent), and its market share recovered to over 60 percent.[11] Generally speaking, when a few firms dominate a market, any major competitor can expect that if it were to raise prices, the competition would not match such a raise, fearing that increased prices would have too dramatic an impact on volumes sold. Conversely, if any major competitor were to reduce prices, the reduction would be quickly matched again, because otherwise the lowest-priced competitor would capture a disproportionately large gain in market share.

The significant factor in such a situation is that no competitor can price unilaterally. Instead, pricing strategy must be developed with special consideration of competitors' pricing tactics and their expected reactions to any price changes initiated. In oligopolistic markets, price stability often occurs because lower prices would cause diminished margins and lost profits for everyone. However, as we saw in the preceding Bausch & Lomb example, the dominant competitor may desire to maintain the largest share of the market in order to maintain lower production costs. Thus decreased margins may be less damaging than lower unit sales volumes. In such situations, a pricing leadership role is often assumed by the competitor with the largest share of the market.

But how should the late-entering competitor price a new product? Even though the innovator firm is in an advantageous position, the late entrant may be able to gain market share. If the new entry has distinctive product features, then pricing at a premium or competitive pricing combined with heavy promotional expenditures may succeed in establishing a position for the late entrant. Conversely, if distinctiveness is lacking, then parity pricing combined with heavy promotional expenditures also may be successful. Papa John's Pizza is an example of a late-entry firm with a product distinctiveness (in this situation, a superior product feature— fresh components versus preprocessed) that wrestled away market share from Pizza Hut by aggressive advertising and other integrated marketing communications (IMC) activities.

Maturity Stage

When a product's rate of sales growth levels off and begins to decline, the maturity stage has been reached. There are usually a large number of competitors in the market, and product distinctiveness does not exist. Many close-substitute products are available to buyers, and margins have reached low levels. In this situation, no competitor can price very much above or below the prevailing market price. Too low a price may result in a price war that benefits no one, whereas too high a price likely will result in substantial loss of market share. The best examples of this situation can be found in the retailing, fast-food, and airline industries. All are currently highly visible examples.

Pricing in the mature stage also may encounter the entrance of an aggressive price-cutter. These late-entering competitors perceive an opportunity to carve out significant market share by re-establishing prevailing competitive prices at a lower level. The new entrant may introduce a "no frills" version of the product or use modified channel structures, private branding, or some other technique designed to minimize its cost structure, thereby allowing some margin for profits even at the new lower price. Therefore, all competitors in a mature market face constant pressure to lower margins while also often being pressured by rising costs.

Decline Stage

Loss leader
A product priced low to attract more buyers.

The decline stage is reached when unit sales volumes have eroded over more than a short term. Frequently, product distinctiveness no longer exists. Some competitors even may face inferior distinctiveness. Marketers of these products often attempt to price just below the market. Sometimes their products may even be priced as a **loss leader** (a product priced low to attract more buyers).[12] However, the continued marketing of such products may be desirable in order to fill out a product line or until a new product is ready to be launched as a replacement. The pricing strategy must be designed to equate with competitors' prices or, if possible, to be just below the market price.

● PSYCHOLOGICAL PRICING

Psychological price
Price that is supposed to produce sales responses as a result of emotional reactions rather than as a result of objective analysis.

When establishing pricing strategy, the marketer must consider not only objective factors such at the relationship of pricing and the product life cycle but also subjective factors[13] such as psychological pricing.[14] A **psychological price** is one that is supposed to produce sales responses as a result of emotional reactions rather than objective analyses. Although used mostly by retailers, some business-to-business marketers also have used psychological pricing. Three types of price adjustments—odd pricing, prestige pricing, and psychological discounting—are commonly used because of their perceived psychological effects.

Odd Pricing

Odd pricing
The practice of establishing resale prices that end in odd numbers.

Odd pricing is the practice of establishing resale prices that end in odd numbers (e.g., $19.97). Visit any retail firm and you will see odd pricing in action. Although all retailers are convinced that odd pricing is effective, there is no commonly recognized body of research that validates this viewpoint. However, although used frequently, odd pricing is probably the least important of the psychological pricing practices and often is used in conjunction with markdowns and discounts designed to elicit additional psychological reactions from purchasers.

Prestige Pricing

Prestige pricing
The practice of setting high prices for products with unique or unusual distinctiveness.

Prestige pricing is the practice of setting high prices for products with unique or unusual distinctiveness. Use of prestige pricing assumes that more units of a prestige item can be sold at a higher price than at a lower price. The use of price as an indicator of customer value suggests that, for example, a new product that has innovative features may not be viewed as a high-customer-value product if it is not prestige priced. The classic example of this is the introduction of the Polaroid camera with its remarkable self-developing film. If the camera had been priced too

IT'S LEGAL BUT IS IT ETHICAL?

Is the Price Right if It's Free?

Music executives blame digital copying for most of a collapse in sales. In 2001 they sold 10.3 percent fewer albums and singles than in 2000, while seizures of counterfeit, pirate, or bootleg labels soared nearly 504 percent in the same period to total 22.2 million according to the Recording Industry Association of America. And sales early in 2002 were down another 12 percent. "It's a monumental problem. Banks won't even let [music companies] in the door. And I was laughed out of every investment house in America," says Miles Copeland, founder of the Copeland Group, a recording, publishing, and management company.

"More than half of the broadband traffic in the U.S. is file-swapping, and it mostly involves copyrighted works," says Richard Doherty, director of The Envisioneering Group. Record companies say a telltale sign of digital copying is the steep drop in an album's sales in its second week out. A few years ago, second-week sales typically fell 25 percent or less. Now, 40 percent is the norm. But it isn't clear that piracy is even a main reason the music industry is in trouble. "In 1977,

11 percent of music was pirated, and 40 percent of computer software was pirated," says Pricewaterhouse-Coopers' Saul Berman. "Who makes more money: Microsoft or the record companies?" Retailers also question whether digital copying is to blame for the industry's woes. "Do we still have a competitively priced product?" asks Pam Horovitz, president of the National Association of Recording Merchandisers. "DVD sales have exploded, and it's a product where the price has come down while the price of CDs has gone up. If our only response as an industry is to stop copying of CDs, we may be missing a consumer message."

Record company supporters and critics alike acknowledge that the industry—in its zeal to kill file-sharing services such as Napster—didn't listen enough to PC owners' desire to get music via download. Miles Copeland says, "But this is the first technological revolution that enables the public to get something for free. And that's something nobody has come to grips with. How do you compete with free?"

Source: David Lieberman, "How dangerous are pirates?" *USA Today* (April 5, 2002), pp. B1–B2.

low, say, at $99, then perhaps the public would have believed that an inexpensive camera at that price could not possibly deliver the promised high-quality self-developing film feature. By pricing the camera close to $200, Polaroid was establishing a prestige price in order to send a psychological message to potential purchasers about the quality and value of the camera's innovative features.

Psychological Discounting

Psychological discounting
The practice of using certain prices that are perceived to give the purchaser the illusion of markdowns from higher prices.

Psychological discounting is the practice of using certain prices that are perceived to give the purchaser the illusion of markdowns from higher prices.[15] For example, a purchaser may perceive that a retail price of $8.99 represents a price that originally was set at $9.99 or that a price of $2.29 indicates a reduction from the original $2.99. As noted previously, there is no recognized body of research that establishes the validity of psychological discounting, but there are many retailers who practice psychological pricing consistently who are thoroughly convinced of its effectiveness.

Closely related to psychological discounting is the use of fictitious comparative-pricing signage or price tags. The Federal Trade Commission, in cooperation with the Better Business Bureaus (BBBs), has vigorously attacked this practice as misleading and dishonest. The misleading signs that some merchants prominently display read: "Original price $24.99, now $12.99," or "Manufacturer's suggested price $19.99, now $9.99," or "Sold by competitors at $39.95, our price $14.99." Unless the merchant can establish with reasonable certainty that the pricing claim is valid, some states have declared such practices illegal and will issue cease and desist orders.

Impact on Manufacturer

With the exception of prestige pricing, most psychological pricing is practiced by retailers and may be viewed as having limited importance to manufacturers. However, since the reseller's price has a substantial impact on the size and profitability of the actual market for goods and services, it is important for marketers to recognize when there is an opportunity or need for resellers to practice psychological pricing and to influence the appropriate use of these practices.

● STRATEGIC PRICING MODELS

Each of the pricing models discussed below has proponents who are convinced that the method they use is the best for their organization and their business environment. We will discuss each model in turn in order to understand the reasoning applicable to these three pricing models.

The Market-Based Pricing Model

Market-based pricing
Establishing a desired target price after considering the targeted customers, key competitors' products, and product benefits provided.

The logic of a **market-based pricing** model begins with understanding three components: the needs and desires of the targeted customers, the features offered by key competitors' products, and the product benefits (product position) provided by the good/service the firm is marketing. Taking these factors into consideration, a

IT'S LEGAL BUT IS IT ETHICAL?

Price Wars

The Wal-Mart juggernaut is rolling into retail gasoline markets across Canada, sparking immediate price wars and perhaps permanently depressing the cost of a fill-up. Wal-Mart and partner Murphy Oil Co. Ltd., which operates the stations, have opened locations on Wal-Mart property. The stations linked to Wal-Mart's "hypermarket" stores through promotional tie-ins. Michael Ervin, president of M.J. Ervin & Associates Inc., which monitors the retail gasoline industry, says, "Wal-Mart ... will bring big-city competition to a host of smaller markets across Canada. It's going to be a national phenomenon." Wal-Mart aims to offer the lowest gasoline prices in any market it enters, and will post that price. It also gives a further 1-cent discount (per liter) to customers who have a Wal-Mart Shopping Card.

The company said its expansion will allow customers to make just one trip to shop at its store, as will as filling up with cheaper gasoline.

Price wars are usually short-lived in gasoline retailing, since thin margins leave little room for sustained cost-cutting. They are also a phenomenon largely limited to big cities where each station needs to keep selling a comparatively huge volume of gasoline, intensifying competitive pressures. In smaller, less volatile markets, prices tend to be more stable and higher over time. But Wal-Mart will upend that traditional situation, and many are predicting the demise of the small-volume locally run stations.

Source: Patrick Brethour, "Wal-Mart Stoking Gas War," *Toronto Globe and Mail* (September 2, 2002), pp. B1–B2.

---

firm establishes a desired target price position. Then, working backward from the target price and incorporating the margins resellers require and any sales commissions applicable, the net price is calculated. From the net price the manufacturer deducts all variable costs to determine the unit contribution margin of the product. If the resulting contribution is not sufficient to meet desired profit objectives, then operating processes are examined to lower costs.[16] Raising the target price is not considered. This market-based pricing model is illustrated in Figure 14.2.

The Cost-Plus Pricing Model

Many firms establish their pricing strategy with a logic that is directly opposed to the market-based pricing model. These firms begin with a desired profit margin and then add the costs of making or providing the good or service and the costs of distributing and marketing the good or service (including the calculation of the cost-based sales commissions and markups required by channel members). The **cost-plus pricing** model is illustrated in Figure 14.3.

Several problems are associated with the cost-plus pricing model. The first problem is that cost-plus pricing may lead to grossly underpricing products and services, causing a firm to forego much higher levels of profitability. If we look at the application side of Figure 14.3, we see that a product that costs $20 to manufacture is priced and sold at $30 to the channel in order to achieve the desired 33 percent margin. As the resellers in the channel each add on their respective margins, a price to

> **Cost-plus pricing**
> A pricing strategy whereby a firm establishes a desired profit margin and adds this amount to the total costs of manufacturing, distributing and marketing a product.

FIGURE 14.2

Market-Based Pricing Model

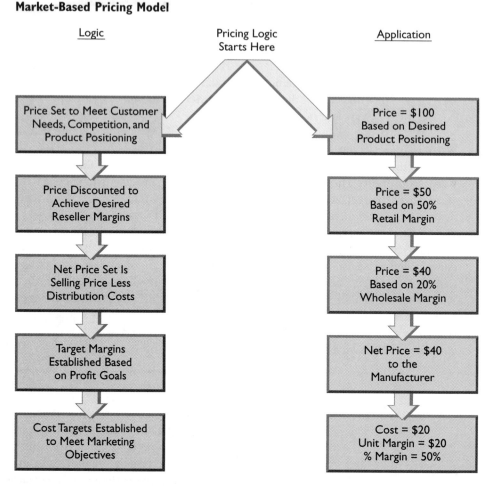

Source: *Market-Based Management Strategies* by Best, Roger, © 1997. Reprinted by permission of Prentice-Hall, Inc., Upper Saddle River, NJ.

customers of $75 is established. But what if customers were willing and expecting to pay $100 because of the overall benefits expected? Working backward from a market-based price set at $100 and allowing for the same reseller margins, we see that the net price to the manufacturer is $40. With total costs of $20, the firm could have achieved a 50 percent unit margin, meaning that profit has been lost because of underpricing.

A second problem of cost-plus pricing is the possibility of overpricing. Cost-plus pricing involves an internally focused viewpoint; that is, the price is set based on internal costs and desired margins. This internal focus may result in setting a price that is too high in terms of expected benefits or value, as perceived by customers relative to competing products. Thus targeted sales volumes are not achieved, nor are expected profits. Any attempt to correct the situation usually begins with a cut in prices. But because the cost of manufacturing is already established, the resulting sales are at reduced margins and the expected profit levels are never reached. If the

FIGURE 14.3

Cost-Plus Pricing Model

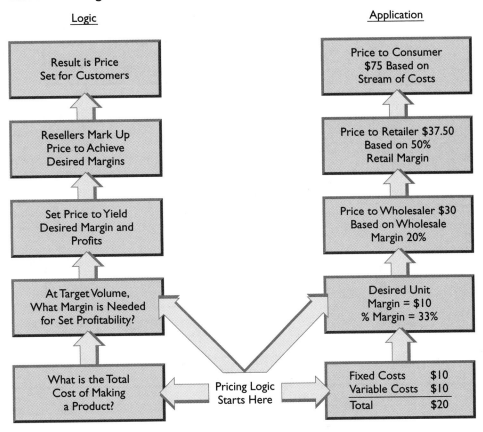

Source: *Market-Based Management Strategies* by Best, Roger, © 1997. Reprinted by permission of Prentice-Hall, Inc., Upper Saddle River, NJ.

pricing process had begun with a market focus (customers, competitors, and product position), the firm would recognize that cost reductions were needed to achieve desired margins and profit levels.

The Value-Based Pricing Model

Value-based pricing
A pricing strategy that maximizes customers' expected value perceptions.

Reference product
A purchased product for which customers can recall perceptions of price paid and benefits derived.

Focal product
A product being considered for purchase.

As illustrated in Figure 14.4, the **value-based pricing** model recognizes that buyers make a comparison between a good's or service's perceived reasonable price (called the **reference product**) and the actual price of the good or service that the consumer is considering for purchase (called the **focal product**). The model assumes that a variety of contextual factors are used by potential purchasers in order to determine perceptions about the product or service attributes of both the reference product and the focal product. Some of these contextual factors could be brand recognition or brand equity, organizational image, reseller or retailer reputation, and past experiences.

FIGURE 14.4

Value-Based Pricing Model

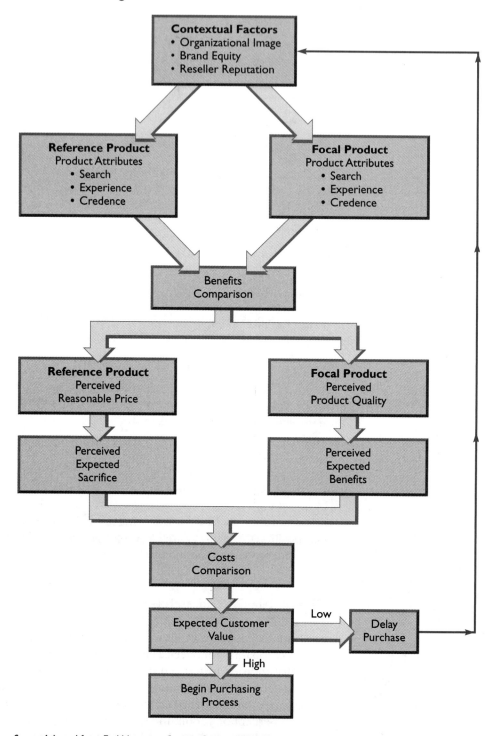

Source: Adapted from Earl Naumann, *Creating Customer Value* (Cincinnati, Ohio: Thomson Executive Press, 1995).

Benefits comparison
A customer comparison of perceived benefits from a focal product relative to a reference product.

Based on the consumer's perceptions of the reference product and focal product, he or she performs a **benefits comparison** to establish two additional perceptions. First, the consumer decides on the reasonableness of a price for the reference product; then he or she forms a perception of the quality of the focal product. For example, well-developed organizational images such as those of IBM, Intel, Microsoft, or Xerox, or reseller reputations such as those of Wal-Mart, Kmart, Sears, and Target, or brand equity such as Tide, Kleenex, Frigidaire, and Sunkist all are used by customers as indicators of quality.

The greater the perceived risks involved in the purchase, the more important become the contextual factors that work as extrinsic cues for the customer. In many service purchases, because there is such an intangible component involved, these contextual factors assume an even greater importance. In conjunction with the good or service attributes, contextual factors and stored attitudes based on past experiences combine to create the perceptual basis on which customers rely to establish both their perceived quality of the focal product and their perceived reasonable price for the reference product.

For example, a customer shopping for shoes initially satisfies the contextual factors by visiting a retailer satisfactorily shopped previously and by examining shoes of a nationally advertised brand with a superior reputation. Trying on a pair of shoes, the customer compares (focal product) attributes with attributes of shoes previously purchased (reference product). This is the "benefits comparison" process (noted in the model), such as: Will they be comfortable, stylish, durable, and so forth? Next, the customer recalls perceptions of price and value received from reference products (past purchases), perhaps remembering having paid $80 the last time this brand was purchased and enjoying comfortable, long-lasting, and stylish benefits. These recalled perceptions are compared with similar perceptions now being formed about the focal product (trial shoes). Perhaps the current price is $95, but the design is more appealing and the customer expects equal durability. This involves the customer in both the "costs comparison" process and the "expected customer value" aspects of the model. Although the price is higher, the durability is equal and the stylishness is superior, so the customer's expected value is high and a purchase is made.

The next stage of the process involves the development of a third set of two parallel perceptions as a result of the benefits comparison stage of the process. One of the two parallel perceptions involves the customer establishing a perception of what is the expected sacrifice based on the reference product's perceived reasonable price. The other parallel perception involves using the already developed perceived quality of the focal product as the basis for developing a perception of the expected benefits. Then the customer performs the cost comparison based on the two parallel perceptions—it is a comparison made between the perceived expected sacrifice and the perceived expected benefits. The result of this comparison is the **expected value** that the customer perceives in the purchase situation. If this expected value is high, a purchase usually is initiated. Conversely, if this expected value is low, the purchase is usually declined. The key to understanding this process is realizing that the purchaser is trading off the known benefits of previously used products against the perceived expected value (benefits) of the next purchase.

Expected value
Results from a benefits comparison; must be high for a purchase to occur.

The potential customer's expected value is the result of comparing the expected benefits to expected sacrifice. This sacrifice may include total life cycle costs of use; however, by increasing expected benefits while holding expected sacrifice constant, sellers are able to enhance perceived customer value and thereby increase the probability of a sale (recall the Palm strategy in the opening scenario). In addition, sellers could decrease the expected sacrifice while holding expected benefits constant, which also results in enhanced customer value. This is the approach used by several retail chains that introduced "everyday low prices" as a competitive pricing strategy in the early 1990s. Whatever methods are used to increase expected customer value, it is imperative to keep clearly in mind that expected customer value is a dynamic concept.[17] As Martyn Straw, an adman at Geer, DuBois, Inc., the agency for Jaguar Ltd., says, "value is the new prestige."[18] What today constitutes a good value may tomorrow or next week or next month become a poor value. If we accept the premise that the greater the expected value, the greater is the willingness to buy, then we must agree with Earl Naumann's observation that sometimes "the sale [price] is just too good to pass up. The consumer may stock up [buy] to 'save money.'"[19]

● PRICING STRATEGY AND BREAK-EVEN ANALYSIS

Although break-even analysis is often viewed as an accounting concept, it is also an extremely useful way to evaluate the profit potential and risk associated with a pricing strategy. We will examine from a marketing viewpoint the usefulness of calculating break-even volume and break-even market share.

Break-Even Volume

Break-even
When net profits equal zero.

It is useful to calculate the break-even volume for any planned pricing strategy (and marketing strategy). Since **break-even** occurs when net profits are zero, what number of units needs to be sold to break even? For example, if we produce a unit of product whose selling price is $100 with a variable cost per unit of $50, the result is a margin of $50. Ordinary business activity incurs fixed expenses (marketing and direct operating expenses) of $5 million. Calculating the break-even volume would result in an answer of 100,000 units.

Net profits = volume (unit price − unit variable cost) − (marketing expenses
+ operating expenses)

$$0 = \text{volume } (\$100 - \$50) - (\$2 \text{ million} + \$3 \text{ million})$$

$$\text{Volume} = (\$2 \text{ million} + \$3 \text{ million})/(\$100 - \$50)$$

$$= \$5 \text{ million}/\$50$$

$$= 100,000 \text{ units}$$

We see from this example that break-even volume is the number of units needed to cover fixed expenses based on a specific margin per unit sold. This break-even calculation can be calculated graphically as indicated in Figure 14.5 but can be computed more directly with the following formula:

$$\text{Break-even volume} = \frac{\text{fixed expenses}}{\text{margin per unit}}$$

FIGURE 14.5

Break-Even Analysis

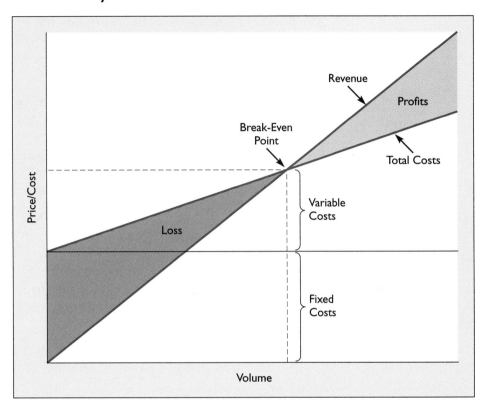

The lower the break-even volume is relative to the expected sales volumes for a firm and its manufacturing capacity, the greater will be the profit potential and the lower will be the risk of a price strategy that does not achieve the firm's planned-for profit levels.

Break-Even Market Share and Risk

Determining the break-even volume is normally an unconstrained calculation; therefore, the reasonableness of the volume figure requires additional insight and calculations to aid understanding. In contrast, market-share calculations are constrained and must fall between zero and 100 percent. Thus, if a market analyst calculates a break-even market share, this will provide a better basis from which to judge profit potential and risk. This computation of break-even market share requires the analyst to divide the break-even volume of the firm by the size of the target market, as shown below:

$$\text{Break-even market share} = \frac{\text{break-even volume (in units)}}{\text{market demand (units)}} \times 100$$

If in our example the total market demand for the industry were 1 million units per year, then the break-even market share would be 10 percent when the firm's break-even volume is 100,000 units. If the firm's targeted market share is only 5 percent, then the risk of achieving sales below break-even is small. However, if the targeted market share is 15 percent, then the risk of not achieving break-even sales is much greater, and the pricing strategy may need to be re-examined.

● PRICING STRATEGY DECISIONS: ISSUES, PROBLEMS, AND LEGAL CONCERNS

Each step in the pricing process may present management with complex issues and problems that require sophisticated analytical techniques. Some of the major issues involved in establishing an effective pricing strategy and some methods for resolving these issues are discussed next.

Product-Line Pricing

Many manufacturers produce a line of products designed to meet the needs of their various targeted customer groups. For example, the manufacturer of power lawn maintenance equipment may offer the following list of seven major products in its line, with some containing a number of models:

> Four staggered-wheel rotary-engine mower models priced from $280 to $480
> Four in-line small-wheeled rotary-engine mower models priced from $300 to $500
> Three in-line large-rear-wheeled rotary-engine mower models priced from $375 to $550
> Four heavy-duty rotary-engine mower models priced from $490 to $600
> Three riding mowers priced from $900 to $2200
> Four commercial/institutional rotary-engine mowers priced from $1100 to $4000
> Three edge-trimmer models priced from $95 to $195

To effectively market a line of products for a particular market segment, pricing differentials must be established for each item in the line. These are all differentials from the base price. The size of the differential established often depends on the differences in costs, product features, and forecasted volume expectations, as well as customers' responses. However, the line also may include one or more promotional items that will be sold at less than average total costs in order to attract potential customers. Resellers would be encouraged to trade up customers to better-performing, higher-priced equipment to achieve higher profits (assuming that this is done in a legal and ethical manner).

The theoretical goal in setting product-line prices is to improve the marketability and profitability of the entire line.[20] However, other pricing goals are to be competitive, to satisfy user needs, and also to satisfy resellers' needs—all of which may require flexibility and willingness to compromise. For example, many retailers use a pricing method known as **price lining.** The merchant may set pricing differentials that are applied to all items sold, such as the following prices for six different levels

Price lining
When a merchant sets price differentials for each model (or variation) in a line of products.

in a line of women's dresses (which vary in terms of design, quality of materials, and construction):

$49.95 $69.95 $89.95 $119.95 $149.95 $199.95

Price lining simplifies the customer's decision by holding constant one key variable in the final selection of style and brand within a line. The customer knows that all dresses sold at $49.95 will be similar in quality—even though the styles and colors may be different. The customer also knows that the higher-priced dresses will be of higher quality.

Manufacturers also use price lining to meet resellers' needs for price lining and to be profitable at the various price levels. This is an excellent example of market-driven pricing. And although price lining is less common in other areas of marketing, it is this pressure of both consumers and resellers that dictates the pricing alternatives that are open to any manufacturer. This market pressure also reaffirms why a cost-plus pricing process may be dysfunctional.

Structuring Discounts

Establishing a set of discounts to adjust the base price for variations in product offerings, customer expectations, and competitive activity constitutes the pricing structure of a firm.[21] Discounts (and extras) can be designed to apply to almost any pricing situation. Typical situations exist, and are discussed in the following paragraphs.

Trade discounts
Discounts granted to customers based on their position (categorization) within the channel of distribution.

Trade Discounts. A customary practice is granting discounts based on a customer's position in the channel of distribution. These discounts are usually referred to as **trade discounts** (or *functional discounts*). The various channel (reseller) positions that are regularly granted discounts include retailer (dealer), jobber (middleman who buys from manufacturers and sells to retailers), and wholesaler (distributor). Discounts granted to resellers for performing their usual tasks as channel members are granted exclusively to all resellers who are categorized as belonging to that specific trade category. For example, if a wholesaler qualifies for a specific discount, then another reseller category such as a retailer will never be granted the discount regardless of how large and important that retailer becomes. Since the various categories of resellers do not theoretically compete with each other, these discounts traditionally have been viewed as not having a restraining effect on competition. Thus they are seen as acceptable from a legal standpoint. Of course, the large-volume and therefore powerful retailer mentioned earlier will negotiate other forms of discounts and concessions from the manufacturer to compensate for not being granted additional trade discount categories.

Cumulative discounts
Quantity discounts granted on the total volume of purchases made by a single customer over some designated time period (often a year).

Quantity Discounts. A common discount granted by many sellers is one based on orders for large volumes. Generally, two types of volume discounts are negotiable: cumulative and noncumulative. **Cumulative discounts** are granted on the total volume of purchases made by a single customer over some designated time period, such as a financial year or a calendar quarter year. The negotiated size of the discount

Noncumulative discounts
Granted to a customer based only on the quantity in a specific single order.

is usually based on past volumes purchased or on expected volumes. **Noncumulative discounts** are based only on the quantity purchased in a specific order.

Important legal requirements must be met when volume discounts are negotiated. The cumulative quantity discount is difficult to defend on the basis of cost savings, and without this factor, it may be in violation of the Robinson-Patman Act, which regulates discounts and allowances that may prevent competition. However, the noncumulative discount usually can be justified via a cost savings argument. The Federal Trade Commission has ruled that no quantity discount schedules can be discriminatory, even though the differences in discount may reflect actual cost savings. For example, if only one or two firms were to be considered qualified for the largest quantity discount category, the FTC might rule (as it has in the past) that the effect of such a discount on competition is unfair.

Promotional Allowances.   There are also two forms of promotional discounts: *permanent* and *special.* Resellers who are regular customers often desire **permanent promotional allowances** because they use IMC (promotional) activities on a consistent basis. For example, a cooperative advertising program may be established by manufacturers who want to encourage all resellers to promote their products. In contrast, **special promotional allowances** usually relate to a particular IMC (promotional) campaign or event. For example, to build up reseller inventory levels prior to a manufacturer-planned and -funded large-scale consumer IMC program, the manufacturer may offer some form of special discount or incentive to resellers. This incentive may be in the form of a direct discount or free goods.

Permanent promotional allowances
Discounts granted to regular customers who consistently are involved in promotional activities suggested by the discounting firm.

Special promotional allowances
Discounts granted to any customer who will cooperate in a particular promotional event or campaign.

The Robinson-Patman Act also regulates promotional allowances. They must be offered to all resellers, they must be proportional to the amount of business done with each reseller, and they must be used by the reseller solely for promotional purposes. The law's intent is to prohibit promotional allowances from becoming convenient disguises for illegal price discrimination.

Location Discounts.   The location of a buyer creates one of the more difficult problems in establishing pricing strategy for a firm. Logically, it seems self-evident that the cost of moving finished products from the place of manufacture to a reseller's location is a marketing cost, which, like other marketing costs, must be recovered from sales revenues for a profitable transaction. However, difficulties arise when considering how to recover such costs. The easiest, and some believe the fairest, method is to add the transportation costs to the selling price, and the result is the delivered price to the buyer. This is a common method and is known as **Free on-board (FOB) pricing.**[22] FOB pricing is easy to understand and to use but difficult to administer, especially for firms with broad product lines and widely geographically dispersed purchasers. Purchasers will expect the firm to ship the merchandise by the most economical method. This means that sellers must maintain a sizable traffic/transportation department in order to arrange timing, scheduling, and routing and to determine charges to be billed to purchasers. The result of FOB pricing, however, is to place certain selling firms at a pricing disadvantage vis-à-vis competitors located closer to buyers. To offset this competitive disadvantage, and to avoid the costly and thankless tasks of determining transportation charges for each transaction, most firms have developed a number of discount arrangements based on customer locations. We will discuss three such arrangements.

Free on-board (FOB) pricing
Adding transportation costs to the selling price to establish the delivered price to the buyer.

Uniform delivered pricing
Where each purchaser is charged the same delivered price.

Uniform Delivered Pricing. A **uniform delivered pricing** system whereby each purchaser is charged the same delivered price technically does not involve a discount based on buyer location. Uniform delivered pricing is effective if transportation costs are low relative to the value of the product and there are competitive advantages to a marketwide one-price policy. The purchase price includes a fixed calculated average cost of transportation and therefore does involve differentials in price based on customer location.

Zone pricing
Where geographic zones are established so that any purchaser located within a particular zone is charged a uniform price for that zone.

Zone Pricing. When transportation charges are large in relation to the value of the purchased goods but sellers want the advantages of uniform delivered pricing, then a **zone pricing** system is used. Geographic zones are established so that any purchaser located in a particular zone is charged the same price. However, pricing differentials are established for each separate zone. For example, if California is a separate zone, then any purchaser located there pays the price established for that zone, whereas a purchaser in Florida (another zone) pays another (perhaps lesser) price. Industrial firms frequently use multiple zones, and often the number of zones corresponds to the territorial sales districts established.

Freight equalization
Meeting competitors' delivered prices in order to maintain market share.

Freight Equalization. **Freight equalization** is the practice of meeting competitors' delivered prices in order to maintain market share. In a highly competitive marketplace, the seller absorbs transportation costs. If used aggressively or in a predatory manner, freight equalization may be considered an unfair pricing practice. However, if used independently rather than in collusion and in order to meet competition, freight equalization is acceptable. It is feasible over the longer term only if the incremental profit from the additional revenue more than offsets the cost of freight absorption.

PRICING STRATEGY AND IMC

As noted previously, all pricing decisions must fit into the overall marketing strategy and be harmonized with the entire marketing mix. In addition, it is imperative that pricing strategy be coordinated with IMC activities. As we have discussed, IMC covers all types of marketing activities designed to stimulate sales. Pricing is also one of a firm's major competitive weapons. Richard Starmann, senior vice-president of McDonald's Corp., when speaking about pricing strategy, said: ". . . value is much more than price, . . . is much more than promotion . . . ," and is a critical component in the fast-food industry.[23] Information about pricing is an important message that must be transmitted to customers. Customers must be knowledgeable about a firm's prices if they are to be influenced by those prices. In today's highly competitive business environment, food retailers, discount stores, department stores, specialty shops, and a host of other firms make extensive use of promotional media of all types to announce pricing decisions. If these efforts are not coordinated, then the effectiveness of the planned IMC activities *and* the planned pricing decisions may be negated. For example, if a furniture retailer has planned to have a 3-day sale that features a substantial reduction from normal pricing but whose planned IMC activities never take place, then the sale event will not be successful. In a similar manner, if the planned pricing discounts are not available to customers who expect such reductions as a result of IMC activities, again the sale will not be successful. Of course, the availability of the product at the planned locations is also important. All the components of the marketing mix must be coordinated in order for special IMC activities to achieve maximum success.

Summary

Price is the monetary amount a buyer pays for a good or service. However, both the buyer and seller have different views on the meaning of price. Pricing conflicts occur within a firm because of differing views of the role of price, within the channels because of the differing needs of buyers and reseller, and within the environment—including competitors, governmental agencies, and public policy.

Pricing strategy decisions are closely related to the position of the good or service in the product life cycle. In the introduction stage, the appropriate pricing strategy depends on the product's degree of distinctiveness. In the growth stage, the pricing strategy must focus on competitors' pricing tactics. As a product matures, pricing tends to stabilize as a result of the similarity of products in the competitive environment. During the decline stage, pricing tends to be lower to attract more buyers or until a replacement product can be introduced.

A psychological price is one that is supposed to produce sales responses as a result of emotional reactions. Odd pricing is the practice of establishing resale prices ending in odd numbers. Prestige pricing is the practice of setting high prices for products with unique or unusual distinctiveness. Psychological discounting is the practice of using certain prices that are perceived to be markdowns from higher prices.

Pricing strategy became increasingly important through the 1990s as a competitive factor. Three strategic approaches to pricing models are market-based pricing, cost-plus pricing, and value-based pricing. Market-based pricing is based on the needs of the target customer, the features of competitive products, and the specific product benefits the firm is marketing. Cost-plus pricing is based on the desired profit margin plus the costs of making and distributing the product. Value-based pricing is based on the concept that customers' willingness to buy is directly related to their perceptions of expected value.

Break-even analysis also relates to pricing strategy. This accounting concept is an extremely useful way to evaluate the profit potential and risk associated with a particular pricing strategy.

A variety of pricing issues, problems, and legal concerns have an impact on a firm's overall marketing strategy, including various discounting methods such as trade, quantity, promotional, and location discounts. It is important to ensure that all pricing decisions fit into the overall marketing plan, are harmonized with the entire marketing mix, and are integrated and coordinated with IMC activities.

Questions

1. A pricing strategy called *skimming* involves charging a high price to early adopters on the premise that they highly value the product. Later the price is dropped. What are the possible negative aspects of price skimming?

2. When videotapes of movies were first sold to the public, they were priced at about $80, but currently, they are priced as low as $5. If a penetration pricing strategy had been used, what do you think would have happened? Who benefited from the early pricing strategy?

3. What is the role of break-even analysis in pricing strategy?

4. Contrast and compare market-based pricing methods with cost-plus pricing methods. What are some of the criticisms of using cost-plus pricing? Do you agree with these criticisms?

5. Explain value-based pricing methods with special concern about "expected value."

6. What is the relationship between pricing strategy and the other aspects of the marketing strategy?

7. How would you describe the relationship between pricing strategy and IMC activities?

8. Explain the differences between cumulative discounts and noncumulative discounts.

9. Explain the difference between uniform delivered pricing and FOB pricing.

Exercises

1. Visit a local clothing specialty store (for either men's or women's apparel), and without questioning any employee, inspect price tags on the merchandise and decide if the store is using psychological pricing. Then attempt to figure out what price-lining strategy is being used (if any) and what the price break points are. Write down your findings for later reference. Next, ask an employee (or the manager or owner, if possible) what the pricing policy is and if the store uses price lining. Make a comparison of your own independently developed figures with those provided by the store. As a closing item, ask if the store uses psychological pricing of any kind.

2. Choose three local mobile phone service providers to telephone. Ask each for an explanation of the costs of their services. Take notes while talking to each service provider, and also complete your notes after the conversation ends. Now compare your notes and be prepared to share your findings with the class, including which service you believe offers the "best" prices.

3. Visit at least three competing supermarkets and record the shelf prices for the same 10 items at each location (or choose more than 10 items if you like). In your list of items, be certain to include 1 gallon of whole milk, 1 pound of bananas, 1 pound of T-bone

(or porterhouse) steak, 1 pound of ground beef (hamburger), 1 pound of butter, one standard-sized can of Niblets brand corn, one 2-liter bottle of regular Coca-Cola, and 1 pound of fresh tomatoes. Compare the prices you find and determine if there is any difference in the pricing strategies being used by the different supermarkets.

Endnotes

1. "Fortune Cookies: Management Wit and Wisdom," *Fortune* magazine, edited by Alan Deutschman (New York: Vintage Books, 1993), p. 28.

2. Laura Mazar, "Why Companies Need to Learn to Manage Pricing?" *Marketing*, London (February 7, 2002); and Thomas Nagle and Reed Holder, *The Strategy and Tactics of Pricing* (Englewood Cliffs, N.J.: Prentice-Hall, 1995).

3. Michael V. Marn and Robert L. Rosiello, "Managing Price, Gaining Profit," *Harvard Business Review* (September–October 1992), pp. 84–94.

4. Christopher Power, Walecia Konrad, Alice Z. Cuneo, James B. Treece, and bureau reports, "Value Marketing: Quality, Service and Fair Pricing Are the Keys to Selling in the '90s," *Business Week* (November 11, 1991), pp. 132–140.

5. Bernard Wysocki, Jr., "Pricing Power: Lost But Not Forgotten," *Wall Street Journal* (March 25, 2002), p. A2.

6. Marios Theodosiu, "Pricing Strategies Depend on Similarity," *Marketing News* (August 27, 2001), p. 29.

7. Bob Donath, "Promise 'em Anything, But Give 'em a Price," *Marketing News* (January 18, 1998), p. 5.

8. Thomas Nagle, "Make Pricing a Key Driver of Your Marketing Strategy," *Marketing News* (November 9, 1998), p. 4.

9. For a discussion of price skimming, see David Besanko and Wayne Winston, "Optimal Price Skimming by a Monopolist Facing Rational Consumers," *Management Science* (May 1990), pp. 555–567.

10. For a summary of elasticity studies, see Dominique M. Hanssens, Leonard J. Parsons, and Randall L. Schultz, *Market Response Models: Econometric and Time Series Analysis* (Boston: Kluwer Academic Publishers, 1990), pp. 187–191.

11. See "Bausch & Lomb: Hardball Pricing Helps It to Regain Its Grip on Contact Lenses," *Fortune* (July 16, 1984), p. 78.

12. Vicki Clift, "'Loss Leaders' Not Just for Retailers Anymore," *Marketing News* (February 1, 1999), p. 7.

13. K. N. Rajendran and Gerard J. Tellis, "Contextual and Temporal Components of Reference Price," *Journal of Marketing* (January 1994), pp. 22–34.

14. Paul Hunt, "Analyzing the Psychology of Pricing," *Marketing* (February 25, 2002), p. 27.

15. Christopher Farrell *et al.*, "Stuck! How Companies Cope When They Can't Raise Prices," *Business Week* (November 15, 1993), pp. 146–155.

16. *Ibid.*

17. Alexander Hiam and Charles D. Schewe, *The Portable MBA in Marketing* (New York: John Wiley & Sons, 1992), p. 314.

18. Power *et al.*, *op. cit.*

19. Earl Naumann, *Creating Customer Value* (Cincinnati, Ohio: Thomson Executive Press, 1995), p. 118.

20. See David J. Reibstein and Hubert Gatignon, "Optimal Product Line Pricing: The Influence of Elasticities and Cross-Elasticities," *Journal of Marketing Research* (August 1984), p. 259.

21. Please note that the pricing structure may include extras as well as discounts. An *extra* is a charge added to the base price to compensate the seller for the cost of unusual buyer requirements. For example, if a special packaging or handling process is required, or if prepriced labels are requested, then unless the buyer has significant purchasing power to offset the additional costs, the seller would attempt to add on an extra charge.

22. Legal title to goods priced FOB passes to the purchaser when the merchandise is accepted by the carrier, and the purchaser is liable for all transportation costs incurred.

23. Richard Gibson, "With Egg on Its Face, McDonald's Cuts the 55-Cent Specials to Breakfast Only," *Wall Street Journal* (June 4, 1997), p. B7.

MARKETING MANAGEMENT IN ACTION: CLOSING CASE

Austin, Texas Challenges Time Warner Cable Pricing Scheme

Austin City Manager Jesus Garza, with the approval of the City Council, on January 31, 2002 sent a letter to the Federal Communications Commission (FCC) saying that Time Warner Cable, the dominant carrier in Austin, offered "tremendously slashed prices" to win back former customers who had switched to cable competitor Grande Communications Inc. or to satellite-based systems. The letter said that Time Warner's rate policies violate the FCC's Uniform Rate Requirement, which calls for discounts and promotions to be "universally available to all consumers in a geographic area served by the provider."

The local V.P. of Time Warner public affairs, Lidia Agraz, confirmed the discount was being offered, but said the FCC law only prohibits such discriminatory actions based on geographics. She said, "We're doing this all over the country, and the FCC is aware of this." The city is sending the letter to the FCC to stop the Commission from labelling Austin a competitive zone as requested by Time Warner. If declared a competitive zone, then Time Warner would no longer need the City of Austin's approval to raise or lower its basic prices.

Garza's letter states the City "has evidence that Time Warner is using an anti-competitive pricing system that, instead of promoting competition, threatens to stunt Grande's growing competitive presence." And for several months Time Warner representatives have been "quietly contacting former Time Warner customers who now purchase their cable services from Grande and other satellite-based systems. The letter continues with the following: "These government representatives are offering . . . a 36 percent reduction for its Digital Value Package, and a whopping 42 percent discount on the same package plus two premium channels." And that "The representatives guarantee these prices will remain the same for at least 12 months."

To discourage the FCC from taking away the city's regulatory power to control Time Warner's rates, the city is telling federal regulators that its discounts to former customers provide "a preview of the new competitive landscape if Time Warner's petition for effective competition is granted. As a result of this price war, a small number of customers living in areas serviced by Grande may enjoy reduced cable rates, but how does this further Congress' goal of franchise-wide competition?"

The letter goes on to state, "Furthermore, what kind of pricing scheme will Time Warner employ once it has destroyed the competition? Upon eliminating Grande, Time Warner will be Austin's sole cable provider and will raise rates once again."

Source: Colin Pope, "City Challenges Time Warner's Pricing Strategy," *Austin Business Journal* (January 28, 2002) online.

Case Study Questions

1. Assuming the pricing scheme is legal, should Time Warner go ahead with this special pricing strategy despite all the talk and the City Manager's letter to the FCC?

2. There is an old saying, "You can't fight City Hall," which implies that Time Warner should back down and attempt to regain "good will" lost in the current situation. Do you agree with this statement?

3. What pricing strategy would you suggest Time Warner substitute for the deep discount offer to former customers?

4. How price sensitive are cable customers?

Managing Marketing Efforts

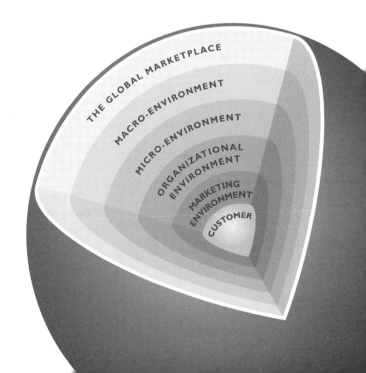

CHAPTER 15

Control and Measurement of Marketing Performance

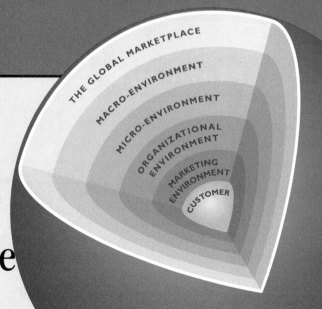

THE GLOBAL MARKETPLACE
MACRO-ENVIRONMENT
MICRO-ENVIRONMENT
ORGANIZATIONAL ENVIRONMENT
MARKETING ENVIRONMENT
CUSTOMER

Overview

Controlling Marketing Efforts

Levels of Analysis

Measuring Performance

While some marketers, using old "tried and true" approaches, are facing a crisis, innovative practitioners are meeting the challenge. With a more comprehensive approach to productivity—effective efficiency—marketers using better measurement techniques, more sensible strategies, and more effective systems of monitoring and evaluating productivity will win the day.[1]

Improving the Score at Nike

The rise of the Nike brand in the 1990s was phenomenal. A particularly impressive run in the mid-1990s peaked with a 50 percent growth in sales during 1997. By 1999, Nike was not scoring as well. Sales had dropped, profits fell to $451 million from a peak of $797 million in 1997, and the Nike brand image had begun to lose its appeal. More than half of Nike's $10 billion in annual sales comes from shoes, but U.S. shoe sales were flat and orders were down by 3 percent in the third quarter of 2002. In the same period, Nike reported a $48.9 million net loss that included a $266 million charge attributed to goodwill on previous acquisitions. Another blow to sales came from order cancellations (worth as much as $250 million) by Foot Locker Inc. due to slow sales of Nike's premium, high-priced shoes. Foot Locker, a key customer of Nike, is responsible for 11 percent of Nike's sales, so this move strained the relationship between the two companies, and left Nike shopping for new retail outlets for its inventory of $160 Vince Carter Shox and $200 Air Jordan shoes.

It will take all the brand strength and fiscal discipline Nike can muster to regain share lost in the United States to competitors such as Adidas and New Balance. The poor performance of Nike's core business was held responsible for a 30 percent drop in the price of its shares since hitting a 2-year high of $63.99 in March 2002. Nike faces another problem in proving that the company can be a major player in the lower-priced shoe market.

Money that teenagers spent on multiple pairs of high-end athletic shoes in the past is now being spent on other trendy items such as cell phones and other gizmos.

Nike's turnaround began when Phil Knight acknowledged in early 2001 that he needed to make changes, beginning with its management. Knight, who held the positions of chairman, CEO, and president, turned day-to-day control over to two Nike veterans, Mark G. Parker and Charlie Denson, who were given the title of co-presidents. In his original position as a shoe designer, Parker introduced innovative new products such as Nike's flexible Presto and spring-soled Shox. Now his attention is on sub-$100 footwear. Denson's background was in sales, which he applied to shrinking nearly $1 billion in inventory that "threatened to implode the supply chain." He also installed new computer systems for better inventory management. Other key managers hired from outside the firm include CFO Donald W. Blair and Mindy Grossman. Blair was hired from PepsiCo Inc. in 1999, and introduced fiscal discipline in a culture that likes to spend heavily on product development and marketing. Grossman joined the firm from Polo Ralph Lauren Corp. in 2000, with experience in the apparel industry.

Nike is making headway with its growth plans in spite of problems, such as Foot Locker's cancelled orders, less-than-spectacular product launches, changing customer preferences, and allegations of ties to Third World sweatshops. The company appears more financially disciplined than before, and is showing that it can achieve growth from categories other than shoes. Gross margin in second quarter 2002 was over 40 percent of revenues for the first time in a decade.

Nike apparel lines have been reinvigorated under Grossman's leadership, including the creation of an active lifestyle fashion line, and cutting lead times to put new outfits in the stores from 18 to 11 months. Retailer Shawn Neville, CEO of Footaction, says, "I think they are bridging lifestyle and sport a lot better and creating more fashionable looks and fabrics." Nike's classic Air Jordan 9 shoe was relaunched at $125 to regain market position. The second edition of the Vince Carter Shox was planned for launch in February

2003 at the NBA All-Star Game. Nike's footwear vice president, Eric Sprunk, said, "We're not going to $200. We probably pushed that too aggressively."

Although the U.S. market is flat, Nike has experienced gradual growth in its overall international revenues that have grown to $4.4 billion, close to the U.S. revenues of $4.7 billion. In third quarter 2002, Nike's sales grew 24 percent in Asia and 15 percent in Europe. Soccer equipment and footwear are expected to be the major catalysts for growth overseas. To capitalize on this trend at the time of the World Cup soccer match, Nike introduced a line of radically designed shoes, jerseys, and equipment. This product introduction was combined with a $100-million advertising campaign, $155 million spent on endorsements, and 13 mini theme parks spread throughout the world. The benefit for Nike is a growing share of the $1 billion global soccer shoe and apparel market, and a renewed enthusiasm for the Nike brand among younger consumers. Other sponsorships that are paying off and seem to be returning the power of the Nike brand include sponsorship of golfer Tiger Woods, and a related lineup of products that include balls, clubs, and shoes.

Nike's efforts to improve performance paid off in fiscal 2002 with a 12 percent increase in net income to $553.3 million. Although sales are expected to grow by 5 percent in the year ending May 31, 2003, profits are expected to grow an additional 13 percent. Nike apparel, once a disappointing contributor to company sales, generated $2.9 billion in sales (30 percent of Nike's total sales) for the fiscal year ended May 31, 2002. Compared to Nike's low acceptance as a soccer shoe manufacturer during the 1994 World Cup, the 2002 World Cup was a different story. Global soccer revenues increased to $450 million, an increase of 24 percent over the previous year.

Nike scored unexpected points during the World Cup soccer match on June 30, 2002 when Ronaldo, a superstar from Brazil, knocked in two goals in the final match to defeat Germany 2-0. Not only was this an honor for his soccer-mad country, but it was also a great marketing script for Nike. Ronaldo, who had overcome previous career-threatening injuries, was wearing a pair of Nike's "special lightweight, silver-coated

'Mercurial Vapor' soccer shoes" at the time of his victory. Nike sponsored the Brazilian national team and its star in an attempt to break into the $2.5 billion global soccer gear business dominated by Adidas-Salomon, a German firm, and could not have scripted a better ending for the game. As one observer noted, "That's just the sort of deft footwork that Nike will need if it's going to break free from a moribund U.S. sneaker market."

When Phil Knight recognized the need to make changes in management and other aspects of his business if it was to grow, he said prior to naming Parker and Denson co-presidents, "We got to be a $9 billion company with a $5 billion management." After many of the changes were implemented, and the turnaround was well on its way in 2002, Knight said, "I think now we're a pretty well-run $10 billion company, and we're ready to grow again."

Source: Stanley Holmes and Christine Tierney, "How Nike Got Its Game Back," *BusinessWeek* (November 4, 2002), pp. 129–131.

As the opening quote indicates, marketing must be both effective and efficient. The importance of marketing and the size of marketing budgets have grown in the face of increasingly higher levels of worldwide competition. Because marketing activities generate revenues, profitability, and visibility, marketing budgets have not been as vulnerable to cost cutting as some other functional areas of a business. In discussing the productivity crisis in today's businesses, Sheth and Sisodia observe that although marketing represents the largest *discretionary* spending area in most companies, it is also an area where many companies would like to devote even more resources. These authors believe that this situation will not persist and see clear indications that CEOs are demanding greater accountability from marketing than ever before.[2]

Throughout this book, the focus has been on marketing operations in a rapidly changing global environment. This chapter addresses the need for accountability in marketing, with a focus on performance and the need for strategic control of marketing efforts at the business-unit level. Assessment of functional level performance was discussed in other chapters in the context of integrated marketing communications (IMC), pricing, marketing intelligence, and other topics.

Excellence in marketing is goal-directed and is driven by the quest for satisfied customers and efficient, effective, and profitable operations. Marketing experts constantly attempt to identify the key success factors that characterize top performers. In general, most of the market leaders emphasize planning and control; use capital, human resources, and technology efficiently and effectively; are market share leaders; and know their markets well. Dynamic, successful marketers obtain synergies from the relationship between performance, excellence, and power. Table 15.1 presents a summary of selected top-performing global firms and most-admired U.S. companies that operate in a variety of industries.

The most innovative and successful marketers prosper because of their ability to manage and use information about their internal operations and external environments. They continuously monitor uncertain and volatile environments that are characterized by intensified competition, industry consolidation, demanding customers, powerful suppliers, and shifting channel power. They develop successful strategies based on an informed analysis of their markets and their own operating results.

TABLE 15.1

Top-Performing Global Firms, 2001, and Most-Admired U.S. Companies, 2002

		a. The Fortune Global 500: The World's Largest Corporations					
Rank 2001	*Rank 2000*	*Company*	*Revenues, $ mil*	*Profits, $ mil*	*Assets, $ mil*	*Stockholders' Equity, $ mil*	*Employees*
1	2	Wal-Mart Stores[1]	219,812.0	6,671.0	83,375.0	35,102.0	1,383,000.0
2	1	Exxon Mobil	191,581.0	15,320.0	143,174.0	73,161.0	97,900.0
3	3	General Motors	177,260.0	601.0	323,969.0	19,707.0	365,000.0
4	7	BP	174,218.0	8,010.0	141,158.0	74,367.0	110,150.0
5	4	Ford Motor	162,412.0	−5,453.0	276,543.0	7,786.0	352,748.0
6	16	Enron[2]	138,718.0	NA	NA	NA	153,888[3]
7	5	DaimlerChrysler	136,897.3	−592.8	184,671.4	34,727.9	372,470.0
8	6	Royal Dutch/Shell Group	135,211.0	10,852.0	111,543.0	56,160.0	91,000.0
9	8	General Electric	125,913.0	13,684.0	495,023.0	54,824.0	310,000.0
10	10	Toyota Motor[4]	120,814.4	4,925.1	150,064.0	55,268.4	246,702.0

	b. The Fortune Global 500: Ranked by 2001 Total Profits		
Rank	*Company*	*2001 Profits, $ mil*	*% Change in Profits from 2000*
1	Exxon Mobil	15,320.0	−13.5
2	CitiGroup	14,126.0	4.5
3	General Electric	13,684.0	7.5
4	Royal Dutch/Shell Group	10,852.0	−14.7
5	Philip Morris	8,560.0	0.6
6	BP	8,010.0	−32.5
7	Pfizer	7,788.0	109.0
8	International Business Machines	7,723.0	−4.6
9	AT&T	7,715.0	65.2
10	Microsoft[5]	7,346.0	−22.0

(continued)

[1]Figures are for fiscal year ended January 31, 2002.
[2]Company filed for bankruptcy December 2, 2001, and financial data for the full year of 2001 were not available at press time. Revenues are for nine months ended September 30, 2001. With Enron eliminated from the list, number 11 Citigroup would move into the top ten with $112,022 in revenues, $14,126 in profits, $1,051,450 in assets, $81,247 in stockholders' equity, and 268,000 employees.
[3]As of June 14, 2002.
[4]Figures are for fiscal year ended March 31, 2002.
[5]Figures are for fiscal year ended June 30, 2001.

TABLE 15.1 *(continued)*

Top-Performing Global Firms, 2001, and Most-Admired U.S. Companies, 2002

		Total Return (%)	
Rank	Company	2001	1996–2001
	c. America's Most Admired Companies		
	(Eight Key Attributes* of Reputation and Overall Return to Shareholders)		
1	General Electric	−15.1	21.2
2	Southwest Airlines	−17.2	33.7
3	Wal-Mart	8.9	39.1
4	Microsoft	52.7	26.2
5	Berkshire Hathaway	6.5	17.3
6	Home Depot	12.1	36.0
7	Johnson & Johnson	14.0	20.5
8	FedEx	29.8	18.4
9	Citigroup	0.0	28.9
10	Intel	4.9	14.1
	Top ten average	**9.7**	**25.5**
	S&P 500	**−11.9**	**10.7**

*The eight attributes are innovativeness, quality of management, employee talent, quality of products/services, long-term investment value, financial soundness, social responsibility, and use of corporate assets.
Source: Part (a) and part (b) reprinted from the July 22, 2002 issue of *Fortune.* Part (c) reprinted from the March 4, 2002 issue of *Fortune.* Copyright © 2002, Time, Inc. All rights reserved.

On the other hand, a lack of understanding of events in the marketing environment can have a negative impact on profitability and customer satisfaction. Several well-known marketers got "off track" with their strategies and suffered losses in revenues and earnings over the past decade.

Target Corporation (formerly Dayton-Hudson Corp.) has been recognized as a successful, well-managed retailer for several decades. However, its Mervyn's apparel and softgoods chain experienced difficulties in 1987. Company executives identified the problem as one of execution rather than strategy and were challenged to develop marketing strategies that would get them back on track and keep them there. The company made a major turnaround following the October 1987 stock market crash and a hostile takeover raid by the Dart Group. By 1989, Dayton-Hudson's earnings, operating margins, and stock price had returned to solid growth. The turnaround was accomplished in part by emphasizing Mervyn's merchandising and purchasing rather than its previous focus on growth and opening new stores.

Mervyn's also created a quality control team and undertook a multimillion-dollar store remodeling program. As a result, operating margins nearly doubled. In 2002 Mervyn's operated about 265 midrange department stores in California and 13 other states, mostly in the West and Midwest. The Target Corporation subsidiary competes with more upscale department stores, including Target's Marshall Field's chain, on one side and discount chains, such as Target Stores, on the other, making it crucial to constantly monitor performance. Growth has been slow but steady in a highly competitive market since the company's difficulties of the 1980s.

Other performance reviews resulted in Target Corporation's decision to improve productivity and profitability of its chains by opening Target Stores subsidiaries Target Greatland and Super Target warehouse-type stores in the 1990s using a profitable low cost-high turnover strategy. The company also launched its own credit card and Web site, both of which provide valuable customer data that can be analyzed for future inventory decisions, merchandising, and promotions. In January 2000, the company's corporate name was officially changed from Dayton Hudson to Target Corporation to reflect the fact that Target Stores represent 80 percent of revenues for the firm, and the company's other chains, Mervyn's and Marshall Fields, contribute about 20 percent. Department store performance throughout the industry had slowed significantly during the 1990s, and in January 2001, Dayton's and Hudson's became part of the Marshall Field brand to leverage the Field's brand name nationally. Measures of Target Corporation's performance in 2002 (in a slower economy) include one-year sales growth of 8.1 percent; one-year net income growth of 8.2 percent; and employee growth of 10.2 percent. The company ranked 34 in the Fortune 500; 14 in Fortune's Global Most Admired Companies; 103 in the FT Global 500; and was listed in the S&P 500 in 2002.[3]

As Target Corporation/Dayton-Hudson Corp.'s experience indicates, marketing performance must be controlled and measured throughout all stages of the managerial process. Managers who understand why results were not as planned have taken a major step toward correcting mistakes.

● CONTROLLING MARKETING EFFORTS

An evaluation of a firm's marketing performance starts with an understanding of the management process and the role that measurement of results plays in that process. The components of the management process work together to generate target levels of productivity and profitability. Performance measurement is an integral part of the strategic planning process, including control, coordination, and value creation. Performance measurement is also an important aspect of the firm's marketing plan, as discussed in Appendix A: Development, Implementation, and Evaluation of a Marketing plan.

The Managerial Process

Management decisions involve basic problems that must be solved, questions that must be asked, and information that is needed to analyze and evaluate operating results. These decisions are driven by a firm's strategic plan and should be evaluated

FIGURE 15.1

The Managerial Process

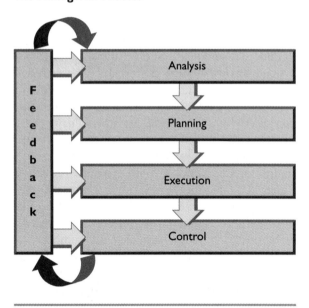

during each stage in the managerial process, which includes (1) analysis related to the problem that is being addressed, (2) planning, (3) execution, and (4) control. The results of this assessment of marketing successes and failures provide feedback for both short- and long-range planning. (See Figure 15.1.) For example, to attain corporate financial goals, the necessary funds for inventory investment must be allocated, buyers must be motivated to select the right products, and the performance of marketing personnel and product lines must be evaluated.

Marketing managers must act quickly and decisively to solve problems that occur in daily business operations, which may lead to a shorter-range perspective. However, when the strategic planning process includes an evaluation of operating results, management must address the implications of developments in the markets where they operate. This includes competitive activities, economic trends, and other relevant environmental factors. This type of analysis helps the marketer anticipate future scenarios and encourages a longer-range strategic view.

Profitability and Productivity

Marketers often find it difficult to measure marketing productivity accurately because marketing expenditures (inputs) cannot easily be related to specific results (outputs) due to their intangibility. Sheth and Sisodia suggest that a definition of marketing productivity should be based on the amount of desirable output obtained for each unit of input, that is, quality as well as quantity.[4] Efficient and effective use of marketing resources should incorporate attention to both customer acquisition and customer retention. (See Figure 15.2.)

Approaches to improving marketing productivity are described in Table 15.2. These include the use of better marketing accounting systems, greater use of collaborative strategies, better domain definition, unbundling and rebundling of services,

MARKETING IN THE GLOBAL VILLAGE

Gaining Altitude: Boeing versus Airbus

Airbus is flying high—and there is excitement at the company's Toulouse, France headquarters where a factory is under construction for production of the newest Airbus plane. The 555-seat superjumbo A380 is scheduled to roll off production lines in 2006, ending the Boeing Co.'s long running hold on the market for the largest aircraft with its Boeing 747. By October 2002, Airbus had 95 orders for its new superjumbo, but estimated it would take 250 orders to break even. The A380's high development costs have a major impact on Airbus' bottom line; over $1.2 billion is budgeted for research and development in 2003. Although the future performance of Airbus looks bright, the company does have its problems. Forecasts for 2002 sales were $19.2 billion, 5 percent lower than the previous year, and operating profits as much as 30 percent lower, at $1.1 billion.

The commercial jet industry has struggled to regain profitable operations for several years, but the post-9/11 era has been particularly difficult for all airline-related businesses, including airplane manufacturers. Boeing, an archrival of Airbus, suffered a severe drop in orders of nearly 50 percent in 2002. With production cut in half, Boeing cut 30,000 jobs from its workforce of 93,000. This, in turn, angered the unions that represent the workers. In October, Boeing Chairman and chief executive, Philip M. Condit reported a 42 percent drop in third-quarter earnings to $372 million, as sales of commercial jets dropped 25 percent to $6.1 billion, compared with the same quarter in 2001.

While other airplane manufacturers were suffering a downturn in their businesses, Airbus announced new orders from airlines such as easyJet Airline Co., a British carrier and former loyal Boeing customer. The easyJet order for 120 Airbus A319s, with an option for 120 more, was a difficult loss for Boeing. The easyJet deal brought Airbus 2002 orders up to 276 compared

with Boeing's 186. Airbus delivered less than half the number of planes delivered by Boeing in 1999, but analysts predicted that Airbus would surpass Boeing by delivering 300 planes in 2003. Boeing has dominated the fast-growing discount airline market with its efficient 737 jet for many years. However, the easyJet deal gave Airbus the impetus it needed to get into this market. The company sold 54 mid-size A330 and A340 planes in 2001, gaining ground on the 69 orders booked by Boeing for its competing 767 and 777. As Airbus CEO Noel Forgeard said, "We have successfully attacked the three bastions of our competitor."

Although Airbus' easyJet sale was a "stunning deal" according to the airline's CEO Ray Webster, analysts questioned whether Airbus was sacrificing profitability to gain market share. The two companies did not disclose terms of the sale, but analysts believe the A319's $50 million list price was cut as much as 40 percent, plus other terms of sale favorable to easyJet. However, Airbus will not finance the deal, and easyJet will make a 20 percent payment upfront. Boeing also gave deep discounts to obtain an order of up to 150 planes from Ryanair, an Irish carrier. The easyJet deal gave Airbus access to the European discount market, just as earlier sales to JetBlue, a no-frills U.S. carrier, gave it access to the U.S. discount market. The easyJet deal also was reflected in the stock market following Airbus' announcement of the sale, and that it was on track to increase operating margins to 10 percent by the end of 2004. Analysts questioned whether this was possible. However, shares in the European Aeronautics Defense & Space Co. (EADS), which owns 80 percent of the unlisted Airbus, rose 11 percent after the agreement. (Airbus was responsible for 64 percent of EADS' $30 billion in sales and nearly 100 percent of EADS' profits in the previous year.)

Slumping sales and aggressive competition in the commercial jet business have had a significant

(continued)

impact on profitability and earnings. As shareholders demand return on their investment, cost-cutting measures are needed. Boeing laid off workers when production slowed. Airbus workers were more fortunate in that the company runs a lean and flexible operation with only 45,000 workers (versus the 60,000 that remain at Boeing's commercial division after layoffs). Airbus uses a large number of temporary and/or part-time workers—about 15 percent of its workforce, and can cut the equivalent of 5,000 jobs by not using these workers. The company also outsources more work than Boeing does, and it is their subcontractors who have to lay off personnel. Most of Airbus' aircraft were introduced in the 1980s and 1990s, and are newer

and more technologically up to date than most of their competitors, giving them an added advantage. Boeing was faced with revitalizing its product line while cutting costs—a difficult task. Two attempts were unsuccessful: no buyers were found for its 747 stretch version that was a match for the Airbus superjumbo; and plans to produce its Sonic Cruiser had to be shelved for lack of customer interest. With less cash flow, Boeing will "have to make money with what they've got, despite shrinking market share," according to one market analyst.

Source: Carol Matlack and Stanley Holmes, "Look Out, Boeing," *BusinessWeek* (October 28, 2002), pp. 50-51.

rationalizing the marketing mix, use of information technology, and better monitoring and control of personnel and marketing practices.[5]

The Control Process and Strategic Planning

A strategic plan without a plan for control and measurement of marketing performance may be doomed to failure. Therefore, performance evaluation should be considered throughout the entire strategic planning process; that is, who is accountable for achieving the strategic goals, and how should the results be measured?

FIGURE 15.2

Marketing Efficiency and Effectiveness

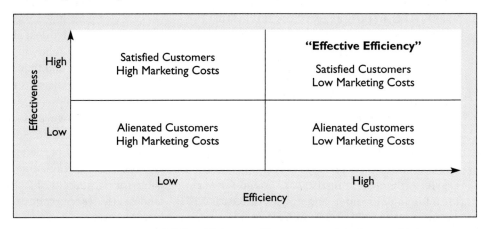

Source: AMA Marketing Encyclopedia (1995), p. 222. Reprinted by permission of the American Marketing Association.

TABLE 15.2

Approaches to Improving Marketing Productivity

Better Marketing Accounting

- *Activity-based costing.* Understand where resources are being spent, where customer value is being created, and where money is being made or lost.

Greater Use of Collaborative Strategies

- *Partnering.* Treat your suppliers and customers as partners in lowering systemwide costs and adding value.
- *Relationship marketing.* Be selective about customers, and take a long-term, win-win perspective.
- *Marketing alliances.* Share resources and opportunities with other companies serving the same customers.

Better Domain Definition

- *Make vs. buy: Insourcing vs. outsourcing.* Focus on your marketing core competencies and let outside experts handle the rest.
- *Getting customers to do more work.* Lower costs and increase customer satisfaction by adding customers to the value chain.

Unbundling and Rebundling of Services

- Uncover the hidden costs of free service, and create new revenue sources.

Rationalizing the Marketing Mix

- *Umbrella branding.* Increase return on branding by developing brand names with broad applicability to multiple products and markets.

- *Rationalizing and recycling advertising.* Remove conflicts of interest in agency compensation methods, unbundle advertising creation and placement, and understand advertising life cycles.
- *Reducing product proliferation.* Variety does not always equate to value; reduce customer confusion and marketing costs by matching product lines with distinct market segments.

Use of Information Technology

- *Data-based marketing.* Target marketing efforts more precisely, but ensure that you are creating additional value for the customer and are acutely sensitive to privacy concerns.
- *Front-line information systems.* Deploy information tools where they have the greatest impact on customer service and satisfaction: at the front line.
- *Marketing and the global information highway.* Prepare now for a radically different, more integrated mode of marketing in the future, predicated on "total customer convenience."

Better Monitoring and Control

- *Adjusting compensation of marketing personnel.* Compensation drivers must be linked to the need for effective efficiency in all marketing activities.
- *Continuous assessment of marketing practices.* Beware of creeping marketing incrementalism; take a periodic "zero-based" view of marketing practices.

Source: Sheth, Jagdish and Rajendra S. Sisodia, (1995), "Improving Marketing Productivity," in *Marketing Encyclopedia: Issues & Trends Shaping the Future.* Jeffrey Heilbrun, ed., Chicago, IL: American Marketing Association, pp. 223–236. Reprinted by permission of the American Marketing Association.

Control and the Managerial Process. Control is an important element of the managerial process, as shown in Figure 15.1. There are a number of issues that managers must resolve in order to design and implement an effective control process: identification of key variables to measure or control, performance standards and measures, assessment and reassessment procedures, and provision for corrective action. Each of these issues is described briefly within the context of strategic control at the business-unit level.

- *Key variables to be measured or controlled.* The selection of key variables should relate to a company's mission statement and strategic objectives. The goals to achieve these objectives generally can be categorized as financial (e.g., return on investment, net profit), efficiency (e.g., productivity in terms of use of assets, personnel performance), or effectiveness (e.g., market leadership, competitive positioning, customer satisfaction). The nature of these variables transcends all functional areas of an organization as they relate to marketing, taking into consideration both internal and external factors.

- *Standards of performance.* Performance expectations are based on a company's strategic goals, the standards that are met or exceeded by leading marketers. Standards may be established on the basis of the company's vision for the future (i.e., its positioning relative to competition or others in the same industry), historical company data and forecasts for future performance, or by benchmarketing against key success factors in the industry. Performance standards are set for the entire company and for subunits that comprise the company. Standards for one organizational level should support the standards of the other levels. Performance standards usually are viewed within the parameters of some time designation, preferably with the ability to compare with previous time periods, industry standards, company goals, and so forth. Many companies today are benchmarking their operations against leading companies within their own industry or in unrelated industries.

- *Performance measures.* Performance generally is controlled by measuring factors such as profitability, sales, market share, shareholder value, employee productivity, and customer satisfaction. Although individual variables are analyzed, managers usually consider a number of standards simultaneously that combine to provide an overall measure of performance. Even though the most common variables that are used to represent an organization's performance are quantitative (e.g., net profit, return on equity), many qualitative measures (e.g., customer satisfaction, attitude change toward the company or its products) are also considered in an overall assessment of performance. For example, a firm might consider the efficiency of its operation based on cost containment and contribution margins and the productivity of its personnel who make goods in the factory, salespeople who call on the company's customers, or the rate of new product introduction into the market.

  Qualitative factors that are more elusive, and hence more subjective, help management gain a better understanding of overall performance. For example, customer satisfaction, product quality (as it is perceived by the customer), and return on investment in advertising can be combined with quantitative factors in measuring performance.

- *Assessment/reassessment.* Data for discrete (one-time) or continuous assessment of marketing performance can be found in the company's financial and accounting reports (financial ratios are discussed later), sales data and salesforce reports (by product, territory, etc.), feedback from customers and employees, and other sources. Assessment can be conducted by individuals within the company or by outside consultants.

- *Correcting identified problems or weaknesses.* Once problem areas have been identified, they should be prioritized for action. Based on an understanding of the problem, management next develops a plan to improve the situation. The most successful plans include input from all stakeholders in the process and its outcomes. A plan for implementation of the corrective measures should be developed, authority and responsibility should be assigned, and actions should be monitored and fine-tuned as needed. At this point it is helpful to continue to seek feedback from all affected parties.

Anaylsis and Strategic Planning: An Ongoing Process. The early chapters of this book represented a broad view of marketing management and strategic planning. They addressed the general question, "What will we do?" ("What objectives does our company want to achieve?" and "What strategies will we use to reach our objectives?") Subsequent chapters concentrated on narrower functional marketing-mix areas, addressing the more specific question, "How will we do it?" ("How shall we use our marketing mix and operate our business on a day-to-day basis?") That is, "What tactics will we use to carry out strategies?" and "What resources are needed for implementation?"

In this chapter the questions addressed in an assessment of marketing performance are, "Did we do, or are we doing, what we set out to do?" and "Why did we or didn't we do it?" During the execution phase, the question "What is/isn't working so far?" also should be addressed. (See Figure 15.3.)

FIGURE 15.3

Analysis and Strategic Planning: An Ongoing Process

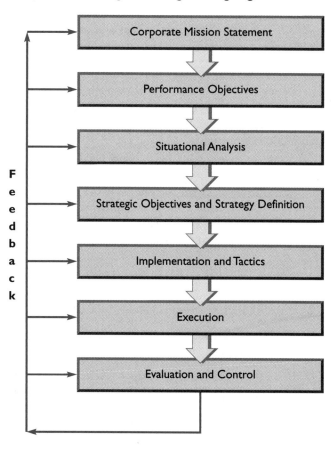

Coordination Across Functions.   As indicated in the discussion of the relationship between the managerial process, control, and strategic planning, marketing cannot be isolated from other areas of an organization. The control process must consider the sources and uses of funds, personnel issues, shared technologies, production schedules, research and development (R&D) expenditures, and other factors as they affect marketing outcomes. Measurement of the efficiency and effectiveness of cross-functional performance provides a method to identify areas that achieve synergy in the ways they work together to achieve a common goal, as well as those areas that need to develop cross-functional synergies.

Measuring Value Creation.   The efficient and effective use of capital is a major concern to marketing organizations, particularly with regard to shareholder value and customer satisfaction. Many firms achieve higher levels of performance and productivity by leveraging customer loyalty and the amount of capital employed to finance the company's investments. While sales growth, profitability, and cash flow from operations are used as indicators of a company's success, the final test is whether the firm's activities and investment in those activities are creating value for its owners. (Customer satisfaction and customer loyalty are important contributors to these measures, but more difficult to link specifically to profitability, and thus are not discussed in this section.) **Economic value added (EVA)** analysis provides a way to measure value creation and evaluate business performance by analyzing profits and the cost and uses of capital, represented by the formula

> **Economic value added (EVA)**
> Method of evaluating business performance by analyzing profits and the cost and uses of capital.

$$\text{EVA} = \text{net operating profit} - (\text{costs of capital} \times \text{capital employed})$$
or $\text{EVA} = \text{net operating profit} - (\text{weighted average cost of capital} \times \text{capital employed})$

where net operating profit = operating profit − taxes.[6]

EVA analysis says that EVA will be positive (or negative) if the firm's return on invested capital is higher (or lower) than the cost of that capital (as measured by the weighted cost of capital). This is related to shareholder value analysis (SVA) that says economic value is added and shareholder value (market value of a company minus its debt) is increased when a company makes sufficient profit to earn a return on its investment, at least equal to its cost of capital.

This formula is based on the idea that every firm will employ capital for uses such as plant, inventory, working capital, and other assets, but recognizing that the capital employed has a cost that should be included when valuing business performance. Aaker[7] identified four routes to increasing EVA:

1. Increase profit by reducing costs or increasing revenue without using more capital.

2. Invest in high-return products—the basis for all marketing strategy.

3. Decrease the cost of capital—with a higher ratio of debt to equity or a less risky business portfolio.

4. Use less capital—many firms have improved their performance dramatically by making better use of existing assets and being less capital-intensive in their operations.

Value creation is clearly related to the key attributes of *Fortune*'s ranking of America's most admired companies, in particular: use of corporate assets; long-term investment value; and financial soundness.[8] Many firms have experienced huge increases in the value of their companies by employing the principles of EVA. Managers from top-performing companies such as these know the answers to the questions: What is the true cost of capital? How much capital is tied up in our operation?

⬤ LEVELS OF ANALYSIS

The performance of an organization can be evaluated at the corporate or strategic, business, and functional or operating levels of the firm. (See Figure 15.4.) Although different factors may be emphasized at different organizational levels, three major concerns generally are addressed: performance versus plan, execution of the plan, and capital expenditures. In each case, the company seeks to determine whether it has made the best use of its resources. Although examples are given of issues to be examined at each organizational level, the emphasis in this section is on analysis of results at the functional level.

At all levels of a company, the question that must be answered is, "How can we better exploit our current internal resources (financial, human, physical, technological, and organizational) to achieve a clear, sustainable competitive advantage?" As Waterman observed in *The Renewal Factor,* opportunity knocks softly and in unpredictable ways.[9] Today's business leaders must face—and manage—constant change, with the goal of prospering from the forces that decimate their competition. Analysis provides critical information for marketers to use in planning, executing, controlling, and revising strategy and to help them to be ready for opportunity when it knocks.

FIGURE 15.4

Levels of Analysis

Corporate Level
Evaluation of Managers and Operations Across Divisions
Emphasis on Logic and Coordination of Businesses Across the Corporation
Longer Term Perspective of Strategies

Business Level
Evaluation of Managers and Operations Across Business Units and Within the Business Division
Emphasis on Effective and Efficient Coordination of Functional Areas
Narrower Perspective Than Corporate and Wider Than Functional Level

Functional Level
Evaluation Within and Across Functional Areas
Emphasis on Dealing with Efficiency of Carrying Out Strategic Intent
Narrowest Perspective, Oriented to Daily Operations

Corporate Level Analysis

At the corporate or strategic level, analysis encompasses all business units or all divisions of a multibusiness organization. Large firms may have several different business formats, operate in multiple industries, or represent different stages in the channels of distribution. Managers and operations are evaluated across divisions to determine their contribution to the corporate bottom line, with the objective of balancing all businesses profitably. Emphasis is on the logic and coordination of the businesses that make up the corporation, taking a longer-term perspective of strategies for organizational effectiveness ("what to do"). One important measure of organizational effectiveness focuses on the use of financial resources, with the objective of achieving the highest possible return for each dollar invested by the firm. This would include, for example, capital expenditures such as expansion activities, major equipment purchases, or acquisitions or merger activities.

Business Level Analysis

Analysis at the business level takes a narrower perspective of the environment than that taken at the corporate level but broader than that at the functional level. Emphasis is on the effective and efficient coordination of all functional areas to ensure maximum impact. Managers, business operations, and other factors are evaluated across all units within the business division to answer the basic question of how each unit performed against its planned performance standards. Results provide inputs to determine the most advantageous allocation of money, personnel, and other assets. For example, Procter & Gamble Co. (P&G) launched a plan in 1998 to redesign its operations in response to pressure from large international retailers. Wal-Mart Stores, Inc., Carrefour USA Inc., and others pushed suppliers such as P&G to standardize worldwide pricing, marketing and distribution. P&G changed its strategy from a country-by-country setup to a limited number of powerful departments organized on a global scale for category management (e.g., hair care, diapers, soap). Implementation of the plan was expected to take two years and relied heavily on increasing sales and market share in international markets—where many countries were experiencing economic crises. Another result of business level analysis was the Organization 2005 plan launched in 1999 to improve performance. Among other changes under this initiative, P&G reorganized the company's corporate structure from four geographic business units into seven global business units based on product categories.[10]

A firm's operating plan establishes performance standards that can be used for comparison with actual results during and after execution. This is an integral part of the strategic planning and control process. If performance is below expectations, analysis may reveal explanations that are not evident otherwise. Evaluation during the early stages reveals strengths and weaknesses and permits management to make necessary revisions in a timely manner. For example, a lower than desired profit level may be caused by a number of interacting factors, such as higher than average advertising expenses and short-run price cuts taken to achieve a high sales volume. Or changes in the firm's operating environment (such as a labor strike in a key supplier's factory) may make it necessary to re-evaluate the original plan.

At the business level, each functional area can be evaluated to determine its role in the execution of marketing strategies and its contribution to overall financial performance. Business level analysis also looks outward to the company's operating environment to assess market opportunities and demand for the firm's products and services. (See discussion of environmental factors in Chapter 1.) An evaluation of information about current conditions and the ability to anticipate future events and activities enable a firm to be proactive in influencing environmental forces rather than merely reacting to them.

Functional (Operating) Level Analysis

At the functional, or operating, level, analysis is concerned with the efficiency of carrying out the strategic intent ("how to do it") within and across the functional areas of a business unit. The planning horizon is shorter term as managers concentrate on the details of carrying out the firm's strategy on a day-to-day basis. The overriding goal is to coordinate all departments and functions in order to execute corporate strategy successfully and achieve corporate objectives. Performance at the functional level can "make or break" performance goals at the business level and therefore should be measured and controlled for its contribution to the overall efficiency and effectiveness of the organization.

The Marketing Mix. All relevant aspects of the marketing mix are evaluated to determine how well the plan has been executed: product and pricing strategies, marketing communications mix, distribution, and customer service. A 30-month-long study by the Marketing Metrics Research Project found that only a small minority of U.K. firms thoroughly assess their marketing performance—although most believe that their assessments are adequate.[11] Marketers are always anxious to measure everything else but are less keen on being measured themselves. The results of this research indicate that those who do not understand their brand equity position have little idea how good—or bad—their marketing is. Most marketers compare sales with plan, with an increased focus on shareholder value, but not customer value. As a major client of Marketing Metrics stated, "One of the most chilling realizations is the recognition of the limitations of financial measurements when an entire business needs to be re-engineered . . . they told the management team nothing about how to manage revenue toward becoming a customer-driven business when help was needed most." Critical success factors include learning what matters most to the customer and how this affects the future.[11] The distinction should be made between marketing performance and expenditure effectiveness when measuring marketing results. Marketing expenditure should be viewed as an investment, not a cost, and the resulting asset and its valuation should be measured by the firm's brand equity.

Unsuccessful execution may be due to ineffective product management, unreliable suppliers, or errors in identifying customer wants. Or adjustments may be needed in the communications mix, pricing, or distribution channels. Conversely, factors responsible for successful tactical execution also can be identified and taken advantage of. Next, we will look briefly at the need for performance evaluation within selected functional areas and the combined effect of these functions as they interact to produce operating results at the strategic level.

Product managers determine market needs and forecast market demand. They determine prices and distribution channels and play a key role in developing integrated communications programs. These tasks must be accomplished within the context of company policies, budgets, competitive pressures, and the interaction of these factors with other functional areas of the firm. There are a number of approaches to this type of analysis, but the most efficient method is to use complex statistical computer models that can handle individual and combined effects. For example, conjoint analysis has been used effectively for product concept testing and consumer reactions for goods and services in a variety of industries, including consumer nondurables, financial services, industrial goods, and transportation. One study involved the adoption of electronic toll collection for the interregional roadways of the area (EZPass). An evaluation of customer wants and needs in the design phase led to identification of attributes that were most important to customers as they used the tollway, and provided a basis for measuring performance in terms of customer satisfaction against these attributes.[12] Table 15.3 suggests various spreadsheet approaches and decision models that can be used to plan and evaluate marketing decisions.[13]

Sales forecasting models are used to estimate demand and sales. Anticipated sales levels are used to determine production and inventory levels for a specified selling period, the amount of salesforce coverage needed, the most effective communication methods, and optimal distribution channels. During and after execution, analysis of sales and inventory data provides information about the accuracy of forecasts and the possible need to adjust original estimates.

Analysis of pricing strategies is needed to determine market response to the selected price points. What is the price elasticity? Does the range of prices offer customers sufficient alternatives? Are the price points psychologically appropriate? Are the gross margins high enough to achieve the firm's profit objectives and/or low enough to achieve sales objectives? What effect do margins and profit objectives have on prices that can be paid to suppliers? Do new price lines or price points need to be introduced?

Channel members need information to plan inventory assortments, determine basic stock needs, and make projections about customer responses to the goods and services offered. Projections may be based on knowledge of characteristics of the firm's customers and how they use products and services, and results can be measured against these projections.

The performance of marketing managers is evaluated in several ways: achievement of sales objectives, expense control, and contribution to profit margins. High performance often results in bonuses or profit-sharing plans. Effective use of assets such as inventory can be evaluated from several interrelated perspectives. The productivity of each dollar invested in inventory is analyzed to determine whether an optimal balance between stock and sales (in dollars and units) is being achieved and whether the investment in inventory is producing the desired level of sales and profits. Stock turnover rates, optimal reorder points, and reorder quantities also are evaluated. The marketer who is concentrating on building market share (e.g., low profit margin to high asset turnover ratio) will have a different philosophy than one who is content with maintaining the status quo (e.g., average profit margin to average asset turnover ratio).

Integrated Marketing Communications (IMC).   Ways to measure the effectiveness of integrated marketing communications programs were discussed in Chapters 11 and 12. Analysis includes an evaluation of the promotional mix (advertising, personal selling, sales promotion, publicity, and public relations), as well as services offered by the firm. The marketer's goal is to obtain the highest return possible from each dollar spent on communication with target customers. Analytical models, often

TABLE 15.3

Marketing Control and Decision Models

The following software programs are computer-based models that may be invaluable to managers concerned with marketing control and/or other marketing decisions. Many are Excel spreadsheet-based but some are stand-alone models that are either commercially available or available in the public domain.

Excel Spreadsheets	Non-Excel Models	Commercial Non-Excel Models
ADBUG	**ADCAD**	**Expert Choice**
Advertising budgeting	Ad copy design	Evaluate alternatives
ADVISOR	**Cluster Analysis**	**Decision Tree**
Communications planning	Market segmentation	Evaluate alternatives
ASSESSOR	**Conjoint Analysis**	**Geodemographics**
Market pretest	Product design	Site planning
CALLPLAN	**Multinomial Logit Analysis**	**Neural Net**
Sales call planning	Market forecasting	Market forecasting
Choice-Based Segmentation	**Positioning Analysis**	
Market segmentation	Market forecasting	
GE: Portfolio		
Product planning		
PIMS		
Marketing strategy		
Promotional Spending Analysis		
Effectiveness of promotions		
Sales Resource Allocation		
Territorial design		
Value-in-Use Pricing		
Total value pricing		
Visual Response Modeling		
Define shape of market		
Yield Management		
Maximize hotel occupancy		
Competitive Bidding		
Preparation of bid pricing		

Source: G. Lilien/A. Rangaswamy, *Marketing Engineering,* (exhibit 1.11, page 25). © 1998 by Gary L. Lilien and Arvind Rangaswamy. Reprinted by permission of Pearson Education, Inc., Upper Saddle River, NJ.

using databases, point-of-sale scanner data, or other customer response information, can be used to identify the most cost-effective communications mix to achieve the highest levels of sales and/or profit goals.

Questions to be addressed include: Are the promotional message, media, and timing effective in achieving the marketer's objectives? Is the intended message reaching the target audience, and with the desired results? An evaluation of the effect of salesforce expenditures is necessary, particularly in comparison with high-technology alternatives and an increasing use of self-service methods. Have the sales personnel been trained properly? Are they carrying out the firm's strategic intent and making their sales goals? Is the compensation plan motivating high levels of performance?

Sales promotion efforts are analyzed to determine whether they are being used appropriately and how they are integrated with IMC. How do customers respond to special events, "giveaways," contests, couponing, trade shows, or other sales promotion tools? Are packaging and other visual factors effective "silent" salespeople?

The effectiveness of publicity and public relations efforts should be evaluated to determine whether they have been directed to the right media and individuals. What results have been obtained from these communication channels? Should other options be explored?

Execution of a marketing strategy often involves services that accompany purchases. Are the right services being offered? Do some services contribute to expenses only and not to sales? Should other services be offered to meet the needs of customers and to differentiate the firm's offerings from competitors?

According to Graham,[14] a successful marketing program can be evaluated in eight tangible ways employing a number of measures:

1. It differentiates a company from the competition.
2. It creates a flow of new business leads.
3. It keeps the company in the minds of customers and prospects.
4. It gives the company a strong hold on the marketplace.
5. It communicates a company's expertise and knowledge.
6. It gives the company a long-term orientation.
7. It is customer-oriented.
8. It is a vital force in customer retention.

Other Functional Areas.   The performance of a company's operations, accounting and control, and human resources functions also should be evaluated relative to their impact on performance of the marketing function and the company as a whole. Control of the operations function includes analysis of factors such as maintenance of physical facilities, efficient space utilization, risk management and security, and in many cases performance of technological applications.

The accounting function is concerned with recording, maintaining, and analyzing data that are used to evaluate financial performance and control marketing operations. One popular approach is activity-based accounting, a method for analyzing where money is being spent, where value is being added for customers, and where the business is operating at a profit (or loss). Other tools used by accounting and finance areas include the marketing information system (MIS) and the marketing decision support system (MDSS) described in Chapter 4. The accounting function conducts an ongoing analysis to compare sales, profits, and other performance indicators across functional areas and business units.

Performance evaluation of the human resources function focuses on employee productivity. Employee compensation is a major expense for most companies, making productivity an issue for personnel at every level of an organization. Measures may vary according to individual responsibilities but generally are based on output and results. For example, top-level marketing executives are evaluated and rewarded according to their ability to generate profits for the company, and entry-level employees may be evaluated on the basis of number of customers served, efficiency on a production line, and so forth. Each of these has an impact on overall marketing performance.

Performance Evaluation Across Functions: An Example. Functional-area decisions are interrelated and must operate within the context of a larger organization, as shown in Figure 15.5. To illustrate, at the operating level of an electronics retail establishment, support for a special sale event featuring television sets will require money, personnel, physical resources, management expertise, and other company assets. Analysis of sales reports, financial statements, and other timely data provides a basis for effective resource allocation among the various departments and functions involved.

When the company's television buyer decides to feature the television sets, managers in other functional areas also must make decisions. Buyers must identify the best suppliers and the best product styles and prices and negotiate favorable terms of sale. Merchandise managers must estimate demand and plan store inventories, perhaps decreasing inventory levels in other areas if the total departmental budget is not increased. Those responsible for designing and delivering an IMC program must decide how to promote and display the televisions—working with other internal departments and outside media sources. Promotion and dates for delivering the television sets must be coordinated. Operations efficiency is concerned with receiving and processing the television deliveries and taking measures to prevent theft. Accounting performance is concerned with recording and analyzing accurate data related to the television inventory and sales from the time the purchase order is placed until the customer pays the final bill for the merchandise. Human resources effectiveness and efficiency measures relate to employee productivity (sales and other support functions), scheduling, customer service, sales performance, and other factors.

FIGURE 15.5

Interrelationship of Functional Areas in Marketing Analysis

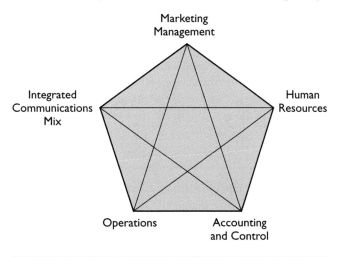

● MEASURING PERFORMANCE

The process of measuring performance starts with deciding which factors to analyze; that is, what are the key questions? Next, criteria must be established as standards for performance, and key ratios should be calculated for comparison with past performance and industry competitors.

Factors to Analyze

Marketing managers are concerned with assessing the results of current efforts, determining why strategies are (or are not) working, identifying environmental changes and their effect on operations, and maximizing opportunities for growth. Control measures are selected in line with the firm's mission and objectives.

The following hierarchy of questions needs to be answered to obtain the type and quality of data needed to evaluate performance at the business-unit level:

1. What is/isn't working? Consider the results of current efforts. This may be the most important question to be answered about the effectiveness of marketing strategies. For example, we might want to know whether lower prices are achieving market-share objectives.

2. Why are strategies working or not working? Take an objective look at the company and its competitors.

3. Have marketing strategies been implemented according to plan? Have all resources (financial, human, physical, etc.) been used efficiently and effectively?

4. What are direct and indirect competitors' current and evolving marketing strategies and tactics? What is their impact on the company's ability to meet its performance objectives?

5. What significant trends and critical events are occurring within the firm's macro- and micro-environment that affect all competitors in the industry? Analyze the effect of these environmental forces on the firm's operations and those of its competitors. Determine whether all firms in the industry are affected in the same way. Develop strategies to control or respond to these forces.

Answers to these questions form a basis for evaluating possible opportunities (or problems), which leads to another level of analysis: Do untapped growth opportunities exist? Are these opportunities in current market segments or in new markets? How much are these opportunities expected to contribute to sales and/or profits? Will the returns justify the investment cost?

Key Performance Criteria

A firm establishes performance criteria consistent with its mission and objectives. Typically, marketing managers are concerned with overall performance in five key areas as they apply to design and implementation of the marketing mix: profitability, activity, productivity, liquidity, and leverage. Each performance measure is described briefly.

- *Profitability* indicates the marketer's success or failure for a specified time period and is a measure of the portion of each dollar of sales or investment that the marketer can retain in the business.

- *Activity,* or *asset turnover,* is analyzed to determine how effectively the marketer is using resources, such as inventory and equipment, to generate sales revenues.

- Whereas *activity* refers to the effective use of assets, *productivity* refers to the efficient use of assets, such as plant capacity, advertising dollars, or personnel, to generate sales and profits.

- Performance criteria also include *liquidity,* which is the marketer's ability to pay maturing debts in the short term.

- *Leverage* is a measure of the relationship between the total value of assets used to operate the business and the amount actually owned by the investors. This ratio varies according to the marketer's operating philosophy and tolerance for risk.

Key Ratios and Their Implications

A firm's financial and accounting records contain readily available data for evaluating performance. It is important to remember, however, that it is the individual products, people, plans, and procedures that make the numbers in these financial ratios "happen."

Key ratios provide a convenient and easily interpreted method for evaluating marketing results. Examples of frequently used ratios are given next for the five key performance areas defined previously: profitability, activity, productivity, liquidity, and leverage. (See Figure 15.6.) Each ratio is calculated and briefly interpreted. Managers also would compare the resulting ratios (1) to industry averages to indicate this marketer's performance relative to competition and (2) to the firm's present and past ratios to determine whether performance is better or worse than in the previous period.

Profitability.   Regardless of the profitability measure that is used, the overriding issue is how to operate effectively (strategic viewpoint) and efficiently (operating plans and tactics). A key problem that arises in measuring profitability is deciding which measure to use. Profit, the amount of money left for the marketer after paying suppliers, employees, landlords, taxes, and all other expenses, is measured relative to other indicators, such as sales, assets, or the owners' equity (net worth). The following indicators of profitability are discussed here: (1) profit on sales, (2) rate of return on total assets, and (3) rate of return on net worth.

A hypothetical income statement and balance sheet are shown in Figure 15.7 to provide data for calculating the ratios below. The resulting ratios are briefly discussed and interpreted.

Profit on sales
Percentage of each dollar of revenue that a firm retains as profit.

The formula for **profit on sales** (net profit margin) is Net profit/net sales.

Calculation: $15,000/140,000 = 10.7$ percent

This ratio represents the percentage of each dollar of revenue that the firm retains as profit. In the example, the firm keeps nearly 11 cents of every dollar after paying all operating expenses. Assuming that the industry average is 9 percent, the firm's performance is above the industry average for this type of business. This may be attributed to a higher markup policy or lower operating costs compared with competitors.

FIGURE 15.6

Using Key Ratios to Evaluate Marketing Performance

1. Profitability:

> Profit on Sales
> Rate of Return on Total Assets
> Rate of Return on Net Worth
> Gross Margin Return on Inventory Investment

2. Activity:

> Inventory Turnover
> Asset Turnover
> Receivables Turnover
> Collection Period

3. Productivity:

> Space
> Personnel
> Accounts Payable to Sales

4. Liquidity:

> Current Ratio
> Quick Ratio
> Current Liabilities to Net Worth
> Current Liabilities to Inventory

5. Leverage:

> Total Assets to Net Worth (Equity)
> Debt to Equity (Net Worth)

Return on assets
Relates profits to the assets required to produce them.

The formula for rate of **return on assets** is Net profit/total assets.

Calculation: 15,000/220,000 = 6.8 percent

This ratio determines the payback on assets used to operate the business by relating profits to the assets required to produce them. For the marketing firm in our example, a total of $1 in assets (e.g., inventory, fixtures, equipment, property, etc.) is required to generate less than 7 cents in profit. In general, the larger this ratio, the better is the marketer's performance. Assuming that the industry average is 10 percent, the firm's return on assets is considerably less than the industry average. This ratio may be due to low sales revenues or to excessive or nonproductive assets.

Return on net worth
Payback on equity (amount the owners have invested in the business).

The formula for rate of **return on net worth** is Net profit/net worth.

Calculation: 15,000/60,000 = 25.0 percent

FIGURE 15.7

Income Statement and Balance Sheet Example

Income Statement			
Net Sales		$140,000	
Less Cost of Goods Sold	80,000		
Gross Margin	60,000		
Less Operating Expenses	45,000		
Net Profit (Before Taxes)		15,000	
Balance Sheet			
Assets			
Total Current Assets		$ 70,000	
Long-term Assets		150,000	
Total Assets			220,000
Liabilities and Owners Equity			
Total Current Liabilities		40,000	
Long-term Liabilities		120,000	
Total Liabilities			160,000
Owners' Equity (Net Worth)		60,000	
Total Liabilities and Owners' Equity			220,000

This ratio represents the payback on equity. The marketer in our example is receiving about 25 cents in profit for each dollar the owners have invested in the business. In general, a larger ratio is related to effective use of the owners' capital. Assuming that industry ratios indicate that return on net worth should be at least 15 percent, the company is performing above the industry average.

Activity. Ratios used to measure activity, or asset turnover, include (1) inventory turnover, (2) asset turnover, (3) receivables turnover, and (4) collection period.

The formula for **inventory turnover** is Cost of goods sold/average inventory at cost.

Inventory turnover
Number of times the average amount of inventory carried is completely sold out during a selling period.

Calculation: 80,000/32,000 = 2.5 times per year

This ratio represents the number of times that the average amount of inventory carried is completely sold out. In general, a stockturn that is too high or too low relative to the industry should be avoided. While high ratios are desirable, they may indicate inventory levels that are too low or ordering that is too frequent. Low ratios may indicate nonproductive or aging inventory. In our example, we assume that the company has an average investment in inventory of $32,000 at cost. If the industry average is 4 stockturns per year, the company is performing below the industry average, signaling a problem for this marketer. Note that the turnover ratio will be the same, whether sales and inventory are valued at cost or retail (net sales/average inventory at retail).

Asset turnover
Measure of marketer's efficiency in using all available assets to generate sales revenues.

The formula for **asset turnover** is Net sales/average total assets.

Calculation: 140,000/220,000 = 0.64 times

This ratio measures the marketer's efficiency in using all available assets to generate sales revenues. Ideally, the highest possible level of sales should be generated with the lowest possible investment in assets. If industry ratios indicate an average asset turnover of 1.5, then this firm's asset turnover of 0.64 times during a year is significantly lower than the industry average. This performance ratio indicates that the firm may have difficulty generating sales with available assets. If sales are lower than expected, analysis should identify nonproductive, inappropriate, or excessive assets.

Receivables turnover
Amount of credit purchases and length of time that customers take to pay for purchases.

The formula for **receivables turnover** is Net sales/average accounts receivable.

Calculation: 140,000/10,000 = 14 times per year

This ratio relates the amount of credit purchases and length of time that customers take to pay for purchases. When a customer purchases goods with credit rather than cash, inventory dollars are converted to accounts receivable. A high percentage of credit purchases will result in a low receivables turnover ratio and the need to finance operations from sources other than cash sales during the average collection period. In our example, if accounts receivable average $10,000, a receivables turnover ratio of 14 times per year means that credit customers take nearly 4 weeks to pay their accounts (52 weeks/14).

Collection period
Average number of days that customers take to pay their accounts.

The formula for **collection period** is (Accounts receivable/net sales) × 365.

Calculation: (10,000/140,000) × 365 = 26.1 days

The collection period is the average number of days that customers take to pay their accounts. This ratio, which is closely related to the receivables turnover calculated earlier, should be consistent with the company's credit terms. If the firm's collection period is much longer than average, this may indicate lenient credit policies or the desire to generate revenues from consumer debt. On the other hand, the marketer may need to have stricter policies for credit authorization and collection.

Productivity.   Productivity ratios may be calculated relative to space, personnel, customer transactions, and other factors. Performance measures used for illustration below include (1) space, that is, sales per square foot of selling space, (2) personnel, that is, selling payroll as a percent of net sales, and (3) accounts payable to sales.

Space productivity
Amount of sales per square foot of selling space (also may be expressed in linear or cubic feet).

The formula to determine **space productivity** is Net sales/square foot of selling space.

Calculation (based on 1100 square feet):   140,000/1100 = $127.27 per square foot

As the final link in the distribution channel for consumer goods, retailers are particularly interested in this ratio. The high cost of retail space has led to a focus on increased productivity in terms of sales per square foot (or linear foot, or cubic foot). This ratio may determine merchandise assortments and their location in a store. In our example, the $127.27 generated for each square foot of selling space would be examined relative to industry averages for the merchandise category or store type that it represents. When sales per square foot are higher than industry averages, the firm is using its space more productively than its competitors, on average. (Profit per square foot is another important productivity ratio. Calculation: Net profit/ square foot of selling space = $15,000/1100 = $13.64.)

The formula used to determine **personnel productivity** is Selling expense/ net sales.

Personnel productivity
Percentage of sales dollars used in payment and benefits given to sales and sales support personnel.

Calculation: 12,000/140,000 = 8.57 percent

Selling expenses may include all forms of payments and benefits given to the salesforce and sales support personnel. The ratio indicates the percentage of each dollar of sales that must be used to pay salaries, wages, commissions, and benefits to employees. Assuming selling expenses of $12,000 and an industry average of 7.5 percent (or 7½ cents of every sales dollar), then the firm's personnel productivity is slightly higher than the industry average, indicating the ability to compete effectively in this area.

The formula used to determine the productivity of **accounts payable to sales** is Accounts payable/net sales.

Accounts payable to sales
Percentage of each sales dollar owed to suppliers.

Calculation: 20,000/140,000 = 14.29 percent

This ratio represents the percentage of each sales dollar that is owed to suppliers. It demonstrates the degree to which sales figures are financed by other businesses. In our example, where accounts payable total $20,000, slightly over 14 cents of each dollar in sales must be used to pay these accounts. If the industry average is 25 percent, for example, the firm's accounts payable to sales ratio indicates that, on average, this marketer owes considerably less to other businesses than its competitors.

Liquidity.   Day-to-day operations are directly affected by the firm's degree of liquidity. Frequently used liquidity ratios are (1) current ratio, (2) quick ratio, (3) current liabilities to net worth, and (4) current liabilities to inventory.

The formula for the **current ratio** is Current assets/current liabilities.

Current ratio
Firm's ability to pay short-term debt (includes inventory).

Calculation: 70,000/40,000 = 1.75

The current ratio is a measure of the firm's ability to pay short-term debt. A ratio of 1.0 indicates that current liabilities equal current assets, which means that the firm should be able to meet its short-range obligations. A ratio of less than 1.0 indicates that liabilities exceed assets and that if the current liabilities are called, the firm cannot readily pay them. A ratio greater than 1.0 indicates the extent of the firm's assets beyond current debt. A benchmark ratio is 2:1; therefore, the marketer in our example has a relatively healthy current ratio. In general, a larger ratio is desirable, although it may suggest a very conservative attitude toward buying inventory and other assets on credit.

The formula for the **quick ratio** is (Current assets − inventory)/current liabilities or (Cash + marketable securities + receivables)/current liabilities.

Quick ratio
Firm's ability to pay short-term debt (excludes inventory).

Calculation: (70,000 − 32,000)/40,000 = 0.95

The quick ratio is similar to the current ratio, except that inventory is excluded from the calculation of assets. The rationale for this exclusion is that if assets need to be liquidated quickly to pay debt, they may need to be sold below the desired margin. Therefore, the real value of this asset may be questionable. In general, a benchmark ratio is 1:1, but the higher this ratio, the better is the marketer's position to pay current debt. In this example, the firm would be able to meet nearly all its creditors' demands for immediate payment on short notice.

Current liabilities to net worth
Relates short-term liabilities to owners' actual investment.

The formula for **current liabilities to net worth** is Current liabilities/net worth.

Calculation: 40,000/60,000 = 66.7 percent

This ratio relates short-term liabilities to the owners' actual investment in the business. In our example, for every dollar the owners have invested in the business, they owe nearly 67 cents to their creditors. In general, the higher the ratio, the greater is the financial risk associated with the firm. That is, creditors actually may own more of the business than the stockholders, placing the owners in a precarious position. The liabilities of the firm in our example should be at or above the industry average when compared with net worth.

Current liabilities to inventory
Relates short-term liabilities to retailer's investment in inventory.

The formula for **current liabilities to inventory** is Current liabilities/inventory.

Calculation: 40,000/32,000 = 1.25

This ratio relates short-term liabilities to the firm's investment in inventory. It is an indication of the company's dependence on inventory as a primary source of revenue to meet current debt. The firm in our example owes more than the amount of inventory that could be sold to cover the amount of current debt if creditors demanded immediate payment. Although prices could be lowered to generate the necessary cash, this would still be insufficient to cover the debt.

Leverage.   The relationship between a firm's assets and debt position can be evaluated with these ratios: (1) total assets to net worth (equity) and (2) debt to equity (net worth).

Total assets to net worth
Relates all of marketer's assets to owners' funds invested in the business.

The formula for determining **total assets to net worth** is Total assets/net worth.

Calculation: 220,000/60,000 = 3.67

This ratio relates all the firm's assets to net worth. It indicates the extent to which assets are financed out of the owners' funds rather than with debt. This performance measure is determined by the firm's capital structure decisions, which may involve growth strategies, tolerance for risk, and other factors. Assuming an industry average for this ratio of 2.0, the firm in our example has assets that are valued at nearly twice the amount invested in the business, that is, assets that are clear of all debt.

Debt to equity
Relates amount owed by the company to amount invested in the company by owners.

The formula for determining **debt to equity** is Total liabilities/net worth.

Calculation: 160,000/60,000 = 2.67

This ratio relates the amount owed by the company to the amount invested in the company by the owners. If this ratio is greater than 1.0, then creditors have a larger investment in the company than the owners. In our example, the marketer owes nearly three times as much as he or she owns. Assuming an industry ratio of 1.5, the company's operations are heavily financed with debt compared with its competitors.

Several key ratios are combined in the next section to illustrate their interaction in achieving target performance levels. They contain four critical factors that determine overall success in a marketing organization: sales, profits, assets, and net worth.

Strategic Profit Model: Framework for Analysis

The strategic profit model (SPM) provides an integrated framework that is useful for analyzing marketing performance. The SPM includes three ratios that were described in the preceding section: profitability, asset turnover, and leverage. These ratios relate net profits to net sales (return on sales), to total assets (return on assets), and to net worth (return on net worth or return on investment). Analysis of profitability, based on these measures or others, revolves around planning profit objectives and evaluating performance against plan. Figure 15.8 uses data from the preceding performance ratios to illustrate how the SPM can be used to evaluate operating results and the financing of capital expenditures. Calculations are based on the following relationship among ratios:

$$\text{(Net profit/net sales)} \times \text{(Net sales/total assets)} = \text{Return on total assets}$$
$$\text{(Total assets/net worth)} = \text{Financial leverage}$$
$$\text{(Return on total assets} \times \text{financial leverage)} = \text{Return on net worth}$$

SPM ratios are used to illustrate the effect of growth objectives on key performance measures. High-quality, accurate data must be used to calculate these ratios if

FIGURE 15.8

SPM Analysis of Capital Expenditures and Operating Results

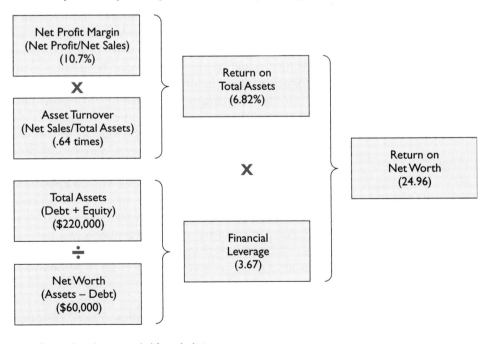

Note: Figures have been rounded for calculation.

they are to provide a sound basis for marketing management decisions. The growth orientation of the marketer and the nature of competition have a major impact on determining and achieving profit goals.

Data Sources and Quality

The marketer's information system (see Chapter 4) generally contains the data and tools necessary to analyze present operations and future opportunities: the database, statistical and mathematical models, qualitative analysis, and the interpretation and conclusions from prior analysis. Statistical and mathematical models are useful for objectively describing, estimating, and predicting events and behavior. Qualitative analysis, although more subjective, can provide in-depth explanations of attitudes and behavior. Whether or not the results of analysis are really useful depends on both the quality of data inputs and management's ability to interpret and apply the findings.

At this point it is important to consider the sources and quality of data used in measuring marketing performance. Since the quality of data is directly related to their accuracy and suitability for the type of analysis needed, the data sources must be chosen carefully. As noted previously, data can be obtained from both primary and secondary information sources. These sources may be either internal or external to the company.

Secondary Data Sources.   *External secondary data* are gathered by someone else for another purpose, making it difficult for marketing managers to control their quality or apply them to new situations. Frequently used sources include U.S. government surveys and documents, industry reports, and trade association data. Government data may be obtained from a wide variety of sources, such as the U.S. Census reports of population at the federal, state, and local levels, and publications that report industry trade data, Commerce Department statistics, and many others. Publications such as Dun & Bradstreet and Standard & Poor's, provide useful data for comparing a company's results with those of its competitors. Trade associations generally disseminate trade-related data to industry members, such as the semiconductor or restaurant industry. Performance ratios, based on aggregate industry statistics, provide a benchmark for evaluating a company's performance compared with the industry. Other indicators of industry performance for large and small firms may be available from books, films and periodicals, or special seminars.

Internal secondary data can be used to identify the existing problems and provide information for daily operations. The marketing decision support system (MDSS), described earlier in this book, should contain high-quality, useful data that apply to both internal and external management concerns.

Operating statements, customer billings, purchase orders, employee records, and other company data are generated routinely as a part of day-to-day business operations or for a specific purpose. They are readily available for marketing management decisions. Operating statements contain a record of the company's profits and losses, cost of goods sold, expenditures, and other accounting and financial indicators of good and bad performance. For example, a decrease in profits may be due to an increase in costs, a decrease in sales, or both. Historical data also can be obtained from operating statements to use as inputs in sales forecasts or for projecting future performance goals. Note that although past data can provide a useful basis for evaluating performance, they should not dictate future strategies.

MARKETING IN THE INFORMATION AGE

Evaluating Advertising Effectiveness: Art or Science?

Advertising effectiveness is an elusive aspect of marketing program evaluation. Financial analysts emphasize the expected value that can be created by a major capital investment (e.g., factory, machinery), generally by making a direct link to the cash flows that it creates. The value of the investment is determined by making assumptions about the most likely economic profit (net income minus charge for invested equity capital) and return on investment.

In advertising, it is difficult to make a direct link between a dollar invested and a dollar earned, because customers are influenced by many other factors. John Wanamaker, a pioneer U.S. retailer, made this classic statement, "Half the money I spend on advertising is wasted; the trouble is, I don't know which half." In spite of the progress made in modern financial analysis, many of the largest companies are not sure whether the hundreds of millions of dollars invested in advertising each year ($100 billion in 2001) are directly creating value for shareholders. These companies would not make major capital investments without first estimating the most likely financial return, but find it difficult to conduct the same type of analysis for advertising. Brand managers often use "rules of thumb, intuition, or other incomplete frameworks" to guide advertising decisions.

Mergy and Lade propose a methodology to identify tangible links between proposed advertising strategies and shareholder value: a strategy-driven resource allocation process that uses economic profit (EP) as the financial metric. This approach provides an in-depth understanding of the most likely return on advertising investment, and considers all costs involved in executing an advertising strategy versus the profits it generates. Marketers can avoid overestimating a brand's contribution to shareholder value by considering all expenses that go into creating gains from advertising. Calculating reliable numbers for anticipated changes in revenue and economic profit is the most difficult part of the "return on advertising" methodology. A six-step process can help marketers choose the best strategy for maximizing long-term economic profit.

Step 1. What is the brand's overall profitability? Many companies do not measure the profitability of individual brands sufficiently to answer the question, "How much of the share price (in $/share) can be attributed to a specific brand?" Profitability is measured at the operating income level, but expenses such as shared overhead, sales force time, and other specific costs are not attributed to the brand at this level. Therefore, it may be necessary to develop a new income statement and balance sheet under different sets of assumptions when developing a new advertising strategy. For example, the level and allocation of salesforce time for a brand might reveal that a so-called "profitable niche" is actually the company's most unprofitable brand. Advertising strategies can be reevaluated to address the identified problems, and maximize economic profit for each brand, and whether to maintain, cut, or increase the current level of advertising investment.

Step 2. Which segments are profitable? An in-depth calculation of return on advertising includes an analysis of the most profitable market segments as measured by type of distribution channel, geography, and customer characteristics. Knowledge of the profitability of each segment helps in ranking its attractiveness, in developing strategies to capitalize on strengths and minimize weaknesses, and in focusing a revised advertising campaign.

Step 3. What are the alternative strategies? Marketers typically propose a single ad strategy and try to obtain funding for it, which does not always create the highest value. Brand managers can propose several alternative advertising campaigns, each with a different focus, objectives, marketing tactics, and level of investment. The best option(s) can be narrowed down by using

(continued)

quantitative strategic and financial analysis, emphasizing maximum economic profit.

Step 4. What's it worth? The value created by the campaign is determined by potential revenue and projected costs. Estimating potential revenue for each campaign alternative is more difficult than estimating costs, but revenue can be calculated using available techniques such as historical analysis and scoring analysis. *Historical analysis* uses a direct estimate of advertising elasticity (increase in volume/change in expenditures) if sufficient data are available. The likelihood of customers switching from one brand to another can also be estimated. *Scoring analysis* uses three market-based variables to predict response to an advertising campaign: customer perception; competitive intensity; and demographic density.

Step 5. Calculating the return on advertising investment. The completed quantitative analysis of each of the proposed ad strategies is used to estimate the economic profit from each advertising strategy. This procedure is similar to the net present value method of valuing investments, but seldom used for investments in advertising. Calculation for each alternative would follow this format: [Cash in (revenue) from each proposed alternative] = [likely effectiveness of the ad campaign (i.e., elasticity)] × [proposed level of investment].

Step 6. Refine strategic alternatives. Attaching numbers to investment alternatives can give insights about how to optimize the strategies to improve returns. Methods, such as sensitivity analysis, can be used to identify the investment with the highest return by inputting different media or levels of investments, for example. While precise measurements cannot be obtained for all aspects of return on advertising calculations, marketers can estimate the expected return more accurately and with better-informed judgment about an ad strategy's ability to create value. The financial model can also be used to track performance, and determine how well a chosen strategy delivers the desired results.

Use of the economic profit process for calculating return on investment in advertising may be time consuming, but it has several advantages: ability to quantify the costs and benefits of different levels of investment in advertising; recognition of costs incurred to achieve potential gains from an ad; and a clear, common metric that can be used as the basis for comparison not only with other ad campaigns, but also with investments in other areas of the business.

Source: Lee Mergy and D. Stewart Lade, "Demystifying Advertising Investments," *Journal of Business Strategy* (November/December 2001), pp. 18–22.

Employee records may include information concerning work schedules, job productivity, training, sales reports, and feedback from customers. These data can be used to identify specific divisions or personnel that represent the best and worst sales performance or highest costs or to make decisions about retention or training programs.

Customer records provide a company with data about its target market (who and where their customers are, what and when they buy, how much they buy, and how they pay for their purchases). This information is useful for market analysis, communications strategies, and other marketing decisions throughout all phases of a marketing program. The type of customer information needed for decision making should be determined in advance by management, and an effective system should be developed for data gathering, recording, and analysis.

Problems with the Use of Secondary Data Sources. Although secondary data are easily obtained and valuable in analyzing marketing situations, managers should be aware of three potential problems associated with the use of secondary sources: (1) units of measurement, (2) class definitions, and (3) publication currency.[15]

1. *Units of measurement.* Although secondary data may be available on the subject being analyzed, they may not be the same as needed for the current situation. For example, the size of a company can be reported in terms of annual sales, profits, or number of employees. If the marketer is interested in comparing sales for one specific product category with its competitors but only has data on total business results, a satisfactory comparison cannot be made. The income of consumers in a particular market may be expressed according to an individual, family, household, or spending unit. A marketer who targets young singles would not find income data meaningful if it were only reported for family units. The unit of measurement must be consistent with the marketer's needs if it is to be useful.

2. *Class definition.* Data may be available in the right units of measurement for the present problem but may not be provided in categories or "class boundaries" that are useful for the marketer's needs. The marketer who wants to compare sales in one trading area of a city with those of competition may have an internal sales database by customers' zip codes, but secondary data may only be available in voting districts or city precincts. Consumer income data for a market may be available for single individuals in increments of $15,000 (0 to $14,999, $15,000 to $29,999, etc.), but the marketer's analysis may require increments of $10,000 (0 to $9999, $10,000 to $19,999, etc.). In these cases, the class definition would be inappropriate, and modifications would diminish the precision of the data used in analysis.

3. *Currency of information.* Although most marketing decisions require up-to-date information, there may be several years between data collection and publication or dissemination. This is particularly true for most government census data and other public data that may be published only every 5 or 10 years. Proprietary data may not be available to outside parties for some period of time, if at all. Rapid shifts in markets, movement of competitors in and out of the market, shifting economic indicators, and other changes in the marketer's environment require current data for analysis. In this case, the only alternative may be to collect primary data.

Criteria for Judging the Accuracy of Secondary Data.   Criteria for determining the accuracy or precision of data include an assessment of (1) the source used, (2) the purpose of publication, and (3) general evidence of quality.[16]

1. *The source used.* Errors may be found in data-collection methods, analysis, and reporting. Secondary sources often obtain data previously gathered from other sources. For example, *The Statistical Abstract of the United States* is a widely used secondary source of secondary data obtained from other government and trade sources. Copying data from one place to another may result in inaccuracies or misinterpretation, making it advisable to consult and evaluate the primary source where the data were first published. Only the primary source of secondary data can provide general evidence of the quality of the research.

2. *The purpose of publication.* One indication of the accuracy of data is related to the purpose of the publication in which they appear. The data may be of questionable quality if they are published by a source that is selling something,

promoting private interests or one side of a controversial issue, or is not identi-fied. Thus it is advisable to determine the motives of the publication's sponsors.

3. *General evidence regarding quality.* The original data source should present the data in context and with fewer errors. Evidence of quality includes the rep-utation of the research group, the organization's ability to collect the data, appropriateness of the sample, method of data collection and analysis, qualifica-tions and training of personnel who gathered the data, extent of nonresponse and other sources of bias, and presentation, as in the accuracy and organization of results.

Primary Data Sources.   Since the analysis of operating results depends mainly on secondary data, a discussion of primary data collection methods is beyond the scope of this chapter. However, there is a relationship between primary data sources and the original design of the marketer's information system. Issues to be addressed within the context of primary data collection include the requirements and format for data concerning sales records, operating costs, capital expenditures, personnel, and other important data. When deciding between secondary and pri-mary data sources, it is important first for a marketing manager to know the specific problems that need to be solved and the questions that need to be answered with the data that are readily available.

Primary data have the advantage of providing timely, in-depth answers to ques-tions that secondary data cannot address satisfactorily. Primary data may be as com-plex as a comprehensive market research study conducted to determine customer response to changes in a product line or as simple as "want lists" created in re-sponse to customer requests. Warranty cards, responses to promotional efforts (such as direct mail, couponing, special offers), and other forms of direct communi-cation with customers also provide valuable primary data.

Grocery retailers obtain volumes of data from store "loyalty" cards that are is-sued to their customers for check-cashing identification and other purposes. Re-searchers examined the use of these cards in the United Kingdom in terms of their commercial effectiveness and as a way to measure and evaluate retail grocers' per-formance.[17] Loyalty cards are part of a strategy aimed at maximizing the potential of the retailers' customer base. The goal is to increase both the number of shopping trips and the amount spent per trip. Loyalty is determined by quantified sales meas-ures and consumer panel data. From these data, retailers can analyze customers' pur-chases and other store-related behavior for different levels of store loyalty. The results are useful for profiling and targeting selected market segments and for assessing response to marketing efforts.

Good-quality primary data can be obtained from professional research firms and subscription services for a fee and/or on a contractual basis. However, the marketer has the most control over data quality when using primary sources. Primary data can be evaluated against most of the criteria described for judging the accuracy, quality, and usefulness of secondary data.

Summary

Marketing must be both effective and efficient; therefore, the focus in this chapter is on the need for accountability in marketing operations. The emphasis is on performance and the need for strategic control of marketing efforts at the business-unit level. An evaluation of a firm's marketing performance starts with an understanding of the managerial process and the role that measurement of results plays in that process and the achievement of profitability and productivity targets. Performance measurement is an integral part of the strategic planning and marketing planning processes, including control, coordination, and value creation.

The control process includes an identification of the key issues to be measured or controlled, performance standards and measures, assessment and reassessment, and correcting identified problems or weaknesses. The control process should be continuous and coordinated across all functional areas and should consider the economic value added by each business unit.

Performance evaluation occurs at all levels of an organization: corporate, business, and functional (operating). Measurement of marketing performance is concerned primarily with all relevant elements of the marketing mix, with a great deal of attention paid to integrated marketing communications. It is also useful to evaluate the performance of other functional areas (e.g., accounting, human resources, operations) as they impact marketing outcomes.

The key questions to be answered in measuring performance are: What is (or is not) working? Why are the strategies working (or not working)? Have marketing strategies been implemented according to plan? Likewise, analysis includes an assessment of competition and the firm's environment. Key performance criteria include measures of profitability, activity, productivity, liquidity, and leverage. Ratio analysis of data in each category provides the marketer with information about the firm's position relative to the industry and its own past performance. The strategic profit model (SPM) is an integrated framework that is useful for planning and analyzing marketing strategies. Profitability, asset turnover, and leverage are the primary ratios used to analyze performance.

The sources and quality of data used to measure performance have a significant impact on the quality of analysis that can be performed. Considerable secondary data are available from either internal or external sources, gathered by another party for another purpose. Problems with the use of secondary data are related to units of measurement, class definition, and currency of information. Criteria for judging the accuracy of secondary data include the source used, the purpose of the publication, and general evidence of quality. Primary data (gathered for the present purpose) have the advantage of being timely and providing in-depth answers and quality control.

Questions

1. Describe the managerial process. Explain the relationship between the managerial process and (a) profitability and productivity and (b) strategic planning.

2. Describe the elements of the control process used to measure marketing performance in a typical firm.

3. Discuss the types of operating results that typically are analyzed at the corporate (strategic), business, and functional (operating) levels of a business. Give specific examples, and indicate why you believe each is useful for making and evaluating marketing management decisions.

4. Describe the relationship between an analysis of the macro- and micro-environments and an analysis of each of the functional areas at the operating level. Include specific applications for the following:

   a. Product mix (sales forecasting, pricing strategy, buying, inventory control)

   b. Integrated communications mix (all aspects of the promotional mix)

   c. Operations (productivity, risk management)

d. Accounting and control (MDSS inputs and use)

e. Human resources (personnel data)

5. A product manager in an electronics manufacturing firm decides to add a line of new, high-tech, high-priced items to the product line. Although this line generally would compete at regular price with comparable brands in the higher-priced home electronics line, the manager plans to enter the market with a penetration pricing strategy to gain volume and market share from competitors. Explain how this decision will impact other functional areas of the business and be affected by them.

6. Marketers must answer a series of questions for a comprehensive evaluation of their overall performance. List these questions, and explain how each is helpful in an analysis of a company's performance results. Compared with a large company, would it be useful for a small company to seek answers to these same questions in evaluating marketing performance? Defend your answer.

7. Discuss the problems that may be encountered when using secondary sources of information for managerial decisions. What criteria can be used to determine the accuracy of secondary data? If the data are published in a reputable publication, is that a guarantee of their accuracy? Why or why not?

8. When is it appropriate to collect primary data? Give a specific example relative to computer software that is targeted to both final consumers and organizational buyers. Assume that the marketer wants to enter new markets with the company's software. Suggest several sources of external secondary data that may be helpful in making the right decision, as well as potential sources of internal secondary data. Give specific examples of how each source can be used for additional insights.

Exercises

1. Review current business media to determine any changes that have occurred in the business operations or industries of the market leaders described in this book. If any of these companies has experienced significant successes or failures, analyze the reasons for these changes.

2. Describe each of the key performance criteria that were discussed in this chapter. Obtain an annual report or other financial statements from a marketing firm and calculate as many of these ratios as possible with available data. Be sure to include each of the following criteria: profitability, activity, productivity, liquidity, and leverage. Compare the results with published industry ratios (see comparative ratios that can be found in Dun's Industry Ratios, Robert Morris, The Almanac of Financial Ratios, or other sources). Interpret your findings in terms of the success of this company's performance relative to the entire industry. Should corporate ethics and social responsibility be measured? If so, how?

3. Using the financial statement(s) that provided the basis for analysis in Exercise 2, analyze the results within the context of the strategic profit model, focusing on each of the individual ratios (profitability, asset turnover, leverage) as well as the return on investment (ROI) calculated for the entire model. Suggest some ways that the resulting ROI figure could be increased by management decisions with regard to any or all components of the strategic profit model.

Endnotes

1. Jagdish N. Sheth and Rajendra S. Sisodia, "Improving Marketing Productivity," in Jeffrey Heilbrun (ed.): *Marketing Encyclopedia: Issues and Trends Shaping the Future* (Chicago: American Marketing Association, 1995), p. 218.

2. *Ibid.,* p. 219.

3. Mary J. Pitzer, Michael Oneal, and Tim Smart, "How Three Master Merchants Fell from Grace," *Business Week* (March 16, 1987), pp. 38–40; Target Corporation, Hoovers Online, www.hoovers.com; Mervyn's, Hoovers Online, www.hoovers.com.

4. Sheth and Sisodia, *op. cit.,* pp. 221–223.

5. *Ibid.,* pp. 223–236.

6. David A. Aaker, *Strategic Market Management*, 5th ed. (New York: John Wiley & Sons, 1998), pp. 119–120; Gabriel Hawawini and Claude Viallet, *Finance for Executives: Managing for Value Creation* (Cincinnati, OH: South-Western Publishing Co., 2002), pp. 30–31, 505–507.

7. David A. Aaker, *op. cit.,* p. 120.

8. "America's Most Admired Companies," *Fortune* (March 4, 2002), pp. 64–86.

9. Robert H. Waterman, Jr., *The Renewal Factor: How the Best Get and Keep the Competitive Edge* (New York: Bantam Books, 1987).

10. Peter Galuszka, Ellen Neuborne, and Wendy Zeller, "P&G's Hottest New Product: P&G," *Business Week* (October 5, 1998), pp. 92, 96; Marianne K. McGee, "P&G Jump-Starts Corporate Change," *InternetWeek* (November 1, 1999), pp. 30–31.

11. Tim Ambler, "Why Is Marketing Not Measuring Up?" *Marketing* (September 24, 1998), pp. 24–25; "What We Do: Client Testimonials," *Marketing Metrics*, www.marketingmetrics.com (November 15, 2002).

12. Paul E. Green, Abba M. Krieger, and Terry G. Vavra, "Evaluating New Products," *Marketing Research* (Winter 1997), pp. 12–21; Terry G. Vavra, Paul E.

Green, and Abba M. Krieger, "Evaluating EZPass," *Marketing Research* (Summer 1999), pp. 5–13, 16.

13. For additional discussion of marketing decision tools, see Gary L. Lilien, Philip Kotler, and K. Sridhar Moorthy, *Marketing Models*, Upper Saddle River, NJ: Prentice Hall (1992); Gary L. Lilien and Arvind Rangaswamy, *Marketing Engineering: Computer-Assisted Marketing Analysis and Planning* (Reading, MA: Addison-Wesley, 1998); and Gary L. Lilien and Arvind Rangaswamy, *Marketing Management and Strategy: Marketing Engineering Applications*, Reading, MA: Addison-Wesley (1999).

14. John R. Graham, "Ways to Evaluate Your Marketing Program," *Nation's Restaurant News* (March 23, 1998), pp. 32, 62.

15. Gilbert A. Churchill, *Marketing Research: Methodological Foundations*, 4th ed., (New York: Dryden Press, 1987); also see Joseph F. Hair, Jr., Robert P. Bush, and David J. Ortinau, *Marketing Research: A Practical Approach for the New Millenium* (Boston, MA: Irwin McGraw-Hill, 2000), pp. 91–99.

16. *Ibid.*

17. Judith Passingham, "Grocery Retailing and the Loyalty Card," *Market Research Society* (January 1998), pp. 55–63.

MARKETING MANAGEMENT IN ACTION: CLOSING CASE

The "Kraft-ing" of Mattel into a More Stable Toy Company

Robert A. Eckert, CEO of Mattel Inc., faces the challenge of how to achieve consistent long-term growth from the fickle—and often volatile—toy business. The success of the largest toy manufacturers in the industry relies "on the whims of customers too young to use a credit card, or even cut their own food with a knife." If the company is lucky in choosing the "next hot thing," kids all over the world—and the company's stockholders—will be happy. If not, there will be a large inventory of markdowns, and no one will be happy.

Mattel, the world's largest toymaker with nearly $5 billion in revenues, has a strong incentive for more consistent performance. It is the company that "sells a perfectly shaped Barbie [doll] some-

where in the world every three seconds." Beyond the Barbie line, Mattel products include Fisher-Price toys, Hot Wheels and Matchbox cars, American Girl dolls and books, and popular licensed items. In spite of its many successes, Mattel suffered some disasters over the past several decades. The most recent blow to the company's bottom line was the acquisition of the money-losing Learning Co., a computer-game company purchased under the previous CEO, Jill Barad. In addition to the ups and downs experienced by the company under Barad's leadership in the 1990s, other major events have had a negative impact on Mattel's performance. Founder Ruth Handler was forced out due to an accounting scandal in the 1970s; and

Mattel was nearly forced into bankruptcy by the demise of the video-game market in the early 1980s.

Eckert, the former head of Philip Morris Co.'s Kraft Foods Inc. division, believes he can improve the stability and predictability of Mattel's business. In his $2^1/_2$ years with the company, Eckert is on the way to achieving his goal of reducing the guesswork that goes into selling toys that can be profitable year after year. He is accomplishing this objective largely by adapting the strategic approaches used by consumer product companies (such as Kraft).

Eckert's divestitures of the Learning Co., plus cost-cutting measures, improved the company's profitability in the short run. Mattel lost $431 million in 2000, but 2002 net income was estimated at $459 million. Without Learning Co., revenues dropped to an estimated $4.7 billion in 2000, down from $5.6 billion in 1998. As of the end of 2002, Mattel's stock price was double the low of $9 in March 2000.

Other strategic changes to improve Mattel's long-term performance include developing more toys in-house; becoming less dependent on licensed properties; improving inventory control; and pursuing strong overseas expansion. Eckert anticipates that these changes will result in the steady growth that an investor could expect at a consumer products company. However, a conservative approach may be a problem if it causes the company to miss a blockbuster toy that will gain significant sales and market share in the shorter run. According to T. K. MacKay, an analyst at Morningstar, "This strategy increases the risk that Mattel could underproduce popular toys." Eckert appears to be willing to take the risk.

Eckert's strategy appears to be paying off. One example is Mattel's approach to managing the Harry Potter toys in the 2001 Christmas holiday season, in contrast to the handling of *Star Wars* merchandise by its archrival Hasbro Inc. Mattel took a conservative approach by producing a much smaller number of items than it had for previous major movie tie-ins. Sales of Harry Potter merchandise reached $160 million, 30 percent more than forecast. The results led Warner Bros. Inc., the licensor, to sign Mattel to a 5 year agreement to produce toys for new movie and TV versions of *Batman* and other favorites. In comparison, Hasbro made a

major commitment to produce toys tied to the *Star Wars* sequels. A blowout *Star Wars* introduction resulted in expensive licensing fees, and sales that were below expectations. As a result of the fallout from this venture, Hasbro decided to emphasize its core brands and stay away from expensive licensing deals.

Eckert's international expansion strategy is also similar to that of a consumer goods company: when the U.S. market is mature, take your product overseas. To implement this strategy, products are released simultaneously worldwide, and packages are inscribed with multiple languages. The outcome is higher sales and lower costs per product introduction. For example, Mattel ran a big advertising campaign for its Hot Wheels brand in Spain, and achieved a 50 percent increase in its share of the toy market there. In the third quarter of 2002, overseas sales increased by 17 percent. Eckert's goal is to raise the percentage of Mattel's sales from international business to 50 percent from the present 31 percent.

Mattel's brand extensions are another adaptation of consumer products company strategies. Mattel's flagship product, Barbie, suffered a 6 percent drop in the first three quarters of 2002. Although Barbie dolls and related items generated $1.5 billion in annual sales, new Barbies are constantly introduced to the market, such as the Rapunzel Barbie, introduced for the Christmas 2002 holiday season. The Barbie name also has been licensed for eyewear.

Mattel reorganized shipping schedules for 2002 holiday selling, by shipping toys later in the year to ensure they would be on store shelves during the peak holiday selling period. In 2001, many stores had to mark down Holiday Barbies that were received in their inventory as early as July. In another move, Mattel is selling through its own catalog and Internet sales to become less reliant on its largest retail customers—Wal-Mart, Toys "R" Us, and Target.

Mattel is not averse to the "next big thing," but wants to minimize the risk of making the wrong choice, through long-term contracts or by early identification of a potentially hot property to avoid expensive licensing bidding wars. Two successful opportunities that were identified early are the rights to *Yu-Gi-Oh!* (monster-themed Japanese television show) before it became popular, and a long-term licensing contract with Nickelodeon for first rights to the popular *SpongeBob SquarePants*.

Eckert also established a development group within the company, Project Platypus, that introduced Ello, a "whimsically shaped construction set for girls."

Robert Eckert is considering the next steps that need to be taken to accomplish his goal of making Mattel Inc. a more stable and predictable business. As he evaluates the results of past performance and considers future opportunities, he is inspired by many options.

Source: Christopher Palmeri, "Mattel's New Toy Story," *BusinessWeek* (November 18, 2002), pp. 72, 74; www.mattel.com; Hoovers Online, www.hoovers.com.

Case Study Questions

1. Describe the relationship between the control and measurement of marketing performance at Mattel, Inc. and the managerial process depicted in Figure 15.1.

2. Determine the key variables that Robert Eckert should analyze when evaluating the results of his strategic decisions, and explain why each is important.

3. Give specific examples of the performance measures that you would use to evaluate Mattel's performance. Justify your answer.

4. Explain how elements of the marketing mix (product, price, place/distribution, IMC) can be evaluated, using the Hot Wheels campaign in Spain as an example.

5. List the questions that Mr. Eckert must answer to obtain the type and quality of data he needs to evaluate performance at the business unit level. Answer each question based on information provided in the case. (Optional: additional information may be obtained from outside research.)

6. Prepare a list of your specific recommendations for Mattel's marketing strategy for the next 2 years (that you will present to Mr. Eckert). Include a detailed plan for implementation.

CHAPTER 16

The Marketing-Oriented Organization

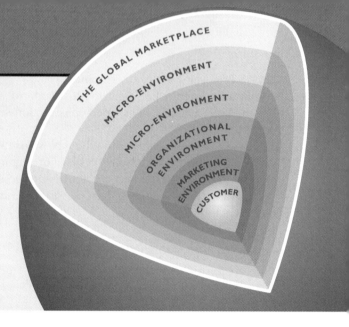

Overview

We know how to invest in technology and machinery, but we're at a loss when it comes to investing in human capital.[1]

Virtual Firms Win Respect

Public relations professionals and clients say that virtual public relations (PR) agencies, which have existed for about a decade, have tremendous advantages over the traditional office-based agency. An example is PerkettPR Inc., a virtual firm since its founding in 1998. PerkettPR employs a network of seven account executives working from their homes in Massachusetts, Colorado, and Michigan. For the most part, they communicate with each other, with clients, and with colleagues via phone, fax, and the Internet. Founder and president Chris Perkett says, "We are about one quarter less (expensive) than the cost of a traditional agency." She says her experiences working for a large PR agency in the Northeast made her realize that many agencies simply spend too much money "on making the office cool and classy."

No one tracks the total number of virtual agencies, but virtual agency directors say their business model is gaining acceptance because of results. To avoid being labelled as merely a loose coalition of freelancers, some virtual firms are insisting that their account executives work only for them and refuse work from outside the firm's client list. Dick Grove is CEO of virtual firm INK Inc., whose 20 employees work from home offices scattered from London to New York to San Francisco. Grove says, "The real key to a virtual agency is you can keep overhead lower and pass that savings on to your clients."

"I would say that on average the client (of a virtual firm) can save anywhere from 15 percent to 40 percent," says Neal Leavitt, president of Leavitt Communications Inc., which has used a virtual organization format since its founding in 1991. "We were paying exorbitant fees to traditional agencies," says Claire Collins, PR manager for nCipher Corp. Ltd., a PerkettPR client. Collins notes she gets the same level of quality in her PR representations since switching to a virtual firm. And, when choosing a new firm in the summer of 2001, Collins says, "It was not important to us to see what kind of desks they had or what their lobby looked like to gauge the level of their work as PR professionals."

Executives at virtual PR firms say they are gaining acceptance because they are successfully sharing information and working as a team via the Internet. PerkettPR uses a service called Salesnet.com to help centralize and organize the firm's prospective client lists. Their account executives can log on to Salesnet.com from their home offices (or other remote locations) anytime and monitor the status of prospective client contacts to avoid overlap. Perkett also finds that monthly e-mail newsletters are effective at keeping her far-flung group working together as a team. Her newsletter features links to pertinent trade magazine stories, descriptions of successful PR tactics by fellow employees, and a "get to know your colleagues" section where they share information on backgrounds and current interests. Of course, virtual firms rely heavily on conference telephone calls for creative team brainstorming, and Perkett says she can show her team any file on her computer while the conference call is in progress, including full Powerpoint presentations.

Source: Steve Jarvis, "Virtual Firms Win Respect for Performance, Savings," *Marketing News* (July 8, 2002), pp. 4–5.

A s the PerkettPR scenario indicates, the adoption of a marketing-oriented viewpoint has profoundly affected the way many firms organize and operate. The impact is visible at every level, from chief executive to marketing trainee, and is seen to some degree in every facet of a firm's activities. We see it in finance, in research and development (R&D), in manufacturing, and of course, in sales. Peter Drucker, the universally acclaimed guru of management thinkers, has said that the purpose of a business is "to create a customer." He also stated that marketing is "a central dimension of the entire business."[2]

THE MARKETING ORGANIZATION'S STRUCTURE

We could say that a marketing organization is one that views its whole business according to its basic function—satisfying the customer. Concern and responsibility for marketing therefore must permeate all areas of the enterprise, and carrying out the marketing task is the responsibility of the entire company, because satisfying customers is everybody's job.[3] However, at each management level, the marketing tasks are slightly different.[4]

The Role of Technology

Technology offers marketers leverage as they reorganize (for current trends) and can help integrate diverse activities, notes Michael Krauss in a recent article. He wondered if there were guidelines for how to organize a marketing firm, because of all the possible ways to design the organization: by product groups, like Palm handheld digital assistants; by brands, like Intel; by product categories, like detergents; by markets, as some firms target small business; by geography, like regional offices; by function, like customer relations and market research; or by customer groups, like P&G's marketing unit just for Wal-Mart.

Krauss doesn't offer specific guidelines. However, based on discussions with Professor Sawhney of Northwestern's J.L. Kellogg Graduate School of Management, he suggests several elements. Customers must be the first consideration, as in the organization of IBM Global Services. But Sawhney also notes that overlay organizational structures, such as a matrix, should be retained because they offer benefits in servicing customers. Third, groupware technology, knowledge management techniques, and other information technology (IT) systems should link decision making to again place customers at the center of all the organization's activities. Sawhney then suggests reinforcing structure through evaluation methods and compensation, because people should be rewarded based on how the customer account does. Lastly, Sawhney suggests that people are the real mechanisms through which links are established.[5]

A recent report by Coopers & Lybrand, Inc. indicated that "Strategic marketing, marketing strategies, and marketing plans which help corporations hold or develop a competitive advantage have become paramount management challenges and major unresolved business issues."[6] According to the head of one executive search firm, clients are increasingly asking to locate chief executive officer (CEO) candidates with "savvy, marketing skills, and vision." John Bassler noted that "profitability-minded boards of directors want CEOs who can establish a strong customer focus and marketing strategy and to clearly communicate it to all reporting managers throughout the company."[7]

Top managers determine the kind and size of company theirs should be. In the very broadest sense, the CEO must answer this question: "Who is our customer, and how do we satisfy him or her—now and in the future?" By defining the customer, it is possible to plan to provide specific goods and services designed to satisfy the targeted groups. Top management can determine which ventures to support and which to abandon. We refer to these kinds of marketing-oriented decisions as *corporate strategic planning*.

The company's top management also gives specific marketing-oriented direction to those at lower levels in the company so that these people can develop appropriate marketing strategies and tactics to carry out the company's mission. Top management establishes objectives for its various divisions. It also may set policies that will guide operating people in making lower-level decisions. Finally, of course, top management establishes an organization capable of carrying out the company's mission and objectives as well as creating a climate conducive to effective performance. To illustrate how important this kind of leadership can be to a company, consider the situation at Club Med Inc. Club Med Inc. was a company that grew dramatically in its early years as a result of the unique operating formula established at its vacation club locations. However, when faced with the reality of a rapidly changing market during the 1990s, the company recruited for its president's office Phillippe Bourguignon. Bourguignon had been CEO of Euro Disney SCA, where he had turned a loss situation into a profit maker in a little more than 2 years.[8]

The Role of Divisional Management

In decentralized companies, the second tier of management often is called the *divisional level*. The divisional level may be an entire company, such as a subsidiary of a large parent corporation. In smaller firms, the second level might be a group of similar products managed by a divisional vice-president. Regardless of nomenclature, a hierarchy exists, and this next-lower management level has a specific marketing role.

The division manager is responsible for developing a long-range marketing strategy consistent with the company's mission—one that will achieve the objectives assigned to the division. Marketing is a most important element in a division's overall plan. The marketing strategy is aimed at a particular group of potential customers (usually labeled a *market segment*). It entails decision making in the four critical areas of marketing management: products, distribution, communications, and pricing. Manufacturing plans, financial plans, and work force plans also are needed. But the principal thrust of a division's program is almost always marketing, because the basic purpose of a company—its very reason for existing—is to develop customers and provide customer satisfaction. Obviously, a marketing strategy is not developed until exhaustive research concerning the consumer, the competition, and all the other external influences has been completed.

> **Strategic business units (SBUs)**
> Operate more or less independently to reach established goals by manufacturing and supplying a product (or product line) to a distinctive market segment that differs from the market served by the remainder of the firm.

As companies have grown, especially through acquisition or by diversification, it has become useful to define another level of strategic management. Within the division or business group there may exist **strategic business units (SBUs).** These business units are operated more or less like individual businesses, and their managers have considerable authority over the manner in which they seek to achieve their objectives. This is the level of management where specific decisions are made about the products or services to be offered and the markets to be served. If an SBU has more than one product or market, it may organize itself around these products and markets. It may have several products/markets in its portfolio of offerings. These products/markets usually are directed by middle managers known as *product* or *market managers.* Although these managers do not have as far-reaching authority as do division or even SBU managers, they often are responsible for developing strategies for the entire marketing program, including those activities performed outside the marketing department.

The Role of Functional Management

At the operational level, many businesses are organized along functional lines. That is, a division or SBU often is divided into at least three specialized areas: manufacturing, marketing, and finance. These functional departments are managed by persons who develop the detailed programs (or tactics) necessary to carry out the divisional strategy. These action-oriented programs usually are associated with the short run, a period of 1 year or less.

The marketing department is the key functional group in a company's effort to implement a marketing orientation focused on customers. It contributes in two very important ways. First, as a functional department specializing in marketing, it has the responsibility of working out the short-term tactical details of a division's long-range marketing plan. Managers of specialized marketing activities, such as product planning, advertising, and personal selling, develop short-run programs for their areas. The manager of the marketing department makes sure that the various tactical plans are integrated.

The marketing department's second contribution to the company's overall marketing effort is in its role as an intelligence-gathering arm of the firm. Corporate strategic planning and divisional and SBU long-range planning require information about customers, competition, and social, economic, and political developments. Similarly, information about the company's past sales and profits is required. It is often the responsibility of the marketing department to gather this marketing research information from external and internal sources. Very large companies with extensive and sophisticated marketing intelligence needs expand the research function into a complete marketing information and control system, often referred to as a *marketing intelligence system.*

In carrying out these two important responsibilities, the marketing department becomes the key group in a company. However, it does not run the company, nor do marketing managers intrude into the domains of other functional managers, dictating how their jobs should be done. Marketing gives purpose and direction, and a company operates best not when marketing people run it but when all those making business decisions do so from a marketing point of view.

The Flow of Authority

In most organizations, power is concentrated in the hands of the owners or their hired managers. Operationally, power is centered in the office of the CEO. To accomplish the organization's objectives, this power is delegated to subordinates within the organization. The delegation of authority is not without constraints. It must take place within the framework of established policies, job descriptions, job relationships, and cultural norms of the organization.

Line authority
The power to issue instructions and delegate authority to others in the organization.

Line Authority.   One type of delegated authority is line authority. **Line authority** involves the power to issue instructions to other designated persons. A plant manager is authorized to operate a factory and may, in turn, delegate authority for performing specialized manufacturing activities to various foremen or department heads. Foremen, in turn, may delegate some authority to production group leaders. Sales authority is delegated to a general sales manager, who usually delegates authority to regional or district sales managers. The regional sales manager, in turn, delegates authority to individual salespeople. Thus the component positions in a business are linked by the flow of line authority.

Responsibility for performing staff (advisory) activities is often delegated to specialists. Staff executives have no power over other functions. A staff executive, however, often requires the support and cooperation of these people. In place of line authority, the power of persuasion and the influence of skill and knowledge must be exercised. In a way, the staff executive must rely on an authority of ideas instead of an authority of position.

The delegation of authority creates a one-on-one, vertical relationship of superior and subordinate. In larger organizations such as the military, authority must be dispersed throughout the various levels within the system before delegation can take place. The dispersion is accomplished by decentralization.

Decentralization.   Decentralization can be accomplished in several ways. First, the responsibility and authority to implement marketing plans may be assigned geographically to district or local managers. This method is used most commonly in organizing the sales department. It also is used in decentralized retail organizations, such as Sears, Roebuck and Co. and J.C. Penney Company, Inc. Marketing responsibilities also may be assigned functionally. Advertising, sales, marketing research, and physical distribution frequently are headed by individual functional managers. A third way to decentralize the marketing management authority is on the basis of products. Occasionally, product decentralization is carried all the way through the organizational structure. The result is that a company may have parallel organizational arrangements for different product lines. For instance, Procter & Gamble Co. has separate marketing organizations servicing retail food stores. One group represents such food products as cake mixes, another group sells soaps and detergents, and still another sells health and beauty products. The product management system generally is used by firms that offer a wide variety of products or brands to a relatively homogeneous group of customers.

A fourth method of decentralizing marketing authority is through the use of marketing managers.[9] The **marketing manager** is the person charged with the task of directing a company's efforts to serve a particular class of customer. For instance, an industrial products company that sells products both to manufacturers called *original equipment manufacturers* (OEMs) and to distributors for use as replacement parts may use separate marketing managers, one for each class of trade. Fractional-horsepower electric motors provide an example. General Electric Co. (GE) sells motors to Maytag for installation in home washing machines and dryers. It also sells motors to electrical wholesalers, who in turn sell them to appliance repair companies. GE may very well use two marketing managers, one for OEM customers (such as Maytag) and another for so-called after-market (resale) customers. The marketing manager system generally is used when a firm has a relatively short and standardized line of products used by customers in a number of different applications.

It is possible to combine two or more of these four methods of decentralization into a single complex method. Basic divisions may be made along either product or market lines. Planning, marketing research, and promotional tasks could be assigned to functional departments. A traditional line organization might be used for the sales department. We refer to this structure as **matrix management** because the various components have overlapping concerns and must coordinate their activities closely.

Another matrix arrangement is shown in Figure 16.1. The basic approach is functional. The marketing manager directs two product managers and also supervises a corporate staff of marketing specialists. These functional managers assist the marketing director in developing overall plans and procedures. They also have functional responsibility for the activities of their counterparts who work for the product managers at the next-lower level of the organization. For example, the product *A* advertising manager would consult with the corporate advertising manager on matters of company policy, such as the use of corporate identification marks, advertising agency selection, and obtaining frequency and space discounts in advertising media. The product *A* advertising manager, however, reports to the product manager, not to the corporate advertising manager.

In Figure 16.1, the **product manager** is a line executive with direct responsibility for the total marketing of a product. However, many product managers are considered to be staff. They have no direct authority over anybody else in the organization, but they nonetheless have responsibility for managing their assigned products at a profit. This is where the "authority of ideas" comes into play. Any organizational conflict that may arise because of a lack of direct authority ultimately must be resolved by the line executives involved. However, if the product manager is doing the job well, such crises are not likely to occur often. This remains one of the most serious drawbacks of the product manager form of organization, though.

Marketing manager
The person charged with the task of directing a firm's efforts to serve (satisfy) a particular class of customer.

Matrix management
Involves dual lines of authority and reporting responsibilities, which results in overlapping concerns.

Product manager
A line executive with direct responsibility for the total marketing of a product.

FIGURE 16.1

Example of a Matrix Structure

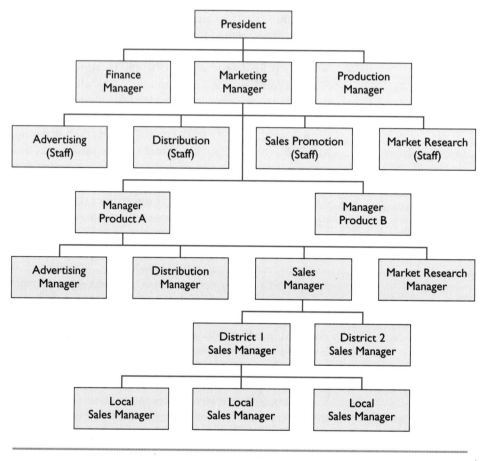

The Flow of Information

The other important flow that traditionally linked the components of an organization is that of information. In the past, much of this flow was related directly to the flow of authority and to the staff's responsibility for preparing instructions and reports. However, the overall information flows within an organization move more freely and in far more complex ways than do those required by the basic organization. As noted earlier, staff executives have no line authority over other functional components within the system, but they do exchange information with them, carrying out assigned responsibilities through this exchange of ideas.

It is largely through this transfer of information that a business system becomes operative. Organizational relationships can be defined and communicated, but in the absence of dynamic information flows, it is impossible for the system to be active. Only by reacting to information about a change in its environment can a company adapt to external threats to its survival or respond to opportunities on which to base its expansion programs. Because of the functional importance of the information flow and the fact that serious management problems are encountered in connection with it, considerable attention has been paid to the management of information. In no area is this more critical than in marketing management.

● THE EVOLVING MARKETING ORGANIZATION

The past 50 years have seen many changes in marketing organization. Contemporary forms bear only a slight resemblance to those that existed prior to World War II. Despite the improvements, problems continue to exist.[10] Because the marketing function changes constantly, it is by no means certain that the best organizational form has yet been developed. The discussion of marketing organization that follows assumes this point of view. The dynamic character of a marketing organization is stressed.

MARKETING IN THE INFORMATION AGE

Structural Flaws Dash Marketing Strategy

Organizational structures have changed in the last few years due to the rise in the quick-response model developed by the Internet. Typified by dot.com firms, many of whom no longer survive, the quick-response model had the impact of breaking down traditional command-and-control structures developed over the last several decades. Many of the so-called old economy firms are struggling with how they can or should organize for the ever-evolving interactive—or at least customer-focused—marketplace.

Professor Adrian Payne, director of the Centre for Relationship Marketing at the Cranfield University School of Management, presents the viewpoint that most organizations currently are structured with separate, disconnected, functional departments. The functions or activities of these units have little or no relationship to one another, and since each unit reports to senior management, they are focused entirely on satisfying senior management. Thus, each functional group is aggressively intent on gaining more of the available organizational resources to enhance size, number of activities, and—most of all—its executives' power base. They are totally disconnected from customers. Payne says customers are off to the side; supposedly everyone's responsibility, they end up as no one's responsibility. Payne argues for the idea of holistic organizations that are not just coordinated but actually organized around processes that totally focus on the customer.

According to Don E. Schultz, Professor of IMC at Northwestern's Medill School of Journalism, firms that are totally committed to focusing on customers, and integrating all marketing and communications activities, often crash on the cruel rocks of organization structure. The rise of electronic communications and interactive media and the advent of customer relationship management has made integrating marketing and communications not only difficult but seemingly impossible in many organizations. There is little question that to succeed in today's highly competitive markets, any firm must be customer focused. However, Schultz suggests that most of today's managers have not been taught to think about customers' needs. Instead, what really matters are volume objectives, market share, cash flows, and "making the numbers." As a result, most marketing managers still manage outputs, such as advertising, sales promotion, direct

(continued)

marketing, events, and sponsorships, and they evaluate success on the basis of efficiency or the new buzz word, optimization. Schultz suggests the real focus should be on outcomes—not what was spent, but what return was achieved.

Unfortunately, neither Payne nor Schultz offers a detailed organizational plan to achieve customer focus. Instead, we are left with the realization that such structures are still experimental and evolving. There is agreement that old organi-

zational structures no longer work, but no organization can yet be suggested to have established the new model for twenty-first century effectiveness.

Sources: Don E. Schultz, "Summit Explores Where IMC, CRM Meet," *Marketing News* (March 4, 2002), pp. 11–12; and "Structural Flaws Dash Marcom Plans," *Marketing News* (August 28, 2001), p. 9.

The Marketing Organization Circa 1946

Figure 16.2 presents an organizational chart of a typical firm engaged in marketing in the immediate post–World War II period. It is generally similar to the structures that prevailed for many years prior to that date.

Three traditional organizational components—manufacturing, finance, and sales—dominate the structure. Two important and distinct entities exist within the manufacturing area: the engineering department, which is responsible for the design and development of products, and the production department, which is responsible

FIGURE 16.2

Marketing Organization Circa 1946

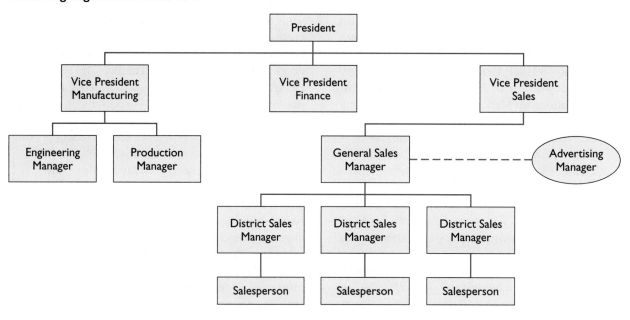

for manufacturing the firm's products. Line authority within the sales division was delegated by the general sales manager to district sales managers. These individuals, in turn, assigned sales authority to individual salespersons in the various territories. One staff marketing position is shown: an advertising manager reporting to the general sales manager. The advertising manager had no authority over others in the organization but was limited to preparing advertising plans and serving as a point of contact with an advertising agency. (The reader should not be surprised to know that this form of organization still exists.)

In the decade following the end of World War II, important developments occurred. First, most companies experienced rapid, and sometimes disruptive, growth. Doubling in size was quite normal, and tenfold increases in the level of business were common. Many firms diversified rapidly, driven partly by profit possibilities and partly to hedge against the uncertainty of single-line manufacture and marketing. Important technologic developments occurred, along with changes in manufacturing methods that were largely the result of automation. There also were changes in the way in which customers used the products and raw materials they purchased, as well as dramatic changes in the level of sophistication in customers' purchasing practices. Another aspect of technologic change was the R&D explosion. The pent-up technology that broke through in the postwar period made many prewar products obsolete. This increased level of R&D resulted in the rapid obsolescence of even some of the newer products, and the life expectancies of all products were cut substantially.

The favorable economic conditions of the postwar period made it possible for many new businesses to get started. Their entry, together with diversification moves by established firms, resulted in increased competition of three distinct types. First, there were new firms selling products similar to those already on the market, and because of technologic improvements, these firms were able to sell their products at lower prices. Second, there was the competition of new products from established companies. Finally, there was the dramatic impact of new product competition from entirely new businesses.

Changing technology, new products, and increased competition demanded tremendous capital outlay, and costs mushroomed. Growth, diversification, adaptation of technologic breakthroughs, massive R&D, and increased competitive pressure forced postwar firms into a period that some writers called *profitless prosperity.* Insistence on profit control, increased skill in selling, and greater attention to productivity became focal points of management's attention. (These same factors re-emerged as key concerns in the 1990s.)

The Marketing Organization Circa 1960

Figure 16.3 presents a hypothetical organization that adapted to the economic and technologic developments between 1946 and 1960. The principal changes in structure occurred in the manufacturing area. Growth and diversification forced the enlargement, and in some cases the decentralization, of manufacturing. The products blocks (*A, B,* and *C*) could represent either product or geographic separation in manufacturing (probably both). Some of the decentralization also was the result of companies searching for lower-cost manufacturing locations. Within the engineering division, activities began to be specialized. Design and methods engineering

FIGURE 16.3

Marketing Organization Circa 1960

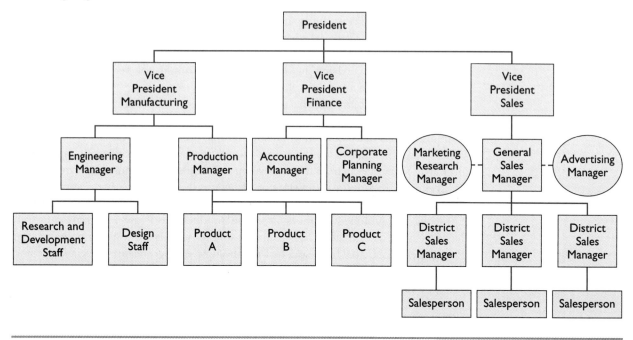

were required to support the manufacturing operation, and a separate engineering activity was dedicated to product R&D. Although R&D groups and departments had existed previously, they became more common in this period. Some specialization also occurred in finance. Corporate financial planning, occasionally headed by a company economist, became a separate department within the financial division. Routine financial work such as accounting and budgeting was handled in another department.

Changes in the sales area were quite modest. In a few firms, a second specialist arose—the marketing research manager. Marketing research as a field was over 50 years old, but it had infrequently been awarded organizational status. Strangely enough, in some of the early organizational arrangements, the marketing research manager actually reported to the company's financial officer, not to the sales manager.

The changes made between 1946 and 1960 did not adequately solve the economic and technologic problems that had developed. Indeed, some of the organizational developments actually aggravated existing situations. Among the principal difficulties encountered in the mid-1950s was the entrenched product and manufacturing orientation in most firms. The changes that had taken place in manufacturing—decentralization, specialization of production, and the emergence of strong R&D groups—often led to a product-oriented company philosophy. The question usually was, "Can we make it?"—not, "Is there a market for it?"

A second major problem was a lack of coordination among sales, engineering, and manufacturing departments. Although engineering and production often reported to a common superior, there was little attempt to coordinate their activities more than was necessary to accommodate the manufacturing needs of the company. Coordination with sales occurred seldom, if ever.

Following a brief post–Korean War slump in the economy, prosperity generally prevailed, and most companies continued to grow. Unfortunately, profit margins became tighter and tighter. In part, this was the result of continuously rising costs. More important, however, was the decline in the number of profitable business opportunities. The cream apparently had been skimmed. Early on, capital had been poured into those projects that offered the best return. Only less profitable or marginal projects remained. It was in this condition that many companies entered the 1960s.

The Marketing Organization Circa 1980

The dynamic changes in competitive activities, customer expectations and demands in the period between 1960 and 1980, and the problems created by them led to some further important changes in the philosophy and structure of business. The philosophical change involved the adoption of the marketing orientation concept, which focused efforts on the customer rather than on production capability. It demanded the integration of all marketing activities within the overall marketing effort and the integration of marketing with nonmarketing activities within the firm. Finally, it emphasized the importance of profit goals rather than sales goals. The organizational impact of the marketing concept is shown in very simple form in Figure 16.4.

FIGURE 16.4

Marketing Organization Circa 1980

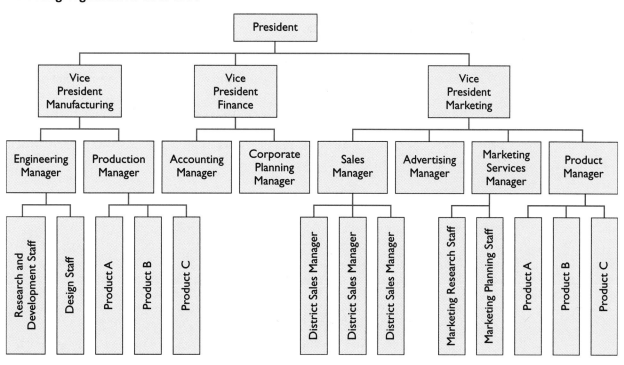

The organizational changes in the period were almost entirely within the old sales department. The name changed. The term *sales* was replaced by *marketing*. However, it was not simply a change in terminology, for a new top-level management post was created. It was a line management position, and its incumbent was charged with the responsibility of carrying out all the marketing activities within the firm and of coordinating such activities with other company functions. This top marketing post carried different names in different companies. Whether titled vice-president of marketing, director of marketing, or simply marketing manager, the post reflected the ascendancy of the marketing concept to a visible position in the organizational structure.

Important developments took place within the new marketing department. The older marketing activities—sales, advertising, and marketing research—now reported to a common supervisor, the top marketing executive. A new marketing staff position was developed to coordinate various aspects of marketing, to work out detailed marketing programs for particular products or markets, and to provide liaison with other parts of the company. As we have already noted, the marketing manager was charged with coordinating all company efforts on behalf of a selected group of customers. The product manager, or brand manager, as the new marketing position commonly was called, was responsible for coordinating all company efforts on behalf of assigned products.

We will use the terms *brand manager* and *product manager* synonymously, although distinctions are sometimes drawn. The most common is to use the term *brand manager* exclusively in connection with consumer packaged-goods marketing. The term *product manager* seems to be used rather generally in both consumer and industrial marketing organizations. Often the product manager was charged with the responsibility of achieving programmed levels of profits.[11]

By 1970, many companies had adopted the product manager system. As might have been expected, companies in the consumer products field were the first to do so. Some industrial firms followed. Unfortunately, the product manager system was unsatisfactory in a number of companies. Uncertainty as to the type of person who should fill the position, failure to define the job carefully, and the inherent difficulties of achieving coordination in organizations long accustomed to operating independently hindered the development of a viable product manager system. Personnel turnover was high, results were slow to materialize, disappointments grew, and some companies returned to traditional organizational methods.[12]

Other companies attempted to find ways to make the product manager system work. For example, as a means of injecting more strategic thinking and concern for profitability into its marketing organization, Ocean Spray Cranberries, Inc., changed its organization from a traditional brand manager system to one that gave profit and strategy responsibilities to division business managers. In general, internal training, careful guidance and supervision by top management, and a great deal of patience have enabled many companies to make the system work satisfactorily. The shakedown seems to have occurred, and it appears that the general form of organization shown in Figure 16.4 was followed by most companies in the 1980s.

Marketing Organizations Currently

It is always difficult to recognize organizational trends in their early stages, and it is almost impossible to generalize about marketing organizations currently and in the future. Companies continually experiment, and only after some passage of time can clear indications of new developments be seen. However, some developments in recent years suggest several new directions. The considerable need for a constant flow of ideas for new products or other ventures has led some management leaders to separate the acquisition and expansion operations from the rest of the business. Often called *new-venture departments,* such units usually are not profit centers. Operating divisions therefore are not burdened with the specific costs of searching for and developing new products. Also, the search for new products or other ventures is not hindered by concern for or vested interests in established products.

The 3M Company is probably the best known of the companies that "disorganize" for new products. The Mac Group at Apple Computer Corp. functioned in almost complete isolation from the rest of the business as it developed Macintosh Office.

Another variant in the marketing-oriented organization appears to have developed in some large industrial companies. Ironically, it represents a return to an organizational form from which the organizational structures of the 1970s evolved. Known as the *strategic business unit,* it constitutes a "business within a business." We have already noted its role in the contemporary management hierarchy. In its earliest forms it was simply thought of as a return to a general management structure in which functional departments reported to the same executive, who in turn was held responsible for the profitable operation of the unit. The initial reason for the return to this basic structural form was to localize responsibility for performance and to achieve better coordination among manufacturing, marketing, and finance. However, it became evident at about the same time that much greater strategic flexibility could be achieved within the general management organizational scheme. Rather than trying to achieve corporate objectives by driving a monster organization in a single strategic direction, it made much more sense to let separate entities within the business develop their own strategic plans within the framework of overall company policy. The concept of the strategic business unit evolved.

In one large firm in this evolutionary period, the Monsanto Company, product managers in one of the divisions (which would be called an SBU) were assigned the task of developing the total business plan for the unit. The plan, of course, was the general manager's plan, but the fact that it was prepared by a marketing person was significant. The importance of marketing was enhanced, because the business plan was a marketing plan. However, it was also a general business plan, embracing all the other functions. Thus marketing assumed its most logical role, not of running the business but of leading it in directions where its capabilities could best be used in serving its customers.

The SBU became the basis for a fundamental change in the way in which many (large) companies developed overall company strategy. Instead of simply being turned loose to maximize their respective positions, the business units were carefully managed as instruments of corporate strategy.

An important concept in architecture as well as management is that form follows function. This concept is directly applicable to marketing management. Organization should be the servant of strategy, not the reverse. As the marketing task changes, new organizational forms will unquestionably evolve to respond to the new assignment.

As we have seen, organizational changes have characterized the development of marketing. They will continue. Just as consumer relations management developed to deal with the challenge of consumerism, and new product departments were created to expedite the development of new offerings, so we can expect to see modifications to the present organizational arrangements in marketing. No organizational structure should be cast in concrete. To permit organization to dictate strategy would be absurd. At the same time, a company cannot be constantly changing its structure, nor should its managers ever fall into the trap of thinking that organizational change can be substituted for strategy. Form should follow function, and the best organizational arrangement is the one that permits a company to implement the most effective marketing plans it can devise. Conformance to this principle has brought the marketing organization to the state in which we find it today. It will surely dictate the organizational forms to be employed in the future.

⬤ INTEGRATED MANAGEMENT SYSTEMS

During the 1980s, several methods to improve organizational performance were embraced by firms eager to improve effectiveness and efficiency. These methods included systematized problem solving, various quality control methods, just-in-time inventory control, and continuous process improvement.[13] All these techniques helped to improve productivity, to develop innovative products, to reduce costs, to improve time to market, to improve quality, and to increase customer satisfaction and shareholder value. However, despite these results, many organizations in the last half of the 1990s were still experiencing an increasingly competitive environment while facing slow growth, declining market share, low return on assets, declining shareholder value, sagging morale, or some combination of these elements.

> **Integrated management system (IMS)**
> Involves re-engineering and restructuring in order to continuously transform and renew strategies, operations, work cultures, people management and development, product development, customer service, mission, and values to ensure continued survival in a highly competitive business environment.

To counteract these negatives, some firms turned to a variety of new solutions such as rapid-response initiatives and strategic alignment that basically seek to achieve customer satisfaction in a dynamic marketplace. However, some organizational writers[14] are suggesting that all these concepts are components to an overarching system called the **integrated management system (IMS).** The rationale is that during the 1980s the major challenge facing most organizations related to the need to significantly enhance the quality of both product and service offerings as well as the quality of internal operations. During the early 1990s, the challenge for managers shifted to re-engineering and restructuring in order to continuously transform and renew strategies, operations, work culture, people management and development, product development, customer service, mission, and values—all before the competition did so. Often the stakes were continued survival, because organizations that did not or could not continually reinvent themselves eventually would fall behind the competition. Xerox Corp., American Telephone & Telegraph Co. (AT&T), and more recently Kodak Co. and International Business Machines Corp. (IBM) are examples of firms that were market leaders but did not keep pace with industry changes. However, IBM and Hewlett-Packard Co. are current examples of firms that have renewed themselves successfully. How is it that some firms seem to be able to constantly renew while others seem less able to accomplish renewal?

Self-assessment and an integrated management system (IMS), when combined with the will and resources to do so, seem to be the key ingredients necessary to manage change on the targeted, leveraged, and accelerated basis necessary for organizational renewal. IMS is a closed-loop management system where all elements are interdependent (thus the need for bidirectional arrows in Figure 16.5). In the following paragraphs we discuss how the typical IMS functions.

FIGURE 16.5

The Integrated Management System

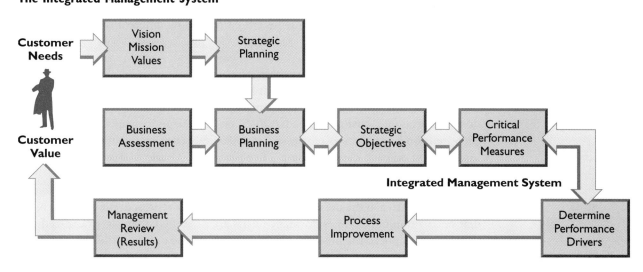

Source: Adapted from Ken Breen, Jerry Pecora, and Tome McCabe, "A New Dimension: Integrated Management Systems," *Quality Digest* (August 1997), pp. 36–41.

Key Elements of the Integrated Management System

The integrated management system (IMS) involves several key elements: attention to customer needs; strong vision, mission, and values; careful strategic planning, business assessment, and business planning; the development of strategic objectives; a determination of critical performance measures and performance drivers; process improvement; and a final management review of the results.

Customer Needs.   Most organizations today proclaim that they are customer-focused and that success is determined by how well the organization gives customers what they want (satisfies customers). However, there is often a big gap between what is professed and what is delivered. Management needs to determine how well the organization surveys customer needs, improves customer value, measures customer satisfaction, resolves disputes, manages customer databases, manages customer relationships, retains customers, and integrates these activities into every aspect of daily operations.

Vision, Mission, and Values.   *Vision* is the firm's perception of where the organization is going (strategic direction), and it is derived from the desire to profitably satisfy customer needs. The vision is translated into a *mission*—what to do, for whom, and why. In combination, the vision and mission direct the organization (employees) toward achieving a set of uniform objectives. The core *values* of the organization provide a common framework for decision making and taking action to achieve the strategic objectives.

Strategic Planning.   Based on vision and mission, *strategic planning* produces measurable goals and objectives that are converted into business strategies, structures, systems, policies, and plans to ensure that everyone is working to achieve the strategic objectives. It determines where the firm is now, where it is going, and how it will get there.

Business Assessment.   The organization should conduct a *business assessment* (determining where the firm is today) at least once yearly that corresponds with the IMS model. Thus each element of the model will have a category of survey questions, for example, customer needs/values or critical performance measures, and each item on the survey is expressed as a desired state. Senior managers rate the organization on each element using a five-point Likert scale from strongly agree to strongly disagree, and each element is viewed in three ways: approach or method, deployment (extent to which the method is deployed), and results (performance). Differences between the desired state and current state represent performance gaps that need attention. Once performance gaps are identified, they are prioritized and then used as input to the business planning process. The output is the business plan.

Business Planning.   In *business planning,* management establishes financial targets for the organization as well as goals and objectives for the various function areas, for example, product development objectives or market expansion objectives or productivity objectives. *Objectives* are quantified 1-year targets, whereas *goals* are 5-year milestones against which progress is measured. The business plan states how resources are allocated and how objectives will be reached.

Strategic Objectives.   The *strategic objectives*—what the organization must achieve—are the basis for the business plan and are monitored continuously throughout the year. The business plan usually attempts to meet all stakeholder needs.

Critical Performance Measures.   To use IMS effectively, management must define the *critical performance measures* that drive the organization. Typical examples of critical performance measures are return on assets, return on equity, yield, defect rate, on-time deliveries, process efficiency, employee productivity, supplier effectiveness, sales plan versus actual, and customer satisfaction index.

Critical Performance Drivers.   Once the critical performance measures are established, management must determine which performance factors have the greatest impact on achieving objectives. For example, if improving the frequency of sales contacts and reducing the time between order placement and order delivery will increase customer satisfaction, then these become *drivers* or top business priorities.

Process Improvement.   The next step is to identify the processes that have the most impact on each performance driver. To achieve quantum performance gains on performance driver processes quickly, rapid-response teams are appointed and trained on a just-in-time basis. The rapid-response teams take action only on those processes deemed to be critically important to achieving strategic goals.

Management Review.   IMS is an iterative method, whereby early stages in the method may need to be repeated if later stages indicate the need to revisit previous stages to ensure effectiveness. Nonetheless, to complete the model, management must review IMS as a complete entity. Management must review all predictive measures and results, assess progress of all key improvement initiatives, make certain all targets are achieved, analyze gaps in performance, and take necessary corrective action. This review should be at each organizational level and at frequent intervals. The actual interval depends on the recent history of the firm in meeting its strategic objectives. If the firm has been unsuccessful recently, a crisis mode of operation exists.

The IMS Organization

Exactly what form of organization will be necessary to use IMS effectively has not yet become clear. Some firms have used self-directed work teams, whereas others have opted for temporary special task forces or rapid-response teams. Part of the answer may lie in determining whether the performance drivers involve only processes that are internal to the organization or also involve processes that have components that are external and thus involve suppliers or customers or other stakeholders. As time passes and more firms gain experience with IMS, the most effective modifications to organizational structure will become clear.

RECENT TRENDS IN MANAGEMENT PRACTICE

To determine the most effective modifications to organizational structure that will be necessary for future effectiveness, one must consider several recent trends in management practice. These trends are discussed in the following paragraphs.

Total Quality Management

Total quality management (TQM) Involves a customer focus, strategic planning and leadership, continuous improvement of all business systems and processes, and empowerment and teamwork in order to pursue quality as a basis for satisfying customers.

During the 1980s and 1990s many organizations embraced the concept of **total quality management (TQM).** Although it is impossible to cover TQM thoroughly with a brief explanation, it is possible to examine its basic attributes: (1) customer focus, (2) strategic planning and leadership, (3) continuous improvement, and (4) teamwork and empowerment.

To maximize the potential benefits of TQM concepts, the organization must take the customer into consideration. The basic tenet of effective marketing is satisfying customers, and today's customers demand quality goods and services. As noted by Dean and Evans, "Today most managers agree that the main reason to pursue quality is to satisfy customers."[15] The American National Standards Institute (ANSI) and the American Society for Quality Control (ASQC) define *quality* as "the totality of features and characteristics of a product or service that bears on its ability to satisfy given needs." However, many organizations and customers now define quality as goods and/or services that meet or exceed customer expectations, and they believe that quality is a requirement for successful global competition. Thus TQM has become a standard requirement for effective marketing and for creating competitive advantage. So what are the basic attributes of TQM?

Customer Focus. Since the customer is the judge of quality, TQM must be concerned with all product attributes that provide value in the eyes of the customer and that lead to customer satisfaction and loyalty. Many factors have an impact on value and satisfaction during purchase and use or consumption of goods and services. These factors include the relationship between the organization and customers. This relationship is based on trust and confidence in the offered goods and services and leads to customer loyalty.

However, the organization that differentiates itself by offering features that enhance the good/service thereby meets or exceeds customer expectations. By exceeding customer expectations, a firm establishes a competitive edge. In this manner, TQM becomes a basic and key element of business strategy used for both customer retention and gaining market share. To be effective, TQM demands constant awareness of emerging customer and market requirements, plus ongoing measurement of those factors that drive customer satisfaction.

Strategic Planning and Leadership.   Market leadership based on TQM requires a long-term viewpoint, commitment of resources, and implementation of TQM concepts as key components to organization strategy. Planning, organizing, and executing TQM activities require a major commitment from all members of an organization. Strategies, plans, and budgets all need to reflect these long-term commitments to customers, employees, stockholders, and suppliers (some of the most important stakeholders). Such aspects as employee training and development, supplier development, and development of technology become key elements of this commitment and need regular review and assessment of progress toward established goals.

Leadership is the most important aspect of this commitment. Top-level managers must publicize internally their belief in TQM, and they must take part in the creation of strategies, systems, and activities designed not only to satisfy customers but also to exceed their expectations. Top managers must be role models for the whole organization. They must exhibit direct guidance of the activities and decisions of all portions of the organization and encourage participation and creativity by all employees. In addition, they must reinforce the corporate TQM values and commitment necessary to achieve satisfied customers even when costs and time schedules conflict with quality—otherwise the employees will view TQM as just another passing fad or the management technique of the month. Over the long run, organizations cannot sustain TQM without strong ongoing top management leadership.

Continuous Improvement.   To achieve the highest level of quality and competitiveness, it is necessary for any organization to have a well-developed and well-executed continuous improvement system. Continuous improvement systems are likely to include at least several of the following approaches:

- Reducing errors, defects, and waste in operating activities, systems, and procedures
- Improving productivity and effectiveness in using resources
- Improving cycle-time performance and responsiveness to customers
- Improving customer value through new and improved products and services

Continuous improvement systems are necessary if the organization is to achieve quality, be efficient, and be responsive to customers, all of which will result in marketplace advantages. Implementing continuous improvement requires a basis (preferably

MANAGING CHANGE

Temp-Work Plan Faces Europe's Rigid Labor Market

 Virtually unheard of in Europe 10 years ago, temporary workers are popular today. The number of registered temporary agencies has grown by roughly 10 percent per year since 1990, and nearly two million temporary jobs have been created in that time. Now there is a European Union (EU) proposal that would give temporary workers extraordinary protections, forcing companies to pay full salaries and benefits to temps after only 6 weeks on the job. "Temporary workers aren't treated fairly. We need this directive to change that," said Wim Bergans, a spokesman for the European Trade Union Confederation, an umbrella group that represents 64 million workers from 34 countries.

But working against the proposal was Europe's largest and most prominent business trade group, the Union of Industrial and Employees Confederations of Europe (UNICE) and also the International Confederation of Temporary Work Businesses, which represents 3.5 million temps in 26 countries.

Few debate the need for labor-market reform in Europe. During the last half of the 1990s, Europe's economy grew 2.6 percent a year on average while the U.S. economy soared at 4.1 percent. In 2001 the European unemployment rate was 7.6 percent, and that exceeded the U.S. rate by 1.8 percent. Economists say making labor laws more flexible is key to creating more jobs and boosting economic growth. But laws in many European countries make layoffs difficult or even impossible. And that is why many companies hire temps—because those workers are more flexible. Businesses see the proposal as a throwback to the 1970s, when many European countries put laws in place that created what economists called "nanny capitalism," giving workers tons of protection and expecting very little out of them in return.

The business argument is that flexible temp rules like those in the United States help companies grow by letting them create short-term jobs when they can't afford to add permanent positions. Paying temps as much as full-timers makes no economic sense, businesses say, because productivity is notoriously low among temps, who often lack the experience or the qualifications of full-timers.

Source: Paul Hofheinz, "Temp-Work Plan Faces Europe's Rigid Labor Market," *Wall Street Journal* (October 2, 2002), p. A3.

---

quantitative) for assessing progress. This quantitative basis also becomes an information base for future improvement cycles. Customer satisfaction, the quality of products, and the effectiveness of internal processes all must be measured in order to meet organizational goals. These measurements must be based on reliable information, data, and analysis. The factors necessary for assessment and improvement include customer demographics and other facts, market surveys, competitor analysis, supplier capabilities and history, employee-related data, operating systems records, product and service performance records, and historical cost and financial records. Analysis of these factors is based on statistical reasoning and forms the basis for continuous improvement.

One approach that many organizations use as a basis to begin continuous improvement is to measure the costs of poor quality (or nonconformance); in this manner they identify improvement opportunities. The cost of poor quality includes items such as costs of scrap and wastage, costs of inspection, costs of rework (in all internal systems, not just production), costs of warranty claims, and costs of customer returns. With experience, most firms can isolate key success factors that are major elements in need of concentrated efforts directed at continuous improvement.

Teamwork and Empowerment.   To achieve organizational quality goals, teamwork must function at all levels. Dean and Evans have suggested that teamwork should be viewed in three distinct dimensions: horizontal, vertical, and interorganizational.[16] *Horizontal teamwork* more commonly takes the form of **cross-functional work teams,** in which team membership is drawn from a cross section of work groups and traditional functional departmental boundaries. Cross-functional work teams bring together persons with a variety of viewpoints and work experiences to foster cooperation in solving problems that transcend multiple departments within the organization.

> **Cross-functional work team**
> Involves membership drawn from a cross section of work groups and traditional functional departments within a firm (and sometimes from external suppliers or customers).

Vertical teamwork involves cooperation between all organization levels of the firm. Team membership includes representatives drawn from top management, supervisory personnel, and shop-floor employees. As with cross-functional teams, one of the major advantages of vertical teamwork is the wealth of work experience and viewpoints that are focused in a cooperative environment designed to enhance the problem-solving capabilities of the team.

> **Vertical teamwork**
> Involves cooperation between all organizational levels of a firm.

For teamwork to be effective, employees must be empowered to participate in making decisions that affect the organization and especially their work area. The individual who best knows the job is the person performing it. Developing and implementing new and improved systems will be most effective when implementation is initiated through employee involvement teams. Organizations should encourage teamwork and risk taking by removing the fear of failure, sharing success stories throughout the organization, implementing suggestion systems that react quickly, providing employee feedback, rewarding employees for implemented suggestions, and providing the necessary technical and financial support required to develop suggestions.

In many firms, empowering employees requires a profound shift in management philosophy. Employees at various levels within the organization will require training in teamwork skills to achieve effectiveness. However, participation in teamwork by everyone in the organization, as well as suppliers and customers, often will lead to creativity and innovation and thereby increase customer satisfaction and market share.

Re-engineering/Process Redesign.   A discussion of TQM would be incomplete without at least a brief reference to re-engineering. **Re-engineering** (also known as *process redesign*) is a type of continuous improvement with the potential for dramatic improvement in quality, speed of work cycle, and reduced costs because it involves fundamentally changing the processes by which the work gets done. When the implementation of incremental changes to operations usually associated with continuous improvement systems proves to be insufficient in enabling an organization to achieve its goals or objectives, then re-engineering is called for. For example, if a 5 percent improvement in speed of work, costs, and quality is insufficient because the leading competitor is already ahead by 50 percent in these factors, then process redesign is necessary.

> **Re-engineering**
> Involves fundamentally changing work processes with the potential for dramatic improvement in quality, speed of work cycle, and reduced costs. Also known as *process redesign*.

Process is what connects customer expectations to the goods or services they receive. Process is what ensures or fails to ensure that goods/services meet or exceed customer expectations. Redesigning processes to reduce waste is the basis of re-engineering. If a process is not driven by customer expectation but is instead driven by cost accounting or a functional specialization, it may be ripe for redesign. The general principles of redesign include reducing handoffs, eliminating steps, performing steps in parallel instead of in sequence, and involving key people early. The results of re-engineering are often startling, and frequently those involved wonder why it was not done this way in the past. But the key aspect of redesign driven by customer expectations is the fact that it leads to increased customer satisfaction and competitive advantage.

Managing Change

Modern organizations confront a turbulent environment that requires rapid, flexible responses to changing conditions. Today, "doing business as usual" is ineffective.[17] Moreover, globalization of business necessitates effective and speedy communications and coordination across multiple time zones and far-flung geographic locations. Time constraints dictate reduction in reaction time as well as necessitating effective business processes such as just-in-time inventory, orders, scheduling, payments, manufacturing, distribution, and so on. Change has become the norm and unpredictable or unforeseen situations the basic reality for many firms.[18]

As a result, organizational theory indicates that in order to achieve sustainability, firms must change or adapt. Such adaptations range from specific responses to complete overhaul of strategic direction.[19] Previously we discussed the evolution of the marketing organization, but here we will re-emphasize that recent major changes in the corporate focus center on how the organization interacts with its environment. Management theories emerged that considered sources of organizational dependence on the business environment to include people, resources, markets, or information and how they could be controlled and influenced.[20] In order to develop mechanisms to support adaptation to change, both intracompany and intercompany coordination is needed. Information technology frequently is regarded as an integral component of these shifts in organizational design.[21] Electronic integration (EI) enabled the formation of new organizations that transcended traditional boundaries, and information technology was a critical force in this transformation of competition, firm structures, and firm boundaries.[22] Such agile, market-driven companies shuffle resources to meet customer needs[23] by implementing strategic alliances and interorganizational collaborations and partnerships.[24]

Guiding the development of new entrepreneurial units or deciding how to reformulate traditional organizational structures is a very difficult task. One new model that is being developed includes a network of corporate units, independent organizations, and entrepreneurs. These new model organizations are lean, flexible, adaptive, and responsive to both customer needs and market requirements. Key features include an understanding of customer needs and product selections that offer value to customers.[25] The term coined to describe such an organization is *dynamic network,* which is a controlled interlinkage of only those work groups required for the creation and marketing of a particular product or service (bundle of benefits) at a particular point in time. Such a highly flexible organizational arrangement can readily adapt to changes in technologies, markets, and demand levels by adding or subtracting work groups to the network.

Members of these work groups do what is called *collaborative work*. Collaborative work often involves increased levels of cooperation and coordination, both within and between organizations. Communications networks and information technology are the tools that make collaborative work possible, and telecommuting (or homework) makes work groups more productive.[26] With modern technology and group software, a work group can function almost like a single entity, even if its members are geographically widely dispersed.[27]

THE VIRTUAL ORGANIZATION[28]

As mentioned previously, information technology is the fundamental supporting tool required to perform the critical activities of modern businesses in a highly competitive environment. Information technology enables organizations to make effective and efficient changes in the way work is performed[29] and offers real potential for changing the way people work.[30] Some companies are forming international collaborative alliances to develop a sustainable competitive advantage.[31] Teams, committees, or work groups are fundamental to these organizations, and thus group behavior becomes a key concern. Some of these electronically linked groups behave like real social groups, even though they share no physical space, their members are invisible, and their interactions are asynchronous.[32] Information technology allows organizations to create more flexible structures designed to maximize the experience and expertise of their employees and to make it available wherever needed. This has led to the **virtual organization.**

Virtual organization
A collaborative network of employees, linked by integrated computer and information technologies, who draw on vital resources as needed and are not constrained by physical locations or by complex contractual arrangements.

Virtual organizations began 15 to 20 years ago as people envisioned the possibility of using technology for work at home.[33] Some now believe that it has become an economic necessity for corporate executives and a research area for business theorists.[34] The virtual organization takes the flexible specialization concept a step further than the dynamic network organization, because it is not constrained by either physical locations or by complex contractual arrangements.[35] Corporations are evolving into virtual enterprises using integrated computer and communications technologies to link all their employees together. Such collaborative networks are not defined by the usual physical walls around a specific space at a designated location. Instead, collaborative networks draw on vital resources as needed, regardless of where they are located physically and regardless of who owns them.[36] This does not mean that such organizations do not occupy a physical space—they do, but physical space need no longer be a fixed site.[37] Slow to modify, traditionally defined, and sharply delineated companies are evolving into virtual organizations with structures and systems that are loose and fuzzy in order that they may assume whatever form is needed to respond to a rapidly changing marketplace.[38] Advocates for Remote Employment and the Virtual Office (AREVO) define the **virtual office** as the operational domain of any business or organization whose work force includes a significant proportion of remote workers.[39]

Virtual office
The operational domain of any firm whose work force includes a significant number of remote workers.

Virtual product
New products or services demanded by customers, which change continuously to satisfy customer needs, wants, and desires.

Virtual organizations are emerging because customers are demanding new goods and services: the **virtual product.** Virtual goods or services include 1-hour prescription eyeglasses, 1-hour development of photographs, overnight delivery, digital cameras, and a growing number of other instant-gratification goods or services. For an entity or object to be *virtual* used to mean that it possessed powers or capabilities of another entity or object. Now the term means that previously well-defined structures begin to lose their edges, seemingly permanent things start to change continuously, and goods and services adapt to match our desires. Virtual products can be made available at any time, in any place, and in any variety; but they can only be offered because of the latest innovation in information processing, organizational dynamics, and marketing and manufacturing systems. Virtual products deliver instant customer gratification in a cost-effective value-added way, can be produced in diverse locations and offered in a great number of models or formats, and ideally are produced instantaneously, customized to the customer's request. Only the virtual organization can deliver these virtual goods and services.[40]

Virtual organizations are reliant on cyberspace (the medium in which electronic communications flow and software operates) and initially will exist only across conventional organizational structures. Barnatt has identified four different versions of the virtual organization:[41]

1. *Telecommuting.* With telecommuting, or working at home, employees use a remote terminal to access their office system.

2. *Hot-desk environment.* In a hot-desk environment, individual desks are abandoned. Employees arriving at work are allocated a desk for the day from which they can access their electronic mail and computer network files.

3. *Hoteling.* Hoteling acknowledges the fact that many workers have no need of a permanent desk at their parent company. Instead, they spend much of their working lives with clients, using client facilities much like a hotel.

4. *Virtual teams.* By working in virtual teams, people collaborate closely but may be physically located in a variety of locations.

The growth of the virtual organization is fueled by three factors:[42]

1. Rapid evolution of electronic technologies, which facilitate digital, wireless transfer of video, audio, and text information

2. Rapid spread of computer networks

3. Growth of telecommuting, which will enable companies to provide faster response to customers, reduce facility expenses, and assist workers to meet their child-care and elder-care responsibilities

In the past, managers were restricted in their choice of organizational form and often used information technology as a tool for downsizing and restructuring.[43] Currently, because computer systems have assumed many of the communications, coordination, and control functions within organizations, managers have the option to choose technology-driven control systems that can support the flexibility and responsiveness of a decentralized organization, as well as the integration and control of a centralized organization. Technology can be used to shape the organization into more flexible and dynamic structures.[44]

Summary

Although satisfying customers must be the concern and responsibility of everyone in the marketing organization, the tasks of top managers, divisional managers, and functional managers are different. Different organizational structures affect the flow of authority, the flow of information, and other linkages within the organization.

Over the past decades, the marketing organization has evolved from one dominated by manufacturing, finance, and sales to one whose focus is on the customer and coordinating marketing activities. Most recently, marketing organizations have added new venture departments to meet the need for new ideas and new business ventures.

The integrated management system (IMS) is one that has been proposed as a method to improve organizational performance. IMS is a closed-loop management system that, when implemented correctly, enables organizations to concentrate their efforts on satisfying their customers' needs in a value-added manner. Key elements of the IMS include customer needs; the organization's vision, mission, and values; strategic planning; business assessment; business planning; strategic objectives; critical performance measures; critical performance drivers; process improvement; and management review.

Total quality management and continuous process improvement have had a significant impact on management practice and organizational design over the past 20 years. Marketers also need to manage change from a global perspective and a look at future trends in organizational functional design. The virtual organization and virtual products may be what the future holds for effective and efficient marketing organizations in the twenty-first century.

Questions

1. Describe in your own words the three tiers of responsibility that occur for marketing managers in marketing-oriented organizations.

2. Contrast and compare how the flow of authority versus the flow of information affects the linkages within organizations and how they in turn affect organizational structure.

3. With reference to the appropriate exhibits within the chapter, describe how the marketing organization within firms evolved from the 1960s to the 1980s.

4. What do you believe are the major advantages for a firm that uses IMS to improve organizational performance?

5. Describe what you believe the impact of TQM has been on marketing management.

6. How has the impact of continuous process improvement on marketing management differed as compared with your answer to Question 5?

7. What are the advantages to a firm of a virtual organization form of functional design?

Exercises

1. Using the resources of the local Chamber of Commerce, establish which local company employs the largest number of people (Note: Omit governmental agencies, universities, and colleges.) Locate this firm's latest five annual reports, and analyze them to see if there has been any reported major reorganization of the firm. Also telephone the firm and contact the human resources manager to ask how the organization of the firm has changed over the last 5 years. If there is no reported reorganization, or if the HR manager says the firm has not changed over the last 5 years, ask the question: "Why do you think there has not been the need to change the organization in the last 5 years given the dramatic advances in information technology and information management?"

2. Contact a large local hospital or similar health care facility, again speak with the manager of human resources, and ask how the organization, compensation, and evaluation of the nursing staff has changed recently (this can be

within the last 10 years). Be particularly careful to ask about changes in the layers of management.

3. Contact the manager of your local bank, and ask how the organization of the bank has changed recently. Ask if these changes have resulted from governmental regulations, from consolidation within the banking industry, or from competitive and market factors.

Endnotes

1. Peter Senge, *The Fifth Discipline: The Art and Practice of the Learning Organization* (New York: Currency/Doubleday, 1990), p. 15.

2. Peter Drucker, *Management: Tasks, Responsibilities, Practices* (New York: Harper & Row, 1974), p. 61.

3. Frederick E. Webster, Jr., "The Changing Role of Marketing in the Corporation," *Journal of Marketing* 56 (October 1992), pp. 1-17.

4. *Ibid.*

5. Michael Krauss, "Marketing Dept. Organization Is Destiny," *Marketing News* (February 18, 2002), p. 14.

6. "Strategic Marketing Priority of Chief Execs," *Marketing News* (January 13, 1986), p. 1.

7. John Bassler, "Companies Want CEOs with Strong Marketing Vision," *Marketing News* 23 (May 1986), p. 17.

8. Cecile Daurat, "Paradise Regained?" *Forbes* (March 22, 1999), pp. 102-104.

9. M. Hanan, "Reorganize Your Company Around Its Markets," *Harvard Business Review* (November-December 1974), p. 63.

10. John P. Workman, Jr., Christian Hombur, and Kjell Gruner, "Marketing Organization: An Integrative Framework of Dimensions and Determinants," *Journal of Marketing* (July 1998), pp. 21-41.

11. The position of the product (brand) manager, its challenges, and its problems have received considerable attention in the literature. See, for example, V. P. Buell, "The Changing Role of the Product Manager in Consumer Goods Companies," *Journal of Marketing* (July 1975), p. 3; G. R. Gremmil and D. L. Wileman, "The Product Manager as an Influence Agent," *Journal of Marketing* (January 1973), p. 26; and Steven Lysonski, "A Boundary Theory Investigation of the Product Managers' Role," *Journal of Marketing* (Winter 1985), p. 26.

12. See, for example, "The Brand Manager: No Longer King," *Business Week* (June 9, 1973), p. 58; and

Robert S. Wollowitz, "Product Management Lagging," *Advertising Age* (January 14, 1985), p. 14.

13. *Ibid.*

14. Ken Breen, Jerry Pecora, and Tome McCabe, "A New Dimension: Integrated Management Systems," *Quality Digest* (August 1997), pp. 36-41.

15. James W. Dean, Jr. and James R. Evans, *Total Quality: Management, Organization, and Strategy* (Minneapolis, Minn.: West Publishing Company, 1994), p. 12.

16. *Ibid.*, pp. 17-19.

17. P. Keen, *Shaping the Future: Business Design Through Information Technology* (Boston: Harvard Business School Press, 1991).

18. Robert F. Hurley and Tomas M. Hult: "Innovation, Market Orientation, and Organizational Learning: An Integration and Empirical Examination," *Journal of Marketing* (July 1998), pp. 42-54.

19. P. D. Jennings and P. A. Zandbergen, "Ecologically Sustainable Organizations: An Institutional Approach," *Academy of Management Review* 20 (1995), pp. 1015-1052.

20. H. J. Leavitt and H. Bahrami, *Managerial Psychology: Managing Behavior in Organizations,* 5th ed. (Chicago: University of Chicago Press, 1996).

21. G. DeSanctis and B. M. Jackson, "Coordination of Information Technology Management: Team-Based Structures and Computer-Based Communication Systems," *Journal of Management Information Systems* 10(4) (1994), pp. 85-110.

22. A. Kambil and J. E. Short, "Electronic Integration and Business Network Redesign: A Roles-Linkage Perspective," *Journal of Management Information Systems* 10(4) (1994), pp. 59-83.

23. R. E. Miles and C. C. Snow, "Causes of Failure in Network Organizations," *California Management Review* 241(5) (1992), pp. 53-72.

24. N. F. Piercy and D. W. Cravens, "The Network Paradigm and the Marketing Organization: Developing a New Management Agenda," *European Journal of Marketing* (1995), pp. 7-34.

25. D. W. Cravens, S. H. Shipp, and K. S. Cravens, "Reforming the Traditional Organization: The Mandate for Developing Networks," *Business Horizons* 37(4) (1994), pp. 19-28.

26. B. W. Stuck, "Collaboration: Working Together Apart," *Business Communications Review (Networking Supplement)* (February 1995), pp. 9-11ff.

27. S. A. Bly, S. R. Harrison, and S. Irwin, "Media Spaces: Bringing People Together in a Video, Audio, and Computing Environment," *Communications at the ACM* 36(1) (1993), pp. 28-47.

28. Much of this section is adapted from Susan E. Yager, "Everything's Coming Up Virtual," *Crossroads*, ACM's first electronic publication, 1997. Reprinted by permission of the author.

29. E. Turban, E. McLean, and J. Wetherbe, *Information Technology for Management* (New York: John Wiley & Sons, 1996).

30. S. Daniels, "The Disorganized Organization," *Work Study* 44(2) (1995), pp. 20–21.

31. A. J. Bailetti and J. R. Callahan, "The Coordination Structure of International Collaborative Technology Arrangements," *R&D Management* 23(2) (1993), pp. 129–146.

32. T. Finholt and L. S. Sproull, "Electronic Groups at Work," *Organization Science* 1(1) (1990), pp. 41–64.

33. H. C. Lucas, Jr. and J. Baroudi, "The Role of Information Technology in Organization Design," *Journal of Management Information Systems* 10(4) (1994), pp. 9–23.

34. B. Caldwell and J. Gambon, "The Virtual Office Gets Real," 1997, available at http://techweb.cmp.com/iw/563/63mtoff.htm.

35. C. Barnatt, "Office Space, Cyberspace and Virtual Organization," *Journal of General Management* 20(4) (1995), pp. 78–91.

36. S. E. Bleecker, "The Virtual Organization," *Futurist* 28(2) (1994), pp. 9–14.

37. T. L. Dixon, "Virtual Organizations: Success Stories," 1995, available at http://mansci1.uwaterloo.ca/~msci604/summaries/virt_org.html.

38. N. Duratta, "Communicating for Real Results in the Virtual Organization," *Communications World* 12(9) (1995), pp. 15–19.

39. Advocates for Remote Employment and the Virtual Office (AREVO), 1996, http://www.globaldialog.com/~morse/arevo/.

40. W. H. Davidow and M. S. Malone, *The Virtual Corporation: Structuring and Revitalizing the Corporation for the 21st Century* (New York: Harper Business Press, 1992).

41. C. Barnatt, *op. cit.*

42. R. Barner, "The New Millennium Workplace: Seven Changes That Will Challenge Managers—and Workers," *Futurist* 30(2) (1996), pp. 14–18.

43. L. M. Applegate, J. I. Cash, Jr., and D. Q. Mills, "Information Technology and Tomorrow's Manager," *Harvard Business Review* 66(6) (1988), pp. 128–136.

44. S. E. Yager, "Everything's Coming Up Virtual," 1997, available at www.acm.org/crossroads/xrds4-1/organ.html.

MARKETING MANAGEMENT IN ACTION: CLOSING CASE

Resurrected Harp Maker Plays to Win!

When Alberto Bertolazzi, a hero among harmonica players, enters the factory his 80-strong staff give him a warm welcome. With quick thinking and bold moves, Bertolazzi has transformed Fabrica de Harmonicas Catarinense (FHC), a musical toy maker located in Blumenau, Brazil, from a firm battered by globalization into a fast-growing, innovative manufacturer of harmonicas (mouth organs). Although a niche market, only four competitors vie for an estimated work market of $130 million. Unlike other "period" products such as juke boxes or pinball machines, demand for harmonicas is growing. In Brazil, there was a boom in cowboy-style Sertanejo music, while abroad there was a renaissance of blues, country, and psychedelic 1960s music.

When Brazil was swamped with cheap imported Chinese harmonicas, the 58-year-old former stockbroker-turned-musical impresario Bertolazzi used globalization to his advantage. Rethinking Hering, as the company is known, he expanded distribution overseas, customized harmonicas for specific consumer markets, and used a little high-tech. "Hering has a good product," said Brian Majeski, editor of New Jersey-based *Music Trades* magazine. "They're quite new to the U.S. market, but they seem to be making good headway." When Brazil opened its borders to international trade in 1994, it was swamped with cheap products, mainly from Asia. FHC was on the brink of bankruptcy with an outdated and unloved range of accordions, toy pianos, and clarinets. Toy makers, which once numbered more than 500 in Brazil, were among the first casualties; in 2001, only 60 were still in operation.

As a stockbroker, Bertolazzi had invested in FHC and had seen an opportunity to buy 80 percent of the company at bargain prices. He decided he either had to take a huge loss or rethink the company. He negotiated to keep the brand name, some of the machinery, and 25 specialists in harmonica production. Bertolazzi's new plan was to "Stop producing loss-making toys and focus on something we were competitive in." Today, FHC, Germany's Hohner, and Japan's Suzuki and Tomba vie for about half the global market. The other half is made up of Chinese-made toy harmonicas and professional grade harmonicas. FHC sold $2.2 million in harmonicas and accessories in 2000, but predicted a 50 percent sales growth in 2001. Market dominant in Latin America, FHC recently signed a contract with Yamaha, under which the world's biggest instrument maker will distribute $1 million worth of FHC harmonicas in Japan. FHC is also marketing "the only true all-American harp" in the United States through a new Miami office. While targeting the two largest markets, Bertolazzi spotted a trend of retail consolidation, noting that multi-brand megastores were gobbling specialty stores by buying directly from manufacturers. Bertolazzi negotiated an exclusive deal with the fast-growing Mars Music, a chain of superstores.

On the factory floor, little has changed. Holes are punched in carefully aged steel plates, brass reeds are fitted, and chrome housing is polished by hand. Finished instruments are tuned on archaic, foot-pumped machines. "We are the only ones in the world who tune our harmonicas three times before packaging," Bertolazzi boasts. But for export markets, changes were necessary. "In the States, people say Hering harmonicas were great but looked cheap, so we upgraded the plates from brass to bronze," he says. "For Yamaha, we had to add three dots marking the octaves. Don't ask why. The Japanese prefer them that way." All this may seem cosmetic, but Bertolazzi also looked for innovation. In 2001, FHC took its first high-tech harmonica to a Los Angeles music industry fair. The new Hering Electronic Harp was developed by British musician Richard Smith, has a funky lime green plastic casing, and is connected to an amplifier. This new harp, played by blues maestro Peter "Mad Cat" Ruth, got a cool reception at the 2000 annual meeting of the U.S. Society for the Preservation and Advancement of the Harmonica in Detroit, where the average age was 70. However, Bertolazzi says, "The harmonica is an instrument that needs to attract younger people. That's what we're trying to do."

Source: Tony Smith, "Resurrected Harp-Maker Plays to Win," *Marketing News* (February 26, 2001), p. 47.

Case Study Questions

1. Can a firm with an old-fashioned type of organization survive in today's global economy?

2. Is a charismatic leader all that is necessary for a firm to be successful?

3. Can a firm be a global competitor if the use of high-tech (or high-tech-based innovations) is limited to just the firm's products while the day-to-day operating procedures remain out of date?

4. In the twenty-first century, to be successful in niche markets, does a firm need to be a global player?

5. Will FHC survive?

6. Is Bertolazzi a "hero" or just lucky?

PART FIVE

Introduction to the Case Method

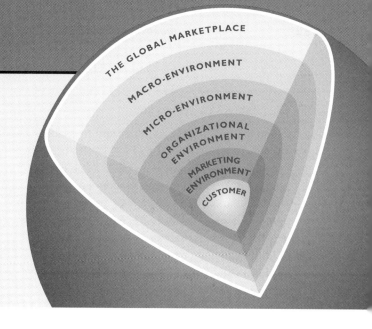

We learn best by doing.

Anonymous

In view of the diverse objectives of courses on strategic marketing management, the specific contents of such courses may vary substantially. This book approaches these subjects through business cases. A case is a description of an organizational situation and frequently contains detailed information about complex issues.

The case method is a Socratic teaching method designed to help you apply theories and concepts that you have learned to actual situations. Most cases focus on some core problem or problems, but the cases can be lengthy and comprehensive. As a student, you are asked to identify those problems and to solve them.* The solution may require you to take advantage of strategic opportunities, and sometimes you may need to propose tactical actions. At other times you will simply be asked to analyze what a firm did correctly, not what its problems were.

Cases are usually written by professors or students or by people involved in the organizational situation. Cases almost always involve real situations. Occasionally, the identity of the organization involved is disguised, but often you will know the identity of the company. Thus you will be able to obtain additional information about the organization if you wish or if your instructor asks you to. However, it is often not wise to research past the date in which the business situation occurred (unless specifically requested by the instructor). For example, if the case describes a situation that occurred in June of 1998, then gathering information that is more current may be dysfunctional. Knowing what the company actually did in the situation is extremely difficult to ignore, and students almost always assume what the company did was the correct thing to do. This knowledge of action taken may render the learning experience offered in the business situation less effective because students think they know the correct answer and fail to consider alternative actions and learn from the discussion of all the alternatives.

Cases may be accompanied by (or contain) industry notes. Your instructor may choose to utilize these industry notes or to ignore them. When used, they are supportive materials for a specific case situation, not a replacement for case materials. As you approach any case, you should obtain as much information on the company's industry as you need to understand the situation described in the case.

*This section is adapted from two sources: James M. Higgins and Julian W. Vincze, *Strategic Management: Text and Cases,* 5th ed. (Orlando, FL: Dryden Press, 1993), pp. 467–472, and Charles W. L. Hill and Gareth R. Jones, *Cases in Strategic Management* (Boston: Houghton Mifflin, 1998), pp. C2–C9. Copyright © 1998 by Houghton Mifflin Company. Used with permission.

OBJECTIVES

The case method's objectives are

1. To add realism to the classroom and to enable students to apply what they have learned
2. To help students to integrate knowledge of the functional areas and to employ concepts of strategic marketing management
3. To improve students' decision-making ability, primarily through practice in making decisions
4. To help students see how actions are related and what they mean in a practical as well as a theoretical sense
5. To encourage students to be effective oral communicators through participation in class, through defense of their ideas, and through the need to "seize the floor" in order to participate
6. To improve students' overall communication skills

APPROACHES

Case analyses may be oral, written, or both. They may be structured or unstructured. Students may be asked to take the role of the CEO, a consultant, or some other person involved in the situation. Normally, the outside consultant's role is preferred because it forces the student to be responsible for communicating his or her basis of analysis, their reasoning that resulted in suggestions, and in addition their complete thinking relative to proposals for action and the implementation of chosen alternatives.

TYPES OF ORGANIZATIONS ENCOUNTERED

Cases cover both goods and services marketing in consumer and business-to-business marketing situations in organizations of various sizes, missions (profit and nonprofit), and geographic market penetration (local, national, multinational, and global). The problems encountered by all these organizations are similar yet distinct.

CASE PROBLEMS ENCOUNTERED

Most of the problems encountered in the cases in this book involve the formulation and control of marketing strategy or tactics. Some require lengthy analysis—which will be explained in detail by your instructor. A few cases involve social responsibility and ethical issues. All require the student analyst to work diligently to acquire an in-depth understanding of the business situation described in the case and, by doing so, to maximize his or her learning opportunity.

Group versus Individual Analysis

Students can engage in preclass and class analysis of a case in either of two ways—in a group or individually. The group method is used when the course is designed to teach people to work in teams and when it is feasible for people to meet in groups. Always be certain of the instructor's expectations relative to individual versus group case analysis. When group analysis is used, the workload should be distributed fairly, but in all groups some people do their fair share and some do not. Appropriate peer-group evaluation should be carried out. Students should resist pressures to conform and be self-reliant in group meetings. Before the group meets, each student should go individually through the steps of analysis outlined in the following section. When the individual method is used, the student prepares all work by himself or herself.

PREPARING A CASE: A SUGGESTED COURSE OF ACTION

1. Read the case; become familiar with the situation. If possible, put the case aside for awhile.
2. Reread the case.
   a. Summarize pertinent information. Use what you have learned in other courses.
   b. Identify vision, mission, goals, objectives, past marketing strategies, current strategies, key success factors, constraints, and SWOT (strengths, weaknesses, opportunities, threats).
   c. Pay special attention to information in exhibits, take notes, and perform analyses:

ratios, financial statements, forecasts, pro forma financial statements.

   d. Answer any questions your instructor has provided.

3. Establish a decision framework.

   a. What are the major problems?

   b. How do you know?

   c. What are the decision constraints?

   d. What are your strategic assumptions?

4. Try to get a comprehensive view of the problem. Do you have the strategic picture in mind? Do you see the interrelationships of the key variables? If not, mull over what you do know until you obtain an overall perspective.

5. Search for and delineate alternatives. Match strengths and weaknesses against opportunities and threats. Be sure to use applicable concepts such as the various product and business matrices, the product lifecycle model, and basic strategic options, and ensure that alternatives address the problems you identify.

6. Choose the appropriate alternatives. Match your choices against vision, mission, goals, objectives, and SWOT. The evaluation process is largely rational but partly intuitive. Once you have finished your analyses, your intuition must function to help you put the complex pieces together.

7. Set priorities for your solution.

8. Be prepared to implement your recommended decisions with a plan of action. You should know how to obtain support for your choices, and you should, if your professor desires, budget for your intended actions.

CLASS PARTICIPATION

The effectiveness of the case method depends in large part on students' contributions in class. Unlike a lecture class, the case method requires the student to assume responsibility for learning, and for the learning of others. Interactions involved in sharing ideas, questioning for understanding, challenging comments, acknowledging issues, and defending positions are important parts of the classroom experience in the case method. In the classroom, you should

1. Participate often and intelligently. A portion of your classroom grade may be based on your participation. An A average on other work may become a B or a C (or worse) for the course if you do not participate appropriately.

2. Substantiate your reasoning and positions with analysis and interpretation of the facts in the business situation.

3. Do not participate just to participate. Contribute. You will soon learn that your professor and your classmates can tell the difference.

4. Respect your peers—you will learn from them. Recognize that others will have thought of issues, analyzed facts, and come to conclusions that you have not.

5. Be prepared to seize the floor. As part of the case method learning experience, you must share your efforts—to do this, you must be heard. If not, how will sharing occur—how will anyone know of your efforts? And your classroom participation grade will suffer significantly.

6. Recognize that your instructor is going to disagree with you, sometimes simply to see if you can defend your position. Furthermore, your classmates are often going to disagree with you to enhance their own situations. You must be prepared to defend your reasoning and analysis.

7. Be willing to take risks. If you make a mistake, you make a mistake, but if you don't try, you'll never get anywhere and you squander a learning opportunity.

8. Avoid use of weak words such as *maybe, I think, I feel, It appears, It tends to.* Be positive and persuasive. Use such words as *It is* and *The analyses reveal that. . . .*

9. Be prepared to change your mind during the discussion of the case. Others may have presented analyses that suggest you missed something. Revising your opinion will not help your written report, since presumably you already will have turned in your written report. But be flexible enough to change your mind in your oral communications if you see you were wrong, because it will help your class participation to do so, and more importantly, it will contribute to your learning experiences.

10. Try to maintain a general manager's orientation to what is going on in the classroom. Think of the way you should respond to the positions of others if you were the CEO of this organization, and react accordingly.

WRITING A CASE STUDY ANALYSIS

Often, as part of your course requirements, you will need to prepare a written case analysis. This may be an individual or a group report. Whatever the situation, there are certain guidelines to follow in writing a case analysis that will improve the evaluation your work will receive from your instructor. Before we discuss these guidelines and before you use them, make sure that they do not conflict with any directions your instructor has given you.

The structure of your written report is critical. Generally, if you follow the steps for analysis discussed in the preceding section, you *already will have a good structure for your written discussion.* All reports begin with an *introduction* to the case. This should explain briefly the organization of your report. Do this sequentially by writing, for example, "First, we discuss the business environment and organizational audit of company X.... Third, we discuss several alternatives that were considered.... Last, we provide recommendations and a detailed plan of action for turning around company X's business."

In the second part of the case write-up, the strategic analysis section (or business audit), do a thorough analysis of past marketing strategies that resulted in past successes both to understand how the organization adds value and to identify past and current key success factors. This should be followed by the SWOT analysis. Next, analyze the organization's structure and control systems, and then analyze and discuss the nature and problems of the company's business-level and corporate strategy. Make sure you use plenty of headings and subheadings to structure your analysis. For example, have separate sections on any important conceptual tool you use. Thus you might have a section on the product lifecycle concept as part of your analysis of the environment. You might offer a separate section on portfolio techniques when analyzing a company's corporate strategy. Tailor the sections and subsections to the specific issues of importance in the case.

In the third part of the case write-up, present your understanding of issues and decisions that managers face within the organization. Also try to state a specific "problem" statement that summarizes all the issues previously identified, and do not forget the time horizon as to when decisions must be made.

The fourth part of the case write-up contains the possible alternative solutions you considered. Some instructors will require that this section of your report contain a brief explanation of the alternative followed by an evaluation of the alternative. Evaluation may be as simple as a list of pros and cons. But it also may be a more detailed discussion of positive and negative aspects of each alternative considered. And some instructors also may expect a discussion of the justification of which alternative is the best given the specifics of the business situation.

The next part of the case write-up contains your solutions in the form of both a set of recommendations of what should be done and also a plan of action that details how to perform the recommended actions. Be comprehensive and as specific as possible, and make sure your proposed activities are in line with the previous analysis so that the recommendations fit together and move logically from one to the next. The recommendations section is very revealing because, as mentioned earlier, your instructor will have a good idea of how much work you put into the case from the quality of your recommendations.

Following this framework will provide a good structure for most written reports, although obviously it must be shaped to fit the individual case being considered. Some cases are about excellent companies experiencing no problems. In such instances, it is hard to write recommendations. Instead, you can focus on analyzing why the company is doing so well, using that analysis to structure the discussion. Following are some minor suggestions that can help make a good analysis even better.

1. Do not repeat in summary form large pieces of factual information from the case. The instructor has read the case and knows what is going on. Rather, use the information in the case to illustrate your statements, to defend your arguments, or to make salient points. Beyond the brief introduction to the company, you must

avoid being *descriptive;* instead, you must be *analytical.*

2. Make sure the sections and subsections of your discussion flow logically and smoothly from one to the next. That is, try to build on what has gone before so that the analysis of the case study moves toward a climax. This is particularly important for group analysis, because there is a tendency for people in a group to split up the work and say, "I'll do the beginning. You take the middle. And I'll do the end." The result is a choppy, stilted analysis because the parts do not flow from one to the next, and it is obvious to the instructor that no real group work has been done.

3. Avoid grammatical and spelling errors. They make the paper sloppy.

4. Some cases dealing with well-known companies end in 1993 or 1994 because the decision was an important one and represents an unusual learning opportunity (also often no later information was available when the case was written). If expected or requested by your instructor, do a library and/or World Wide Web search for more information on what has happened to the company in subsequent years. Following are sources of information for performing this search:

The Internet with its World Wide Web is the place to start your research. Very often you can download copies of a company's annual report from its Web site, and many companies also keep lists of press releases and articles that have been written about them. Thoroughly search the company's Web site for information such as the company's history and performance, and download all relevant information at the beginning of your project. Yahoo is a particularly good search engine to use to discover the address of your company's Web site, although others work as well.

Compact disk sources such as Lotus One Source and InfoTrac provide an amazing amount of good information, including summaries of recent articles written on specific companies that you can then access in the library. *FINS Predicasts* provide a listing on a yearly basis of all the articles written about a particular company. Simply reading the titles gives an indication of what has been happening in the company.

Annual reports on a Form 10-K often provide an organization chart.

Companies themselves provide information if you write and ask for it.

Fortune, BusinessWeek, and *Forbes* have many articles on companies featured in the cases in this book.

Standard & Poor's industry reports provide detailed information about the competitive conditions facing the company's industry. Be sure to look at this journal.

5. Sometimes instructors hand out questions for each case to help you in your analysis. Use these as a guide for writing the case analysis. They often illuminate the important issues that have to be covered in the discussion.

If you follow the guidelines in this section, you should be able to write a thorough and effective evaluation.

ADDITIONAL PERSPECTIVES

As you engage in case analysis, the following additional issues may arise.

Degree of Difficulty

Sometimes the point of the case will be obvious. At other times it will be necessary to read, reread, and reanalyze the case in order to identify the major problem or opportunity. Many cases contain problems of technique that are not the major problems, only symptoms of a major problem.

Viewpoint

One factor to be considered is the viewpoint of the student. Should he or she envision himself or herself as a consultant or as a member of the organization? The ease with which solutions may be implemented is related to the choice of viewpoint. Be certain you understand the viewpoint your instructor expects you to use as a case analyst!

Results

Most of the time your predicted results will be attainable, but in some situations, no matter what the decision, the results may be ineffective. Many factors, especially external environmental factors, are completely beyond the control of an organization. In such situations, the best decisions may be those which allow an organization to minimize its losses.

Strength of Analyses

Most students will not uncover all the factors that eventually will be revealed in the classroom discussions. This constitutes one of the most important learning factors gained from use of the case method—the realization that there is always something the individual will overlook. This is very much like real life.

Perspective

For both the student and the instructor, the case method is a difficult process. In traditional classroom learning situations, students have been assigned the roles of listeners and nonparticipants. To be effective, the case method requires that students think, act, and participate. In order for students to receive good grades, they must achieve these more active levels of learning as opposed to being merely receptive and passive members of a lecturer's audience. The role of a strategic marketing manager, too, demands this kind of behavior.

Case Bias

One must be aware of the inherent bias in a case. The case is related as it is perceived by someone else—the case writer. The reader of a case does not have the benefit of knowing how the information was obtained or what factors the individual considered in writing the case. What is presented as fact may not be as clear-cut as it seems. How facts are presented, which facts are included, and which facts are left out are critical factors. Occasionally, facts may be distorted, especially facts related to statements about the personalities of individuals. Often, individuals' personalities are the key problems in a case, yet the reader can never be sure that the statements about these personalities are exactly accurate.

Answers

There are no right answers in a case situation. Some answers, however, are better than others. The only true test of the decision is in its implementation, and unfortunately, the case method does not allow for implementation of decisions. The right answer, then, is unknown. Only the better answer can be determined. Students whose decisions are based on insufficient analysis usually come up with worse answers and correspondingly worse grades. It is the analysis and interpretation of facts on which decisions are based that are important; several acceptable solutions may be derived from them.

Botton Village

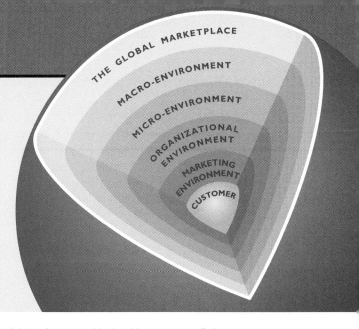

This case was prepared by Adrian Sargeant, Henley Management College.

We have learned never to give up on anyone. Everyone finds their place eventually. All they need is the right chance. We created something new—a working environment supported by a strong social and cultural life where mentally handicapped people can fit in naturally.

Kate Roth, Cofounder of Botton Village

The 45-year history of Botton Village had been built on challenge. Botton had tackled public prejudice against mental handicap; successive funding crises; and even, at one point, a cessation of government funding for their work. All of these issues had been dealt with one by one, and by the late 1990s, the organisation had successfully raised enough funds to secure a long and promising future. It had done so by managing one of the most successful fund-raising campaigns ever to take place in the United Kingdom. Ironically, however, Botton was to become a "victim" of its own success. By the spring of 1998, the organisation was facing the prospect of generating far more income than it would ever be likely to need. The supporter base was proving so loyal that donor attrition was half the sector average, and typical gifts were far in excess of those reported to other similar organisations. It was clear that a change in strategy was necessary, but deciding what exactly this should be was far from easy.

This case is intended as a basis for classroom discussion rather than to illustrate effective or ineffective handling of an administrative situation.

Reprinted by permission from the *Case Research Journal*, volume 21, issue 1. Copyright © 2001 by Adrian Sargeant and the North American Case Research Association. All rights reserved.

The men charged with resolving these problems were John Durham and Lawrence Stroud. By 1998, Durham had worked in the Botton community for over 20 years, playing a variety of roles including houseparent, marketing manager of Botton's cottage industries, and fund-raiser. He had given up a successful marketing career in industry to take up this role.

> When I set out on my career with ICI, I never dreamed I would one day give it all up to live in a place like Botton—and work for no wages!

Lawrence Stroud, by contrast, was not a professional marketer. He had begun his working life in Botton as the village's maintenance man and had stumbled across the fund-raising function almost by accident. However, despite his inexperience, in partnership with Durham he was to design a record-breaking campaign that would ultimately propel him into his own consultancy business. It was in this new role that he met with Durham in the spring of 1998.

> "Whatever we decide to do this year, we can't afford to lose sight of the values of this place,"

said Durham. "They're what make us so special, so unique."

Stroud agreed. From the outset, both men had been struck by the earnestness of Botton's people in striving to fulfill their ideals and the genuine warmth of community spirit that had been generated. Nestling in a particularly picturesque part of the North York moors, Botton Village was a very special community, catering for the needs of mentally handicapped adults from all over Britain. At Botton, they lived with coworkers from around the world, who together combined their talents with care for the villagers. Like any other village, Botton was essentially a varied collection of families, each with a character of its own. There were some 30 houses, roughly grouped in five neighbourhoods, and ranging in size from 6 to 16 people; total population was around 320 people. A typical house was run by a couple who acted as houseparents and, with the help of other coworkers, looked after as many as nine adults with special needs. There was no hierarchy: Everyone worked together to make their house a real home. The warmth this approach generated had been a primary motivator for both men to join the Botton team.

> Community life was all about involvement, and one soon became involved in the cultural, social, and economic facets of village life. We were always very busy. I suspect the 48-hour day was invented at Botton Village!

Indeed, there were many work opportunities, from craftwork and production to candle-making and a modern printing press. A food centre produced a selection of jams, cordials, peanut butter, and many other foodstuffs. There was also a bakery, and work in each of the households involved cooking, cleaning, and ironing. For those who preferred the outdoor life, opportunities also existed to work on one of several farms that formed the hub of their respective neighbourhood.

> Originally, everyone worked in Botton Village. Work was seen as therapy. To be an adult in Botton, you worked; that was what an adult did. At the time we started in 1955, mentally handicapped adults were either at home or in subnormality hospitals and certainly didn't work. So the village impulse was to create an environment where they were needed, where they

contributed, and where they were part of the life of the community.

Although the survival of the community was now assured, the future had not always seemed so bright. There had been times in the early 1980s, in particular, when changes in government policy promised a dramatic shortfall in the community's income. In 1984, for example, the Department of Employment[1] altered its definition of qualification for capital funding. In more recent times, the requirement to register as a "registered home" had also put pressure on the community's finances; buildings and equipment had to be updated rapidly to meet the requirements of the government's new standards.

It was in response to these challenges that the organisation had taken tentative steps towards initiating its first fund-raising program.

> The response we received was remarkable," noted Stroud, "It isn't going to be easy finding some way to modify what has proved to be such a successful recipe. We could well alienate many of the friends we've made over the years and, if we get it really wrong, still jeopardise the long-term survival of the village."

Durham agreed and flicked through the pile of papers on his desk. It was time for both men to review the reasons for their success and the forces that were now making the future so challenging.

BACKGROUND

Botton Village was part of a unique network of communities administered by the Camphill Village Trust, which existed to provide a stimulating, supportive environment for people with a wide range of disabilities. Indeed, Botton was one of nine communities that made up the Trust, which was itself a charity and a nonprofit company. Botton was also a member of the Association of Camphill Communities, which covered all 37 Camphill Centres in the United Kingdom (see Appendix A).

The principles underlying the Camphill movement were first formulated by Karl Konig, an Austrian medical practitioner who came to Britain as a refugee in 1938. When Konig first arrived in Britain, he found refuge on the Camphill estate in Aberdeen, where he founded a school for mentally handicapped children. From these small beginnings, a number of schools were soon established; by the early 1950s, more than 400 children were benefiting from an education designed especially for them. This education was based on the strong Christian ideals of Rudolf Steiner, and an environment was created where those with disabilities could live, learn, and work with others to develop healthy social relationships based on mutual care and respect. A strong emphasis was placed on the development of the whole individual rather than the mere acquisition of skills and knowledge—the common focus of a traditional school curriculum.

Having experienced the care and support they received from these schools, parents of the time began to worry about the prospects for their children upon completion of their studies. In the early 1950s, there were only a few options open to adults with a mental handicap. Parents were fearful that when their children left school they would be sent to a mental hospital or would face the strain and inadequacies of home care.

On a cold Sunday in January 1954, at the headquarters of the Magic Circle Club in London, a group of parents of mentally handicapped adults met. They were there to listen to Dr Karl Konig:

> Your sons and daughters must go to our village. It does not exist yet. You and I have to bring it into existence. Ours is to be a village where mentally handicapped people will be able to support themselves by work.
>
> No fees will be paid. The villagers must not feel that they are still dependents. They must feel that the success of the place depends on them. They will live in small family units, and the housemothers and other helpers will receive no salary.

Then began a very lengthy discussion, a ray of hope, and a committee. On October 4, 1954, the Camphill Village Trust was formed, and the search for a place for the first village was able to begin. By the summer of 1955, the Trust purchased the Botton estate in Danby Dale. At the end of August in the same year, the first villagers took up residence.

From the start, life in the community at Botton was based on Konig's three guiding principles:

1. A cultural life, in which education and learning, appreciation of the arts, concern for the environment, and the fostering of mutual understanding were combined to offer the possibility for all members of the community to realise their full potential.

2. A community life, in which the recognition of the special qualities of every individual and the celebration of the Christian festivals through the year form the basis for daily life. Sharing these ingredients brings people together as equals for a common purpose.

> I was 18 when I came here. Now I am 45. Botton is my home. I hope I can live here forever. If I didn't lived at Botton, I wouldn't be needed.

Lizzie Swift, Resident of Botton Village

3. An economic life, in which there is separation of work and money. Work is carried out according to the needs of the community and the ability of each person; people's financial needs are met on an individual and cooperative basis irrespective of the work done. Rudolf Steiner referred to this as the Fundamental Social Law:

> The well-being of a community of individuals working together becomes greater, the less the individuals demand for themselves the products of their own achievements: that is, the more of those products they pass on to their follow workers, and the more their own needs are satisfied, not out of their own individual achievements, but out of the achievements of others.

Many of those working in the village felt that the adoption of this principle had actually compelled them to work harder than they would had they been paid employees. There was a sense that the work was important not because of the benefit it conveyed to the worker, but rather because of the benefit it conveyed to the wider community. As a result, those who were able often participated in village life in two or more ways.

> Now for work. I am a cleaner and I work at Honey Bee Nest farm in the mornings. I make tea at half past ten, then I do the sink and floors and finally the table for lunch.
>
> In the afternoon, I work in the centre of the village—the Village Store, which is our focal point. Also, especially in the summer, we have large crowds of visitors. Can you imagine keeping your equilibrium properly when you are trying to clean and suddenly lots of ladies from the WI come in on coach parties?

In the evening, different activities are on. Saturday is Bible evening, which I like because of the discussion. I have found my place in Botton Village, and I am very lucky to be here.

Mary Mascaro, Resident of Botton Village

THE WIDER CAMPHILL COMMUNITY

The success of Botton and other such fledgling organisations soon inspired the development of a wider number of Camphill communities.

In the schools within Camphill, pupils have continued since the 1940s to receive a broad education based on the Waldorf curriculum as conceived by Rudolf Steiner. By 1998, pupils could move into further education according to need and ability, many within their original schools or at other Camphill communities that offer training to young people. Emphasis was placed on the maturing of the individual and the strengthening of the element of mutual support in both work and social life. Craftwork plays an important part at this stage of individual development. For those young people who continue to need and wish for a sheltered environment, Camphill communities could also offer an appropriate setting in which a healthy transition to adult life could occur.

The varied locations of the Camphill communities—from villages where production in craft or food workshops generates a substantial proportion of their revenue to smaller rural communities where a quieter rhythm of life is possible—offered possibilities to a broad spectrum of people with different needs. Categories of accommodation also varied, from separate houses distanced from each other in urban surroundings to purpose-built clusters of houses within the environment of a new town. Indeed, there were a variety of communities appropriate for many different people who wished to share their lives with others.

FUND-RAISING AT BOTTON

In 1998, Botton received funding from several different sources. Part of the daily living costs were met by the Department of Employment, which viewed the entire village as a place offering "supported employment." Local authorities and the Department of Social Security[2] contributed towards the residential costs of individual villagers. Botton also received further income from the sale of crafts and produce. In total, these sources of income were sufficient to meet the ongoing running costs of the community. All the money for improvements, new buildings, expansion, and development at Botton had, however, to come from fund-raising. By 1998, the voluntary (i.e., fund-raising) income accruing to Botton was to equal that derived from statutory sources.

The development of Botton's fund-raising activity happened almost by accident. Lawrence Stroud was originally engaged as the village's maintenance man. His role brought him into daily contact with a recently introduced job creation scheme and youth opportunities program, designed primarily to facilitate repairs while giving a number of young people their first work experience.

> Suddenly, it dawned on us that we really didn't have the money to pay for the materials. Quite by accident, I was clearing out an old desk, and I came across a box of old letters from grant-making trusts. I thought it might be a good idea to write to them just to say "hi," thank them for their past support, and let them know we were still in existence.
>
> I think I had £10,000 by return of post. I was so surprised by it that I decided there must be something in this fund-raising!

It was not for some months, however, that any formal strategy began to develop. Indeed, the first concerted attempt at fund-raising occurred as the result of a chance meeting between Lawrence Stroud and Ken Burnett, who had just set himself up as a fund-raising consultant.

> I attended a seminar offered by the Directory of Social Change[3]—I think it was called "Direct Mail—The Last Unexplored Medium," with Ken Burnett as the speaker. I made a point of meeting him at the end of the session, and I invited him to Yorkshire. I told him I couldn't pay him any money, but he came anyway!"

As a result of this meeting, a plan for Botton's first fund-raising mailshot was developed. The first mailshot was targeted at 40,000 recipients and formed part of the recruitment strategy that was planned to span an initial 5-year period.

> It was going to cost £8,000, which was roughly equivalent to the entire annual village expendi-

ture on repairs. It also meant not buying a car for the village that year. Such was the scale of the expenditure that we had a meeting in the community centre where I had to convince everyone that it was a really good idea to spend this money.

The mailshot went out, and I didn't sleep for a week! It was £8,000 that was going, and I wondered how I would ever live it down if it all went wrong. Much to our astonishment, though, we actually made money from our first cold mailing. I thought if we were making money out of cold, this was a real opportunity.

Even at this early stage, the decision was made to seek genuine relationships with donors instead of merely a succession of "one-off" donations. It was felt that donors should be treated as part of a wider Botton community and feel a sense of belonging to their organisation. Donors were encouraged to support the village in whatever manner suited them best. They were encouraged to specify the type of relationship that they wanted with the village. In 1997, donors were additionally offered the opportunity to obtain past issues of *Botton Village Life (BVL)*, the charity's newsletter; information videos; audio cassettes; or even be removed from the mailing list altogether. This opportunity (see Appendix B) was distributed with every appeal, and the information on donor preferences gathered was appended to the database to aid in building the communication program. When the strategy was first developed, Botton was among the first charities to make the conscious decision to move away from segmentation based solely on measures of donor value (such as RFM[4]) and toward a system based largely on donor interest and preference.

It was interesting to note how well people responded to this type of thing, right from the word go. It was quite revolutionary, asking people what they wanted. Donors wrote back and said, "Fantastic, you're actually one of the first charities that offered me a box saying we'd like to receive your newsletters but not be pestered by your appeals."

Alongside this strategy of donor choice, Botton also developed an enhanced approach to market segmentation. When the first segmented mailing was sent in April 1992, there were 12 segments of donors. Initially, each segment was allocated a code identifying whether the donors were grant-making

trusts, corporate organisations, individual givers, committed supporters (e.g., covenantors[5]), high-value givers, or multiple givers. Stroud was eager to use this information to develop a one-to-one dialogue with his supporters.

Steps were also taken to reduce the likelihood of the communication break-downs that had hitherto dogged the sector:

There's nothing I hate more than sending a donation to someone and then two days later getting a letter asking me for money. So at Botton we always trawled back 6 to 7 weeks before a mailshot and sent any recent givers a mailshot saying "thanks again for that recent gift; we thought you might like to know what's going on." This is so much better than saying "thank you very much, but would you like to give again." It's interesting to note that this "recent" segment generated above-average donation levels anyway.

The focus on donor relationships had led Botton to steer clear of what it perceived as the current gimmicks employed by other charities within the sector. Tick boxes suggesting appropriate levels at which individuals might like to give were no longer found in Botton mailings. Although Stroud was initially in favour of experimenting with different levels of prompt for different levels of donor, the fund-raising team eventually decided that this was not right for Botton. It did not fit with the organisation's philosophy of leaving donors free to choose their own level of gift.

Interestingly, because tick boxes are no longer provided, great care has to be taken with the copy so as not to imply appropriate amounts. In one edition of BVL, it was intimated that a set of door handles to be fitted in the course of renovation work would cost the charity £7 per pair:

People who normally donated £10 sent £7, or multiples of £7. We said that this was one thing we would have to beware of again. Someone even wrote in to suggest where we might get them cheaper!

The closeness of the relationship that Botton developed with its supporters was evident from the ever-increasing file of correspondence the charity received.

On one occasion, we said to donors that we were thinking of using a wood-burning generator to provide power to a new complex. Donors wrote in suggesting where we might get advice. We even had one old lady who rang in saying that she was very worried that if we started burning wood in this way the whole complex was going to burn down. I'm therefore on the phone at 10 P.M., saying, "I think its been properly researched, Mrs. Jones, so please don't worry!"

Indeed, recent research indicated that people were so enthusiastic about the Botton cause that they actually believed they had made a donation, even when they had not.

Part of the reason for our success has undoubtedly been the fact that we've always presented a solution rather than a problem. I support that donors can say, psychologically speaking, that they're connected with something that's succeeding.

BOTTON VILLAGE LIFE

A central tenet of Botton's fund-raising strategy had been the village newsletter, *Botton Village Life*. The publication was developed four times a year with help from Burnett Associates and mailed to all of those Botton supporters who had indicated they would like to receive it. The front page of the newsletter had traditionally kept donors abreast of the results of any previous fund-raising campaigns and their impact on the community. Therefore, each edition of *BVL* served a useful purpose in informing donors of how their money had actually been used. There was, however, another and arguably more important purpose to *BVL*.

It's very important to us that our donors feel like valued, respected friends, and to that end we genuinely try to pass on some of the values of the village and the wider Camphill movement. The newsletter actually brings people closer to the village. Although we try to raise money with an appeal each quarter, the mailing also goes out with the purpose of bringing people up to date with the news and helping them to get to know the village better.

Past editions of the newsletter had covered issues such as Botton's philosophy of farming, various views of work, the cultural life, and the way the craft workshops operate. There had even been a

special green issue that explored Botton's approach to the conservation of its environment. Much thought had gone into the content of *BVL,* and the organisation was always thinking about issues that it might explore in future editions. Much of the recent content had focused on the building work taking place, as every home in Botton's community had recently been brought up to the new standards required by the Registered Home Act.

Coverage had also been provided of the organisation's open day, where each year every Botton supporter is encouraged to visit the community. In the first year, 38,000 invitations were sent out and, although only 100 supporters actually arrived, feedback from donors suggested that everyone had appreciated being asked, even if they had ultimately decided that they could not attend. Indeed, it would have been something of a problem had a larger proportion of donors elected to attend; the North York moors could effectively have been brought to a standstill. Visitor numbers of between 100 and 200 were felt to be ideal, given this constraint and the car-parking capacity of the site.

The overall number of Botton's supporters had grown consistently from year to year, certainly until 1996, when the decision was taken to maintain the database at or around its 1998 level (see Exhibit 1). Levels of donor loyalty compared very favourably with other organisations in the sector, and the lifetime of a typical Botton donor was approximately 1.5 times that of the sector norm. Botton's performance in this respect is illustrated in Exhibit 2. The organisation continued to maintain a healthy proportion of active donors. In Exhibit 3, this data has been extrapolated to predict the number of individuals likely to be supporting Botton in the year 2000.

COLD MAILING

Botton had made good use of both cold lists and reciprocal mailings since fund-raising activities had begun in earnest. Historically, the Botton team agonised over list selection, but as the results began to justify the investment, the numbers per mailing grew quite dramatically (at one point approaching nearly 2 million per annum). The available lists were quickly exhausted, and greater reliance had to be placed on the advice of their broker.

EXHIBIT 1

Donors on File Each Year

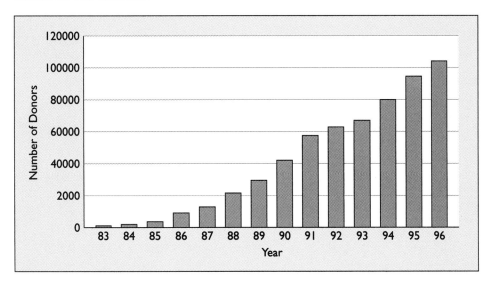

EXHIBIT 2

Donor Progress

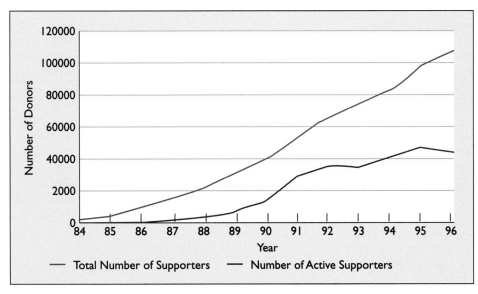

Key
Upper Line = Total Number of Supporters
Lower Line = Number of Active Supporters

EXHIBIT 3

Numbers of Active Botton Supporters (i.e., those who have donated within the past 2-year period)

Year	Cumulative Volume of Donations	Yearly Volume of Donations	Yearly Cumulative Volume of Supporters	Volume of New Supporters	Yearly Lifetime Value
1991	81,871		18,588		
1992	111,543	29,672	23,041	4,453	778,929
1993	147,582	36,039	25,091	2,050	1,198,972
1994	184,385	36,803	26,965	1,874	903,046
1995	226,222	41,837	26,685	2,720	1,148,284
1996	269,465	43,243	30,754	1,069	458,588
1997	314,434	44,969	32,104	1,350	726,520
1998	360,321	45,888	33,322	1,217	694,802
1999	406,462	46,140	34,434	1,112	668,211
2000	452,188	45,726	35,460	1,026	645,445

Botton had always expended considerable effort in testing both its packs and the lists to which they would be addressed. The original strategy had been to go with the list that generated the maximum possible response. The feeling among members of the fund-raising group had been that, once recruited, they then had an excellent chance to convince donors of the need for ongoing support. A more recent analysis employing the statistical technique CHAID[6] had, however, suggested a correlation between the size of the first gift and donor loyalty. It would therefore appear that the more a donor gives initially, the longer they are likely to stay in the program. As a consequence, a change of strategy ensued, and lists were now selected on the basis of the level of the average gift generated. It would, of course, be a few years before the true utility of this change in strategy could be ascertained.

Once recruited, donors were input into a highly focused "welcome cycle," specifically designed to facilitate what Botton regarded as the crucial second gift. Typically, only 50 percent of the donors would elect to give again, a phenome-non common to most charities across the sector. The welcome cycle thus consisted of a series of up to seven mailings, posted at quarterly intervals. The focus of these mailings was to inform the donor about the organisation and the value of its work, and to build the beginnings of a relationship. At any point, donors could make a second donation and be "shifted sideways" into what Botton termed a "code 8." It was not until the organisation received its third donation, however, that the donor was considered a normal donor, because it was at that point that a pattern of loyalty had been built up, and the donor was quite clearly committed to the cause.

It was interesting to note that the response rates from each of the welcome cycle mailings were quite acceptable and well above what could be achieved from a standard cold mailing. The typical response varies from each mailing by 12 percent, 8 percent, 3.6 percent, 4 percent, and 2.5 percent.

Even if a second response was not forthcoming, however, the charity did not drop the donors concerned. Instead, donors continued to receive information, but only on an infrequent basis as time and money permitted. The reason for this was simply that Botton remained uncertain as to how its regular legacy income (typically £500,000) was generated. There was a feeling within the organisation that dropping lapsed supporters from the database might detract from this valuable source of revenue.

WARM MAILING

The original target had been to build a database of 7,500 supporters that could form the core target for future fund-raising activity. In 1998, Botton had a database of some 55,000 people and was generating a net income of around £1.9 million per annum. The returns from Botton's warm mailing program were far in excess of the sector-wide average. Indeed, response rates and levels of average gift were typically twice those that would normally be generated by a typical charity. The "mail at Christmas only" segment of donors, for example, regularly generated a response rate in excess of 50 percent, and the historically best campaign generated a response rate of 32 percent across the file (see Appendix C).

At times, these enhanced patterns of performance had proved to be a source of embarrassment to Botton's fund-raisers. It was, until the mid-1990s, common practice for Botton to engage in reciprocal mailings with other charities.

> This used to be quite embarrassing because we would get between 9 percent and 10 percent on reciprocals and other charities would only get 4 percent to 5 percent. We would get more than they would get from their own donors.

Approximately 70 tests have historically been conducted in the course of an appeals mailing, although Botton had resisted the temptation to hone the precision of their fund-raising much further.

> We were looking at a greater degree of tailoring—trying to lead people into committed giving, considering gender-specific copy, and changing the wording of various packs to address each donor on an increasingly individual basis. We concluded, however, that this was not an approach suited to Botton. We just didn't need (or want) this degree of sophistication.

FUND-RAISING ANALYSIS

Botton conducted a detailed analysis of the results of each campaign. A complete response profile was conducted; this was typically broken down by segment, ACORN[7] category, lifetime value, gender, and so forth. In 1997, the charity also commissioned a detailed study of the historic performance of its fund-raising activity, examining the period 1990 to 1996. The key findings of this report are summarised in Exhibits 4 through 7.

A VICTIM OF SUCCESS?

After Lawrence Stroud left Botton in 1996 to set up his own consultancy business, a new dilemma began to face Botton fund-raisers: where to go next. Historically, the majority of the income generated by Botton's fund-raising had been aimed at meeting the requirements of registration. Because the village buildings had been gradually updated, there was no longer such a need to generate income. John Durham recalled:

> Botton had always been clear that its campaigning should be driven by a genuine need and not by how much money is available, and so we had quite a lot of debate around the level to which Botton should be fund-raising.

As a consequence, Botton's strategy began to focus solely on maintaining the size of the active supporter file. High-volume cold recruitment mailings were no longer felt necessary.

> We must be one of the few charities that actually considered sending a mailing, saying, "Thank you very much, but we don't need any money this time. You've been so generous in the past. We'll just keep in touch with our newsletter and write to you when we need your help again."

Indeed, the Botton team did actively consider wrapping up their fund-raising program and concentrating entirely on other Camphill sites. The potential problem with this option, however, was that Botton's fund-raising team would have had to take on responsibility for a much larger program: None of the other CVT sites had the necessary in-house

EXHIBIT 4

Forecast Lifetime Value by Duration of Supporter Lifetime

Retention	Supporters	Percent of Supporters	Income	Gifts	Average Gift	Average Lifetime Value
Missing	6,221	30.23	164,287	5,981	27	26
One Year	6,478	31.47	181,487	8,753	21	28
1–2 Years	2,042	9.92	124,139	5,675	22	61
2–3 Years	1,530	7.43	161,804	5,502	29	106
3–4 Years	1,236	6.01	197,776	5,886	34	160
4–5 Years	965	4.69	159,771	5,367	30	166
5–6 Years	775	3.77	225,819	5,213	43	291
6–7 Years	517	2.51	118,506	3,969	30	229
7–8 Years	343	1.67	78,299	2,885	27	228
8–9 Years	230	1.12	66,106	2,001	33	287
9–10 Years	154	0.75	64,753	1,548	42	420
Over 10 Years	91	0.44	40,188	1,160	35	442
Total	20,582	100	1,582,924	53,940	29	77

EXHIBIT 5

Category of Giving by Gender

Category	Percent of Supporters	Percent of Gifts	Percent of Income	Average Gift
Noncommitted				
Unknown	9	8	10	35
Female	49	42	34	22
Male	35	28	29	27
Total	93	78	74	26
Committed				
Unknown	1	4	5	34
Female	3	10	11	29
Male	3	8	11	37
Total	7	22	26	33
All Supporters	100	100	100	27

EXHIBIT 6

Analysis of Income by Value Decile

Decile	Number	Income	Percent Income	Gifts	Percent Gifts
Top 10%	11,002	8,008,903	63.82	141,605	32
10–20	11,002	1,845,610	14.71	87,585	20
20–30	11,002	982,136	7.83	58,534	13
30–40	11,002	982,136	4.71	40,186	9
40–50	11,002	590,505	3.09	32,427	7
50–60	11,002	387,131	2.00	21,581	5
60–70	11,002	250,900	1.64	15,140	3
70–80	11,002	205,969	1.09	17,354	4
80–90	11,002	136,950	0.76	14,654	3
90–100	11,002	94,796	0.36	11,989	3
Total	110,020	45,581	100	441,055	100

expertise to run their own fund-raising activities. This breadth of responsibility, it was felt, could lead to numerous conflicts of interest and create unnecessary levels of internal tension. Botton, after all, had no dedicated fund-raisers, only a small team of helpers each with other responsibilities within the site.

A further option that the village considered was the gradual expansion of their own community and the potential fund-raising for the new building work required. There was a strong feeling though that in growing in this way, something of the unique character of Botton life would be lost. There were also very real constraints likely to be imposed by the national park authorities, who would be unlikely to sanction any further building work in the Danby Dale area.

We did feel, though, that it would be a pity to allow what has been a very successful fund-raising mechanism to decline. We, therefore, took the decision not to enlarge it, rather to use it to help others who do still have a need.

With a plethora of other Camphill sites that could potentially stand to benefit from Botton's fund-raising, it seemed appropriate to consider helping Botton's sister organisations. Early attempts at raising funds for the whole Camphill organisation had, however, met with little success. As Durham recalls

Part of our appeal was the word *VILLAGE*. There's a view that it's not something sprawling or bureaucratic. The trustees and most of the people involved in it are actually living in the community. The Camphill Foundation is altogether more nebulous. We were faced with saying that we were responsible for a lot of communities. There just wasn't that ability to connect—not the same magic. We were definitely selling something different.

In the late 1990s, Botton decided to experiment with raising funds for specific Camphill communities. A page of Botton's newsletter was now devoted to following the activities and progress of what they referred to as "Botton's Wider Family." Editions of *BVL* have, therefore, also covered the Russian and Polish communities, together with Larchfield, the Croft and other U.K. sites. *BVL* was also used to trail an appeal for another Camphill

EXHIBIT 7

Numbers of Supporters by LTV Band

LTV Band	Donors	Gifts	Total Income	Total Costs
−£20 to −£50	2	7	10	52
−£10 to −£20	187	495	1,064	3,321
−£5 to −£10	969	1,678	6,000	13,148
Down to −£5	7,209	9,134	38,577	50,074
Nil	3	6	33	33
Up to £5	12,098	16,344	96,002	61,790
£5–£10	10,795	16,418	130,077	58,262
£10–£20	21,753	35,801	423,916	109,426
£20–£50	21,030	63,783	837,377	145,401
£50–£100	13,629	68,295	1,102,823	123,545
£100 to £500	18,460	169,413	4,197,424	236,730
£500 to £1000	2,578	38,052	1,792,782	41,992
£1000 to £5000	1,214	20,109	2,130,523	21,730
£5000 to £10,000	61	1,084	396,718	1,096
Over £10,000	32	436	774,550	534

Note: N. B. lifetime value is calculated by subtracting a supporter's individual recruitment and servicing costs from their total income. A supporter's cost is calculated by adding their recruitment cost in the year of joining plus annual mailing costs until the supporter either leaves the database or is inactive for over 2 years.

site, so that donors were familiar with its work before a request was actually made.

We began by taking a small group of Botton supporters and mailing them quite outside the normal cycle of four mailings per year. We mailed them separately in between mailings with a letter that was from Botton but about another community. We did that twice—just once per year. So for instance when Botton's cheesemaker went off to start a Camphill community in Estonia, *Botton Village Life* followed Christian's leaving and going on to Estonia and monitored his progress. We were then able to write to a group of Botton supporters, just telling them about the situation in Estonia and asking them if they wanted to help him to build a

house. The response we got did not seem to impact our next Botton mailing.

We did that twice, and then about a year ago we decided that Botton was really committed in the longer term to moving its donors much more in the direction of supporting other communities. On the back of that decision, we decided to use our standard warm mailings to raise money for wider communities—and we decided that once a year we would give over one warm appeal to another Camphill community.

In September 1997, the first Botton mailing on behalf of Larchfield was undertaken. The mailing went to all Botton's active supporters, excluding those in the welcome cycle. The results of the campaign can be seen in Appendix C. Although the response from donors was good, the average donation level was smaller than had been the case in previous years. A further analysis of the response suggested the pattern of giving had also been affected by the change. In 1996, when all appeals were made on behalf of Botton, 48 percent of those individuals who gave in September gave again in December. In 1997, only 38 percent of those who gave in September also gave again in December. It was interesting to note that a significant percentage of donors still elected to support Botton, even though the team had led them toward the Larchfield appeal.

A CHANGE IN DIRECTION?

It was this confusion and a general uncertainty over whether Botton should really be fund-raising for other organisations at all that had led to the meeting between Durham and Stroud in 1998. Durham summarised the key issues for the benefit of his former colleague:

> In reality, there is still a lot of work to do on this. We still haven't really resolved how best to go forward. Indeed, to be honest we don't really know how to interpret the results we've just achieved for 1997. Should we continue to fund-raise for our sister organisations and perhaps devote two or more campaigns to this per year, or should we just wind down our fund-raising activity? If so, how exactly should we go about this? It's quite a dilemma we have to address.

Endnotes

1. A department of the U.K. central government.
2. A department of the U.K. central government.
3. An umbrella body, itself a charity, which exists to support the voluntary sector through the provision of research, training, and statistics.
4. Recency, frequency, value. Much modern fund-raising software creates a score for each donor, highlighting the likelihood that they will respond to a given campaign. It is derived from measures of recency, frequency, and value.
5. One of a number of tax-efficient forms of giving in the United Kingdom. Signing a covenant allows the charity to reclaim the tax the donor would have paid on the amount donated.
6. Chi-square automatic interaction detector.
7. One of a number of geodemographic systems available in the United Kingdom. ACORN stands for "a classification of residential neighbourhoods" and is produced by CACI.

APPENDIX A

A Sample of Other Camphill Communities

Cherry Orchards Camphill Community

Cherry Orchards provides a therapeutic environment for people between the ages of 21 and 42 who are suffering from mental illness. Situated on a 17-acre estate within the city of Bristol, community life forms the basis of mutual care, support, and development. Intensive treatment and rehabilitation are offered for a specific period to those who are willing to be coparticipants in their own healing process.

The Croft

The community has sought since 1976 to provide supportive integration into society for adults with learning disabilities. It is an established central resource for 34 residents and several friends who are living independently.

Camphill Devon Community

Hapstead Village was started at the end of 1979 to provide residential care and work for adults with learning difficulties. The work realms are farm garden, estate, weavery, pottery, woodwork, and copperwork.

Grange Village

Grange Village is an estate of 30 acres offering opportunities for adults with social or mental disabilities. Work at Grange Village includes bakery, basketry, pottery, woodwork, farming, and horticulture.

Larchfield

Larchfield is a 156-acre land-based community situated on the outskirts of Teeside. Larchfield was created in response to Middlesborough Borough council's invitation for a Camphill Community within its boundaries to provide employment for people with special needs. Farm, gardens, and workshops produce high-quality goods that are retailed locally and through the Wheelhouse Coffee Bar, which is open to the public. With a strong emphasis on adult education, classes take place throughout the working week.

Mount Camphill Community

Mount Camphill is a therapeutic community for young people age 15 to 25 years who have special needs. Mount Camphill offers upper-school education and a college for further education and training in craft and practical skills.

Pennine Camphill Community

The Pennine Community helps young people (16 years or older) having special needs to develop social maturity and individual direction within a college framework of further education, craft training, and work experience.

The Sheiling School

The Sheiling School is a school for children age 6 to 16 years who have special needs. The Sheiling School offers term or weekly board and some day placements.

Let Botton help you

Your support means a great deal to us and we want to help you in return. Please decide exactly how you want us to stay in touch by ticking the relevant boxes below.

Choose when you want to hear from us

1. At the moment we send you four issues of *Botton Village Life a year:*

☐ *I would prefer to hear from you just once a year, at Christmas.*

☐ *I would like you to keep me up to date with Botton's news through Botton Village Life, but I do not wish to receive appeals.*

2. If you only receive a newsletter once a year, you may like us to contact you more often:

☐ *I would like to receive Botton Village Life four times a year.*

3. If you would rather NOT receive information:

☐ *I would prefer you not to write to me again.*

4. Choose whether you'll help us find new friends:

From time to time we agree with other carefully selected charities to write to some of each other's supporters. This can be a very valuable way to find new friends.

☐ *I would prefer not to hear from any other organisations.*

Choose what you'd like to receive

5. Our video of life in Botton

Our latest video, *Botton Village: This Is Our Home* – set against the changing seasons in the rural beauty of Danby Dale – will help you to get to know us better. It tells the story of our community through the lives of our villagers and is a charming portrait of special people and the challenges they meet in sharing life together.

☐ *Please send me your video on a month's free loan.*

☐ *Please send me my own copy. I enclose a cheque for £7.50.*

6. Our *Sounds of Botton* audio tape

Our tape follows villager Jane Hill as she tours the village and meets her friends. It will give you a unique insight into life at Botton.

☐ *Please send me a free copy of the Sounds of Botton tape.*

7. Our information for visitors

Visitors are always welcome at Botton. If you can, please give us a ring in advance on (01287) 660871. We can supply details of the opening times of our workshops and a map of how to get to Botton.

☐ *Please send me your information for visitors.*

How else can we help?

8. Explaining the methods of giving you can use

Please send me:

☐ *A Deed of Covenant form.*

☐ *A Gift Aid form for gifts of £250 upwards.* Please note our charity is not eligible for Gift Aid 2000.

9. Providing a helpful guide to making a Will

We produce *The Simple Guide to Making a Will* which is full of useful, impartial information. Of course, if you do decide to remember Botton in your Will, we would be very grateful. *Please send me my free copy of* The Simple Guide to Making a Will, *currently applicable only in England and Wales.*

I would like the ☐ *standard print* ☐ *large-print version.*

10. Sending you past issues of our newsletter

Interesting stories from the village's history feature in past issues of our newsletter, *Botton Village Life.* You may ask for any of the past issues you would like, or another copy of ones you may have mislaid or passed on to a friend.

☐ *Please send me a set of back issues (1-20).*

☐ *Please send me issue no_____ (nos 21 upwards).*

11. Giving you details about Camphill in the UK

Botton Village is just one of the many communities which are part of the Camphill movement. If you want to know about other Camphill centres, we will be happy to help.

☐ *Please send me the booklet* An Introduction to Camphill Communities *and a list of centres.*

Above: left to right are shown our Sounds of Botton tape, guide to making a Will, the Botton video, and a back issues set of Botton Village Life newsletter.

Do you want a word with someone?

Our office team of Fran, Jackie, Kelly, Joanne and Sue is here to help you. Just ring our helpline (01287 661294) or our switchboard (01287 660871), 9am to 4pm weekdays, and one of us will be pleased to talk to you. Do let us know if you have moved to a new address, if we are sending you more than one copy of our newsletter by mistake, or if there is anything else you would like to tell us.

Botton Village is part of The Camphill Village Trust Limited, a non-profit-making company limited by guarantee 539694 in England and registered as a charity, number 232402.

APPENDIX C

Botton Average Gifts (warm)

Year	March Quantity	March Av. Gift	June Quantity	June Av. Gift	September Quantity	September Av. Gift	December Quantity	December Av. Gift	Average Quantity	Average Av. Gift
1991	38,420	45.59	38,507	54.95	39,000	40.71	47,000	37.93	40,807	44.80
1992	43,915	43.55	42,893	40.28	41,425	44.55	55,509	47.07	45,936	43.86
1993	38,934	49.47	38,163	67.52	32,163	51.58	44,694	49.82	38,489	54.60
1994	36,854	51.62	36,464	78.23	34,130	50.70	49,160	44.26	39,152	56.20
1995	43,136	49.67	44,718	60.74	46,012	43.38	68,259	41.21	50,531	48.75
1996	46,803	50.61	46,793	51.57	49,404	43.29	91,358	37.52	58,590	45.76
1997	49,616	53.87	46,199	57.83	46,690	27.39	73,469	37.93	53,994	44.26
1998	49,015	48.52								
AVR (91–97)	42,525	49.20	42,005	58.73	41,261	43.09	61,350	42.25	46,785	48.32

Botton Percent Response Rate Achieve (warm)

Year	March Quantity	March Percent	June Quantity	June Percent	September Quantity	September Percent	December Quantity	December Percent	Average Quantity	Average Percent
1991	38,420	17.82	38,507	14.07	39,000	15.95	47,000	23.42	40,807	17.82
1992	43,915	15.38	42,893	20.69	41,425	12.00	55,509	23.38	45,936	17.86
1993	38,934	17.65	38,163	19.16	32,163	19.46	44,694	30.26	38,489	21.63
1994	36,854	20.26	36,464	20.89	34,130	19.10	49,160	31.16	39,152	22.85
1995	43,136	17.07	44,718	15.41	46,012	17.57	68,259	29.42	50,531	19.87
1996	46,803	18.82	46,793	15.05	49,404	20.54	91,358	23.54	58,590	19.49
1997	49,616	17.48	46,199	16.15	46,690	18.33	73,469	32.33	53,994	21.07
1998	49,015	18.55							49,015	18.55
AVR (91–97)	42,525	17.78	42,005	17.35	41,261	17.56	61,350	27.64	46,785	20.08

Botton Campaign Surplus (i.e., revenues–costs)

March Quantity	March Surplus	June Quantity	June Surplus	September Quantity	September Surplus	December Quantity	December Surplus	Average Surplus	Average Quantity	Total Surplus	Year
38,420	297,108	38,507	283,050	39,000	235,327	47,000	397,621	303,277	163,227	1,213,106	1991
43,915	270,113	42,893	327,244	41,425	198,590	55,509	579,616	343,891	183,742	1,375,563	1992
38,934	326,689	38,163	458,323	32,163	322,900	44,694	645,034	438,237	153,954	1,752,946	1993
36,854	354,600	36,464	566,468	34,130	299,737	49,160	617,322	459,532	156,608	1,838,127	1994
43,136	326,743	44,718	359,216	46,012	338,751	68,259	757,129	445,460	202,125	1,781,839	1995
46,803	385,957	46,793	421,461	49,404	361,993	91,358	699,443	467,214	260,403	1,868,854	1996
49,616	410,195	46,199	371,002	46,690	235,546	73,469	812,274	457,254	215,974	1,829,017	1997
49,015	382,209							382,209	49,015	382,209	1998
42,525	338,772	42,005	398,109	41,261	284,692	61,350	644,063	416,409	190,862	1,665,636	AVR (91–97)

Note: September 1997 Surplus (Larchfield) includes £68,448 marked Botton only.

W. L. Gore & Associates, Inc.: Entering 1998

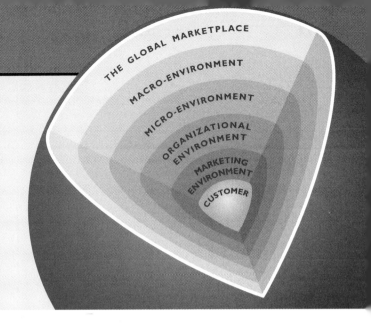

This case was prepared by Frank Shipper of the Department of Management and Marketing at Franklin P. Perdue School of Business at Salisbury State University, and Charles C. Manz, Nirenberg Professor of Business Leadership at the University of Massachusetts, Amherst.

"To make money and have fun."

W. L. Gore

Bursting with resolve, Jack Dougherty, a newly minted MBA from the College of William and Mary, reported to his first day at W. L. Gore & Associates on July 26, 1976. He presented himself to Bill Gore, shook hands firmly, looked him in the eye, and said he was ready for anything.

Jack was not ready, however, for what happened next. Gore replied, "That's fine, Jack, fine. Why don't you look around and find something you'd like to do?" Three frustrating weeks later he found that something: trading in his dark blue suit for jeans, he loaded fabric into the mouth of a machine that laminated the company's patented Gore-Tex[1] membrane to fabric. By 1982, Jack had become responsible for all advertising and marketing in the fabrics group. This story is part of the folklore of W. L. Gore & Associates.

Today, the process is more structured. Regardless of the job for which they are hired, new associates[2] take a journey through the business before settling into their own positions. A new sales associate in the fabrics division may spend 6 weeks rotating through different areas before beginning to concentrate on

Reprinted by permission of the authors.

sales and marketing. Among other things, the newcomer learns how Gore-Tex fabric is made, what it can and cannot do, how Gore handles customer complaints, and how it makes its investment decisions.

Anita McBride related her early experience at W. L. Gore & Associates this way:

Before I came to Gore, I had worked for a structured organization. I came here, and for the first month it was fairly structured because I was going through training, and this is what we do and this is how Gore is and all of that. I went to Flagstaff for that training. After a month, I came down to Phoenix, and my sponsor said, "Well, here's your office; it's a wonderful office" and "Here's your desk," and walked away. And I thought, "Now what do I do?" You know, I was waiting for a memo or something, or a job description. Finally, after another month I was so frustrated, I felt, "What have I gotten myself into?" And so I went to my sponsor, and I said, "What the heck do you want from me? I need something from you." And he said, "If you don't know what you're supposed to do, examine your commitment and opportunities."

COMPANY BACKGROUND

W. L. Gore & Associates was formed by the late Wilbert L. Gore and his wife in 1958. The idea for the business sprang from his personal, organizational, and technical experiences at E. I. DuPont de Nemours and particularly his discovery of a chemical compound with unique properties. The compound, now widely known as Gore-Tex, has catapulted W. L. Gore & Associates to a high ranking on the *Forbes* 1998 list of the 500 largest private companies in the United States, with estimated revenues of more than $1.1 billion. The company's avant-garde culture and people management practices resulted in W. L. Gore being ranked as the seventh best company to work for in America by *Fortune* in a January 1998 article.

Wilbert Gore was born in Meridian, Idaho, near Boise in 1912. By age 6, according to his own account, he was an avid hiker in the Wasatch Mountain Range in Utah. In those mountains, at a church camp, he met Genevieve, his future wife. In 1935, they got married—in their eyes, a partnership. He would make breakfast, and Vieve, as everyone called her, would make lunch. The partnership lasted a lifetime.

He received both a bachelor of science in chemical engineering in 1933 and a master of science in physical chemistry in 1935 from the University of Utah. He began his professional career at American Smelting and Refining in 1936. He moved to Remington Arms Company in 1941 and then to E. I. DuPont de Nemours in 1945. He held positions as research supervisor and head of operations research. While at DuPont, he worked on a team to develop applications for polytetrafluoroethylene, referred to as PTFE in the scientific community and known as "Teflon" by DuPont's consumers. (Consumers know it under other names from other companies.) On this team, Wilbert Gore, called Bill by everyone, felt a sense of excited commitment, personal fulfillment, and self-direction. He followed the development of computers and transistors and felt that PTFE had the ideal insulating characteristics for use with such equipment.

He tried many ways to make a PTFE-coated ribbon cable without success. A breakthrough came in his home basement laboratory while he was explaining the problem to his 19-year-old son Bob. The young Gore saw some PTFE sealant tape made by 3M and asked his father, "Why don't you try this tape?" Bill then explained that everyone knew that you cannot bond PTFE to itself. Bob went on to bed.

Bill Gore remained in his basement lab and proceeded to try what everyone knew would not work. At about 4:00 A.M. he woke up his son, waving a small piece of cable around and saying excitedly, "It works, it works." The following night father and son returned to the basement lab to make ribbon cable coated with PTFE. Because the breakthrough idea came from Bob, the patent for the cable was issued in Bob's name.

For the next 4 months, Bill Gore tried to persuade DuPont to make a new product—PTFE-coated ribbon cable. By this time in his career, Bill Gore knew some of the decision makers at DuPont. After talking to a number of them, he came to realize that DuPont wanted to remain a supplier of raw materials and not a fabricator.

Bill and his wife, Vieve, began discussing the possibility of starting their own insulated wire and cable business. On January 1, 1958, their wedding anniversary, they founded W. L. Gore & Associates. The basement of their home served as their first facility. After finishing dinner that night, Vieve turned to her husband of 23 years and said, "Well, let's clear up the dishes, go downstairs, and get to work."

Bill Gore was 45 years old with five children to support when he left DuPont. He put aside a career of 17 years and a good, secure salary. To finance the first 2 years of the business, he and Vieve mortgaged their house and took $4000 from savings. All their friends told them not to do it.

The first few years were rough. In lieu of salary, some of their employees accepted room and board in the Gore home. At one point 11 associates were living and working under one roof. One afternoon, while sifting PTFE powder, Vieve received a call from the city of Denver's water department. The caller indicated that he was interested in the ribbon cable but wanted to ask some technical questions. Bill was out running some errands. The caller asked for the product manager. Vieve explained that he was out at the moment. Next, he asked for the sales manager and, finally, the president. Vieve explained that they also were out. The caller became outraged and hollered, "What kind of company is this anyway?" With a little diplomacy, the Gores were able eventually to secure an order for $100,000. This order put the company on a profitable footing, and it began to take off.

W. L. Gore & Associates continued to grow and develop new products, primarily derived from PTFE. Its best known product would become Gore-Tex fabric. In 1986, Bill Gore died while backpacking in the Wind River Mountains of Wyoming. He was then chairman of the board. His son Bob continued to occupy the position of president. Vieve remained as the only other officer, secretary-treasurer.

Company Products

In 1998, W. L. Gore & Associates has a fairly extensive line of high-tech products that are used in a variety of applications, including electronic, waterproofing, industrial filtration, industrial seals, and coatings.

Electronic and Wire Products. Gore electronic products have been found in unconventional places where conventional products will not do—in space shuttles, for example, where Gore wire and cable assemblies withstand the heat of ignition and the cold of space. In addition, they have been found in fast computers, transmitting signals at up to 93 percent of the speed of light. Gore cables have even gone underground, in oil drilling operations, and underseas, on submarines that require superior microwave signal equipment and no-fail cables that can survive high pressure. The Gore electronic products division has a history of anticipating future customer needs with innovative products. Gore electronic products have been well received in industry for their ability to last under adverse conditions. For example, Gore has become, according to Sally Gore, leader in human resources and communications, ". . . one of the largest manufacturers of ultrasound cable in the world, the reason being that Gore's electronic cables' signal transmission is very, very accurate and it's very thin and extremely flexible and has a very, very long flex life. That makes it ideal for things like ultrasound and many medical electronic applications."

Medical Products. The medical division began on the ski slopes of Colorado. Bill was skiing with a friend, Dr. Ben Eiseman of Denver General Hospital. As Bill Gore told the story:

> We were just to start a run when I absentmindedly pulled a small tubular section of Gore-Tex out of my pocket and looked at it. "What is that stuff?" Ben asked. So I told him

about its properties. "Feels great," he said. "What do you use it for?" "Got no idea," I said. "Well give it to me," he said, "and I'll try it in a vascular graft on a pig." Two weeks later, he called me up. Ben was pretty excited. "Bill," he said, "I put it in a pig and it works. What do I do now?" I told him to get together with Pete Cooper in our Flagstaff plant and let them figure it out.

Not long after, hundreds of thousands of people throughout the world began walking around with Gore-Tex vascular grafts.

Gore-Tex–expanded PTFE proved to be an ideal replacement for human tissue in many situations. In patients suffering from cardiovascular disease, the diseased portion of arteries has been replaced by tubes of expanded PTFE—strong, biocompatible structures capable of carrying blood at arterial pressures. Gore has a strong position in this product segment. Other Gore medical products have included patches that can literally mend broken hearts by sealing holes and sutures that allow for tissue attachment and offer the surgeon silklike handling coupled with extreme strength. In 1985, W. L. Gore & Associates won Britain's Prince Philip Award for Polymers in the Service of Mankind. The award recognized especially the life-saving achievements of the Gore medical products team.

Two recently developed products by this division are a new patch material that is intended to incorporate more tissue into the graft more quickly and the Gore RideOn[3] cable system for bicycles. According to Amy LeGere of the medical division, "All the top pro riders in the world are using it. It was introduced just about a year ago, and it has become an industry standard." This product had a positive cash flow very soon after its introduction. Some associates who were also outdoor sports enthusiasts developed the product and realized that Gore could make a great bicycle cable that would have 70 percent less friction and need no lubrication. The associates maintain that the profitable development, production, and marketing of such specialized niche products are possible because of the lack of bureaucracy and associated overhead, associate commitment, and use of product champions.

Industrial Products. The output of the industrial products division has included sealants, filter bags, cartridges, clothes, and coatings. Industrial filtration products, such as Gore-Tex filter bags, have reduced air pollution and recovered valuable solids from gases and liquids more completely than alternatives—and they have done so economically. In the future they may make coal-burning plants completely smoke-free, contributing to a cleaner environment. The specialized and critical applications of these products, along with Gore's reputation for quality, have had a strong influence on industrial purchasers.

This division has developed a unique joint sealant—a flexible cord of porous PTFE—that can be applied as a gasket to the most complex shapes, sealing them to prevent leakage of corrosive chemicals, even at extreme temperature and pressure. Steam valves packed with Gore-Tex have been sold with a lifetime guarantee, provided the valve is used properly.

In addition, this division has introduced Gore's first consumer product—Glide[4]—a dental floss. Ray Wnenchak, of the industrial products division, said:

> That was a product that people knew about for a while and they went the route of trying to persuade industry leaders to promote the product, but they didn't really pursue it very well. So out of basically default almost, Gore decided, okay, they're not doing it right. Let's go in ourselves. We had a champion, John Spencer, who took that and pushed it forward through the dentist's offices and it just skyrocketed. There were many more people on the team, but it was basically getting that one champion who focused on that product and got it out. They told him it "Couldn't be done," "It's never going to work," and I guess that's all he needed. It was done, and it worked.

Amy LeGere added:

> The champion worked very closely with the medical people to understand the medical market, like claims and labeling, so that when the product came out on the market it would be consistent with our medical products. And that's where, when we cross divisions, we know whom to work with and with whom we combine forces so that the end result takes the strengths of all of our different teams.

As of 1998, Glide has captured a major portion of the dental floss market, and the mint flavor is the largest selling variety in the U.S. market based on dollar volume.

Fabric Products.   The Gore fabrics division has supplied laminates to manufacturers of foul-weather gear, ski wear, running suits, footwear, gloves, and hunting and fishing garments. Firefighters and U.S. Navy pilots have worn Gore-Tex fabric gear, as have some Olympic athletes. The U.S. Army adopted a total garment system built around a Gore-Tex fabric component. Employees in high-tech clean rooms also wear Gore-Tex garments.

Gore-Tex membrane has 9 billion pores randomly dotting each square inch and is feather light. Each pore is 700 times larger than a water vapor molecule, yet thousands of times smaller than a water droplet. Wind and water cannot penetrate the pores, but perspiration can escape. As a result, fabrics bonded with Gore-Tex membrane are waterproof, windproof, and breathable. The laminated fabrics bring protection from the elements to a variety of products—from survival gear to high-fashion rainwear. Other manufacturers, including 3M, Burlington Industries, Akzo Nobel Fibers, and DuPont, have brought out products to compete with Gore-Tex fabrics. Earlier, the toughest competition came from firms that violated the patents on Gore-Tex. Gore successfully challenged them in court. In 1993, the basic patent on the process for manufacturing ran out. Nevertheless, as Sally Gore explained:

> … what happens is you get an initial process patent and then as you begin to create things with this process you get additional patents. For instance, we have patents protecting our vascular graft, different patents for protecting Gore-Tex patches, and still other patents protecting Gore-Tex industrial sealants and filtration material. One of our patent attorneys did a talk recently, a year or so ago, when the patent expired and a lot of people were saying, "Oh golly, are we going to be in trouble!" We would be in trouble if we didn't have any patents. Our attorney had this picture with a great big umbrella, sort of a parachute, with Gore under it. Next he showed us lots of little umbrellas scattered all over the sky. So you protect certain niche markets and niche areas, but indeed competition increases as your initial patents expire.

Gore, however, has continued to have a commanding position in the active-wear market.

To meet the needs of a variety of customers, Gore introduced a new family of fabrics in the 1990s (Exhibit A). The introduction posed new challenges. According to Bob Winterling:

EXHIBIT A

Gore's Family of Fabrics

Brand Name	Activity/Conditions	Breathability	Water Protection	Wind Protection
Gore-Tex	Rain, snow, cold, windy	Very breathable	Waterproof	Windproof
Immersion technology	For fishing and paddle sports	Very breathable	Waterproof	Windproof
Ocean technology	For offshore and coastal sailing	Very breathable	Waterproof	Windproof
WindStopper	Cool/cold, windy	Very breathable	No water resistance	Windproof
Gore Dryloft	Cold, windy, light precipitation	Extremely breathable	Water resistant	Windproof
Activent	Cool/cold, windy, light precipitation	Extremely breathable	Water resistant	Windproof

. . . we did such a great job with the brand Gore-Tex that we actually have hurt ourselves in many ways. By that I mean it has been very difficult for us to come up with other new brands, because many people didn't even know Gore. We are the Gore-Tex company. One thing we decided to change about Gore 4 or 5 years ago was instead of being the Gore-Tex company, we wanted to become the Gore company and that underneath the Gore company we had an umbrella of products that fall out of being the great Gore company. So it was a shift in how we positioned Gore-Tex. Today, Gore-Tex is stronger than ever as it's turned out, but now we've ventured into such things as WindStopper[5] fabric that is very big in the golf market. It could be a sweater or a fleece piece or even a knit shirt with the Wind-Stopper behind it or closer to your skin, and what it does is it stops the wind. It's not waterproof; it's water resistant. What we've tried to do is position the Gore name and beneath that all the great products of the company.

W. L. Gore & Associates' Approach to Organization and Structure

W. L. Gore & Associates has never had titles, hierarchy, or any of the conventional structures associated with enterprises of its size. The titles of president

and secretary-treasurer continue to be used only because they are required by the laws of incorporation. In addition, Gore has never had a corporatewide mission or code of ethics statement, nor has Gore ever required or prohibited business units from developing such statements for themselves. Thus the associates of some business units who have felt a need for such statements have developed them on their own. When questioned about this issue, one associate stated: "The company belief is that (1) its four basic operating principles cover ethical practices required of people in business; (2) it will not tolerate illegal practices." Gore's management style has been referred to as "unmanagement." The organization has been guided by Bill's experiences on teams at DuPont and has evolved as needed.

For example, in 1965, W. L. Gore & Associates was a thriving company with a facility on Paper Mill Road in Newark, Delaware. One Monday morning in the summer, Bill Gore was taking his usual walk through the plant. All of a sudden he realized that he did not know everyone in the plant. The team had become too big. As a result, he established the practice of limiting plant size to approximately 200 associates. Thus was born the expansion policy of "get big by staying small." The purpose of maintaining small plants was to accentuate a close-knit atmosphere and encourage communication among associates in a facility.

EXHIBIT B

International Locations of W. L. Gore & Associates

At the beginning of 1998, W. L. Gore & Associates consisted of over 45 plants worldwide with approximately 7000 associates. In some cases, the plants are grouped together on the same site (as in Flagstaff, Arizona, with 10 plants). Overseas, Gore's manufacturing facilities are located in Scotland, Germany, and China, and the company has two joint ventures in Japan (see Exhibit B). In addition, it has sales facilities located in 15 other countries. Gore manufactures electronic, medical, industrial, and fabric products. In addition, it has numerous sales offices worldwide, including eastern Europe and Russia.

The Lattice Organization.   W. L. Gore & Associates has been described not only as unmanaged but also as unstructured. Bill Gore referred to the structure as a "lattice organization" (see Exhibit C). The characteristics of this structure are

1. Direct lines of communication—person to person—with no intermediary
2. No fixed or assigned authority
3. Sponsors, not bosses
4. Natural leadership defined by followership
5. Objectives set by those who must "make them happen"
6. Tasks and functions organized through commitments

The structure within the lattice is complex and evolves from interpersonal interactions,

EXHIBIT C

The Lattice Structure

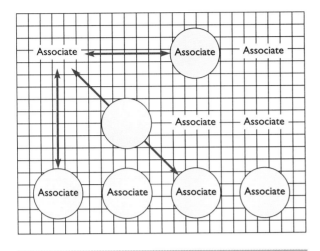

self-commitment to group-known responsibilities, natural leadership, and group-imposed discipline.

Bill Gore once explained the structure this way: "Every successful organization has an underground lattice. It's where the news spreads like lightning, where people can go around the organization to get things done." An analogy might be drawn to a structure of constant cross-area teams—the equivalent of quality circles going on all the time. When a puzzled interviewer told Bill that he was having trouble understanding how planning and accountability worked, Bill replied with a grin: "So am I. You ask me how it works? Every which way."

The lattice structure has not been without its critics. As Bill Gore stated:

> I'm told from time to time that a lattice organization can't meet a crisis well because it takes too long to reach a consensus when there are no bosses. But this isn't true. Actually, a lattice by its very nature works particularly well in a crisis. A lot of useless effort is avoided because there is no rigid management hierarchy to conquer before you can attack a problem.

The lattice has been put to the test on a number of occasions. For example, in 1975, Dr. Charles Campbell of the University of Pittsburgh reported that a Gore-Tex arterial graft had developed an aneurysm. If the bubblelike protrusion continued to expand, it

would explode. Obviously, this life-threatening situation had to be resolved quickly and permanently.

Within only a few days of Dr. Campbell's first report, he flew to Newark to present his findings to Bill and Bob Gore and a few other associates. The meeting lasted 2 hours. Dan Hubis, a former policeman who had joined Gore to develop new production methods, had an idea before the meeting was over. He returned to his work area to try some different production techniques. After only 3 hours and 12 tries, he had developed a permanent solution. In other words, in 3 hours a potentially damaging problem to both patients and the company was resolved. Furthermore, Hubis's redesigned graft went on to win widespread acceptance in the medical community.

Eric Reynolds, founder of Marmot Mountain Works, Ltd., of Grand Junction, Colorado, and a major Gore customer, raised another issue: "I think the lattice has its problems with the day-to-day nitty-gritty of getting things done on time and out the door. I don't think Bill realizes how the lattice system affects customers. I mean after you've established a relationship with someone about product quality, you can call up one day and suddenly find that someone new to you is handling your problem. It's frustrating to find a lack of continuity." He went on to say: "But I have to admit that I've personally seen at Gore remarkable examples of people coming out of nowhere and excelling."

When Bill Gore was asked if the lattice structure could be used by other companies, he answered: "No. For example, established companies would find it very difficult to use the lattice. Too many hierarchies would be destroyed. When you remove titles and positions and allow people to follow who they want, it may very well be someone other than the person who has been in charge. The lattice works for us, but it's always evolving. You have to expect problems." He maintained that the lattice system worked best when it was put in place in start-up companies by dynamic entrepreneurs.

Not all Gore associates function well in this unstructured work environment, especially initially. For those accustomed to a more structured work environment, there can be adjustment problems. As Bill Gore said: "All our lives most of us have been told what to do, and some people don't know how to respond when asked to do something—and have the very real option of saying no—on their job. It's the new associate's responsibility to find out what he or she can do for the good of the operation." The vast majority of the new associates, after some initial floundering, have adapted quickly.

Others, especially those who require more structured working conditions, have found that Gore's flexible workplace is not for them. According to Bill for those few, "It's an unhappy situation, both for the associate and the sponsor. If there is no contribution, there is no paycheck."

As Anita McBride, an associate in Phoenix, noted:

> It's not for everybody. People ask me do we have turnover, and yes we do have turnover. What you're seeking looks like utopia, but it also looks extreme. If you finally figure the system, it can be real exciting. If you can't handle it, you gotta go. Probably by your own choice, because you're going to be so frustrated.

Overall, the associates appear to have responded positively to the Gore system of unmanagement and unstructure. And the company's lattice organization has proven itself to be good for it from a bottom-line perspective. Bill estimated the year before he died that "the profit per associate is double" that of DuPont.

Features of W. L. Gore's Culture

Outsiders have been struck by the degree of informality and humor in the Gore organization. Meetings tend to be only as long as necessary. As Trish Hearn, an associate in Newark, Delaware, said, "No one feels a need to pontificate." Words such as *responsibilities* and *commitments* are commonly heard, whereas words such as *employees, subordinates,* and *managers* are taboo in the Gore culture. This is an organization that has always taken what it does very seriously, without its members taking themselves too seriously.

For a company of its size, Gore has always had a very short organizational pyramid. As of 1995, the pyramid consisted of Bob Gore, the late Bill Gore's son, as president and Vieve, Bill Gore's widow, as secretary-treasurer. He has been the chief executive officer for over 20 years. No second-in-command or named successor has been designated. All the other members of the Gore

EXHIBIT D

Sarah Clifton's card

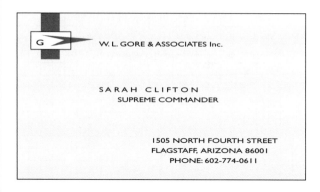

W. L. GORE & ASSOCIATES Inc.

SARAH CLIFTON
SUPREME COMMANDER

1505 NORTH FOURTH STREET
FLAGSTAFF, ARIZONA 86001
PHONE: 602-774-0611

organization were, and continue to be, referred to as associates.

Some outsiders have had problems with the idea of no titles. Sarah Clifton, an associate at the Flagstaff facility, was being pressed by some outsiders as to what her title was. She made one up and had it printed on some business cards: Supreme Commander (see Exhibit D). When Bill Gore learned what she did, he loved it and recounted the story to others.

Leaders, Not Managers. Within W. L. Gore & Associates, the various people who take lead roles are thought of as being leaders, not managers. Bill Gore described in an internal memo the kinds of leadership and the role of leadership as follows:

1. The associate who is recognized by a team as having a special knowledge or experience (e.g., this could be a chemist, computer expert, machine operator, salesman, engineer, lawyer). This kind of leader gives the team *guidance in a special area.*

2. The associate the team looks to for coordination of individual activities in order to achieve the agreed on objectives of the team. The role of this leader is to persuade team members to *make the commitments* necessary for success (commitment seeker).

3. The associate who proposes necessary objectives and activities and seeks agreement and team *consensus on objectives.* This leader is perceived by the team members as having a

good grasp of how the objectives of the team fit in with the broad objective of the enterprise. This kind of leader is often also the "commitment seeking" leader in 2 above.

4. The leader who evaluates relative contribution of team members (in consultation with other sponsors), and reports these contribution evaluations to a compensation committee. This leader also may participate in the compensation committee on relative contribution and pay and *reports changes in compensation* to individual associates. This leader is then also a compensation sponsor.

5. The leader who coordinates the research, manufacturing, and marketing of one product type within a business, interacting with team leaders and individual associates who have commitments regarding the product type. These leaders are usually called *product specialists*. They are respected for their knowledge and dedication to their products.

6. *Plant leaders* who help coordinate activities of people within a plant.

7. *Business leaders* who help coordinate activities of people in a business.

8. *Functional leaders* who help coordinate activities of people in a "functional" area.

9. *Corporate leaders* who help coordinate activities of people in different businesses and functions and who try to promote communication and cooperation among all associates.

10. *Entrepreneuring associates* who *organize new teams* for new businesses, new products, new processes, new devices, new marketing efforts, new or better methods of all kinds. These leaders invite other associates to "sign up" for their project.

It is clear that leadership is widespread in our lattice organization and that it is continually changing and evolving. The situation that leaders are frequently *also* sponsors should not confuse that these are different activities and responsibilities.

Leaders are not authoritarians, managers of people, or supervisors who tell us what to do or forbid us doing things; nor are they "parents" to whom we transfer our own self-responsibility. However, they do often advise us of the consequences of actions we have done or propose to do. Our actions result

in contributions, or lack of contribution, to the success of our enterprise. Our pay depends on the magnitude of our contributions. This is the basic discipline of our lattice organization.

Egalitarian and Innovativeness.   Other aspects of the Gore culture have been at promoting an egalitarian atmosphere, such as parking lots with no reserved parking spaces except for customers and disabled workers or visitors and dining areas—only one in each plant—set up as focal points for associate interaction. As Dave McCarter of Phoenix explained: "The design is no accident. The lunchroom in Flagstaff has a fireplace in the middle. We want people to like to be here." The location of a plant is also no accident. Sites have been selected on the basis of transportation access, a nearby university, beautiful surroundings, and climate appeal. Land cost has never been a primary consideration. McCarter justified the selection by stating: "Expanding is not costly in the long run. The loss of money is what you make happen by stymieing people into a box."

Bob Gore is a champion of Gore culture. As Sally Gore related:

We have managed surprisingly to maintain our sense of freedom and our entrepreneurial spirit. I think what we've found is that we had to develop new ways to communicate with associates because you can't communicate with 6000 people the way that you can communicate with 500 people. It just can't be done. So we have developed a newsletter that we didn't have before. One of the most important communication mediums that we developed, and this was Bob Gore's idea, is a digital voice exchange which we call our Gorecom. Basically everyone has a mailbox and a password. Lots of companies have gone to e-mail, and we use e-mail, but Bob feels very strongly that we're very much an oral culture and there's a big difference between cultures that are predominantly oral and predominantly written. Oral cultures encourage direct communication, which is, of course, something that we encourage.

In rare cases an associate "is trying to be unfair," in Bill's own words. In one case the problem was chronic absenteeism, and in another, an individual was caught stealing. "When that happens, all hell breaks loose," said Bill Gore. "We can get damned authoritarian when we have to."

Over the years, Gore & Associates has faced a number of unionization drives. The company has neither tried to dissuade associates from attending an organizational meeting nor retaliated when flyers were passed out. As of 1995, none of the plants has been organized. Bill believed that no need existed for third-party representation under the lattice structure. He asked the question, "Why would associates join a union when they own the company? It seems rather absurd."

Commitment has long been considered a two-way street. W. L. Gore & Associates has tried to avoid layoffs. Instead of cutting pay, which in the Gore culture would be disastrous to morale, the company has used a system of temporary transfers within a plant or cluster of plants and voluntary layoffs.

Exhibit E contains excerpts of interviews with two Gore associates that further indicates the nature of the culture and work environment at W. L. Gore & Associates.

W. L. Gore & Associates' Sponsor Program

Bill Gore knew that products alone did not a company make. He wanted to avoid smothering the company in thick layers of formal "management." He felt that hierarchy stifled individual creativity. As the company grew, he knew that he had to find a way to assist new people and to follow their progress. This was particularly important when it came to compensation. W. L. Gore & Associates developed its sponsor program to meet these needs.

When people apply to Gore, they are initially screened by personnel specialists. As many as 10 references may be contacted on each applicant. Those who meet the basic criteria are interviewed by current associates. The interviews have been described as rigorous by those who have gone through them. Before anyone is hired, an associate must agree to be his or her sponsor. The sponsor is to take a personal interest in the new associate's contributions, problems, and goals, acting as both a coach and an advocate. The sponsor tracks the new associate's progress, helping and encouraging, dealing with weaknesses, and concentrating on strengths. Sponsoring is not a short-term commitment. All associates have sponsors, and many have more than one. When individuals are hired initially, they are likely to have a sponsor in their immediate

work area. If they move to another area, they may have a sponsor in that work area. As associates' commitments change or grow, they may acquire additional sponsors.

Because the hiring process looks beyond conventional views of what makes a good associate, some anomalies have occurred. Bill Gore proudly told the story of "a very young man" of 84 who walked in, applied, and spent 5 very good years with the company. The individual had 30 years of experience in the industry before joining Gore. His other associates had no problems accepting him, but the personnel computer did. It insisted that his age was 48. The individual success stories at Gore have come from diverse backgrounds.

An internal memo by Bill Gore described three roles of sponsors:

1. *Starting sponsor*—a sponsor who helps a new associate get started on a first job or a present associate get started on a new job.

2. *Advocate sponsor*—a sponsor who sees that an associate's accomplishments are recognized.

3. *Compensation sponsor*—a sponsor who sees to it that an associate is fairly paid for contributions to the success of the enterprise.

A single person can perform any one or all three kinds of sponsorship. Quite frequently, a sponsoring associate is a good friend, and it is not unknown for two associates to sponsor each other.

COMPENSATION PRACTICES

Compensation at W. L. Gore & Associates has taken three forms: salary, profit sharing, and an associates' stock ownership program (ASOP).[6] Entry-level salary has been in the middle for comparable jobs. According to Sally Gore: "We do not feel we need to be the highest paid. We never try to steal people away from other companies with salary. We want them to come here because of the opportunities for growth and the unique work environment." Associates' salaries have been reviewed at least once a year and more commonly twice a year. The reviews are conducted by a compensation team at each facility, with sponsors for the associates acting as their advocates during the review process. Prior to meeting with the compensation committee, the sponsor checks with customers or associates

EXHIBIT E

Excerpts from Interviews with Associates

The first excerpt is from an associate who was formerly with IBM and has been with Gore for 2 years.

Q: What is the difference between being with IBM and Gore?

A. I spent 24 years working for IBM, and there's a big difference. I can go ten times faster here at Gore because of the simplicity of the lattice organization. Let me give you an example. If I wanted to purchase chemicals at IBM (I am an industrial chemist), the first thing I would need to do is get accounting approval, then I would need at least two levels of managers' approval, then a secretary to log in my purchase, and then the purchase order would go to Purchasing, where it would be assigned a buyer. Some time could be saved if you were willing to "walk" the paperwork through the approval process, but even after computerizing the process, it typically would take 1 month from the time you initiated the purchase requisition until the time the material actually arrived. Here they have one simple form. Usually, I get the chemicals the next day, and a copy of the purchase order will arrive a day or two after that. It happens so fast. I wasn't used to that.

Q. Do you find that a lot more pleasant?

A. Yeah, you're unshackled here. There's a lot less bureaucracy that allows you to be a lot more productive. Take lab safety, for example. In my Lab at IBM, we were cited for not having my eyewash taped properly. The first time, we were cited for not having a big enough area taped off. So we taped off a bigger area. The next week the same eyewash was cited again because the area we taped off was 3 inches too short in one direction. We retaped it, and the following week, it got cited again for having the wrong color tape. Keep in mind that the violation was viewed as serious as a pail of gasoline next to a lit Bunsen burner. Another time I had the dubious honor of being selected the functional safety representative in charge of getting the function's labs ready for a corporate safety audit. [The function was a third level in the pyramidal organization: (1) department, (2) project, and (3) function.] At the same time I was working on developing a new surface-mount package. As it turned out, I had no time to work on development, and the function spent a lot of time and money getting ready for the corporate auditors who in the end never showed. I'm not belittling the importance of safety, but you really don't need all that bureaucracy to be safe.

The second interview is with an associate who is a recent engineering graduate.

Q. How did you find the transition coming here?

A. Although I never would have expected it to be, I found my transition coming to Gore to be rather challenging. What attracted me to the company was the opportunity to "be my own boss" and determine my own commitments. I am very goal oriented and enjoy taking a project and running with it—all things that you are able to do and encouraged to do within the Gore culture. Thus I thought, a perfect fit!

However, as a new associate, I really struggled with where to focus my efforts—I was ready to make my own commitments, but to what?! I felt a strong need to be sure that I was working on something that had value, something that truly needed to be done. While I didn't expect to have the "hottest" project, I did want to make sure that I was helping the company to "make money" in some way.

At the time, though, I was working for a plant that was pretty typical of what Gore was like when it was originally founded—after my first project (which was designed to be a "quick win"—a project with meaning, but one that had a definite end point), I was told, "Go find something to work on." While I could have found something, I wanted to find something with at least a small degree of priority! Thus the whole process of finding a project was very frustrating for me—I didn't feel that I had the perspective to make such a choice and ended up in many conversations with my sponsor about what would be valuable.... In the end, of course, I did find that project—and it did actually turn out to be a good investment for Gore. The process to get there, though, was definitely trying for someone as inexperienced as I was—so much ground would have been gained by suggesting a few projects to me and then letting me choose from that smaller pool.

(continued)

EXHIBIT E *(continued)*

Excerpts from Interviews with Associates

What's really neat about the whole thing, though, is that my experience has truly made a difference. Due in part to my frustrations, my plant now provides college grads with more guidance on their first several projects. (This guidance obviously becomes less and less critical as each associate grows within Gore.) Associates still are choosing their own commitments, but they're doing so with additional perspective and the knowledge that they are making a contribution to Gore—which is an important thing within our culture. As I said, though, it was definitely rewarding to see that the company was so responsive and to feel that I had helped to shape someone else's transition!

familiar with the person's work to find out what contribution the associate has made. The compensation team relies heavily on this input. In addition, the compensation team considers the associate's leadership ability and willingness to help others develop to their fullest.

Profit sharing follows a formula based on economic value added (EVA). Sally Gore had the following to say about the adoption of a formula:

It's become more formalized and in a way, I think that's unfortunate because it used to be a complete surprise to receive a profit share. The thinking of the people like Bob Gore and other leaders was that maybe we weren't using it in the right way and we could encourage people by helping them know more about it and how we made profit share decisions. The fun of it before was people didn't know when it was coming, and all of a sudden you could do something creative about passing out checks. It was great fun, and people would have a wonderful time with it. The disadvantage was that associates then did not focus much on, "What am I doing to create another profit share?" By using EVA as a method of evaluation for our profit share, we know at the end of every month how much EVA was created that month. When we've created a certain amount of EVA, we then get another profit share. So everybody knows and everyone says, "We'll do it in January," so it is done. Now associates feel more part of the happening to make it work. What have you done? Go make some more sales calls, please! There are lots of things we can do to improve our EVA, and everybody has a responsibility to do that.

Every month EVA is calculated, and every associate is informed. John Mosko of electronic products commented, "... [EVA] lets us know where we

are on the path to getting one [a profit share]. It's very critical—every associate knows."

Annually, Gore also buys company stock equivalent to a fixed percent of the associates' annual income, placing it in the ASOP retirement fund. Thus an associate can become a stockholder after being at Gore for a year. Gore's ASOP ensures that associates participate in the growth of the company by acquiring ownership in it. Bill Gore wanted associates to feel that they themselves are owners. One associate stated, "This is much more important than profit sharing." In fact, some long-term associates (including a 25-year veteran machinist) have become millionaires from the ASOP.

W. L. GORE & ASSOCIATES' GUIDING PRINCIPLES AND CORE VALUES

In addition to the sponsor program, Bill Gore articulated four guiding principles:

1. Try to be fair.
2. Encourage, help, and allow other associates to grow in knowledge, skill, and scope of activity and responsibility.
3. Make your own commitments, and keep them.
4. Consult with other associates before taking actions that may be "below the water line."

The four principles have been referred to as "Fairness, Freedom, Commitment, and Waterline." The waterline terminology is drawn from an analogy to ships. If someone pokes a hole in a boat above the waterline, the boat will be in relatively little real danger. If someone, however, pokes a hole below the waterline, the boat is in immediate danger of sinking. Waterline issues must be discussed across teams and plants before decisions are made.

The operating principles were put to a test in 1978. By this time, word about the qualities of Gore-Tex fabric was being spread throughout the recreational and outdoor markets. Production and shipment had begun in volume. At first a few complaints were heard. Next, some of the clothing started coming back. Finally, much of the clothing was being returned. The trouble was that the Gore-Tex fabric was leaking. Waterproofing was one of the major properties responsible for Gore-Tex fabric's success. The company's reputation and credibility were on the line.

Peter W. Gilson, who led Gore's fabrics division, recalled: "It was an incredible crisis for us at that point. We were really starting to attract attention; we were taking off—and then this." In the next few months, Gilson and a number of his associates made a number of those below-the-waterline decisions.

First, the researchers determined that oils in human sweat were responsible for clogging the pores in the Gore-Tex fabric and altering the surface tension of the membrane. Thus water could pass through. They also discovered that a good washing could restore the waterproof property. At first, this solution, known as the "Ivory Snow solution," was accepted.

A single letter from "Butch," a mountain guide in the Sierras, changed the company's position. Butch described what happened while he was leading a group: "My parka leaked, and my life was in danger." As Gilson noted, "That scared the hell out of us. Clearly, our solution was no solution at all to someone on a mountain top." All the products were recalled. Gilson remembered: "We bought back, at our own expense, a fortune in pipeline material—anything that was in the stores, at the manufacturers, or anywhere else in the pipeline."

In the meantime, Bob Gore and other associates set out to develop a permanent fix. One month later, a second-generation Gore-Tex fabric had been developed. Gilson, furthermore, told dealers that if a customer ever returned a leaky parka, they should replace it and bill the company. The replacement program alone cost Gore roughly $4 million.

The popularity of Gore-Tex outerwear took off. Many manufacturers now make numerous pieces of apparel such as parkas, gloves, boots, jogging outfits, and wind shirts from Gore-Tex laminate. Sometimes when customers are dissatisfied with a garment, they return it directly to Gore. Gore has always stood behind any product made of Gore-Tex fabric. Analysis of the returned garments found that the problem often was not the Gore-Tex fabric. The manufacturer ". . . had created a design flaw so that the water could get in here or get in over the zipper, and we found that when there was something negative about it, everyone knew it was Gore-Tex. So we had to make good on products that we were not manufacturing. We now license the manufacturers of all our Gore-Tex fabric products. They pay a fee to obtain a license to manufacture Gore-Tex products. In return, we oversee the manufacture, and we let them manufacture only designs that we are sure are guaranteed to keep you dry, that really will work. Then it works for them and for us—it's a win-win for them as well as for us," according to Sally Gore.

To further ensure quality, Gore & Associates has its own test facility, including a rain room for garments made from Gore-Tex. Besides a rain/storm test, all garments must pass abrasion and washing machine tests. Only the garments that pass these tests will be licensed to display the Gore-Tex label.

RESEARCH AND DEVELOPMENT

Like everything else at Gore, research and development (R&D) has always been unstructured. Even without a formal R&D department, the company has been issued many patents, although most inventions have been held as proprietary or trade secrets. For example, few associates are allowed to see Gore-Tex being made. Any associate can, however, ask for a piece of raw PTFE (known as a "silly worm") with which to experiment. Bill Gore believed that all people had it within themselves to be creative.

One of the best examples of Gore inventiveness occurred in 1969. At the time, the wire and cable division was facing increased competition. Bill Gore began to look for a way to straighten out the PTFE molecules. As he said, "I figured out that if we ever unfold those molecules, get them to stretch out straight, we'd have a tremendous new kind of material." He thought that if PTFE could be stretched, air could be introduced into its molecular structure. The result would be greater volume per pound of raw material with no effect on performance. Thus fabricating costs would be reduced, and profit margins would be increased. Going about this search in a scientific manner, Bob Gore heated rods of PTFE to various temperatures and then slowly stretched them. Regardless of the temperature or how carefully he stretched them, the rods broke.

Working alone late one night after countless failures, Bob in frustration stretched one of the rods violently. To his surprise, it did not break. He tried it again and again with the same results. The next morning Bob demonstrated his breakthrough to his father, but not without some drama. As Bill Gore recalled: "Bob wanted to surprise me, so he took a rod and stretched it slowly. Naturally, it broke. Then he pretended to get mad. He grabbed another rod and said, 'Oh, the hell with this,' and gave it a pull. It didn't break—he'd done it." The new arrangement of molecules not only changed the wire and cable division but led to the development of Gore-Tex fabric.

Bill and Vieve did the initial field-testing of Gore-Tex fabric the summer of 1970. Vieve made a hand-sewn tent out of patches of Gore-Tex fabric. They took it on their annual camping trip to the Wind River Mountains of Wyoming. The very first night in the wilderness, they encountered a hail storm. The hail tore holes in the top of the tent, and the bottom filled up like a bathtub from the rain. Undaunted, Bill Gore stated: "At least we knew from all the water that the tent was waterproof. We just needed to make it stronger, so it could withstand hail."

Gore associates have always been encouraged to think, experiment, and follow a potentially profitable idea to its conclusion. At a plant in Newark, Delaware, Fred L. Eldreth, an associate with a third-grade education, designed a machine that could wrap thousands of feet of wire a day. The design was completed over a weekend. Many other associates have contributed their ideas through both product and process breakthroughs.

Even without an R&D department, innovation and creativity continue at a rapid pace at Gore & Associates. The year before he died, Bill Gore claimed that "the creativity, the number of patent applications and innovative products [are] triple" that of DuPont.

DEVELOPMENT OF GORE ASSOCIATES

Ron Hill, an associate in Newark, noted that Gore "will work with associates who want to advance themselves." Associates have been offered many in-house training opportunities, not only in technical and engineering areas but also in leadership development. In addition, the company has established cooperative education programs with universities and other outside providers, picking up most of the costs for the Gore associates. The emphasis in associate development, as in many parts of Gore, has always been that the associate must take the initiative.

MARKETING APPROACHES AND STRATEGY

Gore's business philosophy incorporates three beliefs and principles: (1) that the company can and should offer the best-valued products in the markets and market segments where it chooses to compete, (2) that buyers in each of its markets should appreciate the caliber and performance of the items it manufactures, and (3) that Gore should become a leader with unique expertise in each of the product categories where it competes. To achieve these outcomes, the company's approach to marketing (it has no formally organized marketing department) is based on the following principles:

1. Marketing a product requires a leader, or *product champion*. According to Dave McCarter: "You marry your technology with the interests of your champions, since you've got to have champions for all these things no matter what. And that's the key element within our company. Without a product champion, you can't do much anyway, so it is individually driven. If you get people interested in a particular market or a particular product for the marketplace, then there is no stopping them." Bob Winterling of the fabrics division elaborated further on the role and importance of the product champion:

> The product champion is probably the most important resource we have at Gore for the introduction of new products. You look at that bicycle cable. That could have come out of many different divisions of Gore, but it really happened because one or two individuals said, "Look, this can work. I believe in it; I'm passionate

about it; and I want it to happen." And the same thing with Glide floss. I think John Spencer in this case—although there was a team that supported John, let's never forget that—John sought the experts out throughout the organization. But without John making it happen on his own, Glide floss would never have come to fruition. He started with a little chain of drug stores here, Happy Harry's, I think, and we put a few cases in, and we just tracked the sales, and that's how it all started. Who would have ever believed that you could take what we would have considered a commodity product like that, sell it direct for $3–5 apiece. That is so un-Gore-like it's incredible. So it comes down to people, and it comes down to the product champion to make things happen.

2. *A product champion is responsible for marketing the product through commitments with sales representatives.* Again, according to Dave McCarter:

We have no quota system. Our marketing and our salespeople make their own commitments as to what their forecasts have been. There is no person sitting around telling them that is not high enough, you have to increase it by 10 percent, or whatever somebody feels is necessary. You are expected to meet your commitment, which is your forecast, but nobody is going to tell you to change it.... There is no order of command, no chain involved. These are groups of independent people who come together to make unified commitments to do something, and sometimes when they can't make those agreements ... you may pass up a market-place.... But that's OK, because there's much more advantage when the team decides to do something.

3. *Sales associates are on salary, not commission.* They participate in the profit-sharing and ASOP plans in which all other associates participate.

As in other areas of Gore, individual success stories have come from diverse backgrounds. Dave McCarter related another success of the company relying on a product champion as follows:

I interviewed Sam one day. I didn't even know why I was interviewing him actually. Sam was retired from AT&T. After 25 years, he took the golden parachute and went down to Sun Lakes to play golf. He played golf a few months and got tired of that. He was selling life insurance.

I sat reading the application; his technical background interested me.... He had managed an engineering department with 600 people. He'd managed manufacturing plants for AT&T and had a great wealth of experience at AT&T. He said, "I'm retired. I like to play golf, but I just can't do it every day, so I want to do something else. Do you have something around here I can do?" I was thinking to myself, "This is one of these guys I would sure like to hire, but I don't know what I would do with him." The thing that triggered me was the fact that he said he sold insurance, and here is a guy with a high degree of technical background selling insurance. He had marketing experience, international marketing experience. So the bell went off in my head that we were trying to introduce a new product into the marketplace that was a hydrocarbon leak-protection cable. You can bury it in the ground, and in a matter of seconds it could detect a hydrocarbon like gasoline. I had a couple of other guys working on the product who hadn't been very successful with marketing it. We were having a hard time finding a customer. Well, I thought that kind of product would be like selling insurance. If you think about it, why should you protect your tanks? It's an insurance policy that things are not leaking into the environment. That has implications, big time monetary. So, actually, I said, "Why don't you come back Monday? I have just the thing for you." He did. We hired him; he went to work, a very energetic guy. Certainly a champion of the product, he picked right up on it, ran with it single handed.... Now it's a growing business. It certainly is a valuable one too for the environment.

In the implementation of its marketing strategy, Gore has relied on cooperative and word-of-mouth advertising. Cooperative advertising has been especially used to promote Gore-Tex fabric products. These high-dollar, glossy campaigns include full-color ads and dressing the salesforce in Gore-Tex garments. A recent slogan used in the ad campaigns has been, "If it doesn't Gore-Tex, it's not." Some retailers praise the marketing and advertising efforts as the best. Leigh Gallagher, managing editor of *Sporting Goods Business* magazine, describes Gore & Associates' marketing as "unbeatable."

Gore has stressed cooperative advertising because the associates believe positive experiences with any one product will carry over to purchases of other and more Gore-Tex fabric products. Apparently, this strategy has paid off. When the Grandoe Corporation introduced Gore-Tex gloves, its president, Richard Zuckerwar, noted: "Sports activists have had the benefit of Gore-Tex gloves to protect their hands from the elements.... With this handsome collection of gloves ... you can have warm, dry hands without sacrificing style." Other clothing manufacturers and distributors who sell Gore-Tex garments include Apparel Technologies, Lands' End, Austin Reed, Hudson Trail Outfitters, Timberland, Woolrich, North Face, L. L. Bean, and Michelle Jaffe.

The power of these marketing techniques extends beyond consumer products. According to Dave McCarter, "In the technical end of the business, company reputation probably is most important. You have to have a good reputation with your company." He went on to say that without a good reputation, a company's products would not be considered seriously by many industrial customers. In other words, the sale is often made before the representative calls. Using its marketing strategies, Gore has been very successful in securing a market leadership position in a number of areas, ranging from waterproof outdoor clothing to vascular grafts. Its market share of waterproof, breathable fabrics is estimated to be 90 percent.

ADAPTING TO CHANGING ENVIRONMENTAL FORCES

Each of Gore's divisions has faced from time to time adverse environmental forces. For example, the fabric division was hit hard when the fad for jogging suits collapsed in the mid-1980s. The fabric division took another hit from the recession of 1989. People simply reduced their purchases of high-end athletic apparel. By 1995, the fabric division was the fastest growing division of Gore again.

The electronic division was hit hard when the main-frame computer business declined in the early 1990s. By 1995, that division was seeing a resurgence for its products partially because that division had developed some electronic products for the medical industry. As can be seen, not all the forces have been negative.

The aging population of America has increased the need for health care. As a result, Gore has invested in the development of additional medical products, and the medical division is growing.

W. L. GORE & ASSOCIATES' FINANCIAL PERFORMANCE

As a closely held private corporation, W. L. Gore has kept its financial information as closely guarded as proprietary information on products and processes. It has been estimated that associates who work at Gore own 90 percent of the stock. According to Shanti Mehta, an associate, Gore's returns on assets and sales have consistently ranked it among the top 10 percent of the Fortune 500 companies. According to another source, W. L. Gore & Associates has been doing just fine by any financial measure. For 37 straight years (from 1961 to 1997) the company has enjoyed profitability and positive return on equity. The compounded growth rate for revenues at W. L. Gore & Associates from 1969 to 1989 was more than 18 percent discounted for inflation.[7] In 1969, total sales were about $6 million; by 1989, the figure was $600 million. As should be expected with the increase in size, the percentage increase in sales has slowed over the last 7 years. The company projects sales to reach $1.4 billion in 1998. Gore financed this growth without long-term debt unless it made sense. For example, "We used to have some industrial revenue bonds where, in essence, to build facilities the government allows banks to lend you money tax-free. Up to a couple of years ago we were borrowing money through industrial revenue bonds. Other than that, we are totally debt-free. Our money is generated out of the operations of the business, and frankly we're looking for new things to invest in. I know that's a challenge for all of us today," said Bob Winterling. *Forbes* magazine estimates Gore's operating profits for 1993, 1994, 1995, 1996, and 1997 to be $120, $140, $192, $213, and $230 million, respectively. Bob Gore predicts that the company will reach $2 billion in sales by 2001.

Recently, the company purchased Optical Concepts, Inc., a laser, semiconductor technology company, of Lompoc, California. In addition, Gore & Associates is investing in test marketing a new product, guitar strings, that was developed by its associates.

When asked about cost control, Sally Gore had the following to say:

You have to pay attention to cost or you're not an effective steward of anyone's money, your own or anyone else's. It's kind of interesting, we started manufacturing medical products in 1974 with the vascular graft, and it built from there. The Gore vascular graft is the Cadillac or BMW or the Rolls Royce of the business. There is absolutely no contest, and our medical products division became very successful. People thought this was Mecca. Nothing had ever been manufactured that was so wonderful. Our business expanded enormously, rapidly out there [Flagstaff, Arizona], and we had a lot of young, young leadership. They spent some time thinking they could do no wrong and that everything they touched was going to turn to gold. They have had some hard knocks along the way and discovered it wasn't as easy as they initially thought it was. And that's probably good learning for everyone somewhere along the way. That's not how the business works. There's a lot of truth in that old saying that you learn more from your failures than you do your successes. One failure goes a long way toward making you say, "Oh, wow!"

ACKNOWLEDGMENTS

Many sources were helpful in providing background material for this case. The most important sources of all were the W. L. Gore associates, who generously shared their time and viewpoints about the company. They provided many resources, including internal documents and added much to this case through sharing their personal experiences as well as ensuring that the case accurately reflected the Gore company and culture.

Endnotes

1. Gore-Tex is a registered trademark of W. L. Gore & Associates.
2. In this case, the word *associate* is used because in W. L. Gore & Associates' literature the word is always used instead of employees. In fact, case writers were told that Gore "never had 'employees'—always 'associates.'"
3. Gore RideOn is a registered trademark of W. L. Gore & Associates.
4. Glide is a registered trademark of W. L. Gore & Associates.
5. WindStopper is a registered trademark of W. L. Gore & Associates.
6. Similar legally to an ESOP (employee stock ownership plan). Again, Gore simply has never allowed the word *employee* in any of its documentation.
7. In comparison, only 11 of the 200 largest companies in the Fortune 500 had positive ROE each year from 1970 to 1988, and only 2 other companies missed a year. The revenue growth rate for these 13 companies was 5.4 percent, compared with 2.5 percent for the entire Fortune 500.

Bibliography

Aburdene, Patricia, and John Nasbitt, *Re-inventing the Corporation* (New York: Warner Books, 1985).

Angrist, S. W. "Classless Capitalists," *Forbes*, May 9, 1983, pp. 123–124.

Franlesca, L. "Dry and Cool," *Forbes*, August 27, 1984, p. 126.

Hoerr, J. "A Company Where Everybody Is the Boss," *Business Week*, April 15, 1985, p. 98.

Levering, Robert, *The 100 Best Companies to Work for in America* (New York: Signet, 1985), see the chapter on W. L. Gore & Associates, Inc.

McKendrick, Joseph, "The Employees as Entrepreneur," *Management World*, January 1985, pp. 12–13.

Milne, M. J. "The Gorey Details," *Management Review*, March 1985, pp. 16–17.

Price, Debbie M. "Gore-Tex Style." *Baltimore Sun*, April 20, 1997, pp. 1D & 4D.

Price, Kathy, "Firm Thrives without Boss," *AZ Republic*, February 2, 1986.

Posner, B. G. "The First Day on the Job," *Inc.*, June 1986, pp. 73–75.

Rhodes, Lucien, "The Un-manager," *Inc.*, August 1982, p. 34.

Simmons, J. "People Managing Themselves: Un-management at W. L. Gore, Inc.," *The Journal for Quality and Participation*, December 1987, pp. 14–19.

"The Future Workplace," *Management Review*, July 1986, pp. 22–23.

Trachtenberg, J. A. "Give Them Stormy Weather," *Forbes*, 137(6), March 24, 1986, pp. 172–174.

Ward, Alex. "An All-Weather Idea," *New York Times Magazine*, November 10, 1985, sec. 6.

Weber, Joseph. "No Bosses. And Even 'Leaders' Can't Give Orders," *Business Week*, December 10, 1990, pp. 196–197.

"Wilbert L. Gore," *Industry Week*, October 17, 1983, pp. 48–49.

Service in the Skies: High-Class, Low-Class, and No-Class

A Case Study in Airline Misbehavior

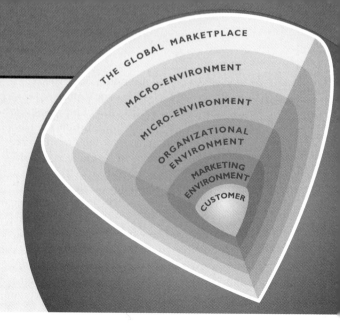

This case was prepared by Carol H. Anderson, Crummer Graduate School of Business, Rollins College, and Alexander T. Wood, Educational Foundations, College of Education, University of Central Florida.

Abstract: This case provides an opportunity to analyze the challenges faced by airlines and airline passengers when individuals become unruly. Airlines, government agencies, and other organizations are concerned about the threat of air rage to air safety and customer satisfaction, and must develop measures to overcome these problems. Passengers share these concerns and want something done about it.

"Passenger's Death Prompts Calls for Improved 'Air Rage' Procedures."[1] "'Air Rage' A Threat On Flights."[2] Numerous headlines about unruly passengers underscore the airline industry's dilemma in trying to ensure safe air travel for customers and crews. Passengers are creating a growing number of critical incidents and potential disasters by "threatening crews, pilots, and the general well-being of everyone on board."[3] Passengers who do not like the cabin service often resort to verbal abuse and assault on crew members.

"Airline misbehavior" often appears to be the product of mounting tensions that are related to pre-flight, in-flight, and post-flight customer service. From the perspective of the airlines, personal safety and service quality suffer due to service disruptions caused by unruly passengers. Airline officials are concerned about increased incidents of passenger frustration and rude behavior, which leads to abuse

of flight attendants and unpleasant service experiences for other passengers. Many incidents occur when passengers have had too much to drink, and get rowdy when told they cannot have more alcohol.[4] A number of other cases involve drugs or mental illness. Drunken passengers have hit, scratched, and shoved flight attendants when they were denied another drink. One passenger was so angry that he defecated on a food-service cart and used the linen napkins as toilet paper. On another flight, 18 British travelers started a food fight aboard a Northwest Airlines flight when they were refused liquor.[5] However, airline passengers also have their side of the story. They have reported numerous indignities suffered at the hands of the airlines, and have called attention to experiences of poor service, discomfort, and lack of consideration.

AIR RAGE

Andrew R. Thomas, President of www.AirRage.org and co-author of the book, *Air Rage: Crisis in the*

Skies, defines air rage as "*the aberrant, abusive, or abnormal behavior of passengers either on aircraft or in airports.*"[6] Research conducted by www.AirRage.com since the September 11, 2001 hijacking and World Trade Center bombing indicates that passenger air rage is on the rise, despite tightened security. The study included reports filed by local police, the FBI, and FAA, at 15 airports across the U.S. Hundreds of other unreported incidents have been occurring at more frequently, and often at a higher level of intensity since September 11, 2001. Thomas maintains that although the more sensational incidents tend to be reported, the media, government agencies, and the airlines themselves have underreported the problem for quite some time. Prior to September 11, there were six cockpit intrusions, and the number escalated after the WTC bombing—a threat to the safety of the 1.5 billion airline passengers who fly each year. Within a little over a month after the WTC incident, several commercial airliners were forced to make an emergency landing—some with military fighter escort planes at their side, due to passengers trying to break into the cockpit. Numerous other air rage incidents have continued to be reported throughout the U.S. and other countries. The reasons behind air rage before and after September 11 are similar. However, Thomas attributes the rise in air rage incidents after the WTC bombing to higher anxiety about air travel, increased alcohol consumption to overcome anxiety, increased number of passengers smoking in the lavatory, increased mistrust of—and anger toward—"dark skinned" passengers, and mounting frustration with the inconveniences of new security measures.

Thomas, and others have called for the U.S. Congress to include the air rage problem in the new aviation security measures. He stresses the need for government, law enforcement agencies, airlines and regulatory authorities to cooperate in finding "common solutions to a common problem."[7]

INCIDENTS PRIOR TO SEPTEMBER 11, 2001

While air rage may be an extreme case of airline passenger misbehavior, it emphasizes the severity of any situation where an agitated customer is out of control in a confined space with hundreds of other people, thousands of feet above the earth. At issue is how airline personnel can deal with a situation, such as the killing of a violent 19-year-old man on Southwest Airlines Co. flight 1763, on August 11, 2000. Mr. Jonathan Burton of Las Vegas began to act wildly and tried to kick through the cockpit door about 20 minutes before landing in Salt Lake City. When he tried a second time, passengers came to the aid of the two stewardesses who were trying to restrain him at the front of the Boeing 737. Mr. Burton ended up in an exit-row seat, but flight attendants decided to move him to the back of the plane because of his comments about wanting to get off the plane. He became agitated and fought violently as six passengers pinned him to the floor in the rear of the airplane. In the end, six to eight passengers subdued and ultimately suffocated Mr. Burton. Southwest defended the action of its crew and passengers, stating that "You don't want anyone to die, but you don't want the plane to go down either."[8] A Southwest spokesman attributed the incident to an attempted hijacking, rather than a case of air rage. Authorities ruled the death a homicide, but stated that it was justified in self-defense.

Southwest Airlines is a consistently successful airline with an enviable performance record. It is the fourth largest U.S. carrier in terms of originating customers boarded, and has received numerous awards and accolades for its on-time performance, baggage handling, and low number of customer complaints compared to competitors. The company is also well known for its outstanding employee culture, "fun" service environment, and respectful attitude toward customers—leading to high levels of customer satisfaction. Southwest's low-cost, no-frills airline service strategy has resulted in 26 consecutive years of profitability, despite two major industry downturns.[9] However, like many other airlines, Southwest does not train its cabin crews in physical restraint. It is common practice for airlines to encourage attendants to summon help from other passengers. The Burton incident and others have raised questions that are being pondered by the airlines, unions representing pilots and flight attendants, the Federal Aviation Administration, and concerned citizen groups, such as the Skyrage

Foundation. In general, there is a call for more training for flight crews on how to handle anything from passengers who are annoying to those who are physically abusive. However, this type of training requires a different approach, and as Colleen Barrett, Southwest's executive vice president of customers, says, "We don't want to turn any employee into a law-enforcement officer."[10] (The effect of the federal Sky Marshall program that was put in place following the September 11, 2001 WTC bombing was unknown at the time of this case.)

The August 2000 Southwest air rage incident is not an isolated case. In June 2000, the NASA Aviation Safety Reporting System stated that unruly airline passengers whose behavior disrupts pilots caused serious flying errors that threatened safety.[11] In a study of 152 passenger-aircraft rage incidents, analysts found that in 40 percent of these cases, pilots left the cockpit to handle a disturbance or had their flight routine interrupted by flight attendants who needed help. One of four of these cases involved errors such as flying too fast, flying at the wrong altitude, or taxiing across runways designated for other aircraft. In a number of recent cases deranged passengers have broken into jet cockpits before they could be subdued. Flight attendants and pilots reported the following causes of rage incidents: alcohol (43 percent), prohibited electronic devices (15 percent), smoking in lavatories (9 percent), drugs or medication (8 percent), bomb/hijack threats (5 percent), and other reasons (18 percent). According to the study, about 10 percent of pilot errors, over a 10-year period, were due to air-rage cases that disturbed the pilot's carefully choreographed routines, particularly during the critical takeoff and landing phases.

The airlines' ability to manage the service process and to deliver high quality customer service affects, and is affected by, a number of players. In order to identify issues related to airline passenger misbehavior and make recommendations for resolving this increasingly widespread problem, a number of viewpoints should be considered. In the following sections, we will consider the perspectives of airline management, front-line employees, and customers. The roles of support personnel, travel agents, and other parties that interface in any way with the airline industry and its customers also should be considered.

AIRLINE MANAGEMENT PERSPECTIVE

The deregulation of the airlines in 1978 set off the beginning of intense competition among America's airlines. Over the past two decades, airlines have added more aircraft, that travel at faster speeds, with greater fuel efficiency and safety than ever before. Operating efficiencies of larger planes that can carry larger passenger loads over greater distances make it possible to lower the cost of passenger air travel. A healthy economy and global business expansion also contribute to increased numbers of both first time and repeat leisure and business airline travelers.

In spite of this apparent success story, there are many service mishaps that must be addressed by marketing managers. Competition is fierce among the airlines as they try to give higher levels of customer service, frequently with limited resources to back it up. They struggle to be profitable, while often operating in a survival mode in an industry where operating costs are escalating and customers are more demanding. Many airlines are attempting to increase profitability by focusing on lucrative market niches, and offering these customers special amenities. Others are forming strategic alliances with other domestic and overseas carriers and adding new routes or pruning existing routes.

AIRLINE FRONT-LINE EMPLOYEE PERSPECTIVE

Observations made by flight crews and airport personnel indicate a widespread lack of consideration by passengers for other people or for established airline procedures, such as the following:[12]

- Passengers board planes in random fashion, not in the orderly fashion prescribed by the airlines.

- Passengers carry on too much luggage, cramming it into overhead bins, under seats, or anywhere they can—leaving the later arriving passengers without the storage space to which they are entitled.

- Passengers use the aisles as their personal playground or workout area, making it difficult for the flight attendants to provide service to other passengers.

- Passengers are often unreasonable—insisting on more alcohol when they have already imbibed too much; asking for special food that should have been ordered in advance; throwing a tantrum when they do not get their way.

- Passengers have physically assaulted and verbally abused flight attendants and other airline employees—often taking out their frustrations on individual employees rather than the airline.

- Pilots express concern about safety issues that are created when they need to leave the cockpit to settle disputes in the cabin.

- Flights are long, layovers are short, and home is … where?

In general, airline front-line employees share concerns about the inconsiderate, unruly, and often dangerous behavior of their customers. The stories of mistreatment of flight crews and other airline personnel by passengers are seemingly endless, and the problem is yet to be resolved in an industry that competes largely on the basis of price and customer service.

AIRLINE CUSTOMER PERSPECTIVE

On the 1999 New Year's weekend, thousands of Northwest Airlines passengers were left stranded on runways at the Detroit Metropolitan Airport. More than 8,000 Northwest travelers were restricted to their seats for as long as 11 hours—mostly without food, water, working toilets, or the use of their own cellular phones (they were restricted to the expensive in-flight phones)—based on airline rules for maintaining order and safety. They also were prohibited from walking around the cabin. Passengers with special needs included families with babies that did not have enough formula to feed them and individuals with medical problems.[13] This fiasco illustrates the frustrations and disappointment of many passengers with the quality of airline service.

Blizzard conditions kept more than 75 planes, most with passengers already aboard, on the field where they had already taxied onto the runways before the flights were canceled. Conditions were considered unsafe to take buses to the plane to pick up the travelers. Northwest apologized to all passengers who were inconvenienced and offered those who were delayed on the ground for more than $2\frac{1}{2}$ hours a free domestic round-trip ticket.

The Department of Transportation and the Federal Aviation Administration were given the responsibility of investigating these actions, which had been performed in the name of passenger "safety." The federal investigation concluded that Northwest Airlines violated no laws, but the Department of Transportation was "sharply critical of Northwest's lack of planning, poor communications, and other failings that resulted in thousands of passengers being trapped in its grounded planes for hours."[14] The report said, "Even if the well-being of passengers had not been an issue, the … stranding of passengers on aircraft queued up on taxiways for up to $8\frac{1}{2}$ hours invites more serious problems and is simply unacceptable." The airline has since implemented changes in its procedures and planning, and attempted to make restitution to the inconvenienced passengers. However, a number of lawsuits have been filed against Northwest Airlines and other defendants, alleging infliction of emotional distress and false imprisonment.

PASSENGER RIGHTS: THE "CUSTOMERS FIRST" INITIATIVE

Passengers and airline employees alike have experienced an escalation in rude behavior, service quality issues, and agitation for most of the past decade, while participating in commercial airline flights. As employees feel more harassed in their work, and passengers experience poorer quality service (or perhaps expect more attention and consideration than is realistic), federal lawmakers and airline industry groups are trying to resolve the problem.

The sheer volume of air travel has increased significantly. In 1999, airlines struggled to provide service to more than 600 million passengers.

Unexplained delays, canceled and overbooked flights, cramped seating, and lost luggage, resulted in consumer outcries and calls for Congressional legislation. "Passenger rights" bills were brought before Congress, and the furor against poor service by the airlines continues to attract the attention of the U.S. government.

In June 1999, the airline industry responded to pressure from the White House and Capitol Hill by instituting a "Customers First" initiative.[15] Twenty-three carriers pledged to:

- inform travelers promptly of delays and cancellations;
- assign a customer service representative to handle complaints and respond to them within 60 days;
- make food, water, and restrooms available when a plane is sitting on the tarmac for an extended period of time;
- ask the Transportation Department to consider raising the liability limit for lost luggage;
- make available information about airline policies on cancellations, restrictions, seat size, and more.[16]

"When you fly, do you feel like the focus of a cattle-herding operation? Cramped seats, endless delays and cheery flight attendants tossing bags of pretzels your way? Sorry—none of that will improve soon. But some things may get better, and an informed traveler is certainly a happier traveler."[17] From this perspective, Customers First attempts to provide the information outlined above to airline travelers. In December 1999, the Air Transport Association (which represents carriers that transport over 95 percent of all air passengers and cargo in the United States) enacted the guidelines that resulted from the Customers First initiative. These guidelines are designed to make air travel more pleasant and passengers better informed.[18] (See Exhibit 1.)

Customer complaints seem to revolve around several issues: inadequate or inaccurate information about airline policies and flight details; lack of planning for unexpected inconveniences (i.e., delayed flights, lost luggage, etc.); and lack of timely responsiveness to passenger complaints and concerns.

AIRLINE MANAGEMENT RESPONSES TO CUSTOMER AND EMPLOYEE CONCERNS

The Customers First pledge by the airline industry, described in the previous section, addresses major customer concerns related to information, unexpected inconveniences, and responsiveness. Individual airlines are pursuing a variety of strategies to improve service performance and customer satisfaction. Some examples follow.

It is interesting to note that while some airlines focus on more comfortable seats, better in-flight food from celebrity chefs, and appealing advertising, these are not at the top of travelers' minds. According to an online study of nearly 21,000 U.S. adults, what travelers want from their airlines is "dependable, no-hassle transportation at a reasonable cost, plus happy employees and strong performance."[19] The number one ranked domestic and international carriers in this study were Southwest Airlines and Singapore Airlines respectively. Southwest's on-time record, low fares, and friendly employees appear to overcome any negative aspects of no-frills service.

Although there have been great advances in package tracking technology, the use of this innovation has not been fully implemented, and airlines still have not found satisfactory answers to lost luggage. United Airlines in the Denver airport and British Airways at London's Heathrow Airport installed new higher-tech systems—but both have met with a number of problems. With heavier passenger loads, the volume of baggage that must be handled has increased greatly. However, most of the time travelers' belongings are still handled in the same way they were a generation ago. In 1997, major carriers mishandled an average of 4.96 bags out of 1,000. In 1999, this number increased to 5.08—figures that have held fairly consistent for the past decade. Today, airlines use minimal technology for luggage handling. Barcodes are put on luggage, but only used to sort at the originating airport, and not to track luggage after that point. The U.S. Department of Transportation says that 99.5 percent of all passengers' bags are handled without any problems. This sounds like a good track record until we consider that one-half of one percent of 500 million passengers traveling through the domestic system represents the mishandling of 2.5 million bags each year.[20]

Electronic ticketing has removed some of the time-consuming details of travel for passengers and is cost-effective for the airlines. United Airlines started selling e-tickets in 1994, and by 2000 about 60 percent of its sales were from e-tickets. Other airlines report similar transitions. However, occasionally travelers are frustrated by computers that crash while they are in the check-in line, computer errors, or lack of a paper ticket if a flight is delayed or canceled and the customer wants to book a flight with another airline.[21]

These are but a few examples of how the airlines are trying to improve the service process for their customers. Some other initiatives include

EXHIBIT I

Air Transport Association Guidelines

According to guidelines enacted by the Air Transport Association (ATA) in December 1999, member airlines pledge the following to their customers:

- *Fares:* Customers will be offered the lowest fare available, and will be told the lowest fare for the date, flight and class of service requested.

- *Information about delays, etc.:* Airline personnel will provide passengers with the "best available information" about delays, cancellations and diversions, in what the association calls a "timely manner." Policies on accommodating passengers who are delayed overnight will be determined by each airline individually.

- *Luggage:* Airlines will "make every reasonable effort" to get checked luggage to a passenger within 24 hours and will attempt to contact a customer whose unclaimed bag bears a name, address or telephone number.

- *Baggage liability:* The airlines petitioned the Department of Transportation to increase their baggage liability limit from $2,350 to $2,500.

- *Reservation penalties:* Airlines will not penalize customers who hold a reservation without payment for 24 hours or who cancel a reservation within 24 hours in the same span. Each airline will determine which of these policies to enact.

- *Refunds:* Refunds will be issued to eligible customers within seven days for credit card purchases or 20 days for cash purchases.

- *Special accommodations:* Each airline will disclose its individual policies for accommodating disabled and special needs passengers (e.g., unaccompanied minors).

- *Delay on runway:* Each airline will develop plans to accommodate the needs of passengers who are delayed on an airliner on a runway, and will make "every reasonable effort" to provide food, water, restrooms, and medical treatment as the situation warrants.

- *Overbooked flights:* When passengers are bumped from overbooked flights, they will be handled with "fairness and consistency," and airlines will disclose policies and procedures (e.g., check-in deadlines).

- *Disclosures:* Airlines will inform customers about changes in travel itinerary, equipment (e.g., type of plane), frequent-flier rules, cancellation policies, etc.

- *Code-sharing:* When airlines use other airlines in a "code-share" arrangement, consumers will be ensured of the partners' commitment to "comparable consumer plans and policies."

- *Customer complaints:* Airlines will respond to written customer complaints within 60 days.

Source: Carden, Lisa, "Airlines' New Guidelines: What Do They Really Mean?" *The Orlando Sentinel* (January 23, 2000), p. L-2. (Also see http://www.airtransport.org/press/1999/99-022.htm for additional information.)

training flight attendants to speak other languages and paying attention to the needs of special customer segments (e.g., children, disabled, college students, etc.). Many airlines are jazzing up their images by adding personal services for business-class passengers, repainting planes, and paying attention to details such as the type of tableware used to serve airplane food. While making these higher-paying passengers more comfortable with larger seats and more services, they are taking space away from the lower-fare coach section and making these seats smaller and more crowded.

The problem of unruly passengers and disruptive air rage incidents is more difficult to remedy. Airlines are generally in agreement that measures must be taken, but training of customer contact employees seems to focus on customer service, with varied approaches to dealing with dangerous passenger behavior. There is not a set policy, but British Airways PLC, for example, uses role-playing and body-language awareness to teach conflict management to its crews. The airline also has stern warning letters on its planes that flight attendants can deliver to passengers who are disruptive to warn them of the consequences of their actions. Several carriers have installed redesigned cockpit doors to keep passengers from breaking in and have equipped airplanes with plastic "flex-cuffs" or wrist restraints. They are also providing more information to passengers about the consequences of unruly behavior on their aircraft.

The U.S. government and the airline industry developed a number of short-term and long-term solutions to the problems that can be attributed to air rage incidents since September 11, 2001. Short-term measures included closure of airports, heightened screening at airport check-ins, banning of carry-on luggage, and other safety precautions. Longer-term remedies included the creation of a federal Sky Marshall program whereby trained and armed individuals would fly as passengers to help to avert serious incidents, improved airport check-in procedures (both personnel and equipment), heightened airport security (including the U.S. National Guard presence in airports), and others that were still being considered at the time of this case.

SUMMARY

The need to balance airline safety, service quality, and profitability is a major challenge for U.S. passenger airlines. Assume that you are Mr. Andrew Thomas, Director of AirRage.org, and that you have been asked to present your solutions to this problem to executives from the major U.S. airlines. What would you tell them about how you would approach this problem? Airline management, front-line employees, customers (as well as the airline industry at large), and law enforcement agencies are all key players in the scenarios described in this case, and each has his or her personal view of the situation that must be considered in arriving at a solution. What can commercial airlines do to improve personal safety and the quality of service experienced by their customers? What role(s) can customers play in this process, if any?

Endnotes

1. Trottman, Melanie and Chip Cummins, "Passenger's Death Prompts Calls for Improved 'Air Rage' Procedures," *Wall Street Journal* (September 26, 2000), pp. B1, B4.
2. Levin, Alan, "'Air Rage' A Threat On Flights," *USA Today* (June 12, 2000), p. A1.
3. Dateline NBC, "Cabin Pressure; Unruly Passengers Pose Threat On Some Domestic Airline Flights" (April 9, 2000, 7 p.m. ET).
4. Nomani, Asra, "Airlines Tell Boozers to Put a Cork in It," *Wall Street Journal* (August 28, 1998), pp. W1, W7; Associated Press, "Flight Attendants Decry Abuse: It's a Jungle Up There," *Orlando Sentinel* (January 31, 1996), p. A-10; Reuters, "Rowdy Passenger Forces Down Another Flight," http://dailynews.netscape.com (June 9, 1999).
5. Associated Press, "Flight Attendants Decry Abuse: It's A Jungle Up There," *Orlando Sentinel* (January 21, 1996), p. A-10; Reuters, "Rowdy Passenger Forces Down Another Flight" (June 9, 1999), Nomani, Asra Q., "Airlines Tell Boozers to Put a Cork in it," *Wall Street Journal* (August 28, 1998), pp. W1, W7.
6. Thomas, Andrew R., "The Number of Air Rage Incidents Has Increased Since the Hijackings of September 11, 2001 Despite Security Crackdowns At Airports and On Airlines Across the US," News Release, www.AirRage.org, October 25, 2001.
7. Thomas, Andrew R., "Congress Must Include Air Rage in New Security Measures," *Aviation Daily*, October 22, 2001.
8. Trottman and Cummins, *op. cit.*, p. B1.
9. Anonymous, "Air Herb's Secret Weapon," *Chief Executive* (July/August 1999), pp. 32–42.
10. Trottman and Cummins, *op. cit.*, p. B4.

11. Levin, Alan, "'Air Rage' A Threat On Flights," *USA Today* (June 12, 2000), p. A1.

12. McCartney, Scott, "Chaos in the Aisles: Airlines Try to Speed Up Boarding," *Wall Street Journal* (March 8, 1996), pp. B1, B6.

13. Carey, Susan, "Fliers Assert Rights After Runway Ordeal," *Wall Street Journal* (January 15, 1999), pp. B1, B4.

14. Carey, Susan, "U.S. Criticizes Northwest Air's Actions in Blizzard," *Wall Street Journal* (June 3, 1999), p. A4.

15. Taylor, Lauren R., "Air Travel: Know Before You Go," *Government Executive* (August 1999), pp. 62–63.

16. For additional information about Customers First, go to http://www.airtransport.org/press/1999/99-022.htm or call the Air Transport Association at (202) 626-4000.

17. Taylor, *op. cit.*

18. Carden, Lisa, "Airlines' New Guidelines: What Do They Really Mean?" *Orlando Sentinel* (January 23, 2000).

19. McCartney, Scott, "Airlines' Reputations Hinge on the Basics, Study Shows," *Wall Street Journal* (April 27, 2000), p. B4.

20. McCartney, Scott, "Baggage Bedlam," *Wall Street Journal* (June 30, 2000), pp. W1, W4.

21. Reynolds, Christopher, "Know the Pitfalls, Pluses of Electronic Ticketing," *Orlando Sentinel* (November 5, 2000), pp. L1, L6.

Cowgirl Chocolates

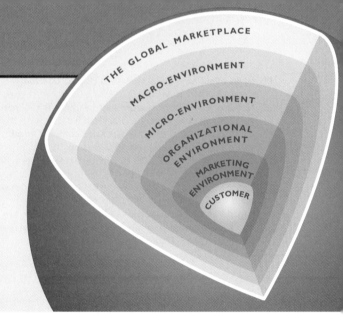

THE GLOBAL MARKETPLACE

MACRO-ENVIRONMENT

MICRO-ENVIRONMENT

ORGANIZATIONAL ENVIRONMENT

MARKETING ENVIRONMENT

CUSTOMER

This case was prepared by John J. Lawrence, Linda J. Morris, and Joseph J. Geiger, University of Idaho.

Marilyn looked at the advertisement—a beautiful woman wearing a cowboy hat in a watering trough full of hot and spicy Cowgirl Chocolates truffles (Exhibit 1). The ad would appear next month in the March/April edition of Chile Pepper *magazine, the leading magazine for people who liked fiery foods. The ad, the first ever for the business, cost $3,000 to run, and Marilyn wondered if it would be her big mistake for 2001. Marilyn allowed herself one $3,000–$6,000 mistake a year in trying to get her now 4-year-old business to profitability. Two years ago, it was the pursuit of an opportunity to get her product into Great Britain on the recommendation of the owner of a British biscuit company who loved her chocolates. Despite significant effort and expense, she could not convince anyone in Great Britain to carry her chocolates. Last year, it was her attempt to use a distributor for the first time. It was a small, regional distributor, and she had provided them with $5,000*

Reprinted by permission from the *Case Research Journal*, volume 22, issue 1. Copyright © 2002 by John J. Lawrence, Linda J. Morris, and Joseph J. Geiger and the North American Case Research Association. All rights reserved.

worth of product and had never gotten paid. She eventually got half her product back, but by the time she did, it had limited remaining shelf life and she already had enough new stock on hand to cover demand. She ended up giving away most of what she got back.

Marilyn knew it took time to make money at something. She was now an internationally celebrated ceramicist, but it had taken 20 years for her ceramic art to turn a profit. She also knew, however, that she could not wait 20 years for her foray into chocolates to make money, especially not at the rate that she was currently losing money. Last year, despite not paying herself a salary and occasionally bartering her art for services, the small business's revenues of $30,000 did not come close to covering her $50,000+ in expenses. Although her art did not make money for a long time, it did not lose that kind of money either. Her savings account was slowly being depleted as she loaned the company money. She knew that the product was excellent—it had won numerous awards from the two main fiery food competitions in the United States—and her packaging was also excellent and had won awards itself. She just was not sure how to turn her award-winning products into a profitable business.

EXHIBIT I

Cowgirl Chocolates Ad to Appear in *Chile Pepper* Magazine

COMPANY HISTORY

Cowgirl Chocolates was started in Moscow, Idaho, in 1997 by Marilyn Lysohir and her husband, Ross Coates. Marilyn and Ross were both artists. Marilyn was a nationally known ceramicist and lecturer; Ross was also a sculptor and a professor of fine arts at a nearby university. They had started publishing a once-a-year arts magazine in 1995 called *High Ground. High Ground* was really a multimedia product—each edition contained more than simply printed words and pictures. For example, past editions had included such things as vials of Mount

St. Helens ash, cassette tapes, seeds, fabric art, and chocolate bunnies in addition to articles and stories. One edition was even packaged in a motion picture canister. With a total production of about 600 copies, however, *High Ground* simply would not pay for itself. But the magazine was a labor of love for Marilyn and Ross, and so they sought creative ways to fund the endeavor. One of the ways they tried was selling hot and spicy chocolate truffles.

The fact that Marilyn and Ross turned to chocolate was no random event. Marilyn's first job, at age 16, was at Daffin's Candies in Sharon, Pennsylvania. The business's owner, Pete Daffin, had been an early mentor of Marilyn's and had encouraged her creativity. He even let her carve a set of animals, including an 8-foot-tall chocolate bunny, for display. Her sculptures proved irresistible to visiting youngsters, who would take small bites out of the sculptures. It was at this point that Marilyn realized the power of chocolate.

In addition to loving chocolate, Marilyn loved things hot and spicy. She also was aware that cayenne and other chilies had wonderful health properties for the heart. But it was her brother who originally gave her the idea of combining hot and spicy with chocolate. Marilyn considered her brother's idea for awhile and could see it had possibilities, so she started experimenting in her kitchen. She recruited neighbors, friends, and acquaintances to try out her creations. Although a few people who tried those early chocolates were not so sure that combining hot and spicy with chocolate made sense, many thought the chocolates were great. Encouraged, and still searching for funding for *High Ground,* Marilyn found a local candy company to produce the chocolates in quantity, and she and her husband established Cowgirl Chocolates.

The name itself came from one friend's reaction the first time she tasted the chocolates. The friend exclaimed, "These are cowboy chocolates!" Marilyn agreed that there was a certain ruggedness to the concept of hot and spicy chocolates that matched the cowboy image, but thought that *Cowgirl* Chocolates was a more appropriate name for her company. Marilyn found the picture of May Lillie that would become the Cowgirl Chocolates logo in a book about cowgirls. May Lillie was a turn of the century, pistol-packing cowgirl, and Marilyn loved the picture of May looking down the barrel of a pistol because May looked so tough. It certainly was not hard to envision May adopting the Cowgirl Chocolates motto—"Sissies Stay Away." That motto had come to Marilyn when a group of friends told her that they really did not like her hot and spicy chocolates. Marilyn was a little disappointed and hurt, and thought to herself, "Well, sissies, stay away. If you don't like them, don't eat them."

THE PRODUCT

Cowgirl Chocolates sold its hot and spicy creations in three basic forms: individually wrapped truffles, chocolate bars, and a hot caramel dessert sauce.

The individually wrapped truffles were available in a variety of packaging options, with most of the packaging designed to set Cowgirl Chocolates apart. The truffles could be purchased in gift boxes, in drawstring muslin bags, and in a collectable tin. According to Marilyn, this packaging made them "more than a candy—they become an idea, an experience, a gift." The truffles were also available in a plain plastic bag from Cowgirl Chocolates' Web site for customers who just wanted the chocolate and did not care about the fancy packaging. The chocolate bars and truffles were offered in several flavors. The chocolate bars were available in either orange espresso or lime tequila crunch. The truffles were available in plain chocolate, mint, orange, lime tequila, and espresso. The plain chocolate, mint, and orange truffles were packaged in gold wrappers; the lime tequila truffles were packaged in green wrappers. The espresso truffles were the hottest, about twice as hot as the other varieties, and were wrapped in a special red foil to give customers some clue that these were extra hot. Cowgirl Chocolates' full line of product offerings is described in Exhibit 2 and are shown in Exhibit 3.

Marilyn was also in the process of introducing "mild-mannered" truffles. Mild-mannered truffles were simply the same fine German chocolate that Marilyn started with to produce all of her chocolates, but without the spice. Marilyn had chosen silver as the wrapper color for the mild-mannered truffles. Although friends teased her about how this did not fit with the company's motto—Sissies Stay Away—which was integrated into the company's logo and printed on the back of company t-shirts and hats, she had decided that even the sissies deserved excellent chocolate. Further, she thought that having the mild-mannered chocolate might allow her to get her product placed in retail locations that had previously rejected her chocolates as being too spicy. Marilyn was the first to admit that her chocolates packed a pretty good kick that not everybody found to their liking. She had developed the hot and spicy chocolates based primarily on her own tastes and the input of friends and acquaintances. She had observed many peoples' reactions upon trying her hot and spicy chocolates at trade shows and at new retail locations. Although many people liked her chocolates, the majority found at least some of the varieties to be too hot. In general, men tended to like the hotter truffles much more than women did. Marilyn

EXHIBIT 2

Cowgirl Chocolates Product Offerings with Price and Cost Figures

Item	Approximate Percentage of Total Revenues	Suggested Retail Price[1]	Wholesale Price[1]	Total Item Cost (a + b)	Cost of Chocolate or Sauce (a)	Cost of Product Packaging[2] (b)
Spicy Chocolate Truffle Bars (available in 2 flavors: orange espresso or lime tequila crunch)	50%	$2.99	$1.50	$1.16	$1.04	$0.12
1/4 Pound Muslin Bag (13 truffles in a drawstring muslin bag-available in 3 flavors: assorted hot, lime tequila, and mild-mannered)	16%	$6.95	$3.50	$2.35	$1.69	$0.66
1/2 Pound Tin (assorted hot and spicy truffles in a collectable tin)	12%	$14.95	$7.50	$4.78	$3.25	$1.53
Hot Caramel Dessert Sauce (9.5 oz. Jar)	10%	$5.95	$3.50	$2.50	$2.00	$0.50
Sampler Bag (4 assorted hot truffles in a small drawstring muslin bag)	7%	$2.95	$1.50	$0.97	$0.52	$0.45
1/4 Pound Gift Box (assorted hot truffles or mild-mannered truffles in a fancy gift box with gift card)	~1%	$8.95	$4.50	$2.95	$1.69	$1.26
1 Pound Gift Box (assorted hot truffles or mild-mannered truffles in a fancy gift box with gift card)	~1%	$24.95	$12.95	$9.05	$6.37	$2.68
Gift Bucket (tin bucket containing 1/4 pound gift box, 2 truffle bars, and 1 jar of caramel sauce)	~1%	$39.95	$20.95	$11.02	$5.77	$5.25
Gift Basket (made of wire and branches and containing 1/2 pound tin, 2 truffle bars, 1 jar of caramel sauce, and a t-shirt)	~1%	$59.95	$30.95	$23.06	$15.29[3]	$7.77
Nothing Fancy (1 pound assorted hot truffles or mild-mannered truffles in a plastic bag)	~1%	$19.50	N.A.	$7.42	$6.37	$1.05

[1]Approximately 1/3 of sales were retail over the Cowgirl Chocolates Web site; the remaining 2/3 of sales were to wholesale accounts (i.e., to other retailers).
[2]Packaging cost includes costs of container (bags, tins, or boxes), labels, and individual truffle wrapping. Packaging cost assumes Marilyn packs the items and does not include the packing and labeling fee charged by Seattle Chocolates if they do the packing ($1.00 per 1/2 pound tin or 1 pound box; $0.75 per 1/4 pound box; $0.25 per 1/4 pound bag; $0.20 per sampler bag).
[3]This cost includes the cost of the t-shirts.

EXHIBIT 3

Picture of Cowgirl Chocolates Products and Packaging

knew her observations were consistent with what information was available on the fiery foods industry. Approximately 15 percent of American consumers were currently eating hot and spicy foods, and men were much more inclined to eat hot and spicy foods than were women. In addition to introducing mild-mannered chocolates, Marilyn was also thinking about introducing a chocolate with a calcium supplement aimed at women concerned about their calcium intake.

All of Cowgirl Chocolates' chocolate products were sourced from Seattle Chocolates, a Seattle-based company that specialized in producing European-style chocolate confections wrapped in an elegant package fit for gift giving. Seattle Chocolates obtained all of its raw chocolate from world-renowned chocolate producer Schokinag of Germany. Seattle Chocolates sold its own retail brand and provided private label chocolate prod-

ucts for a variety of companies including upscale retailers like Nieman Marcus and Nordstrom. Seattle Chocolates was, at least relative to Cowgirl Chocolates, a large company with annual sales in excess of $5 million. Seattle Chocolates took Cowgirl Chocolates on as a private label customer because they liked and were intrigued by the company's product and owners, and they had made some efforts to help Cowgirl Chocolates along the way. Seattle Chocolates provided Cowgirl Chocolates with a small amount of its table space at several important trade shows and produced in half batches for them. A half batch still consisted of 150 pounds of a given variety of chocolate, which was enough to last Cowgirl Chocolates for 6 months at 2000 sales rates. Marilyn hoped that she could one day convince Seattle Chocolates to manage the wholesale side of Cowgirl Chocolates, but Seattle Chocolates simply was not interested in taking this on at the current time, at least in part because they were not really sure where the market was for the product. Marilyn also knew she would need to grow sales significantly before Seattle Chocolates would seriously consider such an arrangement, although she was not sure exactly how much she would have to grow sales before such an arrangement would become attractive to Seattle Chocolates.

The chocolate bars themselves cost Cowgirl Chocolates $1.04 per bar, while the individual chocolate truffles cost $0.13 per piece. Seattle Chocolates also performed the wrapping and packing of the product. The chocolate bar wrappers cost $0.06 per bar. The wrapper design of the bars had recently been changed to incorporate dietary and nutritional information. Although such information was not required, Marilyn felt it helped convey a better image of her chocolates. The change had cost $35 to prepare the new printing plates. Including the materials, wrapping the individual truffles cost $0.02 per piece.

The distinctive muslin bags, collector tins, and gifts boxes also added to the final product cost. The muslin bags cost $0.35 each for the quarter-pound size and $0.32 each for the sampler size. The tamper-proof seals for the bags cost an additional $0.05 per bag. The minimum-size bag order was 500 bags. As with the chocolate bar wrappers, Cowgirl Chocolates had to buy the printing plates to print the bags. The plates to print the bags, however, cost $250 per plate. Each color of each design required a separate plate. Each of her three quarter-pound bag styles (assorted, lime tequila, and mild-mannered) had a 3-color design. One plate that was used to produce the background design was common to all three styles of bags, but each bag required two additional unique plates. There was also a separate plate for printing the sampler bags. Marilyn was planning to discontinue the separate lime tequila bag and just include lime tequila truffles in the assorted bag as a way to cut packaging costs. The lime tequila bags had been introduced a year ago. Although they sold reasonably well, they also appeared to mostly cannibalize sales of the assorted bags.

The collectible tins cost $0.80 each, and the labels for these tins cost $0.19 per tin. The tape used to seal the tins cost $0.04 per tin. The minimum order for the tins was for 800 units. The company that produced the tins had recently modified the tin design slightly to reduce the chance that someone might cut themselves on the edge of the can. Unfortunately, this change had resulted in a very small change to the height of the can, which left Cowgirl Chocolates with labels too big for the can. Each label currently had to be trimmed slightly to fit on the can. The alternative to this was to switch to a smaller label. This would require purchasing a new printing plate at a cost of about $35 and might require the purchase of a new printing die (the die holds the label while it is printed), which would cost $360. Marilyn also had hopes of one day being able to get her designs printed directly on the tins. It would make for even nicer tins and save the step of having to adhere the labels to the tins. The minimum order for such tins, however, was 15,000 units.

The gift boxes, including all of the associated wrapping, ribbon, and labels, cost about $1.70 per box. The gift boxes did not sell nearly as well as the tins or bags and were available primarily through the Cowgirl Chocolates Web site. Marilyn was still using and had a reasonable inventory of boxes from a box order she had placed 3 years ago.

Marilyn currently had more packaging in inventory than she normally would because she had ordered $5,000 worth in anticipation of the possibility of having her product placed in military PX stores at the end of 2000. Seattle Chocolates had been negotiating to get their product into these stores, and there had been some interest on the part of the PX stores in also having Cowgirl Chocolates products. Given the 6- to 8-week lead time on packaging, Marilyn had wanted to be positioned to quickly take advantage of this opportunity if it materialized. Although Marilyn was still hopeful this deal might come about, she was less optimistic than she had been at the time she placed the packaging order.

Marilyn was concerned that the actual packing step was not always performed with the care it should be. In particular, she was concerned that not enough or too many truffles ended up in the bags and tins, and that the seals on these containers, which made the packages more tamper resistant, were not always applied correctly. Each quarter-pound bag and gift box was supposed to contain 13 individual truffles; each half-pound tin was supposed to contain 25 individual truffles; and each 1-pound gift box was supposed to contain 49 individual truffles. The tins, in particular, had to be packed pretty tightly to get 25 truffles into them. Marilyn had done some of the packing herself at times and wondered if she would not be better off hiring local college or high school students to do the packing for her to ensure that the job was done to her satisfaction. It could also save her some money, as Seattle Chocolates charged her extra for packing the tins and bags. The tins, in particular, were expensive because of the time it took to apply the labels to the top and side of the tin and because of the extra care it took to get all 25 truffles into the tin. Seattle Chocolates charged $1 per tin for this step.

Marilyn made the caramel sauce herself with the help of the staff in a commercial kitchen in Sandpoint, Idaho, about a $2\frac{1}{2}$-hour drive north of Moscow. She could make 21 cases of 12 jars each in 1 day, but including the drive it took all day to do. As with the chocolate, she used only the best ingredients, including fresh cream from a local Moscow dairy. Marilyn figured her costs for the caramel sauce at about $2.50 per jar, which included the cost of the ingredients, the jars, the labeling, and the cost of using the Sandpoint kitchen. That figure did not include any allowance for the time it took her to make the sauce or put the labels on the jars. She was considering dropping the caramel sauce from her product line because it was a lot of work to produce, and she was not sure she really made any money on it after her own time was factored in. She had sold 70 cases of the sauce in 2000, however, so she knew there was some demand for the product. She was considering the possibility of offering it only at Christmastime as a special seasonal product. She was also looking into the possibility of having a sauce company in Montana make it for her. The company produced caramel, chocolate, and chocolate-caramel sauces that had won awards from the fancy food industry trade association. Marilyn thought the sauces were quite good, although she did not like their caramel sauce as much as her own. The company would sell her 11-ounce jars of any of the sauces, spiced up to Marilyn's standards, for $2.75 per jar. Marilyn would have to provide the labels, for which she would need to have new label designs made to match the jar style the company was set up for, and she would also have to pay a shipping cost of $70 to $90 per delivery. The company requested a minimum order size of 72 cases, although the company's owner had hinted

that they might be willing to produce in half batches initially.

All of Cowgirl Chocolates' products had won awards, either in the annual Fiery Food Challenges sponsored by *Chile Pepper* magazine or the Scovie Award Competitions sponsored by *Fiery Foods* magazine (the Scovie awards are named after the Scovie measure of heat). All in all, Cowgirl Chocolates had won 11 awards in these two annual competitions. Further, the truffles had won first place in the latest Fiery Food Challenge and the caramel sauce won first place in the latest Scovie competition. The packaging, as distinctive as the chocolate itself, had also won several awards, including the 2000 Award for Excellence for Package Design from American Corporate Identity.

DISTRIBUTION AND PRICING

Marilyn's attempts to get her chocolates into the retail market had met with varying degrees of success. She clearly had been very successful in placing her product in her hometown of Moscow, Idaho. The Moscow Food Co-op was her single best wholesale customer, accounting for 10 percent to 15 percent of her annual sales. The co-op sold a wide variety of natural and/or organic products and produce. Many of its products, like Cowgirl Chocolates, were made or grown locally. The co-op did a nice job of placing her product in a visible shelf location and generally priced her product less than any other retail outlet. The co-op sold primarily the chocolate bars, which it priced at $2.35, and the quarter-pound muslin bags of truffles, which it priced at $5.50. This compared to the suggested retail prices of $2.99 for the bars and $6.99 for the bags. The product was also available at three other locations in downtown Moscow: Wild Women Traders, a store that described itself as a "lifestyle outfitter" and sold high-end women's clothing and antiques; Northwest Showcase, a store that sold locally produced arts and crafts; and Bookpeople, an independent bookstore that catered to customers who liked to spend time browsing an eclectic offering of books and drinking espresso before making a book purchase.

Marilyn was unsure how many of these local sales were to repeat purchasers who really liked the product and how many were to individuals who wanted to buy a locally made product to give as a gift. She was also unsure how much the co-op's lower prices boosted the sales of her product at that location. At the co-op, her product was displayed with other premium chocolates from several competitors, including Seattle Chocolates' own branded chocolate bars, which were priced at $2.99. Marilyn knew Seattle Chocolates' bars were clearly comparable in chocolate quality (although without the spice and cowgirl image). Some of the other competitors' comparably sized bars were priced lower, at $1.99, and some smaller bars were priced at $1.49. Although these products were clearly higher in quality than the inexpensive chocolate bars sold in vending machines and at the average supermarket checkout aisle, they were made with a less expensive chocolate than she used and were simply not as good as her chocolates. Marilyn wondered how the price and size of the chocolate bar affected the consumer's purchase decision, and how consumers evaluated the quality of each of the competing chocolate bars when making their purchase.

Outside of Moscow, Marilyn had a harder time getting her product placed onto store shelves and getting her product to move through these locations. One other co-op, the Boise Food Co-op, carried her products, and they sold pretty well there. Boise was the capital of Idaho and the state's largest city. The Boise Museum of Fine Arts gift shop also carried her product in Boise, although the product did not turn over at this location nearly as well as it did at the Boise Co-op. Other fine art museum gift shops in places like Missoula, Montana; Portland, Oregon; and Columbus, Ohio carried Cowgirl Chocolates, and Marilyn liked having her product in these outlets. She felt that her reputation as an artist helped her get her product placed in such locations, and the product generally sold well in these locations. She thought her biggest distribution coup was getting her product sold in the world-renowned Whitney Museum in New York City. She felt that the fact that it was sold there added to the product's panache. Unfortunately, the product did not sell there particularly well, and it was dropped by the museum. The museum buyer had told Marilyn that she simply thought it was too hot for their customers. Another location in New York City, the Kitchen Market, did much better. The Kitchen Market was an upscale restaurant and gourmet food take-out business. The

Kitchen Market was probably her steadiest wholesale customer other than the Moscow Co-op. The product also sold pretty well at the few similar gourmet markets where she had gotten her product placed, like Rainbow Groceries in Seattle and the Culinary Institute of America in San Francisco.

Marilyn had also gotten her product placed in a handful of specialty food stores that focused on hot and spicy foods. Surprisingly, she found, the product had never sold well in these locations. Despite the fact that the product had won the major fiery food awards, customers in these shops did not seem to be willing to pay the premium price for her product. She had concluded that if her product was located with similarly priced goods, like at the Kitchen Market in New York City, it would sell, but that if it stood out in price then it did not sell as well. Marilyn was not sure, however, just how similarly her product needed to be priced compared to other products the store sold. It seemed clear to her that her $14.95 half-pound tins were standing out in price too much in the hot and spicy specialty stores that thrived on selling jars of hot sauce that typically retailed for $2.99 to $5.99. Marilyn wondered how her product might do at department stores that often sold half-pound boxes of "premium" chocolates for as little as $9.95. She knew her half-pound tins contained better chocolate, offered more unique packaging and logo design, and did not give that "empty-feeling" that the competitor's oversized boxes did, but she wondered if her product would stand out too much in price in such retail locations.

Several online retailers also carried Cowgirl Chocolates, including companies like Salmon River Specialty Foods and Sam McGee's Hot Sauces, although sales from such sites were not very significant. Marilyn had also had her product available through Amazon.com for a short time, but few customers purchased her product from this site during the time it was listed. Marilyn concluded that customers searching the site for music or books simply were not finding her product, and those who did simply were not shopping for chocolates.

Marilyn also sold her products retail through her own Web site. The Web site accounted for about one-third of her sales. She liked Web-based sales, despite the extra work of having to process all the small orders, because she was able to capture both the wholesale and retail profits associated with the sale. She also liked the direct contact with the retail customers, and frequently tossed a few extra truffles into a customer's order and enclosed a note that said "A little extra bonus from the head cowgirl." Marilyn allowed customers to return the chocolate for a full refund if they found it not to their liking. Most of her sales growth from 1999 to 2000 had come from her Web site.

The Web site itself was created and maintained for her by a small local Internet service provider. It was a fairly simple site. It had pages that described the company and its products and allowed customers to place orders. It did not have any of the sophisticated features that would allow her to use it to capture information to track customers. Although she did not know for sure, she suspected that many of her Internet sales were from repeat customers who were familiar with her product. She included her Web site address on all of her packaging and had listed her site on several other sites, like saucemall.com and worldmall.com, that would link shoppers at these sites to her site. Listing on some of these sites, like saucemall.com, was free. Listing on some other sites cost a small monthly fee. For the worldmall.com listing, for example, she paid $25 per month. Some sites simply provided links to her site on their own. For example, one customer had told her she had found the Cowgirl Chocolates site off of an upscale shopping site called Style365.com. She was not sure how much traffic these various sites were generating on her site, and she was unsure how best to attract new customers to her Web site aside from these efforts.

Marilyn had attempted to get her product into a number of bigger name, upscale retailers, like Dean & DeLuca and Coldwater Creek. Dean & DeLuca was known for its high-end specialty foods, and the buyers for the company had seemed interested in carrying Cowgirl Chocolates. The owner, however, had nixed the idea because he found the chocolates too spicy. One of the buyers had also told Marilyn that the owner was more of a chocolate purist or traditionalist who did not really like the idea of adding cayenne pepper to chocolate. Marilyn had also tried hard to get her product sold through Coldwater Creek, one of the largest catalog and online retailers in the country that sold high-end women's apparel and gifts for the home. Coldwater Creek was headquartered just a couple of hours north of Moscow in Sandpoint, Idaho. Like Dean & DeLuca, Coldwater Creek had decided that the chocolate was too spicy. Coldwater Creek had

also expressed some reservations about carrying food products other than at its retail outlet in Sandpoint. Marilyn hoped that the introduction of Mild-mannered Cowgirl Chocolates would help get her product into sites like these two.

PROMOTION

Marilyn was unsure how best to promote her product to potential customers given her limited resources. The ad that would appear in *Chile Pepper* magazine was her first attempt at really advertising her product. The ad itself was designed to grab readers' attention and peak their curiosity about Cowgirl Chocolates. Most of the ads in the magazine were fairly standard in format. They provided a lot of information and images of the product packed into a fairly small space. Her ad was different: It had very little product information and utilized the single image of the woman in the watering trough. It was to appear in a special section of the magazine that focused on celebrity musicians like Willie Nelson and The Dixie Chicks.

Other than the upcoming ad, Marilyn's promotional efforts were focused on trade shows and creating publicity opportunities. She attended a handful of trade shows each year. Some of these were focused on the hot and spicy food market, and it was at these events that she had won all of her awards. Other trade shows were more in the gourmet food market, and she typically shared table space at these events with Seattle Chocolates. She always gave away a lot of product samples at these trade shows and had clearly won over some fans to her chocolate. But although these shows occasionally had led to placement of her product in retail locations, at least on a trial basis, they had as yet failed to land her what she would consider to be a really high-volume wholesale account.

Marilyn also sought ways to generate publicity for her company and products. Several local newspapers had carried stories on her company in the last couple of years. Each time something like that would happen, she would see a brief jump in sales on her Web site. *The New York Times* had also carried a short article about her and her company. The day after that article ran, she generated sales of $1,000 through her Web site. More publicity like the *New York Times* article would clearly help. The recently released movie *Chocolat* about a woman who brings spicy chocolate with somewhat magical powers to a small French town was also generating some interest in her product. A number of customers had inquired if she used the same pepper in her chocolates as was used in the movie. Marilyn wondered how she might best capitalize on the interest the movie was creating in spicy chocolates. She thought that perhaps she could convince specialty magazines like *Art & Antiques* or regional magazines like *Sunset Magazine* or even national magazines like *Good Housekeeping* to run stories on her, her art and her chocolates. But she only had so much time to divide between her various efforts. She had looked into hiring a public relations firm but had discovered that this would cost something on the order of $2,000 per month. She did not expect that any publicity a public relations firm could create would generate sufficient sales to offset this cost, particularly given the limited number of locations where people could buy her chocolates. Marilyn was considering trying to write a cookbook as a way to generate greater publicity for Cowgirl Chocolates. She always talked a little about Cowgirl Chocolates when she gave seminars and presentations about her art, and she thought that promoting a cookbook would create similar opportunities. The cookbook would also feature several recipes using Cowgirl Chocolates products.

In addition to being unsure how best to promote her product to potential customers, Marilyn also wondered what she should do to better tap into the seasonal opportunities that presented themselves to sellers of chocolate. Demand for her product was somewhat seasonal, with peak retail demand being at Christmas and Valentine's Day, but she was clearly not seeing the Christmas and Valentine sales of other chocolate companies. Seattle Chocolates, for example, had around three-quarters of its annual sales in the fourth quarter, whereas Cowgirl Chocolates sales in the second half of 2000 were actually less than in the first half. Likewise, although Cowgirl Chocolates experienced a small increase in demand around Valentine's Day, it was nowhere near the increase in demand that other chocolate companies experienced. Marilyn did sell some gift buckets and baskets through her Web site, and these were more popular at Christmas and Valentine's Day. The Moscow Co-op had also sold some of these gift baskets and buckets during the 2000 Christmas season. Marilyn knew that the gift basket industry in the United States

was pretty large, and that the industry even had its own trade publication called the *Gift Basket Review*. But she was not sure if gift baskets were the best way to generate sales at these two big holidays; she thought that she could probably be doing more. One other approach to spur these seasonal sales that she was planning to try was to buy lists of e-mail addresses that would allow her to send out several e-mails promoting her products right before Valentine's Day and Christmas. She had talked to the owners of a jewelry store about sharing the expense of this endeavor and they had tentative plans to purchase 10,000 e-mail addresses for $300.

WHAT NEXT?

Marilyn looked again at the advertisement that would be appearing soon in *Chile Pepper* magazine. The same friend who had helped her with her award-winning package design had helped produce the ad. It would clearly grab people's attention, but would it bring customers to her products in the numbers she needed?

Next to the ad sat the folder with what financial information she had. Despite having little training in small business accounting and financial management, Marilyn knew it was important to keep good records. She had kept track of revenues and expenses for the year, and she had summarized these in a table (Exhibit 4). Marilyn had shared this revenue and cost information with a friend with some experience in small business financial management, and the result was an estimated income statement for the year 2000 based upon the unaudited information in Exhibit 4. The estimated income statement, shown in Exhibit 5, revealed that Cowgirl Chocolates had lost approximately $6,175 on operations before taxes. Combining the information in both Exhibits 4 and 5, it appeared that the inventory had built up to approximately $16,848 by December 31, 2000. Marilyn had initially guessed that she had $10,000 worth of product and packaging inventory, about twice her normal level of inventory, between what was stored in her garage turned art studio turned chocolate warehouse and what was stored for her at Seattle Chocolates. However, the financial analysis indicated that she either had more inventory than she thought or that she had given away more product than she originally thought. Either way, this represented a significant

EXHIBIT 4

Summary of 2000 Financial Information (unaudited)

Revenues

Product Sales	$26,000	
Revenue from Shipping	4,046	(see Note 1)
Total Revenues	$30,046	

Expenses (related to cost of sales)

Chocolate (raw material)	$16,508	
Caramel (raw material)	2,647	
Packaging (bags, boxes, tins)	9,120	
Printing (labels, cards, etc.)	3,148	
Subtotal	$31,423	(see Note 2)

Other Expenses

Shipping and Postage	$ 4,046	
Brokers	540	
Travel (airfare, lodging, meals, gas)	5,786	
Trade Shows (promotions, etc.)	6,423	
Web Site	1,390	
Phone	981	
Office Supplies	759	
Photography	356	
Insurance, Lawyers, Memberships	437	
Charitable Contributions	200	
Miscellaneous Other Expenses	1,071	
State Taxes	35	
Subtotal	$ 22,024	
Total Expenses	$ 53,447	
Cash Needed to Sustain Operations	$ 23,023	(see Note 3)

Estimated Year-End Inventory (12/31/00)

Product Inventory	$ 9,848	
Extra Packaging and Labels	7,000	
Total Inventory	$16,848	

Notes:

1. The $4,046 revenue from shipping represents income received from customers who are charged shipping and postage up front as part of the order. Cowgirl Chocolates then pays the shipping and postage when the order is delivered. The offsetting operating expense is noted in "Other Expenses."

2. Of this amount, $14,575 is attributed to product actually sold and shipped. The remaining $16,848 represents left over inventory and related supplies (i.e., $16,848 + $14,575 = $31,423).

3. Marilyn made a personal loan to the firm in the year 2000 for approximately $23,000 to sustain the business's operations.

EXHIBIT 5

Cowgirl Chocolates Income Statement (accountant's unaudited estimate for year 2000)

			% of Sales
Revenues			
Product Sales	$26,000		
Miscellaneous Income	$ 4,046		
Total Net Sales		$30,046	100%
Cost of Sales (shipped portion of chocolate, caramel, packaging, and printing)		$14,197	47%
Gross Margin		$15,849	53%
Operating Expenses			
Advertising and Promotions			
Trade Shows	6,423		
Web Site	1,390		
Charitable Contributions	200		
Subtotal		8,013	27%
Travel		5,786	19%
Miscellaneous		1,071	4%
Payroll Expense/Benefits @ 20%	(no personnel charges)	—	0%
Depreciation on Plant and Equipment	(no current ownership of PPE)	—	0%
Continuing Inventory (finished and unfinished)	(not included in income statement)	—	0%
Shipping and Postage		4,046	13%
Insurance, Lawyers, Professional Memberships		437	1.5%
Brokers		540	1.8%
Office Expenses (phone, supplies, photography, taxes)		2,131	7%
Total Operating Expenses		22,024	
Grand Total: All Expenses		$36,221	
Profit Before Interest and Taxes		($6,175) [see note]	
Interest Expense (short term)		—	
Interest Expense (long term)		—	
Taxes Incurred (Credit @ 18%, approximate tax rate)		($1,124)	
Net Profit After Taxes		($5,051.15)	
Net Profit After Taxes/Sales			−17%

Note: The ($6,175) loss plus the $16,848 in inventory buildup approximates the cash needed ($23,023)—see Exhibit 4) to cover the total expenses for year 2000.

additional drain on her resources. In effect, cash expended to cover both the operational loss and the inventory buildup was approximately $23,000 in total. When Marilyn looked at the exhibits, she could better understand why she had to loan the firm money. The bottom line was that the numbers did not look good, and she wondered if the ad would help turn things around for 2001.

If the ad did not have its desired effects, she wondered what she should do next. She clearly had limited resources. She had already pretty much decided that if this ad did not work, she would not run another one in the near future. She was also wary of working with distributors. In addition to her own bad experience, she knew of others in the industry who had bad experiences with distributors, and she did not think she could afford to take another gamble on a distributor. She wondered if she should focus more attention on her online retail sales or on expanding her wholesale business to include more retailers. If she focused more on her own online sales, what exactly should she do? If she focused on expanding her wholesale business, where should she put her emphasis? Should she continue to pursue retailers that specialized in hot and spicy foods; try to get her product placed in more coops; expand her efforts to get the product positioned as a gift in museum gift shops and similar outlets; or focus her efforts on large, high-end retailers like Coldwater Creek and Dean & DeLuca now that she had a nonspicy chocolate in her product mix? Or should she try to do something entirely new? What more should she do to create publicity for her product? Was the cookbook idea worth pursuing? As she thought about it, she began to wonder if things were beginning to spin out of control. Here she was, contemplating writing a cookbook to generate publicity for her chocolate company that she had started to raise money to publish her arts magazine. Where would this end?

Calgene Inc.: Marketing High-Tech Tomatoes

This case was prepared by Julian W. Vincze, Crummer Graduate School of Business, Rollins College.

BRUISED PRODUCT PROBLEM

By the late 1990s, few customers had had the opportunity to taste the bioengineered and trade-marked MacGregor's tomatoes grown from FlavrSavr tomato seeds. MacGregor's tomatoes, which were introduced with a flurry of publicity by Calgene Inc., had not achieved wide distribution. Why had this occurred? The answer was that Calgene's research and development (R&D) department, after overcoming complex technological, regulatory, and environmental obstacles through years of effort and considerable expense, seemed to encounter totally unexpected tomato distribution problems. MacGregor's tomatoes were designed to have several outstanding product features such as longer shelf life, better taste, and juicier flavor. These features were expected to differentiate Mac-Gregor's tomatoes from ordinary fresh tomatoes. Unfortunately, during the growing season, Calgene had realized that its product was not able to withstand the normal rigors of the standard picking, packing, and shipping methods used in the fresh tomato packing industry. Early shipments became

bruised on their way to market, so Calgene had to undertake a costly overhaul of its packing methods (detailed later).

This damage to product, which was both unexpected and very late in the R&D cycle, had a major impact on Calgene's timetable for widespread distribution and market introduction of the MacGregor tomato. Industry analysts believed this difficulty contributed to a cash drain that had forced Calgene to sell assets and cut its workforce by 10 percent. "This tomato has brought them to their knees," said Stan Shimoda, an analyst with Bio-Science Securities Inc. of Orinda, California. "The question is, can they get up again?"[1]

CALGENE'S HISTORY

Calgene Inc., an agricultural biotechnology company involved in developing, through genetic manipulation, a portfolio of genetically engineered plants and plant products for the food, seed, and oleochemical industries, focused operations in three core crop businesses (as detailed below). Headquartered in Davis, California, Calgene was formed in 1982 and became involved in the development of improved plant varieties and plant products and was the first company to introduce genetically engineered products in the fresh tomato, cottonseed, and industrial and edible plant oils (canola) markets, where it believed biotechnology could provide substantial added commercial value in consumer, industrial, and seed markets.

Fresh Market Tomato Core Crop No. 1

Fresh tomatoes currently were the most visible and probably also the most important of Calgene's core crops. After 12 years of R&D efforts, Calgene's first apparent success was when the U.S. Food and Drug Administration (FDA) announced its determination that the MacGregor tomato had not been significantly altered with respect to safety or nutritive value when compared with conventional tomatoes. This FDA approval allowed Calgene to begin to market MacGregor's tomatoes. However, this success was tempered by the apparent ongoing difficulties encountered in achieving widespread distribution and therefore market availability of MacGregor's tomatoes (as noted above). These difficulties caused Calgene's non-genetically engineered tomato production to be scaled back and eventually resulted in curtailment of much of Calgene's Mexican operations. Calgene had made agreements with both Campbell Soup Company and Zeneca A.V.P. (the original financial backers of the R&D that produced MacGregor's tomatoes) whereby Calgene received worldwide, exclusive royalty-free rights to produce and sell fresh market tomatoes containing the FlavrSavr gene. Prior to these agreements, Calgene's commercialization rights were limited to North America and had required royalty payments to Campbell Soup Company.

Tomato Packing Methods

The traditional tomato packing method was called the *gassed-green method,* which began with either mechanical or hand field picking. The field picking occurred while the tomatoes were green and rock hard. This green picking was necessary for traditional tomatoes so that they could withstand the rigors of the remaining steps in the packing process. These additional steps included being moved by conveyor belts, being dumped into large bins, being subjected to high-pressure gas spraying, and then being boxed. If field picking was mistimed until after the tomatoes began to ripen, they would start to soften too quickly as

a result of an enzyme called *polygalacturonase* (PG). If this softening occurred, the tomatoes were prone to being damaged during packing and shipping to retailers and/or by the handling that occurred within retail stores. In addition, late picking lessened the shelf life of the tomatoes at the retail store.

Customers' Reactions of Gassed-Green Tomatoes

However, the problem with the green picking and packing process was that the ultimate consumers did not want to buy green and unripened tomatoes. Therefore, the packing process included the high-pressure gas spraying step. The gas used in the spraying step was ethylene, a hormone that triggered the beginning of the reddening and ripening process. Thus almost all fresh field-grown tomatoes ripened during the packing and shipping process because the ethylene spray eventually caused the green tomatoes to turn red. However, these artificially induced ripe tomatoes did not achieve a deep red color. Instead, they turned a pale red and were somewhat mushy and to many customers were tasteless. These traditional tomato packing methods were considered by the industry to be very efficient because they minimized costs and resulted in relatively low retail prices for consumers. Unfortunately, these traditional packing methods had such a deleterious effect on the taste of tomatoes picked while still green and rock hard that many customers equated this taste with cardboard. The tomatoes certainly did not compare favorably with vine-ripened, freshly picked field tomatoes. In fact, one industry observer noted that a U.S. Department of Agriculture report gave an 84 percent dissatisfaction rate among customers of gassed-green tomatoes.[2]

Development of MacGregor's Tomato

Cognizant of this criticism of tasteless tomatoes, and anxious to capitalize on what they perceived to be a market opportunity, Calgene's geneticists bioengineered the ordinary tomato to delay softening and rotting (the maturation process) in order to enhance taste and lengthen retail shelf life. They used what was then cutting-edge technology of gene splicing. Calgene's scientists developed a procedure that prevented tomatoes from producing PG by creating an antisense, or mirror, image of the gene that carried instructions for producing the enzyme. By then inserting the antisense gene into the tomato's DNA, production of the enzyme was blocked. This began the ripening process, which in turn was responsible for breaking down the wall of tomato cells. This antisense gene also was expected to allow growers to wait until the MacGregor's tomato was turning red before harvesting.[3]

The concept seemed straightforward and rather simple: that is, the stronger the cell walls, the easier it would be to transport tomatoes without damage; the more advanced the maturation process was before picking and packing, the better the flavor and the longer the retail shelf life. However, delayed maturation, which allowed for longer time ripening on the vine, also resulted in a softer tomato when picked. With hindsight, it now seemed that Calgene had rushed to commercialize its MacGregor's Flavr-Savr tomato without considering that its tomato would not tolerate traditional packing house processes without bruising.

Cotton—Calgene's Core Crop No. 2

Calgene's second core crop and genetic engineering program focused on reducing farmers' growing costs through the development of cotton varieties that required fewer pesticides (and also the creation of cotton varieties that produced natural colors). It was estimated that U.S. cotton farmers spent over $200 million annually on herbicides and from $225 to $400 million on insecticides. Therefore, when Calgene could create herbicide resistant and insect resistant cotton varieties, the result would be not only reduced production costs for farmers but also improved crop yields and environmental benefits. Calgene believed that these product features would translate into premium pricing opportunities.

Calgene's BXN trademarked cottonseed received U.S. Department of Agriculture (USDA) deregulation in 1994. Calgene marketed conventional cottonseed varieties and their BXN cotton through its Stoneville subsidiary, which had experienced a revenue growth of 19 percent during the 1994 fiscal year. In April of 1995, Calgene introduced two new genetically engineered varieties of BXN cotton that were

resistant to the herbicide bromoxynil (commonly used cotton crop herbicide) at a 45 percent price premium over Calgene's non-genetically engineered cottonseed. These two new BXN cotton varieties, like all of Calgene's BXN cotton, also were genetically engineered to contain a Bt gene for resistance to *Heliothis,* the principal cotton insect pest.

Plant Oils—Calgene's Core Crop No. 3

Calgene's third core crop was industrial and edible plant oils. This program focused on genetically engineering rapeseed oils with a broad range of food and industrial applications. Calgene's scientists had successfully genetically altered canola rapeseed varieties that produced substantial quantities of laurate, an important ingredient in detergents that was not naturally present in canola or other nontropical oil plants. In March of 1994, Calgene received a U.S. patent on the bay thioesterase gene. This gene in rapeseed plants resulted in the production of laurate, while in June of 1994, Calgene successfully purified the LPAAT enzyme. Introduction of the gene that produced this LPAAT enzyme increased laurate levels significantly beyond the 40 percent level that had been achieved previously. Thus, by July of 1995, Calgene's Laurical trademarked canola sales were reported to be 1 million pounds.

The Plant Oils Division also was conducting its eighth season of field trials with canola plants that had been genetically engineered to produce oil with increased stearate levels. Stearate had the potential to substitute for hydrogenated oils in margarine, shortening, and confectionary products. Therefore, Calgene had begun to establish strategic relationships with Procter & Gamble, Unilever, and Pfizer Food Science to explore the potential commercial opportunities for its plant oil products.

KEY STRENGTHS AND BUSINESS STRATEGY

In a recent president's letter to shareholders included in Calgene's Annual Report, Roderick Stacey said:

> As we look to the future, I believe the key strengths of Calgene are as follows:

1. We are the scientific and regulatory leaders in agricultural biotechnology, particularly in the science of plant oils modification. All technical hurdles are behind us in our first tomato, cotton, and oil products. We have the only FDA and USDA approvals for genetically engineered plant products.

2. Our proprietary position is strong. We resolved all of the issues regarding tomato technology with Zeneca and Campbell and have worldwide royalty-free rights to the FlavrSavr gene in fresh tomatoes. We have successfully negotiated favorable cross-licenses with Monsanto, Mogen International nv, PGS, and Agracetus to obtain freedom to operate in the most important core plant genetic engineering technologies. Seven oils gene modification patents have been issued in Europe, and U.S. counterparts (patents), starting with the Laurate gene patent, are beginning to issue. We remain confident that we will prevail in our litigation with Enzo Biochem, Inc.

3. We are in excellent position to commercialize on our scientific successes. We have a conventional operating business base which generated $35 million in product revenues. We have a seasoned senior management group and an experienced and capable field production team in each of our core crops. The supply of our MacGregor's tomatoes grown from FlavrSavr seeds will be increased in October. Field results of BXN cotton have exceeded expectations, and market launch is set.

We are positioned to realize the promise of our 12 years' investment in plant science, regulatory innovation, and business planning.[4]

However, despite this optimism voiced by Mr. Stacey, several industry observers were skeptical of the basis for his optimism and openly wondered if Calgene could successfully market its high-tech tomatoes. However, in 10-K financial filings, Calgene noted that its business strategy was to build operating businesses in their core crop areas to facilitate the market introduction of genetically engineered proprietary products and to maximize the long-term financial return from such products. Calgene believed that implementing this strategy would provide direct access to markets where Calgene could sell fresh and processed plant products having improved quality traits or cost-of-production advantages or both. For details about Calgene's financial situation, refer to Exhibits A and B.

CALGENE REACTS TO BRUISING PROBLEM

Once aware of the bruising problem, Calgene's first response was to approach experienced packing companies to ask them to devise gentler handling procedures; however, none could meet Calgene's requirements. Calgene then decided to build its own processing plant near Chicago for the purpose of developing gentler handling procedures. However, by the time tomatoes grown in fields in the southern states arrived at the plant, many were bruised or split or both. Finally, Calgene announced that it would spend up to $10 million building three facilities nearer its growing areas. These facilities would be equipped with high-tech "soft touch" machines that included optical sensors to distinguish tomato size, shape, and color and which were designed originally to sort peaches.

The first location, a 90,000 square foot facility in Immokalee, Florida, was proclaimed to be on-line and operational by late March. A second location in Lake Park, Georgia, was a 65,000 square foot packing and distribution facility that was scheduled to begin operations in May. The third location, in Irvine, California, was a modification of an existing structure that was also expected to be on-line for packing and distributing by May. "We now have the facilities in place to supply demand for FlavrSavr tomatoes across the U.S.," said Danilo Lopes, CEO of Calgene Fresh, the wholly owned subsidiary of Calgene Inc. that grows, packs, distributes, and sells fresh produce.[5] In addition, Calgene noted that it would rely more heavily on manual labor in picking and packing its tomatoes grown on approximately 2000 acres in California, Florida, and Georgia. "The combination of increased acreage, new packing and distribution facilities, and an experienced management team should enable us to achieve our target

EXHIBIT A

Calgene Inc. Balance Sheet (000's)[16]

	Year 5	Year 4	Year 3	Year 2	Year 1
Assets					
Cash	11,753	5,286	15,009	9,511	5,548
Marketable securities	10,283	15,457	24,773	31,748	30,632
Receivables	6,697	4,792	2,666	2,864	3,163
Inventories	8,148	5,068	4,774	4,461	5,529
Other current assets	1,699	2,278	6,023	7,814	7,363
Total current assets	38,580	32,881	53,245	56,636	52,235
Property, plant, and equipment	38,044	32,363	26,561	21,982	20,872
Accumulated depreciation	15,524	12,872	11,023	9,909	8,432
Net property and equipment	22,520	19,491	15,538	12,073	12,440
Investment and advances to subs	0	1,415	1,551	3,432	3,710
Intangibles	26,224	23,677	17,308	12,205	14,180
Deposits and other assets	1,907	848	759	877	571
Total assets	89,231	78,312	88,401	85,223	83,136
Liabilities					
Notes payable	7,761	8,650	7,597	9,083	7,039
Accounts payable	6,487	7,916	5,327	1,977	2,457
Current long-term debt	1,494	1,728	1,241	1,037	527
Accrued expenses	2,049	1,803	1,562	3,735	4,278
Other current liabilities	9,968	8,088	3,211	2,502	5,057
Total current liabilities	27,759	28,185	18,938	18,334	19,358
Long-term debt	14,671	4,204	3,694	4,378	5,065
Other long-term liabilities	750	1,500	N/A	N/A	N/A
Total liabilities	43,180	33,889	22,632	22,712	24,423
Minority interests	N/A	N/A	N/A	N/A	948
Preferred stock	N/A	N/A	N/A	29,506	29,627
Common stock (net)	30	27	24	18	15
Capital surplus	223,161	190,934	169,482	111,101	86,488
Retained earnings	−177,140	−146,538	−103,737	−78,114	−58,198
Other equities	N/A	N/A	N/A	N/A	−167
Total shareholder equity	46,051	44,423	65,769	62,511	57,765
Total liabilities and net worth	89,231	78,312	88,401	85,223	83,136

expanded distribution," said Mr. Lopez.[6] Roger Salquist, Calgene's CEO, said the company was on target to have its tomatoes in 2500 stores by June and added that sales of the company's tomatoes in the Midwest were "doing great."[7]

Mr. Shimoda's response to these statements was: "The technology didn't do what they thought it would do, and so they had to reinvent the wheel to deal with a soft tomato."[8] Another industry observer, Andre Garnet, analyst at A. G. Edwards, asserted that "Calgene's distribution system is all screwed up, and it costs more to produce than to sell."[9] Mr. Garnet believed that Calgene would be forced to raise additional cash.

EXHIBIT B

Calgene Inc. Income Statement (000's)[17]

	Year 5	Year 4	Year 3	Year 2	Year 1
Net sales	55,431	38,433	27,237	21,877	26,104
Cost of goods sold	57,114	46,703	26,633	20,316	19,727
Gross profit	−1,683	−8,270	604	1,561	6,377
R&D expenditures	11,937	12,847	10,260	11,256	11,151
Selling, gen. and admin. exp.	16,081	21,279	16,494	11,318	10,161
Income before depreciation	−29,701	−42,396	−26,150	−21,013	−14,935
Nonoperating income	38	389	1,644	3,274	1,515
Interest expense	924	729	673	813	898
Income before taxes	−30,587	−42,736	−25,179	−18,555	−14,318
Provisions for income tax	15	65	44	61	61
Net income before extraord.	−30,602	−42,801	−25,223	−18,616	−14,379
Extraordinary items	N/A	N/A	−400	−1,300	−12,600
Net income	−30,602	−42,801	−25,623	−19,916	−26,979

Key Annual Financial Ratios	*1994*	*1993*	*1991*
Quick ratio	0.91	2.24	2.41
Current ratio	1.17	2.81	3.09
Sales/cash	1.85	0.68	0.53
Receivables turnover	8.02	10.22	7.64
Receivables days sales	44.89	35.24	47.13
Inventories turnover	7.58	5.71	4.90
Net sales/working capital	8.18	0.79	0.57
Net sales/total assets	0.49	0.31	0.26
Net sales/employees	113.707	73.021	77.578
Total liabilities/total assets	0.43	0.26	0.27
Times interest earned	−57.62	−36.41	−21.74
Total debt/equity	0.13	0.08	0.09
Net income/net sales	−1.11	−0.94	−0.91
Net income/total assets	−0.55	−0.29	−0.23

COMPETITOR TOMATO: ENDLESS SUMMER

Although there is currently only one other firm attempting to market genetically engineered fresh market tomatoes, competition is expected to intensify rapidly as existing gassed-green tomato producers react to competitive pressures by growing and marketing traditionally developed vine-ripened tomatoes. The existing direct competitor was DNA Plant Technology Corporation (DNAP) of Oakland, California, which developed a competitor to Mac-Gregor's tomato which they called the Fresh World Farms Endless Summer. FDA clearance to market Endless Summer was granted in early 1995.[10] DNAP claimed that Endless Summer tomatoes required no special handling, even though they too stay ripening longer on the vine than the so-called gassed-green tomatoes. The secret was a more-recent technology that regulated a tomato's ethylene production and slowed down the overall ripening process, including softening. This allowed Endless Summer to be picked earlier than FlavrSavr tomatoes while they were still relatively hard and therefore able to withstand traditional packing house processes. Yet because of the slowed ripening, Endless Summer tomatoes outlasted FlavrSavr on shelf life because they stayed fresh for 30 days after harvest. The relative taste factors of these two competitor high-tech tomatoes had not yet been determined by the market place. However, Carolyn Hayworth, a Calgene spokesperson, said: "It's a huge market—a $3½ billion market for fresh tomatoes in the U.S.; let's just let the consumer decide."[11]

Endless Summer, grown in Florida and California, was in test market in Rochester, New York, and national rollout was predicted for the fall of 1995. DNAP intended to apply its technology to other foods as well. Potential candidate foods for its process were noted to include bananas, pineapples, peas, peppers, and strawberries.[12] Mr. Shimoda thought Endless Summer stood a better chance of success than MacGregor's tomato, and George Dahlman, an analyst with Piper Jaffray Inc. and once a Calgene advocate, seemed to agree. Mr. Dahlman said: "The future of this company [Calgene] is more controversial than ever." However, Carolyn Hayworth, a Calgene spokeswoman, noted: "We're building a business, and we believe we know what we are doing."[13] Roger Salquist, Calgene's CEO, insisted that Calgene would not have to raise more money and that the fiscal year ending in 1996 would be profitable.

CONSUMER REACTIONS UNCERTAIN

Both MacGregor's tomato and Endless Summer were the result of gene-transfer technology used to develop tomatoes that could ripen longer on the vine yet not spoil on the trip to market. The goal appeared to be a year-round tomato with flavor and juiciness. However, consumer reaction to genetically altered foods remained uncertain. When MacGregor's tomatoes were offered in Seattle's Fred Meyer stores (an upscale supermarket chain) in November and December, "We had a very positive response. The stores have been asking for more as a result of requests by shoppers," said assistant vice president Rob Boley.[14] The tomatoes carried a label noting that they were grown from genetically modified seeds and a sign that gave additional details.

However, some industry observers were critical of both Calgene and DNAP for not publicizing any marketing research studies that they may have carried out prior to or during the development of MacGregor's tomato and Endless Summer. This failure to publicize any research relative to the acceptability to customers of bioengineered fresh tomatoes was interpreted by some to indicate that little, if any, actual customer opinion surveys had been carried out by either company and that in their rush to apply the technology, the whole aspect of consumer acceptance was overlooked. If R&D scientists had pressed for quick development and upper management had not expended scarce resources on customer surveys, then, without any indication of customer acceptance of bioengineered fresh tomatoes, the probability of immediate acceptance by consumers was viewed as questionable at best and perhaps improbable in a worst-case scenario. This lack of market research therefore could represent an unexplored opportunity or potentially a tremendous oversight fraught with perils. Still other industry observers were more trusting that good management existed at both Calgene and DNAP and that such a major oversight could not have occurred. They argued that surely these two management teams had not only looked at the supply side of the market but had thoroughly analyzed the demand aspects as well. Since neither company had publicized such demand analyses, actual retail trials would have to be relied on to judge potential customer acceptance rates. And results from trial markets were not being made public by either firm.

Controversy about Genetically Engineered Food

Controversy had surrounded the idea of genetically engineered food. For example, with MacGregor's tomatoes, the use of marker genes added to the tomatoes in order to determine whether the gene for slow ripening was transferred successfully had become a public controversy. The controversial aspect of the process related to the fact that the marker genes were resistant to certain antibiotics, and critics said that such resistance might create antibiotic resistance in people who ate these altered tomatoes. Even though Food and Drug Administration (FDA) scientists had concluded that such development of resistance to antibiotics by people consuming genetically altered foods was not a possibility, the rumor still existed.

In addition, a national coalition of prominent chefs as early as mid-1992 had begun to call for a boycott of genetically engineered foods.[15] This coalition claimed support from some 1000 of their colleagues, including such nationally known figures as Wolfgang Puck of Spago in West Hollywood, Jimmy Schmidt of the Rattlesnake Club in Detroit, Jean Louis Palladin of Jean Louis in Washington, D.C., and Mark Miller of Red Sage in Washington, D.C., and was led by chef Rick Moonen of the Water Club in New York. Despite this protest, the FDA declared that genetically engineered foods were safe and special labeling was unnecessary regardless of customers who had professed to having religious or health concerns.

THE FUTURE

What does the future hold for Calgene and its MacGregor's tomato? Many investors and industry analysts are pondering this question. Stan Shimoda indicated that MacGregor's tomato had brought Calgene to its knees—his question was, Could they get up again? Others held similar views, only differing in degree of pessimism. Countering these views, however, were the optimistic statements of the management of Calgene, which implied that Calgene was on the verge of a huge success in the marketplace. Which view is the correct one? Would the MacGregor's tomato be a marketing success story? What would you predict? If you were to unexpectedly inherit $25,000 would you invest it in Calgene stock?

Questions

1. Do a traditional SWOT (strengths, weaknesses, opportunities, and threats) analysis of Calgene's situation in the spring of 1995.

2. What is your assessment of the product development procedures used by Calgene to develop the MacGregor's FlavrSavr tomato? Were they effective, or could they be improved?

3. What is your assessment of Calgene's knowledge about customer acceptance of bioengineered foods and specifically the FlavrSavr tomato? Do you think there has been an oversight, or do you agree that Calgene management has effectively considered market demand for the product?

4. Diagram the consumer purchasing process you believe is used by the average household when purchasing fresh tomatoes. List what

you believe are the evaluative criteria applied when deciding which alternative fresh tomatoes to purchase?

5. Calgene seems to be planning to introduce MacGregor's FlavrSavr tomatoes to the market by traditional channels of distribution. Is this the best channel to use? What other channels might be used?

6. How much of a technological lead does Calgene enjoy over DNAP? Does the FlavrSavr tomato have a market leadership position over Endless Summer tomatoes?

7. What are the barriers to entry in the fresh tomato producing and marketing industry?

8. Assume that you have unexpectedly inherited $25,000 today. Would you invest it in Calgene?

Endnotes

1. Ralph T. King, Jr., "Low-Tech Woe Slows Calgene's Super Tomato," *Wall Street Journal*, April 11, 1995, pp. B-1, B-6.
2. Barbara DeLollis, "High-Tech Tomato Had Growing Pains; Developing the Technology Was Only Half of the Challenge," *The Fresno Bee*, April 10, 1995.
3. Del I. Hawkins, Roger J. Best, and Kenneth A. Coney, "Calgene, Inc. versus the Pure Food Campaign," *Consumer Behavior: Implications for Marketing Strategy*, 6th ed. (Homewood, IL: Irwin, 1995), p. 384.
4. *1994 Annual Report to Shareholders*, Calgene Inc., Davis, California.
5. "Calgene Tomato Packing and Distribution System Nears Completion; Senior Produce Executives Join Calgene Fresh Team," PR Newswire, March 28, 1995.
6. *Ibid.*
7. Herb Greenberg, "I Say Tomato, Some Say Tomorrow, What's Really Going On?" *San Francisco Chronicle*, January 16, 1995.
8. "Calgene Tomato Packing and Distribution System Nears Completion; Senior Produce Executives Join Calgene Fresh Team," PR Newswire, March 28, 1995.
9. Lauren Dermer, "Calgene Short Seller Stomps on Biotech-Enhanced Tomato," *Portfolio Letter*, February 6, 1995.
10. "Calgene and DNAP Vie in Tomato War," *Industries in Transition*, February 1995.
11. Judith Blake, "High-Tech Tomato May Roll onto Market Soon," *Seattle Times*, February 1, 1995.
12. "Calgene and DNAP Vie in Tomato War," *Industries in Transition*, February 1995.
13. Ralph T. King, Jr., "Low-Tech Woe Slows Calgene's Super Tomato," *Wall Street Journal*, April 11, 1995, pp. B-1, B-6.
14. Judith Blake, "High-Tech Tomato May Roll onto Market Soon," *Seattle Times*, February 1, 1995.
15. "Chefs Vow Boycott of Genetically Engineered Foods," *Nation's Restaurant News*, August 10, 1992.
16. *Annual Reports to Stockholders*, Calgene Inc., Davis, California.
17. *Ibid.*

3DV-LS: Assessing Market Opportunity in the Computer Visualization Market

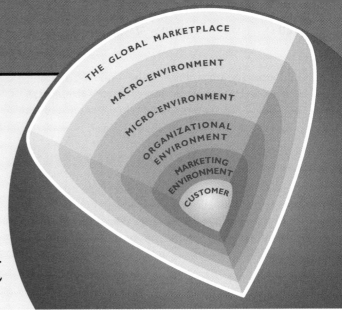

This case was prepared by Robin Habeger and Kay M. Palan, Iowa State University.

As Pat Patterson, Director of the 3DV Litigation Services (3DV-LS)[1] business unit, was reviewing the second quarter sales numbers, he sighed heavily and rubbed his temples in an attempt to avert an impending migraine blooming behind his eyes. The sales numbers were disappointing, to say the least. In fact, sales had been low over the last four quarters. Sales had dried up on the east and west coasts because of increased competition, resulting in an alarming 16 percent average sales decline each of the last four quarters. 3DV had recently reorganized several of its business units, closing some and combining others. To avoid a similar fate, it was imperative that litigation services post increasing sales and profits. The decline in sales, Pat knew, put the business unit in jeopardy.

Pat sighed again as his mind ran through the available options. He could give the marketing and sales efforts more time to increase sales. A new Web page, giving the unit improved Internet presence, would soon be implemented, which might spark some sales activity. But, as he pondered the situation, Pat believed that it would take more than this to reverse the declining sales trend. When he

joined the company in the mid-1990s as a salesman, he shared a cubicle with three other people. He remembered the lean days when it was touch and go as to whether or not he would even get a paycheck. Now, in December 2000, he had his own corner office. He had helped build the litigation services unit into the nationwide competitor it now was. Pat was determined to overcome the recent sales decline. He had invested too much of his own time and energy into the business unit to let it fail now.

Just then, Pat heard a knock on his door. Glancing up, he saw Lance Wolffe, one of 3DV-LS's project managers. Lance had an air of excitement about him. "Pat, I've got to show you this magazine article I came across last night!" He tossed the magazine into Pat's hands and continued, "The article discusses how some construction and transportation projects are beginning to use computer-generated models to help clients visualize finished projects— that's something we could be doing, only better!"

Pat briefly looked at the civil engineering trade magazine turned to the article Lance had marked. Pat, too, could see that the kind of computer visualization process used by 3DV might be transferable to other industries such as the construction and transportation industries illustrated in the article. But any enthusiasm Pat shared with Lance was tempered by the realization that entering a new market would take time and resources and, in the end, might not be any more fruitful than improving the unit's marketing efforts.

To Lance, he said, "It certainly does look like there's some potential for us to expand our efforts into other markets, but there's a lot of information we need to know before we make such a decision. Let's make a list of questions we need to answer."

Pat and Lance created a list of questions to answer regarding this new market opportunity. The list addressed issues such as quantifying market potential, determining 3DV-LS's competitive advantage, and identifying threats and weaknesses to market entry.

As the list grew longer, Lance observed, "What we essentially need to do is a cost/benefit analysis."

Pat agreed, but added, "We need to focus our analysis just on the construction and transportation industries, but we also need to compare the results of the cost/benefit analysis to maintaining the status quo. If we can't demonstrate that entry into this new market will be profitable in a reasonable period of time, then we just won't be able to do it."

Lance felt his bubble burst. He really felt in his gut that expanding 3DV-LS's technological capabilities to the construction and transportation industries with the right thing to do. He grew quiet for a few minutes, trying to settle his desire for immediate market entry.

Finally he said, "We do need to go into this with our eyes open and that means finding as much information as we can. Where do you want me to start?"

"At the beginning," Pat replied. "Find out everything you can about the customers and competitors in the construction and transportation industries, the costs and profits, the attractiveness of the market. You should probably ask Sandy to help you. Because she is in charge of marketing she will have some idea where to find the information you need. Let's plan to meet again in a couple of weeks to review the situation."

As Lance turned to leave, Pat allowed himself a momentary glimmer of hope. Could this be the break 3DV-LS needed to improve sales and profitability?

3DV: HISTORY OF THE COMPANY

3DV, founded in 1988 for the purpose of accurately creating 3-D accident reconstructions, used a revolutionary programming code developed by the founders. Attorneys, representing automobile manufacturers, hired 3DV to construct visual animations of automobile accidents. These visualizations were used in court cases to demonstrate how an automobile accident had most likely occurred.

Although the company's primary focus in the early years was accident reconstruction for automobile manufacturers, by 1999 3DV had several distinct products and services, each targeting a select market. For example, using the basis of the original programming code, 3DV developed several different types of software packages that allowed manufacturing companies to use the Internet for project collaboration and visualization. That is, the software enabled employees in different locations to view, modify, and work with the same 3-D model simultaneously, while at the same time maintaining secure online access. Another product helped companies in various industries improve the ergonomics of product designs and workplace tasks. Companies could use still other 3DV software to cost-effectively model and view an entire 2-D/3-D manufacturing facility by designing optimal factory floor plans and testing efficiency through virtual simulation. 3DV provided software support and training and implementation services for all of its software products.

3DV's software had revolutionized the visualization industry. Relative to other companies that provided computer visualization, 3DV produced animation and 3-D models that were the highest quality visualizations available. Consequently, although 3DV had once been fairly unknown, it now enjoyed an international reputation, having served such customers as General Motors, Ford, Toyota-Honda, Eastman Kodak, Lockheed Martin, Johnson & Johnson, Dow Chemical Company, and Motorola. Moreover, 3DV had benefited from the public-trading frenzy accorded to high-tech companies in the mid-1990s.

But 3DV's fortunes in the last few years had not been good. The stock price had reached a high of $72, but it was currently trading under $20, and the company as a whole had reported a net operating loss of over $40 million in 1999. As a result, 3DV had gone through two major restructurings within the last 2 years. It closed several business units that fell outside of its core competencies. A second reduction in support staff (e.g., human resources and technical support) followed the first by approximately 6 to 8 months. Although 3DV still employed approximately 600 people worldwide, managers were aware that additional staff reductions were possible in unprofitable business units.

3DV: THE LITIGATION SERVICES BUSINESS UNIT

From the outset, 3DV had created a specialized business unit, known as 3DV Litigation Services (3DV-LS), to focus specifically on litigation visualization services. 3DV-LS specialized in animation and 3-D models for attorneys to use as displays or demonstrative evidence in court cases. 3DV-LS offered some additional visualization services, including secure online project management workspace, DVD presentation systems, digitally altered photographs for use as before versus after displays, videotape production, and visuals needed for presentation materials. 3DV-LS differentiated itself from other visualization providers by using computers to hardware-render the frames (individual pictures) used to make an animation (Exhibit 1). This method, relative to the more commonly used

software rendering, created customized animations faster and with more precision and greater detail. For clients, the primary advantage of hardware-rendered animations was the ability to make changes to animations within days, whereas software-rendering processes required weeks to make similar changes. In particular, in the litigation industry, attorneys sometimes requested changes right up to the day before the animations were used in a trial. Hardware rendering, unlike software rendering, accommodated these last-minute changes.

However, the process and, consequently, the advantage of hardware rendering was not well understood by potential clients. Simply put, hardware-rendered visualizations were created directly by computer hardware; software-rendered visualizations were created from software packages. Pat liked to explain the difference between hardware and software rendering to clients as analogous to how the brain functioned in humans. The brain (the "hardware") was programmed to tell the lungs when to breathe, the eyes to blink, or the heart to beat. It did not require any conscious thought to do these

EXHIBIT 1

Definitions for Computer Visualization Terms

Term	Definition
Animation	A group of computer-rendered frames shown in a sequential manner to portray movement or show a specific angle. It takes 1,800 frames to make 1 minute of animation.
3-D Model	A computer-generated picture of a virtual 3-D object usually created in a CAD package that contains all the spatial information (*x, y, z*, and scale) of a real object.
Rendered Frame	A 3-dimensional photograph of the subject material created by a computer, i.e., a picture of a building from a specific angle.
Software Render	A computer image rendered using a software program. The speed is restricted by the central processing unit (CPU) processing speed and available RAM. The rendering of one frame is completed in several minutes to several days depending on image complexity. Ongoing programming throughout the development of a visualization is required.
Hardware Render	A computer image rendered directly by computer hardware with preprogrammed construction sets. The rendering of an average frame can be completed in approximately 5 to 10 seconds using this process. Some highly complex images may take up to 30 seconds to render. Visualizations take less time to develop because ongoing programming with software is not required.

functions and, therefore, no conscious thought ("processing power") was required to complete the tasks. In contrast, Pat would continue, a human activity such as playing chess required a great deal of concentration and conscious thought, thereby slowing down or replacing all brain functions except the preprogrammed tasks like breathing. Software rendering was, therefore, similar to playing chess in that it required the computer to perform higher level processing that required more time and effort than did hardware-coded functions. Software rendering required ongoing programming throughout the development of a visualization, but hardware rendering was preprogrammed.

Despite the advantages of hardware rendering, more and more firms were using software rendering to create computer visualizations. As one salesperson had reported to Pat, "We've been losing lots of cases to small mom and pop shops that are located in the same cities as the law firms. The law firms seem to think that it's important for the visualization firm to be geographically close, so they use local firms that do software rendering. They don't seem to 'get it' that our animation and modeling process is more precise and faster." This was directly impacting 3DV-LS's sales.

Financial Position

By 1999, 3DV-LS had created visualizations and reconstructions for thousands of cases involving patent infringement, product liability, medical malpractice, insurance defense, and aviation and automobile accident reconstruction. In 1998 alone, it produced more than 10,000 minutes of litigation animation. 3DV-LS was the giant in the litigation visualization services market. Despite this success, however, the litigation services unit had slowly lost its place of importance within the company as 3DV developed other areas of specialization. The unit's financial position was also worrisome. Although sales were decreasing, operating expenses remained the same, including the annual $10,000 marketing budget. At the current level of operations, Pat calculated that 3DV-LS needed to generate at least $2.4 million in yearly sales for the unit to break even. If 3DV-LS entered a new market, there was the possibility of additional costs, such as the training and hiring of salespeople. The cost of

hiring just one salesperson was $50,000. Revenues in FY2000 (January 1–December 31) were expected to be $2.7 million.

Contracts for litigation visualizations varied greatly based on the depth and breadth of the case. For example, the animations created for biomedical cases tended to be longer than those created for ground/vehicle accident projects because the information was less common and harder to understand. On average, though, the typical project required approximately 6 to 12 minutes of animation at an average cost of $26,000 to $60,000. For smaller projects, such as still models or storyboards that did not require animation, the cost of the project averaged $5,000 to $15,000. Prices were set at rates that covered variable costs plus a 25 percent to 30 percent profit margin.

Organization Structure and Culture

3DV-LS had 33 employees, most of whom worked on-site. Nearly all of the employees on-site had engineering or technical backgrounds. Pat Patterson, who reported directly to a 3DV vice president, had a Ph.D. in construction engineering and a law degree. Five project managers reported directly to Pat. Two managers had Ph.D.s in mechanical engineering, one had a Ph.D. in biological medicine, one had a master's degree in engineering mechanics, and one had a degree in architecture. The qualifications of the project managers gave 3DV-LS an advantage in the litigation market because attorneys preferred dealing with doctorate-prepared managers.

Underneath the project managers were production crews. These employees were either engineers with bachelor's degrees or "technical animators" who had either a 2- or 4-year degree in graphic arts design. Rounding out the on-site group was an administrative assistant who did secretarial tasks and a marketing coordinator who performed a variety of marketing functions. However, most of the marketing efforts required by the unit were performed or controlled by 3DV, which also handled 3DV-LS's accounting and human resource management needs.

3DV-LS employed five field salespeople. These people were dispersed across the country in large metropolitan centers (two in Chicago and one each in New York, Texas, and California). None of the salespeople had backgrounds in the computer or technology industries, but they all had extensive experience in working with and selling to attorneys. The salespeople reported directly to Pat.

The litigation services unit was different from the rest of the company. Whereas 3DV's culture was formal, 3DV-LS's was markedly informal. There were frequent informal meetings among the production staff and project managers to exchange ideas on individual projects. The project managers also talked informally with Pat on a daily basis and kept him apprised of progress on the various projects. Project managers met weekly to allocate the production staff. Every 2 weeks, the entire business unit met informally over lunch. Nicknamed "Lit Lunch" (for "Litigation Lunch"), it was a time to catch up on personal news as well as to informally discuss projects.

In sharp contrast, however, to this free-flowing exchange of technical and creative ideas was the lack of communication between the production section of the business and the marketing coordinator. The marketing coordinator, Sandy Clarke, had been relocated to headquarters from a remote office during one of the reorganizations about 2 years earlier. The 3DV-LS director tightly controlled and supervised her activities and did not promote interaction with the other employees. About a year later, when Pat Patterson became the 3DV-LS director, his attempts to integrate marketing activities with production failed. Neither the project managers nor the sales staff knew what Sandy did and rarely talked to her about projects. Salespeople independently made decisions about what kind of marketing efforts to use in their region—only rarely would they ask Sandy for help or ideas. Even Sandy, who had extensive experience marketing in the legal industry, was confused about her job responsibilities. Any efforts she made to influence the unit's marketing decisions were ignored.

Marketing Communications

Salespeople generally used either e-mail or direct mail campaigns to generate sales leads. Qualified sales leads then received personal sales calls at which the salesperson showed product demos. The marketing coordinator also maintained a customer database and identified sales leads by staying current with various industry publications.

3DV-LS was dependent on 3DV for publicity, advertising, and marketing support. Publication of marketing materials, which had been designed by Sandy Clarke, had to be approved by and contracted by 3DV. News releases were submitted to 3DV's publicity department for release. Unfortunately, as 3DV-LS's favored status within the company declined, so did the marketing support it received.

A recent addition to 3DV-LS's communications package was development of a Web site, which potential clients could access to view all its products. In addition, the site included a feature that allowed viewers to contact a project manager via the Web site. Other than including information about the Web site in all client contacts, 3DV-LS did not develop any specific strategy detailing how to use the site to develop new business.

Assessing the Market Opportunity

Lance hurried to his desk to start compiling the information he would need to complete the analysis. He had worked at 3DV-LS as a project manager for 2 years, but had yet to complete a task such as this. His usual duties included discussing project-specific concepts and issues with the attorneys that hired 3DV-LS, monitoring the progress of the modeling and animations, and dealing with the production crew. Completing an analysis of the construction and transportation industries in a 2-week period would be difficult considering that some of his projects were reaching drop-dead dates.[2]

Lance decided that this was definitely a situation that required more help. He grabbed his list and went to see Sandy Clarke, the marketing coordinator. Lance knew Sandy, but had never worked with her on a project. Because the market and this type of technology were so new, finding accurate and relevant information would be difficult; he was hopeful that Sandy would be able to help. After Lance shared his list with her, Sandy took a deep breath.

"Whew," Sandy said, when Lance finished, "that's a lot of information to find and make sense of in 2 weeks."

"But is it possible?" Lance queried. "If it helps," he continued, "I've been doing some research on my own, so I already know a little about what's happening in the construction and transportation industries."

"Well, that's a start," Sandy replied. "Tell me what you know."

The Construction and Transportation Industries

The transportation and construction industries utilized hand-drawn renderings (pictures) of buildings and landscapes in the development of projects. These hand-drawn renderings provided general concept ideas in a washed-out, 2-dimensional picture, but they did not allow stakeholders and the public to grasp how the finished project would look in the surrounding environment. Several companies released computer applications that created computer-generated 2-dimensional pictures conveying aesthetics and design concepts. However, because many of these computer software programs relied on software rendering, they were not capable of creating complicated or highly detailed pictures in a short period of time. Using the software required high-end computer equipment and an experienced user who was familiar with computer-aided drafting (CAD).

Lance learned that certain aspects of construction and transportation projects differed depending on whether or not they were publicly or privately funded. Both types of funded projects used a bidding process, starting with RFPs (requests for proposals), to select project consultants. In turn, consultants were responsible for hiring subcontractors, such as 3DV-LS. Any firm could submit bids in response to an RFP, but for public agencies, contracts would only be awarded to firms that had been preapproved by the governing agency. Moreover, the preapproval process extended to subcontractors. In contrast, privately funded large-scale construction projects did not require a preapproval process.

Publicly funded and privately funded projects also differed in the project design phase. Publicly funded designs had to go through a public participation process; although privately funded designs used a marketing process. The public participation process, required by all government agencies for any type of construction project, consisted of several meetings at which the public asked questions and provided input to the governing agency. Frequently, the public had very strong opinions concerning these projects, especially those dealing with land acquisition or condemnation. The government agency's role was often to educate the public about the necessity and value of the project.

In contrast, private large-scale development projects were promoted to governing agencies, the public, and investors. This process was mainly concerned with convincing officials and the public that the project was beneficial to the community and would not have any negative impact. For investors, the promotion process centered on the project design issues and associated costs. For either process, accurate visualization of the finished project enhanced the participants' ability to understand the proposed project and, consequently, could be very important to securing project approval.

In addition to needing computer visualizations of construction and transportation projects, the construction and transportation industries also needed to study human factors in the design of construction and transportation projects. For example, human reaction time to construction zone signing was a concern, as were potential weather effects. The merging of 3-D visualization with geographical information systems (GIS) was a hot topic in many trade publications. GIS was a mapping technology that was the norm in the transportation industry. Light detection and ranging (LIDAR) technology, a revolutionary laser scanning system, could also revolutionize the industry. In fact, Lance had been looking into purchasing LIDAR technology for 3DV-LS, but with a price tag of $250,000 he thought it was cost prohibitive. However, purchase of the technology might be justified if 3DV-LS expanded into the transportation industry.

After Lance briefed Sandy on what he knew, they decided to spend the next several days contacting and questioning firms that had won construction and transportation consulting contracts. As Sandy put it, "We need to know more about the size of the market, whether or not it's growing, and more specific information on the use of computer visualization."

Use of Computer Visualization in Construction and Transportation Projects

Firms reported that computer-generated pictures were beginning to replace the hand-rendered sketches that had been the industry standard. However, after talking with several consultants. Lance and Sandy found that only large consultants were heavy users—there was a reluctance to use animations for anything but large-scale projects (i.e., those involving hundreds of millions of dollars) because acquiring the hardware, software, and personnel capable of creating quality models or pictures was extremely expensive. Even those consultants who subcontracted for visualization services were concerned about the cost of computer-generated pictures. "Unless computer visualizations are required, I avoid using them because they add unnecessary expense to an already expensive project," one consultant observed.

Nonetheless, some of the consultants Lance and Sandy talked to mentioned that the benefit of computer visualizations, though not immediately obvious, was still significant. As one consultant put it, "I can show a group of investors a hand-drawn sketch of how a building will look like when it's done, or I can show them a computer-generated picture of the finished building that's about as close to a real picture of the finished building as possible without actually erecting the building. They're always much more impressed with the computer-generated pictures. It saves a lot of time in securing final project approval. I figure the time I save by using computer-generated pictures more than outweighs the expense of creating the pictures." Another consultant stated that computer visualizations made it easier to respond to "what if" scenarios frequently requested by customers.

Growth in Construction and Transportation Industries

As Sandy delved deeper into the market trends, she found a report released by the American Institute of Architects (AIA). In this report, she found several pieces of interesting information. The AIA projected:

- A 1 percent increase in building activity paralleling population growth, as compared to levels in the first half of the 1990s
- A 13.91 percent increase in the average annual volume of contract awards (Exhibit 2)
- An emphasis on growth in construction spending in the commercial and industrial categories, especially for office buildings
- A growing share of construction spending for building renovations over the next 15 years. By 2010, building renovations would exceed new building construction

The AIA report also reported preliminary results indicating that approximately $24 billion was billed for architectural services in 1999. Roughly one-third of that amount related to the commercial/industrial sector, whereas institutional billings accounted for almost one-half of the billed services.

From a contact in the Department of Transportation, Lance learned that transportation projects would also continue to become available due to the

EXHIBIT 2

Average Volume of Contract Awards (in billions of 2000 dollars)

	1991 to 1995	1996 to 2010	% Change
Educational Facilities	$24.3	$24.1	−1%
Health Care Facilities	13.3	13.3	0
Public Buildings	7.1	7.9	10%
Retail Facilities	23.2	22.7	−2%
Office Buildings	16.4	28.1	42%
Industrial Facilities	19.1	21.7	12%
Total	$103.5	$117.9	

Source: American Institute of Architects 2000 firm survey. Originally given in 1987 dollars; converted to 2000 dollars.

federal government's commitment to rehabilitating the nation's road infrastructure. Billions of dollars were allocated annually for road enhancement projects and large-scale interstate construction.

Perceptions of Computer Visualization

Next, Sandy put together a list of questions and spent several hours on the phone talking to potential clients. Sandy found that consultants networked through a variety of conferences, most held in conjunction with trade organizations. Consultants usually worked on projects in teams, with the same three or four consultants completing several different types of projects for the same government agency or private developer. Often, the consultants who designed projects for government-initiated projects were the same consultants who designed large-scale commercial projects. The designated primary consultant changed depending on the project but had the same subcontractors. Most consultants decided who to work with based on experience, quality, past working relationship, availability, and price.

The consultants Sandy talked to also shared with her some of their perceptions of 3DV-LS. For example, one consultant told her that 3DV-LS had a reputation of charging high fees for standard services. Another reported a concern that 3DV-LS's prices were too high, because it did not provide any expertise concerning design issues. Sandy was surprised by this, because her research showed 3DV-LS's prices, even with a 25 percent to 30 percent profit margin, to be competitive in the litigation market. She was afraid that the perception of high prices derived from the early years in computer visualization when any type of computer generated models or animation had been extremely expensive.

Sandy also queried the consultants on whether or not the visualizations they contracted for were software or hardware rendered. Most were uncertain. "I didn't know that there was more than one way to get pictures," was a typical response.

Pricing

The consultants were reluctant to share what they were paying for visualization services in the construction and transportation industries. However, after some digging, Lance was able to identify the going rates for animation and photo simulations in the transportation industry. The rates did not specify what kind of process was used (i.e., hardware or software rendering) to create the visualizations. But, because Lance knew of no other companies that did hardware rendering besides 3DV-LS, he assumed the prices reflected software rendered visualizations.

- Animation—$3,000 to $6,000 per minute
- Digitally altered photographs—$5,000 to $7,000 per image
- Photo images or 3-D models—$800 to $1,500 per image

In the transportation industry, most of the projects were large-scale transportation projects funded by government agencies. The government agency often specified the amount of money to be spent on visualizations. For example, the allowable costs for visualization on a recently approved $500 million transportation project ranged from $70,000 to $150,000.

Neither Sandy nor Lance was able to find a range of prices in the construction industry, but they assumed that the rates were most likely comparable to those in the transportation industry. Moreover, because many construction projects were also funded by the government, Lance and Sandy surmised that the government would specify the computer visualization budgets for those projects, also.

Competition

After talking to several consultants, Sandy looked into how competitive the market was. She identified two types of competitors and profiled each of these.

The first competitor was typically a large firm that provided a full complement of services desired by the construction and transportation industries. These firms had the ability to design a project, conduct marketing campaigns and public participation workshops, and manage the implementation or construction of the project. Competitors in this group, such as Howard, Needles, Tammen, and Bergendoff (HNTB), the eighth largest architecture firm nationwide and fourth largest in transportation design, had national brand recognition and many years of extensive and varied experience. Not surprisingly, these firms rarely hired subcontractors, relying, instead, on in-house technology departments for their visualization needs. For example, HNTB's Technology Group employed content planners, media designers, 3-D animators, and networking and programming professionals to provide high-tech communication and information solutions to the architecture, transportation, environmental engineering, and construction services industries. However, HNTB relied on software rendering for its visualization projects.

Another firm that fit this competitor profile was Parsons Brinckerhoff, Inc., a global engineering giant. This firm provided planning, engineering, construction management, and operations and maintenance services to a wide variety of clients around the world. Similar to HNTB, Parsons Brinckerhoff had started Parsons and Brinckerhoff 4D Imaging (PB4D) in 1988 as an advanced computer visual simulation business unit. PB4D was the industry leader for the visualization of transportation projects, and it was also a large-scale multimedia and Internet business unit. Like HNTB, PB4D also relied on software rendering.

The second type of competitor was characterized as firms specializing in design visualization services. Typically, these firms were smaller than 3DV and had regional brand recognition. Although these firms' staffs were small, they also had specific experience with architects, landscape architects, planners, and civil engineers. Consequently, these competitors knew how to communicate with these professionals using industry jargon. Interestingly, most of these firms also relied on software rendering and did not provide extensive product or service lines. One firm typical of this type of competitor was Newlands & Co., a consulting firm located in Portland, Oregon, that specialized in design visualization, 3-D animation, and Web development services. Newlands & Co. produced high-quality visual simulations, animations, Web and multimedia presentations for transportation, urban design, and architecture. Its mission was to employ the best in art and technology to facilitate communication between designers and their clients. Its services included photography, 3-D modeling, photo simulation, animation, multimedia presentation creation, Web development, and training.

THE FUTURE

Lance met with Pat 2 weeks later to present the information he and Sandy had uncovered about the construction and transportation industries. When Lance finished the brief overview, he handed over a complete written report of the findings to Pat. "So," Pat said, "based on what you've learned, what do you think we should do?"

Lance, expecting this question, carefully formulated his response. "I think there's an excellent opportunity for 3DV-LS in this new market. The construction and transportation industries are growing, and there's increasing use of computer visualization on projects. Plus, I think the advantage of hardware rendering—that is, being able to quickly create and change visualizations—will be just as important to the construction and transportation industries as it has proven to be in the litigation industry. But we'll have to convince consultants of this fact and at the same time compete against companies that are already firmly established in this market. It won't be easy."

Pat thanked Lance for all his hard work. Left alone with his thoughts, Pat pondered his options. One option was to hire and train one to two new salespeople to focus on developing business in the construction and transportation industries. This would require some investment, but would allow the current sales force to stay focused on the litigation industry. Another option was to allocate the time and efforts of one or two current salespeople to developing small-scale bids for regional projects in the construction and transportation industries. This option was less risky financially, but might further affect sales in the litigation industry.

Pat couldn't help but speculate. What if the sales decline in the last year was just temporary? What if the Web site proved to be an effective tool in cultivating sales? Several times over the last few months, Pat had wondered whether the declining sales were a direct effect of poorly communicating the advantages of hardware rendering relative to software rendering. At especially low moments, he worried that, to the average client, the advantages of hardware rendering were not tangible enough to clearly differentiate it from software rendering.

With respect to the new market opportunity, Pat had other nagging questions. Did 3DV-LS have the necessary skills and resources to enter the construction and transportation market while at the same time maintaining its litigation business? In particular, could the current five salespeople adapt their skills, honed in the litigation market, to the construction and transportation market? Could 3DV-LS successfully differentiate its hardware rendering visualization method from the more commonly used software rendering in the new market? Would entry into the new market pull necessary attention from the litigation industry? Although Pat appreciated Lance's opinion, he knew that whether or not 3DV-LS should enter the construction and transportation market depended on the answers to these questions.

Endnotes

1. The name of the company and the principal players in this case were disguised to protect the competitive interests of 3DV-LS.
2. A drop-dead date was the date that visualizations and materials were due to attorneys. Material that did not arrive by the drop-dead date could not legally be admitted into evidence.

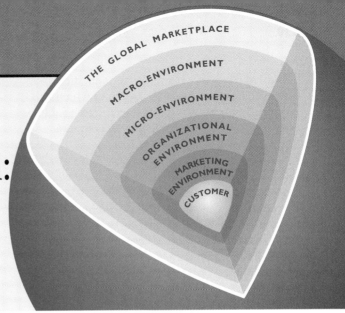

Rayovac Corporation: "Recreating a Proud America Brand"

This case was prepared by Jeff W. Totten, Bemidji State University, and Walter E. Greene, University of Texas Pan American.

One day in June 1998, in Madison, Wisconsin, David A. Jones, chairman and chief executive officer of Rayovac Corporation, shifted in his chair to be more comfortable as the interview began. Ms. Sharon Phillips, senior editor for the Wall Street Corporate Reporter, *did the same and then asked a question about Jones' background.*

"My expertise lies in developing top-notch management teams and business strategies that can win in competitive environments," said Jones. "My skills are in developing strong consumer brands in retail markets." Prior to Rayovac, Mr. Jones worked for GE, Electrolux, Regina, and Thermoscan (from major and small appliances to medical products to batteries). Phillips then asked about Rayovac®.

"Rayovac® was a very old, established consumer brand," Jones responded. "It had not been aggressively marketed or advertised for many years and,

This case is written solely for the basis of stimulating student discussion. All data are based on secondary research and telephone interviews. The decisions, organizations, individuals, and amount of variation in the information are real. The authors acknowledge the valuable comments of the anonymous reviewers and the editor of the *Case Research Journal,* Linda Swayne. The quality of this case was greatly improved as a result of their efforts.

Reprinted by permission from the *Case Research Journal,* volume 21, issue 2. Copyright © 2001 by Jeff W. Totten, and Walter E. Greene and the North American Case Research Association. All rights reserved.

as a result, had fallen behind Duracell® and Energizer®. I was brought in by the Thomas H. Lee Group of Boston in September 1996 to take this fine company and change the marketing, advertising, and distribution strategies to bring it into the twenty-first century. In essence, we are recreating a proud American brand."[1]

Over a year later, John Daggett, director of marketing services and company spokesperson, noted,

Certainly Rayovac has challenges, yet it has turned things around, making impressive inroads in a short time. Our strategy was to look at making distribution gains, bring out new products, and be a global brand. With the [1999] acquisition of ROV Ltd., we reunified the Rayovac® brand worldwide except for Brazil.

In the past few years (1996 to 1999) since Jones had become CEO, the firm had:

- Embarked on an advertising initiative with Michael Jordan
- Increased market share in alkalines, the leading category
- Expanded distribution in the United States as well as worldwide
- Developed new products and revitalized existing brands

Rayovac faced two large rivals (Gillette/ Duracell; Energizer Holdings), each of which had greater resources. Was Rayovac going to be able to continue to compete in the new millennium?

HISTORY

The company was founded as the French Battery Company in Madison, Wisconsin, in 1906. The Rayovac® brand was introduced in 1921. In the mid-1930s, the company was renamed the Rayovac Company. In 1933, the company patented the first portable radio with high-fidelity reception, and in 1937 it patented the first wearable vacuum tube hearing aid. The world's first leak-proof, "sealed in steel," dry cell battery was introduced in 1939, and 1949 saw the company introduce the crown cell alkaline battery for hearing aids and launch the famous stainless steel Sportsman® flashlight. In 1956, Rayovac's stock was listed on the New York Stock Exchange. Rayovac's batteries captured the most or second-most market share in each line. The company was sold to the Electric Storage Battery Company of Philadelphia in 1957.

Rayovac was awarded the patent for silver oxide button cells in 1971. The first heavy-duty all-zinc chloride battery with double the life of general purpose batteries was introduced in 1972. Inco Limited of Toronto acquired Rayovac as part of a hostile takeover in 1974 and moved Rayovac's headquarters back to Madison, Wisconsin, in 1979. Thomas and Judith Pyle and two partners purchased Rayovac in 1982. The Pyles were seeking a new challenge, and Rayovac provided them that challenge. Although the company was ranked third in battery sales, it "was losing $25 million a year and had seen its market share slip from 30 percent in the 1950s to between 4 percent and 5 percent."[2] In 1984, Rayovac introduced the Workhorse® premium flashlight with its lifetime product warranty. The Pyles bought out their partners in 1986. The Pyles solved Rayovac's problems by concentrating on niche markets to dominate and by streamlining operations; for this effort, they were named Wisconsin Entrepreneurs of the Year in 1989.

A new computer clock battery was introduced to power the real-time clocks of personal computers in 1988. Two years later, in 1990, the Heavy Duty®, and Industrial® flashlight product lines were introduced. A new Workhorse® Fluorescent Lantern was introduced in 1992 to provide the consumer with more light and features. Rayovac introduced Renewal® a reusable, long-life alkaline battery in 1993. In 1995, the 2AA flashlight, constructed of durable polypropylene, joined the Workhorse® family. Also, 1995 saw basketball superstar Michael Jordan become the spokesperson for Renewal® Reusable Alkaline batteries and Power Station® chargers. In 1996, a new "hands free" flashlight called the Swivel-Lite® was introduced as well as the Rubber Camo Sportsman® flashlight.

The Thomas H. Lee Group of Boston led a group in buying 80 percent of Rayovac's stock in September 1996. David A. Jones of Thermoscan, Inc., was brought in by Lee to run the company. In 1997, Rayovac entered the market for photo and keyless-entry batteries and in 1998 introduced a line of products to serve the medical instrument and health services markets.

By 1999, Rayovac was:

- The #3 battery manufacturer and distributor in the United States, after Duracell and Energizer
- #1 in hearing aid and rechargeable household batteries
- The leading worldwide manufacturer of hearing aid batteries
- The leading domestic manufacturer of rechargeable household batteries and other specialty batteries, including lantern batteries and lithium batteries for personal computers
- A leading marketer of battery-powered lighting products

Rayovac employed approximately 3,400 individuals worldwide, and its headquarters was located in Madison, Wisconsin. Key officers are listed in Exhibit 1.

INTERNAL ENVIRONMENT

Research and Development

Rayovac's research and development strategy was to purchase or license state-of-the-art manufacturing technology from third parties and to develop such technology through its own research and development efforts. The alkaline battery technology agreement with the Matsushita Battery Industrial

EXHIBIT 1

Key Executive Officers (as of June 2000)

Name	Position
David A. Jones	Chairman of the Board and Chief Executive Officer
Kent J. Hussey	President and Chief Operating Officer
Randall J. Steward	Executive Vice President of Administration and Chief Financial Officer
Merrell M. Tomlin	Executive Vice President of Sales and President Rayovac Canada Inc.
Stephen P. Shanesey	Executive Vice President of Global Brand Management
Kenneth V. Biller	Executive Vice President of Operations
Luis A. Cancio	Senior Vice President/General Manager Latin America
Paula A. Bauer	Vice President—Supply Chain Management
Paul Cheeseman	Vice President—Technology
John P. Ridlehoover	Vice President—Chief Information Officer
Mark R. Joslyn	Vice President—Human Resources

Source: Rayovac Corporation, Hoover's Online, www.hoovers.com/, August 21, 2000.

Company of Japan was extended through the end of March 2003. This agreement allowed Rayovac to license highly advanced battery designs, technology, and equipment owned by Matsushita. In March 1998, Rayovac agreed to purchase a new high-speed alkaline battery production line from Matsushita for its Fennimore, Wisconsin, plant. The new line increased production capacity for AA-size batteries by approximately 50 percent. Rayovac agreed to source some batteries, battery parts, and materials from Matsushita. The licensing partnership with Matsushita had existed since the early 1990s, beginning with groundbreaking alkaline technology that allowed Rayovac to produce environmentally safe (mercury-free) alkaline batteries. Matsushita was the world's largest producer of portable batteries (under the Panasonic trade name) and a recognized leader in alkaline product technology.

Rayovac strongly believed in continual developmental activities as a means of producing competitive products. For example, the R&D group maintained close working relationships with the manufacturers of hearing aid devices. This alliance led to the successful pioneering development of the two smallest hearing aid batteries (5A and 10A size). Rayovac initially developed an on-package battery tester in response to competitors' similar testers. However, its consumer testing "indicated that such testers are difficult to use, prone to failure, and do not represent a significant marketing advantage." Thus the company's management decided not to implement the testers.

All battery manufacturers were watching the efforts of the Israel Institute of Technology's researchers to boost battery life. A new "super-iron" component had been found that potentially could increase battery life by 50 percent. Although still under development, the new batteries had been found in tests to produce 50 percent more energy and to generate extra conductivity, which was useful in "high-drain" electronic devices.[3]

Manufacturing and Raw Materials

In late March 1998, Rayovac announced manufacturing changes that included the consolidation of packaging operations at one Wisconsin plant, the closing of two plants in Wisconsin and the United Kingdom, the sale of a North Carolina plant, and the shifting or outsourcing of operations from the closed and sold plants, which increased plant capacity utilization. Ass part of the restructuring, Rayovac stopped making heavy-duty batteries, concentrating instead on popular types of batteries.[4] Tim Reiland, a Milwaukee stockbroker, lauded the changes. "This is really significant. The changes make Rayovac a more focused company. It gets to the issue of core competencies and distribution [and leads to increased efficiency and more flexibility]."[5] With the push into Latin America, plants and distribution centers were added in the Dominican Republic, Guatemala, Honduras, Mexico, Venezuela, and other Latin American countries.[6]

The most significant raw materials used by the company to manufacture batteries were zinc powder, electrolytic manganese dioxide powder, and steel. There were a number of worldwide sources for all necessary raw materials, and management believed that Rayovac would have continued access to adequate quantities of such materials at competitive prices. The company regularly engaged in commodity swaps, calls, and puts to effectively manage raw material costs and inventory relative to anticipated production requirements.

Product Lines

Rayovac had two broad product lines: (1) general and specialty batteries, and (2) lighting products and lantern batteries. General batteries included alkaline and rechargeable alkaline batteries. Specialty batteries included button cells and lithium coin cells. Lighting products included flashlights and lanterns. General batteries were used in such products as radios, remote controls, pagers, portable compact disc players, video games, and toys. Button cell specialty batteries were used in smaller products like hearing aids and watches. Lithium coin cells were used in cameras, calculators, and communication equipment (e.g., cordless telephones). Exhibit 2 provides percentage of net sales per product category, and Exhibit 3 lists Rayovac's major products and their typical uses.

Positioning and Branding Strategy

Rayovac positioned itself as the leading value brand in the U.S. general alkaline battery market by offering "top-tier quality at a value price," said John Daggett, company spokesman.[7]

Alkaline Batteries.   The Rayovac® brand had wide recognition in all markets where it competed, but had lower awareness than the more highly advertised Duracell® and Energizer® brands. Rayovac was committed to creating top-of-mind awareness of its brand name.[8] Several phone and mall interviews found that more than 80 percent of shoppers nationwide are familiar with the Rayovac name; focus groups identified the company's products through the lightning bolt symbol found on the product and

EXHIBIT 2

Percentage of Net Sales by Product

Product Type	Fiscal Year 6/30/96	Transition Period 9/30/96	Fiscal Year 9/30/97	Fiscal Year 9/30/98	Fiscal Year 9/30/99
Battery Products					
Alkaline	43.6%	41.4%	45.0%	49.1%	50.1%
Heavy Duty	12.2%	12.7%	10.4%	07.8%	09.9%
Rechargeable	07.1%	05.1%	05.5%	05.4%	04.5%
Hearing Aid	14.6%	14.3%	14.8%	14.8%	13.3%
Other Specialty	08.6%	10.1%	09.8%	09.1%	08.6%
Total	86.1%	83.6%	85.5%	86.2%	86.4%
Lighting Prod. & Lantern Batteries	13.9%	16.4%	14.5%	13.8%	13.6%
Total	100%	100%	100%	100%	100%

Sources: Rayovac Corporation, 1999 *Annual Report,* p. 45; Rayovac's 10-K, September 30, 1998, p. 6.

EXHIBIT 3

Battery Products and Typical Uses

Product	Technology	Types	Brand*	Sizes	Typical Uses
General Batteries	Alkaline	Disposable Rechargeable	MAXIMUM Renewal Power Station	D, C, AA, AAA, 9-volt	All standard house-hold applications and wide variety of industrial uses
	Zinc	Heavy Duty	Rayovac	as above	
Hearing Aid Batteries	Zinc Air	n/a	Loud'n Clear ProLine Best Labs Ultracell Xcell and AIRPOWER	5 sizes	Hearing aids
Other Specialty Batteries	Lithium	n/a	Lifex	5 primary sizes	Personal computer clocks and memory back-up
	Silver	n/a	Rayovac	10 primary sizes	Watches
	Lithium Ion, Nickel Metal Hydride, etc.	Rechargeable	Rayovac	35 sizes	Cellular phones, camcorders and cordless phones
Lantern Batteries	Zinc	Lantern	Rayovac	Standard lantern	Beam lanterns, camping lanterns

*Brand name for all is Rayovac®; others listed are sub-brands.
Source: Rayovac Corporation's 10-K, September 30, 1998, p. 7.

packaging.[9] Rayovac had integrated an advertising campaign using significantly higher levels of television and print media. The campaign was designed to increase awareness of the Rayovac® brand and to heighten customers' perceptions of the quality, performance, and value of Rayovac products.[10] The company intended to continue building its brand name to increase sales of all its products.

The alkaline battery market was "very high impulse, very low brand loyalty" and "very distribution driven." Consumers would buy "if they recognized brand name." Consumers liked the "portable lifestyle" such products provided. Rayovac used National Family Opinion diary panels and learned from these diaries that the "biggest reason for battery purchase was pantry inventory—having enough around."[11] Focus group research results indicated that Rayovac® batteries scored high on these product attributes: good value, high quality, long lasting, powerful, reliable.

Rechargeable Batteries. The Renewal® rechargeable battery was the only rechargeable alkaline battery in the U.S. market, commanding a 66 percent market share of the rechargeable household battery market through mass merchandisers, food and drug stores for the 52 weeks ended July 5, 1997.[12] Since the recapitalization, management had lowered the price of Renewal® rechargers by 33 percent to encourage consumers to purchase the system and shifted Renewal's® marketing message from its environmental benefits to its money-saving benefits. Renewal® batteries presented a value proposition to consumers because Renewal® batteries can be recharged over 25 times, providing 10 times the energy of disposable alkaline batteries at only twice the retail price.[13] In addition, alkaline rechargeables were superior to nickel cadmium rechargeables (the competing technology) because they provided more energy between charges, were sold fully charged, retained their charge longer, and were environmentally safer. In late 1997, Rayovac launched the first rechargeable alkaline battery in the United Kingdom. They hoped to double the rechargeable sector of the U.K. battery market from 5 percent to 10 percent. Prize competitions on national and local radio stations, totaling £500,000, were used to launch the new product.[14]

Hearing Aid Batteries. Rayovac acquired BRISCO G.M.B.H. (Germany) and BRISCO B.V. (Holland) on December 1, 1997. The acquired company "packages and distributes hearing aid batteries in unique, customized, environmentally-friendly packaging to hearing health care professionals" in several European countries. Rayovac "plans to use this acquisition to better serve its customers throughout Europe and surrounding regions."[15]

Also in March 1998, Rayovac acquired the battery distribution portion of Best Labs, a Florida manufacturer of hearing instruments and distributor of batteries. This move was made to allow Rayovac to further improve its customer service. "More than 5 million people wear hearing aids in the United States [and that] number is expected to increase to 20 million as baby boomers grow older."[16] Rayovac also established relationships with key Pacific Rim hearing aid battery distributors in a move to take advantage of potential market growth in that part of the world.

Other Specialty Batteries and Lighting Products. In March 1998, Rayovac acquired the retail business of Direct Power Plus of New York, allowing the company to expand into the nonalkaline, rechargeable battery market. "Rayovac will sell rechargeable batteries, battery chargers, and accessories for cellular phones and camcorders to retailers under both Rayovac® and DPP brand names." With this acquisition and the launch of a new line of rechargeable cordless telephone batteries under the Rayovac® brand name, Jones stated, "Rayovac becomes a major player in the rechargeable battery marketplace. These new additions will add more than 100 new items to our product offerings. Customers and consumers can now turn to the Rayovac® brand as their one-stop source for both primary and [alkaline and nonalkaline] rechargeable batteries."[17]

Product graphics and packaging of other specialty batteries were redesigned in order to achieve a uniform brand appearance and build brand awareness and loyalty. Rayovac also saw potential growth in the keyless-entry battery market. They estimated that over 25 million vehicles using keyless-entry systems were on our highways, and that approximately 55 million would be using these systems by the year 2000. Rayovac also estimated that consumer demand for replacement keyless-entry batteries was at least $100 million a year.[18]

No Straying from Our Strategy. Mr. Daggett summed up Rayovac's positioning and branding strategy at the end of 1999:

> We have a real simple message that we haven't strayed from in our strategy—"anyone, anywhere for Rayovac products." Any retailer can use a value brand. We can back up value with performance and get third-party endorsements.

Sales and Distribution Strategy

The sales force was reorganized by distribution channel after Jones took over. Before the change in ownership, the sales force had been organized by product line. Separate sales forces were maintained in the United States to service (1) retail sales and distribution channels, and (2) hearing aid professionals, industrial and original equipment manufacturer (OEM) sales, and distribution channels. Rayovac also used a network of brokers to service selected distribution channels. However, Rayovac reduced the number of independent brokers and sales agents from over 100 to approximately 50 for cost savings. With respect to sales of hearing aid batteries, although most of the sales had historically been through hearing aid professionals, the company was actively engaged in efforts to increase sales through retail channels. In addition, Rayovac maintained its own sales force of approximately 30 employees in Europe, which promoted the sale of all its products.

Retail

The primary retail distribution channels included mass merchandisers (both national and regional); warehouse clubs; food, drug, and convenience stores; electronics specialty retailers; hardware and automotive centers; department stores; automotive aftermarket dealers; military sales; and catalog showrooms. Rayovac worked closely with individual retailers to develop unique product promotions and provided them with the opportunity for attractive profit margins to encourage brand support. Rayovac targeted its Renewal® product line for more suitable distribution channels like electronics specialty stores, such as Radio Shack. Rayovac also attempted to persuade retail stores to promote batteries during the spring and summer months, which were considered to be an untapped opportunity for sales.[19]

Rayovac's sales efforts in the retail channel focused primarily on sales and distribution to national mass merchandisers, in particular the Wal-Mart, Kmart and Target chains, which collectively accounted for over half of industry sales growth in the domestic alkaline battery market over the past 5 years. These three retailers, along with Sears, had been targeted because Rayovac fit their profile (value pricing). Rayovac updated product packaging in an effort to assist retailers in taking advantage of limited shelf space. All stock-keeping units now had the same look. The company also offered different packaging and display concepts that helped the retailer maximize space. In line with this philosophy of space-saving concepts, the company just introduced the Clear Value Pack®, that offered more of the product in less space. Rayovac strived to "allow the retailer to capture value-conscious consumers who would have gone to another retailer" for batteries.[20]

Rayovac's sales strategy was to penetrate further particular retail distribution channels, including home centers, hardware stores, warehouse clubs, and food and drug stores. According to Rayovac's *1998 Annual Report,* 18,000 retail outlets were added during fiscal year 1998. Rayovac® batteries were now available in such stores as Lowe's, A&P, Shaw's, Kerr, Western Auto, Pep Boys, and CompUSA. "Rayovac was in 36,000 retail outlets prior to the initial public offering, and, 2 years later, we are in 77,000 outlets."[21] This represented an increase of about 14,000 outlets since the *1998 Annual Report* was released. Another 100,000 outlets were to be added over the next few years.[22] The company's strategy for these retail channels was to develop creative and focused marketing campaigns that emphasized the performance parity and consumer cost advantage of the Rayovac® brand and tailored specific promotional programs unique to these distribution channels.

Industrial/OEM.   In the industrial battery market, Rayovac had three sales and distribution channels: contract sales to governments and related agencies; maintenance repair organizations; and office product supply companies. The primary products sold to this market included alkaline, heavy duty, and lantern batteries and flashlights. Maintenance repair organizations, the largest of which was W. W. Grainger (to whom Rayovac was a major supplier of battery and lighting products), generally sold to contractors and manufacturers. The office product supply channel included sales to both professional and retail companies in the office product supply business.

Rayovac actively pursued OEM arrangements and alliances with major electronic product manufacturers for its rechargeable batteries. The OEM channel was also used to sell and distribute hearing aid batteries. Jones wanted to continue developing relationships with communication equipment manufacturers in order to expand the company's share of the nonhearing aid button cell market. Jones also wanted to penetrate the portable personal computer market for its lithium coin cell batteries. Telecommunications and medical equipment manufacturers who would use the coin cells were also in the company's target sight.

Advertising and Sales Promotion Strategy

Advertising Spending.   Rayovac increased advertising spending after the change of ownership. Rayovac initially spent $26 million in advertising and promotional efforts on Renewal® in fiscal year 1994. A new $20.3 million promotional campaign featuring Michael Jordan, basketball star with the Chicago Bulls, was undertaken in fiscal year 1996. The product line advertising emphasis was shifted from Renewal® to MAXIMUM® when it was introduced in 1997. According to Rayovac's *1999 Annual Report,* advertising expenses increased from $24.326 million in fiscal year 1997 to $33.292 million in fiscal year 1999.

Alkaline Batteries.   In 1997, the company launched a reformulated alkaline battery, Rayovac MAXIMUM®, supported by new graphics, new packaging, a new advertising campaign, and aggressive introductory retail promotions. This focused marketing approach was specifically designed to raise consumer awareness and increase retail sales.[23] Michael Jordan, normally used to promote

Renewal® rechargeables, was hired to appear in the ads.[24] Daggett noted that "alkaline batteries will play a more dominant role in the future. We think we can offer retailers a complete package of products that will create a unique look for them and help them build their batteries business. We also want to leverage [Jordan's] visibility to help build sales."[25] The price tag for the print ads and Jordan commercial was $25 million.[26]

Rayovac began 1998 with an aggressive promotional effort for MAXIMUM®. Immediate response coupons on the battery packages were tied to candy purchases, while another promotion was tied to music and video products. Several batteries were packaged with a flashlight to make up special Storm Emergency Packs®, and promotions included commercials on the Weather Channel's *Storm Watch Updates.*[27] Another major advertising and promotional campaign was launched in October 1998, with a $30 million price tag. Michael Jordan was featured in the four new television commercials, the new print advertisement, and the point-of-purchase support material. The commercials appeared on numerous network and cable channels, including ABC, WTBS, A&E, TNT, and Lifetime. The print campaign ran in such magazines as *People, Reader's Digest,* and *TV Guide.*[28] Other merchandising programs in 1998 included a money-back trial offer, a national free-standing coupon insert,[29] free flashlights and Halloween stickers, instant rebates of $3 to $5 on toys and $2 off film, and tie-in specials with the feature film, *Rudolph the Red-Nosed Reindeer: The Movie.*[30]

In February 1999, Rayovac announced that it would be the primary sponsor of Jarrett-Favre Motorsports in the 1999 NASCAR Busch Series. Executive vice president Merrell Tomlin said that Rayovac had been looking for the right team with which to enter the racing series. Given the fact that Brett Favre, one of the equity partners in the racing team, was the quarterback of the Green Bay Packers, Rayovac thought that it should not pass up this opportunity to connect the two well-known Wisconsin organizations. The company also ran an in-store promotion where consumers, for the purchase of a 3-pack or two multipacks of batteries, could send away for a free replica of the racing car.[31]

Rayovac's promotional plans for the 1999 holiday season included its instant toy-savings offer, where consumers received $3 off any toy purchase with the purchase of MAXIMUM® batteries, and $1,000 holiday shopping sprees sweepstakes based on game pieces inside MAXIMUM® packages. Special display designs for the instant toy-savings promotion were also available for retailers.[32]

Alkaline Rechargeable Batteries. Michael Jordan was hired as spokesman for Renewal® in 1995. Jordan talked about coming back to basketball (from his brief baseball career) with a "renewed" spirit. Rayovac had Renewal®, so the company approached Jordan. Focus group research showed that Michael Jordan connoted power and performance, as did Renewal® batteries. Limited advertising campaigns in 1996 and 1997 featured Jordan. For example, while used to promote the product, Jordan did not appear in a 30-second television spot for a Father's Day promotion in 1997.[33] As mentioned earlier, Jordan later was hired to promote the new Rayovac MAXIMUM®.

Hearing Aid Batteries. The focus here was on the continued use of a highly successful national print campaign that featured Arnold Palmer. As a user of Rayovac® batteries in his hearing aids, Mr. Palmer effectively promoted the use of hearing aids and, specifically, the benefits of Rayovac's batteries. In addition to this campaign, another national print campaign was developed for use in certain publications like *Modern Maturity* in order to reach the largest potential market for hearing aid batteries. Rayovac also pioneered the use of multipacks for hearing aid batteries and sought to extend distribution of multipacks in professional and retail channels.

Customer Service

On September 10, 1998, Rayovac and 1-800-Batteries announced "an exclusive agreement to create a state-of-the-art telephone hotline ordering system to allow consumers who cannot find the batteries and accessories they need in their regular retail store to order for next-day delivery using their credit card." The agreement also involved the linkage of the two companies' Web sites to allow convenient Internet ordering. "This new system is offered exclusively to retailers that stock Rayovac's new line of rechargeable batteries for cellular and cordless telephones and camcorders." 1-800-Batteries carried an inventory of over 7,000 batteries, rechargers, and mobile gear. This new system was staffed 24 hours a day, 7 days a week. Rayovac's Jones stated,

"The hotline and Internet sales are a win-win for all. Consumers get the right batteries they want when they want them, and retailers can minimize their inventories without compromising customer service."[34] Participating retailers received free installation, point-of-sale support, quarterly reports on frequently requested items, and 15 percent commission on each sale.[35]

FINANCIAL SITUATION

Rayovac returned to stock market trading with an initial public offering in November 1997. The company raised $93.8 million from the sale of 6.7 million shares (approximately 26 percent of itself) to pay off the bonds that were sold in 1996 for the leveraged buyout by the Lee Group.[36] Using the sales proceeds to pay debt put Rayovac "in a better position to compete by allowing us to put more money into our promotions, advertising, and marketing

plans."[37] Stock prices for the two fiscal years (1998 and 1999) since Rayovac went public are provided in Exhibit 4.

Income statements from 1993 to 1996 are found in Exhibit 5. As a result of the buyout by the Lee Group in September 1996, the end of the fiscal year was changed from June 30 to September 30, creating a transitional period. The transitional period statement for 1996 and new fiscal year 1996, 1997, 1998, and 1999 income statements are found in Exhibit 6. Note that advertising, distribution and marketing expenses were included under "Selling Expenses."

Second-quarter net sales in fiscal year 2000 were $142.6 million, and net income was $3.7 million. Strong growth in general batteries and lighting products spurred the increase in sales. The acquisition of ROV Limited brought an additional $25.2 million in sales in Latin America for the second quarter. Third-quarter net sales were $152 million, and net income was $8.1 million. For the first 9 months of fiscal year 2000, net sales were $509.4

EXHIBIT 4

Income Statements, 1993–1996

		Fiscal Year Ended June 30		
	1993	*1994*	*1995*	*1996*
		(in millions)		
Net Sales	$372.4	$403.7	$415.2	$423.4
Cost of Goods Sold	201.4	234.9	237.1	239.4
Gross Profit	171.0	168.8	178.1	184.0
Selling Expense	98.8	121.3	108.7	116.5
General and Admin. Expense	35.4	29.4	32.9	31.8
Recapitalization and Other Charges	—	1.5	—	—
Income from Operations	31.2	10.9	31.5	30.3
Interest Expense	6.0	7.7	8.6	8.4
Other Expense (income), Net	1.2	(0.6)	0.3	0.6
Income Before Taxes	24.0	3.8	22.6	21.3
Income Tax Expense (benefit)	9.0	(0.6)	6.2	7.0
Net Income	$15.0	$4.4	$16.4	$14.3

Source: Rayovac Corporation, 10-K report, www.rayovac.com/, February 6, 1998, p. 16.

EXHIBIT 5

Transition Period and Income Statements, 1996–1999

	Transition Period Ended 9/30/96	Twelve Months Ended 9/30/96	Fiscal Year Ended 9/30/97	Fiscal Year Ended 9/30/98	Fiscal Year Ended 9/30/99
			(in millions)		
Net Sales	$101.9	$417.9	$432.6	$495.7	$564.3
Cost of Goods Sold	59.3	237.9	234.6	258.0	295.2[a]
Gross Profit	42.6	180.0	198.0	237.7	269.1
Selling Expense	27.8	114.4	122.1	148.9	160.2
General and Admin. Expense	8.6	33.0	32.2	35.9	38.4
Research and Dev. Expense	1.5	5.6	6.2	6.2	8.7
Recapitalization and Other Charges	28.4	28.4	3.0	6.2	8.1
Income (loss) from Operations	(23.7)	(1.4)	34.5	40.5	53.7
Interest Expense	4.4	10.5	24.5	15.7	16.4
Other Expense (Income), Net	0.1	0.5	0.4	(0.2)	(0.3)
Income (loss) Before Taxes	(28.2)	(12.4)	9.6	25.0	37.6
Income Tax Expense (benefit)	(8.9)	(3.8)	3.4	8.6	13.5
Income Before Extraordinary Item	(19.3)	(8.6)	6.2	16.4	24.1
Extraordinary Item	(1.6)	(1.6)	—	(2.0)	—
Net Income (loss)	$(20.9)	$(10.2)	$6.2	$14.4	$24.1
Stock Prices:					
High	n/a	n/a	n/a	$24.50	$31.31
Low	n/a	n/a	n/a	13.25	15.50
Close of Fiscal Year	n/a	n/a	n/a	17.13	21.63

[a]Includes other special charges of $1.3 million (FY 99 only).
Sources: Rayovac Corporation, 10-K report, www.rayovac.com/, February 6, 1999, p. 17; Rayovac Corporation, *1999 Annual Report,* p. 28; stock prices from Rayovac Corporation, Hoover's Online, www.hoovers.com/, August 21, 2000, (paid-access).

million, and net income was $25.6 million. Alkaline sales were up 11 percent, lighting products sales were up 17 percent, and hearing aid battery sales declined 5 percent during the third quarter. The hearing aid battery sales decline was due to foreign-exchange fluctuations and a soft period in growth in the hearing aid industry.[38]

COMPETITIVE ENVIRONMENT

Overview

Competition in the U.S. general battery market was based upon brand-name recognition, perceived quality, price, performance, product packaging and

EXHIBIT 6

U.S. Alkaline Market Share Data (% share)

	9/30/96	3/31/97	8/28/98	8/28/99	2/15/00	6/19/00
Duracell®	44.0	41.6	43.9	43.8	38.0	44.4
Energizer®	37.0	36.5	34.2	30.7	30.0	30.8
Rayovac®	11.0	10.2	11.4	14.3	17.8	12.8
All others	08.0	11.7	10.5	11.2	14.2	12.0

Sources: Avrum D. Lank. "Rayovac Enters Battery Fray with New Energy," *The Milwaukee Journal Sentinel,* March 3, 1997, p. 12D; Sean Mehegan. "Air of Electricity," *Brandweek,* June 30, 1997, pp. 1 and 6; John Daggett, Rayovac spokesperson, telephone interview, October 11, 1999; Seth Mendelson. "Keeping the Power On," *Supermarket Business,* February 15, 2000, pp. 81–82; and Cara Beardi. "Rayovac Will Spend $35 Mil to Reinforce Value Position," *Advertising Age,* June 19, 2000, p. 32.

innovation, and creative marketing, promotion, and distribution strategies. Turning to the international general battery market, one saw more competitors and similar methods of competition as that found in the U.S. market. In the international hearing aid battery industry, competition was based upon reliability, quality, performance, packaging, and brand-name recognition.

In the U.S. battery market, Rayovac competed primarily with two well-established companies: Duracell International Inc., a subsidiary of The Gillette Company since 1996 (Duracell®), and Energizer Holdings, Inc. (Energizer®). Ralston Purina, the former owner of what was called Eveready, spend $14 million in the first 9 months of 1999 on advertising Energizer®. Gillette spent $25 million in advertising over that same time period.[39] Alkaline market share data is shown in Exhibit 6.

Primary competitors for the hearing aid market were Duracell®, Energizer® and Panasonic. More competitors, including Black & Decker, Mag-Lite, and Energizer® challenged Rayovac, in the lighting devices marketplace. Rayovac's global market share in the hearing aid market was up to 58 percent to 60 percent in 1999.[40] Rayovac held approximately 75 percent of the U.S. sales for conventional rechargeable batteries and 50% of the sales for the lithium battery/computer clock market.[41]

Category Sales.   The alkaline market accounted for 75.6 percent of the $2.58 billion battery category for the 52 weeks ended April 23, 2000.[42] Rick

Anderson, Duracell's vice president of marketing, noted that the alkaline "category has grown from $200 million in 1974 to over $[2] billion in 1998" and that, in retail stores, the "premium battery segment is replacing the low-end segment—the most significant shift in the category since alkaline batteries appeared."[43] Rayovac's Daggett said that discount stores held "the biggest share at about 40 percent, followed by food stores (16 percent), drug (15 percent), warehouse clubs (14 percent), and all others (14 percent)" for 1998.[44] By the end of November 1999, mass merchandisers (i.e., discount stores) controlled about 50 percent of category sales.[45]

Tom Murray, Duracell Ultra's® product manager, stated that in 1999, the "average American household own[ed] 20 portable electronic devices, compared to owning only two in 1970." Based on industry data, "these high-tech devices account[ed] for approximately 20 percent of total AA and AAA battery consumption and 30 percent of C and D battery use [by mid-1999]."[46] Battery sales shot up 10 percent in 1999 (to over $2.5 billion for 52 weeks ended November 27, 1999), due in part to the "double whammy of one of the worst hurricane seasons in memory and concerns over Y2K knocking out the nationwide power grid." The influx of high-tech consumer electronics products also helped.[47]

According to a study of the U.S. battery market, which included all types of batteries (alkaline, automobile, and others), by The Freedonia Group in

1999, alkaline battery sales grew from $1.44 billion in 1993 to $2.315 billion in 1998. Sales during this 5-year period grew at an annual rate of 10 percent. Alkaline sales were projected to grow to $3.25 billion in 2003 and to $4.5 billion in 2008. The projected annual rate of growth between 1998 and 2003 was 7 percent.[48]

Consumer Market Profiles.   Based on trade magazine interviews with battery competitors' spokespeople, battery consumers had the following profiles in 1998. The average household used 36 batteries a year. The heavy-user segment, about 30 percent of all households, used 65 or more batteries per year. Heavy users tended to be young married couples with children between the ages of 4 and 12, young adults (ages 16 to 24), professionals, and senor citizens. They tended to own the greatest number of electronic devices. The majority of household shopping was done by women who were between the ages of 25 and 54, and who bought anywhere from 58 percent to 70 percent of all batteries. Batteries were considered to be a planned impulse purchase, where shoppers needed promotional merchandising to remind them to buy batteries. About 73 percent of all batteries were bought on impulse.[49]

In the year 2000, *Supermarket Business* magazine hired a Chicago-based research supplier, Spectra, to provide an analysis of the battery buyer. Spectra identified children as being the primary drivers for battery sales, with all the portable electronic devices they used (which required batteries to operate). Heavy users of household batteries were families with parents between the ages of 35 and 54. Heavy users also tended to be Hispanic families, with three or more children (especially teenagers) at home. Heavy users were also educated and affluent, with 32 percent of them having graduated from college and 50 percent of them earning over $50,000 annually. Users also tended to be married, with both parents working full-time. Battery consumers tended to have a personal computer at home, tended to purchase large volumes of recorded music, and enjoyed such outdoor activities as camping, hiking, swimming, and skiing. They also read newspapers and magazines often and listened to the radio often during the daytime.[50]

Duracell® Batteries (Gillette)

Recent History.   Duracell, based out of Bethel, Connecticut, produced alkaline batteries and specialty batteries for cameras, cellular phones, hearing aids, and other medical devices. Duracell took on Eveready in the mid-1980s and successfully dropped Eveready's market share from 60 percent in 1986 to 42 percent in 1989, while reaching a 36 percent market share by 1989. Duracell also battled Germany's Varta in Europe and captured 50 percent of the European alkaline market by 1988.[51] Duracell became a division of The Gillette Company in 1996. Following Gillette's marketing strategy, Duracell used top acquisitions overseas to move into new markets and captured greater market share. Its global plan also included buying foreign battery makers and converting their short-life zinc carbon batteries into longer lasting and more expensive alkaline batteries.

New Products.   A new battery line, introduced by Duracell in February 1998, was designed to complement the current line, not replace it.[52] Duracell® Ultra™ designed for digital cameras and other power-draining products, was supposed to last up to 50 percent longer than regular batteries in such products. Duracell began shipping AA and AAA batteries in May 1998. Prices were higher for the premium product, about $5 for four AAs. The company hoped to convince users of rechargeable batteries to switch for the convenience of disposables.[53] There were some people who questioned the performance claims of new products like Ultra™. An unscientific test done by a newspaper writer found that Energizer® and Rayovac® outperformed the Duracell Copper Top®, and Energizer's new formula battery beat out Ultra™. Also, Jeff Shepard with Darnell Group, a consulting firm that monitors the battery market, stated, "There is not very much magic left in the battery industry. Battery chemistry is fairly well-developed. When someone like Duracell comes out with a new battery, there's not that much improvement."[54]

Promotional Strategy.   Promotional efforts in 1997 included PowerCheck® batteries tied to NHL hockey teams' power plays and NHL gear, sponsoring the Newman/Haas racing team in the PPG CART World Series, Duracell Days at all 12 Six Flags theme parks, and rebate tie-ins with the movie *Batman & Robin*.[55] Movie cross-promotions continued in 1998 with a tie-in with *Godzilla*.

Despite the critics of the new Ultra™ Duracell® spent most of its $52.5 million measured-media budget on Ultra™ in 1999.[56] Gillette applied razor strategies to selling batteries, with ads hinting that "for such 'high-drain' devices as portable stereos and digital cameras, the Ultra™ is the gold standard of battery technology," and given the alkaline sales for the beginning of 1999, "consumers [were] responding to that message." Ultra™'s 7.3 percent dollar market share for the month of June 1999 contributed to the widened market share lead.[57] Ultra™ and Duracell® promotions for the fall 1999 season included tie-ins with major league baseball and players Ken Griffey, Jr., and Roger Clemens; a scratch-and-win game with two grand prizes and 10,000 other prizes; 50-cents-off coupons; and another game featuring the Nickelodeon character CatDog and 50,000 prizes.[58]

Duracell® continued to emphasize its Ultra™ brand in the year 2000. Product manager Tom Murray said, "The company has a new global advertising campaign, focused on power—the power that our product delivers to the consumer and its superior performance, especially in high-drain devices." The core Duracell® brand was not to be forgotten. National promotions with heavy point-of-purchase materials were planned for the year 2000. Trade and consumer promotions were also planned for Duracell's lithium, hearing aid and camcorder battery lines.[59]

Energizer® Batteries (Energizer Holdings)

Recent History. For many years, Eveready was a business unit of the Ralston Purina Company. In June 1999, Ralston Purina announced plans to spin off its Eveready unit in order to focus on its core pet foods business. "Analysts said the decision puts new pressure on the struggling Eveready to deliver favorable results. Eveready has been battling competitors both big and small just to stay afloat as the nation's second-largest battery maker ... (as well as suffering) from economic unrest in Asia, where the unit derives roughly 25 percent of its profits" (refer to Exhibit 6 for share information).[60] Analysts say it is unlikely Energizer will switch from dueling with Duracell to taking on Rayovac. Energizer cannot afford to cut prices; the company's battery division has struggled to maintain profit growth in the face of increased ad costs and soft Asian demand. In fact, the top three brands raised prices between 3 percent and 4 percent [in 1998], partly to cover product and packaging improvements." There was some speculation in 1999 that the spin-off "could result in a more aggressive Energizer."[61] Energizer Holdings was created as a result of the spin-off of Eveready Batteries from Ralston Purina in the spring of 2000.[62]

New Products. Energizer launched a full line of rechargeable batteries for cell phones, camcorders, and computers, called Energizer Rechargeable Power Systems® in 1997.[63] Eveready introduced Energizer® Advanced Formula alkaline batteries in the summer of 1998. The new formula was targeted towards high-drain battery-powered products, as was Duracell Ultra™. In the year 2000, Energizer planned to introduce a new titanium-based super premium battery, e2®. This new battery was designed to last twice as long in high-drain devices.[64]

Promotional Strategy. For the spring of 1997, Energizer ran the "Win on the Spot" promotion, where consumers received $25 checks if the on-battery tester read "win."[65] Over the summer months, the Magic Touch Vacation Photo promotion was launched.[66] The company continued its fire alarm safety promotion, encouraging consumers to change their smoke alarm batteries when they changed their clocks back.[67] A major spring 1998 promotion was with Disney's® *Little Mermaid* video release, involving both immediate and mail-in rebates totaling $8 off the price.[68]

Eveready planned to spend $150 million in the global launch of the new Advanced Formula® alkaline batteries. The 6-month budget was to include packaging changes and advertising both nationally and internationally.[69] In 1999, Eveready joined forces with the Red Cross to create a number of educational materials on the importance of emergency preparedness. The $11 million campaign emphasized that Energizer® batteries and flashlights were an important part of any emergency preparedness plan. Bonus packs of two free batteries were offered to consumers when they purchased multipacks of Energizer® batteries.[70]

For the year 2000, the company planned to heavily promote its recently launched nickel metal hydride rechargeable batteries (which can be recharged up to 1,000 times) and its Advanced Formula® alkaline battery line.[71] Energizer planned to support the new super premium battery's (e2®) global launch with a $100 million campaign. The three television advertising spots were to start in July 2000.[72]

Panasonic Batteries (Matsushita)

Brief History.   Matsushita Battery Industrial Company of Japan was the world's largest producer of portable batteries (under the Panasonic® trade name) and a recognized leader in alkaline product technology. Panasonic, its American business unit, was based in Secaucus, New Jersey.

New Products.   Panasonic entered the high-drain field with its new Panasonic Plus Alkaline® in April 1997. During the winter of 1997–1998, Panasonic joined the rechargeable marketplace with its new High Capacity Rechargeable® AA size and Auto-Off Charger® and spruced up its products in the hearing aid market with new packaging and a customer information booklet.[73] Panasonic decided to enter the high-drain market in March 2000, with the introduction of its new Panasonic Alkaline for Digital® battery line. This new line was designed for electronic devices such as pagers and CD players.[74]

Promotional Strategy.   Panasonic focused on free product and cash-back offers in the spring of 1997. A free soda promotion, very successful in 1996, was repeated in the summer. Other promotions included cash back on vitamin purchases and free issues of TV Guide at the checkout counter with purchase of Panasonic® batteries.[75] Consumer promotionals tied to the new battery included free soda, candy bars and gift wrap, in addition to the use of coupons, advertisements, and free-standing newspaper inserts.[76] New consumer and retailer promotions were rolled out in 1998. These included a co-promotion with Spring (5-minute phone card attached to battery packages), a free-battery offer with the receipt of an empty competitor's battery package and a special certificate, a scratch-and-win game, and the Buy 4, Get 2 Free Family Pack Christmas offer.[77] Back-to-school promotions were part of the company's promotional efforts in 1999.[78]

The print campaign for the Alkaline for Digital® battery line appeared in consumer magazines such as *Time, Newsweek, People,* and *Good Housekeeping,* using the company's tagline, "just slightly ahead of our time." Although not disclosing the cost of the campaign, Suzanne Haines, Panasonic's senior marketing manager, did admit that Matsushita (America) had tripled its ad budget for the year 2000.[79]

Other Competitors

In addition to Panasonic, other foreign companies were involved in the U.S. alkaline battery market. According to The Freedonia Group, "shipments of batteries from U.S. facilities will rise 5.9 percent per year through 2003 to $11.8 billion, slower than demand, as imports continue to account for a larger share of the U.S. market. . . . Japan-based electronics conglomerates such as Matsushita Electric Industrial (via the PANASONIC trade name), Sanyo Electric, Toshiba, and Sony dominate global production." Net imports had grown at a 40.4 percent annual growth rate between 1993 and 1998 (to $535 million in 1998). Net imports were projected to grow at an annual rate of 13.9 percent between 1998 and 2003 (up to $1.025 billion in 2003 and $1.725 billion by 2008).[80]

For example, Sony launched a marketing campaign in St. Louis in August 1997 for its new Stamina™ alkaline battery. Bob Striano, senior vice president of sales for Sony Electronics, said, "Our goal is to establish the Sony name, which has long been a leader in portable electronics, as a player in the battery category as well." The marketing campaign ran through November and included over 1,700 local television spots airing on networks and cable channels, radio ads, and print ads. Sony also sponsored several concerts in the St. Louis area.[81]

A new competitor based on new technology appeared at the World PC Expo in Tokyo in September 1997. A small start-up company in Newark, New Jersey, Ultralife Batteries, Inc., introduced a "new type of lithium battery made from flexible sheets of plastic."[82] This new battery powered the smallest notebook computer, Mitsubishi's Pedion.

A new Canadian battery, Red Cell, was "attempting to break into the U.S. market with alkaline batteries it claims are just as good as the major U.S. brands in high-drain applications. But, [it] first has to get chains in Canada and the United States to carry the brand." It was offering a wide assortment of rechargeable and disposable alkaline batteries as an inducement to retail channels.[83]

In addition to battery producers, retailers and wholesalers also sold private-label batteries. Some of the private-label batteries were produced by major manufacturers like Duracell; however, the brand leaders were reluctant to talk about supplying their products under private labels when asked by industry trade reporters.[84] Earlier in the year 2000, Wal-Mart announced plans to sell batteries under its own name.[85]

Barriers to Entry

Rayovac believed that new market entrants would need significant financial and other resources (especially for advertising) to develop brand recognition and the distribution capability necessary to serve the U.S. marketplace. Substantial capital expenditures would be required to establish U.S. battery manufacturing operations, although potential competitors could import their products into the U.S. market. Rayovac and its primary competitors enjoyed significant advantages in having established brand recognition and distribution channels.

Rayovac and Duracell were even battling each other in the courtroom. Rayovac filed a lawsuit in late April 1999, contending that Duracell infringed upon three of Rayovac's technology patents for longer lasting hearing aid batteries. Rayovac usually conducted its own research on hearing aid technology, rather than licensing such technology. Duracell claimed to have 23 percent of the $150 to $180 million U.S. market. Gillette, in turn, sued Rayovac in July for alleged patent infringement.[86] A year later, in May 2000, a federal jury ruled that the three Rayovac patents were invalid, but also found that Duracell had infringed Rayovac's patents. Given the inconsistency of these findings, Rayovac planned to pursue judicial review of the federal jury's decision.[87]

KEY ELEMENTS TO GROWTH

Rayovac's top management laid out seven key elements to its growth in the future:

1. Continue to reinvigorate the Rayovac® brand name.
2. Leverage the value brand position.
3. Expand retail distribution.

4. Further capitalize on our worldwide leadership in hearing aid batteries.
5. Develop new markets.
6. Introduce new niche products.
7. Reposition the Renewal® Rechargeable Alkaline Battery.

Reinvigorate the Brand

The company increased the amount of advertising spending in an effort to increase awareness of the brand and to positively change consumers' perceptions of the quality, performance, and value of Rayovac's products, with the result being increased retail sales. CEO Jones noted, "We utilize Michael Jordan as a focal point in our alkaline ads and Arnold Palmer in our hearing aid ads. These two gentlemen are among the most recognized celebrities on earth and provide us great visibility in the marketplace."[88] In October 1998, Rayovac designated Marathon Projects as the "exclusive agent to license the Rayovac® brand name in the United States, Canada, and Puerto Rico." This was the first time for brand licensing in the company's history. Marathon targeted automotive batteries, nonflashlight and lantern lighting products, and electric appliances and accessories. This move was seen as a way to enter new markets without upfront investment on Rayovac's part, as well as a way to further build "Brand Rayovac."[89]

Repositioning Renewal®

Rayovac repositioned Renewal® with a better-suited distribution channel, focused now on electronics specialty stores such as Radio Shack. The Renewal® system was also launched in Europe. Rayovac's market share had reached 71 percent by the end of fiscal year 1999. Two major new products were launched in 1999. First, the new ULTRA™ Rechargeable Nickel Metal Hydride battery, which can be recharged up to 1,000 times, was launched at a premium price level. Second, a new universal charger that handled all three rechargeable systems (alkaline, nickel cadmium, and nickel metal hydride) was launched. The charger was designed to sense how much charging each battery needed, charge up to that level, and then shut itself off.

Position Leveraging

Rayovac believed it had a unique position in the general battery market as the value brand in an industry in which the leading three brands accounted for approximately 90 percent of sales. Its strategy was to provide products of quality and performance equal to its major competitors in the general battery market at a lower price, appealing to a large segment of the population desiring a value brand.[90] To demonstrate its value positioning, Rayovac offered comparable battery packages at a lower price or, in some cases, more batteries for the same price. Jones' strategy was "to own the low-priced battery market ignored by Duracell and Eveready, not compete directly with the well-known brands."[91]

Expand Retail Distribution

Over the years, Rayovac focused on the mass merchandiser channel and, as a result, achieved a 21 percent unit share of U.S. alkaline battery sales through this channel (versus 13 percent to 17 percent share overall for the alkaline market; see Exhibit 6). Top management believed it was time to focus on other retail channels and reorganized its sales efforts accordingly.

Hearing Aid Leadership

Rayovac sought to increase its nearly 60 percent worldwide market share in the hearing aid battery segment, as it had done consistently for the past 10 years, by leveraging its leading technology and its dedicated and focused sales and marketing organizations. Rayovac planned to continue to utilize Arnold Palmer as its spokesperson in its print media campaign.

New Markets

Rayovac entered the Chinese battery market in 1999 with its MAXIMUM® alkaline battery through an established distributor and supported the launch with point-of-purchase materials and television advertising that featured Michael Jordan. When asked why China, Jones noted, "With 1.2 billion consumers, China offers a tremendous opportunity for the Rayovac® brand and our value-price strategy. We hope to harness the power and appeal of Michael to the power and pricing advantages of our Rayovac, alkaline brand in our China launch. [With an estimated total market potential of 4 billion units,] the [alkaline] segment has experienced exponential annual growth of more than 35 percent over the past few years."[92] The marketing campaign was estimated to be approximately $4 million, and it was anticipated that the Chinese market would eventually become Rayovac's fourth-largest market. The United States, Europe, and Canada markets were the top three markets for Rayovac.[93]

Rayovac also looked to expand into South America. "We have a very large business in Europe now and are just beginning to develop an emerging business in the Far East. South America is a potential growth area for this company; however, we currently [as of 1998] do not participate in that marketplace. Latin American countries represent high-growth battery markets and, although there is currently instability in the stock market and currency markets in this region, over the long term these markets are going to grow at a much higher rate of growth than the U.S. marketplace. We are looking at various strategies to be able to move into that area of the world opportunistically when conditions improve."[94] In February 1999, Rayovac acquired ROV Limited, one of the leading battery manufacturers in Latin America, through bank borrowings. The $155 million acquisition was completed by early August 1999.[95] ROV Limited had been spun off by Rayovac in 1982. This acquisition unified the Rayovac® brand under one roof and should increase Rayovac's distribution and brand awareness by setting the stage for a global marketing launch.[96]

As a result of this acquisition, Rayovac announced some restructuring initiatives in September 1999 that affected manufacturing, distribution, marketing, and support functions. "The initiatives reflect the restructuring of the organization to streamline and better serve global markets and improve the company's overall operating efficiencies, the restructuring of manufacturing operations to position the company for future growth, and the termination of nonperforming foreign distributors ... Worldwide overcapacity for silver-oxide watch cells has rendered low-volume manufacturing noneconomic. ... Rayovac will cease the manufacture of watch batteries at its Portage plant and will source these products from one of the world's largest manufacturers of watch batteries. This will allow the Portage plant to focus on hearing aid manufacturing as well as expanding capacity to meet surging demand for lithium coin cells sold to the computer, telecommunications, and auto industries."[97]

New Products

Rayovac continued searching out underserved niche markets to exploit as well as entering high-growth specialty battery markets. For example, in late 1999, Rayovac entered a partnership with the Harley Davidson® Motor Company to launch a special product line of chrome and leather-clad flashlights and key-chain lights with the Harley Davidson® brand on the products. The new flashlight line was launched with a Father's Day television advertising campaign between May 29 and June 18 of the year 2000. The ad aired over cable networks and Wal-Mart's in-store channel (PICS).[98] In addition, nickel cadmium and other new styles of battery packs were being developed.[99]

THE POWER TO GROW

According to its *1999 Annual Report,* Rayovac approached the twenty-first century with several targeted areas for growth: (1) a more customer-centered orientation; (2) a focus on value and performance in the alkaline market; (3) a focus on technology in the hearing aid market; (4) a deeper and broader distribution network; and (5) a focus on global expansion.

Customer-Centered Orientation

Rayovac aligned its business into three geographic regions: North America, Latin America, and Europe and the rest of the world. Each region has its own management team to direct marketing initiatives within each particular region. Internally, the functional areas of marketing, sales, supply chain, and support were reorganized into customer-focused teams that were dedicated to major customers and to specific customers in specific distribution channels. Cross-functional product teams were also created to handle global brand management strategies and goals.

Value and Performance in the Alkaline Market

Rayovac continued the focus on providing value to consumers. Rayovac's MAXIMUM® batteries provided the long-lasting performance consumers desired for their high-drain devices, for 15 percent to 20 percent less cost than Duracell® or Energizer®. With access to high-level alkaline technology from Matsushita, Rayovac was able to improve the performance of its AA batteries anywhere from 7 percent to 54 percent, depending on the device, from 1998 to 1999. The life of AAA batteries improved upwards to 23 percent in 1999 versus 1998 performance. Rayovac's "Battery Gobblers" advertising campaign that featured Michael Jordan successfully reached its objectives of improved brand awareness (23 percent increase in total brand awareness since 1999), increased market share, and improved brand perceptions. The company and its advertising agency, Young & Rubicam of Chicago, were rewarded with the top prize in the consumer electronics category, a Silver Effie, from the American Marketing Association in June 2000.[100] Rayovac also announced plans to maintain its value position through a $35 million budget, of which $15 million would be spent in measured media. Most of the budget would be spent in the last 6 months of 2000, with a new print ad for consumer magazines such as *Family Circle* and *Redbook* highlighting reclosable plastic multipacks of MAXIMUM® alkaline batteries. In addition, a new television ad with Jordan would debut in the fall.[101]

Improved Hearing Aid Performance

Investments in research and development led to 31 zinc air patents in fiscal year 1999. The new generation of batteries (ULTRA™), to be introduced in early summer of 2000, were to last 30 percent longer than competitors' current products and 13 percent longer than the company's current generation of hearing aid batteries. Arnold Palmer would again be used to launch the new product in a series of ads. The hearing aid battery market offered much potential for growth, because it was estimated that only 20 percent of people who need hearing aids actually wear them.[102]

Deeper and Broader Distribution

The potential existed to double distribution of Rayovac's products by penetrating existing channels and pursuing new channels. The company had just "broken the surface" with such channels as drugstores, supermarkets, warehouse clubs, office supply chains, and sporting goods stores. The company entered channels that had never sold batteries before, such as Mailboxes, Etc. (4,000 stores). Exclusive distribution agreements were signed with Kmart (hearing aid batteries) and Walgreens (rechargeable alkaline batteries), among others.

Wal-Mart selected Rayovac as "Supplier of the Fourth Quarter" in March 2000 for the second year in a row. Wal-Mart's recognition was for the impulse merchandising category and was based on performance of suppliers in the busiest quarter of the retail year (i.e., fall holiday season).[103] Another honor came Rayovac's way in June 2000. Buyers and merchandise managers from the mass-market retail industry's top 100 retailers awarded Rayovac the 2000 SPARC (Supplier Performance Awards by Retail Category) First Place Award. The company was lauded for its service, innovation, and superior promotional programs that assisted the industry in maximizing profit and achieving other objectives such as quality control.[104]

Global Expansion Opportunities

In fiscal year 1999, sales outside of North America accounted for 15 percent of total Rayovac revenue. Out of $564.3 million in sales in fiscal year 1999 (from Exhibit 5), $66.7 million was generated in Europe and the rest of the world, and $19.3 million was generated in Latin America. International revenue was predicted to reach 30 percent in fiscal year 2000. The worldwide (overall) battery market potential was estimated at $20 billion. This was broken down by region as follows: Europe/Rest of World, $11.5 billion; North America, $6.5 billion; Latin America, $2.0 billion. Rayovac sought continued expansion into Latin America, Europe, and China, among other international markets.

The Latin American expansion continued into the year 2000. Rayovac added 325 major new retail accounts between October 1999 and June 2000. As a result, the company added over 3,000 new stores to its retail accounts, including these chains: OXXO, Farmacias, Gigante, Casa Royal, Carrefour, and Supermercado.[105]

JORDAN'S RETIREMENT

On January 13, 1999, Michael Jordan made it official. He retired from professional basketball after 13 years with the Chicago Bulls and several championship rings. In addition to stunning the sports world, Jordan also stunned the sports business world. What was going to happen to all those companies whose products Jordan endorsed? How durable would his endorsement power be? Stock prices for companies tied to Jordan fell amidst speculation of his retirement. Rayovac's stock price fell 50 cents to $24.50 at that time.[106] Jordan was considered by marketers to be a "powerbrand—a player whose popularity and reach was peerless in the history of sports business."[107] As Seth M. Siegel of Beanstalk Group, a licensing firm, said, "If he's not positioned well, it's just a question of a couple of years before he loses the power of being a credible and meaningful endorser."[108]

Rayovac's Daggett didn't see Jordan losing endorsement power. "When we first got involved with Jordan, we made a conscious effort to portray him as a person rather than a basketball player. His image has transcended the sport."[109] In hindsight, Rayovac made a smart move by not having Jordan wear his uniform. Rather, he appeared in street clothes and in a "home" setting, not on the basketball court. Rayovac continued to use Jordan in its commercials. The company's Web site featured a new Jordan commercial video for the new Clear Value Pack® in late 1999.

Fourteen months later, Jordan made another announcement that affected the sports business world. In a March 22, 2000, interview with the *Chicago Sun-Times,* Jordan announced that he was finished with commercial endorsements. Instead, he wanted a more active role in the businesses he represented. For example, Mr. Jordan partnered with two other sports stars to form the online sporting goods store MVP.com, and he was also president of basketball operations for the NBA's Washington Wizards team. For Rayovac and other clients, Jordan's spokesman said the ex-player would honor current endorsement contracts.[110] Rayovac had Jordan under contract for another 4 years or so, according to CEO Jones.[111]

THE HIGH (-DRAIN) ROAD OR THE LOW (-PRICED) ROAD?

"We are halfway through the year 2000," mused Jones. "We've made major changes and have positioned our brand as the value brand in the alkaline market. We've been successful with our niche strategies in other markets. We are expanding globally. Yet we face strong competitors. How will we respond to the super premium battery challenge presented by Energizer's e²™? How can we remain competitive in our other markets? What is the future for Renewal®? What should our marketing strategy be?"

Endnotes

1. "Market leading technology—Unique niche strategy," *Wall Street Corporate Reporter* (June 22–28, 1998), from the Rayovac Corporation's home page (http://www.rayovac.com/wallst.htm), pp. 1–5, 2/6/99.

2. Avrum D. Lank, "Rayovac enters battery fray with new energy," *Milwaukee Journal Sentinel* (3/3/97): 12D.

3. Lauren Neergaard, "Discovery may lead to better batteries," *Duluth News Tribune* (8/16/99): 1A, 7A.

4. "Rayovac gets out of big batteries," *Batteries International* (July 1998): 17.

5. Avrum D. Lank, "Rayovac plans to restructure," *The Milwaukee Journal Sentinel* (3/26/98): 2D.

6. Rayovac Corporation, Hoover's Online, http://www.hoovers.com/, 8/21/2000 (paid access).

7. John Daggett, Rayovac spokesman, phone interview, 4:00 p.m., 10/11/99.

8. Lank, p. 14D; Tessa Franklin, "Rayovac Introduces…," *Supermarket Business* (April 1996): 47.

9. Judy Newman, "Rayovac Gears Up for Major Marketing Push," *Knight-Ridder/Tribune Business News* (September 4, 1997): 904B1020.

10. Franklin, p. 47.

11. Daggett, phone interview, 10/11/99.

12. Complete citation not yet found; students show the source of this paragraph to be from Levitt, pp. 81–82.

13. T. Covino, "Rayovac Battery," *Cellular Business* (July 1996): 37–39.

14. Yinka Adegoke, "Rayovac takes on NiCad battery," *DIY Week* (November 28, 1997): 3; "Rayovac offers prizes in UKPd500,000 local and national radio campaign," *DIY Week* (December 12, 1997): 19.

15. Current News Releases, http://www.rayovac.com/news/release/buy_brisco.htm, 1/28/98.

16. James E. Causey, "Rayovac acquires battery distribution portion of Florida's Best Labs," *The Milwaukee Journal Sentinel* (4/1/98): 6D.

17. Avrum D. Lank, "Rayovac shares get big charge," *The Milwaukee Journal Sentinel* (3/17/98): 1D, 2D.

18. "Rayovac offers ideas on merchandising," *Chain Drug Review* (June 23, 1997): 204.

19. Craig Levitt, "Charging the battery," *Discount Merchandiser* (May 1997): 81–84; Craig Levitt, "Leading the Charge for Batteries," *Supermarket Business* (May 1997): 137–138, 140.

20. Daggett, phone interview, 10/11/99; also see Rayovac's website for a video ad for Clear Value Pack®, http://www.rayovac.com (accessed 10/9/99).

21. Daggett, phone interview, 10/11/99.

22. Rick Barrett, "Rayovac Plans to Put More Batteries within Shoppers' Reach," *The Wisconsin State Journal* (7/22/99).

23. Craig Levitt, "Power Surge," *Discount Merchandiser* (August 1997): 45–48.

24. Sean Mehegan, "Maximum alkaline batteries," *Mediaweek* (June 30, 1997): 36.

25. Levitt, "Power Surge," p. 47.

26. "State of the Market (Annual Report of Categories): Batteries," *Drug Store News* (5/25/98): 80+.

27. Craig Levitt, "The battery game," *Discount Merchandiser* (February 1998): 55–56.

28. "Rayovac's Greatest Strength Is Specialty Batteries," *MMR* (10/19/98): 50.

29. "Rayovac powering up its alkaline business," *Supermarket Business* (April 1998): 46.

30. Craig Levitt, "Dueling diodes," *Discount Merchandiser* (August 1998): 97–98; "Rayovac and Rudolph Light Up This Holiday Season," *PRNewswire* (11/20/98).

31. Craig Diamond, "Charging ahead," *Discount Merchandiser* (2/1/2000), pp. 46–48.

32. "Power surge," *Discount Merchandiser* (8/1/99), p. 63.

33. Craig Levitt, "Charging the battery," p. 84.

34. "Rayovac and 1-800-Batteries Ink Revolutionary Battery Delivery Deal Featuring In-Store Fulfillment Hotlines, Internet Sales," *PRNewswire* (September 10, 1998): 1–2 [http://www.prnewswire.com/, 2/6/99].

35. "Dialing for Batteries," *Supermarket Business* (November 1998): 53.

36. Avrum D. Lank, "Rayovac would sell 26% of firm," *Milwaukee Journal Sentinel* (September 10, 1997): 1D, 3D; Lank, "Rayovac issues high-voltage IPO," *Milwaukee Journal Sentinel* (November 22, 1997): 1D.

37. Levitt, "The battery game," pp. 55–56.

38. "Strong Sales Drive 14th Straight Quarter of Record Revenue & Earnings," *PR Newswire, Netscape Financial News,* 4/25/2000; "Rayovac: Strong Sales Drive 15th Consecutive Quarter of Record Sales and Earnings," *PR Newswire,* 7/25/2000 (from Rayovac's home page).

39. Cara Beardi, "Panasonic touts digital edge for its batteries," *Advertising Age* (February 21, 2000), p. 16.

40. Daggett, phone interview, 10/11/99; see also Barrett, "Rayovac Plans…" (7/22/99) and "Rayovac Announces Record Fourth Quarter and Fiscal Year Sales and Earnings Results," *PR Newswire* (11/8/99), 4 pages (Internet printout from Rayovac home page).

41. Thane Peterson, "Industry Insider: A Talk with the Man Who Got Rayovac All Charged Up," *Business Week Online* (2/21/00), *Custom E. Prints,* 5/31/2000, p. 2.

42. Beardi (6/19/2000), p. 32.

43. "Batteries remain a mainstay of front-end mix at drug chains," *Chain Drug Review* (9/14/98); 42+.

44. Ibid.; also see Scott Meyer, "More Devices Need More Batteries," *MMR* (1/25/99): 13.

45. Craig Diamond, "Charging ahead," *Discount Merchandiser* (2/1/2000), pp. 46–48.

46. "Power surge," *Discount Merchandiser* (8/1/99), p. 63.

47. Mendelson (2/15/2000), pp. 81–82.

48. The Freedonia Group, "Section I: Executive Summary," Batteries to 2003, 1999, 4 pages (Purchased 8/21/2000).

49. "Batteries remain a mainstay," "Rayovac's Greatest Strength Is Specialty Batteries," *MMR* (10/19/98): 50; "Category Builder Batteries," *U.S. Distribution Journal* (May 1999), pp. 3 + 22.

50. "Battery buyers," *Supermarket Business* (6/15/2000), pp. 109–110.

51. Duracell, company history, Hoover's Online (http://www.hoovers.com/), 8/21/2000 (paid access).

52. Levitt, "Dueling diodes," pp. 97–98.

53. William C. Symonds, "Duracell's Bunny Buster?" *Business Week* (March 2, 1998): 42.

54. K. Oanh Ha, "The Great Battery Race," *San Jose Mercury News* (April 17, 1998) [pages 1–4, printed 2/9/99].

55. Duke Ratliff, "Tricks of the Trade," *Discount Merchandiser* (February 1997): 42; Levitt, "Charging the battery," pp. 81–84; Levitt, "Power surge," pp. 45–48; Jennifer Kulpa, "What's ahead in specialty batteries," *Drug Store News* (10/20/97): 74+.

56. Beardi (6/19/2000), p. 32.

57. Chris Reidy, "Battery Maker Duracell Takes Page Out of Gillette's Razor Playbook," *The Boston Globe* (7/25/99): pp. 1–4 (Internet source printout, 10/11/99).

58. "Power surge," *Discount Merchandiser* (8/1/99), p. 63.

59. Seth Mendelson, "Keeping the power on," *Supermarket Business* (2/15/2000), pp. 81–82.

60. "Ralston Purina To Spin Off Eveready Battery Unit, Focus on Pet Food," *The Wall Street Journal* (6/10/99), dowjones.com archives (10/11/99).

61. Rekha Balu, "Hop Faster, Energizer Bunny: Rayovac Batteries Roll on," *The Wall Street Journal* (6/15/99): B4.

62. Energizer Holdings, company history, Hoover's Online (http://www.hoovers.com/), 8/21/2000 (paid access).

63. Kulpa, "What's ahead in specialty batteries," p. 74+.

64. Cara Beardi, "Energizer powers up e2 with $100 mil campaign," *Advertising Age* (July 24, 2000), pp. 3 + 49; Beardi (6/19/2000), p. 32; and Beardi (2/21/2000), p. 16.

65. Ratliff, "Tricks of the Trade," p. 42.

66. Levitt, "Leading the Charge for Batteries," p. 138.

67. Harbatkin, "Battery makers charge into holidays," pp. 28–29.

68. Levitt, "The battery game," pp. 55–56.

69. "Battery titan turns up the juice with new high-powered model," *Oshkosh Northwestern* (5/27/98): D6; Levitt, "Dueling Diodes," pp. 97–98; and "Batteries remain a mainstay," pp. 42+.

70. "Power surge," *Discount Merchandiser* (8/1/99), p. 63.

71. Seth Mendelson, "Keeping the power on," *Supermarket Business* (2/15/2000), p. 81–82; Craig Diamond, "Charging ahead," *Discount Merchandiser* (2/1/2000), pp. 46–48.

72. Cara Beardi, "Energizer powers up e2 with $100 mil campaign," *Advertising Age* (July 24, 2000), pp. 3 + 49; Beardi (6/19/2000), p. 32; and Beardi (2/21/2000), p. 16.

73. "State of the Market (Annual Report of Categories): Batteries," *Drug Store News* (5/25/98): 80+.

74. Beardi (2/21/2000), p. 16.

75. Ratliff, "Tricks of the Trade," p. 42.

76. Levitt, "Power surge," pp. 45–48; Kulpa, "What's ahead in specialty batteries," p. 74+.

77. Levitt, "The battery game," pp. 55–56; Levitt, "Dueling diodes," pp. 97–98.

78. "Power surge," *Discount Merchandiser* (8/1/99), p. 63.

79. Beardi (2/21/2000), p. 16.

80. The Freedonia Group, "Section I: Executive Summary," Batteries to 2003, 1999, 4 pages (Purchased 8/21/2000).

81. Levitt, "Power surge," pp. 45–48.

82. "Battery Breakthrough," *Business Week* (March 30, 1998): 38.

83. "Premium batteries may further boost sales," *Discount Store News* (3/9/98): 59.

84. Kate Griffin, "Private-label batteries charge low-end sales," *National Home Center News* (1/11/99), pp. 23+.

85. Thane Peterson, "Industry Insider: A Talk with the Man Who Got Rayovac All Charged Up," *Business Week Online* (2/21/00), *Custom E. Prints*, 5/31/2000, p. 1.

86. Judy Newman, "Rayovac Corp. Files Suit Against Duracell over Hearing Aid Technology," *Knight-Ridder/Tribune Business News* (4/29/99); "Gillette Sues Battery Firm Rayovac For Violating Patents," *The Wall Street Journal* (8/5/99), dowjones.com archives (10/11/99).

87. "UPDATE 1-Rayovac hearing aid battery patents found invalid," *Reuters, Netscape Financial News*, 5/31/2000; "Rayovac Maintains Superiority in Hearing Aid Battery Industry," *PR Newswire, Netscape Financial News*, 5/31/2000.

88. "Market leading technology—Unique niche strategy," *Wall Street Corporate Reporter* (June 22–28, 1998), from the Rayovac Corporation's home page (http://www.rayovac.com/wallst.htm), pp. 1–5, 2/6/99.

89. "Rayovac Announces Licensing Agreement With Marathon Projects," *PR Newswire* (10/7/98), http://www.prnewswire.com, 2/6/99.

90. Lank, p. 14D; Don Quinlan, "Industry Report," *Supermarket Business* (February 1996): 63.

91. "Rayovac Increases Market Share on Higher Ad Spending, IBD Says," *Bloomberg News* (12/23/98): A4.

92. "Rayovac Announces China Launch," *PRNewswire* (June 8, 1998), http://www.prnewswire.com, 2/6/99.

93. "Rayovac Prepares Summer Campaign For Push Into China," *The Wall Street Journal* (6/8/98): A15(W).

94. "Market leading technology".

95. "$155 Million Acquisition of ROV Ltd. Completed; Rayovac Launches Global Marketing Initiative," *PR Newswire* (8/9/99), 2 pages (Internet printout from Rayovac's home page).

96. "Rayovac Proceeding With ROV Ltd. Acquisition," *PRNewswire* (1/27/99), http://investing.lycos.com, 1/29/99; "$155 Million Acquisition ..." (8/9/99).

97. "Rayovac Announces Restructuring Initiatives," *PR Newswire* (9/15/99), 2 pages (Internet printout from *Netscape financial news*).

98. "Rayovac Revs Up for Father's Day," *PR Newswire, Netscape Financial News*, 5/30/2000.

99. "CEO David Jones steering Rayovac into new century," *TWICE* (6/29/98): 38.

100. "Rayovac Gobbles Silver Effie Award With Its Successful Battery Campaign," *PR Newswire*, http://www.prnewswire.com/, 6/8/2000.

101. Beardi (6/19/2000), p. 32.

102. "Rayovac Launches World's Longest-Lasting Hearing Aid Battery," *PR Newswire*, http://www.hoovers.com/, 3/21/2000.

103. "Rayovac Recognized by Wal-Mart During Busiest Time of Year," *PR Newswire*, http://www.hoovers.com/, 3/28/2000.

104. "Rayovac Receives Covered SPARC Award," *PR Newswire*, http://www.prnewswire.com/, 6/20/2000.

105. "Rayovac Reports Red-Hot Distribution Gains in Latin America," *PR Newswire*, http://www.prnewswire.com/, 6/14/2000.

106. "Nike's Shares Fall on Jordan's Expected Retirement (Update 2)," *Bloomberg News* (1/12/99), http://www.news.com, 2/9/99.

107. "Yikes! Mike Takes A Hike," *Business Week* (January 25, 1999): 74–76.

108. Ibid., p. 76.

109. Skip Wollenberg, "Will Jordan Keep Air Time?" ABCNEWS.com (1/13/99), http://abcnews.go.com/sections/ business/DailyNews/jordan990113.html, 2/9/99, pp. 1–3.

110. Laura Petrecca, "Jordan trades pitches for piece of the action," *Advertising Age* (3/27/2000), pp. 1, 72.

111. Thane Peterson, "Industry Insider: A Talk with the Man Who Got Rayovac All Charged Up," *Business Week Online* (2/21/00), *Custom E. Prints*, 5/31/2000, p. 1.

DeCopier Technologies, Inc.

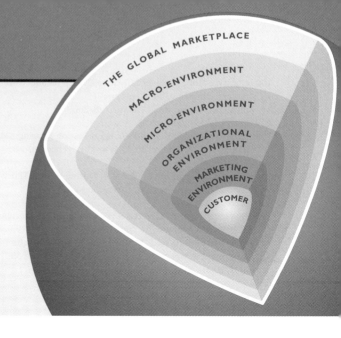

This case was prepared by John H. Friar and Raymond M. Kinnunen, Northeastern University, and Vishal Aggarwal, Principal Consultant, Keane Inc.

We work around the clock. Lauree typically works until 1:30 A.M. and then before she goes to sleep, she sends me several e-mails. I open the e-mails and start work at 4:30 A.M. In my opinion, there is no other way to grow this company. Good things never come easily. You have to work hard.

In December 1998, Dr. Sushil Bhatia, president and CEO, and Lauree Cameron, director of business development, were speaking about DeCopier Technologies, Inc., a start-up company. The company was engaged in the design and development of proprietary "patent-pending" technology that removed ("decopied") toner from laser-printed and photocopied paper and from transparencies. The process rendered the sheets image-free and ready for immediate reuse. The two entrepreneurs were confident that commercialization of the De-Copier™ technology would create a new industry segment that increased the security of confidential printed information, decreased waste, and reduced expenses for paper and transparencies. The

DeCopier™ technology also decopied highlighter, marker, and ballpoint pen and pencil marks. Although confident that the technology would work and that there was a need for their technology, the two also were trying to figure out what steps they needed to take to turn a "neat" technology into a successful business.

THE INSPIRATION FOR THE TECHNOLOGY

The concept for the DeCopier™ technology was born out of Dr. Bhatia's vision for a better way to address office paper waste. After leaving his position as manager of new business development at Avery Dennison (an office products company) in the late summer of 1993, Dr. Bhatia began to investigate options in starting a business of his own. Dr. Bhatia looked at various areas of growth in the marketplace. One area of growth that he found intriguing was the office products market. Dr. Bhatia was primarily intrigued with the proliferation of wastepaper that resulted from the growth in the use of office products such as copiers and laser printers. He became interested in resolving the wastepaper problem as a result of watching tons of office wastepaper accumulate at a local incinerator facility. By 1995, he made a commitment to pursue a solution:

There must be a better way to handle this waste—a better way to save the paper and help the environment.

Dr. Bhatia's initial vision was for an "office paper decopier." He started reading literature on toners, inks, and dyes. He created a chart of a number of different methods for decopying a sheet of paper. He then sketched his concept for a DeCopier™ machine. Dr. Bhatia wanted the decopying process to have universal application—to have the ability to decopy many different types of toner. In the late summer of 1995, Dr. Bhatia did a patent search on his concept for decopying a printed sheet of paper and found nothing significant.

THE TECHNOLOGY AND THE PROCESS

In the spring of 1996, Dr. Bhatia founded Imagex Technologies, Inc., to further develop the DeCopier™ technology. In August 1998, in order to build more equity into the brand, the name of the corporation was changed from Imagex Technologies, Inc., to DeCopier Technologies, Inc. The company was a privately held "C" corporation with principal offices in Framingham, Massachusetts.

Dr. Bhatia explained:

The original design of the DeCopier™ machine was aimed at removing only toner, because 95 percent of office paper is printed with a laser printer or run through the photocopy machine. The company's R&D team is continuing to evolve the technology and broaden its applications. The DeCopier™ technology can also be used to selectively decopy professionally printed (offset-printed) letterhead, decopying the laser printed information and leaving the letterhead printing intact. This is where the cost and waste savings really start to add up.

Ms. Cameron added:

The company has tested and decopied over 40 different types of toners from more than 8,000 sheets of paper and transparencies. Many of these sheets have been decopied, recopied/reprinted, and decopied up to five times with no significant signs of degeneration.

The company had been working with several government agencies and consultants to demonstrate and test the effectiveness of the DeCopier™ technology in decopying confidential printed information. Decopied paper had been tested using high-resolution scanners and other proprietary methods. The results of these tests showed that no traces of the information previously printed on the paper remained.

The best way to describe the decopying process was to think of a reverse photocopier machine. Exhibit 1 provides a sketch of the proposed DeCopier™ machine. The printed sheets were fed into one side of the machine, and the decopied sheets came out the other side. The decopying process involved the application of proprietary formulations that loosened the toner on a sheet of paper. The toner was then brushed from the sheet, and what emerged was a clean sheet ready for immediate reuse. The DeCopier™ machines were being designed as closed-loop systems that recirculated and reused the DeCopier™ fluid and also captured the decopied toner particles so that they could be recycled into plastic filler material. The company had material safety data sheets provided by vendors confirming that the DeCopier™ materials were nontoxic and environmentally safe.

The company's primary focus had been on developing a high-speed industrial DeCopier™ machine with a goal of decopying images from photocopied and laser-printed paper at a rate of 60 sheets per minute. The company's design team (consisting of a machine designer, a control system designer, a chassis enclosure designer, and an industrial designer) had designed the industrial prototype with off-the-shelf parts and subsystems. The initial design work had been finished, and the prototype industrial DeCopier™ machine had been assembled. The development team was working to fine-tune the prototype industrial DeCopier™ machine. Dr. Bhatia said:

We were not interested in reinventing the wheel. The DeCopier™ machine has been designed with off-the-shelf components, which has saved the company time and money. As the company plans to have the DeCopier™ machines contract manufactured, the design work has been done with an eye fixed on manufacturability.

Initially, the machine was to be priced at $45,000. (The first photocopier was priced at approximately $150,000 in today's dollars.) Annual expenses would include a 10 percent maintenance fee and approximately $150,000 in supplies (see Exhibit 2).

EXHIBIT I

DeCopier Technologies, Inc.

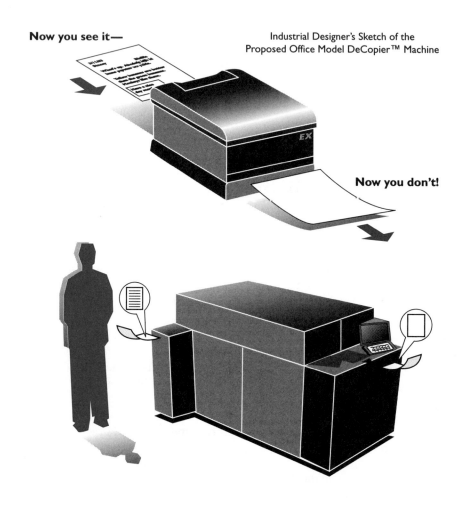

Now you see it—

Industrial Designer's Sketch of the
Proposed Office Model DeCopier™ Machine

Now you don't!

EXHIBIT 2

Financials

Projected Number of Industrial DeCopier™ Machines Sold			
	FY 1999	**FY 2000**	**FY 2001**
New Industrial DeCopier™ Machines	12	58	174
Installed Base	12	70	244

DeCopier Technologies, Inc., 3-Year Revenue Projections (in dollars)

Revenues	FY 1999	FY 2000	FY 2001
DeCopier™ Machines	$ 540,000	$ 2,320,000	$ 6,090,000
DeCopier™ Supplies	301,363	6,002,957	16,813,634
DeCopier™ Machine Maintenance	54,000	232,000	609,000
Total Revenues	**895,363**	**8,554,957**	**23,512,634**
Net Income Before Taxes	**($2,250,170)**	**$ 2,119,251**	**$ 10,372,784**

The company initially expects the following sources of revenue:

- Revenue from the sale of industrial DeCopier™ machines
- Revenue from DeCopier™ supplies
- Revenue from industrial DeCopier™ machine maintenance contracts

In addition to these sources of revenue, other potential sources of revenue include international sales, revenues from the sale of proposed office and desktop DeCopier™ machines, decopying service center franchise fees, and other DeCopier™ technology licensing fees and royalties.

Milestone Goals

- Completion of prototype industrial DeCopier™ machine—Q1 of 1999
- Shipment of beta industrial DeCopier™ machines—Spring 1999
- Receipt of first orders for industrial DeCopier™ machines—Spring 1999
- Production ramp-up of industrial DeCopier™ machines—Spring-Summer 1999
- Lease and/or purchase of space to mix in bulk and package DeCopier™ fluids—Spring 1999
- Delivery of first orders for industrial DeCopier™ machines—Fall 1999

The projected life of the machine would be the same as a copier machine (7 to 10 years) and consume approximately the same amount of electricity. The company also believed that once proven, the shape of the high-speed industrial DeCopier™ machine could be modified and reduced to produce smaller DeCopier™ machines that would decopy up to 30 sheets of paper/transparencies per minute.

INDUSTRY TRENDS AND PROJECTIONS

The information revolution had to date multiplied rather than replaced paper use. According to the International Institute for Environment and Development, paper use had trebled during the last 30 years and could double again by 2001. According to research conducted by Giga Information Group, Inc.,

International Data Corp., and Dataquest, Inc., the number of sheets of paper consumed in U.S. offices was increasing by 20 percent each year and was expected to hit 6 trillion sheets by the year 2000. Dr. Bhatia elaborated:

> Regulation of waste is a major concern not only in the United States but also around the world where landfill space is scarce to nonexistent. In many European countries, landfills are mandated to close by the year 2000. In Hong Kong, where landfill space is nonexistent, waste is often endlessly carried around on a barge.

According to the Association of Records Managers and Administrators, 95 percent of all information was recorded on paper. Compared to the 1994 world average of 97 pounds, the U.S. per capita amount of paper waste was nearly 600 pounds, approximately 1.61 pounds per person per day, 54 percent of which was white sheet paper (interview: North Shore Recycled Fibers, 1996). Since 1980, per capita consumption of paper products in the United States had grown 43 percent (see Exhibit 3).

Paper production and waste were major contributors to the erosion of the environment. Between 1990 and 1997, recovery rates (recycling) in the United States jumped from 19.9 percent to 38.2 percent, but the overall amount of paper produced also jumped. By the year 2000, the American Forest and Paper Association estimated that 50 percent of the paper consumed in the United States would be recovered. The days when a company freely tossed its wastepaper into the basket were gone. Companies paid large sums to either recycle their wastepaper or have it hauled away to a landfill. In Europe and the rest of the world, companies and citizens were much more environmentally conscious than their U.S. counterparts and were forced to recycle at a higher rate because of governmental regulation, limited supplies of wood pulp, and finite landfill space. In Europe, approximately 45 percent of paper was recycled; in Japan, over 55 percent of paper was recycled.

Overhead transparencies could also be recycled by the DeCopier™ technology. After a presentation was completed, the imaged transparencies were often thrown away and entered the waste stream as long-lasting landfill. Although transparencies were categorized as type 1 polyester, which was normally easy to recycle, the recycling of imaged transparencies was very complicated, and most recycling centers did not accept them. 3M Company, a major manufacturer of transparency film, projected that the U.S. transparency market would be over 945 million sheets in 1998 (10,500 tons). It was also estimated that in 1998 approximately 750 million sheets of transparency film (83 percent of what was sold annually) was dumped into U.S. landfills. This was equivalent to 15 million pounds or 6,800 metric tons of polyester. Dr. Bhatia explained:

EXHIBIT 3

The Paperless Office Irony

Although computer use had increased dramatically, the use of paper had also increased:

- In the United States alone, in 1996 over 1.5 trillion sheets (3 million tons) of paper were photocopied and laser printed.
- The number of sheets used in U.S. offices was going up 20 percent each year and was expected to hit 6 trillion sheets by the year 2000.
- Sheets of paper used in laser printers and photocopiers were projected to exceed 3.3 trillion by 2001.
- The installed base of photocopiers and laser and ink-jet printers was projected to reach over 60 million units in the United States alone by 1998.
- Printing skyrocketed 40 percent when e-mail was introduced in an office.
- The paper consumed in U.S. offices by 2001 could wrap around the earth six times.

Source: International Data Corp., Dataquest, Inc., and Giga Information Group, Inc., as quoted in *The Wall Street Journal*, May 12, 1998.

Transparency film is considerably more expensive than a sheet of paper. Prices per new transparency sheet range from approximately $.30 to $1.26, and the cost of a sheet of paper ranges from $.01 to $.03. Assuming the purchase price for transparencies is at the low end of the range, the annual cost to companies, universities, and individuals for purchasing those transparency sheets, not including the costs associated with dumping them into landfill, is over $225 million.

Another common question that is raised is whether the use of transparency film has diminished with the implementation of PowerPoint software and other computerized means of presentation. The company's research suggests that because computers and program compatibility are unpredictable, most people still have transparencies as a backup to the computer presentation.

SECURITY OF CONFIDENTIAL DOCUMENTS

Prior to the introduction of shredders, confidential documents were incinerated or buried. It was rumored that some company executives actually transported confidential documents to the landfill in person. The landfill operator dug a hole, the executive tossed the confidential documents into the hole, and the hole was filled in. In 1999, the United States government and businesses annually spent in excess of $300 million on document destruction equipment, primarily shredders and disintegrators. Despite these precautions, it was estimated by the American Society for Industrial Security and the National Counterintelligence Center that potential losses from intellectual property theft for U.S.-based companies were in the range of $24 billion in 1998. A large percentage of these losses occurred by illegal means: stealing, "dumpster-diving," or by confidential documents just ending up in the wrong hands. Much of this intellectual property was printed on paper and transparencies. Ms. Cameron said:

> Current methods of confidential document destruction are no longer considered to be the most effective means of addressing the issue of document security. Both government and business are in search of a better method of maintaining the security of printed information.

Dr. Bhatia concluded:

> Taken together, these facts describe a very large and lucrative business opportunity for a company like DeCopier Technologies, Inc., which has proprietary technology that decopies printed sheets of paper and transparencies, rendering them image-free and ready for immediate reuse. The DeCopier™ technology provides a solution that addresses both the need to maintain the security of confidential information and the need to decrease the generation of current and future waste.

THE POTENTIAL MARKET

Contrary to speculation that computers would transform the American workplace into a paperless environment, the opposite had occurred. As was evident from the industry trends and projections over the last 20 years, the increased availability of photocopiers, fax machines, and computer printers had resulted in a dramatic increase in the use of office paper and transparencies. Dr. Bhatia assumed that these projections could also be applied to the recovery of laser-printed and photocopied paper and transparencies. Based upon these recovery projections, he estimated that by the year 2000 over 1.38 trillion sheets of laser-printed paper and transparencies would be recovered and that the size of the potential U.S. market for the DeCopier™ technology would be over $18 billion.

Many companies, including banks, law firms, and governmental agencies, routinely threw confidential documents into the wastebasket. These confidential documents often contained names, addresses, phone numbers, social security numbers, patent drafts, and proprietary research. One's entire identity or a proprietary project could often be recreated by sorting through the trash. Ms. Cameron commented:

> There is concern and paranoia about others getting into the trash and reconstructing confidential documents, business plans, even people's identities. Many individuals and companies now shred everything.

The company had identified two initial types of customers for the proposed DeCopier™ products:

1. Entities that were concerned primarily with document security and wanted to decopy

confidential printed information to prevent its dissemination (and were interested in the secondary benefit of being able to immediately reuse the sheets)

2. End users of sheets of paper and transparencies who wanted to reduce waste and save money.

TARGET MARKET

The company's management realized that it would take some time for people to accept the "decopying" concept and to change waste disposal habits. Management was confident, however, that it would not take as long as when recycling efforts were first initiated. Office workers, students, and others were already accustomed to separating white paper into recycle bins. Dr. Bhatia elaborated:

> If one thinks back to when the concept of recycling was first introduced: People had their basketball hoops over their wastepaper baskets in the corner of their offices. More people are now in the habit of putting their white sheet paper in the recycling bin; there is a certain level of guilt associated with not recycling.

There were two major differences between decopying and recycling or shredding. With decopying, there would be (1) additional and/or substitute bins for decopying paper and transparencies and (2) both paper and transparencies would be decopied for immediate reuse rather than be recycled or thrown away. The cost of a shredder ranged from under $100 for personal models to $2,000 for heavy duty all-purpose shredding machines. In addition, it cost approximately $150 to have a large dumpster (30 feet long) with approximately 10 tons of recyclable material taken away by a disposal company. However, disposal companies had recently paid $10 per ton for the recyclable material. Consequently, the net cost to dispose of recyclable material was approximately $5 per ton. To dispose of the same paper as normal trash would cost approximately $110 per ton. Data gathered on U.S. paper recycling has shown that:[1]

- Paper-recycling companies use an industry standard that states for every one administrative employee, companies recycle 1 pound of office paper per day or 0.1825 tons per year.

- A major university recycles approximately 500 tons of office paper per year.

- A major U.S. manufacturing company with 32,000 employees recycles around 128 tons of office paper per year.

Because of this information, the company believed that eventually the cost savings and environmental aspects of the decopying technology would catch on. At that point, the company would begin to pursue educational institutions, *Fortune* 1000 companies, quick printers, and copy shops.

INTERNATIONAL OPPORTUNITIES

The company also believed that the DeCopier™ technology had global market potential. Many inquiries about the company's proposed line of DeCopier™ products had come from around the world (Canada, Europe, the Far East, and the Middle East). The high price of paper and mandates to close landfills in the rest of the world created an immediate international market for the DeCopier™ products. Inquiries had come from customers who wanted to purchase DeCopier™ machines, individuals who wanted to know if the company was publicly traded, others inquiring whether they could buy stock, and from potential distributors who wanted territorial exclusives on selling the DeCopier™ products. The company had to decide where to launch the product first: in the United States or internationally. Dr. Bhatia added:

> From a recycling point of view, Europe might be a starting market for us, but from a security point of view, the U.S. market is the right market on which to focus.

COMPETITION

The company's management strongly believed that the foundation to its competitive edge and value was its intellectual property assets. Although there were substitutes to the company's product—shredder machines, incinerators, disintegrators, recycling and waste management companies—based upon the company's market research and patent searches, the management team did not believe that any other entity had successfully developed, filed for, or received a patent for this type of product. Dr. Bhatia commented on the competition:

> Ricoh Corporation has been working on a machine for some time that decopies Ricoh ink from Ricoh coated paper. It has a very limited application—not universal. Ricoh has been talking about launching this machine, but we have heard nothing definitive: It seems that they are still working on their product. Ricoh's proposed machine decopies at the rate of 3 sheets per minute; ours does 60 sheets per minute. We do not consider that to be competition.

In anticipation of potential competition, the company had built a solid wall of protection around its intellectual property, a wall that created a significant barrier to entry. Through careful strategic planning, the company had field and continued to file for patents on both the DeCopier™ technology and the decopying process; had field for trademark protection; and had instituted strict policies to protect its trade secrets and other know-how. The company intended to continue to pursue patent and other protections for its proprietary DeCopier™ products and technologies to enhance its ability to maintain its competitive advantage.

THE FINANCIAL SITUATION AND THE FUTURE

Thus far, Dr. Bhatia had substantially funded the company's operations. Additionally, the company had received funding from private investors and a U.S. Environmental Protection Agency small business innovation research (SBIR) grant to further fund the development of a prototype. A summary of financial projections for 1999, 2000, and 2001 are presented in Exhibit 2. The selling price of a DeCopier™ machine was expected to decrease to $35,000 in the year 2001.

Dr. Bhatia wanted to focus the company's strength on its ability to design and develop innovative technology. The company preferred to stay an R&D organization. It did not want to build manufacturing and sales capabilities. The company was actively seeking, therefore, one or more strategic partners to manufacture and distribute its proposed line of DeCopier™ machines. With this strategy, the successful manufacture, marketing, distribution, and sale of the DeCopier™ machines

were contingent upon forming alliances with one or more entities with complementary strengths and expertise. An ideal alliance would be with a partner that was vertically integrated from manufacturing through sales. Potential strategic partners included laser printer and photocopier and fax machine manufacturers and distributors; shredder and disintegrator manufacturers and distributors; computer manufacturers; paper and paper-recycling mills; specialty chemical companies that supply chemicals to toner manufacturers; office supply/equipment companies; software companies; and quick copy, printing, and imaging companies. The company had already entered into preliminary discussions with a number of potential strategic partners. Dr. Bhatia explained:

> Instead of investing time and money in building manufacturing plants and buying manufacturing equipment, pursuit of strategic partners will allow the company to reinvest its earnings in research and development to further evolve the DeCopier™ technology.

The company wanted to maintain control of the DeCopier™ supplies business, however. The company's strength and competitive advantage in the marketplace were based on its proprietary decopying formulations. The company intended to use some capital to lease and/or purchase additional space to prepare, mix, and package the DeCopier™ fluid in bulk.

Dr. Bhatia commented on the company infrastructure and company goals:

> We have a strong infrastructure and have assembled an experienced management team to develop and market the proposed DeCopier™ technology. I keep telling Lauree and others that I am fortunate to be surrounded by a good set of people who are helping the project move in the right direction. That is what has given us success today and that is what carries the day at the end of it all. (See Exhibit 4 for a profile of the management team.)
>
> Our initial goal is to further develop and promote the DeCopier™ technology. We intend to form a strategic alliance to manufacture the industrial DeCopier™ machines or license out the DeCopier™ machine technology and maintain control of the DeCopier™ supplies business. The exact shape of our exit strategy is unknown at this point and will depend in part

EXHIBIT 4

Management Team

President and Chairman of the Board   Sushil Bhatia

Dr. Sushil Bhatia had been president of the company since its inception. Dr. Bhatia was also president of the privately held JMD Manufacturing, Inc., a company specializing in contact marking and coding equipment, new product R&D, international technology transfer, and global trading. Previously, Dr. Bhatia had held the positions of manager of new business development and director of international business development at Avery Dennison, a *Fortune* 200 company specializing in the field of printing, labeling, and packaging. Dr. Bhatia holds a Ph.D. in physical chemistry from the University of Liege in Belgium and an MBA from Suffolk University in Boston. He also holds a BS and an MS from universities in India. Dr. Bhatia had over 20 years of senior-level experience in new technologies, business development, research and development, international technology transfer, and licensing. He had been awarded a number of patents for the technologies and new products he had developed individually and jointly. The products that Dr. Bhatia worked to develop have resulted in over $50 million in sales. These products include copier labels, electro-sensitive paper, glue stick products, rub transfer images, a cold seal packaging protection system for electronic goods, high-image labels using UV systems, hot metal adhesive technology for a large number of pressure-sensitive labeling systems (i.e., name tags), a cold glue report binding system, microbind, nonhazardous water-based coating technology at MAC-TAC, (Ohio) and a multicolor roller for marking and coding markets. These products have resulted in Dr. Bhatia's winning an innovation award at Avery Dennison and a recognition award for a new product in a national competition. Dr. Bhatia was a past president of the Framingham Rotary Club. He was also a member of the Metro West Massachusetts Chamber of Commerce board of directors.

Chief Financial Officer   Joseph Faris

Joseph F. Faris had been the company's chief financial officer since its inception. Mr. Faris had been an independent financial consultant and had served as a part-time chief financial officer/controller to companies in several different industries since 1986. From 1984 to 1986, Mr. Faris was controller to Amnet, Inc., a privately held company specializing in developing products for the communications industry. From 1977 to 1984, Mr. Faris was a financial analyst and financial supervisor at Shell Oil Company. Mr. Faris received his BS degree in accounting from Northeastern University and was a certified public accountant.

Director of Business Development and Partnering   Lauree Cameron

Lauree Cameron had served as the director of business development and partnering at the company since 1997. Ms. Cameron had over 10 years of in-depth experience working with both large and small companies to manage and successfully commercialize intellectual property assets. Prior to her position at the company, Ms. Cameron was the director of business development at EKMS, Inc., an intellectual property management-consulting firm in Cambridge, MA. From 1987 through 1996, Ms. Cameron was the director of U.S. operations for CDR International, a London-based consultancy; an intellectual property manager for The Timberland Company; and a senior intellectual property/litigation paralegal for Sherburne, Powers & Needham, PC. Ms. Cameron was part of a management team that started and operated a local microbrewery and currently owns a minority interest in a north-end restaurant. Ms. Cameron has been on the part-time faculty at Northeastern University since 1993 and at Massachusetts Continuing Legal Education (MCLE) since 1992. Ms. Cameron earned her BA in international relations from the University of Maine and did graduate work in international law and German at the University of Salzburg in Austria. Ms. Cameron received her Certificate of International Business German from the Goethe Institute and was a 2000 candidate for her MBA at F. W. Olin Graduate School of Business at Babson College.

EXHIBIT 4 *(continued)*

Management Team

Board of Directors

Edward J. Marino	–	President of DANKA Services International
Edward F. Murphy, Jr.	–	President and CEO of Murphy Associates
Richard L. Pellegrini	–	President of Pilgrim Associates
Steven F. Snyder	–	President of APPLIED, Inc.

Board of Advisors

Samir Desai	—	President and CEO of Systems Resources Corporation
Ashok Kalelkar	—	Corporate Senior VP and CPO of Arthur D. Little, Inc.
Jit Saxena	—	President and CEO of Applix, Inc.

In addition to this, the company retained the services of a sales advisor, a technical advisor, and several professional advisors (including a corporate counsel, a patent counsel, a certified public accountant, and an investment banker).

on strategic partners or licensees. At this time, we can conceive of the following potential avenues of exit: acquisition by one of the strategic partners, an outright sale of the technology, or an IPO.

All of the studies indicated that photocopying numbers were both enormous and rising, resulting in a huge potential market for DeCopier Technologies. In order to become a successful business, however, the management team had to make several important decisions. The financial projections showed that if DeCopier Technologies sold the machines themselves, the company would need to raise at least $2.25 million. This would be difficult to do, however, because the company had yet to determine which market was the best to enter. Investors tended to shy away from companies that could not produce a customer in hand, so the question of which market or markets to target was a major decision that had to be made. There were numerous market opportunities, which included domestic or international recycling and document security for both commercial and government customers.

If the company tried to work through a partner, the question remained as to who would be willing to be that partner. The technology was only at the prototype stage and had yet to be tested at any beta sites. A potential partner would need to be willing to accept the additional technical development risk along with all the market development risk. Either way the company decided to go, selling direct or through a partner, the management team was constrained by its small size and, therefore, realized that it could not develop the product, perform the marketing research, find potential customers, and find potential partners all at the same time. They needed to decide upon the most appropriate first steps.

Endnote

1. This data was gathered via a telephone conversation with a major recycling company.

Circus Circus Enterprises, Inc. (1998)

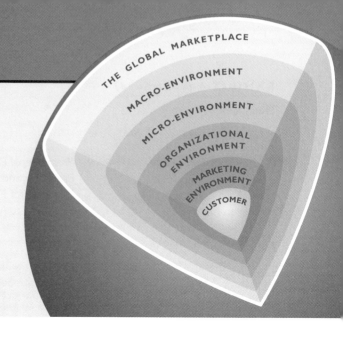

This case was prepared by Professors John K. Ross III, Michael J. Keefe, and Bill J. Middlebrook of Southwest Texas State University.

We possess the resources to accomplish the big projects: the knowhow, the financial power and the places to invest. The renovation of our existing projects will soon be behind us, which last year represented the broadest scope of construction ever taken on by a gaming company. Now we are well-positioned to originate new projects. Getting big projects right is the route to future wealth in gaming; big successful projects tend to prove long staying power in our business. When the counting is over, we think our customers and investors will hold the winning hand.

Annual Report, 1997

Big projects and a winning hand. Circus Circus does seem to have both. And big projects they are, with huge pink and white striped concrete circus tents, a 600-foot-long river boat replica, a giant castle, and a great pyramid. The company's latest project, Mandalay Bay, will include a 3700-room hotel/casino, an 11-acre aquatic environment with beaches, a snorkeling reef, and a swim-up shark exhibit.

COMPANY HISTORY

Circus Circus Enterprises, Inc. (hereafter Circus), describes itself as in the business of entertainment and has been one of the innovators in the theme resort concept popular in casino gaming. Their areas of operation are the glitzy vacation and convention Mecca's of Las Vegas, Reno, and Laughlin, Nevada, as well as other locations in the United States and abroad. Historically, Circus's marketing of its products has been called "right out of the bargain basement" and has catered to "low rollers." Circus has continued to broaden its market and now aims more at the middle-income gambler and family-oriented vacationers as well as the more upscale traveler and player.

Circus was purchased in 1974 for $50,000 as a small and unprofitable casino operation by partners William G. Bennett, an aggressive cost cutter who ran furniture stores before entering the gaming industry in 1965, and William N. Pennington (see Exhibit A for board of directors and top managers). The partners were able to rejuvenate Circus with fresh marketing, went public with a stock offering in October 1983, and experienced rapid growth and high profitability over time. Within the 5-year period between 1993 and 1997, the average return on invested capital was 16.5 percent, and Circus had generated over $1 billion in free cash

EXHIBIT A

Directors and Officers: Circus Circus Enterprises, Inc.

Name	Age	Title
Directors		
Clyde T. Turner	59	Chairman of the Board and CEO, Circus Circus Enterprises
Michael S. Ensign	59	Vice Chairman of the Board and COO, Circus Circus Enterprises
Glenn Schaeffer	43	President and CFO, Circus Circus Enterprises
Yvett Landau		Vice President, General Counsel, and Secretary
Les Martin		Vice President and Chief Accounting Officer
William A. Richardson	50	Vice Chairman of the Board and Executive Vice President, Circus Circus Enterprises
Richard P. Banis	52	Former President and COO, Circus Circus Enterprises
Arthur H. Bilger	44	Former President and COO, New World Communications Group International
Richard A. Etter	58	Former Chairman and CEO, Bank of America–Nevada
William E. Bannen, M.D.	48	Vice President/Chief Medical Officer, Blue Cross-Blue Shield of Nevada
Donna B. More	40	Partner, Law Firm of Freeborn & Peters
Michael D. McKee	51	Executive Vice President, The Irving Company
Officers		
Clyde T. Turner		Chairman of the Board and Chief Executive Officer
Michael S. Ensign		Vice Chairman of the Board and Chief Operating Officer
Glenn Schaeffer		President, Chief Financial Officer, and Treasurer
William A. Richardson		Vice Chairman of the Board and Executive Vice President, Circus Circus Enterprises
Tony Alamo		Senior Vice President, Operations
Gregg Solomon		Senior Vice President, Operations
Kurt D. Sullivan		Senior Vice President, Operations
Steve Greathouse		Senior Vice President, Operations

Source: Annual Report 1998; Proxy statement, May 1, 1998.

flow. Today, Circus is one of the major players in the Las Vegas, Laughlin, and Reno markets in terms of square footage of casino space and number of hotel rooms—despite the incredible growth in both markets. For the first time in company history, casino gaming operations in 1997 provided slightly less than half the total revenue, and that trend continued into 1998 (see Exhibit B). On January 31, 1998, Circus reported a net income of approximately $89.9 million on revenues of $1.35 billion. This was down slightly from 1997's more than $100 million net income on revenues of $1.3 billion. During the same year, Circus invested over $585.8 million in capital expenditures, and another $663.3 million was invested in fiscal year 1998.

CIRCUS CIRCUS OPERATIONS

Circus defines entertainment as pure play and fun, and it goes out of the way to see that customers have plenty of opportunities for both. Each Circus location has a distinctive personality. Circus Circus Las Vegas is the world of the Big Top, where live circus acts perform free every 30 minutes. Kids may cluster around video games while the adults migrate to

EXHIBIT B

Circus Circus Enterprises, Inc.: Sources of Revenues as a Percentage of Net Revenues

	1998	1997	1996	1995
Casinos	46.7%	49.2%	51.2%	52.3%
Food & Beverage	15.9	15.8	15.5	16.2
Hotel	24.4	22.0	21.4	19.9
Other	10.5	11.0	12.2	14.2
Unconsolidated	7.3	6.5	3.5	.5
Less: Complimentary allowances	4.8	4.5	3.8	3.1

Source: Circus Circus 10-k, January 31, 1995–1998.

nickel slot machines and dollar game tables. Located at the north end of the Vegas strip, Circus Circus Las Vegas sits on 69 acres of land with 3744 hotel rooms, shopping areas, two specialty restaurants, a buffet with seating for 1200, fast-food shops, cocktail lounges, video arcades, 109,000 square feet of casino space, and includes the Grand Slam Canyon, a 5-acre glass-enclosed theme park including a four-loop roller coaster. Approximately 384 guests also may stay at nearby Circusland RV Park. For the year ending January 31, 1997, $126.7 million was invested in this property for new rooms and remodeling, with another $35.2 million in fiscal year 1998.

Luxor, an Egyptian-themed hotel and casino complex, opened on October 15, 1993, when 10,000 people entered to play the 2245 slot and video poker games and 110 table games in the 120,000-square-foot casino in the hotel atrium (reported to be the world's largest). By the end of the opening weekend, 40,000 people per day were visiting the 30-story bronze pyramid that encases the hotel and entertainment facilities.

Luxor features a 30-story pyramid and two new 22-story hotel towers including 492 suites and is connected to Excalibur by a climate-controlled skyway with moving walkways. Situated at the south end of the Las Vegas strip on a 64-acre site adjacent to Excalibur, Luxor features a food and entertainment area on three different levels beneath the hotel atrium. The pyramid's hotel rooms can be reached from the four corners of the building by state-of-the-art "inclinators" that travel at a 39-degree angle. Parking is available for nearly 3200 vehicles, including a covered garage that contains approximately 1800 spaces.

The Luxor underwent major renovations costing $323.3 million during fiscal year 1997 and another $116.5 million in fiscal year 1998. The resulting complex contains 4425 hotel rooms, extensively renovated casino space, an additional 20,000 square feet of convention area, an 800-seat buffet, a series of IMAX attractions, five theme restaurants, seven cocktail lounges, and a variety of specialty shops. Circus expects to draw significant walk-in traffic to the newly refurbished Luxor and is one of the principal components of the Masterplan Mile.

Located next to the Luxor, Excalibur is one of the first sights travelers see as they exit interstate highway 15 (management was confident that the sight of a giant, colorful medieval castle would make a lasting impression on mainstream tourists and vacationing families arriving in Las Vegas). Guests cross a drawbridge, with moat, onto a cobblestone walkway where multicolored spires, turrets, and battlements loom above. The castle walls are four 28-story hotel towers containing a total of 4008 rooms. Inside is a medieval world complete with a Fantasy Faire inhabited by strolling jugglers, fire eaters, and acrobats, as well as a Royal Village complete with peasants, serfs, and ladies-in-waiting around medieval theme shops. The 110,000-square-foot casino encompasses 2442 slot machines, more than 89 game tables, a sports book, and a poker and keno area. There are 12 restaurants, capable of feeding more than 20,000 people daily, and a 1000-seat amphitheater. Excalibur, which opened in June 1990, was built for $294 million and primarily financed with internally generated funds. In the year ending January 31, 1997, Excalibur contributed 23 percent of the organization's revenues, down from 33 percent in 1993, yet 1997 was a record year, generating the company's highest margins and over $100 million in operating cash flow. In fiscal year 1998, Excalibur underwent $25.1 million in renovations and was connected to the Luxor by enclosed, moving walkways.

Situated between the two anchors on the Las Vegas strip are two smaller casinos owned and operated by Circus. The Silver City Casino and Slots-A-Fun primarily depend on the foot traffic along the strip for their gambling patrons. Combined, they offer more than 1202 slot machines and 46 gaming tables on 34,900 square feet of casino floor.

Circus owns and operates 10 properties in Nevada and 1 in Mississippi and has a 50 percent ownership in three others (see Exhibit C).

All of Circus' operations do well in the city of Las Vegas. However, Circus Circus 1997 operational earnings for the Luxor and Circus Circus Las Vegas were off 38 percent from the previous year. Management credits the disruption in services due to renovations for this decline.

EXHIBIT C

Circus Circus Enterprises, Inc.: Properties and Percent of Total Revenues

| Properties | Percent Revenues | | | |
	1998	1997	1996	1995
Las Vegas				
Circus Circus Las Vegas	25*	24*	27*	29*
Excalibur	21	23	23	25
Luxor	23	17	20	24
Slots-A-Fun and Silver City				
Reno				
Circus Circus Reno				
Laughlin				
Colorado Bell	12†	12†	13†	16†
Edgewater				
Jean, Nevada				
Gold Strike	6‡	6‡	4‡	NA
Nevada Landing				
Henderson, Nevada				
Railroad Pass				
Tunica, Mississippi				
Gold Strike	4	4	5	3
50% ownership:				
Silver Legacy, Reno, Nevada	7.3	6.5§	3.5	§0.5 §
Monte Carlo, Las Vegas, Nevada				
Grand Victoria Riverboat Casino,				
Elgin, Illinois				

*Combined with revenues from Circus Circus Reno.
†Colorado Bell and Edgewater have been combined.
‡Gold Strike and Nevada Landing have been combined.
§Revenues of unconsolidated affiliates have been combined. Revenues from Slots-A-Fun and Silver City, management fees, and other income were not separately reported.

However, Circus' combined hotel room occupancy rates had remained above 90 percent due, in part, to low room rates ($45 to $69 at Circus Circus Las Vegas) and popular buffets. Each of the major properties contain large, inexpensive buffets that management believes make staying with Circus more attractive. Yet, recently, results show a room occupancy rate of 87.5 percent, due in part to the building boom in Las Vegas.

The company's other big-top facility is Circus Circus Reno. With the addition of Skyway Tower in 1985, this big top now offers a total of 1605 hotel rooms, 60,600 square feet of casino, a buffet that can seat 700 people, shops, video arcades, cocktail lounges, midway games, and circus acts. Circus Circus Reno had several marginal years but has become one of the leaders in the Reno market. Circus anticipates that recent remodeling, at a cost of $25.6 million, will increase this property's revenue-generating potential.

The Colorado Belle and the Edgewater Hotel are located in Laughlin, Nevada, on the banks of the Colorado River, a city 90 miles south of Las Vegas. The Colorado Belle, opened in 1987, features a huge paddle wheel riverboat replica, buffet, cocktail lounges, and shops. The Edgewater, acquired in 1983, has a southwestern motif, a 57,000-square-foot casino, a bowling center, buffet, and cocktail lounges. Combined, these two properties contain 2700 rooms and over 120,000 square feet of casino. These two operations contributed 12 percent of the company's revenues in the year ended January 31, 1997, and again in 1998, down from 21 percent in 1994. The extensive proliferation of casinos throughout the region, primarily on Indian land, and the development of megaresorts in Las Vegas have seriously eroded outlying markets such as Laughlin.

Three properties purchased in 1995 and located in Jean and Henderson, Nevada, represent continuing investments by Circus in outlying markets. The Gold Strike and Nevada Landing service the I-15 market between Las Vegas and southern California. These properties have over 73,000 square feet of casino space, 2140 slot machines, and 42 gaming tables combined. Each has limited hotel space (1116 rooms total) and depends heavily on I-15 traffic. The Railroad Pass is considered a local casino and is dependent on Henderson residents as its market. This smaller casino contains only 395 slot machines and 11 gaming tables.

Gold Strike Tunica (formally Circus Circus Tunica) is a dockside casino located in Tunica, Mississippi, opened in 1994 on 24 acres of land located along the Mississippi River, approximately 20 miles south of Memphis. In 1997, operating income declined by more than 50 percent due to the increase in competition and lack of hotel rooms. Circus decided to renovate this property and add a 1200-room tower hotel. Total cost for all remodeling was $119.8 million.

Joint Ventures

Circus is currently engaged in three joint ventures through the wholly owned subsidiary Circus Participant. In Las Vegas, Circus joined with Mirage Resorts to build and operate the Monte Carlo, a hotel-casino with 3002 rooms designed along the lines of the grand casinos of the Mediterranean. It is located on 46 acres (with 600 feet on the Las Vegas strip) between the New York–New York casino and the soon to be completed Bellagio, with all three casinos to be connected by monorail. The Monte Carlo features a 90,000-square-foot casino containing 2221 slot machines and 95 gaming tables, along with a 550-seat bingo parlor, high-tech arcade rides, restaurants and buffets, a microbrewery, approximately 15,000 square feet of meeting and convention space, and a 1200-seat theater. Opened on June 21, 1996, the Monte Carlo generated $14.6 million as Circus's share in operating income for the first 7 months of operation.

In Elgin, Illinois, Circus is in a 50 percent partnership with Hyatt Development Corporation in The Grand Victoria. Styled to resemble a Victorian riverboat, this floating casino and land-based entertainment complex includes some 36,000 square feet of casino space, containing 977 slot machines and 56 gaming tables. The adjacent land-based complex contains two movie theaters, a 240-seat buffet, restaurants, and parking for approximately 2000 vehicles. Built for a total of $112 million, The Grand Victoria returned to Circus $44 million in operating income in 1996.

The third joint venture is a 50 percent partnership with Eldorado Limited in the Silver Legacy. Opened in 1995, this casino is located between Circus Circus Reno and the Eldorado Hotel and Casino on two city blocks in downtown Reno, Nevada. The Silver Legacy has 1711 hotel rooms, 85,000 square feet of casino, 2275 slot machines, and 89 gaming

EXHIBIT D

Selected Financial Information

	FY98	*FY97*	*FY96*	*FY95*	*FY94*	*FY93*	*FY92*	*FY91*
Earnings per share	0.40	0.99	1.33	1.59	1.34	2.05	1.84	1.39
Current ratio	0.85	1.17	1.30	1.35	0.95	0.90	1.14	0.88
Total liabilities/ total assets	0.65	0.62	0.44	0.54	0.57	0.48	0.58	0.77
Operating profit margin	17.4%	17%	19%	22%	21%	24.4%	24.9%	22.9%

Source: Circus Circus Annual Reports and 10k's, 1991–1998.

tables. Management seems to believe that the Silver Legacy holds promise; however, the Reno market is suffering, and the opening of the Silver Legacy has cannibalized the Circus Circus Reno market.

Circus engaged in a fourth joint venture to penetrate the Canadian market, but on January 23, 1997, it announced that it had been bought out by Hilton Hotels Corporation, one of three partners in the venture.

Circus has achieved success through an aggressive growth strategy and a corporate structure designed to enhance that growth. A strong cash position, innovative ideas, and attention to cost control have allowed Circus to satisfy the bottom line during a period when competitors typically were taking on large debt obligations to finance new projects (see Exhibits D, E, F, and G). Yet the market is changing. Gambling of all kinds has spread across the country; no longer does the average individual need to go to Las Vegas or New Jersey. Instead, gambling can be found as close as the local quick market (lottery), bingo hall, many Indian reservations, the Mississippi River, and others. There are now almost 300 casinos in Las Vegas alone, 60 in Colorado, and 160 in California. In order to maintain a competitive edge, Circus has continued to invest heavily in renovation of existing properties (a strategy common to the entertainment/amusement industry) and continues to develop new projects.

New Ventures

Circus currently has three new projects planned for opening within the near future. The largest project, named Mandalay Bay, is scheduled for completion in the first quarter of 1999 and is estimated to cost

EXHIBIT E

Twelve-Year Summary

Revenues (in thousands)		Net Income
FY 98	$1,354,487	$ 89,908
FY 97	1,334,250	100,733
FY 96	1,299,596	128,898
FY 95	1,170,182	136,286
FY 94	954,923	116,189
FY 93	843,025	117,322
FY 92	806,023	103,348
FY 91	692,052	76,292
FY 90	522,376	76,064
FY 89	511,960	81,714
FY 88	458,856	55,900
FY 87	373,967	28,198
FY 86	306,993	37,375

Source: Circus Circus Annual Reports and 10k's, 1986–1998.

$950 million (excluding land). Circus owns a contiguous mile of the southern end of the Las Vegas strip that it calls the Masterplan Mile and which currently contains the Excalibur and Luxor resorts. Located next to the Luxor, Mandalay Bay will aim for the upscale traveler and player and will be styled as a South Seas adventure. The resort will contain a 43-story hotel/casino with over 3700 rooms and an 11-acre aquatic environment. The aquatic environment will contain a surfing beach, swim-up shark tank, and snorkeling reef. A Four Seasons Hotel with some 400 rooms will complement the remainder of Mandalay Bay. Circus anticipates that the remainder

EXHIBIT F

Circus Circus Enterprises, Inc.: Annual Income (Year Ended January 31, in thousands)

	1/31/98	1/31/97	1/31/96	1/31/95	1/31/94
Revenues					
Casino	$ 632,122	$ 655,902	$ 664,772	$ 612,115	$ 538,813
Rooms	330,644	294,241	278,807	232,346	176,001
Food and beverage	215,584	210,384	201,385	189,664	152,469
Other	142,407	146,554	158,534	166,295	117,501
Earnings of unconsolidated affiliates	98,977	86,646	45,485	5,459	—
	1,419,734	1,393,727	1,348,983	1,205,879	984,784
Less complimentary allowances	(65,247)	(59,477)	(49,387)	(35,697)	(29,861)
Net revenue	1,354,487	1,334,250	1,299,596	1,170,182	954,923
Costs and expenses					
Casino	316,902	302,096	275,680	246,416	209,402
Rooms	122,934	116,508	110,362	94,257	78,932
Food and beverage	199,955	200,722	188,712	177,136	149,267
Other operating expenses	90,187	90,601	92,631	107,297	72,802
General and administrative	232,536	227,348	215,083	183,175	152,104
Depreciation and amortization	117,474	95,414	93,938	81,109	58,105
Preopening expense	3,447	—	—	3,012	16,506
Abandonment loss		48,309	45,148	—	—
	1,083,435	1,080,998	1,021,554	892,402	737,118
Operating profit before corporate expense	271,052	223,252	278,042	277,780	217,805
Corporate expense	34,552	31,083	26,669	21,773	16,744
Income from operations	236,500	222,169	251,373	256,007	201,061
Other income (expense)					
Interest, dividends, and other income (loss)	9,779	5,077	4,022	225	(683)
Interest income and guarantee fees from unconsolidated affiliate	6,041	6,865	7,517	992	—
Interest expense	(88,847)	(54,681)	(51,537)	(42,734)	(17,770)
Interest expense from unconsolidated affiliate	(15,551)	(15,567)	(5,616)		
	(88,578)	(58,306)	(45,614)	(41,517)	(18,453)
Income before provision for income tax	147,922	163,863	205,759	214,490	182,608
Provision for income tax	58,014	63,130	76,861	78,204	66,419
Income before extraordinary loss	—	—	—	—	116,189
Extraordinary loss	—	—	—	—	—
Net income	89,908	100,733	128,898	136,286	116,189
Earnings per share					
Income before extraordinary loss	0.95	0.99	1.33	1.59	1.34
Extraordinary loss	—	—	—	—	—
Net income per share	0.94	0.99	1.33	1.59	1.34

Source: Circus Circus Annual Reports and 10k's, 1994–1998.

EXHIBIT G

Circus Circus Enterprises, Inc.: Consolidated Balance Sheets (in thousands)

	1/31/98	1/31/97	1/31/96	1/31/95	1/31/94
Assets					
Current assets					
Cash and cash equivalents	$ 58,631	$ 69,516	$ 62,704	$ 53,764	$ 39,110
Receivables	33,640	34,434	16,527	8,931	8,673
Inventories	22,440	19,371	20,459	22,660	20,057
Prepaid expenses	20,281	19,951	19,418	20,103	20,062
Deferred income tax	7,871	8,577	7,272	5,463	
Total current	142,863	151,849	124,380	110,921	87,902
Property, equipment	2,466,848	1,920,032	1,474,684	1,239,062	1,183,164
Other assets					
Excess of purchase price over fair market value	375,375	385,583	394,518	9,836	10,200
Notes receivable	1,075	36,443	27,508	68,083	
Investments in unconsolidated affiliates	255,392	214,123	173,270	74,840	
Deferred charges and other assets	21,995	21,081	17,533	9,806	16,658
Total other	653,837	657,230	612,829	162,565	26,858
Total assets	3,263,548	2,729,111	2,213,503	1,512,548	1,297,924
Liabilities and Stockholders Equity					
Current liabilities					
Current portion of long-term debt	3,071	379	863	106	169
Accounts and contracts payable					
Trade	22,103	22,658	16,824	12,102	14,804
Construction	40,670	21,144	—	1,101	13,844
Accrued liabilities					
Salaries, wages and vacations	36,107	31,847	30,866	24,946	19,650
Progressive jackpots	7,511	6,799	8,151	7,447	4,881
Advance room depoists	6,217	7,383	7,517	8,701	6,981
Interest payable	17,828	9,004	3,169	2,331	2,278
Other	33,451	30,554	28,142	25,274	25,648
Income tax payable					3,806
Total current liabilities	166,958	129,768	95,532	82,008	92,061
Long-term debt	1,788,818	1,405,897	715,214	632,652	567,345
Other liabilities					
Deferred income tax	175,934	152,635	148,096	110,776	77,153
Other long-term liabilities	8,089	6,439	9,319	988	1,415
Total other liabilities	184,023	159,074	157,415	111,764	78,568
Total liabilities	2,139,799	1,694,739	968,161	826,424	737,974
Redeemable preferred stock		17,631	18,530		
Temporary equity		44,950			
Commitments and contingent liabilities					
Stockholders equity					
Common stock	1,893	1,880	1,880	1,607	1,603
Preferred stock					

(continued)

EXHIBIT G *(continued)*

Circus Circus Enterprises, Inc.: Consolidated Balance Sheets (in thousands)

	1/31/98	1/31/97	1/31/96	1/31/95	1/31/94
Additional paid-in capital	558,658	498,893	527,205	124,960	120,135
Retained earnings	1,074,271	984,363	883,630	754,732	618,446
Treasury stock	(511,073)	(513,345)	(185,903)	(195,175)	(180,234)
Total stockholders equity	1,123,749	971,791	1,226,812	686,124	559,950
Total liabilities and stockholders equity	3,263,548	2,729,111	2,213,503	1,512,548	1,297,924

Source: Circus Circus Annual Reports and 10k's, 1994–1998.

of the Masterplan Mile eventually will be comprised of at least one additional casino resort and a number of stand-alone hotels and amusement centers.

Circus also plans three other casino projects, provided all the necessary licenses and agreements can be obtained. In Detroit, Michigan, Circus has combined with the Atwater Casino Group in a joint venture to build a $600 million project. Negotiations with the city to develop the project have been completed; however, the remainder of the appropriate licenses will need to be obtained before construction begins.

Along the Mississippi Gulf, at the north end of the Bay of St. Louis, Circus plans to construct a casino resort containing 1500 rooms at an estimated cost of $225 million. Circus has received all necessary permits to begin construction; however, these approvals have been challenged in court, delaying the project.

In Atlantic City, Circus has entered into an agreement with Mirage Resorts to develop a 181-acre site in the Marina District. Land title has been transferred to Mirage; however, Mirage has purported to cancel its agreement with Circus. Circus has filed suit against Mirage, seeking to enforce the contract, while others have filed suit to stop all development in the area.

Most of Circus' projects are being tailored to attract mainstream tourists and family vacationers. However, the addition of several joint ventures and the completion of the Masterplan Mile also will attract the more upscale customer.

THE GAMING INDUSTRY

By 1997, the gaming industry had captured a large amount of the vacation/leisure time dollars spent in the United States. Gamblers lost over $44.3 billion

on legal wagering in 1995 (up from $29.9 billion in 1992), including wagers at racetracks, bingo parlors, lotteries, and casinos. This figure does not include dollars spent on lodging, food, transportation, and other related expenditures associated with visits to gaming facilities. Casino gambling accounts for 76 percent of all legal gambling expenditures, far ahead of second-place Indian Reservations at 8.9 percent and lotteries at 7.1 percent. The popularity of casino gambling may be credited to a more frequent and somewhat higher payout as compared with lotteries and racetracks; however, as winnings are recycled, the multiplier effect restores a high return to casino operators.

Geographic expansion has slowed considerably because no additional states have approved casino-type gambling since 1993. Growth has occurred in developed locations, with Las Vegas, Nevada, and Atlantic City, New Jersey, leading the way.

Las Vegas remains the largest U.S. gaming market and one of the largest convention markets, with more than 100,000 hotel rooms hosting more than 29.6 million visitors in 1996, up 2.2 percent over 1995. Casino operators are building to take advantage of this continued growth. Recent projects include the Monte Carlo ($350 million), New York–New York ($350 million), Bellagio ($1.4 billion), Hilton Hotels ($750 million), and Project Paradise ($800 million). Additionally, Harrah's is adding a 989-room tower and remodeling 500 current rooms, and Caesar's Palace has expansion plans to add 2000 rooms. Las Vegas hotel and casino capacity is expected to continue to expand, with some 12,500 rooms opening within a year. According to the Las Vegas

Convention and Visitor Authority, Las Vegas is a destination market, with most visitors planning their trip more than a week in advance (81 percent), arriving by car (47 percent) or airplane (42 percent), and staying in a hotel (72 percent). Gamblers are typically return visitors (77 percent), averaging 2.2 trips per year, liking to play the slots (65 percent).

For Atlantic City, besides the geographic separation, the primary differences in the two markets reflect the different types of consumers frequenting these markets. While Las Vegas attracts overnight resort-seeking vacationers, Atlantic City's clientele are predominantly day-trippers traveling by automobile or bus. Gaming revenues are expected to continue to grow, perhaps to $4 billion in 1997 split between 10 casino/hotels currently operating. Growth in the Atlantic City area will be concentrated in the Marina section of town, where Mirage Resorts has entered into an agreement with the city to develop 150 acres of the Marina as a destination resort. This development will include a resort wholly owned by Mirage, a casino/hotel developed by Circus, and a complex developed by a joint venture with Mirage and Boyd Corp. Currently, in Atlantic City, Donald Trump's gaming empire holds the largest market share, with Trump's Castle, Trump Plaza, and the Taj Mahal (total market share is 30 percent). The next closest in market share is Caesar's (10.3 percent), Tropicana and Bally's (9.2 percent each), and Showboat (9.0 percent).

There remain a number of smaller markets located around the United States, primarily in Mississippi, Louisiana, Illinois, Missouri, and Indiana. Each state has imposed various restrictions on the development of casino operations within their states. In some cases, e.g., Illinois, where there are only 10 gaming licenses available, this has severely restricted growth opportunities and hurt revenues. In other states, e.g., Mississippi and Louisiana, revenues are up 8 and 15 percent, respectively, in riverboat operations. Native American casinos continue to be developed on federally controlled Indian land. These casinos are not publicly held but do tend to be managed by publicly held corporations. Overall, these other locations present a mix of opportunities and generally constitute only a small portion of overall gaming revenues.

MAJOR INDUSTRY PLAYERS

Over the past several years there have been numerous changes as mergers and acquisitions have reshaped the gaming industry. As of year end 1996, the industry was a combination of corporations ranging from those engaged solely in gaming to multinational conglomerates. The largest competitors, in terms of revenues, combined multiple industries to generate both large revenues and substantial profits (see Exhibit H). However, those engaged primarily in gaming also could be extremely profitable.

In 1996, Hilton began a hostile acquisition attempt of ITT Corporation. As a result of this attempt, ITT merged with Starwood Lodging Corporation and Starwood Lodging Trust. The resulting corporation is one of the world's largest hotel and gaming corporations, owning the Sheraton, The Luxury Collection, the Four Points Hotels, and Caesar's, as well as communications and educational services. In 1996, ITT hosted approximately 50 million customer nights in locations worldwide. Gaming operations are located in Las Vegas, Atlantic City, Halifax and Sydney (Nova Scotia), Lake Tahoe, Tunica (Mississippi), Lima (Peru), Cairo (Egypt), Canada, and Australia. In 1996, ITT had net income of $249 million on revenues of $6.579 billion. In June 1996, ITT announced plans to join with Planet Hollywood to develop casino/hotels with the Planet Hollywood theme in both Las Vegas and Atlantic City. However, these plans may be deferred as ITT becomes fully integrated into Starwood and management has the opportunity to refocus on the operations of the company.

Hilton Hotels owns (as of February 1, 1998) or leases and operates 25 hotels and manages 34 hotels partially or wholly owned by others along with 180 franchised hotels. Eleven of the hotels are also casinos, 6 of which are located in Nevada, 2 in Atlantic City, with the other 3 in Australia and Uruguay. In 1997, Hilton had net income of $250.0 million on $5.31 billion in revenues. Hilton receives some 98 percent of total operating revenues from gaming operations and continues to expand in the market. Recent expansions include the Wild Wild West theme hotel/casino in Atlantic City, the completed acquisition of all the assets of Bally's, and construction on a 2900-room Paris Casino resort located next to Bally's Las Vegas.

EXHIBIT H

Major U.S. Gaming, Lottery, and Parimutuel Companies: 1996 Revenues and Net Income (in millions)

	1997 Revenues	1997 Income	1996 Revenues	1996 Net Income
Starwood/ITT	—	—	$6597.0	$249.0
Hilton Hotels	5316.0	250.0	3940.0	82.0
Harrah's Entertainment	1619.0	99.3	1586.0	98.9
Mirage Resorts	1546.0	207	1358.3	206.0
Circus Circus	1354.4	89.9	1247.0	100.7
Trump Hotel and Casino, Inc.	1399.3	−42.1	976.3	−4.9
MGM Grand	827.5	111.0	804.8	74.5
Aztar	782.3	4.4	777.5	20.6
Int. Game Technology	743.9	137.2	733.5	118.0

Source: Individual companies annual reports and 10k's, 1996 and 1997.

Harrah's Entertainment, Inc., is primarily engaged in the gaming industry with casino/hotels in Reno, Lake Tahoe, Las Vegas, and Laughlin, Nevada, Atlantic City, New Jersey, riverboats in Joliet, Illinois and Vicksburg and Tunica, Mississippi, Shreveport, Louisiana, Kansas City, Kansas, two Indian casinos, and one in Auckland, New Zealand. In 1997, it operated a total of approximately 774,500 square feet of casino space with 19,835 slot machines and 934 tables games. With this and some 8197 hotel rooms, the company had a net income of $99.3 million on $1.619 billion in revenues.

All of Mirage Resorts' gaming operations are currently located in Nevada. It owns and operates the Golden Nugget–Downtown, Las Vegas, the Mirage on the strip in Las Vegas, Treasure Island, and the Golden Nugget–Laughlin. Additionally, it is a 50 percent owner of the Monte Carlo with Circus Circus. Net income for Mirage Resorts in 1997 was $207 million on revenues of $1.546 billion. Current expansion plans include the development of the Bellagio in Las Vegas ($1.6 billion estimated cost) and the Beau Rivage in Biloxi, Mississippi ($600 million estimated cost). These two properties would add a total of 265,900 square feet of casino space to the current Mirage inventory and an additional 252 gaming tables and 4746 slot machines. An additional project is the development of the Marina area in Atlantic City, New Jersey, in partnership with Boyd Gaming.

MGM Grand Hotel and Casino is located on approximately 114 acres at the northeast corner of Las Vegas Boulevard across the street from New York–New York hotel and casino. The casino is approximately 171,500 square feet in size and is one of the largest casinos in the world, with 3669 slot machines and 157 table games. Current plans call for extensive renovation costing $700 million. Through a wholly owned subsidiary, MGM owns and operates the MGM Grand Diamond Beach Hotel and a hotel/casino resort in Darwin, Australia. Additionally, MGM and Primadonna Resorts, Inc., each own 50 percent of New York–New York hotel and casino, a $460 million architecturally distinctive themed destination resort that opened on January 3, 1997. MGM also intends to construct and operate a destination resort hotel/casino, entertainment, and retail facility in Atlantic City on approximately 35 acres of land on the Atlantic City Boardwalk.

THE LEGAL ENVIRONMENT

Within the gaming industry, all current operators must consider compliance with extensive gaming regulations as a primary concern. Each state or country has its own specific regulations and regulatory boards requiring extensive reporting and licensing requirements. For example, in Las Vegas,

Nevada, gambling operations are subject to regulatory control by the Nevada State Gaming Control Board, the Clark County Nevada Gaming and Liquor Licensing Board, and city government regulations. The laws, regulations, and supervisory procedures of virtually all gaming authorities are based on public policy primarily concerned with the prevention of unsavory or unsuitable persons from having a direct or indirect involvement with gaming at any time or in any capacity and the establishment and maintenance of responsible accounting practices and procedures. Additional regulations typically cover the maintenance of effective controls over the financial practices of licensees, including the establishment of minimum procedures for internal fiscal affairs and the safeguarding of assets and revenues, providing reliable record keeping and requiring the filing of periodic reports, the prevention of cheating and fraudulent practices, and providing a source of state and local revenues through taxation and licensing fees. Changes in such laws, regulations, and procedures could have an adverse effect on many gaming operations. All gaming companies must submit detailed operating and financial reports to authorities. Nearly all financial transactions, including loans, leases, and the sales of securities, must be reported. Some financial activities are subject to approval by regulatory agencies. As Circus moves into other locations outside of Nevada, it will need to adhere to local regulations.

FUTURE CONSIDERATIONS

Circus Circus states that it is "in the business of entertainment, with . . . core strength in casino gaming" and that it intends to focus its efforts in Las Vegas, Atlantic City, and Mississippi. Circus further states that the "future product in gaming, to be sure, is the entertainment resort" (Circus Circus 1997 Annual Report).

Circus was one of the innovators of the gaming resort concept and has continued to be a leader in that field. However, the megaentertainment resort industry operates differently than the traditional casino gaming industry. In the past, consumers would visit a casino to experience the thrill of gambling. Now they not only gamble but expect to be dazzled by enormous entertainment complexes

that are costing billions of dollars to build. The competition has continued to increase at the same time growth rates have been slowing.

For years, analysts have questioned the ability of the gaming industry to continue high growth in established markets as the industry matures. Through the 1970s and 1980s, the gaming industry experienced rapid growth. Through the 1990s, the industry began to experience a shakeout of marginal competitors and consolidation phase. Circus Circus has been successful through this turmoil but now faces the task of maintaining high growth in a more mature industry.

Bibliography

"Circus Circus Announces Promotion," *PR Newswire*, June 10, 1997.

"Industry Surveys—Lodging and Gaming," *Standard and Poors Industry Surveys*, June 19, 1997.

"Casinos Move into New Areas," *Standard and Poors Industry Surveys*, March 11, 1993, pp. L35–L41.

Circus Circus Enterprises, Inc., Annual Report to Shareholders, January 31, 1989, January 31, 1990, January 31, 1993, January 31, 1994, January 31, 1995, January 31, 1996.

Circus Circus Enterprises, Inc., Annual Report to Shareholders, January 31, 1997.

Circus Circus Enterprises, Inc., Annual Report to Shareholders, January 31, 1998.

Corning, Blair. "Luxor: Egypt Opens in Vegas," *San Antonio Express News*, October 24, 1993.

Lalli, Sergio. "Excalibur Awaiteth," *Hotel and Motel Management*, June 11, 1990.

"Economic Impacts of Casino Gaming in the United States," by Arthur Anderson for the American Gaming Association, May 1997.

"Harrah's Survey of Casino Entertainment," Harrah's Entertainment, Inc., 1996.

"ITT Board Rejects Hilton's Offer as Inadequate, Reaffirms Belief that ITT's Comprehensive Plan Is in the Best Interest of ITT Shareholders," press release, August 14, 1997.

Mirage Resorts, Inc. *1997 and 1998 10k*, and retrieved from EDGAR Database, http://www.sec.gov/Archives/edgar/data/.

Hilton Hotels Corp. *1997 and 1998 10k*, retrieved from EDGAR Database, http://www.sec.gov/Archives/edgar/data/.

Aztar Corp. *1997 and 1998 10k*, retrieved from EDGAR Database, http://www.sec.gov/Archives/edgar/data/.

ITT Corp. *1997 10k*, retrieved from EDGAR Database, http://www.sec.gov/Archives/edgar/data/.

Harrah's Entertainment, Inc. *1997 and 1998 10k*, retrieved from EDGAR Database, http://www.sec.gov/Archives/edgar/data/.

MGM Grand, Inc. *1997 and 1998 10k*, retrieved from EDGAR Database, http://www.sec.gov/Archives/edgar/data/.

Priceline.com: Act III–From Dot.com to "Real Business"

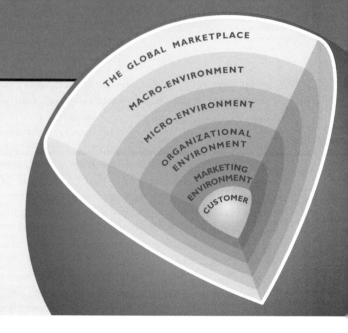

This case was prepared by Carol H. Anderson, Crummer Graduate School of Business, Rollins College, and Alexander T. Wood, University of Central Florida.

Jeffrey Boyd and Richard Braddock were discussing Priceline.com's financial results for the second quarter of 2001. Boyd, Priceline.com's President and Chief Operating Officer, said, "We are pleased that our airline ticket sales have substantially recovered, despite the difficult airline travel market and competition from heavy discounting by the major carriers." "It is also encouraging to see the continued rapid growth of our hotel and rental car products, which we believe have a substantial inventory advantage over the competition, and broad consumer appeal."

Braddock, the company's Chairman and Chief Executive Officer, stated, "We expect Priceline.com to continue the steady growth of customers beyond our current 11 million customers." He added that this could be accomplished through more efficient database marketing tools, and by building on the company's repeat business ratio.[1]

With reference to the future, Mr. Braddock said, "On-line travel appears to be one of the few sweet spots in e-commerce....With our renewed brand strengths, our product offerings robust and expanding, our customer base growing on both new and repeat bases, and our margins well above industry averages and sustainable, we believe Priceline.com is now positioned to be one of the Internet's pre-eminent, profitable, e-commerce brands.[2]

Neither Boyd nor Braddock had any way of knowing that their company and the travel industry would face new challenges in the wake of the September 11, 2001 attacks on the World Trade Center in New York City.

PRICELINE.COM: COMPANY HIGHLIGHTS

Priceline.com, the "Name Your Own Price" Internet pricing system, was introduced in 1998 to sell airline tickets, hotel rooms, and other goods and services to consumers at bargain prices. From its inception, Priceline attracted attention as a leader among the growing number of dot.com competitors who offered bargains on line. Investors were attracted by the promise of founder Jay Walker's patented business model that was designed for a variety of audiences. For consumers, it is a travel agent or collector of bargain offers. For vendors, it is an alternative way to distribute products, or to get rid of distressed inventory without a negative association with cheap prices. Vendors also can use Priceline as a direct marketing channel, and a source of information to assess customers' levels of price elasticity. Investors were attracted to the idea of an easily expandable business platform where there were no physical products, and inventory risks were minimal. (A more detailed description of the Priceline business model follows in a later section.)

JAY WALKER, PRICELINE.COM FOUNDER

According to one observer, Jay Walker is a "self-styled serial inventor, who uses the Internet to devise ways of revolutionizing business much as other inventors use their toolsheds to refine mousetraps or build rockets."[3] Priceline.com, a website for bargain-hunting customers, is the most prominent of the over 300 novel business models registered by Jay Walker's think tank, Walker Digital Corporation. This innovation briefly made an $8 billion fortune on paper, and the company was called the most successful Internet business model of the year in spring 2000.

A year earlier (1999), Mr. Walker said that there was no category in which Priceline's business model could not be successful. However, in late October 2000, the company was forced to close two affiliates, WebHouse Club and Perfect Yardsale, where consumers bid for cut-price groceries, gasoline, and other small-ticket goods. Priceline invested $363 million in about a year in these unsuccessful attempts to extend the name-your-own-price model into new product categories. Investors' confidence in "name-your-own-price" online retailing was badly undermined by the WebHouse Club and Perfect Yardsale closures, and share prices fell to $1.31 by the end of 2000. (WebHouse is discussed further in a later section.)

In December 2000, Jay Walker stepped down from the board of Priceline in order to focus on rebuilding Walker Digital Corporation, his closely-held new business incubator. At that time, Walker was the largest shareholder of Priceline, but did not hold an executive position.[4] He sold a significant number of Priceline.com shares at very low prices, instituted cost-cutting measures at Walker Digital, and stopped construction on his $7.5 million, 24,000 square foot mansion in Connecticut.

THE NAME-YOUR-OWN PRICE BUSINESS MODEL

Jay Walker said that he is " …a theorist who wants to understand the abstract levels at which things operate, then turn those abstractions into commercial value."[5] Walker developed many successful ventures with this philosophy, particularly through his Walker Digital Corporation laboratory. Priceline.com was developed from a system that allows a company to dispose of excess inventory at optimal prices. A double-blind method is used so the provider can maintain brand image and charge full price for non-surplus goods. Investors were so attracted to this model they gave the company $13 million during its IPO in March 1999. Walker Digital's patented business processes were widely believed to be a key to success.

The Priceline model was built on the premise that there were only four ways to create value in the New Economy: information, entertainment, convenience, and savings, and that businesses in an electronic network blend these in some proportion. Walker believed that information and entertainment were not a good basis for business models, but the real battle was over the balance between convenience and savings—and the greatest of these was savings. Further, the Priceline model separated the information component from the physical component in the Information Economy. Information was treated as a separate element, and had its own source of value. For example, FedEx delivers packages physically (as an industrial company), but it's an information company when you can track your package, know your discount and billing, and so forth. Customers can decide which is more important to them— the information component or the industrial component.

Priceline generates revenue in two ways in the airline travel business. (1) It keeps the difference between the consumer's bid and the lowest fare given to Priceline by the airline partner. Both the consumer's bid and the airline's lowest fare are unpublished, although the airline price is visible to Priceline. (2) "Adaptive marketing" and "cross-subsidy" promotional programs give consumers the chance to increase the value of their bids. If an airline ticket customer signs up for a new credit card, for example, Priceline might add $20 to the consumer's bid (no charge to consumer) to improve the odds that the bid will be matched. However, Priceline keeps the difference between the $20 added to the bid and the $50–$75 it gets for each new credit card customer, and so on. (A number of other fees may be obtained from business partners and customers.)[6]

When Priceline introduced Priceline.com in April 1998, Walker's concept was unique, and at first shoppers and investors loved it. Priceline.com expanded its product lines from airlines to other goods and services, including a new car buying service launched in July 1998, hotel rooms launched in October 1998, and rental cars launched in February 2000. Other online services followed. Some were successful and some were not. As of November 2001, Priceline's services spanned four broad product categories: travel service (leisure airline tickets, hotel rooms, rental cars); personal finance service (home mortgages, refinancing and home equity loans through an independent licensee); automotive service that offers new cars; and telecommunications service (long distance telephone services).[7] The primary focus was on travel services.

WEBHOUSE CLUB: AN ATTEMPT TO EXTEND THE PRICELINE.COM BUSINESS MODEL

WebHouse Club was conceived as an extension of the Walker Digital name-your-price model used by Priceline.com, with the idea that large numbers of grocery and gasoline customers would bring in more frequent customers than Priceline. Jay Walker said, "Once you achieve critical mass, you can build a very large and profitable company."[8]

Some analysts predicted that the Priceline model would revolutionize the world of retailing, and there was great excitement late in 1999 when the company opened WebHouse Club, operating as an independent licensee. WebHouse made it possible for customers to bid on gasoline and groceries. The company selected William Shatner (Star Trek's Captain Kirk) as its pitchman for WebHouse Club in a series of "campy" ads on television and radio. Shatner predicted "This is going to be big—really big."[9] (Unfortunately, the appeal seemed to wear off in a matter of months.)

The media enthusiastically hailed WebHouse Club's entry into the name-your-price Internet grocery business during the last months of 1999.[10] The first launch was in the New York metro market, serving millions of residents of the New York–New Jersey–Connecticut region. Members did not pay a fee to belong to WebHouse Club, and could expect to reduce their grocery bills significantly, comparable to shopping at Sam's Club or Costco—but without the need to buy in such large quantities. Customers could register online, and have their card mailed to their home or they could pick it up at participating grocery stores. New York test area stores included A&P, ShopRite, King Kullen, Waldbaum's, D'Augustino's, and Gristede's.

WebHouse's approach was that they deliver prices, not boxes of products. They did not need a distribution facility, just the ability to get prices their customers wanted. How did this work? When a customer wanted to place an order, he or she logged on to Priceline.com and linked to the WebHouse Club site. Next, he named his desired price for national brands of grocery products in any of the 140 categories listed (excluding deli and dairy products). Customers had to pick two acceptable brand names. A minute later, WebHouse was to respond with a match. (Customer's credit card was charged at this point.) Then the customer printed out the statement and took it to his/her participating store where the WebHouse membership card and grocery list were presented at checkout. The manufacturer covered the discounted cost of the groceries directly to the retailer. Many customers were initially sold on this new method of shopping for groceries at a lower price, in spite of the need to shop online, then go to the grocery store to fill an order.

Eventually, questions were raised about the name-your-own-price grocery service. In a December 1999 *Chain Store Age* article,[11] the author described his WebHouse experience one week after the site opened for business as follows: "Consumers … go onto www.priceline.webhouse.com and select from 140 grocery categories. They either choose one of three pre-set bids for items or create a bid of their own. They are then given a list of which bids were accepted [credit cards are charged], and they print out a list of items." "At the store, shoppers take the lists they printed out from the Web site and meander around collecting the groceries. They then hit the checkout line, swipe their WebHouse card and leave." The author had no problems, but identified some critical issues based on his experience:

- Inventory—consumers had to return to the store for out-of-stock items.

- Logistics—consumers who forgot to take their printed out list, or lost the list, had to log back on to the Web and print out another copy.

- Convenience—The WebHouse frequent shopper card made it possible to deduct prepurchased items at checkout, but the customer had to separate these items from regular grocery items.

At the end of 1999, WebHouse managers faced a number of important issues: (1) they had not closed a deal with any major brand manufacturers; (2) member savings were subsidized by WebHouse's company funds, and the early consumer response resulted in significant losses and use of cash; (3) questions were raised about where and how quickly to expand; and (4) Walker was recognized as a brilliant innovator and marketer, but was considered to be an entrepreneur whose strength was in ideas, not in managing a company with complex processes.[12]

By October 2000, headlines were very unfavorable. As one headline announced, "Priceline's WebHouse Club Abandoned as Investors Balk."[13] However, analysts felt that there would be little direct financial impact on Priceline from WebHouse Club's shutdown since it was set up as a separate venture. Another headline proclaimed, "There's just one thing wrong with name-your-own-price businesses: You're not naming your own price."[14] The author maintained that this was a "propose-your-own-price" business, which was a different model. He suggested that people of Western capitalism had agreed over the past few centuries that it is more efficient not to haggle over everyday goods, and that there is a difference between saving several hundred dollars on an airline flight versus pennies on a jar of peanut butter. He questioned the price elasticity in something with a long shelf life (e.g., cereal), and said that for many consumers, the advantage of shopping on the Web is to reduce haggling and bargaining for purchases.

WebHouse discontinued operations in October 2000, after only 10 months of being in business. Investors refused to infuse more money into the company, which was losing money on the deep discounts it was forced to absorb in order to keep its two million price shoppers coming back. Jay Walker and other WebHouse executives attributed the venture's failure to the current investment climate, rather than their business model. They identified their typical WebHouse customer as a female, shopping for her family, who was flexible about brands she would buy, and who wanted to save money.[15]

PRICELINE.COM'S PROFITABILITY PITFALLS

A series of news events illustrate the company's dilemma during the last two quarters of 2000:[16]

- July 2000: Six of Priceline's supplier airlines (America West, American, Continental, Northwest, United, and US Airways) decided to operate their own website, Hotwire.com, to sell vacant airline seats directly to customers at discounted prices. (Hotwire started service in October 2000, and customers found it easier and faster than Priceline's process.)[17]

- September 29, 2000: Priceline warned investors that revenues would not meet expectations due to weak airline ticket sales. Since this represented Priceline's core business, it seemed doubtful the company could become profitable anytime soon.

- October 2000: Walker announced that he was shutting down WebHouse Club, Priceline's innovative online grocery and gasoline business.

- October 2000: The Connecticut Attorney General's Office announced that it was probing complaints of incomplete and inaccurate disclosure of the company's sales policies—particularly in the case of airline tickets.

- Early November 2000: The company reported that fourth-quarter revenue would slow down, and that it was cutting back its work force by laying off 16 percent of its employees (87 of 535 employees were fired).

- November 3, 2000: Priceline chief financial officer, Heidi Miller, resigned—considered a significant loss of a star executive.[18]

- November 3, 2000: Notice was given that a class action lawsuit against Priceline.com, Inc. and its senior executives was being pursued in the U.S. District Court for the District of Connecticut, "seeking to recover damages on behalf of allegedly defrauded investors who purchased Priceline securities between January 31 and October 4, 2000.[19]

- November 18, 2000: Another high-profile executive, Maryann Keller (former auto analyst), resigned as head of Priceline's auto-services business.[20]

- Negative publicity: CBS Television program, "48 Hours," aired consumer complaints about

Priceline.com, and announced that the Connecticut Better Business Bureau had revoked Priceline's membership because the company did not resolve the complaints.

- Fall 2000: Numerous class action suits were filed against Priceline because of declining stock value. This activity was costly and time consuming, and took the company's attention away from running the business.

- Warrants: The company's cash position was threatened by a financial burden in the form of warrants held by Delta Air Lines and other suppliers.

- Challenges to patents: Priceline charged Microsoft's Expedia with patent infringement.[21] Other patent challenges also were in process.

- Brand association: Priceline WebHouse Club's grocery business was on the Priceline.com website, leading WebHouse customers to believe they were dealing directly with Priceline.[22]

Jay Walker and other Priceline executives remained positive in the face of the many challenges that confronted them going into the fourth quarter of 2000. The company had the advantage of being the best-known name in Internet travel sales, with an ample supply of inventory that was available for them to sell. Priceline's customer base was constantly growing, with an estimated 8 million shoppers at that time. It offered an extensive product line, and had experienced significant increases in its core business of airline tickets. In the third quarter 2000, Priceline sold 1.29 million airline seats. This was twice as many as were sold in the same quarter the previous year. However, analysts were not optimistic about Priceline's survival going into the fourth quarter of 2000. At the same time, airlines were discounting their own fares, and headlines contained negative publicity about Priceline.[23]

PRICELINE PERFORMANCE

Wall Street was delighted when Priceline went public in April 1999, and very soon the company's stock traded as high as $162 per share. Then it fell to around $50 during fall 1999, and surged to nearly $100 during spring 2000. By late summer it was down to about $25. By fall 2000, a series of events took the stock down to single digits.

Priceline's much-needed investors were losing confidence in the company.[24] In March 2000, the company's market capitalization reached more than $17 billion, and Wall Street was positive about Priceline's future profitability. Priceline's name-your-own-price model seemed like a sure winner. Three months later, the company's stock fell to an all-time low of $4.28, a 97 percent drop from its April 1999 high of $165.[25]

In the first quarter 2000, Priceline.com's net loss narrowed, as revenue grew to $313 million due to significant increases in demand for airline and hotel booking services. As a result, Wall Street analysts said, "Priceline's performance demonstrated the strength of the company's business." Analysts appeared to favor the idea of patenting a method that allowed customers to name their own prices—which Priceline could accept or not—for purchasing services. The company's executives said that the first quarter 2000 results showed the benefits of its diversified product expansion strategy over the past year, and the ability of every shopping service introduced by Pipeline to take advantage of the company's existing customer-support lines, technology, and other infrastructure. This was believed to give Priceline a better chance to be profitable than more narrowly focused Internet retailers.[26]

At the end of the third quarter 2000, Priceline showed improved performance in revenues and gross profit over the same period for 1999. The company had positive operating cash flow for the second quarter in a row, with $131 million of cash and short-term investments. Comparisons of pro forma results for the first and third quarters of 1999 and third quarter of 2000 indicate improved performance in revenues, gross profit, operating loss, net loss, and loss per share, as the company appeared to be heading toward anticipated profitability. (See Exhibit 1).

Given high expectations and the promise of satisfaction for customers, suppliers, and investors, it is not surprising that the company's results have been both a source of satisfaction and disappointment for each of these groups over the past several years. Although Priceline.com was not profitable until the second quarter of 2001, the company maintained a relatively strong cash position during several years of typical dot.com performance ups and downs. Priceline.com Inc. reported record revenues for second quarter 2001, and its *first-ever profit*. Revenues reached $364.8 million, compared to $352.1 million in second quarter 2000. Pro forma net income reached $11.7 million or $0.06 per basic share. Gross profit for second quarter 2001 was a record $60.1 million. (See comparative data in Exhibits 1 and 2.)

During the first two months of the third quarter 2001, Priceline.com generated about $245 million in revenue and was well on its way to continued growth in revenue and profits. In spite of the infamous 9/11 attack, Priceline was able to generate $302 million in revenues and $50.4 million in gross profits for the third quarter. Pro forma net income was $6.3 million (GAAP net income before preferred stock dividend was $5.0 million), and gross

EXHIBIT 1

Priceline.com Pro Forma Results—1999–2000 (in $thousands)

	1 Q 99	1 Q 00	2 Q 99	2 Q 00	3 Q 99	3 Q 00	4 Q 99	4 Q 00	4 Q 00 vs. 4 Q 99 $ Change	% Change
	49,411	313,798	111,564	352,095	152,222	341,334	169,213	228,169	58,956	34.84%
Gross profit	5,752	49,027	10,900	55,176	18,594	54,435	24,109	35,055	10,946	45.40%
Operating profit/loss	(17,237)	(9,994)	(15,895)	(4,358)	(14,255)	(4,488)	(12,745)	(26,986)	(14,241)	111.74%
Net profit/loss	(16,779)	(7,279)	(13,876)	(1,633)	(11,899)	(2,224)	(9,988)	(25,003)	(15,015)	150.33%
Net profit/loss per share	(0.18)	(0.04)	(-0.10)	(0.01)	(0.08)	(0.01)	(0.06)	(0.15)	(0.09)	150.00%

EXHIBIT 2

Priceline.com Pro Forma Results—2000–2001 (in $thousands)

	1 Q 00	1 Q 01	2 Q 00	2 Q 01	3 Q 00	3 Q 01	4 Q 00	4 Q 01*	3 Q 00 vs. 3 Q 99* $ Change	%Change
Revenues	313,798	269,704	352,095	364,765	341,334	301,989	228,169		(39,345)	−11.53%
Gross profit	49,027	43,115	55,176	60,106	54,435	50,432	35,055		(4,003)	−7.35%
Operating profit/loss	(9,994)	(8,024)	(4,358)	9,919	(4,488)	4,193	(26,986)		8,681	−193.43%
Net profit/ loss	(7,279)	(6,248)	(1,633)	11,735	(2,224)	6,289	(25,003)		8,513	−382.78%
Net profit/ loss per share	(0.04)	(0.03)	(0.01)	0.06	(0.01)	0.03	(0.15)		$0.04	−400.00%

*4 Q 01 not available 11/01.

margin reached 16.7% for the period. Priceline's consumer franchise grew to nearly 12 million customers, and repeat business reached a record 63%. (See Exhibits 1 and 2 for additional financial data.) [27]

According to Priceline.com, demand for travel products recovered substantially after the 9/11 attacks. However, unit sales and revenue from travel product sales were not able to keep up with that demand due to refunds following the attacks, and pressure from deep discounting by airlines, hotel, and rental car companies to stimulate demand. Recovery also was slowed down by schedule changes and disruptions in available air, hotel, and rental car inventories.

In spite of any setbacks caused by the terrorist attacks, Priceline.com's top executives were confident about the future. They expected continued growth and financial success for the fourth quarter 2001, and beyond. President and COO, Jeffrey Boyd, attributed the rapid recovery of consumer demand for the company's travel products to brand equity, customer loyalty, and the value offered to consumers. Hotel and rental car unit sales exceeded airline ticket sales for the first two quarters of 2001, and continued strong during the third period, accounting for 42% of all booked offers (including air), compared to 28% for the same period in 2000. The company's "look-to-book" ratio[28] of 12.8% exceeded that of leading competitors Travelocity (8.0%) and Expedia.com (5.5%). Richard Braddock, Chairman and CEO, stated that the steadily growing customer base, record level of repeat business, and a strong look-to-book ratio have provided a strong customer franchise, and positioned Priceline.com favorably for the future. He said, "Our Name Your Own Price proposition is now a preferred way of purchasing for millions of loyal customers, who come back to Priceline.com again and again for their travel and other purchases." (See Exhibit 3 for comparative data on offers and customer activity for Priceline.com's airline, hotel, and rental car businesses.)

PROBLEMS FACED BY INTERNET MARKETERS[29]

Priceline was not the only rising star dot.com that faced problems in the new economy. Other Internet companies experienced similar difficulties, raising questions about the underlying business models that previously seemed to promise great returns. Fall 2000 saw many examples of this. Healtheon/WebMD Corp. announced that it would cut 1,100 jobs at its Atlanta medical—services site. Amazon.com Inc.'s stock took a downturn on an analyst's questioning whether it could succeed with its huge product assortment, and Yahoo!'s stock plunged on slowing growth and smaller margins related to an expected downturn in advertising expenditures. Webvan Group Inc. decided to delay its launch of delivery services in several key regions (and filed for Chapter 11 bankruptcy protection in July 2001).

Jim Horty, president of a forensic accounting firm that gauges valuations on startups, said: "A lot of these Internet companies view the technology as their business, rather than having a business." Many have realized that making money on the Internet has been more difficult than many expected. This is a problem, because dot.coms traditionally have relied on venture capital and hyped valuations to fund expansion plans, but now many investors have lost enthusiasm and have become wary of promised future earnings.

A number of key problems that have confronted Internet marketers include:

- Lack of control over cash flow issues
- Underestimating capital costs
- Lack of control over suppliers
- Lack of control over the products the company sells (e.g., Priceline finding discount gasoline in the middle of an oil crisis)
- Lack of control over demand—after the novelty of shopping on the Internet had worn off for some customers
- Scrambling—while Internet companies struggled to redefine themselves, traditional established businesses with "deep pockets and staying power" were rallying (e.g., Toys 'R' Us.com). John Barbour, CEO of Toys 'R' Us said (referring to WebHouse Club), "But they didn't have a business model, they don't have a path to profitability and they don't have a compelling consumer benefit." Target's president of financial services and new business, Gerry Storch, added, "The stupid era of the Internet is over. It's time to start doing things that make business sense." While "old economy" methods and business models were considered passé by

EXHIBIT 3

Offer and Customer Activity (in thousands)—By Segment (Jan. 1999–Sept. 2001)

	1Q99	2Q99	3Q99	4Q99	1Q00	2Q00	3Q00	4Q00	1Q01	2Q01	3Q01
Priceline.com: ***Airline Tickets***											
Tickets Sold	186,521	440,339	623,848	707,343	1,250,416	1,288,592	1,290,096	809,327	1,075,555	1,435,936	1,183,981
Net Unique Offers	570,947	822,887	1,077,111	1,129,711	1,820,918	1,753,273	1,290,096	1,242,967	1,392,747	1,683,661	1,445,575
Offers Booked	108,917	280,471	397,355	442,089	801,204	869,408	1,756,236	590,088	709,576	963,167	779,319
Bind Rate (%)	19.1	34.1	36.9	39.1	44.0	49.6	50.5	47.5	50.9	57.2	53.9
Air product was launched 4/6/98											
Priceline.com: ***Hotel Rooms***											
Room Nights Sold	45,580	92,134	179,508	192,795	409,514	432,463	526,450	367,372	432,884	680,604	879,922
Net Unique Offers	68,740	168,543	220,613	208,991	383,708	431,249	511,396	319,501	351,952	516,816	647,446
Offers Booked	15,717	36,854	78,047	83,824	180,343	195,517	244,655	176,712	432,884	680,604	879,922
Bind Rate (%)	22.9	21.9	35.4	40.1	47.0	45.3	47.8	55.3	53.5	60.2	61.0
Hotel product was launched 10/28/98											
Priceline.com: ***Rental Cars***											
Days Sold					229,998	429,622	579,866	522,242	607,336	922,545	895,601
Net Unique Offers					90,639	175,878	217,760	207,436	229,581	325,235	313,389
Offers Booked					37,706	70,351	107,058	93,757	105,970	162,053	160,603
Bind Rate (%)					41.6	40.0	49.2	45.2	46.2	49.8	51.2
Rental car product was launched 2/3/00											

Explanation of terms:

Net Unique Offers = New customer offers + repeat customer offers.

Bind Rate = offers booked/net unique offers.

the dot.com innovators, it appears that some of the experience and wisdom of the past may help dot.coms become profitable.

Priceline once seemed to symbolize the Internet's limitless potential as a place to invent new ways of doing business—not just a new place to do business. It has become evident, however, that just inventing a new business model is insufficient. "Innovative pricing mechanisms are useless without the ability to figure out when 'new' also means 'better.'" Another new startup, iDerive, offered another model: name your own price. If you don't save, the company pays you a predetermined amount. Most customers of price-oriented companies like Priceline and iDerive are savvy about gathering information online that will help them with their asking prices.

PRICELINE.COM'S INITIATIVES FOR IMPROVED PERFORMANCE

The Star Trek image of going boldly where no man had gone before was severely challenged for Priceline.com. Jay Walker has been referred to as an "indefatigable entrepreneur."[30] Many successful entrepreneurial ventures preceded Walker Digital Corporation, which is Walker's laboratory developed for the sole purpose of developing strategic theories and concepts that eventually could be converted into businesses, and patented. The focus was on Internet applications.[31] By the fourth quarter of 2000, Priceline.com had suffered serious setbacks that threatened to cause its demise. However, it was hoped that Walker's past successes and fervent belief in his name-your-own-price model would attract the necessary capital to keep the business afloat until it could achieve profitability.

At the end of the third quarter 2000, Daniel H. Schulman, president and chief executive officer of Priceline.com, reviewed positive aspects of the business, and presented a number of initiatives that were expected to improve Priceline.com's performance.[32] He cited the positive cash flow experienced by the company for the second consecutive quarter. While disappointed in airline ticket sales for the third quarter, he reported that the customer base grew to 8 million, and that more than half of the purchase offers were made by an increasing number of repeat customers. He further stated that

19 percent of revenues for the period came from Priceline.com's non-air business, versus 12 percent the previous year. An increase in cross selling resulted in Priceline.com's airline ticket customers making up about half of hotel and rental car sales, as well as a large number of long distance sales from existing Priceline.com customers.

According to Mr. Schulman, a number of initiatives to improve cost structures and achieve long-term profitability by the end of 2000 were being implemented by Priceline. Customer satisfaction and service were being given top priority. This initiative included an educational program to demonstrate the Priceline value proposition more clearly to customers. This was to be accomplished through an improved website, product delivery, and consumer and third-party feedback.

The company realigned its operating management, and implemented a new compensation program designed to motivate and retain key employees (consisting primarily of equity-based compensation). Other initiatives included significant reduction in staffing, and amended terms of warrants held by Delta Air Lines. (These measures had a negative impact on fourth quarter 2000 results.) Mr. Schulman concluded at this time that although recent results were hurt by a weakness in airline ticket sales, the company was confident that customer metrics and performance on other fronts indicated a positive outlook for the business. He said, "We believe we are taking the right steps to position Priceline.com for future profitable growth in our core businesses." By spring 2001, analysts were favorable toward Priceline's chances for profitability. As an analyst for Goldman Sachs wrote on May 2, 2001, "Priceline has successfully 'right sized' its cost structure and now better controls its destiny."[33] On May 8, the company announced that Richard Braddock would reassume the position of chief executive, replacing Mr. Schulman, since Mr. Braddock was a "more seasoned executive who could turn the company around." At this time, Jeffery Boyd, chief operating officer, was promoted to the position of president.[34]

The clearest signal of a turnaround for Priceline was its first-ever profit report for the third quarter of 2001. This was attributed to "cutting costs, tempering advertising spending, and reviving sales in an economic environment that appears to favor its discount-driven model" ... after being "counted among the nearly dead dot-coms six months ago."

The third quarter profitability figures reflect items such as a $5.4 million charge for severance pay and forgiven loans for Mr. Schulman. The downturn in the travel industry had a positive effect on profits. Revenue was increased by more airlines and hotels who offered discounted seats and rooms through Priceline.com during the quarter—but the economic downturn also exerts pressure on prices throughout the industry and increases competition for customers.[35]

Richard Braddock outlined the company's plan for an improved earnings outlook in the fourth quarter of 2001 and on into 2002.[36] He credited this outlook to key operating efficiencies that were instituted over the past year as part of Priceline's turnaround plan. He outlined the reasons why he believes that priceline.com will continue to be a winning e-commerce company, despite the current challenges in the travel business:

- demand driven recovery in Priceline.com's U.S. travel business.

- strong, loyal consumer franchise.

- broadened product scope to reduce reliance on air product (e.g., increased strength of hotel and rental car business, and progress to date in building its mortgage business).

Braddock also cited significant developments for Priceline.com during the 3rd quarter 2001:

- customer care following the 9/11 crisis; exceptional customer service at emergency response levels.

- deepening strategic relationship with Cheung Kong (Holdings) Limited and Hutchison Whampoa Limited. These companies purchased over 7 million additional shares of Priceline.com stock in September 2001, and raised their equity to 30%; provides opportunity to introduce similar service in the Asian markets.[37]

- expansion of Priceline.com's travel products (e.g., hotel service in Mexico, Bahamas, Caribbean; beta test in 50 cities and towns in Europe; online test for cruise product; software developed for vacation package product).

- acquisition of 49 percent equity stake in PricelineMortgage.

- broadening of key supplier relationships (e.g., VISA USA).

THE MARKETING CONSULTANT'S CHALLENGE

Priceline.com has hired you as a marketing consultant. You have been asked to determine the following:

1. the optimal service mix for the company.

2. the most important actions that the company should take to achieve profitability in each of its industries.

3. a short-term marketing plan for the 4th quarter 2001 and 1st quarter 2002.

You have an appointment to meet with Richard Braddock and Jeffery Boyd tomorrow morning to present your recommendations for continued growth and prosperity.

Endnotes

1. Repeat business ratio is defined as the number of unique purchase offers coming from repeat customers divided by the number of total unique purchases.
2. Business Wire, "Priceline.com Reports Profitability and Record Revenue for 2nd Quarter 2001 (July 31, 2001).
3. Edgecliffe-Johnson, Andrew, "Under the Hammer: Priceline Preached A Revolution. Consumers Were Not Ready, Says Andrew Edgecliffe-Johnson," *Financial Times (London)*, Comment and Analysis Section (October 9, 2000), p. 27.
4. Angwin, Julia, "Priceline.com Founder Leaves Board To Focus on Incubator Walker Digital," *Wall Street Journal* (December 29, 2000), p. A13.
5. Rothenberg, Randall, "Jay Walker: The Thought Leader Interview," *Strategy + Business* (Second Quarter 2000), pp. 87–94.
6. Eisenmann, Thomas and Jon K. Rust, "Case Study: Priceline WebHouse Club," *Journal of Interactive Marketing* (Volume 14, Number 4, Autumn 2000), pp. 47–72.
7. Business Wire, "Priceline.com Reports 3rd Quarter 2000 Financial Results; Announces Measures to Strengthen Core Business," (November 2, 2000); Business Wire, "Priceline.com Reports Pro Forma Earnings Per Share of $0.03 for 3rd Quarter 2001 (November 1, 2001).
8. Angwin, Julia and Nick Wingfield, "Discounted Out: How Jay Walker Built WebHouse on a Theory That He Couldn't Prove—Priceline Offshoot Ended Up Eating Millions in Costs to Subsidize Customers—Savvy Schemes at the Pumps," *Wall Street Journal* (October 16, 2000), p. A.1+.
9. Lavoie, *op. cit.*
10. Corral, Cecile B., "WebHouse Club Puts Priceline In Grocery Biz," *Discount Store News* (October 4, 199), pp. 3, 48; Anonymous, "Priceline Strategy Extends to Online Grocery Shopping," *Supermarket Business* (October 15, 1999), p. 11+.
11. Hanover, Dan, "WebHouse Is Good, but Could Be Better," *Chain Store Age* (December 1999), p. 224.
12. Eisenmann, Thomas and Jon K. Rust, *op. cit.*, p. 49.

13. Hansell, Saul, "Priceline's WebHouse Club Abandoned as Investors Balk," *New York Times* (October 6, 2000), p. C.1.

14. Race, Tim, "New Economy: There's Just One Thing Wrong With Name-Your-Own-Price Businesses: You're Not Naming Your Own Price," *Wall Street Journal* (October 23, 2000), p. 4.

15. Race, *op. cit.*

16. Ali, "Priceline Shares Hit All-Time Low as E-Commerce Firm Struggles to Survive," *The Star Ledger*, http://www.nj.com/news (November 8, 2000).

17. Loomis, Carol J., "Inside Jay Walker's House of Cards," *Fortune* (November 13, 2000), pp. 127-138.

18. Also see Angwin, Julia and Joann Lublin, "Priceline Loses Finance Chief, Issues Warning," *Wall Street Journal* (November 3, 2000), pp. A3, A12.

19. *Business Wire*, "Dyer & Shuman, LLP Announces Shareholder Class Action Against Priceline.com, Inc. (November 3, 2000); Priceline.com is charged with violations of the antifraud provisions of the Securities Exchange Act of 1934, and alleges that Priceline issued a series of materially false and misleading statements that resulted in artificially inflated Priceline securities prices during the class period. Note that other lawsuits against the company also are pending.

20. Angwin, Julia and Karen Lundegaard, "Priceline Auto-Services Executive Quits," *Wall Street Journal* (November 18, 2000), p. B6.

21. Loomis, *op. cit.*, p. 138.

22. Loomis, *op. cit.*, p. 134.

23. Ali, *op. cit.*

24. Lavoie, Denise, "Priceline.com—The Rise and Fall of the Perfect Internet Company," *Associated Press State and Local Wire, Business News Section* (November 8, 2000).

25. Ali, Sam, *op. cit.*

26. Wingfield, Nick, "Priceline Loss Narrows as Revenue Soars Amid Demand for Bookings," *Wall Street Journal* (April 25, 2000), p. B6.

27. *Business Wire*, "Priceline.com Reports Pro Forma Earnings Per Share of $0.03 for 3rd Quarter 2001."

28. The "look-to-book" ratio is a metric used in the travel industry to measure the percentage of people who actually buy a product after visiting or contacting the travel company.

29. Most of this section is based on Kerstetter, Jim, Linda Himelstein, Rob Hof, Louise Lee, and Pamela Moore, "Analysis and Commentary: The Internet," *Business Week* (October 23, 2000), pp. 44-45.

30. Loomis, *op. cit.*, p. 138.

31. Rothenberg, *op. cit.*

32. Business Wire, "Priceline.com Reports 3rd Quarter 2000 Financial Results….," *op. cit.*

33. Angwin, Julia, "Priceline Surges on Turnaround Progress," *Wall Street Journal*. (May 2, 2001), p. A3.

34. Sandberg, Jared, "Priceline Replaces CEO With Chairman," *Wall Street Journal* (May 8, 2001), p. B7.

35. Angwin, Julia, "Priceline.com Posts a Profit, Crediting Stringent Cost Cuts, Escalating Demand," *Wall Street Journal* (August 1, 2001), p. A3.

36. *Business Wire*, "Priceline.com Reports Pro Forma Earnings Per Share of $0.03 For 3rd Quarter," (November 1, 2001).

37. See *Business Wire*, "Priceline.com Agrees to Connect Its Name Your Own Price Travel Services to the Amadeus Global Travel Distribution System," (November 6, 2000) for other opportunities to expand globally through Priceline.com's November 2000 agreement with Amadeus Global Travel Distribution, whereby its international Global Distribution System (GDS) could be used to process ticket purchase requests from Priceline.com's customers and international licensees.

Black Diamond, Ltd.: Hanging on the Cutting Edge

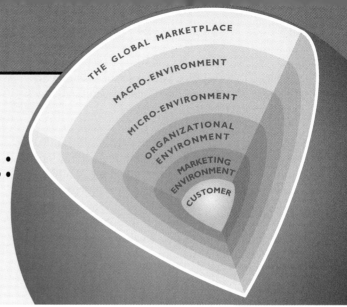

This case was prepared by Steven J. Maranville, Assistant Professor of Strategic Management, University of St. Thomas, and Madeleine E. Pullman of Southern Methodist University.

Jeff Jamison looked above at the glistening ice and snow of the frozen waterfalls. He had waited 3 weeks for the ice to get to this perfect condition, thick enough to support body weight, and the correct consistency for holding the picks of the two axes in his hands and the tooth-covered crampons on his feet. On this day in early January of 1993, he was trying out a new axe, the Black Prophet, a state-of-the-art climbing tool with a light weight, composite handle, and innovative head design produced by Black Diamond Equipment, Ltd. Everyone in the mountaineering world was talking about the Black Prophet's novel design and waiting for the tool to enter the stores in the coming months. Jeff was lucky enough to have a connection with one of Black Diamond's sales representatives, giving Jeff access to the new Black Prophet before its formal release to the market.

At the top of the last pitch of the climb, he sunk the Black Prophet into the ice and suddenly felt a disconcerting snap. Jeff watched with trepidation as pieces of the broken axe plummeted thousands of feet to the canyon floor. As panic swept in, Jeff realized that he would be forced to descend with only one axe, a doable but challenging feat. During the long, arduous descent, all Jeff

could think about was how could a tool like that one have left Black Diamond's factory.

The following Monday, January 4, 1993, Mellie Abrahamsen, Black Diamond's new quality assurance manager, a recent MBA graduate from the University of Utah, entered her office and turned on her computer to scan her e-mail. The news of the axe incident was echoing from all over the plant. Research & Development, Production, Customer Service, Marketing, and the president were all demanding an explanation and a plan. With all the excitement over the new design, preseason orders for the Black Prophet had exceeded expectations. Although the tool was on back order for many customers, the first production run of the axe had already been shipped to mountaineering stores throughout the world. Highlighted at the top of Abrahamsen's e-mail listing was a priority message from Peter Metcalf, president of Black Diamond, calling an emergency meeting with all department heads to develop a plan for handling the crisis.

MONDAY MORNING MEETING

By 9:00 A.M., Black Diamond's top management team was huddled around the square butcher-block table that filled the center of Metcalf's congested corner office. As Abrahamsen approached, she could see into Metcalf's office through the two large windows that faced the shop floor. Because she was new to the company, many of the artifacts peculiar to Black Diamond still caught her attention.

Metcalf's office walls were decorated with framed photographs of mountain-climbing and skiing adventures. The management team members sitting around the table were dressed casually; many were wearing Black Diamond sportswear—tee-shirts and sweaters with the Black Diamond insignia. Abrahamsen squeezed through the office and found a seat next to Metcalf, from which she had a view out the windows.

Metcalf anxiously spoke to the group. "This incident is a devastating blow. Thank goodness the guy didn't get hurt, but now every one of our axes out there is suspect. If we have to issue a recall on the product, that will kill our axe business. If we have to discontinue our axe program, all the European competitors will step in and copy the technology that we worked so long to perfect. Yet, think of the liability implications of an accident from this tool! How could this have happened? I thought this axe had the latest and greatest technology! We've never had problems like this with our regular mountaineering axes."

Cranor, the marketing manager, added to Metcalf's fervent speech. "If customers see this axe as being of poor quality, we'll be forced to cease the axe program. But worse, if customers think Black Diamond is a company that markets unsafe products, our whole business is in jeopardy! Black Diamond must not lose its leadership image."

"My sales representatives are having a fit," Stan Smith, manager of customer service, proclaimed loudly. "They have huge back orders for the axe, and the retail shops have several customers a day asking about the tool. You folks know how this industry is—rumors about tool failures and accidents get around fast."

In a despondent tone, the designer of the Black Prophet, Chuck Brainard, said, "I can't believe this nightmare. Just as we were sitting on top of the world with the most innovative design to enter the market in years—all the competition taken by surprise, and a good ice climbing season ahead—a major stroke of bad luck hits."

"I can't help but think" said Stan Brown, the production manager, "that the cause of the axe's failure is in its design. It's great to be innovative, but I think the design is so innovative that it just doesn't work."

"Now wait a minute, Stan," Metcalf interjected, "I don't want this to deteriorate into finger pointing."

Brainard spoke, "No, no, that's all right Peter. Stan might be right. Maybe we did go too far."

Metcalf went on: "We don't know all the facts. So let's stay focused and not jump to conclusions. This is a companywide problem."

Trying to refocus the group, Cranor said, "We tried to cut the lead time on this project so that we would have at least a year of sales before the French, Swiss, and other U.S. competitors could copy our concept and steal our market share. We have the reputation as the quality and innovative design company. This incident is potentially very damaging to our reputation as the market leader for innovation."

"We've got to nip this one in the bud and find a way to reassure our customer base," contended Smith. "I need an answer as soon as possible."

John Bercaw, manager of research and development, said, "Stan, I appreciate the urgent need that you're feeling with regard to handling customer concerns, but we need more than a quick fix. We need to find out why the failure occurred and put systems in place to prevent this from happening again."

"I agree," Metcalf applauded. "As I said, this is a companywide problem."

Brainard attempted to clarify the situation: "As I see it, the possible sources of the failure are design, materials, and/or assembly."

"I can speak about the development phase of the project," stated Bercaw. "We worked hard to develop this axe and cut down on the lead time between the conceptualization and production of the final tool. Peter, you know we've been under tremendous pressure to have this new axe into the production phase and on the market in under 2 years."

Metcalf nodded. "That's been our strategy," he said, "being the firstest with the mostest."

Bercaw continued: "This project has been a real struggle; we've been working with all sorts of new technologies like composite construction and modular tool design. The vendors normally don't make tools for these types of applications. They've had a hard time meeting our specifications, and many of the vendors don't want to work on our products because of potential liability implications."

"What about the assembly?" asked Metcalf.

Brown spoke, "Well, the shop worked like crazy to get those axes out for the winter season, and I put my best people on the rush assembly. The shop has been really taxed, what with the increasing growth rate for all our climbing and mountaineering products. We're always scrambling to meet the back orders. We need more people and new machines to keep up with this demand and improve our quality."

Metcalf persisted: "Do you know of anything in particular that may have been out of the ordinary during assembly?"

Brown replied: "I'd have to talk to Brian, our lead assembler, to see if he has any clues about why that axe could have failed in the field."

Metcalf turned to his left, where Black Diamond's newest management team member was sitting. "I realize that this is all new to you and that you came in after the fact, so I doubt the Quality Assurance Department can do much about this situation now."

Caught somewhat by surprise, Abrahamsen pulled her thoughts together. "Since this job is a newly created position, I wasn't here during the design development and testing phase. I would like to see the procedures and testing information on the production lot of axes. Black Diamond wants to be ISO 9000-certified, and we would need to have all those documents for ISO 9000 certification anyway, so this is a good starting place. Meanwhile, I think we should bring all the field axes back for inspection to reinforce customer confidence and prevent what happened on Saturday from happening again."

Looking out of his office's windows, Metcalf pointed to the shop floor and remarked, "Isn't that Brian walking through the shop? Ask him to come in."

Brian Palmer, the lead assembler, entered Metcalf's office. There was no place to sit, so he remained standing. Metcalf explained to Brian the purpose for bringing him into the meeting. Brian indicated that he had heard about the climbing incident involving the Black Prophet.

Metcalf continued: "Brian, we're not on a witch hunt; we're trying to understand the full range of factors that could have contributed to the tool's failure. What can you tell us about the assembly?"

Brian spoke frankly: "I personally put together all those axes. We didn't have any procedures, because it was the first time we had made a production lot. Normally when we work on a new product, we go through a learning curve trying to

figure out the best assembly method. We make so many different types of products in the shop, it's really like a craft shop. And I'm not even sure if I have the most up-to-date prints right now. The vendor had a lot of trouble casting all those parts to the exact dimensions. But I was able to find enough parts that seemed to fit, and with a little extra elbow grease, I hammered the pieces together. I had to work overtime to meet the deadline and get all the preliminary orders out to the customers. But that's what matters—pleasing the customer."

"But is creating a defective axe really pleasing the customer?" questioned Abrahamsen. "What good is it to be first to market if the product fails in the field. Sure, we have to get to market fast, but we also have to make the axe right the first time. The way we deal in the short term with the Black Prophet situation will have some long-term implications for Black Diamond's strategy. I think we should examine the new product introduction process as well as the ongoing production processes to see how we can prevent this type of thing from happening in the future."

THE MARKET FOR MOUNTAINEERING EQUIPMENT

The established customer for mountaineering products, including mountaineering skis, had traditionally been the serious international mountaineer—professionals as well as expert amateurs. Some dedicated mountaineers worked as professional guides and explorers; nonprofessionals had other jobs, but both professionals and amateurs spent their vacations and weekends climbing in their local areas and traveling throughout the world attempting to conquer remote peaks. This traditional customer base had been primarily in North America, eastern and western Europe, Japan, and Korea, although limited numbers of participants were from other countries.

Mountaineering was as popular in Europe as basketball was in the United States, with mountaineering stars earning high incomes through competitions, product endorsements, and other media exposure. Because of the long history of climbing in Europe, the European market was the biggest segment in the world climbing market, with 10 percent of the market in France alone. Not only did the adult urban European population prefer to spend vacations in mountain villages, but increasingly, younger generations of Europeans were forsaking crowded beaches for mountain holidays revolving around mountain sports.

Starting in the 1980s, media exposure had brought mountain sports to previously ignored market segments throughout the world. Rock climbing and mountaineering images had become popular for advertising many types of products and for adding "color" to music videos and movie plots. Because of this exposure, teenage and recreational customers—predominantly in the U.S. market—were high-growth segments, with noticeable growth in the mid-1980s erupting into an explosive growth rate of 40 percent in the early 1990s. Customers in this growing market segment had no intention of traveling the world looking for untouched and ever more challenging peaks; instead, this recreational segment climbed and skied purely for fun in their local and national resort areas.

Customarily, people wishing to learn mountain sports would employ guide services and schools for acquiring the necessary skills. The newer converts, however, were bypassing this conventional route by going to indoor climbing gyms or learning skills from friends. Many industry experts speculated that this breakdown of the conventional training methods would contribute to an increased lack of knowledge regarding mountaineering safety and lead to increased accident rates. In turn, accidents would increase the chances of litigation for all firms involved in the industry. These trends were a concern to mountain-sports firms worldwide.

COMPETITION IN THE MOUNTAINEERING EQUIPMENT INDUSTRY

Located in Salt Lake City, Utah, Black Diamond Equipment, Ltd., was a major player in the burgeoning international mountaineering industry, on both domestic and global fronts. Black Diamond manufactured and distributed a full range of products for mountain sports, from rock-climbing gear to mountaineering and backcountry skis, and faced few domestic or global competitors whose business was on a similar scale. (Exhibit A is a company/product profile of the mountaineering industry.)

The industry that served the mountaineering market consisted of three groups: retailers, wholesalers, and manufacturers.

Retailers

The retail businesses serving the market's diverse variety of mountaineering customers were one of three types. The first group, the "core" mountaineering shops, were small retail operations specializing in products specific to mountaineering such as ropes, climbing protection, climbing axes, expedition clothing, packs, harnesses, and information guides for local and national areas. Because these shops were usually located in mountain areas such as the Rocky Mountains or the Alps, the shop personnel were experts in the special tools and applications for their regions. In addition, these shop personnel often had personal knowledge of other international locations.

These shops usually carried products made in their region with specialized products from other countries. The core shops competed on the basis of the expertise of their personnel and their stock of technically appropriate tools. These retailers specialized in high-quality, cutting-edge-technology products. Prices were relatively high. The majority of their customers were highly skilled mountaineers. Black Diamond operated a small retail shop in this category located next to its Salt Lake City manufacturing facility. Black Diamond's full product range sold well in this type of shop.

Because of their remote locations, many core shops made effective use of catalogues as a direct-marketing tool. Several mail-order companies, including Black Diamond's mail-order division, competed in this core area, selling products both nationally and internationally.

The second group, "mom and pop" stores, also consisted of small retail outlets, but they sold all types of equipment from camping and backpacking equipment to bikes and skis. The product mix varied depending on the geographic location. Most of these stores carried a limited assortment of climbing products—usually ropes, harnesses, and carabiners, small clips used in all climbing applications to attach the climber to rock or snow. The personnel in mom and pop stores usually had limited technical knowledge of the products being sold.

EXHIBIT A

Mountaineering Industry Competitive Product Profile

Product Category/ Manufacturers	National Market Share, %	International Market Share, %
Carabiners		
Black Diamond	50	10
Omega	10	3
SMC	10	3
Wild Country	10	20
DMM	10	20
Petzl	5	30
MSR (REI)	5	4
Climbing protections		
Black Diamond	50	20
Metolius	20	10
Lowe	10	10
Wild Country	10	25
DMM50	10	25
Harnesses		
Black Diamond	50	20
Petzl	20	50
REI	20	
Blue Water	10	10
Wild Country	5	20
Plastic boots		
Scarpa*	40	30
Merrell	25	5
Koflach	25	40
Lowe	15	5
Adjustable ski poles		
Black Diamond	60	5
Life Link	40	5
Mountaineer skis		
Rossignol	30	50
Hagen*	20	10
Climbing accessories		
Black Diamond	55	15
Omega	25	10
Petzl	20	75
Gloves		
Black Diamond	50	5
Snow climbing axes		
Charlie Moser	50	10
Black Diamond	20	5

(continued)

EXHIBIT A *(continued)*

Mountaineering Industry Competitive Product Profile

Product Category/ Manufacturers	National Market Share, %	International Market Share, %
Ice climbing axes		
Black Diamond	30	10
Charlie Moser	30	15
DMM	25	30
Grivel	15	30
Rock shoes		
Scarpa*	25	20
Sportiva	25	35
Boreal	25	35
Five Ten	15	5
Ropes		
Mamutt	30	50
PMI*	20	40
New England	20	
Blue Water	20	10

*European manufacturers producing Black Diamond designs.
Source: Estimates of industry representatives.

The third group consisted of sporting goods and department store chains, ranging in size from regional chains such as Eastern Mountain Sports (7 stores) to national chains such as Recreational Equipment, Inc. (REI) (40 stores). These stores, which were located in major cities with access to mass markets, had extensive outdoor clothing departments, tents, stoves, canoes and kayaks, sleeping bags, bikes, skis, etc. Products in each category were selected for volume sales. Thus, in the climbing department, the product line covered the needs of entry-level or intermediate recreational climbers. The expertise of department store personnel was, however, generally limited.

In the United States, REI was the dominant firm in this group of retailers. REI operated department stores in Seattle, Boston, Los Angeles, and Washington, D.C., with limited national competition on this level. Because of its large size and wide scope, REI could buy in volume for all its stores and offered very competitive prices. The Canadian retailer, Mountain Equipment Coop (MEC), served a similar market in Canada, with a large store in each of Canada's major cities. In France, Au Vieux Campeur

owned multiple department stores in major French cities, serving a broad customer base.

Wholesalers

Retail outlets bought their product lines from wholesalers during semiannual outdoor equipment shows held throughout the world. The wholesaler category of firms consisted of companies that either manufactured their own products or subcontracted the manufacturing of their designs and distributed their own product lines and companies licensed to distribute the products of other companies in certain geographic areas, as well as various combinations of these two. Black Diamond was in this last category. The company distributed equipment designed and manufactured in its Utah plant, equipment manufactured for Black Diamond by other firms, and merchandise designed by Black Diamond and distributed under other manufacturers' names. In all, Black Diamond offered over 250 different items, covering most mountain sports (see Exhibit B).

REI was Black Diamond's biggest wholesale customer, making up almost 10 percent of Black

EXHIBIT B

Black Diamond Product Categories

Climbing protection	Ropes and rope bags
Camming devices	Packs
Nuts	Hip packs
Stoppers	Backpacks
Pitons	Tents
Piton hammers	Snow and ice tools
Slings	Axes
Runners	Crampons
Daisy chains	Ice screws and
Etriers	hooks
Webbing	Ski tools
Belay devices	Skis
Carabiners	Bindings
Harnesses	Poles
Sport climbing	Climbing clothing
Alpine	Tee-shirts
mountaineering	Sweatshirts
Big wall	Shorts
Footwear	Pants
Mountaineering	Hats
boots	Belts
Ski boots	Chalk bags
Rock climbing shoes	

Diamond's total sales. The next biggest customer, Lost Arrow—Japan, was a Japanese distributor comprising 5 percent of Black Diamond's sales. The other major wholesale customers were North American outdoor sports department store chains, mail-order companies, and Black Diamond's own retail shop and mail-order business. Combined, the top 20 percent of Black Diamond's retail customers—roughly 60 companies—accounted for about 80 percent of total sales.

Domestically, Black Diamond's wholesaling competition came from Omega Pacific, which manufactured and distributed its own metal products, and Blue Water, which wholesaled its own lines of ropes and harnesses. Neither of these companies, however, carried a product line as extensive as Black Diamond's.

The international wholesaling segment included strong competition from two U.K. firms, Denny Morehouse Mountaineering and Wild Country, and a French company, Petzl. These firms wholesaled a full range of mountaineering products manufactured by companies with strong international reputations. Additional competition came from more regional firms. Most countries had several smaller manufacturers of specific products such as carabiners or climbing axes that were successful in wholesaling their own products.

Several issues influenced sales in the international marketplace. First, the International Organization of Standards had mandated that by 1997 "personal protective equipment" would have to meet ISO 9000 quality certification standards in order to be sold in Europe. Companies with certification stamped their products with a symbol showing that the product's manufacturer had met the relevant ISO 9000 standards. This certification was intended to give the consumer more confidence in a product's quality. Most of the European mountaineering manufacturers had initiated the certification process and were well on their way to obtaining certification. In contrast, very few American companies, including Black Diamond, had even begun the certification process. (Exhibit C provides an overview of the ISO 9000 standards.)

Second, some European countries had a long history of climbing and mountaineering, and certain manufacturers, Grivel, for example, dated back to the late 1800s. Although several European companies had well-established worldwide reputations for quality and innovative products, others relied on home country support, producing lower-quality, lower-priced products. All mountainous European countries had small factories for carabiners, skis, axes, or shoes that produced, at relatively low cost, simple products in high volume for domestic consumption.

Third, the European market was predominantly ethnocentric in purchasing behavior. French climbers preferred to buy French products, while German climbers preferred German products. Because of the risks involved in climbing and mountaineering, customers chose equipment they knew the most about and had the most confidence in. Usually, these products were from the buyers' respective countries.

Manufacturers

As a manufacturer, Black Diamond faced both domestic and international competition. Domestic manufacturing firms ran the gamut from small garage operations to large machine shops with 50 or more employees, and most produced either

EXHIBIT C

ISO 9000 Standards

The ISO 9000 standards provide the requirements for documenting processes and procedures. The intent of the standards mandates an organization "do what they say and say what they do." The standards offer three quality system models—ISO 9001, ISO 9002, and ISO 9003—with increasing levels of stringency. 9003 covers documentation and procedure requirements for final inspection and testing, 9002 adds production and installation, and 9001 includes design and development. An organization chooses the appropriate standard depending on the strategically important functional areas requiring quality procedures. In most cases, manufacturers use 9001 for covering all areas.

In order to receive ISO 9000 certification, a company will spend several years complying with the requirements in the standards. This compliance usually requires extensive documentation of the existing quality program and training for all employees involved in processes related to quality. Individual auditors, who work for the international ISO registration organization, evaluate the company for requirement compliance. The certified companies are reevaluated every two years to ensure continuing compliance.

A brief overview of the 9001 requirements are provided below:
• The entire quality system must be defined and documented to ensure each product meets specifications.
• The contractual requirements for quality between company and the customer must be defined and documented.
• Procedures are required to ensure that critical processes are under control.
• Procedures are required for inspection at all levels and for identification of nonconforming parts or products.
• Procedures are required to prevent nonconforming parts from getting damaged in storage, delivery, or packing.
• Training is required for all personnel affecting quality.
• The quality system must be audited internally to ensure effectiveness and compliance.

"software" or "hardware." The software firms worked with textile products such as ropes and harnesses. The majority of the software firms, including Blue Water, Sterling Rope, and Misty Mountain, were located in the southeastern United States. These more specialized manufacturing firms expanded their market by catering to the needs of nonmountaineering industries, such as construction safety, military applications, and spelunking. The hardware group manufactured or assembled metal products such as carabiners and other climbing tools and protection. This group of manufacturers included Friends, Rock Hardware, and Rock Exotica. These firms had reputations as producers of innovative and high-quality equipment.

REI had recently started up a small manufacturing facility for carabiners. The manager of this REI facility had many years of engineering experience with Boeing Aircraft and had designed a highly automated manufacturing system capable of both production and quality testing.

Because Black Diamond had begun as a machine shop, the company had strong capabilities in metalworking. Specifically, the Salt Lake facility manufactured cold-forged metal parts associated with carabiners, axes, and other climbing accessories and protection. Hot-forging and casting were subcontracted by Black Diamond to manufacturers specializing in this area. Black Diamond was beginning to expand into simple soft goods, such as slings and other webbing products, and intended to continue developing its in-house sewing capabilities.

Black Diamond had plans to become vertically integrated. Management believed that in-house performance of operations related to core products would enhance Black Diamond's competitiveness. Consequently, Black Diamond had started reviewing some of its subcontracting practices to determine what functions could be brought in-house. In particular, the company wanted to bring in-house all sewing of climbing gear and some metal treatments such as heat-treating.

Other products, such as skis, ski poles, foot gear, and ropes, required very specific technologies, production skills, and economies of scale for competitive pricing and quality. Black Diamond entered into subcontracting agreements with international manufacturers to design and manufacture such products. The company also subcontracted the production of its harnesses to a technically sophisticated harness manufacturer located next door to the Salt Lake City facility that made the harnesses on a semiautomated assembly line. This process required minimal human involvement, in contrast to a "garment industry" sewing process by which one person sews the complete harness from start to finish.

By the late 1980s, European competition was becoming a more significant factor in the U.S. market. In particular, Petzl, a French company with a full range of products, had taken an aggressive position in the U.S. market. Petzl, like several of the European competitors, had a well-established reputation as a producer of high-quality, innovative products. Petzl had set up a manufacturing facility in the United States within 60 miles of Black Diamond's manufacturing facility and had sponsored several professional U.S. climbers. Black Diamond, of course, was making efforts to sell its own products in Europe but faced the problem of ISO 9000 certification.

Some international manufacturing activity went on in Korea and Japan. Products produced by these manufacturers were marketed and distributed through other international companies. The majority of these products were low-cost, mass-produced items such as carabiners.

The continuing growth of copyright violations and product privacy—especially prevalent within international markets—added a further dimension to global competition. Several U.S. and European companies had used machine shops in Korea and Japan as subcontractors, supplying dies and other technological knowhow. Consequently, unlicensed clones of more expensive items were expected to appear soon in the international market.

BLACK DIAMOND'S OPERATIONS

Black Diamond Equipment, Ltd., opened for business in 1989 after a group of former managers with employee support bought the assets of Chouinard Equipment from Lost Arrow Corporation during Chapter 11 bankruptcy proceedings. The bankruptcy resulted from four lawsuits related to climbing equipment accidents during the 1980s. Chouinard

Equipment was the first U.S. company to develop and manufacture rock-climbing gear. From its inception and for the following decade, Chouinard Equipment had a reputation for innovation and quality unmatched by any national competitors.

After the purchase, the new owners chose a new name for the company that would reflect its roots yet would project a fresh beginning. The insignia of a diamond was Chouinard Equipment's previous logo. The new company decided to keep the diamond image and chose the name "black diamond" because of the different associations the name might evoke: "diamond in the rough," "rogue," "bad boy," and "unusual" (see Exhibit D for the Black Diamond Logo). Furthermore, a "black diamond" was used to identify the most difficult type of run in ski areas, and the company owners hoped the name would appeal to the "extreme" athlete, their primary targeted customer base. Black Diamond's management believed that "if you target the extremities, the recreational customer will follow."

The mission of Black Diamond was "to design, manufacture, and bring to market, in a profitable and on-time manner, innovative and technical products of high quality, high performance, and exemplary durability that are targeted toward our primary customers—climbers and backcountry skiers." The company was committed to 10 guiding principles:

1. Being the market leader, synonymous with the sports we serve and are absolutely passionate about

EXHIBIT D

Black Diamond Logo

2. Having a truly global presence

3. Supporting the specialty retailer

4. Creating long-term partnerships with companies we do business with

5. Being very easy to do business with

6. Being a fierce competitor with the highest ethical standards

7. Developing sustainable, competitive advantage

8. Sharing the company's success with its employees

9. Creating a safe, personally fulfilling work environment for all employees

10. Championing the preservation of and access to our mountain environments

In 1991, the owner-employees relocated the business from Ventura, California, to Salt Lake City, Utah, where they would be closer to the targeted customer. Black Diamond began operations with a staff of roughly 40, covering all functional areas. (See Exhibit E for Black Diamond's organizational structure.) Black Diamond was 50 percent owned by employees; the remaining 50 percent of the stock was held by outside investors, predominately distributors, customers, and friends and family of the main employee stockholders. Of the 50 percent that was employee owned, 75 percent was held by Metcalf, the CEO; Cranor, head of marketing; and Kawakami, the chief financial officer.

In 1993, Black Diamond's annual sales were expected to be approximately $12 million with a gross profit margin of about 40 percent (grossing about $4.8 million) and with a net profit margin of about 10 percent (netting around $1.2 million). From 1990 through 1993, the climbing industry had experienced tremendous sales growth of 20 to 40 percent per year. The market demanded more innovative products and faster delivery. Black Diamond struggled to keep up with the exploding customer demand by hiring more employees and upgrading shop machinery to increase productivity. Slowly, the original machinery was being replaced by automated machining centers and testing devices. By 1993, the company employed more than 100 people.

Like other metalworking shops, Black Diamond specialized in certain types of metalworking; the areas of specialization consisted of cold-forging metal parts, stamping and forming, computer numerically

controlled (CNC) machining, and assembly or fabrication. Forging, stamping, and forming, along with the assembly processes, had been done for 20 years by the original Chouinard Company, and these processes were considered to be Black Diamond's technical core. These core processes used the same multiton presses that forced metal stock into a die or mold to obtain the desired shape.

Since moving to Salt Lake City, the company had expanded into CNC machines—large programmable machine tools capable of producing small to medium-sized batches of intricate parts—in an effort to reduce costs and to move more production processes in-house. These machines were expensive, although they provided the advantages of capacity and product flexibility. Many of Black Diamond's processes, however, required machinery that was too costly to justify purchase for the manufacturing of a limited number of parts. Consequently, Black Diamond subcontracted with other vendors for aluminum hot-forging, investment casting, laser-cutting steel, preshearing metals, anodizing, heat treating, welding, screw machining, wire forming such as springs, and aluminum extrusion. These processes were subcontracted to achieve economies of scale (e.g., aluminum extrusion) or because the specialized equipment and skills required were beyond Black Diamond's capabilities (e.g., hot-forging).

Black Diamond's production facility was divided into several functional areas: the machine shop, which built prototypes and constructed and maintained tool and die apparatus; the punch press room, where parts were pressed out at a rate of one per second by several multiton presses; a room with assorted machines, each operated by one person doing drilling, milling, grinding, or operating CNC machines; a tumbling and polishing room, where large batches of parts were polished; the assembly room, where parts were assembled by individuals or teams; and finally, a room for materials and shipping.

Supported by a material requirements planning (MRP) system, materials were ordered several months in advance for a full batch of products—for example, 5000 carabiners or 500 axes. When fairly common parts such as springs and aluminum rod stock were involved, the orders arrived on time and met standard quality requirements. The more complex and customized parts, such as investment-cast

EXHIBIT E

Black Diamond Organizational Structure

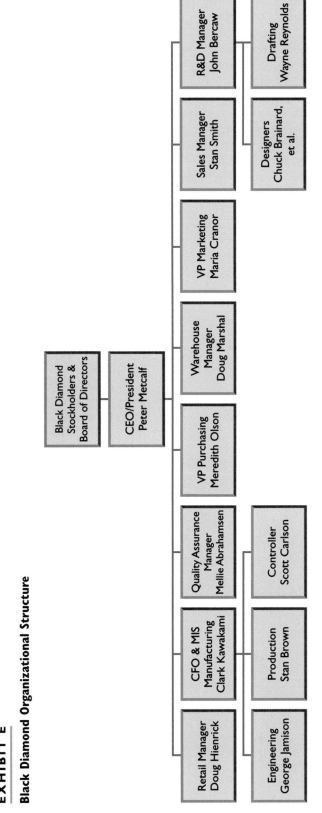

axe parts, were difficult for vendors to make to specifications and thus often did not meet the assembly deadline.

When the parts arrived in the materials supply area, one person was responsible for spot-checking the order to see if the parts met specifications. For example, when 500 axe heads arrived, the inspector would randomly select 15 parts and would measure 20 different key dimensions on each part to determine if the tolerances met specifications. If one dimension was out of tolerance, the quality manager was summoned for an evaluation. Depending on the impact on other assembly processes, a larger meeting, involving all potentially affected parties, might be necessary to determine a course of action.

Most of Black Diamond's products began as a sheet of steel or aluminum rod. After receiving the metal, the incoming inspector would pull a sample of the metal to check hardness and dimensions. When production on an order was ready to begin, the metal was moved from a hallway to the press room. The press operator would receive an order for 5000 parts and would set up the press to begin cutting and smashing parts to shape. Once the dies were in place, the operator would smash a few sample parts and check with an inspector for approval.

As the dies wore down, the parts might turn out to have excess metal, or the logo engraving might be substandard. Depending on the demand for the parts, the inspector might feel pressure to pass on these cosmetically imperfect parts. Once approval was given, the operator would proceed to press out as many parts as possible in the shortest time. Often chips of metal would settle in the die and these chips would be imbedded into many parts before being discovered by the operator. When this occurred, thousands of parts needed to be scrapped.

After the smashing process, the parts usually were sent out for heat-treating to harden the metal. The heat-treatment plant was located in California, and so this procedure had a turnaround time of several weeks. When the parts returned, they went to the tumbling and drilling rooms for further processing. When color was needed, the parts would be shipped out again for anodizing, an electrolytic process by which metal is covered with a protective and/or decorative oxide film.

Finally, when the main body of a part was finished, the materials department would issue batches of all the other components needed to finish the product batch under production. All these parts would proceed to a group of assemblers, seated around tables, who were responsible for assembling the final product. The assembly room was the epitome of a craft shop environment. Large and expensive products such as axes were assembled in small batches by one individual, while products such as carabiners were assembled in larger batches by teams of people who often rotated jobs. The finished products would go through individual testing and inspection before passing to the shipping area. During inspection, one inspector might evaluate thousands of parts in a day.

Originally, the company had one employee responsible for quality assurance, and several shop employees performed quality control functions. The quality assurance person worked for the R&D department and focused on testing new products, prototypes, and work in production. As the company grew and ISO 9000 certification loomed in the future, several members of the management team decided that quality issues needed more prominent attention. Not only was testing required, but a plantwide program to ensure that defects did not occur in the first place was needed.

Black Diamond's original quality assurance officer had left the company to guide climbing expeditions, after which Black Diamond's management created a stand-alone Quality Assurance Department and hired Mellie Abrahamsen as the manager. At the time of Abrahamsen's hiring, the organization lacked a companywide quality assurance program. The members of R&D and the shop functioned along craft-shop lines. Product designers built prototypes on the shop floor, iterating between field testing and lab testing until they felt the design was ready. When the new design went into production, the shop personnel used trial and error to develop an assembly procedure. Out-of-tolerance parts often were accepted by shop personnel, who invented creative ways of adapting the parts or the procedures for assembling the products.

Implementing a quality control program would mean the introduction of formal testing and assembly procedures for both designers and shop workers. As Andrew McLean, a head designer, said:

"We are like artists here, and you just can't restrain or rush creativity and get good results." Chuck Brainard complained: "If we have to write procedures for every step of production, we'll be changing those things a million times."

Like most machine-shop workers, Black Diamond's shop employees labored under comparatively unglamorous working conditions, involving, for example, noise, grease, and monotony. Many shop workers lacked a high school education, and some could not read or write in English. Although the shop workers were the lowest-paid employees at Black Diamond, the company offered a generous profit-sharing bonus to all workers and tried to involve all of them in monthly meetings concerning the financial performance of the company. Despite these measures, the shop had a high rate of job turnover.

Because quality control programs require training in procedure writing, blueprint reading, and statistical techniques, the shop employees needed elementary math and language training before they could learn more complicated subjects. Stan Brown acknowledged that the workers needed training but said: "I can't let those people miss too much work for training; we really need everyone working nonstop to get products out the door."

Many of the professional employees at Black Diamond were avid climbers and users of the products, taking great pride in trying to make the very best products available. Marketing was concerned about keeping up the company's innovative image with new products every season. Production worried about vendor costs, delivery of parts, and the shop's ability to meet sales forecasts. R&D attempted to simultaneously develop buildable new products, reduce lead time for new product development, and improve existing products. Customer service tried to keep retailers pacified with partial deliveries and promises.

Finally, quality assurance was charged with implementing quality control procedures, conducting training, testing products, and resolving problems attributed to parts or products not meeting specifications. All functional areas faced the problems inherent in trying to achieve the simultaneous goals of meeting customer demand and ensuring the highest-quality products, and the different areas often clashed on the best means and methods of achieving these goals.

THE BLACK PROPHET

The concept for the Black Prophet axe was developed originally to round out Black Diamond's product line of axes. The product line had two other axes: the Alpamayo, a glacier-walking and snow-climbing axe, and the X-15, a versatile axe for both snow and ice climbing. The Black Prophet was designed specifically for ice climbing and incorporated an innovative ergonomic shape to reduce arm fatigue, a composite, rubber-bonded shaft construction for gripability and weight reduction, and interchangeable modular components allowing the use of different types of tools—a hammer head, picks, or an adze—for miscellaneous ice applications. (Exhibit F is a drawing of the Black Prophet and its component parts.)

Designing and producing the axe entailed several years of working with different vendors to develop the appropriate production process for each component. The axe was designed as a prototype and field tested with different constructions until R&D agreed on a specific configuration. This configuration was then reviewed by sales representatives considered to be mountaineering experts and by other company members at the quarterly meetings. If the tool did not pass the scrutiny of those examiners, R&D would begin a new phase of prototype development and field tests. This development process would continue until a company-wide consensus was reached.

The axe required five parts: shaft, head, hammer, pick, and adze. Three parts were cast metal, requiring a casting subcontractor with the ability to meet strict specifications. The composite shaft was produced by a composite and bonding manufacturer. The ice pick was manufactured in Black Diamond's plant. Black Diamond received the parts from each vendor, inspected them for conformance to specifications, and assembled the axes.

The Black Prophet, which cost approximately $80 to produce, sold as an axe with two tool accessories. The total retail price was $200; the wholesale price was $140. The initial shipment of Black Prophets for winter season 1993 was approximately 200 axes. The company expected yearly sales of the axe to reach at least 2500 units, making a significant contribution to winter sales.

Management expected the Black Prophet to be one of Black Diamond's top 10 selling winter

EXHIBIT F

The Black Prophet

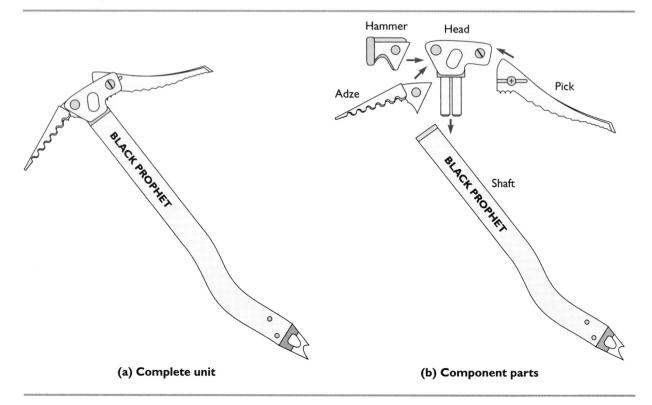

(a) Complete unit	**(b) Component parts**

products, and the entire company regarded it as a very big image item on the world mountaineering scene. Every competitor in this industry had an axe for glacier walking. Axes were especially popular in Europe, where Black Diamond foresaw superb potential for the new axe.

The axe had been well received at the previous year's outdoor product show. At that time, no other axes like it were in the wings, and the climbing industry anticipated the Black Prophet's arrival with great excitement. All major U.S. and European industry magazines had published articles about the Black Prophet, and famous mountaineers had called Black Diamond requesting Black Prophets for their upcoming expeditions.

THE DILEMMA

As the Monday morning meeting continued, Black Diamond's top management team members struggled to find answers to the questions raised by the axe crisis. They knew that the situation required both short- and long-term solutions. In the short term, management needed to address the pressure for immediate delivery confronting customer service. Should management recall all the Black Prophet axes currently on the market? A recall would come with high shipping, testing, and opportunity costs. Or should Black Diamond basically ignore the incident, assuming the accident was a one-time freak, and continue to sell the axes while refuting any rumors about the axe's questionable performance? The possibility of lawsuits had to be considered. For any accident causing injury, legal fees could be expected to run $500,000, and a catastrophic accident could bring a suit for several million dollars. While Black Diamond's insurer would pay legal expenses and any settlement involved, with a cap of $1 million, Black Diamond could expect to pay at least $25,000—the company's insurance deductible—for each legal action. In addition, there would be the costs of lost time by the employees who had to go to court (such costs might involve one or two managers' salaries for a year—at $40,000 to $60,000 per person). Several catastrophic accident cases won by the plaintiffs in a single year could put the company into bankruptcy.

Another option was to continue the sale of Black Prophets—including the axes already released as well as those in production—but require all units to be sold with a cautionary label? Or should Black Diamond just quietly and quickly sell those Black Prophets already in retail outlets and only undertake a critical view of the axes still in production?

Management's response to the short-term issue of customer service would have major implications for Black Diamond's competitive strategy. Would Black Diamond be able to meet the market's rapidly growing demand for all products while improving—or at the very least maintaining—product quality? Would Black Diamond be able to maintain an image as the recognized industry leader in the manufacture of innovative tools and equipment? Would Black Diamond be able to balance the realities of increased risk associated with innovative product design and of increased liability corresponding to the greater potential for accidents, while still establishing a dominant competitive position? Even though various members held strong—and in some cases, divergent—opinions, the management team was willing to consider enterprising alternatives.

Nevertheless, management also knew that a more long-term plan needed to be put into place. "When crises strike," Metcalf said, "there will always be some degree of needing to react to the surprise of the situation. But we need to institute a system of managing crises proactively—that means organizing the business to prevent the preventable crises."

Even though the management team thought the Quality Assurance Department should be a constructive resource in this long-term effort, the department was so new that no one had a clear idea of the Quality Assurance Department's role. Abrahamsen also questioned her role: "I was hired to implement a plantwide quality control program and to specifically work on ISO 9000 certification. Representing QA, I'm supposed to improve the efficiency of the company by reducing or eliminating defects in the whole production chain, but I'm not sure that a TQM [total quality management] approach will completely solve Black Diamond's problems. Perhaps the whole process of new product development and on-going operations would be more effective if a BPR [business process reengineering] approach were used. Either way, my challenge is to get all these other employees and departments to change the way they do things so they're both more efficient and effective."

Philip Morris, Inc. ("Big Mo"): The Consumer Brand Powerhouse Plans Its Future (2001)

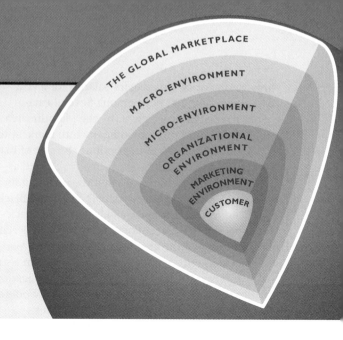

THE GLOBAL MARKETPLACE
MACRO-ENVIRONMENT
MICRO-ENVIRONMENT
ORGANIZATIONAL ENVIRONMENT
MARKETING ENVIRONMENT
CUSTOMER

This case was prepared by Carol H. Anderson, Crummer Graduate School of Business, Rollins College, and Alexander T. Wood, Educational Foundations, College of Education, University of Central Florida.

Abstract: This case describes the challenges faced by a successful multi-national leading consumer products company when its lawfully marketed adult products are met with legal, ethical, and social responsibility concerns by the public. Philip Morris Companies Inc. must develop strategies for profitable long-term corporate growth across all subsidiaries, while dealing with tobacco litigation and anti-smoking sentiments.

Hal, a hypothetical college student, is feeling hungry and is ready to take a break from studying. He looks in his refrigerator and kitchen cabinets for a likely repast. What do you think he sees? In his refrigerator he finds Cracker Barrel cheese, Oscar Mayer wieners, Claussen pickles, and Miracle Whip salad dressing. There are also several bottles of Icehouse, Red Dog, and Miller High Life beer. Hal's freezer contains a DiGiorno pizza with pepperoni. In his kitchen cabinet he spots Jell-O pudding mix, a package of Kool-Aid drink mix, and an open can of Maxwell House coffee. He finds a Toblerone chocolate bar hidden behind a box of Grape-Nuts cereal, and notices a Taco Bell dinner kit and a box of Kraft macaroni and cheese. Finally, he spies a half-empty pack of Marlboro cigarettes on the kitchen table.

We are not sure which food or beverage will appeal to Hal in this situation, or what his attitude toward smoking might be. However, we do know that all of these products and many more are among the extensive food, beverage, and tobacco products offered to the consumer market by the multinational corporation that is the focus of this case study: The Philip Morris Companies Inc.

PHILIP MORRIS COMPANIES, INC.

Geoffrey Bible, chairman of the board and CEO of Philip Morris Companies Inc., told shareholders at the company's annual meeting on April 26, 2001:[1]

"...Philip Morris entered 2001 with momentum and expects 'solid results again this year.' Our strategies have served us well, and we intend to stay the course and adhere to them as our guideposts for the future.... Our corporate infrastructure is powerful and sound, and we are successfully managing our litigation challenges

EXHIBIT I

Philip Morris Companies Inc.

Delivering on Our Promise...
...to Be the Most Successful Consumer Products Company in the World

Philip Morris has been guided for many years by a number of fundamental strategies that drive our growth, our profitability and our vision for the future. Together, these strategies enable us to continue delivering on our promise:

✓ To invest in the development, retention and motivation of our talented employees, and to provide a workplace where creativity, respect and diversity are valued and encouraged.

✓ To conduct our businesses as a responsible manufacturer and marketer of consumer products, including those intended for adults.

✓ To profitably grow our worldwide tobacco, food and beer businesses.

✓ To reinvest in our businesses and brands and meet the changing demands of consumers through innovation and new product development.

✓ To pursue a disciplined program of acquisitions, while pruning businesses that no longer offer a strategic fit.

✓ To enhance shareholder value through a balanced program of dividends and share repurchases.

✓ To steadfastly safeguard our credit rating.

✓ To successfully manage our litigation challenges and play an active and constructive role in regulatory issues.

Source: Philip Morris Companies Inc., *2000 Annual Report*, Inside front cover.

and we are changing the way we conduct our businesses in concert with societal expectations."

Mr. Bible expressed confidence in the future, with growth coming from adherence to a set of fundamental strategies. (See Exhibit 1.) He also stated "that both Philip Morris Incorporated (PM USA) and Philip Morris International (PMI) are reaching out to critics and others regarding regulation of tobacco products. Mr. Bible also said that the company is looking forward to taking part in the process of creating a new and rational regulatory environment for the manufacture, sale, and marketing of cigarettes— one that addresses health issues while respecting the principle of freedom of choice among adults."

The big question on the minds of many shareholders, financial analysts, and others is whether Philip Morris Companies Inc. can continue its history of growth across all divisions in the face of tobacco litigation and a growing anti-smoking culture.

Philip Morris Companies Inc. (or "Big MO" as it is known on Wall Street) is the world's largest

manufacturer and marketer of consumer packaged goods, and is ranked in the top ten in net income in the *Fortune* 500 listing of U.S. companies. This corporate powerhouse has one of the most valuable portfolios of premium brands in the entire consumer packaged goods industry. Although many people associate the Philip Morris name with only the tobacco industry (and with the issues faced by the tobacco industry over the past several decades), this is but one of the company's major product lines. The company's extensive food (Kraft) and beer (Miller) businesses also consist of an impressive array of leading global brands. In 2000, revenues for the combined tobacco, food, and beer subsidiaries exceeded $80 billion, compared to $78 billion in 1999. Ninety-one of the company's brands (including 16 acquired from Nabisco) each generated over $100 million in revenues. Fifteen "mega-brands" each exceeded $1 billion. Among these were: Marlboro, Kraft, Oscar Mayer, Miller Lite, Basic, L&M, Virginia Slims, Post, Parliament, Jacobs, Maxwell House, Philip Morris,

EXHIBIT 2

Philip Morris Brands (2001)

List of Products

Tobacco

- Marlboro
- Virginia Slims
- Parliament
- Merit
- Benson & Hedges

- Basic
- L&M
- Chesterfield
- Lark
- Cambridge

Selected International Brands
- Apollo Soyuz
- Bond Street
- Caro
- Diana

- f6
- Kazakstan
- Klubowe
- Longbeach
- Multifilter
- Muratti

- Peter Jackson
- Petra
- Philip Morris
- Polyot
- SG
- Vatra

Food

Chinese, Meals and Enhancers

Cheese
- Athenos
- Cheez Whiz
- Churny
- Cracker Barrel
- Deli Deluxe
- DiGiorno
- Easy Cheese
- Hoffman's
- Kraft
- Philadelphia
- Polly-O
- Velveeta

Dairy Products
- Breakstone's sour cream, cottage cheese
- Knudsen sour cream, cottage cheese
- Kraft dips
- Light n' Lively lowfat cottage cheese

Meals
- Kraft macaroni & cheese and other dinners
- Minute
- Stove Top
- Taco Bell†
- Velveeta shells & cheese

Enhancers
- A.1.
- Bull's-Eye
- Good Seasons
- Grey Poupon
- Kraft barbecue sauce, mayonnaise, salad dressings
- Miracle Whip
- Oven Fry
- Sauceworks
- Seven Seas
- Shake 'N Bake

Biscuits, Snacks and Confectionery

Cookies & Crackers
- Better Cheddars
- Cheese Nips
- Chips Ahoy!
- Handi-Snacks
- Honey Maid
- Newtons
- Nilla
- Nutter Butter
- Oreo
- Premium
- Ritz
- SnackWell's
- Stella D'oro
- Teddy Grahams
- Triscuit
- Wheat Thins

Snacks
- Cornnuts
- Planters

Pet Snacks
- Milk-Bone

Confectionery
- Altoids
- Callard & Bowser**
- Creme Savers
- Farley's
- Gummi Savers
- Jet-Puffed
- Life Savers
- Milka L'il Scoops
- Now and Later
- Sather's
- Terry's
- Tobler
- Toblerone
- Trolli

Beverages, Desserts and Cereals
Beverages
- Capri Sun†
- Country Time
- Crystal Light
- Kool-Aid
- Tang

Coffee
- General Foods
- International Coffees
- Gevalia
- Maxwell House

- Sanka
- Starbucks†
- Yuban

Desserts
- Baker's
- Balance Bar
- Breyers yogurt†
- Calumet
- Certo
- Cool Whip
- Dream Whip
- Ever-Fresh
- Handi-Snacks
- Jell-O
- Knox
- Light n' Lively lowfat yogurt
- Minute
- Sure-Jell

Cereals
- Alpha-Bits
- Banana Nut Crunch
- Blueberry Morning
- Cranberry Almond Crunch
- Cream of Wheat
- Cream of Rice
- Fruit & Fibre
- Golden Crisp
- Grape-Nuts
- Great Grains
- Honey Bunches of Oats
- Honeycomb
- Oreo O's
- Pebbles†
- Raisin Bran
- Shredded Wheat
- Toasties
- Waffle Crisp

Oscar Mayer and Pizza
Meats
- Louis Rich
- Louis Rich Carving Board
- Lunchables
- Oscar Mayer

Meat Alternatives
- Boca

Pickles and Sauerkraut
- Claussen

Pizza
- California Pizza Kitchen†
- DiGiorno
- Jack's
- Tombstone

Selected International Brands*
Snacks
- Aladdin
- Artic
- Cerealitas
- Chips Ahoy!
- Club Social
- Côte d'Or
- Daim
- Diamante Negro
- Estrella
- Express
- Figaro
- Freia
- Guayabita
- Korono
- Lacta
- Laka
- Lucky
- Maarud
- Marbu
- Marabou
- Merries
- Milan
- Milka
- Oreo
- Ouro Branco
- Pacific Soda
- Peanøtt
- Planters
- Poiana
- Prince Polo
- Rhodesia
- Ritz
- Royal
- Shot
- Sonho de Valsa
- Suchard
- Sugus
- Tapita
- Terrabusi
- Terry's
- Trakinas
- Toblerone
- Tita

Coffee
- Blendy
- Carte Noire
- Dadak
- Gevalia
- Grand' Mère
- Kaffee HAG
- Jacobs Krönung
- Jacobs Milea
- Jacobs Monarch
- Jacques Vabre
- Kenco
- Maxim
- Maxwell
- Nabob
- Onko
- Saimaza
- Splendid

Powdered Soft Drinks
- Clight
- Fresh
- Frisco
- Kool-Aid
- Mañanita
- Q-Refres-Ko
- Ki-Suco
- Royal
- Tang
- Verao

Cheese
- Dairylea
- Eden
- El Caserio
- Invernizzi
- Kraft Cracker Barrel
- Kraft Lindenberger
- Kraft Singles
- Kraft Sottilette
- Mama Luise
- Philadelphia
- P'tit Québec

Convenient Meals and Grocery
- Dairylea Lunchables
- Fleischmann's
- Kraft Delissiopizza
- Kraft Lunchables
- Kraft ketchup
- Kraft peanut butter
- Kraft pourables
- Magic Moments
- Miracle Whip
- Mirácoli
- Simmenthal
- Vegemite

Beer

- Miller Lite
- Miller Genuine Draft
- Miller Genuine Draft Light
- Miller High Life

- Miller High Life Light
- Milwaukee's Best
- Milwaukee's Best Light
- Icehouse

- Foster's†
- Red Dog
- Southpaw Light
- Leinenkugel's
- Henry Weinhard's

- Henry's Hard Lemonade
- Hamm's
- Mickey's
- Olde English 800

- Magnum
- Presidente
- Sharp's non-alcohol brew

*Not generally available in the U.S.   **International products available in some specialty stores and supermarkets.   †Licensed trademark.
Source: Philip Morris Companies, Inc., *2001 Fact Book.*

Philadelphia, and Merit. Marlboro, one of the world's best-selling consumer packaged products, had sales of $30 billion in 1999.[2] (See Exhibit 2 for a listing of major Philip Morris brands.)

The company's production and marketing efforts are supported by an extensive network of manufacturing plants and distribution channels throughout the world, thus enabling it to meet consumer demand quickly in each of the markets in which it operates. Philip Morris subsidiaries operate in nearly 200 countries, and employ 137,000 people worldwide.[3]

Philip Morris has a major impact on many aspects of the global economy. The company is the largest purchaser of U.S.-grown tobacco, and leads all other consumer packaged goods companies in the world in the purchase of dairy products, grains, wheat, poultry, coffee, cocoa, and sugar. The company's economic impact is felt in other areas as well. Philip Morris is a major U.S. taxpayer, and a major contributor to profitable business transactions in other industries. In 2000, the company generated nearly $15 billion in taxes,[4] making it one of the largest taxpayers in the U.S. A recent study indicates that the total combined economic impact of Philip Morris and its thousands of U.S. business partners reached over $55 billion in the U.S. (in addition to its overseas economic impact). The company and its business partners in agriculture, construction, wholesale and retail trade, transportation, utilities, insurance and real estate, and other industries together generated over 490,000 jobs in the U.S., and $11 billion in wages, benefits and other compensation.[5]

PHILIP MORRIS 2000 ANNUAL MEETING OF STOCKHOLDERS

Geoffrey C. Bible, Chairman of the Board and Chief Executive Officer of Philip Morris Companies Inc. opened the 2000 Annual Meeting of Stockholders on April 27, 2000, with this statement[6] (see Exhibit 3 for company press release concerning this meeting):

> …First I would like to make it clear that while 1999 was a year of transition, our businesses came through the year in very good shape and we are beginning 2000 with strong momentum across all our operating companies.

Unfortunately, the performance of our stock has not reflected this strength. I know that you are all deeply concerned about this situation. The Board and I share your concern.

Clearly, the primary reason for the low stock price is investor concern about the legal challenges and societal perceptions surrounding the domestic tobacco industry. I am convinced that these concerns are based on an extremely pessimistic reading of our company's situation. When you examine the facts, the story is quite compelling. Yes, we are facing a lot of litigation. However, the litigation environment has improved in significant ways since we last met.

Mr. Bible cited a number of reasons for his optimism regarding the litigation that plagued the company's tobacco business during the previous year:[7]

- A positive trend in class-action suit dismissals, for a total of 23 cases brought against Philip Morris in the U.S.—representing the overwhelming majority of decisions in these cases.

- Juries found in favor of the defense in six individual smoking and health lawsuits tried in 1999.

- The jury voted unanimously in favor of the Company in the Ohio *Iron Workers* case. (As of the date of the Stockholders Meeting, this is the only case concerning a third-party payor to proceed to a jury verdict.)

- Lawsuits brought by other third-party payors of healthcare costs were rejected by five federal circuit courts of appeal, and numerous cases were dismissed at the trial court level. The U.S. Supreme Court turned down a request by labor funds to review three of these decisions, and rejected the FDA's attempt to regulate tobacco.

- An important source of litigation risk to Philip Morris was removed with the Tobacco Settlement reached with the State Attorneys General in 1998.

Counteracting these successes, the *Engle* class-action case in Florida dominated the attention of investment analysts and others at the time of the 2000 Annual Stockholders Meeting, because of the magnitude of potential punitive damage awards and their impact on industry stocks.[8] In addition, Mr. Bible noted that another source of investor concern is a lawsuit brought by the Clinton

EXHIBIT 3

Philip Morris Annual Shareholders Meeting (2000)

Philip Morris Companies, Inc., Press Release (April 27, 2000)

PHILIP MORRIS
COMPANIES INC.
120 PARK AVENUE, NEW YORK, NY. 10017

FOR IMMEDIATE RELEASE

PHILIP MORRIS HOLDS 2000 ANNUAL MEETING

Chairman Says Company Has Strong Business Momentum Going Forward Notes

Improved Litigation Environment

Notes Improved Litigation Environment

Reaffirms Commitment To "Constructive Engagement" With The Public

RICHMOND, Va., April 27, 2000

Geoffrey C. Bible, chairman of the board and chief executive officer of Philip Morris Companies Inc. (NYSE: MO), told an audience of approximately 1,100 shareholders at the company's annual meeting today that Philip Morris "came through the year in very good shape" in a "litigation environment that has improved in significant ways." He also reaffirmed the company's commitment to "engage in a constructive dialogue" with the company's critics as well as the general public.

Mr. Bible opened the meeting by noting that "while 1999 was a year of transition," the company performed well during the year and "we are beginning 2000 with strong momentum across all of our operating companies." He acknowledged that "unfortunately, the performance of our stock has not reflected this strength."

Mr. Bible attributed the company's low stock price primarily to "investor concern about the legal challenges and societal perceptions surrounding the domestic tobacco industry. Highlighting improvements in the litigation environment, he cited a number of favorable legal developments during the year, as well as the 1998 Tobacco Settlement Agreement with the State Attorneys General, which removed a significant source of litigation risk to the company.

Despite these successes, Mr. Bible said that two lawsuits, the Engle class-action case in Florida and the Department of Justice suit to recover health care costs, have "added to investor concerns." He noted that the Engle case is now proceeding to the next phase, and that the Department of Justice suit is one in which "we believe we have a good chance of prevailing" if the case proceeds to trial.

Mr. Bible emphasized that Philip Morris is "ready and eager to engage in a constructive dialogue about strong, meaningful and reasonable regulation of cigarettes." He said that the company wants to be "at the table and part of the process of creating a regulatory framework that is fair for smokers, the general public and for the industry."

Administration's Department of Justice. The purpose of this lawsuit is to recover Medicare costs paid out by the U.S. government for alleged tobacco-related illnesses.

PHILIP MORRIS 2001 ANNUAL MEETING OF STOCKHOLDERS

Mr. Geoffrey Bible reported positive financial and strategic results for the year 2000. In addition to portions of this speech that were included at the beginning of the case, Mr. Bible discussed (among other topics) the following themes that underlie expectations of growth in 2001 and beyond:[9]

- Continued development of talented employees around the world.
- People of Philip Morris work to make a difference in their communities.
- Continued growth in businesses and increased earning per share.
- Completed acquisition of Nabisco, and integration of Nabisco with Kraft worldwide.
- IPO of common stock for Kraft Foods, reinvestment in businesses and brands.
- Progress in aligning global businesses to meet high expectations of society (including "reasonable and practical" positions regarding tobacco regulation, and leadership in food safety).
- Favorable actions concerning the litigation environment (Engle verdict appeal, dismissed cases, and other legal actions).
- Continued social responsibility emphasis.

HISTORICAL HIGHLIGHTS OF A GROWING FAMILY OF BRANDS

The corporate timeline of the Philip Morris Company's business growth began in 1847 when Philip Morris, Esq., a tobacconist and importer of fine cigars, opened a shop on Bond Street in London. The histories of many other companies that eventually became part of Philip Morris' consumer brands in the tobacco, food, and beer industries have evolved simultaneously over the past century and a half. As stated in the Corporate Timeline published by the Company, "The key to our past has

been the power of our brands and the energy and creativity of our people. Our success in the years ahead will depend on continuing that legacy."[10] This legacy includes the following selected corporate highlights:

- Mid-1800s—Philip Morris establishes Bond Street shop in London.
- 1902—Philip Morris & Co., Ltd. is incorporated in New York.
- 1919—The U.S. Philip Morris Company is acquired by a new company owned by U.S. stockholders, and incorporated in Virginia under the name of Philip Morris & Co. Ltd., Inc.
- 1929—Philip Morris begins manufacturing its own cigarettes by purchasing a factory in Richmond, Virginia.
- Mid-1950s—Philip Morris & Co. Ltd, Inc. acquires Benson & Hedges, sets up first affiliate outside U.S. (Australia), sets up an overseas division, introduces the Marlboro brand with a special filter in a flip-top box.
- 1960s—Organizes as three operating companies to manage the business of Philip Morris Incorporated; 1968 operating revenues top $1 billion.
  - The Surgeon General issues report on Smoking and Health.
  - Tobacco industry creates advertising code (voluntary agreement not to promote cigarettes to young people, and to avoid implying that cigarettes have health or social benefits).
  - U.S. Federal Cigarette Labeling Act (1966) takes effect to require warning label on all cigarette packages.
- 1970s—Acquires 100% each of Miller Brewing Company, Mission Viejo Company, and the Seven-Up Company, and the international cigarette business of the Liggett Group Inc.
  - TV and radio cigarette advertising ban takes effect in 1971.
  - Miller Brewing Company introduces Miller Lite nationally to create a new beer category.
- 1980s—In 1980 Philip Morris celebrates its 125th anniversary; revenues are nearly $10 billion, and grow to nearly $45 billion by 1989, largely through acquisitions.

- More changes in the corporate structure, and Philip Morris Credit Corporation is incorporated.

- Philip Morris acquires General Foods Corporation (1985) and Kraft (1988)—later to be renamed Kraft General Foods (KGF), the largest U.S. food company; sells most of Philip Morris Industrial, Seven-Up International and Seven-Up Canada, and the U.S. franchise business of Seven-Up.

- General Foods forms three separate operating companies: General Foods, USA; General Foods, Coffee & International; and Oscar Mayer Foods; also buys Freihofer Baking Company.

- Miller Brewing Company introduces Miller Genuine Draft and Sharp's (nonalcoholic), and acquires Jacob Leinenkugel Brewing Company.

- 1990s—Philip Morris acquires Jacobs Suchard AG, Swiss-based coffee and confectionery company.

  - KGF introduces seven categories of fat-free products; acquires Capri Sun, Inc. and Jack's Frozen Pizza; completes purchase of U.S. and Canadian ready-to-eat cold cereal businesses of RJR Nabisco; and acquires foreign confectionery manufacturers while expanding existing brands.

- 1998—U.S. tobacco industry settlement with the Attorney Generals of 46 states—payout of $206 billion over 25 years for tobacco-related claims and lawsuits; agreement includes advertising and marketing restrictions.

- 1999—Corporate communications initiatives include launching of corporate online website at http:/www.philipmorris.com.

  - 1999 revenues are over $78 billion, and operating companies income reaches $15.2 billion.

- 2000—Kraft Foods acquires Balance Bar and Boca Burger.

  - Litigation issues continue in the tobacco industry.

  - August 2000—World Health Organization investigators claim that for many years Philip Morris and other multinational cigarette manufacturers have systematically attempted to discredit the agency and undermine its global anti-smoking efforts.[11]

- December 2000—Philip Morris acquires all outstanding shares of Nabisco Group Holdings Corp. for $19.2 billion (to be combined with Kraft Foods, Inc.).[12]

- June 2000—Philip Morris Companies Inc. and Kraft Foods, Inc. issued an initial public offering (IPO) of 280 million shares of Kraft Foods Inc. stock. (This financial move was designed to help the company pay down the debt incurred with the purchase of Nabisco, and to overcome some of the investors' negative sentiment due to ongoing liability in tobacco lawsuits.)[13]

CURRENT SITUATION AT PHILIP MORRIS: CIRCA 2000

Litigation

Philip Morris Companies Inc.'s food and beer industry businesses are enjoying tremendous growth and success. However, litigation and health and social concerns related to smoking plague the financial and marketing successes of the tobacco business. Legal battles against the tobacco industry started in 1954 with a tobacco liability lawsuit brought by a lung cancer victim (case was dropped 13 years later). In 1964 the Surgeon General released reports stating that smoking causes lung cancer. The pace and pressure of lawsuits escalated in the 1990s, along with tighter restrictions on the marketing of cigarettes—particularly to the nation's youth. Tobacco companies face legal battles in the form of class action suits, suits by individuals, federal claims, and insurer and third-party claims.[14]

Perhaps the most famous tobacco litigation is the Engle case in Florida, which was appealed by Philip Morris. In June 2001, a Los Angeles jury awarded a $3 billion verdict to a 56-year-old man with lung cancer. Philip Morris said it would appeal the verdict if the trial judge did not overturn it. Many other claims have been rejected in favor of the company and the industry. While there are legal challenges against tobacco companies throughout the world (including actions by the World Health Organization), Philip Morris believes it has shown that litigation is manageable over time, and that the company can remain profitable.

Corporate Communications

Philip Morris Companies Inc. launched a new long-term corporate communications initiative in 1999. This ongoing program, entitled *Working to Make a Difference: The People of Philip Morris,* is designed to tell the public "who we are and what we do." As stated in the 1999 Annual Report: "This domestic communications program is reinforced by a policy of 'constructive engagement' worldwide, which commits us to engaging the media, government, the public and our critics to seek constructive solutions to the issues surrounding our businesses." This includes advertising, education and community partnership and outreach, and active participation with governments, schools, parents, civic groups, and distributors, wholesalers, retailers and suppliers. A major part of the initiative is the Philip Morris Web site, launched in 1999, to enable the company to communicate with the public about its company and products over the Internet.[15] This site includes links to a number of national and worldwide health organizations, such as the World Health Organization, the American Cancer Society, the U.S. Centers for Disease Control and Prevention, and the U.S. Surgeon General.[16]

Social Responsibility

Philip Morris Companies Inc. is actively involved in philanthropy, and has been one of the world's most generous corporate philanthropists for more than four decades. The company has supported programs in the areas of food and hunger; AIDS awareness and treatment; prevention of domestic violence and shelter for victims, humanitarian aid, and the arts. In response to concerns related to smoking, the company has committed major resources to youth smoking prevention (over 100 programs in 60 countries), and is addressing drunk driving and underage drinking issues through education and community involvement.

The company follows a set of environmental principles that are designed to reduce a negative impact on the environment and sustain the world's natural resources, while providing quality products for consumers. For example, Miller Brewing Company has used resources more efficiently by reducing the consumption of water and electricity, and lowering wastewater discharge. Kraft Foods North America recycles or reuses more than 90 percent of its total solid waste and by-products. Packaging has been improved for the company's brands through reduced package size and the use of recycled materials. Performance is measured regularly for these and other environmental efforts.[17]

For many consumers, social responsibility issues related to the tobacco and beer industries include both corporate and individual responsibility. The dilemma is magnified when a company sells legal products in a quasi-regulated environment. In the Philip Morris Companies Inc. 2000 Annual Report, CEO Geoffrey Bible describes the company's proactive programs for prevention of youth smoking, underage drinking, and drunk driving. Mr. Bible states: "Let me make it clear that we do not want youth to smoke, we do not market our products to youth and we are fully committed to making a difference on this issue." He further states: "It is a fact, however, that a large part of our business involves selling adult products. And we continue to believe very strongly that adults have a right to choose to use tobacco and beer products, just as they have the freedom to make a range of choices in their lives."[18]

FINANCIAL CONDITION: CONSOLIDATED AND BY SUBSIDIARIES

Philip Morris Companies Inc. has enjoyed steady growth for over 150 years, primarily through strategic acquisitions in growth categories, and strong brand equity throughout the world. In spite of legal issues in the tobacco industry, all company subsidiaries have prospered. Although the company met its earnings-per-share growth target for 1999 and 2000, stock performance was a disappointment—primarily attributable to litigation. Year 1999 and 2000 financial results are presented in Exhibits 4 and 5, including both a consolidated statement and results by business segment.

In August, 2000, Goldman Sachs analysts predicted that shares of Philip Morris "could 'nearly triple in two years' if the company follows through with the 2001 partial spin-off of its Kraft foods operations, and if aggravated claims cases disappear."[19] The success of the Kraft IPO and acquisition of Nabisco should help this prediction become a reality.

EXHIBIT 4

2000 Financial Highlights

Philip Morris Companies, Inc. 2000 Annual Report

(in millions of dollars, except per share data)

Consolidated Results

	Reported			Underlying		
	2000	**1999**	**% Change**	**2000**	**1999**	**% Change**
Operating revenues	$80,356	$78,596	2.2%	$80,316	$77,829	3.2%
Operating companies income	16,228	14,825	9.5%	16,045	15,144	5.9%
Net earnings	8,510	7,675	10.9%	8,427	7,926	6.3%
Basic earnings per share	3.77	3.21	17.4%	3.73	3.31	12.7%
Diluted earnings per share	3.75	3.19	17.6%	3.71	3.30	12.4%
Dividends declared per share	2.02	1.84	9.8%	2.02	1.84	9.8%

Compounded Average Annual Growth Rates

	2000–1995	2000–1990	2000–1985	2000–1995	2000–1990	2000–1985
Operating revenues	4.0%	4.6%	11.3%	4.0%	4.6%	11.3%
Net earnings	9.3%	9.2%	13.6%	9.0%	9.1%	13.5%
Basic earnings per share	11.7%	11.4%	15.4%	11.3%	11.3%	15.3%
Diluted earnings per share	11.8%	11.4%	15.4%	11.4%	11.3%	15.3%

Results by Business Segment

	Reported			Underlying		
	2000	**1999**	**% Change**	**2000**	**1999**	**% Change**
Tobacco						
Domestic						
Operating revenues	$22,658	$19,596	15.6%	$22,658	$19,596	15.6%
Operating companies income	5,350	4,865	10.0%	5,350	5,048	6.0%
International						
Operating revenues	26,374	27,506	(4.1%)	26,503	27,377	(3.2%)
Operating companies income	5,211	4,968	4.9%	5,270	5,045	4.5%
Food						
North American						
Operating revenues	$18,461	$17,897	3.2%	$18,522	$17,801	4.1%
Operating companies income	3,547	3,190	11.2%	3,570	3,312	7.8%

EXHIBIT 4 *(continued)*

2000 Financial Highlights
Philip Morris Companies, Inc. 2000 Annual Report

	Reported			Underlying		
	2000	**1999**	**% Change**	**2000**	**1999**	**% Change**
International						
Operating revenues	8,071	8,900	(9.3%)	7,966	8,547	(6.8%)
Operating companies income	1,208	1,063	13.6%	1,050	996	5.4%
Beer						
Operating revenues	$4,375	$4,342	0.8%	$4,250	$4,153	2.3%
Operating companies income	650	511	27.2%	543	515	5.4%
Financial Services						
Operating revenues	$417	$355	17.5%	$417	$355	17.5%
Operating companies income	262	228	14.9%	262	228	14.9%
Total						
Operating revenues	$80,356	$78,596	2.2%	$80,316	$77,829	3.2%
Operating companies income	16,228	14,825	9.5%	16,045	15,144	5.9%

Notes:
Underlying results reflect the results of our business operations, excluding significant one-time items for employee separation programs, write-downs of property, plant and equipment, sales made in advance of the century date change and gains on sales of businesses. Underlying operating revenues and operating companies income also exclude the results of businesses that have been sold.

Operating revenues and operating companies income for 1999 have been restated to reflect the transfer of managerial responsibility for Mexico and Puerto Rico to North American food from international food.

Source: Philip Morris Companies Inc., *2000 Annual Report,* p.1.

PHILIP MORRIS MANAGEMENT FACES THE CHALLENGE OF THE FUTURE WHILE DEALING WITH THE PAST

Philip Morris plans to drive future growth by taking advantage of its strengths and key business strategies, including:[20]

1. Developing new products consistent with emerging consumer trends.

2. Building leadership position in key categories.

3. Creating opportunities in new, high-growth categories through strategic acquisitions and partnerships.

4. Driving businesses at retail through superior marketing expertise and sales execution.

5. Improving margins by lowering costs.

6. Generating growth and enhancing efficiency by capitalizing on new technology.

Senior management of Philip Morris Companies Inc. and its major subsidiaries in the food, beer, and tobacco industries are faced with a number of related decisions. They must determine both short- and long-term strategies that will help the company achieve the six corporate objectives listed above, as well as the expectations of financial analysts and stockholders for higher stock prices. The outcomes of these corporate strategies will have a significant effect on consumers, employees, stockholders, suppliers, government entities, and all other constituencies of the company.

Assuming that you are in the position of Mr. Geoffrey Bible, CEO of Philip Morris Companies Inc., what will you be prepared to say to stockholders about the company's strategies and performance at the next Annual Meeting of Stockholders?

EXHIBIT 5

Philip Morris, Inc. 2001 Second Quarter Fact Sheet

Consolidated Financial Review

(in millions, except per share data)

	Second Quarter	
Reported Selected Earnings Highlights	2001	2000
Operating revenues	$23,188	$20,844
Cost of sales	8,599	7,517
Excise taxes on products	4,319	4,421
Operating companies income(A)	4,626	4,131
Earnings before income taxes and minority interest	3,766	3,587
Net earnings	2,288	2,171
Basic EPS	1.04	0.96
Diluted EPS	1.03	0.95

(A)Operating companies income is income before amortization of goodwill, general corporate expenses, minority interest, interest and other debt expense, net, and income taxes.

	Operating Revenues		Operating Companies Income	
	Second Quarter		Second Quarter	
Underlying Earnings Highlights	2001	2000	2001	2000
Consolidated Totals	$23,188	$20,744	$4,626	$4,116
% of Total: Tobacco	57%	60%	59%	63%
Food	37%	33%	36%	31%
Beer	5%	6%	4%	5%
Financial Services	1%	1%	1%	1%

	2001	2000
Net earnings	$2,288	$2,171
Basic EPS	$1.04	$0.96
Diluted EPS	$1.03	$0.95

Underlying operating revenues and operating companies income exclude the results of businesses that have been sold.

	June 30,	December 31,
Balance Sheet Highlights and Ratios	2001	2000
Property, plant and equipment, net (consumer products)	$15,064	$15,303
Inventories (consumer products)	8,724	8,765
Total assets	79,467	79,067
Total debt (consumer products)	18,623	27,196
Total debt (financial services)	1,809	1,926
Stockholders' equity	19,535	15,005
Ratio of total debt to stockholders' equity	1.05 to 1	1.94 to 1
Ratio of consumer products debt to stockholders' equity	0.95 to 1	1.81 to 1
Net return on average stockholders' equity	48.5%	56.2%

EXHIBIT 5 (*continued*)

Philip Morris, Inc. 2001 Second Quarter Fact Sheet

	Six Months Ended June 30,	
Cash Flow Statement Highlights	2001	2000
Net cash provided by operating activities	$4,626	$5,849
Capital expenditures (consumer products)	790	700
Dividends paid	2,342	2,229

Domestic Tobacco

(in millions, with % change vs. prior year)

	Second Quarter	
Philip Morris Inc. (Philip Morris U.S.A.)	2001	2000
Operating revenues	$6,425, up 12.6%	$5,706, up 20.5%
Operating companies income	$1,383, up 8.6%	$1,274, up 6.5%

International Tobacco

(in millions, with % change vs. prior year)

	Second Quarter	
Philip Morris International Inc.	2001	2000
Operating revenues	$6,753, down 0.7%	$6,801, down 1.8%
Operating companies income	$1,348, up 2.9%	$1,310, up 4.6%

North American Food

(in millions, with % change vs. prior year)

	Second Quarter	
Kraft Foods North America, Inc.	2001	2000
Operating revenues—underlying*	$6,518, up 32.9%	$4,906, up 4.1%
Operating companies income—underlying*	$1,353, up 31.6%	$1,028, up 5.9%

*Underlying operating revenues and operating companies income exclude the results of businesses that have been sold since the beginning of 2000.
During the fourth quarter of 2000, managerial responsibility for the Company's food operations in Mexico and Puerto Rico was transferred from the international food segment to the North American food segment. Prior period amounts have been reclassified to reflect the transfer.

International Food

(in millions, with % change vs. prior year)

	Second Quarter	
Kraft Foods International, Inc.	2001	2000
Operating revenues—underlying*	$2,174, up 8.2%	$2,009, down 0.4%
Operating companies income—underlying*	$ 298, up 21.6%	$ 245, up 2.9%

*Underlying operating revenues and operating companies income exclude the results of businesses that have been sold since the beginning of 2000.
During the fourth quarter of 2000, managerial responsibility for the Company's food operations in Mexico and Puerto Rico was transferred from the international food segment to the North American food segment. Prior period amounts have been reclassified to reflect the transfer.

(continued)

EXHIBIT 5 (*continued*)

Philip Morris, Inc. 2001 Second Quarter Fact Sheet

Beer

(in millions, with % change vs. prior year)

| | Second Quarter | |
Miller Brewing Company	2001	2000
Operating revenues—underlying*	$1,207, down 0.7%	$1,215, up 4.7%
Operating companies income—underlying*	$168, down 11.6%	$190, up 14.5%

*Underlying operating revenues and operating companies income exclude the results of businesses that have been sold since the beginning of 2000.

Financial Services

(in millions, with % change vs. prior year)

| | Second Quarter | |
Philip Morris Capital Corporation	2001	2000
Operating revenues	$111, up 3.7%	$107, up 10.3%
Operating companies income	$ 76, up 10.1%	$ 69, up 15.0%

Source: Philip Morris Companies Inc., *2001 Fact Book.*

Endnotes

1. Transcript of speech: "Remarks of Geoffrey C. Bible, Chairman of the Board and Chief Executive Officer, Philip Morris Companies, Inc., 2001 Annual Meeting of Stockholders" (April 26, 2001), Richmond, VA.
2. *Philip Morris Companies, Inc., 2000 Fact Book; Philip Morris Companies Inc., 1999 Annual Report* (February 22, 2000); *Philip Morris Companies, Inc., 2001 Fact Book; Philip Morris Companies Inc., 2000 Annual Report* (February 27, 2001).
3. *Ibid.*
4. Taxes include federal and state excise taxes; federal and state income taxes; and sales, property, payroll and other taxes.
5. Transcript of speech: "Remarks of Geoffrey C. Bible, Chairman of the Board and Chief Executive Officer, Philip Morris Companies, Inc., 2000 Annual Meeting of Stockholders" (April 27, 2000), Richmond, VA.
6. *Ibid.*
7. *Ibid.*
8. On Friday, July 14, 2000, a six-member state-court jury in Miami, Florida, ordered the tobacco industry to pay $145 billion in punitive damages to plaintiffs who sued the industry for their tobacco-related illnesses. (Geyelin, Milo and Gordon Fairclough, "Taking a Hit: Yes, $145 Billion Deals Tobacco a Huge Blow, but Not a Killing One," *Wall Street Journal* (July 17, 2000), pp. A1, A8; "Damage Award in Florida Case Took the Wind Out of Big Tobacco's New Repentance Tactic," New York Times News Service, *St. Louis Post-Dispatch* (July 16, 2000), pp. A1, A3; "$145 Billion Award Doesn't Mean End of Tobacco Industry," Associated Press, *The Southern Illinoisan* (July 16, 2000), pp. 1C, 3C.)

9. *Ibid*, 2001 Annual Meeting to Shareholders.
10. "Philip Morris Through the Years," *Corporate Timeline*, http://philipmorris.com/corporate/corp_over/timeline/index.html, and "The Philip Morris History," (1765–1987), Philip Morris Inc. publication.
11. Fairclough, Gordon, "Philip Morris and Other Cigarette Firms Tried to Foil WHO, Agency's Staff Says," *Wall Street Journal* (August 2, 2000), pp. A3, A6.
12. "Philip Morris Acquires Nabisco for $55.00 Per Share in Cash and Plans for IPO of Kraft," Philip Morris Companies Inc, Press Release (June 25, 2000); *Philip Morris Companies Inc. 2001 Fact Book.*
13. Schoen, John W., "Big Appetite for Kraft Foods IPO," http://msnbc.com/news/585852.asp.
14. Geyelin, Milo and Gordon Fairclough, "Taking a Hit: Yes, $145 Billion Deals Tobacco a Huge Blow, but Not a Killing One," *Wall Street Journal* (July 17, 2000), pp. A1, A8.
15. *Philip Morris Companies Inc., 1999 Annual Report* (February 22, 2000), p. 4.
16. *Working to Make a Difference: The People of Philip Morris,* Corporate Pamphlet (More Than a Tobacco Company), Philip Morris Companies, Inc., p. 20.
17. *Working to Make a Difference: The People of Philip Morris,* Corporate Pamphlet (Environmental Principles), Philip Morris Companies, Inc.
18. *Philip Morris Companies Inc., 2000 Annual Report,* p. 4.
19. "Goldman: Tobacco Stock Valuations to Improve, MO Could Triple," *Newstraders* (August 11, 2000), Hoovers Online, http:/www.hoovers.com.
20. Letter to Shareholders from Geoffrey C. Bible, Chairman of the Board and CEO, *Philip Morris Companies Inc: 1999 Annual Report* (February 22, 2000), p. 5.

Frigidaire Company: Launching the Front-Loading Washing Machine

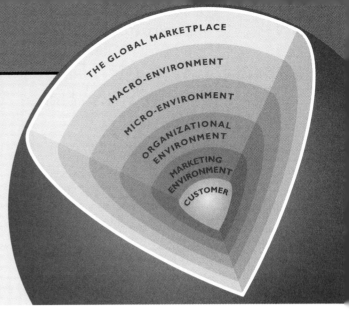

This case was prepared by Kay M. Palan and Timothy T. Dannels of Iowa State University.

The Frigidaire Company, Laundry Products Division, in Webster City, Iowa, was a high-volume manufacturer of washing machines and dryers. In October of 1996, after several years of intense development, Frigidaire introduced a new front-loading (horizontal axis) washing machine in the United States. This new machine was designed and developed to offer U.S. consumers an alternative laundry product that was superior to conventional, top-loading (vertical axis) washing machines in terms of energy consumption, water conservation, and washing performance. Although an eager and receptive market for the front-loading washer did not exist, Frigidaire intended to use the new product to expand its position in the marketplace and to establish itself as the industry leader in energy-saving, environmentally sound laundry products.

Despite a $20 million investment, exhaustive development efforts, and detailed marketing plans, however, Bill Topper, vice president and general manager of the Laundry Products Division, was concerned. Initial sales were sluggish; results for the first 3 months of sales were 30 to 40 percent below projected levels. Although this early dismal per-

formance was not a cause for panic, it triggered some serious concerns for the Frigidaire management staff. As Bill Topper reviewed data for the first 3 months' performance, he pondered several questions that he would need to review with the key players in his management team—Chris Kenner, market manager; John Jergens, market planner; and Dave Modtland, manager of washer engineering and project leader. Could Frigidaire create and grow a market for horizontal-axis washing machines in the United States? How could Frigidaire best encourage product adoption?

THE FRIGIDAIRE COMPANY

The Frigidaire Company, owned by AB Electrolux of Sweden, was the fourth largest producer of household appliances in the United States, behind Whirlpool, General Electric, and Maytag (see Exhibit A for a summary of the U.S. appliance market). Frigidaire had 10 operating sites within the United States, with its corporate headquarters located in Dublin, Ohio. The company manufactured all major appliances—washers and dryers, refrigerators and freezers, ranges, dishwashers, and air conditioners—under the popular brand names of Frigidaire, White-Westinghouse, Gibson, Kelvinator, and Tappan. In addition, Frigidaire manufactured appliances for the General Electric Company (under the GE label) and for Sears (under the Kenmore label).

This case, originally presented at the North American Case Research Association's annual meeting in 1997, is based on field research and was written solely as a basis for class discussion rather than to illustrate either effective or ineffective marketing management. All other rights reserved jointly to the authors and the North American Case Research Association (NACRA). Copyright © 1998 by the *Case Research Journal* and Kay M. Palan and Timothy T. Dannels. Used by permission.

EXHIBIT A

1996 Major Appliance Market Share in the United States*

Company	Percent Market Share
Whirlpool	35.9
General Electric	30.4
Maytag	14.8
Frigidaire (Electrolux)	11.0
Amana (Raytheon)	6.4
Others	1.5
TOTAL	100.0

*Major appliances include dishwashers, ranges, washers/dryers, and refrigerators.

Source: Appliance Magazine, September 1997.

Laundry Products Division

The Laundry Products Division, located in Webster City, Iowa, produced washers, dryers, laundry centers (stacked, full-size washer-dryer combinations), and now, the front-loading washing machine. Transmission assemblies for washing machines were made at a smaller plant in nearby Jefferson, Iowa. The facility in Webster City had gradually been expanded and had the capacity to produce 6500 units a day (over 1.5 million units per year).

THE FRONT-LOADING WASHING MACHINE

Background

The U.S. laundry market was dominated by the top-loading (vertical axis) washing machine—it was estimated that over 95 percent of the washing machines in the United States were of this type. Top-loading machines were developed in the late 1940s and had been the primary method of washing clothes ever since. In contrast, the horizontal-axis, front-loading washer had experienced very little success with U.S. consumers. In 1945, Westinghouse started to market a front-loading machine. These machines were often referred to as "tumble action" washers because they simply tumbled clothes clean (versus cleaning with the "agitation motion" caused by the presence of an agitator in top-loaders). However, the early front-loading machines were plagued with many problems. Aside from the many mechanical problems that were reported (front-loaders were much more technologically complex than top-loaders), consumers perceived that front-loaders did not clean very well and even tangled clothes. Furthermore, front-loaders were more costly to purchase and service. Not surprisingly, in light of all these problems, the front-load market failed to materialize, and top-loading machines evolved as the dominant laundry product in the United States.

In Europe, however, high energy costs had driven the market toward front-loading technology because front-loading washers required less water and less energy to operate. In addition, Europeans believed that front-loading machines cleaned better and were gentler on clothes, relative to top-loading washers. The European market was dominated by front-loading machines.

Aware of the success of the front-loading washing machines in Europe, Sears and Magic Chef attempted, in 1981, to market front-loading washing machines in the United States by carrying foreign-made units. However, their attempts failed to produce significant results. Westinghouse, despite the disappointment associated with the original introduction of front-loading washers in the United States, continued to carry a front-loading machine, only to cease manufacturing in 1994 due to recurring service issues and customer complaints.

Despite these setbacks and problems, Bill Topper believed that the demand for front-loading machines in the United States would increase over the next several years. Initially, the management team believed that governmental influence would lead to a new market for this style of washing machine. It had been rumored for several years that the U.S. Department of Energy (DOE) was preparing to unleash new, rigid efficiency standards that would apply to household appliances. These regulations would lead to the design and introduction of new energy-efficient machines by all appliance makers and would create consumer demand for energy-efficient appliances. Furthermore, the team believed that the growth in environmental awareness and energy/water conservation in the United States would support the presence of an energy-efficient washing machine. After all, similar machines had been used in Europe for years for reasons of energy conservation, and it was felt that this trend would eventually drift into U.S. markets. Topper hoped that the company could stimulate this market by being the first domestic appliance manufacturer to successfully produce and sell a reliable, high-quality front-loading washing machine. If the front-loading washer functioned as intended, it would cost less to operate (use less water and energy), it would be gentler on clothes, and most important, it would clean better. Likewise, it would provide Frigidaire with much needed product differentiation in an industry where differentiation and competitive advantage were very difficult to attain.

With these considerations in mind, a $20 million project to design, develop, and produce a new and better front-loading washing machine was begun by Frigidaire in 1989. The project experienced a setback in 1994, however, when the government announced that the much-anticipated DOE changes would be delayed indefinitely. Industry speculations included the possibility that the delayed DOE regulations eventually might set energy-efficiency standards that could easily be met by either revolutionary vertical-axis designs or the more conventional top-loading machines currently available. Consequently, many appliance manufacturers had chosen to discontinue development of front-loading machines. Frigidaire, however, continued with the project because the management team believed that the benefits of differentiation, combined with increasing environmental awareness, ultimately would lead to a demand for the front-loading washer.

With the delay of the DOE regulations, the market manager, Chris Kenner, could no longer be assured that a ready-made market would exist for the front-loading washer. Instead, Kenner and his team were forced to focus on the difficulties and unknowns associated with market creation.

Exactly *who* would buy a front-loader?

How much would consumers pay for a front-loader?

How could loyal consumers of top-loading washers be converted to the use of front-loaders? Could consumers be converted?

What were the direct competitors doing with respect to the development and introduction of front-loaders?

The Product

Dave Modtland, manager of washer engineering and project leader for the front-loader, was tasked with overseeing the design of this revolutionary washing machine. The front-loading washing machine represented the first major technological innovation in several years in the industry. The horizontal-axis washer used tumble action—top-loading washers used an agitator that actually forced clothes to beat against each other, while the front-loader lifted and tumbled clothes in and out of the water without rough agitation. The new washer had more capacity than previous front-loaders and used approximately 20 less gallons of water per load than conventional top-loaders, or about 8000 gallons a year. Likewise, the front-loader saved on energy costs. Using national averages, water and energy savings were calculated to be at least $86 per year. Additional savings would be gained from reduced drying time due to the higher spin speeds achieved in front loaders. The front-loader also offered many features—automatic dispensing (of detergent, bleach, and fabric softener), an extra rinse option (i.e., for infant clothing), automatic water fill (fills to needed level and eliminates waste), and dryer clothes due to its high-rpm motor. Moreover, the front-loading washer offered versatility in installation—it could be installed under a counter, stacked with a dryer, or used in a free-standing position. The washer had a unique look, and the glass door allowed the viewing of machine operation. A matching clothes dryer complemented the new washer very well.

There were, however, some disadvantages associated with the front-loading washer. The washer was very heavy and more difficult to install (due to extra internal packing needed to protect critical components during shipment). Also, the front-loading washer was more costly to service than conventional top-loaders.

COMPETITION

The laundry market represented a very competitive and demanding environment. Frigidaire currently competed with four other major appliance manufacturers in the United States—Whirlpool, General Electric, Maytag, and Amana—all of whom managed

EXHIBIT B

Major Appliance Industry Brands by Company, 1996

Frigidaire	Maytag	Whirlpool	General Electric	Amana
Frigidaire	Maytag	Whirlpool	General Electric	Amana
Frigidaire Gallery	Jenn Aire	KitchenAid	GE Profile	Speed Queen
White-Westinghouse	Admiral	Roper	Hotpoint	
Gibson	Magic Chef	Estate	RCA	
Tappan	Norge	Kenmore (Sears)		
Kelvinator				
O'Keefe & Merrett				
Kenmore (Sears)				
GE (General Electric)				

Source: Frigidaire Product Planning Department, Webster City, Iowa.

several different brand names (see Exhibit B). At the present time, Frigidaire's market share for the home laundry market was about 7.9 percent, down from 9.2 percent in 1995. However, the Frigidaire brand name itself represented only about 2 percent of the washer market (see Exhibit C). The Laundry Division's market planner, John Jergens, believed the front-loader represented a tremendous opportunity for Frigidaire to expand its position in the marketplace.

Despite delayed DOE regulations, both Maytag and Amana had announced plans to introduce their own versions of horizontal-axis machines in 1997; Frigidaire managers had noted, though, that news releases on Maytag's new washer indicated that it might not be front-loading. In addition, Whirlpool was in the process of developing a new-generation washing machine, which was rumored to be neither traditional vertical nor horizontal axis, and GE had recently released a new, redesigned vertical-axis machine. Because of the new products being developed by competitors, Jergens felt that early presence in the marketplace would be vital to the success of the front-loader.

CUSTOMER ANALYSIS

Bill Topper and his management team knew that a key to market creation was to understand the needs and wants of potential consumers with respect to washing machines. Several pieces

EXHIBIT C

1996 Washing Machine Market Share in the United States

Brand Name	Percent Market Share
Kenmore	29.0
Whirlpool	21.6
Maytag	14.7
GE	13.1
Amana	4.9
Roper	2.4
Frigidaire	2.3
Admiral	1.9
Others	10.1
TOTAL	100.0

Source: Industrial Marketing Research, Inc.

of information were available to the management team, including survey and focus group data and personal feedback from consumers who had tried early prototypes of the front-loader.

Survey Data

Results of a 1991 consumer/environmental profile suggested to Chris Kenner, marketing manager, that a potential market existed for the front-loader. Over half of surveyed households (53 percent) purchased energy-efficient appliances, while 28 percent used water-conservation devices in their homes; 46 percent of households reported considering environmental impact when purchasing products. Consumers in several geographic regions in the United States were rated above average for considering environmental issues when purchasing appliances; cities included Denver, Minneapolis–St. Paul, Houston, Washington, D.C., Salt Lake City, Seattle, San Francisco, Dallas–Fort Worth, and Hartford.

Kenner also reviewed information related to current Frigidaire users. The majority of Frigidaire brand purchasers were families (79.3 percent), followed by single females (14.5 percent), and single males (6.1 percent). Brand sales were highest in the East North Central (26.8 percent) and South Atlantic (22.0 percent) regions; New England posted the fewest brand sales (1.2 percent). Sales in the other regions of the United States varied from 4.9 to 12.2 percent. Sales of washing machines were subject to fluctuations—for example, sales tended to be lowest in January and April. However, Kenner did not find evidence of seasonal sales. Of more concern to Kenner was Frigidaire's low ranking in brand acceptability relative to major competitors (see Exhibit D).

Focus Groups

Chris Kenner also reviewed a 1993 market research focus study, which exposed consumers to the front-loading washer. Several concerns about the washer had been identified in the study:

1. Water leakage through the front door
2. Small load capacities
3. Cleaning performance without an agitator

EXHIBIT D

1996 Brand Acceptability among U.S. Households

Brand Name	Acceptability
Maytag	97%
General Electric	95%
Whirlpool	93%
Frigidaire	92%
Amana	87%

Source: Frigidaire Market Research Department, Webster City, Iowa.

4. Insufficient water savings and energy conservation to merit purchase
5. Difficult loading and unloading of the washer
6. Brand loyalty to current (i.e., familiar and proven) washing technologies

Another study, conducted by Kenner's Market Research Department, had shown that pricing of the front-loader was a potential problem. Consumer interest in the washer did not increase significantly until the price was reduced to $599 or less. Many consumers reported that a lower price and/or a manufacturer's rebate would offer the best incentive for purchase. Even with an incentive, 35 percent of those consumers surveyed indicated that they would not buy the washer.

Consumer Feedback

In 1995, Bill Topper had implemented a controlled sales program in Iowa, Wisconsin, and California. The purpose of the program was to obtain consumer feedback on the new washer prior to national introduction. Several hundred units were sold to target consumers; they were given large rebates and were asked to work with the design and marketing teams to identify the strengths and weaknesses of the product. Engineers and other manufacturing personnel stayed in close contact with these consumers—reading surveys, answering telephone calls, and visiting actual homes to discuss performance and problems. Problems were identified and corrected, and more important, Frigidaire found that many of the customers reported high levels of satisfaction with the close personal contact and attention they received from manufacturing personnel.

Market Segmentation

Using historical data obtained on previous buyers of front-loading machines (White-Westinghouse), Kenner and his marketing group identified six target segments of potential customers. Although the information was dated, the profiles were used to estimate demand potential and sales forecasts for the new washers. The six segments, representing only 16.7 percent of U.S. households, had generated nearly half the demand for the previous White-Westinghouse front-loading machines. Frigidaire's marketing department calculated that the same segments would produce a potential demand of 134,000 units per year for the new front-loading machine (the estimate included a conversion factor that assumed a 14-year life for each horizontal washer). The segmentation data is summarized in Exhibit E on pages 718 and 719.

MARKETING PLAN FOR HORIZONTAL-AXIS, FRONT-LOADING WASHER

Bill Topper and his management team concluded that in order for the front-loading machine to be successful, the company would have to implement a marketing plan that would (1) overcome consumers' negative perceptions about the Frigidaire brand name and about the front-loading technology, (2) take advantage of the environmental and energy concerns of consumers, and (3) provide close personal contact and attention to customers.

Product Introduction

The front-loader washer initially would be marketed under the Frigidaire Gallery brand name, a new professional series line recently launched by Frigidaire. This tactic allowed the new washer to take advantage of the market synergies created by the recent large-scale Gallery introduction. Introduction focused on one model, available in either white or almond. This approach streamlined production, inventory levels, and distribution.

The management team believed that it was imperative to convey the potential benefits of the front-loader to consumers, dealers, and within the company itself. Failure to do so would hamper successful introduction of the washer. Consequently, Kenner and his marketing department developed a summary of benefits to guide product introduction:

Consumer Benefits	Dealer Benefits	Frigidaire Benefits
Better washing performance	High profit potential	Increased market share
Gentler on clothes	Improved product offering	Increased profitability
Saves energy, saves water	Improved visibility/traffic	Improved product offering
Flexible installation	New laundry room options	First-mover advantages

Although the initial product introduction involved only one model, the engineering department, under the direction of Dave Modtland, continued to develop additional features and product offerings. Negotiations were underway with GE and Whirlpool to possibly manufacture front-loading washers for these major appliance companies. Commercial versions and coin-operated machines also were under development. Finally, a line of horizontal machines, with varying features and price points, was planned for future introduction. Eventual plans called for an ultra-high-end model and a low-end model that could compete with traditional top-loader price points.

Pricing

Topper wanted to competitively price the new washing machine—not so high that consumers would not even consider the washer but also not so low that profit objectives could not be attained. Consequently, a suggested retail price range for the new horizontal-axis machine was established at $749 to $849, with a target retail selling price of $799. Built into the price was a very appealing profit margin for dealers (30 percent) relative to dealer margins for top-loading washing machines (10 percent). Frigidaire's profit margin was set at about 26 percent. Frigidaire's profit margin accounted for all variable and fixed costs allocated to the front-loading washer. The price also allowed for a 12 percent return on investment (ROI) to be obtained.

Even at this price, however, the management team knew that the front-loader faced a tough challenge. There were (and would continue to be) many conventional washing machines on the market that cost much less than the front-loading washer; most top-of-the-line washers sold for less than the front-loader would sell for. In fact, only about 0.8 percent of the available washing machines on the market were priced above $700. Thus, at the targeted retail selling price of $799, consumers had the very attractive option of purchasing a conventional top-loading machine *and* a dryer or just a front-loading washer.

Merchandising

The front-loader washing machine would be marketed through existing distribution channels, catalogues, and the Internet (www.frigidaire.com). In addition, a dedicated sales manager was assigned to the new washer to help push it through the new distribution channels. High priority also would be given to the dealers. According to Chris Kenner:

> A critical step in growing this market is to educate and convince dealers of the benefits of front-load technology.

Consequently, several steps were implemented to educate dealers about the new washer and to assist dealers in sales of the washer.

First, the manufacturing facility in Webster City hosted an open house and training for dealers and district managers as a kickoff for the front-loading washing machine introduction. Dealers and district managers also received free sales and training kits to help stimulate sales. Those who could not attend the training at the Webster City facility received a free formal introduction presentation at their own facilities. Dealers and retailers also received a free floor plan to assist in the visual display of the new washer. Retailers were equipped with a variety of sales aids to enhance in-store sales efforts; for example, a sliding rule showing energy and water savings was made available to retailers.

An Inside Line Consumer Direct program was established for fully trained, certified retailers. These retailers had access to an upscale consumer database to capitalize on target markets.

Financial incentives were initiated. Dealers would earn a higher profit margin for the front-loader than for conventional washers. Discounted pricing would be implemented throughout the first year of sales, creating an even larger profit margin. District managers would receive premium commissions for their sales efforts and results. Both retail sales personnel and district managers were enrolled in the Earn a Free Washer sales contest program—free front-loading washers would be awarded based on number of units sold.

Consumer-oriented strategies aimed at assisting dealers and district managers also were implemented. Free financing for 6 months (no pay, no interest) was made available to consumers; moreover, because installing a front-loading washer was more difficult and costly than that required for conventional machines, an installation allowance would be provided to purchasers. The front-loading washer carried a full 2-year warranty, the longest available in the industry, and consumers were promised a 30-day money back guarantee if they were not fully satisfied with the cleaning performance—The Cleaner/Gentler Promise. Consumer promotions included free "low suds" detergent samples of Wisk (Frigidaire and Lever Brothers were partners in developing and marketing this low-sudsing detergent), and those customers who purchased both a new front-loading washer and a matching dryer received a free Braun steam iron.

There was a contest for consumers, too. A Watch & Win program enabled interested customers to watch an "infomercial" videotape about the front-loading washer and then answer some questions about the washer on a contest entry form. Completing the entry form provided a chance for the consumer to win free Frigidaire Gallery appliances. But the contest actually had a broader aim, which was to educate consumers about the benefits of the new washing machine.

Marketing Communications

The management team believed that the benefits of the front-loader were best conveyed to potential customers through personal communications. Although mass media reached a large number of consumers quickly, explaining the front-loading machine necessitated a complex message. Plus Frigidaire's experience with the controlled sales program had revealed that personal contact with consumers was crucial to creating satisfied customers. Consequently, mass-media advertising was limited to a brief television advertisement, to be aired in national markets in early 1997. The primary thrust of the communications plan rested on the ability of retailers and dealers to communicate and educate consumers on the benefits of the front-loader at the point of sale. Besides training all salespeople, floor displays and literature were designed to enhance and complement sales efforts.

EXHIBIT E

Potential Market Segments for Front-Loading Washing Machines

Segment	Age Group	Ethnic Background	Affluence	Psychographics	Ecological Orientation	Motivation to Buy	Expected Demand
Urban Gold Coast Elite urban singles and couples	25–34 35–54	White, Asian	High	Egocentric, amicable, conforming, self-assured. Not style-conscious, impulsive, or cautious	Below Average	Space Savings	0.51%
Gray Power Affluent retirees in sunbelt cities	65+	White	Middle	Cautious, egocentric, broad-minded, reserved, brand loyal. Not experimenters, ad-believers, or conformists	Low	Energy Savings	2.09%
A. *Money & Brains* Sophisticated townhouse couples	55–64 65+	White, Asian	High	Amicable, broad-minded, efficient, intelligent, creative. Not reserved, impulsive, or economy-minded	Above Average	Space Savings Performance Environment	3.08%
B. *Young Literan* Upscale urban singles and couples	25–34 35–54	White, Asian	Middle				
C. *Bohemian Mix* Bohemian singles and couples	Under 24 25–34	Ethnic Diversity	Middle				

EXHIBIT E *(continued)*

Potential Market Segments for Front-Loading Washing Machines

Segment	Age Group	Ethnic Background	Affluence	Psychographics	Ecological Orientation	Motivation to Buy	Expected Demand
A. *Kids & Cul-de-Sacs* Upscale suburban families	35–54	White, Asian	High	Amicable, intelligent, efficient, reserved, style-conscious, cautious	Above Average	Performance Fashion	4.76%
B. *Winner's Circle* Executive suburban families	35–54 55–64	White, Asian	High	Not conformists, brand loyal, impulsive, or economy-minded			
A. *Executive Suites* Upscale white-collar couples	25–34 55–64	White, Asian	High	Amicable, efficient, brand loyal, intelligent, cautious, creative, style-conscious	Below Average	Performance Fashion	4.75%
B. *Pools & Patios* Established empty nesters	55–64 65+	White, Asian	High	Not experimenters, conformists, ad-believers, economy-minded, or impulsive			
C. *Second City Elite* Upscale executive families	35–54 55–64	White	High	Amicable, cautious, intelligent, refined, efficient, self-assured, frank, brand loyal			
Blue Blood Estates Elite super-rich families	35–54	White, Asian	High	Not experimenters, impulsive, ad-believers, or economy-minded	Above Average	Performance Fashion	0.78%

Source: Claritas, PRIZM Profiles, 1994.

All communications emphasized a performance-driven product that resulted in superior cleaning, delicate handling, better efficiency, and flexible installation.

To promote postpurchase satisfaction, a Use and Care video was issued with every purchased front-loading washing machine to educate the buyer and to prevent service calls related to the installation and/or use of the product. The Watch & Win contest provided an incentive to purchasers to watch the video if they had not done so prior to purchase. Also, a 1-800 customer line was established to address customer complaints, concerns, or comments.

An After-Sales Call program would be established, although not until 1998. This would be a continuation of the earlier experiment that allowed customers to talk directly to the manufacturing personnel who had actually built their washing machine. The management team believed that this interaction not only would result in satisfied customers but also would pinpoint product problems and areas for product improvement.

EARLY SALES PERFORMANCE AND CONCERNS

The front-loading washer was released to the public on October 1, 1996. The initial project release date had been May 1995; however, due to several late design changes and some unanticipated component failures, the introduction was delayed. The development of the washer had taken considerably longer to complete than any other machine Frigidaire had ever produced. The primary reason for the delay was that the front-loader represented a much more complex design than the top-loading machine, and it was mandatory that this machine be "perfect"—it could not have the problems that so many of the early front-loading machines had. Despite these setbacks, the front-loader was a design success—it met initial design specifications and, more important, met the high quality and reliability standards established during the infant stages of the development process.

Unfortunately, initial sales volumes for the horizontal-axis machine were sluggish. Based on the target market analysis, previous sales, industry projections, brand positioning factors, and future DOE

EXHIBIT F

Sales Volume Forecast—Horizontal-Axis Washer (000s of units)

Brand	1996	1997	1998	1999
Frigidaire	60	70	100	120
Kenmore	20	30	30	30
Private Label	10	10	10	10
International	8	12	20	30
TOTAL	98	122	160	190

Source: Frigidaire Marketing Department, Webster City, Iowa.

regulations, Bill Topper and his team had developed a sales volume forecast for the front-loading washer for 1996 through 1999. The forecast incorporated Frigidaire's plans to sell the washer not only under its own brand name but also under Sears' Kenmore label and other private-label agreements being negotiated; international sales also were projected. However, because the forecast was based on several market variables that were not yet truly understood, Topper believed sales tracking would be critical to the determination of market reaction. Details of the forecast are located in Exhibit F.

Sales for October, November, and December of 1996, the first three months that the front-loading machine was on the market, were up to 30 percent below projected levels (see Exhibit G). In fact, sales projections for the first year had been decreased from 98,000 units to 60,000 units because Frigidaire had been unable to finalize negotiations with Sears to manufacture the horizontal-axis washer under the Kenmore name.

The reasons for this unanticipated dismal performance were unclear. Some managers believed the retail price was to blame for slow sales; as a result of the delayed introduction (delayed from May 1995 to October 1996), the target retail price had been increased from $799 to $999. The delay, everyone agreed, had been necessary to correct quality and reliability problems. However, costs increased, driving the retail price higher. In addition, it was speculated that Maytag's competing front-loading washer, due out in 1997, would be priced in the range of $1200 to $1300. Because of Maytag's high association with quality, Frigidaire managers worried that their washer priced at $799

EXHIBIT G

**Horizontal-Axis Front-Loading Washing Machine Sales,
October 1, 1996–December 27, 1996**

Month	Monthly Production Budget	Monthly Sales Forecast	Monthly Sales	Sold/ Forecast (%)
October	5750	4503	4876	108.28
November	4750	3456	2433	70.40
December	4500	2483	1894	76.28
TOTAL	15,000	10,442	9203	88.13

Notes: (1) Production budget = (units produced/day) × (# of available work days per month). Current production schedule is to build 250 units/day (equivalent to 60,000 units/year). (2) Monthly sales forecast is the original forecast.
Source: Frigidaire Marketing Department, Webster City, Iowa.

would be perceived as inferior relative to Maytag. Consequently, the price was increased to $999 in order to still be competitive with Maytag's product and at the same time to be close enough to Maytag's price that consumers would perceive Frigidaire as a quality washing machine. Managers reasoned that if a price adjustment was necessary, it would be easier to decrease the price than to increase it. However, other factors also may have been responsible for the lackluster sales. For example, managers questioned the decision to limit mass-media advertising, especially in light of the fact that Maytag was known to effectively use television and print media to mass advertise its products. It also was possible that demand for the front-loading washer had been overestimated.

In response to the initial sales volumes, the management team began to review its marketing strategies and objectives. The dominant question on their minds was, "How do we develop a market that has failed to take off for over 50 years?" Bill Topper knew they had to do something quickly to create a market for the front-loading washer if Frigidaire wanted to establish itself as the dominant player and industry leader in this new sector of the laundry market.

Target Is Hot! What's Next for the "Upscale Discounter" (2001)

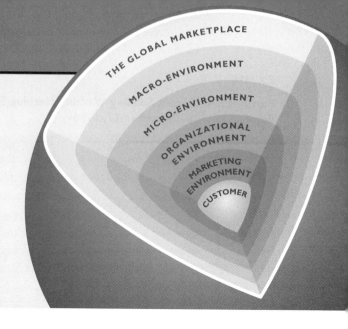

THE GLOBAL MARKETPLACE
MACRO-ENVIRONMENT
MICRO-ENVIRONMENT
ORGANIZATIONAL ENVIRONMENT
MARKETING ENVIRONMENT
CUSTOMER

This case was prepared by Carol H. Anderson, Crummer Graduate School of Business, Rollins College.

In a January 17, 2001 interview with the Star Tribune in Minneapolis, Bob Ulrich, Chairman and CEO of Target Corporation and Target Stores, expressed his confidence that Target was prepared for a soft economy. "In 25 years, Target's comp-store sales [sales from stores open at least a year] haven't fallen below a 3 percent increase in any single year, and we've had several recessions," he said. "I think we're well positioned to survive a recession, if there is one."[1] Ulrich has weathered a number of economic ups and downs during his 34-year career with Target. In recent years most of the revenue and profits for the parent company have come from the rapid growth of the Target discount store division (the focus of this case), and from the national brand recognition that is associated with the Target bullseye logo. The department store chains, Mervyn's and Marshall Field's, have not been as immune to a slowing economy, but Target Corporation has made a number of changes in these divisions that are expected to improve their performance.

Following the September 11, 2001 attacks on the World Trade Center in New York City, many retailers saw their market plunge drastically. Fewer customers were shopping in the stores and malls, and those who did shop tended to buy less and to seek greater value in their purchases. Although each of the major discount retail chains was affected by this event, Target Stores and Wal-Mart Stores, Inc. rallied as customers returned. Kmart Corp. was the hardest hit, and did not seem to recover from this financial blow during the 2001 fall and holiday selling season. By January 2002, Kmart's stock had dropped to its lowest closing price since 1970. A contributing factor was the company's decision to cut advertising expenditures during the holidays. Target Stores and Wal-Mart were able to pull out of the downslide following the events of September 11. By January 2002, Target's share prices had gained 54 percent over the September 21 low, and Wal-Mart's shares had risen 30 percent during the same period. Kmart shares dropped 25 percent during this period, compared to a 155 percent increase in share price from the end of 2000 to their peak in August 2001.[2]

Target's performance has been outstanding in the face of past economic downturns and disasters. Bob Ulrich has many challenges ahead in 2002 and beyond. He and his company must continue to develop strategies for growth of the Target Stores division, and be able to reach the firm's desired financial goals in a slowing economy.

TARGET CORPORATION (FORMERLY DAYTON HUDSON)

Target Corporation's headquarters are in Minneapolis, Minnesota, with regional offices and distribution centers located in other cities/states. The history of the corporation dates back to the

Reprinted by permission of the author.

founding of J.L. Hudson Company in Detroit in 1881, the founding of the Dayton Company in Minneapolis in 1902, and the merger of the two chains in 1969. Target Corporation ranks as America's fourth largest retailer among general merchandisers in the 2001 *Fortune* 500,[3] and includes three divisions: Target Stores (upscale discounter), Mervyn's California (midrange department store), and Marshall Field's (upscale department store chain consisting of Marshall Field's and the former Dayton's and Hudson's stores). The company also owns Rivertown Trading (a catalog company), and Associated Merchandising (apparel supplier). Target Corporation entered the year 2002 with a total of 1,383 stores: 1,055 Target Stores (including 62 SuperTargets) in 47 states, 264 Mervyn's California stores in 14 states, and 64 Marshall Field's stores in 8 states.[4] Corporate revenue and net income for the three chains combined in 2000 were $36.9 billion (9.5% growth) and $1.26 billion (10.5% growth), respectively. Target Corporation has 255,000 employees, an 18.7% growth over the previous year.[5] Target is consistently ranked high among all U.S. firms by industry analysts, such as number 37 in the 2001 *Fortune* 500 rankings, and number 46 in Hoover's 500.

Target Stores Division

Target Stores is the largest division of Target Corporation, generating 80 percent of corporate income, while the two department store divisions contribute about 20 percent each. Target Stores is community oriented, and contributes 5 percent of its federally taxable income to its local communities through grants, special programs, team member participation, partnerships with nonprofits, and other means.

Profile of Target Stores Shoppers ("Guests")[6]

Target shoppers tend to be the youngest among major retailers, with a median age of 44. They have a median household income of $51,000, compared to the median American household income of $39,000. Eighty percent are female and approximately 43 percent have children at home. About 39 percent are college graduates.[7] According to the company,

Target guests recognize the "difference between price and the more enduring concept of value." "Target guests are smart about their purchases, savvy to trends and conscientious about their communities. They're a unique crowd for a unique store."

Some of the Major Brands Available In Target Stores—2001

Calphalon (cookware)

Michael Graves (décor; housewares)

Philips (coffee maker)

Martex (bed and bath)

Waverly (home textiles, etc.)

Mossimo (apparel)

Carter's Baby Tykes (children's apparel)

Eddie Bauer (camping products)

And many other national and store brands with a fashion emphasis (e.g., Cherokee, Merona)

Target continues to add new brands to its merchandise mix to provide more value for its customers. For example, in January 2002, the Stride Rite Corporation announced the introduction of two new footwear brands ("Kid Smart?" and "Baby Smart?") that would be available in Target stores in Spring 2002. Stride Rite's Chairman and CEO said, "We are excited to expand our brand lineup to fill the needs of Target guests looking for stylish, value-priced children's shoes." Prices of the shoes will range from $12.99 to $16.99.[8]

Target Stores' Merchandising Approach

Store design consists of wide aisles, bright lighting, and layouts that make merchandise easy to find. Customers are able to move through checkout lanes easily. The store is operated from the perspective of a service-driven attitude, and supported with an innovative distribution network. Target's philosophy is to provide its shoppers with "Trend-driven merchandise with the everyday basics, a unique shopping experience, and a commitment to the community. It is this vision for value that has taken Target from its department store roots and made it into *the* upscale discount retailer."[9]

SELECTED HISTORY OF TARGET STORES (1962 – 2001)

1960s:

- First store opened in Roseville, Minnesota, in 1962.
- End of 1960s: Target operated 17 stores in 4 states; sales $100 million.

1970s

- 1975—Target became top revenue producer for parent Dayton Hudson Corp., and has kept that position ever since.
- End of 1970s: Target operated 80 stores in 11 states, over 18,000 team members, and $1.12 billion in sales.

1980s

- Continued expansion into many new states.
- End of 1980s: Target operated 399 stores in 33 states, and reached $7.52 in sales.

1990s

- 1990—opened first Target Greatland store in Apple Valley, Minnesota.
- 1995—opened first SuperTarget store.
  —launched the Target Guest Card, and Club Wedd bridal registry.
- 1997—began building Target House, for long-term patients and their families at St. Jude Children's hospital.
  —entered New York City metropolitan market.
- 1999—continued expansion in the Northeast in Massachusetts and Rhode Island.
- 1999—target.com established in August 1999—a Web site where both merchandise and information about the company are available. By the end of 1999, the site had almost 2,000 items and a growing number of loyal customers.
- End of 1990s: Target operated 907 stores in 44 states, and sales reached $26.02 billion.

2000

- January 2000—Corporate name was changed from Dayton Hudson Corporation to Target Corporation[10]
- February 2000—Target Corporation formed a new e-commerce unit, called "Target Direct," with responsibility for all of the company's electronic retailing and direct marketing efforts for all of the corporation's store brands and catalogs.[11]
- May 2000—Target announced that it had entered into a strategic multi-channel marketing alliance with E*TRADE. The agreement includes an in-store E*TRADE financial service center at a SuperTarget store, and the creation of a co-branded Target/E*TRADE website for Target guests (launched August 24, 2000 to offer financial services and free investment information).[12]
- August 2000—Target Stores and America Online, Inc. (AOL) announced the roll-out of joint marketing and promotional initiatives. Special edition AOL CD-ROMs are now available in over 900 Target stores.[13]
- Year 2000 sales reached $29.28 billion; pre-tax profits reached $2.223 billion.

2001

Target Stores

- January 2001—Target's corporate brand strengthened by changing names of Dayton's and Hudson's to Marshall Field's to leverage the Field's brand name nationally.
- Number of stores as of March 2001:[14] 992 Target Stores in 46 states, including 95 Target Greatland stores, 37 SuperTarget stores, 507 pharmacies, 136 optical centers, and 9 multilevel stores.
- Total number of Target Stores as of August 31, 2001 increased to 1,019.[15]
- Typical store size of 90,000—125,000 square feet; and company's total store square footage of about 125,000 square feet.
- Approximately 195,000 team members are employed by Target Stores.
- May 2001—Target Corporation announced plans to double the number of its discount

stores over the next few years, rather than expand Marshall Field's or Mervyn's.[16]

- June 2001—Target announced a partnership with VISA U.S.A. to offer a chip-embedded smart card. Cardholders can access special offers and build points toward rewards on a national basis.[17]

- July 2001—Target announced an agreement with Tupperware to sell plastic containers in SuperTarget stores. [18]

- August 2001—Target claimed victory over Kmart Corp. in a slugfest over comparative price claims by Kmart in its Dare to Compare promotion. Target claimed that 74% of the Kmart ads it surveyed not only included the wrong prices, but also referenced items that Target did not stock. Kmart denied any wrongdoing, but stopped the promotion.[19]

- September 2001—Target Stores and Nickelodeon announced an exclusive marketing partnership for the fall 2001 retail launch of SpongeBob SquarePants (a popular Nickelodeon animated character) merchandise, including school supplies, apparel for all ages, toys, and other items.[20]

- September 2001—Attack on World Trade Center took its toll on retail sales throughout the U.S. However, Target was able to recover and sustain its profitability more quickly than its competitors. Target's value proposition and sense of fashion attracted many shoppers who were concerned about the economy during the fall and holiday 2001 selling season.

- Target continued to open new stores, particularly SuperTarget Stores, as the company moved into 2002. For example, a new SuperTarget Store will open in New Tampa, Florida, in March 2002. In early January, the company attracted about 3,000 job seekers for 300 positions starting at $7 an hour as cashiers, bakers, sales, and stock personnel. (This store will offer a full line of groceries, a deli and bakery, a Starbucks coffee house, and a Krispy Kreme Doughnuts shop—in addition to clothing, electronics, music, and other products.)[21]

- January 2002—In a rare publicized complaint about Target Stores policies, a customer in Wichita, Kansas, took exception to an unpopular return policy that only allowed her to receive current clearance prices for items now on sale—although the item she returned shortly after

Christmas, was purchased at full price during the holidays. Although Target had posted signs throughout the store and at every checkout lane, customers complained that this was an unfair policy. Management listened to these complaints and revised their return policy. They still require a receipt for returns, but the company has a new receipt lookup service to help consumers who have lost their proof of purchase.[22]

Target Greatland

- Store size averages 135,000 square feet, with over 1.5 miles of shelf space

- Stores have 2,200 feet of aisles throughout the store (equivalent of 7 football fields)

- Stockroom space measures about $1/_4$ mile.

SuperTarget Stores

- A SuperTarget store is "a 175,000-square-foot box" designed with three distinct segments: clothing and furniture; grocery area; and more traditional items found in grocery stores and traditional Targets, such as health and beauty aids, and cleaning products.

- There were 62 SuperTarget stores in 14 states at the end of 2001. Longer-range plans are to open 200 SuperTargets by 2010, although some think this number could be as high as 400.

- The grocery area is stocked with name-brand groceries plus Target's house brand, "Archer Farms." At the front of the grocery area are several outlets, such as D'Amico & Sons deli, Wuollet Bakery, Starbucks Coffee, and Famous Dave's ribs. (An analyst says the way to look at this area is "that it's a lifestyle-based destination for food.") For example, the produce section has sushi, edible flowers, imported cheeses, organic foods, and other specialty foods—all part of the concept of bringing "fashion to food."[23]

Target.com Web Site

- October 2000—announced a redesigned website, www.target.com, to leverage its successful offline brand online, offering nearly 15,000 products—some are also available in Target stores; some are only available from target.com; successfully launched during the 2000 holiday season.[24]

• target.com was ranked by Net Nielsen Ratings among the top 10 online shopping sites.

• Convenient online access to Club Wedd and Lullaby Club.

• Online purchases may be returned to any Target store location.

• July 2001—Target announced that it was selling windmills and other energy-saving products online at target.com to help combat high energy prices.[25]

• August 2001—The Target Town House was opened in Manhattan—a 6,000 square foot Tribeca townhouse, styled with Target merchandise throughout. In each room, Target previewed the best of home, fashion, and beauty. (A virtual tour of the townhouse was also made available online at target.com.) The Town House opened with a gala celebration, and featured Target designers such as Sonia Kashuk, Mossimo Giannulli, and Michael Graves. At the close of the Target Town House, all of the furnishings and a charitable grant were given to the Coalition for the Homeless.[26]

• August 2001—Target Corporation launched Bullseye, a new website destination devoted exclusively to teenagers at www.target.com/ bullseye. Target's senior marketing manager said that "Bullseye is at the center of today's pop culture." Bullseye has seven key site features to engage a growing teen audience: Horoscopes, Music, Quizzes (interactive), Advice, Fashion, Beauty, and Events.[27]

Target Stores Performance

See Exhibit 1 for end-of-August through December 2001 monthly sales and year-to-date sales for Target Corporation and each of its divisions. *Fortune* 500 rankings are presented in Exhibit 2 for the years 1999 and 2000. For further financial information, refer to the company's 2000 Annual Report and website (www.target.com, or www.targetcorp.com). Data from previous years also is included in the Target (A) case (1999):"Target Is Hot! What's Next for the 'Upscale Discounter'?"

HOW TO SUSTAIN SUCCESS

Assume that you are a consultant to Bob Ulrich, Chairman and CEO of Target Corporation and Target Stores. What advice would you give Mr. Ulrich about strategies for continued growth and profitability over the next 5 to 10 years? What are some specific ways that the company can sustain its success?

EXHIBIT I

Target Corporation Sales: August—December 2001 and Year-to-Date

TARGET CORPORATION AUGUST SALES UP 9.8 PERCENT

MINNEAPOLIS, September 6, 2001—Target Corporation today reported that its net retail sales for the four weeks ended September 1, 2001 increased 9.8 percent to $3.010 billion from $2.741 billion for the four-week period ended August 26, 2000. Comparable-store sales increased 2.4 percent from August 2000.

"For the Corporation overall, August sales were essentially in line with our plan," said Bob Ulrich, chairman and chief executive officer of Target Corporation.

	Sales (millions)	Total Sales % Change	Comparable Stores % Change
August			
Target	$2,454	13.4	3.9
Mervyn's	328	(3.4)	(3.0)
Marshall Field's	190	(4.0)	(4.0)
Other	38	(7.9)	na
Total	$3,010	9.8	2.4

EXHIBIT 1 *(continued)*

Target Corporation Sales: August—December 2001 and Year-to-Date

Year-to-Date

Target	$16,374	11.5	3.2
Mervyn's	2,056	(1.9)	(1.4)
Marshall Field's	1,381	(6.3)	(6.3)
Other	201	(8.4)	na
Total	$20,012	8.3	1.9

Source: Target Corporation news releases at www.target.com or www.prnewswire.com.

TARGET CORPORATION SEPTEMBER SALES UP 7.4 PERCENT

MINNEAPOLIS, Oct 11, 2001—Target Corporation (NYSE:TGT) today reported that its net retail sales for the five weeks ended October 6, 2001 increased 7.4 percent to $3.286 billion from $3.060 billion for the five-week period ended September 30, 2000. Comparable-store sales increased 0.2 percent from September 2000.

"Sales for the corporation were below plan in September, particularly in the second week," said Bob Ulrich, chairman and chief executive officer of Target Corporation. "Profit trends remain very good at Target Stores, and are somewhat weak at Mervyn's and Marshall Field's. As a result, we now expect third quarter earnings per share (before unusual items) to be in the range of $0.24 to $0.25, compared with $0.24 a year ago." The company previously disclosed that it will record an unusual charge of approximately $0.05 per share in this year's third quarter related to accounting for previously sold receivables.

	Sales (millions)	Total Sales % Change	Comparable Stores % Change
September			
Target	$2,672	10.6	1.3
Mervyn's	306	(9.1)	(8.7)
Marshall Field's	268	1.9	1.9
Other	40	(8.1)	na
Total	$3,286	7.4	0.2
Year-to-Date			
Target	$19,045	11.4	3.0
Mervyn's	2,362	(2.9)	(2.4)
Marshall Field's	1,649	(5.0)	(5.0)
Other	243	(8.3)	na
Total	$23,299	8.2	1.7

(continued)

Source: Target Corporation news releases at http://www.target.com or http://www.prnewswire.com

EXHIBIT 1 *(continued)*

Target Corporation Sales: August—December 2001 and Year-to-Date

TARGET CORPORATION OCTOBER SALES UP 8.9 PERCENT

MINNEAPOLIS, Nov 8, 2001/PRNewswire via COMTEX/—Target Corporation (NYSE:TGT) today reported that its net retail sales for the four weeks ended November 3, 2001 increased 8.9 percent to $2.873 billion from $2.638 billion for the four-week period ended October 28, 2000. Comparable-store sales increased 2.0 percent from October 2000.

"Sales for the corporation were below plan in October, reflecting particular weakness at Marshall Field's," said Bob Ulrich, chairman and chief executive officer of Target Corporation.

	Sales (millions)	Total Sales % Change	Comparable Stores % Change
October			
Target	$2,336	12.8	4.1
Mervyn's	283	(1.6)	(1.0)
Marshall Field's	226	(10.1)	(10.1)
Other	28	2.5	na
Total	$2,873	8.9	2.0
Third Quarter			
Target	$7,461	12.2	3.0
Mervyn's	917	(4.8)	(4.4)
Marshall Field's	685	(4.0)	(4.0)
Other	107	(5.3)	na
Total	$9,170	8.7	1.5
Year-to-Date			
Target	$21,381	11.5	3.1
Mervyn's	2,645	(2.7)	(2.2)
Marshall Field's	1,875	(5.7)	(5.7)
Other	270	(7.3)	na
Total	$26,172	8.3	1.7

Source: Target Corporation news releases at http://www.target.com or http://www.prnewswire.com

TARGET CORPORATION NOVEMBER SALES UP 19.4 PERCENT

MINNEAPOLIS, Dec 6, 2001/PRNewswire via COMTEX/—Target Corporation (NYSE:TGT) today reported that its net retail sales for the four weeks ended December 1, 2001 increased 19.4 percent to $3.902 billion from $3.269 billion for the four-week period ended November 25, 2000. Comparable-store sales increased 11.4 percent from fiscal November 2000.

"Sales for the corporation were slightly below plan in November," said Bob Ulrich, chairman and chief executive officer of Target Corporation.

EXHIBIT 1 *(continued)*

Target Corporation Sales: August—December 2001 and Year-to-Date

	Sales (millions)	Total Sales % Change	Comparable Stores % Change	Comparable Sales % (adjusted calendar*)
November				
Target	$3,211	23.2	13.5	1.1
Mervyn's	388	2.4	3.0	(3.0)
Marshall Field's	252	2.6	2.6	(8.8)
Other	51	34.0	na	na
Total	3,902	19.4	11.4	(0.1)
Year-to-Date				
Target	$24,592	12.9	4.3	
Mervyn's	3,034	(2.1)	(1.6)	
Marshall Field's	2,127	(4.8)	(4.8)	
Other	321	(2.6)	na	
Total	$30,074	9.6	2.9	

*Compares four weeks ended December 1, 2001 to four weeks ended December 2, 2000. Target Corporation news releases at http://www.target.com or http://www.prnewswire.com

TARGET CORPORATION DECEMBER SALES UP 7.5 PERCENT

MINNEAPOLIS, Jan. 10/PRNewswire-FirstCall/—Target Corporation (NYSE:TGT) today reported that its net retail sales for the five weeks ended January 5, 2002 increased 7.5 percent to $6.550 billion from $6.093 billion for the five-week period ended December 30, 2000. Comparable-store sales increased 0.6 percent from fiscal December 2000.

"Sales for the corporation were well above plan in December, primarily due to exceptional strength at Target Stores," said Bob Ulrich, chairman and chief executive officer of Target Corporation. "As a result of this sales performance, we now expect our fourth quarter EPS to be moderately higher than the current First Call median estimate of $0.65."

	Sales (millions)	Total Sales % Change	Comparable Stores % Change	Comparable Sales % (adjusted calendar*)
December				
Target	$5,399	10.3	1.81	0.1
Mervyn's	639	(1.3)	(0.6)	6.1
Marshall Field's	442	(10.0)	(10.0)	(2.3)
Other	70	14.9	na	na
Total	6,550	7.5	0.6	8.6

(continued)

EXHIBIT 1 *(continued)*

Target Corporation Sales: August—December 2001 and Year-to-Date

Year-to-Date			
Target	$29,992	12.4	3.9
Mervyn's	3,673	(1.9)	(1.4)
Marshall Field's	2,569	(5.7)	(5.7)
Other	390	0.0	na
Total	$36,624	9.2	2.5

*Compares five weeks ended January 5, 2002 to five weeks ended January 6, 2001. Target Corporation news releases at http://www.target.com or http://www.prnewswire.com

EXHIBIT 2

Target Corporation—*Fortune* 500 Rankings (1999–2000)

Year	Rank	Revenues		Profits			Assets		Stkhldrs Equity	
		$ mil.	% change	$ mil.	Rank	% change	$ mil.	Rank	$ mil.	Rank
2000	37	36,903	9.5	1,264	90	10.5	19,490	159	6,519	114
1999	32	33,702	8.9	1,144	92	22.4	17,143	156	5,862	113

Mkt. Value 3/15/01* 3/14/00**		Profits As % Of...			Earnings Per Share			Total Return to Investors		
$ mil.	Rank	Revenues	Assets	Stkhldrs Equity	2000 $	% change	1990–2000 ann'l grwth	2000 %	Rank	1990–2000 annual rate
31,861*	80	3.4	6.5	19.4	1.38	12.7	11.8	(11.5)	307	23.1
27,166**	83	3.4	6.7	19.5	2.45	23.7	10.6	36.2	86	23.5

Endnotes

1. Moore, Janet, "Target's Ulrich Is Confident Despite Soft Economy," *Star Tribune*, Minneapolis (January 17, 2001).
2. Chicago Tribune Market Report Column, *Knight Ridder Tribune Business News* (January 3, 2002), p. 1.
3. "2001 Five Hundred," *Fortune* (April 16, 2001), pp. F-1, F-32, F-54.
4. *Target Corporation Fact Card,* Sales and Corporate Data, http://www.corporate-ir.net (January 10, 2002). Store data given were the latest available at the time of writing this case. Financial data were not available for the year 2001 as of January 2002.
5. Sources include www.target.com, www.targetcorp.com, *Target Corporation Annual Report 2000,* and http://hoovers.com.
6. Patty Morris, Target Media Relations, March 2001, and company information.
7. *Ibid. Target Corporation Fact Card.*
8. "New Children's Footwear Brands From Stride Rite Introduced at Target Stores in the U.S.; Stride Rite Continues Strategy of Bringing Expertise to Wider Audience," *Hoover's Online,* http://hoovnews.hoovers.com/ (January 7, 2002).
9. *Ibid.* Patty Morris.
10. "Dayton Hudson Corporation to Change Its Name to Target Corporation," Target Corporation News Release, www.iredge.com (January 13, 2000).
11. "Target Corp. Forms New E-Commerce Unit; Names Nitschke President of 'Target Direct,'" Target Corporation News Release, www.iredge.com (February 1, 2000).
12. "Target Announces Strategic Multi-Channel Marketing Alliance With E*TRADE," Target Corporation News Release, www.iredge.com (May 11, 2000); "Target and E*TRADE® Launch Co-branded Web Site Offering Financial Services and Free Investment Information," Target Corporation News Release, www.iredge.com (August 24, 2000).

13. "Target and America Online Launch Marketing and Promotion Initiatives," Target Corporation News Release, www.iredge.com (August 22, 2000).

14. *Ibid.*

15. Note: due to rapid growth of Target Stores, number of stores reported here may be much greater.

16. Brumback, Nancy, "Target Aims to Double Number of Stores," *Business and Industry* 75(22) (May 28, 2001), p. 3.

17. Mills, Karen, "Target Partners With Visa to Offer Smart Card," *Associated Press* (June 19, 2001).

18. Goldman, Abigail, "Tupperware Still Parties—But It's Spreading to Target," *Los Angeles Times* (July 18, 2001), Part 3, page 1.

19. D'Innocenzio, Anne, "Big Discounters Turn Warlike In Fight for Customers," *Associated Press* (August 24, 2001).

20. "Nickelodeon's SpongeBob SquarePants Makes a Splash With Major Retail Debut at Target Stores," *PR Newswire* (September 5, 2001).

21. "Thousands Apply for Chance to Work at SuperTarget Store in New Tampa, Fla.," *Tampa Tribune* (January 14, 2002).

22. "Target Stores Overturn Unpopular Return Policy," *Wichita Eagle* (January 7, 2002).

23. Moore, Janet and Ann Merrill, "Target Market; The Concept that People Will Pay More for What's Fashionable—Including Food—Is Being Tested In SuperTarget Stores," *Star Tribune* (July 27, 2001), p. 1D.

24. "target.com Redesign Leverages Successful Offline Brand Online," Target Corporation News Release, www.iredge.com (October 27, 2000); "target.com Expands Merchandise Offerings to Include Exclusive Branded Products," Target Corporation News Release, www.iredge.com (September 5, 2000).

25. "Target Selling Windmills On-line to Combat High Energy Prices: Become Your Own Utility!" *Business Wire* (July 30, 2001).

26. "Target Takes Manhattan—An Inside Look at Life and Style for Real People," *PR Newswire* (August 7, 2001).

27. "Target Aims for Teens with Bullseye Online; Bullseye Offers Cool News, Tips and Advice for Teen Guests," *PR Newswire* (August 16, 2001).

Outback Goes International

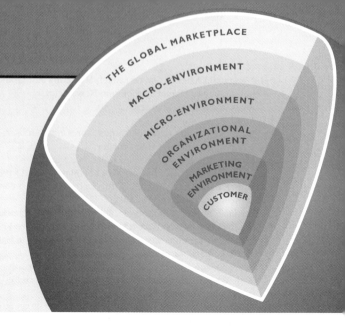

THE GLOBAL MARKETPLACE
MACRO-ENVIRONMENT
MICRO-ENVIRONMENT
ORGANIZATIONAL ENVIRONMENT
MARKETING ENVIRONMENT
CUSTOMER

This case was prepared by Marilyn L. Taylor of the Bloch School of Business and Public Administration, University of Missouri at Kansas City, George M. Puia of the College of Business Administration, Indiana State University, Krishnan Ramaya of the School of Business Administration, University of Southern Indiana, and Madelyn Gengelbach of the Bloch School of Business and Public Administration, University of Missouri at Kansas City.

In early 1995, Outback Steakhouse enjoyed the position as one of the most successful restaurant chains in the United States. Entrepreneurs Chris Sullivan, Bob Basham, and Tim Gannon, each with more than 20 years' experience in the restaurant industry, started Outback Steakhouse with just two stores in 1988. In 1995, the company was the fastest growing U.S. steakhouse chain with over 200 stores throughout the United States.

Outback achieved its phenomenal success in an industry that was widely considered as one of the most competitive in the United States. Fully 75 percent of entrants into the restaurant industry failed within the first year. Outback's strategy was driven by a unique combination of factors atypical of the foodservice industry. As Chairman Chris Sullivan put it, "Outback is all about a lot of different experiences that has been recognized as entrepreneurship." Within 6 years of commencing operations, Outback was voted as the best steakhouse chain in the country. The company also took top honors along with Olive Garden as America's favorite restaurant. In December 1994, Outback was awarded Inc.'s prestigious

This case was developed with support from the Ewing Marion Kauffman Foundation and was presented to North American Case Research Association. Reprinted by permission of the authors.

Entrepreneur of the Year award. In 1994 and early 1995, the business press hailed the company as one of the biggest success stories in corporate America in recent years.

In late 1994, Hugh Connerty was appointed president of Outback International. In early 1995, Connerty, a highly successful franchisee for Outback, explained the international opportunities facing Outback Steakhouse as it considered its strategy for expansion abroad:

> We have had hundreds of franchise requests from all over the world. [So] it took about two seconds for me to make that decision [to become president of Outback International].... I've met with and talked to other executives who have international divisions. All of them have the same story. At some point in time the light goes off and they say, "Gee we have a great product. Where do we start?" I have traveled quite a bit on holiday. The world is not as big as you think it is. Most companies who have gone global have not used any set strategy.

Despite his optimism, Connerty knew that the choice of targeted markets would be critical. Connerty wondered what strategic and operational changes the company would have to make to ensure success in those markets.

HISTORY OF OUTBACK STEAKHOUSE, INC.

Chris Sullivan, Bob Basham, and Tim Gannon met in the early 1970s shortly after they graduated from college. The three joined Steak & Ale, a Pillsbury subsidiary and restaurant chain, as management trainees as their first postcollege career positions. During the 1980s, Sullivan and Basham became successful franchisees of 17 Chili's restaurants in Florida and Georgia with franchise headquarters in Tampa, Florida.[1] Meanwhile, Tim Gannon played significant roles in several New Orleans restaurant chains. Sullivan and Basham sold their Chili's franchises in 1987 and used the proceeds to fund Outback, their start-from-scratch entrepreneurial venture. They invited Gannon to join them in Tampa in the fall of 1987. The trio opened their first two restaurants in Tampa in 1988.

The three entrepreneurs recognized that in-home consumption of meat, especially beef, had declined.[2] Nonetheless, upscale and budget steakhouses were extremely popular. The three concluded that people were cutting in-home red meat consumption but were still very interested in going out to a restaurant for a good steak. They saw an untapped opportunity between high-priced and budget steakhouses to serve quality steaks at an affordable price.

Using an Australian theme associated with the outdoors and adventure, Outback positioned itself as a place providing not only excellent food but also a cheerful, fun, and comfortable experience. The company's Statement of Principles and Beliefs referred to employees as "Outbackers" and highlighted the importance of hospitality, sharing, quality, fun, and courage.

Catering primarily to the dinner crowd,[3] Outback offered a menu that featured specially seasoned steaks and prime rib. The menu also included chicken, ribs, fish, and pasta entrees in addition to the company's innovative appetizers.[4] CFO Bob Merritt cited Outback's food as a prime reason for the company's success. As he put it:

> One of the important reasons for our success is that we took basic American meat and potatoes and enhanced the flavor profile so that it fit with the aging population. . . . Just look at what McDonald's and Burger King did in their market segment. They [have] tried to add things to their menu that were more flavorful. [For example] McDonald's put the Big Mac on the menu. . . . as

people age, they want more flavor . . . higher flavor profiles. It's not happenstance. It's a science. There's too much money at risk in this business not to know what's going on with customer taste preferences.

The company viewed suppliers as "partners" in the company's success and was committed to work with suppliers to develop and maintain long-term relationships. Purchasing was dedicated to obtaining the highest-quality ingredients and supplies. Indeed, the company was almost fanatical about quality. As Tim Gannon, vice president and the company's chief chef, put it, "We won't tolerate less than the best." One example of the company's quality emphasis was its croutons. Restaurant kitchen staff made the croutons daily on site. The croutons had 17 different seasonings, including fresh garlic and butter. The croutons were cut by hand into irregular shapes so that customers would recognize they were handmade. At about 40 percent of total costs, Outback had one of the highest food costs in the industry. On Friday and Saturday nights, customers waited up to 2 hours for a table. Most felt that Outback provided exceptional value for the average entree price of $15 to $16.

Outback focused not only on the productivity and efficiency of "Outbackers" but also on their long-term well-being. Executives referred to the company's employee commitment as "tough on results, but kind with people." A typical Outback restaurant staff consisted of a general manager, an assistant manager, and a kitchen manager plus 50 to 70 mostly part-time hourly employees. The company used aptitude tests, psychological profiles, and interviews as part of the employee selection process. Every applicant interviewed with two managers. The company placed emphasis on creating an entrepreneurial climate where learning and personal growth were strongly emphasized. As Chairman Chris Sullivan explained:

> I was given the opportunity to make a lot of mistakes and learn, and we try to do that today. We try to give our people a lot of opportunity to make some mistakes, learn, and go on.

In order to facilitate ease of operations for employees, the company's restaurant design devoted 45 percent of restaurant floor space to kitchen area. Wait staff were assigned only three tables at any time. Most Outback restaurants were only open

4:30 to 11:30 P.M. daily. Outback's wait staff enjoyed higher income from tips than in restaurants that also served lunch. Restaurant management staff worked 50 to 55 hours per week in contrast to the 70 or more common in the industry. Company executives felt that the dinner-only concept had led to effective utilization of systems, staff, and management. "Outbackers" reported that they were less worn out working at Outback and that they had more fun than when they worked at other restaurant companies.

Outback executives were proud of their "B-locations [with] A-demographics" location strategy. They deliberately steered clear of high-traffic locations targeted by companies that served a lunch crowd. Until the early 1990s, most of the restaurants were leased locations, retrofits of another restaurant location. The emphasis was on choosing locations where Outback's target customer would be in the evening. The overall strategy payoff was clear. In an industry where a sales-to-investment ratio of 1.2:1 was considered strong, Outback's restaurants generated $2.10 for every $1 invested in the facility. The average Outback restaurant unit generated $3.4 million in sales.

In 1995, management remained informal. Headquarters were located on the second floor of an unpretentious building near the Tampa airport. There was no middle management—top management selected the joint-venture partners and franchisees who reported directly to the president. Franchisees and joint-venture partners, in turn, hired the general managers at each restaurant.

Outback provided ownership opportunities at three levels of the organization: at the individual restaurant level, though multiple-store arrangements (joint-venture and franchise opportunities), and through a stock ownership plan for every employee. Health insurance also was available to all employees, a benefit not universally available to restaurant industry workers. Outback's restaurant-level general managers' employment and ownership opportunities were atypical in the industry. A restaurant general manager invested $25,000 for a 10 percent ownership stake in the restaurant, a contract for 5 years in the same location, a 10 percent share of the cash flow from the restaurant as a yearly bonus, opportunity for stock options, and a 10 percent buyout arrangement at the end of the 5 years. Outback store managers typically

earned an annual salary and bonus of over $100,000 as compared with an industry average of about $60,000 to $70,000. Outback's management turnover of 5.4 percent was one of the lowest in its industry, in which the average was 30 to 40 percent.

Community involvement was strongly encouraged throughout the organization. The corporate office was involved in several nonprofit activities in the Tampa area and also sponsored major national events such as the Outback Bowl and charity golf tournaments. Each store was involved in community participation and service. For example, the entire proceeds of an open house held just prior to every restaurant opening went to a charity of the store manager's choice.

Early in its history the company had been unable to afford any advertising. Instead, Outback's founders relied on their strong relationships with local media to generate public relations and promotional efforts. One early relationship developed with Nancy Schneid who had extensive experience in advertising and radio. Schneid later became Outback's first vice president of marketing. Under her direction, the company developed a full-scale national media program that concentrated on television advertising and local billboards. The company avoided couponing, and its only printed advertising typically came as part of a package offered by a charity or sports event.

Early financing for growth had come from limited-partnership investments by family members, close friends, and associates. The three founders' original plan did not call for extensive expansion or franchising. However, in 1990, some friends, disappointed in the performance of several of their Kentucky-based restaurants, asked to franchise the Outback concept. The converted Kentucky stores enjoyed swift success. Additional opportunities with other individuals experienced in the restaurant industry arose in various parts of the country. These multistore arrangements were in the form of franchises or joint ventures. Later in 1990, the company turned to a venture capital firm for financing for a $2.5 million package. About the same time, Bob Merritt joined the company as CFO. Merritt's previous IPO[5] experience helped the company undertake a quick succession of three highly successful public equity offerings. During 1994, the price of the company's stock ranged from $22.63 to a high of $32.00. The

EXHIBIT A

Consolidated Statements of Income

	Years Ended December 31,		
	1994	*1993*	*1992*
Revenues	$451,916,000	$309,749,000	$189,217,000
Costs and expenses			
Costs of revenues	175,618,000	121,290,000	73,475,000
Labor and other related expenses	95,476,000	65,047,000	37,087,000
Other restaurant operating expenses	93,265,000	64,603,000	43,370,000
General and administrative expenses	16,744,000	12,225,000	9,176,000
(Income) from oper. of unconsol. affl.	(1,269,000)	(333,000)	
	379,834,000	262,832,000	163,108,000
Income from operations	72,082,000	46,917,000	26,109,000
Nonoperating income (expense)			
Interest income	512,000	1,544,000	1,428,000
Interest expense	(424,000)	(369,000)	(360,000)
	88,000	1,175,000	1,068,000
Income before elimination			
Minority partners interest and income taxes	72,170,000	48,092,000	27,177,000
Elimination of minority partners' interest	11,276,000	7,378,000	4,094,000
Income before provision for income taxes	60,894,000	40,714,000	23,083,000
Provision for income taxes	21,602,000	13,922,000	6,802,000
Net income	$39,292,000	$26,792,000	$16,281,000
Earnings per common share	$0.89	$0.61	$0.39
Weighted average number of common shares outstanding	43,997,000	43,738,000	41,504,000
Pro forma:			
Provision for income taxes	22,286,000	15,472,000	8,245,000
Net income	$38,608,000	$25,242,000	$14,838,000
Earnings per common share	$0.88	$0.58	$0.36

company's income statements, balance sheets, and a summary of the stock price performance appear as Exhibits A, B, and C, respectively.

OUTBACK'S INTERNATIONAL ROLLOUT

Outback's management believed that the U.S. market could accommodate at least 550 to 600 Outback steakhouse restaurants. At the rate the company was growing (70 stores annually), Outback would near the U.S. market's saturation within 4 to 5 years. Outback's plans for longer-term growth hinged on a multipronged strategy. The company planned to roll out an additional 300 to 350 Outback stores, expand into the lucrative Italian dining segment through its joint venture with the successful Houston-based Carrabbas Italian Grill, and develop new dining themes.

At year-end 1994, Outback had 164 restaurants in which the company had direct ownership interest. The company had 6 restaurants that it operated through joint ventures in which the company had a 45 percent interest. Franchisees operated another 44 restaurants. Outback operated the company-owned

EXHIBIT B

Consolidated Balance Sheets

	December 31,				
	1994	*1993*	*1992*	*1991*	*1990*
Assets					
Current assets					
Cash and cash equivalents	$18,758,000	$24,996,000	$60,538,000	$17,000,700	$2,983,000
Short-term municipal securities	4,829,000	6,632,000	1,316,600		
Inventories	4,539,000	3,849,000	2,166,500	1,020,800	319,200
Other current assets	11,376,000	4,658,000	2,095,200	794,900	224,100
Total current assets	39,502,000	40,135,000	66,116,700	18,816,400	3,526,300
Long-term municipal securities	1,226,000	8,903,000	7,071,200		
Property, fixtures, and equipment, net	162,323,000	101,010,000	41,764,500	15,479,000	6,553,200
Investments in and advances to unconsolidated affiliates	14,244,000	1,000,000			
Other assets	11,236,000	8,151,000	2,691,300	2,380,700	1,539,600
	$228,531,000	$159,199,000	$117,643,700	36,676,100	11,619,100
Liabilities and stockholders' equity					
Current liabilities					
Accounts payable	$10,184,000	$1,053,000	$3,560,200	643,800	666,900
Sales taxes payable	3,173,000	2,062,000	1,289,500	516,800	208,600
Accrued expenses	14,961,000	10,435,000	8,092,300	2,832,300	954,800
Unearned revenue	11,862,000	6,174,000	2,761,900	752,800	219,400
Current portion of long-term debt	918,000	1,119,000	326,600	257,000	339,900
Income taxes payable			369,800	1,873,200	390,000
Total current liabilities	41,098,000	20,843,000	16,400,300	6,875,900	2,779,600
Deferred income taxes	568,000	897,000	856,400	300,000	260,000
Long-term debt	12,310,000	5,687,000	1,823,700	823,600	1,060,700
Interest of minority partners in consolidated partnerships	2,255,000	1,347,000	1,737,500	754,200	273,000
Total liabilities	56,231,000	28,774,000	20,817,900	8,753,700	4,373,300
Stockholders' equity					
Common stock, $0.01 par value, 100,000,000 shares authorized for 1994 and 1993; 50,000,000 authorized for 1992 42,931,344 and 42,442,800 shares issues and outstanding as of December 31, 1994z and 1993, respectively. 39,645,995 shares issued and outstanding as of December 31, 1992.	429,000	425,000	396,500	219,000	86,300
Additional paid-in capital	83,756,000	79,429,000	74,024,500	20,296,400	4,461,100
Retained earnings	88,115,000	50,571,000	22,404,800	7,407,000	2,698,400
Total stockholders' equity	172,300,000	130,425,000	96,825,800	27,922,400	7,245,800
	$228,531,000	$159,199,000	$117,643,700	$36,676,100	$11,619,100

EXHIBIT C

Selected Financial and Stock Data

Year	Systemwide Sales	Co. Revenues	Net Income	EPS	Co. Stores	Franchises and JVS	Total
1988	2,731	2,731	47	0.01	2	0	2
1989	13,328	13,328	920	0.04	9	0	9
1990	34,193	34,193	2,260	0.08	23	0	23
1991	91,000	91,000	6,064	0.17	49	0	49
1992	195,508	189,217	14,838	0.36	81	4	85
1993	347,553	309,749	25,242	0.58	124	24	148
1994	548,945	451,916	38,608	0.88	164	50	214

OUTBACK Stock Data	High	Low
1991		
Second quarter	$4.67	$4.27
Third quarter	6.22	4.44
Fourth quarter	10.08	5.5
1992		
First quarter	13.00	9.17
Second quarter	11.41	8.37
Third quarter	16.25	10.13
Fourth quarter	19.59	14.25
1993		
First quarter	22.00	15.50
Second quarter	26.16	16.66
Third quarter	24.59	19.00
Fourth quarter	25.66	21.16
1994		
First quarter	29.50	23.33
Second quarter	28.75	22.75
Third quarter	30.88	23.75
Fourth quarter	32.00	22.63

restaurants as partnerships in which the company was general partner. The company owned from 81 to 90 percent. The remainder was owned by the restaurant managers and joint-venture partners. The 6 restaurants operated as joint ventures also were organized as partnerships in which the company owned 50 percent. The company was responsible for 50 percent of the costs of these restaurants.

The company organized the joint venture with Carrabbas in early 1993. The company was responsible for 100 percent of the costs of the new Carrabba's Italian Grills, although it owned a 50 percent share. As of year-end 1994, the joint venture operated 10 Carrabba's restaurants.

The franchised restaurants generated 0.8 percent of the company's 1994 revenues as franchise fees. The portion of income attributable to restaurant managers and joint-venture partners amounted to $11.3 million of the company's $72.2 million 1994 income.

By late 1994, Outback's management also had begun to consider the potential of non-U.S. markets for the Outback concept. As Chairman Chris Sullivan put it:

...we can do 500 to 600 [Outback] restaurants, and possibly more over the next 5 years.... [However] the world is becoming one big market, and we want to be in place so we don't miss that opportunity. There are some problems, some challenges with it, but at this point there have been some casual restaurant chains that have gone [outside the United States] and their average unit sales are way, way above the sales level they enjoyed in the United States. So the potential is there. Obviously, there are some distribution issues to work out, things like that. But we are real excited about the future internationally. That will give us some potential outside the United States to continue to grow as well.

In late 1994, the company began its international venture by appointing Hugh Connerty as president of Outback International. Connerty, like Outback's three founders, had extensive experience in the restaurant industry. Prior to joining Outback, he developed a chain of successful Hooter's restaurants in Georgia. He used the proceeds from the sale of these franchises to fund the development of his franchise at Outback restaurants in northern Florida and southern Georgia. Connerty's success as a franchisee was well recognized. Indeed, in 1993 Outback began to award a large crystal trophy with the designation "Connerty Franchisee of the Year" to the company's outstanding franchisee.

Much of Outback's growth and expansion were generated through joint-venture partnerships and franchising agreements. Connerty commented on Outback's franchise system:

> Every one of the franchisees lives in their areas. I lived in the area I franchised. I had relationships that helped with getting permits. That isn't any different than the rest of the world. The loyalties of individuals that live in their respective areas [will be important]. We will do the franchises one by one. The biggest decision we have to make is how we pick that franchise partner.... That is what we will concentrate on. We are going to select a person who has synergy with us, who thinks like us, who believes in the principles and beliefs.

Outback developed relationships very carefully. As Hugh Connerty explained:

> ...trust...is foremost and sacred. The trust between [Outback] and the individual franchisees is not to be violated.... Company grants fran-

chises one at a time.[6] It takes a lot of trust to invest millions of dollars without any assurance that you will be able to build another one.

However, Connerty recognized that expanding abroad would present challenges. He described how Outback would approach its international expansion:

> We have built Outback one restaurant at a time. ...There are some principles and beliefs we live by. It almost sounds cultish. We want international to be an opportunity for our suppliers. We feel strongly about the relationships with our suppliers. We have never changed suppliers. We have an undying commitment to them and in exchange we want them to have an undying commitment to us. They have to prove they can build plants [abroad]....

He explained:

> I think it would be foolish of us to think that we are going to go around the world buying property and understanding the laws in every country, the culture in every single country. So the approach that we are going to take is that we will franchise the international operation with company-owned stores here and franchises there so that will allow us to focus on what I believe is our pure strength, a support operation.

U.S. RESTAURANTS IN THE INTERNATIONAL DINING MARKET

Prospects for international entry for U.S. restaurant companies in the early 1990s appeared promising. Between 1992 and 1993 alone, international sales for the top 50 restaurant franchisers increased from US$15.9 billion to US$17.5 billion. Franchising was the most popular means for rapid expansion. Exhibit D provides an overview of the top U.S. restaurant franchisers, including their domestic and international revenues and number of units in 1993 and 1994.

International expansion was an important source of revenues for a significant number of players in the industry. International growth and expansion in the U.S. restaurant industry over the 1980s and into the 1990s was driven largely by major fast-food restaurant chains. Some of these companies, for example, McDonald's, Wendy's, Dairy Queen,

EXHIBIT D

Top 50 U.S. Restaurant Franchises Ranked by Sales

Rank	Firm	Total Sales		International Sales		Total Stores		International Stores	
		1994	1993	1994	1993	1994	1993	1994	1993
1	McDonald's	25986	23587	11046	9401	15205	13993	5461	4710
2	Burger King	7500	6700	1400	1240	7684	6990	1357	1125
3	KFC	7100	7100	3600	3700	9407	9033	4258	3905
4	Taco Bell	4290	3817	130	100	5615	4634	162	112
5	Wendy's	4277	3924	390	258	4411	4168	413	377
6	Hardee's	3491	3425	63	56	3516	3435	72	63
7	Dairy Queen	3170	2581	300	290	3516	3435	628	611
8	Domino's	2500	2413	415	275	5079	5009	840	550
9	Subway	2500	2201	265	179	9893	8450	944	637
10	Little Caesar	2000	2000	70	70	4855	4754	155	145
Average of firms 11-20		1222	1223	99	144	2030	1915	163	251
Average of firms 21-30		647	594	51	26	717	730	37	36
Average of firms 31-40		382	358	7	9	502	495	26	20
Average of firms 41-50		270	257	17	23	345	363	26	43

Non-Fast Food in Top 50

Rank	Firm	Total Sales		International Sales		Total Stores		International Stores	
		1994	1993	1994	1993	1994	1993	1994	1993
11	Denny's	1779	1769	63	70	1548	1515	58	63
13	Dunkin Donuts	1413	1285	226	209	3453	3047	831	705
14	Shoney's	1346	1318	0	0	922	915	0	0
15	Big Boy	1130	1202	100	0	940	930	90	78
17	Baskin-Robbins	1008	910	387	368	3765	3562	1300	1278
19	T.G.I. Friday's	897	1068	114	293	314	NA	37	NA
20	Applebee's	889	609	1	0	507	361	2	0
21	Sizzler	858	922	230	218	600	666	119	116
23	Ponderosa	690	743	40	38	380	750	40	38
24	Int'l House of Pancakes	632	560	32	29	657	561	37	35
25	Perkins	626	588	12	10	432	425	8	6
29	Outback Steakhouse	549	348	0	0	NA	NA	NA	NA
30	Golden Corral	548	515	1	0	425	425	2	1
32	TCBY Yogurt	388	337	22	15	2801	2474	141	80
37	Showbiz/Chuck.E Cheese	370	373	7	8	332	NA	8	NA
39	Round Table Pizza	357	340	15	12	576	597	29	22
40	Western Sizzlin	337	351	3	6	281	NA	2	NA
41	Ground Round	321	310	0	0	NA	NA	NA	NA
42	Papa John's	297	NA	0	NA	632	NA	0	NA
44	Godfather's Pizza	270	268	0	0	515	531	0	0
45	Bonanza	267	327	32	47	264	NA	30	NA
46	Village Inn	266	264	0	0	NA	NA	NA	NA
47	Red Robin	259	235	27	28	NA	NA	NA	NA
48	Tony Roma's	254	245	41	36	NA	NA	NA	NA
49	Marie Callender	251	248	0	0	NA	NA	NA	NA

Note: NA: Not ranked in the top 50 for that category.
Source: "Top 50 Franchises," *Restaurant Business,* November 1, 1995, pp. 35–41.

and Domino's Pizza, were public and free-standing. Others, such as Subway and Little Caesars, remained private and free-standing. Some of the largest players in international markets were subsidiaries of major consumer products firms such as PepsiCo[7] and Grand Metropolitan PLC.[8] Despite the success enjoyed by fast-food operators in non-U.S. markets, casual dining operators were slower about entering the international markets. (See Appendix A for brief overviews of the publicly available data on the top 10 franchisers and casual dining chains that had ventured abroad as of early 1995.)

One of the major forces driving the expansion of the U.S. foodservice industry was changing demographics. In the United States, prepared foods had become the fastest-growing category because they relieved the cooking burdens on working parents. By the early 1990s, U.S. consumers were spending almost as much on restaurant fare as for prepared and nonprepared grocery store food. U.S. food themes were very popular abroad. U.S. food themes were common throughout Canada as well as western Europe and East Asia. As a result of the opening of previously inaccessible markets such as eastern Europe, the former Soviet Union, China, India, and Latin America, the potential for growth in U.S. food establishments abroad was enormous.

In 1992 alone, there were more than 3000 franchisers in the United States operating about 540,000 franchised outlets—a new outlet of some sort opened about every 16 minutes. In 1992, franchised business sales totaled $757.8 billion, about 35 percent of all retail sales. Franchising was used as a growth vehicle by a variety of businesses, including automobiles, petroleum, cosmetics, convenience stores, computers, and financial services. However, foodservice constituted the franchising industry's largest single group. Franchised restaurants generally performed better than free-standing units. For example, in 1991 franchised restaurants experienced per-store sales growth of 6.2 percent versus an overall restaurant industry growth of 3.0 percent. However, despite generally favorable sales and profits, franchisor-franchisee relationships often were difficult.

Abroad, franchisers operated an estimated 31,000 restaurant units. The significant increase in restaurant franchising abroad was driven by universal cultural trends, rising incomes, improved international transportation and communications, rising educational levels, increasing numbers of women entering the workforce, demographic concentrations of people in urban areas, and the willingness of younger generations to try new products.[9] However, there were substantial differences in these changes between the United States and other countries and from country to country.

FACTORS AFFECTING COUNTRY SELECTION

Outback had not yet formed a firm plan for its international rollout. However, Hugh Connerty indicated the preliminary choice of markets targeted for entry:

> The first year will be Canada. . . . Then we'll go to Hawaii. . . . Then we'll go to South America and then develop our relationships in the Far East, Korea, Japan, . . . the Orient. At the second year we'll begin a relationship in Great Britain and from there a natural progression throughout Europe. But we view it as a very long-term project. I have learned that people think very different than Americans.

There were numerous considerations that U.S. restaurant chains had to take into account when determining which non-U.S. markets to enter. Some of these factors are summarized in Exhibit E. Issues regarding infrastructure and demographics are expanded below. Included are some of the difficulties that U.S. restaurant companies encountered in various countries. Profiles of Canada, South Korea, Japan, Germany, Mexico, and Great Britain appear as Appendix B.

Infrastructure

A supportive infrastructure in the target country is essential. Proper means of transportation, communication, basic utilities such as power and water, and locally available supplies are important elements in the decision to introduce a particular restaurant concept. A restaurant must have the ability to get resources to its location. Raw materials for food preparation, equipment for manufacture of food served, employees, and customers must be able to enter and leave the establishment. The network that brings these resources to a firm is commonly called a *supply chain.*

The level of economic development is closely linked to the development of a supportive

EXHIBIT E

Factors Affecting Companies' Entry into International Markets

External Factors

Country market factors

Size of target market, competitive structure—atomistic, oligopolistic to monopolistic, local marketing infrastructure (distribution, etc.)

Country production factors

Quality, quantity, and cost of raw materials, labor, energy, and other productive agents in the target country as well as the quality and cost of the economic infrastructure (transportation, communications, port facilities, and similar considerations)

Country environmental factors

Political, economic, and sociocultural character of the target country—government policies and regulations pertaining to international business

Geographic distance—impact on transportation costs

Size of the economy, absolute level of performance (GDP per capita), relative importance of economic sectors—closely related to the market size for a company's product in the target country

Dynamics including rate of investment, growth in GDP, personal income, changes in employment. Dynamic economies may justify entry modes with a high break-even point even when the current market size is below the break-even point.

Sociocultural factors—cultural distance between home country and target country societies. Closer the cultural distance, quicker entry into these markets, e.g., Canada.

Home country factors

Big domestic market allows a company to grow to a large size before it turns to foreign markets. Competitive structure. Firms in oligopolistic industries tend to imitate the actions of rival domestic firms that threatens to upset competitive equilibrium. Hence, when one firm invests abroad, rival firms commonly follow the lead. High production costs in the home country is an important factor.

Internal Factors

Company product factors

Products that are highly differentiated with distinct advantages over competitive products give sellers a significant degree of pricing discretion.

Products that require an array of pre- and postpurchase services makes it difficult for a company to market the product at a distance.

Products that require considerable adaptation.

Company resource/commitment factors

The more abundant a company's resources in management, capital, technology, production skills, and marketing skills, the more numerous its entry mode options. Conversely, a company with limited resources is constrained to use entry modes that call for only a small resource commitment. Size is therefore a critical factor in the choice of an entry mode. Although resources are an influencing factor, it must be joined with a willingness to commit them to foreign market development. A high degree of commitment means that managers will select the entry mode for a target from a wider range of alternative modes than managers with a low commitment.

The degree of a company's commitment to international business is revealed by the role accorded to foreign markets in corporate strategy, the status of the international organization, and the attitudes of managers.

Source: Franklin Root: Entry Strategies for International Markets. Lexington, MA: D.C. Heath (1987).

infrastructure. For example, the U.S. International Trade Commission said:

> Economic conditions, cultural disparities, and physical limitations can have substantial impact on the viability of foreign markets for a franchise concept. In terms of economics, the level of infrastructure development is a significant factor. A weak infrastructure may cause problems in transportation, communication, or even the provision of basic utilities such as electricity.... International franchisers frequently encounter problems finding supplies in sufficient quantity, of consistent quality, and at stable prices.... Physical distance also can adversely affect a franchise concept and arrangement. Long distances create communication and transportation problems, which may complicate the process of sourcing supplies, overseeing operations, or providing quality management services to franchisees.[10]

Some food can be sourced locally, some regionally or nationally, and some must be imported. A country's transportation and distribution capabilities may become an element in the decision of the country's suitability for a particular restaurant concept.

Sometimes supply-chain issues require firms to make difficult decisions that affect the costs associated with the foreign enterprise. Family Restaurants, Inc., encountered problems providing brown gravy for its CoCo's restaurants in South Korea. "If you want brown gravy in South Korea," said Barry Krantz, company president, "you can do one of two things. Bring it over, which is very costly. Or, you can make it yourself. So we figure out the flavor profile, and make it in the kitchen." Krantz concedes that a commissary is "an expensive proposition but the lesser of two evils."[11]

In certain instances, a country may be so attractive for long-term growth that a firm dedicates itself to creating a supply chain for its restaurants. An excellent illustration is McDonald's expansion into Russia in the late 1980s:

> ...supply procurement has proved to be a major hurdle, as it has for all foreign companies operating in Russia. The problem has several causes: the rigid bureaucratic system, supply shortages caused by distribution and production problems, available supplies not meeting McDonald's quality standards.... To handle these problems, McDonald's scoured the country for supplies,

contracting for such items as milk, cheddar cheese, and beef. To help ensure ample supplies of the quality products it needed, it undertook to educate Soviet farmers and cattle ranchers on how to grow and raise those products. In addition, it built a $40 million food-processing center about 45 minutes from its first Moscow restaurant. And because distribution was [and still is] as much a cause of shortages as production was, McDonald's carried supplies on its own trucks.[12]

Changing from one supply chain to another can affect more than the availability of quality provisions—it can affect the equipment that is used to make the food served. For example:

> ...Wendy's nearly had its Korean market debut delayed by the belatedly discovered problem of thrice-frozen hamburger. After being thawed and frozen at each step of Korea's cumbersome three-company distribution channel, ground beef there takes on added water weight that threw off Wendy's patty specifications, forcing a hasty stateside retooling of the standard meat patty die used to mass-produce its burgers.[13]

Looking at statistics such as the number of ports, airports, quantity of paved roads, and transportation equipment as a percentage of capital stock per worker can give a bird's eye view of the level of infrastructure development.

Demographics

Just like the domestic market, restaurants in a foreign market need to know who their customers will be. Different countries will have different strata in age distribution, religion, and cultural heritage. These factors can influence the location, operations, and menus of restaurants in the country.

A popular example is India, where eating beef is contrary to the beliefs of the 80 percent of the population that is Hindu.[14] Considering that India's population is nearly 1 billion people, companies find it hard to ignore this market even if beef is a central component of the firm's traditional menu. "We're looking at serving mutton patties," says Ann Connolly, a McDonald's spokeswoman.[15]

Another area where religion plays a part in affecting the operation of a restaurant is the Middle East. Dairy Queen expanded to the region and found that during the Islamic religious observance of Ramadan, no business was conducted; indeed, the windows of shops were boarded up.[16]

Age distribution can affect who should be the target market. "The company [McDonald's in Japan] also made modifications [not long after entering the market], such as targeting all advertising to younger people, because the eating habits of older Japanese are very difficult to change."[17] Age distribution also can affect the pool of labor available. In some countries, over 30 percent of the population is under 15 years old; in other countries, over 15 percent is 65 or older. These varying demographics could create a change in the profile for potential employees in the new market.

Educational level may be an influence on both the buying public and the employee base. Literacy rates vary, and once again, this can change the profile of an employee as well as who comprises the buying public.

Statistics can help compare countries using demographic components such as literacy rates, total population and age distribution, and religious affiliations.

Income

Buying power is another demographic that can provide clues to how the restaurant might fare in the target country, as well as how the marketing program should position the company's products or services. Depending on the country and its economic development, the firm may have to attract a different segment than in the domestic market. For example, in Mexico:

> … major U.S. firms have only recently begun targeting the country's sizable and apparently burgeoning middle class. For its part, McDonald's has changed tactics from when it first entered Mexico as a prestige brand aimed almost exclusively at the upper class, which accounts for about 5 percent of Mexico's population of some 93 million. With the development of its own distribution systems and improved economies of scale, McDonald's lately has been slashing prices to aid its penetration into working-class population strongholds. "I'd say McDonald's pricing now in Mexico is 30 percent lower, in constant dollar terms, than when we opened in '85," says Moreno [Fernando Moreno, now international director of Peter Piper Pizza], who was part of the chain's inaugural management team there.[18]

There are instances where low disposable income does not translate to a disinterest in dining out in a Western-style restaurant. While Americans dine at a fast-food establishment such as McDonald's one or two times per week, lower incomes in the foreign markets make eating at McDonald's a special, once-a-month occurrence. "These people are not very wealthy, so eating out at a place like McDonald's is a dining experience."[19] China provides another example:

> … at one Beijing KFC last summer, [the store] notched the volume equivalent of nine U.S. KFC branches in a single day during a $1.99 promotion of a two-piece meal with a baseball cap. Observers chalk up that blockbuster business largely to China's ubiquitous "spoiled-brat syndrome" and the apparent willingness of indulgent parents to spend one or two months' salaries on splurges for the only child the government allows them to rear.[20]

Statistics outlining the various indexes describing the country's gross domestic product, consumer spending on food, consumption and investment rates, and price levels can assist in evaluating target countries.

Trade Law

Trade policies can be friend or foe to a restaurant chain interested in expanding to other countries. Trade agreements such as NAFTA (North American Free Trade Agreement) and GATT (General Agreement on Tariffs and Trade) can help alleviate the ills of international expansion if they achieve their aims of "reducing or eliminating tariffs, reducing non-tariff barriers to trade, liberalizing investment and foreign exchange policies, and improving intellectual property protection. . . . The recently signed Uruguay Round Agreements [of GATT] include the General Agreement on Trade in Services (GATS), the first multilateral, legally enforceable agreement covering trade and investment in the services sector. The GATS is designed to liberalize trade in services by reducing or eliminating governmental measures that prevent services from being freely provided across national borders or that discriminate against firms with foreign ownership."[21]

Franchising, one of the most popular modes for entering foreign markets, scored a win in the GATS agreement. For the first time, franchising was addressed directly in international trade talks. However, most countries have not elected to make their restrictions on franchising publicly known. The U.S. International Trade Commission pointed out:

> Specific commitments that delineate barriers are presented in Schedules of Commitments [Schedules]. As of this writing, Schedules from approximately 90 countries are publicly available. Only 30 of these countries specifically include franchising in their Schedules.... The remaining two-thirds of the countries did not schedule commitments on franchising. This means that existing restrictions are not presented in a transparent manner and additional, more severe restrictions may be imposed at a later date.... Among the 30 countries that addressed franchising in the Schedules, 25 countries, including the United States, have committed themselves to maintain no limitations on franchising except for restrictions on the presence of foreign nationals within their respective countries.[22]

Despite progress, current international restaurant chains have encountered a myriad of challenges because of restrictive trade policies. Some countries make the import of restaurant equipment into their country difficult and expensive. The Asian region possesses "steep tariffs and [a] patchwork of inconsistent regulations that impede imports of commodities and equipment."[23]

OUTBACK'S GROWTH CHALLENGE

Hugh Connerty was well aware that there was no mention of international opportunities in Outback's 1994 Annual Report. The company distributed that annual report to shareholders at the April 1995 meeting. More than 300 shareholders packed the meeting to standing room only. During the question and answer period, a shareholder had closely questioned the company's executives as to why the company did not pay a dividend. The shareholder pointed out that the company made a considerable profit in 1994. Chris Sullivan responded that the company needed to reinvest the cash that might be used as dividends in order to achieve the targeted growth. His response was a public and very visible commitment to continue the company's fast-paced growth. Connerty knew that international had the potential to play a critical role in that growth. His job was to help craft a strategy that would ensure Outback's continuing success as it undertook the new and diverse markets abroad.

Endnotes

1. All three Outback founders credited casual dining chain legend and mentor Norman Brinker with his strong mentoring role in their careers. Brinker played a key role in all the restaurant chains Sullivan and Basham were associated with prior to Outback.
2. American consumption of meat declined from the mid-1970s to the early 1990s primarily as a result of health concerns about red meat. In 1976, Americans consumed 131.6 pounds of beef and veal, 58.7 pounds of pork, and 12.9 pounds of fish. In 1990, the figures had declined to 64.9 pounds of beef and veal, 46.3 of pork, and 15.5 of fish. The dramatic decrease was attributed to consumer attitudes toward a low-fat, healthier diet. Menu items that gained in popularity were premium baked goods, coffees, vegetarian menu items, fruits, salsa, sauces, chicken dishes, salad bars, and spicy dishes. [George Thomas Kurian, *Datapedia of the United States 1790–10000* (Maryland: Bernan Press, 1994), p. 113.]
3. Outback's original Henderson Blvd. (Tampa, Florida) restaurant was one of the few open for lunch. By 1995, the chain also had begun to open in some locations for Sunday lunch or for special occasions such as Mother's Day lunch.
4. Outback's signature trademark was its best-selling "Aussie-Tizer," the Bloomin' Onion. The company expected to serve 9 million Bloomin' Onions in 1995.
5. Merritt had worked as CFO for another company that had come to the financial markets with its IPO (initial public offering).
6. Outback did not grant exclusive territorial franchises. Thus, if an Outback franchisee did not perform, the company could bring additional franchisees into the area. Through 1994, Outback had not had territorial disputes between franchisees.
7. PepsiCo owned Kentucky Fried Chicken, Taco Bell, and Pizza Hut.
8. Grand Met owned Burger King.
9. Ref. AME 76 (KR).
10. "Industry and Trade Summary: Franchising," U.S. International Trade Commission, Washington, D.C., 1995, pp. 15–16.
11. "World Hunger," *Restaurant Hospitality*, November 1994, p. 97.
12. *International Business Environments and Operations*, 7th ed. 1995), pp. 117–119.
13. "U.S. Restaurant Chains Tackle Challenges of Asian Expansion," *Nation's Restaurant News*, February 14, 1994, p. 36.
14. *CIA World Factbook*, India, 1995.
15. "Big McMuttons," *Forbes*, July 17, 1995, p. 18.
16. Interview with Cheryl Babcock, professor, University of St. Thomas, October 23, 1995.

17. "Franchise Management in East Asia," *Academy of Management Executive*, 4(2) (1990), p. 79.

18. "U.S. Operators Flock to Latin America," *Nation's Restaurant News*, October 17, 1994, p. 47.

19. Interview with Cheryl Babcock, professor, University of St. Thomas, October 23, 1995.

20. "U.S. Restaurant Chains Tackle Challenges of Asian Expansion," *Nation's Restaurant News*, February 14, 1994, p. 36.

21. "Industry and Trade Summary: Franchising," U.S. International Trade Commission, Washington, D.C., 1995, p. 30.

22. *Ibid.*

23. "U.S. Restaurant Chains Tackle Challenges of Asian Expansion," *Nation's Restaurant News*, February 14, 1994, p. 36.

APPENDIX A: PROFILES OF CASUAL DINING AND FAST-FOOD CHAINS*

This appendix provides summaries of the 1995 publicly available data on (1) the two casual dining chains represented among the top 50 franchisers that had operations abroad (Applebee's and T.G.I. Friday's/Carlson Companies, Inc.) and (2) the top ten franchisers in the restaurant industry, all of which are fast-food chains (Burger King, Domino's, Hardee's, International Dairy Queen, Inc., Little Caesar's, McDonald's, PepsiCo including KFC, Taco Bell and Pizza Hut, Subway, and Wendy's).

(1) *Casual Dining Chains with Operations Abroad*

Applebee's

Applebee's was one of the largest casual chains in the United States. It ranked twentieth in sales and thirty-sixth in stores for 1994. Like most other casual dining operators, much of the company's growth had been fueled by domestic expansion. Opening in 1986, the company experienced rapid growth and by 1994 had 507 stores. The mode of growth was franchising, but in 1992 management began a program of opening more company-owned sites and buying restaurants from franchisees. The company positioned itself as a neighborhood bar and grill and offered a moderately priced menu including burgers, chicken, and salads.

In 1995 Applebee's continued a steady program of expansion. Chairman and CEO Abe Gustin set a target of 1200 U.S. restaurants and also had begun a slow push into international markets. In 1994 the company franchised restaurants in Canada and Curacao and signed an agreement to franchise 20 restaurants in Belgium, Luxembourg, and the Netherlands.

	1989	1990	1991	1992	1993	1994ᵃ
Sales ($m)	29.9	38.2	45.1	56.5	117.1	208.5
Net income ($m)	0.0	1.8	3.1	5.1	9.5	16.9
EPS ($)	(0.10)	0.13	0.23	0.27	0.44	0.62
Stock price close ($)	4.34	2.42	4.84	9.17	232.34	13.38
Dividends ($)	0.00	0.00	0.01	0.02	0.03	0.04
No. of employees	1,149	1,956	1,714	2,400	46,600	8,700

ᵃ1994: Debt ratio 20.1%; R.O.E. 19.2; cash $17.2m; current ratio 1.13; LTD $23.7

T.G.I. Friday's/Carlson Companies, Inc.

T.G.I. Friday's was owned by Carlson Companies, Inc., a large, privately held conglomerate that had interests in travel (65 percent of 1994 sales), hospitality (30 percent) plus marketing, employee training and incentives (5 percent). Carlson also owned a total of 345 Radisson Hotels and Country Inns plus 240 units of Country Kitchen International, a chain of family restaurants.

Most of Carlson's revenues came from its travel group. The company experienced an unexpected surprise in 1995 when U.S. airlines announced that it would put a cap on the commissions it would pay to book U.S. flights. Because of this change, Carlson decided to change its service to a fee-based arrangement and expected sales to drop by US$100 million in 1995. To make up for this deficit, Carlson began to focus on building its hospitality group of restaurants and hotels through expansion in the United States and overseas. The company experienced significant senior management turnover in the early

---

*Unless otherwise noted, the information from this Appendix was drawn from "Top 50 Franchisers," *Restaurant Business,* November 1, 1995, pp. 35–41; and Hoover's Company profile Database 1996, Reference Press, Inc., Austin, TX (from American Online Service), various company listings.

1990s, and founder Curtis Carlson, age 80, had announced his intention to retire at the end of 1996. His daughter was announced as next head of the company.

T.G.I. Friday's grew 15.7 percent in revenue and 19.4 percent in stores in 1994. With 37 restaurants overseas, international sales were 12.7 percent of sales and 11.8 percent of stores systemwide. Carlson operated a total of 550 restaurants in 17 countries. About one-third of overall sales came from activities outside the U.S.

	1985	1986	1987	1988	1989	1990	1991	1992	1993	1994
Sales[a]	.9	1.3	1.5	1.8	2.0	2.2	2.3	2.9	2.3	2.3

[a]$b; no data available on income; excludes franchisee sales

(2) The Top Ten Franchisers in the Restaurant Industry

Burger King

In 1994, Burger King was number two in sales and number four in stores among the fast-food competitors. Burger King did not have the same presence in the global market as McDonald's and KFC. For example, McDonald's and KFC had been in Japan since the 1970s. Burger King opened its first Japanese locations in 1993. By that time, McDonald's already had over 1000 outlets there. In 1994, Burger King had 1357 non-U.S. stores (17.7 percent of systemwide total) in 50 countries, and overseas sales (18.7 percent) totaled US$1.4 billion.

Burger King was owned by the British food and spirits conglomerate Grand Metropolitan PLC. Among the company's top brands were Pillsbury, Green Giant, and Haagen-Dazs. Grand Met's situation had not been bright during the 1990s, with the loss of major distribution contracts like Absolut vodka and Grand Marnier liqueur, as well as sluggish sales for its spirits in major markets. Burger King was not a stellar performer either and undertook a major restructuring in 1993 to turn the tide including reemphasis on the basic menu, cuts in prices, and reduced overhead. After quick success, BK's CEO James Adamson left his post in early 1995 to head competitor Flagston Corporation.

	1985	1986	1987	1988	1989	1990	1991	1992	1993	1994
Sales[a]	5,590	5,291	4,706	6,029	9,298	9,394	8,748	7,913	8,120	7,780
Net income[a]	272	261	461	702	1,068	1,069	616	412	450	
EPS ($)	14	16	19	24	28	32	33	28	30	32
Stock price close ($)	199	228	215	314	329	328	441	465	476	407
Dividend/ share ($)	5.0	5.1	6.0	7.5	8.9	10.2	11.4	12.3	13.0	14.0
Employees (K)	137	131	129	90	137	138	122	102	87	64

[a]Millions of Sterling; 1994: debt ratio 47.3%; R.O.E. 12.4%; Cash (Ster.) 986M; LTD (Ster.) 2322M. 1994 Segments sales (profit): North America: 62% (69%); U.K. & Ireland 10% (10%); Africa & Middle East 2% (1%); Other Europe: 21% (18%); Other Countries: 5% (2%). Segment sales (profits) by operating division: drinks 43% (51%); food 42% (26%); retailing 14% (22%); other 1% (1%).

Domino's

Domino's Pizza was eighth in sales and seventh in stores in 1994. Sales and store unit growth had leveled off; from 1993 to 1994 sales grew 3.6 percent and units only 1.4 percent. The privately held company registered poor performance in 1993, with a 0.6 percent sales decline from 1992. Observers suggested that resistance to menu innovations contributed to the share decline. In the early 1990s the company did add deep dish pizza and buffalo wings.

Flat company performances and expensive hobbies were hard on the owner and founder Thomas Monaghan. He attempted to sell the company in 1989 but could not find a buyer. He then replaced top management and retired from business to pursue a growing interest in religious activities. Company performance began to slide, and the founder emerged from retirement to retake the helm in the early 1990s. Through extravagant purchases of the Detroit Tigers, Frank Lloyd Wright pieces, and antique cars, Monaghan put the company on the edge of financial ruin. He sold off many of his holdings (some at a loss), reinvested the funds to stimulate the firm, and once again reorganized management.

Despite all its problems, Domino's had seen consistent growth in the international market. The company opened its first foreign store in 1983 in Canada. Primary overseas expansion areas were eastern Europe and India. By 1994, Domino's had 5079 stores, with 823 of these in 37 major international markets. International brought in 17 percent of 1994 sales. Over the next 10 to 15 years the company had contracts for 4000 additional international units. These units would give Domino's more international than domestic units. International sales were 16.6 percent of total, and international stores were 16.5 percent of total in 1994.

	1985	1986	1987	1988	1989	1990	1991	1992	1993	1994
Sales[a]	1,100	1,430	2,000	2,300	2,500	2,600	2,400	2,450	2,200	2,500
Stores	2,841	3,610	4,279	4,858	5,185	5,342	5,571	5,264	5,369	5,079
Employees (K)	na	na	na	na	na	100	na	na	na	115

[a]$000,000

Hardee's

Hardee's was number 6 in sales and 11 in stores for 1994. In 1981, the large, diversified Canadian company Imasco purchased the chain. Imasco also owned Imperial Tobacco (Player's and du Maurier, Canada's top two sellers), Burger Chef, two drug store chains, the development company Genstar, and CT Financial.

Hardee's had pursued growth primarily in the United States. Of all the burger chains in the top 10 franchises, Hardee's had the smallest international presence, with 72 stores generating US$63 million (1.8 and 2.0 percent of sales and stores, respectively) in 1994.

Hardee's sales grew by about 2 percent annually for 1993 and 1994. A failed attempt by Imasco to merge its Roy Roger's restaurants into the Hardee's chain forced the parent company to maintain both brands. Hardee's attempted to differentiate from the other burger chains by offering an upscale burger menu, which received a lukewarm reception by consumers.

	1985	1986	1987	1988	1989	1990	1991	1992	1993	1994
Sales[a]	3,376	5,522	6,788	7,311	8,480	9,647	9,870	9,957	9,681	9,385
Net income[a]	262	184	283	314	366	205	332	380	409	506
EPS ($)	1.20	0.78	1.12	1.26	1.44	1.13	0.64	0.68	0.74	0.78
Stock price close ($)	13.94	16.25	12.94	14.00	18.88	13.81	18.25	20.63	20.06	19.88

	1985	1986	1987	1988	1989	1990	1991	1992	1993	1994
Dividends ($)	0.36	0.42	0.48	0.52	0.56	0.64	0.64	0.68	0.74	0.78
Employees (K)	na	na	na	na	190	190	180	na	200	200

[a]$M—all $ in Canadian; 1994: debt ratio: 38.4%; R.O.E. 16.1%; current ratio: 1.37; LTD (M): $1927; 1994 Segment sales (operating income): CT Financial Services 47%; (28%); Hardee's 32% (11%); Imperial Tobacco 16% (50%); Shoppers Drug Mart 2% (9%); Genstar Development 1% (2%).

International Dairy Queen, Inc.

Dairy Queen was one of the oldest fast-food franchises in the United States; the first store was opened in Joliet, Illinois, in 1940. By 1950, there were over 1100 stores, and by 1960, Dairy Queen had locations in 12 countries. Initial franchise agreements focused on the right to use the DQ freezers, an innovation that kept ice cream at the constant 23°F necessary to maintain the soft consistency. In 1970, a group of investors bought the franchise organization, but the group has been only partly successful in standardizing the fast-food chain. In 1994 a group of franchisees filed an antitrust suit in an attempt to get the company to loosen its control on food supply prices and sources. DQ franchises cost $30,000 initially plus continuing payments of 4 percent of sales.

The company's menu consisted of ice cream, yogurt, and brazier (hamburgers and other fast food) items. Menu innovations had included Blizzard (candy and other flavors mixed in the ice cream). The company also had acquired several companies, including the Golden Skillet (1981), Karmelkorn (1986), and Orange Julius (1987).

In 1994, Dairy Queen ranked number 7 in sales and 6 in stores. By that same year, the company had expanded its presence into 19 countries with 628 stores and US$300 million in international sales. 1994 was an excellent year for DQ; sales were up 22.8 percent over 1993. This dramatic change (1993 scored an anemic 3.0 percent gain) was fueled by technology improvements for franchisees and international expansion. In 1992 Dairy Queen opened company-owned outlets in Austria, China, Slovenia, and Spain. DQ announced in 1995 that they had a plan to open 20 stores in Puerto Rico over a 4-year period.

	1985	1986	1987	1988	1989	1990	1991	1992	1993	1994
Sales[a]	158	182	210	254	282	287	287	296	311	341
Net income[a]	10	12	15	20	23	27	28	29	30	31
EPS ($)	0.33	0.42	0.51	0.70	0.83	0.97	1.05	1.12	1.79	1.30
Stock price close ($)	5.20	7.75	8.00	11.50	14.75	16.58	21.00	20.00	18.00	16.25
Dividends ($)	-0-	-0-	-0	-0-	-0-	-0-	-0-	-0-	-0-	-0-
Employees (K)	430	459	503	520	549	584	592	672	538	564

[a]$M; 1994: debt ratio 15.3%; R.O.E. 24.4%; current ratio 3.04; LTD $23M. 1994 restaurants: U.S. 87%; Canada 9%; other 4%; restaurants by type: DQs franchised by company, 62%; franchised by territorial operators, 27%; foreign, 3%; Orange Julius, 7%; Karmelkorn, 1%; Golden Skillet less than 1%; sales by source: good supplies and equipment to franchises, 78%; service fees, 16%; franchise sales and other fees, 3%; real-estate finance and rental income, 3%.

Little Caesar's

Little Caesar's ranked 10 in sales and 8 in stores for 1994. Sales growth had slowed to a halt; a 1992–1993 increase of 12.2 percent evaporated into no increase for 1993–1994.

These numbers were achieved without a significant overseas presence. Of the top 10 franchises, only Hardee's had a smaller number of stores in foreign lands. Little Caesar's received 3.5 percent of sales from foreign stores. Only 3.2 percent of the company's stores were in non-U.S. locations, namely, Canada, Czech and Slovak Republics, Guam, Puerto Rico, and the United Kingdom.

	1985	1986	1987	1988	1989	1990	1991	1992	1993	1994
Sales	340	520	725	908	1,130	1,400	1,725	2,050	2,150	2,000
No. of stores	900	1,000	1,820	2,000	2,700	3,173	3,650	4,300	5,609	4,700
Employees	18,000	26,160	36,400	43,600	54,000	63,460	73,000	86,000	92,000	95,000

McDonald's

At the top in 1994 international sales and units, McDonald's, Inc., was the most profitable retailer in the United States during the 1980s and into the 1990s. The company opened its first store in California in 1948, went public in 1965, and by 1994 had over 20 percent of the U.S. fast-food business. McDonald's opened its first international store in Canada in 1967. Growing domestic competition in the 1980s gave impetus to the company's international expansion. By 1994 there were over 15,000 restaurants under the golden arches in 79 countries. The non-U.S. stores provided about one-third of total revenues and half the company's profits. McDonald's planned to open 1200 to 1500 new restaurants in 1995—most outside the United States. International markets had grown into an attractive venue for the burger giant because there was "less competition, lighter market saturation, and high name recognition" in international markets.

The company's growth was fueled by aggressive franchising. In the early 1990s, two-thirds of the McDonald's locations were franchised units, and franchisees remained with the company an average of 20 years. McDonald's used heavy advertising ($1.4 billion in 1994) and frequent menu changes and other innovations (1963, Filet-O-Fish sandwich and Ronald McDonald; 1968, Big Mac and first TV ads; 1972, Quarter Pounder, Egg McMuffin (breakfast); 1974, Ronald McDonald House; 1975, drive thru; 1979, Happy Meals; 1983, Chicken McNuggets; 1986, provided customers with list of products' ingredients; 1987, salads; 1980s, "value menus"; 1991, McLean DeLuxe, a low-fat hamburger (not successful) and experimentation with decor and new menu items at local level; 1993, first restaurants inside another store (Wal-Mart). The company planned to open its first restaurants in India in 1996 with menus featuring chicken, fish sandwiches, and vegetable nuggets. There would be no beef items.

From 1993–1994, McDonald's grew 10.2 percent in sales and 8.7 percent in stores. Because of its extensive experience in international markets, international sales had grown to 42.5 percent of total revenues and half its profits. Indeed, McDonald's was bigger than the 25 largest full-service chains put together.

	1985	1986	1987	1988	1989	1990	1991	1992	1993	1994
Sales[a]	3,695	4,144	4,894	5,566	6,142	6,640	6,695	7,133	7,408	8,321
Net income[a]	433	480	549	656	727	802	860	959	1,083	1,224
EPS ($)	0.56	0.63	0.73	0.86	0.98	1.10	1.18	1.30	1.46	1.68
Stock price close ($)	9.00	10.16	11.00	12.03	17.25	14.56	19.00	24.38	28.50	29.25
Dividends ($)	0.10	0.11	0.12	0.14	0.16	0.17	0.18	0.20	0.21	0.23
Employees (K)	148	159	159	169	176	174	168	166	169	183

[a]$M; 1994: debt ratio 41.2%; R.O.E. 20.7%; cash: $180M; current ratio: 0.31; LTD $2.9M; market value: $20B.

PepsiCo: KFC and Taco Bell (also Includes Pizza Hut; Latter Is Not in the Top 50)

Pepsico owned powerful brand names such as Pepsi-Cola and Frito-Lay and also was the world's no. 1 fast-food chain—with its ownership of KFC, Taco Bell, and Pizza Hut. KFC was third in sales and stores of the top 50 franchises in 1994. Active in the international arena since the late 1960s, KFC had been a major McDonald's competitor in non-U.S. markets. In 1994, the company had US$3.6 billion in sales and 4258 stores in other countries. McDonald's had been commonly number one in each country it entered, but KFC had been number two in international sales and had the number one sales spot in Indonesia. In 1994, KFC international revenues were 50.7 percent of sales with 45.3 percent of stores in international locations.

Taco Bell was fourth in sales and fifth in stores of the top 50 franchises in 1994. This ranking had been achieved with minimal international business to date. Taco Bell had US $130 million sales and 162 stores internationally. The company attempted to enter the Mexican market in 1992 with a kiosk and cart strategy in Mexico City. The venture did not fare well, and Taco Bell soon pulled out of Mexico. In 1994, international revenues were 3.0 percent of sales and 2.9 percent of stores were international locations.

	1985	1986	1987	1988	1989	1990	1991	1992	1993	1994
Sales[a]	8,057	9,291	11,485	13,007	15,242	17,803	19,608	21,970	25,021	28,474
Net income[a]	544	458	595	762	901	1,077	1,080	1,302	1,588	1,784
EPS ($)	0.65	0.58	0.76	0.97	1.13	1.35	1.35	1.61	1.96	2.22
Stock price close ($)	8.06	8.66	11.11	13.15	21.31	26.00	22.88	31.40	40.88	36.25
Div./share ($)	0.15	0.21	0.22	0.25	0.31	0.37	0.44	0.50	0.58	0.68
Employees (K)	150	214	225	235	266	308	338	372	423	471

[a]$M; 1994: debt ratio 48.1%, R.O.E. 27.0%; cash(M) $1,488; current ratio 0.96; LTD (M) $8.841. 1994 segment sales (operating income): restaurants: 37% (22%); beverages 34% (37%); snack foods 29% (41%).

Subway

Founded more than 29 years ago, Subway remained privately held in 1994. The company had experienced explosive growth during the 1990s. It ranked ninth in sales and second in stores for 1994. Sales grew 13.6 percent from 1993 to 1994 and 26 percent from 1992 to 1993. Stores grew 17.1 percent from 1993 to 1994 and 15.3 percent from 1992 to 1993. In 1994, Subway overtook KFC as the number two chain in number of stores behind McDonald's. The company attributed its growth at least partially to an exceptionally low-priced and well-structured franchise program. In addition, store sizes of 500 to 1500 square feet were small. Thus the investment for a Subway franchise was modest.

The company's growth involved a deliberate strategy. The formula involved no cooking on site, except for the baking of bread. The company promoted the "efficiency and simplicity" of its franchise and advertised its food as "healthy, delicious, [and] fast." The company advertised regularly on TV with a $25 million budget and planned to increase that significantly. All stores contributed 2.5 percent of gross sales to the corporate advertising budget. Subway's goal was to equal or exceed the number of outlets operated by the largest fast-food company in every market that it entered. In most cases the firm's benchmark was burger giant McDonald's.

International markets played an emerging role in Subway's expansion. In 1994, international sales were 10.6 percent of sales, compared with 8.9 percent the previous year. International stores were 9.5 percent of total in 1994 and 7.5 percent in 1993. Subway boasted a total of 9893 stores in all 50 states and 19 countries.

Wendy's

Wendy's was number five in sales and number nine in stores for 1994. In 1994, after 25 years of operation, Wendy's had grown to 4411 stores. This growth had been almost exclusively domestic until 1979, when Wendy's ventured out of the United States and Canada to open its first outlets in Puerto Rico, Switzerland, and West Germany. Wendy's granted J.C. Penney the franchise rights to France, Belgium, and Holland and had one store opened in Belgium by 1980.

Wendy's still saw opportunities for growth in the United States. Industry surveys had consistently ranked Wendy's burgers number one in quality but poor in convenience (Wendy's had one store for every 65,000 people, while McDonald's, in contrast, had one for every 25,000). Growth was driven primarily by franchising. In 1994, 71 percent of the stores were operated by franchisees and 29 percent by the company. Company restaurants provided 90 percent of total sales, while franchise fees provided 8 percent. The company had made menu and strategic changes at various points in history. For example, in 1977 the company first began TV advertising; 1979 introduced its salad bar; 1985 experimented with breakfast; 1986 and 1987 introduced Big Classic and SuperBar buffet (neither very successful); 1990 grilled chicken sandwich and 99 cent Super Value Menu items; and 1992 packaged salads.

Wendy's planned to add about 150 restaurants each year in foreign markets. With a presence of 236 stores in 33 countries in 1994, international was 9.1 percent of sales and 9.4 percent of stores in 1994.

	1985	1986	1987	1988	1989	1990	1991	1992	1993	1994
Sales[a]	1,126	1,140	1,059	1,063	1,070	1,011	1,060	1,239	1,320	1,398
Net income[a]	76	(5)	4	29	24	39	52	65	79	97
EPS ($)	0.82	(0.05)	0.04	0.30	0.25	0.40	0.52	0.63	0.76	0.91
Stock price close ($)	13.41	10.25	5.63	5.75	4.63	6.25	9.88	12.63	17.38	14.38
Div./share ($)	0.17	0.21	0.24	0.24	0.24	0.24	0.24	0.24	0.24	0.24
Employees (K)	40	40	45	42	39	35	39	42	43	44

[a]$M; 1994: debt ratio 36.6%; R.O.E. 5.2%; current ratio 0.98; LTD(M) $145.

APPENDIX B: Country Summaries*

Canada

In the 1990s, Canada was considered an ideal first stop for U.S. business seeking to begin exporting. Per capita output, patterns of production, market economy, and business practices were similar to the United States. U.S. goods and services were well received in Canada; 70 percent of all Canadian imports were from the United States. Canada's market conditions were stable, and U.S. companies continued to see Canada as an attractive option for expansion.

Canada had one of the highest real growth rates among the OECD during the 1980s, averaging about 3.2 percent. The Canadian economy softened during the 1990s, but Canadian imports of U.S. goods and services were expected to increase about 5 percent in fiscal year 1996.

Although Canada sometimes mirrored the United States, there are significant cultural and linguistic differences from the United States and between the regional markets in Canada. These differences were evident in the mounting friction between the English- and French-speaking areas of Canada. The conflict had potential for splitting of territory between the factions, slicing Canada into two separate countries. The prospect of this outcome left foreign investors tense.

Germany

In the mid-1990s, Germany was the largest economy in Europe, and the fifth largest overall importer of U.S. goods and services. Since reunification in 1990, the eastern part of Germany had continued to receive extensive infusions of aid from western Germany, and these funds were only just beginning to show an impact. The highly urbanized and skilled western German population enjoyed a very high standard of living with abundant leisure time. In 1994, Germany emerged from a recession and scored a GDP of US$2 trillion.

A unique feature of Germany was the unusually even distribution of both industry and population—there was no single business center for the country. This was a challenge for U.S. firms. They had to establish distribution networks that adequately covered all areas of the country. In Germany there was little opportunity for regional concentration around major population centers as in the United States.

The country was a good market for innovative high-tech goods and high-quality food products. Germans expected high-quality goods and would reject a less expensive product if quality and support were not in abundance. Strongest competition for U.S. firms were the German domestic firms not only because of their home-grown familiarity of the market but also because of the consumers' widely held perception that German products were "simply the best."

A recurring complaint from Germans was the prevalent "here today, gone tomorrow" business approach of American firms. Germans viewed business as a long-term commitment to support growth in markets and did not always receive the level and length of attention necessary from U.S. companies to satisfy them.

Conditions in the former area of East Germany were not the doomsday picture often painted, nor were they as rosy as the German government depicts. It would take 10 to 15 years for the eastern region of the country to catch up to the western region in terms of per capita income, standard of living, and productivity.

Japan

Japan had the second largest economy in the world. Overall economic growth in Japan over the past 35 years had been incredible: 10 percent average annual growth during the 1960s, 5 percent in the 1970s and 1980s. Growth ground to a halt during the 1990s due to tight fiscal policy. The government tightened fiscal constraints in order to correct the significant devaluation of the real estate markets. The

---

*Note that the material in this Appendix is adapted from the Department of Commerce *Country Commercial Guides* and the *CIA World Fact Book*.

economy posted a 0.6 growth in 1994 largely due to consumer demand. The overall economic outlook remained cloudy, but the outlook for exports to Japan remained positive.

Japan was a highly homogeneous society with business practices characterized by long-standing close relationships among individuals and firms. It took time for Japanese businessmen to develop relationships, and for non-Japanese businesspeople the task of relationship building in Japan was formidable. It was well known that Japan's market was not as open as the United States, but the U.S. government had mounted multifaceted efforts to help U.S. businesspeople to "open doors." While these efforts were helpful, most of the responsibility in opening the Japanese market to U.S. goods or services remained with the individual firm. Entering Japan was expensive and generally required four things: (1) financial and management capabilities and a Japanese-speaking staff residing within the country, (2) modification of products to suit Japanese consumers, (3) a long-term approach to maximizing market share and achieving reasonable profit levels, and (4) careful monitoring of Japanese demand, distribution, competitors, and government. Despite the challenges of market entry, Japan ranked as the second largest importer of U.S. goods and services.

Historically, Japanese consumers were conservative and brand conscious, although the recession during the 1990s nurtured opportunities for "value" entrants. Traditional conformist buying patterns were still prominent, but more individualistic habits were developing in the younger Japanese aged 18 to 21. This age cohort had a population of 8 million people and boasted a disposable income of more than US$35 billion.

Japanese consumers were willing to pay a high price for quality goods. However, they had a well-earned reputation for having unusually high expectations for quality. U.S. firms with high-quality, competitive products had to be able to undertake the high cost of initial market entry. For those who were willing, Japan could provide respectable market share and attractive profit levels.

Mexico

Mexico had experienced a dramatic increase in imports from the United States since the late 1980s. During 1994, the country experienced 20 percent growth over 1993. In 1994, Mexico's peso experienced a massive devaluation brought on by investor anxiety and capital flight. Although the Mexican government implemented tight fiscal measures to stabilize the peso, its efforts could not stop the country from plunging into a serious recession.

Inflation rose as a result of the austerity policies, and it was expected to be between 42 and 54 percent in 1995. Negative economic growth was anticipated in 1995 as well. The U.S. financial assistance package (primarily loans) provided Mexico with nearly US$50 billion and restored stability to the financial markets by mid-1995. The government was taking measures to improve the country's infrastructure. Mexico's problems mask that its government had, on the whole, practiced sound economic fundamentals.

Mexico was still committed to political reform despite the current economic challenges. After ruling the government uninterrupted for 60 years, the PRI party had begun to lose some seats to other political parties. Mexico was slowly evolving into a multiparty democracy.

Despite the economic misfortunes of recent years, Mexico remained the United States' third largest trading partner. Mexico still held opportunities for U.S. firms able to compete in the price-sensitive recessionary market. Mexico had not wavered on the NAFTA agreement since its ratification, and in the mid-1990s, 60 percent of U.S. exports to Mexico entered duty-free.

South Korea

South Korea had been identified as one of the U.S. Department of Commerce's 10 "Big Emerging Markets." The country's economy overcame tremendous obstacles after the Korean War in the 1950s left the country in ruins. The driving force behind South Korea's growth was export-led development and energetic emphasis on entrepreneurship. Annual real GDP growth from 1986 to 1991 was over 10 percent. This blistering pace created inflation, tight labor markets, and a rising current account deficit. Fiscal policy in 1992 focused on curbing inflation and reducing the deficit. Annual growth, reduced to a still enviable 5 percent in 1992, rose to 6.3 percent in 1993. Fueled by exports, 1994s growth was a heady 8.3 percent. South Korea's GDP was larger than those of Russia, Australia, and Mexico.

The American media had highlighted such issues as student demonstrations, construction accidents, and North Korean nuclear problem and trade disputes. Investors needed to closely monitor developments related to North Korea. However, the political landscape in South Korea had been stable enough over the 1980s to fuel tremendous economic expansion. The country was undertaking significant infrastructure improvements. Overall, South Korea was a democratic republic with an open society and a free press. It was a modern, cosmopolitan, fast-paced, and dynamic country with abundant business opportunities for savvy American businesses.

There had been staggering development of U.S. exports to South Korea: US$21.6 billion in 1994 and over US$30 billion expected in 1995. While South Korea was 22 times smaller than China in terms of population, it imported two times more U.S. goods and services than China in 1994.

Although South Korea ranked as the United States' sixth largest export market, obstacles for U.S. firms still remained. Despite participation in the Uruguay Round of GATT and related trade agreements, customs clearance procedures and regulations for labeling, sanitary standards, and quarantine often served as significant nontariff barriers.

United Kingdom (or Great Britain)

The United Kingdom (U.K.) was the United States' fourth largest trading partner and the largest market for U.S. exports in Europe. Common language, legal heritage, and business practices facilitated U.S. entry into the British market.

The United Kingdom had made significant changes to their taxation, regulation, and privatization policies that changed the structure of the British economy and increased its overall efficiency. The reward for this disciplined economic approach had been sustained, modest growth during the 1980s and early 1990s. GDP grew 4.2 percent in 1994, the highest level in 6 years. The United Kingdom trimmed its deficit from US$75 billion in fiscal 1994 to US$50 billion in fiscal 1995.

The United Kingdom had no restrictions on foreign ownership and movement of capital. There was a high degree of labor flexibility. Efficiencies had soared in the United Kingdom, and in the mid-1990s, the country boasted the lowest real per unit labor cost of the Group of Seven (G7) industrialized countries.

The United Kingdom's shared cultural heritage and warm relationship with the United States translated into the British finding U.S. goods and services as attractive purchases. These reasons, coupled with British policy emphasizing free enterprise and open competition, made the United Kingdom the destination of 40 percent of all U.S. investment in the EU.

The U.K. market was based on a commitment to the principles of free enterprise and open competition. Demand for U.S. goods and services was growing. The abolition of many internal trade barriers within the European Common market enabled European-based firms to operate relatively freely. As a result, U.S. companies used the United Kingdom as a gateway to the rest of the EU. Of the top 500 British companies, one in eight was a U.S. affiliate. Excellent physical and communications infrastructure combined with a friendly political and commercial climate were expected to keep the United Kingdom as a primary target for U.S. firms for years to come.

Perdue Farms Inc.: Responding to Twenty-first Century Challenges

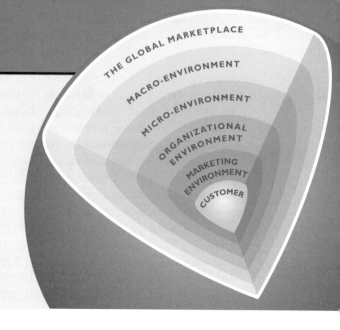

THE GLOBAL MARKETPLACE
MACRO-ENVIRONMENT
MICRO-ENVIRONMENT
ORGANIZATIONAL ENVIRONMENT
MARKETING ENVIRONMENT
CUSTOMER

This case was prepared by George C. Rubenson, Salisbury University, and Frank Shipper, Salisbury University.

Background/Company History

"I have a theory that you can tell the difference between those who have inherited a fortune and those who have made a fortune. Those who have made their own fortune forget not where they came from and are less likely to lose touch with the common man."

Bill Sterling, "Just Browsin" column in Eastern Shore News, March 2, 1988

This history of Perdue Farms Inc. is dominated by seven themes: quality, growth, geographic expansion, vertical integration, innovation, branding, and service. Arthur W. Perdue, a Railway Express Agent and descendent of a French Huguenot family named Perdeaux, founded the company in 1920 when he left his job with Railway Express and entered the egg business full-time near the small town of Salisbury, Maryland. Salisbury is located in a region immortalized in James Michener's Chesapeake *that is also*

known as "the Eastern Shore" or "Delmarva Peninsula." It includes parts of DELaware, MARyland and VirginiA. Arthur Perdue's only child, Franklin Parsons Perdue, was also born in 1920.

A quick look at Perdue Farms' mission statement (Exhibit 1) reveals the emphasis the company has always put on quality. In the 1920s, "Mr. Arthur," as he was called, bought leghorn breeding stock from Texas to improve the quality of his flock. He soon expanded his egg market and began shipments to New York. Practicing small economies such as mixing his own chicken feed and using leather from his old shoes to make hinges for his chicken coops, he stayed out of debt and prospered. He tried to add a new chicken coop every year.

By 1940, Perdue Farms was already known for quality products and fair dealing in a tough, highly competitive market. The company began offering chickens for sale when "Mr. Arthur" realized that the future lay in selling chickens, not eggs. In 1944,

ACKNOWLEDGMENTS: The authors are indebted to Frank Perdue, Jim Perdue, and the numerous associates at Perdue Farms, Inc., who generously shared their time and information about the company. In addition, the authors would like to thank the anonymous librarians at Blackwell Library, Salisbury State University, who routinely review area newspapers and file articles about the poultry industry—the most important industry on the Delmarva Peninsula. Without their assistance, this case would not be possible.

Reprinted by permission of the authors.

EXHIBIT I

Perdue Mission 2000

Stand on Tradition

*Perdue was built upon a foundation of quality,
a tradition described in our Quality Policy . . .*

Our Quality Policy

**"We shall produce products and provide services
at all times which meet or exceed the expectations of our customers."**

**"We shall not be content to be of
equal quality to our competitors."**

"Our commitment is to be increasingly superior."

**"Contribution to quality is a responsibility
shared by everyone in the Perdue organization."**

Focus on Today

Our mission reminds us of the purpose we serve. . .

Our Mission

"Enhance the quality of life with great food and agricultural products."

While striving to fulfill our mission, we use our values to guide our decisions. . .

Our Values

- **Quality:** We value the needs of our customers. Our high standards require us to work safely, make safe food and uphold the Perdue name.

- **Integrity:** We do the right thing and live up to our commitments. We do not cut corners or make false promises.

- **Trust:** We trust each other and treat each other with mutual respect. Each individual's skill and talent are appreciated.

- **Teamwork:** We value a strong work ethic and ability to make each other successful. We care what others think and encourage their involvement, creating a sense of pride, loyalty, ownership and family.

EXHIBIT 1 *(continued)*

Perdue Mission 2000

Look to the Future

*Our vision describes what we will become and the qualities
that will enable us to succeed . . .*

Our Vision

"To be the leading quality food company with $20 billion in sales in 2020."

Perdue in the Year 2020

- **To our customers:** We will provide food solutions and indispensable services to meet anticipated customer needs.

- **To our consumers:** A portfolio of trusted food and agricultural products will be supported by multiple brands throughout the world.

- **To our associates:** Worldwide, our people and our workplace will reflect our quality reputation, placing Perdue among the best places to work.

- **To our communities:** We will be known in the community as a strong corporate citizen, trusted business partner and favorite employer.

- **To our shareholders:** Driven by innovation, our market leadership and our creative spirit will yield industry-leading profits.

Mr. Arthur made his son Frank a full partner in A. W. Perdue and Son, Inc.

In 1950, Frank took over leadership of the company, that employed 40 people. By 1952, revenues were $6,000,000 from the sale of 2,600,000 broilers. During this period, the company began to vertically integrate, operating its own hatchery, starting to mix its own feed formulations, and operating its own feed mill. Also in the 1950s, Perdue Farms began to contract with others to grow chickens for them. By furnishing the growers with peeps (baby chickens) and the feed, the company was better able to control quality.

In the 1960s, Perdue Farms continued to vertically integrate by building its first grain receiving and storage facilities and Maryland's first soybean processing plant. By 1967, annual sales had increased to about $35,000,000. However, it became clear to Frank that profits lay in processing chickens. Frank recalled in an interview for *Business Week* (Septem-

ber 15, 1972) "... processors were paying us 10¢ a live pound for what cost us 14¢ to produce. Suddenly, processors were making as much as 7¢ a pound."

A cautious, conservative planner, Arthur Perdue had not been eager for expansion and Frank Perdue himself was reluctant to enter poultry processing. But economics forced his hand, and in 1968 the company bought its first processing plant, a Swift and Company operation in Salisbury.

From the first batch of chickens that it processed, Perdue's standards were higher than those of the federal government. The state grader on the first batch has often told the story of how he was worried that he had rejected too many chickens as not Grade A. As he finished his inspections for that first day, he saw Frank Perdue headed his way and he could tell that Frank was not happy. Frank started inspecting the birds and never argued over one that was rejected. Next, he saw Frank start to go through the ones that the state grader had passed, and began to toss some of them over with the rejected birds. Finally, realizing that few met his standards, Frank put all of the birds in the reject pile. Soon, however, the facility was able to process 14,000 broilers per hour.

From the beginning, Frank Perdue refused to permit his broilers to be frozen for shipping, arguing that it resulted in unappetizing black bones and loss of flavor and moistness when cooked. Instead, Perdue chickens were (and some still are) shipped to market packed in ice, justifying the company's advertisements at that time that it sold only "fresh, young broilers." However, this policy also limited the company's market to those locations that could be serviced overnight from the Eastern Shore of Maryland. Thus, Perdue chose for its primary markets the densely populated towns and cities of the East Coast, particularly New York City, which consumes more Perdue chicken than all other brands combined.

Frank Perdue's drive for quality became legendary both inside and outside the poultry industry. In 1985, Frank and Perdue Farms, Inc. were featured in the book, *A Passion for Excellence*, by Tom Peters and Nancy Austin.

In 1970, Perdue established its primary breeding and genetic research programs. Through selective breeding, Perdue developed a chicken with more white breast meat than the typical chicken. Selective breeding has been so successful that Perdue Farms chickens are desired by other processors. Rumors have even suggested that Perdue chickens have been stolen on occasion in an attempt to improve competitor flocks.

In 1971, Perdue Farms began an extensive marketing campaign featuring Frank Perdue. In his early advertisements, he became famous for saying things like "If you want to eat as good as my chickens, you'll just have to eat my chickens." He is often credited with being the first to brand what had been a commodity product. During the 1970s, Perdue Farms also expanded geographically to areas north of New York City such as Massachusetts, Rhode Island, and Connecticut.

In 1977, "Mr. Arthur" died at the age of 91, leaving behind a company with annual sales of nearly $200,000,000, an average annual growth rate of 17 percent compared to an industry average of 1 percent a year, the potential for processing 78,000 broilers per hour, and annual production of nearly 350,000,000 pounds of poultry per year. Frank Perdue said of his father simply "I learned everything from him."

In 1981, Frank Perdue was in Boston for his induction into the Babson College Academy of Distinguished Entrepreneurs, an award established in 1978 to recognize the spirit of free enterprise and business leadership. Babson College President Ralph Z. Sorenson inducted Perdue into the academy which, at that time, numbered 18 men and women from four continents. Perdue had the following to say to the college students:

> "There are none, nor will there ever be, easy steps for the entrepreneur. Nothing, absolutely nothing, replaces the willingness to work earnestly, intelligently towards a goal. You have to be willing to pay the price. You have to have an insatiable appetite for detail, have to be willing to accept constructive criticism, to ask questions, to be fiscally responsible, to surround yourself with good people and, most of all, to listen." (Frank Perdue, speech at Babson College, April 28, 1981)

The early 1980s saw Perdue Farms expand southward into Virginia, North Carolina, and Georgia. It also began to buy out other producers such as Carroll's Foods, Purvis Farms, Shenandoah Valley Poultry Company, and Shenandoah Farms. The latter two acquisitions diversified the company's markets to include turkey. New Products included value-added items such as "Perdue Done It!," a line of fully cooked fresh chicken products.

James A. (Jim) Perdue, Frank's only son, joined the company as a management trainee in 1983 and became a plant manager. The later 1980s tested the mettle of the firm. Following a period of considerable expansion and product diversification, a consulting firm recommended that the company form several strategic business units, responsible for their own operations. In other words, the firm should decentralize. Soon after, the chicken market leveled off and then declined for a period. In 1988, the firm experienced its first year in the red. Unfortunately, the decentralization had created duplication and enormous administrative costs. The firm's rapid plunge into turkeys and other food processing, where it had little experience, contributed to the losses. Characteristically, the company refocused, concentrating on efficiency of operations, improving communications throughout the company, and paying close attention to detail.

On June 2, 1989, Frank celebrated 50 years with Perdue Farms, Inc. At a morning reception in downtown Salisbury, the governor of Maryland proclaimed "Frank Perdue Day." The governors of

Delaware and Virginia did the same. In 1991, Frank was named Chairman of the Executive Committee and Jim Perdue became Chairman of the Board. Quieter, gentler, and more formally educated, Jim Perdue focuses on operations, infusing the company with an even stronger devotion to quality control and a bigger commitment to strategic planning. Frank Perdue continued to do advertising and public relations. As Jim Perdue matured as the company leader, he took over the role of company spokesperson and began to appear in advertisements.

Under Jim Perdue's leadership, the 1990s were dominated by market expansion into Florida and west to Michigan and Missouri. In 1992, the international business segment was formalized, serving customers in Puerto Rico, South America, Europe, Japan, and China. By fiscal year 1998, international sales were $180 million per year. International markets are beneficial for the firm because U.S. customers prefer white meat while customers in most other countries prefer dark meat.

Food service sales to commercial consumers has also become a major market. New retail product lines focus on value-added items, individually quick frozen items, home meal replacement items, and products for the delicatessen. The "Fit'n Easy" label continues as part of a nutrition campaign using skinless, boneless chicken and turkey products.

The 1990s also saw the increased use of technology and the building of distribution centers to better serve the customer. For example, all over-the-road trucks were equipped with satellite two-way communications and geographic positioning, allowing real-time tracking, rerouting if needed, and accurately informing customers when to expect product arrival. Currently, nearly 20,000 associates have increased revenues to more than $2.5 billion.

Photo of (left to right) Jim, Frank, and Mr. Arthur

MANAGEMENT AND ORGANIZATION

From 1950 until 1991, Frank Perdue was the primary force behind Perdue Farms' growth and success. During Frank's years as the company leader, the industry entered its high growth period. Industry executives typically had developed professionally during the industry's infancy. Many had little formal education and started their careers in the barnyard, building chicken coops and cleaning them out. They often spent their entire careers with one company, progressing from supervisor of grow-out facilities to management of processing plants to corporate executive positions. Perdue Farms was not unusual in that respect. An entrepreneur through and through, Frank lived up to his marketing image of "it takes a tough man to make a tender chicken." He mostly used a centralized management style that kept decision-making authority in his own hands or those of a few trusted, senior executives whom he had known for a lifetime. Workers were expected to do their jobs.

In later years, Frank increasingly emphasized employee (or "associates" as they are currently referred to) involvement in quality issues and operational decisions. This later emphasis on employee participation undoubtedly eased the transfer of power in 1991 to his son, Jim, which appears to have been unusually smooth. Although Jim grew up in the family business, he spent almost 15 years earning an undergraduate degree in biology from Wake Forest University, a master's degree in marine biology from the University of Massachusetts at Dartmouth, and a doctorate in fisheries from the University of Washington in Seattle. Returning to Perdue Farms in 1983, he earned an EMBA from Salisbury State University and was assigned positions as plant manager, divisional quality control manager, and vice president of Quality Improvement Process (QIP) prior to becoming Chairman.

Jim has a people-first management style. Company goals center on the three P's: People, Products, and Profitability. He believes that business success rests on satisfying customer needs with quality products. It is important to put associates first because "If [associates] come first, they will strive to assure superior product quality—and satisfied customers." This view has had a profound impact on the company culture, which is based on Tom Peters' view that "Nobody knows a person's 20 square feet better than the person who works there." The idea is to gather ideas and information from everyone in the organization and maximize productivity by transmitting these ideas throughout the organization.

Key to accomplishing this "employees first" policy is workforce stability, a difficult task in an industry that employs a growing number of associates working in physically demanding and sometimes stressful conditions. A significant number of associates are Hispanic immigrants who may have a poor command of the English language, are sometimes undereducated, and often lack basic health care. In order to increase these associates' opportunity for advancement, Perdue Farms focuses on helping them overcome these disadvantages.

For example, the firm provides English-language classes to help non-English-speaking employees assimilate. Ultimately, employees can earn the equivalent of a high-school diploma. To deal with physical stress, the company has an ergonomics committee in each plant that studies job requirements and seeks ways to redesign those jobs that put workers at the greatest risk. The company also has an impressive wellness program that currently includes clinics at 10 plants. The clinics are staffed by professional medical people working for medical practice groups under contract to Perdue Farms. Employees can visit a doctor for anything from a muscle strain, to prenatal care, to screening tests for a variety of diseases, and they have universal access to all Perdue-operated clinics. Dependent care is available. While benefits to the employees are obvious, the company also benefits through a reduction in lost time for medical office visits, lower turnover, and a happier, healthier, more productive and stable work force.

MARKETING

In the early days, chicken was sold to butcher shops and neighborhood groceries as a commodity, that is, producers sold it in bulk and butchers cut and wrapped it. The customer had no idea what firm grew or processed the chicken. Frank Perdue was convinced that higher profits could be made if the firm's products could be sold at a premium price. But, the only reason a product can command a premium price is if customers ask for it by name—and that means the product must be differentiated and "branded." Hence, the emphasis over the years on superior quality, broader breasted chickens, and a healthy golden color (actually the result of adding marigold petals in the feed to enhance the natural yellow color that corn provided).

EXHIBIT 2

Perdue Farms Incorporated Senior Management

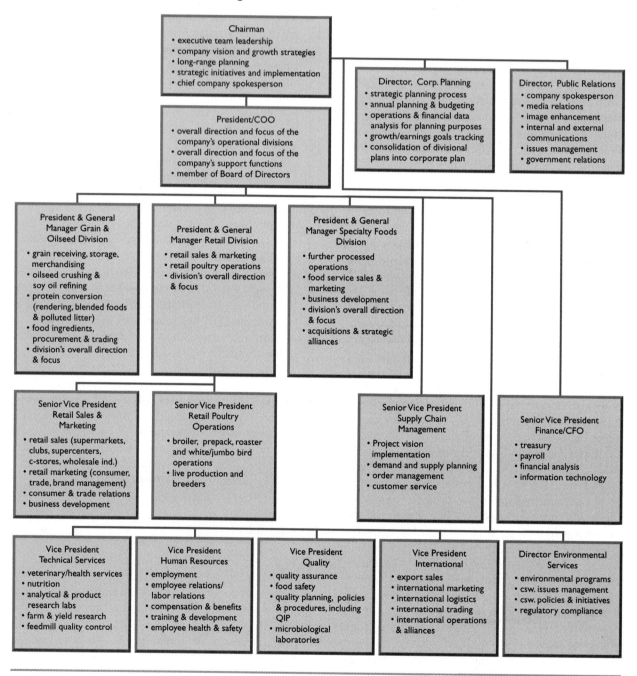

In 1968, Frank Perdue spent $50,000 on radio advertising. In 1969, he added $80,000 in TV advertising to his radio budget—against the advice of his advertising agency. Although his early TV ads increased sales, he decided the agency he was dealing with didn't match one of the basic Perdue tenets: "The people you deal with should be as good at what they do as you are at what you do." That decision set off a storm of activity on Frank's part. In order to select an ad agency that met his standards, Frank learned more about advertising than any poultry man before him and, in the process, catapulted Perdue Farms into the ranks of the top poultry producers in the country.

He began a 10-week immersion on the theory and practice of advertising. He read books and papers on advertising. He talked to sales managers of every newspaper, radio, and television station in the New York area, consulted experts, and interviewed 48 ad agencies. During April 1971, he selected Scali, McCabe, Sloves as his new advertising agency. As the agency tried to figure out how to successfully "brand" a chicken—something that had never been done—they realized that Frank Perdue was their greatest ally, because "He looked a little like a chicken himself, and he sounded a little like one, and he squawked a lot!"

McCabe decided that Perdue should be the firm's spokesman. Initially Frank resisted. But, in the end, he accepted the role, and the campaign based on "It takes a tough man to make a tender chicken" was born. The firm's very first television commercial showed Frank on a picnic in the Salisbury City Park saying:

> A chicken is what it eats ... And my chickens eat better than people do ... I store my own grain and mix my own feed ... And give my Perdue chickens nothing but pure well water to drink ... That's why my chickens always have that healthy golden yellow color ... If you want to eat as good as my chickens, you'll just have to eat my chickens.

Additional ads, touting high quality and the broader breasted chicken, read as follows:

> Government standards would allow me to call this a grade A chicken ... but my standards wouldn't. This chicken is skinny ... It has scrapes and hairs ... The fact is, my graders reject 30

Television Ad

SCALI, McCABE, SLOVES INC.

CLIENT: PERDUE FOODS INC.

PRODUCT: PERDUE CHICKENS

TITLE: "MY CHICKENS EAT BETTER THAN PEOPLE"

LENGTH: 30 SECONDS

COMMERCIAL NO.: TV-PD-30-2C

1. FRANK PERDUE: A chicken is what it eats. And my chickens eat better than ...

2. people do. I store my own grain and mix my own feed.

3. And give my Perdue chickens nothing but pure well water to drink.

4. That's why my chickens always have that healthy golden-yellow color.

5. If you want to eat as good as my chickens, you'll just have to eat my chickens.

6. That's really good.

percent of the chickens government inspectors accept as grade A ... That's why it pays to insist on a chicken with my name on it ... If you're not completely satisfied, write me and I'll give you your money back ... Who do you write in Washington? ... What do they know about chickens?

The Perdue Roaster is the master race of chickens.

Never go into a store and just ask for a pound of chicken breasts ... Because you could be cheating yourself out of some meat ... Here's an ordinary one-pound chicken breast, and here's a one-pound breast of mine ... They weigh the same. But as you can see, mine has more meat, and theirs has more bone. I breed the broadest breasted, meatiest chicken you can buy ... So don't buy a chicken breast by the pound ... Buy them by the name ... and get an extra bite in every breast.

The ads paid off. In 1968, Perdue held about 3 percent of the New York market. By 1972, one out of every six chickens eaten in New York was a Perdue chicken, and 51 percent of New Yorkers recognized the label. Scali, McCabe, Sloves credited Perdue's "believability" for the success of the program. "This was advertising in which Perdue had a personality that lent credibility to the product. If Frank Perdue didn't look and sound like a chicken, he wouldn't be in the commercials."

Frank had his own view. As he told a Rotary audience in Charlotte, North Carolina, in March 1989, "the product met the promise of the advertising and was far superior to the competition. Two great sayings tell it all: 'nothing will destroy a poor product as quickly as good advertising,' and 'a gifted product is mightier than a gifted pen!'"

Today, branded chicken is ubiquitous. The new task for Perdue Farms is to create a unified theme to market a wide variety of products (e.g., fresh meat to fully prepared and frozen products) to a wide variety of customers (e.g., retail, food service, and international). Industry experts believe that the market for fresh poultry has peaked while sales of value-added and frozen products continue to grow at a healthy rate. Although domestic retail sales accounts for about 60 percent of Perdue Farms revenues in FY2000, food service sales now account for 20 percent-international sales account for 5 percent, and grain and oilseed contribute the remaining 15 percent. The com-

pany expects food service, international, and grain and oilseed sales to continue to grow as a percentage of total revenues.

Domestic Retail

Today's retail grocery customer is increasingly looking for ease and speed of preparation, that is, value-added products. The move toward value-added products has significantly changed the meat department in the modern grocery. There are now five distinct meat outlets for poultry:

1. The fresh meat counter—traditional; fresh meat, includes whole chicken and parts.

2. The delicatessen—processed turkey, rotisserie chicken.

3. The frozen counter—individually quick-frozen items such as frozen whole chickens, turkeys, and Cornish hens.

4. Home meal replacement—fully prepared entrees such as Perdue brand "Short Cuts" and Deluca brand entrees (the Deluca brand was acquired and is sold under its own name) that are sold along with salads and desserts so that you can assemble your own dinner.

5. Shelf stable—canned products.

Because Perdue Farms has always used the phrase "fresh young chicken" as the centerpiece of its marketing, value-added products and the retail frozen counter create a possible conflict with past marketing themes. Are these products compatible with the company's marketing image and, if so, how does the company express the notion of quality in this broader product environment? To answer that question, Perdue Farms has been studying what the term "fresh young chicken" means to customers who consistently demand quicker and easier preparation and who admit that they freeze most of their fresh meat purchases once they get home. One view is that the importance of the term "fresh young chicken" comes from the customer's perception that "quality" and "freshness" are closely associated. Thus, the real issue may be "trust," that is, the customer must believe that the product, whether fresh or frozen, is the freshest, highest quality possible, and future marketing themes must develop that concept.

EXHIBIT 3

International Volume

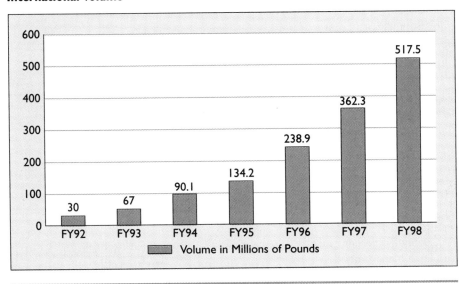

Volume in Millions of Pounds

Food Service

The food-service business consists of a wide variety of public and private customers including restaurant chains, governments, hospitals, schools, prisons, transportation facilities, and the institutional contractors who supply meals to them. Historically, these customers have not been brand conscious, requiring the supplier to meet strict specifications at the lowest price, thus making this category a less than ideal fit for Perdue Farms. However, as Americans continue to eat a larger percentage of their meals away from home, traditional grocery sales have flattened while the food-service sector has shown strong growth. Across the domestic poultry industry, food service accounts for approximately 50 percent of total poultry sales, while approximately 20 percent of Perdue Farms revenues come from this category. Clearly, Perdue Farms is playing catchup in this critical market.

Because Perdue Farms has neither strength nor expertise in the food-service market, management believes that acquiring companies that already have food-service expertise is the best strategy. An acquisition already completed is the purchase in September 1998 of Gol-Pak Corporation based in Monterey, Tennessee. A further processor of products for the food-service industry, Gol-Pak had about 1600 employees and revenues of about $200 million per year.

International

International markets have generally been a happy surprise. In the early 1990s, Perdue Farms began exporting specialty products such as chicken feet (known as "paws") to customers in China. Although not approved for sale for human consumption in the United States, paws are considered a delicacy in China. By 1992, international sales, consisting principally of paws, had become a small, but profitable, business of about 30 million pounds per year. Building on this small "toehold," by 1998 Perdue Farms had quickly built an international business of more than 500 million pounds per year (see Exhibit 3) with annual revenues of more than $140 million, selling a wide variety of products to China, Japan, Russia, and the Ukraine.

In some ways, Japan is an excellent fit for Perdue Farms products because customers demand high quality. However, all Asian markets prefer dark meat, a serendipitous fit with the U.S. preference for white breast meat, because it means that excess (to America) dark meat can be sold in Asia at a premium price. On the downside, Perdue Farms gains

EXHIBIT 4

Milestones in the Quality Improvement Process at Perdue Farms

1924	—	Arthur Perdue buys leghorn roosters for $25
1950	—	Adopts the company logo of a chick under a magnifying glass
1984	—	Frank Perdue attends Philip Crosby's Quality College
1985	—	Perdue recognized for its pursuit of quality in *A Passion for Excellence*
		200 Perdue Managers attend Quality College
		Adopted the Quality Improvement Process (QIP)
1986	—	Established Corrective Action Teams (CAT's)
1987	—	Established Quality Training for all associates
		Implemented Error Cause Removal Process (ECR)
1988	—	Steering Committee formed
1989	—	First Annual Quality Conference held
		Implemented Team Management
1990	—	Second Annual Quality Conference held
		Codified Values and Corporate Mission
1991	—	Third Annual Quality Conference held
		Customer Satisfaction defined
1992	—	Fourth Annual Quality Conference held
	—	How to implement Customer Satisfaction explained to team leaders and Quality Improvement Teams (QIT)
	—	Created Quality Index
	—	Created Customer Satisfaction Index (CSI)
	—	Created "Farm to Fork" quality program
1999	—	Launched Raw Material Quality Index
2000	—	Initiated High Performance Team Process

much of its competitive advantage from branding (e.g., trademarks, processes, and technological and biological know-how), which has little value internationally because most of Asia has not yet embraced the concept of branded chicken.

To better serve export markets, Perdue Farms has developed a portside freezing facility in Newport News, Virginia. This permits poultry to be shipped directly to the port, reducing processing costs and helping to balance ocean shipping costs to Asia which are in the range of 2/3 cents per pound (contracting an entire ship equal to 300 to 500 truckloads).

Shipping poultry to Asia is not without problems. For example, in China, delivery trucks are seldom refrigerated. Thus, the poultry can begin to thaw as it is being delivered, limiting the distance it can be transported prior to sale. One shipload of Perdue Farms chicken bound for Russia actually vanished. It had been inappropriately impounded using forged documents. Although most of its dollar value was eventually recovered, it is important for firms to be aware of the possible difficulties of ocean shipping and the use of foreign ports.

Initial demand for product in Russia, Poland, and Eastern Europe was huge. By FY1998, a signifi-

EXHIBIT 5

Perdue Farms Integrated Operations

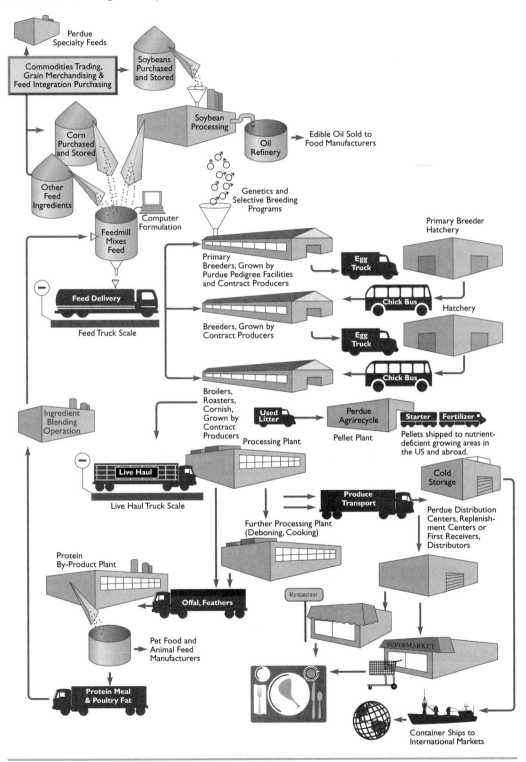

cant portion of international volume was being purchased by Russia. Unfortunately, the crumbling of Russia's economy has had a devastating effect on imports and sales are currently off significantly. Such instability of demand, coupled with rampant corruption, makes risking significant capital unacceptable.

Import duties and taxes are also a barrier. In China, according to the U.S. Department of Agriculture (USDA), import duty rates for poultry are a whopping 45 percent for favored countries and 70 percent for unfavored countries. And, there is a 17 percent value-added tax for all countries. Import duties and taxes in Russia have been similarly high. Hence, profits can be expected to be slim.

Perdue Farms has created a joint partnership with Jiang Nan Feng (JNF) brand to develop a small processing plant in Shanghai. Brand recognition is being built through normal marketing tools. The products use the first "tray pack" wrapping avail-able in Shanghai supermarkets. This new business shows promise because the sale in China of home-grown, fresh dark meat is a significant competitive advantage. Additionally, although government regulations do not presently permit importation to the United States of foreign-grown poultry, the future possibility of importing excess white meat from Shanghai to the United States is attractive since Asian markets, which prefer dark meat, will have difficulty absorbing all of the white breast meat from locally grown poultry. Perdue Farms' management believes that investments in processing facilities in Asia require the company to partner with a local company. Attempting to go it alone is simply too risky due to the significant cultural differences.

OPERATIONS

Two words sum up the Perdue approach to operations—quality and efficiency—with emphasis on

---

EXHIBIT 6

Quality Policy

< WE SHALL produce products and provide services at all times that meet or exceed the expectations of our customers.

< WE SHALL not be content to be of equal quality to our competitors.

< OUR COMMITMENT is to be increasingly superior.

< CONTRIBUTION TO QUALITY is a responsibility shared by everyone in the Perdue organization.

EXHIBIT 7

Perdue Farms Inc. Technological Accomplishments

- Conducts more research than all competitors combined
- Breeds chickens with consistently more breast meat than any other bird in the industry
- First to use digital scales to guarantee weights to customers
- First to package fully cooked chicken products in microwaveable trays
- First to have a box lab to define quality of boxes from different suppliers
- First to test both its chickens and competitors' chickens on 52 quality factors every week
- Improved on time deliveries 20 percent between 1987 and 1993
- Built state of the art analytical and microbiological laboratories for feed and end product analysis
- First to develop best management practices for food safety across all areas of the company
- First to develop commercially viable pelletized poultry litter

the first. Perdue more than most companies represents the Total Quality Management (TQM) slogan, "Quality, a journey without end." Some of the key events are listed in Exhibit 4.

Both quality and efficiency are improved through the management of details. Exhibit 5 depicts the structure and product flow of a generic, vertically integrated broiler company. A broiler company can choose which steps in the process it wants to accomplish in-house and which it wants suppliers to provide. For example, the broiler company could purchase all grain, oilseed, meal, and other feed products. Or, it could contract with hatcheries to supply primary breeders and hatchery supply flocks.

Perdue Farms chose maximum vertical integration in order to control every detail. It breeds and hatches its own eggs (19 hatcheries), selects its contract growers, builds Perdue-engineered chicken houses, formulates and manufactures its own feed (12 poultry feedmills, one specialty feedmill, two ingredient blending operations), oversees the care and feeding of the chicks, operates its own processing plants (21 processing/further processing plants), distributes via its own trucking fleet, and markets the products—(see Exhibit 5). Total process control formed the basis for Frank Perdue's early claims that Perdue Farms poultry is, indeed, higher quality than other poultry. When he stated in his early ads that "A chicken is what it eats . . . I store my own grain and mix my own feed . . . and give my Perdue chickens nothing but well water to drink," he knew that his claim was honest and he could back it up.

Total process control also enables Perdue Farms to ensure that nothing goes to waste. Eight measurable items—hatchability, turnover, feed conversion, livability, yield, birds per man-hour, utilization, and grade—are tracked routinely.

Perdue Farms continues to ensure that nothing artificial is fed to or injected into the birds. No shortcuts are taken. A chemical-free and steroid-free diet is fed to the chickens. Young chickens are vaccinated against disease. Selective breeding is used to improve the quality of the stock. Chickens are bred to yield more white breast meat because that is what the consumer wants.

To ensure that Perdue Farms poultry continues to lead the industry in quality, the company buys and analyzes competitors' products regularly. Inspection associates grade these products and share the information with the highest levels of management. In addition, the company's Quality Policy is displayed at all locations and taught to all associates in quality training (Exhibit 6).

RESEARCH AND DEVELOPMENT

Perdue is an acknowledged industry leader in the use of research and technology to provide quality products and service to its customers. The company spends more on research as a percent of revenues than any other poultry processor. This practice goes back to Frank Perdue's focus on finding ways to differentiate his products based on quality and value. Research into selective breeding resulted in the broader breast, an attribute of Perdue Farms chicken that was the basis of his early advertising. Although other processors have also improved their stock, Perdue Farms believes that it still leads the industry. A list of some of Perdue Farms[2] technological accomplishments is given in Exhibit 7.

As with every other aspect of the business, Perdue Farms tries to leave nothing to chance. The company employs specialists in avian science, microbiology, genetics, nutrition, and veterinary science. Because of its research and development capabilities, Perdue Farms is often involved in USDA field tests with pharmaceutical suppliers. Knowledge and experience gained from these tests can lead to a competitive advantage. For example, Perdue has the most extensive and expensive vaccination program in the industry. Currently, the company is working with and studying the practices of several European producers who use completely different methods. The company has used research to significantly increase productivity. For example, in the 1950s, it took 14 weeks to grow a 3-pound chicken. Today, it takes only 7 weeks to grow a 5-pound chicken. This gain in efficiency is due principally to improvements in the conversion rate of feed to chicken. The current rate of conversion is about 2 pounds of feed to produce 1 pound of chicken. Feed represents about 65 percent of the cost of growing a chicken. Thus, if additional research can further improve the conversion rate of feed to chicken by just 1 percent, it would represent estimated additional income of $2.5 to 3 million per week or $130 to 156 million per year.

FINANCE

Perdue Farms, Inc., is privately held and considers financial information to be proprietary. Hence, avail-

EXHIBIT 8

Annual Compound Growth Rate Through FY2000

	Revenue	Associates	Sales/Associate
Past 20 years	10.60%	6.48%	3.87%
Past 15 years	8.45%	4.48%	4.48%
Past 10 years	7.39%	4.75%	2.52%
Past 5 years	8.39%	0.99%	7.33%

able data are limited. Stock is primarily held by the family with a limited amount held by Perdue Management. Common numbers used by the media and the poultry industry peg Perdue Farm's revenues for FY2000 at about $2.5 billion and the number of associates at nearly 20,000. Forbes magazine has estimated FY2000 operating profits at about 160 million and net profits at about 22 million.

The firm's compound sales growth rate has been slowly decreasing during the past 20 years, mirroring the industry, which has been experiencing market saturation and overproduction. However, Perdue has compensated by using manpower more efficiently through improvements such as automation. For example, 20 years ago, a 1 percent increase in associates resulted in a 1.6 percent increase in revenue. Currently, a 1 percent increase in associates results in an 8.5 percent increase in revenue (see Exhibit 8).

Poultry operations can be divided into four segments: Retail Chicken (growth rate 5 percent), Food-service Chicken and Turkey (growth rate 12 percent), International Sales (growth rate 64 percent over past 6 years), and Grain and Oilseed (growth rate 10 percent). The bulk of Perdue Farms sales continues to come from retail chicken—the sector with the slowest growth rate. The greatest opportunity appears to lie in food-service sales, where the company is admittedly behind, and international sales, where political and economic instability in target countries make the risk to capital significant.

Perdue Farms has been profitable every year since its founding, with the exception of 1988 and 1996. Company officials believe the loss in 1988 was caused by overproduction by the industry and higher administrative costs resulting from a decen-

tralization effort begun during the mid-eighties. At that time, there was a concerted effort to push decisions down through the corporate ranks to provide more autonomy. When the new strategy resulted in significantly higher administrative costs due to duplication of effort, the company responded quickly by returning to the basics, reconsolidating and downsizing. The loss in 1996 was due to the impact of high corn prices. Currently, the goal is to constantly streamline in order to provide cost-effective business solutions.

Perdue Farms approaches financial management conservatively, using retained earnings and cash flow to finance most asset replacement projects and normal growth. When planning expansion projects or acquisitions, long-term debt is used. The target debt limit is 55 percent of equity. Such debt is normally provided by domestic and international bank and insurance companies. The debt strategy is to match asset lives with liability maturities, and have a mix of fixed-rate and variable-rate debt. Growth plans require about two dollars in projected incremental sales growth for each dollar in invested capital.

ENVIRONMENT

Environmental issues present a constant challenge to all poultry processors. Growing, slaughtering, and processing poultry is a difficult and tedious process that demands absolute efficiency in order to keep operating costs at an acceptable level. Inevitably, detractors argue that the process is dangerous to workers, inhumane to the poultry, and hard on the environment, and results in food that may not be safe. Thus media headlines such as

"Human Cost of Poultry Business Bared," "Animal Rights Advocates Protest Chicken Coop Conditions," "Processing Plants Leave a Toxic Trail," or "EPA Mandates Poultry Regulations" are routine.

Perdue Farms tries to be proactive in managing environmental issues. In April 1993, the company created an Environmental Steering Committee. Its mission is "... to provide all Perdue Farms work sites with vision, direction, and leadership so that they can be good corporate citizens from an environmental perspective today and in the future." The committee is responsible for overseeing how the company is doing in such environmentally sensitive areas as waste water, storm water, hazardous waste, solid waste, recycling, bio-solids, and human health and safety.

For example, disposing of dead birds has long been an industry problem. Perdue Farms developed small composters for use on each farm. Using this approach, carcasses are reduced to an end-product that resembles soil in a matter of a few days. The disposal of hatchery waste is another environmental challenge. Historically, manure and unhatched eggs were shipped to a landfill. However, Perdue Farms developed a way to reduce the waste by 50 percent by selling the liquid fraction to a pet food processor that cooks it for protein. The other 50 percent is recycled through a rendering process. In 1990, Perdue Farms spent $4.2 million to upgrade its existing treatment facility with a state-of-the-art system at its Accomac, Virginia, and Showell, Maryland, plants. These facilities use forced hot air heated to 120 degrees to cause the microbes to digest all traces of ammonia, even during the cold winter months.

More than 10 years ago, North Carolina's Occupational Safety and Health Administration cited Perdue Farms for an unacceptable level of repetitive stress injuries at its Lewiston and Robersonville, North Carolina, processing plants. This sparked a major research program in which Perdue Farms worked with Health and Hygiene Inc. of Greensboro, North Carolina, to learn more about ergonomics, the repetitive movements required to accomplish specific jobs. Results have been dramatic. Launched in 1991 after 2 years of development, the program videotapes employees at all of Perdue Farms' plants as they work in order to describe and place stress values on the various tasks. Although the cost to Perdue Farms has been significant, results have been dramatic, with workers'

compensation claims down 44 percent, lost-time recordables just 7.7 percent of the industry average, an 80 percent decrease in serious repetitive stress cases, and a 50 percent reduction in lost time or surgery back injuries (Shelley Reese, "Helping Employees Get a Grip," *Business and Health*, August 1998).

Despite these advances, serious problems continue to develop. In 1997, the organism *Pfiesteria* burst into media headlines when massive numbers of dead fish with lesions turned up along the Chesapeake Bay in Maryland. Initial findings pointed to manure runoff from the poultry industry. Political constituencies quickly called for increased regulation to ensure proper manure storage and fertilizer use. The company readily admits that "... the poultry process is a closed system. There is lots of nitrogen and phosphorus in the grain, it passes through the chicken and is returned to the environment as manure. Obviously, if you bring additional grain into a closed area such as the Delmarva Peninsula, you increase the amount of nitrogen and phosphorus in the soil unless you find a way to get rid of it." Nitrogen and phosphorus from manure normally make excellent fertilizer that moves slowly in the soil. However, scientists speculate that erosion speeds up runoff, threatening the health of nearby streams, rivers, and larger bodies of water such as the Chesapeake Bay. The problem for the industry is that proposals to control the runoff are sometimes driven more by politics and emotion than research, which is not yet complete.

Although it is not clear what role poultry-related nitrogen and phosphorus runoff played in the *Pfiesteria* outbreak, regulators believe the microorganism feasts on the algae that grows when too much of these nutrients are present in the water. Thus, the U.S. Environmental Protection Agency (EPA) and various states are considering new regulations. Currently, contract growers are responsible for either using or disposing of the manure from their chicken houses. But, some regulators and environmentalists believe that (1) it is too complicated to police the utilization and disposal practices of thousands of individual farmers, and (2) only the big poultry companies have the financial resources to properly dispose of the waste. Thus, they want to make poultry companies responsible for all waste disposal, a move that the industry strongly opposes.

Some experts have called for conservation measures that might limit the density of chicken houses

EXHIBIT 9

Perdue Farms Environmental Policy Statement

Perdue Farms is committed to environmental stewardship and shares that commitment with its farm family partners. We're proud of the leadership we're providing our industry in addressing the full range of environmental challenges related to animal agriculture and food processing. We've invested—and continue to invest—millions of dollars in research, new technology, equipment upgrades, and awareness and education as part of our ongoing commitment to protecting the environment.

- Perdue Farms was among the first poultry companies with a dedicated Environmental Services department. Our team of environmental managers is responsible for ensuring that every Perdue facility operates within *100 percent compliance of all applicable environmental regulations and permits.*

- Through our joint venture, Perdue AgriRecycle, Perdue Farms is investing $12 million to build in Delaware a first-of-its-kind pellet plant that will convert surplus poultry litter into a starter fertilizer that will be marketed internationally to nutrient deficient regions. The facility, which will serve the entire Delmarva region, is scheduled to begin operation in April, 2001.

- We continue to explore new technologies that will reduce water usage in our processing plants without compromising food safety or quality.

- We invested thousands of man-hours in producer education to assist our family farm partners in managing their independent poultry operations in the most environmentally responsible manner possible. In addition, all our poultry producers are required to have nutrient management plans and dead-bird composters.

- Perdue Farms was one of four poultry companies operating in Delaware to sign an agreement with Delaware officials outlining our companies' voluntary commitment to help independent poultry producers dispose of surplus chicken litter.

- Our Technical Services department is conducting ongoing research into feed technology as a means of reducing the nutrients in poultry manure. We've already achieved phosphorous reductions that far exceed the industry average.

- We recognize that the environmental impact of animal agriculture is more pronounced in areas where development is decreasing the amount of farmland available to produce grain for feed and to accept nutrients. That is why we view independent grain *and* poultry producers as vital business partners and strive to preserve the economic viability of the family farm.

At Perdue Farms, we believe that it is possible to preserve the family farm; provide a safe, abundant and affordable food supply; and protect the environment. However, we believe that can best happen when there is cooperation and trust between the poultry industry, agriculture, environmental groups and state officials. We hope Delaware's effort will become a model for other states to follow.

in a given area or even require a percentage of existing chicken houses to be taken out of production periodically. Obviously, this would be very hard on the farm families who own existing chicken houses and could result in fewer acres devoted to agriculture. Working with AgriRecycle Inc. of Springfield, Missouri, Perdue Farms has developed a possible solution. The plan envisions the poultry companies processing excess manure into pellets for use as fertilizer. This would permit sale outside the poultry-growing region, better balanc-ing the input of grain. Spokesmen estimate that as much as 120,000 tons, nearly one third of the surplus nutrient from manure produced each year on the Delmarva Peninsula, could be sold to corn growers in other parts of the country. Prices would be market driven, but could be $25 to 30 per ton, suggesting a potential small profit. Nevertheless, almost any attempt to control the problem potentially raises the cost of growing chickens, forcing poultry processors to look elsewhere for locations where the chicken population is less dense.

In general, solving industry environmental problems presents at least five major challenges to the poultry processor:

- How to maintain the trust of the poultry consumer,
- How to ensure that the poultry remain healthy,
- How to protect the safety of the employees and the process,
- How to satisfy legislators who need to show their constituents that they are taking firm action when environmental problems occur, and
- How to keep costs at an acceptable level.

Jim Perdue sums up Perdue Farms' position as follows: "...we must not only comply with environmental laws as they exist today, but look to the future to make sure we don't have any surprises. We must make sure our environmental policy statement (see Exhibit 9) is real, that there's something behind it and that we do what we say we're going to do."

LOGISTICS AND INFORMATION SYSTEMS

The explosion of poultry products and increasing number of customers during recent years placed a severe strain on the existing logistics system, which was developed when there were far fewer products, fewer delivery points, and lower volume. Hence, the company had limited ability to improve service levels, could not support further growth, and could not introduce innovative services that might provide a competitive advantage.

In the poultry industry, companies are faced with two significant problems—time and forecasting. Fresh poultry has a limited shelf life—measured in days. Thus, forecasts must be extremely accurate and deliveries timely. On the one hand, estimating requirements too conservatively results in product shortages. Mega-customers such as Wal-Mart will not tolerate product shortages that lead to empty shelves and lost sales. On the other hand, if estimates are overstated, the result is outdated products that cannot be sold and losses for Perdue Farms. A common expression in the poultry industry is "you either sell it or smell it."

Forecasting has always been extremely difficult in the poultry industry because the processor needs to know approximately 18 months in ad-vance how many broilers will be needed in order to size hatchery supply flocks and contract with growers to provide live broilers. Most customers (e.g., grocers, food-service buyers) have a much shorter planning window. Additionally, there is no way for Perdue Farms to know when rival poultry processors will put a particular product on special (reducing Perdue Farms sales), or when bad weather and other uncontrollable problems may reduce demand.

Historically, poultry companies have relied principally on extrapolation of past demand, industry networks, and other contacts to make their estimates. Although product complexity has exacerbated the problem, the steady movement away from fresh product to frozen product (which has a longer shelf life) offers some relief.

In the short run, information technology (IT) has helped by shortening the distance between the customer and Perdue Farms. As far back as 1987, PCs were placed directly on each customer service associate's desk, allowing them to enter customer orders directly. Next, a system was developed to put dispatchers in direct contact with every truck in the system so that they would have accurate information about product inventory and truck location at all times. Now, IT is moving to further shorten the distance between the customer and the Perdue Farms service representative by putting a PC on the customer's desk. All of these steps improve communication and shorten the time from order to delivery.

In the longer run, these steps are not enough due to the rapidly expanding complexity of the industry. For example, today, poultry products fall into four unique channels of distribution:

1. Bulk fresh—*Timeliness and frequency of delivery are critical to ensure freshness*. Distribution requirements are high volume and low-cost delivery.

2. Domestic frozen and further processed products—*Temperature integrity is critical*; distribution requirements are frequency and timeliness of delivery. This channel lends itself to dual-temperature trailer systems and load consolidation.

3. Export—*Temperature integrity, high volume, and low cost are critical*. This channel lends itself to inventory consolidation and custom loading of vessels.

4. Consumer packaged goods (packaged fresh, prepared, and deli products)—*Differentiate via innovative products and services*. Distribution requirements are reduced lead time and low cost.

Thus, forecasting now requires the development of a sophisticated **supply chain management system** that can efficiently integrate all facets of operations including grain and oilseed activities, hatcheries and growing facilities, processing plants (which now produce more than 400 products at more than 20 locations), distribution facilities, and finally, the distributors, supermarkets, food-service customers, and export markets (see Exhibit 5). Perdue Farms underlined the importance of the successful implementation of supply chain management by creating a new executive position, Senior Vice President for Supply Chain Management.

A key step in overhauling the distribution infrastructure is the building of replenishment centers that will, in effect, be buffers between the processing plants and the customers. The portside facility in Norfolk, Virginia, which serves the international market, is being expanded and a new domestic freezer facility added.

Conceptually, products are directed from the processing plants to the replenishment and freezer centers based on customer forecasts that have been converted to an optimized production schedule. Perdue Farms trucks deliver these bulk products to the centers in finished or semi-finished form. At the centers, further finishing and packaging is accomplished. Finally, specific customer orders are custom palletized and loaded on trucks (either Perdue owned or contracted) for delivery to individual customers. All shipments are made up from replenishment center inventory. Thus, the need for accurate demand forecasting by the distribution centers is key.

In order to control the entire supply chain management process, Perdue Farms purchased a multi-million dollar IT system that represents the biggest nontangible asset expense in the company's history. This integrated, state-of-the-art information system required total process re-engineering, a project that took 18 months and required training 1200 associates. Major goals of the system were to (1) make it easier and more desirable for the customer to do business with Perdue Farms, (2) make it easier for Perdue Farms associates to get the job done, and (3) take as much cost out of the process as possible.

INDUSTRY TRENDS

The poultry industry is affected by consumer, industry, and governmental regulatory trends. Currently, chicken is the number one meat consumed in the United States with 40 percent market share (Exhibits 10 & 11). Typical Americans consume about 81 pounds of chicken, 69 pounds of beef, and 52 pounds of pork annually (USDA data). Additionally, chicken is becoming the most popular meat in the world. In 1997, poultry set an export record of $2.5 billion. Although exports fell 6 percent in 1998, the decrease was attributed to Russia's and Asia's financial crisis, and food industry experts expect this to be only a temporary setback. Hence, the world market is clearly a growth opportunity for the future.

The popularity and growth of poultry products is attributed to both nutritional and economic issues. Poultry products contain significantly less fat and cholesterol than other meat products. In the United States, the demand for boneless, skinless breast meat, the leanest meat on poultry, is so great that dark meat is often sold at a discount in the United States or shipped overseas where it is preferred over white meat.

Another trend is a decrease in demand for whole birds to be used as the base dish for home meals and an increase in demand for products that have been further processed for either home or restaurant consumption. For example, turkey or chicken hot dogs, fully cooked sliced chicken or turkey, and turkey pastrami—which neither looks nor tastes like turkey—can be found in most deli cases. Many supermarkets sell either whole or parts of hot rotisserie chicken. Almost all fast food restaurants have at least one sandwich based on poultry products. Many upscale restaurants feature poultry products that are shipped to them frozen and partially prepared to simplify restaurant preparation. All these products have been further processed, adding value and increasing the potential profit margin.

The industry is consolidating, that is, the larger companies in the industry are continuing to buy smaller firms. Currently there are about 35 major poultry firms in the United States, but this number is expected to drop to 20 to 25 within the next 10 years. There are several reasons for this. Stagnant

EXHIBIT 10

Consumption per Capita of Chicken, Beef, and Pork in the 1990s and Projected Consumption for 2000, 2001

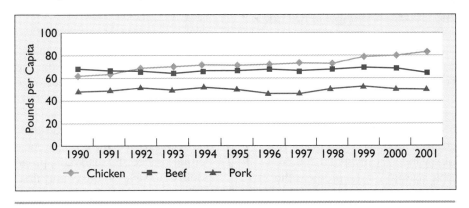

EXHIBIT 11

Going Up: Chicken as a Percentage Overall Meat Consumption, 1960–2000

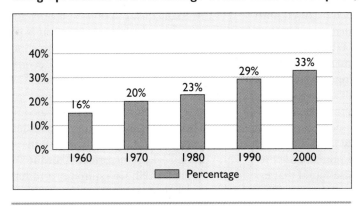

U.S. demand and general product oversupply create downward price pressure that makes it difficult for smaller firms to operate profitably. In addition, pressure for efficiency improvements requires huge capital outlays. Finally, mega-retailers such as Sam's Club and Royal Ahold (the Dutch owner of several U.S. supermarket chains) do not like to manage individual contracts with numerous smaller processors. Mega-retailers prefer to deal with mega-suppliers.

The industry is heavily regulated. The U.S. Food and Drug Administration (FDA) monitors product safety. The USDA inspects poultry as it arrives at the processing plant. After it is killed, each bird is again inspected by a USDA inspector for avian diseases, contamination of feces, or other foreign material. All poultry that does not meet regulations is destroyed under USDA supervision. USDA inspectors also examine the plant, equipment, operating procedures, and personnel for compliance with sanitary regulations. The U.S. Congress has mandated that the USDA make this information available online. Additional intensive inspections of statistically selected samples of poultry products have been recommended by the National Academy of Sciences. Thus, additional FDA regulations for product quality are anticipated.

Although poultry produces less waste per pound of product than cattle or hogs, all meat industries are experiencing increased EPA scrutiny regarding the disposal of waste. In general, waste generated at processing plants is well controlled by regulation, monitoring, and fines. When an EPA violation occurs, the company that operates the plant can receive a substantial fine, potentially millions of dollars.

Still, the most difficult problems to deal with are those that occur as a cumulative result of numerous processors producing in a relatively limited area. For example, increasing poultry production in a given area intensifies the problem of disposal of manure. In manmade fertilizer, phosphorus and nitrogen exist in approximately a 1 to 8 ratio, whereas in poultry manure the ratio can be 1 to 1. Thus, too much poultry manure can result in serious phosphorus runoff into streams and rivers, potentially resulting in aquatic disease and degradation of water quality. In 1997, an outbreak of *Pfiesteria,* a toxic microbe, occurred in the tributaries of the Chesapeake Bay. Although the poultry industry insisted that there were many possible reasons for the problem, the media and most regulatory spokespersons attributed it primarily to phosphorus runoff from chicken manure. After much negative publicity and extensive investigation by both poultry processors and state regulatory agencies, the State of Maryland passed the Water Quality Act of 1998, which required nutrient management plans. However, many environmentalists continue to believe that the EPA must create additional, stricter federal environmental regulations. Recent regulatory activity has continued to focus on Eastern Shore agriculture, especially the poultry industry. However, new studies from the U.S. Geological Survey suggest that the vast majority of nutrients affecting the Chesapeake Bay come from rivers that do not flow through the poultry-producing regions of the Eastern Shore. The studies also found that improved agricultural management practices have reduced nutrient runoff from farmlands. Jim Perdue says, "While the poultry industry must accept responsibility for its share of nutrients, public policy should view the watershed as a whole and address all the factors that influence water quality."

Other government agencies whose regulations impact the industry include the Occupational Safety and Health Administration (OSHA) for employee safety and the Immigration and Naturalization Service (INS) for undocumented workers. OSHA enforces its regulations via periodic inspections, and levies fines when noncompliance is found. For example, a Hudson Foods poultry plant was fined more than a million dollars for alleged willful violations causing ergonomic injury to workers. The INS also uses periodic inspections to find undocumented workers. It estimates that undocumented aliens working in the industry vary from 3 percent to 78 percent of the workforce at individual plants. Plants that are found to use undocumented workers, especially those that are repeat offenders, can be heavily fined.

THE FUTURE

The marketplace for poultry in the twenty-first century will be very different from the past. Understanding the wants and needs of generation Xers and echo-boomers will be key to responding successfully to these differences.

Quality will continue to be essential. In the 1970s, quality was the cornerstone of Frank Perdue's successful marketing program to "brand" his poultry. However, in the twenty-first century, quality will not be enough. Today's customers expect—even demand—all products to be high quality. Thus, Perdue Farms plans to use customer service to further differentiate the company. The focus will be on learning how to become indispensable to the customer by taking cost out of the product and delivering it exactly the way the customer wants it, where and when the customer wants it. In short, as Jim Perdue says, "Perdue Farms wants to become so easy to do business with that the customer will have no reason to do business with anyone else."

In the poultry business, customer purchase decisions, as well as company profitability, hinge on mere pennies. Thus, the location of processing facilities is key. Historically, Perdue Farms has been an Eastern Shore company and has maintained major processing facilities on the Eastern Shore. However, it currently costs about $1^1/_2$ cents more per pound to grow poultry on the Eastern Shore versus Arkansas. This difference results from the cost of labor, compliance with federal and state environmental laws, resource costs (e.g., feed grain), and other variables. Clearly, selecting favorable sites for future growing and processing facilities is key. In the future, assuming regulations will permit the importation of foreign-grown poultry, producers could even use inexpensive international labor markets to further reduce costs. The opportunity for large growers to capture these savings puts increased pressure on small poultry companies. This suggests further consolidation of the industry.

Grocery companies are also consolidating in order to compete with huge food industry newcomers such as Wal-Mart and Royal Ahold. These new competitors gain efficiency by minimizing the number of their suppliers and buying huge amounts from each at the lowest possible price. In effect, both mega-companies—the supplier and the buyer—become dependent on each other. Further, mega-companies expect their suppliers to do more for them. For example, Perdue Farms considers it possible that, using sophisticated distribution information programs, they will soon be able to manage the entire meat department requirements for several supermarket chains. Providing this service would support Perdue Farms' goal of becoming indispensable to their first-line retail customer, the grocer.

The twenty-first century consumer will demand many options. Clearly, the demand for uncooked, whole chickens purchased at the meat counter has peaked. Demand is moving toward further processed poultry. To support this trend, Perdue Farms plans to open several additional cooking plants. In addition, a criterion for future acquisitions will be whether they support value-added processing. Products from these plants will fill food-service requirements and grocery sales of prepared foods such as delicatessen, frozen, home meal replacement, and shelf-stable items. Additionally, the twenty-first century customer will be everywhere. Whether at work, at a sports event, in school, or traveling on the highway, customers expect to have convenient refreshment machines available with a wide selection of wholesome, ready-to-eat products.

Designing a distribution system that can handle all of these options is extremely difficult. For example, the system must be able to efficiently organize hundreds of customer orders that are chosen from more than 400 different products, which are processed and further prepared at more than 20 facilities throughout the southeast for delivery by one truck—a massive distribution task. As executives note, the company survived until now using distribution techniques created as many as 20 years ago, when there were a handful of products and

processing facilities. However, the system approached gridlock during the late 1990s. Thus, Perdue Farms invested in a state-of-the-art information processing system—a tough decision because "we could build two new processing plants for the price of this technology package."

International markets are a conundrum. On the one hand, Perdue Farms' international revenue has grown from an insignificant side business in 1994 to about $140 million in 1999, approximately 5 percent of total revenues. Further, its contribution to profits is significant. Poultry is widely accepted around the world, providing opportunities for further growth. But, trying to be global doesn't work. Different cultures value different parts of the chicken and demand different meat color, preparation, and seasoning. Thus, products must be customized. Parts that are not in demand in a particular country must be sold at severely reduced prices, used as feed, or shipped frozen to a different market where demand exists. While this can be done, it is a distribution problem that significantly complicates an already difficult forecasting model.

International markets can also be very unstable, exposing Perdue Farms to significant demand instability and potential losses. For example, in 1997, about 50 percent of Perdue Farms' international revenues came from Russia. However, political and economic problems in Russia reduced 1999 revenues significantly. This high level of instability, coupled with corruption that thrives in a country experiencing severe political and economic turmoil, introduces significant risk to future investment.

Clearly, the future holds many opportunities. But, none of them comes without risk, and Perdue Farms must carefully choose where it wants to direct its scarce resources.

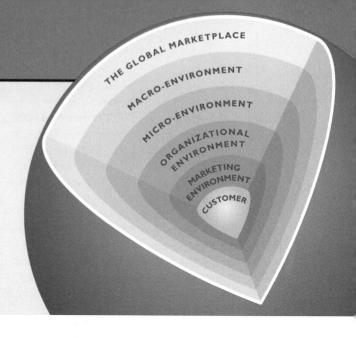

CASE 17

Nike, Inc. (1999)

This case was prepared by Robert J. Mockler of St. John's University, Dorothy G. Dologite of the City University of New York–Baruch College, and Paul Poppler of St. John's University. Edited by Julian W. Vincze.

Beaverton, Oregon–based Nike, Inc., has grown dramatically during the last decade. Nike, which designs, develops, and markets high-quality footwear, apparel, and accessory products worldwide, had consolidated revenues in 1988 of $1.2 billion but reached $9.5 billion by 1998 and has expectations for near-term growth to $15 billion. Their "swoosh" logo has become as familiar as McDonald's "golden arches," and much of the growth has been international. Nike's quality products are designed in-house after extensive research and development that uses high-tech innovations, but they also respond to fashion trends. They have stringently searched for sources of cheap but disciplined labor and are noted for sophisticated outsourcing of production to firms in developing nations.

However, the present economic crisis in Asia, when combined with changing customer taste in footwear, indicated that industry growth would be minimal over the next few years. These factors as well as Nike's 1998 financial results had management concerned.

NIKE'S HISTORY

Phil Knight, cofounder and CEO, while an undergraduate runner at the University of Oregon, was coached by William J. Bowerman (also a cofounder of Nike), who redesigned a made-in-Japan running shoe and hired a band of students to hawk the shoes at track meets.[1] In 1962, Knight wrote a term paper about a business opportunity to create a better track shoe. Adidas shoes, made in West Germany, were then the best, but they were expensive and hard to come by in the United States. Knight reasoned that with cheap Japanese labor but American distribution and marketing, he could sell track shoes that rivaled Adidas in quality and undercut them in price and take over the market. After graduation in 1962, Knight and Bowerman each invested $500 so that Knight could travel to Japan and (using the name Blue Ribbon Sports) represent himself as a shoe importer to Onitsuka, the manufacturer of Tiger brand shoes. They were granted exclusive rights to distribute Tiger shoes in the western United States in 1964. By 1968, they had begun designing their own shoes and searching for Asian manufacturing sources.[2]

Nike's performance-oriented product innovations and outsourcing of production resulted in shoes that athletes wanted to wear and could afford. Knight and Bowerman's track connections got their shoes onto the feet of real runners just as jogging emerged as a new national pastime. In 1968, Blue Ribbon Sports became Nike, and the "swoosh" logo was born. Jon Anderson won the Boston Marathon wearing Nike shoes, Jimmy Conners won Wimbledon and the U.S. Open wearing Nike shoes, Henry Rono set four track and field records in Nike shoes, and members of the Boston Celtics and Los Angeles Lakers basketball teams were wearing Nike products. Sales and profits were doubling every year during the 1970s.

In the mid-1980s, after more than a decade of fast growth, Nike hit $1 billion in revenue. However, Nike misjudged the aerobics market, outgrew its own capacity to manage, and made a disastrous move into casual shoes. How? By making an aerobics shoe functionally superior to Reebok's but missing on styling. This also happened to Nike's casual shoes—viewed as funny looking. Nike confused consumers who viewed it as a running shoe company. Casual shoes sent a different message. Nike began to lose its magic. Retailers were unenthusiastic, athletes were looking at the alternatives, and sales slowed.

For three years ending in 1989, Nike wallowed in second place behind Reebok, whose sneakers became synonymous with aerobics. Nike lost its footing, and the company was forced to make a subtle but important shift. Instead of emphasizing just design and manufacture of their products, Nike focused more on the consumer and the brand. In a short time, it learned to be marketing oriented. Since then, Nike has resumed its leadership of the athletic footwear industry.[3]

Image

Nike built its brand through advertising slogans—"Bo Knows," "Just Do It," "There Is No Finish Line"—many became popular expressions.[4] The Nike brand became well known around the world. Through an exclusive agreement with The Athletics Congress, Nike became the sole provider of competitive uniforms for the U.S. track and field team until the twenty-first century. As a global brand franchise, Nike focused on distinct, culturally relevant messages that reflected the minds of sports and fitness enthusiasts everywhere. This focus allowed Nike to develop a consistent worldwide brand image, using the "swoosh" logo to enhance the perception of sneakers as upbeat,

fun products, signifying the energy stored within, evoking images of technology, and being a visual shorthand for what was hip and meaningful. Nike's marketing themes—health, fitness, and self-empowerment—remained consistent.[5]

The Company

Nike designs, develops, and markets worldwide high-quality footwear, apparel, and accessory products. Distribution is through approximately 14,000 retailers in the United States and through a mix of independent distributors, licensees, and subsidiaries in approximately 82 countries. Manufacturing of most products (except Cole Haan) is outsourced to independent contractors—most located outside the United States. Apparel, however, is produced both domestically and abroad. The company's financial performance for the 3-year period ending in 1997 was remarkable, with revenues moving from $3.8 billion to $9.2 billion. Until 1998, the company believed it had great management, tremendous opportunities internationally, superb marketing ability, and brand-name appeal that was unparalleled in the industry.[6]

Product Offerings[7]

By the mid-1990s, consumers had gravitated to quality, one of Nike's strengths, but by 1998, they had become more value-oriented. Nike's revenue figures are reported by these categories: U.S. footwear, U.S. apparel, non-U.S. footwear, non-U.S. apparel, and other brands.

U.S. footwear products emphasized quality construction and innovative design, but U.S. footwear revenues in 1998 decreased 7 percent, or $255 million. The five largest footwear categories were training, basketball, running, kids, and Brand Jordan (which was reintroduced in 1998), together totaling approximately 80 percent of revenue. During 1998, Brand Jordan revenues increased 57 percent, but the others experienced decreases between 4 and 17 percent. However, the company also marketed shoes designed for aerobics, tennis, golf, soccer, baseball, football, bicycling, volleyball, wrestling, cheerleading, aquatic activities, and general outdoor activities. Golf and soccer showed increases of 71 and 74 percent in 1998.

U.S. apparel included active sports apparel as well as athletic bags and accessory items designed to complement Nike's footwear products, featuring the same trademarks and sold through the same marketing and distribution channels. Frequent use of "collections" of similar design or for specific purposes resulted in a revenue increase of 11 percent in 1998, with nearly all categories reporting growth: training up 10 percent, accessories up 6 percent, kids up 41 percent, tee-shirts up 5 percent, and golf up 57 percent. Team sports apparel was the only decrease, at 8 percent.

For non-U.S. footwear, despite the Asian economic crisis in 1998, revenues increased by 12 percent.

Non-U.S. apparel revenues increased by 21 percent in 1998 and represented 41 percent of Nike's total revenues. Europe increased 6 percent in footwear and 35 percent in apparel, Asia-Pacific had footwear down 8 percent but apparel up 34 percent, and the Americas reported footwear up 20 percent and apparel up 78 percent. Overall, the biggest country markets were Japan, United Kingdom, Canada, France, Italy, and Spain. The biggest declines were in Korea (minus 29 percent) and Germany (minus 6 percent).

Several lines of merchandise were sold under other brand names. Nike had a line of dress and casual footwear and accessories for men, women, and children under the brand name Cole Haan using a wholly owned subsidiary, Cole Haan Holdings, Inc. In January 1993, Nike had acquired Sports Specialties, Inc., which marketed a line of headwear with licensed team logos under the brand name Sports Specialties. The company also sold small amounts of various plastic products to other manufacturers through its wholly owned subsidiary, Tetra Plastics, Inc.

Product R&D

Nike's research and development (R&D) was a cornerstone of past successes. Technical innovations in footwear and apparel design received continued emphasis—striving for products that reduced injuries, aided athletic performance, and maximized comfort. In addition to its own staff specialists in the areas of biomechanics, exercise physiology, engineering, industrial design, and related fields, Nike also used research committees and advisory boards made up of athletes, coaches, trainers, equipment managers, orthopedists, podiatrists, and other experts who consulted with the company and reviewed designs, materials, and concepts for product improvement.

Logistics and Distribution

Nike had concentrated on the domestic (U.S.) market until 1981, when international strategies were formulated to service a growing foreign market. Nike initially reached more than 40 countries and, by 1993, had became the world's largest athletic footwear manufacturer, marketing in 82 countries.[8] Domestic sales through approximately 14,000 retailers accounted for approximately 59 percent of total revenues in 1998. Domestic retailers included a mix of department stores, footwear stores, sporting goods stores, tennis and golf shops, and other retail accounts. During the high growth years of 1995 to 1997, Nike made substantial use of its innovative "Futures" ordering program. Retailers could order 5 to 6 months in advance of delivery with the guarantee that 90 percent of their orders would be delivered within a set time period at a fixed price. However, in 1998, it became evident that during economic declines, this program resulted in overinventory positions for many retailers both domestically and especially in Asia. It necessitated large-scale sell-offs.

Nike had 17 company sales offices in the United States to market shoes and apparel, as well as 28 independent sales representatives for the sale of specialty products, such as golf, cycling, water sports, and outdoor wear. In addition, it operated 60 wholly owned retail outlets: 31 carried primarily closeout merchandise, 18 were Cole Haan stores, and 4 were Nike Town stores designed to showcase the company's products. High-profile Nike Town locations, called "concept shops," showcased the complete Nike line. The stores occupied 20,000 to 30,000 square feet and were designed as half art gallery and half walk-in advertisement. The concept was successful. Nike reported attracting on average 5000 people a week, with average spending of $50 from each customer.[9] The company's domestic distribution centers for footwear were located in Beaverton, Oregon, Wilsonville, Oregon, Memphis, Tennessee, Greenland, New Hampshire, and Yarmouth, Maine. Apparel products were shipped from the Memphis distribution center and from Greenville, North Carolina. Sports Specialties headwear was shipped from Irvine, California.

The largest volume category in retailers was discount stores, with 32 percent of the market. Shoe stores had 10 percent, department stores had 9 percent, athletic shoe stores had 9 percent, and sporting goods stores had 8 percent in the early 1990s. Discount stores carried many low-priced shoes but not the high-end, high-cost athletic footwear. Department stores, athletic footwear stores, and shoe stores, on the other hand, would carry more fashionable shoes with more varieties of choices. And for high-technology, high-performance and high-end athletic shoes, sporting goods stores and athletic shoe stores would have more to offer. All the stores were widely scattered, and they were the consumer's most preferred stores when they thought of buying a pair of athletic shoes.

In 1992, Nike opened its first 2000-square-foot concept shop at Macy's (San Francisco) and reported "pretty strong" sales gains. As a result, it quickly opened more of the Nike Town concept stores. Nike believed opportunities for increased sales depended on how its product met different retailers' needs. Nike placed more emphasis on in-store displays and offered less expensive shoes in discount stores and more fashionable, functional, and high-end shoes in department stores, sporting goods stores, and specialty athletic stores. Nike also adopted competitive distribution to retailers by selling through a direct ownership method designed not only to influence retail pricing but also to improve retailer relations.[10]

International Activities

Nike marketed internationally through independent distributors, licensees, subsidiaries, and branch offices. It operated 24 distribution centers in Europe, Asia, Canada, Latin America, and Australia and also distributed through independent distributors and licensees. International branch offices and subsidiaries of Nike were located in Australia, Austria, Belgium, Brazil, Canada, Chile, Costa Rica, Denmark, Finland, France, Germany, Hong Kong, Indonesia, Italy, Korea, Malaysia, Mexico, New Zealand, Norway, People's Republic of China, Spain, Sweden, Singapore, Switzerland, Taiwan, Thailand, The Netherlands, and the United Kingdom.

International operations in the footwear industry also were subject to risks such as possible revaluation of currencies, export tariffs, quotas, restrictions on the transfer of funds, and political instability. NAFTA provided an incentive for more investments in Mexico, and U.S. footwear companies were interested in Latin American markets.

FOOTWEAR INDUSTRY

In the 1970s, jogging, health and fitness, and sports had become national pastimes, particularly among the youth, leading to the dramatic growth of the industry. In the 1980s, the increasing popularity of aerobics brought a great number of women into the market.[11] Industry sales peaked in 1990 at $12.1 billion and had decreased to $11.6 billion in 1992 because of the worldwide recession and the changing habits of consumers, such as buying more all-purpose outdoor footwear and less expensive athletic shoes.

During the high growth 1980s, the leading companies were Nike, Reebok, L.A. Gear, Converse, Keds, Adidas, and Puma. The biggest two, Nike and Reebok, used aggressive advertising, cost reduction, and quality control as successful strategies. However, the athletic footwear industry reached a difficult point in the early 1990s.[12] A saturated male-oriented market, a weak economy, an upswing in nonathletic casual shoes, and a growing popularity of hikers, deck shoes, and other casual shoes contributed to the slowdown. Customers were buying less traditional athletic footwear.[13] Some industry experts expected that a market that consisted of casual, nonfunctional athletic footwear for outdoor activities would exist in the middle to late 1990s. The sales of hiking shoes, for example, had more than doubled, while the sales of athletic footwear had been declining in 1991. However, this prediction was not totally accurate in that Nike was able to achieve revenue growth of 24 percent in 1995, 32 percent in 1996, and an amazing 43 percent in 1997 just prior to the 1998 decrease.[14]

CUSTOMERS AND MARKETS

Customers, either domestic or international, could be classified into men, women, children, teenagers, and the elderly. To position their products effectively required companies to fully understand customers' needs as well as market trends.[15]

Domestic Market

Men. Surveys showed that only 14 percent of purchases were used for sports, 43 percent for everyday street wear, 26 percent for work or school, 3 percent for lounging or relaxing, and over 2 percent for visiting or entertaining. In the early 1990s, some people felt that the declining growth rate in the men's market and the high cost of promotion made the market much more competitive. However, since most men's sneakers were purchased for everyday street wear, manufacturers might respond by producing more high-quality athletic shoes in different colors and more casual styles.

Women. Only 8 percent of women's athletic shoes were used for sports, 40 percent for everyday street wear, 25 percent for work or school, and 4 percent for lounging or relaxing. Women usually spent more money and bought more pairs of athletic shoes than men, but this had begun to change. For the first time since the early 1980s, when women's buying habits were first tracked, women bought fewer athletic shoes and spent less in 1992[16] than in the previous year, and this trend continued. However, Nike designed a new footbed for women's shoes and in the fall of 1998 introduced it using women's concept shops within Nike's retail partners such as Dick's and The Finish Line.[17]

Children. Sixty percent were used for sports (80 percent of boys). Children's athletic shoes were the majority of the total number of pairs of children's footwear sold. Children in the 1990s influenced purchasing decisions of the family, ranging from what type of cars were purchased, to where families vacationed, to which restaurants they patronized. Although mothers still controlled buying, they were influenced by their children, who, in turn, were influenced by television commercials, other forms of advertisement, and peers. Often children preferred to dress in sweats and activewear, and so mothers would buy shoes that provided comfort and aided development of children's feet.[18]

Teenagers. Sixteen-year-old males were the primary consumers of the latest, and often the most expensive, products. Teens often could not buy without parental permission, but in an era of immediate gratification—"what you want is what you get"—teenagers paid high prices and were more influenced by styles and trends than comfort and fit. They owned from three to seven pairs. They purchased almost every 3 months. About one-third of teenagers said they wore only one athletic label.[19] Companies that provided current, fashionable, and stylish products and used intensive advertisement were targeting teenagers.

Elderly. Customers aged 65 and over were interested in soft and comfortable shoes with more functions and less fashion. Most athletic footwear sold to elderly was walking shoes.

International Market

International market expansion was expected to offer the greatest long-term growth potential, while the domestic athletic footwear market could be considered mature. Valued at $12 billion, this market was untapped in the early 1980s.[20] International operations had fueled overall growth of the U.S. footwear industry in the early 1990s, and although Nike's domestic sales had decreased in 1998, its international revenues grew by 12 percent. That fueled Nike's overall revenue growth of 4 percent in 1998. Customers in Europe, the Asia-Pacific region, Latin America, and Canada were interested in Nike's athletic footwear and apparel.

TECHNOLOGY AND FASHION

Technology, which was critical to product diversity and integrity, was one of the key ingredients driving the industry. Athletic footwear had become a super-sleek construction of multiengineered materials using space-age technologies that cushioned the foot and had arch supports and waffled soles to allow the foot to exert its natural torque. First came Nike's Air shoe in 1979, and then came Reebok's Pump (replaced in 1998 by DMX cushioning technology) and Puma's Disc system sneaker.[21] Well-designed shoes addressed a major consumer concern—performance and preventing injury—for example, footwear developed for running would aid performance while preventing injury. Although technology was critical, however, fashion also became an important factor. The athletic look became socially acceptable, indeed fashionable, for a wide range of activities.

APPAREL AND ACCESSORIES

In the late 1960s, Adidas was the first footwear company to exploit its brand name by introducing sports clothing. By 1982, most companies with a strong brand image took the plunge into apparel. However, apparel was clearly different from shoes because it was driven primarily by fashion, not technical performance. Products became popular quickly but died quickly also, and there were many competitors waiting to duplicate popular designs.

Several footwear companies sold both performance leisure-wear and accessories. At the performance end of the spectrum, they competed with numerous small specialty outfits that focused on high-performance clothing for athletes. Performance-wear included tennis shirts and shorts, bicycle racing shorts and tops, snow-skiing apparel, and running shorts and pants. At the leisure end of the spectrum, they competed with hundreds of small sportswear firms that aggressively developed leisure-wear lines. Leisure-wear included t-shirts, light jackets, sweatsuits, shorts, socks, and long-sleeve shirts.

MANUFACTURING

The principal materials used were natural and synthetic rubber, vinyl and plastic compounds, nylon, leather, and canvas. To lower manufacturing cost, almost all sneakers were manufactured overseas, mainly in Asia,[22] often by independent contractors using designs from the United States, Japan, or Germany. U.S. companies and their contractors and suppliers bought raw materials in bulk because of ready availability in manufacturing countries.[23]

Labor costs and customs duties were constant concerns of companies that used overseas manufacturing operations. They were unable to predict whether additional customs duties, quotas, or other restrictions might be imposed on the importation of their products. The enactment of any such duties, quotas, or restrictions could result in increases in the cost of their products and adversely affect sales and profitability of a company and the industry. For example, in October 1997, the EU Commission imposed definitive antidumping duties on certain textile upper footwear imported from China and Indonesia. And then, in February of 1998, the EU Commission imposed definitive antidumping duties on certain synthetic and leather upper footwear originating in China, Indonesia, and Thailand. Such antidumping duties could have had considerable impact except that the textile footwear duties did not cover sports footwear, and in the case of synthetic and leather upper footwear duties, the so-called special technology footwear, which was for use in sporting activities, was expressly excluded.

Mainland China was expected by some industry observers to become the biggest footwear exporter due to its abundant supplies of cheap, easily trained workers. Until 1997, the economies of most East Asian countries were booming. However, Latin America and Eastern Europe also might become major manufacturing regions because they were nearer the U.S. and European markets and had lower transportation costs. Also, the labor costs in these regions were considered as low as those in Asia.

MARKETING

Although in many ways Nike's marketing had been driven by developing technologically advanced products, this alone did not account for its past success and envious growth. Effective logistics and distribution combined with effective integrated marketing communications (including advertising and the "swoosh") had enabled Nike to develop strong image and brand equity. Past marketing efforts had enabled Nike to achieve sales objectives while maintaining image and brand recognition. Like its competitors, Nike spent millions on brand advertising. The company used television, print advertisement, trade shows, sponsorships, and point-of-purchase (POP) displays. TV ads often featured top athletes or famous movie and singing artists. For many consumers, it was not the shoe's performance but the image as presented by popular sports celebrities in TV commercials that counted. Point of purchase (POP) was almost essential, because a powerful in-store presentation and display could help customers identify which technology belonged to which brand and persuade customers to purchase a certain product.

By 1998, Nike had begun reviewing all sponsorship contracts for professional and amateur athletes. The company preferred to have fewer spokespeople who would do more frequent ads. This would help to control advertising costs and create a more exclusive image for the company's products. Nike also contracted with coaches who made promotional appearances and who also could offer suggestions on product improvement. In addition, they often distributed sneakers to their student-athletes.[24]

But Nike did not restrict itself only to the use of "pull" marketing techniques. Widespread availability in a variety of retail outlets was a requirement for volume sales to occur. Nike's salesforce was noted for enthusiasm and effectiveness in setting up in-store displays, training retail sales clerks, and explaining any Nike-funded contests or special awards designed to motivate retailers.

COMPETITION

Much of the athletic footwear sales in the United States were controlled by Nike and Reebok. However, there were several other companies, including L.A. Gear, Asics Tiger Corp., Keds, Converse, Inc., Fila Footwear USA, Inc., and Adidas USA, Inc., all seeking to increase demand for their brands.

Reebok

Reebok International, Ltd., located in Stoughton, Massachusetts, experienced an 11.5 percent sales decline to $3.2 billion in 1998 from $3.6 billion in 1997. (For complete details, the reader should access Reebok's 1998 annual report at their Web location: www.reebok.com.)

Reebok and its subsidiaries designed and marketed active lifestyle and performance products, including footwear and apparel. The company's principal operating units included the Reebok Division, the Rockport Company, Inc., Greg Norman Collection, and RLS Polo Sport, the company having sold the AVIA Group International, Inc. division in 1998. They concentrated on the Reebok division and recently hired Mr. Carl Yankowski as president and CEO to rebuild Reebok. In early 1999, he created six global strategic business units: Classic Footwear, Performance and Fitness Footwear, Global Apparel, Kids Products, Retail Operations, and Licensing/New Business.

Dominating operation, the Rockport division was positioned as a leader in quality, comfort, and performance in its walking, outdoors, boating, casual, and dress shoes but also markets a broad range of other products.[25] Sales in 1998 increased to $460 million, with U.K. sales continuing to improve as a result of an advertising campaign named "Uncompromise" that featured contemporary personalities such as famous drag queen RuPaul dressed as a man ("I am comfortable being a man"). The Greg Norman Collection division, which started out as an assortment of golf attire in 1991, currently included a variety of men's lifestyle clothing and accessories—from fashionable blazers, outerwear, socks, and belts to beach and volleyball gear. Sales reached $90 million in 1998.

The RLS Polo Sport division (previously called Polo Ralph Lauren) was based on Reebok International being the exclusive licensee for Ralph Lauren Footwear in North America. The portfolio of brands includes Polo Ralph Lauren, Ralph Lauren Collection, Lauren by Ralph Lauren, Polo Sport Ralph Lauren, and RLS/Polo Sport Ralph Lauren. 1998 sales totaled $73 million, and in February of 1999 the division introduced the RLX/Polo Sport brand, which was designed and manufactured to enhance performance and will be marketed for world-class athletes.

L.A. Gear

L.A. Gear, Inc., based in Los Angeles, California, until 1998 had designed, developed, and marketed a broad range of high-quality athletic and athletic-style and casual/lifestyle footwear for men, women, and children, primarily under the L.A. Gear brand name. However, after suffering a series of years of negative earnings,[26] L.A. Gear had reorganized as a privately owned company focusing solely on licensing its trademarks and brand names worldwide. It had signed a licensing agreement with ACI International to produce women's, children's, and men's footwear in the United States and Canada. ACI International's collection of L.A. Gear branded shoes was introduced at the WSA convention in Las Vegas in February of 1999. (For details, the reader should access the company's Web site at www.lagear.com.)

Asics Tiger Corp.

Asics had been successful in the early 1990s, becoming the number five U.S. branded athletic shoe company by 1992. Its sales had increased at an average annual rate of 38 percent since 1990. However, like L.A. Gear, the mid-1990s brought declining sales and losses instead of profits so that by 1999 Asics was being sold through only one major retailing organization and was struggling to survive. (For details, please access the company's Web site at www.asicstiger.com.)

Converse

Converse, Inc., of North Reading, Massachusetts, in 1998 reported that revenues decreased 31.5 percent to $308 million compared with $450 million in 1997. This resulted in a net loss for 1998 of $14 million, and the company noted that the reduction in revenues was primarily attributable to an industrywide oversupply of inventory and the related promotional activities necessary to move these excess quantities. Glenn Rupp, chairman and CEO, commented in the annual report, "Although dissatisfied with the financial performance, we are pleased with our substantial cost cutting efforts which, coupled with our substantially reduced inventory levels, place us in a favorable position upon a resurgence in the athletic footwear industry. We are also very encouraged by our recently announced development of an innovative new footwear technology containing helium." (For complete details, the reader is requested to access the company's Web site at www.converse.com.)

Keds

Keds is a part of the Stride Rite Corp., headquartered in Lexington, Massachusetts, which markets Keds, Stride Rite, Sperry Top-Sider, Tommy Hilfiger Footwear, and Nine West Kids brands of footwear in U.S. shoe stores, department stores, sporting goods stores, and marine supply stores. In Canada and internationally it markets through independent distributors and licensees. Stride Rite reported 1998 revenues of $539 million and noted that Keds posted its first sales increase since 1992. (For more details, the reader should access either of the following: www.keds.com or www.striderite.com.)

Fila

In his 1998 letter to shareholders (a part of the annual report), CEO Michele Scannovini noted that it was a difficult year for Fila—revenue fell for the first time after years of steady growth. Fila Holding S.P.A., the Italian company of which Fila USA is a part, reported that revenues declined approximately 23 percent from 1997 levels. Scannovini noted that for the first time in the past two decades, the U.S. athletic footwear market suffered a contraction as wholesale sales were reduced by over $500 million (equivalent to over 6 percent). (Complete details from Web site: www.fila.com.)

Adidas

Headquartered in Herzogenaurach, Germany, Adidas-Salomon AG in 1998 reported that it was the second-largest company in the sporting goods industry with an estimated 12 percent market share as measured in terms of worldwide sales. The company reported the second best results in its history, with global sales up 48 percent to total 9.9 billion Deutsche marks (approximately U.S. $5.7 billion). Marketing globally through almost 100 subsidiaries in all major markets, it had the following brand names: *Adidas*—footwear, apparel and accessories; *Erima*—teamsport apparel, swimwear, and accessories; *Salomon*—skis, snowboards, snowblades, ski boots and bindings, summer sports product, hiking boots, and trekking equipment; *Taylor Made*—golf equipment; *Mavic*—cycle components; and *Bonfire*—winter sports apparel. In predicting the 1999 global market environment, Adidas forecasted no growth—with the U.S. market in poor condition due to "too fast" expansion and thus expecting consolidation. (The reader interested in complete details should access Web site www.adidas.com.)

SOCIAL AND PUBLIC ISSUES

Due to the lavish endorsement deals between large footwear companies and top athletes, as well as promotional deals with coaches, public concern about the industry's influence and/or control of professional sports developed.[27] In 1990, Operation PUSH, an activist group, called for a public boycott of all Nike products because of some violent incidents in which inner-city youths appeared to have killed a youth just to steal Air Jordan or similar expensive shoes and apparel.[28] The activist group also presented the viewpoint that because the black community was Nike's primary U.S. market, the company did not employ enough black businesses as suppliers or hire enough black workers.[29] Nike reacted to these situations by holding lengthy negotiation sessions with leaders of inner-city minorities and pledged significant monetary resources to fund activities aimed at inner-city youths and also to increase the number of minority-owned suppliers it used and to increase the numbers of minorities it employed.

Nike and Reebok (in fact, almost all athletic footwear companies) imported their athletic footwear products from off-shore manufacturers. Many of these imported goods were purported to be manufactured in sweatshop environments or by prison labor. Importing prison products was illegal, and Congress seemed poised to impose crippling penalties on importers of forced-labor goods.[30] However, the largest public reaction was generated by TV journalists who reported that Nike and some well-known retailers were supporting the use of child labor. By interviewing on TV women workers and underage children employed by firms doing contracted manufacturing for Nike and other firms, it was suggested that Nike was thereby supporting both the exploitation of women, who were required to work in sweat-shop conditions that were unsafe, and also condoning the use of child labor. These social issues were difficult to refute and almost seemed to take on lives of their own. One public figure caught in this situation (due to her TV endorsements of the line of branded merchandise) was Kathy Lee Gifford.

FINANCIALS

Nike's financial results for the past 10 years are shown in Exhibit A. Even a quick glance at this table will indicate that Nike's financial results until fiscal year 1997 had placed it in an enviable position. However, fiscal year 1998 indicated a significant reversal. But Nike, although hurting, is not in financial difficulties of any kind, although return on assets is at a 10-year low. (For complete details, the reader should access Nike's complete annual report available to the public at www.nike.com.)

THE FUTURE

Philip H. Knight, chairman of the board and CEO, in his annual letter to stockholders noted that 1998 produced considerable pain, by far the worst of which was the laying off of 1600 friends and coworkers. (For complete details, the reader should access www.nike.com.) Knight cited the Asian economic meltdown, the popularity of brown shoes (i.e., nonathletic shoes), the labor practices social issue (mentioned above), past boring advertising aired by Nike, resignations of experienced employees (who often had become millionaires by owning Nike stock), and the layoffs as the factors that caused the 1998 results.

He also added that he had been criticized for expansion of headquarters. However, he answered this last criticism by saying, "Most of our troubles are really symptoms of a larger, more difficult problem: We are a very well-managed $5 billion company. Right now, though, we are a $10 billion company trying to get to $15 billion." Over the past 3 years Nike had grown from 9500 employees to 21,800, and Knight thought perhaps that this unchecked growth had likely obscured the ability to look objectively at what was happening to Nike. Now, he believed, it was time to stop adding employees and concentrate on training and assimilation.

Knight observed that Nike also needed to think about redundancies and inefficiencies in its structure. To facilitate international market expansion, Nike had built strong international regional headquarters designed to support the fledgling country businesses. Many of these countries grew into substantial businesses. Knight decided to reduce the size of the international regional headquarters and to bolster in-country organizations and thereby align costs more directly to in-country revenues. This also would permit a better focus on customer differences and peculiarities within country markets. At the same time, Knight moved to consolidate the warehouses servicing international markets. All these activities, including the exiting of certain manufacturing operations, resulted in a restructuring charge of $129.9 million in the fourth quarter of 1998.

However, Knight also pointed out what he believed were the bright spots of 1998 by noting that he believed Nike's had the best production process in the industry, and that it had taken

EXHIBIT A

Nike's Financial History, Year Ended May 31 (In Millions, Except Per-Share Data and Financial Ratios)

	1998	1997	1996	1995	1994	1993	1992	1991	1990	1989
Revenues	$9,553.1	$9,186.5	$6,470.6	$4,760.8	$3,789.7	$931.0	$3,405.2	$3,003.6	$2,235.2	$1,710.8
Gross margin	3,487.6	3,683.5	2,563.9	1,895.6	1,488.2	1,544.0	1,316.1	1,153.1	851.1	636.0
Gross margin %	36.5%	40.1%	39.6%	39.8%	39.3%	39.3%	38.7%	38.4%	38.1%	37.2%
Restructuring charge	129.9	—	—	—	—				—	
Net income	399.6	795.8	553.2	399.7	298.8	365	329.2	287.0	243.0	167.0
Basic earnings per common share	1.38	2.76	1.93	1.38	1.00	1.20	1.09	0.96	0.81	0.56
Diluted earnings per common share	1.35	2.68	1.88	1.36	0.99	1.18	1.07	0.94	0.80	0.56
Average common shares outstanding	288.7	288.4	286.6	289.6	298.6	302.9	301.7	300.4	299.1	297.7
Diluted average common shares outstanding	295	297	293.6	294	301.8	308.3	306.4	304.3	302.7	300.6
Cash dividends declared per common share	0.46	0.38	0.29	0.24	0.20	0.19	0.15	0.13	0.10	0.07
Cash flow from operations	517.5	323.1	339.7	254.9	576.5	265.3	435.8	11.1	127.1	169.4
Price range of common stock										
High	64.125	76.375	52.063	20.156	18.688	22.563	19.344	13.625	10.375	4.969
Low	37.750	47.875	19.531	14.063	10.781	13.750	8.781	6.500	4.750	2.891
At May 31:										
Cash and equivalents	$108.6	$445.4	$262.1	$216.1	$518.8	$291.3	$260.1	$119.8	$90.4	$85.7
Inventories	1,396.6	1,338.6	931.2	629.7	470.0	593	471.2	586.6	309.5	222.9
Working capital	1,828.8	1,964.0	1,259.9	938.4	1,208.4	1,165.2	964.3	662.6	561.6	419.6
Total assets	5,397.4	5,361.2	3,951.6	3,142.7	2,373.8	2,186.3	1,871.7	1,707.2	1,093.4	824.2
Long-term debt	379.4	296.0	9.6	10.6	12.4	15	69.5	30	25.9	34.1
Redeemable preferred stock	0.3	0.3	0.3	0.3	0.3	0.3	0.3	0.3	0.3	0.3
Common shareholders' equity	3,261.6	3,155.9	2,431.9	1,964.7	1,740.9	1,642.8	1,328.5	1,029.6	781.0	558.6
Year-end stock price	46.000	57.500	50.188	19.719	14.750	18.125	14.500	9.938	9.813	4.750
Market capitalization	13,201.1	16,633.0	14,416.8	5,635.2	4,318.8	5,499.3	4,379.6	2,993.0	2,942.7	1,417.4

(continued)

EXHIBIT A (*continued*)

Nike's Financial History, Year Ended May 31 (In Millions, Except Per-Share Data and Financial Ratios)

	1998	1997	1996	1995	1994	1993	1992	1991	1990	1989
Financial Ratios										
Return on equity	12.5%	28.5%	25.2%	21.6%	17.7%	24.5%	27.9%	31.7%	36.3%	34.5%
Return on assets	7.4%	17.1%	15.6%	14.5%	13.1%	18.0%	18.4%	20.5%	25.3%	21.8%
Inventory turns	4.4	4.8	5	5.2	4.3	4.5	3.9	4.1	5.2	5.1
Current ratio at May 31	2.1	2.1	1.9	1.8	3.2	3.6	3.3	2.1	3.1	2.9
Current ratio at May 31 (diluted)	34.1	21.5	16.6	14.5	14.9	15.3	13.5	10.5	12.2	8.6
Geographic Revenues										
United States	$5,452.5	$5,529.1	$3,964.7	$2,997.9	$2,432.7	$2,528.8	$2,270.9	$2,141.5	$1,755.5	$1,362.2
Europe	2,143.7	1,833.7	1,334.3	980.4	927.3	1,085.7	919.8	664.7	334.3	241.4
Asia/Pacific	1,255.7	1,245.2	735.1	515.6	283.4	178.2	75.7	56.2	29.3	32
Canada, Latin America, and other	701.2	578.5	436.5	266.9	146.3	138.3	138.8	141.2	116.1	75.2
Total revenues	$9,553.1	$9,186.5	$6,470.6	$4,760.8	$3,789.7	$3,931.0	$3,405.2	$3,003.6	$2,235.2	$1,710.8

decades to develop. And he suggested that in the last 6 months of 1998 it had gotten even better. But he also noted that "Inventory is where you can get really killed in this industry. And, we got our bell rung pretty good in the fiscal '98. But we responded very quickly in our sales problems so that, as we go to press, our inventories are 'in line,' several months ahead of our original estimates." In the spring of 1998, Nike introduced the first line of Tiger Woods footwear and apparel, which helped the golf segment of Nike's business post a healthy global increase of 81 percent, while in October of 1998, Nike presented the first products in its Sports Timing category—the Triax running watch. Knight also noted that Nike continued to make strides in growing its women's business. But, he said, the clear winner in fiscal year 1998 had been European apparel, which was up 35 percent.

Nike clearly faced a situation that it had not foreseen nor expected and now faced the challenge of choosing an effective strategy for continued growth.

Endnotes

1. Susan Hauser, "To the Top," *People Weekly*, May 4, 1992, p. 142.
2. Stresser, J. B., and Laurie Becklund, "Swoosh, The Unauthorized Story of Nike and the Men Who Played There," *Harper Business*, 1993, p. 17.
3. Geraldine E. Willigan, "High-Performance Marketing: An Interview with Nike's Phil Knight," *Harvard Business Review*, July-August 1992, pp. 91–101.
4. *Ibid.*
5. Steve E. Holt, "Limousines for the Feet," *Graphic*, March 1993, pp. 89–98.
6. 1998 Annual Report—President's Letter to Stockholders, www.nike.com.
7. Please note that all sales revenue and percentages noted in this section of the case were taken directly from Nike's 1998 Annual Report, available at www.nike.com.
8. Kevin Goldman, "Reebok Signs Up the Newest Star in Basketball in $15 Million Pact," *Wall Street Journal*, January 6, 1993, p. B8.
9. Elizabeth Comte, "Art for Shoes' Sake," *Forbes*, September 28, 1992, pp. 128–130.
10. Nike's 1998 Annual Report.
11. Staff writer, "Farewell …," *Sports Illustrated*, February 19, 1990, pp. 77–82.
12. Rich Wilner, "The Battle for #3," *Footwear News*, February 1, 1993, pp. 12, 13, 47.
13. Rich Wilner, "Change, Though Inevitable, Never Comes Easily," *Footwear News*, July 26, 1993, pp. 28–29.
14. Nike's 1998 Annual Report.
15. Many of the figures in this section of the case were taken from Dick Silverman, "The Numbers Game," *Footwear News*, February 1, 1993, p. 54.
16. Staff writer, "Women's Total Athletic Shoe Sales Slip in '92," *Footwear News*, April 19, 1993, p. 19.
17. Nike 1998 Annual Report.
18. Michael Kormos, "Back to School Report, Doing the 'Rithmatic'," *Footwear News*, March 15, 1993, p. 14.
19. Laurie Sohng, "The Athletic Consumer, Age 14," *Footwear News*, February 1, 1993, pp. 44–45.
20. Staff writer, "Shoes," *Standard and Poor's Industry Reports*, October 1993, p. 77.
21. Joseph Perrira, "From Air to Pump to Puma's Disc System, Sneaker Gimmicks Bound to New Heights," *Wall Street Journal*, 1991, p. B5.
22. Staff writer, "Farewell …," *Sports Illustrated*, February 19, 1990, pp. 77–82.
23. Mark Clifford, "Spring in Their Step," *Far Eastern Economic Review*, November 5, 1992, pp. 56–57.
24. Bill Brubaker, "In Shoe Companies' Competition, the Coaches Are the Key Players," *Washington Post*, March 11, 1991, p. A1.
25. Kevin Goldman, "Reebok Signs Up the Newest Star in Basketball in $15 Million Pact," *Wall Street Journal*, January 6, 1993, p. 88.
26. Staff writer, "L.A. Gear Posts Wider than Expected Loss for Fiscal 4th Period," *Wall Street Journal*, February 22, 1993, p. B6.
27. David Thigpen, "Is Nike Getting Too Big for Its Shoes," *Time*, April 26, 1993, p. 55.
28. Laurie Freeman, "Flat-Footed Ad Campaigns Try to Spark Sales as Sports Shoes Hit Plateau," *Stores*, August 1991, pp. 67, 82.
29. *Ibid.*
30. Amy Borrus, "Staunching the Flow of China's Gulag Exports," *Business Week*, April 13, 1992, pp. 51–52.

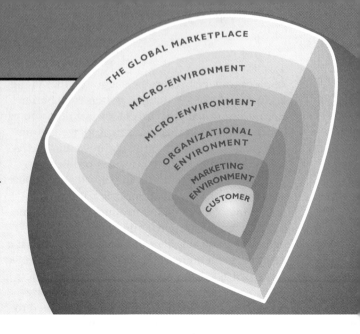

CASE 18

Nike's Dispute with the University of Oregon

This case was prepared by Rebecca J. Morris, University of Nebraska at Omaha, and Anne T. Lawrence, San Jose State University.

On April 24, 2000, Philip H. Knight, CEO of athletic shoe and apparel maker Nike Inc., publicly announced that he would no longer donate money to the University of Oregon (UO). It was a dramatic and unexpected move for the high-profile executive. A former UO track and field star, Knight had founded Nike's predecessor in 1963 with his former UO coach and mentor, Bill Bowerman. Over the years, Knight had maintained close ties with his alma mater, giving more than $50 million of his personal fortune to the school over a quarter century. In 2000, he was in active discussion with school officials about his biggest donation yet—millions for renovating the football stadium. But suddenly it was all called off. Said Knight in his statement: "[F]or me personally, there will be no further donations of any kind to the University of Oregon. At this time, this is not a situation that can be resolved. The bonds of trust, which allowed me to give at a high level, have been shredded."[1]

This case was written on the basis of publicly available information solely for the purpose of stimulating student discussion. All individuals and events are real. An earlier version of this case was presented at the 2000 annual meeting of the North American Case Research Association. The comments of reviewers at that meeting and of three anonymous reviewers for the *Case Research Journal* are greatly appreciated. All rights reserved jointly to the authors and the North American Case Research Association.

Reprinted by permission from the *Case Research Journal*, volume 21, issue 3. Copyright © 2001 by Rebecca J. Morris and Anne T. Lawrence and the North American Case Research Association. All rights reserved.

At issue was the University of Oregon's intention, announced April 14, 2000, to join the Worker Rights Consortium (WRC). Like many universities, UO was engaged in an internal debate over the ethical responsibilities associated with its role as a purchaser of goods manufactured overseas. Over a period of several months, UO administrators, faculty, and students had been discussing what steps they could take to ensure that products sold in the campus store, especially university-logo apparel, were not manufactured under sweatshop conditions. The university had considered joining two organizations, both of which purported to certify goods as "no sweat." The first, the Fair Labor Association (FLA), had grown out of President Clinton's Apparel Industry Partnership (AIP) initiative and was vigorously backed by Nike, as well as several other leading apparel makers. The second, the Worker Rights Consortium, was supported by student activists and several U.S.-based labor unions that had broken from the AIP after charging it did not go far enough to protect workers. Knight clearly felt that his alma mater had made the wrong choice. "[The] University [has] inserted itself into the new global economy where I make my living," he charged. "And inserted itself on the wrong side, fumbling a teachable moment."

The dispute between Phil Knight and the University of Oregon captured much of the furor swirling about the issue of the role of multinational corporations in the global economy and the effects of their far-flung operations on their many thousands of workers, communities, and other *stakeholders. In part because of its high-profile brand name, Nike had become a lightening rod for activists concerned about worker rights abroad. Like many U.S.-based shoe and apparel makers, Nike had located its manufacturing operations overseas, mainly in Southeast Asia, in search of low wages. Almost all production was carried out by subcontractors rather than by Nike directly. Nike's employees in the United States, by contrast, directed their efforts to the high-end work of research and development, marketing, and retailing. In the context of this global division of labor, what responsibility, if any, did Nike have to ensure adequate working conditions and living standards for the hundreds of thousands of workers, mostly young Asian women, who made its shoes and apparel? If this was not Nike's responsibility, then whose was it? Did organizations like the University of Oregon have any business pressuring companies through their purchasing practices? If so, how should they best do so? In short, what were the lessons of this "teachable moment"?*[5]

NIKE, INC.

In 2000, Nike, Inc., was the leading designer and marketer of athletic footwear, apparel, and equipment in the world. Based in Beaverton, Oregon, the company's "swoosh" logo, its "Just Do It!" slogan, and its spokespersons Michael Jordan, Mia Hamm, and Tiger Woods were universally recognized. Nike employed around 20,000 people directly, and *half a million* indirectly in 565 contract factories in 46 countries around the world.[2] Wholly-owned subsidiaries included Bauer Nike Hockey Inc. (hockey equipment), Cole Haan (dress and casual shoes), and Nike Team Sports (licensed team products). Revenues for the 12 months ending November 1999 were almost $9 billion.[3] With a 45 percent global market share, Nike was in a league of its own.[4] Knight owned 34 percent of the company's stock and was believed to be the sixth-richest individual in the United States.[5]

Knight had launched this far-flung global empire shortly after completing his MBA degree at Stanford University in the early 1960s. Drawing on his firsthand knowledge of track and field, he decided to import low-priced track shoes from Japan in partnership with his former college coach. Bowerman would provide design ideas, test the shoes in competition, and endorse the shoes with other coaches; Knight would handle all financial and day-

to-day operations of the business. Neither man had much money to offer, so for $500 each and a handshake, the company (then called Blue Ribbon Sports) was officially founded in 1963. The company took the name Nike in 1978; two years later, with revenues topping $269 million and 2,700 employees, Nike became a publicly-traded company.[6]

From the beginning, marketing had been a critical part of Knight's vision. The founder defined Nike as a "marketing-oriented company." During the 1980s and early 1990s, Nike aggressively sought endorsements by celebrity athletes to increase brand awareness and foster consumer loyalty. Early Nike endorsers included marathoners Alberto Salazar and Joan Benoit, Olympic gold medalist Carl Lewis, Wimbledon champion Andre Agassi, and six members of the 1992 Olympic basketball "Dream Team." Later Nike endorsers included tennis aces Pete Sampras and Monica Sales, basketball great Michael Jordan, and golf superstar Tiger Woods.

Nike became the world's largest athletic shoe company in 1991 when revenues soared to $3 billion, but that was only the beginning.[7] Continued development of "cool shoes," aggressive geographic expansion, and the world dominance of Nike-endorsing athletes resulted in record-breaking performance year after year. By 1998, Nike's total revenues exceeded $9.5 billion.[8] Although the Asian economic crisis and sluggish U.S. sales caused revenues to dip slightly in 1999, Nike easily led the athletic footwear industry, outpacing the number two firm (Adidas) by 1.5 times.[9] Key events in Nike's history are summarized in Exhibit 1.

CUTTING-EDGE PRODUCTS

An important element in Nike's success was its ability to develop cutting-edge products that met the needs of serious athletes, as well as set fashion trends. Research specialists in Nike's Sports Research Labs conducted extensive research and testing to develop new technologies to improve the performance of Nike shoes in a variety of sports. Tom McQuirk, head of the company's Sports Research Labs stated, "Our job here in sports research is to define human movement in terms of biomechanics and physiology. Our job is to translate activities into a set of performance-enhancing and injury-reducing needs."[10] For example, research specialists studied the causes of ankle injuries in

EXHIBIT I

Key Events in Nike's History

1957	Phil Knight and Coach Bill Bowerman met for the first time at the University of Oregon.
1959	Phil Knight graduated from the University of Oregon with a BBA degree in accounting.
1962	Knight wrote the marketing research paper outlining the concept that became "Blue Ribbon Sports" (BRS).
1963	The first shipment of 200 Tiger shoes arrived from Japan.
1966	The first retail store was opened.
1969	Knight left the accounting field to devote his full-time efforts to building the company.
1970	Nike's legal dispute with the Japanese supplier resulted in the exploration of manufacturing in Mexico, Puerto Rico, and Canada.
1971	Nike contracted for the production of shoes in Mexico; however, the shoes were a disaster—cracking when used in cold weather.
1972	The first shoes bearing the Nike brand were sold.
1977	Nike contracted with factories in Taiwan and Korea, ending the manufacturing relationship with the Japanese firm.
1978	The split between Blue Ribbon Sports and their Japanese supplier became final. BRS changed to the Nike name for all operations.
1980	Nike sold the first shares of common stock to the public.
1981	Revenues were $457.7 million, and Nike had 3,000 employees.
1982	Phil Knight received the Pioneer Award. The Pioneer Award was given annually by the University of Oregon to a person "whose character places him/her in a position of leadership." The award recognized individuals who led in business, philanthropy, communications, government, or the arts.
1986	For the first time, Nike revenues surpassed the billion-dollar mark.
1990	Growth in international sales helped Nike reach $2 billion in revenues. Nike employed 5,300 employees in the United States. The Nike World Campus opened in Beaverton, Oregon.
1991	Revenues reached $3 billion with $869 million in international revenues. Michael Jordan wears Nike shoes while leading the Chicago Bulls to their first NBA championship.
1995	Nike's revenues were $4.8 billion. Nike shoes using the patented Nike Air system were introduced, radically changing shoe design.
1996	Nike's revenues were $6.5 billion. In the Atlanta Olympics, Michael Johnson became the fastest man in the world while wearing a pair of specially designed gold metallic Nike's. Phil Knight donated $25 million to the Oregon Campaign. His gift designated $15 million to the creation of endowed chairs. The remaining $10 million helped finance the construction of a new law school building that was named the William W. Knight Law Center after Phil Knight's father. The $25 million gift was the largest single gift to a university in the Pacific Northwest. Knight's earlier gifts to UO totaled $25 million. Knight funds supported athletics, and the university library was named for his family in the 1980's.
1998	Nike's revenues were $9.5 billion. Basketball shoes slumped as Michael Jordan retired and the NBA played a shortened season due to a labor dispute. Nike's international trading partner, Nissho Iwai of Japan, donated an undisclosed "generous" amount to the UO Knight Library to "honor Mr. Knight's great commitment to supporting the University of Oregon." Nissho Iwai had made a donation to the renovation of the library in 1990. One floor of the library was named for the Japanese company.[a]
1999	Nike's revenues dipped to $8.8 billion. Revenue decline was attributed to the "brown shoes" movement in the United States and the Asian economic slump.
2000	Phil Knight withdrew his pledge for a $30 million contribution for the University of Oregon's football stadium.

[a]*Trading Firm Makes Gift to UO Knight Library Endowment.* (June 11, 1998). University of Oregon (press release). Accessed: March 27, 2000, at comm. uoregon.edu/newsreleases/official/jun98/Go61198_1.html.

Sources: Based on the following sources: *Our History.* (n.d.). Nike, Inc. Accessed: February 3, 2000 at www.nikebiz.com/story/chrono.shtml; Katz, D. R. (1995), *Just Do It: The Nike Spirit in the Corporate World.* Holbrook, MA: Adams Media Corporation; Nike, Inc. (1995–1999). *Form 10-K.* Securities and Exchange Commission. Accessed: February 5, 2000.

basketball players to develop shoes that would physically prevent injuries as well as signal information to the user to help him or her resist turning the ankle while in the air. Other specialists developed new polymer materials that would make the shoes lighter, more aerodynamic, or more resistant to the abrasions incurred during normal athletic use.

Findings from the Sports Research Labs were then passed on to design teams that developed the look and styling of the shoes. Drawing heavily from trends in popular culture, shoe designers in the Jordan Building of Nike's Beaverton, Oregon, corporate campus blended the technological with the "romance and imagery and all those subliminal characteristics that make an object important to people in less utilitarian ways."[11] Put more simply, the Nike designers took a technologically sophisticated piece of sporting equipment and gave it attitude.

The Making of Athletic Shoes

Although it was the leading athletic footwear company in the world, Nike never manufactured shoes in any significant number. Rather, from its inception, the company had outsourced production to subcontractors in Southeast Asia, with the com-

pany shifting production locations within the region when prevailing wage rates became too high. In the early years, it had imported shoes from Japan. It later shifted production to South Korea and Taiwan, then to Indonesia and Thailand, and later yet to Vietnam and China, as shown in Exhibit 2.[12]

The reasons for locating shoe production mainly in Southeast Asia were several, but the most important was the cost of labor. The availability of component materials and trade policies were also factors. Modern athletic shoes were composed of mesh, leather, and nylon uppers that were hand-assembled, sewn, and glued to composite soles.[13] Mechanization had not been considered effective for shoe manufacturing due to the fragile materials used and the short life spans of styles of athletic shoes.[14] Therefore, shoe production was highly labor-intensive. Developing countries, primarily in Southeast Asia, offered the distinct advantage of considerably lower wage rates. For example, in the early 1990s, when Nike shifted much of its shoe production to Indonesia, daily wages there hovered around $1 a day (compared to wages in the U.S. shoe industry at that time of around $8 an hour).[15]

Along with lower labor costs, Asia provided the additional advantage of access to raw materials suppliers.[16] Very few rubber firms in the United States, for example, produced the sophisticated composite

EXHIBIT 2

Location of Shoe Production in Nike Subcontractor Factories, 1995–1999 Percent of Athletic Shoe Production by Country

	1995	1996	1997	1998	1999
China	31	34	37	37	40
Indonesia	31	38	37	34	30
South Korea	16	11	5	2	1
Thailand	14	10	10	10	11
Taiwan	8	5	3	2	2
Vietnam		2	8	11	12
Philippines			4	4	2
Italy					2

Source: Nike 10-K statements, 1995–1999.

soles demanded in modern athletic shoe designs. Satellite industries necessary for modern shoe production, plentiful in Asia, included tanneries, textiles, and plastic and ironwork moldings.[17]

A third factor in determining where to locate production was differential tariffs that applied to athletic shoes. The tariffs were determined by the manner in which the upper was attached to the sole of the shoe. The three types—nonmolded, molded, and fox-banded (where a strip of material was applied over the joint of the sole and upper, as in canvas sneakers)—were assessed different tariffs for importation. Variations in the materials used for the uppers also determined the tariff rate. In general, canvas sneakers were assessed higher tariffs than leather molded footwear, such as basketball or running shoes. As a result, differential tariffs prompted shoe companies to outsource higher margin high-tech athletic shoes while sometimes producing low-margin canvas shoes domestically.[18]

The economic reality for many firms in the athletic footwear industry involved balancing consumer demand for new and innovative styles with pressures to improve the profit picture. Manufacturing new high-technology styles in Southeast Asia permitted the firms to take advantage of lower labor costs, lower tariffs, and a better-developed supplier network. Many of Nike's factories in Asia were operated by a small number of Taiwanese and Korean firms that specialized in shoe manufacturing, many owned by some of the wealthiest families in the region. When Nike moved from one location to another, often these companies followed, bringing their managerial expertise with them.

Nike's Subcontractor Factories

In 2000, Nike contracted with over 500 different footwear and apparel factories around the world to produce its shoes and apparel.[19] Although there was no such thing as a typical Nike plant, a factory operated by the Korean subcontractor Tae Kwang Vina (TKV) in the Bien Hoa City industrial zone near Ho Chi Minh City in Vietnam provided a glimpse into the setting in which many Nike shoes were made.[20]

TKV employed approximately 10,000 workers in the Bien Hoa City factory. The workforce consisted of 200 clerical workers, 355 supervisors, and 9,465 production workers, all making athletic shoes for Nike. Ninety percent of the workers were women between the ages of 18 to 24. Production workers were employed in one of three major areas within the factory: the chemical, stitching, and assembly sections. Production levels at the Bien Hoa City factory reached 400,000 pairs of shoes per month; Nike shoes made at this and other factories made up fully 5 percent of Vietnam's total exports.[21]

A second-generation South Korean shoe worker employed by Nike described the challenges of work in the typical shoe factory as the "three D's." "It's dirty, dangerous, and difficult," explained T. H. Lee. "Making shoes on a production line is something people only do because they see it as an important and lucrative job. Nobody who could do something else for the same wage would be here. It's less dirty, dangerous, and difficult than it was in the past—but it's not an easy way to spend a day."[22]

The Chemical Section.[23]   Over 1,000 natural and man-made materials were used in the factory to produce shoes from scratch. Workers in the chemical or polyurethane (PU) plant were responsible for producing the high-technology outsoles. Production steps in the chemical division involved stretching and flattening huge blobs of raw rubber on heavy-duty rollers and baking chemical compounds in steel molds to form the innovative 3-dimensional outsoles. The chemical composition of the soles changed constantly in response to the cutting-edge formulations developed by the Beaverton, Oregon, design teams, requiring frequent changes in the production process.

The smell of complex polymers, the hot ovens, and the changing of the steel molds resulted in a working environment that was louder, hotter, and had higher concentrations of chemical fumes than allowed by Vietnamese law.[24] Chemicals used in the section were known to cause eye, skin, and throat irritations; damage to liver and kidneys; nausea; anorexia; and reproductive health hazards through inhalation or in some cases through absorption through the skin.[25] Workers in the chemical section were thought to have high rates of respiratory illnesses, although records kept at the TKV operations did not permit the tracking of illnesses by factory section.

Workers in the chemical section were issued gloves and surgical-style masks. However, they often discarded the protective gear, complaining that it was too hot and humid to wear them in the plant.

Cotton masks and gloves also were ineffective in protecting workers from solvent fumes and exposure to skin-damaging chemicals.[26]

The Stitching Section.[27]   In a space the size of three football fields, row after row of sewing machines operated by young women hummed and clattered. One thousand stitchers worked on a single floor of the TKV factory, sewing together nylon, leather, and other fabrics to make the uppers. Other floors of the factory were filled with thousands of additional sewing machines producing different shoe models.

The stitching job required precision and speed. Workers who did not meet the aggressive production goals did not receive a bonus. Failing to meet production goals three times resulted in the worker's dismissal. Workers were sometimes required to work additional hours without pay to meet production quotas.[28] Supervisors were strict, chastising workers for excessive talking or spending too much time in the restrooms. Korean supervisors, often hampered by language and cultural barriers, sometimes resorted to hard-nosed management tactics, hitting or slapping slower workers. Other workers in need of discipline were forced to stand outside the factory for long periods in the tropical sun. The Vietnamese term for this practice was "phoi nang," or sun-drying.[29]

The Assembly Section.[30]   Women worked side by side along an assembly line to join the uppers to the outsoles through the rapid manipulation of sharp knives, skivers,[31] routers, and glue-coated brushes. Women were thought to be better suited for the assembly jobs because their hands were smaller and more capable of the manual dexterity needed to fit the shoe components together precisely. During the assembly process, some 120 pairs of hands touched a single shoe.

A strong, sweet solvent smell was prominent in the assembly area. Ceiling-mounted ventilation fans were ineffective because the heavy fumes settled to the floor. Assembly workers wore cotton surgical masks to protect themselves from the fumes; however, many workers pulled the masks below their noses, saying they were more comfortable that way.[32]

Rows and rows of shoes passed along a conveyor before the sharp eyes of the quality control inspectors. The inspectors examined each of the thousands of shoes produced daily for poor stitching or crooked connections between soles. Defective shoes were discarded. Approved shoes continued on the conveyor to stations where they were laced by assembly workers and finally put into Nike shoe boxes for shipment to the United States.[33]

Despite the dirty, dangerous, and difficult nature of the work inside the Bien Hoa factory, there was no shortage of applicants for positions. Although entry-level wages averaged only $1.50 per day (the lowest of all countries where Nike manufactured), many workers viewed factory jobs as being better than their other options, such as working in the rice paddies or pedaling a pedicab along the streets of Ho Chi Minh City.[34] With overtime pay at one and a half times the regular rate, workers could double their salaries—generating enough income to purchase a motorscooter or to send money home to impoverished rural relatives. These wages were well above national norms. An independent study by researchers from Dartmouth University showed that the average annual income for workers at two Nike subcontractor factories in Vietnam was between $545 and $566, compared to the national average of between $250 and $300.[35] Additionally, workers were provided free room and board and access to on-site health care facilities.

Many Vietnamese workers viewed positions in the shoe factory as transitional jobs—a way to earn money for a dowry or to experience living in a larger city. Many returned to their homes after working for Nike for 2 or 3 years to marry and begin the next phase of their lives.[36]

THE CAMPAIGNS AGAINST NIKE

In the early 1990s, criticism of Nike's global labor practice began to gather steam. *Harper's Magazine,* for example, published the pay stub of an Indonesian worker, showing that the Nike subcontractor had paid the woman just under 14 cents per hour, and contrasted this with the high retail price of the shoes—and the high salaries paid to the company's celebrity endorsers.[37] The Made in the U.S.A. Foundation, a group backed by American unions, used a million-dollar ad budget to urge consumers to send their "old, dirty, smelly, worn-out Nikes" to Phil Knight in protest of Nike's Asian manufacturing practices.[38] Human rights groups and Christian organizations joined the labor unions in targeting the labor practices of the athletic shoes firm. Many felt that Nike's antiauthority corporate image ("Just Do It") and message of social betterment through fitness were incompatible with press photos of slight Asian women hunched over sewing machines 70 hours a week, earning just pennies an hour.

By mid-1993, Nike was being regularly pilloried in the press as an imperialist profiteer. A CBS news segment airing on July 2, 1993, opened with images of Michael Jordan and Andre Agassi, two athletes who had multimillion-dollar promotion contracts with Nike. Viewers were told to contrast the athletes' paychecks with those of the Chinese and Indonesian workers who made "pennies" so that Nike could "Just Do It."[39]

In 1995, *The Washington Post* reported that a pair of Nike Air Pegasus shoes that retailed for $70 cost Nike only $2.75 in labor costs, or 4 percent of the price paid by consumers. Nike's operating profit on the same pair of shoes was $6.25; the retailer pocketed $9.00 in operating profits, as shown in Exhibit 3. Also that year, shareholder activists organized by the Interfaith Center on Corporate Responsibility submitted a shareholder proposal at Nike's annual meeting, calling on the company to review labor practices by its subcontractors; the proposal garnered 3 percent of the shareholder vote.

Things were to get worse. A story in *Life*.[40] magazine documented the use of child labor in Pakistan to produce soccer balls for Nike, Adidas, and other companies. The publicity fallout was intense. The public could not ignore the photographs of small children sitting in the dirt, carefully stitching together the panels of a soccer ball that would become the plaything of some American child the same age.[41] Nike moved quickly to work with its Pakistani subcontractor to eliminate the use of child labor, but damage to Nike's image had been done.

In October 1996, CBS News *48 Hours* broadcast a scathing report on Nike's factories in Vietnam. CBS reporter Roberta Baskin focused on low wage rates, extensive overtime, and physical abuse of workers. Several young workers told Baskin how a Korean supervisor had beaten them with a part of a shoe because of problems with production.[42] A journalist in Vietnam told the reporter that the phrase "to Nike someone" was part of the Vietnamese vernacular. It meant to "take out one's frustration on a fellow worker." Vietnamese plant managers refused to be interviewed, covering their faces as they ran inside the factory. CBS news anchor Dan Rather concluded the damaging report by saying, "Nike now says it plans to hire outside observers to talk to employees and examine working conditions in its Vietnam factories, but the company just won't say when that might happen."[43]

EXHIBIT 3

The Cost of a Pair of Nike Air Pegasus Shoes

Subcontractor → A → Nike → B → Retailer → C → Consumer

A. Cost to Nike		B. Cost to Retailer		C. Cost to Consumer	
Materials	$ 9.00	Nike's Operating Profit	$ 6.25	Retail Sales Personnel	$ 9.50
Tariffs	3.00	Sales, Distribution, and Administration	5.00	Rent of Retail Space	9.00
Rent and Equipment	3.00	Promotion/Advertising	4.00	Retailer's Operating Profit	9.00
Production Labor	2.75	Research and Development	0.25	Other Expenses	7.00
Subcontractor's Operating Profit	1.75				
Shipping	0.50				
Cost to Nike	$20.00	Cost to Retailer	$35.50	Cost to Consumer	$70.00

Source: Adapted from "Why It Costs $70 for a Pair of Athletic Shoes." *The Washington Post,* May 3, 1995.

The negative publicity was having an effect. In 1996, a marketing research study authorized by Nike reported the perceptions of young people age 13 to 25 of Nike as a company. The top three perceptions, in the order of their response frequency, were athletics, cool, and bad labor practices.[44] Although Nike maintained that its sales were never affected, company executives were clearly concerned about the effect of criticism of its global labor practices on the reputation of the brand they had worked so hard to build.

THE EVOLUTION OF NIKE'S GLOBAL LABOR PRACTICES

In its early years, Nike had maintained that the labor practices of its foreign subcontractors—like TKV—were simply not its responsibility. "When we started Nike," Knight later commented, "it never occurred to us that we should dictate what their factor[ies] should look like, which really didn't matter because we had no idea what a shoe factory should look like anyway."[45] The subcontractors, not Nike, were responsible for wages and working conditions. Dave Taylor, Nike's vice president of production, explained the company's position: "We don't pay anybody at the factories, and we don't set policy within the factories; it is their business to run."[46]

When negative articles first began appearing in the early 1990s, however, Nike managers realized that they needed to take some action to avoid further bad publicity. In 1992, the company drafted its first code of conduct (Exhibit 4), which required every subcontractor and supplier in the Nike network to honor all applicable local government labor and environmental regulations, or Nike would terminate the relationship.[47] The subcontractors were also required to allow plant inspections and complete all necessary paperwork. Despite the compliance reports the factories filed every 6 months, Nike insiders acknowledged that the code of conduct system might not catch all violations. Tony Nava, Nike's country coordinator for Indonesia, told a *Chicago Tribune* reporter, "We can't know if they're actually complying with what they put down on paper."[48] In short, Nike required its subcontractors to comply with existing labor laws, but did not feel it was the firm's duty to challenge local policies that suppressed worker rights or kept wages low in order to attract manufacturing.

In 1994, Nike tried to address this problem by hiring Ernst & Young, the accounting firm, to independently monitor worker abuse allegations in Nike's Indonesian factories. Later, Ernst & Young also audited Nike's factories in Thailand and Vietnam. Although these audits were not made public, a copy of the Vietnam audit leaked to the press showed that workers were often unaware of the toxicity of the compounds they were using and ignorant of the need for safety precautions.[49] In 1998, Nike implemented important changes in its Vietnamese plants to reduce exposure to toxins—substituting less harmful chemicals, installing ventilation systems, and training personnel in occupational health and safety issues.

In 1996, Nike established a new Labor Practices Department, headed by Dusty Kidd, formerly a public relations executive for the company. Later that year, Nike hired GoodWorks International, headed by former U.S. ambassador to the United Nations Andrew Young, to investigate conditions in its overseas factories. In January 1997, GoodWorks issued a glossy report, stating that "Nike is doing a good job in the application of its Code of Conduct. But Nike can and should do better." The report was criticized by activists for its failure to look at the issue of wages. Young demurred, saying he did not have expertise in conducting wage surveys. Said one critic, "This was a public relations problem, and the world's largest sneaker company did what it does best: It purchased a celebrity endorsement."[50]

Over the next few years, Nike continued to work to improve labor practices in its overseas subcontractor factories, as well as the public perception of them. In January 1998, Nike formed a Corporate Responsibility Division, combining the Labor Practices, Global Community Affairs, and Environmental Action Teams under the leadership of former Microsoft executive Maria S. Eitel, hired to be Nike's new vice president for Corporate and Social Responsibility. Nike subsequently doubled the staff of this division. In May of that year, Knight gave a speech at the National Press Club, at which he announced several new initiatives. At that time, he committed Nike to raise the minimum age for employment in its shoe factories to 18 and in its apparel factories to 16. He also promised to achieve OSHA standards for indoor air quality in all its factories by the end of the year, mainly by eliminating the use of the solvent toluene; to expand educational programs for workers and its

EXHIBIT 4

Nike's 1992 Code of Conduct

Nike Inc, was founded on a handshake.

Implicit in that act was the determination that we would build our business with all our partners upon trust, teamwork, honesty, and mutual respect. We expect all of our business partners to operate on the same principles.

At the core of the Nike corporate ethic is the belief that we are a company comprised of many different kinds of people, appreciating individual diversity, and dedicated to equal opportunity for each individual.

Nike designs, manufactures, and markets sports and fitness products. At each step in that process we are dedicated to minimizing our impact on the environment. We seek to implement to the maximum extent possible the three "R's" of environmental action—reduce, reuse, and recycle.

There is No Finish Line.

Memorandum of Understanding

Wherever Nike operates around the globe, we are guided by our Code of Conduct and bind our business partners to those principles with a signed Memorandum of Understanding.

Government Regulation of Business (subcontractor/supplier) certifies compliance with all applicable local government regulations regarding minimum wage; overtime; child labor laws; provisions of pregnancy, menstrual leave; provisions for vacation and holidays; and mandatory retirement benefits.

Safety and Health (subcontractor/supplier) certifies compliance with all applicable local government regulations regarding occupational health and safety.

Worker insurance (subcontractor/supplier) certifies compliance with all applicable local laws providing health insurance, life insurance and worker's compensation.

Forced Labor (subcontractor/supplier) certifies that it and its suppliers and contractors do not use any form of forced labor—prison or otherwise.

Environment (subcontractor/supplier) certifies compliance with all applicable local environmental regulations and adheres to Nike's own broader environmental practices, including the prohibition on the use of chloro-fluoro-carbons (CFCs), the release of which could contribute to the depletion of the earth's ozone layer.

Equal Opportunity (subcontractor/supplier) certifies that it does not discriminate in hiring, salary, benefits, advancement, termination, or retirement on the basis of gender, race, religion, age, sexual orientation, or ethnic origin.

Documentation and Inspection (subcontractor/supplier) agrees to maintain on file such documentation as may be needed to demonstrate compliance with the certifications in this Memorandum of Understanding and further agrees to make these documents available for Nike's inspection upon request.

Source: Code of Conduct. (n.d.). Nike Inc. Accessed: November 18, 2000, at www.nikebiz.com/labor/code.shtml

microenterprise loan program; and to fund university research on responsible business practices. Nike also continued its use of external monitors, hiring Pricewaterhouse-Coopers to join Ernst & Young in a comprehensive program of factory audits, checking them against Nike's code. At the conclusion of his speech Knight said,

At the end of the day, we don't have all the answers. Nobody has all the answers. We want to be the best corporate citizens we can be. If we continue to improve, and our industry colleagues and people interested in these issues join in our efforts, the workers are the ultimate beneficiaries.[51]

APPAREL INDUSTRY PARTNERSHIP

One of Nike's most ambitious social responsibility initiatives was its participation in the Apparel Industry Partnership. It was this involvement that would lead, eventually, to Knight's break with the University of Oregon.

In August 1996, President Clinton launched the White House Apparel Industry Partnership on Workplace Standards (AIP). The initial group was comprised of 18 organizations. Participants included several leading manufacturers, such as Nike, Reebok, and Liz Claiborne. Also in the group were several labor unions, including the Union of Needletrades, Industrial, and Textile Employees (UNITE) and the Retail, Wholesale and Department Store Union; and several human rights, consumer, and shareholder organizations, including Business for Social Responsibility, the Interfaith Center on Corporate Responsibility, and the National Consumers League. The goal of the AIP was to develop a set of standards to ensure that apparel and footwear were not made under sweatshop conditions. For companies, it held out the promise of certifying to their customers that their products were "no sweat." For labor and human rights groups, it held out the promise of improving working conditions in overseas factories.[52]

In April 1997, after months of often-fractious meetings, the AIP announced that it had agreed on a workplace code of conduct that sought to define decent and humane working conditions.[53] Companies agreeing to the code would have to pledge not to use forced labor—that is, prisoners or bonded or indentured workers. They could not require more than 60 hours of work a week, including overtime. They could not employ children younger than 15 years old, or the age for completing compulsory schooling, whichever was older—except they could hire 14-year-olds if local law allowed. The code also called on signatory companies to treat all workers with respect and dignity; to refrain from discrimination on the basis of gender, race, religion, age, disability, sexual orientation, nationality, political opinion, or social or ethnic origin; and to provide a safe and healthy workplace. Employees' rights to organize and bargai0n collectively would be respected. In a key provision, the code also required companies to pay at least the local legal minimum wage or the prevailing industry wage, whichever was higher. All standards would apply not only to a company's own facilities but also to their subcontractors or suppliers.

Knight, who prominently joined President Clinton and others at a White House ceremony announcing the code, issued the following statement:

> Nike agreed to participate in this Partnership because it was the first credible attempt, by a diverse group of interests, to address the important issue of improving factories worldwide. It was worth the effort and hard work. The agreement will prove important for several reasons. Not only is our industry stepping up to the plate and taking a giant swing at improving factory conditions, but equally important, we are finally providing consumers some guidance to counter all of the misinformation that has surrounded this issue for far too long.[54]

THE FAIR LABOR ASSOCIATION

But this was not the end of the AIP's work; it also had to agree on a process for monitoring compliance with the code. Although the group hoped to complete its work in 6 months, over a year later it was still deeply divided on several key matters. Internal documents leaked to *The New York Times* in July 1998 showed that industry representatives had opposed proposals, circulated by labor and human rights members, calling for the monitoring of 30 percent of plants annually by independent auditors. The companies also opposed proposals that would require them to support workers' rights to organize independent unions and to bargain collectively, even in countries—like China—where workers did not have such rights by law. Said one nonindustry member, "We're teetering on the edge of collapse."[55]

Finally, a subgroup of nine centrist participants, including Nike, began meeting separately in an attempt to move forward. In November 1998, this subgroup announced that it had come to agreement on a monitoring system for overseas factories of U.S.-based companies. The AIP would establish a new organization, the Fair Labor Association (FLA), to oversee compliance with its workplace code of conduct. Companies would be required to monitor their own factories, and those of their subcontractors, for compliance; all would have to be checked within the first 2 years. In addition, the FLA would select and certify independent external monitors, who would inspect 10 percent of each firm's factories each year. Most of these monitors were expected to be accounting firms, which had expertise in conducting audits. The monitors' reports would be kept private. If a company was found to be out of compliance, it would be given a chance to correct the problem. Eventually, if it did not, the company would be dropped from the FLA, and its termination would be announced to the public. Companies would pay for most of their own monitoring.[56]

The Clinton administration quickly endorsed the plan. Secretary of Labor Alexis Herman said, "[We are] convinced this agreement lays the foundation to eliminate sweatshop labor, here and abroad. It is workable for business and creates a credible system that will let consumers know the garments they buy are not produced by exploited workers."[57]

Both manufacturers and institutional buyers stood to benefit from participation in the Fair Labor Association. Companies, once certified for 3 years, could place an FLA service mark on their brands, signaling to both individual consumers and institutional buyers that their products were "sweatshop-free." It was expected that the FLA would also serve the needs of institutional buyers, particularly universities. By joining the FLA and agreeing to contract only with certified companies, universities could warrant to their students and others that their logo apparel and athletic gear were manufactured under conditions conforming to an established code of fair labor standards.[58] Both parties would pay for these benefits. The FLA was to be funded by dues from participating companies ($5,000 to $100,000 annually, depending on revenue) and by payments from affiliated colleges and universities (based on 1 percent of their licensing income from logo products, up to a $50,000 annual cap).

Criticism of the Fair Labor Association

Although many welcomed the agreement—and some new companies signed on with the FLA soon after it was announced—others did not. Warnaco, a leading apparel marker that had participated in the AIP, quit, saying that the monitoring process would require it to turn over competitive information to outsiders. The American Apparel Manufacturing Association (AAMA), an industry group representing

350 companies, scoffed at the whole idea of monitoring. "Who is going to do the monitoring?" asked a spokesperson for the AAMA, apparently sarcastically. "Accountants or Jesuit priests?" The FLA monitoring scheme was also attacked as insufficient by some partnership participants that had not been part of the subgroup. In their view, companies simply could not be relied upon to monitor themselves objectively. Said Jay Mazur, president of UNITE, "The fox cannot watch the chickens. If they want the monitoring to be independent, it can't be controlled by the companies."[59] FLA critics believed that a visit from an external monitor once every 10 years would not prevent abuses. In any case, as a practical matter, they stated that most monitors would be drawn from the major accounting firms that did business with the companies they were monitoring and were, therefore, unlikely to seek out lapses. Companies would not be required to publish a list of their factories, and any problems uncovered by the monitoring process could be kept from the public under the rules governing nondisclosure of proprietary information.

One of the issues most troubling to critics was the code's position on wages. The code called on companies to pay the minimum wage or prevailing wage, whichever was higher. In many of the countries of Southeast Asia, though, these wages fell well below the minimum considered necessary for a decent standard of living for an individual or family. For example, *The Economist*[60] reported that Indonesia's average minimum wage—paid by Nike subcontractors—was only two-thirds of what a person needed for basic subsistence. An alternative view was that a code of conduct should require that companies pay a *living wage,* that is, compensation for a normal workweek adequate to provide for the basic needs of an average family, adjusted for the average number of adult wage earners per family. One problem with this approach, however, was that many countries did not systematically study the cost of living, relative to wages, so defining a living wage was difficult. The partnership asked the U.S. Department of Labor to conduct a preliminary study of these issues; the results were published in 2000 (see Exhibit 5).

The code also called on companies to respect workers' rights to organize and bargain collectively. Yet a number of FLA companies outsourced production to nondemocratic countries, such as China and Vietnam, where workers had no such rights. Finally,

EXHIBIT 5

Wages, Minimum Wages, and Poverty Lines for Selected Countries in U.S. Dollars

Country	Year (latest available)	National Poverty Line	Minimum Wage	Prevailing Wage in Apparel and Footwear Industries
China	1997	$21–$27/cap/mo[a]	$12–$39/mo	$115–$119/mo
Indonesia	1999	$5–$6/cap/mo	$15–$34/mo	$15–$42/mo
South Korea	1999	$182/mo	$265/mo	$727–$932/mo
Thailand	1999	$22/cap/mo	$93–$109/mo	$106/mo
Taiwan	1998	$214–$334/mo	$476/mo	$690–$742/mo
Vietnam[b]	1997	$27–$29/mo	$35–$45/mo	$47–$56/mo
Philippines	1999	$26/cap/mo	$150/mo	$150/mo
Italy	1998	$390/cap/mo	$949–$1,445/mo	$1,280–$1,285/mo
United States	1998	$693/cap/mo	$858–$1,083/mo	$1,420–$1,488/mo

National Poverty Line: Poverty measures reflect an estimate of absolute poverty thresholds based on some specified set of basic needs. Opinions differ as to whether the poverty line should reflect mere physical subsistence levels or sufficient income to provide for a nutritious diet, safe drinking water, suitable housing, energy, transportation, health care, child care, education, savings, and discretionary income. Comparability between countries is difficult because the basis for establishing the poverty level usually differs across countries.

Minimum Wage: The minimum wage-fixing system differs according to the country's objectives and criteria. It is usually set by striking a balance between the needs of the worker and what employers can afford or what economic conditions will permit. A range for minimum wage indicates that the country has differential minimums based on the region, often differing for urban and rural regions.

Prevailing Wage: The prevailing wage reflects the "going rate" or average level of wages paid by employers for workers in the apparel or footwear industries. Positions requiring greater skills, supervisory responsibilities, or workers with longer years of employment typically earn more than the wage reported. Nonwage benefits such as access to health care, paid vacations, supplementary pay, or training are not included in the prevailing wage.

[a]Per capita per month.
[b]Canada NewsWire. (October 16, 1997). "Nike Factory Workers in SE Asia Help Support Their Families and Have Discretionary Income, According to Preliminary Findings of Study by MBA Team from Dartmouth's Tuck School."
Source: U.S. Department of Labor. (February, 2000). "Wages, Benefits, Poverty Line and Meeting Workers' Needs in the Apparel and Footwear Industries of Selected Countries," www.dol.gov/ilab/public/media/reports/oiea/main.htm.

some criticized the agreement on the grounds that it provided companies, as one put it, "a piece of paper to use as a fig leaf." Commented a representative of the needle trades unions. "The problem with the partnership plan is that it tinkers at the margins of the sweatshop system but creates the impression that it is doing much more. This is potentially helpful to companies stung by public condemnation of their labor practices, but it hurts millions of workers and undermines the growing antisweatshop movement."[61]

THE WORKER RIGHTS CONSORTIUM

Some activists in the antisweatshop movement decided to chart their own course, independent of the FLA. On October 20, 1999, students from more than 100 colleges held a press conference to announce formation of the Worker Rights Consortium (WRC) and called on their schools to withdraw from, or not to join, the FLA. The organization would be formally launched at a founding convention in April 2000.[62]

The Worker Rights Consortium differed radically in its approach to eliminating sweatshops. First, the WRC did not permit corporations to join; it was comprised exclusively of universities and colleges, with unions and human rights organizations playing an advisory role. In joining the WRC, universities would agree to "require decent working conditions in factories producing their licensed products." Unlike the FLA, the WCA did not endorse a single, comprehensive set of fair labor standards. Rather, it called on its affiliated universities to develop their own codes. However, it did establish minimum standards that such codes should meet—ones that were, in some respects, stricter than the FLA's. Perhaps most significantly, companies would have to pay a living wage. Companies were also required to publish the names and addresses of all of their manufacturing facilities, in contrast to FLA rules. Universities could refuse to license goods made in countries where compliance with fair labor standards was "deemed impossible," whatever efforts companies had made to enforce their own codes in factories there.

By contrast with the FLA, monitoring would be carried out by "a network of local organizations in regions where licensed goods are produced," generally nongovernmental organizations, independent human rights groups, and unions. These organizations would conduct unannounced "spot investigations," usually in response to worker complaints; WRC organizers called this the "fire alarm" method of uncovering code violations. Systematic monitoring would not be attempted.

The consortium's governance structure reflected its mission of being an organization by and for colleges and universities. Its 12-person board was composed of three representatives of United Students Against Sweatshops, three university administrators from participating schools, and six members drawn from an advisory board of persons with "expertise in the issues surrounding worker abuses in the apparel industry and independent verification of labor standards in apparel factories." No seats at the table were reserved for industry representatives. The group would be financed by 1 percent of licensing revenue from participating universities, as well as foundation grants.

THE UNIVERSITIES TAKE SIDES

Over the course of the spring semester 2000, student protests were held on a number of campuses, including the University of Oregon, to demand that their schools join the WRC. By April, around 45 schools had done so. At UO, the administration encouraged an open debate on the issue so that all sides could be heard on how to ensure that UO products were made under humane conditions. Over a period of several months, the Academic Senate passed a resolution in support of the WRC. In a referendum sponsored by the student government, three-quarters of voters supported a proposal to join the WRC. A committee of faculty, students, administrators, and alumni appointed by the president voted unanimously to join the consortium.[63] Finally, after concluding that all constituents had an opportunity to be heard, on April 12, 2000, University of Oregon president David Frohnmayer announced that UO would join the WRC for 1 year. Its membership would be conditional, he said, on the consortium's agreement to give companies a voice in its operations and universities more power in governance. Shortly after the university's decision was announced in the press, Phil Knight withdrew his philanthropic contribution. In his public announcement, he started his main disagreements with the Worker Rights Consortium:

> Frankly, we are frustrated that factory monitoring is badly misconstrued. For us, one of the great hurdles and real handicaps in the dialogue has been the complexity of the issue. For real progress to be made, all key participants have to be at the table. That's why the FLA has taken so long to get going. The WRC is supported by the AFL-CIO and its affiliated apparel workers' union, UNITE. Their main aim, logically and understandably, however, misguided, is to bring apparel jobs back to the United States. Among WRC rules, no company can participate in setting

standards, or monitoring. It has an unrealistic living wage provision. And its "gotcha" approach to monitoring doesn't do what monitoring should—measure conditions and make improvements.[64]

Endnotes

1. "Knight's Statement," by Philip H. Knight, via press release, www.oregonlive.com

2. Greenhouse, S. (January 26, 2000). "Anti-Sweatshop Movement Is Achieving Gains Overseas," *The New York Times*, Section A, p. 10.

3. Lee, L. (February 21, 2000). "Can Nike Still Do It," *Business Week*, p. 120.

4. Martinson, J. (July 8, 2000). "Brand Values: Nike: The Sweet Swoosh of Success," *The Guardian* (London), Guardian City Pages, p. 26.

5. Anonymous. (October 11, 1999). "The Forbes 400: America's Richest People," *Forbes*, p. 296.

6. *Our History: BRS Becomes Nike.* (n.d.). Nike Inc. Accessed: February 3, 2000, www.nikebiz.com/story/before.shtml

7. *Our History: In Our Own League.* (n.d.). Nike, Inc. Accessed: February 3, 2000, www.nikebiz.com/story/chrono.shtml

8. Nike, Inc. (1999, May 31—filing date). *Form 10-K.* Securities and Exchange Commission. Accessed: February 5, 2000.

9. Gellene, D. (April 8, 1999). "Ad Reviews: Adidas," *The Los Angeles Times*, Part C, p. 6.

10. Katz, D. R. (1995). *Just Do It: The Nike Spirit in the Corporate World.* Holbrook, MA: Adams Media Corporation, p. 132.

11. *Just Do It*, p. 130.

12. Although Nike operated shoe factories in New England in the 1970s and 1980s, Nike's annual U.S. production never accounted for more than 1 week of demand annually. Later, these plants were closed, and Nike stopped producing shoes in the United States, other than prototypes.

13. Nike, Inc. (1999, May 31—filing date). *Form 10-K.* Securities and Exchange Commission. Accessed: February 5, 2000.

14. Vanderbilt, T. (1998). *The Sneaker Book.* NY: The New Press, p. 77.

15. *Just Do It*, p. 162.

16. *The Sneaker Book*, p. 81.

17. *The Sneaker Book*, p. 90.

18. Austen, J., and Barff, R. (1993). "It's Gotta Be Da Shoes," *Environment and Planning*, 25, pp. 48–52.

19. Greenhouse, S. (January 26, 2000). "Antisweatshop Movement Is Achieving Gains Overseas," *The New York Times*, Section A, p. 10.

20. Descriptions of the Tae Kwang Vina factory in Bien Hoa City were derived from the following: Manning, J. (November 9, 1997). "Nike: Tracks Across the Globe" (Three-part newspaper series originally appearing in *The Oregonian*.) Online source at oregonlive.com/series/nike11091.html; Katz, D. R. (1995). *Just Do It: The Nike Spirit in the Corporate World.* Holbrook, MA: Adams Media Corporation; Vanderbilt, T. (1998). *The Sneaker Book.* New York: The New Press; Ernst & Young. (January 13, 1997); *Ernst & Young Environmental and Labor Practice Audit of the Tae Kwang Vina Industrial Ltd. Co., Vietnam.* (Copy of the audit available at www.corpwatch.org/trac/nike/ audit.html).

21. Greenhouse, S. (November 8, 1997). "Nike Shoe Plant in Vietnam Is Called Unsafe for Workers," *The New York Times*, Section A, p. 1.

22. *Just Do It*, p. 161.

23. Manning, J. (November 9, 1997). "Nike: Tracks Across the Globe" (Three-part newspaper series originally appearing in *The Oregonian*.) Online source, oregonlive.com/series/nike11091.html

24. Manning, J. (November 11, 1997). "Poverty's Legions Flock to Nike," *The Oregonian*, www.oregonlive.com/series/nikel11103.html

25. *Ernst & Young Audit.* (n.d.). Corporate Watch. Accessed: March 26, 2000, www.corpwatch.org/trac/nike/audit.html

26. *Ernst & Young Audit.* (n.d.). Corporate Watch. Accessed: March 26, 2000, www.corpwatch.org/trac/nike/audit.html

27. Manning, J. (November 9, 1997). "Nike: Tracks Across the Globe" (Three-part newspaper series originally appearing in *The Oregonian*.) Online source at oregonlive.com/series/nike11091.html

28. Manning J. (November 9, 1997). "Nike's Asian Machine Goes on Trial" (Part 1 of a three-part newspaper series originally appearing in *The Oregonian*.) Online source at oregonlive.com/series/nike11091.html

29. Manning, J. (November 10, 1997). "Poverty's Legions Flock to Nike" (Part 2 of a three-part newspaper series originally appearing in *The Oregonian*.) Online source at oregonlive.com/series/nike11091.html

30. *The Sneaker Book*, p. 84.

31. Skivers are cutting tools that are used to split leather. In athletic shoe manufacturing, skivers are used to cut away the excess leather when bonding the upper to the sole.

32. *Ernst & Young Audit.* (n.d.). Corporate Watch. Accessed: March 26, 2000, www.corpwatch.org/trac/nike/audit.html

33. *Just Do It*, p. 160.

34. Lamb, D. (April 18, 1999). "Job Opportunity or Exploitation?" *The Los Angeles Times*, Part C. p. 1.

35. Baum, B. (August 27, 1999). "Study Concludes That Nike Workers Can More Than Make Ends Meet," *Athenaeum*. (Online version available at ww.athensnewspapers.com/1997/101797/1017.a3nike.html).

36. Manning, J. (November 10, 1997). "Poverty's Legions Flock to Nike" (Part 2 of a three-part newspaper series originally appearing in *The Oregonian*.) Online source at oregonlive.com/series/nike11091.html

37. Ballinger, J. (August 1992). "Nike: The New Free Trade Hell," *Harper's*, p. 119.

38. *Just Do It*, p. 166.

39. *Just Do It*, p. 187.

40. Schanberg, S. (June 1996). "Six Cents an Hour," *Life Magazine*, pp. 38–47.

41. Holstein, W. J., Palmer, B., Ur-Rehman, S., and Ito, T. (December 23, 1996). "Santa's Sweatshops," *U.S. News and World Report*, p. 50.

42. The *48 Hours* report, however, neglected to mention that the supervisor had subsequently been fired and was later criminally convicted in Vietnamese court (*Just Do It*, p. 188).

43. CBS News *48 Hours* (October 17, 1996), transcript.

44. Manning, J. (November 10, 1997). "Poverty's Legions Flock to Nike" (Part 2 in "Nike: Tracks Across the Globe" series). *The Oregonian* at www.oregonlive.com/series/nike11101.html

45. Philip Knight, Speech to the National Press Club, May 12, 1998.

46. *Just Do It*, p. 191.

47. *Just Do It*, p. 191.

48. Goozner, M. (November 7, 1994). "Nike Manager Knows Abuses Do Happen," *The Chicago Tribune*, p. 6.

49. Hammond, K. (November 7, 1997). "Leaked Audit: Nike Factory Violated Worker Laws," *Mother Jones*, www.motherjones.com/news_wire/nike.html

50. Glass, S. (August 25, 1997). "The Young and the Feckless," *The New Republic* (online source at www.corpwatch.org/trac/feature/sweatshops/newprogressive.html; Glass was later fired by *The New Republic*, which charged that Glass had fabricated some of his sources for this and other articles.

51. Federal News Service. (May 12, 1998). National Press Club luncheon address by Philip Knight, Chief Executive Officer, Nike. LEXIS-NEXIS Academic Universe, Category: News. Accessed: August 27, 2000, web.lexis-nexis.com/universe

52. "Companies Agree to Meet on Sweatshops," *Washington Post*, August 3, 1996.

53. For the full text of the Fair Labor Association Workplace Code of Conduct, see www.fairlabor.org/html/amendctr.html#workplace

54. Philip H. Knight, statement released to the press April 14, 1997.

55. Steven Greenhouse, "Antisweatshop Coalition Finds Itself at Odds on Garment Factory Code," *New York Times*, July 3, 1998.

56. For a description of the monitoring process, see www.fairlabor.org/html/amendctr.html#monitoringprocess

57. "Plan to Curtain Sweatshops Rejected by Union," *The New York Times*, November 5, 1998.

58. For a list of signatory companies, universities, and other organizations, see www.fairlabor.org/html/affiliat.html

59. *The New York Times*, November 21, 1997.

60. Anonymous. (June 15, 1991). "Indonesia: Staying Alive," *The Economist*, p. 38.

61. Alan Howard, "Partners in Sweat," *The Nation*, December 29, 1998.

62. The Web site for the WRC is www.workersrights.org. Further material on disagreements within the FLA that led to the WRC's founding may be found at www.sweatshopwatch.org.

63. Sarah Edith Jacobson, "Nike's Power Game" [editorial page letter], *The New York Times*, May 16, 2000.

64. "Knight's Statement," by Philip H. Knight, via press release, www.oregonlive.com

Kellogg Company

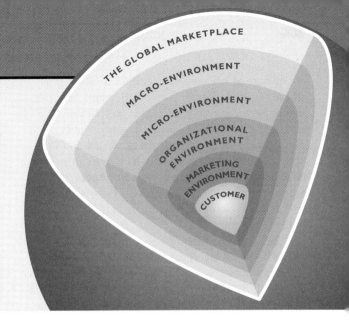

THE GLOBAL MARKETPLACE
MACRO-ENVIRONMENT
MICRO-ENVIRONMENT
ORGANIZATIONAL ENVIRONMENT
MARKETING ENVIRONMENT
CUSTOMER

This case was prepared by Craig A. Hollingshead, W. Blaker Bolling, Richard L. Jones, and Ashli White of Marshall University.

From a news item in the *New York Times:*

> Battle Creek, January 25, 1995—Since the Kellogg Company posted fourth-quarter earnings on Friday, investors and analysts have become concerned that the company might be forced to adopt discounting measures to defend market share, weakening its profit margins. Last spring, Kellogg significantly cut back on discounting measures such as "buy one—get one free" offers on some of its best-selling cereals to lower costs and raise profits. The strategy succeeded at first, but then sales in Kellogg's core domestic cereal business fell, continuing a decline in market share that has seen Kellogg's brands go from over 40 percent of the $8 billion market in the late 1980s to 35 percent today.[1] Kellogg has assured investors that it will not reintroduce promotions. However, in response to Kellogg chairman and chief executive officer Arnold Langbo's remark that Kellogg is "extremely sensitive toward further volume decline," Kellogg shares dropped by $2.75 on Friday to close at $54.25 on the New York Stock Exchange.

Reprinted by permission of Craig A. Hollingshead.

In Battle Creek, Michigan, headquarters of Kellogg Company, Chief Executive Officer and Chairman of the Board Arnold G. Langbo reflected back on the company's performance in 1994. Although Kellogg's sales increased for the fiftieth consecutive year and earnings increased for the forty-first time in 42 years, the company did not meet its growth objectives for the year. Kellogg remained the world's leading producer of ready-to-eat cereal products and controlled 43 percent of the global market. Even though Kellogg continued to lead the industry in 1994, it faced many challenges. Langbo was concerned with how the company would reach its marketing objectives and continue leading the industry, how it could maintain profit margin, and how it might increase its stock price, which was near a 3-year low in early 1995.

THE CEREAL INDUSTRY

Cereal grains milled into breakfast cereal is an $8 billion business worldwide. The worldwide demand for ready-to-eat cereal is in a long-term upward trend. Annual per capita cereal consumption in North America is 10.3 pounds, while the world's leading consumer of cereal, Ireland, topped at 17 pounds. However, cereal for breakfast is not part of the cultural tradition in many parts of the world. For example, in Africa and Asia, per capita cereal consumption runs well below 1 pound per year, offering a great opportunity for market development. In North America and Europe, an increasing consciousness of healthy diet and nutrition needs drives increased demand among adults. U.S. annual growth is estimated at 2 to 3 percent, with worldwide growth in the 5 to 7 percent range.

Competition within the industry centers around several companies. Kellogg Company is the worldwide leader with a 35 percent U.S. market share, 43 percent worldwide. Of the 10 most popular breakfast cereals in the world, six wear a Kellogg label. The number two player, and Kellogg's primary competitor, is General Mills, with a 25 percent U.S. market share. General Mills was a messy conglomerate in the early 1980s. Since 1985, however, it has sought to focus more on cereal products. Worldwide, General Mills formed joint ventures with Nestlé (Cereal Partners Worldwide) and PepsiCo (Snack Ventures Europe). Both are relatively new, and neither of these enterprises has scored significant success. General Mills' recent performance has been marred by disappointing returns from its Big G cereal business and violations of Food and Drug Administration (FDA) regulations. Unregistered pesticide traces were found in the company's raw oat supply. Although not a particular health hazard, this disrupted General Mills' production and marketing plans. Traditionally more broadly diversified than Kellogg, General Mills had recently sold off its three restaurant chains: Red Lobster, Olive Garden, and China Coast. The company retained Betty Crocker, Gold Medal, and Yoplait Products Divisions.

Other companies seeking market share were Quaker Oats, Ralston Purina, Kraft, General Foods, and Nabisco. With a growing worldwide demand, these companies had a chance to build markets and increase profits.

KELLOGG COMPANY

Kellogg Company and its subsidiaries are involved primarily in the manufacture and marketing of con-

venience foods. The main products of the company are ready-to-eat cereals, including Frosted Flakes, Corn Flakes, Apple Jacks, Frosted Mini-Wheats, Rice Krispies, Raisin Bran, Cracklin' Oat Bran, and Nut & Honey Crunch. These products are manufactured in 18 countries and distributed in more than 150. These cereals are sold primarily to grocery stores for resale to consumers and are marketed globally. In addition to ready-to-eat cereals, Kellogg produces or processes and distributes frozen dessert pies, toaster pastries, waffles, snacks, and other convenience foods in the United States, Canada, and other limited areas outside the United States. Some of these products include Pop-Tarts, Eggo waffles, Nutri-Grain Bars, Croutettes, and Corn Flake Crumbs.

The corporate culture at Kellogg is focused on the long-term well-being of the business. Management's primary objective is to increase shareholders' value over time. In order to reach this objective, the Kellogg Strategy was formed:

> Continued aggressive investment in new cereal markets, increased returns on existing investments, maximizing cash flows, and minimizing the cost of capital through appropriate financial policies.

At Kellogg, it was believed that the 16,000 employees were the company's most important competitive advantage.

Kellogg Company History

Kellogg Company's worldwide leadership came from the accidental invention of flaked cereal at the Battle Creek Sanitarium in 1894. The sanitarium was a famous Seventh Day Adventist hospital and health spa where exercise, fresh air, and a strict diet were offered. Sanitarium Superintendent Dr. John Harvey Kellogg and Will Keith Kellogg, his younger brother and business manager, invented many grain-based foods served at the facility.

The sanitarium served hard and tasteless bread. The Kellogg brothers conducted experiments to develop a better-tasting alternative. Wheat was cooked, forced through granola rollers, and then rolled into long sheets of dough.

One day the brothers experienced a fortunate accident. A batch of wheat was cooked but then set aside, neglected. Later, the brothers decided to process the stale dough. Instead of producing long sheets of dough, the rollers flattened the wheat mixture into small, thin flakes. Toasted, these flakes tasted light and crispy.

The patients at the sanitarium liked these new flakes so well that they wanted to eat them at home. To satisfy that demand, the Kellogg brothers started the Sanitas Nut Food Company, selling the toasted wheat flakes by mail order. In 1898, Will Keith Kellogg extended the process to flaking corn. Seeing his brother's lack of interest in expanding the food company, W. K. Kellogg went into business for himself.

On April 1, 1906, the Battle Creek Toasted Corn Flake Company started production. W. K. Kellogg used his manufacturing and marketing ideas to promote his product. He added malt flavoring to the corn flakes to make them unique. He advertised to healthy people the benefits of a product with flavor, freshness, value, and convenience. Kellogg used most of his working capital to buy a full-page ad in *The Ladies Home Journal* in 1906. Results were amazing. Sales quickly went from 33 cases to 2900 cases per day. With continued advertising, the company's annual sales surged to more than a million cases by 1909. W. K. Kellogg became known for his innovative sales promotions, which included free samples and premiums. The company was renamed Kellogg Company in 1922.

Effective marketing led to the company's success. In addition, Kellogg constantly sought ways to improve the product. He was committed to providing consumers with information about diet and nutrition. Kellogg was the first company to print nutrition messages, recipes, and product information on cereal packages in the 1930s. By that time, products such as All-Bran and Rice Krispies had been introduced. Kellogg became an international business when it built facilities in Canada, Australia, and England. In 1930, the W. K. Kellogg Foundation was established. Today, it is one of the largest philanthropic institutions in the world, funding projects in health, education, agriculture, leadership, and youth.

During the 1950s, products such as Corn Pops, Frosted Flakes, and Honey Smacks were introduced. Television also became an important part of advertising in the 1950s. As the mid-1960s approached, Pop Tarts and Product 19 were added.

Consumers began showing more interest in health and nutrition in the 1960s. So Kellogg Company provided information programs for schools, health organizations, and consumers. During the 1970s, Kellogg provided more detailed package labels, including amounts of sodium and dietary fiber. By the mid-1980s, packages included cholesterol, potassium, and nutrient information. New product introductions included Nutri-Grain, Crispix, Just Right, and Mueslix.

In Kellogg's continued commitment to health, the company led an All-Bran/National Cancer Institute campaign that produced more than 80,000 contacts to the National Cancer Institute (NCI) for information about the role of diet in reducing the risk of some kinds of cancers. Recently, Kellogg took pride in providing information to consumers about healthy lifestyles, cholesterol, and heart disease.

Production

Kellogg Company traditionally sought market leadership through production efficiency and product quality control, product innovation, and marketing effectiveness. The company spent considerable capital to maintain high-tech, high-capacity production capability. The result was low production costs but considerable excess capacity. To take advantage of possible economies of scale in production, there was constant pressure to build and maintain markets. New product innovations were an important part of this strategy. Kellogg moved Nutri-Grain from the health food store to the supermarket in 1981 and modified the production process to gain extended shelf life for the product.

Kellogg practiced Japanese-style total quality management (TQM) principles. The company strictly monitored product quality control. It made sure that new automated manufacturing machinery was thoroughly tested before it went on-line to serve a market. Worker teams monitored quality, controlled costs, and suggested improvements. Kellogg sought to improve inbound logistics by developing stronger relations with a limited number of suppliers.

Marketing

One of the roots of Kellogg's success was a strong marketing program. This was logical considering that the company marketed a low-priced, convenience good and that high volumes of repeat sales were necessary to maintain market share. The foundation of Kellogg's marketing strategy had been to offer a good product backed with high-performance promotion. The company used a mix of price and sales promotion to build and maintain market share. It believed that money spent to introduce good products would build market share. This was a successful strategy until the early 1990s. Success, for Kellogg, traditionally had been measured by market share.

The primary consumers of breakfast cereal products in the United States were children. Kellogg sought to serve this target market with its mainstay brands: Corn Flakes, Rice Krispies, Corn Pops, Honey Smacks, Froot Loops, Apple Jacks, and Raisin Bran had heavy consumption by kids. These products were in the maturity stage of their product lifecycle, but the market constantly renewed itself as younger children moved into the school-age years. Kellogg sought to maintain brand loyalty with a good-tasting product, vigorously promoted through advertising and coupon offers. In the past, Kellogg was known for new product innovation, rolling out four or five brand extensions a year. This rate of introduction was reduced recently to one, maybe two, per year.

One high-potential market niche was health-conscious adults. In the late 1980s, oat-bran products offered the promise of minimizing blood cholesterol and reducing the chances of heart attack. Oat bran was "by far the most dramatic thing that has ever happened to the cereal industry," said one high-level industry executive. Oat

bran and oat products doubled their market share to 18 percent in 1989, while the ready-to-eat cereal market grew only 1 to 2 percent. Kellogg, with only about 20 percent of its product line based on oats, was late to market with an acceptable brand. The company never really caught up. When it did offer a product, it cannibalized share from its existing offerings. Then the balloon burst. The health benefits of oat bran were placed in doubt. Consumers rebelled. Sales plummeted. Oat bran tasted like cattle feed—if it wasn't *really* good for you, people wouldn't eat it. Kellogg's Common Sense Oat Bran dropped from a 2 percent share to 0.7 percent. Cracklin' Oat Bran fell from 1.4 percent in 1990 to 0.4 percent in 1991.

Market share for Kellogg's domestic products had been slipping for a decade (see Table below). Kellogg's declining market share was the result of two factors: (1) product price increases accompanied by a heavy reliance on price-promotion spending and (2) increased competition. Kellogg raised prices six times, accompanied by heavy couponing in the 3 years preceding 1994. In 1994, the company cut back on coupons, maintained restraint on pricing, and spent money on increased advertising. Kellogg was concerned about the effect on its strategy when General Mills decreased prices. Low-priced private-label cereals, mostly from Ralston Purina, also were a concern. Kellogg's choice: Keep prices high and risk a further loss of market share or lower prices at the expense of profits—with no assurance that market share would increase. For the meantime, the focus was on profitability. Arnold Langbo calculated that price maintenance and selective couponing would increase profits more than simply cutting prices across the board. He thought that Kellogg's brand equity and consumer loyalty were great enough that the public would tolerate price increases with no added value to the product. Langbo told a meeting of Wall Street analysts:

Kellogg Company Domestic Market Share

Year	1986	1987	1988	1989	1990	1991	1992	1993	1994
%	42	41	42	40	37	39	37	37	35

"There are 140 brands of cereal being bought by very loyal consumers. Some of the fastest-growing brands are the most expensive, so it's not all about price."

In the early 1990s, Kellogg and its major U.S. competitors sought to maintain higher pricing and profitability by steadily increasing their use of price-promotion spending, including lots of buy-one-get-one-free offers, known as "bogos." However, this strategy failed to stop Kellogg's continued slide in U.S. market share. In 1994, Kellogg CEO Arnold Langbo said: "In the long run, bogos don't work. They borrow share. They don't earn share."

Kellogg also was hurt by its lack of appealing new cereal products that were needed to pull up U.S. volume. Kellogg's Healthy Choice cereals, introduced in early 1994, have performed well, but the overall new-product performance by Kellogg and its competitors since the early 1980s has been, at best, unspectacular.

Kellogg's Global Markets

Unlike some companies that sought product diversification to build profits, Kellogg concentrated on marketing cereal and other food products. Eighty percent of its worldwide sales came from cereal. The company's market development took the form of expanding to foreign markets. The company entered Canada in 1914 and by 1991 had 17 cereal plants located in 15 foreign countries. Since then, the company has added Argentina, Latvia, India, and China. In 1994, Kellogg controlled 43 percent of worldwide cereal sales.

Kellogg North America led its market with a 37 percent share in 1993. It enjoyed both good product quality control and high labor productivity. It also led the market in advertising expenditures. In addition to ready-to-eat cereals, Kellogg North America offered other grain-based convenience foods: frozen dessert pies, toaster pastries, waffles, granola bars, and snacks. In 1993, new product roll-outs included Low Fat Granola Bars, Nutri-Grain Bars, new Eggo versions, Mini Eggos, and new flavors of Pop Tarts.

The best of the overseas beachheads seemed to be in the old British Empire (Britain, Ireland, Australia), where eating breakfast cereal was culturally accepted. Kellogg Europe controlled 50 percent of the market, six times the share of its nearest competitor. During 1993, the company was selected first in customer service among all British manufacturers for the fourth year in a row. Ireland was the world's top cereal consumer, but market growth potential was still great. Kellogg gained 5 percent in sales volume in Ireland during 1993. A promising new market in this division was the Republic of Latvia. In a joint venture with Adazi Food Products, Kellogg opened a new cereal plant in 1993. This was the first Western cereal enterprise in the former Soviet Union. Cereal for breakfast was not a tradition in this region, so market potential could be great. Initially, demand would be low, but competition would be zero. Kellogg was substantially increasing advertising expenditures throughout Europe, trying to interest younger people in testing the convenience of cereal for breakfast or a snack instead of a croissant or *schwartzbrot*. This strategy was successful, resulting in a strong growth in the cereal business in continental Europe in the late 1980s and early 1990s.

So far as market potential was concerned, some countries had a very low market penetration rate. Worldwide cereal consumption averaged around 2 pounds per year, compared with North America's 10 pounds. Cereal for breakfast was not yet culturally accepted in certain areas. Kellogg marketing people thought it was merely a matter of education to get these consumers turned on to eating breakfast cereal. In some countries, there also was the matter of obtaining dairy products for topping. Some countries didn't drink a lot of milk and/or have an established dairy industry or an established channel of distribution that offered refrigeration. People did not have facilities to keep milk to pour over their Corn Flakes. Kellogg had a few cultural and infrastructure problems to solve before its market potential estimates could be realized.

Kellogg Asia Pacific controlled a 47 percent market share. New plants in India and China would serve millions of potential customers, more than one-third of the world's population. Here again, market development would require effecting significant changes in the traditional tastes and preferences of local consumers. Kellogg developed specific cereal products for niche foreign markets. A high-mineral multigrain cereal was developed for the health-conscious Australians, while in Japan, where fish and rice made a traditional breakfast,

Kellogg was offering Genmai Flakes, made from whole-grain rice.

Operations in the Latin America Division covered Mexico, Central America, and South America, and Kellogg dominated this market with 78 percent market share. This market share placed Kellogg in control of the developing markets as well. A new plant was under construction near Buenos Aires, Argentina, and capacity increases occurred at the plants in Bogota, Colombia; Maracay, Venezuela; and São Paulo, Brazil. Performance for the year in Latin America was favorable for the most part. However, disappointing results in Mexico had a negative impact on the overall performance of the division.

Opportunities for future growth were quite favorable with the increased interest in health and nutrition in Latin America. Kellogg had performed many different activities in order to make consumers more aware of the importance of nutrition. Some of the activities included school nutrition education programs, which covered 300,000 children in Mexico alone, fiber symposia, and nutritional newsletters to health professionals.

In an attempt to provide consumers with additional value in its products, Kellogg added extra vitamins to the cereals in Latin Americans' diets and added zinc to products in other selected countries. This adaptation of products to the culture was one of Kellogg's ways to boost cereal consumption.

THE COMPANY TODAY

Even with intense competition and many challenges faced by Kellogg during 1993, worldwide revenues increased by 2 percent. This was the forty-ninth consecutive year for increases. In the United States alone, sales rose by 6 percent. There were 24 new product introductions worldwide. Kellogg received 40 percent of its revenues from outside the United States.

In Europe, sales decreased 8 percent due to unfavorable foreign currency exchange rates. If this problem had not occurred, sales would have been up by 4 percent. Dividends increased for the thirty-seventh consecutive year, with 10 percent growth in 1993. Price-earnings multiple remained at one of the highest levels in the food industry. However, the performance of stock was disappointing.

In 1993, Kellogg decided to divest units that did not fit with long-term strategic plans. So the British carton container and Argentinian snack food businesses were sold for a total pretax gain of $65.9 million. (Other results of operations may be found in the financial statements provided at the end of the case.)

In 1994, Kellogg followed a price-maintenance policy to provide value to consumers. The company also cut back on coupons. Since then, the company's market share has been steady.

THE FUTURE

The future for Kellogg and the ready-to-eat cereal industry looked quite favorable at the end of 1995. Demand continued in a long-term upward trend, with growth estimated at 2 to 3 percent in the United States and 5 to 7 percent overseas. This continued growth would come with the increasing recognition by consumers of the nutritional value of cereal. Domestic growth also would come with the increasing ages of Baby-Boomers from young adulthood to middle age, where cereal consumption had grown steadily.

It also appeared that the trend among competitors in the industry was to cut promotional spending. These competitors could have unbounded opportunities to establish a position in the new markets that were being entered, such as India and China.

CEO Langbo has come to the conclusion: "If this business was ever easy, it isn't anymore."

EXHIBIT A

Kellogg Company and Subsidiaries: Consolidated Balance Sheet (At December 31, in millions)

	1993	1992
Current assets		
Cash and temporary investments	$ 98.1	$ 126.3
Accounts receivable, less allowances of $6.0 and $6.2	536.8	519.1
Inventories:		
Raw materials and supplies	148.5	167.7
Finished goods and materials in process	254.6	248.7
Deferred income taxes	85.5	66.2
Prepaid expenses	121.6	108.6
Total current assets	1,245.1	1,236.6
Property		
Land	40.6	40.5
Buildings	1,065.7	1,021.2
Machinery and equipment	2,857.6	2,629.4
Construction in progress	308.6	302.6
Accumulated depreciation	(1,504.1)	(1,331.0)
Property, net	2,768.4	2,662.7
Intangible assets	59.1	53.3
Other assets	164.5	62.4
Total assets	$4,237.1	$4,015.0
Current liabilities		
Current maturities of long-term debt	$ 1.5	$ 1.9
Notes payable	386.7	210.0
Accounts payable	308.8	313.8
Accrued liabilities:		
Income taxes	65.9	104.1
Salaries and wages	76.5	78.0
Advertising and promotion	233.8	228.0
Other	141.4	135.2
Total current liabilities	1,214.6	1,071.0
Long-term debt	521.6	314.9
Nonpension postretirement benefits	450.9	407.6
Deferred income taxes	188.9	184.6
Other liabilities	147.7	91.7
Shareholders' equity		
Common stock, $.25 par value		
Authorized: 330,000,000 shares		
Issued: 310,292,753 shares in 1993 and 310,193,228 in 1992	77.6	77.5
Capital in excess of par value	72.0	69.2
Retained earnings	3,409.4	3,033.9
Treasury stock, at cost: 82,372,409 and 72,874,738 shares	(1,653.1)	(1,105.0)
Minimum pension liability adjustment	(25.3)	
Currency translation adjustment	(167.2)	(130.4)
Total shareholders' equity	1,713.4	1,945.2
Total liabilities and shareholders' equity	$4,237.1	$4,015.0

EXHIBIT B

Kellogg Company and Subsidiaries: Consolidated Earnings and Retained Earnings
(Year ended December 31, in millions, except per share amounts)

	1993	1992	1991
Net Sales	$6,295.4	$6,190.6	$5,786.6
Other revenue (deductions), net	(1.5)	36.8	14.6
	6,293.9	6,227.4	5,801.2
Cost of goods sold	2,989.0	2,987.7	2,828.7
Selling and administrative expense	2,237.5	2,140.1	1,930.0
Interest expense	33.3	29.2	58.3
	5,259.8	5,157.0	4,817.0
Earnings before income taxes and cumulative effect of accounting change	1,034.1	1,070.4	984.2
Income taxes	353.4	387.6	378.2
Earnings before cumulative effect of accounting change	680.7	682.8	606.0
Cumulative effect of change in method of accounting for postretirement benefits other than pensions—$1.05 a share (net of income tax benefit of $144.6)		(251.6)	
Net earnings—$2.94, $1.81, $2.51 a share	680.7	431.2	606.0
Retained earnings, beginning of year	3,033.9	2,889.1	2,542.4
Dividends paid—$1.32, $1.20, $1.075 a share	(305.2)	(286.4)	(259.3)
Retained earnings, end of year	$3,409.4	$3,033.9	$2,889.1

Bibliography

Cohen, Waren, "A Crunch for Cereal Makers," *U.S. News & World Report*, March 28, 1994.

Elliott, Stuart, "Consumers Take Center Stage in a Campaign to Promote the Value of a Kellogg Breakfast," *New York Times*, July 20, 1994.

Erickson, Julie Liesse, "Schroeder: Kellogg Is Popping," *Advertising Age*, August 14, 1989, p. 3.

Erickson, Julie Liesse, "Why Schroeder Is Leaving Kellogg," *Advertising Age*, September 25, 1989, p. 6.

General Mills 1994 Annual Report.

Gibson, Richard, "Head of Kellogg's U.S. Cereal Business Resigns as Part of Management Shuffle," *Wall Street Journal*, July 5, 1994, p. B7.

Gibson, Richard, "Kellogg Tries to Keep Cereal Sales Crisp as Rivals Nibble Away at Market Share," *Wall Street Journal*, November 9, 1993, p. A5B.

Gibson, Richard, "Kellogg Earnings Increased 3.5% in Third Quarter," *Wall Street Journal*, October 24, 1994, p. A9A.

Kahn, Mir Maqbool Alam, "Kellogg Reports Brisk Cereal Sales in India," *Advertising Age*, November 14, 1994, p. 60.

"Kellogg Says It Plans to Further Cut Use of Discount Programs," *Wall Street Journal*, November 14, 1994, p. B5A.

Kellogg Company 1993 Annual Report.

Kellogg Company, Value Line, Edition 10, August 1994, pp. 1468, 1476, 1485.

Liesse, Julie, "Kellogg, Alpo Top Hot New Product List," *Advertising Age*, January 4, 1993, p. 66.

Liesse, Julia, and Judann Degnoll, "Kellogg's Golden Era Flakes Away," *Advertising Age*, August 31, 1990, p. 4.

Liesse, Julia, "Gen. Mills 1, Kellogg 0," *Advertising Age*, September 20, 1993, p. 2.

Liesse, Julie, "Kellogg's Prices Go Up, Up, Up," *Advertising Age*, August 9, 1993, p. 1.

Mitchell, Russell, "Big G Is Growing Fat on Oat Cuisine," *Business Week*, September 18, 1989, p. 29.

Mitchell, Russell, "The Health Craze Has Kellogg Feeling G-R-R-Reat," *Business Week*, March 30, 1987, pp. 52–53.

Moody's Industrial Manual, Vol. 2 (New York: Moody's Investors Service, Inc., 1993), pp. 4001–4004.

"The History of Kellogg Company," Kellogg Company pamphlet, 1992.

"¿Tiene usted los Corn Flakes?" *Forbes*, January 4, 1991, p. 168.

Sellers, Patricia, "How King Kellogg Beat the Blahs," *Fortune*, August 29, 1988, pp. 55–64.

Serwer, Andrew E., "What Price Brand Loyalty," *Fortune*, January 10, 1994, pp. 103–104.

Treece, James B., and Greg Burns, "The Nervous Faces Around Kellogg's Breakfast Table," *Business Week*, July 18, 1994, p. 33.

Woodruff, David, "Winning the War of Battle Creek," *Business Week*, May 31, 1991, p. 80.

Endnote

1. A conversation with Richard E. Lovell, manager, corporate communications, Kellogg's Company Corporate Headquarters, indicated a factual error in the news item. Kellogg's strategy of reducing price-promotion spending resulted in a 1 percent market share drop at first. This leveled off at 35 percent and has remained constant since then. The authors appreciate the great assistance provided by Mr. Lovell in the preparation of this case.

Women's Undergarment Factory #8

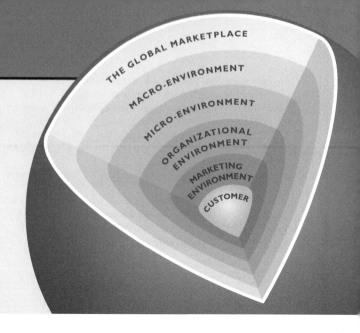

THE GLOBAL MARKETPLACE
MACRO-ENVIRONMENT
MICRO-ENVIRONMENT
ORGANIZATIONAL ENVIRONMENT
MARKETING ENVIRONMENT
CUSTOMER

This case was prepared by Katherine Campbell and Duane Helleloid, University of Maryland.

As Mr. Toomas Ruus walked down the snow-covered sidewalk toward his sixth-floor apartment in Tallinn, Estonia, he reflected on the afternoon's weekly staff meeting. The preliminary financial results for 1999 looked very good. Production was near capacity and demand was strong. The plant had successfully managed the transition from a controlled economy under the Soviet system to free markets. Nevertheless most sales were to customers from the former Soviet Union, and changing demands and new competition caused managers to constantly review their operations. (Exhibit 1 contains financial information.)

A space utilization issue was the primary topic at the meeting. During the previous summer, the managers had shut down silk-weaving operations. In the meeting, the staff expressed a wide variety of opinions regarding how the vacated 12,000-square-meter space should be utilized:

I do not think there are many opportunities for us to make use of this space. If we look to West-

ern markets, we could perhaps increase our orders, but this is still only a very small portion of our business. To be honest, the only way to increase sales in Western markets is via quality improvement—not the quantity growth that utilizing this space would allow. Although there is strong demand from Eastern markets, these are not very profitable, and results would probably not justify investment in the additional equipment required. We are already such a large plant that we probably have diseconomies of scale. Perhaps we could lease it to some other firm that would perform a manufacturing process that would provide valuable inputs for our production activities, but I do not know what that would be.

Ardo Oll, Western Marketing Manager

There are few costs involved with leaving the space idle. Although we could earn some rent by leasing this space to another firm, because it is in the middle of our factory, having strangers working under the same roof would be disruptive to our business and potentially to our employees. Rather, we should use this space to locate new equipment for narrow-woven elastic ribbons or some other profitable product.

Paul Melli, Chief Accountant

We have a huge unsatisfied Eastern market where we could sell more than we are selling today, but this market is cyclical and difficult to

EXHIBIT I

Financial Data

Balance Sheet (in million kroons[a])	As of 12/31/99	As of 12/31/98	As of 12/31/97
Assets			
Fixed Assets	167	165	171
Inventory	88	85	81
Accounts Receivable	62	50	36
Cash and Liquid Assets	66	53	42
Total Assets	383	353	330
Liabilities			
Long-Term Debt	2	2	2
Accounts Payable	9	9	10
Other Short-Term Liabilities	3	5	6
Provision for Bad Debt	10	6	6
Total Liabilities	24	22	24
Reserve Capital (owners' equity)	359	331	306

Income Statement (in million kroons[a])	1999	1998	1997
Revenue			
Garment Production	338	310	291
Sale of Equipment, Income from Heat/Water Services	38	35	20
Total Revenue	376	345	311
Expenses			
Payments to Suppliers of Materials and Services	104	96	94
Expenses of the Factory	205	195	167
Total Expenses	309	291	261
Gross Profits	67	54	50
Taxes on Profits	30	24	23
Net Profit	37	30	27

[a]Approximate exchange rates: 12 kroons per U.S. dollar
                                    19 kroons per British pound
                                    8 kroons per German mark

Source: Audited financial statements for 1997 and 1998; internal numbers for 1999.

forecast. Thus, I would be reluctant to encourage investment in new machinery that would increase production in any department—it is just too hazardous. For the time being, we should concentrate all investments in improving and modernizing our existing facilities. Our Eastern customers are beginning to become more picky about quality issues, and we need to be able to meet their future expectations. Perhaps it would be possible to convert the space from the silk mills into a more thorough quality department.

Aare Mullen, Eastern Marketing Manager

For me as a technologist, it is very painful to see such a large production space idle when we have inventory and material crowding our machinery elsewhere. These old machines produced very good products for many years and were very well maintained. Now they are becoming rusty and serving only as a home for spiders. We should either find some way to use them, or sell them as scrap and use this space for other machines that can be used productively. We have been thinking of purchasing circular knitting machines that could make briefs and some other products without the need to sew individual panels of fabric together. This would not only allow us to make higher quality products, but it would reduce the work-in-process inventory between the component manufacturing and sewing. Alternatively, we could use this space to expand production of our cash cow—elastic lace.

Siim Kangas, Technical Director

I know this sounds odd coming from me, but I think we should be producing less and not more. Since we gained our freedom from the State Planning Authorities, we have decreased production and employment and increased our profits. By closing operations that consumed more valuable resources than they produced, like the silk-weaving department, we have become a better organization. We should get rid of the idle equipment and generate revenue from the space. I think if we do more careful analyses we will find that other operations should also be closed. We must become more focused in what we do. Just recently I reduced our machinery shop from 45 people to 10. It simply makes no sense anymore for us to make our own carts and bicycles when these goods can be purchased more cheaply. Under central planning, it was easier to make our own bicycles for use within the factory than it was to obtain them from Gosplan. We could sell some of the machine shop equipment for a nice profit today. If we do a better job of determining which resources are productive and which are wasted, we can increase our profits even more.

Uno Tammerk, Manufacturing Manager

Toomas enjoyed the opportunity to reflect during his long commute home. The factory was located 20 km outside of Estonia's capital city of Tallinn, in the small town of Paldiila. The factory was the town for all practical purposes. Most residents worked at the factory. During Soviet times, the factory supplied heat and water as well as daycare facilities and most other municipal services for the entire town. Toomas liked the excitement of

Tallinn and enjoyed being away from issues that would be constantly just out his window if he lived in Paldiila. On this day, however, like many others recently, the issues were following him home. In many ways, it was easier for the plant's former managers who had worked under the Soviet system: Just follow the plan, or figure out how to get around the plan. Now he was responsible for working with employees to figure out what the plan should be. This was both liberating and stressful. (Exhibit 2 shows the factory's layout. Exhibit 3 presents the organization chart. Background information on Estonia, including a map, is found in Appendix 1.)

FACTORY BACKGROUND

Women's Undergarment Factory #8 (hereafter referred to as "WUF#8" or "the factory") was built from 1962 to 1968. It produced knitted materials (components) that were supplied as inputs to other factories producing complete women's undergarments. The central planning authorities viewed production of the components (e.g., cloth, lace, and elastic) as capital intensive and affording significant economies of scale. Thus, they deemed a large plant as appropriate for this operation. Sewing these components into garments was more labor intensive and took place at many smaller geographically dispersed facilities throughout the country. A secondary purpose of the factory was to produce finished goods for local sale.

The factory was one of the largest undergarment facilities in the world. It was probably also the most vertically integrated. Workers took thread with various chemical properties and produced lace, fabric, elastic, and completed garments. In 1999, the plant produced 4 million finished undergarments under the Agata brand and was the primary supplier for undergarment components to about 300 sewing factories in the Soviet Union. These sewing factories produced another 91 million finished undergarments. The factory had started selling some finished undergarments to firms in Western Europe, but it sold only 600,000 such items in 1999. The plant employed just over 3,000 people involved in everything from sewing and machinery operation to support services like shipping, facility maintenance, and accounting. All production took place in a one-floor, 100,000-square-meter, windowless building.

EXHIBIT 2

Factory Layout

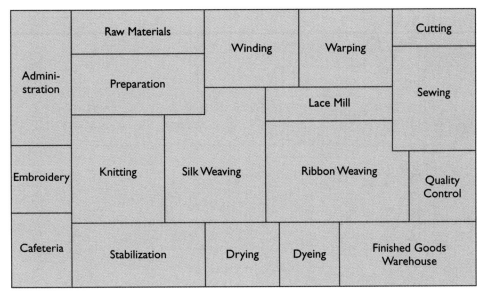

Note: Total building size is approximately 100,000 square meters (250 meters wide and 400 meters long).
Source: Author's sketch.

Given its monopoly position in the production of undergarment components under the Soviet system, the main objective of the plant was quantity of production. Quality concerns were secondary, and there was no need for the plant to make marketing decisions or obtain customer feedback. The central Soviet planning authority made all product mix and sales decisions, as well as determined suppliers. Nevertheless, a strong informal network existed between the factory's managers and its suppliers and sewing factory customers. Together they developed new fabrics and designs. They often collaborated in supplying central authorities with the (mis)information that would best serve their mutual purposes.

INDEPENDENCE AND RESTRUCTURING

The independence of Estonia caused minimal disruptions for WUF#8. Its monopoly position insulated WUF#8 from the dramatic changes and tumultuous upheaval many other enterprises experienced.

Demand for undergarments was strong, and most of the sewing factories remained loyal customers of bulk materials. The loyalty was partially the result of historic relationships and familiarity with the factory's products and partly because few other suppliers were able to offer similar components. Although individual components like lace or elastic were available from other sources, consistent dyes and similar stretching characteristics from multiple manufacturers' components would be difficult to achieve. Without matched components, quality would suffer. The factory had not experienced much difficulty with its suppliers. Many suppliers did not produce sufficient quality for export to Western markets and wanted to keep existing customers.

The managers closed the silk-weaving department during the summer of 1999 due to low profitability and declining sales. An economic analysis showed that silk fabric could be purchased for about 20 percent of the factory's production cost. Weakening demand for silk products motivated the analysis, suggesting that the factory received some market feedback. Whether the end consumers

EXHIBIT 3

Factory Organization

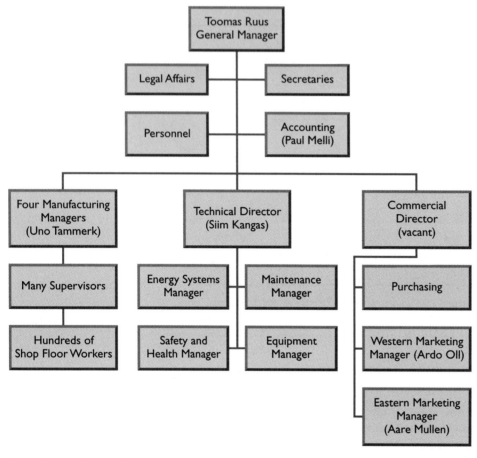

Source: Company documents.

were in general preferring other fabrics to silk, or whether they were instead purchasing imported silk products, was unclear. Several members of the marketing staff were concerned, however, that at the "high" end of the market consumers were purchasing finished undergarments from foreign manufacturers. In the most exclusive shops in Moscow and St. Petersburg, foreign-made products with foreign labels (typically French) were becoming more common. Some of these were fine French products; others were high-quality products from Asian manufacturers that bore a French-sounding name and packaging. After the silk-weaving department closed, some supervisors felt the equipment and space should be left unutilized to provide a symbolic reminder of what could happen to other

jobs if the factory was not responsive to market demands for high quality and competitively priced goods.

OPERATING CONDITIONS

Toomas Ruus reported to a board of directors that included himself, the factory's commercial director, two representatives from the employees' union, and five outside directors. The outside directors were senior managers at other Estonian firms and banks. The chairman of the board was the president of one of Estonia's largest banks, which held approximately 5 percent of the outstanding shares. The board met quarterly to review performance and generally supported the views and proposals of Toomas and his management team. (The decision to close the silk-weaving department was reported to the board after the fact, with little discussion. A decision to reallocate the space for some other use would not likely be reviewed by the board, unless it involved a significant expenditure.) Toomas also sat on the boards of three of the factory's directors' firms.

Procurement

The primary raw materials used were cotton thread and three types of synthetic fibers: nylon, polyurethane, and polyester. A chemical fiber plant in Latvia that was known for its poor quality supplied over 80 percent of the nylon; approximately one-third of all nylon shipments were barely useable. Poor-quality nylon was used for inexpensive products. Several Western companies provided the rest, which was used for the highest quality products and for all products that were produced for Western markets. Nylon from Western sources was three times as expensive, although the factory had attempted to enter into long-term contracts with several Western firms to supply a higher portion of its nylon requirements.

Similarly, polyurethane with marginal quality was supplied by a Russian plant. Around a quarter of the polyurethane, with both higher quality and price, was purchased from DuPont. Although all polyurethane could be obtained from Western sources, the added cost wasn't worth it. In the words of the manufacturing manager, Uno Tammerk, "The poor quality of the nylon overshadows any improvements that could be made by switching suppliers of polyurethane. So, we might as well save the money." Cotton, polyester, silk, as well as all other materials, chemicals, and dyes were generally available at acceptable quality levels.

Production

Turning thread into garments involved eight separate operations: winding, warping, knitting, weaving, dyeing, stabilization/preparation, cutting, and sewing. During the warping and winding processes, fibers were checked for quality and wound onto large spools. From the spools, the thread was either knitted (for fabrics and laces) or woven (ribbons and elastic), with fully automated machinery. All material was then dyed, dried, stretched, and stabilized. The dyeing process presented challenges, because different fibers and fabrics accepted dye and retained color somewhat differently. Similar coloration for all components (e.g., lace, elastic, fabric) was important in the final product.

After fabric preparation was complete, materials sold to sewing factories in the East were bundled for shipment. Material that WUF#8 sewed into final goods was measured, cut to the appropriate size, and sent to the sewing department. About 1,000 women worked in the sewing department, with each doing a specific function (e.g., sewing lace onto the edges of a brassiere). Most had been working at the factory for over 20 years, and tended to think and act as if they were still in Soviet times. It was hard to get them to focus on quality, or to improve efficiency. Wages were around 3,500 kroons per month (about $300), and there was an ample supply of similarly unskilled labor in the area. During Soviet times, workers were strictly paid by salary, with no incentives for either quality or quantity of production.

Capital Equipment

The factory's machinery ranged in age from 1 to 25 years. Because of the factory's scale and the cost of downtime, it was not feasible to bring entirely new machinery into a department all at once. The cutting area was a good example of the consequences of this replacement strategy. Cutting machines that were 20 years old and manually operated were located right next to new computer-controlled laser cutting machines that worked automatically with algorithms for optimizing fabric utilization. Other machines in the cutting department fell within this range, all with slightly different technology. This mix created difficulties. First, the machines had greatly different cycle times, making coordination and flow between machines difficult. Second, they often required slightly different grades of input. A fine thin fabric could tear in the older machines, for example, which were designed for thicker, sturdier fabrics. In contrast, a fabric of uneven thickness (i.e., low quality) could work well in an older machine, but jam a new one. The quality of output also varied, with some machines producing much rougher edges. Depending upon the lace or ribbon that would be sewn onto the fabric, rough edges might or might not matter in the end. Regardless of the machinery used, when one color batch of material was being cut, the full range of sizes needed to be cut. Because this was virtually impossible to schedule perfectly, excess components of various colors and sizes were typically sitting around until they could be matched with another batch. Similar situations occurred in knitting, weaving, and other departments, although perhaps the consequences were not quite as pronounced.

The factory had a strong balance sheet and could obtain additional debt if it wanted to undertake extensive modernization. The strong demand, while creating an incentive to invest in new machinery, had also made Toomas reluctant to shut down existing equipment and suffer the lost sales that would result from downtime. If WUF#8 proved unable to meet the sewing factories' demand, they might turn to other sources in Asia for components. Once they had found other sources, it might be difficult to recapture their business.

A factory in western Russia that made canvas tarps and heavy-duty clothes for fishermen and construction workers had recently closed. The equipment in the plant was available for purchase at scrap metal prices. Toomas and two of the production managers visited the plant and found most of the equipment to be very usable, but generally 10 to 20 years old. They purchased 300 sewing machines, because the models were similar to those used at WUF#8. As their own machines broke, they thought they might use these for replacement parts. They could also use them to increase production of finished goods. Additional sewing and cutting machines were available, but there was no place to store them. Toomas was reluctant to purchase or install much of this equipment, preferring that time and effort instead be focused on selecting and installing new, state-of-the-art equipment.

Eastern Markets

The former Soviet Union was the primary market for WUF#8. (Exhibit 4 presents data on the prod-

EXHIBIT 4

Sales Distribution

Revenue by Product Type	
Fabric and Embroidered Fabric	31%
Elastic Material	18%
Other Components (e.g., ribbon, decorative lace)	23%
Finished Undergarments	28%
Revenue by Geographic Region	
Baltic Countries	28%
Russia	21%
Ukraine	16%
Belarus	15%
Western Europe	11%
Other Countries of the Former Soviet Union	9%

Source: Company documents.

uct mix and geographic location of sales.) Sales of bulk materials to sewing factories comprised the majority of sales. Once sold to the sewing factories, most of the materials supplied by WUF#8 were cut and sewn to make undergarments. The sewing factories typically produced a wide range of finished goods, including outer garments (e.g., shirts, blouses, pants, dresses) for local retailers. Over the past few years, some of these sewing factories changed their overall pattern of orders, choosing to focus on a more narrow product line. A couple of sewing factories closed due to inefficiency and competition from Asian firms.

WUF#8 also produced about 4 million Agata brand finished undergarments per year for direct sale to stores in western Russia, Estonia, Latvia, and Lithuania. Thus, it competed with several sewing factories in western Russia and one in Latvia. These sewing factories purchased bulk materials from WUF#8 and made virtually identical products (although under different labels). In Soviet times, competition between WUF#8 and its customer sewing factories was not a problem—demand generally exceeded supply. Products were marketed under different brands, and stores preferred providing the appearance of competition. The director of Eastern marketing, Aare Mullen, described the arrangement as follows:

> There is no real competition between our Agata products and the goods produced from our components by local sewing firms—the market is still very large and unfilled. As long as there is excess demand, we can all make money. We have also attempted to position the Agata brand as higher quality, with slightly higher prices than most Eastern products. By doing so, we also minimize direct competition. We generally take the better quality bulk materials for our own use and sell the lesser quality materials to the other sewing factories. Of course we do not sell them garbage—quality levels that they have historically accepted are used as a minimum. We are now working very hard to improve overall quality of production, and some sewing factories have mentioned that they notice an improvement in quality. Although we earn much larger margins on finished articles than the bulk material, we are hesitant to increase production of finished articles too much. We do not want to make our bulk material customers upset, because the majority of profits are earned from these sales.

Western Markets

Since Estonian independence, WUF#8 had tried to increase sales of finished undergarments to Western countries. It was most successful in selling to several large retailers in Sweden and Finland. The retailers required that the articles be labeled with their own store brands. The retailers viewed WUF#8 as one of many suppliers that competed on cost and delivery time. If the factory was able to continue to meet customers' expectations, it might be able to double or triple orders from these retailers.

Undergarment demand in the West was relatively stable and proportional to the population in each country. Western women purchased six to eight new undergarments per year; historic shortages meant that the average in the former Soviet Union was less than half this number. The manufacturing cost at a Western plant ran from $5 to $10, and retail prices were two to four times cost. Western prices varied by season, however, and discounts dramatically lowered prices. The same article with the same brand name could be three to four times more expensive in a fancy Swedish store than in a discount shop in Britain. In contrast, Agata products sold by Eastern retailers for about $3.

From its efforts to sell products in Western markets, WUF#8 picked up some interesting ideas. Samples given to Western buyers had come back with letters detailing required improvements. Sometimes these involved dyes or sewing technique; other times, they involved basic aspects of the design and materials. Even if an order never came from the exchange, it provided valuable information about customer expectations in the West. By being in contact with Western customers, WUF#8 expected it could be in a leading position in Eastern markets when these customers demanded similar improvements.

Competitors

The sewing factories in the former Soviet Union continued to be loyal customers. Although several Asian firms produced similar bulk materials, these suppliers had not actively marketed their products to the sewing factories. Through improved product quality and more efficient machinery, WUF#8's managers intended to stay ahead of competitors in the bulk materials market. If wage demands and other costs in Estonia rose too high, however, Asian firms could gain a cost advantage.

In finished goods, the factory's primary competitors in Eastern markets were its customers. The managers realized that they must maintain a careful balance, and by positioning Agata at the higher end, hoped to avoid conflict.

Western markets presented a more challenging environment. The Agata brand was unrecognized outside the local area. WUF#8 couldn't produce more than a few million articles at the quality required by Western buyers. For the private-label buyers, the primary competitors were Asian firms. The factory's scale gave it some advantages over these firms, because it could easily supply the entire demand of a large retailer. (Typically retailers negotiated with many different Asian firms, or utilized a broker.)

The managers had no direct knowledge of WUF#8's Eastern customers' selling finished undergarments in the West. Like WUF#8, however, these factories could export to the higher margin Western markets if their quality were sufficient. WUF#8 had noticed a recent large increase in orders from a Ukrainian sewing factory, and having no reason to believe that demand in the Ukraine had suddenly risen, Aare was concerned that this plant might be selling finished goods outside the Ukraine.

Atbalsts

Atbalsts, a Latvian firm, was both a customer and competitor of WUF#8. A Swedish company, Tetonia AB, purchased Atbalsts in 1993. Relations between WUF#8 and Atbalsts remained very good. Lately, however, Atbalsts' strategic decisions came from Sweden. Some of the Latvian managers had joked that this was like old times, only orders came from Swedes rather than Russians.

Atbalsts manufactured about 3 million articles per year and was running at about 80 percent of capacity. Aare Mullen estimated that 70 percent of Atbalsts' sales were to Baltic markets with bulk materials purchased from WUF#8. The remaining 30 percent of Atbalsts' sales were to Tetonia, which then sold the articles in Scandinavia under its brand names. The bulk material input for garments going to Tetonia was supplied from Sweden. Whereas Tetonia's factories in Sweden were automated, the Atbalsts factory was still quite labor intensive.

Toomas was under the general opinion that Tetonia purchased Atbalsts to take advantage of low labor costs. It was able to purchase an entire plant full of workers only a 1-hour flight away for less than the cost of a few machines. Although Atbalsts was likely to continue making and marketing products in the Baltic countries, Tetonia earned much higher margins by selling products through its Swedish distribution system. If Tetonia changed Atbalsts' production to more articles for Western markets, Atbalsts would become a less important competitor for WUF#8 in the East. Unless WUF#8's quality of bulk goods improved, however, it would lose Atbalsts as a customer.

SPACE ALLOCATION CONCERNS

What to do with the space from the silk-weaving department had been foremost in managers' minds. If the space had been at one corner of the factory, another firm could easily rent the space, but its location in the center of the factory complicated matters.

Toomas personally wanted to see shining new computer-controlled machines purring away, producing some high-margin product in the space. What that product would be, however, he didn't know. In addition, such an investment would mean at least a 10- to 20-year commitment. Given uncertainties in the Eastern and Western markets, he wondered if it was rational to make such a big financial commitment. Bulk materials would only be profitable as long as the sewing factories' finished goods were competitive with imported articles from low-wage countries. WUF#8 could invest in more sewing capacity for the Eastern market, but that could potentially harm relations with its sewing factory customers. Investing in sewing capacity for Western markets was also risky because the marketing team still had not made any

EXHIBIT 5

Profit Margins

Average Profit Margins by Product Type and Market	
Finished Undergarments to Western Europe	60%
Finished Undergarments in Eastern Markets[a]	
Brassieres	27%
Briefs	21%
Body Shapers and Exotic Articles	39%
Bulk Materials in the Eastern Markets	
Fabric	12%
Ribbons and Strap Material	14%
Lace	17%
Elastic Material	19%

[a]Profit margins in the Baltic countries tend to be higher than in other Eastern markets. This is a result of higher sales prices, lower transportation costs, and less significant "facilitating payments" to customs or shipping officials.
Source: Company documents.

significant inroads in the West. (Exhibit 5 presents estimated margins on different products.)

One of the best and worst things about the Estonian economy was its rapid growth and modernization. Of all the countries of the former Soviet Union, Estonia had made the most progress toward westernization. It was the only country in the former Soviet Union on the fast track for inclusion in the European Union. This was good for the economy and his employees. But, as Estonian wages and prices of other inputs rose toward Western European levels, WUF#8's cost advantages could diminish.

Decisions could also have unintended consequences. Toomas had often worried that if the factory increased production of the Agata brand, consumers might demand higher quality from the sewing factories, who in turn would demand higher quality bulk materials from WUF#8. Yet the quality of bulk materials only partly depended on WUF#8's operations, people, and equipment; the quality of the externally purchased basic thread inputs affected operations and the quality of the end product.

He really could not afford, though, to wait and just see what happened: He and his managers needed to make decisions that would help them create and define their future competitive position. What was needed right now was some decision on what to do with the equipment and space from the silk-weaving department. As much as he tried to push responsibility down and make decisions collaboratively, old habits from the Soviet times remained; the boss ultimately was expected to make a decision. His management team had given him their input, and they were now looking to him for leadership in reallocating this space.

APPENDIX I

Background on Estonia

In the 800 years leading up to the twentieth century, portions of Estonia were ruled by Germans, Russians, Danes, Swedes, and Poles at various points in its history. In 1918, following the Bolshevik Revolution in Russia, Estonia declared its independence and fought a War of Independence against Russian and German troops. For the next 22 years, Estonia was governed by a variety of leaders and parties, and did not have a particularly stable democracy. The economic depression in the West, and the politically charged environment in the years leading to World War II, buffeted the small country. Estonia was invaded by Russia in 1940 and remained under Soviet rule until 1991. During this time, the government and economy were largely controlled by Russian nationals sent by Moscow. The Estonian language, which is most similar to Finnish, became secondary to Russian in most formal settings.

Estonia regained its independence in 1991 as a result of the breakup of the Soviet Union. Since then it has been generally seen as the most Western and free-market oriented of the former Soviet territories. It maintains close ties with Finland to the north and has attracted foreign investment from Scandinavia and Western Europe. Given its proximity to St. Petersburg, and a large Russian minority, it still has strong economic and political ties to western Russia. It is likely to be the first of the former Soviet territories to be admitted to the European Union, and it has become a member of the UN, WTO, and numerous other intergovernmental organizations.

A good source of additional information is the official Estonian government Web site, in English: www.riik.ee/en. This Web pages also provides links to English newspapers. The following data is from the CIA *World Fact Book:* www.cia.gov/cia/publications/factbook/geos/en.html

Geography

Location: Eastern Europe, bordering the Baltic Sea and Gulf of Finland, between Latvia and Russia

Area: *total:* 45,226 sq km

  land: 43,211 sq km (includes 1,520 islands in the Baltic Sea)

  water: 2,015 sq km

Area—comparative: slightly smaller than New Hampshire and Vermont combined

Climate: maritime, wet, moderate winters, cool summers

Terrain: marshy, lowlands

Natural resources: shale oil, peat, phosphorite, amber, cambrian blue clay, limestone, dolomite, arable land

Land use: *arable land:* 25%

  permanent crops: 0%

  permanent pastures: 11%

  forests and woodland: 44%

  other: 20% (1996 est.)

Irrigated land: 110 sq km (1996 est.)

Natural hazards: flooding occurs frequently in the spring

Environment—current issues: air heavily polluted with sulfur dioxide from oil-shale burning power plants in northeast; contamination of soil and groundwater with petroleum products, chemicals at former Soviet military bases; Estonia has more than 1,400 natural and manmade lakes, the smaller of which in agricultural areas are heavily affected by organic waste; coastal sea water is polluted in many locations.

People

Population: 1,431,471 (July 2000 est.)

Age structure:

  0–14 years: 18% (male 129,204; female 124,269)

  15–64 years: 68% (male 466,960; female 503,233)

  65 years and over: 14% (male 67,781; female 140,024) (2000 est.)

Population growth rate: −0.59% (2000 est.)

Life expectancy at birth:

>*male:* 63.4 years
>
>*female:* 75.79 years (2000 est.)

Total fertility rate: 1.19 children born/woman (2000 est.)

Ethnic groups: Estonian 65.1%, Russian 28.1%, Ukrainian 2.5%, Byelorussian 1.5%, Finn 1%, other 1.8% (1998)

Religions: Evangelical Lutheran, Russian Orthodox, Estonian Orthodox, Baptist, Methodist, Seventh-Day Adventist, Roman Catholic, Pentecostal, Word of Life, Jewish

Languages: Estonian (official), Russian, Ukrainian, English, Finnish, other

Literacy: 100%

Government

Government type: parliamentary democracy

Capital: Tallinn

Administrative divisions: 15 counties

Independence: 6 September 1991 (from Soviet Union)

National holiday: Independence Day, 24 February (1918)

Constitution: adopted 28 June 1992

Legal system: based on civil law system; no judicial review of legislative acts

Suffrage: 18 years of age; universal for all Estonian citizens

Executive branch:

>*chief of state:* President Lennart MERI (since 5 October 1992)
>
>*head of government:* Prime Minister Mart LAAR (since 29 March 1999)
>
>*cabinet:* Council of Ministers appointed by the prime minister, approved by Parliament
>
>*elections:* president elected by Parliament for a five-year term

Legislative branch: unicameral Parliament or Riigikogu (101 seats; elected by popular vote to serve 4 year terms)

Judicial branch: National Court, chairman appointed by Parliament for life

International organization participation: BIS, CBSS, CCC, CE, EAPC, EBRD, ECE, EU (applicant), FAO, IAEA, IBRD, ICAO, ICFTU, ICRM, IFC, IFRCS, IHO, ILO, IMF, IMO, Interpol, IOC, IOM (observer), ISO (correspondent), ITU, OPCW, OSCE, PFP, UN, UNCTAD, UNESCO, UNMIBH, UNMIK, UNTSO, UPU, WEU (associate partner), WHO, WIPO, WMO, WTO

Economy

Economy—overview: In 1999, Estonia experienced its worst year economically since it regained independence in 1991 largely because of the impact of the August 1998 Russian financial crisis. Estonia joined the WTO in November 1999—the second Baltic state to join—and continued its EU accession talks. GDP is forecast to grow 4% in 2000. Privatization of energy, telecommunications, railways, and other state-owned companies will continue in 2000. Estonia expects to complete its preparations for EU membership by the end of 2002.

GDP: purchasing power parity −$7.9 billion (1999 est.)

GDP—real growth rate: −0.5% (1999 est.)

GDP—per capita: purchasing power parity −$5,600 (1999 est.)

GDP—composition by sector:

>*agriculture:* 3.6%
>
>*industry:* 30.7%
>
>*services:* 65.7% (1999)

Population below poverty line: 6.3% (1994 est.)

Inflation rate (consumer prices): 3.7% (1999 est.)

Labor force: 785,500 (1999 est.)

Labor force—by occupation: industry 20%, agriculture and forestry 11%, services 69% (1999 est.)

Unemployment rate: 11.7% (1999 est.)

Budget: *revenues:* $1.37 billion

        expenditures: $1.37 billion, including capital expenditures

Industries: oil shale, shipbuilding, phosphates, electric motors, excavators, cement, furniture, clothing, textiles, paper, shoes, apparel

Industrial production growth rate: 3% (1996 est.)

Agriculture—products: potatoes, fruits, vegetables; livestock and dairy products; fish

Exports: $2.5 billion (f.o.b., 1999)

Exports—commodities: machinery and appliances 19%, wood products 15%, textiles 13%, food products 12%, metals 10%, chemical products 8% (1999)

Exports—partners: Sweden 19.3%, Finland 18.8%, Russia 8.8%, Latvia 8.8%, Germany 7.3%, US 2.5% (1999)

Imports: $3.4 billion (f.o.b., 1999)

Imports—commodities: machinery and appliances 26%, foodstuffs 15%, chemical products 10%, metal products 9%, textiles 8% (1999)

Imports—partners: Finland 23%, Russia 13.2%, Sweden 10%, Germany 9.1%, US 4.7% (1999)

Debt—external: $270 million (January 1996)

Economic aid—recipient: $137.3 million (1995)

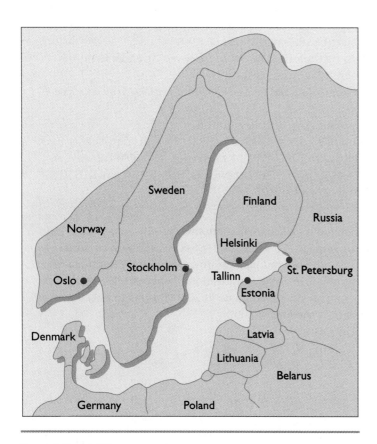

Source: Author sketch.

America Online

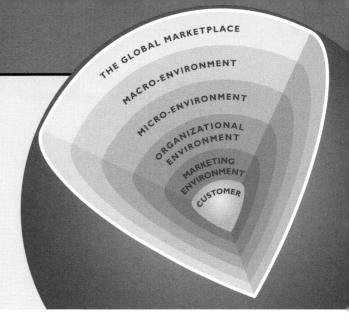

THE GLOBAL MARKETPLACE
MACRO-ENVIRONMENT
MICRO-ENVIRONMENT
ORGANIZATIONAL ENVIRONMENT
MARKETING ENVIRONMENT
CUSTOMER

This case was prepared by Natalya V. Delcoure, Lawrence R. Jauch, and John L. Scott of Northeast Louisiana University.

America Online, Inc. (NYSE: AOL), was founded in 1985. This media company, with headquarters in Dulles, Virginia, has more than 10 million members and currently operates in the United States, Canada, the United Kingdom, France, and Germany. AOL provides on-line services including electronic mail, on-line conferencing, Internet access, news, magazines, sports, weather, stock quotes, mutual fund transactions, software files, games, computing support, and on-line classes.

According to the company, its mission is "to lead the development of a new interactive medium that eliminates traditional boundaries between people and places to create a new kind of interactive global community that holds the potential to change the way people obtain information, communicate with one another, buy products and services, and learn."

To accomplish this mission, the company's strategy is to continue investment in the growth of its subscriber base, pursue related business opportunities often through joint ventures and acquisitions, provide a full range of interactive services, and maintain technological flexibility.

AOL's rapid growth and community orientation have made it the most popular, easiest, and well-known way for consumers to get on-line. In December 1996, AOL had 8.5 million member sessions a day, 7 million e-mails sent to 12 million recipients a day, and it accounted for approximately $750,000 per day in merchandise transactions.

However, AOL has not been trouble-free. On August 7, 1996, AOL threw 6 million subscribers off line for 19 hours due to software problems. America Online revealed that the glitch resulted from an error made by its working subsidiary, ANS Co., in reconfiguring software and from a bug in router software. The error cost AOL $3 million in rebates. On January 8, 1997, America Online suffered a partial outage that forced it to shut down half its system for 4 hours to find a problem. The problem was with an interface in a router device, which manages the flow of data in the network. The outage drew front-page headlines around the world, as millions of users were unable to access electronic mail, the Internet, and a variety of services and publications on-line for nearly a day.

AMERICA ONLINE COMPANY PROFILE

America Online emerged from a firm founded in the early 1980s as Control Video Corp., aimed to create an on-line service that specialized in games.

It failed to meet strong competition from the Apple II and Commodore 64. Control Video was reorganized as Quantum Computer Services and became a custom developer of online services for other companies. Over time, Quantum managed to persuade Tandy Corp. and Apple Computers to offer a new service called Applelink Personal Edition. At the last minute, Apple withdrew from the deal and left Quantum holding a lot of software it had developed expressly for Applelink. In 1989, Quantum was only scraping by, and it did not have much money for splashy ad campaigns to attract computer users to its new service—America Online. So it came on the market with a unique approach, which was to blanket the countryside with diskettes containing America Online software. As the years went by, the company changed the way it accounted for the costs of acquiring subscribers and its pricing plans, but America Online, Inc., had never actually made any money in its entire history. At the same time, America Online had positioned itself apart from traditional print and television companies as the first "digital media company." Similar to television, the company produces digital content and distributes it digitally and allows a customer to interact digitally.

AOL Organization

AOL Corporation now oversees the operations of several subsidiaries and three divisions: AOL Networks, ANS Access, and AOL Studios. The corporation comprises the core business functions of finance, human resources, legal affairs, corporate communications, corporate development, and technology. AOL Technologies is responsible for delivering research, development, network/data-center operations, and member support to the other America Online divisions, technology licensees, and joint-venture partners. The group is also responsible for support functions—including technical support, billing, and sales.

AOL Networks is responsible for extending the AOL brand into the market, developing new revenue streams, advertising, and online transactions. AOL Networks is led by Robert Pittman, president, formerly managing partner and CEO of Century 21 and cofounder of MTV Network.

ANS Access is responsible for the telecommunications network. The network consists of more than 160,000 modems connecting 472 cities in the United States and 152 cities internationally. Nearly 85 percent of the American population can dial into AOLNet on a local number. For America Online's members who travel, GlobalNet offers access in approximately 230 additional cities in 83 countries. The ANS technical team is responsible for architecture, design, development, installation, management, and maintenance of hardware and software for the nationwide corporate data networks and Internet backbone by which communications take place.

AOL Studios, formerly AOL Productions, runs AOL's innovative chat (iChatco), games (INN), local (Digital City), and independent (Greenhouse) programming properties. AOL Studios is the newest division in AOL. It is working on development of leading-edge technology for broadband and midband distribution, interactive brands that can be extended into other media properties such as TV and radio, and managing joint ventures with companies including Time-Warner and CapCities/ABC. WorldPlay, built from ImagiNation Network entertainment, is the provider of computer on-line games for AOL. ImagiNation Network was founded in 1991 and became an independent subsidiary of AOL in 1996.

Digital City provides local programming, news, services, chat rooms, and commerce to AOL members as well as to the Internet at large. To date, Digital City has been launched nationally in Washington, D.C., Boston, Philadelphia, Atlanta, San Francisco, and Los Angeles. Digital City planned to expand to over 40 cities in 1997. Digital City, Inc., is owned by Digital City LP. AOL owns a majority interest in that entity, and the Tribune Company owns the remaining interest.

Advanced CO+RE Systems, Inc., a wholly owned subsidiary of America Online, provides network services for AOLnet, together with Sprint Corporation and BBN Corporation. Through this subsidiary, America Online designs, develops, and operates high-performance wide-area networks for business, research, education, and government organizations.

In February 1996, AOL merged with the Johnson-Grace Company, a leading developer of compression technology and multimedia development and delivery tools. Using the Johnson-Grace technology, America Online is able to deliver the data-intensive graphics and audio and video capabilities using narrow-band technologies, even over the slower-speed modems currently used by most AOL members.

2Market, Inc., is a joint venture of America Online, Apple Computer, and Medior. It provides retail catalog shopping CD-ROMs that include on-line ordering capabilities. In 1997, America Online, along with Netscape Communications and Disney's ABC unit, announced plans to launch ABCNEWS.com, a 24-hour news service.

Since the beginning of 1995, the company also acquired Advanced Network and Services, Inc. (ANS), Ubique, Ltd., Navisoft, Inc., Global Network Navigator, Inc. (GNN), BookLink Technologies, Inc., and Redgate Communications Corporation. ANS was used to build the AOLNet telephone network and has now been traded to WorldCom in return for CompuServe. (This transaction is discussed more fully later.) Ubique, Ltd., was an Israeli company that developed unique and personable ways to interact over the Internet, notably Virtual Places. Navisoft, Inc., made software such as that which allowed AOL's users to author Web pages. GNN was AOL's flat-rate full Web service provider. However, AOL's flat-rate pricing scheme rendered GNN redundant. BookLink Technologies, Inc., produced software to browse the Web. Redgate Communications Corporation was a multimedia services corporation with a specialization in using multimedia in marketing.

AOL is also planning to go in to the bookselling business in a joint venture with Barnes & Noble, but the timing is still uncertain.

AOL Marketing

The goals of the firm's consumer marketing programs are to increase the general visibility of America Online and to make it easy for customers to experiment with and subscribe to its services. AOL attracts new subscribers through independent marketing programs such as direct mail, disk inserts and inserts in publications, advertising, and a variety of comarketing efforts. The company has entered into comarketing agreements with numerous personal computer hardware, software, and peripheral production companies, as well as with certain of its media partners. These companies bundle America Online software with their products and cater to the needs of a specific audience.

America Online also has been expanding into business-to-business markets, using AOL's network

to provide customized network solutions to both individual businesses and professional communities and industries. These private AOLs (the PAOLs) offer the ease of use America Online is known for, as well as customized features and functionality accessible only by preauthorized users, access to the fleet of AOL distribution platforms, secure communications, and information. The company offers these products using a direct salesforce and direct marketing and through resellers and system integrators.

America Online uses specialized retention programs designed to increase customer loyalty and satisfaction and to maximize customer subscription life. These retention programs include regularly scheduled on-line events and conferences; the regular addition of new content, services, and software programs; and on-line promotions of upcoming on-line events and new features. The firm also provides a variety of support mechanisms such as on-line technical support and telephone support services.

In May 1995, America Online introduced its Web browser, which provides integrated World Wide Web access within the AOL services. The integrated approach allows the user to seamlessly use the full suite of America Online features, including chat room, e-mail gateways and mailing lists, File Transfer Protocol, USENET newsgroups, WAIS, and Gopher.

In the summer of 1997, America Online planned to offer its 8 million members a three-dimensional gaming world, CyberPark. The company will try to compete with such heavyweights as Microsoft, the Internet Gaming Zone site, and MCI, which will launch a service in 1997 that allows computer users to play their favorite CD-ROM games. The projected earnings are expected to reach $127 million in 1997, but there are still some technical problems to overcome and the uncertainty of how much to charge future users.

America Online has included international market expansion in its strategy to gain competitive advantage. In April 1995, AOL entered into a joint venture with Bertelsmann, one of the world's largest media companies, to offer interactive services in Europe: Germany (November 1995), the United Kingdom (January 1996), and France (March 1996). Bertelsmann agreed to contribute up to $100 million to fund the launch of the European services, provided access to its book and music club membership base of over 30 million, and offered its publishing content to the joint venture on a most favored customer basis. In addition, Bertelsmann acquired approximately a 5 percent interest in America Online and designated a member of the company's board of directors. AOL contributed interactive technology and management expertise, proprietary software licenses and development services, and staff training and technical support in order to develop, test, and launch the interactive services in Europe. Subscribers to the European services enjoy access to America Online's services in the United States, and U.S. subscribers enjoy access to the European services.

AOL Canada, launched in January 1996, features local content and services. In Ocober 1996, AOL Canada offered Canadian members software, thirteen local channels, billing in Canadian dollars, e-mail, message boards, and easy access to the Internet through a Web browser. AOL Canada's key partners include Citytv, an internationally renowned broadcaster and program producer; MuchMusic, Canada's first national music television channel; *Shift Magazine,* Canada's hottest publication in media; Intuit Canada, makers of the world's leading personal finance software, Quicken; and Southam New Media, a wholly owned subsidiary of Southam, Inc., Canada's largest news organization.

In May 1996, America Online announced a partnership with Mitsui & Co., one of the world's largest international trading companies, and Nikkei, one of Japan's leading media companies with respected business and computer publications. The joint venture consists of Mitsui & Co. owning 40 percent, Nikkei 10 percent, and AOL 50 percent. Japanese partners contributed more than 120 years of experience and credibility in the Japanese market, a strong management team, and $56 million to fund the launch of the Japanese service. America Online brings to the venture its ability to develop, manage, and execute interactive on-line services in the United States, Europe, and Canada.

America Online's wildly successful marketing ploy of flat-rate pricing in the United States turned out to contribute to AOL's latest problem. About 75 percent of AOL's customers took the flat-rate offer. As a result, total daily AOL customer use soared from 1.6 million hours on-line in October 1996 to more than 4 million hours in January 1997. (These problems are described more fully later in this case.)

Meeting Customer Needs

The company provides tools to its members so that they can control their child's or teen's experience on-line without cramping the adults who enjoy using AOL's services to talk to other adults. Parental controls can block or limit the use of chat, instant messages, e-mail, binary files, newsgroups, or the Web. Different on-line areas support different values. For instance:

- *ACLU Forum:* This encourages lively yet responsible debate. Illegal activities (harassment, distribution of illegal materials) are not permitted in this area.
- *Womens' Network:* This is a women-friendly and safe space for chatting, learning, teaching, and networking, but men are still welcome to join the communication.
- *Christian Chat Room:* This allows fellowship among Christian members. In this space, proselytizing is forbidden.
- *Kids Only:* This gives children their own space on-line for searching help with homework, sending e-mail, and hanging out in chat rooms. Parental control can be set up in this area.

The average adult spends about an hour on-line, but the average kid spends three. Currently, there are 4.1 million kids surfing the Net. By 2000, it is expected that there will be 19.2 million. Kids, who spent $307 million in 1996 on on-line services, will spend $1.8 billion by 2002, and this is why media and Web giants are scrambling to offer new kid-friendly sites. Fox TV features cartoons and kid shows. Disney gave AOL first crack at hosting Daily Blast, which offers kids games, comics, and stories for $4.95 per month or $39.95 per year. "But," says Rob Jennings, vice president for programming for AOL networks, "We felt we had a good mix already." Yahooligans! offers kids-friendly Web sites for free. AOL still has partnerships with other media giants such as Disney rival Viacom, Inc.'s Nickelodeon unit for other offerings.

Since 1994, AOL has offered a Kids Only area featuring homework help, games, and on-line magazines, as well as the usual fare of software, games, and chat rooms. The area gets about 1 million 8- to 12-year-old visitors monthly.

In April 1996, America Online began to see the effect of seasonality in both member acquisitions and in the amount of time spent by customers using its services. The company expects that member acquisition is to be highest in the second and third fiscal quarters, when sales of new computers and computer software are highest due to holiday seasons (AOL's fiscal year ends June 30.) Customer usage is expected to be lower in the summer months, due largely to extended daylight hours and competing outdoor leisure activities.

AOL Employees

As of June 30, 1996, America Online had 5828 employees, including 1058 in software and content development, 3271 in customer support, 199 in marketing, 1099 in operations, and 291 in corporate operations. None of AOL's employees is represented by a labor union, and America Online has never experienced a work stoppage.

AOL employs numerous part-time workers around the world known as "remote staff." These are volunteer staff who develop content and provide both marketing and operations functions. Remote staff write informational articles, produce graphics, host chat rooms, provide technical assistance, and fulfill various support functions. Remote staff duties vary. Some may work as little as 10 hours per week or more than 40 hours per week. AOL's remote staff is compensated for these services with "community leader accounts"—a membership for which the staff members are not charged. Relatively few remote staff members are paid as independent contractors.

AOL's flat-rate pricing plan had a serious impact on its remote staff. Prior to the flat rate, members paid about $3 per hour of on-line access. Hence a "free" account would have a monthly value of approximately $300 for a staff member who spent 3 hours per day online.

After the flat-rate pricing plan, this account's value fell to $20. This enormous decrease in incentives led many remote staff members to resign their positions. The positions hardest hit were those for which the job pressures were highest, including AOL's guides and Techlive. Guides served to police AOL's chat rooms and to assist users with whom they came in contact. Techlive assisted users with computer problems, computer use, and navigation of AOL. Techlive is now buried beneath menu options that do not hint that real-time online help is available.

AOL Finance

Exhibits A and B present the financial statements for fiscal years 1995 and 1996. About 90 percent of the firm's revenues are generated from on-line subscription fees. AOL's other revenues are generated from sales of merchandise, data network services, online transactions and advertising, marketing and production services, and development and licensing fees. The increase of over $600 million in service revenues from 1995 to 1996 was attributed primarily to a 93 percent increase in AOL subscribers.

This is expected to undergo radical change, due to the flat rate pricing, with much less revenue coming from subscriber fees, which AOL hopes to make up by increases in the other revenue streams.

Cost of revenue, which includes network-related costs, consists of data and voice communication costs and costs associated with operating the data centers and providing customer support. These increased almost $400 million from 1995 to 1996. This increase was related to a growth of data communication costs, customer support costs, and royalties paid to information and service providers.

For fiscal year 1996, marketing expenses increased 176 percent over fiscal year 1995. This was attributed primarily to an increase in the size and number of marketing programs designed to expand the subscriber base.

Product development costs include research and development, other product development, and the amortization of software. For fiscal year 1996, these costs increased 277 percent over fiscal year 1995 and increased as a percentage of total revenues from 3.6 to 4.9 percent. The increases in product development costs were attributable primarily to an increase in the number of technical employees. Product development costs, before capitalization and amortization, increased by 242 percent.

For fiscal year 1996, general and administrative costs increased 159 percent over fiscal year 1995 and decreased as a percentage of total revenues from 10.8 to 10.1 percent. The increase in general and administrative costs was related to higher personnel, office, and travel expenses related to an increase in the number of employees. The decrease in general and administrative costs as a percentage of total revenues was a result of the substantial growth in revenues, which more than offset the

EXHIBIT A

Income Statement (Year Ended June 30; Amounts in Thousands, Except per Share Data)

	1997	1996	1995
Revenues			
On-line service revenues	$1,429,445	$991,656	$344,309
Other revenues	255,783	102,198	49,981
Total revenues	1,685,228	1,093,854	394,290
Costs and expenses			
Cost of revenues	1,040,762	638,025	232,318
Marketing	409,260	212,710	77,064
Write-off of deferred subscriber acquisition costs	385,221	—	—
Product development	58,208	43,164	11,669
General and administrative	193,537	110,653	42,700
Acquired research and development	—	16,981	50,335
Amortization of goodwill	6,549	7,078	1,653
Restructuring charge	48,627	—	—
Contract termination charge	24,506	—	—
Settlement charge	24,204	—	—
Total costs and expenses	2,190,874	1,028,611	415,739
Income (loss) from operations	(505,646)	65,243	(21,449)
Other income (expense), net	6,299	(2,056)	3,074
Merger expenses	—	(848)	(2,207)
Income (loss) before provision for income taxes	(499,347)	62,339	(20,582)
Provision for income taxes	—	(32,523)	(15,169)
Net income (loss)	$ (499,347)	$ 29,816	$ (35,751)
Earnings (loss) per share			
Net income (loss)	$(5.22)	$0.28	$(0.51)
Weighted average shares outstanding	95,607	108,097	69,550

additional general and administrative costs, combined with the semivariable nature of many of the general and administrative costs.

Acquired research and development costs relate to in-process research and development purchased with the acquisition of Ubique, Ltd., in September 1995. Acquired research and development costs relate to in-process research and development purchased as part of the acquisitions of BookLink Technologies, Inc. (Booklink), and Navisoft, Inc. (Navisoft).

The amortization of goodwill increase relates primarily to America Online's fiscal 1995 acquisitions of Advanced Network & Services, Inc., and Global Network Navigator, Inc., which resulted in approximately $56 million of goodwill. The goodwill related to these acquisitions is being amortized on a straight-line basis over periods ranging

from 5 to 10 years. The increase in amortization of goodwill results from a full year of goodwill recognized in fiscal year 1996 compared with only a partial year of goodwill recognized in fiscal year 1995.

Other income (expenses) consists of interest expense and nonoperating charges net of investment income and nonoperating gains. The change in other income (expenses) was attributed to the $8 million settlement of a class action lawsuit partially offset by an increase in investment income.

Nonrecurring merger expenses totaling $848,000 were recognized in fiscal year 1996 in connection with the merger of America Online with Johnson-Grace Company. Nonrecurring merger expenses totaling $2,207,000 were recognized in fiscal year 1995 in connection with the mergers of AOL with Redgate Communications Corporation, Wide Area Information Servers, Inc., and Medior, Inc.

EXHIBIT B

Consolidated Balance Sheet (June 30; Amounts in Thousands; Except per Share Data)

	1997	1996	1995
Assets			
Current assets			
Cash and cash equivalents	$124,340	$118,421	$ 45,877
Short-term investments	268	10,712	18,672
Trade accounts receivable	65,306	49,342	32,176
Other receivables	26,093	23,271	11,381
Prepaid expenses and other current assets	107,466	65,290	25,527
Total current assets	323,473	267,036	133,633
Property and equipment at cost, net	233,129	111,090	70,919
Other assets			
Restricted cash	50,000	—	—
Product development costs, net	72,498	44,330	18,949
Deferred subscriber acquisition costs, net	—	314,181	77,229
License rights, net	16,777	4,947	5,579
Other assets	84,618	29,607	9,121
Deferred income taxes	24,410	135,872	35,627
Goodwill, net	41,783	51,691	54,356
Total assets	$846,688	$958,754	$405,413
Liabilities and stockholders' equity			
Current liabilities			
Trade accounts payable	$ 69,703	$105,904	$ 84,640
Other accrued expenses and liabilities	297,298	127,876	23,509
Deferred revenue	166,007	37,950	20,021
Accrued personnel costs	20,008	15,719	2,863
Current portion of long-term debt	1,454	2,435	2,329
Total current liabilities	554,470	289,884	133,362
Long-term liabilities			
Notes payable	50,000	19,306	17,369
Deferred income taxes	24,410	135,872	35,627
Deferred revenue	86,040	—	—
Minority interests	2,674	22	—
Other liabilities	1,060	1,168	2,243
Total liabilities	$718,654	$446,252	$188,601
Stockholders' equity			
Preferred stock, $.01 par value; 5,000,000 shares authorized, 1,000 shares issued and outstanding at June 30, 1997 and 1996	1	1	—
Common stock, $.01 par value; 300,000,000 and 100,000,000 shares authorized, 100,188,971 and 92,626,000 shares issued and outstanding at June 30, 1997 and 1996, respectively	1,002	926	767
Unrealized gain on available-for-sale securities	16,924	—	—
Additional paid-in capital	617,221	519,342	252,668
Accumulated deficit	(507,114)	(7,767)	(36,623)
Total stockholders' equity	128,034	512,502	216,812
Total liabilities and equity	$846,688	$958,754	$405,413

In December 1993, the company completed a public stock offering of 8 million shares of common stock, which generated net cash proceeds of approximately $62.7 million. In April 1995, the joint venture with Bertelsmann AG to offer interactive on-line services in Europe, netted approximately $54 million through the sale of approximately 5 percent of its common stock to Bertelsmann. In October 1995, AOL completed a public offering of 4,963,266 shares of common stock, which generated net cash proceeds of approximately $139.5 million. In May 1996, America Online received approximately $28 million through the sale of convertible preferred stock to Mitsui in its joint venture with Mitsui & Co., Ltd., and Nohon Keizai Shimbun, Inc., to offer interactive on-line services in Japan. The preferred stock has an aggregate liquidation preference of approximately $28 million and accrues dividends at a rate of 4 percent per annum. Accrued dividends can be paid in the form of additional shares of preferred stock. Exhibit C shows the history of share prices of AOL's common stock.

America Online has financed its operations through cash generated from operations and the sale of its capital stock. AOL has financed its investments in facilities and telecommunications equipment principally through leasing. American Online leases the majority of its facilities and equipment under noncancelable operating leases. The communications network requires a substantial investment in telecommunications equipment, which America Online plans to finance principally through leasing. The company has never declared, nor has it paid, any cash dividends on its common stock. AOL currently intends to retain its earnings to finance future growth.

The company uses its working capital to finance ongoing operations and to fund marketing and content programs and the development of its products and services. American Online plans to continue to invest in computing and support infrastructure. Additionally, AOL expects to use a portion of its cash for the acquisition and subsequent funding of technologies, products, or businesses complementary to the company's current business.

For example, America Online is investing in the development of alternative technologies to deliver its services. AOL has entered into agreements with several manufacturers of personal digital assistants (PDAs are low-powered, hand-held computers), including Sony, Motorola, Tandy, and Casio, to bundle a palmtop edition of America Online's client software with their PDAs. AOL is participating in early cable trials using cable as the conduit into PCs and has announced future support of ISDN, which allows digital transmission, as opposed to the analog transmission of telephones, and wireless, similar to cell phone and satellite transmission. By the time that cable modems are poised for market penetration, a new generation of competitive telephone modems may be available. In the paging market, AOL has entered into agreements with AT&T Wireless Services and MobileMedia to provide their paging customers who subscribe to AOL with mobile access to certain America Online services.

EXHIBIT C

Market Price of Common Stock

For the Quarter Ended	High	Low
September 30, 1994	$10.28	$ 6.88
December 31, 1994	14.63	7.47
March 31, 1995	23.69	12.31
June 30, 1995	24.06	16.75
September 30, 1995	37.25	21.38
December 31, 1995	46.25	28.25
March 31, 1996	60.00	32.75
June 30, 1996	71.00	36.63
September 30, 1996	37.75	34.65
December 31, 1996	33.38	32.25

AOL'S ENVIRONMENT

AOL is subject to federal and state regulations applicable to business in general. However, America Online must keep up with changes in the regulatory environment relating to telecommunications and the media. Additional legislative proposals from international, federal, and state government bodies in the areas of content regulations, intellectual property, privacy rights, and state tax issues could impose additional regulations and obligations on all online service providers. For a long time, such companies as AT&T, Western Union, and RCA dominated the telecommunications industry.

The courts deregulated the telephone industry in the 1980s. Although technology and market development made passage of new telecommunications legislation inevitable, it took about 10 years to frame it. Even though the Telecommunications Reform Act of 1996 meant to remove many of the regulatory barriers and make it easier for telecom companies to invest in the information superhighway, so far it has made little difference.

The Department of Commerce and the U.S. Trade Representative have pushed the World Trade Organization to open up the telecom sector to more service and equipment competition. As a result of trade negotiations in Singapore, tariffs on many telecommunications products and services will be reduced, with great potential benefit to U.S. firms. Additional talks were under way in Switzerland in 1997 that may permit U.S. telecommunications companies to compete on equal footing with providers in Europe and elsewhere.

Telephone companies are collecting high revenues as computer and on-line services expand. One study found that local carriers collected revenues totaling $1.4 billion in 1995 from second phone lines used mainly for Net links while spending only $245 million to upgrade their networks for the additional usage. Phone companies experienced 8 to 9 percent profit growth in 1996 since second phone line installations at homes grew 25 percent. Both local carriers and on-line service providers agree that there is a necessity to build higher-capacity networks to satisfy the increasing demand for public phone networks to meet the growing trend in cybersurfing.

The future of technology is difficult to predict but can affect AOL's future strategy. Some speculate that interactive TV is going to be replaced by network computers (such as those from Sun). Some argue that Internet connections should be available to people who want to use them and that public monies should be provided to ensure access for all. There is a growing place for satellite and fiber in the new communication system. Technology trends are sometimes born of social change. Here are some of the most important trends to watch for the next 5 years:

- The world phone could be a satellite wireless phone that uses digital technology. A combination of Global System for Mobilization (GSM) and satellite technologies could be the model for the world phone. Pioneers such as Wildfire Communications, Lucent Technologies, Dialogic, and VDOnet are among hundreds of alternative carriers that try to unite PCs, phone, e-mail, fax, and video into a seamless fabric. They are designing software that sends phone calls around the world on the Internet very cheaply. The line dividing computers and telephones, voice and data is blurring. Building on the union of data networks and computers, the Internet has become the new global communications infrastructure for businesses.

- Personal communication systems (PCSs) could broadside local telecom carriers. Projections are that local exchange carriers must brace for a loss of 35 percent of high-margin business customers and 25 percent or more of their residential shares to PCS providers. Mobile subscribers could represent 17 percent of traditional wireline carrier business by 2010. VocalTec, Ltd., leading maker of Internet telephony products, recently broadened the appeal by introducing gateways that connect the Internet to standard phone systems—allowing PC users to call non-PC users on their phones, and vice versa. VocalTec claims it saves $10,000 a month on phone bills between the company's New Jersey and Israeli offices.

- Wireless convergence. Commercial mobile wireless will include mobile satellite, and satellite communication will overlap coverage and mobility with cellular/PCS. Cordless telephony will play major roles. Several years ago, Microsoft Corp. and Novell, Inc., tried to apply computer-telephony integration technology to any desktop by creating competing standards for connecting phone systems to PC networks. But the products, TAPI and TSAPI, which allowed desktop computer users to receive and manage phone calls through their PCs, went nowhere. Now, a wave of products built on TAPI and TSAPI that work with standard telecom equipment is hitting the market. Users can select a handful of names from a database and command the phone switch to set up a conference call with all of them. Pacific Bell is testing a sophisticated messaging service on 300 wireless-phone customers in San Diego. It answers incoming phone calls, screens them, and automatically routes them to wherever you are—a conference room, your home office, or a shopping mall. For a richer media experience, many companies are concentrating on desktop video-conferencing products from Intel, C-Phone, and VDOnet, among others. These products are very cost-efficient and price-compatible.

- Asynchronous transfer mode. ATM carrier services are still expensive. Originally developed by Bell Laboratories for high-speed voice networks, ATM has now been adapted for data applications. They are able to move data at 155 mb/s, whereas advanced modems top out at 56 kb/s. The Defense Department uses a fiberoptic ATM network between the United States and Germany. The Mayo Clinic in Rochester, Minnesota, uses ATM for "telemedicine"—doctors can videoconference with patients. ATM switches account for an estimated savings of $200,000 per month for the American Petroleum Institution, which uses this tool to transmit drilling-site data over satellite. This technology is moving quickly into the public phone network, which increases the speed of the global communications network.

- Residential gateways will let customers plug in telecom carriers and cable companies' networks and give users more control.

Increased competition makes it hard to make money by selling unlimited online access. Service providers have to upgrade their equipment to handle higher modem speeds and install separate equipment and phone lines for rival technologies. Sales of new modems are expected to be huge, driven by the Internet boom. AOL signed a deal with U.S. Robotics, which was scheduled to start turning on telephone access numbers on February 27, 1997, to give subscribers log-on access at a faster speed. Currently, the only high-speed (56 kb/s) modems that America Online customers can use are made by U.S. Robotics, which now controls a quarter of the market. Modems from the Open 56K Forum Group—available in March 1997—cannot talk to those of U.S. Robotics. Most of the Open 56K Group will have modems out in March 1997. U.S. Robotics has dominated the market; thus it appears that AOL chose well. The number 2 modem maker, Hayes Microcomputer Products, Inc., registered more than 40,000 people for a deal it offered on the company's Web page: Customers can get their high-speed modems

for $99 by sending in any brand modem. U.S. Robotics sells its superfast modems for $199 for a version that is installed into the computer or $239 for an external model.

Use of the Net has increased dramatically the demand for techies. An estimated 760,000 people are working for Net-related companies alone. The Internet is full of companies' ads wanting programmers. A new study by the Information Technology Association of America estimates that 190,000 "infotech" jobs stand vacant in U.S. companies—half in the information industry. The situation can get worse, because the number of college students in computer science has fallen 43 percent in the past decade. Net-related companies are spending millions of dollars recruiting employees. In 1996, pay for infotech workers rose by 12 percent to 20 percent, while average annual pay for software architects rose to $85,600.

The on-line services market is highly competitive. Major direct competitors include Prodigy Services Company, a joint venture of International Business Machines Corp. and Sears, Roebuck and Co.; e-World, a service of Apple Computer, Inc.; GEnie, a division of General Electric Information Services; Delphi Internet Services Corporation, a division of News Corp.; Interchange, a service of AT&T Corp.; and Microsoft Corp., which launched its on-line service under the name Microsoft Network. Microsoft has been devoting considerable resources and energy to focus the firm and its products squarely on the Internet. The Internet directory services are another source of competition, including NETCOM On-Line Communication Services, Inc., Bolt, Beranek & Newman, Inc., Performance System International, UUNET Technologies with Internet MCI, Yahoo, Inc., Excite, Inc., Infoseek Corporation, and Lycos, Inc. Finally, software providers such as Intuit, Inc., and Netscape Communication Corporation are another category of competitors.

America Online is by far the largest on-line service, with 10 million American members as of 1997. CompuServe was the second largest service prior to AOL acquiring it. The Microsoft Network is the second largest online service, with 2.3 million subscribers. But a great deal of the competition comes from the small local Internet providers, who were the catalyst that drove AOL to the flat-rate pricing plan.

The imperatives for global communications look very promising. Telecom and data networks should become a lifeline for nations, businesses, and individuals. The Internet is pushing world financial markets and the flow of goods and services. The Net has the potential to revolutionize business and human lives, but it also has the danger that the network can be a vehicle of isolation. Communication by fax, modem, wireless handset, videoconferencing, or telecommuting can create personal isolation. A high-tech world may need to be counterbalanced by community, family, and person-to-person contacts.

The Internet and more advanced computing, plus training for people to understand and participate in the network, have obvious educational potential.

THE FLAT-RATE DEBACLE

Through December 31, 1994, America Online's standard monthly membership fee for its service, which included 5 hours of services, was $9.95, with a $3.50 hourly fee for usage in excess of 5 hours per month. Effective January 1, 1995, the hourly fee for usage in excess of 5 hours per month decreased from $3.50 to $2.95, while the monthly membership fee remained the same.

In October 1995, AOL launched its Internet Service, Global Network Navigator (GNN), which was aimed at consumers who wanted a full-featured Internet-based service but without the full-service quality of AOL. The monthly fee for GNN was $14.95. This fee included 20 hours of service per month with a $1.95 hourly fee for usage in excess of 20 hours per month. In May 1996, AOL announced an additional pricing plan, which was oriented to its heavier users and called Value Plan. It became

effective July 1, 1966, and included 20 hours of services for $19.95 per month with a $2.95 hourly fee for usage in excess of 20 hours per month.

AOL usage increased dramatically when the company announced its plans to offer flat-rate unlimited pricing in October 1996. AOL switched its more than 7 million members to unlimited access for $19.95 a month. Its network was deluged by subscribers, many of whom could not log onto the system during peak evening hours or on weekends. Exhibit D shows comparative data before and after this new pricing policy.

Following the second shutdown of its system in January 1997, the company's chairman and CEO, Steve Case, emphasized that AOL took full responsibility for the "busy signals":

> When we decided . . . to introduce unlimited use pricing, we were well aware that usage would increase substantially. We did some consumer testing and operations modeling to generate usage forecasts, and we began building extra capacity in advance of the December launch of unlimited pricing. We thought that there would be some problems with busy signals during our peak periods in some cities. . . . But we expected those problems to be modest, and not too long in duration.

AOL has tried to decrease the "busy signal" by increasing the size and pace of the system capacity expansion by bringing in new hardware, installing circuits, adding 150,000 new modems, increasing the number of customer service representatives to 4000, offering a toll-free line, and reducing marketing efforts. Mr. Case even asked the customers for help by moderating their own use of AOL during peak hours.

EXHIBIT D

AOL System Use Before and After Flat-Rate Pricing

Average AOL	*January 1997*	*September 1996*
Member daily usage	32 minutes	14 minutes
Daily sessions	10 million	6 million
Total hours daily	4.2 million	1.5 million
Total hours per month	125 million (est.), (Dec.: 102 million)	45 million
Peak simultaneous usage	260,000	140,000
Average minutes per session	26 minutes	16 minutes

Even so, AOL became fodder for comics and lawsuits. In one comic strip, the customer is shown on the telephone conversing with "customer service":

Caller: "I am not getting my money's worth with your online service."

Service: "Good news, sir! We have just cut our rates."

Caller: "Your lines are always busy. . . . I can't get online!"

Service: "Don't forget you get unlimited time online for no extra charge."

A number of AOL customers filed lawsuits against the company in more than 37 states, charging the firm with civil fraud, breach of contract, negligence, and violation of state consumer-protection statutes. The negative publicity from the "busy signals" allowed other online providers the opportunity to expand their number of subscribers and increase their revenues from advertising and merchandising fees.

America Online began a refund offer to its members, and the attorneys general in several states agreed to support its proposed plan to members. The plan involved the following refund policy: Customers had a choice of a free month online or up to $39.90—the cost of 2 months of its unlimited service. In addition, AOL increased customer service staffing to handle member cancellations so that calls were answered within 2 minutes. Also, AOL gave customers the opportunity to cancel their membership through mail, fax, or toll-free number.

In the meantime America Online was facing another legal problem, this time from its shareholders. On February 24, 1997, shareholders sued in U.S. District Court in Virginia alleging that AOL directors and outside accountants violated securities laws in the way the company did its accounting. The online giant took a $385 million charge in October 1996, for marketing expenses it had capitalized.

The various problems facing America Online raised serious doubts among analysts about its ability to meet its goal to earn $60 million in fiscal year 1998 (ending in June) without more revenues from sources outside of operations. An analyst with Smith, Barney & Company believed that the $1.7 billion company had a cash flow problem that could force AOL to raise cash through bank loans or another stock offering— which would be the company's fourth. "The worst time to go to the market is when you need to," notes Abe Mastbaum, money manager of American Securities.

Prior to 1997, AOL was able to maintain its positive cash flow through the addition of new members. Due to overload of the system, brought on by flat-rate pricing, new members cannot be added as aggressively as needed. The company will have to develop new sources of revenue, such as on-line advertising and fees on electronic transfers, or charge additional fees for premium channels. AOL launched its first premium channel in July of 1997. Its premium games channel allows people from around the world to play both traditional games, such as hearts, and new games against each other. It charges $2 per hour for the premium games channel.

Since AOL did not have the infrastructure in place to handle the increased usage that came with the revised pricing structure, America Online planned to hold its membership at 8 million and spend $350 million to expand system capacity and customer support. Then a large acquisition substantially changed system capacity.

In April 1997, rumors were heard about AOL acquiring CompuServe from WorldCom. America Online declined to comment. CompuServe said the company is in "external discussions" regarding a deal. Buying CompuServe would add much-needed network capacity to AOL's strained system. These speculations gave a boost to both companies' stock: CompuServe's shares jumped 12 percent to $11; AOL's stock was up 7.6 percent to $45.75. A month before, CompuServe Corp. had quietly cut 500 jobs, or 14 percent of its workforce, which was the latest evidence of the on-line company's troubles as it lost members in an intense competition with America Online and other rivals. The cuts left CompuServe's home office in Columbus, Ohio, with about 3200 employees who were primarily on-line content and service specialists. At the same time, CompuServe posted a $14 million quarterly loss, and 3 days later the company's president and chief executive, Robert J. Massey, resigned. In September 1997, AOL bought CompuServe.

CompuServe was acquired in exchange for AOL's ANS Communications Subsidiary. AOL also received $175 million in cash. This added 100,000 modems to AOL's system for the short term. AOL also received long-term network commitments from WorldCom. AOL expected that the exchange would allow it to focus on its core assets—AOL Networks and AOL Studios. CompuServe would be retained as a brand name with continued marketing to small business and professional markets but with AOL's expanded content and ease of use. The companies plan to collaborate on the future development of a broadband communications network, as opposed to the current narrow-band network that consists mainly of telephone lines.

Kentucky Fried Chicken and the Global Fast-Food Industry

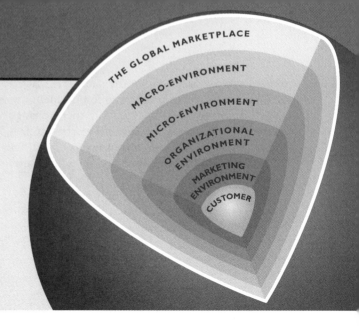

This case was prepared by Jeffrey A. Krug of the Department of Business Administration, University of Illinois at Urbana-Champaign.

Kentucky Fried Chicken Corporation (KFC) was the world's largest chicken restaurant chain and third largest fast-food chain. KFC held over 55 percent of the U.S. market in terms of sales and operated over 10,200 restaurants worldwide in 1998. It opened 376 new restaurants in 1997 (more than one restaurant a day) and operated in 79 countries. One of the first fast-food chains to go international during the late 1960s, KFC has developed one of the world's most recognizable brands.

Japan, Australia, and the United Kingdom accounted for the greatest share of KFC's international expansion during the 1970s and 1980s. During the 1990s, KFC turned its attention to other international markets that offered significant opportunities for growth. China, with a population of over one billion, and Europe, with a population roughly equal to the United States, offered such opportunities. Latin America also offered a unique opportunity because of the size of its markets, its common language and culture, and its geographic proximity to the United States. Mexico was of particular interest because of the North American Free Trade Agreement (NAFTA), a free-trade zone between Canada, the United States, and Mexico that went into effect in 1994.

Reprinted by permission of the author, Jeffrey A. Krug, University of Illinois at Urbana-Champaign.

Prior to 1990, KFC expanded into Latin America primarily through company-owned restaurants in Mexico and Puerto Rico. Company-owned restaurants gave KFC greater control over its operations than franchised or licensed restaurants. By 1995, KFC also had established company-owned restaurants in Venezuela and Brazil. In addition, it had established franchised units in numerous Caribbean countries. During the early 1990s, KFC shifted to a two-tiered strategy in Latin America. First, it established 29 franchised restaurants in Mexico following enactment of Mexico's new franchise law in 1990. This allowed KFC to expand outside its company restaurant base in Mexico City, Guadalajara, and Monterrey. KFC was one of many U.S. fast-food, retail, and hotel chains to begin franchising in Mexico following the new franchise law. Second, KFC began an aggressive franchise building program in South America. By 1998, it was operating franchised restaurants in 32 Latin American countries. Much of this growth was in Brazil, Chile, Colombia, Ecuador, and Peru.

COMPANY HISTORY

Fast-food franchising was still in its infancy in 1952 when Harland Sanders began his travels across the United States to speak with prospective franchisees about his "Colonel Sanders Recipe Kentucky Fried

Chicken." By 1960, "Colonel" Sanders had granted KFC franchises to over 200 take-home retail outlets and restaurants across the United States. He had also succeeded in establishing a number of franchises in Canada. By 1963, the number of KFC franchises had risen to over 300, and revenues had reached $500 million.

By 1964, at the age of 74, the Colonel had tired of running the day-to-day operations of his business and was eager to concentrate on public relations issues. Therefore, he sought out potential buyers, eventually deciding to sell the business to two Louisville businessmen—Jack Massey and John Young Brown, Jr.—for $2 million. The Colonel stayed on as a public relations man and goodwill ambassador for the company.

During the next 5 years, Massey and Brown concentrated on growing KFC's franchise system across the United States. In 1966, they took KFC public, and the company was listed on the New York Stock Exchange. By the late 1960s, a strong foothold had been established in the United States, and Massey and Brown turned their attention to international markets. In 1969, a joint venture was signed with Mitsuoishi Shoji Kaisha, Ltd., in Japan, and the rights to operate 14 existing KFC franchises in England were acquired. Subsidiaries also were established in Hong Kong, South Africa, Australia, New Zealand, and Mexico. By 1971, KFC had 2450 franchises and 600 company-owned restaurants worldwide and was operating in 48 countries.

Heublein, Inc.

In 1971, KFC entered negotiations with Heublein, Inc., to discuss a possible merger. The decision to seek a merger candidate was partially driven by Brown's desire to pursue other interests, including a political career (Brown was elected governor of Kentucky in 1977). Several months later, Heublein acquired KFC. Heublein was in the business of producing vodka, mixed cocktails, dry gin, cordials, beer, and other alcoholic beverages. However, Heublein had little experience in the restaurant business. Conflicts quickly erupted between Colonel Sanders, who continued to act in a public relations capacity, and Heublein management. Colonel Sanders became increasingly distraught over quality control issues and restaurant cleanliness. By 1977, new restaurant openings had slowed to about 20 per year. Few restaurants were

being remodeled, and service quality had declined.

In 1977, Heublein sent in a new management team to redirect KFC's strategy. A "back-to-the-basics" strategy was immediately implemented. New unit construction was discontinued until existing restaurants could be upgraded and operating problems eliminated. Restaurants were refurbished, an emphasis was placed on cleanliness and service, marginal products were eliminated, and product consistency was reestablished. By 1982, KFC had succeeded in establishing a successful strategic focus and was again aggressively building new units.

R. J. Reynolds Industries, Inc.

In 1982, R. J. Reynolds Industries, Inc. (RJR), merged Heublein into a wholly owned subsidiary. The merger with Heublein represented part of RJR's overall corporate strategy of diversifying into unrelated businesses, including energy, transportation, food, and restaurants. RJR's objective was to reduce its dependence on the tobacco industry, which had driven RJR sales since its founding in North Carolina in 1875. Sales of cigarettes and tobacco products, while profitable, were declining because of reduced consumption in the United States. This was mainly the result of an increased awareness among Americans about the negative health consequences of smoking.

RJR had no more experience in the restaurant business than did Heublein. However, it decided to take a hands-off approach to managing KFC. Whereas Heublein had installed its own top management at KFC headquarters, RJR left KFC management largely intact, believing that existing KFC managers were better qualified to operate KFC's businesses than were its own managers. In doing so, RJR avoided many of the operating problems that plagued Heublein. This strategy paid off for RJR as KFC continued to expand aggressively and profitably under RJR ownership. In 1985, RJR acquired Nabisco Corporation for $4.9 billion. Nabisco sold a variety of well-known cookies, crackers, cereals, confectioneries, snacks, and other grocery products. The merger with Nabisco represented a decision by RJR to concentrate its diversification efforts on the consumer foods industry. It subsequently divested many of its nonconsumer food businesses. RJR sold KFC to PepsiCo, Inc., one year later.

PEPSICO, INC.

Corporate Strategy

PepsiCo, Inc., was formed in 1965 with the merger of the Pepsi-Cola Co. and Frito-Lay, Inc. The merger of these companies created one of the largest consumer products companies in the United States. Pepsi-Cola's traditional business was the sale of soft drink concentrates to licensed independent and company-owned bottlers that manufactured, sold, and distributed Pepsi-Cola soft drinks. Pepsi-Cola's best known trademarks were Pepsi-Cola, Diet Pepsi, Mountain Dew, and Slice. Frito-Lay manufactured and sold a variety of snack foods, including Fritos Corn Chips, Lay's Potato Chips, Ruffles Potato Chips, Doritos, Tostitos Tortilla Chips, and Chee-tos Cheese Flavored Snacks. PepsiCo quickly embarked on an aggressive acquisition program similar to that pursued by RJR during the 1980s, buying a number of companies in areas unrelated to its major businesses. Acquisitions included North American Van Lines, Wilson Sporting Goods, and Lee Way Motor Freight. However, success in operating these businesses failed to live up to expectations, mainly because the management skills required to operate these businesses lay outside of PepsiCo's area of expertise.

Poor performance in these businesses led then-chairman and chief executive officer Don Kendall to restructure PepsiCo's operations in 1984. First, businesses that did not support Pepsi-Co's consumer product orientation, such as North American Van Lines, Wilson Sporting Goods, and Lee Way Motor Freight, were divested. Second, PepsiCo's foreign bottling operations were sold to local businesspeople who better understood the culture and business environment in their respective countries. Third, Kendall reorganized PepsiCo along three lines: soft drinks, snack foods, and restaurants.

Restaurant Business and Acquisition of KFC

PepsiCo first entered the restaurant business in 1977 when it acquired Pizza Hut's 3200-unit restaurant system. Taco Bell was merged into a division of PepsiCo in 1978. The restaurant business completed PepsiCo's consumer product orientation. The marketing of fast food followed many of the same patterns as the marketing of soft drinks and snack foods. Therefore, PepsiCo believed that its management skills could be easily transferred among its three business segments. This was compatible with PepsiCo's practice of frequently moving managers among its business units as a way of developing future top executives. PepsiCo's restaurant chains also provided an additional outlet for the sale of Pepsi soft drinks. Pepsi-Cola soft drinks and fast-food products also could be marketed together in the same television and radio segments, thereby providing higher returns for each advertising dollar. To complete its diversification into the restaurant segment, PepsiCo acquired Kentucky Fried Chicken Corporation from RJR-Nabisco for $841 million in 1986. The acquisition of KFC gave PepsiCo the leading market share in chicken (KFC), pizza (Pizza Hut), and Mexican food (Taco Bell), three of the four largest and fastest-growing segments within the U.S. fast-food industry.

Management

Following the acquisition by PepsiCo, KFC's relationship with its parent company underwent dramatic changes. RJR had operated KFC as a semiautonomous unit, satisfied that KFC management understood the fast-food business better than they. In contrast, PepsiCo acquired KFC in order to complement its already strong presence in the fast-food market. Rather than allowing KFC to operate autonomously, PepsiCo undertook sweeping changes. These changes included negotiating a new franchise contract to give PepsiCo more control over its franchisees, reducing staff in order to cut costs, and replacing KFC managers with its own. In 1987, a rumor spread through KFC's headquarters in Louisville that the new personnel manager, who had just relocated from PepsiCo's headquarters in New York, was overheard saying that "there will be no more home grown tomatoes in this organization."

Such statements by PepsiCo personnel, uncertainties created by several restructurings that led to layoffs throughout the KFC organization, the replacement of KFC personnel with PepsiCo managers, and conflicts between KFC and PepsiCo's corporate cultures created a morale problem within KFC. KFC's culture was built largely on Colonel Sanders' laid-back approach to management. Employees enjoyed relatively good employment stability and security. Over the years, a strong loyalty had been created among KFC employees and franchisees, mainly because of the efforts of Colonel Sanders to provide for his employees' benefits, pension, and other non-income needs. In addition, the southern environment of Louisville resulted in a friendly, relaxed atmosphere at KFC's corporate offices. This corporate culture was left essentially unchanged during the Heublein and RJR years.

In stark contrast to KFC, Pepsi-Co's culture was characterized by a strong emphasis on performance. Top performers expected to move up through the ranks quickly. PepsiCo used its KFC, Pizza Hut, Taco Bell, Frito Lay, and Pepsi-Cola divisions as training grounds for its top managers, rotating its best managers through its five divisions on average every 2 years. This practice created immense pressure on managers to continuously demonstrate their managerial prowess within short periods, in order to maximize their potential for promotion. This practice also left many KFC managers with the feeling that they had few career opportunities with the new company. One PepsiCo manager commented, "You may have performed well last year, but if you don't perform well this year, you're gone, and there are 100 ambitious guys with Ivy League MBAs at PepsiCo who would love to take your position." An unwanted effect of this performance-driven culture was that employee loyalty often was lost, and turnover tended to be higher than in other companies.

Kyle Craig, president of KFC's U.S. operations, was asked about KFC's relationship with its corporate parent. He commented:

> The KFC culture is an interesting one because I think it was dominated by a lot of KFC folks, many of whom have been around since the days of the Colonel. Many of those people were very intimidated by the PepsiCo culture, which is a very high performance, high accountability, highly driven culture. People were concerned about whether they would succeed in the new culture. Like many companies, we have had a couple of downsizings which further made people nervous. Today, there are fewer old KFC people around and I think to some degree people have seen that the PepsiCo culture can drive some pretty positive results. I also think the PepsiCo people who have worked with KFC have modified their cultural values somewhat and they can see that there were a lot of benefits in the old KFC culture.

PepsiCo pushes its companies to perform strongly, but whenever there is a slip in performance, it increases the culture gap between PepsiCo and KFC. I have been involved in two downsizings over which I have been the chief architect. They have been probably the two most gut-wrenching experiences of my career. Because you know you're dealing with peoples' lives and their families, these changes can be emotional if you care about the people in your organization. However, I do fundamentally believe that your first obligation is to the entire organization.

A second problem for PepsiCo was its poor relationship with KFC franchisees. A month after becoming president and chief executive officer in 1989, John Cranor addressed KFC's franchisees in Louisville in order to explain the details of the new franchise contract. This was the first contract change in 13 years. It gave PepsiCo greater power to take over weak franchises, relocate restaurants, and make changes in existing restaurants. In addition, restaurants would no longer be protected from competition from new KFC units, and it gave PepsiCo the right to raise royalty fees on existing restaurants as contracts came up for renewal. After Cranor finished his address, there was an uproar among the attending franchisees, who jumped to their feet to protest the changes. The franchisees had long been accustomed to relatively little interference from management in their day-to-day operations (a tradition begun by Colonel Sanders). This type of interference, of course, was a strong part of PepsiCo's philosophy of demanding change. KFC's franchise association later sued PepsiCo over the new contract. The contract remained unresolved until 1996, when the most objectionable parts of the contract were removed by KFC's new president and CEO, David Novak. A new contract was ratified by KFC's franchisees in 1997.

PepsiCo's Divestiture of KFC, Pizza Hut, and Taco Bell

PepsiCo's strategy of diversifying into three distinct but related markets—soft drinks, snack foods, and fast-food restaurants—created one of the world's largest consumer products companies and a portfolio of some of the world's most recognizable brands. Between 1990 and 1996, PepsiCo grew at an annual rate of over 10 percent, surpassing $31 billion in sales in 1996. However, PepsiCo's sales

EXHIBIT A

Tricon Global Restaurants, Inc.—Organizational Chart (1998)

growth masked troubles in its fast-food businesses. Operating margins (profit as a percent of sales) at Pepsi-Cola and Frito Lay averaged 12 and 17 percent between 1990 and 1996, respectively. During the same period, margins at KFC, Pizza Hut, and Taco Bell fell from an average of over 8 percent in 1990 to a little more than 4 percent in 1996. Declining margins in the fast-food chains reflected increasing maturity in the U.S. fast-food industry, more intense competition among U.S. fast-food competitors, and the aging of KFC and Pizza Hut's restaurant base. As a result, PepsiCo's restaurant chains absorbed nearly one-half of PepsiCo's annual capital spending during the 1990s. However, they generated less than one-third of PepsiCo's cash flows. Therefore, cash was diverted from PepsiCo's soft drink and snack food businesses to its restaurant businesses. This reduced PepsiCo's return on assets, made it more difficult to compete effectively with Coca-Cola, and hurt its stock price. In 1997, PepsiCo spun off its restaurant businesses into a new company called Tricon Global Restaurants, Inc. (see Exhibit A). The new company was based in KFC's headquarters in Louisville, Kentucky. PepsiCo's objective was to reposition itself as a packaged goods company, to strengthen its balance sheet, and to create more consistent earning growth. PepsiCo received a one-time distribution from Tricon of $4.7 billion, $3.7 billion of which was used to pay off short-term debt. The balance was earmarked for stock repurchases.

FAST-FOOD INDUSTRY

According to the National Restaurant Association (NRA), food-service sales topped $320 billion for the approximately 500,000 restaurants and other food outlets making up the U.S. restaurant industry in 1997. The NRA estimated that sales in the fast-food segment of the food service industry grew 5.2 percent to $104 billion, up from $98 billion in 1996. This marked the fourth consecutive year that fast-food sales either matched or exceeded sales in full-service restaurants, which grew 4.1 percent to $104 billion in 1997. The growth in fast-food sales reflected the long, gradual change in the restaurant industry from an industry once dominated by independently operated sit-down restaurants to an industry fast becoming dominated by fast-food restaurant chains. The U.S. restaurant industry as a whole grew by approximately 4.2 percent in 1997.

Major Fast-Food Segments

Six major business segments made up the fast-food segment of the food service industry. Sales data for the leading restaurant chains in each segment are shown in Exhibit B. Most striking is the dominance of McDonald's, which had sales of over $16 billion in 1996. This represented 16.6 percent of U.S. fast-food sales, or nearly 22 percent of sales among the nation's top 30 fast-food chains. Sales at McDonald's restaurants average $1.3 million per year, compared with about $820,000 for the average U.S. fast-food restaurant. Tricon Global Restaurants (KFC, Pizza Hut, and Taco Bell) had U.S. sales of $13.4 billion in 1996. This represented 13.6 percent of U.S. fast-food sales and 17.9 percent of the top 30 fast-food chains.

Sandwich chains made up the largest segment of the fast-food market. McDonald's controlled 35 percent of the sandwich segment, while Burger King ran a distant second with a 15.6 percent market share. Competition had become particularly intense within the sandwich segment as the U.S. fast-food market became more saturated. In order to increase sales, chains turned to new products to win customers away from other sandwich chains, introduced products traditionally offered by nonsandwich chains (such as pizzas, fried chicken, and tacos), streamlined their menus, and upgraded product quality. Burger King recently introduced its Big King, a direct clone of the Big Mac. McDonald's quickly retaliated by introducing its Big 'n Tasty, a direct clone of the Whopper. Wendy's introduced chicken pita sandwiches, and Taco Bell introduced sandwiches called "wraps," breads stuffed with various fillings. Hardee's successfully introduced fried chicken in most of its restaurants. In addition to new products, chains lowered pricing, improved customer service, cobranded with other fast-food chains, and established restaurants in nontraditional locations (e.g., McDonald's installed restaurants in Wal-Mart stores across the country) to beef up sales.

The second largest fast-food segment was dinner houses, dominated by Red Lobster, Applebee's, Olive Garden, and Chili's. Between 1988 and 1996, dinner houses increased their share of the fast-food market from 8 to over 13 percent. This increase came mainly at the expense of grilled buffet chains, such as Ponderosa, Sizzler, and Western Sizzlin'. The market share of steak houses fell from 6 percent in 1988 to under 4 percent in 1996. The

rise of dinner houses during the 1990s was partially the result of an aging and wealthier population that increasingly demanded higher-quality food in more upscale settings. However, rapid construction of new restaurants, especially among relative newcomers, such as Romano's Macaroni Grill, Lone Star Steakhouse, and Outback Steakhouse, resulted in overcapacity within the dinner house segment. This reduced per-restaurant sales and further intensified competition. Eight of the sixteen largest dinner houses posted growth rates in excess of 10 percent in 1996. Romano's Macaroni Grill, Lone Star Steakhouse, Chili's, Outback Steakhouse, Applebee's, Red Robin, Fuddruckers, and Ruby Tuesday grew at rates of 82, 41, 32, 27, 23, 14, 11, and 10 percent, respectively.

The third largest fast-food segment was pizza, long dominated by Pizza Hut. While Pizza Hut controlled over 46 percent of the pizza segment in 1996, its market share has slowly eroded because of intense competition and its aging restaurant base. Domino's Pizza and Papa John's Pizza have been particularly successful. Little Caesars is the only pizza chain to remain predominantly a takeout chain, although it recently began home delivery. However, its policy of charging customers $1 per delivery damaged its perception among consumers as a high-value pizza chain. Home delivery, successfully introduced by Domino's and Pizza Hut, was a driving force for success among the market leaders during the 1970s and 1980s. However, the success of home delivery drove competitors to look for new methods of increasing their customer bases. Pizza chains diversified into nonpizza items (e.g., chicken wings at Domino's, Italian cheese bread at Little Caesars, and stuffed crust pizza at Pizza Hut), developed nontraditional items (e.g., airport kiosks and college campuses), offered special promotions, and offered new pizza variations with an emphasis on high-quality ingredients (e.g., Roma Herb and Garlic Crunch pizza at Domino's and Buffalo Chicken Pizza at Round Table Pizza).

Chicken Segment

KFC continued to dominate the chicken segment, with 1997 sales of $4 billion (see Exhibit C). Its nearest competitor, Boston Market, was second with sales of $1.2 billion. KFC operated 5120 restaurants in the United States in 1998, eight fewer restaurants than in 1993. Rather than building new restaurants

EXHIBIT B

Leading U.S. Fast-Food Chains (Ranked by 1996 Sales, $000s)

Sandwich Chains	Sales	Share	Family Restaurants	Sales	Share
McDonald's	16,370	35.0%	Denny's	1,850	21.2%
Burger King	7,300	15.6%	Shoney's	1,220	14.0%
Taco Bell	4,575	9.8%	Big Boy	945	10.8%
Wendy's	4,360	9.3%	Int'l House of Pancakes	797	9.1%
Hardee's	3,055	6.5%	Cracker Barrel	734	8.4%
Subway	2,700	5.8%	Perkins	678	7.8%
Arby's	1,867	4.0%	Friendly's	597	6.8%
Dairy Queen	1,225	2.6%	Bob Evans	575	6.6%
Jack-in-the-Box	1,207	2.6%	Waffle House	525	6.0%
Sonic Drive-In	985	2.1%	Coco's	278	3.2%
Carl's Jr.	648	1.4%	Steak 'n Shake	275	3.2%
Other chains	2,454	5.2%	Village Inn	246	2.8%
Total	46,745	100.0%	Total	8,719	100.0%

Dinner Houses	Sales	Share	Pizza Chains	Sales	Share
Red Lobster	1,810	15.7%	Pizza Hut	4,927	46.4%
Applebee's	1,523	13.2%	Domino's Pizza	2,300	21.7%
Olive Garden	1,280	11.1%	Little Caesars	1,425	13.4%
Chili's	1,242	10.7%	Papa John's	619	5.8%
Outback Steakhouse	1,017	8.8%	Sbarros	400	3.8%
T.G.I. Friday's	935	8.1%	Round Table Pizza	385	3.6%
Ruby Tuesday	545	4.7%	Chuck E. Cheese's	293	2.8%
Lone Star Steakhouse	460	4.0%	Godfather's Pizza	266	2.5%
Bennigan's	458	4.0%	Total	10,614	100.0%
Romano's Macaroni Grill	344	3.0%			
Other dinner houses	1,942	16.8%			
Total	11,557	100.0%			

Grilled Buffet Chains	Sales	Share	Chicken Chains	Sales	Share
Golden Corral	711	22.8%	KFC	3,900	57.1%
Ponderosa	680	21.8%	Boston Market	1,167	17.1%
Ryan's	604	19.4%	Popeye's Chicken	666	9.7%
Sizzler	540	17.3%	Chick-fil-A	570	8.3%
Western Sizzlin'	332	10.3%	Church's Chicken	529	7.7%
Quincy's	259	8.3%	Total	6,832	100.0%
Total	3,116	100.0%			

Source: Nation's Restaurant News.

EXHIBIT C

Top U.S. Chicken Chains

Sales ($ M)	1992	1993	1994	1995	1996	1997	Growth Rate (%)
KFC	3,400	3,400	3,500	3,700	3,900	4,000	3.3
Boston Market	43	147	371	754	1,100	1,197	94.5
Popeye's	545	569	614	660	677	727	5.9
Chick-fil-A	356	396	451	502	570	671	11.9
Church's	414	440	465	501	526	574	6.8
Total	4,758	4,952	5,401	6,118	6,772	7,170	8.5
U.S. restaurants							
KFC	5,089	5,128	5,149	5,142	5,108	5,120	0.1
Boston Market	83	217	534	829	1,087	1,166	69.6
Popeye's	769	769	853	889	894	949	4.3
Chick-fil-A	487	545	534	825	717	762	9.0
Church's	944	932	937	953	989	1,070	2.5
Total	7,372	7,591	8,007	8,638	8,795	9,067	4.2
Sales per unit ($000s)							
KFC	668	663	680	720	764	781	3.2
Boston Market	518	677	695	910	1,012	1,027	14.7
Popeye's	709	740	720	743	757	767	1.6
Chick-fil-A	731	727	845	608	795	881	3.8
Church's	439	472	496	526	531	537	4.1
Total	645	782	782	782	782	782	3.9

Source: Tricon Global Restaurants, Inc., *1997 Annual Report;* Boston Chicken, Inc., *1997 Annual Report;* Chick-fil-A, corporate headquarters, Atlanta; AFC Enterprises, Inc., *1997 Annual Report.*

in the already saturated U.S. market, KFC focused on building restaurants abroad. In the United States, KFC focused on closing unprofitable restaurants, upgrading existing restaurants with new exterior signage, and improving product quality. The strategy paid off. While overall U.S. sales during the last 10 years remained flat, annual sales per unit increased steadily in 8 of the last 9 years.

Despite KFC's continued dominance within the chicken segment, it has lost market share to Boston Market, a new restaurant chain emphasizing roasted rather than fried chicken. Boston Market has successfully created the image of an upscale deli offering healthy, "home style" alternatives to fried chicken and other "fast foods." It has broadened its menu beyond rotisserie chicken to include ham, turkey, meat loaf, chicken pot pie, and deli

sandwiches. In order to minimize its image as a fast-food restaurant, it has refused to put drive-thrus in its restaurants and has established most of its units in outside shopping malls rather than in freestanding units at intersections so characteristic of other fast-food restaurants.

In 1993, KFC introduced its own rotisserie chicken, called Rotisserie Gold, to combat Boston Market. However, it quickly learned that its customer base was considerably different from that of Boston Market's. KFC's customers liked KFC chicken despite the fact that it was fried. In addition, customers did not respond well to the concept of buying whole chickens for take-out. They preferred instead to buy chicken by the piece. KFC withdrew its rotisserie chicken in 1996 and introduced a new line of roasted chicken called Tender

Roast, which could be sold by the piece and mixed with its Original Recipe and Extra Crispy Chicken.

Other major competitors within the chicken segment included Popeye's Famous Fried Chicken and Church's Chicken (both subsidiaries of AFC Enterprises in Atlanta), Chick-fil-A, Bojangle's, El Pollo Loco, Grandy's, Kenny Rogers Roasters, Mrs. Winner's, and Pudgie's. Both Church's and Popeye's had similar strategies—to compete head on with other "fried chicken" chains. Unlike KFC, neither chain offered rotisserie chicken, and nonfried chicken products were limited. Chick-fil-A focused exclusively on pressure-cooked and char-grilled skinless chicken breast sandwiches, which it served to customers in sit-down restaurants located predominantly in shopping malls. As many malls added food courts, often consisting of up to 15 fast-food units competing side by side, shopping malls became less enthusiastic about allocating separate store space to food chains. Therefore, in order to complement its existing restaurant base in shopping malls, Chick-fil-A began to open smaller units in shopping mall food courts, hospitals, and colleges. It also opened free-standing units in selected locations.

Demographic Trends

A number of demographic and societal trends contributed to increased demand for food prepared away from home. Because of the high divorce rate in the United States and the fact that people married later in life, single-person households represented about 25 percent of all U.S. households, up from 17 percent in 1970. This increased the number of individuals choosing to eat out rather than eat at home. The number of married women working outside the home also has increased dramatically during the last 25 years. About 59 percent of all married women have careers. According to the Conference Board, 64 percent of all married households will be double-income families by 2000. About 80 percent of households headed by individuals between the ages of 25 and 44 (both married and unmarried) will be double-income. Greater numbers of working women increased family incomes. According to *Restaurants & Institutions* magazine, more than one-third of all households had incomes of at least $50,000 in 1996. About 8 percent of all households had annual incomes over $100,000. The combination of higher numbers of dual-career families and rising incomes meant that fewer families had time to prepare food at home. According to Standard & Poor's *Industry Surveys,* Americans spent 55 percent of their food dollars at restaurants in 1995, up from 34 percent in 1970.

Fast-food restaurant chains met these demographic and societal changes by expanding their restaurant bases. However, by the early 1990s, the growth of traditional free-standing restaurants slowed as the U.S. market became saturated. The major exception was dinner houses, which continued to proliferate in response to Americans' increased passion for beef. Since 1990, the U.S. population has grown at an average annual rate of about 1 percent and reached 270 million people in 1997. Rising immigration since 1990 dramatically altered the ethnic makeup of the U.S. population. According to the Bureau of the Census, Americans born outside the United States made up 10 percent of the population in 1997. About 40 percent were Hispanic, while 24 percent were Asian. Nearly 30 percent of Americans born outside the United States arrived since 1990. As a result of these trends, restaurant chains expanded their menus to appeal to the different ethnic tastes of consumers, expanded into nontraditional locations such as department stores and airports, and made food more available through home delivery and take-out service.

Industry Consolidation and Mergers and Acquisitions

Lower growth in the U.S. fast-food market intensified competition for market share among restaurant chains and led to consolidation, primarily through mergers and acquisitions, during the mid-1990s. Many restaurant chains found that market share could be increased more quickly and cheaply by acquiring an existing company rather than building new units. In addition, fixed costs could be spread across a larger number of restaurants. This raised operating margins and gave companies an opportunity to build market share by lowering prices. An expanded restaurant base also gave companies greater purchasing power over supplies. In 1990, Grand Metropolitan, a British company, purchased Pillsbury Co. for $5.7 billion. Included in the purchase was Pillsbury's Burger King chain. Grand Met strengthened the franchise by upgrading existing restaurants and eliminated several levels of management in order to cut costs. This gave Burger King a long-needed boost in improving its position against McDonald's, its largest competitor. In 1988, Grand Met had purchased Wienerwald, a West German chicken chain, and the Spaghetti Factory, a Swiss chain.

Perhaps most important to KFC was Hardee's acquisition of 600 Roy Rogers restaurants from Marriott Corporation in 1990. Hardee's converted a large number of these restaurants to Hardee's units and introduced "Roy Rogers" fried chicken to its menu. By 1993, Hardee's had introduced fried chicken into most of its U.S. restaurants. Hardee's was unlikely to destroy the customer loyalty that KFC long enjoyed. However, it did cut into KFC's sales, because it was able to offer consumers a widened menu selection that appealed to a variety of family eating preferences. In 1997, Hardee's parent company, Imasco, Ltd., sold Hardee's to CKE Restaurants, Inc. CKE owned Carl's Jr., Rally's Hamburgers, and Checker's Drive-In. Boston Chicken, Inc., acquired Harry's Farmers Market, an Atlanta grocer that sold fresh quality prepared meals. The acquisition was designed to help Boston Chicken develop distribution beyond its Boston Market restaurants. AFC Enterprises, which operated Popeye's and Church's, acquired Chesapeake Bagel Bakery of McLean, Virginia, in order to diversify away from fried chicken and to strengthen its balance sheet.

The effect of these and other recent mergers and acquisitions on the industry was powerful. The top 10 restaurant companies controlled almost 60 percent of fast-food sales in the United States. The consolidation of a number of fast-food chains within larger, financially more powerful parent companies gave restaurant chains strong financial and managerial resources that could be used to compete against small chains in the industry.

International Quick-Service Market

Because of the aggressive pace of new restaurant construction in the United States during the 1970s and 1980s, opportunities to expand domestically through new restaurant construction in the 1990s were limited. Restaurant chains that did build new restaurants found that the higher cost of purchasing prime locations resulted in immense pressure to increase annual per-restaurant sales in order to cover higher initial investment costs. Many restaurants began to expand into international markets as an alternative to continued domestic expansion. In contrast to the U.S. market, international markets offered large customer bases with comparatively little competition. However, only a few U.S. restaurant chains had defined aggressive strategies for penetrating international markets by 1998.

Three restaurant chains that had established aggressive international strategies were McDonald's, KFC, and Pizza Hut. McDonald's operated the largest number of restaurants. In 1998, it operated 23,132 restaurants in 109 countries (10,409 restaurants were located outside the United States). In comparison, KFC, Pizza Hut, and Taco Bell together operated 29,712 restaurants in 79, 88, and 17 countries, respectively (9126 restaurants were located outside the United States). Of these four chains, KFC operated the greatest percentage of its restaurants (50 percent) outside the United States. McDonald's, Pizza Hut, and Taco Bell operated 45, 31, and 2 percent of their units outside the United States. KFC opened its first restaurant outside the United States in the late 1950s. By the time PepsiCo acquired KFC in 1986, KFC was already operating restaurants in 55 countries. KFC's early expansion abroad, its strong brand name, and its managerial experience in international markets gave it a strong competitive advantage vis-à-vis other fast-food chains that were investing abroad for the first time.

Exhibit D shows *Hotels'* 1994 list of the world's 30 largest fast-food restaurant chains (*Hotels* discontinued reporting these data after 1994). Seventeen of the 30 largest restaurant chains (ranked by number of units) were headquartered in the United States. There were a number of possible explanations for the relative scarcity of fast-food restaurant chains outside the United States. First, the United States represented the largest consumer market in the world, accounting for over one-fifth of the world's gross domestic product (GDP). Therefore, the United States was the strategic focus of the largest restaurant chains. Second, Americans were more quick to accept the fast-food concept. Many other cultures had strong culinary traditions that were difficult to break down. Europeans, for example, had histories of frequenting more midscale restaurants, where they spent hours in a formal setting enjoying native dishes and beverages. While KFC was again building restaurants in Germany by the late 1980s, it previously failed to penetrate the German market, because Germans were not accustomed to take-out food or to ordering food over

EXHIBIT D

The World's 30 Largest Fast-Food Chains (Year-End 1993, Ranked by Number of Countries)

	Franchise	Location	Units	Countries
1	Pizza Hut	Dallas, Texas	10,433	80
2	McDonald's	Oakbrook, Illinois	23,132	70
3	KFC	Louisville, Kentucky	9,033	68
4	Burger King	Miami, Florida	7,121	50
5	Baskin Robbins	Glendale, California	3,557	49
6	Wendy's	Dublin, Ohio	4,168	38
7	Domino's Pizza	Ann Arbor, Michigan	5,238	36
8	TCBY	Little Rock, Arkansas	7,474	22
9	Dairy Queen	Minneapolis, Minnesota	5,471	21
10	Dunkin' Donuts	Randolph, Massachusetts	3,691	21
11	Taco Bell	Irvine, California	4,921	20
12	Arby's	Fort Lauderdale, Florida	2,670	18
13	Subway Sandwiches	Milford, Connecticut	8,477	15
14	Sizzler International	Los Angeles, California	681	14
15	Hardee's	Rocky Mount, North Carolina	4,060	12
16	Little Caesar's	Detroit, Michigan	4,600	12
17	Popeye's Chicken	Atlanta, Georgia	813	12
18	Denny's	Spartanburg, South Carolina	1,515	10
19	A&W Restaurants	Livonia, Michigan	707	9
20	T.G.I. Friday's	Minneapolis, Minnesota	273	8
21	Orange Julius	Minneapolis, Minnesota	480	7
22	Church's Fried Chicken	Atlanta, Georgia	1,079	6
23	Long John Silver's	Lexington, Kentucky	1,464	5
24	Carl's Jr.	Anaheim, California	649	4
25	Loterria	Tokyo, Japan	795	4
26	Mos Burger	Tokyo, Japan	1,263	4
27	Skylark	Tokyo, Japan	1,000	4
28	Jack in the Box	San Diego, California	1,172	3
29	Quick Restaurants	Berchem, Belgium	876	3
30	Taco Time	Eugene, Oregon	300	3

Source: Hotels, May 1994; 1994 PepsiCo, Inc., Annual Report.

the counter. McDonald's had greater success penetrating the German market because it made a number of changes in its menu and operating procedures in order to better appeal to German culture. For example, German beer was served in all of McDonald's German restaurants. KFC had more success in Asia and Latin America, where chicken was a traditional dish.

Aside from cultural factors, international business carried risks not present in the U.S. market.

Long distances between headquarters and foreign franchises often made it difficult to control the quality of individual restaurants. Large distances also caused servicing and support problems. Transportation and other resource costs were higher than in the domestic market. In addition, time, cultural, and language differences increased communication and operational problems. Therefore, it was reasonable to expect U.S. restaurant chains to expand domestically as long as they achieved corporate profit and growth objectives. As the U.S. market became saturated and companies gained expertise in international markets, more companies could be expected to turn to profitable international markets as a means of expanding restaurant bases and increasing sales, profits, and market share.

KENTUCKY FRIED CHICKEN CORPORATION

KFC's worldwide sales, which included sales of both company-owned and franchised restaurants, grew to $8.0 billion in 1997. U.S. sales grew 2.6 percent over 1996 and accounted for about one-half of KFC's sales worldwide. KFC's U.S. share of the chicken segment fell 1.8 points to 55.8 percent (see Exhibit E). This marked the sixth consecutive year that KFC sustained a decline in market share. KFC's market share has fallen by 16.3 points since 1988, when it held a 72.1 percent market share. Boston Market, which established its first restaurant in 1992, increased its market share from 0 to 16.7 percent over the same period. On the surface, it appeared as though Boston Market's market-share gain was achieved by taking customers away from KFC. However, KFC's sales growth has remained fairly stable and constant over the last 10 years. Boston Market's success was largely a function of its appeal to consumers who did not regularly patronize KFC or other chicken chains that sold fried chicken. By appealing to a market niche that was previously unsatisfied, Boston Market was able to expand the existing consumer base within the chicken segment of the fast-food industry.

Refranchising Strategy

The relatively low growth rate in sales in KFC's domestic restaurants during the 1992–1997 period was largely the result of KFC's decision in 1993 to begin selling company-owned restaurants to franchisees. When Colonel Sanders began to expand the Kentucky Fried Chicken system in the late 1950s, he established KFC as a system of independent franchisees. This was done in order to minimize his involvement in the operations of individual restaurants and to concentrate on the things he enjoyed the most—cooking, product development, and public relations. This resulted in a fiercely loyal and independent group of franchisees. PepsiCo's strategy when it acquired KFC in 1986 was to integrate KFC's operations in the PepsiCo system, in order to take advantage of operational, financial, and marketing synergies. How-

EXHIBIT E

Top U.S. Chicken Chains—Market Share (%)

	KFC	Boston Market	Popeye's	Chick-fil-A	Church's	Total
1988	72.1	0.0	12.0	5.8	10.1	100.0
1989	70.8	0.0	12.0	6.2	11.0	100.0
1990	71.3	0.0	12.3	6.6	9.8	100.0
1991	72.7	0.0	11.4	7.0	8.9	100.0
1992	71.5	0.9	11.4	7.5	8.7	100.0
1993	68.7	3.0	11.4	8.0	8.9	100.0
1994	64.8	6.9	11.3	8.4	8.6	100.0
1995	60.5	12.3	10.8	8.2	8.2	100.0
1996	57.6	16.2	10.0	8.4	7.8	100.0
1997	55.8	16.7	10.1	9.4	8.0	100.0
Change	−16.3	16.7	−1.9	3.6	−2.1	0.0

Source: Nation's Restaurant News.

ever, such a strategy demanded that PepsiCo become more involved in decisions over franchise operations, menu offerings, restaurant management, finance, and marketing. This was met by resistance with KFC franchises, who fiercely opposed increased control by the corporate parent. One method for PepsiCo to deal with this conflict was to expand through company-owned restaurants rather than through franchising. PepsiCo also used its strong cash flows to buy back unprofitable franchised restaurants, which could then be converted into company-owned restaurants. In 1986, company-owned restaurants made up 26 percent of KFC's U.S. restaurant base. By 1993, they made up about 40 percent (see Exhibit F).

While company-owned restaurants were relatively easier to control compared with franchises, they also required higher levels of investment. This meant that high levels of cash were diverted from PepsiCo's soft drink and snack food businesses into its restaurant businesses. However, the fast-food industry delivered lower returns than the soft drink and snack foods industries. Consequently, increased investment in KFC, Pizza Hut, and Taco Bell had a

negative effect on PepsiCo's consolidated return on assets. By 1993, investors became concerned that PepsiCo's return on assets did not match returns delivered by Coca-Cola. In order to shore up its return on assets, PepsiCo decided to reduce the number of company-owned restaurants by selling them back to franchisees. This strategy lowered overall company sales but also lowered the amount of cash tied up in fixed assets, provided PepsiCo with one-time cash flow benefits from initial fees charged to franchisees, and generated an annual stream of franchise royalties. Tricon Global continued this strategy after the spin off in 1997.

Marketing Strategy

During the 1980s, consumers began to demand healthier foods, greater variety, and better service in a variety of nontraditional locations such as grocery stores, restaurants, airports, and outdoor events. This forced fast-food chains to expand menu offerings and to investigate nontraditional distribution channels and restaurant designs. Families also demanded greater value in the food they

EXHIBIT F

KFC Restaurant Count (U.S.)

	Company-Owned	% Total	Franchised/Licensed	% Total	Total
1986	1,246	26.4	3,474	73.6	4,720
1987	1,250	26.0	3,564	74.0	4,814
1988	1,262	25.8	3,637	74.2	4,899
1989	1,364	27.5	3,597	72.5	4,961
1990	1,389	27.7	3,617	72.3	5,006
1991	1,836	36.6	3,186	63.4	5,022
1992	1,960	38.8	3,095	61.2	5,055
1993	2,014	39.5	3,080	60.5	5,094
1994	2,005	39.2	3,110	60.8	5,115
1995	2,026	39.4	3,111	60.6	5,137
1996	1,932	37.8	3,176	62.2	5,108
1997	1,850	36.1	3,270	63.9	5,120
1986–1993 Compounded annual growth rate	7.1%		−1.7%		1.1%
1993–1997 Compounded annual growth rate	−2.1%		1.5%		0.1%

Source: Tricon Global Restaurants, Inc., 1997 Annual Report; PepsiCo, Inc., Annual Reports, 1994, 1995, 1996, 1997.

bought away from home. This increased pressure on fast-food chains to reduce prices and to lower operating costs in order to maintain profit margins.

Many of KFC's problems during the late 1980s surrounded its limited menu and inability to quickly bring new products to market. The popularity of its Original Recipe Chicken allowed KFC to expand without significant competition from other chicken competitors through the 1980s. As a result, new product introductions were never an important element of KFC's overall strategy. One of the most serious setbacks suffered by KFC came in 1989 as KFC prepared to add a chicken sandwich to its menu. While KFC was still experimenting with its chicken sandwich, McDonald's test marketed its McChicken sandwich in the Louisville market. Shortly thereafter, it rolled out the Mc-Chicken sandwich nationally. By beating KFC to the market, McDonald's was able to develop strong consumer awareness for its sandwich. This significantly increased KFC's cost of developing awareness of its own sandwich, which KFC introduced several months later. KFC eventually withdrew its sandwich because of low sales.

In 1991, KFC changed its logo in the United States from Kentucky Fried Chicken to KFC in order to reduce its image as a fried chicken chain. It continued to use the Kentucky Fried Chicken name internationally. It then responded to consumer demands for greater variety by introducing several products that would serve as alternatives to its Original Recipe Chicken. These included Oriental Wings, Popcorn Chicken, and Honey BBQ Chicken. It also introduced a dessert menu that included a variety of pies and cookies. In 1993, it rolled out Rotisserie Chicken and began to promote its lunch and dinner buffet. The buffet, which included 30 items, was introduced into almost 1600 KFC restaurants in 27 states by year-end. In 1998, KFC sold three types of chicken—Original Recipe and Extra Crispy (fried chicken) and Tender Roast (roasted chicken).

One of KFC's most aggressive strategies was the introduction of its Neighborhood Program. By mid-1993, almost 500 company-owned restaurants in New York, Chicago, Philadelphia, Washington, D.C., St. Louis, Los Angeles, Houston, and Dallas had been outfitted with special menu offerings to appeal exclusively to the black community. Menus were beefed up with side dishes such as greens, macaroni and cheese, peach cobbler, sweet-potato pie, and red beans and rice. In addition, restaurant employees wore African-inspired uniforms. The introduction of the Neighborhood Program increased sales by 5 to 30 percent in restaurants appealing directly to the black community. KFC followed by testing Hispanic-oriented restaurants in the Miami area, offering side dishes such as fried plantains, flan, and tres leches.

One of KFC's most significant problems in the U.S. market was that overcapacity made expansion of free-standing restaurants difficult. Fewer sites were available for new construction, and those sites, because of their increased cost, were driving profit margins down. Therefore, KFC initiated a new three-pronged distribution strategy. First, it focused on building smaller restaurants in nontraditional outlets such as airports, shopping malls, universities, and hospitals. Second, it experimented with home delivery. Home delivery was introduced in the Nashville and Albuquerque markets in 1994. By 1998, home delivery was offered in 365 U.S. restaurants. Other nontraditional distribution outlets being tested included units offering drive-thru and carry-out service only, snack shops in cafeterias, scaled-down outlets for supermarkets, and mobile units that could be transported to outdoor concerts and fairs.

A third focus of KFC's distribution strategy was restaurant cobranding, primarily with its sister chain, Taco Bell. By 1997, 349 KFC restaurants had added Taco Bell to their menus and displayed both the KFC and Taco Bell logos outside their restaurants. Cobranding gave KFC the opportunity to expand its business dayparts. While about two-thirds of KFC's business was dinner, Taco Bell's primary business occurred at lunch. By combining the two concepts in the same unit, sales at individual restaurants could be increased significantly. KFC believed that there were opportunities to sell the Taco Bell concept in over 3900 of its U.S. restaurants.

Operating Efficiencies

As pressure continued to build on fast-food chains to limit price increases, restaurant chains searched for ways to reduce overhead and other operating costs in order to improve profit margins. In 1989, KFC reorganized its U.S. operations to eliminate overhead costs and increase efficiency. Included in this reorganization was a revision of KFC's crew training programs and operating standards. A re-

newed emphasis was placed on improving customer service, cleaner restaurants, faster and friendlier service, and continued high-quality products. In
1992, KFC reorganized its middle-management
ranks, eliminating 250 of the 1500 management positions at KFC's corporate headquarters. More responsibility was assigned to restaurant franchisees
and marketing managers and pay was more closely
aligned with customer service and restaurant performance. In 1997, Tricon Global signed a 5-year
agreement with PepsiCo Food Systems (which was
later sold by PepsiCo to AmeriServe Food Distributors) to distribute food and supplies to Tricon's
29,712 KFC, Pizza Hut, and Taco Bell units. This provided KFC with significant opportunities to benefit
from economies of scale in distribution.

INTERNATIONAL OPERATIONS

Much of the early success of the top 10 fast-food
chains was the result of aggressive building strategies. Chains were able to discourage competition by
building in low-population areas that could only
support a single fast-food chain. McDonald's was
particularly successful because it was able to
quickly expand into small towns across the United
States, thereby preempting other fast-food chains. It
was equally important to beat a competitor into
more largely populated areas where location was of
prime importance. KFC's early entry into international markets placed it in a strong position to benefit from international expansion as the U.S. market
became saturated. In 1997, 50 percent of KFC's
restaurants were located outside the United States.
While 364 new restaurants were opened outside
the United States in 1997, only 12 new restaurants
were added to the U.S. system. Most of KFC's international expansion was through franchises, although some restaurants were licensed to operators
or jointly operated with a local partner. Expansion
through franchising was an important strategy for
penetrating international markets because franchises were owned and operated by local entrepreneurs with a deeper understanding of local
language, culture, and customs, as well as local law,
financial markets, and marketing characteristics.
Franchising was particularly important for
expansion into smaller countries such as the
Dominican Republic, Grenada, Bermuda, and Suri-
name, which could only support a single restau-

rant. Costs were prohibitively high for KFC to operate company-owned restaurants in these smaller
markets. Of the 5117 KFC restaurants located outside the United States in 1997, 68 percent were
franchised, while 22 percent were company-
owned, and 10 percent were licensed restaurants
or joint ventures.

In larger markets such as Japan, China, and
Mexico, there was a stronger emphasis on building
company-owned restaurants. By coordinating purchasing, recruiting and training, financing, and advertising, fixed costs could be spread over a large
number of restaurants, and lower prices on products and services could be negotiated. KFC also
was better able to control product and service
quality. In order to take advantage of economies of
scale, Tricon Global Restaurants managed all the international units of its KFC, Pizza Hut, and Taco Bell
chains through its Tricon International Division located in Dallas, Texas. This enabled Tricon Global
Restaurants to leverage its strong advertising expertise, international experience, and restaurant management experience across all its KFC, Pizza Hut,
and Taco Bell restaurants.

Latin-American Strategy

KFC's primary market presence in Latin America
during the 1980s was in Mexico, Puerto Rico, and
the Caribbean. KFC established subsidiaries in
Mexico and Puerto Rico, from which it coordinated
the construction and operation of company-owned
restaurants. A third subsidiary in Venezuela was
closed because of the high fixed costs associated
with running the small subsidiary. Franchises were
used to penetrate other countries in the Caribbean
whose market size prevented KFC from profitably
operating company restaurants. KFC relied
exclusively on the operation of company-owned
restaurants in Mexico through 1989. While franchising was popular in the United States, it was
virtually unknown in Mexico until 1990, mainly
because of the absence of a law protecting
patents, information, and technology transferred
to the Mexican franchise. In addition, royalties
were limited. As a result, most fast-food chains
opted to invest in Mexico using company-owned
units.

In 1990, Mexico enacted a new law that provided for the protection of technology transferred
into Mexico. Under the new legislation, the fran-

chisor and franchisee were free to set their own terms. Royalties also were allowed under the new law. Royalties were taxed at a 15 percent rate on technology assistance and knowhow and 35 percent for other royalty categories. The advent of the new franchise law resulted in an explosion of franchises in fast-food, services, hotels, and retail outlets. In 1992, franchises had an estimated $750 million in sales in over 1200 outlets throughout Mexico. Prior to passage of Mexico's franchise law, KFC limited its Mexican operations primarily to Mexico City, Guadalajara, and Monterrey. This enabled KFC to better coordinate operations and minimize costs of distribution to individual restaurants. The new franchise law gave KFC and other fast-food chains the opportunity to expand their restaurant bases more quickly into more rural regions of Mexico, where responsibility for management could be handled by local franchisees.

After 1990, KFC altered its Latin American strategy in a number of ways. First, it opened 29 franchises in Mexico to complement its company-owned restaurant base. It then expanded its company-owned restaurants into the Virgin Islands and reestablished a subsidiary in Venezuela. Third, it expanded its franchise operations into South America. In 1990, a franchise was opened in Chile, and in 1993, a franchise was opened in Brazil. Franchises were subsequently established in Colombia, Ecuador, Panama, and Peru, among other South American countries. A fourth subsidiary was established in Brazil, in order to develop company-owned restaurants. Brazil was Latin America's largest economy and McDonald's primary Latin American investment location. By June 1998, KFC operated 438 restaurants in 32 Latin American countries. By comparison, McDonald's operated 1091 restaurants in 28 countries in Latin America.

Exhibit G shows the Latin American operations of KFC and McDonald's. KFC's early entry into Latin America during the 1970s gave it a leadership position in Mexico and the Caribbean. It also had gained an edge in Ecuador and Peru, countries where McDonald's had not yet devel-

EXHIBIT G

Latin American Restaurant Count: KFC and McDonald's (as of December 31, 1997)

	KFC Company Restaurants	KFC Franchised Restaurants	KFC Total Restaurants	McDonald's
Argentina	—	—	—	131
Bahamas	—	10	10	3
Barbados	—	7	7	—
Brazil	6	2	8	480
Chile	—	29	29	27
Columbia	—	19	19	18
Costa Rica	—	5	5	19
Ecuador	—	18	18	2
Jamaica	—	17	17	7
Mexico	128	29	157	131
Panama	—	21	21	20
Peru	—	17	17	5
Puerto Rico & Virgin Islands	67	—	67	115
Trinidad & Tobago	—	27	27	3
Uruguay	—	—	—	18
Venezuela	6	—	6	53
Other	—	30	30	59
Total	207	231	438	1,091

Source: Tricon Global Restaurants, Inc.; McDonald's, 1997 Annual Report.

oped a strong presence. McDonald's focused its Latin American investment in Brazil, Argentina, and Uruguay, countries where KFC had little or no presence. McDonald's also was strong in Venezuela. Both KFC and McDonald's were strong in Chile, Colombia, Panama, and Puerto Rico.

Economic Environment and the Mexican Market

Mexico was KFC's strongest market in Latin America. While McDonald's had aggressively established restaurants in Mexico since 1990, KFC retained the leading market share. Because of its close proximity to the United States, Mexico was an attractive location for U.S. trade and investment. Mexico's population of 98 million people was approximately one-third as large as the United States and represented a large market for U.S. companies. In comparison, Canada's population of 30.3 million people was only one-third as large as Mexico's. Mexico's close proximity to the United States meant that transportation costs between the United States and Mexico were significantly lower than to Europe or Asia. This increased the competitiveness of U.S. goods in comparison with European and Asian goods, which had to be transported to Mexico across the Atlantic or Pacific Ocean at substantial cost. The United States was, in fact, Mexico's largest

trading partner. Over 75 percent of Mexico's imports came from the United States, while 84 percent of its exports were to the United States (see Exhibit H). Many U.S. firms invested in Mexico in order to take advantage of lower wage rates. By producing goods in Mexico, U.S. goods could be shipped back into the United States for sale or shipped to third markets at lower cost.

While the U.S. market was critically important to Mexico, Mexico still represented a small percentage of overall U.S. trade and investment. Since the early 1900s, the portion of U.S. exports to Latin America had declined. Instead, U.S. exports to Canada and Asia, where economic growth outpaced growth in Mexico, increased more quickly. Canada was the largest importer of U.S. goods. Japan was the largest exporter of goods to the United States, with Canada a close second. U.S. investment in Mexico also was small, mainly because of past government restrictions on foreign investment. Most U.S. foreign investment was in Europe, Canada, and Asia.

The lack of U.S. investment in and trade with Mexico during this century was mainly the result of Mexico's long history of restricting trade and foreign direct investment. The Institutional Revolutionary Party (PRI), which came to power in Mexico during the 1930s, had historically pursued protectionist economic policies in order to shield Mexico's

EXHIBIT H

Mexico's Major Trading Partners—% Total Exports and Imports

	1992		1994		1996	
	Exports	Imports	Exports	Imports	Exports	Imports
U.S.	81.1	71.3	85.3	71.8	84.0	75.6
Japan	1.7	4.9	1.6	4.8	1.4	4.4
Germany	1.1	4.0	0.6	3.9	0.7	3.5
Canada	2.2	1.7	2.4	2.0	1.2	1.9
Italy	0.3	1.6	0.1	1.3	1.2	1.1
Brazil	0.9	1.8	0.6	1.5	0.9	0.8
Spain	2.7	1.4	1.4	1.7	1.0	0.7
Other	10.0	13.3	8.0	13.0	9.6	12.0
% Total	100.0	100.0	100.0	100.0	100.0	100.0
Value ($M)	46,196	62,129	60,882	79,346	95,991	89,464

Source: International Monetary Fund, *Direction of Trade Statistics Yearbook,* 1997.

economy from foreign competition. Many industries were government-owned or controlled, and many Mexican companies focused on producing goods for the domestic market without much attention to building export markets. High tariffs and other trade barriers restricted imports into Mexico, and foreign ownership of assets in Mexico was largely prohibited or heavily restricted.

Additionally, a dictatorial and entrenched government bureaucracy, corrupt labor unions, and a long tradition of anti-Americanism among many government officials and intellectuals reduced the motivation of U.S. firms for investing in Mexico. The nationalization of Mexico's banks in 1982 led to higher real interest rates and lower investor confidence. Afterward, the Mexican government battled high inflation, high interest rates, labor unrest, and lost consumer purchasing power. Investor confidence in Mexico, however, improved after 1988, when Carlos Salinas de Gortari was elected president. Following his election, Salinas embarked on an ambitious restructuring of the Mexican economy. He initiated policies to strengthen the free-market components of the economy, lowered top marginal tax rates to 36 percent (down from 60 percent in 1986), and eliminated many restrictions on foreign investment. Foreign firms can now buy up to 100 percent of the equity in many Mexican firms. Foreign ownership of Mexican firms was previously limited to 49 percent.

Privatization

The privatization of government-owned companies came to symbolize the restructuring of Mexico's economy. In 1990, legislation was passed to privatize all government-run banks. By the end of 1992, over 800 of some 1200 government-owned companies had been sold, including Mexicana and AeroMexico, the two largest airline companies in Mexico, and Mexico's 18 major banks. However, more than 350 companies remained under government ownership. These represented a significant portion of the assets owned by the state at the start of 1988. Therefore, the sale of government-owned companies, in terms of asset value, was moderate. A large percentage of the remaining government-owned assets were controlled by government-run companies in certain strategic industries such as steel, electricity, and petroleum. These industries had long been protected

by government ownership. As a result, additional privatization of government-owned enterprises until 1993 was limited. However, in 1993, President Salinas opened up the electricity sector to independent power producers, and Petroleos Mexicanos (Pemex), the state-run petrochemical monopoly, initiated a program to sell off many of its nonstrategic assets to private and foreign buyers.

North American Free Trade Agreement (NAFTA)

Prior to 1989, Mexico levied high tariffs on most imported goods. In addition, many other goods were subjected to quotas, licensing requirements, and other nontariff trade barriers. In 1986, Mexico joined the General Agreement on Tariffs and Trade (GATT), a world trade organization designed to eliminate barriers to trade among member nations. As a member of GATT, Mexico was obligated to apply its system of tariffs to all member nations equally. As a result of its membership in GATT, Mexico dropped tariff rates on a variety of imported goods. In addition, import license requirements were dropped for all but 300 imported items. During President Salinas' administration, tariffs were reduced from an average of 100 percent on most items to an average of 11 percent.

On January 1, 1994, the North American Free Trade Agreement (NAFTA) went into effect. The passage of NAFTA, which included Canada, the United States, and Mexico, created a trading bloc with a larger population and gross domestic product than the European Union. All tariffs on goods traded among the three countries were scheduled to be phased out. NAFTA was expected to be particularly beneficial for Mexican exporters because reduced tariffs made their goods more competitive in the United States compared with goods exported to the United States from other countries. In 1995, one year after NAFTA went into effect, Mexico posted its first balance of trade surplus in 6 years. Part of this surplus was attributed to reduced tariffs resulting from the NAFTA agreement. However, the peso crisis of 1995, which lowered the value of the peso against the dollar, increased the price of goods imported into Mexico and lowered the price of Mexican products exported to the United States. Therefore, it was still too early to

EXHIBIT I

Selected Economic Data for Canada, the United States, and Mexico

Annual Change (%)	1993	1994	1995	1996	1997
GDP growth					
Canada	3.3	4.8	5.5	4.1	—
United States	4.9	5.8	4.8	5.1	5.9
Mexico	21.4	13.3	29.4	38.2	—
Real GDP growth					
Canada	2.2	4.1	2.3	1.2	—
United States	2.2	3.5	2.0	2.8	3.8
Mexico	2.0	4.5	−6.2	5.1	—
Inflation					
Canada	1.9	0.2	2.2	1.5	1.6
United States	3.0	2.5	2.8	2.9	2.4
Mexico	9.7	6.9	35.0	34.4	20.6
Depreciation against $U.S.					
Canada (C$)	4.2	6.0	−2.7	0.3	4.3
Mexico (NP)	−0.3	71.4	43.5	2.7	3.6

Source: International Monetary Fund, *International Financial Statistics,* 1998.

assess the full effects of the NAFTA agreement. (See Exhibit I for further details.)

Foreign Exchange and the Mexican Peso Crisis of 1995

Between 1982 and 1991, a two-tiered exchange-rate system was in force in Mexico. The system consisted of a controlled rate and a free-market rate. A controlled rate was used for imports, foreign debt payments, and conversion of export proceeds. An estimated 70 percent of all foreign transactions were covered by the controlled rate. A free-market rate was used for other transactions. In 1989, President Salinas instituted a policy of allowing the peso to depreciate against the dollar by one peso per day. The result was a grossly overvalued peso. This lowered the price of imports and led to an increase in imports of over 23 percent in 1989. At the same time, Mexican exports became less competitive on world markets.

In 1991, the controlled rate was abolished and replaced with an official free rate. In order to limit the range of fluctuations in the value of the peso, the government fixed the rate at which it would buy or sell pesos. A floor (the maximum price at

which pesos could be purchased) was established at Ps 3056.20 and remained fixed. A ceiling (the maximum price at which the peso could be sold) was established at Ps 3056.40 and allowed to move upward by Ps 0.20 per day. This was later revised to Ps 0.40 per day. In 1993, a new currency, called the *new peso,* was issued with three fewer zeros. The new currency was designed to simplify transactions and to reduce the cost of printing currency.

When Ernesto Zedillo became Mexico's president in December 1994, one of his objectives was to continue the stability of prices, wages, and exchange rates achieved by ex-President Carlos Salinas de Gortari during his 5-year tenure as president. However, Salinas had achieved stability largely on the basis of price, wage, and foreign-exchange controls. While giving the appearance of stability, an overvalued peso continued to encourage imports, which exacerbated Mexico's balance of trade deficit. Mexico's government continued to use foreign reserves to finance its balance of trade deficits. According to the Banco de Mexico, foreign currency reserves fell from $24 billion in January 1994 to $5.5 billion in January 1995. Anticipating a devaluation of the peso, investors began to move capital into U.S. dollar investments. In order to relieve pressure on the peso, Zedillo announced on December 19, 1994 that the peso would be allowed to depreciate by an additional 15 percent per year against the dollar compared with the maximum allowable depreciation of 4 percent per year established during the Salinas administration. Within 2 days, continued pressure on the peso forced Zedillo to allow the peso to float freely against the dollar. By mid-January 1995, the peso had lost 35 percent of its value against the dollar, and the Mexican stock market plunged 20 percent. By November 1995, the peso had depreciated from 3.1 pesos per dollar to 7.3 pesos per dollar.

The continued devaluation of the peso resulted in higher import prices, higher inflation, destabilization within the stock market, and higher interest rates. Mexico struggled to pay its dollar-based debts. In order to thwart a possible default by Mexico, the U.S. government, International Monetary Fund, and World Bank pledged $24.9 billion in emergency loans. Zedillo then announced an emergency economic package called the pacto that included reduced government spending, increased sales of government-run businesses, and a freeze on wage increases.

Labor Problems

One of KFC's primary concerns in Mexico was the stability of labor markets. Labor was relatively plentiful, and wages were low. However, much of the workforce was relatively unskilled. KFC benefited from lower labor costs, but labor unrest, low job retention, high absenteeism, and poor punctuality were significant problems. Absenteeism and punctuality were partially cultural. However, problems with worker retention and labor unrest also were the result of workers' frustration over the loss of their purchasing power due to inflation and government controls on wage increases. Absenteeism remained high at approximately 8 to 14 percent of the labor force, though it was declining because of job security fears. Turnover continued to be a problem and ran at between 5 and 12 percent per month. Therefore, employee screening and internal training were important issues for firms investing in Mexico.

Higher inflation and the government's freeze on wage increases led to a dramatic decline in dis-posable income after 1994. Further, a slowdown in business activity, brought about by higher interest rates and lower government spending, led many businesses to lay off workers. By the end of 1995, an estimated 1 million jobs had been lost as a result of the economic crisis sparked by the peso devaluation. As a result, industry groups within Mexico called for new labor laws giving them more freedom to hire and fire employees and increased flexibility to hire part-time rather than full-time workers.

RISKS AND OPPORTUNITIES

The peso crisis of 1995 and resulting recession in Mexico left KFC managers with a great deal of uncertainty regarding Mexico's economic and political future. KFC had benefited from economic stability between 1988 and 1994. Inflation was brought down, the peso was relatively stable, labor unrest was relatively calm, and Mexico's new franchise law had enabled KFC to expand into rural areas using franchises rather than company-owned restaurants. By the end of 1995, KFC had built 29 franchises in Mexico. The foreign-exchange crisis of 1995 had severe implications for U.S. firms operating in Mexico. The devaluation of the peso resulted in higher inflation and capital flight out of Mexico. Capital flight reduced the supply of capital and led to higher interest rates. In order to reduce inflation, Mexico's government instituted an austerity program that resulted in lower disposable income, higher unemployment, and lower demand for products and services.

Another problem was Mexico's failure to reduce restrictions on U.S. and Canadian investment in a timely fashion. Many U.S. firms experienced problems getting required approvals for new ventures from the Mexican government. A good example was United Parcel Service (UPS), which sought government approval to use large trucks for deliveries in Mexico. Approvals were delayed, forcing UPS to use smaller trucks. This put UPS at a competitive disadvantage vis-à-vis Mexican companies. In many cases, UPS was forced to subcontract delivery work to Mexican companies that were allowed to use larger, more cost-efficient trucks. Other U.S. companies such as Bell Atlantic and TRW faced similar problems. TRW, which signed a joint-venture agreement with a Mexican partner, had to wait 15 months longer than anticipated before the Mexican government released rules on how it could receive credit data from banks. TRW claimed that the Mexican government slowed the approval process in order to placate several large Mexican banks.

A final area of concern for KFC was increased political turmoil in Mexico during the last several years. On January 1, 1994, the day NAFTA went into effect, rebels (descendants of the Mayans) rioted in the southern Mexican province of Chiapas on the Guatemalan border. After 4 days of fighting, Mexican troops had driven the rebels out of several towns earlier seized by the rebels. Around 150—mostly rebels—were killed. The uprising symbolized many of the fears of the poor in Mexico. While ex-President Salinas' economic programs had increased economic growth and wealth in Mexico, many of Mexico's poorest felt that they had not benefited. Many of Mexico's farmers, faced with lower tariffs on imported agricultural goods from the United States, felt that they might be driven out of business because of lower-priced imports. Therefore, social unrest among Mexico's Indians, farmers, and the poor could potentially unravel much of the economic success achieved in Mexico during the last 5 years.

Further, ex-President Salinas' hand-picked successor for president was assassinated in early 1994 while campaigning in Tijuana. The assassin was a 23-year-old mechanic and migrant worker believed to be affiliated with a dissident group upset with the PRI's economic reforms. The possible existence of a dissident group raised fears of political violence in the future. The PRI quickly named Ernesto Zedillo, a 42-year-old economist with little political experience, as their new presidential candidate. Zedillo was elected president in December 1994. Political unrest was not limited to Mexican officials and companies. In October 1994, between 30 and 40 masked men attacked a McDonald's restaurant in the tourist section of Mexico City to show their opposition to California's Proposition 187, which would have curtailed benefits to illegal aliens (primarily from Mexico). The men threw cash registers to the floor, cracked them open, smashed windows, overturned tables, and spray-painted slogans on the walls such as "No to Fascism" and "Yankee Go Home."

KFC faced a variety of issues in Mexico and Latin America in 1998. Prior to 1995, few restaurants had been opened in South America. However, KFC was now aggressively building new restaurants in the region. KFC halted openings of franchised restaurants in Mexico, and all restaurants opened since 1995 were company-owned. KFC was more aggressively building restaurants in South America, which remained largely unpenetrated by KFC through 1995. Of greatest importance was Brazil, where McDonald's had already established a strong market-share position. Brazil was Latin America's largest economy and a largely untapped market for KFC. The danger in ignoring Mexico was that a conservative investment strategy could jeopardize its market-share lead over McDonald's in a large market where KFC long enjoyed enormous popularity.

Development, Implementation, and Evaluation of a Marketing Plan

WHAT IS A MARKETING PLAN?

A formal marketing plan is a detailed, written document that contains the guidelines for the business unit's marketing programs and allocations over a specified planning period. The planning period is usually 1 year, but the time may vary depending on the plan's purpose (e.g., new product introduction; seasonal patterns). The term "marketing plan" often is used interchangeably with "business plan" or other terms, but the marketing plan generally is viewed as a subset of the business plan.

Proactive marketing planning reflects both customer and competitor orientation, and is a continuous process that anticipates and responds to changing market conditions. While the marketing plan must be creative and innovative, it also must be realistic and actionable. A marketing plan should answer three basic questions, assuming that you have first answered the fundamental question of "What business are we in—and what do we really sell?" (1) Where are we now? (situation analysis); (2) Where do we want to be? (financial and marketing objectives); and (3) How will we get there? (strategies and tactics; action plan).

WHY DO WE NEED A MARKETING PLAN?

Many managers consider the planning process to be the most valuable aspect of developing a marketing plan. An in-depth situation analysis reveals useful insights about your product or service, your market and industry (and the opportunities and threats they present), your customer markets and your position in these markets, and your company's internal strengths and weaknesses versus those of competitors. This analysis will provide a deeper understanding of the "big picture" that includes the interaction of your product/service, customers, and competitors in the greater environment. Preparation of the plan provides a better understanding of the company's internal strengths and weaknesses and external opportunities and threats. It leads to insights and creative thinking about opportunities that can capitalize on core competencies and strengths, and minimize weaknesses and threats. Finally, a written marketing plan provides detailed directions for implementing the plan and reaching your strategic objectives.

GETTING STARTED WITH OUR MARKETING PLAN: PRELIMINARY TASKS AND TIMETABLE

I. Proposal

The first step in developing a marketing plan is to write a proposal that will provide direction for the planning process, and serve as a basis for the more detailed plan to follow:

A. Name and description of company/organization (for-profit or nonprofit) for which your marketing plan is being developed. Include the North American Industry Classification System (NAICS) code (formerly Standard Industrial Classification (SIC). This will help you find information about your company and its industry.

B. Clear description of the product, service, or SBU that is the focus of your marketing plan.

C. Objectives of the marketing plan for the organization (i.e., what should your plan do for the company?)

D. List of *specific* background information needed to complete the plan (i.e., questions to be answered to complete each section). Knowing the questions will help to expedite the research necessary to find the answers.

E. List of possible information sources to answer each "question" listed in (D). (A detailed list at this point will expedite the search process.) Include complete names of publications, Web sites, company sources, etc. Do not just name broad databases, such as "Internet" or Lexis/Nexis," although you will find many specific publications and references in these databases. Note that you will probably use both primary sources (information gathered first hand for this marketing plan, including interviews, surveys, etc.), and secondary sources (information gathered for some other purpose, generally found in publications, existing databases, company records, etc.).

F. List of all activities/tasks necessary to complete the marketing plan.

G. Estimated timetable or schedule for completion of all activities identified in (F). This can be set up on a weekly basis through the completion and presentation of your final plan. (If you are working in a group, indicate who will be responsible for each task.)

II. Tentative Outline

Once your marketing plan proposal has been approved, prepare a tentative working outline of your completed marketing plan. Include all major headings and subheadings, along with a brief description of the specific topics to be included in each section. This should be a detailed outline of topics that are relevant to the marketing planning process and your selected target company, product, market, etc. The outline should not be just a "rehash" of the generic topics in the recommended table of contents.

III. Table of Contents for Completed Marketing Plan

A recommended outline for your completed marketing plan is presented in this section, although each marketing plan is unique and the format and content may vary. Use the following table of contents as an outline, and as a *general guideline* for content and length. Marketing plans may be a few pages or many, and may be specified by your professor. Length should be determined by the nature and quality of content needed. Appendices and/or exhibits may be attached if they are needed for further explanation or clarification. With judicious editing, a comprehensive marketing plan can be presented in 20 to 30 pages total. This can include some detailed outlining or bullet points, and indications of further issues to be addressed at a later time (i.e., "next steps"). Supporting materials may be included in a separate section. The emphasis in this assignment is on understanding *how to develop an effective marketing plan*. This means that *all necessary components should be acknowledged*, even if beyond the scope of the term project.

See Exhibit 1 for a basic Table of Contents for a marketing plan. Exhibit 2 is an expanded version of the Table of Contents, with suggestions for each section.

EXHIBIT 1

Table of Contents for a Marketing Plan

Title page
Executive Summary
Table of Contents
Introduction
Situational analysis
Objective(s)
Strategy
Action Plan
   Target Market
   Marketing Mix
      Product/Service
      Pricing
      Distribution/Location
      Integrated Marketing Communications
   Budget
Implementation Plan
Control and Evaluation
Appendices/Exhibits
References

EXHIBIT 2

Annotated Table of Contents for a Marketing Plan

A. Title page
B. Executive summary (2–3 page "abstract" of complete marketing plan)
C. Table of contents—with page numbers
D. Introduction: Brief background information, issues, and purpose of the plan (1 page)
E. Situational analysis (including macro- and micro-environments; strengths/weaknesses and opportunities/threats [SWOT] analysis)
    Focus on the most relevant information (Refer to parts (D) and (E) in your proposal.)
    1. Length will vary due to uniqueness of each plan. For example, if the emphasis is on the tactical action plan (see H below), the situation analysis section may be edited to 3–4 pages. If the situation analysis is the major part of the marketing plan (e.g., feasibility study), then this section may be 6–8 pages. Suggestion: use a business format, summary tables, exhibits, and/or appendices as needed to present information effectively.
    2. Create a checklist of factors to consider when conducting the situation analysis. (See Chapter 4 for suggestions related to a marketing audit.) Choose those areas of analysis that are most relevant. In general, consider the nature of the product/ service/idea that you are marketing, the competitive environment, and customer markets (final consumers, industrial, institutional, etc.), company resources, and other external and internal environmental forces that can affect your marketing planning and implementation.
    3. Include *headings* and *subheadings* for each section of the situational analysis.
F. Measurable objectives to be achieved by the marketing plan
    1. Marketing objectives (e.g., sales, market share, awareness, etc.)
    2. Financial objectives (e.g., net profit, operating profit, return on investment, etc.)
    3. Include pro forma income statement and balance sheet as appropriate
G. Marketing strategy
    This should be a broad statement of the overall strategy that will be used to achieve the marketing and financial objectives listed in (F).
H. Action (tactical) plan
    This is the tactical part of the marketing plan that guides operating level decisions and activities. This may require 10–12 pages if your emphasis is on an action plan; or 6–8 pages if your emphasis is on the situational analysis (such as that used for a feasibility study for a new venture, as noted in Section E-1). *Include supporting exhibits of details such as media campaign examples and rate cards, pricing strategy with breakeven or other financial analysis, etc., product specifications, or other tactical information.* The quality of this section will have a major impact on the success of your marketing plan, and the information provided must be clearly understood by those who are responsible for carrying it out.
    1. Target market(s) to be reached by action plan
        Identification of the customer segment(s) that will be targeted by your plan.
    2. Marketing mix (this can be adapted to goods or service)
        a. good/service identification and description
        b. pricing strategy (e.g., cost-based, value-based, below market, etc.)
        c. distribution/location (place of business, Internet, catalog, direct, etc.)
        d. promotion (all pertinent tools in the integrated communications mix (IMC), selected from advertising, personal selling, direct marketing, sales promotion, publicity and public relations)
    3. Proposed (realistic!) marketing budget for implementation of marketing plan). Include details, such as estimated sales, media costs, etc.
I. Implementation (1–2 pages)
    1. Schedule/chart/timeline of execution of each element of action plan
    2. Responsibility for each task (who will do it?)
J. Control and Evaluation (2 pages)
    1. Methods for measuring actual performance versus planned objectives
    2. Include illustration(s) of measurement of progress during the campaign, and upon its completion
K. Brief summary of tactical plan and conclusions ($\frac{1}{2}$ to 1 page)
L. Appendices/Exhibits
    1. Use titles to identify these in the text as well as on the exhibits
    2. Cite reference(s) and data sources on each table, figure or other exhibit and use exhibit names when they are referenced in the text.
M. Reference/Bibliography (*use complete citations and indicate in text where each is used*)

Index